MULTICOLOUR ILLUSTRATIVE EDITION

PRINCIPLES OF
ELECTRICAL ENGINEERING AND ELECTRONICS

[FOR B.E/B. TECH AND OTHER ENGINEERING EXAMINATIONS]

V.K. MEHTA
ROHIT MEHTA

S. CHAND & COMPANY LTD.

(AN ISO 9001 : 2000 COMPANY)

RAM NAGAR, NEW DELHI - 110 055

S. CHAND & COMPANY LTD.
(An ISO 9001 : 2000 Company)
Head Office: 7361, RAM NAGAR, NEW DELHI - 110 055
Phone: 23672080-81-82, 9899107446, 9911310888
Fax: 91-11-23677446
Shop at: **schandgroup.com**; e-mail: **info@schandgroup.com**

Branches :

AHMEDABAD : 1st Floor, Heritage, Near Gujarat Vidhyapeeth, Ashram Road, **Ahmedabad** - 380 014, Ph: 27541965, 27542369, ahmedabad@schandgroup.com

BENGALURU : No. 6, Ahuja Chambers, 1st Cross, Kumara Krupa Road, **Bengaluru** - 560 001, Ph: 22268048, 22354008, bangalore@schandgroup.com

BHOPAL : Bajaj Tower, Plot No. 243, Lala Lajpat Rai Colony, Raisen Road, **Bhopal** - 462 011, Ph: 4274723. bhopal@schandgroup.com

CHANDIGARH : S.C.O. 2419-20, First Floor, Sector - 22-C (Near Aroma Hotel), **Chandigarh** -160 022, Ph: 2725443, 2725446, chandigarh@schandgroup.com

CHENNAI : 152, Anna Salai, **Chennai** - 600 002, Ph: 28460026, 28460027, chennai@schandgroup.com

COIMBATORE : No. 5, 30 Feet Road, Krishnasamy Nagar, Ramanathapuram, **Coimbatore** -641045, Ph: 0422-2323620 coimbatore@schandgroup.com **(Marketing Office)**

CUTTACK : 1st Floor, Bhartia Tower, Badambadi, **Cuttack** - 753 009, Ph: 2332580; 2332581, cuttack@schandgroup.com

DEHRADUN : 1st Floor, 20, New Road, Near Dwarka Store, **Dehradun** - 248 001, Ph: 2711101, 2710861, dehradun@schandgroup.com

GUWAHATI : Pan Bazar, **Guwahati** - 781 001, Ph: 2738811, 2735640 guwahati@schandgroup.com

HYDERABAD : Padma Plaza, H.No. 3-4-630, Opp. Ratna College, Narayanaguda, **Hyderabad** - 500 029, Ph: 24651135, 24744815, hyderabad@schandgroup.com

JAIPUR : A-14, Janta Store Shopping Complex, University Marg, Bapu Nagar, **Jaipur** - 302 015, Ph: 2719126, jaipur@schandgroup.com

JALANDHAR : Mai Hiran Gate, **Jalandhar** - 144 008, Ph: 2401630, 5000630, jalandhar@schandgroup.com

JAMMU : 67/B, B-Block, Gandhi Nagar, **Jammu** - 180 004, (M) 09878651464 **(Marketing Office)**

KOCHI : Kachapilly Square, Mullassery Canal Road, Ernakulam, **Kochi** - 682 011, Ph: 2378207, cochin@schandgroup.com

KOLKATA : 285/J, Bipin Bihari Ganguli Street, **Kolkata** - 700 012, Ph: 22367459, 22373914, kolkata@schandgroup.com

LUCKNOW : Mahabeer Market, 25 Gwynne Road, Aminabad, **Lucknow** - 226 018, Ph: 2626801, 2284815, lucknow@schandgroup.com

MUMBAI : Blackie House, 103/5, Walchand Hirachand Marg, Opp. G.P.O., **Mumbai** - 400 001, Ph: 22690881, 22610885, mumbai@schandgroup.com

NAGPUR : Karnal Bag, Model Mill Chowk, Umrer Road, **Nagpur** - 440 032, Ph: 2723901, 2777666 nagpur@schandgroup.com

PATNA : 104, Citicentre Ashok, Govind Mitra Road, **Patna** - 800 004, Ph: 2300489, 2302100, patna@schandgroup.com

PUNE : 291/1, Ganesh Gayatri Complex, 1st Floor, Somwarpeth, Near Jain Mandir, **Pune** - 411 011, Ph: 64017298, pune@schandgroup.com **(Marketing Office)**

RAIPUR : Kailash Residency, Plot No. 4B, Bottle House Road, Shankar Nagar, **Raipur** - 492 007, Ph: 09981200834, raipur@schandgroup.com **(Marketing Office)**

RANCHI : Flat No. 104, Sri Draupadi Smriti Apartments, East of Jaipal Singh Stadium, Neel Ratan Street, Upper Bazar, **Ranchi** - 834 001, Ph: 2208761, ranchi@schandgroup.com **(Marketing Office)**

SILIGURI : 122, Raja Ram Mohan Roy Road, East Vivekanandapally, P.O., **Siliguri**-734001, Dist., Jalpaiguri, (W.B.) Ph. 0353-2520750 **(Marketing Office)**

VISAKHAPATNAM: Plot No. 7, 1st Floor, Allipuram Extension, Opp. Radhakrishna Towers, Seethammadhara North Extn., **Visakhapatnam** - 530 013, (M) 09347580841, visakhapatnam@schandgroup.com **(Marketing Office)**

© 1996, V.K. Mehta and Rohit Mehta

All rights reserved. No part of this publication may be reproduced or copied in any material form (including photo copying or storing it in any medium in form of graphics, electronic or mechanical means and whether or not transient or incidental to some other use of this publication) without written permission of the copyright owner. Any breach of this will entail legal action and prosecution without further notice.

Jurisdiction : All desputes with respect to this publication shall be subject to the jurisdiction of the Courts, tribunals and forums of New Delhi, India only.

First Edition 1996
Subsequent Edition and Reprints 1998, 99, 2000, 2001, 2003, 2004, 2006
First Multicolour Edition 2006, Reprint 2007, 2008 (Twice) 2009 (Twice),
2010 (Twice), 2011
Reprint 2012

ISBN : 81-219-2729-3   **Code : 10 324**

PRINTED IN INDIA
By Rajendra Ravindra Printers Pvt. Ltd., 7361, Ram Nagar, New Delhi -110 055
and published by S. Chand & Company Ltd., 7361, Ram Nagar, New Delhi -110 055.

PREFACE TO THE SECOND EDITION

The general response to the first edition of the book was very encouraging. The authors feel that their work has been amply rewarded and wish to express their deep sense of gratitude, in common to the large number of readers who have used it, and in particular to those of them who have sent helpful suggestions from time to time for the improvement of the book.

In the present edition, the authors have made sincere efforts to make the book up-to-date. A large number of practical problems are given to make the book more useful to the students. A notable feature is the inclusion of **multiple-choice questions** at the end of each chapter. It is hoped that the readers will enjoy reading this text and benefit from its contents.

To ehance the utility of the book, it has been decided to bring out the **multicolour edition** of the book. There are three salient features of this **multicolour edition**. First, the colour scheme has been designed in such a way that there is an easy understanding of the text. Secondly, it significantly improves the striking power of the reader. Thirdly, the pictorial views of electrical/electronic devices given in the book bridges the gap between the theoretical and practical aspects of the subject.

Errors might have crept in despite best efforts to remove them and the authors shall be grateful if these are pointed out alongwith other suggestions for the improvement of the book.

V.K. MEHTA
ROHIT MEHTA

CONTENTS

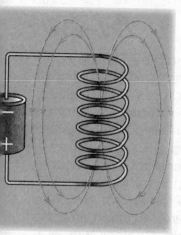
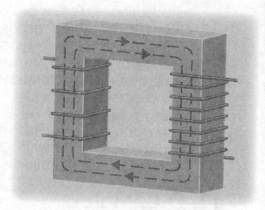

E.M.F.—Self-Inductance (L) —Other Expressions for L—
Inductors—Mutual Inductance (M)—Other Expressions
for Mutual Inductance—Co-efficient of Coupling—
Inductances in Series—Inductances in Parallel—Closing
and Braking and Inductive circuit—Rise of current in an
inductive circuit—Time constant—Decay of current in
an Inductive Circuit—Energy Stored in a Magnetic
Field—Magnetic Energy Stored per unit volume—Lifting
Power of a Magnet—Eddy Current Loss—Formula for
Eddy Current Loss —Stray Inductance—Multiple-Choice
Questions .

Regulation—Losses in a D.C. Motor—Efficiency of a D.C. Motor—Power Stages—Armature Reaction in D.C. Motors—Magnetic Circuit of D.C. Machines—D.C. Motor Characteristics—Characteristics of Shunt Motors—Characteristics of Series Motors—Cumpound Motors—Characteristics of Comulative Compound Motors—Comparison of Three Types of Motors—Applications of D.C. Motors—Troubles in D.C. Motors—Multiple Choice Questions.

Values of Alternating Voltage and Current—Average Value—Average Value of Sinusoidal Current—R.M.S. or Effective Value—R.M.S. Value of Sinusoidal Current—Form Factor and Peak Factor—Phase—Phase Difference—Representation of Alternating Voltages and Currents—Phasor Representation of Sinusoidal Quantities—Phasor Diagram of Sine Waves of Same Frequency—Addition of Alternating Quantities—Subtraction of Alternating quantities—Phasor Diagram Using r.m.s. Values—A.C. Circuit—A.C. Circuit Containing Resistance Only—A.C. Circuit Containing Inductance Only—A.C. Circuit Containing Capacitance Only—Multiple Choice Questions.

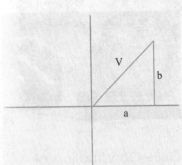

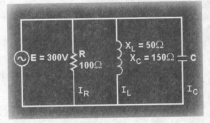

Load—Phasor Diagram of a Loaded Alternator—Voltage Regulation—Parallel operation of Alternators—Advantages of Parallel Operation of Alternators—Hunting—Multiple-Choice Questions.

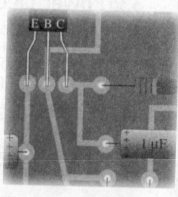
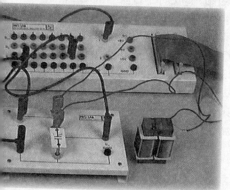 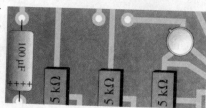

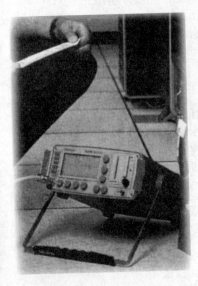

1

Fundamentals of Current Electricity

INTRODUCTION

The study of nature of electricity has been attracting the attention of scientists for hundreds of years. Several theories about electricity were developed through experiments and by observation of its behaviour. The only theory that has survived over the years to explain the nature of electricity is the *Modern Electron Theory of Matter.* This theory has been the result of research work conducted by scientists like Sir William Crooks, J.J. Thomson, Robert A. Millikan, Sir Earnest Rutherford and Neils Bohr. In this chapter, we shall deal with some basic concepts concerning electricity.

1.1. MODERN ELECTRON THEORY

The nature of electricity can be beautifully explained on the basis of *Modern Electron Theory of Matter. According to this theory, all matter whether solid, liquid or gas is composed of minute particles called *molecules.* A molecule is in turn made up of atoms. Those substances whose molecules consist of

---

*   When this theory was stated, it was believed that all atoms were made up of electrons and protons. Hence, the name electron theory. Although it is well known today that an atom contains a number of other particles such as neutrons, mesons, positrons etc. yet the term electron theory has been retained.

the same kind of atoms are called *elements* while those whose molecules consist of atoms of different kinds are called *compounds*. The number of known stable elements is 105 while the number of compounds is unlimited.

Atoms are the building blocks of all matter. An atom consists of a central part called *nucleus* and around the nucleus (called *extra-nucleus*), there are a number of electrons revolving in different paths or orbits. The size of the nucleus is very small as compared to the size of the atom. The diameter of an atom is of the order of 10^{-10} metre compared to the diameter of the nucleus of the order of 10^{-15} metre. Thus, there is vast empty space existing in an atom.

1. Nucleus. It is the central part of an atom and contains *protons* and *neutrons*. A proton is a positively charged particle having mass 1837 times that of an electron. A neutron has the same mass as proton but no charge. Obviously, the nucleus of an atom bears a positive charge. Since the mass of an electron is very small as compared to that of a proton or neutron, the nucleus of an atom constitutes the entire weight of atom *i.e.*,

Atomic Weight = No. of protons + No. of neutrons

2. Extra-nucleus. It is the outer part of an atom and contains electrons only. An electron is a negatively charged particle having negative charge equal to the positive charge on a proton. The electrons move around the nucleus in different paths or orbits obeying the following rules :

(*i*) The maximum number of electrons that can be accommodated in an orbit is given by $2n^2$ where n is the number of orbit. Thus, the first orbit can accommodate $2 \times 1^2 = 2$ electrons; the second orbit $2 \times 2^2 = 8$ electrons ; third orbit $2 \times 3^2 = 18$ electrons and so on.

(*ii*) The last orbit cannot accommodate more than 8 electrons.

(*iii*) The last but one orbit cannot accommodate more than 18 electrons.

Under normal conditions, the number of electrons is equal to the number of protons in an atom. Therefore, an atom is neutral as a whole ; the negative charge on the electrons cancelling the positive charge on the protons. The number of protons or electrons in an atom is called atomic number *i.e.*

Atomic number = No. of protons or electrons in an atom

**Fig. 1.1 (*i*) shows the structure of a copper atom. The atomic weight and atomic number of copper are 64 and 29 respectively. Therefore, a copper atom has 29 protons, 29 electrons and 35 neutrons. The 29 electrons are distributed among the various orbits as : first orbit will have 2 electrons ; second 8 electrons, 3rd 18 electrons and fourth orbit 1 electron. Fig. 1.1 (*ii*) shows the structure of an aluminium atom. It has 13 electrons which are distributed in the first, second and third orbits as 2, 8 and 3 electrons respectively.

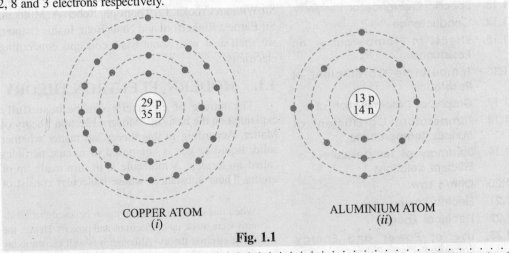

COPPER ATOM
(*i*)

ALUMINIUM ATOM
(*ii*)

Fig. 1.1

* For example, oxygen is an element and its molecule has two atoms of the same kind. On the other hand, water is a compound and its molecule contains two atoms of hydrogen and one atom of oxygen.
** Copper and aluminium have been intentionally chosen because these two elements are widely used in electrical engineering.

Conclusion. The reader may note the following points carefully :

(*i*) Every matter is electrical in nature *i.e.*, it contains particles of electricity *viz.*, protons and electrons.

(*ii*) In the normal state, the number of electrons is equal to the number of protons in an atom. Therefore, an atom is neutral as a whole. This explains why a body does not exhibit any charge under ordinary conditions.

(*iii*) One substance differs from another in the number and arrangement of particles of atom *viz.* protons, neutrons and electrons. Thus the number of these particles for copper and aluminium atoms is different (See Fig. 1.1). Hence, the two substances are different.

1.2. NATURE OF ELECTRICITY

The above discussion shows that matter is electrical in nature *i.e.*, it contains particles of electricity *viz.* protons and electrons. Whether a given body exhibits electricity (*i.e.*, charge) or not depends upon the relative number of these particles of electricity.

(*i*) If the number of protons is equal to the number of electrons in a body, the resultant charge is zero and the body will be electrically neutral. Thus, the paper of this book is electrically neutral (*i.e.*, paper exhibits no charge) because it has the same number of protons and electrons.

(*ii*) If from a neutral body, some *electrons are removed, there occurs a deficit of electrons in the body. Consequently, the body attains a *positive charge*.

(*iii*) If a neutral body is supplied with electrons, there occurs an excess of electrons. Consequently, the body attains a *negative charge*.

1.3. UNIT OF CHARGE

The charge on an electron is so small that it is not conveneient to select it as the unit of charge. In practice, *coulomb* is used as the unit of charge. One *coulomb* of charge is equal to the charge on 625×10^{16} electrons *i.e.*,

$$1 \text{ coulomb} = \text{Charge on } 625 \times 10^{16} \text{ electrons}$$

Thus, when we say that a body has a positive charge of 1 coulomb, it means that it has a deficit of 625×10^{16} electrons.

Note. Charge on one electron (*i.e.* number of coulombs per electron) is given by;

Charge on electron, $e = \dfrac{1 \text{ coulomb}}{625 \times 10^{16} \text{ electrons}} = 1.6 \times 10^{-19} \text{ C}$

1.4. FREE ELECTRONS

It has been shown above that electrons move around the nucleus of an atom in different orbits. The electrons in the inner orbits (*i.e.*, orbits close to the nucleus) are tightly bound to the nucleus. As we move away from the nucleus, this binding goes on decreasing so that electrons in the last orbit (called valence electrons) are quite loosely bound to the nucleus. In certain substances, especially metals (*e.g.*, copper, aluminium *etc.*), the valence electrons are so weakly attached to their nuclei that they can be easily removed or detached. Such electrons are called free electrons.

Those valence electrons which are very loosely attached to the nucleus of an atom are called free electrons.

The free electrons move at random from one atom to another in the material. In fact, they are so loosely attached that they do not know the atom to which they belong. It may be noted here that all valence electrons in a metal are not free electrons. It has been found that one atom of a metal can provide at the most one free electron. Since a small piece of metal has billions of atoms, one can except a very large number of free electrons in metals. For instance, one cubic centimetre of copper has about 8.5×10^{22} free electrons at room temperature.

---

*   Electrons have very small mass and, therefore, are much more mobile than protons. On the other hand, protons are powerfully held in the nucleus and cannot be removed or detached.

(*i*) A substance which has a large number of free electrons at room temperature is called a *conductor* of electricity *e.g.* all metals. If a voltage source (*e.g.* a cell) is applied across the wire of a conductor material, free electrons readily flow through the wire, thus constituting electric current. The best conductors are silver, copper and gold in that order. Since copper is the least expensive out of these materials, it is widely used in electrical and electronic industries.

(*ii*) A substance which has very few free electrons is called an **insulator** of electricity. If a voltage source is applied across the wire of insulator material, practically no current flows through the wire. Most substances including plastics, ceramics, rubber, paper and most liquids and gases fall in this category. Of course, there are many practical uses for insulators in the electrical and electronic industries including wire coatings, safety enclosures and power-line insulators.

(*iii*) There is a third class of substances, called **semiconductors**. As their name implies, they are neither conductors nor insulators. These substances have crystalline structure and contain very few free electrons at room temperature. Therefore, at room temperature, a semiconductor practically behaves as an insulator. However, if suitable controlled impurity is imparted to a semiconductor, it is possible to provide controlled conductivity. Most common semiconductors are silicon, germanium, carbon *etc.* However, *silicon* is the principal material and is widely used in the manufacture of electronic devices (*e.g.* crystal diodes, transistors etc.) and integrated circuits.

1.5. ELECTRIC CURRENT

The flow of free electrons is called *electric current.* The flow of electric current can be beautifully explained by referring to Fig. 1.2. The copper strip has a large number of free electrons. When electric pressure or voltage is applied, then free electrons, being negatively charged, will start moving towards the positive terminal around the circuit as shown in Fig. 1.2. This directed flow of free electrons is called *electric current.*

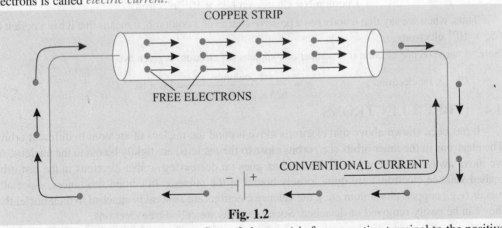

COPPER STRIP

FREE ELECTRONS

CONVENTIONAL CURRENT

Fig. 1.2

The actual direction of current (*i.e.*, flow of electrons) is from negative terminal to the positive terminal through that part of the circuit external to the cell. However, prior to Electron Theory, it was assumed that current flowed from positive terminal to the negative terminal of the cell *via* the circuit. This convention* is so firmly established that it is still in use. This assumed direction is now called *conventional current.*

Unit of Current. The strength of electric current I is the rate of flow of electrons *i.e.*, charge flowing per second.

* This convention was adopted because prior to electron theory, it was believed that electric current was the movement of positive electricity from the positive to the negative terminal. Now, it is well established that electric current is the movement of free electrons which bear negative charge.

$$\therefore \qquad \text{Current, } I = \frac{Q}{t}$$

The charge Q is measured in coulombs and time t in seconds. Therefore, the unit of electric current will be *coulomb/sec* or *ampere*. If $Q = 1$ coulomb, $t = 1$ sec, then $I = 1/1 = 1$ ampere.

One ampere *of current is said to flow through a wire if at any section one coulomb of charge flows in one second.*

Thus, if 5 amperes current is flowing through a wire, it means that 5 coulombs per second flow past any section of the wire.

Note. If n is the number of electrons passing through any section of the wire, then,

$$\text{Current, } I = \frac{Q}{t} = \frac{ne}{t} \quad \text{where } e = 1.6 \times 10^{-19}\,\text{C}$$

Example 1.1. *How much current is flowing through a conductor if 625×10^{16} electrons pass through any cross-section in 1s?*

Solution. Current, $\qquad I = \dfrac{Q}{t} = \dfrac{ne}{t} = \dfrac{(625 \times 10^{16}) \times (1.6 \times 10^{-19})}{1} = \mathbf{1A}$

Example 1.2. *How much current is flowing in a circuit where 1.27×10^{15} electrons move past a given point in 100 ms?*

Solution. Current, $\qquad I = \dfrac{ne}{t} = \dfrac{(1.27 \times 10^{15}) \times (1.6 \times 10^{-19})}{100 \times 10^{-3}}$

$$= 2.03 \times 10^{-3}\,\text{A} = \mathbf{2.03\ mA}$$

Example 1.3. *How long does it take 50 µC of charge to pass a point in a circuit if the current flow is 15 mA?*

Solution. Time, $\qquad t = \dfrac{Q}{I} = \dfrac{50 \times 10^{-6}}{15 \times 10^{-3}} = 3.33 \times 10^{-3}\,s = \mathbf{3.33\ ms}$

Example 1.4. *The current in a certain conductor is 40 mA.*

(i) Find the total charge in coulombs that passes through the conductor in 1.5 s.

(ii) Find the total number of electrons that pass through the conductor in that time.

Solution.

(i) $\qquad\qquad Q = It = (40 \times 10^{-3}) \times (1.5) = 60 \times 10^{-3}\,\text{C} = \mathbf{60\ mC}$

(ii) $\qquad\qquad n = \dfrac{Q}{e} = \dfrac{60 \times 10^{-3}}{1.6 \times 10^{-19}} = \mathbf{3.745 \times 10^{17}}$ **electrons**

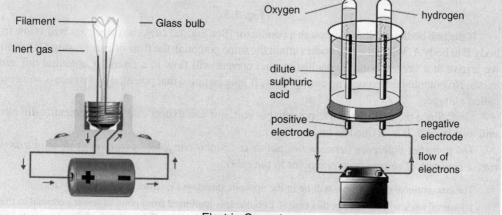

Electric Current

TUTORIAL PROBLEMS

1. Find the current in a conductor when 10^{17} electrons pass through it in 50 ms.   [0.3204 A]
2. How much charge will be delivered per minute by a current flow of 375 mA?   [22.5 C]
3. How long will it take a battery to deliver a 0.5C charge if current flow is 10 mA?   [5 ms]

1.6. ELECTRIC POTENTIAL

When a body is charged, work is done in charging it. This work done is stored in the body in the form of potential energy. The charged body has the capacity to do work by moving other charges either by attraction or repulsion. The ability of the charged body to do work is called electric potential.

The capacity of a charged body to do work is called **electric potential.**

The greater the capacity of a charged body to do work, the greater is its electric potential. Obviously, the work done to charge a body to 1 coulomb will be a measure of its electric potential *i.e.*,

Electric potential, $$V = \frac{\text{Work done}}{\text{Charge}} = \frac{W}{Q}$$

The work done is measured in joules and charge in coulombs. Therefore, the unit of electric potential will be *joule/coulomb* or *volt*. If $W = 1$ joule, $Q = 1$ coulomb, then, $V = 1/1 = 1$ volt.

Hence a body is said to have an electric potential of **1 volt** *if 1 joule of work is done to give it a charge of 1 coulomb.*

Thus, when we say that a body has an electric potential of 5 volts, it means that 5 joules of work has been done to charge the body to 1 coulomb. The greater the joules/coulomb on a charged body, the greater is its electric potential.

1.7. POTENTIAL DIFFERENCE

The difference in the potentials of two charged bodies is called **potential difference.**

If two bodies have different electric potentials, a potential difference exists between the bodies. Consider two bodies A and B having potentials of 5 volts and 3 volts respectively as shown in Fig. 1.3 (*i*). Each coulomb of charge on body A has an energy of 5 joules while each coulomb of charge on body B has an energy of 3 joules. Clearly, body A is at higher potential than the body B.

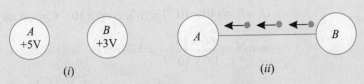

| (*i*) | (*ii*) |

Fig. 1.3

If the two bodies are joined through a conductor [See Fig. 1.3 (*ii*)], then electrons will *flow from body B to body A. When the two bodies attain the same potential, the flow of current stops. Therefore, we arrrive at a very important conclusion that current will flow in a circuit if potential difference exists. No potential difference, no current flow. It may be noted that potential difference is sometimes called voltage.

Unit. Since the unit of electric potential is volt, one can expect that unit of potential difference will also be *volt*. It is defined as under :

The potential difference between two points is **1 volt** *if one joule of work is* ** *done in transferring 1 coulomb of charge from one point to the other.*

* The conventional current flow will be in the opposite direction *i.e.*, from body A to body B.
** 1 joule of work will be done in this case if 1 coulomb is tranferred from point of lower potential to that of higher potential. However, 1 joule of work will be released (as heat) if 1 coulomb of charge moves from a point of higher potential to a point of lower potential.

1.8. MAINTAINING POTENTIAL DIFFERENCE

A device that maintains potential difference between two points is said to develop electromotive force (e.m.f.). A simple example is that of a cell. Fig. 1.4 shows the familiar voltaic cell. It consists of a copper plate (called anode) and a zinc rod (called cathode) immersed in dilute H_2SO_4.

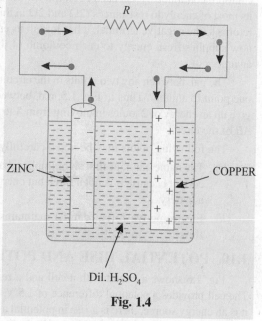

The chemical action taking place in the cell removes electrons from copper plate and transfers them to the zinc rod. This transference of electrons takes place through the agency of dil. H_2SO_4 (called electrolyte). Consequently, the copper plate attains a positive charge of $+Q$ coulombs and zinc rod a charge of $-Q$ coulombs. The chemical action of the cell has done a certain amount of work (say W joules) to do so. Clearly, the potential difference between the two plates will be W/Q volts. If the two plates are joined through a wire, some electrons from zinc rod will be attracted through the wire to copper plate. The chemical action of the cell now transfers an equal amount of electrons from copper plate to zinc rod internally through the cell to maintain original potential difference (*i.e.*, W/Q). This process con-

Fig. 1.4

tinues so long as the circuit is complete or so long as there is chemical energy. The flow of electrons through the external wire from zinc rod to copper plate is the electric current.

Thus potential difference causes current to flow while an e.m.f. maintains the potential difference. Although both e.m.f. and p.d. are measured in volts, they do not mean exactly the same thing.

1.9. CONCEPT OF E.M.F. AND POTENTIAL DIFFERENCE

There is a distinct difference between e.m.f. and potential difference. The e.m.f. of a device, say a battery, is a measure of the energy the battery gives to each coulomb of charge. Thus if a battery supplies 4 joules of energy per coulomb, we say that it has an e.m.f. of 4 volts. The energy given to each coulomb in a battery is due to the chemical action.

The potential difference between two points, say A and B, is a measure of the energy used by one coulomb in moving from A to B. Thus if potential difference between points A and B is 2 volts, it means that each coulomb will give up an energy of 2 joules in moving from A to B.

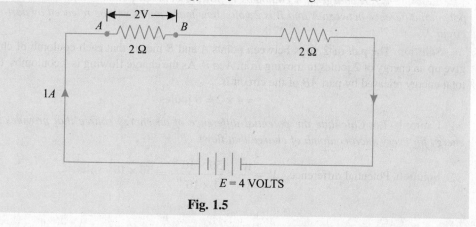

Fig. 1.5

Illustration. The difference between e.m.f. and p.d. can be made more illustrative by referring to Fig. 1.5. Here battery has an e.m.f. of 4 volts. It means that battery supplies 4 joules of energy to each coulomb continuously. As each coulomb travels from the positive terminal of the battery, it gives up its most of energy to resistances (2Ω and 2Ω in this case) and remaining to connecting wires. When it returns to the negative terminal, it has lost all its energy originally supplied by the battery. The battery now supplies fresh energy to each coulomb (4 joules in the present case) to start the journey once again.

The p.d. between any two points in the circuit is the energy used by one coulomb in moving from one point to another. Thus in Fig. 1.5, p.d. between A and B is 2 volts. It means that 1 coulomb will give up an energy of 2 joules in moving from A to B. This energy will be released as heat from the part AB of the circuit.

The following points may be noted carefully :

(*i*) The name e.m.f. at first sight implies that it is a force that causes current to flow. This is not correct because it is not a force but energy supplied to charge by some active device such as a battery.

(*ii*) Electromotive force (e.m.f.) maintains potential difference while p.d. causes current to flow.

1.10. POTENTIAL RISE AND POTENTIAL DROP

Fig. 1.6 shows a circuit with a cell and a resistor. The cell provides a potential difference of 1.5 V. Since it is an energy source, there is a *rise* in potential associated with a cell. The cell's potential difference represents an e.m.f. so that symbol E could be used. The resistor is also associated with a potential difference. Since it is a consumer (converter) of energy, there is a *drop* in potential across the resistor. We can combine the idea of potential rise or drop with the popular term "voltage". It is customary to refer to the potential difference across the cell as a *voltage rise* and to the potential difference across the resistor as a *voltage drop*.

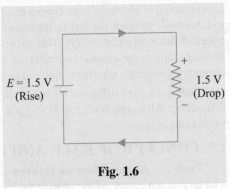

Fig. 1.6

Note. The term voltage refers to a potential difference across two points. There is no such thing as a voltage at one point. In cases where a single point is specified, some reference must be used as the other point. Unless stated otherwise, the ground or common point in any circuit is the reference when specifying a voltage at some other point.

Example 1.5. *A charge of 4 coulombs is flowing between points A and B of a circuit. If the potential difference between A and B is 2 volts, how many joules will be released by part AB of the circuit?*

Solution. The p.d. of 2 volts between points A and B means that each coulomb of charge will give up an energy of 2 joules in moving from A to B. As the charge flowing is 4 coulombs, therefore, total energy released by part AB of the circuit is

$$= 4 \times 2 = 8 \text{ joules}$$

Example 1.6. *Calculate the potential difference of an energy source that provides 50 mJ of energy for every microcoulomb of charge that flows.*

Solution. Potential difference, $V = \dfrac{W}{Q} = \dfrac{50 \times 10^{-3}}{1 \times 10^{-6}} = 50 \times 10^{3}$ **volts**

Example 1.7. *What quantity of charge must be delivered by a battery with a potential difference of 100 V to do 500 J of work?*

Solution. Total charge, $Q = \dfrac{W}{V} = \dfrac{500}{100} = 5\,C$

Example 1.8. *How much work will be done by an electric energy source with a potential difference of 3kV that delivers a current of 1A for 1 minute?*

Solution. We know that 1A of current represents a charge transfer rate of 1C/s. Therefore, the total charge for a period of 1 minute is $Q = It = 1 \times 60 = 60$ C.

Total work done, $W = Q \times V = 60 \times (3 \times 10^3) = 180 \times 10^3 \ J = 180 \ kJ$

TUTORIAL PROBLEMS

1. Calculate the potential difference of an energy source that provides 6.8 J for every milli-coulomb of charge that it delivers.
   [6.8 kV]
2. The potential difference across a battery is 9V. How much charge must it deliver to do 50 J of work?
   [5.56 C]
3. A 300 V energy source delivers 500 mA for 1 hour. How much energy does this represent?
   [540 kJ]

1.11. RESISTANCE

The opposition offered by a substance to the flow of electric current is called resistance.

Since current is the flow of free electrons, resistance is the opposition offered by the substance to the flow of free electrons. This opposition occurs because atoms and molecules of the substance obstruct the flow of these electrons. Certain substances (*e.g.*, metals such as silver, copper, aluminium *etc.*) offer very little opposition to the flow of electric current and are called conductors. On the other hand, those substances which offer high opposition to the flow of electric current (*i.e.*, flow of free electrons) are called insulators *e.g.*, glass, rubber, mica, dry wood *etc.*

It may be noted here that resistance is the electric friction offered by the substance and causes production of heat with the flow of electric current. The moving electrons collide with atoms or molecules of the substance ; each collision resulting in the liberation of minute quantity of heat.

Unit of resistance. The practical unit of resistance is ohm and is represented by the symbol Ω. It is defined as under :

A wire is said to have a resistance of 1 ohm if a p.d. of 1 volt across its ends causes 1 ampere of current to flow through it.

1.12. FACTORS UPON WHICH RESISTANCE DEPENDS

The resistance R of a conductor

(*i*)   is directly proportional to its length (l).

(*ii*)   is inversely proportional to its area of cross-section (a).

(*iii*)   depends upon the nature of material.

(*iv*)   changes with temperature.

From the first three points (leaving temperature for the time being), we have,

$$R \propto \frac{l}{a}$$

or

$$R = \rho \frac{l}{a}$$

where ρ (Greek letter 'Rho') is a constant and is known as *resistivity* or *specific resistance* of the material. Its value depends upon the nature of material.

1.13. SPECIFIC RESISTANCE OR RESISTIVITY

We have seen above that

$$R = \rho \frac{l}{a}$$

If $l = 1m$, $a = 1m^2$, then $R = \rho$

Hence **specific resistance** *of a material is the resistance offered by 1 m length of wire of material having an area of cross-section of 1 m^2 [See Fig. 1.7 (i)].*

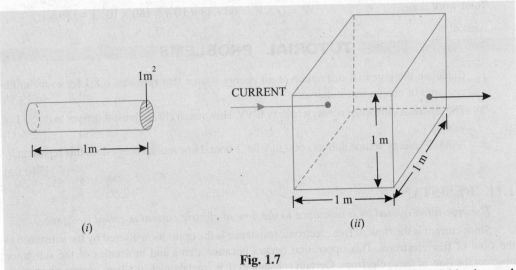

$$\text{(i)} \qquad\qquad\qquad \text{(ii)}$$

Fig. 1.7

Specific resistance can also be defined in another way. Take a cube of the material having each side 1 m. Considering any two opposite faces, the area of cross-section is 1 m^2 and length is 1 m [See Fig. 1.7 (ii)] *i.e.* $l = 1$ m, $a = 1$ m^2.

Hence **specific resistance** *may be defined as the resistance between the opposite faces of a metre cube of the material.*

Unit of resistivity

We know

$$R = \frac{\rho l}{a}$$

or

$$\rho = \frac{R a}{l}$$

In SI units, length is measured in metres and area of x-section in m^2 so that the unit of resistivity will be ohm-m.

$$\text{Unit of } \rho = \frac{\text{ohm} \times \text{m}^2}{\text{m}} = \text{ohm–m}$$

1.14. CONDUCTANCE

Conductance (G) is the reciprocal of resistance.

We know

$$R = \rho \frac{l}{a}$$

∴

$$G = \frac{1}{R} = \frac{1}{\rho} \frac{a}{l}$$

or
$$G = \sigma \frac{a}{l}$$

where σ (Greek letter 'sigma') is called the conductivity or specific conductance of the material. The unit of conductance is mho *i.e.*, ohm spelt backward. A little reflection shows that SI unit of conductivity will be mho/m. Now-a-days, the siemen (S) is used as the unit of conductance and conductivity is expressed as siemen/metre.

Example 1.9. *If 10 metres of manganin-wire, 0.13 cm in diameter has a resistance of 3.4 ohms, find the specific resistance of the material.*

Solution. Length of wire,
$$l = 10 \text{ m} = 1000 \text{ cm}$$

Area of wire,
$$a = \frac{\pi}{4}d^2 = \frac{\pi}{4}(0.13)^2 = 132.8 \times 10^{-4} \text{ cm}^2$$

Resistance of wire,
$$R = 3.4 \ \Omega$$

Resistivity of wire,
$$\rho = ?$$

We know
$$R = \rho\frac{l}{a}$$

or
$$\rho = \frac{Ra}{l} = \frac{3.4 \times 132.8 \times 10^{-4}}{1000} = 45 \times 10^{-6} \ \Omega \text{ cm}$$

Example 1.10. *Find the resistance of 1000 metres of a copper wire 25 sq. mm in cross-section. The resistance of copper is 1/58 ohm per metre length and 1 sq-mm cross-section. What will be the resistance of another wire of the same material, three times as long and one-half the cross-sectional area?*

Solution. For the first case,
$$R_1 = ?; \ a_1 = 25 \text{ mm}^2; \ l_1 = 1000 \text{ m}$$

For the second case,
$$R_2 = 1/58\Omega; \ a_2 = 1 \text{ mm}^2; \ l_2 = 1\text{m}$$
$$R_1 = \rho(l_1/a_1) ; \ R_2 = \rho(l_2/a_2)$$

∴
$$\frac{R_1}{R_2} = \frac{l_1}{l_2} \times \frac{a_2}{a_1} = \left(\frac{1000}{1}\right) \times \left(\frac{1}{25}\right) = 40$$

or
$$R_1 = 40 \ R_2 = 40 \times \frac{1}{58} = \frac{20}{29} \ \Omega$$

For the third case,
$$R_3 = ? ; a_3 = a_1/2 ; \ l_3 = 3l_1$$

∴
$$\frac{R_3}{R_1} = \left(\frac{l_3}{l_1}\right) \times \left(\frac{a_1}{a_3}\right) = (3) \times (2) = 6$$

or
$$R_3 = 6R_1 = 6 \times \frac{20}{29} = \frac{120}{29} \ \Omega$$

Example 1.11. *A length of wire has a resistance of 4.5 ohms. Find the resistance of another wire of the same material three times as long and twice the cross-sectional area.*

Solution. For the first case,
$$R_1 = 4.5 \ \Omega; \ l_1 = l; a_1 = a$$

For the second case,
$$R_2 = ? ; \ l_2 = 3l; \ a_2 = 2a$$

Now
$$R_1 = \rho\frac{l_1}{a_1}; \ R_2 = \rho\frac{l_2}{a_2}$$

∴
$$\frac{R_2}{R_1} = \left[\frac{l_2}{l_1}\right] \times \left[\frac{a_1}{a_2}\right] = \left[\frac{3l}{l}\right] \times \left[\frac{a}{2a}\right] = 1.5$$

or
$$R_2 = 1.5 \ R_1 = 1.5 \times 4.5 = 6.75 \ \Omega$$

Example 1.12. *10 c.c. of copper are (i) drawn into a wire 100 metres long (ii) rolled into a square sheet of 10 cm side. Find the reistance of wire and the resistance between opposite faces of the sheet if specific resistance of copper is 1.7×10^{-6} Ω–cm.*

Solution. (*i*) As seen from Fig. 1.8 (*i*), in this case,

Length of wire, $\qquad\qquad\qquad\qquad\qquad\qquad l = 100 \text{ m} = 10^4 \text{ cm}$

Area of cross-section, $\qquad\qquad\qquad a = \dfrac{\text{volume}}{\text{length}} = \dfrac{10}{10^4} = 0.001 \text{ cm}^2$

∴ Resistance of wire, $\qquad\qquad\qquad R = \dfrac{\rho l}{a} = \dfrac{1.7 \times 10^{-6} \times 10^4}{0.001} = 17 \text{ Ω}$

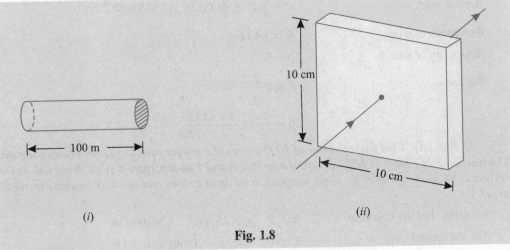

(*i*) $\qquad\qquad\qquad\qquad\qquad\qquad\qquad\qquad\qquad\qquad\qquad\qquad$ (*ii*)

Fig. 1.8

(*ii*) As seen from Fig. 1.8 (*ii*), in this case,

Area of cross-section, $a = 10 \times 10 = 100 \text{ cm}^2$

Length (i.e., thickness), $l = \text{volume/area} = 10/100 = 0.1 \text{ cm}$

∴ Resistance between opposite faces of square sheet is

$$R = \rho \frac{l}{a} = 1.7 \times 10^{-6} \times \frac{0.1}{100} = 17 \times 10^{-10} \text{ Ω}$$

Example 1.13. *A copper wire of diameter 1 cm had a resistance of 0.15 Ω. It was drawn under pressure so that its diameter was reduced to 50%. What is the new resistance of the wire?*

Solution. Area of wire before drawing, $a_1 = \dfrac{\pi}{4}(1)^2 = 0.785 \text{ cm}^2$

Area of wire after drawing, $\qquad\qquad\qquad a_2 = \dfrac{\pi}{4}(0.5)^2 = 0.196 \text{ cm}^2$

As the volume of wire remains the same before and after drawing,

∴ $\qquad\qquad\qquad\qquad a_1 l_1 = a_2 l_2 \text{ or } l_2/l_1 = a_1/a_2 = 0.785/0.196 = 4$

For the first case, $\qquad\qquad R_1 = 0.15 \text{ Ω}; \ a_1 = 0.785 \text{ cm}^2; \ l_1 = l$

For the second case, $\qquad\qquad R_2 = ?; \ a_2 = 0.196 \text{ cm}^2; \ l_2 = 4l$

Now $\qquad\qquad\qquad\qquad\qquad R_1 = \rho \dfrac{l_1}{a_1}; \ R_2 = \rho \dfrac{l_2}{a_2}$

$$\therefore \qquad \frac{R_2}{R_1} = \left(\frac{l_2}{l_1}\right) \times \left(\frac{a_1}{a_2}\right) = (4) \times (4) = 16$$

or $\qquad R_2 = 16\,R_1 = 16 \times 0.15 = \mathbf{2.4\ \Omega}$

Example 1.14. *A rectangular metal strip has the dimensions* $x = 10$ cm, $y = 0.5$ cm *and* $z = 0.2$ cm. *Determine the ratio of the resistances* R_x, R_y *and* R_z *between the respective pairs of opposite faces.*

Solution. $\qquad R_x : R_y : R_z = \dfrac{\rho x}{yz} : \dfrac{\rho y}{zx} : \dfrac{\rho z}{xy}$

$$= \frac{10}{0.5 \times 0.2} : \frac{0.5}{0.2 \times 10} : \frac{0.2}{10 \times 0.5}$$

$$= \frac{10}{0.1} : \frac{1}{4} : 0.04$$

$$= 2500 : 6.25 : 1$$

Example 1.15. *Calculate the resistance of a copper tube 0.5 cm thick and 2 m long. The external diameter is 10 cm. Given that resistance of copper wire 1m long and 1mm^2 in cross-section is 1/58 Ω.*

Solution. External diameter, $\qquad D = 10$ cm

Internal diameter, $\qquad\qquad\quad d = 10 - 2 \times 0.5 = 9$ cm

Area of cross-section, $\qquad\quad a = \dfrac{\pi}{4}\left(D^2 - d^2\right) = \dfrac{\pi}{4}\left[(10)^2 - (9)^2\right]$ cm^2

$$= \frac{\pi}{4}\left[(10)^2 - (9)^2\right] \times 100 \text{ mm}^2$$

$\therefore$ Resistance of copper tube $\quad = \dfrac{\rho l}{a} = \dfrac{1}{58} \times \dfrac{\text{length in metres}}{\text{area of } X\text{-section in mm}^2}$

$$= \frac{1}{58} \times \frac{2}{\dfrac{\pi}{4}\left[(10)^2 - (9)^2\right] \times 100}$$

$$= 23.14 \times 10^{-6}\ \Omega = \mathbf{23.14\ \mu\Omega}$$

Example 1.16. *A copper wire is stretched so that its length is increased by 0.1%. What is the percentage change in its resistance?*

Solution. $\qquad\qquad\qquad\qquad R = \rho\,\dfrac{l}{a}\ ; \quad R' = \rho\,\dfrac{l'}{a'}$

Now $\qquad\qquad\qquad\qquad\quad l' = l + \dfrac{0.1}{100} \times l = 1.001\,l$

As the volume remains the same, $al = a'l'$.

$\therefore \qquad\qquad\qquad\qquad\quad a' = a\dfrac{l}{l'} = \dfrac{a}{1.001}$

$\therefore \qquad\qquad\qquad\quad \dfrac{R'}{R} = \left(\dfrac{l'}{l}\right) \times \left(\dfrac{a}{a'}\right) = (1.001) \times (1.001) = 1.002$

or $\qquad\qquad\qquad\qquad \dfrac{R' - R}{R} = 0.002$

$\therefore \qquad$ Percentage increase $\quad = \dfrac{R' - R}{R} \times 100 = 0.002 \times 100 = \mathbf{0.2\ \%}$

Example 1.17. *A lead wire and an iron wire are connected in parallel. Their respective specific resistances are in the ratio 49 : 24. The former carries 80% more current than the latter and the latter 47% longer than the former. Determine the ratio of their cross-sectional areas.*

Solution. Let us represent lead and iron by suffixes 1 and 2 respectively. Then as per the conditions of the problem, we have,

$$\frac{\rho_1}{\rho_2} = \frac{49}{24} \; ; \; I_1 = 1.8 \, I_2 \; ; \; l_2 = 1.47 \, l_1$$

Now

$$R_1 = \rho_1 \frac{l_1}{a_1} \; ; \; R_2 = \rho_2 \frac{l_2}{a_2}$$

$$I_1 = \frac{V}{R_1} \; \text{and} \; I_2 = \frac{V}{R_2}$$

∴

$$\frac{I_2}{I_1} = \frac{R_1}{R_2} = \frac{\rho_1 l_1}{a_1} \times \frac{a_2}{\rho_2 l_2} = \left(\frac{\rho_1}{\rho_2}\right) \times \left(\frac{l_1}{l_2}\right) \times \left(\frac{a_2}{a_1}\right)$$

or

$$\frac{1}{1.8} = \frac{49}{24} \times \frac{1}{1.47} \times \frac{a_2}{a_1}$$

∴

$$\frac{a_2}{a_1} = \frac{1}{1.8} \times \frac{24}{49} \times 1.47 = 0.4$$

TUTORIAL PROBLEMS

1. Calculate the resistance of 915 metres length of a wire having a uniform cross-sectional area of 0.77 cm^2 if the wire is made of copper having a resistivity of 1.7×10^{-6} Ω cm.
   [0.08 Ω]

2. A wire of length 1 m has a resistance of 2 ohms. What is the resistance of second wire, whose specific resistance is double of the first, if the length of wire is 3 metres and the diameter is double of the first?
   [3 Ω]

3. A rectangular copper strip is 20 cm long, 0.1 cm wide and 0.4 cm thick. Determine the resistance between (i) opposite ends (ii) opposite sides. The resistivity of copper is 1.7×10^{-6} Ω cm.
   [(i) 0.85×10^{-4} Ω (ii) 0.212×10^{-6} Ω]

4. A cube of a material of side 1 cm has a resistance of 0.001 Ω between its opposite faces. If the same material has a length of 9 cm and a uniform cross-sectional area 1 cm^2, what will be the resistance of this length?
   [0.009 Ω]

5. An aluminium wire 10 metres long and 2 mm in diameter is connected in parallel with a copper wire 6 metres long. A total current of 2 A is passed through the combination and it is found that current through the aluminium wire is 1.25 A. Calculate the diameter of copper wire. Specific resistance of copper is 1.6×10^{-6} Ω cm and that of aluminium is 2.6×10^{-6} Ω cm.
   [0.94 mm]

   Hint. As the currents are inversely proportional to the resistances through which they flow,

   ∴ Resistance of copper = $\frac{5}{3} \times$ Resistance of aluminium

1.15. EFFECT OF TEMPERATURE ON RESISTANCE

In general, the resistance of a material changes with the change in temperature. The effect of temperature upon resistance varies according to the type of material as discussed below :

(i) The resistance of pure metals (e.g., copper, aluminium) increases with the increase of temperature. The change in resistance is fairly regular for normal range of temperatures so that temperature/resistance graph is a straight line as shown in Fig. 1.9 (for *copper). Since the resistance of metals increases with the rise in temperature, they have *positive temperature co-efficient of resistance.*

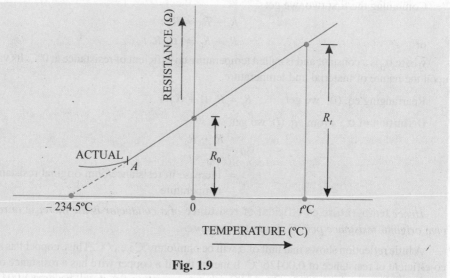

Fig. 1.9

(*ii*) The resistance of electrolytes, insulators (*e.g.*, glass, mica, rubber *etc.*) and semiconductors (*e.g.*, germanium, silicon etc.) decreases with the increase in temperature. Hence these materials have *negative temperature co-efficient of resistance.*

(*iii*) The resistance of alloys increases with the rise in temperature but this increase is very small and irregular. For some high resistance alloys (*e.g.*, Eureka, manganin, constantan *etc.*), the change in resistance is practically negligible over a wide range of temperatures.

The above behaviour of materials can be explained as follows. When the temperature of a substance increases, the molecules vibrate more rapidly, impeding the movement of free electrons through the substance. This causes the resistance of the substance to rise. With the rise in temperature of a conductor (*e.g.*, metals), there is no increase in the number of free electrons and the sole effect of temperature rise is to increase resistance due to the increased molecular vibration. On the other hand, a temperature rise in insulators and semiconductors creates many more free electrons than existed in the cooler state. Often this increase in the number of free electrons more than offsets the interference to the drift movement caused by the increased molecular activity. Hence, the reisistance of such materials decreases with the increase in temperature. In case of alloys, these two effects alomost cancel each other so that there is negligible increase in resistance due to rise in temperature.

1.16. TEMPERATURE CO-EFFICIENT OF RESISTANCE

Consider a conductor having resistance R_0 at 0°C and R_t at t°C. It has been found that in the normal range of temperatures, the increase in resistance (*i.e.*, $R_t - R_0$)

(*i*) is directly proportional to the initial resistance *i.e.*,

$$R_t - R_0 \propto R_0$$

* Fig. 1.9 shows temperature/resistance graph for copper which is a straight line. If this line is extended backward, it would cut the temperature axis at – 234.5° C. However, in actual practice, the curve departs (point A) from the straight line path at very low temperatures.

(ii) is directly proportional to the rise in temperature *i.e.*,

$$R_t - R_0 \propto t$$

(iii) depends upon the nature of material.

Combining the first two, we get,

$$R_t - R_0 \propto R_0\, t$$

or

$$R_t - R_0 =^* \alpha_0\, R_0\, t \qquad\qquad\qquad ...(i)$$

where α_0 is a constant and is called temperature co-efficient of resistance at 0°C. Its value depends upon the nature of material and temperature.

Rearranging eq. (*i*), we get, $\qquad R_t = R_0\, (1 + \alpha_0 t) \qquad\qquad\qquad ...(ii)$

Definition of α_0. From eq. (*i*), we get,

$$\alpha_0 = \frac{R_t - R_0}{R_0 \times t}$$

= Increase in resistance/ohm original resistance/°C rise in temperature

Hence **temperature co-efficient of resistance** *of a conductor is the increase in resistance per ohm original resistance per °C rise in temperature.*

A little reflection shows that unit of α will be ohm/ohm/°C i.e., /°C. Thus, copper has a temperature co-efficient of resistance of 0.00426/°C. It means that if a copper wire has a resistance of 1 Ω at 0°C, then it will increase by 0.00426 Ω for 1 °C rise in temperature *i.e.*, it will become 1.00426 Ω at 1 °C. Similarly, if temperature is raised to 10°C, then resistance will become $1 + 10 \times 0.00426 = 1.0426$ ohms.

If a conductor has a resistance R_0, R_1 and R_2 at 0°C, t_1 °C and t_2 °C respectively, then,

$$R_1 = R_0\, (1 + \alpha_0 t_1)\ ; \qquad R_2 = R_0\, (1 + \alpha_0 t_2)$$

∴

$$\frac{R_2}{R_1} = \frac{1 + \alpha_0 t_2}{1 + \alpha_0 t_1}$$

1.17. GRAPHICAL DETERMINATION OF α

The value of temperature co-efficient of resistance can also be determined graphically from temperature/resistance graph of the conductor. Fig. 1.10 shows the temperature/resistance graph for a conductor. The graph is a straight line AX as is the case with all conductors. The resistance of the conductor is R_0 (represented by OA) at 0°C and it becomes R_t at t°C. By definition,

$$\alpha_0 = \frac{R_t - R_0}{R_0 \times t}$$

But $\qquad R_t - R_0 = BC$

and $\qquad t =$ rise in temp. $= AB$

∴

$$\alpha_0 = \frac{BC}{R_0 \times AB}$$

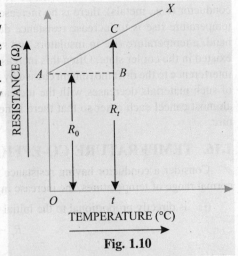

Fig. 1.10

---

* It will be shown in Art. 1.18 that value of α depends upon temperature. Therefore, it is referred to the original temperature i.e., 0°C in this case. Hence, the symbol α_0.

But BC/AB is the slope of temperature/resistance graph.

$$\therefore \qquad \alpha_0 = \frac{\text{Slope of temp./resistance graph}}{\text{Original resistance}}$$

Hence, **temperature co-efficient of resistance** *of a conductor at 0°C is the slope of temp./resistance graph divided by resistance at 0°C (i.e., R_0).*

The following points may be particularly noted :

(*i*) The value of α depends upon temperature. At any temperature, α can be calculated by using eq. (*i*).

Thus $\qquad \alpha_0 = \dfrac{\text{Slope}^* \text{ of temp./resistance graph}}{R_0}$

and $\qquad \alpha_t = \dfrac{\text{Slope of temp./resistance graph}}{R_t}$

(*ii*) The value of α_0 is maximum and it decreases as the temperature is increased. This is clear from the fact that the slope of temperature/resistance graph is constant and R_0 has the minimum value.

1.18. TEMPERATURE CO-EFFICIENT AT VARIOUS TEMPERATURES

Consider a conductor having resistances R_0 and R_1 at temperatures 0°C and t_1°C respectively. Let α_0 and α_1 be the temperature co-efficients of the conductor at 0°C and t$_1$°C respectively. It is desired to establish the relationship between α_1 and α_0. Fig. 1.11 shows the temperature/resistance graph of the conductor. As proved in Art. 1.17,

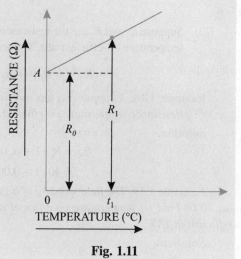

Fig. 1.11

$$\alpha_0 = \frac{\text{Slope of graph}}{R_0}$$

$\therefore$ Slope of graph $= \alpha_0 R_0$

Similarly, $\qquad \alpha_1 = \dfrac{\text{Slope of graph}}{R_1}$

or Slope of graph $= \alpha_1 R_1$

Since the slope of temperature/resistance graph is constant,

$$\therefore \qquad \alpha_0 R_0 = \alpha_1 R_1$$

or $\qquad \alpha_1 = \dfrac{\alpha_0 R_0}{R_1}$

$$= \frac{\alpha_0 R_0}{R_0 (1 + \alpha_0 t_1)} \qquad\qquad [\because R_1 = R_0 (1 + \alpha_0 t_1)]$$

$$\therefore \qquad \alpha_1 = \frac{\alpha_0}{1 + \alpha_0 t_1} \qquad\qquad\qquad ...(i)$$

* The slope of temp/resistance graph of a conductor is always constant (slope of a straight line).

Similarly,* $\qquad\qquad \alpha_2 = \dfrac{\alpha_0}{1 + \alpha_0 t_2}$ ...(ii)

Subtracting the reciprocal of Eq. (i) from the reciprocal of Eq. (ii),

$$\frac{1}{\alpha_2} - \frac{1}{\alpha_1} = \frac{1 + \alpha_0 t_2}{\alpha_0} - \frac{1 + \alpha_0 t_1}{\alpha_0} = t_2 - t_1$$

$\therefore \qquad\qquad \alpha_2 = \dfrac{1}{\dfrac{1}{\alpha_1} + (t_2 - t_1)}$ ...(iii)

Eq. (i) gives the relation between α_1 and α_0 while Eq. (iii) gives the ralation between α_2 and α_1.

1.19. SUMMARY OF TEMPERATURE CO-EFFICIENT RELATIONS

(i) If R_0 and α_0 are the resistance and temperature co-efficient of a conductor at 0°C, then its resistance R_t at t°C is given by ;

$R_t = R_0 (1 + \alpha_0 t)$

(ii) If α_0, α_1 and α_2 are the temperature co-efficients at 0°C, t_1°C and t_2°C respectively, then,

$$\alpha_1 = \frac{\alpha_0}{1 + \alpha_0 t_1} \quad ; \quad \alpha_2 = \frac{\alpha_0}{1 + \alpha_0 t_2} \quad ; \quad \alpha_2 = \frac{1}{\dfrac{1}{\alpha_1} + (t_2 - t_1)}$$

(iii) Suppose R_1 and R_2 are the resistances of a conductor at t_1°C and t_2°C respectively. If α_1 is the temperature co-efficient at t_1°C, then,

$$R_2** = R_1 [1 + \alpha_1 (t_2 - t_1)]$$

Example 1.18. *A copper coil has a resistance of 40 ohms at 0°C. Find the resistance of the coil at 50°C. Resistance temperature co-efficient of copper is 0.0043/°C at 0°C.*

Solution.

$$R_{50} = R_0 (1 + \alpha_0 t)$$
$$= 40 (1 + 0.0043 \times 50) = 48.6 \ \Omega$$

Example 1.19. *The field winding of a generator has a resistance of 12.7 Ω at 18°C and 14.3 Ω at 50°C. Find (i) temperature co-efficient at 0°C (ii) resistance at 0°C, and (iii) temperature co-efficient at 18°C.*

Solution.

(i) $\qquad\qquad R_{18} = R_0 (1 + \alpha_0 \times 18)$

$\qquad\qquad R_{50} = R_0 (1 + \alpha_0 \times 50)$

- -

* $\alpha_0 R_0 = \alpha_2 R_2$, where R_2 is the resistance at t_2 °C.

or $\qquad\qquad \alpha_2 = \dfrac{\alpha_0 R_0}{R_2} = \dfrac{\alpha_0 R_0}{R_0 (1 + \alpha_0 t_2)} = \dfrac{\alpha_0}{1 + \alpha_0 t_2}$

** Slope of graph, $\tan \theta = R_0 \alpha_0 = R_1 \alpha_1 = R_2 \alpha_2$

Increase in resistance as temperature is raised from t_1°C to t_2°C

$\qquad\qquad = \tan \theta (t_2 - t_1) = R_1 \alpha_1 (t_2 - t_1)$

$\therefore$ Resistance at t_2°C, $R_2 = R_1 + R_1 \alpha_1 (t_2 - t_1) = R_1 [1 + \alpha_1 (t_2 - t_1)]$

or $$\frac{R_{18}}{R_{50}} = \frac{1 + 18\alpha_0}{1 + 50\alpha_0}$$

or $$\frac{12.7}{14.3} = \frac{1 + 18\alpha_0}{1 + 50\alpha_0}$$

On solving, $\alpha_0 = \frac{1}{236}/^\circ C$

(ii) $$R_{18} = R_0 (1 + \alpha_0 \times 18)$$

∴ $$R_0 = \frac{R_{18}}{1 + 18\alpha_0} = \frac{12.7}{1 + 18 \times (1/236)} = 11.8 \ \Omega$$

(iii) $$\alpha_{18} = \frac{\alpha_0}{1 + \alpha_0 \times 18} = \frac{1}{(1/\alpha_0) + 18} = \frac{1}{236 + 18} = \frac{1}{254}/^\circ C$$

Example 1.20. *A certain length of aluminium wire has a resistance of 28.3 Ω at 20°C. What is its resistance at 60°C? The temperature co-efficient of resistance of aluminium is 0.00403/°C at 20°C.*

Solution.

$$R_{60} = R_{20}[1 + \alpha_{20}(t_2 - t_1)]$$

$$= 28.3[1 + 0.00403(60 - 20)] = 32.86\Omega$$

Example 1.21. *The shunt winding of a motor has a resistance of 80 Ω at 15°C. Find its resistance at 50° C. Resistance temperature co-efficient of copper is 0.004/°C at 0°C.*

Solution.

$$R_{15} = R_0 (1 + \alpha_0 \times 15)$$

∴ $$R_0 = \frac{R_{15}}{1 + 15\alpha_0} = \frac{80}{1 + 15 \times 0.004} = 75.47 \ \Omega$$

Now, $$R_{50} = R_0 (1 + \alpha_0 \times 50)$$

$$= 75.47 (1 + 0.004 \times 50) = 90.56 \ \Omega$$

Example 1.22. *The resistance of the field coils of a dynamo is 173 Ω at 16°C. After working for 6 hours on full load, the resistance of the coil increases to 212 Ω. Calculate the mean temperature rise of field coils. Assume temperature co-efficient of resistance of copper to be 0.00426/°C at 0°C.*

Solution. Let *t*°C be the final temperature.

∴ $$\frac{R_{16}}{R_t} = \frac{R_0(1 + \alpha_0 \times 16)}{R_0(1 + \alpha_0 \times t)}$$

or $$\frac{173}{212} = \frac{1 + 0.00426 \times 16}{1 + 0.00426 \times t}$$

or $$0.816 = \frac{1.068}{1 + 0.00426 \ t}$$

∴ $$t = 72.5°C$$

Rise in temperature = $t - 16 = 72.5 - 16 = 56.5°C$

Example 1.23. *The field circuit of a 440V shunt motor took 2.3 A when first switched on, the ambient temperature being 17°C. Later the field current was found to remain steady at 1.9 A. Determine the temperature of the winding, assuming $\alpha_0 = 1/234.5$ per °C at 0°C.*

Solution. Let $t°C$ be the final temperature of the winding.

$$R_{17} = 440/2.3 = 191.3 \ \Omega \ ; \quad R_t = 440/1.9 = 231.5 \ \Omega$$

$$\therefore \qquad \frac{R_t}{R_{17}} = \frac{R_0 \, (1 + \alpha_0 \times t)}{R_0 \, (1 + \alpha_0 \times 17)}$$

or

$$\frac{231.5}{191.3} = \frac{1 + (t/234.5)}{1 + (17/234.5)}$$

$$\therefore \qquad t = 69.85° \ C$$

Example 1.24. *The filament of a 60-watt, 230 V lamp has a normal working temperature of 2000°C. Find the current flowing in the filament at the instant of switching, when the lamp is cold. Assume the temperature of cold lamp to be 15°C and $\alpha_{15} = 0.005/°C$.*

Solution. Resistance of lamp at 2000°C, $R_{2000} = V^2/W = (230)^2/60 = 881.67 \ \Omega$

$$R_{2000} = R_{15} \, [1 + \alpha_{15} \, (2000 - 15)]$$

$$\therefore \qquad R_{15} = \frac{R_{2000}}{1 + 0.005 \, (1985)} = \frac{881.67}{10.925} = 80.7 \ \Omega$$

∴ Current taken by cold lamp (*i.e.,* at the time of switching) is

$$I = V/R_{15} = 230/80.7 = \textbf{2.85 A}$$

Example 1.25. *Two coils connected in series have resistances of 600 Ω and 300 Ω and temperature co-efficients of 0.001 and 0.004 respectively at 20°C. Find the resistance of combination at 50°C. What is the effective temperature co-efficient of the combination at 20°C?*

Solution.

Resistance of 600 Ω coil at 50°C	$= 600 \, [1 + \alpha_{20} \, (50 - 20)]$
	$= 600 \, [1 + 0.001 \times 30] = 618 \ \Omega$
Resistance of 300 Ω coil at 50° C	$= 300 \, [1 + \alpha_{20} \, (50 - 20)]$
	$= 300 \, [1 + 0.004 \times 30] = 336 \ \Omega$

∴ Resistance of the combination at 50°C $= 618 + 336 = \textbf{954 } \Omega$

Let β be the temperature co-efficient of the combination at 20°C. Since the equivalent resistance of the combination is 954 Ω and 900 Ω at 50°C and 20°C respectively,

$$\therefore \qquad 954 = 900 \, [1 + \beta \, (50 - 20)]$$

or

$$954/900 = 1 + 30 \, \beta$$

$$\therefore \qquad \beta = \textbf{0.002/°C}$$

Example 1.26. *Two materials, A and B, have resistance temperature coefficients of 0.004 and 0.0004 respectively at a given temperature. In what proportion must A and B be joined in series to produce a circuit having a temperature coefficient of 0.001?*

Solution. Let the resistance of A be 1Ω and that of B be $x\Omega$ *i.e.* $R_A = 1\Omega$ and $R_B = x\Omega$.

Resistance of series combination $= R_A + R_B = (1 + x) \ \Omega$

Suppose the temperature rises by $t°C$.

Resistance of series combination at the raised teimperature

$$= (1 + x) \, (1 + 0.001 \, t) \qquad \qquad ...(i)$$

Resistance of A at the raised temperature

$$= 1 \, (1 + 0.004 \, t) \qquad \qquad ...(ii)$$

Resistance of B at the raised temperature

$$= x \, (1 + 0.0004 \, t) \qquad \qquad ...(iii)$$

As per the conditions of the problem, we have,

$$(ii) + (iii) = (i)$$

or $$1 (1 + 0.004\ t) + x (1 + 0.0004\ t) = (1 + x) (1 + 0.001\ t)$$

or $$0.004\ t + 0.0004\ t\ x = (1 + x) \times 0.001\ t$$

Dividing by t and multiplying throughout by 10^4, we have,

$$40 + 4x = 10 (1 + x)$$

$$\therefore \qquad x = 5$$

$$\therefore \qquad R_A : R_B = 1 : 5$$

i.e. R_B should be 5 times R_A.

Example 1.27. *Two conductors, one of copper and the other of iron, are connected in parallel and carry equal currents at 25°C. What proportion of current will pass through each if the temperature is raised to 100°C? The temperature co-efficients of resistance at 0°C are 0.0043/°C and 0.0063/°C for copper and iron respectively.*

Solution. Since copper and iron conductors carry equal currents at 25°C, their resistances are the same at this temperature. Let their resistance be R ohms at 25°C. If R_1 and R_2 are the resistances of copper and iron conductors respectively at 100° C, then,

$$R_1 = R [1 + 0.0043 (100 - 25)] = 1.3225\ R$$

$$R_2 = R [1 + 0.0063 (100 - 25)] = 1.4725\ R$$

If I is the total current at 100°C, then ,

$$\text{Current in copper conductor} = I \times \frac{R_2}{R_1 + R_2} = I \times \frac{1.4725\ R}{1.3225\ R + 1.4725\ R} = 0.5268\ I$$

$$\text{Current in iron conductor} = I \times \frac{R_1}{R_1 + R_2} = I \times \frac{1.3225\ R}{1.3225\ R + 1.4725\ R} = 0.4732\ I$$

Therefore, at 100°C, the copper conductor will carry **52.68%** of total current and the remaining **47.32%** will be carried by iron conductor.

TUTORIAL PROBLEMS

1. A platinum coil has a resistance of 3.146 Ω at 40°C and 3.767 Ω at 100°C. Find the resistance at 0°C and the temperature co-efficient of resistance at 40°C.
   [2.732 Ω; 1/280 per °C]

2. A copper coil has a resistance of 0.4 Ω at 12°C. Find its resistance at 52°C. Resistance-temperature co-efficient of copper is given to be 0.004/°C at 0°C. [0.4612 Ω]

3. A copper coil has a resistance of 50 Ω at 15°C and 58 Ω at 55° C. Calculate the temperature co-efficient of resistance at 0°C. [1/235 per°C]

4. The field coils of a shunt motor have resistance of 45 Ω at 20°C. Find the average temperature of the winding at the end of the run when the resistance is increased to 48.5 Ω. Temperature co-efficient of resistance is 0.004/°C at 0°C. [41°C]

5. A coil which has an initial temperature of 20°C, is connected to a 180-V supply and the initial current is found to be 4A. Sometime later, the current is found to have decreased to 3.4A, the supply voltage being unchanged at 180 V. Determine the temperature rise of the coil. Assume the temperature co-efficient of copper to be 0.0043/°C at 0°C. [44.6°C]

6. A nichrome heater is operated at 1500°C. What is the percentage increassse in its resistance over that at room temperature (20°C)? Temperature co-efficient of resistance of nichrome is 0.00016/°C at 20° C. [23.6%]

7. A copper coil has a resistance of 200 Ω at 80°C. Find the resistance at 20°C. The tempera-ture co-efficient of resistance of copper is 0.0039/°C at 20°C. [162 Ω]

8. A piece of resistance wire 15.6 m long and of cross-sectional area 12 mm² at a temperature of 0°C passes a current of 7.9 A when connected to a *d.c.* supply at 240 V. Calculate (*i*) resistivity of wire (*ii*) the current which will flow when the temperature rises to 55°C. Temperature co-efficient of resistance of wire is 0.00029/°C.
    [(*i*) 23.37 × 10⁻⁶ Ω m; (*ii*) 7.78 A]

9. When working normally, the temperature of the filament in a 230 V, 150 W gas-filled tung-sten lamp is 2750°C. Assuming a room temperature of 16°C, calculate (*i*) the normal current taken by the lamp (*ii*) the current taken at the moment of switching on. Temperature co-efficient of tungsten is 0.0047/°C. [(*i*) 0.652 A; (*ii*) 8.45 A]

10. The field coil of a motor has a resistance of 250 Ω at 15°C. By how much will the resistance increase if the motor attains an average temperature of 45°C when running? Take $\alpha_0 = 0.00428/°C$. [30 Ω]

1.20. OHM'S LAW

The relationship between voltage (*V*), the current (*I*) and resistance (*R*) in a d.c. circuit was first discovered by German scientist George Simon Ohm. This relationship is called Ohm's law and may be stated as under :

The ratio of potential difference (V) between the ends of a conductor to the current (I) flowing between them is constant, provided the physical conditions (e.g., temperature etc.) do not change i.e.

$$\frac{V}{I} = \text{Constant} = R$$

where *R* is the resistance of the conductor between the two points considered.

For example, if in Fig. 1.12, the voltage between points *A* and *B* is *V* volts and current flowing is *I* amperes, then *V/I* will be constant and equal to *R*, the resistance between points *A* and *B*. If the voltage is doubled up, the current will also be doubled up, so that the ratio *V/I* remains con-stant. It may be noted here that if voltage is mea-sured in volts and current in amperes, then re-sistance will be in *ohms. Ohm's law can be expressed in three forms *viz.*

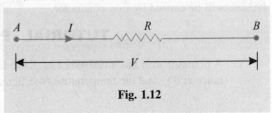

Fig. 1.12

$$I = V/R \; ; \quad V = IR \; ; \quad R = V/I$$

Example 1.28. *A battery has an e.m.f. of 12.8 volts and supplies a current of 3.2 A. What is the resistance of the circuit? How many coulombs leave the battery in 5 minutes?*

Solution.

Circuit resistance, $R = V/I = 12.8/3.2 = 4\ \Omega$

Charge flowing in 5 minutes = current × time in seconds

$$= 3.2 \times 5 \times 60 = 960 \text{ C}$$

Example 1.29. *A metal filament lamp takes 0.3A at 230V. If the voltage is reduced to 115 V, will the current be halved? Explain your answer.*

Solution. No. It is because Ohm's law is applicable only if the resistance of the circuit does not change. In the present case, when voltage is reduced from 230 V to 115 V, the temperature of the lamp

_____

* The unit of resistance (i.e., ohm) was named in honour of George Simon Ohm.

will decrease too much, resulting in an enormous decrease of lamp resistance. Consequently, Ohm's law ($I = V/R$) cannot be applied. To give an idea to the reader, the hot resistance (*i.e.,* at normal operating temperature) of an incandescent lamp is more than 10 times its cold resistance.

Example 1.30. *An incandescent lamp has a resistance of 10 Ω when not burning. When burning with a voltage of 120 V, its resistance is 144 Ω. Find the current at the instant of switching and the normal current when burning. What is the wattage of the lamp?*

Solution.

Current at the instant of switching, $I_1 = V/R_1 = 120/10 =$ **12 A**

Normal current when burning, $I_2 = V/R_2 = 120/144 =$ **0.833 A**

Wattage of lamp $= VI_2 = 120 \times 0.833 =$ **100 W**

The reader may note that when lamp is first connected to supply, the current is very high (12 A in this case). This current raises the temperature of the filament rapidly and the resistance increases due to the increased temperature. By the time normal operating temperature of the lamp is reached, the resistance is increased many times (144 Ω in this case) the cold resistance. If the resistance of the filament did not increase, the power input would remain $P = VI_1 = 120 \times 12 = 1440$ W and the lamp would be destroyed by its own heat.

1.21. ELECTRIC POWER

The rate at which work is done in an electric circuit is called **electric power** *i.e.,*

$$\text{Electric power} = \frac{\text{Work done in electric circuit}}{\text{Time}}$$

When voltage is applied to a circuit, it causes current (*i.e.*, electrons) to flow through it. Clearly, work is being done in moving the electrons in the circuit. This work done in moving the electrons in a unit time is called the electric power. Thus refering to the part *AB* of the circuit (See Fig. 1.13),

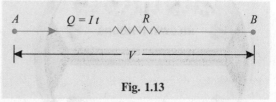

Fig. 1.13

$V =$ P.D. across *AB* in volts

$I =$ Current in amperes

$R =$ Resistance of AB in Ω

$t =$ Time in sec. for which current flows

The total charge that flows in *t* seconds is $Q = I \times t$ coulombs and by definition (See Art. 1.6),

$$V = \frac{\text{Work}}{Q}$$

or $\qquad\qquad \text{Work} = VQ = VIt \qquad\qquad (\because Q = It)$

∴ Electric power, $\qquad P = \dfrac{\text{Work}}{t} = \dfrac{VIt}{t} = VI$ joule / sec or watt

∴ $$P = VI = I^2 R = \frac{V^2}{R}$$

$$^*(\because V = IR \ \text{ or } \ I = \frac{V}{R})$$

The above three formulae are equally valid for calculation of electric power in a d.c. circuit. Which one is to be used depends simply on which quantities are known or most easily determined.

Unit of electric power. The basic unit of electric power is *joule/sec* or *watt*. The power consumed in a circuit is 1 watt if a p.d. of 1 *V* causes 1*A* current to flow through the circuit.

Power in watts = Voltage in volts × Current in amperes

The bigger units of electric power are kilowatts (kW) and megawatts (MW).

$$1 \text{ kW} = 1000 \text{ watts} ; 1 \text{ MW} = 10^6 \text{ watts or } 10^3 \text{ kW}$$

1.22. ELECTRICAL ENERGY

The total work done in an electric circuit is called **electrical energy** *i.e.,*

Electrical energy, W = Electrical power × time

$$= VIt = I^2Rt = \frac{V^2}{R}t$$

In practice, electrical energy is measured in kilowatt hour (kWh).

Energy in kWh = Power in kW × Time in hours

One kilowatt-hour (kWh) *of electrical energy is expended in a circuit if 1 kW (1000 watts) of power is supplied for 1 hour.*

The electricity bills are made on the basis of total electrical energy consumed by the consumer. The unit for charge of electricity is 1 kWh. One kWh is also called Board of Trade (B.O.T.) unit or simply unit. Thus when we say that a consumer has consumed 100 units of electricity, it means that electrical energy consumption is 100 kWh.

Energy meters

1.23. USE OF POWER AND ENERGY FORMULAS

It has already been discussed that electric power as well as electrical energy consumed can be expressed by three formulas. While using these formulas, the following points may be kept in mind :

(*i*) Electric power, $\qquad P = I^2R = \dfrac{V^2}{R}$ watts

Electrical energy consumed, $\quad W = I^2Rt = \dfrac{V^2}{R}t$ joules

The above formulas apply *only* to resistors and to devices (*e.g.* electric bulb, heater, electric kettle *etc*) where all electrical energy consumed is converted into heat.

(*ii*) Electric power, $\qquad P = VI$ watts

Electrical energy consumed, $\quad W = VIt$ joules

These formulas apply to any type of load including the one mentioned in point (*i*).

Example 1.31. *A heating element supplies 300 kilojoules in 50 minutes. Find the p.d. across the element when current is 2 amperes.*

Solution.

Total charge,
$$Q = I \times t = 2 \times 50 \times 60 = 6000 \text{ C}$$

P.D.,
$$V = \frac{\text{Work}}{\text{Charge}} = \frac{300 \times 10^3}{6000} = 50 \text{ V}$$

Example. 1.32. *The following are the details of load on a circuit connected through a supply meter :*

(i)   *Six lamps of 40 watts each working for 4 hours per day*

(ii) *Two fluorescent tubes 125 watts each working for 2 hours per day.*

(iii) *One 1000 watt heater working for 3 hours per day.*

If each unit of energy costs 70 P, what will be the electricity bill for the month of June?

Solution.

Total wattage of lamps   = 40 × 6 = 240 watts

Total wattage of tubes   = 125 × 2 = 250 watts

Wattage of heater   = 1000 watts

Energy consumed by the appliances per day

$$= (240 \times 4) + (250 \times 2) + (1000 \times 3)$$
$$= 4460 \text{ watt-hours} = 4.46 \text{ kWh}$$

Total energy consumed in the month of June (*i.e.*, in 30 days)

$$= 4.46 \times 30 = 133.8 \text{ kWh}$$

Bill for the month of June = Rs 0.7 × 133.8 = **Rs 93.66**

Example 1.33. *A current of 80 A flows for 1 hour in a resistance across which there is a voltage of 2 V. Determine the velocity with which a stone of mass 1000 kg must move in order that its kinetic energy shall be equal in amount to the energy dissipated in the resistance.*

Solution. Let *v* m/s be the required velocity of the stone. As per conditions of the problem, we have,

$$V I t = \frac{1}{2} mv^2$$

or
$$2 \times 80 \times 3600 = \frac{1}{2} \times 1000 \times v^2$$

or
$$v^2 = \frac{2 \times 2 \times 80 \times 3600}{1000} = 1152$$

∴
$$v = \sqrt{1152} = \mathbf{34 \text{ m/s}}$$

Example 1.34. *What must be the useful rating of tin-smelting furnace in order to smelt 50 kg of tin per hour? Smelting temperature of tin = 235°C; specific heat = 0.055 kcal/kg/°C ; latent heat of liquification = 13.31 kcal/kg. Take initial temperature of metal as 15°C.*

Solution.

Energy input/hour $= m [c\theta + L_{liq}]$

Here $c = 0.055$ kcal/kg/°C; $m = 50$ kg; $\theta = (235 - 15)$°C; $L_{liq} = 13.31$ kcal/kg

∴ Energy input/hour $= 50 [0.055 (235 - 15) + 13.31] = 1270.5$ kcal

$$= \frac{1270.5}{860} \text{ kWh} = 1.47 \text{ kWh} \qquad [\because 1\text{kWh} = 860 \text{ kcal}]$$

∴ Useful rating $= \dfrac{1.47}{1} = \mathbf{1.47 \text{ kW}}$

CORNWALL COLLEGE
LEARNING CENTRE

TUTORIAL PROBLEMS

1. A resistor of 50 Ω has a p.d. of 100 volts d.c. across it for 1 hour. Calculate (*i*) power and (*ii*) energy.   **[(*i*) 200 watts; (*ii*) 7.2 × 10⁵ J]**

2. A current of 10 A flows through a resistor for 10 minutes and the power dissipated by the resistor is 100 watts. Find the p.d. across the resistor and the energy supplied to the circuit.   **[10 V; 6 × 10⁴ J]**

3. A factory is supplied with power at 210 volts through a pair of feeders of total resistance 0.0225 Ω. The load consists of 250V, 60-watt lamps and 4 motors each taking 40 amperes. Find :

    (*i*) total current required   (*ii*) voltage at the station end of feeders

    (*iii*) power wasted in feeders.   **[(*i*) 231.4 A ; (*ii*) 215.78 V ; (*iii*) 1.4 kW]**

4. The electrical load in a small workshop consists of 14 lamps, each rated at 240 V, 60 W and 3 electric fires, each rated at 240 V, 1 kW. What is the effective resistance of the load?   **[15 Ω]**

1.24. CARBON RESISTORS

A component whose function in a circuit is to provide a specified value of resistance is called a resistor. The most commonly used resistors in electrical and electronics circuits are the *carbon resistors*. A carbon resistor is made from powdered carbon mixed with a binding material and baked into a small tube with a wire attached to each end. These small-sized resistors are manufactured in values from a fraction of an ohm to several million ohms. Note that power rating of a carbon resistor depends upon the physical size of the resistor. A large resistor is able to throw off (dissipate) more heat than a smaller one.

Colour code for carbon resistors. Since a carbon resistor is physically quite small, it is more convenient to use a *colour code* indicating the resistance value than to imprint the numerical value on the case. In this scheme, there are generally four colour bands printed on the body of the resistor as shown in Fig. 1.14. The first three colour bands give the value of the resistance while

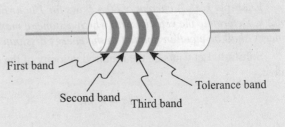

First band

Second band   Third band

Tolerance band

Fig. 1.14

the fourth band tells about the *tolerance in percentage. The table below shows the colour code for resistance values and colour code for tolerance.

Colour code for Resistance values				Colour code for Tolerance	
Black	0	Green	5	Gold	± 5%
Brown	1	Blue	6	Silver	± 10%
Red	2	Violet	7	No colour	± 20%
Orange	3	Grey	8		
Yellow	4	White	9		

(*i*) To read the resistance value, we refer to the first three colour bands. The first two colour bands specify the first two digits of the resistance value and the third colour band gives the number of zeros that follow the first two digits. Suppose the first three colour bands on the resistor are red, brown and orange respectively. Then resistance value is 21000 Ω.

* Due to manufacturing variations, the resistance value may not be the same as indicated by colour code. Thus a resistor marked 100 Ω; ± 10% tolerance means that resistance value is between 90 Ω and 110 Ω.

Red	:	2
Brown	:	1
Orange	:	000

∴ Resistance value = 21000 Ω

(*ii*) The fourth band gives the value of tolerance in percentage. If the colour of the fourth band is gold, tolerance is ± 5% and if silver, then tolerance is ± 10%. If fourth band is omitted, the tolerance is assumed to be ± 20%.

Note. The resistance indicated by the colour code (*i.e.* by first three bands) is called *nominal value*. The actual value of a resistor can vary above or below its nominal value by an amount equal to its tolerance.

Example 1.35. *Find the nominal value of resistance and tolerance from the following colour codes :*

(*i*)   yellow, violet, orange, silver

(*ii*)   brown, black, red

(*iii*)   blue, grey, black, gold

Solution.

(*i*) yellow,   violet,   orange,   silver
          4   7   000   ± 10%

∴ Nominal value of resistance = **47000 Ω** ; Tolerance = **± 10%**

(*ii*) Brown,   black,   red,   none
          1   0   00   ± 20%

∴ Nominal value of resistance = **1000 Ω** ; Tolerance = **± 20%**

(*iii*) Blue,   grey,   black,   gold
          6   8   –   ± 5%

∴ Nominal value of resistance = **68 Ω**; Tolerance = **± 5%**

Example 1.36. *What colour bands will be found on a resistor with a nominal value of 390 Ω and a tolerance of ± 10%?*

Solution.

          3   9   0   ± 10%
      Orange   White   Brown   Silver

The colour bands will be **orange, white, brown** and **silver.**

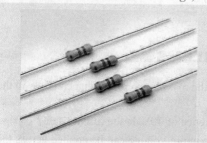 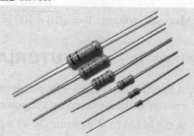

Carbon resistors

TUTORIAL PROBLEMS

1. A resistor has the following order of colour bands :

    Red, Red, Red, gold

    Find its nominal resistance and its range of resistance values.   [2200 Ω; 2090 Ω to 2310 Ω]

2. Find the nominal value of resistance and tolerance of a resistor having colour bands : yellow, violet, orange, gold.   [47 kΩ; ± 5%]

3. What colour bands will be found on a resistor with a nominal value of 1 MΩ and a tolerance of ± 5%?   [brown, black, green, gold]

1.25. POWER RATING OF A RESISTOR

The ability of a resistor to dissipate power as heat without destructive temperature build-up is called power rating of the resistor.

Power rating of resistor = I^2R or V^2/R

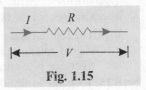

Fig. 1.15

Suppose the power rating of a resistor is 2W. It means that I^2R or V^2/R should not exceed 2W. Suppose the quantity I^2R (or V^2/R) for this resistor becomes 4W. The resistor is able to dissipate 2W as heat and the remaining 2W will start building up the temperature. In a matter of seconds, the resistor will burn out.

The physical size of a resistor is not necessarily related to its resistance value but rather to its *power rating*. A large resistor is able to dissipate (throw off) more heat because of its large physical size. In general, the greater the physical size of a resistor, the greater is its power rating and vice-versa.

Example 1.37. *A 0.1Ω resistor has a power rating of 5W. Is this resistor safe when conducting a current of 10A?*

Solution. Power developed in the resistor is

$$P = I^2R = (10)^2 \times 0.1 = 10 \text{ W}$$

The resistor is **not safe** since the power developed in the resistor exceeds its dissipating rating.

Example 1.38. *What is the maximum safe current flow in a 47 Ω, 2W resistor?*

Solution. Power rating   = I^2R

or $2 = I^2 \times 47$

∴ Maximum safe current, $I = \sqrt{\dfrac{2}{47}} = 0.21\text{A}$

Example 1.39. *What is the maximum voltage that can be applied across a 100 Ω, 10 W resistor in order to keep within the resistor's power rating?*

Solution.

Power rating   = V^2/R

or $10 = V^2/100$

∴ Max. safe voltage, $V = \sqrt{10 \times 100} = \textbf{31.6 volts}$

TUTORIAL PROBLEMS

1. A 200 Ω resistor has a 2 W power rating. What is the maximum current that can flow in the resistor without exceeding the power rating?   [100 mA]

2. A 6.8 kΩ, 0.25 W resistor shows a potential difference of 40V. Is the resistor safe?   [Yes]

3. A 1.5 kΩ resistor has 1W power rating. What maximum voltage can be applied across the resistor without exceeding the power rating?   [38.73 V]

MULTIPLE-CHOICE QUESTIONS

1. The electrons in the last orbit of an atom are called
   - (a) free electrons
   - (b) bound electrons
   - (c) valence electrons
   - (d) thermionic electrons

2. If the number of valence electrons of an atom is less than 4, the substance is usually
   - (a) a conductor
   - (b) an insulator
   - (c) a semiconductor
   - (d) none of the above

3. If the number of valence electrons of an atom is more than 4, the substance is usually

   (a) a conductor

   (b) an insulator

   (c) a semiconductor

   (d) none of the above

4. If the number of valence electrons of an atom is 4, the substance is usually

   (a) a conductor

   (b) an insulator

   (c) a semiconductor

   (d) none of the above

5. A billion electrons pass through a cross-section of a conductor in 10^{-3} s. The current is

   (a) 10^{-7} A   (b) 1.6×10^{-7} A

   (c) 2×10^{-4} A   (d) 2.6×10^{-3} A

6. The specific resistance of a wire depends upon

   (a) its length

   (b) its cross-sectional area

   (c) its dimensions

   (d) its material

7. A length of wire has a resistance of 6Ω. The resistance of a wire of the same material three times as long and twice the cross-sectional area will be

   (a) $9\,\Omega$

   (b) $36\,\Omega$

   (c) $1\,\Omega$

   (d) $12\,\Omega$

8. The potential difference of an energy source that provides 50 mJ of energy for every microcoulomb of charge that flows is

   (a) 5 V

   (b) 50 V

   (c) 50 kV

   (d) 500 V

9. A piece of aluminium wire is streched to reduce its diameter to half of its original value. Its resistance will become

   (a) two times

   (b) sixteen times

   (c) eight times

   (d) four times

10. The resistance of a material 2 m long and 2m^2 in area of X-section is $1.6 \times 10^{-8}\,\Omega$. Its specific resistance will be

    (a) $1.6 \times 10^{-8}\,\Omega\text{m}$

    (b) $6.4 \times 10^{-8}\,\Omega\text{m}$

    (c) $3.2 \times 10^{-8}\,\Omega\text{m}$

    (d) $0.16 \times 10^{-8}\,\Omega\text{m}$

11. A copper wire of resistance R_0 is stretched till its length is increased n times of its original length. Its resistance will now be

    (a) R_0/n^2 (b) $n^2 R_0$

    (c) nR_0 (d) $n^3 R_0$

12. A copper wire is stretched so that its length is increased by 0.1%. The change in its resistance is

    (a) 0.2%   (b) 0.1%

    (c) 0.3%   (d) 0.4%

13. Fig. 1.16 shows the temperature/resistance graph of a conductor. The value of α_0 is

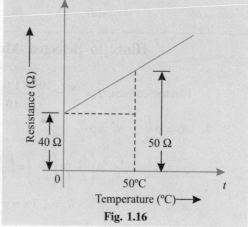

Fig. 1.16

    (a) 0.05/°C   (b) 0.004/°C

    (c) 0.4/°C   (d) 0.005/°C

14. Referring to Fig. 1.16, the value of α_{50} will be

    (a) 0.005/°C   (b) 0.05/°C

    (c) 0.004/°C   (d) 0.4/°C

15. The value of α_0 of a conductor is 1/236 per °C. The value of α_{18} will be

    (a) 1/218 per °C   (b) 1/254 per °C

    (c) 1/272 per °C   (d) 1/216 per °C

16. The number of free electrons passing through the filament of an electric lamp in one hour when current through the filament is 0.32 A will be

    (a) 7.2×10^{21} (b) 7.2×10^{19}

    (c) 3×10^{22} (d) 2×10^{26}

17. What voltage drop will be there across a 1 kW heater whose resistance when hot is $40\,\Omega$?

    (a) 100 V   (b) 50 V

    (c) 150 V   (d) 200 V

18. Two electric bulbs rated for the same voltage have powers of 200 W and 100 W. If their resistances are R_1 and R_2 respectively, then,

    (a) $R_1 = 2R_2$ (b) $R_2 = 4R_1$

    (c) $R_2 = 2R_1$ (d) $R_1 = 4R_2$

19. A carbon electrode has a resistance of 0.125 Ω at 20°C. The temperature coefficient of carbon is – 0.0005 at 20°C. What will be the resistance of electrode at 85°C?

    (a) 4 Ω
    (b) 0.121 Ω
    (c) 1.2 Ω
    (d) 0.5 Ω

20. The percentage by which the incandescence of lamp decreases due to drop of current by 3% is

    (a) 6%   (b) 3%
    (c) 9%   (d) 12%

Answers to Multiple-Choice Questions

1. (c)	2. (a)	3. (b)	4. (c)	5. (b)
6. (d)	7. (a)	8. (c)	9. (b)	10. (a)
11. (b)	12. (a)	13. (d)	14. (c)	15. (b)
16. (a)	17. (d)	18. (c)	19. (b)	20. (a)

Hints to Selected Multiple-Choice Questions

5. Electric current, $I = \dfrac{ne}{t} = \dfrac{10^9 \times 1.6 \times 10^{-19}}{10^{-3}} = 1.6 \times 10^{-7}$ A

7. $R_1 = \rho \dfrac{l_1}{a_1}$; $R_2 = \rho \dfrac{l_2}{a_2}$

   $\therefore \qquad \dfrac{R_2}{R_1} = \left(\dfrac{l_2}{l_1}\right) \times \left(\dfrac{a_1}{a_2}\right) = \left(\dfrac{3l}{l}\right) \times \left(\dfrac{a}{2a}\right) = 1.5$

   or $\qquad R_2 = 1.5\, R_1 = 1.5 \times 6 = 9\Omega$

8. $V = \dfrac{W}{Q} = \dfrac{50 \times 10^{-3}}{1 \times 10^{-6}} = 50 \times 10^3$ V = 50 kV

9. $R_1 = \rho \dfrac{l_1}{a_1}$; $R_2 = \rho \dfrac{l_2}{a_2}$

   $\therefore \qquad \dfrac{R_2}{R_1} = \left(\dfrac{l_2}{l_1}\right) \times \left(\dfrac{a_1}{a_2}\right)$

   Now $\qquad l_1 a_1 = l_2 a_2$ or $l_1 a_1 = l_2 \left(\dfrac{a_1}{4}\right) \qquad \therefore l_2 = 4l_1$

   $\therefore \qquad \dfrac{R_2}{R_1} = \left(\dfrac{4l_1}{l_1}\right) \times \dfrac{a_1}{(a_1/4)} = 16$ or $R_2 = 16R_1$

10. $R = \rho \dfrac{l}{a}$ or $1.6 \times 10^{-8} = \rho \times \dfrac{2}{2} \quad \therefore \rho = 1.6 \times 10^{-8}$ Ωm

11. $R_0 = \rho \dfrac{l_0}{a_0}$; $R = \rho \dfrac{l}{a}$

    It is given that $l = nl_0$. Since volume remains the same,

$$\therefore \quad a_0 l_0 = (n l_0) a \quad \text{or} \quad a = a_0/n$$

$$\therefore \quad \frac{R}{R_0} = \frac{l}{l_0} \times \frac{a_0}{a} = n \times n = n^2 \quad \text{or} \quad R = n^2 R_0$$

12. $R = \rho \dfrac{l}{a} \; ; \; R' = \rho \dfrac{l'}{a'}$

Now $l' = l + \dfrac{0.1}{100} \times l = 1.001\, l$

Since volume remains the same, $al = a'l'$ or $a' = a\dfrac{l}{l'} = \dfrac{a}{1.001}$

$$\therefore \quad \frac{R'}{R} = \left(\frac{l'}{l}\right) \times \left(\frac{a}{a'}\right) = (1.001) \times (1.001) = 1.002$$

or $\qquad \dfrac{R' - R}{R} = 0.002$

$$\therefore \quad \text{Percentage increase} = \frac{R' - R}{R} \times 100 = 0.002 \times 100 = 0.2\,\%$$

13. $\alpha_0 = \dfrac{\text{slope of temperature/resistance graph}}{R_0} = \dfrac{10/50}{40} = 0.005/^\circ C$

14. $\alpha_{50} = \dfrac{\text{slope of temperature/resistance graph}}{R_{50}} = \dfrac{10/50}{50} = 0.004/^\circ C$

15. $\alpha_{18} = \dfrac{\alpha_0}{1 + \alpha_0 \times 18} = \dfrac{1}{(1/\alpha_0) + 18} = \dfrac{1}{236 + 18} = \dfrac{1}{254}/^\circ C$

16. $I = \dfrac{q}{t} = \dfrac{ne}{t}$

$$\therefore \quad n = \frac{It}{e} = \frac{0.32 \times 3600}{1.6 \times 10^{-19}} = 7.2 \times 10^{21}$$

17. $P = \dfrac{V^2}{R} \quad \therefore V = \sqrt{PR} = \sqrt{1000 \times 40} = 200 \text{ volts}$

18. $R_1 = \dfrac{V^2}{200}; \; R_2 = \dfrac{V^2}{100}$

$$\therefore \qquad \frac{R_2}{R_1} = \frac{V^2}{100} \times \frac{200}{V^2} = 2 \quad \text{or} \quad R_2 = 2R_1$$

19. $R_{85} = R_{20}\left[1 + \alpha_{20}(t_2 - t_1)\right] = 0.125\left[1 + (-0.0005 \times 65)\right] = 0.121\ \Omega$

20. $P = I^2 R$ or $\Delta P = 2I(\Delta I)R$

$$\therefore \qquad \frac{\Delta P}{P} = 2\frac{\Delta I}{I} = 2 \times 3\% = 6\%$$

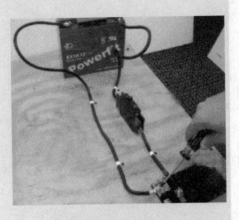

D.C. Circuits

INTRODUCTION

The closed path followed by direct current (*d.c.*) is called a d.c. circuit. A d.c. circuit essentially consists of a source of d.c. power (*e.g.*, battery, d.c. generator *etc.*), the conductors used to carry current and the load. The source supplies electrical energy to the load which converts it into heat or other forms of energy. The load for a d.c. circuit is usually a *resistance. In a d.c. circuit, loads (*i.e.*, resistances) may be connected in series, parallel or series-parallel. In this chapter, we shall confine our discussion to d.c. circuits only.

2.1. RESISTANCES IN SERIES

The circuit in which resistances are connected end to end so that the same current flows through all the resistances is called a series circuit as shown in Fig. 2.1 (*i*). By Ohm's law, voltages across various resistances are:

$$V_1 = IR_1 ; \ V_2 = IR_2 ; \ V_3 = IR_3$$

. . . .

*   Other passive elements *viz.* inductance and capacitance are relevant only in a.c. circuits.

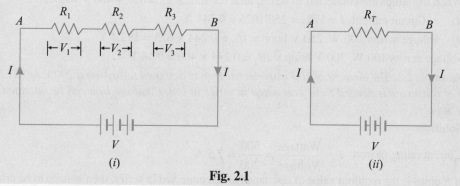

Fig. 2.1

Now, $$V = V_1 + V_2 + V_3 = IR_1 + IR_2 + IR_3$$
$$= I (R_1 + R_2 + R_3)$$

or $$\frac{V}{I} = R_1 + R_2 + R_3$$

But V/I is the total resistance R_T between points A and B. R_T is called the * total or equivalent resistance of the three resistances.

∴ $$R_T = R_1 + R_2 + R_3$$

Hence when a number of resistances are connected in series, the total resistance is equal to the sum of individual resistances.

Note. A series resistor circuit can be considered to be a *voltage divider circuit* because the potential difference across any one resistor is a fraction of the total voltage applied across the series combination; the fraction being determined by the values of the resistances. Thus referring to Fig. 2.1 (*i*), the p.d. across R_1 is $V_1 = IR_1$ and the total voltage across the series combination is $V = I (R_1 + R_2 + R_3)$.

∴ $$\frac{V_1}{V} = \frac{R_1}{R_1 + R_2 + R_3}$$

Example 2.1. *Two filament lamps A and B take 0.8 A and 0.9 A respectively when connected across 110 V supply. Calculate the value of current when they are connected in series across a 220-V supply, assuming the filament resistances to remain unaltered. Also find the voltage across each lamp.*

Solution.

For lamp A, $R_A = 110/0.8 = 137.5 \ \Omega$; For lamp B, $R_B = 110/0.9 = 122.2 \ \Omega$

When the lamps are connected in series, total resistance $R_T = 137.5 + 122.2 = 259.7 \ \Omega$

∴ Circuit current, $I = V/R_T = 220/259.7 = $ **0.847 A**

Voltage across lamp $A = IR_A = 0.847 \times 137.5 = $ **116.5 V**

Voltage across lamp $B = IR_B = 0.847 \times 122.2 = $ **103.5 V**

Example 2.2. *A 100-watt, 250 V lamp is connected in series with a 100 watt, 200 V lamp across 250 V supply. Calculate (i) circuit current and (ii) voltage across each lamp. Assume the lamp resistances to remain unaltered.*

Solution.

Resistance, $R = V^2 / W$

Resistance of 100 watt, 250 V lamp, $R_1 = (250)^2/100 = 625 \ \Omega$

Resistance of 100 watt, 200 V lamp, $R_2 = (200)^2/100 = 400 \ \Omega$

* Total or equivalent resistance is the single resistance, which, if substituted for the series resistances, would provide the same current in the circuit.

When the lamps are connected in series, total resistance $R_T = 625 + 400 = 1025\Omega$

(*i*) ∴ Circuit current, $I = V/R_T = 250/1025 = \textbf{0.244 A}$

(*ii*) Voltage across 100 W, 250 V lamp $= IR_1 = 0.244 \times 625 = \textbf{152.4 V}$

Voltage across 100 W, 200 V lamp $= IR_2 = 0.244 \times 400 = \textbf{97.6 V}$

Example 2.3. *The element of 500-watt electric iron is designed for use on a 200 V supply. What value of resistance is needed to be connected in series in order that the iron can be operated from 240 V supply?*

Solution.

Current rating of iron, $I = \dfrac{\text{Wattage}}{\text{Voltage}} = \dfrac{500}{200} = 2.5 \text{ A}$

If *R* ohms is the required value of resistance to be connected in series, then voltage to be dropped across this resistance $= 240 - 200 = 40$ V

∴ $\qquad R = 40/2.5 = \textbf{16}\Omega$

Example 2.4. *A generator of e.m.f. E volts and internal resistance r ohms supplies current to a water heater. Calculate the resistance R of the heater so that three-quarter of the total energy developed by the generator is absorbed by the water.*

Solution.

Current supplied by generator, $I = \dfrac{E}{R + r}$

Power developed by generator $= E I = \dfrac{E^2}{R + r}$

Power dissipated by heater $= I^2 R = R \times \dfrac{E^2}{(R + r)^2} = \dfrac{E^2 R}{(R + r)^2}$

As per the conditions of the problem, we have,

$$\frac{E^2 R}{(R + r)^2} = \frac{3}{4} \times \frac{E^2}{R + r}$$

or $\qquad \dfrac{R}{R + r} = \dfrac{3}{4}$

∴ $\qquad R = 3r$

Example 2.5. *A direct current arc has a voltage/current relation expressed as:*

$$V = 44 + \frac{30}{I} \text{ volts}$$

It is connected in series with a resistor across 100 V supply. If voltages across the arc and resistor are equal, find the ohmic value of the resistor.

Solution. Let *R* ohms be the resistance of the resistor. The voltage across the arc as well as resistor = 50 volts.

Now $\qquad 50 = 44 + \dfrac{30}{I} \qquad$ ∴ $I = 5A$

∴ $\qquad R = \dfrac{V}{I} = \dfrac{50}{5} = 10 \ \Omega$

2.2. RESISTANCES IN PARALLEL

When one end of each resistance is joined to a common point and the other end of each resistance is joined to another common point so that there are as many paths for current flow as the number of resistances, it is called a **parallel circuit** as shown in Fig. 2.2 (*i*). Note that voltage across each resistance is the same (*i.e.* V volts in this case) and there are as many current paths as the number of resistances. By Ohm's law, current through each resistance is:

$$I_1 = V/R_1, I_2 = V/R_2; I_3 = V/R_3$$

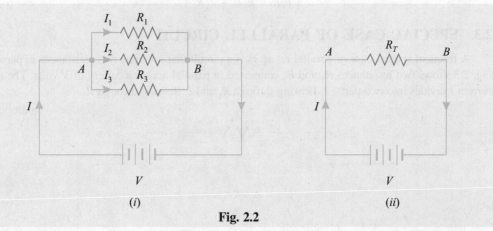

Fig. 2.2

Now,
$$I = I_1 + I_2 + I_3 = \frac{V}{R_1} + \frac{V}{R_2} + \frac{V}{R_3}$$
$$= V\left(\frac{1}{R_1} + \frac{1}{R_2} + \frac{1}{R_3}\right)$$

or
$$\frac{I}{V} = \frac{1}{R_1} + \frac{1}{R_2} + \frac{1}{R_3}$$

But V/I is the total resistance R_T of the parallel resistances [See Fig. 2.2 (*ii*)] so that $I/V = 1/R_T$.

∴
$$\frac{1}{R_T} = \frac{1}{R_1} + \frac{1}{R_2} + \frac{1}{R_3}$$

Hence when a number of resistances are connected in parallel, the reciprocal of total resistance is equal to the sum of reciprocals of individual resistances.

Note.

(*i*) The total resistance of a parallel circuit is always less than the smallest of the resistances.

(*ii*) If *n* resistors, each of R Ω, are connected in parallel, then, $R_T = R/n$.

(*iii*) A parallel resistor circuit can be considered to be a *current divider circuit* because the current through any one resistor is a fraction of the total circuit current; the fraction depending on the values of the resistors. Thus referring to Fig. 2.2 (*i*), the current through resistor R_1 is $I_1 = V/R_1$ and the total current is $I = V/R_T$.

$$\frac{1}{R_T} = \frac{1}{R_1} + \frac{1}{R_2} + \frac{1}{R_3}$$

∴
$$R_T = \frac{R_1 R_2 R_3}{R_2 R_3 + R_3 R_1 + R_1 R_2}$$

∴
$$\frac{I_1}{I} = \frac{V/R_1}{V/R_T} = \frac{R_T}{R_1} = \frac{R_2 R_3}{R_1 R_2 + R_2 R_3 + R_3 R_1}$$

or
$$I_1 = I\left(\frac{R_2 R_3}{R_1 R_2 + R_2 R_3 + R_3 R_1}\right)$$

Similarly,

$$I_2 = I\left(\frac{R_1 R_3}{R_1 R_2 + R_2 R_3 + R_3 R_1}\right)$$

and

$$I_3 = I\left(\frac{R_1 R_2}{R_1 R_2 + R_2 R_3 + R_3 R_1}\right)$$

2.3. SPECIAL CASE OF PARALLEL CIRCUIT

A frequent special case of parallel resistors is a circuit that contains two resistances in parallel. Fig. 2.3 shows two resistances R_1 and R_2 connected in parallel across a battery of V volts. The total current I divides into two parts; I_1 flowing through R_1 and I_2 flowing through R_2.

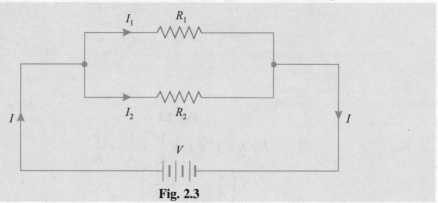

Fig. 2.3

(*i*) **Total resistance R_T**

$$\frac{1}{R_T} = \frac{1}{R_1} + \frac{1}{R_2} = \frac{R_2 + R_1}{R_1 R_2}$$

∴

$$R_T = \frac{R_1 R_2}{R_1 + R_2} \quad i.e., \quad \frac{Product}{sum}$$

Hence the total value of two resistors connected in parallel is equal to the product divided by the sum of two resistors.

(*ii*) **Branch Currents**

$$R_T = \frac{R_1 R_2}{R_1 + R_2}$$

$$V = IR_T = I\,\frac{R_1 R_2}{R_1 + R_2}$$

Current through R_1, $\quad I_1 = \dfrac{V}{R_1} = I\,\dfrac{R_2}{R_1 + R_2} \qquad \left[\text{Putting } V = I\,\dfrac{R_1 R_2}{R_1 + R_2}\right]$

Current through R_2, $\quad I_2 = \dfrac{V}{R_2} = I\,\dfrac{R_1}{R_1 + R_2}$

Hence in a parallel circuit of two resistors, the current in one resistor is the line current (i.e., total current) times the opposite resistor divided by the sum of two resistors.

Example 2.6. *Two coils connected in series have a resistance of 18 Ω and when connected in parallel have a resistance of 4Ω. Find the value of resistances.*

Solution. Let R_1 and R_2 be the resistances of the coils. When resistances are connected in series, $R_T = 18\,\Omega$.

$$\therefore \qquad\qquad R_1 + R_2 = 18 \qquad\qquad\qquad\qquad ...(i)$$

When resistances are connected in parallel, $R_T = 4\,\Omega$.

$$\therefore \qquad\qquad \frac{R_1 R_2}{R_1 + R_2} = 4 \qquad\qquad\qquad\qquad ...(ii)$$

Multiplying Eqns. (i) and (ii), we get, $R_1 R_2 = 18 \times 4 = 72$

Now

$$R_1 - R_2 = \sqrt{(R_1 + R_2)^2 - 4R_1R_2} = \sqrt{(18)^2 - 4 \times 72}$$

$$\therefore \qquad\qquad R_1 - R_2 = \pm 6 \qquad\qquad\qquad\qquad ...(iii)$$

Solving Eqns. (i) and (iii), we get,

$$R_1 = 12\,\Omega \quad \text{or} \quad 6\,\Omega; \ R_2 = 6\,\Omega \text{ or } 12\,\Omega$$

Example 2.7. *A 100-watt, 250 V lamp is connected in parallel with an unknown resistance R across a 250 V supply. The total power dissipated in the circuit is 1100 watts. Find the value of unknown resistance. Assume the resistance of lamp remains unaltered.*

Solution. The total power dissipated in the circuit is equal to the sum of powers consumed by the lamp and unknown resistance R.

∴ Power consumed by R = 1100 − 100 = 1000 watts

$$\text{Value of resistance } R = \frac{V^2}{\text{Power consumed}} = \frac{(250)^2}{1000} = 62.5\ \Omega$$

Example 2.8. *A battery having an e.m.f. of 12 V is connected across terminals AB of the circuit shown in Fig. 2.4. Find (i) current flowing in each resistance and (ii) total power absorbed by the circuit.*

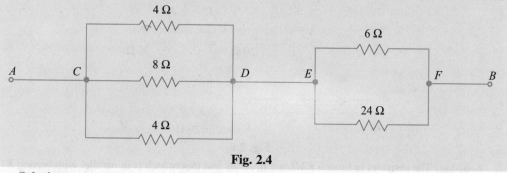

Fig. 2.4

Solution.

Resistance between C and D is given by:

$$\frac{1}{R_{CD}} = \frac{1}{4} + \frac{1}{8} + \frac{1}{4} = \frac{5}{8}\ \Omega$$

$$\therefore \qquad\qquad R_{CD} = 8/5 = 1.6\ \Omega$$

Resistance between E and F, $\qquad R_{EF} = \dfrac{6 \times 24}{6 + 24} = 4.8\ \Omega$

Resistance between A and B, $\qquad R_{AB} = R_{CD} + R_{EF} = 1.6 + 4.8 = 6.4\ \Omega$

Total circuit current, $\qquad\qquad I = V/R_{AB} = 12/6.4 = 1.875\ \text{A}$

Voltage between C and D, $V_{CD} = I R_{CD} = 1.875 \times 1.6 = 3$ V

Voltage between E and F, $V_{EF} = I R_{EF} = 1.875 \times 4.8 = 9$ V

(*i*) Current through 4 Ω resistors $= 3/4 = 0.75$ A

Current through 8 Ω resistor $= 3/8 = 0.375$ A

Current through 6 Ω resistor $= 9/6 = 1.5$ A

Current through 24 Ω resistor $= 9/24 = 0.375$ A

(*ii*) Power absorbed $= I^2 R_{AB} = (1.875)^2 \times 6.4 = 22.5$ watts

Example 2.9. *Three resistors* 4Ω, 12 Ω *and* 6Ω *are connected in parallel. If the total current taken is 12A, find the current through each resistor.*

Solution.

Fig. 2.5 shows the circuit arrangement.

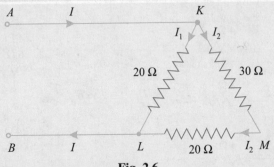

$$\frac{1}{R_T} = \frac{1}{4} + \frac{1}{12} + \frac{1}{6} = \frac{6}{12}$$

∴ $R_T = 12/6 = 2\Omega$

P.D. across the parallel circuit $= I R_T = 12 \times 2$

$= 24$ V

Current through 4 Ω $= 24/4 = $ **6A**

Current through 12 Ω $= 24/12 = $ **2A**

Current through 6 Ω $= 24/6 = $ **4A**

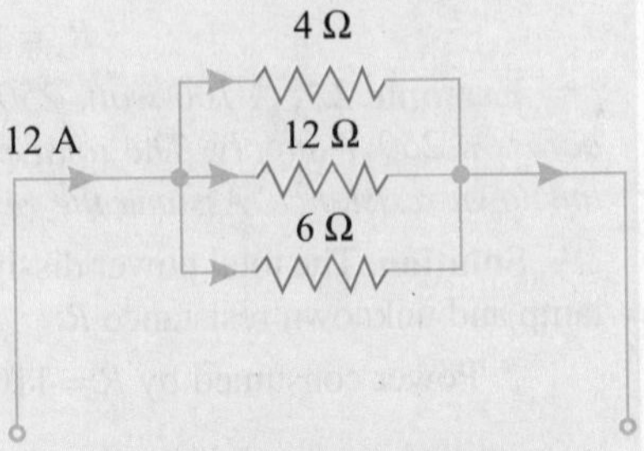

Fig. 2.5

Example 2.10. *A battery connected across AB in Fig. 2.6 is delivering 28 watts into the network of resistors. Calculate the voltage across AB. If the e.m.f. of the battery is 22 V, find the internal resistance of the battery.*

Fig. 2.6

Solution. The resistors in branch *KML* are in series and this branch is in parallel with branch *KL*.

∴ Total resistance between A and B, $R_T = \dfrac{20 \times (30 + 20)}{20 + (30 + 20)} = \dfrac{100}{7}$ Ω

If V is the voltage across *AB*, then power delivered to the network of resistors is V^2/R_T.

∴ $V^2/R_T = 28$ or $V^2 = 28 \times R_T = 28 \times 100/7 = 400$ volts

∴ $V = \sqrt{400} = $ **20 volts**

Current in branch *KL*, $I_1 = 20/20 = 1$A; Current in branch *KML*, $I_2 = 20/50 = 0.4$ A

∴ Total current, $I = 1 + 0.4 = 1.4$ A

Now, $E = V + Ir$

∴ Internal resistance of supply, $r = \dfrac{E - V}{I} = \dfrac{22 - 20}{1.4} = $ **1.429 Ω**

Example 2.11. *In the circuit shown in Fig. 2.7, find the voltage and the current in each element.*

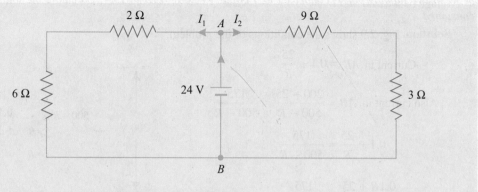

Fig. 2.7

Solution. There are two parallel paths between points A and B.

$$I_1 = \frac{24}{2+6} = \frac{24}{8} = 3\,\text{A} \,;\, I_2 = \frac{24}{9+3} = \frac{24}{12} = 2\,\text{A}$$

Voltage across $2\,\Omega = 3 \times 2 = 6\,\text{V}$; Voltage across $6\,\Omega = 3 \times 6 = 18\,\text{V}$

Voltage across $9\,\Omega = 2 \times 9 = 18\,\text{V}$; Voltage across $3\,\Omega = 2 \times 3 = 6\,\text{V}$

Example 2.12. *A current of 20 A flows through two ammeters A and B joined in series. The p.d. across A is 0.2 V while that across B is 0.3 V. Find how the same current will divide between A and B when they are joined in parallel.*

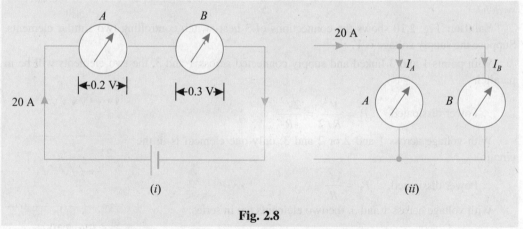

Fig. 2.8

Solution. We can find the resistances of the ammeters from Fig. 2.8 (*i*).

$$R_A = 0.2/20 = 0.01\,\Omega; R_B = 0.3/20 = 0.015\Omega$$

When the two ammeters are joined in parallel [See Fig. 2.8 (*ii*)], 20 A current will be shared as under:

$$I_A = 20 \times \frac{0.015}{0.01 + 0.015} = 12\,\text{A}; \quad I_B = 20 \times \frac{0.01}{0.01 + 0.015} = 8\,\text{A}$$

Example 2.13. *A voltage of 200 V is applied to a tapped resistor of 500 Ω. Find the resistance between two tapping points connected to a circuit needing 0.1A at 25 V. Calculate the total power consumed.*

Solution. Fig. 2.9 shows the conditions of the problem.

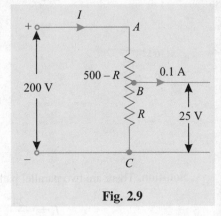

$$\text{Current in } AB = 0.1 + \frac{25}{R}$$

$$\text{Also current in } AB = \frac{200 - 25}{500 - R} = \frac{175}{500 - R}$$

∴
$$0.1 + \frac{25}{R} = \frac{175}{500 - R}$$

or
$$\frac{0.1R + 25}{R} = \frac{175}{500 - R}$$

or $(500 - R)(0.1R + 25) = 175\,R$

Fig. 2.9

or $0.1\,R^2 + 150\,R - 12500 = 0$

On solving and taking the positive value, $R = \mathbf{79\ \Omega}$

$$\text{Total current, } I = \text{Current in } AB = 0.1 + \frac{25}{79} = 0.4165 \text{ A}$$

∴ Total power = $200 \times I = 200 \times 0.4165 = \mathbf{83.5\ W}$

Example 2.14. *A heater has two similar elements controlled by a 3-heat switch. Draw a connection diagram of each position of the switch. What is the heat developed for each position of the switch?*

Solution. Fig. 2.10 shows the connections of 3-heat switch controlling two similar elements. Suppose the supply voltage is *V*.

With points 1 and 3 linked and supply connected across 1 and 3, the two elements will be in parallel.

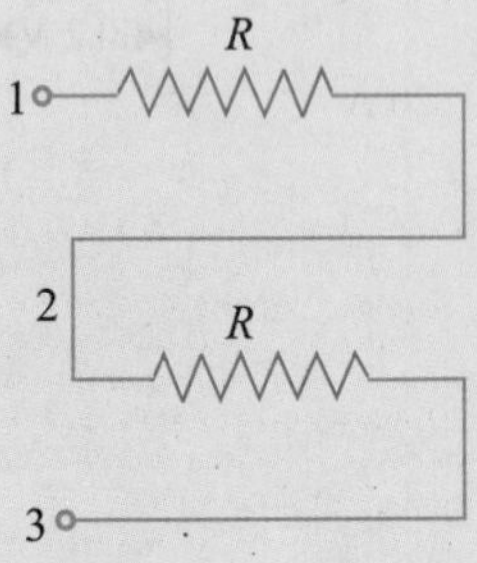

∴ Power dissipated, $P_1 = \dfrac{V^2}{R/2} = \dfrac{2V^2}{R}$

With voltage across 1 and 2 or 2 and 3, only one element is in the circuit.

∴ Power dissipated, $P_2 = \dfrac{V^2}{R}$

With voltage across 1 and 3, the two elements are in series.

Fig. 2.10

∴ Power dissipated, $P_3 = \dfrac{V^2}{2R}$

∴
$$P_1 : P_2 : P_3 = \frac{2V^2}{R} : \frac{V^2}{R} : \frac{V^2}{2R} = 2 : 1 : \frac{1}{2} = 4 : 2 : 1$$

Example 2.15. *The frame of an electric motor is connected to three earthing plates having resistance to earth of 10 Ω, 20 Ω and 30 Ω respectively. Due to a fault, the frame becomes live. What proportion of total fault energy is dissipated at each earth connection?*

Solution. The three resistances are in parallel. During the fault, suppose voltage to ground is V. Then ratios of energy dissipated is

$$\frac{V^2}{10} : \frac{V^2}{20} : \frac{V^2}{30} = \frac{1}{10} : \frac{1}{20} : \frac{1}{30} = 6:3:2$$

% of fault energy dissipated in 10 Ω $= \dfrac{6}{6+3+2} \times 100 = 54.5\%$

% of fault energy dissipated in 20 Ω $= \dfrac{3}{6+3+2} \times 100 = 27.2\%$

% of fault energy dissipated in 30 Ω $= \dfrac{2}{6+3+2} \times 100 = 18.2\%$

TUTORIAL PROBLEMS

1. Two resistors of 4 Ω and 6 Ω are connected in parallel. If the total current is 30 A, find the current through each resistor. **[18 A; 12 A]**

2. Four resistors are in parallel. The currents in the first three resistors are 4 mA, 5 mA and 6 mA respectively. The voltage drop across the fourth resistor is 200 volts. The total power dissipated is 5 watts. Determine the values of the resistances of the branches and the total resistance. **[50 kΩ, 40 kΩ, 33.33 kΩ, 8 kΩ; 5 kΩ]**

3. Four resistors of 2Ω, 3Ω, 4Ω,and 5Ω respectively are connected in parallel. What potential difference must be applied to the group in order that total power of 100 watts may be absorbed? **[8.826 Volts]**

4. Three resistors are in parallel. The current in the first resistor is 0.1 A. The power dissipated in the second is 3 watts. The voltage drop across the third is 100 volts. Determine the ohmic values of resistors and the total resistance if total current is 0.2 A. **[1000 Ω, 3333.3 Ω, 1428.5 Ω ; 500 Ω]**

5. Two coils each of 250Ω resistance are connected in series across a constant voltage mains. Calculate the value of resistance to be connected in parallel with one of the coils to reduce the p.d. across its terminals by 1%. **[12,375Ω]**

6. When a resistor is placed across a 230-volt supply, the current is 12 A. What is the value of resistor that must be placed in parallel to increase the load current to 16 A? **[57.5 Ω]**

7. A 50-ohm resistor is in parallel with a 100-ohm resistor. The current in 50 Ω resistor is 7.2 A. What is the value of third resistance to be added in parallel to make the line current 12.1 A? **[276.9 Ω]**

2.4. SERIES-PARALLEL CIRCUIT

As the name suggests, this circuit is a combination of series and parallel circuits. A simple example of such a circuit is illustrated in Fig. 2.11. Note that R_2 and R_3 are connected in parallel with each other and that both together are connected in series with R_1. One simple rule to solve such circuits is to first reduce the parallel branches to an equivalent series branch and then solve the circuit as a simple series circuit.

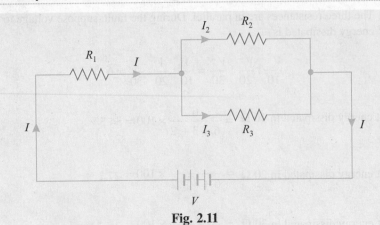

Fig. 2.11

Referring to the series-parallel circuit shown in Fig. 2.11,

$$R_T \text{ for parallel combination } = \frac{R_2 R_3}{R_2 + R_3}$$

$$\text{Total circuit resistance } = R_1 + \frac{R_2 R_3}{R_2 + R_3}$$

$$\text{Voltage across parallel combination } = I \times \frac{R_2 R_3}{R_2 + R_3}$$

The reader can now readily find the values I, I_2 and I_3.

2.5. INTERNAL RESISTANCE OF A SUPPLY

All supplies (*e.g.*, a cell) must have some internal resistance, however small. This is shown as a series resistor external to the supply. Fig. 2.12 shows a cell of *e.m.f. E* volts and internal resistance *r*. When the cell is delivering no current (*i.e.*, on no load), the p.d. across the terminals will be equal to *e.m.f. E* of the cell as shown in Fig. 2.12 (*i*).

When some load resistance *R* is connected across the terminals of the cell, then current I starts flowing in the circuit. This current causes a voltage drop across internal resistance *r* of the cell so that terminal voltage *V* available will be less than *E*. The relationship between *E* and *V* can be easily established [See Fig. 2.12 (*ii*)].

Dry cells

$$I = \frac{E}{R + r}$$

or $\qquad\qquad I R = E - I r$

But $\qquad\qquad I R = V$, the terminal voltage of the cell.

∴ $\qquad\qquad V = E - I r$

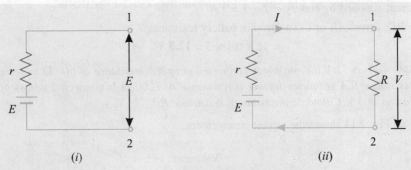

Fig. 2.12

Example 2.16. *A battery having an e.m.f. of E volts and internal resistance 0.1 Ω is connected across terminals A and B of the circuit shown in Fig. 2.13. Calculate the value of E in order that p____ dissipated in 2Ω resistor shall be 2 W.*

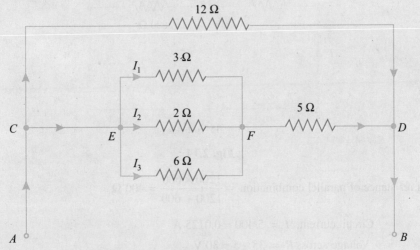

Fig. 2.13

Solution. Resistance between *E* and *F* is given by:

$$\frac{1}{R_{EF}} = \frac{1}{3} + \frac{1}{2} + \frac{1}{6} = \frac{6}{6}$$

∴ $R_{EF} = 6/6 = 1\ \Omega$

Resistance of branch *CEFD* $= 1 + 5 = 6\ \Omega$

$$\text{Current through } 2\ \Omega = \sqrt{\frac{\text{Power loss}}{\text{Resistance}}} = \sqrt{\frac{2}{2}} = 1\,\text{A}$$

P.D. across *EF* $= 1 \times 2 = 2\ \text{V}$

Current through $3\ \Omega = 2/3 = 0.67\ \text{A}$

Current through $6\ \Omega = 2/6 = 0.33\ \text{A}$

Current in branch *CED* $= 1 + 0.67 + 0.33 = 2\ \text{A}$

P.D across *CD* $= 6 \times 2 = 12\ \text{V}$

Current through $12\ \Omega = 12/12 = 1\ \text{A}$

Current supplied by battery = 2 + 1 = 3 A

∴ E = P.D. across AB or CD + Drop in battery resistance

$$= 12 + 0.1 \times 3 = \textbf{12.3 V}$$

Example 2.17. *A 35 V d.c. supply is connected across a resistance of 600 Ω in series with an unknown resistance R.A voltmeter having a resistance of 1200 Ω is connected across 600 Ω and shows a reading of 5 V. Calculate the value of resistance R.*

Solution. Fig. 2.14 shows the circuit arrangement.

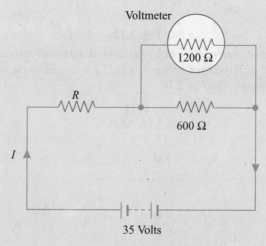

Fig. 2.14

Total resistance of parallel combination $= \dfrac{1200 \times 600}{1200 + 600} = 400 \ \Omega$

∴ Circuit current, I = 5/400 = 0.0125 A

Voltage across R = 35 – 5 = 30 V

∴ Value of R = 30/0.0125 = **2400 Ω**

Example 2.18. *Six resistors are connected as shown in Fig. 2.15. If a battery having an e.m.f. of 24 volts and internal resistance of 1 Ω is connected to the terminals A and B, find (i) the current from the battery (ii) p.d. across 8 Ω and 4 Ω resistors (iii) the current taken from the battery if a conductor of negligible resistance is connected in parallel with 8 Ω resistor.*

Solution. Resistance between E and F,

$$R_{EF} = \frac{(4 + 2) \times 6}{(4 + 2) + 6} = 3 \ \Omega$$

Resistance between C and D,

$$R_{CD} = \frac{(5 + 3) \times 8}{(5 + 3) + 8} = 4 \ \Omega$$

Resistance between A and B, $R_{AB} = 3 + 4 = 7 \ \Omega$

Total circuit resistance, $R_T = R_{AB}$ + Supply resistance = 7 + 1 = 8 Ω

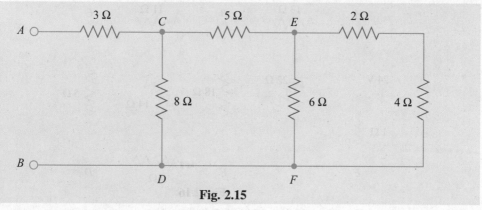

Fig. 2.15

(i) Current from battery, $I = E/R_T = 24/8 = 3A$

(ii) P.D. across $8\,\Omega = E - I(3 + 1) = 24 - 3(4) = 12\text{ V}$

Current through $8\Omega = 12/8 = 1.5$ A

Current through $5\,\Omega = 3 - 1.5 = 1.5$ A

P.D. across $EF = 12 - 1.5 \times 5 = 4.5$ V

Current through $6\,\Omega = 4.5/6 = 0.75$ A

∴ Current through $4\,\Omega = 1.5 - 0.75 = 0.75$ A

∴ Voltage across $4\,\Omega = 0.75 \times 4 = 3\text{ V}$

(iii) When a conductor of negligible resistance is connected across $8\,\Omega$, then resistance between C and D is zero. Therefore, total resistance in the circuit is now 3Ω resistor in series with $1\,\Omega$ internal resistance of battery.

∴ Current from battery $= \dfrac{24}{3 + 1} = 6\text{ A}$

Example 2.19. *An electrical network is arranged as shown in Fig. 2.16. Find (i) the current in branch AF (ii) the power absorbed in branch BE and (iii) p.d. across branch CD.*

Solution. Resistance between E and C,

$$R_{EC} = \frac{(5 + 9) \times 14}{(5 + 9) + 14} = 7\ \Omega$$

Resistance between B and E,

$$R_{BE} = \frac{(11 + 7) \times 18}{(11 + 7) + 18} = 9\ \Omega$$

Resistance between A and E,

$$R_{AE} = \frac{(13 + 9) \times 22}{(13 + 9) + 22} = 11\ \Omega$$

Total circuit resistance, $R_T = 11 + 1 = 12\ \Omega$

(i) Current in branch $AF = 24/12 = 2A$

(ii) P.D. across $AE = 24 - 2 \times 1 = 22$ V

Current in $22\ \Omega = 22/22 = 1$ A

Current in $13\ \Omega = 2 - 1 = 1$ A

P.D. across $BE = 22 - 13 \times 1 = 9$ V

Power in branch $BE = (9)^2 /18 = 4.5\text{ watts}$

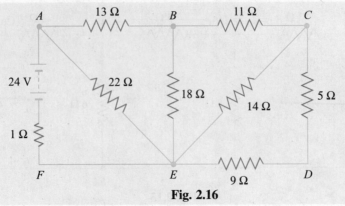

Fig. 2.16

(iii)   Current in 18 Ω = 9/18 = 0.5 A

Current in 11 Ω = 1 – 0.5 = 0.5 A

At point C, current finds two parallel paths viz. path CE of 14 Ω and path CDE of 9 + 5 = 14 Ω.

∴   Current in branch CDE = 0.5/2 = 0.25 A

∴   P.D. across CD = 0.25 × 5 = **1.25 V**

Example 2.20. *Find the value of R and the current flowing through it in Fig. 2.17 (i) if current through branch AO is zero.*

Solution. The circuit shown in Fig. 2.17 (*i*) can be redrawn as shown in Fig. 2.17 (*ii*). It is a Wheatstone bridge. Since current through branch *AO* is zero, the bridge is balanced. For balanced Wheatstone bridge, the products of the resistances of the opposite arms of the bridge are equal.

∴ $R \times 1 = 4 \times 1.5$ or $R = 6\Omega$

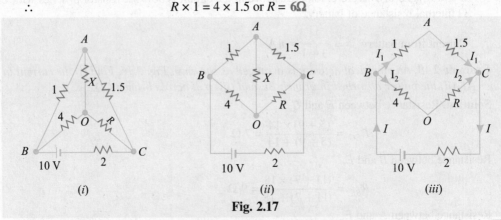

(i)   (ii)   (iii)

Fig. 2.17

Since branch *AO* carries no current, it is ineffective and can be removed from the circuit. The circuit then reduces to Fig. 2.17 (*iii*). The resistance of branch *BAC* = 1 + 1.5 = 2.5 Ω and resistance of branch *BOC* = 4 + R = 4 + 6 = 10Ω. The two branches are in parallel.

∴ $$R_{BC} = \frac{2.5 \times 10}{2.5 + 10} = 2 \ \Omega$$

Total circuit resistance = 2 + 2 = 4 Ω

Circuit current, $I = 10/4 = 2.5$ A

At junction *B*, circuit current *I* (= 2.5 A) divides into two parts; I_1 flowing through branch *BAC* and I_2 flowing through branch *BOC*.

Current through R = Current through branch *BOC*

$$= I_2 = I \times \frac{R_{BAC}}{R_{BAC} + R_{BOC}} \qquad \text{[Current divider rule]}$$

$$= 2.5 \times \frac{2.5}{2.5 + 10} = 0.5 \text{ A}$$

Example 2.21. *Two resistors $R_1 = 2500\Omega$ and $R_2 = 4000\Omega$ are joined in series and connected to a 100 V supply. The voltage drops across R_1 and R_2 are measured successively by a voltmeter having a resistance of 50000Ω. Find the sum of two readings.*

Solution. When voltmeter is connected across resistor R_1 [See Fig. 2.18 (i)], it becomes a series-parallel circuit.

Total circuit resistance $= 4000 + \dfrac{2500 \times 50000}{2500 + 50000} = 4000 + 2381 = 6381 \ \Omega$

Circuit current, $I = \dfrac{100}{6381}$ A

Voltmeter reading, $V_1 = I \times 2381 = \dfrac{100}{6381} \times 2381 = 37.3$ V

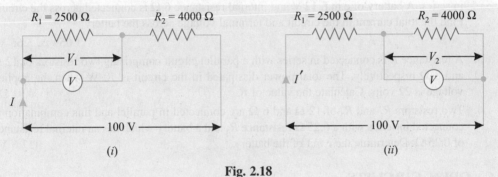

Fig. 2.18

When voltmeter is connected across R_2 [See Fig. 2.18 (ii)], it becomes a series-parallel circuit.

Total circuit resistance $= 2500 + \dfrac{4000 \times 50000}{4000 + 50000}$

$= 2500 + 3703.7 = 6203.7 \ \Omega$

Circuit current, $I' = \dfrac{100}{6203.7}$ A

Voltmeter reading, $V_2 = I' \times 3703.7 = \dfrac{100}{6203.7} \times 3703.7 = 59.7$ V

∴ Sum of two readings $= V_1 + V_2 = 37.3 + 59.7 = \mathbf{97V}$

Example 2.22. Find the voltage V_{AB} in the circuit shown in Fig. 2.19.

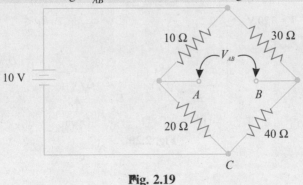

Fig. 2.19

Solution. The resistors 10 Ω and 20 Ω are in series and voltage across this combination is 10 V.

$$\therefore \qquad V_{AC} = \frac{20}{10 + 20} \times 10 = 6.667 \text{ V}$$

The resistors 30 Ω and 40 Ω are in series and voltage across this combination is 10 V.

$$\therefore \qquad V_{BC} = \frac{40}{30 + 40} \times 10 = 5.714 \text{ V}$$

The point A is positive *w.r.t.* point B.

$$\therefore \qquad V_{AB} = V_{AC} - V_{BC} = 6.667 - 5.714 = 0.953 \text{ V}$$

TUTORIAL PROBLEMS

1. A resistor of 3.6 Ω is connected in series with another of 4.56 Ω. What resistance must be placed across 3.6 Ω so that the total resistance of the circuit shall be 6Ω? **[2.4 Ω]**

2. A circuit consists of three resistors of 3 Ω, 4 Ω and 6 Ω in parallel and a fourth resistor of 4Ω in series. A battery of e.m.f. 12 V and internal resistance 6 Ω is connected across the circuit. Find the total current in the circuit and terminal voltage across the battery.

   [1.059 A, 5.65 V]

3. A resistance R is connected in series with a parallel circuit comprising two resistors of 12 Ω and 8 Ω respectively. The total power dissipated in the circuit is 70 W when the applied voltage is 22 volts. Calculate the value of R. **[0.91 Ω]**

4. Two resistors R_1 and R_2 of 12 Ω and 6 Ω are connected in parallel and this combination is connected in series with a 6.25 Ω resistance R_3 and a battery which has an internal resistance of 0.25 Ω. Determine the e.m.f of the battery. **[12.6 V]**

2.6. OPEN CIRCUITS

As the name implies, an *open* is a gap or break or interruption in a circuit path.

When there is a break in any part of a circuit, that part is said to be **open-circuited.**

No current can flow through an open. Since no current can flow through an open, according to Ohm's law, an open has infinite resistance ($R = E/I = E/0 = \infty$). An open circuit may be as a result of component failure or disintegration of a conducting path such as the breaking of a wire.

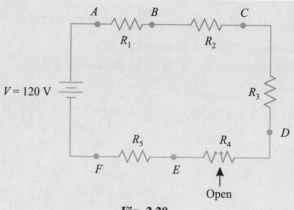

Fig. 2.20

Illustrations

(*i*)   Fig. 2.20 shows an open circuit fault in a **series circuit.** Here resistor R_4 is burnt and an open develops. Because of the open, no current can flow in the circuit.

When an open occurs in a series circuit, the following symptoms can be observed:

(*a*)   The circuit current becomes zero.

(*b*)   There will be no voltage drop across the resistors that are normal.

(*c*)   *The entire voltage drop appears across the open.* This can be readily proved. Applying Kirchhoff's voltage law to the loop *ABCDEFA,* we have,

$$-0 \times R_1 - 0 \times R_2 - 0 \times R_3 - V_{DE} - 0 \times R_5 + 120 = 0$$
$$\therefore V_{DE} = 120 \text{ V}$$

(*d*)   Since the circuit current is zero, there is no voltage drop in the internal resistance of the source. Therefore, terminal voltage may measure higher than the normal.

(*ii*)   One or more branches of a **parallel circuit** may develop an open. Fig. 2.21 shows a parallel circuit with an open. Here resistor R_3 is burnt out and now has infinite resistance.

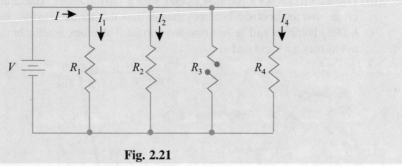

Fig. 2.21

The following symptoms can be observed:

(*a*)   Branch current I_3 will be zero because R_3 is open.

(*b*)   The total current I will be less than the normal.

(*c*)   The operation of the branches without opens will be normal.

(*d*)   The open device will not operate. If R_3 is a lamp, it will be out. If it is a motor, it will not run.

2.7.   SHORT CIRCUITS

A short circuit or short is a path of low resistance. *A* short circuit *is an unwanted path of low resistance.*

When a short circuit occurs, the resistance of the circuit becomes low. As a result, current greater than the normal flows which can cause damage to circuit components. The short circuit may be due to insulation failure, components get shorted etc.

Illustrations

(*i*)   Fig. 2.22 (*i*) shows a **series circuit** with a **partial short.** An unwanted path has connected R_1 to R_3 and has eliminated R_2 from the circuit. Therefore, the circuit resistance decreases and the circuit current becomes greater than normal. The voltage drop across components that are not shorted will be higher than normal. Since current is increased, the power dissipation in the components that are not shorted will be greater than the normal. A partial short circuit may cause healthy component to burn out due to abnormally high dissipation.

Fig. 2.22 (*ii*) shows a **series circuit** with a **dead short.** Here all the loads (i.e. resistors in this case) have been removed by the unwanted path. Therefore, the circuit resistance is almost zero and the circuit current becomes extremely high. If there are no protective devices (fuse, circuit breaker etc.) in the circuit, drastic results (smoke, fire, explosions etc.) may occur.

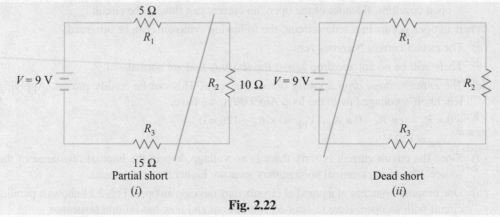

Fig. 2.22

(*ii*) Fig. 2.23 (*i*) shows a **parallel circuit** with a **partial short.** The circuit resistance will decrease and total current becomes greater than the normal. Further, the current flow in the healthy branches will be less than the normal. Therefore, healthy branches may operate but not as they are supposed to.

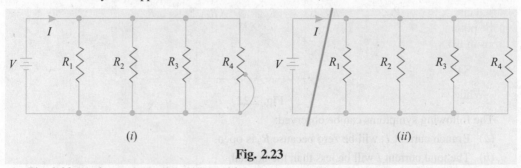

Fig. 2.23

Fig. 2.23 (*ii*) shows a **parallel circuit** with a **dead short.** Note that all the loads are eliminated by the short circuit so that the circuit resistance is almost zero. As a result, the circuit current becomes abnormally high and may cause extensive damage unless it has protective devices (*e.g.* fuse, circuit breaker etc.).

2.8. KIRCHHOFF'S LAWS

Gustav Kirchhoff (1824—1887), an eminent German Physicist did a considerable amount of work on the principles governing the behaviour of electric circuits. He gave his findings in a set of two laws—a current and a voltage law—which together are known as *Kirchhoff's laws*. It is upon these laws that electric theory is based.

First law. This law relates to the currents at the junction points of a circuit and is stated below:

The algebraic sum of currents flowing towards a junction in an electric circuit is zero.

An algebraic sum is one in which the sign of the quantity is taken into account. For example, consider four conductors carrying currents I_1, I_2, I_3 and I_4 and meeting at point O as shown in Fig. 2.24. If we take the signs of currents flowing towards O as positive, then currents flow-

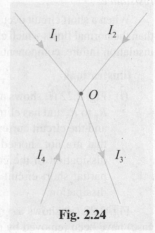

Fig. 2.24

ing away from point O will be assigned negative sign. Thus applying Kirchhoff's first law to junction O in Fig. 2.24,

$$(I_1) + (I_2) + (I_4) + (-I_3) = 0$$

or
$$I_1 + I_2 + I_4 = I_3$$

i.e.,   **Incoming currents = Outgoing currents**

Hence Kirchhoff's first law can also be stated as under:

The sum of the currents flowing towards any junction in an electric circuit is equal to the sum of currents flowing away from the junction.

Kirchhoff's first law is true because electric current is merely the flow of electrons and they cannot accumulate at any point in the circuit. Thus in Fig. 2.24, currents I_1, I_2 and I_4 are flowing towards point O and naturally $(I_1 + I_2 + I_4)$ must flow out of point O. Therefore, $I_1 + I_2 + I_4 = I_3$.

Second Law. This law relates to e.m.f.s and voltage drops in a circuit and is sometimes called voltage law. It is stated as follows:

In any closed circuit or mesh, the algebraic sum of all the electromotive forces (e.m.f.s) and the voltage drops is equal to zero i.e.

In any closed circuit or mesh,

Algebraic sum of e.m.f.s + Algebraic sum of voltage drops = 0

The validity of Kirchhoff's second law can be readily established. If we start from any point in a closed circuit and go back to that point after going round the circuit, there is no increase or decrease in the potential. This means that the sum of e.m.f.s of all the sources met on the way plus the voltage drops in the resistances must be zero.

2.9. SIGNS OF E.M.F.S AND VOLTAGE DROPS

While applying Kirchhoff's second law to a closed circuit, it is very important to assign proper signs to e.m.f.s and voltage drops in the closed circuit. The following sign convention may be followed:

A *rise in potential should be considered **positive** while a **fall in potential** should be considered **negative**.

(*i*) Thus if we go from the positive terminal of battery or source to the negative terminal [See Fig. 2.25 (*i*)], there is a fall in potential and the e.m.f. should be assigned negative sign. On the other hand, if we go from the negative terminal of the battery or source to the positive terminal [See Fig. 2.25 (*ii*)], there is a rise in potential and the e.m.f. should be given positive sign. *It may be noted that sign of e.m.f. is independent of the direction of current through that branch.*

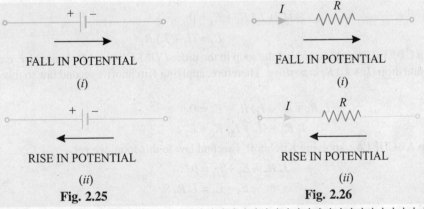

FALL IN POTENTIAL   FALL IN POTENTIAL

(*i*)   (*i*)

RISE IN POTENTIAL   RISE IN POTENTIAL

(*ii*)   (*ii*)

Fig. 2.25   **Fig. 2.26**

* The reverse convention is equally valid *i.e.*, rise in potential may be considered negative and fall in potential as positive.

(*ii*) When current flows through a resistor, there is a voltage drop across it. If we go through the resistor in the same direction as the current [See Fig. 2.26 (*i*)], there is a fall in potential because current flows from higher potential to lower potential. Hence this voltage drop should be given negative sign. On the other hand, if we go against the current flow [See Fig. 2.26 (*ii*)], there is a rise in potential and the voltage drop should be given positive sign. *It may be noted that sign of voltage drop depends upon the direction of current and is independent of the polarity of the e.m.f. in the circuit under consideration.*

2.10. ILLUSTRATION OF KIRCHHOFF'S LAWS

Kirchhoff's Laws can be beautifully explained by referring to Fig. 2.27. Mark the direction of currents as indicated. The direction in which currents are assumed to flow is unimportant, since if wrong direction is chosen, it will be indicated by a negative sign in the result.

(*i*) The magnitude of current in any branch of the circuit can be found by applying Kirchhoff's first law. Thus at junction *C* in Fig. 2.27, the incoming currents to the junction are I_1 and I_2. Obviously, the current in branch *CF* will be $I_1 + I_2$.

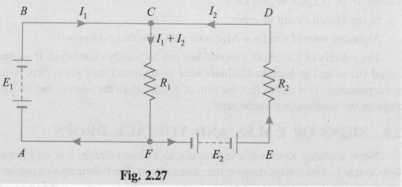

Fig. 2.27

(*ii*) There are three closed loops in Fig. 2.27 *viz. ABCFA, CDEFC* and *ABCDEFA*. Kirchhoff's second law can be applied to these closed loops to get the desired equations.

Loop ABCFA. In this loop, e.m.f. E_1 will be given *positive* sign. It is because as we consider the loop in the order *ABCFA*, we go from $-ve$ terminal to the positive terminal of the battery in the branch *AB* and hence there is a rise in potential. The voltage drop in branch *CF* is $(I_1 + I_2) R_1$ and shall bear *negative* sign. It is because as we consider the loop in the order *ABCFA*, we go with current in branch *CF* and there is a fall in potential. Applying Kirchhoff's second law to the loop *ABCFA*,

$$- (I_1 + I_2) R_1 + E_1 = 0$$

or
$$E_1 = (I_1 + I_2) R_1$$

Loop CDEFC. As we go around the loop in the order *CDEFC*, drop $I_2 R_2$ is *positive,* e.m.f. E_2 is *negative* and drop $(I_1 + I_2) R_1$ is *positive.* Therefore, applying Kirchhoff's second law to this loop, we get,

$$I_2 R_2 + (I_1 + I_2) R_1 - E_2 = 0$$

or
$$I_2 R_2 + (I_1 + I_2) R_1 = E_2$$

Loop ABCDEFA. Applying Kirchhoff's second law to this loop, we get,

$$I_2 R_2 - E_2 + E_1 = 0$$

or
$$E_2 - E_1 = I_2 R_2$$

2.11. METHOD TO SOLVE CIRCUITS BY KIRCHHOFF'S LAWS

(i)   Assume unknown currents in the given circuit and show their directions by arrows.

(ii) Choose any closed circuit or loop and find the algebraic sum of voltage drops *plus* the algebraic sum of e.m.f.s in that loop.

(iii) Put the algebraic sum of voltage drops plus the algebraic sum of e.m.f.s equal to zero.

(iv) Write equations for as many loops as the number of unknown quantities.

(v)   If the value of the assumed current comes out to be negative, it means that actual direction of current is opposite to that of assumed direction.

Example 2.23. *Calculate the current in 2 Ω resistor in Fig. 2.28.*

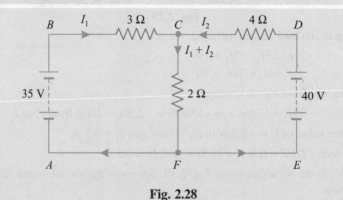

Fig. 2.28

Solution. Mark the currents in the various branches as shown in Fig. 2.28. Since there are two unknown quantities I_1 and I_2, two equations must be formed by considering two loops.

Loop ABCFA $35 - 3I_1 - 2(I_1 + I_2) = 0$

or $5I_1 + 2I_2 = 35$ ...(i)

Loop ABCDEFA $35 - 3I_1 + 4I_2 - 40 = 0$

or $3I_1 - 4I_2 = -5$ ...(ii)

Multiplying eq. (i) by 2 and then adding it to eq. (ii), we get,

$\quad\quad 13I_1 = 65 \quad\quad\quad \therefore I_1 = 65/13 = 5\ A$

Substituting the value of $I_1 = 5$ A in eq. (i), we get, $I_2 = 5$ A

$\therefore$ Current in 2 Ω resistor $= I_1 + I_2 = 5 + 5 = 10\ A$

Example 2.24. *For the circuit shown in Fig. 2.29, find the current flowing in all branches.*

Solution. Mark the currents in various branches as shown in Fig. 2.29. Since there are two unknown quantities I_1 and I_2, two loops will be considered.

Loop ABCFA $30 - 2I_1 - 10 + 5I_2 = 0$

or $2I_1 - 5I_2 = 20$ ...(i)

Loop FCDEF $-5I_2 + 10 - 3(I_1 + I_2) - 5 - 4(I_1 + I_2) = 0$

or $7I_1 + 12I_2 = 5$ ...(ii)

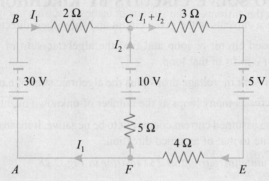

Fig. 2.29

Multiplying eq. (*i*) by 7 and eq. (*ii*) by 2, we get,

$$14I_1 - 35I_2 = 140 \qquad \qquad ...(iii)$$
$$14I_1 + 24I_2 = 10 \qquad \qquad ...(iv)$$

Subtracting eq. (*iv*) from eq. (*iii*), we get,

$$-59I_2 = 130 \quad \therefore \quad I_2 = -130/59 = -2.2A = \textbf{2.2 A} \text{ from } C \text{ to } F$$

Substituting the value of $I_2 = -2.2$ A in eq. (*i*), we get, $I_1 = \textbf{4.5 A}$

Current in branch $CDEF = I_1 + I_2 = (4.5) + (-2.2) = \textbf{2.3 A}$

Example 2.25. *In the circuit shown in Fig. 2.30, determine the direction and value of current in each of the batteries.*

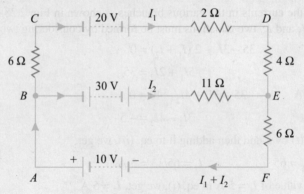

Fig. 2.30

Solution. Mark the currents in the various branches as shown in Fig. 2.30.

Loop ABEFA $\qquad \qquad 30 - 11 I_2 - 6 (I_1 + I_2) + 10 = 0$

or $\qquad \qquad \qquad \qquad 6I_1 + 17I_2 = 40 \qquad \qquad ...(i)$

Loop BCDEB $\qquad -6I_1 + 20 - 2I_1 - 4I_1 + 11I_2 - 30 = 0$

or $\qquad \qquad \qquad \qquad 12 I_1 - 11 I_2 = -10 \qquad \qquad ...(ii)$

From eqs. (*i*) and (*ii*), $\qquad I_1 = \textbf{1A} ; I_2 = \textbf{2A}; I_1 + I_2 = \textbf{3 A}$

Example 2.26. *Two batteries E_1 and E_2, having e.m.f.s of 6 V and 2V respectively and internal resistances of 2Ω and 3Ω respectively, are connected in parallel across a 5 Ω resistor. Calculate (i) the current through each battery (ii) terminal voltage and (iii) energy dissipated in 5Ω resistor in 10 minutes.*

Solution. (*i*) Mark the currents in the various branches as shown in Fig. 2.31.

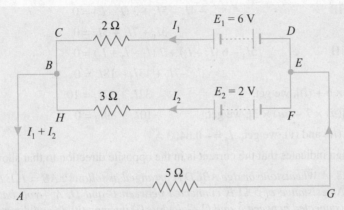

Fig. 2.31

Loop HCDFH $2I_1 - 6 + 2 - 3I_2 = 0$

or $2I_1 - 3I_2 = 4$ ...(*i*)

Loop ABHFEGA $3I_2 - 2 + 5(I_1 + I_2) = 0$

or $5I_1 + 8I_2 = 2$ ...(*ii*)

Multiplying eq. (*i*) by 8 and eq. (*ii*) by 3 and then adding them,

$$31I_1 = 38 \qquad \therefore I_1 = 38/31 = \textbf{1.226 A}$$

i.e., battery E_1 is being *discharged* at 1.226 A.

Substituting $I_1 = 1.226$ A in eq. (*i*), we get, $I_2 = -\,\textbf{0.516 A}$ *i.e.*, battery E_2 is being *charged* at 0.516 A.

(*ii*)   Terminal voltage, $V = (I_1 + I_2) \times 5 = (1.226 - 0.516) \times 5 = \textbf{3.55 V}$

(*iii*)   Energy dissipated in 10 min. $= V \times (I_1 + I_2) \times t$

$$= (3.55)\,(0.71)\,(10 \times 60) \text{ watt-sec or joules} = \textbf{1512 joules}$$

Example 2.27. *Calculate the current in 5 Ω resistor shown in Fig.2.32 (i).*

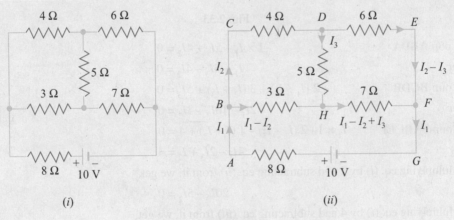

(*i*)   (*ii*)

Fig. 2.32

Solution. Mark the direction of currents in the branches as shown in Fig. 2.32 (*ii*).

Loop ABHFGA $-3(I_1 - I_2) - 7(I_1 - I_2 + I_3) + 10 - 8I_1 = 0$

or $\qquad\qquad\qquad\qquad\qquad\qquad\quad 18I_1 - 10I_2 + 7I_3 = 10$ $\qquad\qquad$ ...(i)

Loop BCDHB $\qquad\qquad\qquad\quad -4I_2 - 5I_3 + 3\,(I_1 - I_2) = 0$

or $\qquad\qquad\qquad\qquad\qquad\qquad\quad -3I_1 + 7I_2 + 5I_3 = 0$ $\qquad\qquad$ ...(ii)

Loop HDEFH $\qquad\quad 5I_3 - 6\,(I_2 - I_3) + 7\,(I_1 - I_2 + I_3) = 0$

or $\qquad\qquad\qquad\qquad\qquad\qquad\quad -7I_1 + 13I_2 - 18I_3 = 0$ $\qquad\qquad$ ...(iii)

Adding [(ii) × 6 + (i)], we get, $\qquad\qquad 32I_2 + 37I_3 = 10$ $\qquad\qquad$ ...(iv)

Subtracting [(ii) × 7 − (iii) × 3], we get, $\qquad 10I_2 + 89I_3 = 0$ $\qquad\qquad$ ...(v)

Solving eqs. (iv) and (v), we get, $I_3 = -0.0403$ A

The minus sign indicates that the current is in the opposite direction to that shown.

Example 2.28. *A Wheatstone bridge ABCD is arranged as follows : AB = 1Ω: BC = 2 Ω; CD = 3 Ω; DA = 4Ω. A resistance of 5 Ω is connected between B and D. A 4-volt battery of internal resistance 1 Ω is connected between A and C. Calculate (i) the magnitude and direction of current in 5 Ω resistor and (ii) the resistance between A and C.*

Solution. (i) Fig. 2.33 shows the Wheatstone bridge *ABCD*. Mark the currents in the various branches as shown. Since there are three unknown quantities (*viz.* I_1, I_2 and I_3), three loops will be considered.

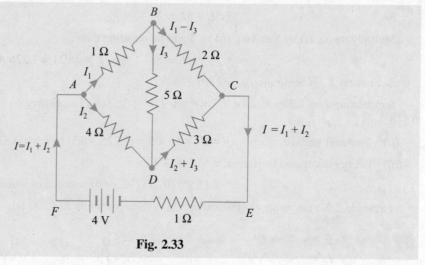

Fig. 2.33

Loop ABDA $\qquad\qquad\qquad\qquad -1 \times I_1 - 5I_3 + 4I_2 = 0$

or $\qquad\qquad\qquad\qquad\qquad\qquad\quad I_1 + 5I_3 - 4I_2 = 0$ $\qquad\qquad$ ...(i)

Loop BCDB $\qquad\qquad -2\,(I_1 - I_3) + 3\,(I_2 + I_3) + 5I_3 = 0$

or $\qquad\qquad\qquad\qquad\qquad\qquad\quad 2I_1 - 10I_3 - 3i_2 = 0$ $\qquad\qquad$ ...(ii)

Loop FABCEF $\qquad -I_1 \times 1 - 2\,(I_1 - I_3) - 1\,(I_1 + I_2) + 4 = 0$

or $\qquad\qquad\qquad\qquad\qquad\qquad\quad 4I_1 - 2I_3 + I_2 = 4$ $\qquad\qquad$ ...(iii)

Multiplying eq. (i) by 2 and subtracting eq. (ii) from it, we get,

$$20I_3 - 5I_2 = 0 \qquad\qquad ...(iv)$$

Multiplying eq. (i) by 4 and subtracting eq. (iii) from it, we get,

$$22I_3 - 17I_2 = -4 \qquad\qquad ...(v)$$

Multiplying eq. (*iv*) by 17 and eq. (*v*) by 5, we get,

$$340I_3 - 85I_2 = 0 \qquad \qquad ...(vi)$$

$$110I_3 - 85I_2 = -20 \qquad \qquad ...(vii)$$

Subtracting eq. (*vii*) from eq. (*vi*), we get, $\qquad 230I_3 = 20$ or $I_3 = 20/230 = 0.087$ A

i.e., $\qquad\qquad\qquad\qquad$ Current in 5 Ω, $I_3 = $ **0.087 A** from *B* to *D*.

(*ii*) Substituting the value of $I_3 = 0.087$ A in eq. (*iv*), we get, $I_2 = 0.348$ A.

Substituting values of $I_3 = 0.087$ A and $I_2 = 0.348$ A in eq. (*ii*), $I_1 = 0.957$ A.

Current supplied by battery, $I = I_1 + I_2 = 0.957 + 0.348 = 1.305$ A.

P.D. between *A* and *C* $\qquad\qquad = $ E.M.F. of battery – Drop in battery

$$= 4 - 1.305 \times 1 = 2.695 \text{ V}$$

∴ Resistance between *A* and $C = \dfrac{\text{P.D. Across } AC}{\text{Battery current}} = \dfrac{2.695}{1.305} = 2.065 \ \Omega$

Example 2.29. *In the Wheatstone bridge network shown in Fig. 2.34, find the current in each resistor.*

Solution. Fig. 2.34 shows the Wheatstone bridge network. Mark the currents in various branches as shown. Since there are three unknown quantities (*viz.* I_1, I_2 and I_3), three loops will be considered.

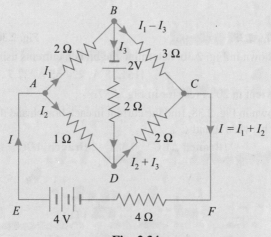

Fig. 2.34

Loop ABDA $\qquad\qquad\qquad -2I_1 + 2 - 2I_3 + I_2 = 0$

or $\qquad\qquad\qquad\qquad\qquad 2I_1 + 2I_3 - I_2 = 2 \qquad\qquad\qquad ...(i)$

Loop BCDB $\qquad -3(I_1 - I_3) + 2(I_2 + I_3) + 2I_3 - 2 = 0$

or $\qquad\qquad\qquad\qquad\qquad 3I_1 - 7I_3 - 2I_2 = -2 \qquad\qquad\qquad ...(ii)$

Loop EABCFE $\qquad -2I_1 - 3(I_1 - I_3) - 4(I_1 + I_2) + 4 = 0$

or $\qquad\qquad\qquad\qquad\qquad 9I_1 - 3I_3 + 4I_2 = 4 \qquad\qquad\qquad ...(iii)$

Multiplying eq. (*i*) by 2 and subtracting eq. (*ii*) from it, we get,

$$I_1 + 11I_3 = 6 \qquad\qquad\qquad ...(iv)$$

Multiplying eq. (*i*) by 4 and adding eq. (*iii*) to it, we get,

$$17I_1 + 5I_3 = 12 \qquad\qquad\qquad ...(v)$$

Multiplying eq.(iv) by 17 and subtracting eq. (v) from it, we get,

$$182 I_3 = 90 \quad or \quad I_3 = 90 / 182 = 0.494 \text{ A}$$

Substituting $I_3 = 0.494$ A in eq. (iv), we get, $I_1 = 0.566$ A

Substituting $I_1 = 0.566$ A and $I_3 = 0.494$ A in eq. (i); $I_2 = 0.12$ A

Current in branch $BC = I_1 - I_3 = 0.566 - 0.494 = 0.072$ A

Current in branch $DC = I_2 + I_3 = 0.12 + 0.494 = 0.614$ A

Total current, $\qquad I = I_1 + I_2 = 0.566 + 0.12 = 0.686$ A

TUTORIAL PROBLEMS

1. Using Kirchhoff's laws, find the current in various resistors in the circuit shown in Fig. 2.35. **[6.574 A, 3.611 A, 10.185 A]**

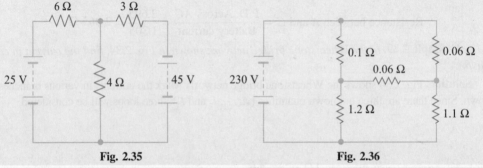

Fig. 2.35 **Fig. 2.36**

2. For the circuit shown in Fig. 2.36, determine the branch currents using Kirchhoff's laws.
[151.35 A, 224.55 A, 27.7 A, 179.05 A, 196.84 A]

3. Calculate the current in 20 Ω resistor in Fig. 2.37. **[26.67 mA]**

4. In the circuit shown in Fig. 2.38, find the current in each branch and the current in the battery. What is the p.d. between A and C ?
[Branch $ABC = 0.581$ A; Branch $ADC = 0.258$ A; $V_{AC} = 0.45$ V]

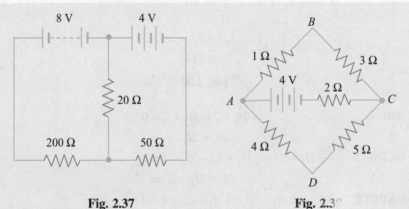

Fig. 2.37 **Fig. 2.3**

5. Two batteries A and B having e.m.fs of 20 V and 21 V respectively   ernal resistances of 0.8 Ω and 0.2 Ω respectively, are connected in parallel across 50 Ω resistor. Calculate (i) the current through each battery and (ii) the terminal voltage.
[(i) Battery A = 0.4725 A; Battery $B = 0.0714$ A (ii) 20 V]

6. A battery having an e.m.f. of 10 V and internal resistance 0.01 Ω is connected in parallel with a second battery of e.m.f. 10 V and internal resistance 0.008 Ω. The two batteries in parallel are properly connected for charging from a d.c. supply of 20 V through a 0.9 Ω resistor. Calculate the current taken by each battery and the current from the supply.

[**4.91 A, 6.14 A, 11.05 A**]

7. Two batteries A and B having e.m.fs. 12 V and 8 V respectively and internal resistances of 2Ω and 1Ω respectively, are connected in parallel across 10 Ω resistor. Calculate (*i*) the current in each of the batteries and the external resistor and (*ii*) p.d. across external resistor.

[(*i*) I_A = **1.625 A discharge** ; I_B = **0.75 A charge, 0.875 A** (*ii*) **8.75 V**]

8. A Wheatstone bridge $ABCD$ is arranged as follows: $AB = 20\Omega$, $BC = 5\ \Omega$, $CD = 4\ \Omega$ and $DA = 10\ \Omega$. A galvanometer of resistance 6 Ω is connected between B and D. A 100-volts supply of negligible resistance is connected between A and C with A positive. Find the magnitude and direction of galvanometer current. [**0.667 A, from** D **to** B]

9. A network $ABCD$ consists of the following resistors: $AB = 5$ kΩ, $BC = 10$ kΩ, $CD = 15$ kΩ and $DA = 20$ kΩ. A fifth resistor of 10 kΩ is connected between A and C. A dry battery of e.m.f. 120 V and internal resistance 500 Ω is connected across the resistor AD. Calculate (*i*) the total current supplied by the battery (*ii*) the p.d. across points C and D and (*iii*) the magnitude and direction of current through branch AC.

[(*i*) **11.17 mA** (*ii*) **81.72 V** (*iii*) **3.27 mA** *from* A *to* C]

10. A Wheatstone bridge $ABCD$ is arranged as follows, $AB = 10\ \Omega$, $BC = 30\ \Omega$, $CD = 15\ \Omega$ and $DA = 20\ \Omega$. A 2 volt battery of internal resistance 2 Ω is connected between A and C with A positive. A galvanometer of resistance 40 Ω is connected between B and D. Find the magnitude and direction of galvanometer current. [**11.5 mA** *from* B *to* D]

2.12. GROUPING OF CELLS

The e.m.f. and current obtained from a single cell are generally small. For instance, an oridnary dry cell has an e.m.f. of 1.5 volts and can deliver about 1/8 ampere continuously. Such a cell can, therefore, supply electrical energy to a circuit requiring 1.5 volts and not more than 1/8 ampere. Many occasions arise where higher voltage or higher current or both are required. To meet these needs, a number of cells are suitably connected or grouped. The combination of cells thus obtained is called a *battery*. The following are the three methods of grouping of cells to form a battery:

(*i*) Series grouping; (*ii*) Parallel grouping; (*iii*) Series-parallel grouping.

Batteries

2.13. SERIES GROUPING OF CELLS

In series grouping, the negative terminal of one cell is connected to the positive terminal of the next cell and so on. Consider n cells, each of e.m.f. E and internal resistance r, connected in series across an external resistance R as shown in Fig. 2.39.

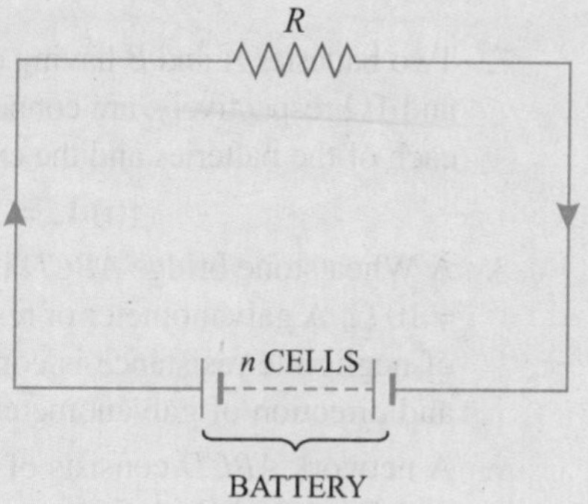

Total battery e.m.f. $= nE$ volts

Internal resistance of battery $= nr\ \Omega$

Total circuit resistance $= R + nr$

∴ Circuit current, $I = \dfrac{nE}{R + nr}$

Fig. 2.39

(i) If R is negligible as compared to nr, then,

Circuit current, $I = \dfrac{nE}{nr} = \dfrac{E}{r}$ = Current due to one cell

(ii) If nr (i.e., battery resistance) is negligible as compared to R, then,

Circuit current, $I = \dfrac{nE}{R} = n \times \dfrac{E}{R} = n \times$ current due to one cell

Hence, series grouping is useful when battery resistance is negligible as compared to external resistance.

Example 2.30. *Twelve cells, each of e.m.f. 2 volts and internal resistance 0.5 Ω, are connected in series across an external resistance of 4.5 Ω. Determine (i) the current supplied by the battery (ii) terminal voltage of the battery and (iii) fall in voltage per cell.*

Solution.

E.M.F. of each cell, $E = 2$ V; Internal resistance of each cell, $r = 0.5\ \Omega$;

Number of cells, $n = 12$; External resistance, $R = 4.5\ \Omega$

Total e.m.f. of battery $= nE = 12 \times 2 = 24$ V; Internal resistance of battery $= nr = 12 \times 0.5 = 6\ \Omega$

Total circuit resistance $= R + nr = 4.5 + 6 = 10.5\ \Omega$

(i) Current supplied by battery, $I = 24/10.5 =$ **2.286 A**

(ii) Terminal voltage of battery $= IR = 2.286 \times 4.5 =$ **10.287 V**

(iii) Fall in voltage per cell $= Ir = 2.286 \times 0.5 =$ **1.143 V**

Example 2.31. *A battery consisting of 10 cells in series has two of the cells reversed. E.M.F. of each cell is 1.5 V and internal resistance 0.1 Ω. The resistance of the external circuit is 4Ω. Find the reduction in current due to the two cells being reverse connected.*

Solution.

When 10 cells are properly connected in series,

Total e.m.f. of battery $= nE = 10 \times 1.5 = 15$ V

Total circuit resistance $= R + nr = 4 + 10 \times 0.1 = 5\ \Omega$

∴ Circuit current $= 15/5 = 3$ A

When two of the cells are reverse connected,

Total e.m.f. of battery $= 8 \times 1.5 - 2 \times 1.5 = 9$ V

Total circuit resistance $= 5\ \Omega$ *i.e.,* same as before

∴ Circuit current $= 9/5 = 1.8$ A

∴ Reduction in current $= 3 - 1.8 =$ **1.2 A**

Example 2.32. *A battery is formed by five cells in series. When the external resistance is 4 Ω, the current is 1.5 A and when it is 9 Ω, the current falls to 0.75 A. Find the e.m.f. and internal resistance of each cell.*

Solution. In series grouping of cells, $I = \dfrac{nE}{R + nr}$ or $nE = I(R + nr)$

When $R = 4\,\Omega, I = 1.5$ A $\quad \therefore 5E = 1.5(4 + 5 \times r)$

or $\quad 5E - 7.5r = 6$ ...(*i*)

When $R = 9\,\Omega; I = 0.75$ A $\quad \therefore 5E = 0.75(9 + 5 \times r)$

or $\quad 5E - 3.75r = 6.75$ ...(*ii*)

Solving eqs. (*i*) and (*ii*), we get, $E = 1.5$ V and $r = 0.2\,\Omega$

2.14. PARALLEL GROUPING OF CELLS

In parallel grouping, positive terminals of all the cells are joined together and in like manner, all the negative terminals are connected together. Consider m rows in parallel, each containing one cell. Let E and r be the e.m.f. and internal resistance respectively of each cell. Further, let this parallel group be connected across an external resistance R as shown in Fig. 2.40.

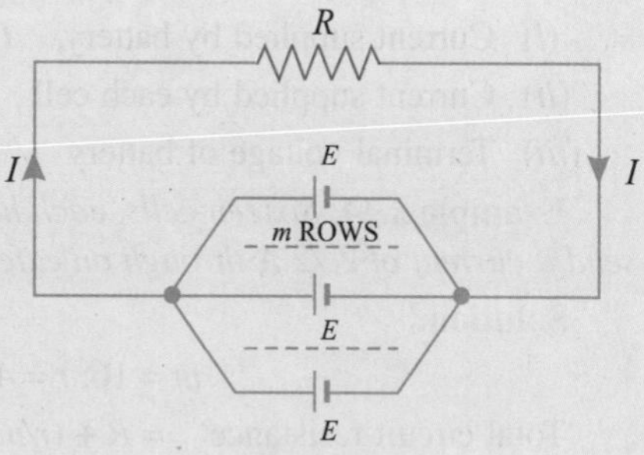

E.M.F. of battery $= E$

Since the cells are connected in parallel, their internal resistances are also in parallel. If r_T is the total resistance of the battery, then,

Fig. 2.40

$$\frac{1}{r_T} = \frac{1}{r} + \frac{1}{r} + \frac{1}{r} + \ \dots m \text{ terms}$$

$$= \frac{1 + 1 + 1 + \dots m \text{ terms}}{r} = \frac{m}{r}$$

$\therefore \qquad r_T = \dfrac{r}{m}\,\Omega$

Total circuit resistance $= R + (r/m)$

$\therefore$ Circuit current, $I = \dfrac{E}{R + (r/m)}$

(*i*) If r/m (*i.e.*, battery resistance) is negligible as compared to R, then,

Circuit current, $I = \dfrac{E}{R}$ = current due to one cell.

(*ii*) If R is negligible as compared to r/m (*i.e.*, battery resistance), then,

Circuit current, $I = \dfrac{E}{r/m} = m \times \dfrac{E}{r} = m \times$ current due to one cell

Hence, parallel grouping is useful when external resistance is negligible as compared to battery resistance.

Example 2.33. *Four cells, each of e.m.f. 1.5 V and internal resistance 0.5 Ω, are connected in parallel across an external resistance of 2.5 Ω. Determine (i) the current supplied by the battery (ii) current supplied by each cell and (iii) the terminal voltage of the battery.*

Solution. Fig. 2.41 shows the arrangement of cells in parallel.

E.M.F. of each cell, $E = 1.5$ V; Resistance of each cell, $r = 0.5\,\Omega$

No. of rows of cells, $m = 4$; Battery e.m.f. $= 1.5$ V

Resistance of battery $= r/m = 0.5/4 = 0.125\ \Omega$

Total circuit resistance $= R + r/m = 2.5 + 0.125 = 2.625\ \Omega$

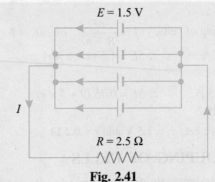

$E = 1.5\ V$

I

$R = 2.5\ \Omega$

Fig. 2.41

(i)   Current supplied by battery, $I = 1.5/2.625 = \mathbf{0.571\ A}$

(ii)   Current supplied by each cell $= 0.571/4 = \mathbf{0.1427\ A}$

(iii)   Terminal voltage of battery $= IR = 0.571 \times 2.5 = \mathbf{1.4275\ V}$

Example 2.34. *Sixteen cells, each having an internal resistance of 4 Ω, when joined in parallel send a current of 2.72 A through an external resistance of 0.3 Ω. Find the e.m.f. of each cell.*

Solution.

$$m = 16;\ r = 4\Omega;\ I = 2.72\ A;\ R = 0.3\ \Omega;\ E = ?$$

Total circuit resistance $= R + (r/m) = 0.3 + (4/16) = 0.55\ \Omega$

$\therefore$ Circuit current, $I = E/0.55$

or $2.72 = E/0.55$

$\therefore$ Battery e.m.f., $E = 2.72 \times 0.55 = \mathbf{1.496\ V}$

Since the cells are connected in parallel, battery e.m.f. is equal to e.m.f. of each cell.

2.15.   SERIES-PARALLEL GROUPING OF CELLS

In series-parallel grouping, a number of cells are connected in series and a number of sets of such series connected cells are in parallel, as shown in Fig. 2.42. Let there be n cells connected in series and m such rows connected in parallel across an external resistance R. Further, let E and r be the e.m.f. and internal resistance respectively of each cell.

Resistance of one row of cells

$$= r + r + r +\dots\ n\ \text{terms} = nr$$

Now, there are m rows in parallel, each having a resistance of nr. If r_T is the total resistance of the battery,

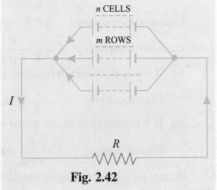

n CELLS

m ROWS

I

R

Fig. 2.42

then, $\dfrac{1}{r_T} = \dfrac{1}{nr} + \dfrac{1}{nr} + \dfrac{1}{nr} + \dots m\ \text{terms}$

$$= \dfrac{1 + 1 + 1 +\dots m\ \text{terms}}{nr} = \dfrac{m}{nr}$$

$\therefore$ $r_T = nr/m$

Total circuit resistance $= R + r_T = R + (nr/m)$

Battery e.m.f. = E.M.F. of one row $= nE$

$\therefore$ Circuit current, $I = \dfrac{nE}{R + (nr/m)} = \dfrac{mnE}{mR + nr}$

Example 2.35. *Thirty two cells are arranged in rows of eight in series and four rows in parallel. The e.m.f. of each cell is 2 V and internal resistance of each cell is 2 Ω. Determine (i) the current supplied to an external resistance of 8 Ω and (ii) maximum power that can be delivered to the load.*

Solution. Fig. 2.43. shows the arrangement of cells.

No. of cells per row, $n = 8$; Number of rows, $m = 4$

E.m.f. of each cell, $E = 2$ V; Internal resistance/cell, $r = 2\ \Omega$

External resistance, $R = 8\ \Omega$; Battery e.m.f. $= nE = 8 \times 2 = 16$ V

Battery resistance $= nr/m = 8 \times 2/4 = 4\ \Omega$

Total circuit resistance $= R + (nr/m) = 8 + 4 = 12\ \Omega$

(i) Circuit current, $I = 16/12 = \textbf{1.33 A}$

(ii) The power delivered to the load (8 Ω) will be maximum when the load $R = nr/m =$ internal resistance of battery $= 4\ \Omega$.

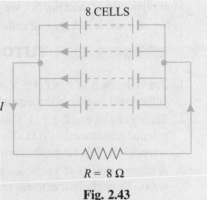

Fig. 2.43

Therefore, total circuit resistance for maximum power delivered to load is $= 4 + 4 = 8\ \Omega$

$\therefore$ Maximum power to load $= (2)^2 \times 4 = \textbf{16 watts}$

Example 2.36. *Find the minimum number of cells connected in two rows in parallel required to pass a current of 6 A through an external resistance of 0.7 Ω. The e.m.f. and internal resistance of each cell are 2.1 V and 0.5 Ω respectively.*

Solution. Let there be n cells in series in each row.

Battery e.m.f. $= nE = 2.1\ n$; Total circuit resistance $= R + (nr/m) = 0.7 + 0.25\ n$

Circuit current $= \dfrac{2.1\ n}{0.7 + 0.25\ n}$

or $6 = \dfrac{2.1\ n}{0.7 + 0.25\ n}$ $\therefore n = 7$

Since there are two rows in parallel, the total number of cells is $= 7 \times 2 = \textbf{14}$

Example 2.37. *A battery of twelve cells is required to send the largest possible current through a resistance of 10 ohms. Find the type of grouping which will give the largest current and estimate its value. The resistance of each cell is 6.3 Ω and its e.m.f. is 1.4 volt.*

Solution. According to maximum power transfer theorem, maximum power (and hence current) is transferred to a load if load resistance is equal to the intenal resistance of source (*i.e.,* battery in this case). Therefore, to solve such problems, find the internal resistance of the battery and see how much it deviates from external resistance (*i.e.,* load).

For series grouping, battery resistance $= nr = 12 \times 6.3 = 75.6\ \Omega$

For parallel grouping, battery resistance $= r/m = 6.3/12 = 0.525\ \Omega$

The reader may note that internal resistance of battery for series as well as parallel grouping is far different from external resistance of 10 Ω. Hence these types of groupings cannot provide strong current. This leaves series–parallel grouping to be used.

Let $n =$ number of cells in series in each row

$m =$ number of rows in parallel

Internal resistance of battery $= nr/m$

For maximum current in series-parallel grouping,

$$R = nr/m$$

or $\quad 10 = n \times 6.3/m$

$\therefore \qquad \dfrac{m}{n} = \dfrac{6.3}{10} = 0.63$ ...(*i*)

But total number of cells is $m \times n$, i.e., $m \times n = 12$ ...(*ii*)

Multiplying Eq. (*i*) and Eq. (*ii*), we get, $m^2 = 12 \times 0.63$ *or* $m = \sqrt{12 \times 0.63} \approx 3$

$\therefore$ No. of rows, $m = 3$; No. of cells per row, $n = 12/3 = 4$

▓▓▓ TUTORIAL PROBLEMS ▓▓▓

1. Ten cells, each of e.m.f. 1.5 V and internal resistance 0.2 Ω are connected in series. What current will they send through an external resistance of 4 Ω? [2.5 A]

2. Three cells of e.m.f. 1.1, 1.3 and 1.5 volts are connected in series to supply current to an external resistance of 1.6 Ω. The internal resistances of three cells are 0.25, 0.35 and 0.4 Ω respectively. Determine the current through the external resistance. [1.5 A]

3. A battery consists of 5 cells, each of e.m.f. 1.5 V and internal resistance 0.25 Ω, connected in series. Through what external resistance will it send a current of 2 A? [2.5 Ω]

4. Six cells, each of e.m.f. 1.5 volts and internal resistance of 2 Ω are joined in parallel and connected to an external resistance of 5 Ω. What current will flow? [0.529 A]

5. A battery consists of 4 cells, each of e.m.f. 1.46 volts. The cells are connected in parallel to an external resistance of 0.525 Ω. If the current supplied by the battery is 0.8 A, find the internal resistance of each cell. [5.2 Ω]

6. Two cells each having e.m.f. of 2 V and internal resistance of 1 Ω are given. Show how will you connect them to a resistance of 0.5 Ω so that current through external resistance is 2 A. [in parallel]

7. Four cells, each of e.m.f. 1.5 V and resistance 0.5 Ω, are connected in series-parallel across an external resistance of 2.5 Ω. Find the current in external resistance. [1 A]

8. 24 cells each having an e.m.f. of 2.1 V and internal resistance of 2 Ω are to supply the maximum current to a 12 Ω external resistance. Show how the cells are to be connected and what is the value of current to external resistance ? [Series-parallel, m = 3; n = 8; 1.625 A]

9. Four secondary cells each having an e.m.f. of 1.3 V and internal resistance 0.025 Ω are to supply the maximum current to a 12 Ω external resistance. Show how the cells are to be connected and what will be the value of maximum current? [Series group; 0.43 A]

10. Twenty-four cells are arranged in rows of six in series and the four rows in parallel. The battery sends a current of 2.53 A through an external resistance of 3.2 Ω. If the internal resistance of each cell is 0.08 Ω, find the e.m.f. of each cell. [1.4 V]

2.16. IDEAL VOLTAGE AND CURRENT SOURCES

Before discussing real voltage and current sources, it is profitable to discuss ideal voltage and current sources.

(*i*) **Ideal voltage source.** *An ideal voltage source (also called constant voltage source) is one that maintains a constant terminal voltage no matter how much current is drawn from it.*

Fig. 2.44 shows an ideal voltage source of 10 V. Regardless of the value of load resistance R_L, the terminal voltage will remain 10 V. An ideal voltage source has zero or negligible internal resistance so that there is a negligible voltage drop in the internal resistance due to change in current. Consequently, terminal voltage remains constant. For example, the internal resistance of a lead-acid cell is very small (0.01 Ω) so that it can be regarded as a constant voltage source for all practical purposes.

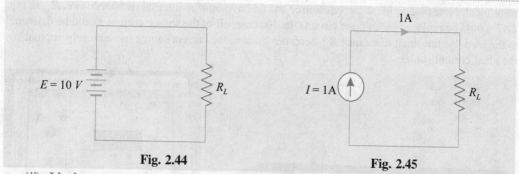

Fig. 2.44   **Fig. 2.45**

(*ii*) **Ideal current source.** *An* ideal current source (*also called constant-current source*) *is one which will supply the same current to any resistance connected across its terminals.*

Fig. 2.45 shows an ideal current source of 1A. Regardless of the value of load resistance R_L, the source will supply a current of 1 A. The schematic symbol for a current source is a circle with an arrow in it. The arrow shows the direction of the current (conventional) produced by the source.

2.17. REAL VOLTAGE AND CURRENT SOURCES

Ideal voltage and current sources are never realised in practice.

(*i*) **Real voltage source.** A real (non-ideal) voltage source has internal resistance that causes its terminal voltage to decrease when current is drawn from it.

A real voltage source can be represented as an ideal voltage source in series with a resistance equal to its internal resistance (R_{int}) as shown in Fig. 2.46.

This representation can be used to calculate the true terminal voltage of a voltage source when current is drawn from it. Note that internal resistance is an inherent property of a source; it is not a discrete component that can be measured with an ohmmeter. As R_{int} becomes small, the voltage source more closely approaches the ideal voltage source.

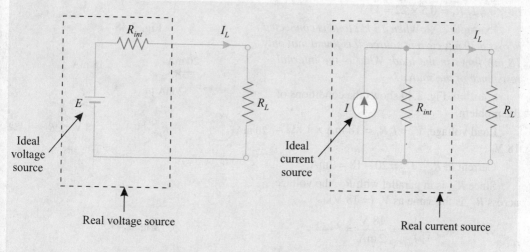

Fig. 2.46   **Fig. 2.47**

(*ii*) **Real current source.** *A real current source can be represented as an ideal current source in parallel with an internal resistance (R_{int}) as shown in Fig. 2.47.*

When load resistance R_L is connected across the terminals, the current (I) produced by the source divides between R_{int} and R_L. Consequently, the load current is less than it would be if the source were ideal. Note that an ideal current source would have *infinite* internal resistance (*i.e.* R_{int} in Fig. 2.47 would be replaced by an open circuit). In that case, all of the source current would be delivered to the load. As the shunt resistance R_{int} becomes greater, the current source more closely approaches the ideal current source.

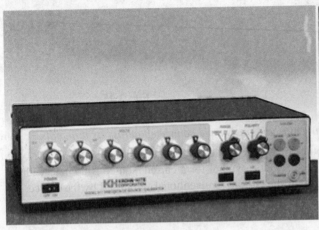

Voltage source   Current source

Example 2.38. *A 12 V voltage source has an internal resistance of 2Ω. Find (i) the terminal voltage when a 22 Ω load is connected across its terminals (ii) the current that flows in the load.*

Solution. Fig. 2.48 shows the conditions of the problem.

(*ii*) Load current, $I_L = \dfrac{12}{2 + 22} = 0.5$ A

(*i*) Terminal voltage, $V_T =$ Load voltage, $V_L =$
$I_L R_L = 0.5 \times 22 = $ **11 V**

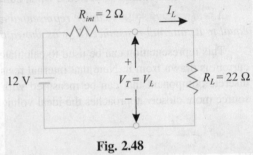

Fig. 2.48

Example 2.39. *When a 1 kΩ load is connected across a 20 mA current source, it is found that only 18 mA flows in the load. What is the internal resistance of the source?*

Solution. Fig. 2.49 shows the conditions of the problem.

Load voltage, $V_L = I_L R_L = 18$ mA $\times 1$ kΩ $=$ 18 V

Current in R_{int}, $I_{int} = 20 - 18 = 2$mA

Since R_{int} is in parallel with R_L, the voltage across R_{int} is the same as V_L (= 18 V).

∴ $\qquad R_{int} = \dfrac{V_L}{I_{int}} = \dfrac{18 \text{ V}}{2 \text{ mA}} = 9 \text{ k}\Omega$

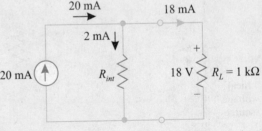

Fig. 2.49

2.18. SOURCE CONVERSIONS

A real voltage source can be converted into *equivalent* real current source and vice-versa. Fig. 2.50 shows a real voltage source connected across load R_L. The value of current of equivalent current source is $I = E/R_{int}$. The value of R_{int} is the same but in parallel with the current source as shown in Fig. 2.51.

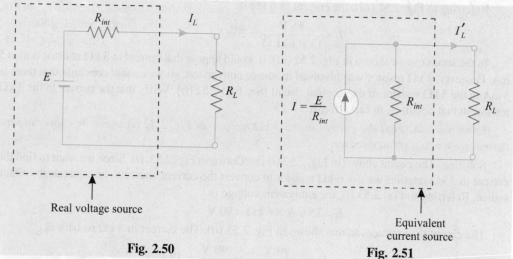

Real voltage source

Fig. 2.50

Equivalent
current source

Fig. 2.51

That the two circuits are equivalent can be easily proved.

In Fig. 2.50, load current, $I_L = \dfrac{E}{R_{int} + R_L}$

In Fig. 2.51, load current, $I'_L = I \times \dfrac{R_{int}}{R_{int} + R_L}$ ...current -divider rule

$$= \dfrac{E}{R_{int} + R_L} \qquad\qquad (\because E = I\,R_{int})$$

$\therefore \qquad\qquad I'_L = I_L$

Hence the equivalence of two circuits stands proved. The source conversion (voltage source into equivalent current source and vice-versa) often simplifies the analysis of many circuits. Any resistance that is in series with a voltage source, whether it be internal or external resistance, can be included in its conversion to an equivalent current source. Similarly, any resistance in parallel with a current source can be included when it is converted to an equivalent voltage source. However, the voltage across or current through any such resistance cannot be computed if that resistance is included in the source conversion.

Example 2.40. *Find the current in 6 kΩ resistor in Fig. 2.52 (i) by converting the current source to a voltage source.*

Solution. Since we want to find the current in 6 kΩ resistor, we use 3 kΩ resistor to convert the current source to an equivalent voltage source. Referring to Fig. 2.52 (*ii*), the equivalent voltage is

$$E = 15\ mA \times 3\ k\Omega = 45\ V$$

The circuit then becomes as shown in Fig. 2.52 (*iii*). Note that polarity of the equivalent voltage source is such that it produces current in the same direction as the original current source.

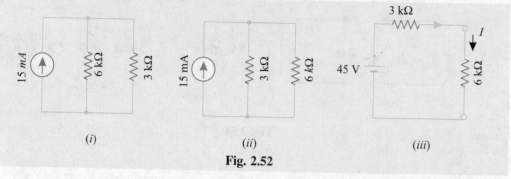

(*i*)   (*ii*)   (*iii*)

Fig. 2.52

Referring to Fig. 2.52 (*iii*), the current in 6 kΩ is

$$I = \frac{45 \text{ V}}{(3 + 6) \text{ k}\Omega} = 5 \text{mA}$$

In the series circuit shown in Fig. 2.52 (iii), it would appear that current in 3 kΩ resistor is also 5 mA. However, 3 kΩ resistor was involved in source conversion, so we *cannot* conclude that there is 5 mA in the 3 kΩ resistor of the original circuit [See Fig. 2.52 (*i*)]. Verify that the current in the 3 kΩ resistor in that circuit is, in fact, 10 mA.

Example 2.41. *Find the current in the 3 kΩ resistor in Fig. 2.52 (i) above by converting the current source to a voltage source.*

Solution. The circuit shown in Fig. 2.52 (*i*) is redrawn in Fig. 2.53. (*i*). Since we want to find the current in 3 kΩ resistor, we use 6 kΩ resistor to convert the current source to an equivalent voltage source. Referring to Fig. 2.53 (*i*), the equivalent voltage is

$$E = 15 \text{ mA} \times 6 \text{ k}\Omega = 90 \text{ V}$$

The circuit then reduces to that shown in Fig. 2.53 (*ii*). The current in 3 kΩ resistor is

$$I = \frac{90 \text{ V}}{(6 + 3) \text{ k}\Omega} = \frac{90 \text{ V}}{9 \text{ k}\Omega} = 10 \text{ mA}$$

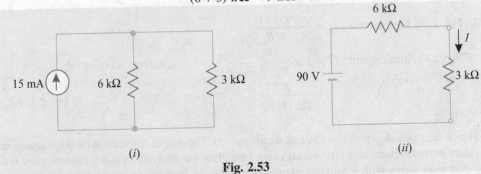

(*i*)   (*ii*)

Fig. 2.53

Example 2.42. *Find the current in various resistors in the circuit shown in Fig. 2.54 (i) by converting voltage sources into current sources.*

Solution. Referring to Fig. 2.54 (*i*), the 100 Ω resistor can be considered as the internal resistance of 15 V battery. The equivalent current is

$$I = \frac{15 \text{ V}}{100 \text{ }\Omega} = 0.15 \text{ A}$$

Similarly, 20 Ω resistor can be considered as the internal resistance of 13 V battery. The equivalent current is

$$I = \frac{13 \text{ V}}{20 \text{ }\Omega} = 0.65 \text{ A}$$

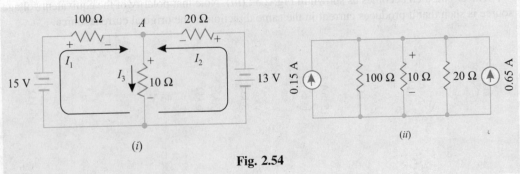

(*i*)   (*ii*)

Fig. 2.54

Replacing the voltage sources with current sources, the circuit becomes as shown in Fig. 2.54 (ii). The current sources are parallel-aiding for a total flow = 0.15 + 0.65 = 0.8 A. The parallel resistors can be combined:

$$100 \, \Omega \, \| \, 10 \, \Omega \, \| \, 20 \, \Omega = 6.25 \, \Omega$$

The total current flowing through this resistance produces the drop:

0.8 A × 6.25 Ω = 5 V

This 5V drop can now be "transported" back to the original circuit. It appears across 10 Ω resistor [See Fig. 2.55]. Its polarity is negative at the bottom and positive at the top. Applying Kirchhoff's voltage law (KVL), the voltage drop across 100 Ω resistor = 15 – 5 = 10 V and drop across 20 Ω resistor = 13 – 5 = 8 V.

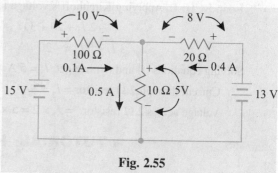

Fig. 2.55

∴   Current in 100 Ω resistor $= \dfrac{10}{100} = 0.1 \, \text{A}$

Current in 10 Ω resistor $= \dfrac{5}{10} = 0.5 \, \text{A}$

Current in 20 Ω resistor $= \dfrac{8}{20} = 0.4 \, \text{A}$

Example 2.43. *Find the current in and voltage across 2 Ω resistor in Fig. 2.56.*

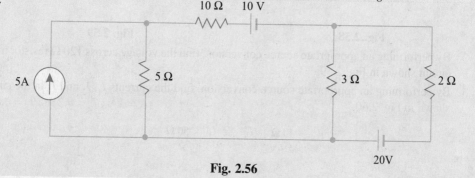

Fig. 2.56

Solution. We use 5 Ω resistor to convert the current source to an equivalent voltage source. The equivalent voltage is

$$E = 5A \times 5\Omega = 25 \, V$$

The circuit shown in Fig. 2.56 then becomes as shown in Fig. 2.57.

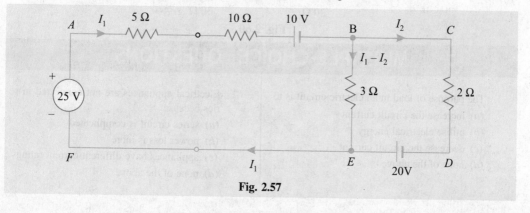

Fig. 2.57

Loop ABEFA. Applying Kirchhoff's voltage law to loop ABEFA, we have,

$$-5I_1 - 10\,I_1 - 10 - 3\,(I_1 - I_2) + 25 = 0$$

or

$$-18\,I_1 + 3\,I_2 = -15 \qquad \qquad \ldots(i)$$

Loop BCDEB. Applying Kirchhoff's voltage law to loop BCDEB, we have,

$$-2\,I_2 + 20 + 3\,(I_1 - I_2) = 0$$

or

$$3\,I_1 - 5\,I_2 = -20 \qquad \qquad \ldots(ii)$$

Solving equations (i) and (ii), we get, $I_2 = 5$ A

∴   Current through 2 Ω resistor $= I_2 = 5$A

Voltage across 2 Ω resistor $= I_2 \times 2 = 5 \times 2 = 10$ V

TUTORIAL PROBLEMS

1. By performing an appropriate source conversion, find the voltage across 120 Ω resistor in the circuit shown in Fig. 2.58.   **[20 V]**

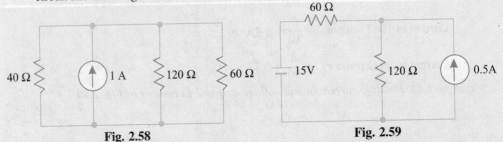

Fig. 2.58   **Fig. 2.59**

2. By performing an appropriate source conversion, find the voltage across 120 Ω resistor in the circuit shown in Fig. 2.59.   **[30 V]**

3. By performing an appropriate source conversion, find the currents I_1, I_2 and I_3 in the circuit shown in Fig. 2.60.   **[$I_1 = 1$A ; $I_2 = 0.2$ A ; $I_3 = 0.8$ A]**

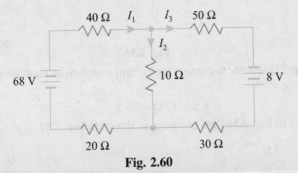

Fig. 2.60

MULTIPLE-CHOICE QUESTIONS

1. The purpose of load in an electric circuit is to
   (a) increase the circuit current
   (b) utilise electrical energy
   (c) decrease the circuit current
   (d) none of the above

2. Electrical appliances are not connected in series because
   (a) series circuit is complicated
   (b) power loss is more
   (c) appliances have different current ratings
   (d) none of the above

3. Electrical appliances are connected in parallel because it
   (a) is a simple circuit
   (b) draws less current
   (c) results in reduced power loss
   (d) makes the operation of appliances independent of each other

4. In Fig. 2.61,

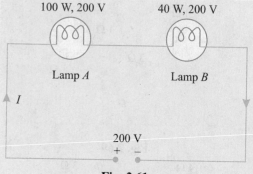

Fig. 2.61

   (a) the lamp A will be brighter than lamp B
   (b) the lamp B will be brighter than lamp A
   (c) the two lamps will be equally bright
   (d) none of the above

5. If a d.c. supply of 180 V is connected across terminals AB in Fig. 2.62, then current in 6 Ω resistor will be

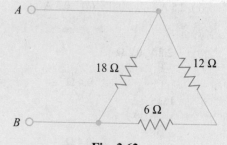

Fig. 2.62

   (a) 10 A   (b) 5 A
   (c) 12 A   (d) 6 A

6. A battery of 24 V is applied across the terminals AB of the circuit shown in Fig. 2.63. The current in 2 Ω resistor will be

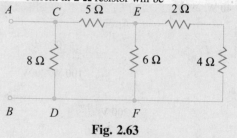

Fig. 2.63

   (a) 3A
   (b) 6 A
   (c) 2.5 A
   (d) 1.5 A

7. A wire has a resistance of 12 Ω. It is bent in the form of a circle. The effective resistance between the two points on any diameter of the circle is
   (a) 6 Ω   (b) 12 Ω
   (c) 24 Ω   (d) 3 Ω

8. The total conductance of the circuit shown in Fig. 2.64 is
   (a) 13 S   (b) 1.6 S
   (c) 6 S   (d) 2.5 S

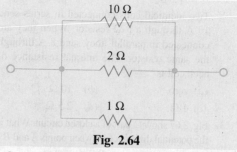

Fig. 2.64

9. A 200 W and 100 W bulb both meant for operation at 220 V are connected in series. When connected to a 220 V supply, the power consumed by them is
   (a) 33 W   (b) 66 W
   (c) 100 W   (d) 300 W

10. The effective resistance between B and C of the letter A containing resistances as shown in Fig. 2.65 is

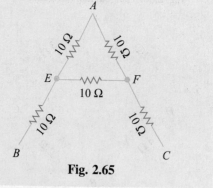

Fig. 2.65

   (a) 80/3 Ω
   (b) 40 Ω
   (c) 160/9 Ω
   (d) 60 Ω

11. In the circuit shown in Fig. 2.66, the final voltage drop across the capacitor C is

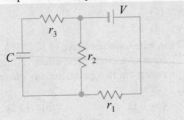

Fig. 2.66

(a) $\dfrac{V\,r_1}{r_1 + r_2}$

(b) $\dfrac{V\,(r_1 + r_2)}{r_2}$

(c) $\dfrac{V\,r_2}{r_1 + r_2}$

(d) $\dfrac{V\,(r_1 + r_2)}{r_1 + r_2 + r_3}$

12. Two identical cells connected in series send 10 A through a 5 Ω resistor. When they are connected in parallel, they send 8 A through the same resistor. The internal resistance of each cell is

(a) zero

(b) 10 Ω

(c) 1 Ω

(d) 2.5 Ω

13. Fig. 2.67 shows a part of a closed circuit. What is the potential difference between points A and B ?

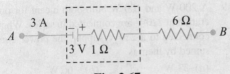

Fig. 2.67

(a) 6 V

(b) 18 V

(c) 24 V

(d) 12 V

14. A current of 2A flows in the circuit shown in Fig. 2.68. The potential difference $V_A - V_B$ is

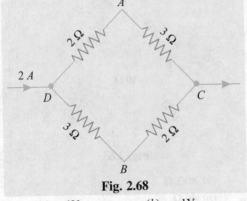

Fig. 2.68

(a) + 1V

(b) – 1V

(c) 4 V

(d) 2V

15. For what value of unknown resistance X, the potential difference between points B and D will be zero in the circuit shown in Fig. 2.69?

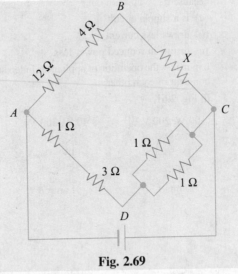

Fig. 2.69

(a) 4 Ω

(b) 3 Ω

(c) 2 Ω

(d) 6 Ω

16. A cell having an e.m.f. of 2.2 V and internal resistance 0.2 Ω is connected to a circuit comprising an ammeter and a resistance of 4 Ω in series with a combination of two resistances of 0.4 Ω each in parallel. What will be the reading of ammeter (See Fig. 2.70)?

(a) 0.25 A

(b) 1.5 A

(c) 2.5 A

(d) 0.5 A

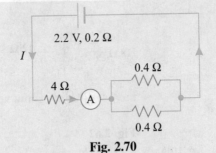

Fig. 2.70

17. In Fig. 2.71, switches S_1 and S_2 are closed and the supply voltage is increased to 400 V. Then,

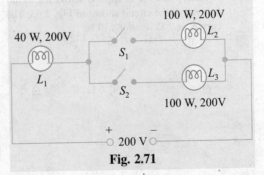

Fig. 2.71

(a) lamp L_1 will burn out

(b) lamp L_2 will burn out

(c) both lamps L_2 and L_3 will burn out

(d) all the lamps will be safe

18. In the circuit shown in Fig. 2.72, a battery of e.m.f. 10 V and negligible internal resistance is connected across two resistances of 500 Ω each in series. A voltmeter of 1000 Ω resistance is connected across one resistance. What is the reading of the voltmeter?

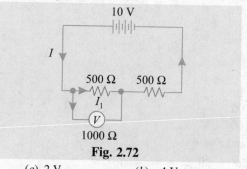

Fig. 2.72

(a) 2 V   (b) 4 V

(c) 3 V   (d) 1 V

19. Two similar cells whether joined in series or parallel have the same current through an external resistance of 2 Ω. The internal resistance of each cell is

(a) 1 Ω   (b) 0.5 Ω

(c) 2 Ω   (d) 1.5 Ω

20. A torch bulb rated at 4.5 W, 1.5 V is connected as shown in Fig. 2.73. The e.m.f. of the cell needed to make the bulb glow at full intensity is

(a) 4.5 V   (b) 1.5 V

(c) 2.56 V   (d) 13.5 V

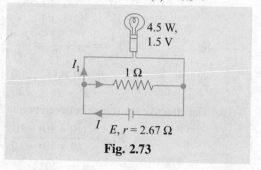

Fig. 2.73

Answers to Multiple-Choice Questions

1. (b)	2. (c)	3. (d)	4. (b)	5. (a)	6. (c)	7. (d)	8. (b)
9. (b)	10. (a)	11. (c)	12. (d)	13. (b)	14. (a)	15. (c)	16. (d)
17. (a)	18. (b)	19. (c)	20. (d)				

Hints to Selected Multiple-Choice Questions

4. The resistance ($= V^2/P$) of 40 W lamp is much more (2.5 times) than that of 100 W lamp. Therefore, a greater part of supply voltage will appear across 40 W lamp. As a result, the lamp B will be brighter than lamp A.

5. So far as terminals AB are concerned, 12 Ω and 6 Ω are in series and this series combination is in parallel with 18 Ω resistor.

$$\therefore \quad R_{AB} = \frac{(12+6) \times 18}{(12+6)+18} = \frac{18 \times 18}{36} = 9 \, \Omega$$

Circuit current, $I = \dfrac{V}{R_{AB}} = \dfrac{180}{9} = 20 \, A$

Since there are two parallel paths of equal resistance, current in each parallel path is 10 A.

6. $R_{EF} = \dfrac{6 \times 6}{6+6} = 3 \, \Omega$; $R_{CD} = R_{AB} = \dfrac{(5+3) \times 8}{(5+3)+8} = \dfrac{8 \times 8}{8+8} = 4 \, \Omega$

$\therefore$ Circuit current $= \dfrac{24}{R_{AB}} = \dfrac{24}{4} = 6 \, A$

Current in 5Ω $= 6/2 = 3$ A

Current in 2 Ω $= 3/2 = 1.5$ A

7. Fig. 2.74 shows the conditions of the problem. Each parallel path has a resistance of 6 Ω.

∴ Effective resistance between two points on the diameter

$$= 6 \| 6 = \frac{6 \times 6}{6 + 6} = \frac{36}{12} = 3\Omega$$

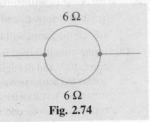

6 Ω

6 Ω

Fig. 2.74

8. Conductance G is the reciprocal of resistance R i.e. $G = 1/R$.

$$\frac{1}{R_T} = \frac{1}{R_1} + \frac{1}{R_2} + \frac{1}{R_3}$$

or

$$G_T = G_1 + G_2 + G_3 = \frac{1}{10} + \frac{1}{2} + \frac{1}{1} = 1.6S$$

9. $R_T = R_1 + R_2$

or

$$\frac{R_T}{V^2} = \frac{R_1}{V^2} + \frac{R_2}{V^2}$$

or

$$\frac{1}{P_T} = \frac{1}{P_1} + \frac{1}{P_2} = \frac{P_1 + P_2}{P_1 P_2}$$

∴

$$P_T = \frac{P_1 P_2}{P_1 + P_2} = \frac{200 \times 100}{200 + 100} = 66\,\text{W}$$

10. The effective resistance between points E and F is

$$R_{EF} = \frac{(10 + 10) \times 10}{(10 + 10) + 10} = \frac{200}{30} = \frac{20}{3}\,\Omega$$

∴

$$R_{BC} = 10 + \frac{20}{3} + 10 = \frac{80}{3}\,\Omega$$

11. In the steady state, the capacitor offers infinite reactance to direct current. Therefore, no current flows through the branch containing r_3 and C. As a result, the potential difference across C is that across r_2.

Current through $r_2 = \dfrac{V}{r_1 + r_2}$

∴ P.D. across r_2 = P.D. across $C = \left(\dfrac{V}{r_1 + r_2}\right) \times r_2 = \dfrac{V\,r_2}{r_1 + r_2}$

12. Let E and r be the e.m.f. and internal resistance respectively of each cell.

For series grouping, $\qquad 2E = (5 + 2\,r) \times 10 \qquad\qquad\qquad\qquad\qquad ...(i)$

For parallel grouping, $\qquad E = \left(5 + \dfrac{r}{2}\right) \times 8 \qquad\qquad\qquad\qquad\qquad ...(ii)$

Solving eqs. (i) and (ii), we get, $r = 2.5\,\Omega$

13. Applying Kirchhoff's voltage law to the circuit, we have,

$$V_A + 3 - 3 \times 1 - 3 \times 6 = V_B$$

or

$$V_A + 3 - 3 - 18 = V_B$$

∴

$$V_A - V_B = 18\,\text{V}$$

14. Branches DAC and DBC have the same resistance. Therefore, current in branch DAC as well as in branch DBC is 1 A.

∴

$$V_D - 2 \times 1 = V_A \text{ and } V_D - 3 \times 1 = V_B$$

∴

$$V_A - V_B = (V_D - 2) - (V_D - 3) = +1\text{V}$$

15. When points B and D are at the same potential, this Wheatstone bridge is balanced. Under balanced conditions of the bridge, the products of resistances of opposite arms are equal.

∴

$$(3 + 1)\,X = (12 + 4) \times \left(\frac{1 \times 1}{1 + 1}\right)$$

or

$$X = 2\Omega$$

16. We consider the ammeter to be ideal so that its resistance is zero.

Total circuit resistance, $\quad R_T = 0.2 + 4 + \dfrac{0.4 \times 0.4}{0.4 + 0.4} = 0.2 + 4 + 0.2 = 4.4\,\Omega$

Circuit current, $\quad I = \dfrac{E}{R_T} = \dfrac{2.2}{4.4} = 0.5\,\text{A}$

Therefore, the reading of ammeter will be **0.5 A**.

17. The resistance of each 100 W lamp is 400 Ω. Therefore, the total resistance of the parallel circuit will be 200 Ω. The resistance of 40 W lamp is 1000 Ω. The applied voltage of 400 V will appear across 40 W lamp and the parallel circuit in the ratio of 1000 : 200 = 5 : 1. Consequently, **voltage across 40 W lamp far exceeds 200 V and it will burn.**

18. Effective resistance of parallel resistances of 500 Ω and 1000Ω is

$$R_P = \dfrac{1000 \times 500}{1000 + 500} = \dfrac{1000}{3}\,\Omega$$

Total circuit resistance, $\quad R_T = \dfrac{1000}{3} + 500 = \dfrac{2500}{3}\,\Omega$

Circuit current, $\quad I = \dfrac{E}{R_T} = \dfrac{10}{2500/3} = \dfrac{3}{250}\,\text{A}$

Current in 500 Ω resistor across which voltmeter is connected is

$$I_1 = I \times \dfrac{1000}{500 + 1000} = \dfrac{3}{250} \times \dfrac{1000}{1500} = \dfrac{1}{125}\,\text{A}$$

∴ P.D. across 500 Ω resistor $\quad = I_1 \times 500 = \dfrac{1}{125} \times 500 = 4\,\text{V}$

Therefore, the voltmeter will read **4V**.

19. Let E and r be the e.m.f. and internal resistance of each cell respectively.

∴ $\qquad \dfrac{2E}{2 + 2r} = \dfrac{E}{2 + r/2}$

or $\qquad \dfrac{2}{2 + 2r} = \dfrac{1}{2 + r/2}$

On solving, we get, $\qquad r = 2\,\Omega$

20. Resistance of bulb, $\qquad R_b = \dfrac{V^2}{P} = \dfrac{(1.5)^2}{4.5} = 0.5\,\Omega$

Rated current of bulb, $\qquad I_1 = \dfrac{4.5}{1.5} = 3\,\text{A}$

In order that bulb glows at full intensity, 3A must pass through it.

Total circuit resistance, $\qquad R_T = 2.67 + \dfrac{0.5 \times 1}{0.5 + 1} = 2.67 + 0.33 = 3\,\Omega$

∴ Current supplied by cell, $\qquad I = E/R_T = E/3$

Now $\qquad I_1 = I \times \dfrac{1}{1 + 0.5} = \dfrac{E}{3} \times \dfrac{1}{1.5}$

or $\qquad 3 = \dfrac{E}{3} \times \dfrac{1}{1.5}$

∴ $\qquad E = 3 \times 3 \times 1.5 = 13.5\,\text{V}$

CORNWALL COLLEGE
LEARNING CENTRE

D.C. Network Theorems

INTRODUCTION

Any arrangement of electrical energy sources, resistances and other circuit elements is called an electrical network. The terms *circuit* and *network* are used synonymously in electrical literature. Thus Fig. 3.1 may be referred to as an electrical circuit or network. In the text so far we employed two network laws *viz.* Ohm's law and Kirchhoff's laws to solve network problems. Occasions arise when these laws applied to certain networks do not yield quick and easy solution. To overcome this difficulty, other network theorems and techniques have been developed which are very useful in analysing both simple and complex electrical circuits. Through the use of these theorems and techniques, it is possible either to simplify the network itself or render the analytical solution easy. In this chapter, we shall focus our attention on important netwrok theorems and techniques with special reference to their utility in solving network problems.

3.1. NETWORK TERMINOLOGY

While discussing network theorems and techniques, one often comes across the following terms:

(*i*) **Active element.** An active element is one which supplies electrical energy to the circuit. Thus in Fig. 3.1, E_1 and E_2 are the active elements because they supply energy to the circuit.

(*ii*) **Passive element.** A passive element is one which receives electrical energy and then either converts it into heat (resistance) or stores in an electric field (capacitance) or magnetic field (inductance). In Fig. 3.1, there are three passive elements, namely R_1, R_2 and R_3. These passive elements (*i.e.* resistances in this case) receive energy from the active elements (*i.e.* E_1 and E_2) and convert it into heat.

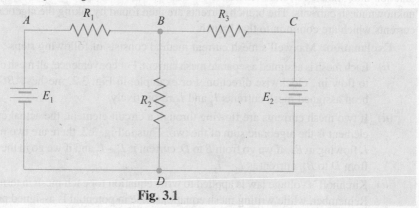

Fig. 3.1

(*iii*) **Node.** A node of a network is an equipotential surface at which *two or more* circuit elements are joined. Thus in Fig. 3.1, circuit elements R_1 and E_1 are joined at A and hence A is the node. Similarly B, C and D are nodes.

(*iv*) **Junction.** A junction is that point in a network where *three or more* circuit elements are joined. In Fig. 3.1, there are only two junction points *viz.* B and D. That B is a junction is clear from the fact that three circuit elements R_1, R_2 and R_3 are joined at it. Similarly, point D is a junction because it joins three circuit elements R_2, E_1 and E_2.

(*v*) **Branch.** A branch is that part of a network which lies between two junction points. Thus referring to Fig. 3.1, there are a total of three branches *viz.* BAD, BCD and BD. The branch BAD consists of R_1 and E_1; the branch BCD consists of R_3 and E_2 and branch BD merely consists of R_2.

(*vi*) **Loop.** A loop is any closed path of a netwrok. Thus in Fig. 3.1, $ABDA$, $BCDB$ and $ABCDA$ are the loops.

(*vii*) **Mesh.** A mesh is the most elementary form of a loop and cannot be further divided into other loops. In Fig. 3.1, both loops $ABDA$ and $BCDB$ qualify as meshes because they cannot be further divided into other loops. However, the loop $ABCDA$ cannot be called a mesh because it encloses two loops $ABDA$ and $BCDB$.

3.2. NETWORK THEOREMS AND TECHNIQUES

Having acquainted himself with network terminology, the reader is set to study the various network theorems and techniques. In this chapter, we shall discuss the following network theorems and techniques :

(*i*) Maxwell's mesh current method   (*ii*) Nodal analysis

(*iii*) Superposition theorem   (*iv*) Thevenin's theorem

(*v*) Norton's theorem   (*vi*) Max. power transfer theorem

(*vii*) Millman's theorem   (*viii*) Delta/star or star/delta transformation.

The network theorem or technique to be used will depend upon the network arrangement. The general rule is this. Use that theorem or technique which requires a smaller number of independent equations to obtain the solution or which can yield easy solution.

3.3. MAXWELL'S MESH CURRENT METHOD

In this method, Kirchhoff's voltage law is applied to a network to write mesh equations in terms of *mesh currents* instead of branch currents. Each mesh is assigned a separate mesh current. This mesh current is assumed to flow *clockwise* around the perimeter of the mesh without splitting at a junction into branch currents. Kirchhoff's voltage law is then applied to write equations in terms of unknown mesh currents. The branch currents are then found by taking the algebraic sum of the mesh currents which are common to that branch.

Explanation. Maxwell's mesh current method consists of following steps :

(*i*) Each mesh is assigned a separate mesh current. For convenience, all mesh currents are assumed to flow *clockwise direction. For example, in Fig. 3.2, meshes *ABDA* and *BCDB* have been assigned mesh currents I_1 and I_2 respectively.

(*ii*) If two mesh currents are flowing through a circuit element, the actual current in the circuit element is the algebraic sum of the two. Thus in Fig. 3.2, there are two mesh currents I_1 and I_2 flowing in R_2. If we go from *B* to *D*, current is $I_1 - I_2$ and if we go in the other direction (*i.e.* from *D* to *B*), current is $I_2 - I_1$.

(*iii*) Kirchhoff's voltage law is applied to write equation for each mesh in terms of mesh currents. Remember, while writing mesh equations, rise in potential is assigned positive sign and fall in potential negative sign.

(*iv*) If the value of any mesh current comes out to be negative in the solution, it means that true direction of that mesh current is anticlockwise *i.e.* opposite to the assumed clockwise direction.

Applying Kirchhoff's voltage law to Fig. 3.2, we have,

Mesh ABDA

$$-I_1 R_1 - (I_1 - I_2) R_2 + E_1 = 0$$

or
$$I_1 (R_1 + R_2) - I_2 R_2 = E_1 \qquad \qquad ...(i)$$

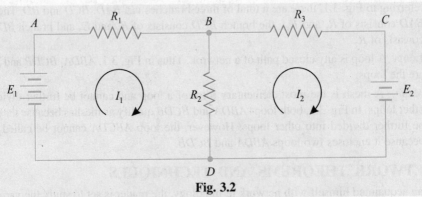

Fig. 3.2

Mesh BCDB

$$-I_2 R_3 - E_2 - (I_2 - I_1) R_2 = 0$$

or
$$-I_1 R_2 + (R_2 + R_3) I_2 = -E_2 \qquad \qquad ...(ii)$$

Solving eq. (*i*) and eq. (*ii*) simultaneously, mesh currents I_1 and I_2 can be found out. Once the mesh currents are known, the branch currents can be readily obtained. The advantage of this method is that it usually reduces the number of equations to solve a network problem.

. . . .

* It is convenient to consider all mesh currents in one direction (clockwise or anticlockwise). The same result will be obtained if mesh currents are given arbitrary directions.

3.4. MATRIX ALGEBRA

The solution of two or three simultaneous equations can be achieved by a method that uses *determinants*. A determinant is a numerical value assigned to a square arrangement of numbers called a *matrix*. The advantage of determinant method is that it is less difficult for three unknowns and there is less chance of error. The theory behind this method is not presented here but is available in any number of mathematics books.

Second-order determinant : A 2×2 matrix has four numbers arranged in two rows and two columns. The value of such a matrix is called a *second-order determinant* and is *equal to the product of the principal diagonal minus the product of the other diagonal*. For example, value of the matrix $= ad - cb$.

Second-order determinants can be used to solve simultaneous equations with two unknowns. Consider the following equations :

$$a_1 x + b_1 y = c_1$$
$$a_2 x + b_2 y = c_2$$

Other diagonal

Principal diagonal

The unknowns are x and y in these equations. The numbers associated with the unknowns are called *coefficients*. The coefficients in these equations are a_1, a_2, b_1 and b_2. The right hand number (c_1 and c_2) of each equation is called a *constant*. The coefficients and constants can be arranged as a *numerator matrix* and as a *denominator matrix*. The matrix for the numerator is formed by replacing the coefficient of the unknown by the constant. The denominator matrix is called *characteristic matrix* and is the same for each fraction. It is formed by the coefficients of the simultaneous equations.

$$x = \frac{\begin{vmatrix} c_1 & b_1 \\ c_2 & b_2 \end{vmatrix}}{\begin{vmatrix} a_1 & b_1 \\ a_2 & b_2 \end{vmatrix}} \quad ; \quad y = \frac{\begin{vmatrix} a_1 & c_1 \\ a_2 & c_2 \end{vmatrix}}{\begin{vmatrix} a_1 & b_1 \\ a_2 & b_2 \end{vmatrix}}$$

Note that the characteristic determinant (denominator) is the same in both cases and needs to be evaluated only once. Also note that the coefficients for x are replaced by the constants when solving for x and that the coefficients for y are replaced by the constants when solving for y.

Third-order determinant : A third-order determinant has 9 numbers arranged in 3 rows and 3 columns. Simultaneous equations with three unknowns can be solved with third-order determinants. Consider the following equations :

$$a_1 x + b_1 y + c_1 z = d_1$$
$$a_2 x + b_2 y + c_2 z = d_2$$
$$a_3 x + b_3 y + c_3 z = d_3$$

The characteristic matrix forms the denominator and is the same for each fraction. It is formed by the coefficients of the simultaneous equations.

$$\text{Denominator} = \begin{vmatrix} a_1 & b_1 & c_1 \\ a_2 & b_2 & c_2 \\ a_3 & b_3 & c_3 \end{vmatrix}$$

The matrix for each numerator is formed by replacing the coefficient of the unknown with the constant.

$$x = \frac{\begin{vmatrix} d_1 & b_1 & c_1 \\ d_2 & b_2 & c_2 \\ d_3 & b_3 & c_3 \end{vmatrix}}{\text{Denominator}} \quad ; \quad y = \frac{\begin{vmatrix} a_1 & d_1 & c_1 \\ a_2 & d_2 & c_2 \\ a_3 & d_3 & c_3 \end{vmatrix}}{\text{Denominator}}$$

$$z = \frac{\begin{vmatrix} a_1 & b_1 & d_1 \\ a_2 & b_2 & d_2 \\ a_3 & b_3 & d_3 \end{vmatrix}}{\text{Denominator}}$$

Example 3.1. *In the network shown in Fig. 3.3, find the magnitude and direction of each branch current by mesh current method.*

Solution. Assign mesh currents I_1 and I_2 to meshes ABDA and BCDB respectively as shown in Fig. 3.3 (i).

Mesh ABDA

$$-40\,I_1 - 20\,(I_1 - I_2) + 120 = 0$$

or

$$60\,I_1 - 20\,I_2 = 120 \qquad\qquad ...(i)$$

Mesh BCDB

$$-60\,I_2 - 65 - 20\,(I_2 - I_1) = 0$$

or

$$-20\,I_1 + 80\,I_2 = -65 \qquad\qquad ...(ii)$$

Multiplying eq. (*ii*) by 3 and adding it to eq. (*i*), we get,

$$220\,I_2 = -75 \qquad\qquad \therefore \quad I_2 = -75/220 = -0.341 \text{ A}$$

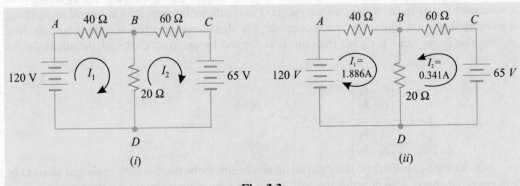

Fig. 3.3

The minus sign shows that true direction of I_2 is anticlockwise. Substituting $I_2 = -0.341$ A in eq. (*i*), we get, $I_1 = 1.886$A. The actual direction of flow of currents is shown in Fig. 3.3 (*ii*).

By determinant method

$$60\,I_1 - 20\,I_2 = 120$$
$$-20\,I_1 + 80\,I_2 = -65$$

$$I_1 = \frac{\begin{vmatrix} 120 & -20 \\ -65 & 80 \end{vmatrix}}{\begin{vmatrix} 60 & -20 \\ -20 & 80 \end{vmatrix}} = \frac{(120 \times 80) - (-65 \times -20)}{(60 \times 80) - (-20 \times -20)} = \frac{8300}{4400} = 1.886 \text{ A}$$

$$I_2 = \frac{\begin{vmatrix} 60 & 120 \\ -20 & -65 \end{vmatrix}}{\text{Denominator}} = \frac{(60 \times -65) - (-20 \times 120)}{4400} = \frac{-1500}{4400} = -0.341 \text{ A}$$

Referring to Fig. 3.3 (*ii*),

Current in branch $DAB = I_1 = \textbf{1.886 A}$; Current in branch $DCB = I_2 = \textbf{0.341A}$

Current in branch $BD = I_1 + I_2 = 1.886 + 0.341 = \textbf{2.227A}$

Example 3.2. *Calculate the current in each branch of the circuit shown in Fig. 3.4.*

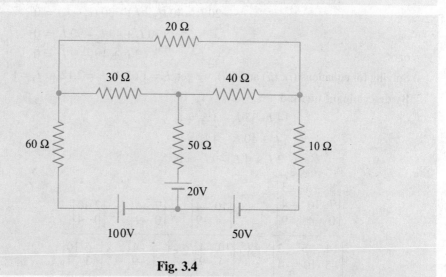

Fig. 3.4

Solution. Assign mesh currents I_1, I_2 and I_3 to meshes *ABHGA*, *HEFGH* and *BCDEHB* respectively as shown in Fig. 3.5.

Mesh ABHGA

$$-60\,I_1 - 30\,(I_1 - I_3) - 50\,(I_1 - I_2) - 20 + 100 = 0$$

or

$$140\,I_1 - 50\,I_2 - 30\,I_3 = 80$$

or

$$14\,I_1 - 5\,I_2 - 3\,I_3 = 8 \qquad \ldots (i)$$

Mesh GHEFG

$$20 - 50\,(I_2 - I_1) - 40\,(I_2 - I_3) - 10\,I_2 + 50 = 0$$

or

$$-50\,I_1 + 100\,I_2 - 40\,I_3 = 70$$

or

$$-5\,I_1 + 10\,I_2 - 4\,I_3 = 7 \qquad \ldots (ii)$$

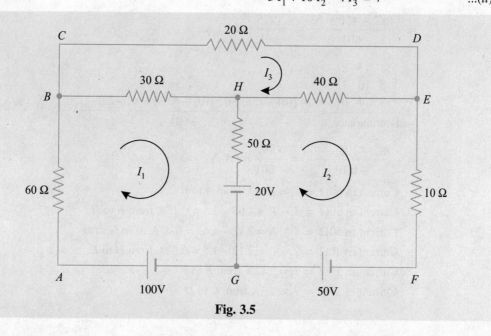

Fig. 3.5

Mesh BCDEHB

$$-20 I_3 - 40 (I_3 - I_2) - 30 (I_3 - I_1) = 0$$

or

$$30 I_1 + 40 I_2 - 90 I_3 = 0$$

or

$$3 I_1 + 4 I_2 - 9 I_3 = 0 \qquad ...(iii)$$

Solving for equations (i), (ii) and (iii), we get, $I_1 = 1.65$ A; $I_2 = 2.12$ A; $I_3 = 1.5$ A

By determinant method

$$14 I_1 - 5 I_2 - 3 I_3 = 8$$
$$-5 I_1 + 10 I_2 - 4 I_3 = 7$$
$$3 I_1 + 4 I_2 - 9 I_3 = 0$$

$$I_1 = \frac{\begin{vmatrix} 8 & -5 & -3 \\ 7 & 10 & -4 \\ 0 & 4 & -9 \end{vmatrix}}{\begin{vmatrix} 14 & -5 & -3 \\ -5 & 10 & -4 \\ 3 & 4 & -9 \end{vmatrix}} = \frac{8\begin{vmatrix} 10 & -4 \\ 4 & -9 \end{vmatrix} + 5\begin{vmatrix} 7 & -4 \\ 0 & -9 \end{vmatrix} - 3\begin{vmatrix} 7 & 10 \\ 0 & 4 \end{vmatrix}}{14\begin{vmatrix} 10 & -4 \\ 4 & -9 \end{vmatrix} + 5\begin{vmatrix} -5 & -4 \\ 3 & -9 \end{vmatrix} - 3\begin{vmatrix} -5 & 10 \\ 3 & 4 \end{vmatrix}}$$

$$= \frac{8\left[(10 \times -9) - (4 \times -4)\right] + 5\left[(7 \times -9) - (0 \times -4)\right] - 3\left[(7 \times 4) - (0 \times 10)\right]}{14\left[(10 \times -9) - (4 \times -4)\right] + 5\left[(-5 \times -9) - (3 \times -4)\right] - 3\left[(-5 \times 4) - (3 \times 10)\right]}$$

$$= \frac{-592 - 315 - 84}{-1036 + 285 + 150} = \frac{-991}{-601} = 1.65 \text{ A}$$

$$I_2 = \frac{\begin{vmatrix} 14 & 8 & -3 \\ -5 & 7 & -4 \\ 3 & 0 & -9 \end{vmatrix}}{\text{Denominator}} = \frac{14\left[(-63) - (0)\right] - 8\left[(45) - (-12)\right] - 3\left[(0) - (21)\right]}{-601}$$

$$= \frac{-882 - 456 + 63}{-601} = \frac{-1275}{-601} = 2.12 \text{ A}$$

$$I_3 = \frac{\begin{vmatrix} 14 & -5 & 8 \\ -5 & 10 & 7 \\ 3 & 4 & 0 \end{vmatrix}}{\text{Denominator}} = \frac{14\left[(0) - (28)\right] + 5\left[(0) - (21)\right] + 8\left[(-20) - (30)\right]}{-601}$$

$$= \frac{-392 - 105 - 400}{-601} = \frac{-897}{-601} = 1.5 \text{ A}$$

∴

Current in 60Ω $= I_1 = $ **1.65A** from A to B

Current in 30Ω $= I_1 - I_3 = 1.65 - 1.5 = $ **0.15A** from B to H

Current in 50Ω $= I_2 - I_1 = 2.12 - 1.65 = $ **0.47A** from G to H

Current in 40Ω $= I_2 - I_3 = 2.12 - 1.5 = $ **0.62A** from H to E

Current in 10Ω $= I_2 = $ **2.12A** from E to F

Current in 20Ω $= I_3 = $ **1.5A** from C to D

Example 3.3 : *Solve the circuit shown in Fig. 3.6 using mesh analysis and calculate the current in 50 Ω resistor.*

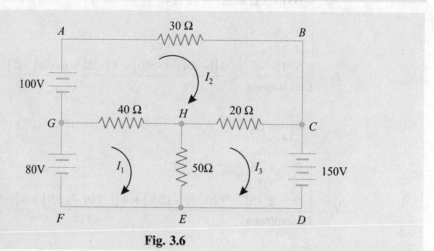

Fig. 3.6

Solution : Assign mesh currents I_1, I_2 and I_3 to meshes *GHEFG*, *ABCHGA* and *HCDEH* respectively as shown in Fig. 3.6.

Mesh GHEFG

$$-40(I_1 - I_2) - 50(I_1 - I_3) + 80 = 0$$

or
$$-90 I_1 + 40 I_2 + 50 I_3 = -80$$

or
$$90 I_1 - 40 I_2 - 50 I_3 = 80$$

or
$$9 I_1 - 4 I_2 - 5 I_3 = 8 \qquad \qquad ...(i)$$

Mesh ABCHGA

$$-30 I_2 - 20(I_2 - I_3) - 40(I_2 - I_1) + 100 = 0$$

or
$$-40 I_1 + 90 I_2 - 20 I_3 = 100$$

or
$$-4 I_1 + 9 I_2 - 2 I_3 = 10 \qquad \qquad ...(ii)$$

Mesh HCDEH

$$-20(I_3 - I_2) - 150 - 50(I_3 - I_1) = 0$$

or
$$50 I_1 + 20 I_2 - 70 I_3 = 150$$

or
$$5 I_1 + 2 I_2 - 7 I_3 = 15 \qquad \qquad ...(iii)$$

Solving eqs. (*i*), (*ii*) and (*iii*), we have,

$$I_1 = 0.5 \text{ A}; \quad I_2 = 1 \text{ A}; \quad I_3 = -1.5 \text{ A}$$

By determinant method

$$9 I_1 - 4 I_2 - 5 I_3 = 8$$
$$-4 I_1 + 9 I_2 - 2 I_3 = 10$$
$$5 I_1 + 2 I_2 - 7 I_3 = 15$$

$$I_1 = \frac{\begin{vmatrix} 8 & -4 & -5 \\ 10 & 9 & -2 \\ 15 & 2 & -7 \end{vmatrix}}{\begin{vmatrix} 9 & -4 & -5 \\ -4 & 9 & -2 \\ 5 & 2 & -7 \end{vmatrix}} = \frac{8[(-63) - (-4)] + 4[(-70) - (-30)] - 5[(20) - (135)]}{9[(-63) - (-4)] + 4[(28) - (-10)] - 5[(-8) - (45)]}$$

$$= \frac{-472 - 160 + 575}{-531 + 152 + 265} = \frac{-57}{-114} = 0.5 \text{ A}$$

$$I_2 = \frac{\begin{vmatrix} 9 & 8 & -5 \\ -4 & 10 & -2 \\ 5 & 15 & -7 \end{vmatrix}}{\text{Denominator}} = \frac{9\left[(-70) - (-30)\right] - 8\left[(28) - (-10)\right] - 5\left[(-60) - (50)\right]}{-114}$$

$$= \frac{-114}{-114} = 1 \text{ A}$$

$$I_3 = \frac{\begin{vmatrix} 9 & -4 & 8 \\ -4 & 9 & 10 \\ 5 & 2 & 15 \end{vmatrix}}{\text{Denominator}} = \frac{9\left[(135) - (20)\right] + 4\left[(-60) - (50)\right] + 8\left[(-8) - (45)\right]}{-114}$$

$$= \frac{1035 - 440 - 424}{-114} = \frac{171}{-114} = -1.5 \text{ A}$$

Current in 50Ω resistor = $I_1 - I_3$ (downward)

$$= 0.5 - (-1.5) \text{ downward}$$

$$= 2 \text{ A } \textit{downward}$$

Note : Current in 50Ω resistor = $I_3 - I_1$ upward

$$= -1.5 - 0.5 \text{ upward} = -2\text{A upward}$$

$$= 2 \text{ A downward}$$

TUTORIAL PROBLEMS

1. Use mesh analysis to find the current in each resistor in Fig. 3.7.

   [in 100Ω = 0.1 A *from L to R* ; in 20Ω = 0.4 A *from R to L* ; in 10Ω = 0.5 A *downward*]

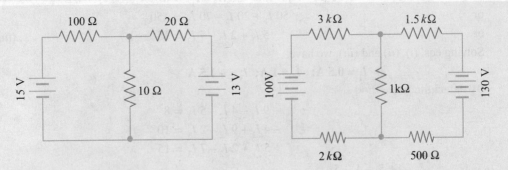

Fig. 3.7   **Fig. 3.8**

2. Using mesh analysis, find the voltage drop across the 1kΩ resistor in Fig. 3.8.   [50 V]

3. Using mesh analysis find the currents in 50Ω, 250Ω and 100Ω resistors in the circuit shown in Fig. 3.9.

   [I (50Ω) = 0.171 A → ; I (250Ω) = 0.237 A ← ; I (100Ω) = 0.408 A ↓]

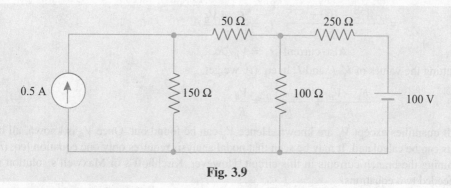

Fig. 3.9

3.5. NODAL ANALYSIS

Consider the circuit shown in Fig. 3.10. The branch currents in the circuit can be found by Kirchhoff's laws or Maxwell's mesh current method. There is another method, called *nodal analysis*, for determining the branch currents in the circuit. In this method, one of the nodes (Remember a node is a point in a network where two or more circuit elements meet) is taken as the *reference node*. The potentials of all the points in the circuit are measured *w.r.t.* this reference node. In Fig. 3.10, *A*, *B*, *C* and *D* are four nodes and node *D* has been taken as the *reference node. A glance at the circuit shows that voltages at nodes *A* and *C w.r.t.* reference node *D* are known. These are $E_1 = $ 120V and $E_2 = 65$V respectively. The only potential of node *B w.r.t. D* (call it V_B) is unknown. If this potential V_B can be found, each branch current can be determined because the voltage across each resistor will then be known.

*Hence **nodal analysis** essentially aims at choosing a reference node in the network and then finding the unknown voltages at the nodes w.r.t. reference node.*

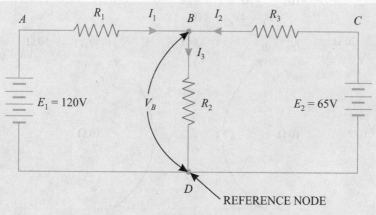

Fig. 3.10

The voltage V_B can be found by applying Kirchhoff's current law at point *B*.

$$I_1 + I_2 = I_3 \qquad \qquad ...(i)$$

In mesh *ABDA*, the voltage drop across R_1 is $E_1 - V_B$.

$$\therefore \qquad \qquad I_1 = \frac{E_1 - V_B}{R_1}$$

In mesh *CBDC*, the voltage drop across R_3 is $E_2 - V_B$.

---

* An obvious choice would be ground or common, if such a point exists.

$\therefore$ $$I_2 = \frac{E_2 - V_B}{R_3}$$

Also current $I_3 = V_B / R_2$

Putting the values of I_1, I_2 and I_3 in eq. (i), we get,

$$\frac{E_1 - V_B}{R_1} + \frac{E_2 - V_B}{R_3} = \frac{V_B}{R_2} \qquad \qquad ...(ii)$$

All quantities except V_B are known. Hence V_B can be found out. Once V_B is known, all branch currents can be calculated. It may be seen that nodal analysis requires only one equation [eq. (ii)] for determining the branch currents in this circuit. However, Kirchhoff's or Maxwell's solution would have needed two equations.

Example 3.4. *Find the currents in the various branches of the circuit shown in Fig. 3.11 by nodal analysis.*

Solution. Mark the currents in the various branches as shown in Fig. 3.11. If the value of any current comes out to be negative in the solution, it means that actual direction of current is opposite to that of assumed. Take point E (or F) as the reference node. We shall find the voltages at nodes B and C.

At node B $\qquad \qquad I_2 + I_3 = I_1$

or $$\frac{V_B}{10} + \frac{{}^*V_B - V_C}{15} = \frac{100 - V_B}{20}$$

or $$13V_B - 4V_C = 300 \qquad \qquad ...(i)$$

At node C $\qquad \qquad I_4 + I_5 = I_3$

or $$\frac{V_C}{10} + \frac{V_C + 80}{10} = \frac{V_B - V_C}{15}$$

or $$V_B - 4V_C = 120 \qquad \qquad ...(ii)$$

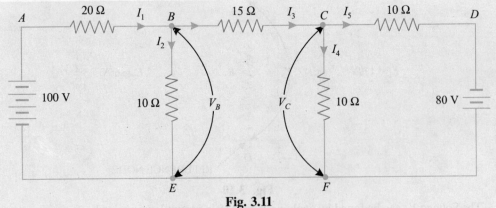

Fig. 3.11

Subtracting eq. (ii) from eq. (i), we get, $12V_B = 180$ $\qquad \therefore$ $V_B = 180/12 = 15$ V

Putting $V_B = 15$ volts in eq. (i), we get, $V_C = -26.25$ volts.

By determinant method

$$13\,V_B - 4\,V_C = 300$$
$$V_B - 4\,V_C = 120$$

* Note that the current I_3 is assumed to flow from B to C. Therefore, with this assumption, $V_B > V_C$.

$$V_B = \frac{\begin{vmatrix} 300 & -4 \\ 120 & -4 \end{vmatrix}}{\begin{vmatrix} 13 & -4 \\ 1 & -4 \end{vmatrix}} = \frac{(300 \times -4) - (120 \times -4)}{(13 \times -4) - (1 \times -4)} = \frac{-720}{-48} = 15 \text{ V}$$

$$V_C = \frac{\begin{vmatrix} 13 & 300 \\ 1 & 120 \end{vmatrix}}{\text{Denominator}} = \frac{(13 \times 120) - (1 \times 300)}{-48} = \frac{1260}{-48} = -26.25 \text{ V}$$

∴ Current $I_1 = \dfrac{100 - V_B}{20} = \dfrac{100 - 15}{20} = \textbf{4.25 A}$

Current $I_2 = V_B / 10 = 15/10 = \textbf{1.5 A}$

Current $I_3 = \dfrac{V_B - V_C}{15} = \dfrac{15 - (-26.25)}{15} = \textbf{2.75 A}$

Current $I_4 = V_C / 10 = -26.25 / 10 = \textbf{-2.625 A}$

Current $I_5 = \dfrac{V_C + 80}{10} = \dfrac{-26.25 + 80}{10} = \textbf{5.375 A}$

The negative sign for I_4 shows that actual current flow is opposite to that of assumed.

Example 3.5. *For the circuit shown in Fig. 3.12, find (i) node pair voltages V_B and V_C and (ii) currents in various branches.*

Solution. (i) Mark the currents in the various branches as shown in Fig. 3.12. Take point D (or E) as the reference node.

At node B $\qquad\qquad I_1 + I_3 = I_2$

or $\qquad \dfrac{12 - V_B}{2} + \dfrac{V_C + 4 - V_B}{4} = \dfrac{V_B}{10}$

or $\qquad (6 - 0.5V_B) + (0.25V_C + 1 - 0.25V_B) = 0.1V_B$

or $\qquad 0.85V_B - 0.25V_C = 7$ ...(i)

At node C $\qquad\qquad I_3 + I_4 = I_5$

or $\qquad \dfrac{V_C + 4 - V_B}{4} + \dfrac{V_C}{20} = \dfrac{8 - V_C}{16}$

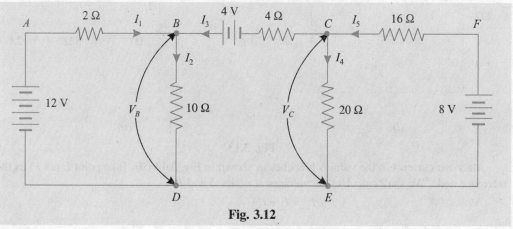

Fig. 3.12

or $\qquad (0.25V_C + 1 - 0.25V_B) + 0.05V_C = 0.5 - 0.0625V_C$

or $\qquad\qquad -0.25 V_B + 0.362 V_C = -0.5$ ...(ii)

From eqs. (i) and (ii), we get, $V_B = 9.82$ V; $V_C = 5.40$V

By determinant method

$$0.85 \, V_B - 0.25 \, V_C = 7$$
$$-0.25 \, V_B + 0.362 \, V_C = -0.5$$

$$V_B = \frac{\begin{vmatrix} 7 & -0.25 \\ -0.5 & 0.362 \end{vmatrix}}{\begin{vmatrix} 0.85 & -0.25 \\ -0.25 & 0.362 \end{vmatrix}} = \frac{(2.534)-(0.125)}{(0.3077)-(0.0625)} = \frac{2.409}{0.2452} = 9.82 \text{ V}$$

$$V_C = \frac{\begin{vmatrix} 0.85 & 7 \\ -0.25 & -0.5 \end{vmatrix}}{\text{Denominator}} = \frac{(-0.425)-(-1.75)}{0.2452} = \frac{1.325}{0.2452} = 5.40 \text{ V}$$

(ii) $\therefore$ Current $I_1 = \dfrac{12 - V_B}{2} = \dfrac{12 - 9.82}{2} = 1.09$ A

Current $I_2 = V_B / 10 = 9.82 / 10 = 0.982$ A

Current $I_3 = \dfrac{V_C + 4 - V_B}{4} = \dfrac{5.40 + 4 - 9.82}{4} = -0.105$ A

Current $I_4 = V_C / 20 = 5.40 / 20 = 0.27$ A

Current $I_5 = \dfrac{8 - V_C}{16} = \dfrac{8 - 5.40}{16} = 0.162$ A

The negative sign for I_3 simply means that current is in opposite direction to that assumed.

Example 3.6 : *Use nodal analysis to find the voltage across and current through 4Ω resistor in Fig. 3.13 (i).*

Solution : We must first convert the 2V voltage source to an equivalent current source. The value of the equivalent current source is $I = 2V/2\Omega = 1A$. The circuit then becomes as shown in Fig. 3.13 (ii).

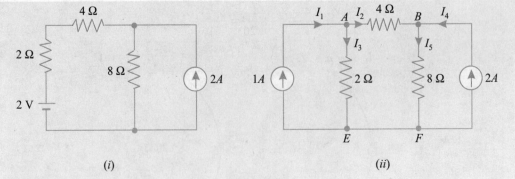

(i)   (ii)

Fig. 3.13

Mark the currents in the various branches as shown in Fig. 3.13 (ii). Take point E (or F) as the reference node. We shall calculate the voltages at nodes A and B.

At node A $\qquad\qquad I_1 = I_2 + I_3$

or
$$1 = {}^*\frac{V_A - V_B}{4} + \frac{V_A}{2}$$

or
$$3V_A - V_B = 4 \qquad \qquad \dots(i)$$

At node B

$$I_2 + I_4 = I_5$$

or
$$\frac{V_A - V_B}{4} + 2 = \frac{V_B}{8}$$

or
$$2V_A - 3V_B = -16 \qquad \qquad \dots(ii)$$

Solving eqs. (i) and (ii), we find $V_A = 4V$ and $V_B = 8V$. Note that $V_B > V_A$, contrary to our initial assumption. Therefore, actual direction of current is from node B to node A.

By determinant method

$$3V_A - V_B = 4$$
$$2V_A - 3V_B = -16$$

$$V_A = \frac{\begin{vmatrix} 4 & -1 \\ -16 & -3 \end{vmatrix}}{\begin{vmatrix} 3 & -1 \\ 2 & -3 \end{vmatrix}} = \frac{(-12)-(16)}{(-9)-(-2)} = \frac{-28}{-7} = 4 \text{ V}$$

$$V_B = \frac{\begin{vmatrix} 3 & 4 \\ 2 & -16 \end{vmatrix}}{\text{Denominator}} = \frac{(-48)-(8)}{-7} = \frac{-56}{-7} = 8 \text{ V}$$

Voltage across 4Ω resistor = $V_B - V_A = 8 - 4 = $ **4 V**

Current through 4Ω resistor = $\dfrac{4V}{4\Omega} = $ **1 A**

We can also find the currents in other resistors.

$$I_3 = \frac{V_A}{2} = \frac{4}{2} = 2 \text{ A}$$

$$I_5 = \frac{V_B}{8} = \frac{8}{8} = 1 \text{ A}$$

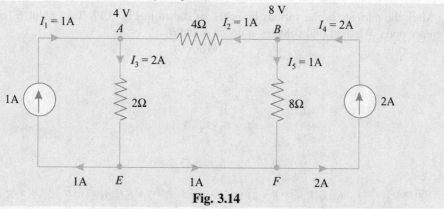

Fig. 3.14

Fig. 3.14 shows the various currents in the circuit. You can verify Kirchhoff's current law at each node.

. . . .
* We assume that $V_A > V_B$. On solving the circuit, we shall see whether this assumption is correct or not.

Note: Sometimes, it is more convenient to express node currents in terms of *conductance* than expressing them in terms of resistance. Thus referring to Fig. 3.15,

$$G = \frac{1}{R} = \frac{1}{10} = 0.1\,S$$

∴ Current, $I = G(V_1 - V_2) = 0.1(V_1 - V_2)$

This is illustrated in the next example.

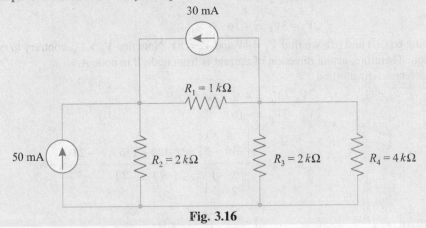

$R = 10\,\Omega$

Fig. 3.15

Example 3.7. *Use nodal analysis to find current in the 4kΩ resistor shown in Fig. 3.16.*

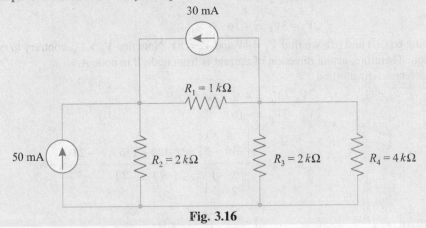

Fig. 3.16

Solution. We shall solve this example by expressing node currents in terms of conductance than expressing them in terms of resistance. The conductance of each resistor can be computed as under:

$$G_1 = \frac{1}{R_1} = \frac{1}{1 \times 10^3} = 10^{-3}\,S$$

$$G_2 = \frac{1}{R_2} = \frac{1}{2 \times 10^3} = 0.5 \times 10^{-3}\,S$$

$$G_3 = \frac{1}{R_3} = \frac{1}{2 \times 10^3} = 0.5 \times 10^{-3}\,S$$

$$G_4 = \frac{1}{R_4} = \frac{1}{4 \times 10^3} = 0.25 \times 10^{-3}\,S$$

Mark the currents in the various branches as shown in Fig. 3.17. Take point E (or F) as the reference node. We shall find voltages at nodes A and B.

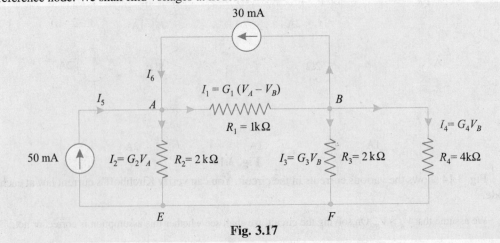

Fig. 3.17

At node A

$$I_5 + I_6 = I_1 + I_2$$

or $\quad 50 \times 10^{-3} + 30 \times 10^{-3} = G_1 (V_A - V_B) + G_2 V_A$

or $\quad\quad\quad 80 \times 10^{-3} = 10^{-3} (V_A - V_B) + 0.5 \times 10^{-3} V_A$

or $\quad\quad\quad 1.5 V_A - V_B = 80$ $\quad\quad\quad\quad\quad\quad\quad\quad$ ...(i)

At node B $\quad\quad\quad I_1 = I_6 + I_3 + I_4$

or $\quad\quad\quad G_1 (V_A - V_B) = 30 \times 10^{-3} + G_3 V_B + G_4 V_B$

or $\quad 10^{-3} (V_A - V_B) = 30 \times 10^{-3} + 0.5 \times 10^{-3} V_B + 0.25 \times 10^{-3} V_B$

or $\quad\quad\quad V_A - 1.75 V_B = 30$ $\quad\quad\quad\quad\quad\quad\quad\quad$ ...(ii)

Solving eqs. (i) and (ii), we get, $V_B = 21.54 V$

By determinant method

$$1.5 V_A - V_B = 80$$

$$V_A - 1.75 V_B = 30$$

$$V_B = \frac{\begin{vmatrix} 1.5 & 80 \\ 1 & 30 \end{vmatrix}}{\begin{vmatrix} 1.5 & -1 \\ 1 & -1.75 \end{vmatrix}} = \frac{(45) - (80)}{(-2.625) - (-1)} = \frac{-35}{-1.625} = 21.54 \text{ V}$$

∴ Current in $4k\Omega$ resistor, $\quad I_4 = G_4 V_B = 0.25 \times 10^{-3} \times 21.54 = 5.39 \times 10^{-3} \text{ A} = \textbf{5.39 mA}$

TUTORIAL PROBLEMS

1. Using nodal analysis, find the voltages at nodes A, B and C w.r.t. the reference node shown by the ground symbol. $\quad\quad\quad$ $[V_A = -30V; \ V_B = -20V; \ V_C = -2V]$

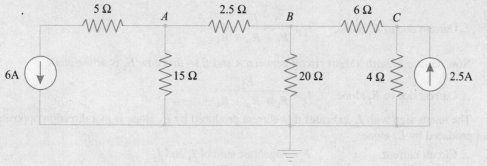

Fig. 3.18

2. Using nodal analysis, find the current through $0.05 \ S$ conductance in Fig. 3.19.

$$[0.264 \text{ A}]$$

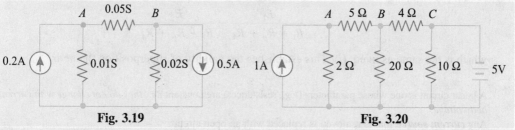

Fig. 3.19 $\quad\quad\quad\quad\quad\quad\quad\quad\quad\quad\quad$ Fig. 3.20

3. Using nodal analysis, find the current flowing in the battery in Fig. 3.20. $\quad\quad$ [1.21 A]

3.6. SUPERPOSITION THEOREM

The essence of superposition theorem is that an e.m.f. acting in a *linear network produces the same effect whether it acts alone or in conjunction with other e.m.f.s. The theorem may be stated as under:

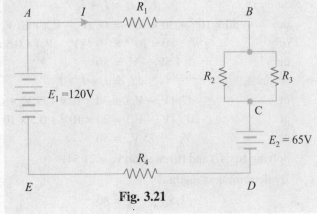

Fig. 3.21

*In a linear network containing more than one source of e.m.f., the resultant current in any branch is the algebraic sum of the currents that would be produced by each e.m.f. acting alone, all other sources of e.m.f., being ***replaced meanwhile by their respective internal resistances.*

Explanation. To show that this statement is true, consider the circuit shown in Fig. 3.21. The total circuit resistance R_T is given by :

$$R_T = R_1 + R_p + R_4 \text{ where } R_p = \frac{R_2 R_3}{R_2 + R_3}$$

Circuit current,
$$I = \frac{\text{Net e.m.f.}}{R_T} = \frac{E_1 - E_2}{R_1 + R_p + R_4}$$

or
$$I = \frac{E_1}{R_1 + R_p + R_4} - \frac{E_2}{R_1 + R_p + R_4} \qquad ...(i)$$

Let us now find the circuit current by superposition theorem. Consider that e.m.f. E_1 is acting alone by replacing E_2 with a short circuit between C and D.

∴ Current due to E_1 alone, $\quad I_1 = \dfrac{E_1}{R_1 + R_p + R_4}$

Now replace E_1 with a short circuit between A and E so that now E_2 is acting alone.

∴ Current due to E_2 alone, $\quad I_2 = \dfrac{-E_2}{R_1 + R_p + R_4}$

The minus sign with I_2 indicates that current produced by E_2 alone is in a direction opposite to that produced by E_1 alone.

∴ Circuit current, $\qquad I = $ Algebraic sum of I_1 and I_2

$$= \left(\frac{E_1}{R_1 + R_p + R_4} \right) + \left(\frac{-E_2}{R_1 + R_p + R_4} \right)$$

$$= \frac{E_1}{R_1 + R_p + R_4} - \frac{E_2}{R_1 + R_p + R_4}$$

which is the same as in eq. (*i*). This establishes the validity of superposition theorem.

* A linear circuit is one whose parameters (*e.g.*, resistances) are constant *i.e.*, they do not change with current and voltage.
** Any *current source* that is removed is replaced with an open circuit.

Example 3.8. *In the network shown in Fig. 3.22 (i), find the different branch currents by super-position theorem.*

Solution. Since there are two sources of e.m.f., two circuits [Figs. 3.22 (*ii*) and 3.23] are required for analysis by superposition theorem.

In Fig. 3.22 (*ii*), 40V source is replaced by a short so that e.m.f. of 35V is acting alone. The various currents can be found as under [Refer to Fig. 3.22 (*ii*)] :

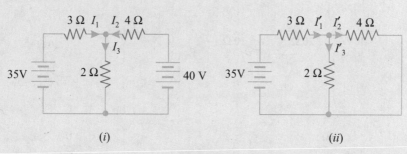

(i)   (ii)

Fig. 3.22

Total resistance across source $= 3 + \dfrac{2 \times 4}{2 + 4} = 4.33 \; \Omega$

Total circuit current, $\quad I_1' = 35 / 4.33 = 8.08 \; A$

Current in 4 Ω resistor, $\quad *I_2' = 8.08 \times 2 / (2 + 4) = 2.69A$

Current in 2 Ω resistor, $\quad I_3' = 8.08 \times 4 / (2 + 4) = 5.39A$

In Fig. 3.23, 35V source is replaced by a short so that now 40V source is acting alone.

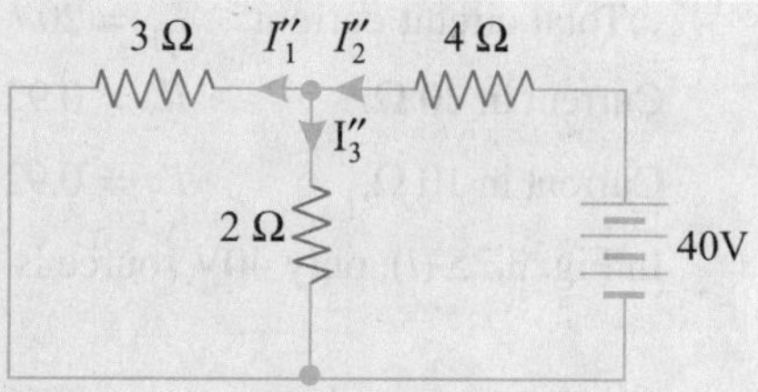

Total resistance across source

$$= 4 + \dfrac{3 \times 2}{3 + 2} = 5.2 \; \Omega$$

Total circuit current, $\quad I''_2 = 40/5.2 = 7.69 \; A$

Current in 3Ω, $\quad I''_1 = 7.69 \times 2 / (2 + 3) = 3.08 \; A$

Current in 2Ω, $\quad I''_3 = 7.69 \times 3 / (2 + 3) = 4.61 \; A$

Fig. 3.23

The actual current values of I_1, I_2 and I_3 shown in Fig. 3.22 (*i*) can be found by algebraically adding the component values.

$\therefore$

$$I_1 = I_1' - I''_1 = 8.08 - 3.08 = 5 \; A$$

$$I_2 = I''_2 - I_2' = 7.69 - 2.69 = 5 \; A$$

$$I_3 = I_3' + I''_3 = 5.39 + 4.61 = 10 \; A$$

* Remember (Refer back to Art. 2.3) current distribution in parallel circuit is as under :

Current in one of the two parallel resistors = Total current × $\dfrac{\text{Resistance of other resistor}}{\text{Sum of two resistances}}$

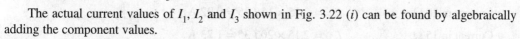

Example 3.9. *Using superposition theorem, find the current in each branch of the network shown in Fig. 3.24 (i).*

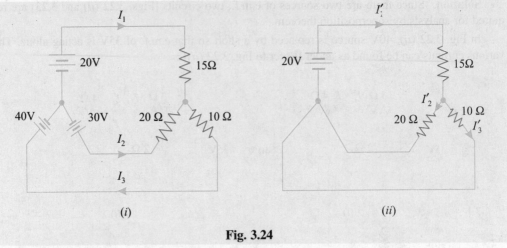

Fig. 3.24

Solution. Since there are three sources of e.m.f., three circuits [Fig. 3.24 (*ii*), Fig. 3.25 (*i*) and (*ii*)] are required for analysis by superposition theorem.

In Fig. 3.24 (*ii*), it is shown that only 20V source is acting.

Total resistance across source $= 15 + \dfrac{20 \times 10}{20 + 10} = 21.67 \ \Omega$

∴ Total circuit current, $\quad I'_1 = 20 / 21.67 = 0.923$ A

Current in 20 Ω, $\qquad I'_2 = 0.923 \times 10 / 30 = 0.307$ A

Current in 10 Ω, $\qquad I'_3 = 0.923 \times 20 / 30 = 0.616$ A

In Fig. 3.25 (*i*), only 40V source is acting in the circuit.

Total resistance across source $= 10 + \dfrac{20 \times 15}{20 + 15} = 18.57 \ \Omega$

Total circuit current, $\qquad I''_3 = 40 / 18.57 = 2.15$ A

Current in 20 Ω, $\qquad I''_2 = 2.15 \times 15 / 35 = 0.92$ A

Current in 15 Ω, $\qquad I''_1 = 2.15 \times 20 / 35 = 1.23$ A

In Fig. 3.25 (*ii*), only 30 V source is acting in the circuit.

Total resistance across source $= 20 + 10 \times 15 / (10 + 15) = 26 \ \Omega$

Total circuit current, $\qquad I'''_2 = 30 / 26 = 1.153$ A

Current in 15 Ω, $\qquad I'''_1 = 1.153 \times 10 / 25 = 0.461$ A

Current in 10 Ω, $\qquad I'''_3 = 1.153 \times 15 / 25 = 0.692$ A

The actual values of currents I_1, I_2 and I_3 shown in Fig. 3.24 (*i*) can be found by algebraically adding the component values.

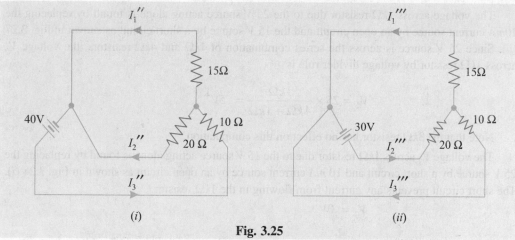

Fig. 3.25

$$I_1 = I_1' - I_1'' - I_1''' = 0.923 - 1.23 - 0.461 = -0.768 \text{ A}$$
$$I_2 = -I_2' - I_2'' + I_2''' = -0.307 - 0.92 + 1.153 = -0.074 \text{ A}$$
$$I_3 = I_3' - I_3'' + I_3''' = 0.616 - 2.15 + 0.692 = -0.842 \text{ A}$$

The negative signs with I_1, I_2 and I_3 show that their actual directions are opposite to that assumed in Fig. 3.24 (*i*).

Example 3.10. *Using superposition principle, find the voltage across 1kΩ resistor in Fig. 3.26.*

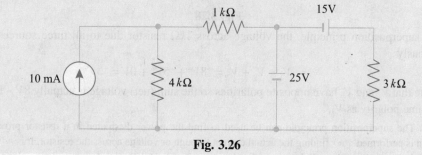

Fig. 3.26

Solution. The voltage across $1k\Omega$ resistor due to the current source acting alone is found by replacing the 25V and 15V sources by short circuits as shown in Fig. 3.27 (*i*). Since the $3k\Omega$ resistor is shorted out, the current in $1k\Omega$ resistor (by current-divider rule) is

$$\text{Current in } 1 \ k\Omega \text{ resistor} = 10 \ mA \times \frac{4 \ k\Omega}{1k\Omega + 4k\Omega} = 8 \ mA$$

∴ Voltage across $1k\Omega$ resistor, $V_1 = 8 \ mA \times 1 \ k\Omega = {}^+8V^-$

The + and – symbols indicate the polarity of voltage due to current source acting alone as shown in Fig. 3.27 (*i*).

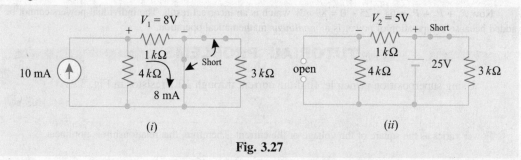

Fig. 3.27

The voltage across $1k\Omega$ resistor due to the 25 V source acting alone is found by replacing the 10mA current source by an open circuit and the 15 V source by a short circuit as shown in Fig. 3.27 (ii). Since 25 V source is across the series combination of $1k\Omega$ and $4k\Omega$ resistors, the voltage V_2 across $1k\Omega$ resistor by voltage divider rule is

$$V_2 = 25 \times \frac{1k\Omega}{4k\Omega + 1k\Omega} = {}^-5V^+$$

Note that the $3k\Omega$ resistor has no effect on this computation.

The voltage V_3 across $1k\Omega$ resistor due to the 15 V source acting alone is found by replacing the 25 V source by a short circuit and 10 mA current source by an open circuit as shown in Fig. 3.28 (i). The short circuit prevents any current from flowing in the $1k\Omega$ resistor.

∴ $$V_3 = 0V$$

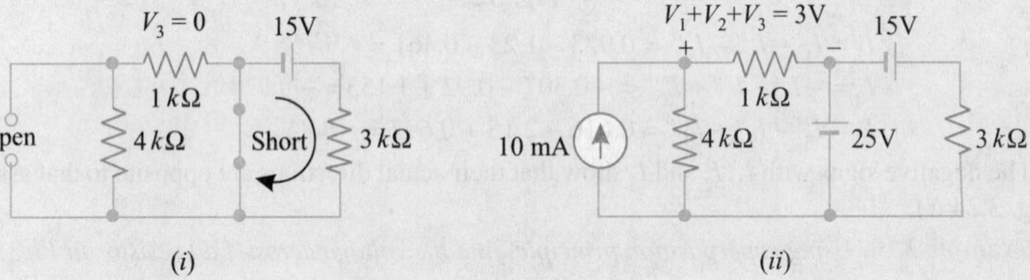

(i)   (ii)

Fig. 3.28

By superposition principle, the voltage across $1k\Omega$ resistor due to all three sources acting simultaneously

$$= V_1 + V_2 + V_3 = {}^+8V^- + {}^-5V^+ + 0V = {}^+3V^-$$

Note that V_1 and V_2 have opposite polarities so the sum (net) voltage is actually $8V - 5V = 3V$ with the same polarity as V_1.

Note : The superposition principle can be used to find the power dissipated in a resistor provided the computation is performed *after* finding the actual current through or voltage across the resistor. It is *not* permissible to find the power by adding all the power dissipations computed when each source is acting alone. Thus in the above example,

Power dissipated in $1k\Omega$ resistor $= \dfrac{(3)^2}{1 \times 10^3} = 9 \times 10^{-3} W = 9\ mW$

It is *incorrect* to compute the power in the $1k\Omega$ resistor by adding the powers P_1, P_2 and P_3 due to each source acting alone :

$$P_1 = \frac{V_1^2}{R} = \frac{(8)^2}{10^3} = 64\ mW; \quad P_2 = \frac{V_2^2}{R} = \frac{(5)^2}{10^3} = 25\ mW; \quad P_3 = \frac{V_3^2}{R} = \frac{(0)^2}{10^3} = 0$$

Now $P_1 + P_2 + P_3 = 64 + 25 + 0 = 89\ mW$ which is an incorrect result. The individual powers cannot be added because computation of power is a *nonlinear* mathematical operation.

TUTORIAL PROBLEMS

1. Using superposition principle, find the current through 10Ω resistor in Fig. 3.29.

[0.5A↓]

. . . .

* Power varies as the square of the voltage or the current. Therefore, this relationship is nonlinear.

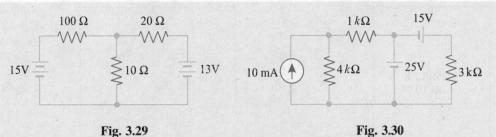

Fig. 3.29   Fig. 3.30

2. Using superposition principle, find the voltage across 4kΩ resistor in Fig. 3.30.

$$\left[28 \; V_{-}^{+} \right]$$

3. Referring to Fig. 3.31, the internal resistance R_S of the current source is 100Ω. The internal resistance R_S of the voltage source is 10Ω. Use superposition principle to find the power dissipated in 50Ω resistor.   [8.26 W]

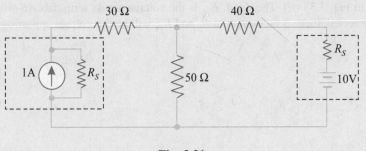

Fig. 3.31

3.7. THEVENIN'S THEOREM

Fig. 3.32 (*i*) shows a network enclosed in a box with two terminals A and B brought out. The network in the box may consist of any number of resistors and e.m.f. sources connected in any manner. But according to Thevenin, the entire circuit behind terminals A and B can be replaced by a single source of e.m.f. E_{Th} (called Thevenin voltage) in series with a single resistance R_{Th} (called Thevenin resistance) as shown in Fig. 3.32 (*ii*). The values of E_{Th} and R_{Th} are determined as mentioned in Thevenin's theorem. Once Thevenin's equivalent circuit is obtained [See Fig. 3.32 (*ii*)], then current through any load resistance R_L connected across AB is given by ;

$$I = \frac{E_{Th}}{R_{Th} + R_L}$$

Hence Thevenin's theorem as applied to d.c. circuits may be stated as under :

Any network having terminals A and B can be replaced by a single source of e.m.f. E_{Th} in series with a single resistance R_{Th}.

(*i*) *The e.m.f. E_{Th} is the voltage obtained across terminals A and B with load, if any, removed i.e., it is the open-circuited voltage between A and B.*

(*ii*) *The resistance R_{Th} is the resistance of the network measured between A and B with load removed and sources of e.m.f.* *replaced by their internal resistances.*

---

* A current source is replaced with open-circuit.

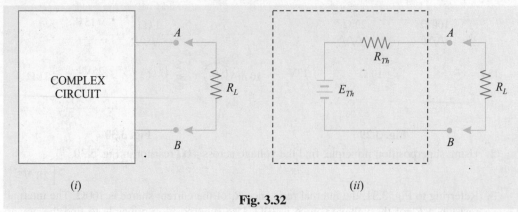

(i)   (ii)

Fig. 3.32

Illustration. Consider the circuit shown in Fig. 3.33 (*i*). As far as the circuit behind terminals *AB* is concerned, it can be replaced by a single source of e.m.f. E_{Th} in series with a single resistance R_{Th} as shown in Fig. 3.33 (*ii*). The e.m.f. E_{Th} is the voltage across terminals *AB* with R_L removed. With R_L disconnected, there is no current in R_2 and E_{Th} will be the voltage appearing across R_3.

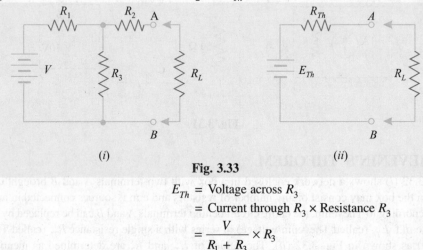

(i)   (ii)

Fig. 3.33

$$\therefore \qquad E_{Th} = \text{Voltage across } R_3$$
$$= \text{Current through } R_3 \times \text{Resistance } R_3$$
$$= \frac{V}{R_1 + R_3} \times R_3$$

To find R_{Th}, remove the load R_L and replace the battery by a short-circuit because its internal resistance is assumed zero. Then resistance measured between *A* and *B* is equal to R_{Th}. Obviously, looking back into the terminals *AB*, R_1 and R_3 are in parallel and this parallel combination is in series with R_2.

$$\therefore \qquad R_{Th} = R_2 + \frac{R_1 R_3}{R_1 + R_3}$$

When load R_L is connected between terminals *A* and *B*, then current in R_L is given by ;

$$I = \frac{E_{Th}}{R_{Th} + R_L}$$

One of the principal advantages of a Thevenin's equivalent circuit is that it greatly simplifies computation when it is necessary to find several values of voltage or current corresponding to several different resistance values in a circuit. For example, suppose we want to find voltage across a resistor in a complex circuit when the resistance is changed several times. Then it is much easier to replace the remaining circuitry with its Thevenin's equivalent than it is to repeat a series of involved computations each time the resistance is changed. Example 3.16 illustrates this point.

Example 3.11. *Using Thevenin's theorem, find the current in 8 Ω resistor in Fig. 3.34 (i). Given that battery has an internal resistance of 1 Ω.*

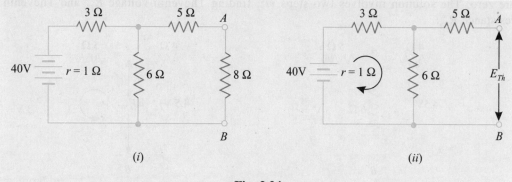

Fig. 3.34

Solution. It is required to find current in 8 Ω resistor by Thevenin's theorem. The solution involves two steps :

(*i*) The first step is to find the open-circuited voltage E_{Th} at terminals AB. It is the voltage appearing across AB when 8 Ω resistor is removed as shown in Fig. 3.34 (*ii*). With 8 Ω resistor removed, there is no drop in 5 Ω and E_{Th} will be the voltage appearing across 6 Ω resistor. Referring to Fig. 3.34 (*ii*),

$$\text{Circuit current} = \frac{40}{1 + 3 + 6} = 4\text{A}$$

Voltage across 6Ω, $E_{Th} = 4 \times 6 = 24$ V

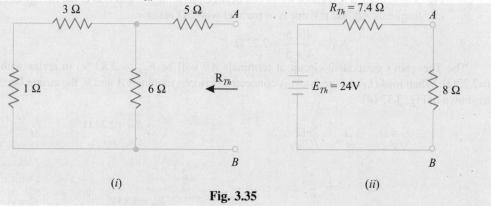

Fig. 3.35

(*ii*) The second step is to find Thevenin's resistance R_{Th}. For this purpose, remove the load (*i.e* 8 Ω) and replace the battery by its internal resistance of 1 Ω as shown in Fig. 3.35 (*i*). The resistance now measured between A and B is equal to R_{Th}. Looking into the terminals AB, 5 Ω resistor is in series with parallel combination of (3 + 1) Ω and 6 Ω.

$$\therefore \qquad R_{Th} = 5 + \frac{4 \times 6}{4 + 6} = 7.4\Omega$$

The Thevenin's equivalent circuit behind terminals AB is E_{Th} (= 24V) in series with R_{Th} (= 7.4 Ω). When load of 8 Ω is connected between terminals A and B, the circuit becomes as shown in Fig. 3.35 (*ii*).

$$\therefore \qquad \text{Current in 8 }\Omega = \frac{E_{Th}}{R_{Th} + 8} = \frac{24}{7.4 + 8} = 1.56 \text{ A}$$

Example 3.12. *Using Thevenin's theorem, find the current in 6 Ω resistor in Fig. 3.36 (i).*

Solution. Since internal resistances of batteries are not given, it will be assumed that they are zero. The solution involves two steps *viz.* finding Thevenin voltage E_{Th} and Thevenin resistance R_{Th}.

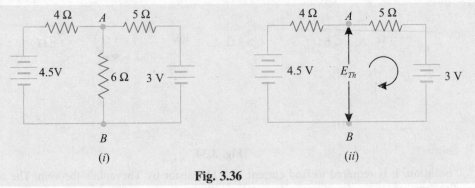

Fig. 3.36

(*i*) To find E_{Th}, remove 6 Ω resistor as shown in Fig. 3.36 (*ii*). The voltage between terminals *A* and *B* is equal to E_{Th}. Now in Fig. 3.36 (*ii*), the net e.m.f. is 4.5 − 3 = 1.5 V and total circuit resistance is 9 Ω.

∴   Circuit current = 1.5/9 = 0.167 A

The voltage across *AB* is equal to 4.5 V *less* drop in 4 Ω resistor.

∴   Voltage across *AB*, E_{Th} = 4.5 − 0.167 × 4 = 3.83 *V*

(*ii*) To find R_{Th}, remove the load (*i.e.* 6Ω resistor) and replace the battery by a short as shown in Fig. 3.37 (*i*). Then resistance measured between terminals *A* and *B* is equal to R_{Th}. Looking into terminals *AB*, 4Ω resistor is in parallel with 5Ω resistor.

∴ $$R_{Th} = \frac{4 \times 5}{4 + 5} = 2.22\,\Omega$$

The Thevenin's equivalent circuit at terminals *AB* will be E_{Th} (= 3.83 V) in series with R_{Th} (=2.22Ω). When load (*i.e.* 6 Ω resistor) is connected between terminals *A* and *B*, the circuit becomes as shown in Fig. 3.37 (*ii*).

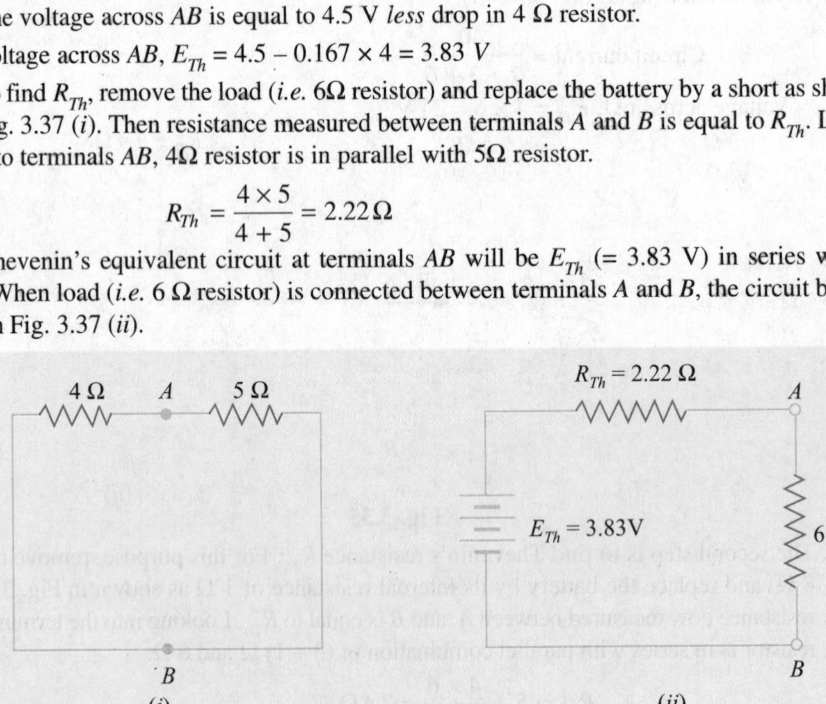

Fig. 3.37

∴ Current in 6Ω = $\dfrac{E_{Th}}{R_{Th} + 6} = \dfrac{3.83}{2.22 + 6} = 0.466$ A

Example 3.13. *Find the p.d. across AB in the circuit shown in Fig. 3.38 (i). Use Thevenin's theorem.*

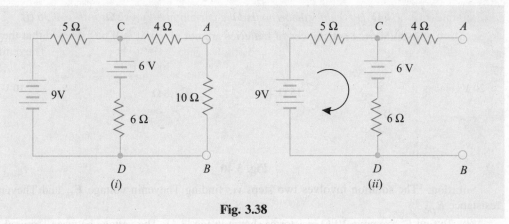

Fig. 3.38

Solution. In order to find open-circuited voltage E_{Th} at terminals AB, remove 10 Ω resistor as shown in Fig. 3.38 (*ii*). The net e.m.f. in the loop is now $9 - 6 = 3$ V and total resistance is $5 + 6 = 11 \, \Omega$.

$\therefore$ Circuit current $= 3/11 = 0.27$ A

Voltage across AB or CD, $E_{Th} = 9 - 5 \times 0.27 = 7.64$ V

In order to find Thevenin resistance R_{Th}, remove the load (*i.e.* 10Ω resistor) and replace the batteries by short as shown in Fig. 3.39 (*i*). The resistance measured between terminals A and B is equal to R_{Th}. Looking into terminals AB, 4Ω resistor is in series with parallel combination of 5Ω and 6Ω resistors.

$\therefore$ $$R_{Th} = 4 + \frac{5 \times 6}{5 + 6} = 6.72 \, \Omega$$

The Thevenin's equivalent circuit at terminals AB is E_{Th} (=7.64V) in series with R_{Th} (= 6.72 Ω). When load (*i.e.* 10Ω resistor) is connected between terminals A and B, the circuit becomes as shown in Fig. 3.39 (*ii*).

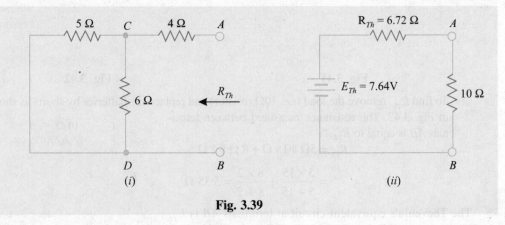

Fig. 3.39

$\therefore$ Current in 10 $\Omega = \dfrac{E_{Th}}{R_{Th} + 10} = \dfrac{7.64}{6.72 + 10} = 0.457 \, \text{A}$

$\therefore$ P.D. across 10 $\Omega = 0.457 \times 10 = \textbf{4.57V}$

Example 3.14. *Find the current in the 10 Ω resistor in the network shown in Fig. 3.40. Use Thevenin's theorem.*

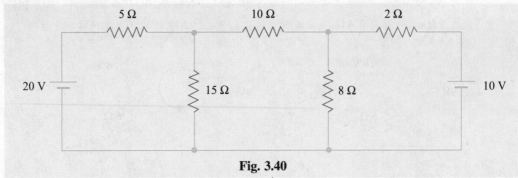

Fig. 3.40

Solution. The solution involves two steps *viz* finding Thevenin voltage E_{Th} and Thevenin resistance R_{Th}.

(*i*) To find E_{Th}, remove 10 Ω resistor as shown in Fig. 3.41. The voltage between terminals A and B is equal to E_{Th}. Referring to Fig. 3.41, we have,

$$I_1 = \frac{20}{5+15} = 1\,A \qquad \therefore \ V_{AC} = 1 \times 15 = 15V$$

$$I_2 = \frac{10}{2+8} = 1\,A \qquad \therefore \ V_{BC} = 1 \times 8 = 8V$$

$$\therefore \qquad V_{AB} = E_{Th} = V_{AC} - V_{BC} = 15 - 8 = 7V$$

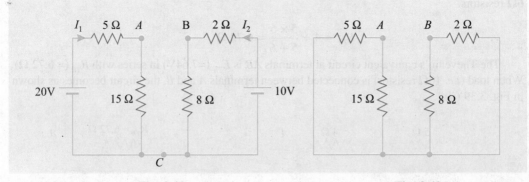

Fig. 3.41   **Fig. 3.42**

(*ii*) To find R_{Th}, remove the load (*i.e.* 10Ω resistor) and replace the batteries by shorts as shown in Fig. 3.42. The resistance measured between terminals *AB* is equal to R_{Th}.

$$\therefore \qquad R_{Th} = 5\Omega \| 15\,\Omega + 8\,\Omega \| 2\,\Omega$$

$$= \frac{5 \times 15}{5+15} + \frac{8 \times 2}{8+2} = 5.35\,\Omega$$

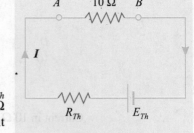

Fig. 3.43

The Thevenin's equivalent circuit at terminals *AB* is E_{Th} (= 7V) in series with R_{Th} (= 5.35 Ω). When load (*i.e.* 10Ω resistor) is connected between terminals *A* and *B*, the circuit becomes as shown in Fig. 3.43.

$$\text{Current in } 10\Omega = \frac{E_{Th}}{R_{Th}+10}$$

$$= \frac{7}{5.35 + 10} = 0.46\,A \ (\textit{from A o B})$$

Example 3.15. *A Wheatstone bridge ABCD has the following details : AB = 10 Ω ; BC = 30 Ω ; CD = 15 Ω and DA = 20 Ω. A battery of e.m.f. 2V and negligible internal resistance is connected between A and C with A positive. A galvanometer of 40 Ω resistance is connected between B and D. Determine the magnitude and direction of current in the galvanometer using Thevenin's theorem.*

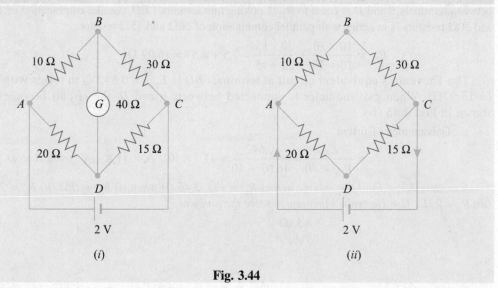

Fig. 3.44

Solution. Fig. 3.44 (*i*) shows the Wheatstone bridge. To find the open-circuited voltage E_{Th} at terminals *BD*, remove 40 Ω resistor as shown in Fig. 3.44 (*ii*). Then voltage between terminals *B* and *D* is equal to E_{Th}.

Current in branch *ABC* $= 2/(10 + 30) = 0.05$A

P.D. between *A* and *B*, $V_{AB} = 10 \times 0.05 = 0.5$V

Current in branch *ADC* $= 2/(20 + 15) = 0.0571$A

P. D. between *A* and *D*, $V_{AD} = 0.0571 \times 20 = 1.142$V

∴   P.D. between *B* and *D*, $E_{Th} = V_{AD} - V_{AB}$

$= 1.142 - 0.5 = 0.642$V

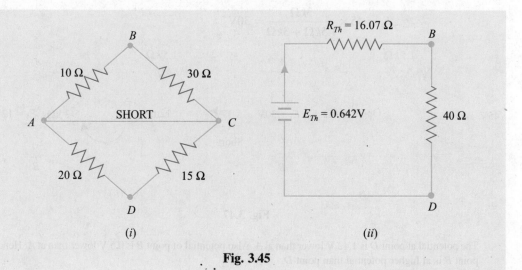

Fig. 3.45

Obviously, point B^* is positive w.r.t. D i.e. current in galvanometer, when connected between B and D, will flow from B to D.

In order to find Thevenin resistance R_{Th}, remove 40Ω resistor and replace the battery by a short (as internal resistance of battery is assumed zero) as shown in Fig. 3.45 (i). Then resistance measured between terminals B and D is equal to R_{Th}. Looking into terminals BD, parallel combination of 10Ω and 30Ω resistors is in series with parallel combination of 20Ω and 15Ω resistors.

$$\therefore \qquad R_{Th} = \frac{10 \times 30}{10 + 30} + \frac{20 \times 15}{20 + 15} = 7.5 + 8.57 = 16.07 \ \Omega$$

The Thevenin's equivalent circuit at terminals BD is E_{Th} (= 0.642V) in series with R_{Th} (= 16.07Ω). When galvanometer is connected between B and D, the circuit becomes as shown in Fig. 3.45 (ii).

$\therefore$ Galvanometer Current

$$= \frac{E_{Th}}{R_{Th} + 40} = \frac{0.642}{16.07 + 40} = 11.5 \times 10^{-3} \,\text{A} = \textbf{11.5 mA} \quad \textit{from B to D}$$

Example 3.16. *Find the voltage across R_L in Fig. 3.46 (i) when (i) $R_L = 1k\Omega$ (ii) $R_L = 2 \ k\Omega$ (iii) $R_L = 9 \ k\Omega$. Use Thevenin's theorem to solve the problem.*

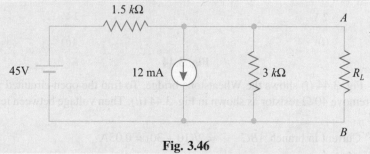

Fig. 3.46

Solution : It is required to find the voltage across R_L when R_L has three different values. We shall find Thevenin's equivalent circuit to the left of the terminals AB. The solution involves two steps.

The first step is to find the open-circuited voltage E_{Th} at terminals AB. For this purpose, we shall use the superposition principle. With the current source removed (opened), we find voltage E_1 due to the 45V source acting alone as shown in Fig. 3.47 (i). Since E_1 is the voltage across the $3k\Omega$ resistor, we have by voltage divider rule :

$$E_1 = 45 \times \frac{3k\Omega}{1.5k\Omega + 3k\Omega} = 30V^+_-$$

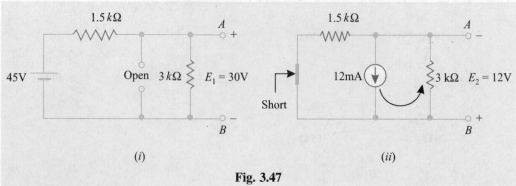

(i)   (ii)

Fig. 3.47

* The potential at point D is 1.42 V lower than at A. Also potential of point B is 0.5 V lower than at A. Hence, point B is at higher potential than point D.

The voltage E_2 due to the current source acting alone is found by shorting 45V voltage source as shown in Fig. 3.47 (*ii*). By current divider rule,

Current in 3kΩ resistor $= 12 \times \dfrac{1.5k\Omega}{1.5k\Omega + 3k\Omega} = 4\,mA$

∴ $\qquad E_2 = 4\ mA \times 3\ k\Omega = 12V_+^-$

Note that E_1 and E_2 have opposite polarities.

∴ Thevenin's voltage, $E_{Th} = E_1 - E_2 = 30 - 12 = 18\ V_-^+$

The second step is to find Thevenin's resistance R_{Th}. For this purpose, we replace the 45V voltage source by a short circuit and the 12 *mA* current source by an open circuit as shown in Fig. 3.48. As can be seen in the figure, R_{Th} is equal to parallel equivalent resistance of 1.5 $k\Omega$ and 3 $k\Omega$ resistors.

∴ $\qquad R_{Th} = 1.5\ k\Omega\ ||\ 3k\Omega = 1\ k\Omega$

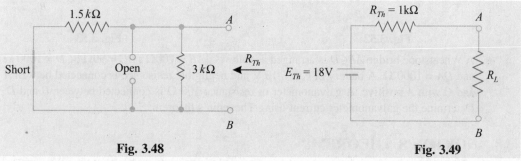

Fig. 3.48　　　　　　　　　　　　　　　　**Fig. 3.49**

Fig. 3.49 shows Thevenin's equivalent circuit.

Voltage across R_L, $V_L = 18 \times \dfrac{R_L}{1k\Omega + R_L}$

(*i*) When $R_L = 1k\Omega$; $V_L = 18 \times \dfrac{1k\Omega}{1k\Omega + 1k\Omega} = 9V$

(*ii*) When $R_L = 2k\Omega$; $V_L = 18 \times \dfrac{2k\Omega}{1k\Omega + 2k\Omega} = 12V$

(*iii*) When $R_L = 9k\Omega$; $V_L = 18 \times \dfrac{9k\Omega}{1k\Omega + 9k\Omega} = 16.2V$

TUTORIAL PROBLEMS

1. Using Thevenin's theorem, find the current in 10 Ω resistor in the circuit shown in Fig. 3.50.　　　　　　　　　　　　　　　　　　　　　　　　　　　　　　**[0.481A]**

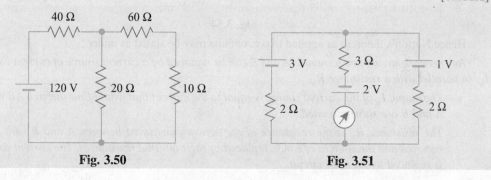

Fig. 3.50　　　　　　　　　　　　　　　　　**Fig. 3.51**

2. Using Thevenin's theorem, find the current in the ammeter shown in Fig. 3.51. **[1A]**

3. Use Thevenin's theorem to find the p.d. across *AB* branch of the network shown in Fig. 3.52. **[4.16V]**

4. Determine Thevenin's equivalent circuit to the left of *AB* in Fig. 3.53.

[A 6V source in series with 3 Ω]

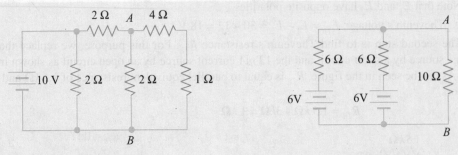

Fig. 3.52	**Fig. 3.53**

5. A Wheatstone bridge *ABCD* is arranged as follows : $AB = 100\Omega$; $BC = 99\Omega$; $CD = 1000$ Ω and $DA = 1000$ Ω. A battery of e.m.f. 10 V and negligible resistance is connected betwen *A* and *C* with *A* positive. A galvanometer of resistance 100 Ω is connected between *B* and *D*. Determine the galvanometer current using Thevenin's theorem. **[38.6 µA]**

3.8. NORTON'S THEOREM

Fig. 3.54 (*i*) shows a network enclosed in a box with two terminals *A* and *B* brought out. The network in the box may contain any number of resistors and e.m.f. sources connected in any manner. But according to Norton, the entire circuit behind *AB* can be replaced by a current source I_N in parallel with a resistance R_N as shown in Fig. 3.54 (*ii*). The resistance R_N is the same as Thevenin resistance R_{Th}. The value of I_N is determined as mentioned in Norton's theorem. Once Norton's equivalent circuit is determined [See Fig. 3.54 (*ii*)], then current through any load R_L connected across *AB* can be readily obtained.

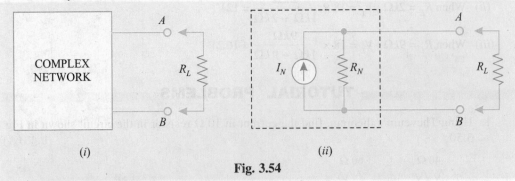

(*i*)	(*ii*)

Fig. 3.54

Hence Norton's theorem as applied to d.c. circuits may be stated as under :

Any network having two terminals A and B can be replaced by a current source of current output I_N in parallel with a resistance R_N.

(*i*) *The output I_N of the current source is equal to the current that would flow through AB when A and B are short-circuited.*

(*ii*) *The resistance R_N is the resistance of the network measured between A and B with load removed and the sources of e.m.f., replaced by their internal resistances. The current source is replaced by an open circuit.*

Norton's theorem is *converse* of Thevenin's theorem in that Norton equivalent circuit uses a current generator instead of voltage generator and the resistance R_N (which is the same as R_{Th}) in parallel with the generator instead of being in series with it.

Illustration. Fig. 3.55 illustrates the application of Norton's theorem. As far as the circuit behind terminals AB is concerned [See Fig. 3.55 (*i*)], it can be replaced by a current source I_N in parallel with a resistance R_N as shown in Fig. 3.55 (*iv*). The output I_N of the current generator is equal to the current that would flow when terminals A and B are short-circuited as shown in Fig. 3.55 (*ii*). The load on the source when terminals AB are short-circuited is given by ;

$$R' = R_1 + \frac{R_2 R_3}{R_2 + R_3} = \frac{R_1 R_2 + R_1 R_3 + R_2 R_3}{R_2 + R_3}$$

Source current,
$$I' = \frac{V}{R'} = \frac{V (R_2 + R_3)}{R_1 R_2 + R_1 R_3 + R_2 R_3}$$

Short-circuit current, I_N = Current in R_2 in Fig. 3.55 (*ii*)

$$= I' \times \frac{R_3}{R_2 + R_3} = \frac{V R_3}{R_1 R_2 + R_1 R_3 + R_2 R_3}$$

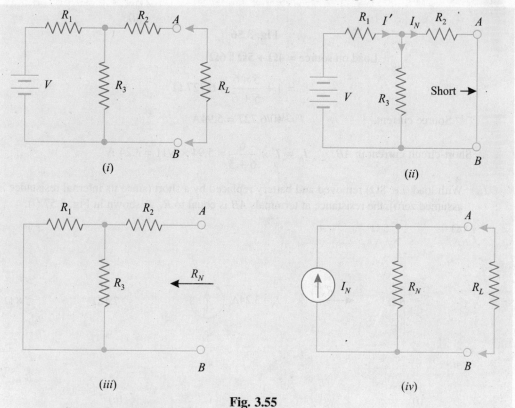

Fig. 3.55

To find R_N, remove the load R_L and replace battery by a short because its internal resistance is assumed zero [See Fig. 3.55 (*iii*)].

∴ R_N = Resistance at terminals AB in Fig. 3.55 (*iii*)

$$= R_2 + \frac{R_1 R_3}{R_1 + R_3}$$

Thus the values of I_N and R_N are known. The Norton equivalent circuit will be as shown in Fig. 3.55 (*iv*).

Example 3.17. *Using Norton's theorem, find the current in 8Ω resistor of the network shown in Fig. 3.56 (i).*

Solution. We shall reduce the network to the left of *AB* in Fig. 3.56 (*i*) to Norton equivalent circuit. For this purpose, we are required to find I_N and R_N.

(*i*) With load removed (*i.e.* 8Ω) and terminals *AB* short-circuited [See Fig. 3.56 (*ii*)], the current that flows through *AB* is equal to I_N. Referring to Fig. 3.56 (*ii*),

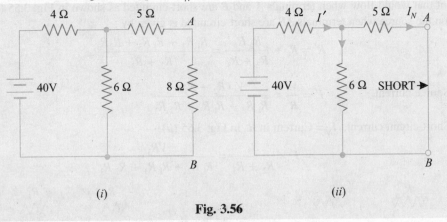

(*i*)   (*ii*)

Fig. 3.56

Load on source = 4Ω + 5Ω ‖ 6Ω

$$= 4 + \frac{5 \times 6}{5 + 6} = 6.727 \ \Omega$$

Source current, $I' = 40/6.727 = 5.94A$

∴ Short-circuit current in *AB*, $I_N = I' \times \dfrac{6}{6 + 5} = 5.94 \times 6/11 = 3.24 \text{ A}$

(*ii*) With load (*i.e.* 8Ω) removed and battery replaced by a short (since its internal resistance is assumed zero), the resistance at terminals *AB* is equal to R_N as shown in Fig. 3.57 (*i*).

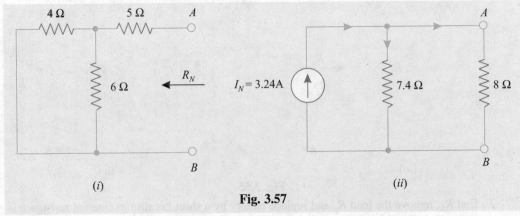

(*i*)   (*ii*)

Fig. 3.57

∴ $R_N = 5\Omega + 4\Omega \, \| \, 6\Omega = 5 + \dfrac{4 \times 6}{4 + 6} = 7.4 \ \Omega$

The Norton equivalent circuit behind terminals *AB* is I_N (=3.24A) in parallel with R_N (= 7.4Ω). When load 8Ω is connected across terminals *AB*, the circuit becomes as shown in Fig. 3.57 (*ii*). The current source is supplying two resistors 7.4 Ω and 8 Ω in parallel.

∴ $\qquad$ Current in $8\,\Omega = 3.24 \times \dfrac{7.4}{8 + 7.4} = 1.55\,A$

Example 3.18. *Using Norton's theorem, find the current in the branch AB containing 6 Ω resistor of the network shown in Fig. 3.58 (i).*

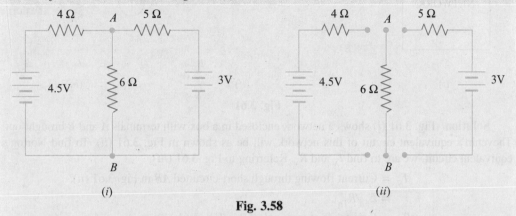

(i) $\qquad\qquad\qquad\qquad\qquad\qquad\qquad\qquad\qquad$ (ii)

Fig. 3.58

Solution. The load of 6 Ω is supplied by two sources. We shall find Norton's equivalent circuit for each source. Applying Norton's theorem to the left of AB in Fig. 3.58 (ii),

$$I_N = 4.5/4 = 1.125A \; ; \qquad\qquad R_N = 4\,\Omega$$

Applying Norton's theorem to the right of AB in Fig 3.58 (ii),

$$I_N = 3/5 = 0.6A \; ; \qquad\qquad R_N = 5\,\Omega$$

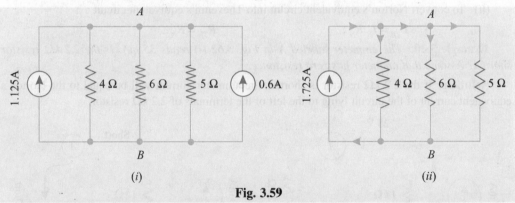

(i) $\qquad\qquad\qquad\qquad\qquad\qquad\qquad\qquad\qquad$ (ii)

Fig. 3.59

The circuit shown in Fig. 3.59 (i) has been redrawn, replacing voltage sources by Norton's equivalent circuits.

We can now replace the two current sources by a single current source supplying $1.125 + 0.6 = 1.725A$ as shown in Fig. 3.59 (ii). The parallel combination of 4 Ω and 5 Ω can be replaced by a single resistor equal to $4 \times 5/(4 + 5) = 2.22\Omega$ as shown in Fig. 3.60. The current source is supplying two resistors 2.22Ω and 6Ω in parallel.

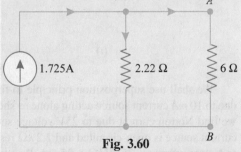

Fig. 3.60

∴ Current in $6\Omega = 1.725 \times \dfrac{2.22}{6 + 2.22} = 0.466\,A$

Example 3.19. *Show that when Thevenin equivalent circuit of a network is converted into Norton equivalent circuit, $I_N = E_{Th}/R_{Th}$ and $R_N = R_{Th}$.*

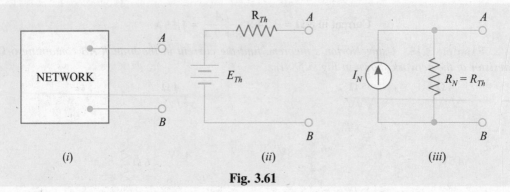

Fig. 3.61

Solution. Fig. 3.61 (*i*) shows a network enclosed in a box with terminals *A* and *B* brought out. Thevenin's equivalent circuit of this network will be as shown in Fig. 3.61 (*ii*). To find Norton's equivalent circuit, we are to find I_N and R_N. Referring to Fig. 3.61 (*iii*),

I_N = Current flowing through short-circuited *AB* in Fig. 3.61 (*ii*).

$\quad = E_{Th}/R_{Th}$

R_N = Resistance at terminals *AB* in Fig. 3.61 (*ii*).

$\quad = R_{Th}$

Hence we arrive at the following important conclusions :

(*i*) To convert Thevenin's equivalent circuit into Norton's equivalent circuit :

$$I_N = E_{Th}/R_{Th} ; \qquad\qquad R_N = R_{Th}$$

(*ii*) To convert Norton's equivalent circuit into Thevenin's equivalent circuit :

$$E_{Th} = I_N R_N ; \qquad\qquad R_{Th} = R_N$$

Example 3.20. *The ammeter labeled A in Fig. 3.62 (i) reads 35 mA. Is the 2.2 kΩ resistor shorted? Assume that ammeter has zero resistance.*

Solution. If the 2.2 *kΩ* resistor is shorted, the ammeter current will be equal to the Norton's equivalent current of the circuit lying to the left of the terminals of 2.2 *kΩ* resistor.

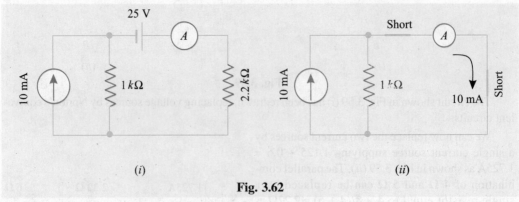

Fig. 3.62

We shall use superposition principle to find Norton current. First, we calculate Norton current due to 10 *mA* current source acting alone as shown in Fig. 3.62 (*ii*). This value is clearly 10 *mA*. Then we find Norton current due to 25*V* voltage source acting alone as shown in Fig. 3.63 (*i*). Note that current source is open-circuited and 2.2 *kΩ* resistor is shorted. The contribution of 25*V* source alone to Norton current = 25*V*/1*kΩ* = 25 *mA*. By superposition principle,

$$I_N = 10\ mA + 25\ mA = 35\ mA$$

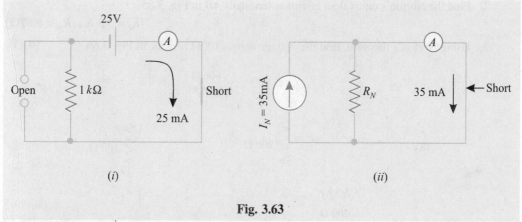

(i)   *(ii)*

Fig. 3.63

Fig. 3.63 (*ii*) shows that a short connected across the terminals of Norton's equivalent circuit draws the entire current of 35*mA* through the ammeter. *Therefore, 2.2 kΩ resistor is shorted.*

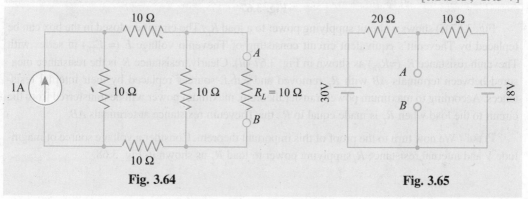

Voltage source   Current Source

TUTORIAL PROBLEMS

1. Using Norton's theorem, find the current through and voltage across load R_L in Fig. 3.64.

   [0.143 A ; 1.43 V]

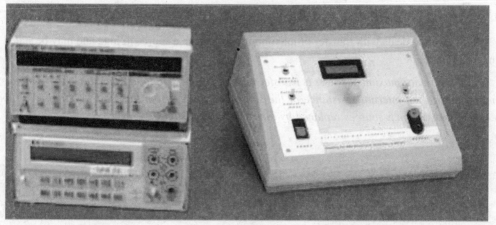

Fig. 3.64   **Fig. 3.65**

2. Find the Norton's equivalent circuit at terminals AB in Fig. 3.65.

$$[I_N = 3.3 \text{ A} \; ; \; R_N = 6.67\Omega]$$

3. Using Norton's theorem, find the voltage across 100Ω resistor in Fig. 3.66. **[0.9V]**

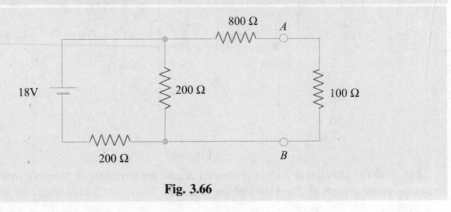

Fig. 3.66

3.9. MAXIMUM POWER TRANSFER THEOREM

This theorem deals with transfer of maximum power from a source to load and may be stated as under :

In d.c. circuits, maximum power is transferred from a source to load when the load resistance is made equal to the internal resistance of the source as viewed from the load terminals with load removed and all e.m.f. sources replaced by their internal resistances.

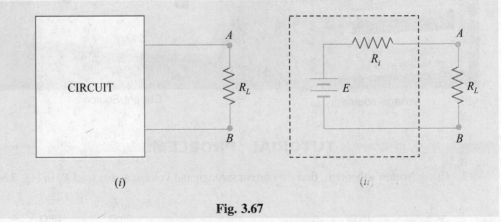

Fig. 3.67

Fig. 3.67 (*i*) shows a circuit supplying power to a load R_L. The circuit enclosed in the box can be replaced by Thevenin's equivalent circuit consisting of Thevenin voltage E (= E_{Th}) in series with Thevenin resistance R_i (=R_{Th}) as shown in Fig. 3.67 (*ii*). Clearly, resistance R_i is the resistance measured between terminals AB with R_L removed and e.m.f. sources replaced by their internal resistances. According to maximum power transfer theorem, maximum power will be transferred from the circuit to the load when R_L is made equal to R_i, the Thevenin resistance at terminals AB.

Proof : We now turn to the proof of this important theorem. Consider a voltage source of magnitude V and internal resistance R_i supplying power to load R_L as shown in Fig. 3.68.

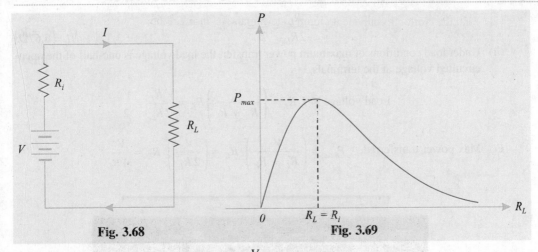

Fig. 3.68   **Fig. 3.69**

Circuit current,
$$I = \frac{V}{R_L + R_i}$$

Power delivered to load,
$$P = I^2 R_L = \left(\frac{V}{R_L + R_i}\right)^2 R_L \qquad \qquad ...(i)$$

For a given source, the generated voltage V and internal resistance R_i are constant. Therefore, power delivered to the load depends upon the value of R_L. In order to find the value of R_L for which the value of P is maximum, differentiate eq. (i) w.r.t. R_L and set the result equal to zero.

Thus
$$\frac{dP}{dR_L} = V^2 \left[\frac{(R_L + R_i)^2 - 2R_L (R_L + R_i)}{(R_L + R_i)^4}\right] = 0$$

or $\qquad (R_L + R_i)^2 - 2R_L (R_L + R_i) = 0$

or $\qquad (R_L + R_i) (R_L + R_i - 2 R_L) = 0$

or $\qquad (R_L + R_i) (R_i - R_L) = 0$

Since $R_L + R_i$ cannot be zero,

∴ $\qquad \qquad R_i - R_L = 0$

or $\qquad \qquad R_L = R_i$

or $\qquad \qquad$ *Load resistance = Internal resistance of source*

Thus, for maximum power transfer, the load resistance R_L should be equal to the internal resistance R_i of the source. Fig. 3.69 shows the graph of load power versus load resistance.

We may extend the maximum power transfer theorem to a linear circuit rather than a single source by means of Thevenin's theorem as under :

The maximum power is obtained from a linear circuit at a given pair of terminals when terminals are loaded by the Thevenin's resistance (R_{Th}) of the circuit.

The above statement is obviously true since by Thevenin's theorem, the circuit is equivalent to a practical voltage source in series with internal resistance R_{Th}.

The following points may be noted carefully :

(*i*) The efficiency at maximum power transfer is only 50% as one-half of the total power generated is dissipated in the internal resistance R_i of the source.

$$\text{Efficiency} = \frac{\text{Output power}}{\text{Input power}} = \frac{I^2 R_L}{I^2 (R_L + R_i)}$$

$$= \frac{R_L}{2R_L} = \frac{1}{2} = 50\%$$ $(\because R_L = R_i)$

(*ii*) Under load conditions of maximum power transfer, the load voltage is one-half of the open-circuited voltage at the terminals.

$$\text{Load voltage} = I \, R_L = \left(\frac{V}{R_L + R_i}\right) R_L = \frac{V R_L}{2 R_L} = \frac{V}{2}$$

(*iii*) Max power transferred, $\quad P_{max} = \left(\frac{V}{R_L + R_i}\right)^2 R_L = \left(\frac{V}{2 R_L}\right)^2 R_L = \frac{V^2}{4 R_L}$

Amplifier uses maximum power transfer theorem

Example 3.21. *Calculate the value of load resistance R_L to which maximum power may be transferred from the circuit shown in Fig. 3.70 (i). Determine also the value of maximum power.*

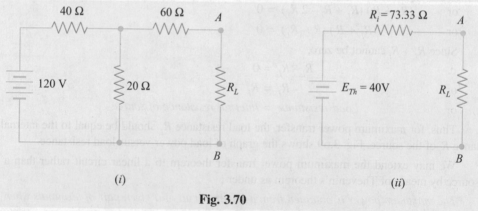

Fig. 3.70

Solution. We shall first find Thevenin's equivalent circuit to the left of terminals *AB*.

E_{Th} = Voltage at *AB* with R_L removed

$$= \frac{120}{40 + 60} \times 20 = 40 \text{ volts}$$

R_i = Resistance at *AB* with R_L removed and 120 V source replaced by a short

$= 60\Omega + 40\Omega \parallel 20\Omega$

$= 60 + 40 \times 20/60 = 73.33\Omega$

The Thevenin's equivalent circuit to the left of AB in Fig. 3.70 (i) will be E_{Th} (= 40V) in series with R_i (= 73.33Ω). When R_L is connected between A and B, the circuit becomes as shown in Fig. 3.70 (ii). It is clear that maximum power will be transferred when :

$$R_L = R_{Th} = 73.33Ω$$

$$\text{Max. power to load} = \frac{(E_{Th})^2}{4\,R_L} = \frac{(40)^2}{4 \times 73.33} = \textbf{5.45 watts}$$

Example 3.22. *Determine the maximum power that can be delivered by the circuit shown in Fig. 3.71 (i).*

Solution. Fig. 3.71 (ii) shows the Norton's equivalent circuit. Maximum power transfer occurs when $R_L = R_N = 300Ω$.

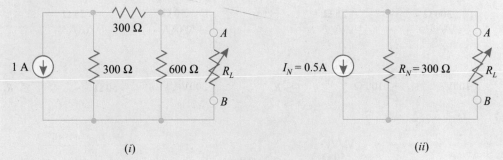

(i)   (ii)

Fig. 3.71

Referring to Fig. 3.71 (ii), current in R_L (= 300Ω) $= I_N / 2 = 0.5/2 = 0.25$ A

∴ Max power transferred $= (0.25)^2 \times R_L = (0.25)^2 \times 300 = \textbf{18.8 W}$

Example 3.23. *What percentage of maximum possible power is delivered to R_L in Fig. 3.72 (i) when $R_L = 2\,R_{Th}$?*

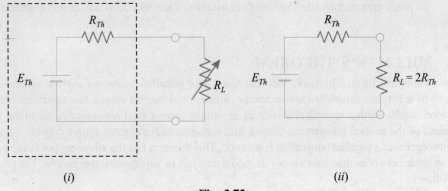

(i)   (ii)

Fig. 3.72

Solution. Fig. 3.72 (ii) shows the circuit when $R_L = 2R_{Th}$.

$$\text{Circuit current} = \frac{E_{Th}}{R_{Th} + 2R_{Th}} = \frac{E_{Th}}{3R_{Th}}$$

Voltage across load,
$$V_L = \frac{E_{Th}}{3R_{Th}} \times 2\,R_{Th} = \frac{2}{3}\,E_{Th}$$

Power delivered to load,
$$P_L = \frac{V_L^2}{R_L} = \frac{\left(\frac{2}{3}\,E_{Th}\right)^2}{2\,R_{Th}} = \frac{4\,E_{Th}^2}{18\,R_{Th}}$$

Since $P_{max} = E_{Th}^2/4R_{Th}$, the ratio of P_L / P_{max} is

$$\frac{P_L}{P_{max}} = \frac{4E_{Th}^2/18R_{Th}}{E_{Th}^2/4R_{Th}} = \frac{16}{18}$$

∴

$$P_L = \frac{16}{18}\, P_{max} \times 100 = 88.89\% \ of \ P_{max}$$

TUTORIAL PROBLEMS

1. Find the value of R_L in Fig. 3.73 necessary to obtain maximum power in R_L. Also find the maximum power in R_L.
   [150Ω ; 1.042 W]

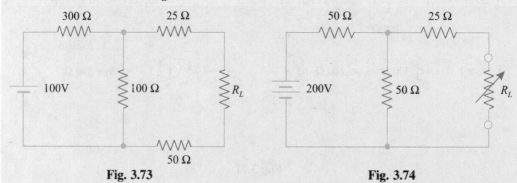

Fig. 3.73   Fig. 3.74

2. Determine the maximum power that can be delivered to the load by the circuit shown in Fig. 3.74. Also find the value of load resistance required to achieve this maximum power.
   [50W ; 50Ω]

3. What percent of the maximum possible power is delivered to a load if the load resistance is 10 times greater than the Thevenin's resistance of the source to which it is connected ?
   [33.06%]

3.10. MILLMAN'S THEOREM

In its simplest form, Millman's theorem *states that parallel connected current sources can be replaced by a single equivalent current source.* Since a real current source has a parallel-connected resistance, it follows that several real sources in parallel have a total resistance equal to the parallel equivalent of the several resistances. Thus a Millman equivalent current source consists of an ideal current source and a parallel equivalent resistance. This theorem has the advantage of being easier to apply to some networks than mesh analysis, nodal analysis or superposition principle. The procedure is as follows :

(i) Convert each parallel-connected voltage source to an equivalent current source. The result is a set of parallel connected current sources.

(ii) Replace the parallel-connected current sources by a single equivalent current source. The equivalent current source is found by *algebraically* adding the individual sources.

(iii) Draw an equivalent circuit with the equivalent current source, the equivalent resistance and the load connected in parallel.

(iv) Solve the equivalent circuit for the desired result.

Example 3.24. *Find the Millman equivalent current source with respect to terminals x – y in Fig. 3.75.*

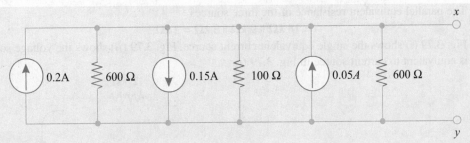

Fig. 3.75

Solution. The resultant current of the three sources

$$= 0.2A\uparrow + 0.15A\downarrow + 0.05A\uparrow$$
$$= 0.1A\uparrow$$

The equivalent resistance of the three parallel resistors

$$= 600\Omega \parallel 100\Omega \parallel 600\Omega$$
$$= 75\Omega$$

Thus the single equivalent current source has a value 0.1A and parallel connected resistance 75Ω as shown in Fig. 3.76.

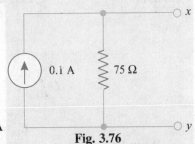

Fig. 3.76

Example 3.25. *Find the current in 1kΩ resistor in Fig. 3.77 by finding Millman equivalent voltage source with respect to terminals x − y.*

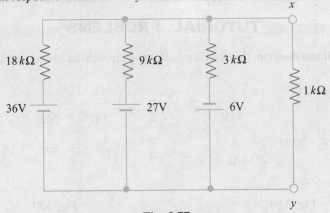

Fig. 3.77

Solution. As shown in Fig. 3.78, each of the three voltage sources is converted to an equivalent current source. For example, the 36V source in series with 18kΩ resistor becomes a 36V/18kΩ = 2 *mA* current source in parallel with 18 kΩ. Note that the polarity of each current source is such that it produces current in the same direction as the voltage source it replaces.

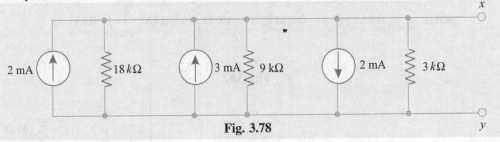

Fig. 3.78

The resultant current of the three current sources

$$= 2\ mA\uparrow + 3\ mA\uparrow + 2\ mA\downarrow = 3\ mA\uparrow$$

The parallel equivalent resistance of the three sources

$$= 18\ k\Omega \parallel 9\ k\Omega \parallel 3\ k\Omega = 2\ k\Omega$$

Fig. 3.79 (*i*) shows the single equivalent current source. Fig. 3.79 (*ii*) shows the voltage source that is equivalent to current source in Fig. 3.79 (*i*).

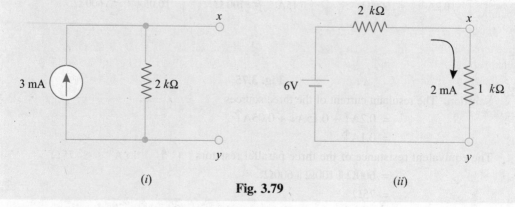

(*i*)　　　　　　　　　　(*ii*)

Fig. 3.79

$$E_{Th} = 3\ mA \times 2\ k\Omega = 6V$$

When 1$k\Omega$ resistor is connected across the $x - y$ terminals, the current is

$$I = \frac{6V}{3k\Omega} = 2\,\text{mA}$$

TUTORIAL PROBLEMS

1. Using Millman theorem, find the current flowing through the load resistance R_L in Fig. 3.80.

   [2.25 mA]

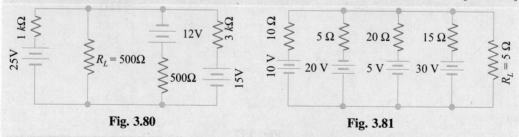

Fig. 3.80　　　　　　　　　　**Fig. 3.81**

2. Using Millman theorem, find the current in the load resistance R_L in Fig. 3.81.　　[0.243 A]
3. Find the single equivalent current source for the circuit shown in Fig. 3.82.

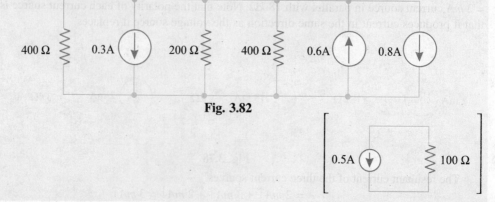

Fig. 3.82

3.11. DELTA / STAR AND STAR / DELTA TRANSFORMATION

There are some networks in which the resistances are neither in series nor in parallel. A familiar case is a three terminal network *e.g.* delta network or star network. In such situations, it is not possible to simplify the network by series and parallel circuit rules. However, converting delta network into star and *vice-versa* often simplifies the network and makes it possible to apply series-parallel circuit techniques.

Delta/Star Transformation. Consider three resistors R_{AB}, R_{BC} and R_{CA} connected in delta to three terminals A, B and C as shown in Fig 3.83 (*i*). It is desired to replace these three delta-connected resistors by three resistors R_A, R_B and R_C connected in star [See Fig. 3.83 (*ii*)] so that the two networks are electrically equivalent. The two arrangements will be electrically equivalent if resistance between any two terminals of one network is equal to the resistance between the corresponding terminals of the other network.

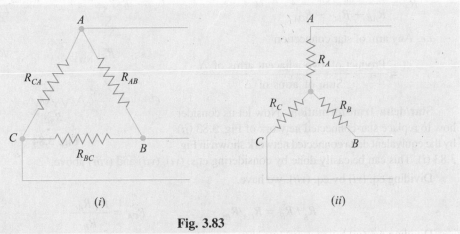

Fig. 3.83

Referring to Delta network shown in Fig. 3.83 (*i*),

Resistance between A and B = $R_{AB} \parallel (R_{BC} + R_{CA})$

$$= \frac{R_{AB}(R_{BC} + R_{CA})}{R_{AB} + R_{BC} + R_{CA}} \qquad ...(i)$$

Referring to star network shown in Fig. 3.83 (*ii*),

Resistance between A and B = $R_A + R_B$ ...(*ii*)

Since the two arrangements are electrically equivalent,

$\therefore \qquad\qquad R_A + R_B = \dfrac{R_{AB}(R_{BC} + R_{CA})}{R_{AB} + R_{BC} + R_{CA}}$ ...(*iii*)

Similarly it can be shown that between terminals B and C and terminals C and A,

$$R_B + R_C = \frac{R_{BC}(R_{CA} + R_{AB})}{R_{AB} + R_{BC} + R_{CA}} \qquad ...(iv)$$

and $\qquad\qquad R_C + R_A = \dfrac{R_{CA}(R_{AB} + R_{BC})}{R_{AB} + R_{BC} + R_{CA}}$ ...(*v*)

Subtracting eq. (*iv*) from eq. (*iii*) and adding the result to eq. (*v*), we get,

$$R_A = \frac{R_{AB}\, R_{CA}}{R_{AB} + R_{BC} + R_{CA}} \qquad ...(vi)$$

Similarly,
$$R_B = \frac{R_{BC}\ R_{AB}}{R_{AB} + R_{BC} + R_{CA}} \qquad \qquad ...(vii)$$

and
$$R_C = \frac{R_{CA}\ R_{BC}}{R_{AB} + R_{BC} + R_{CA}} \qquad \qquad ...(viii)$$

How to remember ? There is an easy way to remember it. Referring to Fig. 3.84, star-connected resistances R_A, R_B and R_C are electrically equivalent to delta connected resistances R_{AB}, R_{BC} and R_{CA}. We have seen above that :

$$R_A = \frac{R_{AB}\ R_{CA}}{R_{AB} + R_{BC} + R_{CA}}$$

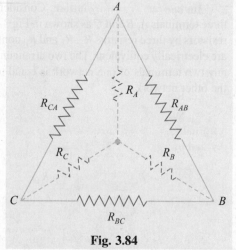

Fig. 3.84

i.e. Any arm of star connection

$$= \frac{\text{Product of two adjacent arms of }\Delta}{\text{Sum of arms of }\Delta}$$

Star/delta Transformation. Now let us consider how to replace star-connected network of Fig. 3.83 *(ii)* by the equivalent delta connected network shown in Fig. 3.83 *(i)*. This can be easily done by considering eqs. *(vi)*, *(vii)* and *(viii)* above.

Dividing eq. *(vi)* by eq. *(vii)*, we have,

$$R_A / R_B = R_{CA}/R_{BC} \qquad \qquad \therefore\ R_{CA} = \frac{R_A\ R_{BC}}{R_B}$$

Dividing eq. *(vi)* by eq. *(viii)*, we have,

$$R_A / R_C = R_{AB}/R_{BC} \qquad \qquad \therefore\ R_{AB} = \frac{R_A\ R_{BC}}{R_C}$$

Substituting the values of R_{CA} and R_{AB} in eq. *(vi)*, we have,

$$R_A = \frac{\left(\dfrac{R_A}{R_C} R_{BC}\right)\left(\dfrac{R_A}{R_B} R_{BC}\right)}{\dfrac{R_A}{R_C} R_{BC} + R_{BC} + \dfrac{R_A}{R_B} R_{BC}}$$

$$= \frac{R_A^2 / R_C R_B}{(R_A / R_C) + 1 + (R_A / R_B)} \times R_{BC}$$

$$= \frac{R_A^2}{R_A R_B + R_C R_B + R_A R_C} \times R_{BC}$$

or
$$R_{BC} = \frac{R_A R_B + R_C R_B + R_A R_C}{R_A}$$

$\therefore$
$$R_{BC} = R_B + R_C + \frac{R_B\ R_C}{R_A}$$

Similarly,
$$R_{CA} = R_C + R_A + \frac{R_C\ R_A}{R_B}$$

and $\qquad R_{AB} = R_A + R_B + \dfrac{R_A\,R_B}{R_C}$

How to remember ? There is an easy way to remember it. Referring to Fig. 3.85, star-connected resistances R_A, R_B and R_C are electrically equivalent to delta connected resistances R_{AB}, R_{BC} and R_{CA}. We have seen

$$R_{AB} = R_A + R_B + \dfrac{R_A\,R_B}{R_C}$$

i.e. Resistance between two terminals of delta

= Sum of star resistances connected to those terminals *plus* product of the same two resistances divided by the third star resistance.

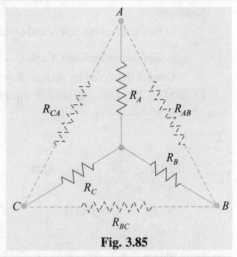

Fig. 3.85

Example 3.26. *A Wheatstone bridge ABCD has the following details : AB = 20Ω; BC = 24Ω ; CD = 5Ω ; DA = 50Ω and BD = 30Ω. A d.c. source of 220V is connected between A and C with A positive. Determine the current delivered by the source using star/delta transformation.*

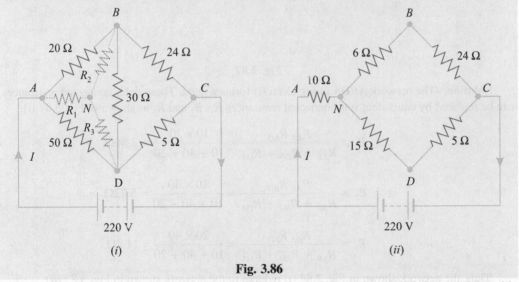

Fig. 3.86

Solution. The network *ABDA* consisting of resistances 20Ω, 30Ω and 50Ω forms a delta with corners at *A*, *B* and *D*. These delta connected resistances can be replaced by equivalent star-connected resistances R_1, R_2 and R_3 as shown in Fig. 3.86 (*i*).

$$R_1 = \frac{R_{AB}\,R_{DA}}{R_{AB} + R_{BD} + R_{DA}} = \frac{20 \times 50}{20 + 30 + 50} = 10\Omega$$

$$R_2 = \frac{R_{AB}\,R_{BD}}{R_{AB} + R_{BD} + R_{DA}} = \frac{20 \times 30}{20 + 30 + 50} = 6\Omega$$

$$R_3 = \frac{R_{DA}\,R_{BD}}{R_{AB} + R_{BD} + R_{DA}} = \frac{50 \times 30}{20 + 30 + 50} = 15\Omega$$

Thus the network shown in Fig. 3.86 (*i*) reduces to the network shown in Fig. 3.86 (*ii*). As seen from Fig. 3.86 (*ii*), there are two parallel paths between *N* and *C*.

∴ Resistance between N and C = $(6 + 24)\,\Omega \parallel (15 + 5)\,\Omega = \dfrac{30 \times 20}{30 + 20} = 12\Omega$

Resistance between A and C = $10 + 12 = 22\,\Omega$

∴ Current delivered by source, $I = 220/22 = \mathbf{10A}$

Example 3.27. *Using delta/star transformation, find the galvanometer current in the Wheatstone bridge shown in Fig. 3.87 (i).*

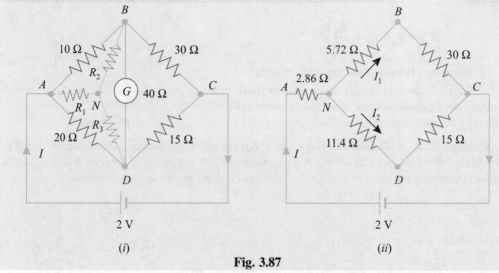

Fig. 3.87

Solution. The network $ABDA$ in Fig. 3.86 (i) forms a delta. These delta connected resistances can be replaced by equivalent star-connected resistances R_1, R_2 and R_3 as shown in Fig. 3.87 (i).

$$R_1 = \frac{R_{AB}\,R_{AD}}{R_{AB} + R_{BD} + R_{DA}} = \frac{10 \times 20}{10 + 40 + 20} = 2.86\Omega$$

$$R_2 = \frac{R_{AB}\,R_{BD}}{R_{AB} + R_{BD} + R_{DA}} = \frac{10 \times 40}{10 + 40 + 20} = 5.72\Omega$$

$$R_3 = \frac{R_{DA}\,R_{BD}}{R_{AB} + R_{BD} + R_{DA}} = \frac{20 \times 40}{10 + 40 + 20} = 11.4\Omega$$

Thus, the network shown in Fig. 3.87 (i) reduces to the network shown in Fig. 3.87 (ii).

Total resistance between A and C

$$= 2.86 + \frac{(30 + 5.72)\,(15 + 11.4)}{(30 + 5.72) + (15 + 11.4)} = 18.04\,\Omega$$

∴ Battery current, $I = 2/18.04 = 0.11$ A

The battery current at N divides into two parallel paths [See Fig. 3.87 (ii)].

∴ Current in branch NBC, $I_1 = 0.11 \times \dfrac{26.4}{26.4 + 35.72} = 0.047\text{A}$

Current in branch NDC, $I_2 = 0.11 \times \dfrac{35.72}{26.4 + 35.72} = 0.063\text{A}$

Potential of *B w.r.t. C* = 30 × 0.047 = 1.41V

Potential of *D w.r.t. C* = 15 × 0.063 = 0.945V

Clearly, point *B* is at a higher potential than point *D* by 1.41 − 0.945 = 0.465V.

$$\therefore \text{ Galvanometer current} = \frac{\text{P. D. between } B \text{ and } D}{\text{Galvanometer resistance}} = 0.465/40 = 11.6 \times 10^{-3} \text{ A}$$

$$= \textbf{11.6 mA } from \ B \ to \ D.$$

Example 3.28. *Determine the load current in branch EF in the circuit shown in Fig. 3.88 (i).*

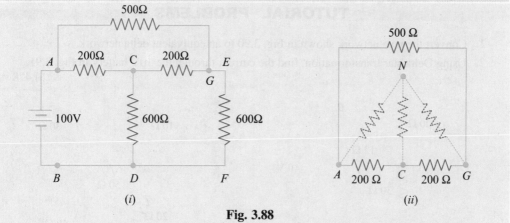

Fig. 3.88

Solution. The circuit *ACGA* forms delta and is shown separately in Fig. 3.88 (*ii*) for clarity. Changing this delta connection into equivalent star connection [See Fig. 3.88 (*ii*)], we have,

$$R_{AN} = \frac{500 \times 200}{500 + 200 + 200} = 111.11\Omega; \quad R_{CN} = \frac{200 \times 200}{500 + 200 + 200} = 44.44\Omega$$

$$R_{GN} = \frac{500 \times 200}{500 + 200 + 200} = 111.11\Omega$$

Thus the circuit shown in Fig. 3.88 (*i*) reduces to the circuit shown is Fig. 3.89 (*i*). The branch *NEF* (= 111.11 + 600 = 711.11Ω) is in parallel with branch *NCD* (= 44.44 + 600 = 644.44 Ω) and the equivalent resistance of this parallel combination is

$$= \frac{711.11 \times 644.44}{711.11 + 644.44} = 338\Omega$$

The circuit shown in Fig. 3.89 (*i*) reduces to the circuit shown in Fig. 3.89 (*ii*).

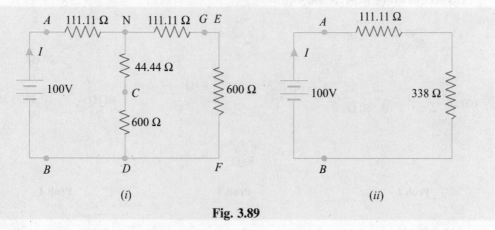

Fig. 3.89

∴ Battery current, $I = \dfrac{100}{338 + 111.11} = 0.222\,A$

This battery current divides into two parallel paths [See Fig. 3.89 (*i*)] *viz.* branch *NEF* and branch *NCD*.

∴ Current in branch *NEF i.e.* in branch *EF*

$$= 0.222 \times \dfrac{644.44}{711.11 + 644.44} = \mathbf{0.1055A}$$

TUTORIAL PROBLEMS

1. Convert the wye network shown in Fig. 3.90 to an equivalent delta network.
2. Using Delta/star transformation, find the current through the 10V battery in Fig. 3.91.

[0.478 A]

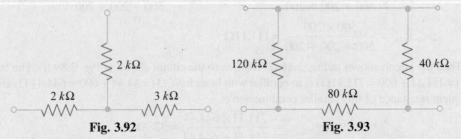

Fig. 3.90   **Fig. 3.91**

3. Convert the Wye network shown in Fig. 3.92 into equivalent delta network.

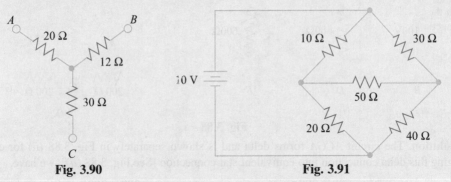

Fig. 3.92   **Fig. 3.93**

4. Convert the delta network shown in Fig. 3.93 into equivalent Wye network.

Answers to Problems 1, 3 and 4

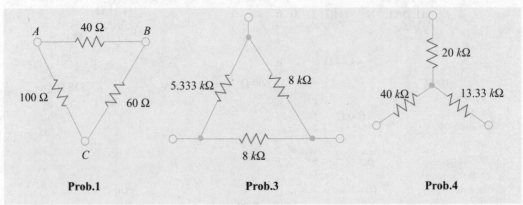

Prob.1   **Prob.3**   **Prob.4**

MULTIPLE-CHOICE QUESTIONS

1. An active element in a circuit is one which
   (a) receives energy
   (b) supplies energy
   (c) both receives and supplies energy
   (d) none of the above

2. A passive element in a circuit is one which
   (a) receives energy
   (b) supplies energy
   (c) both supplies and receives energy
   (d) none of the above

3. In the circuit shown in Fig. 3.94, there are .... junctions.

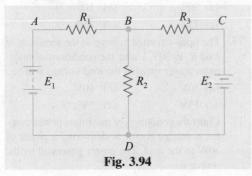

Fig. 3.94

   (a) three   (b) four
   (c) two   (d) none of the above

4. In the circuit shown in Fig. 3.94, the number of nodes is
   (a) one   (b) two
   (c) three   (d) four

5. The circuit shown in Fig. 3.94 has ..... branches.
   (a) two
   (b) three
   (c) four
   (d) none of the above

6. The circuit shown in Fig. 3.94 has .... loops.
   (a) three
   (b) two
   (c) four
   (d) none of the above

7. In the circuit shown in Fig. 3.94, there are ..... meshes.
   (a) two   (b) three
   (c) four   (d) five

8. In the circuit shown in Fig. 3.95, the voltage at the node B w.r.t. node D is calculated to be 15V. The current in 3Ω resistor will be

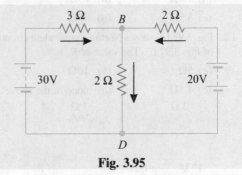

Fig. 3.95

   (a) 2A   (b) 2.5A
   (c) 5A   (d) 10A

9. Fig. 3.96 (ii) shows Thevenin's equivalent circuit of Fig. 3.96 (i). The value of Thevenin's voltage E_{Th} is
   (a)12V   (b) 36V
   (c)20V   (d) 24V

10. The value of R_{Th} in Fig. 3.96 (ii) is
   (a) 15Ω (b) 7.4Ω
   (c) 6.4Ω (d) 3.5Ω

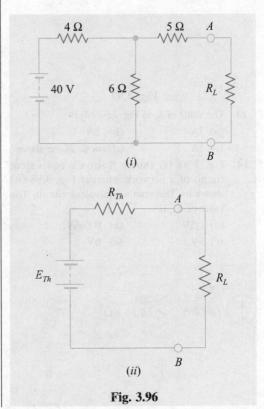

Fig. 3.96

11. For transfer of maximum power in the circuit shown in Fig. 3.96 (*i*), the value of R_L should be

   (*a*) 7.4Ω   (*b*) 6.4Ω

   (*c*) 3.5Ω   (*d*) 15Ω

12. Fig. 3.97 (*ii*) shows Norton's equivalent circuit of Fig. 3.97 (*i*). The value of R_N is

   (*a*) 5Ω   (*b*) 10Ω

   (*c*) 4.5Ω   (*d*) none of the above

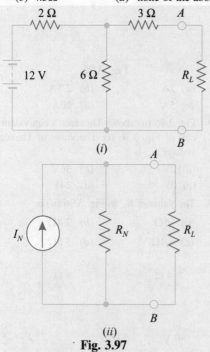

(*i*)

(*ii*)
Fig. 3.97

13. The value of I_N in Fig. 3.97 (*ii*) is

   (*a*) 3A   (*b*) 2A

   (*c*) 1A   (*d*) none of the above

14. Fig. 3.98 (*i*) shows Norton's equivalent circuit of a network whereas Fig. 3.98 (*ii*) shows its Thevenin's equivalent circuit. The value of E_{Th} is

   (*a*) 1.5V   (*b*) 0.866V

   (*c*) 3V   (*d*) 6V

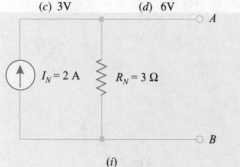

(*i*)

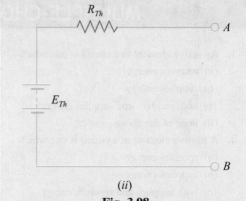

(*ii*)
Fig. 3.98

15. Under the conditions of maximum power transfer, the efficiency is

   (*a*) 50%   (*b*) 100%

   (*c*) 75%   (*d*) 25%

16. The open-circuited voltage at the terminals of load R_L is 30V. Under the conditions of maximum power transfer, the load voltage will be

   (*a*) 30V   (*b*) 10V

   (*c*) 15V   (*d*) 5V

17. Under the conditions of maximum power transfer, a voltage source is delivering a power of 30W to the load. The power generated by the source is

   (*a*) 30W   (*b*) 60W

   (*c*) 45W   (*d*) 90W

18. The output resistance of a voltage source is 4Ω. Its internal resistance will be

   (*a*) 2Ω   (*b*) 1Ω

   (*c*) infinite   (*d*) 4Ω

19. When a load of 1 $k\Omega$ is connected across a 20 *mA* current source, it is found that only 18 *mA* flows in the load. What is the internal resistance of the source?

   (*a*) 9 $k\Omega$ (*b*) 6 $k\Omega$

   (*c*) 3 $k\Omega$ (*d*) 18 $k\Omega$

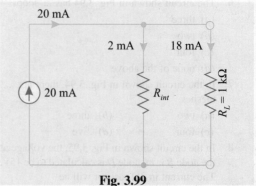

Fig. 3.99

20. A voltage source has a terminal voltage of 28 V when its terminals are open-circuited. When a load of 12 Ω is connected across the terminals, the terminal voltage drops to 24 V. What is the internal resistance of the source ?

(a) 0.5 Ω (b) 1 Ω

(c) 2 Ω (d) 2.5 Ω

21. By performing an appropriate source conversion, find the voltage across 120 Ω resistor in Fig. 3.100.

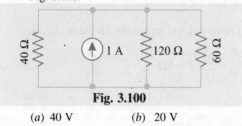

Fig. 3.100

(a) 40 V (b) 20 V

(c) 18 V (d) 30 V

22. Find Thevenin equivalent circuit to the left of terminals $x - y$ in Fig. 3.101.

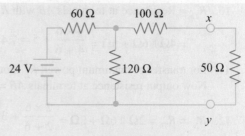

Fig. 3.101

(a) $E_{Th} = 16\ V$; $R_{Th} = 140\ \Omega$

(b) $E_{Th} = 8\ V$; $R_{Th} = 120\ \Omega$

(c) $E_{Th} = 18\ V$; $R_{Th} = 72\ \Omega$

(d) none of the above

Answers to Multiple-Choice Questions

1. (b)	2. (a)	3. (c)	4. (d)	5. (b)	6. (a)	7. (a)	8. (c)
9. (d)	10. (b)	11. (a)	12. (c)	13. (b)	14. (d)	15. (a)	16. (c)
17. (b)	18. (d)	19. (a)	20. (c)	21. (b)	22. (a)		

Hints to Selected Multiple-Choice Questions

3. A junction is that point in a network where three or more circuit elements are joined. In Fig. 3.94, there are only **two** junctions *viz B* and *D*. That *B* is a junction is clear from the fact that there are three circuit elements R_1, R_2 and R_3 joined at it. Similarly, *D* is a junction because it joins three circuit elements R_2, E_1 and E_2.

4. A node of a network is an equipotential surface at which two or more circuit elements are joined. Thus in Fig. 3.94, the circuit elements R_1 and E_1 are joined at *A* and hence *A* is the node. Similarly, *B*, *C* and *D* are the nodes. Therefore, the number of nodes in the given circuit is **4**.

5. A branch is that part of a circuit which lies between two junction points. Thus referring to Fig. 3.94, there are a total of **three branches** *viz BAD, BCD* and *BD*.

6. A loop is any closed path of network. Thus in Fig. 3.94, there are only **three loops** *viz ABDA, BCDB* and *ABCDA*.

7. A mesh is the most elementary form of a loop and cannot be further subdivided into other loops. In Fig. 3.94, both loops *ABDA* and *BCDB* qualify as meshes because they cannot be further divided into other loops. Therefore, there are only **two** meshes in the given circuit. It may be noted that loop *ABCDA* cannot be called a mesh because it encloses two loops *ABDA* and *BCDB*.

8. Current in 3Ω resistor $= \dfrac{30 - 15}{3} = 5\,A$

9. E_{Th} = open-circuited voltage at terminals AB

   = current in $6\Omega \times 6\Omega = 4A \times 6\Omega = 24V$

10. R_{Th} = Resistance at terminals AB with R_L removed and battery replaced by a short

$$= 4\Omega \parallel 6\Omega + 5\Omega = \frac{4 \times 6}{4 + 6} + 5 = 7.4\Omega$$

11. For transfer of maximum power, R_L should be equal to the output resistance at terminals AB. Now output resistance at terminals $AB = R_{Th} = 7.4\Omega$

12. $R_N = R_{Th} = 2\Omega \parallel 6\Omega + 3\Omega = \dfrac{2 \times 6}{2 + 6} + 3 = 4.5\Omega$

13. I_N = current through terminals AB with load removed and terminals AB short-circuited

   Load on source $= 2\Omega + 3\Omega \parallel 6\Omega = 2 + \dfrac{3 \times 6}{3 + 6} = 2 + 2 = 4\Omega$

   Source current, $I = 12/4 = 3A$

$$\therefore \qquad I_N = I \times \frac{6}{3 + 6} = 3 \times \frac{6}{3 + 6} = 2A$$

14. $E_{Th} = I_N R_N = 2A \times 3\Omega = 6V$

15. Suppose a source of voltage V and internal resistance R_i is supplying a current of I to load R_L under maximum power transfer conditions.

$$\text{Efficiency} = \frac{I^2 R_L}{I^2 (R_L + R_i)} = \frac{I^2 R_L}{I^2 \times 2R_L} \qquad (\because R_L = R_i)$$

$$= \frac{1}{2} = 50\%$$

16. Load voltage under maximum power transfer

$$= IR_L = \left(\frac{V}{R_L + R_i} \right) R_L$$

$$= \frac{V}{2R_L} \times R_L = \frac{V}{2} = \frac{30}{2} = 15V \qquad (\because R_L = R_i)$$

17. Under maximum power transfer conditions, one-half of the total power generated is dissipated in the internal resistance R_i of the source *i.e.* the efficiency is 50%.

   $\therefore$ Total power generated $= 2 \times 30 = 60$ **W**

18. The output resistance of a source means its internal resistance. Therefore, the internal resistance of the source is 4Ω.

19. Voltage across load, $V_L = I_L R_L = 18 \ mA \times 1k\Omega = 18V$

   Current in R_{int}, $I_{int} = 20 - 18 = 2 \ mA$

$$\therefore \qquad R_{int} = \frac{V_L}{I_{int}} = \frac{18V}{2 \ mA} = 9k \ \Omega$$

20. When a load of 12Ω is connected across the terminals of the source, the circuit current is

$$I = \frac{V}{R_L + R_{int}} = \frac{28}{12 + R_{int}}$$

Voltage drop across internal resistance = 28 – 24 = 4 V

$$\therefore \qquad 4 = \left(\frac{28}{12 + R_{int}}\right) R_{int}$$

or $\qquad R_{int} = 2\Omega$

21. Since we want to find voltage across 120Ω resistor, we use 40Ω resistor to convert current source into equivalent voltage source. As shown in Fig. 3.102,

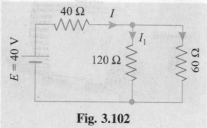

$$E = IR = 1A \times 40\Omega = 40V$$

Referring to Fig. 3.102, the total circuit resistance is

$$R_T = 40 + \frac{120 \times 60}{120 + 60} = 40 + 40 = 80 \ \Omega$$

Circuit current, $I = E/R_T = 40/80 = 0.5$ A

Fig. 3.102

Current in 120Ω resistor, $I_1 = I \times \dfrac{60}{120 + 60} = 0.5 \times \dfrac{60}{180} = 0.1666$ A

Voltage across 120Ω resistor $= I_1 \times 120 = 0.1666 \times 120 = $ **20V**

22. Fig. 3.103 shows the solution of the problem.

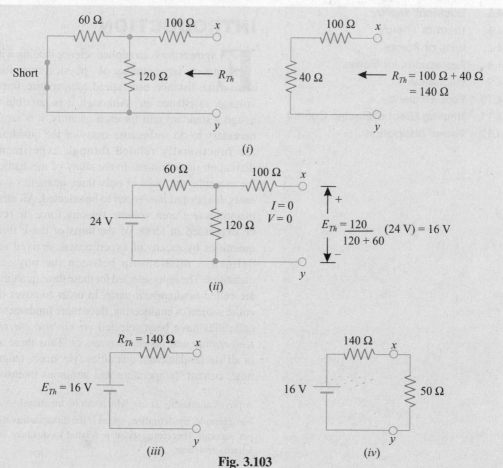

Fig. 3.103

4

Units—Work, Power and Energy

INTRODUCTION

Engineering is an applied science dealing with a very large number of *physical quantities like distance, time, speed, temperature, force, voltage, resistance *etc.* Although it is possible to assign a standard unit for each quantity, it is rarely necessary to do so because many of the quantities are functionally related through experiment, derivation or definition. In the study of mechanics, for example, the units of only three quantities (*viz. mass, length* and *time*) need to be selected. All other quantities (*e.g.* area, volume, velocity, force *etc.*) can be expressed in terms of the units of these three quantities by means of experimental, derived and defined **relationship between the physical quantities. The units selected for these three quantities are called *fundamental units*. In order to cover the entire subject of engineering, three more fundamental quantities have been selected *viz electric current, temperature* and *luminous intensity*. Thus there are in all six fundamental quantities (*viz.* mass, length, time, current, temperature and luminous intensity)

. . . .

*   A physical quantity is one which can be measured.
**   For example, by definition, speed is the distance travelled per second. Therefore, speed is related to distance (*i.e.* length) and time.

which need to be assigned proper and standard units. The units of all other physical quantities can be derived from the units of these six fundamental quantities. In this chapter, we shall focus our attention on the mechanical, electrical and thermal units of work, power and energy.

4.1. INTERNATIONAL SYSTEM OF UNITS

Although several systems were evolved to assign units to the above mentioned six fundamental quantities, only international system of units (abbreviated as SI) has been universally accepted. The units assigned to these six fundamental quantities in this system are given below in the tabular form :

Quantity	Symbol	Unit name	Unit symbol
Length	l, L	metre	m
Mass	m	kilogram	kg
Time	t	second	s
Electric Current	I	ampere	A
Temperature	T	degree kelvin	K
Luminous Intensity	I	candela	Cd

The units of all other physical quantities in science and engineering (*i.e.* other than six fundamental quantities above) can be derived from the above six units. Thus the unit of velocity (= 1m/s) results when unit of length (= 1m) is divided by the unit of time (= 1s).

Similarly, the unit of force (= 1 newton) results when the unit of mass (= $1kg$) is multiplied by the unit of acceleration (= 1m/s²).

4.2. IMPORTANT PHYSICAL QUANTITIES

It is profitable to give a brief description of the following physical quantities much used in science and engineering :

(*i*) **Mass.** It is the quantity of matter possessed by a body. The SI unit of mass is kilogram (kg). The mass of a body is a constant quantity and is independent of place and position of the body. Thus the mass of a body is the same whether it is on Earth's surface, the Moon's surface, on the top of a mountain or down a deep well.

(*ii*) **Force.** It is the product of mass (kg) and acceleration (m/s²). The unit of force is newton (N) ; being the force required to accelerate a mass of 1kg through an acceleration of 1m/s².

∴ $F = m\,a$ newtons

where m = mass of the body in kg

                a = acceleration in m/s²

(*iii*) **Weight.** The force with which a body is attracted towards the centre of Earth is called the weight of the body. Now, force = mass × acceleration. If m is the mass of a body in kg and g is the acceleration due to gravity in m/s², then,

Weight, $W = m\,g$ newtons

As the value of g^* varies from place to place on earth's surface, therefore, the weight of the body varies accordingly. However, for practical purposes, we take $g = 9.81$ m/s² so that weight of body = 9.81 m newtons. Thus if a mass of 1 kg rests on a table, the downward force on the table *i.e.* weight of the body is $W = 9.81 × 1 = 9.81$ newtons.

The following points may be noted carefully :

(*a*) The mass of a body is a constant quantity whereas its weight depends upon the place or

---

* The value of g is about 9.81 m/s² at sea level whereas at equator, it is about 9.78 m/s² and at each pole it is about 9.832 m/s².

position of the body. However, it is reasonably accurate to express weight $W = 9.81\, m$ newtons where m is the mass of the body in kg.

(b) Sometimes weight is given in kg. wt. units. One kg. wt. means weight of mass of 1 kg *i.e.* $9.81 \times 1 = 9.81$ newtons. Therefore, 1 kg. wt. = 9.81 newtons.

Thus when we say that a body has a weight of 100 kg, it means that it has a mass of 100 kg and that it exerts a downward force of $100 \times 9.81 = 981$ newtons.

4.3. UNIT OF WORK OR ENERGY

Work is said to be done on a body when a force acts on it and the body moves through some distance. This work done is stored in the body in the form of energy. Therefore, work and energy are measured in the same units. The SI unit of work or energy is *joule* or *newton-metre* and is defined as under :

The work done on a body is **one joule** *if a force of one newton moves the body through 1m in the direction of force.*

It may be noted that work done or energy possessed in an electrical circuit or mechanical system or thermal system is measured in the same units *viz.* joules. This is expected because mechanical, electrical and thermal energies are interchangeable. For example, when mechanical work is transferred into heat or heat into work, the quantity of work in joules is equal to the quantity of *heat in joules.

4.4. SOME CASES OF MECHANICAL WORK OR ENERGY

It may be helpful to give a few important cases of work done or energy possessed in a mechanical system :

(i) When a force of F newtons is exerted on a body through a distance 'd' metres in the direction of force, then,

Work done = $F \times d$ joules or Nm

(ii) Suppose a force of F newtons is maintained tangentially at a radius r metres from O as shown in Fig. 4.1. In one revolution, the point of application of force travels through a distance of $2\pi\, r$ metres.

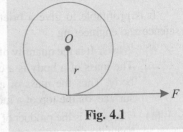

Fig. 4.1

∴ Work done in one revolution

= Force × Distance moved in 1 revolution

= $F \times 2\pi\, r$

= $2\pi \times T$ joules or Nm

where $T = Fr$ is the torque. Clearly, the SI unit of torque will be joules or Nm. If the body makes N revolutions per minute, then,

Work done/minute = $2\pi\, NT$ joules

(iii) If a body of mass m kg is moving linearly with a speed of v m/s, then kinetic energy possessed by the body is given by ;

K.E. of the body = $\dfrac{1}{2}mv^2$ joules

(iv) If a body having a mass of m kg is lifted vertically through a height of h metres and g is acceleration due to gravity in m/s^2, then,

---

* Although heat energy was assigned a separate unit *viz.* calorie but the reader remembers that 1 calorie = 4.186 joules. In fact, the thermal unit calorie is obsolete and now-a-days heat is expressed in joules.

Potential energy of body = Work done in lifting the body

$$= \text{Force required} \times \text{height}$$
$$= \text{Weight of body} \times \text{height}$$
$$= mg \times h$$
$$= mgh \text{ joules}$$

4.5. ELECTRICAL ENERGY

The SI unit of electrical work done or electrical energy expended in a circuit is also joule— exactly the same as for mechanical energy. It is defined as under :

One joule of energy is expended electrically when one coulomb is moved through a p.d. of 1 volt.

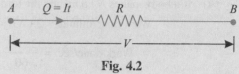

Fig. 4.2

Suppose a charge of Q coulomb moves through a p.d. of V volts as shown in Fig. 4.2. Then electrical energy expended is given by :

Electrical energy expended

$$= VQ = VIt = I^2Rt = \frac{V^2t}{R} \text{ joules} \qquad (\because Q = It \ ; \ V = IR \ ; \ I = V/R)$$

It may be mentioned here that joule is also known as watt-second *i.e.* 1 joule = 1 watt-sec. When we are dealing with large amount of electrical energy, it is often convenient to express it in *kilowatt hours* (*kWh*).

$$1 \text{ kWh} = 1000 \text{ watt–hours} = 1000 \times 3600 \text{ watt-sec or joules}$$
$$\therefore \qquad 1 \text{ kWh} = 36 \times 10^5 \text{ joules or watt-sec}$$

Although practical unit of electrical energy is kWh, yet it is easy to see that this unit is readily convertible to joules with the help of above relation.

4.6. THERMAL ENERGY

The thermal energy was originally assigned the unit 'calorie'. One calorie is the amount of heat required to raise the temperature of 1 gm of water through 1°C. If S is the specific heat of a body, then amount of heat required to raise the temperature of m gm of body through θ°C is given by :

$$\text{Heat gained} = m \, S \, \theta \text{ calories}$$

It has been found experimentally that 1 calorie = 4.186 joules so that heat energy in calories can be expressed in joules as under :

$$\text{Heat gained} = (m \, S \, \theta) \times 4.186 \text{ joules}$$

The reader may note that SI unit of heat is also joule. In fact, the thermal unit calorie is obsolete and unit joule is preferred these days.

4.7. UNITS OF POWER

The rate of doing work is called power. In other words, power is the work done per unit time. Since work is measured in joules and time in seconds, the unit of power will be *joule/sec* or *watt*.

(*i*)   In practice, watt is often found to be inconveniently small, consequently kilowatt (kW) is used. One kW is equal to 1000 watts *i.e.*

$$1 \text{ kW} = 1000 \text{ watts}$$

For larger powers, the unit megawatt (*MW*) is used. One megawatt is equal to 1000 kW *i.e.*

$$1 \text{ MW} = 1000 \text{ kW} = 1000 \times 1000 \text{ watts}$$

$$\therefore \qquad 1 \text{ MW} = 10^6 \text{ watts}$$

(*ii*) Sometimes power is measured in *horse power (H.P.).

$$1 \text{ H.P.} = 746 \text{ watts}$$

4.8. EXPRESSIONS FOR POWER

(*i*) Power = Work done/sec.

= Force × distance/sec.

= Force × velocity

(*ii*) If a body makes N *r.p.m.* and the torque acting is T newton-metre, then,

Work done/minute = $2\pi NT$ joules   [See Art. 4.4]

$$\text{Work done/sec} = \frac{2\pi NT}{60} \text{ joules/sec or watts}$$

i.e. $$\text{Power} = \frac{2\pi NT}{60} \text{ watts}$$

Since 746 watts = 1. *H.P.*, we have,

$$\text{Power} = \frac{2\pi NT}{60 \times 746} \text{ H.P.}$$

where T is in newton-m and N is in *r.p.m.*

4.9. EFFICIENCY

The efficiency of a device or of a circuit is the ratio of useful output to the input *i.e.*

$$\text{Efficiency}, \eta = \frac{\text{Useful output}}{\text{Input}} = \frac{W_o}{W_i}$$

The law of conservation of energy states that "energy cannot be created or destroyed but can be converted from one form to another". Some of the energy in electric circuits may be converted into a form that is not useful. For example, consider an electric motor shown in Fig. 4.3. The purpose of the motor is to convert electric energy into mechanical energy. It does this, but it also converts a part of input energy into heat. The heat produced is not useful. Therefore, the useful output energy is less than the input energy. In other words, the efficiency of the motor is less than 100%.

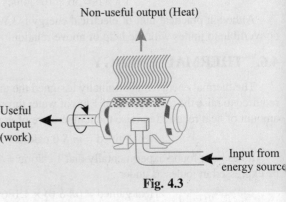

Non-useful output (Heat)

Useful output (work)

Input from energy source

Fig. 4.3

Some electrical devices are nearly 100% efficient. An electric heater is an example. In a heater, practically all the input electric energy is converted into heat energy. In this case, the heat is useful output.

4.10. POOR EFFICIENCY

The poor (or low) efficiency of a device or of a circuit has the following harmful effects :

(*i*) Poor efficiency means waste of energy on non-useful output.

---

*   This unit for power was conceived by James Watt, a Scottish scientist who invented the steam engine. In his experiments, he compared the output of his engine with the power a horse could put out. He found that an average horse could do work at the rate of 746 joules/sec. Although power can be expressed in watts or kW, the unit H.P. is still used.

(ii) Non-useful output of a device or circuit usually appears in the form of heat. Therefore, poor efficiency means a significant temperature rise. High temperature is one of the major limiting factors in producing reliable electric and electronic devices. Circuits and devices that run hot are more likely to fail.

(iii) The heat produced as a result of poor efficiency has to be dissipated *i.e.* heat has to be transferred to the atmosphere or some other mass. Heat removal can become quite difficult in high power circuits and adds to the cost and size of the equipment.

Air Conditioner

Electric Motor

Example 4.1. *A mass of 10 kg is raised by means of rope passing round a pulley wheel of 0.5 m diameter. Calculate the work done when the pulley makes 50 revolutions.*

Solution.

Force required, $\qquad F = mg = 10 \times 9.81 = 98.1$ N

Torque exerted, $\qquad T = F \times r = 98.1 \times 0.5/2 = 24.525$ joules

Distance covered in N revolutions $\quad = 2\pi \, r \times N$

∴ Total work done $\qquad = F \times 2\pi \, rN$

$\qquad\qquad = T \times 2\pi \, N = (24.525) \times (2\pi \times 50) = \mathbf{7704.75 \ joules}$

Example 4.2. *An electric motor is developing 10 H.P. at a speed of 1200 r.p.m. Calculate the torque in newton-metre.*

Solution. $\qquad H.P. = \dfrac{2\pi \times NT}{60 \times 746}$ (See Art. 4.8)

or $\qquad\qquad 10 = \dfrac{2\pi \times 1200 \times T}{60 \times 746}$

∴ Torque, $\qquad T = \dfrac{10 \times 60 \times 746}{2\pi \times 1200} = \mathbf{59.4 \ Nm}$

Exmple 4.3. *A lift of 250 kg mass is raised with a velocity of 5 m/s. If the driving motor has an efficiency of 85%, calculate the input power to the motor.*

Solution.

Weight of lift, $F = mg = 250 \times 9.81$ N

Output power of motor = Force × Velocity = $(250 \times 9.81) \times 5 = 12260$ W

∴ $\qquad$ Input power to motor $= \dfrac{\text{Output power}}{\text{Efficiency}} = 12260/0.85 = \mathbf{14420 \ W}$

Example 4.4. An electrically driven pump lifts 80 m³ of water per minute through a height of 12 m. Allowing an overall efficiency of 70% for the motor and pump, calculate the input power to motor. If the pump is in operation for an average of 2 hours per day for 30 days, calculate the energy consumption in kWh and the cost of energy at the rate of 50 P per kWh. Assume 1 m³ of water has a mass of 1000 kg and g = 9.81 m/s².

Solution.

Mass of 80 m^3 of water, $\qquad\qquad m = 80 \times 1000 = 8 \times 10^4 \, \text{kg}$

Weight of water lifted, $\qquad\qquad W = mg = 8 \times 10^4 \times 9.81 \, \text{N}$

Height through which water lifted, $h = 12$ m

W.D. by motor/minute $\qquad\qquad = mgh = 8 \times 10^4 \times 9.81 \times 12 \, \text{joules}$

W.D. by motor/second $\qquad\qquad = \dfrac{8 \times 10^4 \times 9.81 \times 12}{60} = 156960 \, \text{watts}$

∴ Output power of motor $\qquad\qquad = 156960 \, \text{watts}$

Input power to motor $= \dfrac{\text{Motor output}}{\text{Efficiency}} = \dfrac{156960}{0.7}$

$\qquad\qquad\qquad\qquad = 2,24,228 \, \text{W} = \textbf{224.228 kW}$

Total energy consumption = Input power × Time of operation

$\qquad\qquad\qquad\qquad = (224.228) \times (2 \times 30) \, \text{kWh} = \textbf{13453 kWh}$

Total cost of energy $\qquad\qquad = \text{Rs } 0.5 \times 13453 = \textbf{Rs 6726.5}$

Example 4.5. An electric-motor driven pump lifts 10 m³ of water per minute to a height of 20 metres. The efficiencies of the pump and motor are 80% and 90% respectively. Calculate the current taken by the motor at 440 V. Mass of 1 m³ of water is 1000 kg.

Solution. Mass of 10 m^3 of water, $\quad m = 10 \times 1000 = 10^4 \, \text{kg}$

$\qquad\qquad$ Wt. of water lifted $\qquad = mg = 10^4 \times 9.81 \, \text{N}$

$\qquad\qquad$ Work done/minute $\qquad = mgh = 10^4 \times 9.81 \times 20 = 196.2 \times 10^4 \, \text{joules}$

$\qquad\qquad$ Work done/second $\qquad = 196.2 \times 10^4/60 = 32.7 \times 10^3 \, \text{watts}$

∴ $\qquad\qquad$ Power output $\qquad\qquad = 32.7 \, \text{kW}$

$\qquad\qquad$ Input to pump $\qquad\qquad = 32.7/0.8 = 40.87 \, \text{kW}$

$\qquad\qquad$ Motor input $\qquad\qquad = 40.87/0.9 = 45.41 \, \text{kW}$

$\qquad\qquad$ Current taken by motor $\quad = \dfrac{45.41 \times 1000}{440} = 103.2 \text{A}$

Example 4.6. A 100 MW hydro-electric station is supplying full-load for 10 hours a day. Calculate the volume of water which has been used. Assume effective head of station as 200m and overall efficiency of the station as 80%.

Solution.

Energy supplied by the station in 10 hours

$\qquad\qquad\qquad\qquad = (100 \times 10^3) \times 10 = 10^6 \, \text{kWh}$

$\qquad\qquad\qquad\qquad = 36 \times 10^5 \times 10^6 = 36 \times 10^{11} \, \text{joules}$

Energy input of station $\quad = 36 \times 10^{11}/0.8 = 45 \times 10^{11} \, \text{joules}$

Suppose m kg is the mass of water used in 10 hours.

Then, $\qquad\qquad mgh = 45 \times 10^{11}$

or $\qquad\qquad\qquad m = \dfrac{45 \times 10^{11}}{9.81 \times 200} = 22.93 \times 10^8 \, \text{kg}$

Since 1 m³ of water has a mass of 1000 kg,

Volume of water used $= 22.93 \times 10^8/10^3 = 22.93 \times 10^5$ m³

Example 4.7. *A hydro-electric power station has a reservoir of area 2.4 square kilometres and capacity 5×10^6 m³. The effective head of water is 100 m. The penstock, turbine and generator efficiencies are 95%, 90%, and 85% respectively.*

(i) *Calculate the total energy in kWh which can be generated from the power station.*

(ii) *If a load of 15,000 kW has been supplied for 3 hours, find the fall in reservoir level.*

Solution.

(i) Wt. of water available, W = Volume of reservoir $\times 1000 \times 9.81$ N

$$= (5 \times 10^6) \times (1000) \times (9.81) = 49.05 \times 10^9 \text{ N}$$

Overall effieiency, $\eta_{overall} = 0.95 \times 0.90 \times 0.85 = 0.726$

Electrical energy that can be generated from the station

$$= W \times \text{Effective head} \times \eta_{overall}$$

$$= (49.05 \times 10^9) \times (100) \times (0.726) = 35.61 \times 10^{11} \text{ watt-sec}$$

$$= \frac{35.61 \times 10^{11}}{1000 \times 3600} \doteq \mathbf{9,89,166 \text{ kWh}}$$

(ii)   Level of reservoir $= \dfrac{\text{Volume of reservoir}}{\text{Area of reservoir}} = \dfrac{5 \times 10^6}{2.4 \times 10^6} = 2.083$ m

kWh generated in 3 hrs $= 15000 \times 3 = 45,000$ kWh

Using unitary method, we get,

Fall in reservoir level $= \dfrac{2.083}{9,89,166} \times 45,000 = 0.0947$ m $= \mathbf{9.47 \text{ cm}}$

Example 4.8. *Calculate the current required by a 500 V d.c. locomotive when drawing 100 tonne load at 25 km/hr with a tractive resistance of 7 kg/tonne along (i) level road and (ii) a gradient 1 in 100. Given that the efficiency of motor and gearing is 70%.*

Solution.

Weight of locomotive, $W = 100$ tonne $= 100,000$ kg

Tractive resistance, $F = 7 \times 100 = 700$ kg-wt $= 700 \times 9.81 = 6867$ N

(i) **Level Track.** In this case, the force required is equal to the tractive resistance F [See Fig. 4.4 (i)].

$$\text{Distance travelled/sec} = \frac{25 \times 1000}{3600} = 6.94 \text{ m}$$

Work done/sec = Force $\times$ Distance/sec

or   Motor output $= 6867 \times 6.94 = 47,657$ watts

Motor input $= 47,657/0.7 = 68,081$ watts

∴   Current drawn $= 68,081/500 = \mathbf{136.16 \text{ A}}$

(ii) **Inclined plane.** In this case, the total force required is the sum of tractive resistance F and component $W \sin\theta$ of locomotive weight. Clearly $\sin\theta = 1/100 = 0.01$.

∴   Force required $= W \sin\theta + F$

$$= (100,000 \times 0.01 + 700)\, 9.81 \text{ N} = 16,677 \text{ N}$$

Work done/sec = Force $\times$ distance travelled/sec

$$= 16,677 \times 6.94 = 1,15,738 \text{ watts}$$

$$\therefore \qquad \text{Motor output} = 1,15,738 \text{ watts}$$

$$\text{Motor input} = 1,15,738/0.7 = 1,65,340 \text{ watts}$$

$$\therefore \qquad \text{Current drawn} = 1,65,340/500 = \mathbf{330.68A}$$

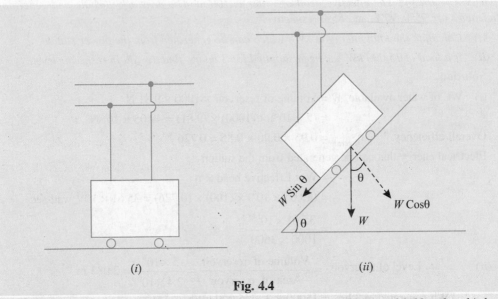

(i)   (ii)

Fig. 4.4

Example 4.9. *A steam power station has an overall efficiency of 20% and 0.6 kg of coal is burnt per kWh of electrical energy generated. Calculate the calorific value of fuel.*

Solution.

Let x kcal/kg be the calorific value of the fuel.

Heat produced by 0.6 kg of coal = 0.6 x kcal

Heat equivalent of 1 kWh = 860 kcal

$$\therefore \qquad \text{Overall efficiency} = \frac{\text{Electrical output in heat units}}{\text{Heat of combustion}}$$

or
$$0.2 = \frac{860}{0.6x}$$

$$\therefore \qquad x = \mathbf{7166.67 \ kcal/kg}$$

Example 4.10. *A generating station has a daily output of 280 MWh and uses 500 tonne of coal in the process. The coal releases 7×10^6 J/kg when burnt. Calculate the overall efficiency.*

Solution.

Input energy/day, $\qquad W_i = (7 \times 10^6) \times (500 \times 1000) = 35 \times 10^{11}$ J

Output energy/day, $\qquad W_0 = 280$ MWh $= (280 \times 10^3) \times (36 \times 10^5)$ J $= 10.1 \times 10^{11}$ J

$$\therefore \qquad \text{Overall efficiency} = \frac{10.1 \times 10^{11}}{35 \times 10^{11}} \times 100 = \mathbf{28.8\%}$$

Example 4.11. *What must be the horse-power of an engine to drive by means of a belt a generator supplying 7000 lamps each taking 0.5 A at 250 V ? The line drop is 5V and the efficiency of the generator is 95%. There is a 2.5% loss in the belt drive.*

Solution. Total current supplied by generator, $I = 0.5 \times 7000 = 3500$ A

Generated voltage, $E = $ Load voltage + Line drop $= 250 + 5 = 255$ V

Generator output = $EI = 255 \times 3500$ W

∴   Engine output = $\dfrac{255 \times 3500}{0.95 \times 0.975}$ = 963562 W

$= \dfrac{963562}{746}$ H.P. = **1292 H.P.**

Example 4.12. *Find the amount of electrical energy expended in raising the temperature of 50 litres of water by 75°C. To what height could a weight of 5000 kg be raised with the same expenditure of energy? Assume that heater has an efficiency of 90% and the lifting equipment has an efficiency of 70%.*

Solution.

Heat required to raise the temperature of water by 75°C = $m\,S\,\theta = 50 \times 10^3 \times 1 \times 75$ cal = 3750 kcal

Electrical energy expended = $\dfrac{3750}{0.9}$ kcal = 4167 kcal

$= \dfrac{4167}{860}$ kWh = **4.845 kWh**   (∵ 1kWh = 860 kcal)

Energy available for lifting the load

$= 4.845 \times 0.7 = 3.39$ kWh

$= 3.39 \times 3.6 \times 10^6$ J   (∵ 1 kWh = 3.6×10^6 J)

Now $mgh = 3.39 \times 3.6 \times 10^6$

∴ $h = \dfrac{3.39 \times 3.6 \times 10^6}{mg} = \dfrac{3.39 \times 3.6 \times 10^6}{5000 \times 9.81} = $ **248.8 m**

Example 4.13. *Find the head in metres of a hydroelectric generating station in which the reservoir of area 4000 m² falls by 30 cm when 75 kWh is developed in the turbine. The efficiency of the turbine is 70%.*

Solution.

Volume of water used, $V = 4000 \times 0.3 = 1200\text{m}^3$

Mass of water used, $m = 1200 \times 10^3 = 1.2 \times 10^6$ kg

Useful energy developed in turbine $= mgh \times \eta = 1.2 \times 10^6 \times 9.81 \times h \times 0.7$

But useful energy developed in turbine $= 75$ kWh $= 75 \times 3.6 \times 10^6$ J

∴ $1.2 \times 10^6 \times 9.81 \times h \times 0.7 = 75 \times 3.6 \times 10^6$

or $h = $ **32.76 m**

Example 4.14. *A room measures 3m × 4m × 4.75m and air in it has to be always kept 10°C higher than that of the incoming air. The air inside has to be renewed every 30 minutes. Neglecting radiation losses, find the necessary rating of electric heater for this purpose. Take specific heat of air as 0.24 and density as 1.28 kg/m³.*

Solution.

Volume of air to be changed/second $= \dfrac{3 \times 4 \times 4.75}{30 \times 60} = 0.032$ m^3

Mass of air to be changed/second $= 0.032 \times 1.28 = 0.041$ kg

Heat required/second $=$ mass/second $\times$ specific heat $\times$ Rise in temp.

$= 0.041 \times 0.24 \times 10$ kcal

$= 0.041 \times 0.24 \times 10 \times 4186$ W = **411 W** $\left(\because \dfrac{1\text{kcal}}{\text{sec.}} = 4186 \text{ W}\right)$

Example 4.15. *Find the current taken by a 480 V d.c. motor driving a pump to raise 14000 litres of water per minute to a height of 27 m. The efficiencies of motor and pump are 90% and 75% respectively. Allow a head of 3m for pipe friction.*

Solution.

Total head, $\qquad\qquad h = 27 + 3 = 30 \ m$

Work done by pump/second $\quad = \dfrac{mgh}{60} = \dfrac{14000 \times 9.81 \times 30}{60} = 68670 \ J/s$ or *watts*

Motor output $\qquad\qquad\qquad = 68670/0.75 = 91560$ W

Motor input $\qquad\qquad\qquad = 91560/0.9 = 101733$ W

Current taken by motor $\qquad = 101733/480 = $ **212A**

Example 4.16. *An electric hoist makes 10 double journeys per hour. In each journey, a load of 6000 kg is raised to a height of 60 m in 90 seconds and the hoist returns empty in 75 seconds. The hoist cage weighs 500 kg and has a balance weight of 3000 kg. The efficiency of the hoist is 80% and that of the driving motor 88%. Calculate (i) the electrical energy absorbed per double journey (ii) the hourly consumption in kWh (iii) the horse-power of the motor.*

Solution. When the hoist cage goes up, the balance weight goes down and when the cage goes down, the balance weight goes up.

Total mass lifted on upward journey = Load + mass of cage – mass of balance weight

$\qquad\qquad\qquad\qquad\qquad\qquad\qquad = 6000 + 500 - 3000 = 3500$ kg

Work done during upward journey $\qquad = mgh = 3500 \times 9.8 \times 60$ J

Total mass moved on downward journey $\ = $ Mass of balance wt. – Mass of cage

$\qquad\qquad\qquad\qquad\qquad\qquad\qquad = 3000 - 500 = 2500$ kg

Work done during downward journey $\quad = mgh = 2500 \times 9.8 \times 60$ J

Work done during each double journey $\ = 9.8 \times 60 \ (3500 + 2500)$ J $= 353 \times 10^4$ J

$\qquad\qquad\qquad$ Overall $\eta = 0.8 \times 0.88 = 0.704$

(i) Input energy per double journey $\qquad = 353 \times 10^4/0.704 = 501 \times 10^4$ J

$\qquad\qquad\qquad\qquad\qquad\qquad\qquad = \dfrac{501 \times 10^4}{3.6 \times 10^6} \ kWh = $ **1.4 kWh**

(ii) Hourly consumption $\qquad\qquad\qquad = 1.4 \times$ No. of double journeys/hr

$\qquad\qquad\qquad\qquad\qquad\qquad\qquad = 1.4 \times 10 = $ **14 kWh**

(iii) The maximum rate of working is during upward journey.

$\qquad \therefore\qquad$ H.P. rating of motor $= \dfrac{\text{Work done in upward journey}}{\text{Hoist efficiency} \times \text{Time for up journey} \times 746}$

$\qquad\qquad\qquad\qquad\qquad\qquad = \dfrac{3500 \times 9.8 \times 60}{0.8 \times 90 \times 746} = $ **38.4 H.P.**

TUTORIAL PROBLEMS

1. An electric motor is developing 2 kW at a speed of 1000 r.p.m. Calculate the shaft torque.

$\qquad\qquad\qquad\qquad\qquad\qquad\qquad\qquad\qquad\qquad\qquad\qquad\qquad\qquad$ **[19.1 Nm]**

2. An electrically driven pump lifts 1500 litres of water per minute through a height of 25m. Allowing an overall efficiency of 75%, calculate the input power to the motor. If the pump is in operation for an average of 8 hours per day for 30 days, calculate the energy consumed in kWh and the cost of energy at the rate of 50 P/kWh. Assume 1 litre of water has a mass of 1000 kg and g = 9.81 m/s^2.

$\qquad\qquad\qquad\qquad\qquad\qquad\qquad\qquad\qquad\qquad\qquad\qquad$ **[8.167 kW, 1960 kWh, Rs 980]**

3. A 440-volt motor is used to drive an irrigation pump. The efficiency of motor is 85% and the efficiency of pump is 66%. The pump is required to lift 240 tonne of water per hour to a height of 30 metres. Calculate the current taken by the motor. **[79.48A]**

4. A 250 V d.c. electric motor operates a lift and raises a mass of 1 tonne through a vertical distance of 17m in 8 seconds. If the overall efficiency of motor and lift mechanism is 64%, calculate the current taken by the motor. **[130.3A]**

5. The effective water head for a 100 MW station is 200 metres. The station supplies full-load for 12 hours a day. If the overall efficiency of the station is 86.4%, find the volume of water used. **[25.48 × 10⁵ m³]**

4.11. HEATING EFFECT OF ELECTRIC CURRENT

When electric current (*i.e.* flow of free electrons) passes through a conductor, there is a considerable 'friction' between the moving electrons and the molecules of the conductor. The electrical energy supplied to the conductor to overcome this 'electrical friction' (which we refer to as electrical resistance) is converted into heat. This is known as heating effect of electric current. For example, if I amperes is flowing through a conductor of resistance R ohms for t seconds, then electrical energy supplied is I^2Rt joules. This energy is not destroyed but the whole of I^2Rt joules is changed into heat.

The heating effect of electric current is utilised in the manufacture of many heating appliances such as electric heater, electric toaster, electric kettle, soldering iron *etc*. The basic principle of all these appliances is the same. Electric current is passed through a high resistance (called heating element), thus producing the required heat. There are a number of substances used for making a heating element. One that is commonly used is an alloy of nickel and chromium, called **nichrome.** This alloy has a resistance more than 50 times that of copper. The heating element may be either nichrome wire or ribbon wound on some insulating material that is able to withstand heat. While dealing with problems on heating appliances, the following points may be kept in mind :

(*i*) The electrical energy in kWh can be converted into joules by the following relation :

$$1kWh = 36 \times 10^5 \text{ joules}$$

(*ii*) The heat energy in calories can be converted into joules by the following relation :

$$1 \text{ calorie} = 4.186 \text{ joules} ; 1 \text{ kcal} = 4186 \text{ joules}$$

(*iii*) The electrical energy in kWh can be converted into calories (or kilocalories) by the following relation:

$$1kWh = 36 \times 10^5 \text{ joules} = \frac{36 \times 10^5}{4.186} \text{ calories} = 860 \times 10^3 \text{ calories}$$

$$\therefore \qquad 1kWh = 860 \text{ kcal}$$

(*iv*) The electrical energy supplied to the heating appliance forms the *input energy*. The heat obtained from the device is the *output energy*. The difference between the two, if any, represents the loss of energy during conversion from electrical into heat energy.

Electric heaters

4.12. POWER DISSIPATION

Power dissipation usually refers to the rate at which electric energy is converted into heat. A resistor in an active circuit may feel warm to touch. This is due to the conversion of electric energy into heat energy. The resistor dissipates the heat energy by transferring it to surrounding structure and to the atmosphere. A resistor that is dissipating a large power may become hot enough to burn a finger. If the power dissipation is high, there will be a rapid conversion of electric energy into heat energy. As a result, the resistor reaches an excessive temperature and is damaged. Resistors and other equipment have maximum power dissipation ratings. For example, a resistor may have a power dissipation rating of 5 W. It means that maximum current through the resistor should be such that power developed ($P = I^2 R$) does not exceed 5 W otherwise the resistor will be damaged due to excessive heat.

Illustration. Let us illustrate the power dissipation of a resistor (or any other electrical device) with numerical examples.

(i) *A 0.1 Ω resistor is rated at 5 W. Is this resistor safe when conducting a current of 10 A ?*

$$P = I^2 R = (10)^2 \times 0.1 = 10\text{W}$$

The resistor is not safe since the calculated power exceeds the dissipation rating.

(ii) *What is the maximum safe current flow in a 47 Ω, 2–W resistor ?*

$$P = I^2 R$$

or $$I = \sqrt{\frac{P}{R}} = \sqrt{\frac{2}{47}} = 0.21\text{A}$$

If the current through this resistor exceeds 0.21 A, the resistor is likely to be damaged due to excessive heat.

(iii) *What is the maximum voltage that can be applied across a 100 Ω, 10 - W resistor in order to keep within resistor's power rating ?*

$$P = \frac{V^2}{R}$$

or $$V = \sqrt{P \times R} = \sqrt{10 \times 100} = 31.6\text{V}$$

If the voltage across this resistor exceeds 31.6 V, the resistor is likely to be damaged due to excessive heat.

Example 4.17. *A soldering iron is rated at 50 watts when connected to a 250 V supply. If the soldering iron takes 5 minutes to heat to a working temperature of 190°C from 20°C, find its mass, assuming it to be made of copper. Given specific heat capacity of copper is 390 J/Kg°C.*

Solution. Let *m* kg be the mass of soldering iron.

Heat gained by the soldering iron = $mS\theta = m \times 390 \times (190 - 20) = 66,300\ m$ joules

Heat released by the heating element = power × time = $(50) \times (5 \times 60) = 15,000$ joules

Assuming all the heat released by the element is absorbed by the copper *i.e.* soldering iron is 100% efficient,

$$15,000 = 66,300\ m$$

∴ $$m = 15,000/66,300 = 0.226\text{ kg}$$

Example 4.18. *An electric kettle marked 1kW, 230 V, takes 7.5 minutes to bring 1 kg of water at 15°C to boiling point (100°C). Find the efficiency of the kettle.*

Solution. Heat received by water (*i.e.* output energy)

$$= \text{mass} \times \text{specific heat} \times \text{rise in temp.}$$
$$= 1 \times 1 \times (100 - 15) = 85\text{ kcal}$$

Electrical energy supplied to the kettle (*i.e.* input energy)

$$= \text{wattage} \times \text{time} = 1\text{kW} \times 7.5/60 \text{ hr} = 0.125 \text{ kWh}$$
$$= 0.125 \times 860 \text{ kcal} = 107.5 \text{ kcal} \quad (\because 1\text{kWh} = 860 \text{ kcal})$$

∴   Efficiency of kettle $= \dfrac{85}{107.5} \times 100 = \mathbf{79.07\%}$

Example 4.19. *The cost of boiling 2 kg of water in an electric kettle is 12 paise. The kettle takes 6 minutes to boil water from an ambient temperature of 20°C. Calculate (i) the efficiency of kettle and (ii) the wattage of kettle if cost of 1 kWh is 40 paise.*

Solution.

(*i*) Heat received by water (*i.e.* output energy) $= 2 \times 1 \times 80 = 160 \text{ kcal}$

Electrical energy supplied (*i.e.* input energy) $= 12/40 \text{ kWh} = 860 \times 12/40 = 258 \text{ kcal}$

∴   Kettle efficiency $= \dfrac{160}{258} \times 100 = \mathbf{62\%}$

(*ii*) Let *W* kilowatt be the power rating of the kettle.

Input energy $= W \times$ time in hours

or $12/40 = W \times 6/60$

∴   Wattage of kettle, $W = \dfrac{12}{40} \times \dfrac{60}{6} = \mathbf{3kW}$

Example 4.20. *How long will it take to raise the temperature of 880 gm of water from 16°C to boiling point ? The heater takes 2 amperes at 220 V and its efficiency is 90%.*

Solution. Heat received by water (*i.e.* output energy)

$$= 0.88 \times 1 \times (100 - 16) = 73.92 \text{ kcal} = 73.92/860 = 0.086 \text{ kWh}$$

Electrical energy supplied to the heater (*i.e.* input energy)

$$= 0.086/0.9 = 0.096 \text{ kWh}$$

The heater is supplying a power of $220 \times 2 = 440$ watts $= 0.44$ kW. Let *t* hours be the required time.

Input energy $=$ wattage $\times$ time

or $0.096 = 0.44 \times t$

∴ $t = 0.096/0.44 = 0.218$ hours $= \mathbf{13.08 \text{ minutes}}$

Example 4.21. *An electric heater contains 40 litres of water initially at a mean temperature of 15°C. The heater supplies an energy of 2.5 kWh to water. Assuming no heat losses, what is the final mean temperature of water ?*

Solution. Let θ°C be the final mean temperature of water.

Electrical energy supplied to water (*i.e.* input energy)

$$= 2.5 \text{ kWh} = 2.5 \times 36 \times 10^5 = 9 \times 10^6 \text{ J}$$

Heat received by water (*i.e.* output energy)

$$= mS (\theta - 15) = 40 \times 4186 (\theta - 15) \text{ J}$$

As there are no heat losses, input energy is equal to the output energy.

∴ $40 \times 4186 (\theta - 15) = 9 \times 10^6$

or $\theta - 15 = \dfrac{9 \times 10^6}{40 \times 4186} = 53.8$

∴ $\theta = 53.8 + 15 = \mathbf{68.8°C}$

Example 4.22. *An electric kettle is required to raise the temperature of 2 kg of water from 20°C to 100°C in 15 minutes. Calculate the resistance of the heating element if the kettle is to be used on a 240 volts supply. Assume the efficiency of the kettle to be 80%.*

Solution.

Heat received by water (*i.e.* output energy)

$$= 2 \times 1 \times (100 - 20) = 160 \text{ kcal} = 160/860 \text{ kWh} = 0.186 \text{ kWh}$$

Electrical energy supplied to the kettle

$$= 0.186/0.8 = 0.232 \text{ kWh}$$

The electrical energy of 0.232 kWh is supplied in 15/60 = 0.25 hours.

∴ Power rating of kettle $= 0.232/0.25 = 0.928 \text{ kW} = 928 \text{ watts}$

Let R ohms be the resistance of the heating element.

∴ $V^2/R = 928$ or $R = \dfrac{240 \times 240}{928} = 62\Omega$

Example 4.23. *An electric kettle contains 1.5 kg of water at 15°C. It takes 2.5 hours to raise the temperature to 90°C. Assuming the heat losses due to radiation and heating the kettle to be 15 kcal, find (i) wattage of kettle and (ii) current taken if supply voltage is 230 V.*

Solution. Heat received by water (*i.e.* output energy)

$$= 1.5 \times 1 \times (90 - 15) = 112.5 \text{ kcal}$$

Electrical energy supplied to the kettle

$$= 112.5 + 15 = 127.5 \text{ kcal} = 127.5/860 \text{ kWh} = 0.1482 \text{ kWh}$$

(*i*) Input energy   = Wattage in kW × time in hours

  or $0.1482 = \text{Wattage} \times 2.5$

  ∴   Wattage of kettle $= 0.1482/2.5 = 0.0592 \text{ kW} = \textbf{59.2 watts}$

(*ii*) Current taken $= 59.2/230 = \textbf{0.257A}$

Example 4.24. *Two heaters A and B are in parallel across the supply voltage V. Heater A produces 500 kcal in 20 minutes and B produces 1000 kcal in 10 minutes. The resistance of heater A is 10 Ω. What is the resistance of heater B ? If the same heaters are connected in series, how much heat will be produced in 5 minutes ?*

Solution.

  Heat produced $= \dfrac{V^2 t}{R \times J} \text{ kcal}$

  For heater A, $500 = \dfrac{V^2 \times (20 \times 60)}{10 \times J}$ ...(*i*)

  For heater B, $1000 = \dfrac{V^2 \times (10 \times 60)}{R \times J}$ ...(*ii*)

Dividing Eq. (*i*) by (*ii*), we get,

$$\frac{500}{1000} = \frac{20 \times 60}{10 \times 60} \times \frac{R}{10}$$

∴ $R = \textbf{2.5 } \Omega$

When the heaters are connected in series, the total resistance becomes 10 + 2.5 = 12.5 Ω.

∴ Heat produced in 5 minutes

$$= \frac{V^2 t}{R \times J} = \frac{V^2}{J} \times \frac{t}{R}$$

$$= \frac{5{,}000}{20 \times 60} \times \frac{5 \times 60}{12.5} \qquad \left[\text{From Eq. } (i),\ \frac{V^2}{J} = \frac{5000}{20 \times 60}\right]$$

$$= \textbf{100 kcal}$$

TUTORIAL PROBLEMS

1. Calculate the time taken for a 3 kW electrical immersion heater to raise the temperature of 136 litres of water from 10°C to 70°C. Assume that overall efficiency of the equipment is 90%. Given that 1 litre of water has a mass of 1kg. **[3 hours, 30 minutes, 54 seconds]**

2. An electrical heater takes 5 minutes to convert 1 kg of water at room temperature of 18°C into steam at 100°C. Calculate the power rating of the heater. Assume the heating equipment to have an efficiency of 90%. Take the latent heat of evaporation of water as 2.257 MJ/kg. **[9.63 kW]**

3. An electric heater rated at 2 kW contains 68 kg of water at 20°C. Assuming the heat losses to be 15% of the input, find the temperature of water after the heater has been switched for 2.5 hours. **[73.75°C]**

4. Find the amount of electrical energy expended in raising the temperature of 45 litres of water by 75°C. To what height could a weight of 5 tonnes be raised with the expenditure of the same energy? Assume efficiencies of heating and lifting equipment to be 90% and 70% respectively. **[4.36 kWh, 224m]**

5. Calculate the time taken for a 25 kW furnace, having an overall efficiency of 80% to melt 20 kg of aluminium. Take the specific heat capacity, melting point and latent heat of fusion of aluminium as 896 J/kg °C, 657°C and 402 kJ/kg respectively. **[16 min, 13 sec]**

MULTIPLE-CHOICE QUESTIONS

1. If potential difference across a conductor of a material of resistivity ρ remains constant, then heat produced in the conductor is proportional to

   (a) ρ (b) ρ^2

   (c) $\dfrac{1}{\sqrt{\rho}}$ (d) $\dfrac{1}{\rho}$

2. The heater element in an electric iron is made of

   (a) nichrome (b) iron

   (c) tungsten (d) constantan

3. Two electric bulbs have tungsten filament of the same length. If one of them gives 60 W and the other 100 W, then,

   (a) 60 W bulb has thicker filament

   (b) 100 W bulb has thicker filament

   (c) both filaments are of same thickness

   (d) information insufficient

4. Two electric lamps of 40 W each are connected in parallel across a.c. mains. The power consumed by the combination is

   (a) 20 W (b) 60 W

   (c) 80 W (d) 100 W

5. Two electric lamps 40 W, 220 V each are connected in series across 220 V. The power consumed by the combination is

   (a) 80 W (b) 160 W

   (c) 40 W (d) 20 W

6. Three bulbs B_1, B_2 and B_3 are connected to the mains as shown in Fig. 4.5. If B_3 is disconnected from the circuit by opening switch S, then incandescence of bulb B_1 will

   (a) decrease (b) increase

   (c) no change (d) cannot say

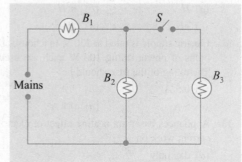

Fig. 4.5

7. The power of a heater is 500 W at 800°C. What will be its power at 200°C ? Temperature coefficient of resistance is $4 \times 10^{-4}/°C$.

   (a) 484 W (b) 620 W

   (c) 526 W (d) 672 W

8. A heater coil rated at 1000 W, 220 V is connected to 110 V line. Power consumed is

   (a) 500 W (b) 400 W

   (c) 250 W (d) 200 W

9. In the circuit shown in Fig 4.6, the heat produced in 5 Ω resistor is 10 cal/sec. The heat produced in 4 Ω resistor will be

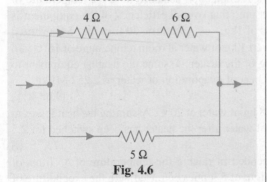

Fig. 4.6

   (a) 3 cal/sec   (b) 1 cal/sec

   (c) 4 cal/sec   (d) 2 cal/sec

10. A constant voltage is applied between the ends of a metallic wire of uniform area of cross-section. The heat is doubled if

   (a) both length and radius are doubled

   (b) both length and radius are halved

   (c) the radius of wire in doubled

   (d) the length of wire in doubled

11. A uniform wire when connected directly across a 200 V line produces heat H per second. If the wire is divided into n equal parts and all the parts are connected in parallel across 200 V line, the heat produced per second is

   (a) H (b) n^2H

   (c) nH (d) H/n^2

12. Electric supply is rated at 220 V. In a house, 11 bulbs of power rating 100 W each are used. The rating of the fuse should be

   (a) 0.5 A   (b) 1 A

   (c) 5 A   (d) 0.1 A

13. Appliances based on heating effect of electric current work on

   (a) d.c. only

   (b) a.c. only

   (c) both d.c. and a.c.

   (d) none of the above

14. A house is served by a 220 V line. In a circuit protected by a fuse marked 9 A, the maximum number of 60 W lamps in parallel that can be turned on is

   (a) 33   (b) 44

   (c) 22   (d) 20

15. A tap supplies water at 22°C. A man takes 1 litre of water per minute at 37°C from the gey-

ser. The power of the geyser is

   (a) 2100 W   (b) 1575 W

   (c) 525 W   (d) 1050 W

16. A battery supplies 150 W and 196 W power to two resistors of 6 Ω and 4 Ω when they are connected separately to it. The internal resistance of the battery is

   (a) 0.5 Ω   (b) 1 Ω

   (c) 1.5 Ω   (d) 2 Ω

17. An electric kettle boils 1 kg of water in time t_1 and another kettle boils the same amount of water in time t_2. When they are joined in series, the time t required to boil 1 kg of water is

   (a) $\dfrac{t_1 t_2}{t_1 + t_2}$ (b) $\dfrac{t_1 + t_2}{2}$

   (c) $t_1 + t_2$ (d) $\dfrac{2 t_1 t_2}{t_1 + t_2}$

18. A 24 V battery of internal resistance 4 Ω is connected to a variable resistor. At what value of current drawn from the battery is heat produced in the resistor maximum ?

   (a) 3 A   (b) 1.5 A

   (c) 2.5 A   (d) 1 A

19. A cell sends current through a resistance R_1 for time t. Next the same cell sends current through another resistance R_2 for the same time t. If the same heat is produced in both cases, then internal resistance of the cell is

   (a) $\dfrac{R_1 + R_2}{2}$ (b) $\dfrac{R_1 - R_2}{2}$

   (c) $\dfrac{\sqrt{R_1 R_2}}{2}$ (d) $\sqrt{R_1 R_2}$

20. In the circuit shown in Fig. 4.7, the cell has internal resistance of 1 Ω. The heat produced in 8 Ω coil is 32 cal/sec. The heat produced in one second in 4 Ω coil is

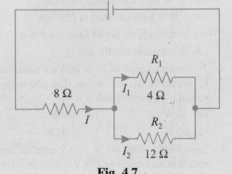

Fig. 4.7

   (a) 3 cal   (b) 9 cal

   (c) 6 cal   (d) 12 cal

Answers to Multiple-Choice Questions

1. (d)	2. (a)	3. (b)	4. (c)	5. (d)	6. (a)	7. (b)	8. (c)
9. (d)	10. (a)	11. (b)	12. (c)	13. (c)	14. (a)	15. (d)	16. (b)
17. (c)	18. (a)	19. (d)	20. (b)				

Hints to Selected Multiple-Choice Questions

1. Rate of heat produced, $H = \dfrac{V^2}{R} = \dfrac{V^2}{\rho l / a} = \dfrac{V^2 a}{\rho l}$

   $\therefore \qquad\qquad H \propto \dfrac{1}{\rho}$ $\qquad\qquad$ ($\because$ V, a and l are constant)

3. $R = \rho\, l/a$. The filament of that bulb is thicker which has low resistance ($\because$ l is constant in the two cases). Now 100 W bulb has smaller resistance than that of 60 W bulb. Therefore, **100 W bulb has thicker filament.**

4. $\dfrac{1}{R_T} = \dfrac{1}{R_1} + \dfrac{1}{R_2}$

   or $\qquad\qquad \dfrac{V^2}{R_T} = \dfrac{V^2}{R_1} + \dfrac{V^2}{R_2}$

   or $\qquad\qquad P_T = P_1 + P_2 = 40 + 40 = 80\ \text{W}$

5. $R_T = R_1 + R_2 \qquad$ or $\qquad \dfrac{R_T}{V^2} = \dfrac{R_1}{V^2} + \dfrac{R_2}{V^2}$

   or $\qquad \dfrac{1}{P_T} = \dfrac{1}{P_1} + \dfrac{1}{P_2} \qquad \therefore\ P_T = \dfrac{P_1\, P_2}{P_1 + P_2} = \dfrac{40 \times 40}{40 + 40} = 20\ \text{W}$

6. When bulb B_3 is disconnected from the circuit, the total circuit resistance is increased and the total circuit current decreases. As power dissipation = I^2R, therefore, the incandescence of bulb B_1 **decreases.**

7. Power, $P \propto 1/R$ so that

   $P_{200} = P_{800}\,[1 + \alpha\,(\theta_2 - \theta_1)] = 500\,[1 + 4 \times 10^{-4} \times 600] = 620\ \text{W}$

8. It is understood that resistance of heater coil is constant.

   Resistance of heater coil, $R = \dfrac{V^2}{P} = \dfrac{(220)^2}{1000} = \dfrac{484}{10} = 48.4\,\Omega$

   Power consumed at 110 V $= \dfrac{(110)^2}{48.4} = 250\ \text{W}$

9. Rate of heat produced, $P = V^2/R$. Since V (=voltage across the parallel combination) is the same, $P \propto 1/R$.

   $\therefore$ Rate of heat produced in the series combination of 4 Ω and 6 Ω resistors = 10/2 = 5 cal/sec. Rate of heat produced in the series combination is in the ratio of 4 : 6 or 2 : 3.

   $\therefore$ Rate of heat produced in 4 Ω resistor $= 5 \times \dfrac{2}{2 + 3} = 2$ cal/sec.

10. For constant applied voltage, heat produced/sec, $H \propto 1/R$.

    $\therefore H \propto \dfrac{a}{\rho l} \propto \dfrac{r^2}{\rho l}$. **If both radius (r) and length (l) are doubled, H becomes doubled.**

11. Heat produced per second $\propto 1/R$

For the first case, $H \propto 1/R$; For the second case, $H' \propto 1/R'$

$$\therefore \qquad \frac{H'}{H} = \frac{R}{R'} = n^2 \quad \text{or} \quad H' = n^2 H \qquad \left[\because R' = \frac{R}{n} \times \frac{1}{n} = \frac{R}{n^2} \right]$$

12. $P = VI$. Therefore, total current, $I = P/V = 11 \times 100/220 = 5A$

13. $P = I^2R$. As the heating effect of electric current is independent of the direction of current, therefore, heating appliances can be used for **both d.c. and a.c. work.**

14. Let n be the required number of 60 W lamps connected in parallel.

Total power, $P = 60\,n$. Now $P = VI$ or $60n = 220 \times 9$

$$\therefore \qquad n = \frac{220 \times 9}{60} = 33$$

15. The heat output of the geyser in joules per second is the power of the device (provided efficiency is 100%).

Power of geyser $= mS\theta \times 4.2\,\text{J/sec} = \dfrac{1000}{60} \times 1 \times (37 - 22) \times 4.2 = \mathbf{1050\ W}$

Note that $m = 1000/60 =$ mass of water per second.

16. Current supplied by battery, $I = \dfrac{E}{R + r}$

Power supplied by battery, $P = I^2R = \dfrac{E^2 R}{(R + r)^2}$

$$\therefore \qquad \frac{P_1}{P_2} = \frac{R_1}{R_2} \times \frac{(R_2 + r)^2}{(R_1 + r)^2}$$

$$\text{or} \qquad \frac{150}{196} = \frac{6}{4} \left(\frac{4 + r}{6 + r} \right)^2$$

On solving, $r = 1\Omega$.

17. When electric kettles are connected in series, the total power P is given by;

$$P = \frac{P_1 P_2}{P_1 + P_2}$$

Let Q be the heat required to boil 1 kg of water. Then,

$$Q = P_1 t_1 = P_2 t_2 = Pt$$

$$\therefore \qquad \frac{Q}{t} = \frac{(Q/t_1) \times (Q/t_2)}{Q/t_1 + Q/t_2} = \frac{Q}{t_1 + t_2}$$

$$\text{or} \qquad t = t_1 + t_2$$

18. According to maximum power transfer theorem, the power dissipated (or heat developed) in an external resistor is maximum when the external resistance is made equal to the internal resistance of the voltage source. Therefore, to satisfy the given conditions, external resistance should be 4Ω.

$$\therefore \quad \text{Required current,} \qquad I = \frac{E}{R + r} = \frac{24}{4 + 4} = 3A$$

19. $Q = \left(\dfrac{E}{R_1 + r} \right)^2 R_1 = \left(\dfrac{E}{R_2 + r} \right)^2 R_2$

or
$$\frac{R_1}{(R_1 + r)^2} = \frac{R_2}{(R_2 + r)^2}$$

On solving, $r = \sqrt{R_1 R_2}$

20. The total resistance R_T of parallel combination of 4Ω and 12Ω resistors is
$$R_T = \frac{R_1 R_2}{R_1 + R_2} = \frac{4 \times 12}{4 + 12} = 3\Omega$$

Since heat produced in 8Ω resistor is 32 cal/sec,

∴ Heat produced in $3\Omega = \frac{32}{8} \times 3 = 12$ cal/sec

The total heat produced in parallel combination of R_1 and R_2 is 12 cal/sec. Since $H \propto 1/R$, the heat produced in 4Ω and 12Ω resistors will be in the ratio $12 : 4 = 3 : 1$.

∴ Heat produced in 4Ω resistor $= 12 \times \dfrac{3}{3 + 1} = $ **9 cal/sec.**

Electrostatics

INTRODUCTION

A charged body has either deficiency or excess of electrons and is said to possess *electricity*. If two oppositely charged bodies are connected through a conductor, electrons will flow from the negative charge (excess of electrons) to the positive charge (deficit of electrons). This flow of electrons is called electric current. The electric current will continue to flow so long as 'excess' and 'deficiency' of electrons exist in the bodies. The branch of electrical engineering which deals with the flow of electrons (*i.e.*, current) is called *current electricity* and is important in many ways. For example, it is the electric current by means of which electrical energy can be transferred from one point to another for utilisation.

There can be another situation where charges (*i.e.*, electrons) do not move but remain static or stationary on the bodies. Such a situation will arise when the charged bodies are separated by some insulating medium, disallowing the movement of electrons. This is called *static electricity* and the branch of engineering which deals with static electricity is called *electrostatics*. Although current electricity is of greater practical use, yet the importance of static electricity cannot be ignored.

Many of the advancements made in the field of electricity owe their developments to the knowledge scientists obtained from electrostatics. The most useful outcomes of static electricity are the development of lightning rod and the capacitor. In this chapter, we shall confine our attention to the behaviour and applications of static electricity.

5.1. COULOMB'S LAWS OF ELECTROSTATICS

First law. This law relates to the nature of force between two charged bodies and may be stated as under :

Like charges repel each other while unlike charges attract each other.

Second law. This law tells about the magnitude of force between two charged bodies and may be stated as under :

The force between two *point charges is directly proportional to the product of their magnitudes and inversely proportional to the square of distance between them.

Mathematically,

$$F \propto \frac{Q_1 Q_2}{d^2}$$

or $$F = k \frac{Q_1 Q_2}{d^2} \qquad ...(i)$$

where k is a constant whose value depends upon the medium in which the charges are placed and the system of units employed. In SI units, force is measured in newtons, charge in coulombs, distance in metres and the value of k is given by :

$$k = \frac{1}{4\pi \varepsilon_0 \varepsilon_r}$$

where ε_0 = Absolute permittivity of vacuum or air

ε_r = Relative permittivity of the medium in which the charges are placed. For vacuum or air, its value is 1.

The value of $\varepsilon_0 = 8.854 \times 10^{-12}$ *F/m* and the value of ε_r is different for different media.

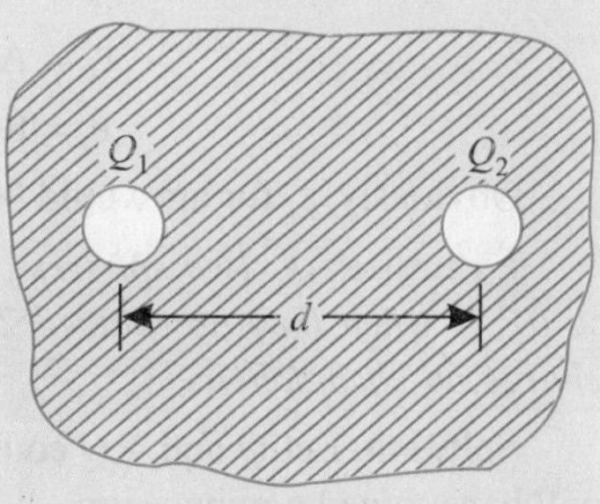

Fig. 5.1

$\therefore \qquad F = \frac{Q_1 Q_2}{4\pi \varepsilon_0 \varepsilon_r d^2} \qquad ...(ii)$

Now $\qquad \dfrac{1}{4\pi\varepsilon_0} = \dfrac{1}{4\pi \times 8.854 \times 10^{-12}} = 9 \times 10^9$

$\therefore \qquad F = 9 \times 10^9 \dfrac{Q_1 Q_2}{\varepsilon_r d^2} \qquad ...in\ a\ medium$

$\qquad = 9 \times 10^9 \dfrac{Q_1 Q_2}{d^2} \qquad ...in\ air$

Unit charge. The unit of charge (*i.e.*, 1 coulomb) can also be defined from Coulomb's second law of electrostatics. Suppose two equal charges placed 1 m apart in *air* exert a force of 9×10^9 newtons *i.e.*,

$$Q_1 = Q_2 = Q; \quad d = 1\,\text{m}; \quad F = 9 \times 10^9\ \text{N}$$

* Charged bodies approximate to point charges if they are small compared to the distance between them.

$$\therefore \qquad F = 9 \times 10^9 \, \frac{Q_1 Q_2}{d^2}$$

or
$$9 \times 10^9 = 9 \times 10^9 \, \frac{Q^2}{(1)^2}$$

or
$$Q^2 = 1$$

or
$$Q = \pm 1 = 1 \text{ coulomb}$$

Hence, one coulomb is that charge which when placed in air at a distance of one metre from an equal and similar charge repels it with a force of 9×10^9 N.

5.2. ABSOLUTE AND RELATIVE PERMITTIVITY

Permittivity is the property of a medium and affects the magnitude of force between two point charges. The greater the permittivity of a medium, the lesser the force between the charged bodies placed in it. Air or vacuum has a minimum value of permittivity. The absolute (or actual) permittivity ε_0 (Greek letter 'epsilon') of air or vacuum is 8.854×10^{-12} F/m. The absolute (or actual) permittvity ε of all other insulating materials is greater than ε_0. The ratio $\varepsilon/\varepsilon_0$ is called the *relative permittivity* of the material and is denoted by ε_r i.e.,

$$\varepsilon_r = \frac{\varepsilon}{\varepsilon_0}$$

ε = Absolute (or actual) permittivity of material

ε_0 = Absolute (actual) permittivity of air or vacuum (8.854×10^{-12} F/m)

ε_r = Relative permittivity of material.

Obviously, ε_r for air would be $\varepsilon_0/\varepsilon_0 = 1$.

Example 5.1. *Two spheres charged with equal but opposite charges experience a force of 25 × 10^5 N when they are placed 2 cm apart in a medium of relative permittivity 5. Determine the charge on each sphere.*

Solution. Let Q and $-Q$ coulomb be the charges on the spheres. Since the force is attractive, it will be assigned a minus sign.

$$F = 9 \times 10^9 \, \frac{Q_1 Q_2}{\varepsilon_r \, d^2}$$

or
$$-25 \times 10^5 = 9 \times 10^9 \, \frac{Q(-Q)}{5 \times (0.02)^2}$$

or
$$Q = \sqrt{\frac{25 \times 10^5 \times 5 \times (0.02)^2}{9 \times 10^9}} = 0.0745 \times 10^{-2} \text{ C} = 745 \text{ } \mu\text{C}$$

Example 5.2. *A small sphere is given a charge of + 20 μC and a second sphere of equal diameter is given a charge of – 5 μC. The two spheres are allowed to touch each other and are then spaced 10 cm apart. What force exists between them? Assume air as the medium.*

Solution. When the two spheres touch each other, the resultant charge = (20) + (– 5) = 15 μC. When the spheres are separated, charge on each sphere, $Q_1 = Q_2 = 15/2 = 7.5$ μC.

$$\therefore \quad \text{Force,} \qquad F = 9 \times 10^9 \times \frac{Q_1 Q_2}{d^2}$$

* Thus when we say that relative permittivity of a material is 10, it means that its absolute or actual permittivity $\varepsilon = \varepsilon_0 \, \varepsilon_r = 8.854 \times 10^{-12} \times 10 = 8.854 \times 10^{-11}$ F/m.

$$= 9 \times 10^9 \times \frac{(7.5 \times 10^{-6})(7.5 \times 10^{-6})}{(0.1)^2} = 50.62 \text{ N} \ \textit{repulsive}$$

Example 5.3. *Find the force between two charges 10 cm apart in vacuum. The charges are 4 × 10⁻⁵ C and 6 × 10⁻⁸ C. If the same charges are separated by the same distance in kerosene (ε$_r$ = 2), what is the force between them?*

Solution.

$$F = 9 \times 10^9 \ \frac{Q_1 Q_2}{d^2} = 9 \times 10^9 \ \frac{(4 \times 10^{-5})(6 \times 10^{-8})}{(0.1)^2} = \textbf{2.16 N} \qquad \textit{...in vacuum}$$

$$= 9 \times 10^9 \ \frac{Q_1 Q_2}{\varepsilon_r \, d^2} = \frac{1}{2}(2.16) = \textbf{1.08 N} \qquad \textit{...in a medium}$$

Example 5.4. *Calculate the force on a unit positive charge at P on X-axis whose co-ordinates are (x = 2 m, y = 0) due to the following two charges :*

(i) a positive charge of 10⁻⁹ C situated in air at the origin (x = 0, y = 0).

(ii) a negative charge of – 2 × 10⁻⁹ C situated on X-axis (x = 1 m, y = 0).

Solution. The conditions of the problem are represented in Fig. 5.2.

Repulsive force on unit positive charge at *P* due to + 10⁻⁹ C charge

$$= 9 \times 10^9 \ \frac{1 \times 10^{-9}}{(2)^2}$$

$$= 2.25 \text{ N}$$

Attractive force on unit positive charge at *P* due to – 2 × 10⁻⁹ C charge

$$= 9 \times 10^9 \times \frac{2 \times 10^{-9}}{(1)^2} = 18 \text{ N}$$

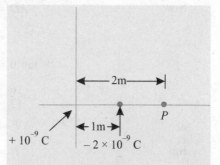

Fig. 5.2

∴ Resultant attractive force on unit positive charge at *P* = 18 – 2.25 = **15.75 N**

Example 5.5. *Three point charges of + 5 μC, + 5 μC and + 5μC are placed at the vertices of an equilateral triangle which has sides 10 cm long. Find the force on each charge.*

Solution. Fig. 5.3 shows the equilateral triangle with the three charges placed at the vertices. Consider the charge + 5μ *C* placed at corner *C*. It is being repelled by charges placed at *A* and *B* along *ACD* and *BCE* respectively. These two forces are equal, each being given by ;

$$F = 9 \times 10^9 \times \frac{(5 \times 10^{-6}) \times (5 \times 10^{-6})}{(0.1)^2}$$

$$= 22.5 \text{ N}$$

Since the angle between these two equal forces is 60°, their resultant is

$$= 2 \ F \cos 30° = 2 \times 22.5 \times \sqrt{3}/2 = \textbf{38.97 N}$$

The force acting on the charges placed at corners *A* and *B* will also be the same.

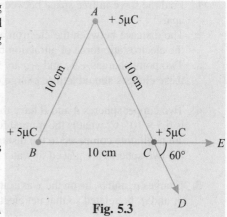

Fig. 5.3

Example 5.6. *Two small spheres, each having a mass of 0.1 g are suspended from a point by threads 20 cm long. They are equally charged and they repel each other to a distance of 24 cm. What is the charge on each sphere?*

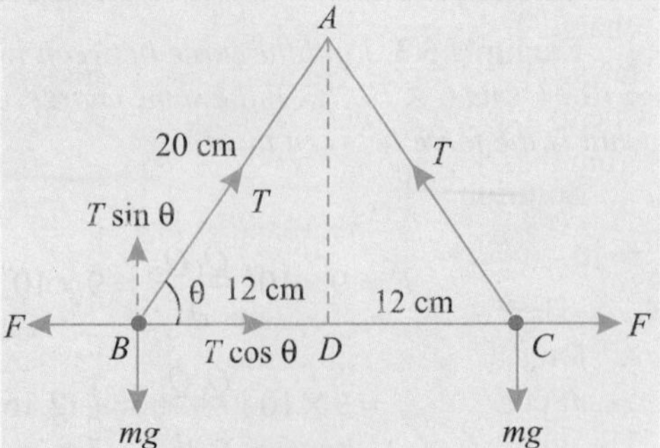

Solution. Fig. 5.4 shows the conditions of the problem. Let B and C be the spheres, each carrying a charge Q. The force of repulsion between the spheres is given by;

$$F = 9 \times 10^9 \frac{Q^2}{(0.24)^2} = 156.25 \times 10^9 \, Q^2$$

Each sphere is under the action of three forces :

(*i*) Weight *mg* acting vertically downward, (*ii*) tension T and (*iii*) electrostatic force F. Considering the sphere B and resolving T into rectangular components, we have,

Fig. 5.4

$$mg = T \sin \theta \; ; \; F = T \cos \theta$$

∴ $$\tan \theta = \frac{mg}{F}$$

Now, $$AD = \sqrt{AB^2 - BD^2}$$

$$= \sqrt{(20)^2 - (12)^2} = 16$$

∴ $$\tan \theta = \frac{AD}{BD} = \frac{16}{12}$$

∴ $$\frac{16}{12} = \frac{mg}{F}$$

or $$F = \frac{12}{16} mg = 0.75 \, mg = 0.75 \times 10^{-4} \times 9.8 = 7.4 \times 10^{-4} \text{ N}$$

But $$F = 156.25 \times 10^9 \, Q^2$$

∴ $$156.25 \times 10^9 \, Q^2 = 7.4 \times 10^{-4}$$

or $$Q^2 = \frac{7.4 \times 10^{-4}}{156.25 \times 10^9} = 4.8 \times 10^{-15}$$

or $$Q = 6.9 \times 10^{-8} \text{ C}$$

TUTORIAL PROBLEMS

1. Find the force in free space between two like point charges of one coulomb each placed 1m apart. [9×10^9 N]

2. The distance between the electron and proton in hydrogen atom is 5.3×10^{-11} m. Calculate the electrostatic force of attraction between them.

3. Two point charges $+ 9q$ and $+ q$ are separated by a distance of 16 cm. At what point between these charges should a third charge Q be placed so that it remains in equilibrium?
[12 cm from $+9q$]

4. Two copper spheres A and B have their centres separated by 50 cm. If charge on each sphere is 6.5×10^{-7} C, what is the mutual force of repulsion between them? The radii of the spheres are negligible compared to the distance of separation. What will be the magnitude of force if the two spheres are placed in water? (Dielectric constant of water = 80).
[1.52×10^{-2} N ; 1.9×10^{-4} N]

5. Charges q_1 and q_2 lie on the x-axis at points $x = -4$ cm and $x = +4$ cm respectively. How must q_1 and q_2 be related so that net electrostatic force on a charge placed at $x = +2$ cm is zero?
[$q_1 = 9q_2$]

5.3. ELECTRIC FIELD

The region surrounding a charged body is always under stress and strain because of the electrostatic charge. If a small charge is placed in this region, it will experience a force according to Coulomb's laws. This stressed region around a charged body is called electric field. Theoretically, electric field due to a charge extends upto infinity but its effect practically dies away very quickly as the distance from the charge increases.

The space (or field) in which a charge experiences a force is called an **electric field** *or* **electrostatic field.**

The electric field around a charged body is represented by imaginary lines, called *electric lines of *force.* By convention, the direction of these lines of force at any point is the direction along which a unit positive charge (*i.e.*, positive charge of 1C) placed at that point would move or tend to move. The unit positive charge is sometimes called a *test charge* because it is used as an indicator to find the direction of electric field. Following this convention, it is clear that electric lines of force would always originate from a positive charge and end on a negative charge. The electric lines of force leave or enter the charged surface** normally.

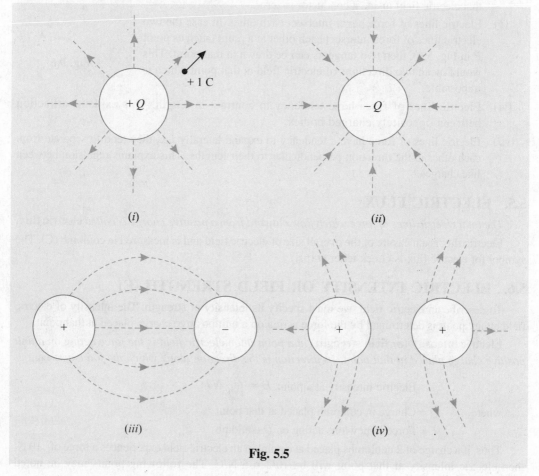

Fig. 5.5

---

*   So called because forces are experienced by charges in this region.
**   If a line of force is at an angle other that 90°, it will have a tangential component. This tangential component would cause redistribution (*i.e.*, movement) of charge. By definition, electrostatic charge is static and hence tangential component cannot exist.

Fig. 5.5 shows typical field distribution. Fig. 5.5 (*i*) shows electric field due to an isolated positively charged sphere. A unit positive charge placed near it will experience a force directed radially away from the sphere. Therefore, the direction of electric field will be radially outward as shown in Fig. 5.5 (*i*). For the negatively charged sphere [See Fig. 5.5 (*ii*)], the force acting on the unit positive charge would be directed radially towards the sphere. Fig. 5.5 (*iii*) shows the electric field between a positive charge and a negative charge while Fig. 5.5 (*iv*) shows electric field between two similarly charged (*i.e.*, + vely charged) bodies.

5.4. PROPERTIES OF ELECTRIC LINES OF FORCE

(*i*) The electric field lines are directed away from a positive charge and towards a negative charge so that at any point, the tangent to a field line gives the direction of electric field at that point.

(*ii*) Electric lines of force start from a positive charge and end on a negative charge.

(*iii*) Electric lines of force leave or enter the charged surface normally.

(*iv*) Electric lines of force cannot pass through a conductor. This means that electric field inside a conductor is zero.

(*v*) Electric lines of force never intersect each other. In case the two electric lines of force intersect each other at a point (such as point *P* in Fig. 5.6), then two tangents can be drawn at that point. This would mean two directions of electric field at that point which is impossible.

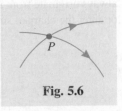

Fig. 5.6

(*vi*) Electric lines of force have tendency to contract in length. This explains attraction between oppositely charged bodies.

(*vii*) Electric lines of force have a tendency to expand laterally *i.e.*, they tend to separate from each other in the direction perpendicular to their lengths. This explains repulsion between like charges.

5.5. ELECTRIC FLUX

The total electric lines of force which flow outward from a positive charge is called **electric flux.**

Electric flux is a measure of the overall size of electric field and is measured in coulomb (C). The symbol for electric flux is Greek letter ψ (psi).

5.6. ELECTRIC INTENSITY OR FIELD STRENGTH (E)

To describe an electric field, we must specify its intensity or strength. The intensity of electric field at any point is determined by the force acting on a unit positive charge placed at that point.

Electric intensity (*or* **field strength**) *at a point in an electric field is the force acting on a unit positive charge placed at that point. Its direction is the direction along which the force acts i.e.,*

$$\text{Electric intensity at a point, } E = \frac{F}{+Q} \ N/C$$

where Q = Charge in coulomb placed at that point

          F = Force in newtons acting on Q coulomb

Thus, if a charge of 2 coulombs placed at a point in an electric field experiences a force of 10 N, then electric intensity at that point will be 10/2 = 5 N/C. The following points may be noted carefully :

(*i*) Since electric intensity is a force, it is a vector quantity possessing both magnitude and direction.

(*ii*) Electric intensity can also be *described in terms of electric lines of force. Where the lines of force are close together, the intensity is high and where the lines of force are widely separated, intensity will be low.

(*iii*) Electric intensity can also be expressed in V/m.

$$1 \text{ V/m} = 1 \text{ N/C (See foot note at page 168)}$$

5.7. ELECTRIC INTENSITY AT A POINT IN ELECTRIC FIELD

The value of electric intensity at any point in an electric field due to a point charge can be calculated by Coulomb's laws. Suppose it is required to find the electric intensity at point *P* situated at a distance *d* metres from a charge of + *Q* coulomb (See Fig. 5.7). Imagine a unit positive charge (*i.e.*, + 1C) is placed at point *P*. Then, by definition, electric intensity at *P* is the force acting on + 1 C placed at *P* *i.e.*,

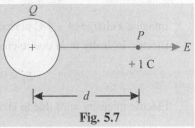

Fig. 5.7

Electric intensity at *P*, $E = $ Force on + 1 C placed at *P*

$$= 9 \times 10^9 \frac{Q \times 1}{\varepsilon_r d^2}$$

∴ $$E = 9 \times 10^9 \frac{Q}{\varepsilon_r d^2} \qquad \qquad ...in \ a \ medium$$

$$= 9 \times 10^9 \frac{Q}{d^2} \qquad \qquad ...in \ air$$

Note the direction of electric intensity. It is acting radially away from + *Q*. For a negative charge (*i.e.*, – *Q*), its direction would have been radially towards the charge.

Example 5.7. (*i*) *A charge of 2 μC placed in an electric field experiences a force of 0.08 N. What is the magnitude of electric intensity?*

(*ii*) *A charge of 0.52 μC is placed in an electric field where field intensity is 4.5 × 10⁵ N/C. What is the magnitude of force acting on the charge?*

Solution. (*i*) Charge, $Q = 2\mu C = 2 \times 10^{-6} \text{ C}$

Force acting, $F = 0.08 \text{ N}$

∴   Electric intensity, $E = \dfrac{F}{Q} = \dfrac{0.08}{2 \times 10^{-6}} = 4 \times 10^4 \text{ N/C}$

(*ii*) If electric intensity at a point in an electric field is *E*, it means that a force of *E* newtons acts on a charge of 1 C placed at that point. If a charge of *Q* coulomb is placed at that point, then force (*F*) acting on the charge is

$$F = EQ = (4.5 \times 10^5) \times (0.52 \times 10^{-6}) = \mathbf{0.23 \ N}$$

Example 5.8. *Two equal and opposite charges of magnitude 2 × 10⁻⁷ C are placed 15 cm apart. What is the magnitude and direction of electric intensity (E) at a point mid-way between the charges? What force would act on a proton (charge = + 1.6 × 10⁻¹⁹ C) placed there?*

Solution. Fig. 5.8 shows two equal and opposite charges separated by a distance of 15 cm *i.e.*, 0.15 m. Let *M* be the mid point *i.e.*, *AM* = *MB* = 0.075 m.

---

*   It may be noted that electric lines of force do not actually exist. It is only a way of representing an electric field. However, it is a useful method of representation. It is a usual practice to indicate high field strength by drawing lines of force close together and low field strength by widely spaced lines.

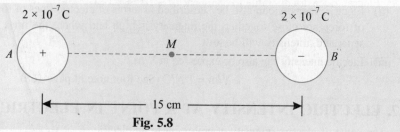

Fig. 5.8

Imagine a charge of + 1 C placed at M.

Electric intensity at M due to charge $+ 2 \times 10^{-7}$ C is

$$E_1 = 9 \times 10^9 \times \frac{2 \times 10^{-7}}{(0.075)^2} = 0.32 \times 10^6 \text{ N/C } along \ AM.$$

Electric intensity at M due to charge $- 2 \times 10^{-7}$ C is

$$E_2 = 9 \times 10^9 \times \frac{2 \times 10^{-7}}{(0.075)^2} = 0.32 \times 10^6 \text{ N/C } along \ MB.$$

Since electric intensities are acting in the same direction, the resultant intensity E is the sum of E_1 and E_2.

∴ Resultant intensity at point M is

$$E = 0.32 \times 10^6 + 0.32 \times 10^6 = \mathbf{0.64 \times 10^6 \text{ N/C } along \ AB}$$

Electric intensity E at M is 0.64×10^6 N/C. Therefore, force F acting on a proton (charge, $Q = + 1.6 \times 10^{-19}$ C) placed at M is

$$F = EQ = (0.64 \times 10^6) \times (1.6 \times 10^{-19}) = \mathbf{1.024 \times 10^{-13} \text{ N } along \ AB}$$

Example 5.9. *Three point charges of $+ 8 \times 10^{-9}$ C, $+ 32 \times 10^{-9}$ C and $+ 24 \times 10^{-9}$ C are placed at the corners A, B and C of a square ABCD having each side 4 cm. Find the electric intensity at the corner D. Assume the medium is air.*

Solution. The various charges are shown in Fig. 5.9. In order to find electric intensity at the corner D, imagine a unit positive charge (*i.e.*, + 1 C) is placed at D. It is clear from Fig. 5.9 that $BD = \sqrt{2} \times 0.04$ m.

Electric intensity at D due to charge $+ 8 \times 10^{-9}$ C

$$= 9 \times 10^9 \times \frac{8 \times 10^{-9} \times 1}{(0.04)^2} \text{ N/C} = 4.5 \times 10^4 \text{ N/C } along \ AX$$

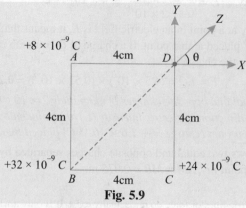

Fig. 5.9

Electric intensity at D due to charge $+ 32 \times 10^{-9}$ C

$$= 9 \times 10^9 \times \frac{32 \times 10^{-9} \times 1}{(\sqrt{2} \times 0.04)^2} \text{ N/C} = 9 \times 10^4 \text{ N/C } along \ DZ$$

Electric intensity at D due to charge $+ 24 \times 10^{-9}$ C

$$= 9 \times 10^9 \times \frac{24 \times 10^{-9} \times 1}{(0.04)^2} \text{ N/C} = 13.5 \times 10^4 \text{ N/C along } DY$$

The three forces are acting at D ; θ being 45°. In order to find the resultant, resolve the forces along X-axis and Y-axis.

Total X-component, $\quad X = 4.5 \times 10^4 + 9 \times 10^4 \cos 45° + 0 = 10.86 \times 10^4$ N/C

Total Y-component, $\quad Y = 13.5 \times 10^4 + 9 \times 10^4 \cos 45° + 0 = 19.86 \times 10^4$ N/C

Resultant intensity at $D = \sqrt{(10.86 \times 10^4)^2 + (19.86 \times 10^4)^2} = \mathbf{22.63 \times 10^4}$ **N/C**

Let the resultant intensity make an angle ϕ with DX.

$$\therefore \qquad \tan \phi = \frac{Y}{X} = \frac{19.86 \times 10^4}{10.86 \times 10^4} = 1.828$$

or $\qquad\qquad \phi = \tan^{-1} 1.828 = \mathbf{61.32°}$

Example 5.10. *The diameter of a hollow metallic sphere is 60cm and the sphere carries a charge of 500μC. Find the electric field intensity (i) at a distance of 100 cm from the centre of the sphere and (ii) at the surface of the sphere.*

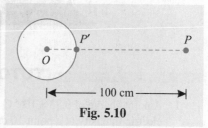

Fig. 5.10

Solution. The electric field due to a charged sphere has spherical symmetry. Therefore, a charged sphere behaves for external points as if the whole charge is placed at its centre.

(i) $\qquad d = OP = 100 \text{ cm} = 1 \text{ m}; \ Q = 500 \ \mu C = 500 \times 10^{-6} C$

$$\therefore \qquad E = 9 \times 10^9 \frac{Q}{d^2} = 9 \times 10^9 \times \frac{500 \times 10^{-6}}{(1)^2} = 4.5 \times 10^6 \text{ N/C}$$

(ii) $\qquad d = OP' = 30 \text{ cm} = 0.3 \text{ m}; \ Q = 500 \times 10^{-6} C$

$$\therefore \qquad E = 9 \times 10^9 \frac{Q}{d^2} = 9 \times 10^9 \times \frac{500 \times 10^{-6}}{(0.3)^2} = \mathbf{5 \times 10^7} \text{ N/C}$$

Example 5.11. *A pendulum bob of mass 80 milligram and carrying a charge of 2×10^{-8} C is at rest in a horizontal uniform electric field of 2×10^4 V/m. Find the tension in the thread of the pendulum and the angle it makes with the vertical.*

Solution. Suppose the tension in the thread is T and the thread makes an angle θ with the vertical. Three forces are acting on the bob *viz.* (*i*) weight mg of bob acting vertically downward (*ii*) electric force QE acting horizontally and (*iii*) tension T along AO. Since the bob is in equilibrium [See Fig. 5.11],

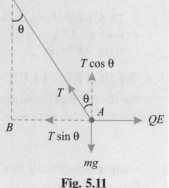

Fig. 5.11

$$T \sin \theta = QE ; \qquad T \cos \theta = mg$$

$$\therefore \qquad \tan \theta = \frac{QE}{mg} = \frac{(2 \times 10^{-8}) \times (2 \times 10^4)}{(80 \times 10^{-6}) \times 9.8} = 0.51$$

or $\qquad\qquad \theta = \tan^{-1} 0.51 = \mathbf{27°}$

Also $\qquad T = \frac{QE}{\sin \theta} = \frac{(2 \times 10^{-8}) \times (2 \times 10^4)}{\sin 27°} = \mathbf{8.81 \times 10^{-4}}$ **N**

Lightning rods

TUTORIAL PROBLEMS

1. A point charge of 0.33×10^{-8} C is placed in a medium of relative permittivity 5. Calculate the electric intensity at a point 10 cm from the point charge. **[0.525 × 10³ N/C]**

2. What is the magnitude of a point charge chosen so that electric field 20 cm away has a magnitude of 18×10^{6} N/C ? **[80 µC]**

3. Three point charges of $+ 0.33 \times 10^{-8}$ C, $+ 0.33 \times 10^{-8}$ C and $- 0.165 \times 10^{-8}$ C are placed at the corners of a square of 5 cm side. Calculate the electric intensity at the fourth corner.
   [1.635 × 10⁴ N/C]

4. A vacuum tube contains two plane parallel plate electrodes 7.5 mm apart. If a p.d. of 150 V (d.c.) is maintained between them, what is the electric field strength in the gap? What is the force acting on an electron in the gap? Charge on an electron = 1.6×10^{-19} C.
   [2 × 10⁴ N/C ; 3.2 × 10⁻¹⁵ N]

5. A tiny charged droplet carries a surplus electron (1.6×10^{-19} C). If this droplet is balanced between two parallel plates in a field of 10^{5} N/C, find the mass of droplet.
   [1.63 × 10⁻¹⁵ kg]

6. Three equal charges of $+ 4 \times 10^{-7}$ C are located at the corners of a right triangled ABC whose sides are $AB = 6$ cm, $BC = 8$ cm and $CA = 10$ cm. Find the force exerted on the charge located at the 90° angle. **[0.459 N repulsion at 29.4°]**

5.8. ELECTRIC FLUX DENSITY

The electric flux density at any section in an electric field is the electric flux crossing normally per unit area of that section i.e.

$$\text{Electric flux density, } D = \frac{\psi}{A} \text{ C/m}^2$$

where ψ is the electric flux in coulombs passing normally through an area A m^2.

For example, when we say that electric flux density in an electric field is 4 C/m², it means that 4 C of electric flux passes normally through an area of 1 m². Electric flux density is a vector quantity; possessing both magnitude and direction. Its direction is the same as the direction of electric intensity.

Relation between D and E. Consider a charge of $+ Q$ coulombs placed in a medium of relative permittivity ε_r as shown in Fig. 5.12. The electric flux density at P at a distance d metres from centre of the charge can be found as follows. With centre at the charge and radius d metres, an imaginary sphere can be considered. The electric flux of Q coulombs will pass normally through this imaginary sphere. Now area of sphere is $= 4\pi d^2$.

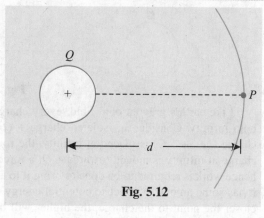

Fig. 5.12

$\therefore$ Electric flux density at P is

$$D = \frac{\text{electric flux}}{\text{area}} = \frac{Q}{4\pi d^2}$$

Also Electric intensity at P, $\quad E = \dfrac{Q}{4\pi\varepsilon_0\varepsilon_r d^2} = \dfrac{Q}{4\pi d^2} \times \dfrac{1}{\varepsilon_0\varepsilon_r} = \dfrac{D}{\varepsilon_0\varepsilon_r} \qquad \left[\because D = \dfrac{Q}{4\pi d^2} \right]$

$\therefore \qquad\qquad\qquad\qquad D = \varepsilon_0\varepsilon_r E$

Hence electric flux density at any point in an electric field is $\varepsilon_0\varepsilon_r$ times the electric intensity at that point.

It may be noted that in a uniform electric field (*e.g.*, between the plates of a capacitor), the electric flux density $D (= \varepsilon_0\varepsilon_r E)$ remains the same and is independent of relative permittivity of the medium.

Example 5.12. *In the electric field of a parallel plate air capacitor, the values of D and E are 0.885 µC/m² and 10⁵ N/C respectively. If area of each plate is 1m², find (i) electric flux (ii) value of absolute permittivity of free space.*

Solution.

(*i*) Electric flux, $\quad \psi = D \times A = (0.885 \times 10^{-6}) \times 1 = \mathbf{0.885 \times 10^{-6}}$ **C**

(*ii*) Now, $\qquad\qquad D = \varepsilon_0\varepsilon_r E \qquad\qquad\qquad\qquad\qquad\qquad$ [See Art. 5.8]

$\qquad\qquad\qquad\quad = \varepsilon_0 E \qquad\qquad\qquad\qquad\qquad\qquad\quad$ (For air, $\varepsilon_r = 1$)

$\therefore \qquad\qquad \varepsilon_0 = \dfrac{D}{E} = \dfrac{0.885 \times 10^{-6}}{10^5} = \mathbf{8.85 \times 10^{-12}}$ **F/m**

Example 5.13. *Two parallel plates are charged to have a p.d. of 100 V. Each has an area of 0.05 m² and they are separated 0.5 mm apart. Calculate the electric charge on each plate.*

Solution.

Electric intensity, $\qquad E = \dfrac{V}{d} = \dfrac{100}{0.5 \times 10^{-3}} = 2 \times 10^5$ V/m

Electric flux density, $\qquad D = \varepsilon_0\varepsilon_r E = (8.854 \times 10^{-12}) \times 1 \times 2 \times 10^5 = 17.7 \times 10^{-7}$ C/m²

Charge on each plate, $\qquad Q = D \times A = (17.7 \times 10^{-7}) \times (0.05) = \mathbf{0.885 \times 10^{-7}}$ **C**

5.9. ELECTRIC POTENTIAL

We know that earth has gravitational field which attracts the bodies towards earth. When a body is raised above the ground level, it possesses mechanical potential energy which is equal to the amount of work done in raising the body to that point. The greater the height to which the body is raised, the greater will be its potential energy. Thus the potential energy of the body depends upon its position in the gravitational field ; being zero on earth's surface. Strictly speaking, sea level is chosen as the place of zero potential.

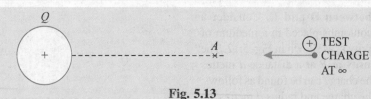

Fig. 5.13

Like earth's gravitational field, every charge has electric field which theoretically extends upto infinity. Consider an isolated charge + Q fixed in space as shown in Fig. 5.13. If a test charge (*i.e.*, + 1 C) is placed at infinity, the force on it due to charge + Q is *zero. If the test charge at infinity is moved towards + Q, a force of repulsion acts on it (like charges repel) and hence work is required to be done to bring it to a point like *A*. Hence when the test charge is at *A*, it has some amount of electric potential energy which we commonly call electric potential. The closer the point to the charge, the higher will be the electric potential at that point. Therefore, electric potential at a point due to a charge depends upon the position of the point ; being zero if the point is situated at infinity. Obviously, in electric field, infinity is chosen as the point of **zero potential.

Hence **electric potential** *at a point in an electric field is the amount of work done in bringing a unit positive charge (i.e., + 1 C) from infinity to that point i.e.*

$$\text{Electric potential} = \frac{\text{Work}}{\text{Charge}} = \frac{W}{Q}$$

where W is the work done to bring a charge of Q coulombs from infinity to the point under consideration.

Unit. The *SI* unit of electric potential is ***volt and may be defined as under :

The potential at a point in an electric field is **1 volt** *if 1 joule of work is done in bringing a unit positive charge (i.e., + 1 C) from infinity to that point* ****against the electric field.

Thus when we say that potential at a point in an electric field is 5V, it simply means that 5 joules of work has been done in bringing a unit positive charge from infinity to that point.

5.10. ELECTRIC POTENTIAL DIFFERENCE

In practice, we are more concerned with potential difference between two points rather than their †absolute potentials. The potential difference (p.d.) between two points may be defined as under :

The potential difference between two points is the amount of work done in moving a unit positive charge (i.e., + 1 C) from the point of lower potential to the point of higher potential.

Consider two points *A* and *B* in the electric field of a charge + Q as shown in Fig. 5.14. Let V_2 and V_1 be the absolute potentials at *A* and *B* respectively. Clearly $V_2 > V_1$. The potential V_1 at *B* means that V_1 joules of work has been done in bringing a unit positive charge from infinity to point *B*. Let the extra work done to bring the unit positive charge from *B* to *A* be W joules.

∴   Potential at $A = V_1 + W$

- -

* $F = 9 \times 10^9 \times \dfrac{Q \times 1}{d^2}.$ As $d \to \infty$, $F \to 0$

**   In practice, earth is chosen as zero potential. It is because earth is such a huge conductor that its potential practically remains constant.

*** Electric potential = W/Q = joules/coulomb. Now joule/coulomb has been given a special name *viz.* volt.

**** Note if the field is due to a positive charge (as is in this case), work will be done against the electric field. However, if the field is due to a negative charge, work is done by the electric field.

†   The potential at a point with infinity as reference is termed as absolute potential.

∴   P.D. between A and $B = (V_1 + W) - V_1$

or $V_2 - V_1 = W = W.D.$ to move $+ 1$ C from B
to A

The SI unit of potential difference is volt and may be defined as under :

*The p.d. between two points is **1V** if 1 joule of work is done in bringing a unit positive charge (i.e., + 1 C) from the point of lower potential to the point of higher potential.*

Thus when we say that p.d. between two points is 5 volts, it simply means that 5 joules of work will

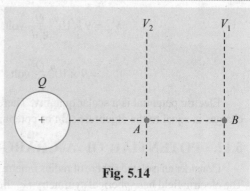

Fig. 5.14

have to be done to bring $+ 1$ C of charge from the point of lower potential to the point of higher potential. Conversely, 5 joules of work or energy will be released if $+ 1$C charge moves from the point of higher potential to the point of lower potential.

5.11. POTENTIAL AT A POINT DUE TO SINGLE CHARGE

Consider an isolated positive charge of Q coulombs placed in a medium of relative permittivity ε_r. It is desired to find the electric potential at point P due to this charge. Let P be at a distance d metres from the charge. Imagine a unit positive charge (*i.e.*, $+ 1$ C) placed at A and situated x metres from the charge. Then the force acting on this unit charge (*i.e.*, electric intensity) is given by ;

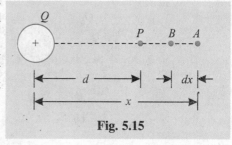

Fig. 5.15

$$F = E = \frac{Q}{4\pi\varepsilon_0\varepsilon_r x^2}$$

If this unit positive charge at A is moved through a small distance dx towards the charge $+ Q$, then work done is given by :

$$dW = \frac{Q}{4\pi\varepsilon_0\varepsilon_r x^2} \times (-* dx) = -\frac{Q}{4\pi\varepsilon_0\varepsilon_r x^2} dx$$

Total work done in bringing a unit positive charge from infinity to point P is

Total work done, $W = \int_{\infty}^{d} -\frac{Q}{4\pi\varepsilon_0\varepsilon_r x^2} dx = -\frac{Q}{4\pi\varepsilon_0\varepsilon_r} \int_{\infty}^{d} \frac{1}{x^2} dx$

$$= -\frac{Q}{4\pi\varepsilon_0\varepsilon_r} \left[-\frac{1}{x}\right]_{\infty}^{d} = \frac{-Q}{4\pi\varepsilon_0\varepsilon_r} \left[-\frac{1}{d} - \left(-\frac{1}{\infty}\right)\right] = \frac{Q}{4\pi\varepsilon_0\varepsilon_r d}$$

$$= 9 \times 10^9 \, \frac{Q}{\varepsilon_r d} \text{ joules} \qquad \left[\because \, \frac{1}{4\pi\varepsilon_0} = 9 \times 10^9\right]$$

By definition, the work done in joules to bring a unit positive charge from infinity to P is equal to potential at P in volts.

---

*   The negative sign is taken because dx is considered in the negative direction of distance (x).

$$\therefore \qquad V_p = 9 \times 10^9 \, \frac{Q}{\varepsilon_r d} \text{ volts} \qquad \qquad ...in\ a\ medium$$

$$= 9 \times 10^9 \, \frac{Q}{d} \text{ volts} \qquad \qquad ...in\ air$$

Electric potential is a scalar quantity. Therefore, electric potential at a point due to a number of charges is equal to the algebraic sum of potentials due to each charge.

5.12. POTENTIAL OF A CHARGED SPHERE

Consider an isolated sphere of radius r metres placed in air and charged uniformly with Q coulombs. The electric field has spherical symmetry *i.e.*, lines of force spread out normally from the surface and meet at the centre of the sphere if produced backward. Outside the sphere, the electric field is exactly the same as though the charge Q on sphere were concentrated at its centre.

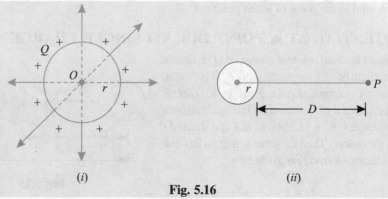

(i) (ii)

Fig. 5.16

(i) *Potential at the sphere surface.* Due to spherical symmetry of the field, we can imagine the charge Q on the sphere as concentrated at its centre O [See Fig. 5.16 (*i*)]. The problem then reduces to find the potential at a point r metres from a charge Q.

$$\therefore \qquad \text{Potential at the surface of sphere} = \frac{Q}{4\pi\varepsilon_0 r} \text{ volts} \qquad \qquad \text{[See Art. 5.11]}$$

$$= 9 \times 10^9 \, \frac{Q}{r} \overset{*}{} \text{ Volts}$$

(ii) *Potential outside the sphere.* Consider a point P outside the sphere as shown in Fig. 5.16 (*ii*). Let this point be at a distance of D metres from the surface of sphere.

$$\text{Then potential at } P = 9 \times 10^9 \, \frac{Q}{(D+r)} \text{ volts}$$

(iii) *Potential inside the sphere.* Since there is no electric flux inside the sphere, electric intensity inside the sphere is zero.

Now,   electric intensity $= \dfrac{\text{change in potential}}{r}$

or $0 = \text{change in potential}$

Hence all the points inside the sphere are at the same potential as the points on the surface.

* If sphere is placed in a medium (ε_r), then potential is $= 9 \times 10^9 \, \dfrac{Q}{\varepsilon_r r}$.

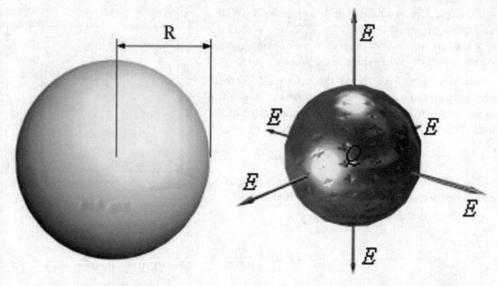

Charged sphere   Field due to charged sphere

Example 5.14. *A point charge of 1 μC is placed between points A and B 3 m apart. Point A is 2 m from the charge and point B is 1 m from the charge. What is the potential difference $V_A - V_B$?*

Solution.

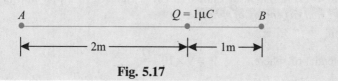

Fig. 5.17

Potential at A due to the charge, $V_A = 9 \times 10^9 \times \dfrac{1 \times 10^{-6}}{2} = 4.5 \times 10^3$ V

Potential at B due to the charge, $V_B = 9 \times 10^9 \dfrac{1 \times 10^{-6}}{1} = 9 \times 10^3$ V

∴ $V_A - V_B = 4.5 \times 10^3 - 9 \times 10^3 = -4.5 \times 10^3$ V

Example 5.15. *Two positive point charges of 16×10^{-10} C and 12×10^{-10} C are placed 10 cm apart. Find the work done in bringing the two charges 4 cm closer.*

Solution. Suppose the charge 16×10^{-10} C to be fixed.

Potential of a point 10 cm from the charge 16×10^{-10} C $= 9 \times 10^9 \dfrac{16 \times 10^{-10}}{0.1} = 144$ V

Potential of a point 6 cm from the charge 16×10^{-10} C $= 9 \times 10^9 \dfrac{16 \times 10^{-10}}{0.06} = 240$ V

∴ Potential difference $= 240 - 144 = 96$ V

Work done = Charge × p.d. $= 12 \times 10^{-10} \times 96 = \mathbf{11.52 \times 10^{-8}}$ **joules**

Example 5.16. *A square ABCD has each side of 1 m. Four point charges of + 0.01 μC, – 0.02 μC, + 0.03 μC and + 0.02 μC are placed at A, B, C and D respectively. Find the potential at the centre of the square.*

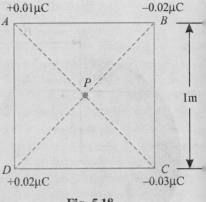

Solution. Fig. 5.18 shows the square *ABCD* with charges placed at its corners. The diagonals of the square intersect at point *P*. Clearly, point *P* is the centre of the square. The distance of each charge from point *P* is

$$= \frac{1}{2}\sqrt{1^2 + 1^2} = \frac{1}{2} \times \sqrt{2} = 0.07 \text{ m}$$

The potential at point *P* due to all charges is equal to the algebraic sum of potentials due to each charge.

∴ Potential at *P* due to all charges

Fig. 5.18

$$= 9 \times 10^9 \left[\frac{Q_1}{0.707} + \frac{Q_2}{0.707} + \frac{Q_3}{0.707} + \frac{Q_4}{0.707} \right]$$

$$= \frac{9 \times 10^9}{0.707} \left[(0.01 - 0.02 + 0.03 + 0.02) \, 10^{-6} \right]$$

$$= \frac{9 \times 10^9}{0.707} \times 0.04 \times 10^{-6} = 509.2 \text{ V}$$

Example 5.17. *A sphere of radius 10 cm is charged to a potential of 4500 volts. Calculate (i) the charge and (ii) energy of sphere.*

Solution.

(*i*) Potential of sphere, $V = 9 \times 10^9 \dfrac{Q}{r}$

∴ Charge on sphere, $Q = \dfrac{4500 \times 0.1}{9 \times 10^9} = 0.05 \times 10^{-6} \text{ C} = 0.05 \text{ μC}$

(*ii*) Energy of sphere $= \dfrac{1}{2} QV = \dfrac{1}{2} \times (0.05 \times 10^{-6}) \times 4500 = 112.5 \times 10^{-6} \text{ joules}$

Example 5.18. *24×10^{-3} J of energy is required to move 400 μC positive charge shown in Fig. 5.19 from the negatively charged plate to the positively charged plate.*

(*i*)   *What is the potential difference between the two charged plates ?*
(*ii*) *What is the electric intensity in the region between the plates?*

Solution.

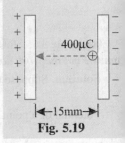

Fig. 5.19

(*i*)   P.D. between plates, $V = \dfrac{W}{Q} = \dfrac{24 \times 10^{-3}}{400 \times 10^{-6}} = 60 \text{ V}$

(*ii*) Electric intensity *E* between plates is given by ;

$$E = \frac{V}{d} = \frac{60}{15 \times 10^{-3}} = 4000 \text{ V/m}$$

TUTORIAL PROBLEMS

1. A charge of -4.5×10^{-7} C is carried from a distant point upto a charged metal sphere. What is the electrical potential of the body if the work done is 1.8×10^{-3} joule? **[4×10^3 V]**

2. The difference of potentials between two points in an electric field is 6 volts. How much work is required to move a charge of 300 μC between these points? **[1.8×10^{-3} joule]**

3. A force of 0.032 N is required to move a charge of 42 μC in an electric field between two points 25 cm apart. What potential difference exists between the two points?

   [1.9×10^2 V]

4. What is the magnitude of an isolated positive charge to give an electric potential of 100 V at 10 cm from the charge? **[1.11×10^{-9} C]**

5. A square ABCD has each side of 1 m. Four charges of + 0.02 μC, + 0.04 μC, + 0.06 μC and + 0.02 μC are placed at A, B, C and D respectively. Find the potential at the centre of square.
   [1000 V]

6. A sphere of radius 0.1 m has a charge of 5×10^{-8} C. Determine the potential (*i*) at the surface of sphere, (*ii*) inside the sphere and (*iii*) at a distance of 1 m from the surface of the sphere. Assume air as the medium. **[(*i*) 4500 V (*ii*) 4500 V (*iii*) 409 V]**

5.13. POTENTIAL GRADIENT

The change of potential per unit distance is called **potential gradient** *i.e.,*

$$\text{Potential gradient} = \frac{V_2 - V_1}{S}$$

where $V_2 - V_1$ is the change in potential (or p.d.) between two points S metres apart. Obviously, the unit of potential gradient will be volts/m.

Consider a charge $+ Q$ and let there be two points A and B situated S metres apart in its electric field as shown in Fig. 5.20. Clearly, potential at point A is more than the potential at point B. If distance S is small, then the electric intensity will be approximately the same in this small distance. Let it be E newtons/coulomb. It means that a force of E newtons will act on a unit positive charge (*i.e.*, + 1

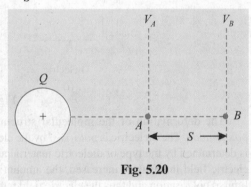

Fig. 5.20

C) placed anywhere between A and B. If a unit positive charge is moved from B to A, then work done to do so is given by;

$$\text{Work done} = E \times S \text{ joules}$$

But work done in bringing a unit positive charge from B to A is the potential difference $(V_A - V_B)$ between A and B.

∴ $$E \times S = V_A - V_B$$

or $$E = \frac{V_A - V_B}{S} = \text{Potential gradient}$$

In differential form, $$E = -\frac{^*dV}{dS}$$

----

* Since work done in moving + 1 C from B to A is against electric field, a negative sign must be used to make the equation technically correct.

Hence electric intensity at a point is numerically equal to the potential gradient at that point.

Since electric intensity is numerically equal to potential gradient at any point, both must be measured in the same units. Clearly, electric intensity can also be measured in V/m. For example when we say that potential gradient at a point is 1000 V/m, it means that electric intensity at that point is *1000 V/m or 1000 N/C.

5.14. DIELECTRICS

An insulator placed in an electric field is called a *dielectric*. The electric field stresses the molecular structure of the dielectric and causes static charges to build up within the dielectric. As shown in Fig. 5.21 (*i*), the surface of the dielectric nearest the positive plate becomes negatively charged while the surface nearest the negative plate becomes positively charged. These induced charges on the dielectric produce an electric field E_i that *opposes* the field E_0 set up by the charged plates. Note that prefix *di* in dielectric means *opposing* because dielectric sets up an electric field in opposition to that created by the charged plates. The result is that the electric field within the dielectric is less than in the air. It has been found that electric field in the dielectric becomes E_0/ε_r where ε_r is the relative permittivity of the dielectric. This is illustrated in Fig. 5.21 (*ii*).

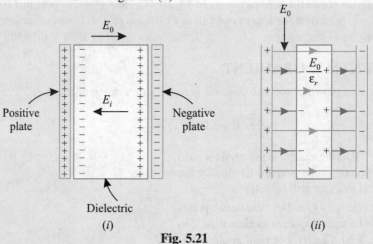

Fig. 5.21

The deformation of the molecular structure of the dielectric by the electric field is called *polarisation*. The dielectric is *polarised* by the electric field. The amount of polarisation of a dielectric is determined by the type of dielectric material and electric field intensity between the plates. As the electric field intensity is increased, the amount of polarisation also increases. However, there is a limit to polarisation and thus the electric field intensity that a given dielectric can tolerate. If this limit is exceeded, electrons are pulled free of the parent atoms and destructive current starts to flow through the dielectric. This may overheat and destroy the dielectric material.

5.15. BREAKDOWN VOLTAGE OR DIELECTRIC STRENGTH

In an insulator or dielectric, the valence electrons are tightly bound so that no free electrons are available for current conduction. However, when voltage applied to a dielectric is gradually increased, a point is reached when these electrons are torn away, a large current (much larger than the usual leakage current) flows through the dielectric and the material loses its insulating properties. Usually

---

* It can be shown that 1 V/m = 1 N/C as under :

$$1 \text{ V/m} = \frac{\text{joule/coulomb}}{\text{metre}} = \frac{\text{newton} \times \text{metre}}{\text{metre} \times \text{coulomb}} = 1 \text{ N/C}$$

spark or arc occurs which burns up the material. The mininum voltage required to breakdown a electric is called breakdown voltage or dielectric strength.

The maximum voltage which a unit thickness of a dielectric can withstand without being punctured a spark discharge is called **dielectric strength** *of the material.*

The dielectric strength (or breakdown voltage) is generally measured in kV/cm or kV/mm. For ample, air has a dielectric strength of 30 kV/cm. It means that maximum p.d. which 1 cm thickness air can withstand across it without breaking down is 30 kV.

Breakdown of air

Example 5.19. *A parallel plate capacitor has plates 1 mm apart and a dielectric with relative rmittivity of 3.39. Find (i) electric intensity and (ii) the voltage between plates if the surface charge 3 × 10^{-4} C/m^2.*

Solution. (*i*) The surface charge is equal to electric flux density D.

Now $\qquad\qquad\qquad\qquad D = \varepsilon_0 \varepsilon_r\, E$

∴ Electric intensity, $\qquad E = \dfrac{D}{\varepsilon_0 \varepsilon_r} = \dfrac{3 \times 10^{-4}}{8.854 \times 10^{-12} \times 3.39} = 10^7$ V/m

(*ii*) P.D. between plates, $\qquad V = E \times dx = 10^7 \times (1 \times 10^{-3}) = 10^4$ V

Example 5.20. *It is found that an electric field of 3 × 10^6 V/m in air will cause electrical eakdown of air. What is the greatest charge that can be placed on the sphere of 1m diameter? What the potential of the sphere for that charge?*

Solution. Electric intensity E is equal to the breakdown voltage (= 3 × 10^6 V/m).

Let Q coulomb be the maximum charge that can be placed on the sphere.

Electric intensity at the surface of sphere, $E = 9 \times 10^9\, \dfrac{Q}{r^2}$ $\qquad\qquad$ (*medium is air*)

or $\qquad\qquad Q = \dfrac{E \times r^2}{9 \times 10^9} = \dfrac{(3 \times 10^6) \times (0.5)^2}{9 \times 10^9} = 83.3 \times 10^{-6}\,C = 83.3\ \mu C$

Potential of Sphere, $\qquad V = 9 \times 10^9\, \dfrac{Q}{r} = 9 \times 10^9 \times \dfrac{83.3 \times 10^{-6}}{0.5} = 15 \times 10^5$ V

Example 5.21. *A sheet of glass 1.5 cm thick and of relative permittivity 7 is introduced between o parallel brass plates 2 cm apart. The remainder of the space between the plates is occupied by r. If a p.d. of 10,000 V is applied between the plates, calculate (i) electric intensity of air film tween glass and plate and (ii) in the glass sheet.*

Solution. Fig. 5.22 shows the arrangement. Let V_1 and V_2 be the p.d. across air and glass respectively and E_1 and E_2 the corresponding electric intensities.

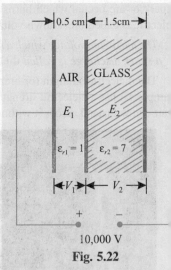

Now, $V_1 = E_1 x_1$

$\quad\quad\quad = E_1 \times (0.5 \times 10^{-2})$

and $\quad V_2 = E_2 x_2$

$\quad\quad\quad = E_2 \times (1.5 \times 10^{-2})$

Now $\quad V = V_1 + V_2$

or $\quad 10,000 = (0.5\,E_1 + 1.5\,E_2)\,10^{-2}$

or $\quad E_1 + 3\,E_2 = 2 \times 10^6$ ...(i)

Now electric flux density $D\,(= \varepsilon_0 \varepsilon_r\,E)$ is the same in the two media because it is independent of the surrounding medium.

$\therefore \quad\quad \varepsilon_0\,\varepsilon_{r1}\,E_1 = \varepsilon_0\,\varepsilon_{r2}\,E_2$

or $\quad\quad\quad E_1 = 7\,E_2$ ...(ii)

Fig. 5.22

From exps. (i) and (ii), we get,

(i) Electric intensity in air $= \mathbf{1.4 \times 10^6}$ V/m ; (ii) Electric intensity in glass $= \mathbf{0.2 \times 10^6}$ V/m

Example 5.22. *A capacitor has two dielectrics 1 mm and 2 mm thick. The relative permittivit of these dielectrics are 3 and 6 respectively. Calculate the potential gradient along the dielectr if a p.d. of 1000 V is applied between the plates.*

Solution. Fig. 5.23 shows the arrangement. Finding the potential gradient means to find the electric intensity (or electric stress).

$\quad\quad\quad V_1 = E_1 x_1$

$\quad\quad\quad\quad = E_1 \times (1 \times 10^{-3})$

$\quad\quad\quad V_2 = E_2 x_2$

$\quad\quad\quad\quad = E_2 \times (2 \times 10^{-3})$

Now $\quad V = V_1 + V_2$

or $\quad\quad 1000 = (E_1 + 2E_2)\,10^{-3}$

or $\quad\quad E_1 + 2E_2 = 10^6$ ...(i)

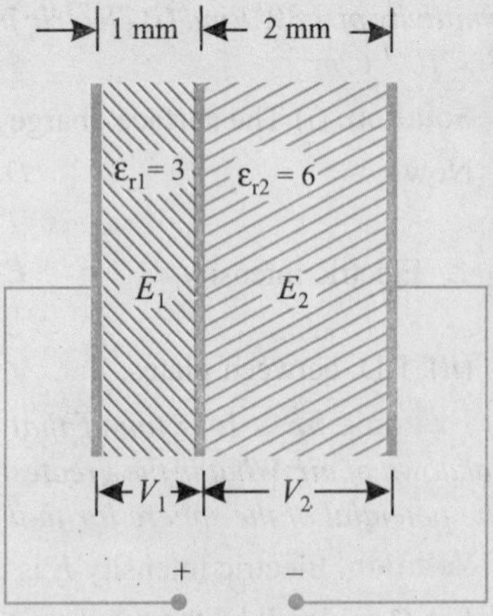

Since electric flux density $D\,(= \varepsilon_0 \varepsilon_r E)$ is the same in the two media,

$\therefore \quad\quad \varepsilon_0 \varepsilon_{r1} E_1 = \varepsilon_0 \varepsilon_{r2} E_2$

or $\quad\quad\quad 3\,E_1 = 6\,E_2$ ...(

From exps. (i) and (ii), we get,

$$E_1 = 0.5 \times 10^6 \text{ V/m} ; \quad E_2 = 0.25 \times 10^6 \text{ V/m}$$

Fig. 5.23

Example 5.23. *Two parallel plates are charged to have a potential difference of 100 V. Each h an area of 0.05 m^2 and they are separated by 1.0 mm of air. Assuming that all electric flux is contain between the plates, calculate the electric charge on each plate.*

Solution.

Electric field intensity, $\quad E = \dfrac{dV}{dS} = \dfrac{100}{1 \times 10^{-3}} = 10^5$ V/m

Electric flux density, $D = \varepsilon_0 \varepsilon_r E = 8.854 \times 10^{-12} \times 1 \times 10^5 = 8.854 \times 10^{-7} \ C/m^2$

Charge on each plate, $Q = DA = 8.854 \times 10^{-7} \times 0.05 = 4.427 \times 10^{-8} \ C$

TUTORIAL PROBLEMS

1. A parallel plate capacitor is built up from two metal plates, each of area 0.05 m^2, separated 0.02 mm by a dielectric. If the p.d. between plates is 200 V, and charge on each plate is 10 μC, find (*i*) the electric flux density between the plates and (*ii*) absolute permittivity of dielectric.
   [(*i*) $2 \times 10^{-4} \ C/m^2$ (*ii*) 20 pF/m]

2. A capacitor consists of two parallel plates 5 mm apart. The space between the plates is filled with a layer of paper 2 mm thick and a sheet of glass 3 mm thick. The relative permittivities of paper and glass are 2 and 8 respectively. A p.d. of 5 kV is applied between the plates. Find the potential gradient in each dielectric.   [1.82 kV/mm in paper ; 0.453 kV/mm in glass]

3. Two parallel metal plates of large area are spaced at a distance of 1 cm from each other in air and a p.d. of 5 kV is maintained between them. If a sheet of glass, 0.5 cm thick and having a relative permittivity of 6, is introduced between the plates, what will be the maximum electric stress and where will it occur?   [8.58 kV/cm in air gap]

4. A capacitor is composed of two plates separated by three dielectrics each of thickness 1 mm and relative permittivity 2, 4 and 5 respectively. A p.d. of 1000 V is applied between the plates. Calculate the potential gradient in each dielectric.
   [5.26×10^5 V/m; 2.63×10^5 V/m; 2.11×10^5 V/m]

MULTIPLE-CHOICE QUESTIONS

1. Which of the following appliance will be studied under electrostatics?
   (*a*) incandescent lamp   (*b*) electric iron
   (*c*) lightning rod   (*d*) electric motor

2. The relative permittivity of a material is 10. Its absolute permittivity will be
   (*a*) 8.854×10^{-11} F/m   (*b*) 9×10^8 F/m
   (*c*) 5×10^{-5} F/m   (*d*) 9×10^5 F/m

3. Another name for relative permittivity is
   (*a*) dielectric constant
   (*b*) dielectric strength
   (*c*) potential gradient
   (*d*) none of the above

4. There are two charges of + 1 μC and + 5 μC. The ratio of the forces acting on them will be
   (*a*) 1 : 5   (*b*) 1 : 1
   (*c*) 5 : 1   (*d*) 1 : 25

5. A soap bubble is given a negative charge. Its radius
   (*a*) decreases
   (*b*) increases
   (*c*) remains unchanged
   (*d*) information is incomplete to say anything

6. If the relative permittivity of the medium increases, the electric intensity at a point due to a given charge
   (*a*) decreases   (*b*) increases
   (*c*) remains the same
   (*d*) none of the above

7. A charge Q_1 exerts some force on a second charge Q_2. A third charge Q_3 is brought near. The force of Q_1 exerted on Q_2
   (*a*) decreases   (*b*) increases
   (*c*) remains unchanged
   (*d*) increases if Q_3 is of the same sign as Q_1 and decreases if Q_3 is of opposite sign

8. The potential at a point due to a charge is 9 V. If the distance is increased three times, the potential at that point will
   (*a*) 27 V   (*b*) 3 V
   (*c*) 12 V   (*d*) 18 V

9. The force between two charges separated by a distance *d* in air is 10 N. When the charges are placed same distance apart in a medium of dielectric constant ε_r, the force between them is 2 N. What is the value of ε_r?
   (*a*) 0.5   (*b*) 20
   (*c*) 5   (*d*) none of above

10. Two equal and similar charges are placed a finite distance apart. A third equal and dissimilar charge is placed mid-way between them. The third charge will be

   (a) in stable equilibrium

   (b) in unstable equilibrium

   (c) neutralised (d) oscillating

11. A tiny particle carrying a charge of 0.3 C is accelerated through a potential difference of 1000 V. The kinetic energy acquired by the particle is

   (a) 900 J (b) 400 J

   (c) 100 J (d) 300 J

12. When a charge is brought from infinity along the perpendicular bisector of a dipole, the work done is

   (a) positive (b) negative

   (c) zero (d) none of above

13. An α-particle is accelerated through a potential difference of 10^4 V. The gain in kinetic energy of the α-particle is

   (a) 2×10^{-4} eV (b) 2×10^4 J

   (c) 2×10^4 eV (d) none of above

14. The ratio of force between two small conducting spheres charged to constant potentials in air and a medium of dielectric constant 2 is

   (a) 1 : 2 (b) 2 : 1

   (c) 1 : 4 (d) 4 : 1

15. A cloud is at a potential of 8×10^6 V relative to the ground. A charge of 40 C is transferred in lightning stroke between the cloud and the ground. The energy dissipated is

   (a) 3.2×10^{-7} J (b) 6.4×10^8 J

   (c) 5×10^{-6} J (d) 3.2×10^8 J

16. Two parallel metal plates maintained at a potential difference of 1000 V are separated by 0.02 m. An electron is placed between the two plates. The force experienced by the electron is

   (a) 1.6×10^{-19} N (b) 8×10^{-15} N

   (c) 1000 N (d) none of above

17. An oil drop carries 6 electronic charges and falls with a terminal velocity in air. What magnitude of vertical electric field is required to make the drop move upward with the same speed as it was formerly moving downward? Mass of oil drop = 1.6×10^{-15} kg.

   (a) 32.7 kNC^{-1} (b) 600 NC^{-1}

   (c) 31.7 kNC^{-1} (d) none of above

18. Two plates are 1 cm apart and the potential difference between them is 10 V. The electric field between the plates is

   (a) 500 N/C (b) 1000 N/C

   (c) 10 N/C (d) 250 N/C

19. n drops each of radius r and carrying charge are combined to form a bigger drop of radius R. What is the ratio of potentials of bigger to that of the smaller?

   (a) $n^{3/2} : 1$ (b) $n^{1/3} : 1$

   (c) $n^{3/4} : 1$ (d) $n^{2/3} : 1$

20. A metal sphere of radius 15 cm hangs from a thread in a very large room. What must be the absolute potential of the sphere if the electric field at its surface is to be equal to the break down strength of air (3 MVm^{-1})?

   (a) 450 kV (b) 50 kV

   (c) 90 kV (d) 30 kV

Answers to Multiple-Choice Questions

1. (c) 2. (a) 3. (a) 4. (b) 5. (b) 6. (a) 7. (c) 8. (b)

9. (c) 10. (b) 11. (d) 12. (c) 13. (c) 14. (a) 15. (d) 16. (b)

17. (a) 18. (b) 19. (d) 20. (a)

Hints to Selected Multiple-Choice Questions

2. $\varepsilon_r = \varepsilon/\varepsilon_0$ $\therefore$ Absolute permittivity, $\varepsilon = \varepsilon_0 \varepsilon_r = 8.854 \times 10^{-12} \times 10 = 8.854 \times 10^{-11}$ F/m

6. Electric intensity (E) at a point in a medium due to charge Q is

$$E = 9 \times 10^9 \frac{Q}{\varepsilon_r d^2}$$

Therefore, as the relative permittivity (ε_r) of the medium increases, the electric field intensity decreases.

7. Superposition principle.
8. Electric potential at a point due to charge Q is

$$V = 9 \times 10^9 \frac{Q}{\varepsilon_r d} \text{ volts}$$

It is clear that electric potential is inversely proportional to the distance of the point from the given charge.

9.

$$\varepsilon_r = \frac{F_{air}}{F_m} = \frac{10}{2} = 5$$

10. If the third charge is moved slightly towards one of charges, it would experience greater attraction due to that charge compared to the other one. Therefore, the third charge is in unstable equilibrium.
11. K.E. acquired = charge × p.d. = 0.3 × 1000 = **300 joules**
12. There is no electric field inside a charged conductor.
13. K.E. = charge × p.d. = **2 × 10⁴ eV**

14.

$$F_{air} = \frac{1}{4\pi\varepsilon_0} \frac{Q_1 Q_2}{d^2}$$

In order to keep potential same in the medium, charges shall have to be increased ε_r (= 2) times.

∴

$$F_m = \frac{1}{4\pi\varepsilon_0 \varepsilon_r} \times \varepsilon_r^2 \frac{Q_1 Q_2}{d^2} = \frac{1}{4\pi\varepsilon_0} \times \varepsilon_r \frac{Q_1 Q_2}{d^2}$$

∴

$$\frac{F_{air}}{F_m} = \frac{1}{\varepsilon_r} = \frac{1}{2}$$

15. Energy dissipated = charge × p.d. = 40 × (8 × 10⁶) = **3.2 × 10⁸ J**

16.

$$E = \frac{V}{d} = \frac{1000}{0.02} = 5 \times 10^4 \text{ V/m}$$

Force experienced by the electron is

$$F = qE = (1.6 \times 10^{-19}) \times 5 \times 10^4 = 8 \times 10^{-15} \text{ N}$$

17. Since the drop falls with a terminal velocity, the upward force on it is equal to weight mg of the drop. In order that the drop moves upward with the same speed, a force of $2mg$ must act on it in the upward direction.

∴

$$2mg = qE \text{ or } E = \frac{2mg}{q} = \frac{2mg}{6e} = \frac{2 \times 1.6 \times 10^{-15} \times 9.8}{6 \times 1.6 \times 10^{-19}}$$

$$= 32.7 \times 10^3 \text{ NC}^{-1} = 32.7 \text{ kNC}^{-1}$$

18.

$$E = \frac{V}{d} = \frac{10}{1 \times 10^{-2}} = 1000 \text{ N/C}$$

19.

$$n \times \frac{4}{3} \pi r^3 = \frac{4}{3} \pi R^3 \text{ or } R = r n^{1/3}$$

Now $V_1 \propto q/r$ and $V_2 \propto nq/R$

∴

$$\frac{V_2}{V_1} = \frac{nr}{R} = \frac{nr}{n^{1/3} \times r} = \frac{n^{2/3}}{1}$$

20. Since the room is very large, the surroundings are essentially at infinity.

∴

$$V = E \times r = 3 \times 10^6 \times (15 \times 10^{-2}) = 450 \times 10^3 \text{ V} = \text{450 kV}$$

Capacitance

INTRODUCTION

It is well known that different bodies hold different charge when given the same potential. This charge holding property of a body is called *capacitance* or *capacity* of the body. In order to store sufficient charge, a device called capacitor is purposely constructed. A capacitor essentially consists of two conducting surfaces (say metal plates) separated by an insulating material (*e.g.*, air, mica, paper *etc.*). It has the property to store electrical energy in the form of electrostatic charge. The capacitor can be connected in a circuit so that this stored energy can be made to flow in a desired circuit to perform a useful function. Capacitance plays an important role in d.c. as well as a.c. circuits. In many circuits (*e.g.*, radio and television circuits), capacitors are intentionally inserted to introduce the desired capacitance. In this chapter, we shall confine our attention to the role of capacitance in d.c. circuits only.

6.1. CAPACITOR

Any two conducting surfaces separated by an insulating material is called a capacitor or condenser.

The conducting surfaces are called the *plates* of the capacitor and the insulating material is called the *dielectric*. The most commonly used dielectrics are air, mica, waxed paper, ceramics *etc*. The following points may be noted carefully :

(i)   The ability of a capacitor to store charge (*i.e.*, its capacitance) depends upon the area of plates, distance between plates and the nature of insulating material (or dielectric).

(ii) A capacitor is generally named after the dielectric used *e.g.* air capacitor, paper capacitor, mica capacitor *etc*.

(iii) The capacitor may be in the form of parallel plates, concentric cylinder or other arrangement.

6.2.   HOW DOES A CAPACITOR STORE CHARGE ?

Fig. 6.1 shows how a capacitor stores charge when connected to a d.c. supply. The parallel plate capacitor having plates *A* and *B* is connected across a battery of *V* volts as shown in Fig. 6.1 (*i*). With the switch *S* open as shown in Fig. 6.1 (*i*), the capacitor plates are neutral *i.e.*, there is no charge on the plates. When the switch is closed as shown in Fig. 6.1 (*ii*), the electrons from plate *A* will be attracted by the +ve terminal of the battery and these electrons start **accumulating on plate *B*. The result is that plate *A* attains more and more positive charge and plate *B* gets more and more negative charge. This action is referred to as charging a capacitor because the capacitor plates are becoming charged. This process of electron flow or charging (*i.e.*, detaching electrons from plate *A* and accumulating on *B*) continues till p.d. across capacitor plates becomes equal to battery voltage *V*. When the capacitor is charged to battery voltage *V*, the current flow ceases as shown in Fig. 6.1 (*iii*). If now the switch is opened as shown in Fig. 6.1 (*iv*), the capacitor plates will retain the charges. Thus the capacitor plates which were neutral to start with now have charges on them. This shows that a capacitor stores charge.

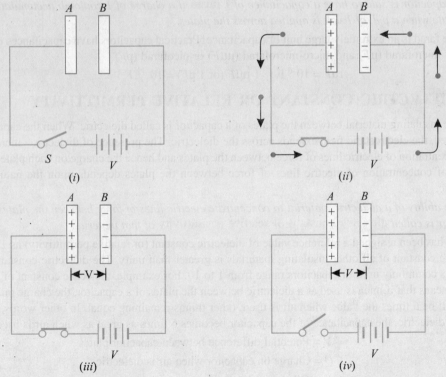

Fig. 6.1

* A steady current cannot pass through an insulator but an electric field can. For this reason, an insulator is often referred to as a dielectric.

** The electrons cannot flow from plate *B* to *A* as there is insulating material between the plates. Hence electrons detached from plate *A* start piling up on plate *B*.

Note. When a capacitor is charged, the two plates carry equal and opposite charges (say $+Q$ and $-Q$). This is expected because one plate loses as many electrons as the other plate gains. Thus charge on a capacitor means charge on *either* plate.

6.3. CAPACITANCE

The ability of a capacitor to store charge is known as its capacitance. It has been found experimentally that charge Q stored in a capacitor is directly proportional to the p.d. across it *i.e.*

$$Q \propto V$$

or

$$\frac{Q}{V} = \text{Constant} = C$$

The constant C is called the capacitance of the capacitor. Hence, capacitance of a capacitor can be defined as under :

The ratio of charge on capacitor plates to the p.d. across the plates is called **capacitance** *of the capacitor.*

Unit of Capacitance

We know that $\qquad C = Q/V$

The SI unit of charge is 1 coulomb and that of voltage is 1 volt. Therefore, the SI unit of capacitance is 1 coulomb/volt which is also called *farad* (Symbol F) in honour of Michael Faraday.

$$1 \text{ farad} = 1 \text{ coulomb/volt}$$

A capacitor is said to have a capacitance of **1 farad** *if a charge of 1 coulomb accumulates on each plate when a p.d. of 1 volt is applied across the plates.*

The farad is an extremely large unit of capacitance. Practical capacitors have capacitances of the order of microfarad (μF) and micro-microfarad ($\mu\mu F$) or picofarad (pF).

$$1\mu F = 10^{-6} \text{ F} \; ; \quad 1 \text{ } \mu\mu F \text{ (or 1 } pF) = 10^{-12} \text{ } F$$

6.4. DIELECTRIC CONSTANT OR RELATIVE PERMITTIVITY

The insulating material between the plates of a capacitor is called dielectric. When the capacitor is charged, the electrostatic field extends across the dielectric. The presence of dielectric* increases the concentration of electric lines of force between the plates and hence the charge on each plate. The degree of concentration of electric lines of force between the plates depends upon the nature of dielectric.

The ability of a dielectric material to concentrate electric lines of force between the plates of a capacitor is called **dielectric constant** *or* **relative permittivity** *of that material.*

Air has been assigned a reference value of dielectric constant (or relative permittivity) as 1. The dielectric constant of all other insulating materials is greater than unity. The dielectric constants of materials commonly used in capacitors range from 1 to 10. For example, dielectric constant of mica is 6. It means that if mica is used as a dielectric between the plates of a capacitor, the charge on each plate will be 6 times the value when air is used; other things remaining equal. In other words, with mica as dielectric, the capacitance of the capacitor becomes 6 times as great as when air is used.

Let $\qquad V = $ Potential difference between capacitor plates

$\qquad Q = $ Charge on capacitor when air is dielectric

Then $\qquad C_{air} = Q/V$

---
* Normally the electrons of the atoms of the dielectric revolve round their nuclei in their regular orbits. When the capacitor is charged, the electro-static field causes distortion of the orbits of the electrons of the dielectric. This distortion of orbits causes more electrons to be transferred from one plate to the other. Hence, the presence of dielectric increases the charge on the capacitor plates and hence the capacitance.

When mica is used as a dielectric in the same capacitor and the same p.d. is applied, the capacitor will now hold a charge of $6\,Q$.

$$\therefore \qquad C_{mica} = \frac{6\,Q}{V} = 6\,\frac{Q}{V} = 6\,C_{air}$$

or $\qquad \dfrac{C_{mica}}{C_{air}} = 6 = $ Dielectric constant of mica

Hence **dielectric constant** (*or* **relative permittivity**) of a dielectric material is the ratio of capacitance of a capacitor with that material as a dielectric to the capacitance of the same capacitor with air as dielectric.

6.5. PARALLEL PLATE CAPACITOR WITH UNIFORM MEDIUM

Consider a parallel plate capacitor consisting of two plates, each of area A square metres and separated by a *uniform* dielectric of thickness d metres and relative permittivity ε_r as shown in Fig. 6.2. Let a p.d. of V volts applied between the plates place a charge of $+\,Q$ and $-\,Q$ on the plates. Suppose E and D respectively are the electric intensity and electric flux density between the plates.

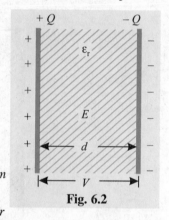

Fig. 6.2

Now, $\qquad D = Q/A$ coulomb/m^2

and $\qquad E = V/d$

But $\qquad D = \varepsilon_0 \varepsilon_r E$

$\therefore \qquad \dfrac{Q}{A} = \varepsilon_0 \varepsilon_r \dfrac{V}{d}$

or $\qquad \dfrac{Q}{V} = \dfrac{\varepsilon_0 \varepsilon_r\, A}{d}$

The ratio Q/V is the capacitance C of the capacitor.

$\therefore \qquad C = \dfrac{\varepsilon_0 \varepsilon_r\, A}{d} \qquad$ ...*in a medium*

$\qquad\qquad = \dfrac{\varepsilon_0\, A}{d} \qquad\qquad$ ...*in air*

It may be seen that capacitance is directly proportional to relative permittivity of the medium (ε_r) and area (A) of capacitor plate. However, it is inversely proportional to the distance (d) between the plates.

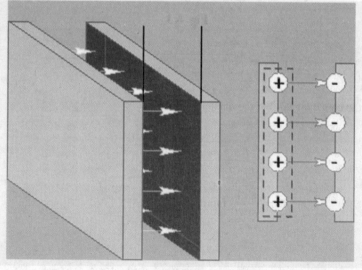

Parallel Plate Capacitor

6.6. PARALLEL-PLATE CAPACITOR WITH COMPOSITE MEDIUM

Suppose the space between the plates is occupied by three dielectrics of thickness d_1, d_2 and d_3 metres and relative permittivities ε_{r1}, ε_{r2} and ε_{r3} respectively as shown in Fig. 6.3. The electric flux density D in the dielectrics remains the *same and is equal to Q/A. However, the electric intensities in the three dielectrics will be different and are given by ;

$$E_1 = \frac{D}{\varepsilon_0\,\varepsilon_{r1}} ; \qquad E_2 = \frac{D}{\varepsilon_0\,\varepsilon_{r2}} ; \qquad E_3 = \frac{D}{\varepsilon_0\,\varepsilon_{r3}}$$

If V is the total p.d. across the capacitor and V_1, V_2 and V_3 the p.d.s across the three dielectrics respectively, then,

$$V = V_1 + V_2 + V_3 = E_1 d_1 + E_2 d_2 + E_3 d_3$$

$$= \frac{D}{\varepsilon_0\,\varepsilon_{r1}}\,d_1 + \frac{D}{\varepsilon_0\,\varepsilon_{r2}}\,d_2 + \frac{D}{\varepsilon_0\,\varepsilon_{r3}}\,d_3 = \frac{D}{\varepsilon_0}\left[\frac{d_1}{\varepsilon_{r1}} + \frac{d_2}{\varepsilon_{r2}} + \frac{d_3}{\varepsilon_{r3}}\right]$$

$$= \frac{Q}{\varepsilon_0 A}\left[\frac{d_1}{\varepsilon_{r1}} + \frac{d_2}{\varepsilon_{r2}} + \frac{d_3}{\varepsilon_{r3}}\right] \qquad \left(\because D = \frac{Q}{A}\right)$$

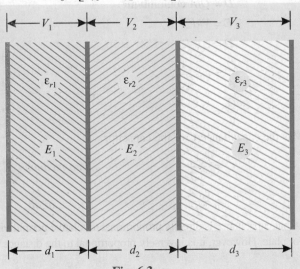

Fig. 6.3

or

$$\frac{Q}{V} = \frac{\varepsilon_0 A}{\left(\dfrac{d_1}{\varepsilon_{r1}} + \dfrac{d_2}{\varepsilon_{r2}} + \dfrac{d_3}{\varepsilon_{r3}}\right)}$$

But Q/V is the capacitance C of the capacitor.

$$\therefore \qquad C = \frac{\varepsilon_0 A}{\left(\dfrac{d_1}{\varepsilon_{r1}} + \dfrac{d_2}{\varepsilon_{r2}} + \dfrac{d_3}{\varepsilon_{r3}}\right)} \text{ farad}$$

In general, $\qquad C = \dfrac{\varepsilon_0 A}{\sum \dfrac{d}{\varepsilon_r}}$ farad $\qquad\qquad …(i)$

....

* The total charge on each plate is Q. Hence Q coulombs is also the total electric flux through each dielectric.

DIFFERENT CASES

(i) **Medium partly air.** Fig. 6.4 shows a parallel plate capacitor having plates d metres apart. Suppose the medium between the plates consists partly of air and partly of dielectric of thickness t metres and relative permittivity ε_{r2}. Then thickness of air is $d - t$. Using the relation (i) above, we have,

$$C = \frac{\varepsilon_0 A}{\dfrac{d-t}{1} + \dfrac{t}{\varepsilon_{r2}}} = \frac{\varepsilon_0 A}{d - \left(t - \dfrac{t}{\varepsilon_{r2}}\right)} \text{ farad}$$

(ii) **When dielectric slab introduced.** Fig. 6.5 shows a parallel-plate air capacitor having plates d metres apart. Suppose a dielectric slab of thickness t metres and relative permittivity ε_{r2} is introduced between the plates of the capacitor.

Using the relation (i) above, we have,

$$C = \frac{\varepsilon_0 A}{\dfrac{d-t}{1} + \dfrac{t}{\varepsilon_{r2}}} = \frac{\varepsilon_0 A}{d - \left(t - \dfrac{t}{\varepsilon_{r2}}\right)} \text{ farad}$$

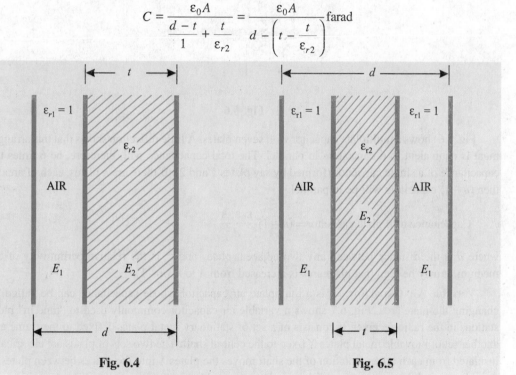

Fig. 6.4   Fig. 6.5

6.7. MULTIPLATE CAPACITOR

The most *convenient way of achieving large capacitance is by using large plate area. Increasing the plate area may increase the physical size of the capacitor enormously. In order to obtain a large area of plate surface without using too bulky a capacitor, multiplate construction is employed. In this construction, the capacitor is built up of alternate sheets of metal foil (i.e., plates) and thin sheets of dielectric. The odd-numbered metal sheets are connected together to form one terminal T_1 and even-numbered metal sheets are connected together to form the second terminal T_2.

* The capacitance of a capacitor can also be increased by (i) using a dielectric of high ε_r and (ii) decreasing the distance between plates. High cost limits the choice of dielectric and dielectric strength of the insulating material limits the reduction in spacing between the plates.

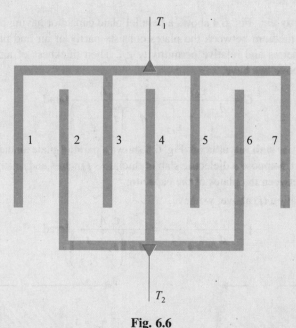

Fig. 6.6

Fig. 6.6 shows a multiplate capacitor with seven plates. A little reflection shows that this arrangement is equivalent to 6 capacitors in parallel. The total capacitance will, therefore, be 6 times the capacitance of a single capacitor (formed by say plates 1 and 2). If there are n plates, each of area A, then $(n-1)$ capacitors will be in parallel.

∴ Capacitance of n plate capacitor $= (n-1) \dfrac{\varepsilon_0 \varepsilon_r A}{d}$

where d is the distance between any two adjacent plates and ε_r is the relative permittivity of the medium. It may be seen that plate area is increased from A to $A(n-1)$.

Variable Air Capacitor. It is a multiplate air capacitor whose capacitance can be varied by changing the plate area. Fig. 6.7 shows a variable air capacitor commonly used to "tune in" radio stations in the radio receiver. It consists of a set of stationary metal plates Y fixed to the frame and another set of movable metal plates X fixed to the central shaft. The two sets of plates are electrically insulated from each other. Rotation of the shaft moves the plates X into the spaces between plates Y, thus changing the *common (or effective) plate area and hence the capacitance. The capacitance of such a capacitor is given by ;

$$C = (n-1) \frac{\varepsilon_0 A}{d} \qquad (\because \ \varepsilon_r = 1)$$

When the movable plates X are completely rotated in (*i.e.*, the two sets of plates completely overlap each other), the common plate area 'A' is maximum and so is the capacitance of the capacitor. Minimum capacitance is obtained when the movable plates X are completely rotated out of stationary plates Y. The capacitance of such variable capacitors is from zero to about 4000 pF.

. . . .

* Remember in the formula for capacitance, A is the common plate area *i.e.*, plate area facing the opposite polarity plate area.

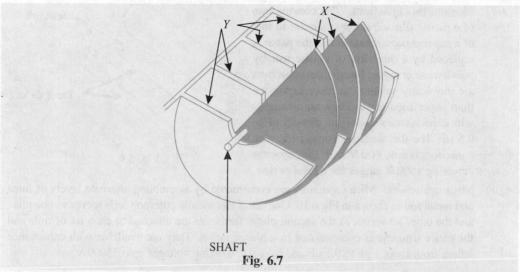

SHAFT
Fig. 6.7

Note. In all the formulas derived for capacitance, capacitance will be in farad if area is in m² and the distance between plates is in *m*.

Variable air capacitors

6.8. TYPES OF CAPACITORS

The capacitor's dielectric is largely responsible for determining its important characteristics. Therefore, capacitors are usually classified by the type of dielectric used. The important types of capacitors are :

(*i*) **Air capacitors.** An air capacitor uses air as the dielectric. Most air capacitors are of the variable type and are constructed as shown in Fig. 6.7 above. In such capacitors, the effective plate area and hence the capacitance ($C = \varepsilon_0 A/d$) is changed. Fig. 6.8 shows the symbol for a variable capacitor, which like the symbols of other variable devices, has an arrow drawn through it.

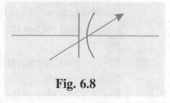

Fig. 6.8

(*ii*) **Paper capacitors.** A paper capacitor uses paper as the dielectric. In its simplest form, a paper capacitor consists of a layer of paper between two layers of metal foil as shown in Fig. 6.9. The arrangement is then rolled into a cylinder and dipped in plastic or wax. Paper capacitors are available with capacitance values ranging from about 500 pF to 50 μF and have d.c. working voltage ratings upto 600 V.

(*iii*) **Plastic film capacitors.** The construction of a plastic film capacitor is similar to that of a paper capacitor except that the paper is replaced by a thin film of plastic usually polystyrene or mylar. Plastic film capacitors are physically smaller but more expensive than paper capacitors. They are available with capacitance values from about 5 pF to 0.5 μF. The d.c. working voltage for such capacitors is upto 600 V with the capacitor surviving 1500 V surges for a brief period.

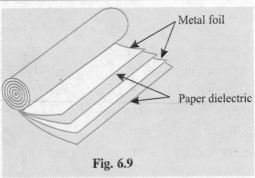

Fig. 6.9

(*iv*) **Mica capacitors.** Mica capacitors are constructed by assembling alternate layers of mica and metal foil as shown in Fig 6.10. One set of electrically common foils serves as one plate and the other set serves as the second plate. Terminals are attached to each set of foils and the entire structure is encapsulated in a plastic jacket. They are available with capacitance values from about 1 pF to 0.1 μF and have d.c. working voltages upto 35000 V.

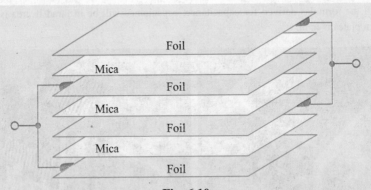

Fig. 6.10

(*v*) **Ceramic capacitors.** A ceramic capacitor is formed by depositing a metal film on each side of a ceramic base that serves as the dielectric as shown in Fig. 6.11. Because of very large permittivity of cermaics, we can obtain high values of capacitance. They are available in capacitance values from about 1 pF to 1 μF. Ceramic capacitors are also designed to serve as small variable capacitors called *trimmer* capacitors. These are screwdriver-adjustable devices with maximum capacitance values that are typically less than 100 pF.

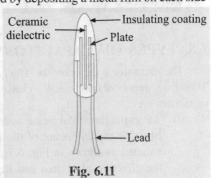

Fig. 6.11

(*vi*) **Electrolytic capacitors.** The most important feature of electrolytic capacitors is their very large capacitance in a physically small container. Fig. 6.12 (*i*) shows the essential parts of an aluminium electrolytic capacitor. It consists of two aluminium foils, one with aluminium oxide (Al_2O_3) film and the one without ; the foils being interleaved with a material such as a paper saturated with an electrolyte (*e.g.* ammonium borate). The oxide film is an insulator and acts as a dielectric. As a result, capacitance is formed between the positive aluminium electrode and the electrolyte in the gauge separator. The negative aluminium plate simply provides connection to the electrolyte. Generally, the metal can itself is the negative terminal of the capacitor as shown in Fig. 6.12 (*ii*). Because of the extremely thin dielectric film, very large capacitance values can be obtained.

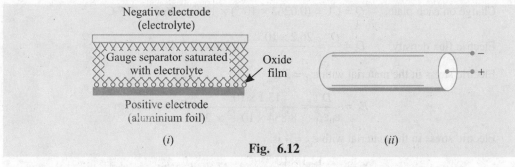

Negative electrode
(electrolyte)

Gauge separator saturated
with electrolyte

Oxide
film

Positive electrode
(aluminium foil)

(i)

Fig. 6.12

(ii)

It is very important that electrolytic capacitors be connected with correct polarity. The positive terminal of an electrolytic capacitor is always identified on the body of the capacitor. If the electrolytic capacitor is connected with reverse polarity, the electrochemical action reverses and the oxide film is removed. As a result, a very large current flows and the capacitor may **explode**. This could have **tragic consequences**.

Paper Capacitor

Electrolytic Capacitor

Example 6.1. *Calculate the capacitance of two metal plates of area 30 m^2 and separated by a dielectric 2 mm thick and of relative permittivity 6. If the electric field strength in the dielectric is 500 V/mm, calculate the total charge on each plate.*

Solution.

Capacitance,
$$C = \frac{\varepsilon_0 \, \varepsilon_r \, A}{d} = \frac{8.854 \times 10^{-12} \times 6 \times 30}{2 \times 10^{-3}} = 0.797 \times 10^{-6} \text{ F} = 0.797 \text{ } \mu F$$

Voltage across plates, $V = E \times d = 500 \times 2 = 1000 \text{ V}$

Charge on each plate, $Q = CV = (0.797 \times 10^{-6}) \times (1000) = 0.797 \times 10^{-3} \text{ C} = 0.797 \text{ mC}$

Example 6.2. *A parallel plate capacitor has plates of area 2 m^2 spaced by three layers of different dielectric materials. The relative permittivities are 2, 4, 6 and thicknesses are 0.5, 1.5 and 0.3 mm respectively. Calculate the combined capacitance and the electric stress in each material when applied voltage in 1000 V.*

Solution.

Capacitance,
$$C = \frac{\varepsilon_0 \, A}{\dfrac{d_1}{\varepsilon_{r1}} + \dfrac{d_2}{\varepsilon_{r2}} + \dfrac{d_3}{\varepsilon_{r3}}}$$

$$= \frac{8.854 \times 10^{-12} \times 2}{\dfrac{0.5 \times 10^{-3}}{2} + \dfrac{1.5 \times 10^{-3}}{4} + \dfrac{0.3 \times 10^{-3}}{6}} = 0.0262 \times 10^{-6} \text{ F}$$

Charge on each plate, $\quad Q = CV = (0.0262 \times 10^{-6}) \times 1000 = 26.2 \times 10^{-6}$ C

Electric flux density, $\quad D = \dfrac{Q}{A} = \dfrac{26.2 \times 10^{-6}}{2} = 13.1 \times 10^{-6}$ C/m^2

Electric stress in the material with $\varepsilon_{r1} = 2$ is

$$E_1 = \frac{D}{\varepsilon_0 \varepsilon_{r1}} = \frac{13.1 \times 10^{-6}}{8.854 \times 10^{-12} \times 2} = 74 \times 10^4 \text{ V/m}$$

Electric stress in the material with $\varepsilon_{r2} = 4$ is

$$E_2 = \frac{13.1 \times 10^{-6}}{8.854 \times 10^{-12} \times 4} = 37 \times 10^4 \text{ V/m}$$

Electric stress in the material with $\varepsilon_{r3} = 6$ is

$$E_3 = \frac{13.1 \times 10^{-6}}{8.854 \times 10^{-12} \times 6} = 24.67 \times 10^4 \text{ V/m}$$

It is clear from the above example that electric stress is greatest in the material having the least relative permittivity. Since air has the lowest relative permittivity, efforts should be made to avoid air pockets in the dielectric materials.

Example 6.3. *A capacitor is composed of two plates separated by 3 mm of dielectric of permittivity 4. An additional piece of insulation 5 mm thick is now inserted between the plates. If the capacitor now has capacitance one-third of its original capacitance, find the relative permittivity of the additional dielectric.*

Solution. Fig. 6.13 (*i*) and Fig. 6.13 (*ii*) respectively show the two cases.

For the first case, $\qquad C = \dfrac{\varepsilon_0 \varepsilon_r A}{d} = \dfrac{\varepsilon_0 \times 4 \times A}{3 \times 10^{-3}}$ $\qquad\qquad$ ...(*i*)

For the second case, $\quad \dfrac{C}{3} = \dfrac{\varepsilon_0 A}{\dfrac{d_1}{\varepsilon_{r1}} + \dfrac{d_2}{\varepsilon_{r2}}} = \dfrac{\varepsilon_0 A}{\dfrac{3 \times 10^{-3}}{4} + \dfrac{5 \times 10^{-3}}{\varepsilon_{r2}}}$ $\qquad$ ...(*ii*)

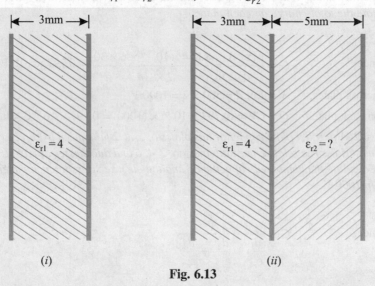

(*i*) $\qquad\qquad\qquad\qquad\qquad\qquad$ (*ii*)

Fig. 6.13

Dividing eq. (*i*) by eq. (*ii*), we get,

$$3 = \frac{4}{3}\left(\frac{3}{4} + \frac{5}{\varepsilon_{r2}}\right)$$

or $\qquad 9 = 3 + 20/\varepsilon_{r2} \qquad\qquad \therefore \ \varepsilon_{r2} = 20/6 = 3.33$

Example 6.4. *An air capacitor has two parallel plates of 1500 cm² in area and 5 mm apart. If a dielectric slab of area 1500 cm², thickness 2 mm and relative permittivity 3 is now introduced between the plates, what must be the new separation between the plates to bring the capacitance to the original value ?*

Solution. This is a case of introduction of dielectric slab into an air capacitor. As proved in Art. 6.6, the capacitance under this condition becomes :

$$C = \frac{\varepsilon_0 A}{d - (t - t/\varepsilon_r)} \qquad\qquad ...(i)$$

If the medium were totally air, capacitance would have been

$$C_{air} = \frac{\varepsilon_0 A}{d} \qquad\qquad ...(ii)$$

Inspection of eqs. (*i*) and (*ii*) shows that with the introduction of dielectric slab between the plates of air capacitor, its capacitance increases. The distance between the plates is effectively reduced by $t - (t/\varepsilon_r)$. In order to bring the capacitance to the original value, the plates must be separated by this much distance in air.

∴ New separation between the plates = $d + (t - t/\varepsilon_r) = 5 + (2 - 2/3) = 6.33$ mm

Example 6.5. *A parallel plate capacitor has three similar parallel plates. Find the ratio of capacitance when the inner plate is mid-way between the outers to the capacitance when inner plate is three times as near one plate as the other.*

Solution. Fig. 6.14 (*i*) shows the condition when the inner plate is mid-way between the outer plates. This arrangement is equivalent to two capacitors in parallel.

Capacitance of the capacitor $\quad C_1 = \dfrac{\varepsilon_0 \varepsilon_r A}{d/2} + \dfrac{\varepsilon_0 \varepsilon_r A}{d/2} = \dfrac{4\varepsilon_0 \varepsilon_r A}{d}$

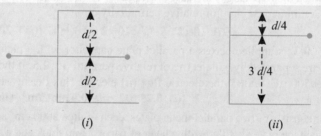

(*i*) $\qquad\qquad\qquad\qquad\qquad$ (*ii*)

Fig. 6.14

Fig 6.14 (*ii*) shows the condition when inner plate is three times as near as one plate as the other.

Capacitance of the capacitor $\quad C_2 = \dfrac{\varepsilon_0 \varepsilon_r A}{d/4} + \dfrac{\varepsilon_0 \varepsilon_r A}{3d/4} = \dfrac{16\varepsilon_0 \varepsilon_r A}{3d}$

∴ $\qquad\qquad\qquad \dfrac{C_1}{C_2} = 0.75$

Example 6.6. *A mica dielectric parallel plate capacitor has 21 plates each having an effective area of 5 cm² and each separated by a gap of 0.005 mm. Find the capacitance. Take the relative permittivity of mica as 6.*

Solution. For a multiplate capacitor, the capacitance is given by (See Art. 6.7) ;

$$C = (n-1) \frac{\varepsilon_0 \varepsilon_r A}{d} = (21-1) \frac{(8.854 \times 10^{-12}) \times 6 \times (5 \times 10^{-4})}{0.005 \times 10^{-3}}$$

$$= 0.1062 \times 10^{-6} \text{ F} = 0.1062 \text{ μF}$$

Example 6.7. *A variable air capacitor has 11 movable plates and 12 stationary plates. The area of each plate is 0.0015 m^2 and separation between opposite plates is 0.001 m. Determine the maximum capacitance of this variable capacitor.*

Solution. The capacitance will be maximum when the moveable plates are completely rotated in *i.e.*, when the two sets of plates completely overlap each other. Under this condition, the common (or effective) area is equal to the physical area of each plate.

$$C = (n-1) \frac{\varepsilon_0 \varepsilon_r A}{d}$$

Here $\qquad n = 11 + 12 = 23$; $\varepsilon_r = 1$; $A = 0.0015 \text{ m}^2$; $d = 0.001$ m

∴ $\qquad C = (23-1) \times \frac{8.854 \times 10^{-12} \times 1 \times 0.0015}{0.001} = 292 \times 10^{-12} \text{ F} = 292 \text{ pF}$

TUTORIAL PROBLEMS

1. A capacitor consisting of two parallel plates 0.5 mm apart in air and each of effective area 500 cm^2 is connected to a 100 V battery. Calculate (*i*) the capacitance and (*ii*) the charge.

    [(*i*) **885 pF** (*ii*) **0.0885 μC**]

2. A capacitor consisting of two parallel plates in air, each of effective area 50 cm^2 and 1 mm apart, carries a charge of 1770×10^{-12} C. Calculate the p.d. between the plates. If the distance between the plates is increased to 5 mm, what will be the electrical effect ?

    [**40 V** ; **p.d. across plates is increased to 200 V**]

3. Two insulated parallel plates each of 600 cm^2 effective area and 5 mm apart in air are charged to a p.d. of 1000 V. Calculate (*i*) the capacitance and (*ii*) the charge on each plate. The source of supply is now disconnected, the plates remaining insulated. Calculate (*iii*) the p.d. between the plates when their spacing is increased to 10 mm and (*iv*) the p.d. when the plates, still 10 mm apart, are immersed in oil of relative permittivity 5.

    [(*i*) **106.2 pF** (*ii*) **106.2 × 10⁻¹² C** (*iii*) **2000 V** (*iv*) **400 V**]

4. A p.d. of 500 V is applied across a parallel plate capacitor with a plate area of 0.025 m^2. The plates are separated by a dielectric of relative permittivity 2.5. If the capacitance of the capacitor is 500 μF, find (*i*) the electric flux (*ii*) electric flux density and (*iii*) the electric intensity. [(*i*) **0.25 μC** (*ii*) **0.01 mC/m²** (*iii*) **45.3 × 10⁶ V/m**]

5. A capacitor consists of two parallel metal plates, each of area 2000 cm^2 and 5 mm apart. The space between the plates is filled with a layer of paper 2 mm thick and a sheet of glass 3 mm thick. The relative permittivities of paper and glass are 2 and 8 respectively. A p.d. of 5 kV is applied across the plates. Calculate (*i*) the capacitance of the capacitor and (*ii*) the potential gradient in each dielectric. [(*i*) **1290 pF** (*ii*) **1820 V/mm (paper)** ; **453 V/mm (glass)**]

6. A parallel plate capacitor has a plate area of 20 cm^2 and the plates are separated by three dielectric layers each 1 mm thick and of relative permittivity 2, 4 and 5 respectively. Find the capacitance of the capacitor and the electric stress in each dielectric if applied voltage is 1000 V. [**18.6 pF** ; **5.26 × 10⁵ V/m** ; **2.63 × 10⁵ V/m** ; **2.11 × 10⁵ V/m**]

7. A 1 μF parallel plate capacitor that can just withstand a p.d. of 6000 V uses a dielectric having a relative permittivity 5, which breaks down if the electric intensity exceeds 30×10^6 V/m. Find (*i*) the thickness of dielectric required and (*ii*) the effective area of each plate.

    [(*i*) **0.2 mm** (*ii*) **4.5 m²**]

8. An air capacitor has two parallel plates 10 cm² in area and 5 mm apart. When a dielectric slab of area 10 cm² and thickness 5 mm was inserted between the plates ; one of the plates has to be moved by 0.4 cm to restore the capacitance. What is the dielectric constant of the slab? [5]

9. A multiplate parallel capacitor has 6 fixed plates connected in parallel interleaved with 5 similar plates; each plate has an effective area of 120 cm². The gap between the adjacent plates is 1 mm. The capacitor is immersed in oil of relative permittivity 5. Calculate the capacitance. [5.31 pF]

10. Calculate the number of sheets of tin foil and mica for a capacitor of 0.33 μF capacitance if area of each sheet of tin foil is 82 cm², the mica sheets are 0.2 mm thick and have relative permittivity 5.

[182 sheets of mica ; 183 sheets of tin foil]

6.9. CYLINDRICAL CAPACITOR

A cylindrical capacitor consists of two co-axial cylinders separated by an insulating medium. This is an important practical case since a single core cable is in effect a capacitor of this kind. The conductor (or core) of the cable is the inner cylinder while the outer cylinder is represented by lead sheath which is at earth potential. The two co-axial cylinders have insulation between them.

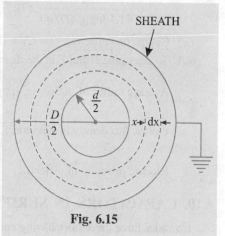

Fig. 6.15

Consider a single core cable with conductor diameter d metres and inner sheath diameter D metres (See Fig. 6.15). Let the charge per metre axial length of the cable be Q coulombs and ε_r be the relative permittivity of the insulating material. Consider a cylinder of radius x metres. According to Gauss's theorem, electric flux passing through this cylinder is Q coulombs. The surface area of this cylinder is

$$= 2\pi x \times 1 = 2\pi x \text{ m}^2$$

∴ Electric flux density at any point P on the considered cylinder is

$$D_x = \frac{Q}{2\pi x} \text{ C/m}^2$$

Electric intensity at point P is

$$E_x = \frac{D_x}{\varepsilon_0 \varepsilon_r} = \frac{Q}{2\pi x \varepsilon_0 \varepsilon_r} \text{ V/m}$$

The work done in moving a unit positive charge from point P through a distance dx in the direction of electric field is $E_x \, dx$. Hence the work done in moving a unit positive charge from conductor to sheath which is the p.d. V between the conductor and sheath is given by :

$$V = \int_{d/2}^{D/2} E_x \, dx = \int_{d/2}^{D/2} \frac{Q}{2\pi x \varepsilon_0 \varepsilon_r} \, dx = \frac{Q}{2\pi \varepsilon_0 \varepsilon_r} \log_e \frac{D}{d}$$

Capacitance of cable, $C = \dfrac{Q}{V} = \dfrac{Q}{\dfrac{Q}{2\pi \varepsilon_0 \varepsilon_r} \log_e \dfrac{D}{d}}$ F/m $= \dfrac{2\pi \varepsilon_0 \varepsilon_r}{\log_e (D/d)}$ F/m

$$= \frac{2\pi \times 8.854 \times 10^{-12} \times \varepsilon_r}{2.303 \log_{10} (D/d)} \text{ F/m} = \frac{\varepsilon_r}{41.4 \log_{10} (D/d)} \times 10^{-9} \text{ F/m}$$

If the cable has a length of l metres, then capacitance of the cable is

$$= \frac{\varepsilon_r l}{41.4 \log_{10}(D/d)} \times 10^{-9} \text{ F} = \frac{24\varepsilon_r l}{\log_{10}(D/d)} \text{ pF}$$

Example 6.8. *In a concentric cable 20 cm long, the diameters of inner and outer cylinders are 15 cm and 15.4 cm respectively. The relative permittivity of the insulation is 5. If a p.d. of 5000 V is maintained between the two cylinders, calculate :*

(i) *capacitance of cylindrical capacitor*

(ii) *the charge*

(iii) *the electric flux density and electric intensity in the dielectric.*

Solution.

(i) Capacitance of the cylindrical capacitor is

$$C = \frac{\varepsilon_r l}{41.4 \log_{10}(D/d)} \times 10^{-9} = \frac{5 \times 0.2}{41.4 \log_{10}(15.4/15)} \times 10^{-9} \text{ F} = 2.11 \times 10^{-9} \text{ F}$$

(ii) Charge on capacitor, $Q = CV = (2.11 \times 10^{-9}) \times 5000 = 10.55 \times 10^{-6} \text{ C} = 10.55 \text{ μC}$

(iii) To determine D and E in the dielectric, we shall consider the average radius of dielectric *i.e.*

Average radius of dielectric, $\quad x = \frac{1}{2}\left[\frac{15}{2} + \frac{15.4}{2}\right] = 7.6 \text{ cm} = 0.076 \text{ m}$

Electric flux density in dielectric, $\quad D = \frac{Q}{2\pi x l} \text{ C/m}^2 = \frac{10.55 \times 10^{-6}}{2\pi \times 0.076 \times 0.2} = 110.47 \times 10^{-6} \text{ C/m}^2$

Electric intensity in dielectric, $\quad E = \frac{D}{\varepsilon_0 \varepsilon_r} = \frac{110.47 \times 10^{-6}}{8.854 \times 10^{-12} \times 5} = 2.5 \times 10^6 \text{ V/m}$

6.10. CAPACITORS IN SERIES

Consider three capacitors having capacitances C_1, C_2 and C_3 farad respectively, connected in series across a p.d. of V volts [See Fig. 6.16 (i)]. In series connection, charge on each capacitor is the *same (i.e., + Q on one plate and – Q on the other) but p.d. across each is different.

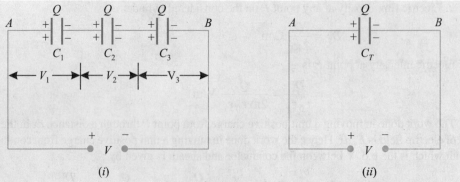

Fig. 6.16

Now, $\qquad V = V_1 + V_2 + V_3 = \frac{Q}{C_1} + \frac{Q}{C_2} + \frac{Q}{C_3} = Q\left(\frac{1}{C_1} + \frac{1}{C_2} + \frac{1}{C_3}\right)$

or $\qquad \frac{V}{Q} = \frac{1}{C_1} + \frac{1}{C_2} + \frac{1}{C_3}$

* When voltage V is applied, a similar electron movement occurs on each plate. Hence the same charge is stored by each capacitor. Alternatively, current (charging) in a series circuit is the same. Since $Q = It$ and both I and t are the same for each capacitor, the charge on each capacitor is the same.

But Q/V is the total capacitance C_T between points A and B so that $V/Q = 1/C_T$ [See Fig. 6.16 (ii)].

$$\therefore \qquad \frac{1}{C_T} = \frac{1}{C_1} + \frac{1}{C_2} + \frac{1}{C_3}$$

Thus capacitors in series are treated in the same manner as are resistors in parallel.

Special Case. Frequently we come across two capacitors in series. The total capacitance in such a case is given by ;

$$\frac{1}{C_T} = \frac{1}{C_1} + \frac{1}{C_2} = \frac{C_1 + C_2}{C_1 \, C_2}$$

or $$C_T = \frac{C_1 \, C_2}{C_1 + C_2} \quad i.e., \quad \frac{\text{Product}}{\text{sum}}$$

Distribution of voltage across capacitors in series. When capacitors are connected in series, the charge Q on each capacitor is the same. Now $Q = C_T \, V$ where C_T is the total capacitance of the series-connected capacitors.

$\therefore$ Voltage across C_1, $\qquad V_1 = \dfrac{Q}{C_1} = \dfrac{C_T \, V}{C_1}$

Voltage across C_2, $\qquad V_2 = \dfrac{Q}{C_2} = \dfrac{C_T \, V}{C_2}$

Voltage across C_3, $\qquad V_3 = \dfrac{Q}{C_3} = \dfrac{C_T \, V}{C_3}$

In general, $\qquad V_n = \dfrac{C_T \, V}{C_n}$

where the subscript n identifies any one of the capacitors in the series grouping.

6.11. CAPACITORS IN PARALLEL

Consider three capacitors having capacitances C_1, C_2 and C_3 farad respectively, connected in parallel across a p.d. of V volts [See Fig. 6.17 (i)]. In parallel connection, p.d. across each capacitor is the same but charge on each is different.

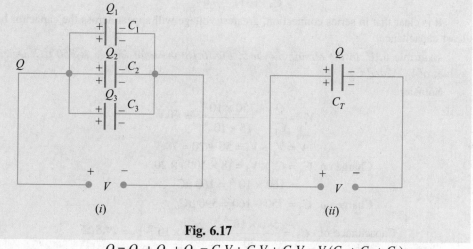

Fig. 6.17

Now, $\qquad Q = Q_1 + Q_2 + Q_3 = C_1 V + C_2 V + C_3 V = V (C_1 + C_2 + C_3)$

or
$$\frac{Q}{V} = C_1 + C_2 + C_3$$

But Q/V is the total capacitance C_T of the parallel combination.

∴
$$C_T = C_1 + C_2 + C_3$$

Thus capacitors in parallel are treated in the same manner as are resistors in series.

Example 6.9. *Three capacitors of capacitance 2 μF, 4 μF and 6 μF respectively are connected in series to a 220 V d.c. supply. Find (i) the total capacitance (ii) charge on each capacitor and (iii) p.d. across each capacitor.*

Solution.

(*i*)
$$\frac{1}{C_T} = \frac{1}{2} + \frac{1}{4} + \frac{1}{6} = \frac{6 + 3 + 2}{12} = \frac{11}{12}$$

∴
$$C_T = 12/11 = \textbf{1.091 μF}$$

(*ii*) In series connection, charge on each capacitor is the same.

∴ Charge on each capacitor, $Q = C_T V = (1.091 \times 10^{-6}) \times 220 = 240 \times 10^{-6}$ C

(*iii*) P.D. across 2μF, $V_1 = \dfrac{Q}{C_1} = \dfrac{240 \times 10^{-6}}{2 \times 10^{-6}} = \textbf{120 V}$

P.D. across 4μF, $V_2 = \dfrac{Q}{C_2} = \dfrac{240 \times 10^{-6}}{4 \times 10^{-6}} = \textbf{60 V}$

P.D. across 6μF, $V_3 = \dfrac{Q}{C_3} = \dfrac{240 \times 10^{-6}}{6 \times 10^{-6}} = \textbf{40 V}$

Alternatively

$$V_1 = \frac{C_T V}{C_1} = \frac{12}{11} \times \frac{220}{2} = 120 \, V$$

$$V_2 = \frac{C_T V}{C_2} = \frac{12}{11} \times \frac{220}{4} = 60 \, V$$

$$V_3 = \frac{C_T V}{C_3} = \frac{12}{11} \times \frac{220}{6} = 40 \, V$$

It is clear that in series connection, greatest voltage will appear across the capacitor having the least capacitance.

Example 6.10. *In the circuit shown in Fig. 6.18, the total charge is 750 μC. Determine the values of V_1, V and C_2.*

Solution.

$$V_1 = \frac{Q}{C_1} = \frac{750 \times 10^{-6}}{15 \times 10^{-6}} = 50 \, V$$

$$V = V_1 + V_2 = 50 + 20 = \textbf{70 V}$$

Charge on $C_3 = C_3 \times V_2 = (8 \times 10^{-6}) \times 20$
$$= 160 \times 10^{-6} = 160 \, μC$$

∴ Charge on $C_2 = 750 - 160 = 590 \, μC$

∴ Capacitance of $C_2 = \dfrac{590 \times 10^{-6}}{20} = 29.5 \times 10^{-6}$ F $= \textbf{29.5 μF}$

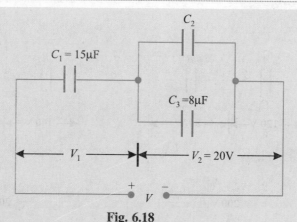

Fig. 6.18

Example 6.11. *A 5µF capacitor is charged to a p.d. of 100 V and then connected in parallel with an uncharged 3µF capacitor. Calculate the p.d. across the parallel capacitors.*

Solution.

Charge on 5 µF capacitor, $Q = CV = (5 \times 10^{-6}) \times 100 = 0.0005$ C

When the capacitors are connected in parallel, the total capacitance is $C_T = 5 + 3 = 8$ µF. The charge 0.0005 C is distributed between the two capacitors to have a common p.d.

$$\therefore \text{P.D. across parallel capacitors} = \frac{Q}{C_T} = \frac{0.0005}{8 \times 10^{-6}} = \textbf{62.5 V}$$

Example 6.12. *Two capacitors of capacitance 4 µF and 6 µF respectively are connected in series across a p.d. of 250 V. The capacitors are disconnected from the supply and are reconnected in parallel with each other. Calculate the new p.d. and charge on each capacitor.*

Solution.

Series connection. Let V_1 and V_2 be the voltages across the capacitors.

Charge on each capacitor $= C_1 V_1 = C_2 V_2$

$\therefore \qquad\qquad 4V_1 = 6 V_2$

or $\qquad\qquad V_1 = 1.5 V_2$ ...(i)

Also $\qquad\qquad V_1 + V_2 = 250$ ...(ii)

From eqs. (i) and (ii), we have, $V_1 = 150$ volts and $V_2 = 100$ volts

Charge on each capacitor $= C_1 V_1 = (4 \times 10^{-6}) \times 150 = 0.0006$C

Charge on both capacitors $= 2 \times 0.0006 = 0.0012$ C

Parallel connection. When the capacitors are connected in parallel, the total capacitance $C_T = 4 + 6 = 10$ µF. The total charge 0.0012 C is distributed between the two capacitors to have a common p.d.

P.D. across capacitors $= \dfrac{0.0012}{10 \times 10^{-6}} = \textbf{120 V}$

Charge on 4µF capacitor $= (4 \times 10^{-6}) \times 120 = 480 \times 10^{-6}$ C $= \textbf{480 µC}$

Charge on 6µF capacitor $= (6 \times 10^{-6}) \times 120 = 720 \times 10^{-6}$ C $= \textbf{720 µC}$

Example 6.13. *Two capacitors A and B are connected in series across a 200 V d.c. supply. The p.d. across A is 120 V. This p.d. is increased to 140 V when a 3 µF capacitor is connected in parallel with B. Calculate the capacitances of A and B.*

Solution. Let C_1 µF and C_2 µF be the capacitances of capacitors A and B respectively.

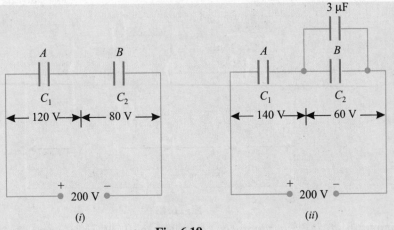

(i)   (ii)

Fig. 6.19

When the capacitors are connected in series [See Fig. 6.19 (*i*)], charge on each capacitor is the same.

∴ $C_1 \times 120 = C_2 \times 80$

or $C_2 = 1.5\, C_1$ ...(*i*)

When a 3 µF capacitor is connected in parallel with *B* [See Fig. 6.19 (*ii*)], the combined capacitance of this parallel branch is ($C_2 + 3$). Thus the circuit shown in Fig. 6.19 (*ii*) can be thought as a series circuit consisting of capacitances C_1 and ($C_2 + 3$) connected in series.

∴ $C_1 \times 140 = (C_2 + 3)\, 60$

or $7C_1 - 3\, C_2 = 9$ ...(*ii*)

Solving eqs. (*i*) and (*ii*), we get, $C_1 = 3.6 \, \mu F$; $C_2 = 5.4 \, \mu F.$

Example 6.14. *Given some capacitors of 0.1 µF capable of withstanding upto 15 V. Calculate the number of capacitors needed if it is desired to obtain a capacitance of 0.1 µF for use in a circuit involving 60 V.*

Solution.

Capacitance of each capacitor, $C = 0.1 \, \mu F$

Voltage rating of each capacitor, $V_C = 15 \, V$

Supply voltage, $V = 60 \, V$

Since each capacitor can withstand 15 V only, the number of capacitors to be connected in series = 60/15 = 4.

Capacitance of 4 series-connected capacitors, $C_S = C/4 = 0.1/4 = 0.025 \, \mu F$

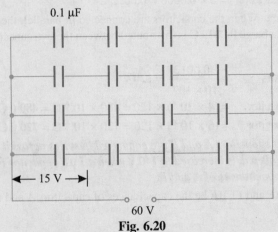

Fig. 6.20

Since it is desired to have total capacitance of 0.1 μF, number of such rows = $C/C_S = 0.1/0.025 = 4$.

∴ Total number of capacitors = $4 \times 4 = 16$

Fig. 6.20 shows the arrangement of capacitors.

Example 6.15. *Two parallel-plate capacitors A and B are connected in series. Capacitor A has a plate area of 5000 mm², an air dielectric and the distance between the plates is 1 mm. Capacitor B has a plate area of 2000 mm², a solid dielectric of relative permittivity 4 and of thickness 0.5 mm. Find the voltage across the combination if potential gradient associated with capacitor A is 100 kV/ m.*

Solution. Fig. 6.21 shows the conditions of the problem.

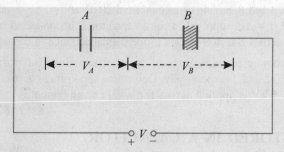

Fig. 6.21

$$V_A = E_A \times d_A = (100 \times 10^3) \times (1 \times 10^{-3}) = 100 \text{ V}$$

$$C_A = \frac{\varepsilon_0 A}{d_A} = \frac{\varepsilon_0 \times 5000 \times 10^{-6}}{1 \times 10^{-3}}$$

$$C_B = \frac{\varepsilon_0 \varepsilon_r A}{d_B} = \frac{\varepsilon_0 \times 4 \times 2000 \times 10^{-6}}{0.5 \times 10^{-3}}$$

∴ $$\frac{C_A}{C_B} = \frac{2.5}{8}$$

Since the two capacitors are in series, the charge on each capacitor is the same *i.e.*,

$$C_A V_A = C_B V_B$$

or $$V_B = V_A \times \frac{C_A}{C_B} = 100 \times \frac{2.5}{8} = 31.25 \text{ V}$$

∴ Total voltage, $$V = V_A + V_B = 100 + 31.25 = \mathbf{131.25 \text{ V}}$$

TUTORIAL PROBLEMS

1. Three capacitors have capacitances of 2, 3 and 4 μF respectively. Calculate the total capacitance when they are connected (*i*) in series (*ii*) in parallel. **[0.923 μF ; 9 μF]**

2. Three capacitors of values 8 μF, 12 μF and 16 μF respectively are connected in series across a 240 V d.c. supply. Calculate (*i*) the resultant capacitance and (*ii*) p.d. across each capacitor. **[(*i*) 3.7 μF (*ii*) $V_1 = 111$ V, $V_2 = 74$ V, $V_3 = 55$ V]**

3. How can three capacitors of capacitance 3 μF, 6 μF and 9 μF respectively be arranged to a system of capacitance 11 μF ?

   [3 μF and 6 μF in series, with 9 μF in parallel with both]

4. Two capacitors of capacitance 0.5 μF and 0.3 μF are joined in series. What value of capacitance joined in parallel with this combination would give a capacitance of 0.5 μF ?

   [0.31 μF]

5. Three capacitors A, B and C are connected in series across a 200 V d.c. supply. The p.d.s. across the capacitors are 40 V, 70 V and 90 V respectively. If the capacitance of A is 8 μF, what are the capacitances of B and C ? [4.57 μF, 3.56 μF]

6. A capacitor of 4 μF capacitance is charged to a p.d. of 400 V and then connected in parallel with an uncharged capacitor of 2 μF capacitance. Calculate the p.d. acros the parallel capacitors. [267 V]

7. Circuit ABC is made up as follows. AB consists of a 3 μF capacitor. BC consists of a 3 μF capacitor in parallel with 5 μF capacitor. If a d.c. supply of 100 V is connected between A and C, determine the charge on each capacitor. [160 μC (AB) ; 60 μC (3μF in BC) ; 100 μC]

8. Two capacitors, A and B, having capacitances of 20 μF and 30 μF respectively, are connected in series to a 600 V d.c. supply. If a third capacitor C is connected in parallel with A, it is found that p.d. across B is 400 V. Determine the capacitance of capacitor C. [40 μF]

9. Three series-connected capacitors of equal dimensions have dielectrics of relative permittivities 1, 2 and 3 respectively. Determine the voltage across each capacitor given that a p.d. of 1.5 kV is applied across the whole arrangement.

[820 V ; 410 V ; 270 V]

6.12. ENERGY STORED IN A CAPACITOR

Charging a capacitor means transferring electrons from one plate of the capacitor to the other. This involves expenditure of energy because electrons have to be moved against the *opposing forces. This energy is stored in the electrostatic field set up in the dielectric medium. On discharging the capacitor, the field collapses and the stored energy is released.

Consider a capacitor of C farad being charged from a d.c. source of V volts as shown in Fig. 6.22. Suppose at any stage of charging, the charge on the capacitor is q coulombs and p.d. across the plates is v volts.

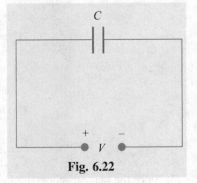

Fig. 6.22

Then $\qquad C = \dfrac{q}{v}$

At this instant, v joules (by definition of V) of work will be done in transferring 1 C of charge from one plate to the other. If further small charge dq is transferred, then work done is

$$dW = v\, dq = Cv\, dv \qquad \begin{bmatrix} q = Cv \\ \therefore\ dq = Cdv \end{bmatrix}$$

∴ Total work done in raising the potential of uncharged capacitor to V volts is

$$W = \int_0^V Cv\, dv = C\left[\frac{v^2}{2}\right]_0^V$$

or $\qquad W = \dfrac{1}{2}\, CV^2$ joules

This work done is stored in the electrostatic field set up in the dielectric.

---

*   Electrons are being pushed to the negative plate which tends to repel them. Similarly electrons are removed from the positive plate which tends to attract them. In either case, forces oppose the transfer of electrons from one plate to the other. This opposition increases as the charge on the plates increases.

∴ Energy stored in the capacitor

$$E = \frac{1}{2} CV^2 = \frac{1}{2}^* QV = \frac{Q^2}{2C}^\dagger \text{ joules}$$

Example 6.16. *A capacitor consists of two metal plates, each 40 cm × 40 cm, spaced 6 mm apart. The space between the metal plates is filled with a glass plate 5 mm thick and a layer of paper 1 mm thick. The relative permittivities of glass and paper are 8 and 2 respectively. Find the capacitance of the system. If a p.d. of 10 kV is applied to the capacitor, determine the energy stored in it.*

Solution.

$$C = \frac{\varepsilon_0 A}{\dfrac{d_1}{\varepsilon_{r1}} + \dfrac{d_2}{\varepsilon_{r2}}}$$

Here $\qquad A = 0.4 \times 0.4 = 0.16 \text{ m}^2 \; ; \; d_1 = 5 \text{ mm} = 5 \times 10^{-3} \text{ m}$

$d_2 = 1 \text{ mm} = 10^{-3} \text{ m} \; ; \; \varepsilon_{r1} = 8 \; ; \; \varepsilon_{r2} = 2$

∴ $\qquad C = \dfrac{8.854 \times 10^{-12} \times 0.16}{10^{-3} \left(\dfrac{5}{8} + \dfrac{1}{2} \right)} = \mathbf{0.001259 \times 10^{-6} \; F}$

Energy stored, $\qquad E = \dfrac{1}{2} CV^2 = \dfrac{1}{2} (0.001259 \times 10^{-6}) \times (10^4)^2 = 62.95 \times 10^{-3} \text{ J}$

Example 6.17. *A 16 μF capacitor is charged to 100 V. After being disconnected, it is immediately connected in parallel with an uncharged capacitor of capacitance 4 μF. Determine (i) the p.d. across the combination and (ii) the electrostatic energies before and after the capacitors are connected in parallel.*

Solution.

$$C_1 = 16 \text{ μF} \; ; \; C_2 = 4 \text{ μF}$$

Before joining

Charge on 16 μF capacitor, $\quad Q = C_1 V_1 = (16 \times 10^{-6}) \times 100 = 1.6 \times 10^{-3} \text{ C}$

Energy stored, $\qquad E_1 = \dfrac{1}{2} C_1 V_1^2 = \dfrac{1}{2} (16 \times 10^{-6}) \times 100^2 = 0.08 \text{ J}$

After joining

When the capacitors are connected in parallel, the total capacitance $C_T = C_1 + C_2 = 16 + 4 = 20 \text{ μF}$. The charge 1.6×10^{-3} C distributes between the two capacitors to have a common p.d. of V volts.

P.D. across parallel combination is

$$V = \frac{Q}{C_T} = \frac{1.6 \times 10^{-3}}{20 \times 10^{-6}} = 80 \text{ V}$$

Energy stored, $\qquad E_2 = \dfrac{1}{2} C_T V^2 = \dfrac{1}{2} (20 \times 10^{-6}) \times (80)^2 = 0.064 \text{ J}$

It may be noted that there is a loss of energy. This is due to the heat dissipated in the conductor connecting the capacitors.

. . . .

* $\quad$ Putting $C = Q/V$ in the exp. $E = \dfrac{1}{2} CV^2$

$\dagger$ $\quad$ Putting $V = Q/C$ in the exp. $E = \dfrac{1}{2} CV^2$

Example 6.18. *A metal sphere 4 m in diameter is charged to a potential of 3 MV. Calculate the heat generated when the sphere is earthed through a long resistance wire.*

Solution.

Potential at the surface of sphere, $V = 9 \times 10^9 \dfrac{Q}{r}$

∴ Charge on sphere, $Q = \dfrac{V \times r}{9 \times 10^9} = \dfrac{(3 \times 10^6) \times 2}{9 \times 10^9} = 0.67 \times 10^{-3}$ C

Energy stored in sphere $= \dfrac{1}{2} QV = \dfrac{1}{2} (0.67 \times 10^{-3}) \times (3 \times 10^6) = \mathbf{1005\ J}$

Energy stored in the sphere will be dissipated as heat in the resistance wire.

Example 6.19. *Two capacitors A and B are placed (i) in series (ii) in parallel. Capacitor C_A = 100 μF and C_B = 50 μF. Find the maximum energy stored in the circuit when 240 V, 50 Hz supply is applied.*

Solution. $V_{max} = 240\sqrt{2}$ volts

(i) $C_S = \dfrac{C_A C_B}{C_A + C_B} = \dfrac{100 \times 50}{100 + 50} = \dfrac{100}{3}$ μF

$E_{max} = \dfrac{1}{2} C_S V_{max}^2 = \dfrac{1}{2}\left(\dfrac{100}{3} \times 10^{-6}\right)(240\sqrt{2})^2 = \mathbf{1.92\,J}$

(ii) $C_P = C_A + C_B = 100 + 50 = 150$ μF

$E_{max} = \dfrac{1}{2} C_P V_{max}^2 = \dfrac{1}{2} (150/10^6)(240\sqrt{2})^2 = \mathbf{8.64\,J}$

6.13. FORCE ON CHARGED PLATES

When two plates carry opposite charges, a force of attraction exists between the plates. Thus the plates of a capacitor are attracted towards one another. Consider two parallel conducting plates *x* metres apart and carrying constant charges of + Q and – Q coulombs respectively as shown in Fig. 6.23. Let the force of attraction between the two plates be *F* newtons.

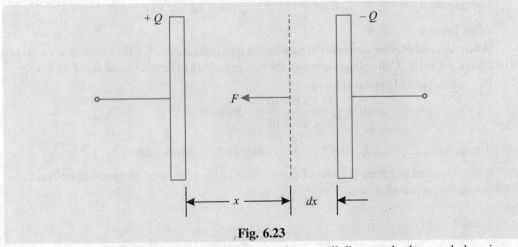

Fig. 6.23

If one of the plates is moved away from the other by a small distance *dx*, then work done is

$= F \times dx$ joules ...(i)

Since the charges on plates remain constant, no electrical energy can enter or leave the system during the movement dx.

∴ Work done = Change in stored energy

$$\text{Initial stored energy} = \frac{1}{2}\frac{Q^2}{C} \text{ joules}$$

Since the separation of the plates has increased, the capacitance will decrease by dC. The final capacitance is, therefore, $(C - dC)$.

$$\text{Final stored energy} = \frac{1}{2}\frac{Q^2}{(C-dC)} = \frac{Q^2\,(C+dC)\,*}{2[C^2 - (dC)^2]}$$

Since dC is small as compared to C, $(dC)^2$ can be neglected compared to C^2.

$$\therefore \quad \text{Final stored energy} = \frac{Q^2\,(C+dC)}{2C^2} = \frac{Q^2}{2C} + \frac{Q^2}{2C^2}\,dC$$

$$\therefore \text{Change in stored energy} = \left(\frac{Q^2}{2C} + \frac{Q^2}{2C^2}\,dC\right) - \frac{Q^2}{2C} = \frac{Q^2}{2C^2}\,dC \qquad ...(ii)$$

Equating eqs. (i) and (ii), we get,

$$F \times dx = \frac{Q^2}{2C^2}\,dC$$

or

$$F = \frac{Q^2}{2C^2}\frac{dC}{dx} = \frac{1}{2}V^2\frac{dC}{dx} \qquad ...(iii)$$

$$(\because V = Q/C)$$

Now

$$C = \frac{\varepsilon_0\varepsilon_r A}{x}$$

∴

$$\frac{dC}{dx} = -\frac{\varepsilon_0\varepsilon_r A}{x^2}$$

Substituting the value of dC/dx in eq. (iii), we get,

$$F = -\frac{1}{2}V^2\frac{\varepsilon_0\varepsilon_r A}{x^2} = -\frac{1}{2}\varepsilon_0\varepsilon_r A\,(V/x)^2$$

$$= -\frac{1}{2}\varepsilon_0\varepsilon_r AE^2 \qquad \text{... in a medium}$$

$$= -\frac{1}{2}\varepsilon_0 AE^2 \qquad \text{... in air}$$

The negative sign indicates that the force acts in the opposite direction to that in which the plate separation was measured. This tallies with the concept that the force is one of attraction.

Example 6.20. *A parallel plate capacitor having plates of 100 cm² area is immersed in oil of relative permittivity 10. The plates are charged to a p.d. of 5 kV and the distance between them is 2 cm. Permittivity of free space = 8.854 × 10⁻¹² F/m. Determine the force between the plates.*

* Note this step. Multiply the numerator and denominator by $(C + dC)$.

Solution.

Force of attraction between the plates of capacitor is

$$F = \frac{1}{2} \varepsilon_0 \varepsilon_r A E^2 \text{ newtons}$$

Here $\varepsilon_r = 10 \; ; A = 100 \text{ cm}^2 = 0.01 \text{ m}^2$

Now $E = \frac{V}{d} = \frac{5 \times 10^3}{2 \times 10^{-2}} = 2.5 \times 10^5 \text{ V/m}$

∴ $F = \frac{1}{2} (8.854 \times 10^{-12}) \times 10 \times 0.01 \times (2.5 \times 10^5)^2 = 2.77 \times 10^{-2} \text{ N}$

Example 6.21. *A parallel plate capacitor has its plates separated by 0.5 mm of air. The area of plates is 2 m^2 and they are charged to a p.d. of 100 V. The plates are pulled apart until they are separated by 1 mm of air. Assuming the p.d. to remain unchanged, what is the mechanical force experienced in separating the plates ?*

Solution.

Before plate movement

Capacitance, $C_1 = \frac{\varepsilon_0 A}{d} = \frac{8.854 \times 10^{-12} \times 2}{0.5 \times 10^{-3}} = 35.4 \times 10^{-9} \text{ F}$

Stored energy, $E_1 = \frac{1}{2} C_1 V^2 = \frac{1}{2} (35.4 \times 10^{-9}) \times (100)^2 = 17.7 \times 10^{-5} \text{ J}$

After plate movement

Capacitance, $C_2 = \frac{1}{2} C_1 = \frac{1}{2} (35.4 \times 10^{-9}) = 17.7 \times 10^{-9} \text{ F}$

Stored energy, $E_2 = \frac{1}{2} C_2 V^2 = \frac{1}{2} (17.7 \times 10^{-9}) \times (100)^2 = 8.85 \times 10^{-5} \text{ J}$

Change in stored energy $= (17.7 - 8.85) \times 10^{-5} = 8.85 \times 10^{-5} \text{ J}$

Suppose F newtons is the average mechanical force between the plates. The plates are separated by a distance $dx = 1 - 0.5 = 0.5$ mm.

∴ $F \times dx = $ Change in stored energy

or $F = \frac{8.85 \times 10^{-5}}{0.5 \times 10^{-3}} = 17.7 \times 10^{-2} \text{ N}$

6.14. CHARGING OF A CAPACITOR

Consider an uncharged capacitor of capacitance C connected in series with a resistor R to a d.c. supply of V volts as shown in Fig. 6.24. When the switch is closed, the capacitor starts charging up and charging current flows in the circuit. The charging current is maximum at the instant of switching and decreases gradually as the voltage across the capacitor increases. When the capacitor is charged to applied voltage V, the charging current becomes zero.

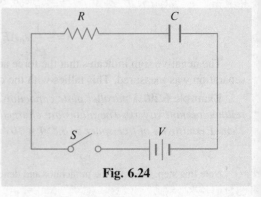

Fig. 6.24

1. At switching instant. At the instant the switch is closed, the voltage across capacitor is zero since we started with an uncharged capacitor. The entire voltage V is dropped across resistance R and charging current is maximum (Call it I_m).

∴ Initial charging current, $I_m = V/R$

Voltage across capacitor = 0

Charge on capacitor = 0

2. At any instant. After having closed the switch, the charging current starts decreasing and the voltage across capacitor gradually increases. Let at any instant during charging :

i = Charging current

v = P.D. across C

q = Charge on capacitor = Cv

(i) Voltage across capacitor

According to Kirchhoff's voltage law, the applied voltage V is equal to the sum of voltage drops across resistor and capacitor.

∴
$$V = v + iR \qquad \qquad ...(i)$$

or
$$V = v + CR^* \frac{dv}{dt}$$

or
$$-\frac{dv}{V-v} = -\frac{dt}{RC}$$

Intergrating both sides, we get,

$$\int -\frac{dv}{V-v} = \int -\frac{dt}{RC}$$

or
$$\log_e (V-v) = -\frac{t}{RC} + K \qquad \qquad ...(ii)$$

where K is a constant whose value can be determined from the initial conditions. At the instant of closing the switch S, $t = 0$ and $v = 0$.

Substituting these values in eq. (*ii*), we get, $\log_e V = K$.

Putting the value of $K = \log_e V$ in eq. (*ii*), we get,

$$\log_e (V-v) = -\frac{t}{RC} + \log_e V$$

or
$$\log_e \frac{V-v}{V} = -\frac{t}{RC}$$

or
$$\frac{V-v}{V} = e^{-t/RC}$$

∴
$$v = V[1 - e^{-t/RC}] \qquad \qquad ...(iii)$$

This is the expression for variation of voltage across the capacitor (v) w.r.t. time (t) and is represented graphically in Fig. 6.25 (*i*). Note that growth of voltage across the capacitor follows an exponential law. An inspection of eq. (*iii*) reveals that as t increases, the term $e^{-t/RC}$ gets smaller and voltage v across capacitor gets larger.

. . . .

* $i = \dfrac{dq}{dt} = \dfrac{d}{dt}(q) = \dfrac{d}{dt}(Cv) = C\dfrac{dv}{dt}$

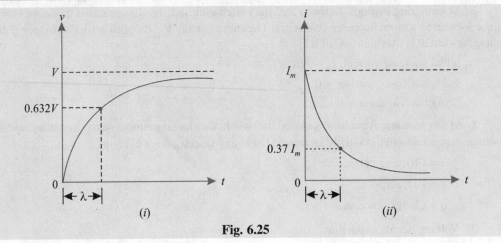

Fig. 6.25

(ii) *Charge on Capacitor*

$$q = \text{Charge at any time } t$$
$$Q = \text{Final charge}$$

Since $v = q/C$ and $V = Q/C$, the exp. (*iii*) becomes :

$$\frac{q}{C} = \frac{Q}{C} [1 - e^{-t/RC}]$$

or $\qquad q = Q\,(1 - e^{-t/RC})$ \hfill ...(*iv*)

Again the increase of charge on capacitor plates follows exponential law.

(iii) *Charging current*

From exp. (*i*), $\qquad V - v = i\,R$

From exp. (*iii*), $\qquad V - v = V\,e^{-t/RC}$

∴ $\qquad\qquad iR = V\,e^{-t/RC}$

or $\qquad\qquad i = \dfrac{V}{R}\,e^{-t/RC}$

∴ $\qquad\qquad i = I_m\,e^{-t/RC}$

where $I_m\,(= V/R)$ is the initial charging current. Again the charging current decreases following exponential law. This is also represented graphically in Fig. 6.25 (*ii*).

(iv) *Rate of rise of voltage across capacitor*

We have seen above that:

$$V = v + CR\,\frac{dv}{dt}$$

At the instant the switch is closed, $v = 0$.

∴ $\qquad\qquad V = CR\,\dfrac{dv}{dt}$

or Initial rate of rise of voltage across capacitor is

$$\frac{dv}{dt} = \frac{V}{CR} \text{ volts/sec} \hspace{3cm} ...(v)$$

Note. The capacitor is almost fully charged in a time equal to 5 RC *i.e.* 5 time constants.

6.15. TIME CONSTANT

Consider the eq. (*iii*) above showing the rise of voltage across the capacitor :

$$v = V (1 - e^{-t/RC})$$

The exponent of *e* is t/RC. The quantity RC has the *dimensions of time so that exponent of *e* is a number. The quantity RC is called the *time constant* of the circuit and affects the charging (or discharging) time. It is represented by λ (or T or τ).

∴   Time constant, $\lambda = RC$ seconds

Time constant may be defined in one of the following ways :

(*i*) At the instant of closing the switch, p.d. across capacitor is zero. Therefore, putting $v = 0$ in

the expression $V = v + CR \dfrac{dv}{dt}$, we have,

$$V = CR \frac{dv}{dt}$$

or $\dfrac{dv}{dt} = \dfrac{V}{CR}$

If this rate of rise of voltage could continue, the capacitor voltage will reach the final value V in time $= V \div V/CR = RC$ seconds $=$ time constant λ.

Hence time constant may be defined as the time required for the capacitor voltage to rise to its final steady value V if it continued rising at its initial rate (i.e. V/CR).

(*ii*) If the time interval $t = \lambda$ (or RC), then,

$$v = V (1 - e^{-t/t}) = V (1 - e^{-1}) = 0.632\ V$$

Hence time constant can also be defined as the time required for the capacitor voltage to reach 0.632 of its final steady value V.

(*iii*) If the time interval $t = \lambda$ (or RC), then,

$$i = I_m e^{-t/t} = I_m e^{-1} = 0.37\ I_m$$

Hence time constant can also be defined as the time required for the charging current to fall to 0.37 of its initial maximum value I_m.

6.16. DISCHARGING OF A CAPACITOR

Consider a capacitor of C farad charged to a p.d. of V volts and connected in series with a resistance R through a switch S as shown in Fig. 6.26 (*i*). When the switch is open, the voltage across the capacitor is V volts. When the switch is closed, the voltage across capacitor starts decreasing. The discharge current rises instantaneously to a value of V/R ($= I_m$) and then decays gradually to zero.

Let at any instant during discharging

$v = $ p.d. across the capacitor

$i = $ discharging current

$q = $ charge on capacitor

. . . .

* $RC = \left(\dfrac{\text{Volt}}{\text{Ampere}} \right) \times \left(\dfrac{\text{Coulomb}}{\text{Volt}} \right) = \dfrac{\text{Volt}}{(\text{Coulomb/sec})} \times \left(\dfrac{\text{Coulomb}}{\text{Volt}} \right) = $ seconds

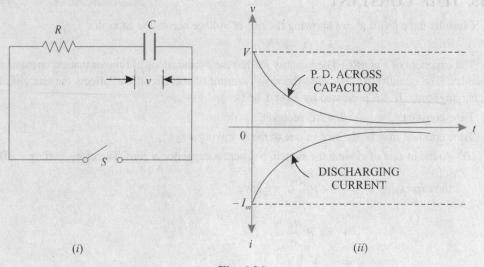

Fig. 6.26

By Kirchhoff's voltage law, we have,

$$0 = v + RC \frac{dv}{dt}$$

or

$$\frac{dv}{v} = -\frac{dt}{RC}$$

Integrating both sides, we get,

$$\int \frac{dv}{v} = -\frac{1}{RC} \int dt$$

∴

$$\log_e v = -\frac{t}{RC} + K \qquad ...(i)$$

At the instant of closing the switch, $t = 0$ and $v = V$. Putting these values in eq. (i), we get,

$$\log_e V = K$$

∴ equation (i) becomes : $\log_e v = (-t/RC) + \log_e V$

or

$$\log_e \frac{v}{V} = -\frac{t}{RC}$$

or

$$\frac{v}{V} = e^{-t/RC}$$

∴

$$v = V e^{-t/\lambda} \qquad ...(ii)$$

Again $RC (= \lambda)$ is the time constant and has the dimensions of time.

Similarly

$$q = Q e^{-t/RC}$$

and

$$i = -I_m e^{-t/RC}$$

Note that negative sign is attached to I_m. This is because the discharging current flows in the opposite direction to that in which the charging current flows.

Example 6.22. *A 2 μF capacitor is connected, by closing a switch, to a supply of 100 volts through a 1 MΩ series resistance. Calculate (i) the time constant (ii) initial charging current (iii) the initial rate of rise of p.d. across capacitor (iv) voltage across the capacitor 6 seconds after the switch has been closed and (v) the time taken for the capacitor to be fully charged.*

Solution.

(*i*) Time constant, $\lambda = RC = (10^6) \times (2 \times 10^{-6}) = 2$ seconds

(*ii*) Initial charging current, $I_m = \dfrac{V}{R} = \dfrac{100}{10^6} \times 10^6 = 100 \ \mu A$

(*iii*) Initial rate of rise of voltage across capacitor is

$$\frac{dv}{dt} = \frac{V}{CR} = \frac{100}{(2 \times 10^{-6}) \times 10^6} = 50 \text{ V/s}$$

(*iv*) $\qquad\qquad\qquad v = V(1 - e^{-t/RC})$

Here $\quad V = 100$ volts ; $\qquad t = 6$ seconds ; $RC = 2$ seconds

$\therefore \qquad\qquad\qquad v = 100(1 - e^{-6/2})$

$$= 100(1 - e^{-3}) = 95.1 \text{ V}$$

(*v*) Time taken for the capacitor to be fully charged

$$= 5 \, RC = 5 \times 2 = 10 \text{ seconds}$$

Example 6.23. *A capacitor of 8 μF capacitance is connected to a d.c. source through a resistance of 1 megaohm. Calculate the time taken by the capacitor to receive 95% of its final charge. How long will it take the capacitor to be fully charged ?*

Solution.

$$q = Q(1 - e^{-t/RC})$$

Here $\qquad\qquad RC = (10)^6 \times 8 \times 10^{-6} = 8$ seconds ; $q/Q = 0.95$

$\therefore \qquad\qquad\qquad 0.95 = 1 - e^{-t/8}$

or $\qquad\qquad\qquad e^{-t/8} = 0.05$

or $\qquad\qquad\qquad e^{t/8} = 1/0.05 = 20$

or $\qquad\qquad (t/8) \log_e e = \log_e 20$

$\therefore \qquad\qquad\qquad t = 8 \log_e 20 = 23.96$ seconds

Time taken for the capacitor to be fully charged

$$= 5 \, RC = 5 \times 8 = 40 \text{ seconds}$$

Example 6.24. *A resistance R and a 4 μF capacitor are connected in series across a 200 V d.c. supply. Across the capacitor is connected a neon lamp that strikes at 120 V. Calculate the value of R to make the lamp strike after 5 seconds.*

Solution. The voltage across the neon lamp has to rise to 120 *V* in 5 seconds.

Now $\qquad\qquad\qquad v = V(1 - e^{-t/\lambda})$

or $\qquad\qquad\qquad 120 = 200(1 - e^{-5/\lambda})$

or $\qquad\qquad\qquad e^{-5/\lambda} = 1 - (120/200) = 0.4$

or $\qquad\qquad\qquad e^{5/\lambda} = 1/0.4 = 2.5$

or $\qquad\qquad (5/\lambda) \log_e e = \log_e 2.5$

$\therefore \qquad\qquad\qquad \lambda = \dfrac{5}{\log_e 2.5} = 5.457$ seconds

or $\qquad\qquad\qquad RC = 5.457$

$\therefore \qquad\qquad\qquad R = \dfrac{5.457}{4 \times 10^{-6}} = 1.364 \times 10^6 \ \Omega = 1.364 \text{ M}\Omega$

Example 6.25. *A capacitor of 1 μF and resistance 82 kΩ are connected in series with an e.m.f. of 100 V. Calculate the magnitude of energy and the time in which energy stored in the capacitor will reach half of its equilibrium value.*

Solution.

Equilibrium value of energy $= \dfrac{1}{2} CV^2$

$\therefore$ Energy stored $\propto V^2$

Half energy of the equilibrium value will be stored when voltage across capacitor is $v = 100/\sqrt{2} = 70.7$ volts.

$\therefore$ Energy stored $= \dfrac{1}{2} Cv^2 = \dfrac{1}{2} (1 \times 10^{-6}) \times (70.7)^2 = \mathbf{0.0025\ J}$

Now $v = V (1 - e^{-t/RC})$

Here, $RC = (82 \times 10^3) \times (1 \times 10^{-6}) = 0.082\ s\ ; \ v = 70.7 V\ ; \ \ V = 100\ V$

$\therefore$ $70.7 = 100\ (1 - e^{-t/0.082})$

or $e^{-t/0.082} = 1 - (70.7/100) = 0.293$

or $e^{t/0.082} = 1/0.293 = 3.413$

or $(t/0.082)\ \log_e e = \log_e 3.413$

$\therefore$ $t = 0.082 \times \log_e 3.413 = \mathbf{0.1\ second}$

Example 6.26. *A capacitor of capacitance C farad is being charged from a d.c. supply of V volts through a resistance of R ohms.*

   (i)   *Show that most of the voltage across the capacitor builds up during the first time constant.*

  (ii) *Show that capacitor is almost fully charged after time equal to 5 time constants.*

Solution : The voltage build up across the capacitor during charging is

$$v = V (1 - e^{-t/RC})$$

  (i)   During the first time constant, *i.e.*, at $t = R\,C$ seconds,

$$v = V (1 - e^{-RC/RC}) = V (1 - e^{-1}) = \mathbf{0.632\ V}\ \textbf{volts}$$

Hence most of the voltage (*i.e.* 63.2%) builds up across the capacitor during first time constant.

  (ii) After time equal to 5 time constants, *i.e.* at $t = 5RC$,

$$v = V (1 - e^{-5RC/RC}) = V (1 - e^{-5}) = \mathbf{0.993\ V}\ \textbf{volts}$$

Hence capacitor is almost fully charged (*i.e.* 99.3%) after time equal to 5 time constants.

TUTORIAL PROBLEMS

1. A capacitor is being charged from a d.c. source through a resistance of 2 MΩ. If it takes 0.2 second for the charge to reach 75% of its final value, what is the capacitance of the capacitor ?   **[18 × 10⁻⁴ F]**

2. An 8 μF capacitor is connected in series with 0.5 MΩ resistance across 200V supply. Calculate (*i*) initial charging current (*ii*) the current and p.d. across capacitor 4 seconds after it is connected to the supply.   **[(*i*) 400 μA (*ii*) 147 μA, 126.4 V]**

3. What resistance connected in series with a capacitance of 4 μF will give the circuit a time constant of 2 seconds ?   **[500 kΩ]**

4. A series *RC* circuit is to have an initial charging current of 4 mA and a time constant of 3.6 seconds when connected to 120 V d.c. supply. Calculate the values of *R* and *C*. What will be the energy stored in the capacitor ?   **[30 kΩ ; 120 μF ; 0.864 J]**

5. A 20 μF capacitor initially charged to a p.d. of 500 V is discharged through an unknown resistance. After one minute, the p.d. at the terminals of the capacitor is 200 V. What is the value of the resistance ?   **[3.274 MΩ]**

6.17. STRAY CAPACITANCE

The unwanted capacitance existing between any two conductors separated by an insulator is called **stray capacitance.**

Thus all pairs of adjacent conductors have capacitance between them and every conductor has a capacitance to ground. This unwanted capacitance is termed as stray capacitance. Stray capacitance exists everywhere in electric and electronic circuits. Fortunately, the magnitude of stray capacitances are usually very small, often less than 1 pF and they have negligible effect on d.c. and low frequency a.c. circuits. However, in high-frequency circuits, such as those used in radio and television systems, stray capacitance can be a severe problem. In designing and constructing such circuits, every precaution is taken to minimise the stray capacitance. Since capacitance is inversely proportional to dielectric thickness ($C = \varepsilon_0 \varepsilon_r\, A/d$), stray capacitance is most easily minimised by keeping conductors as far apart as possible.

MULTIPLE-CHOICE QUESTIONS

1. The capacitance of a capacitor is .... relative permittivity.
   (a) directly proportional to
   (b) inversely proportional to
   (c) independent of
   (d) directly proportional to square of

2. An air capacitor has the same dimensions as that of a mica capacitor. If the capacitance of mica capacitor is 6 times that of air capacitor, then relative permittivity of mica is
   (a) 36   (b) 12
   (c) 3   (d) 6

3. The most convenient way of achieving large capacitance is by using
   (a) multiplate construction
   (b) decreased distance between plates
   (c) air as dielectric
   (d) dielectric of low permittivity

4. The capacitance of three-plate capacitor [See Fig. 6.27 (ii)] is .... that of 2-plate capacitor.
   (a) 3 times   (b) 6 times
   (c) 4 times   (d) 2 times

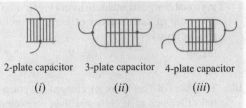

2-plate capacitor   3-plate capacitor   4-plate capacitor
     (i)   (ii)   (iii)

Fig. 6.27

5. Two capacitors of capacitances 3 μF and 6 μF in series will have a total capacitance of

(a) 9 μF
(b) 2 μF
(c) 18 μF
(d) 24 μF

6. The force between the plates of a parallel plate capacitor of capacitance C and distance of separation of plates d with a potential difference V between the plates is
   (a) $\dfrac{CV^2}{2d}$
   (b) $\dfrac{C^2 V^2}{2d^2}$
   (c) $\dfrac{C^2 V^2}{d^2}$
   (d) $\dfrac{V^2 d}{C}$

7. Four capacitors are connected as shown in Fig. 6.28. What is the equivalent capacitance between A and B ?

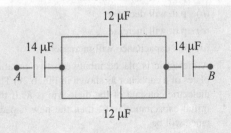

Fig. 6.28

(a) 36 μF
(b) 5.4 μF
(c) 52 μF
(d) 11.5 μF

8. 64 drops of radius r combine to form a bigger drop of radius R. The ratio of capacitances of bigger to smaller drop is

   (a) 1 : 4

   (b) 2 : 1

   (c) 1 : 2

   (d) 4 : 1

9. A capacitor of 20 μF charged to 500 V is connected in parallel with another capacitor of 10 μF capacitance and charged to 200 V. The common potential is

   (a) 200 V

   (b) 250 V

   (c) 400 V

   (d) 300 V

10. Three parallel plates each of area A with separation d_1 between first and second and d_2 between second and third are arranged to form a capacitor. If the dielectric constants are K_1 and K_2, the capacitance of this capacitor is

    (a) $\dfrac{\varepsilon_0 K_1 K_2}{A (d_1 + d_2)}$

    (b) $\dfrac{\varepsilon_0}{A\left(\dfrac{d_1}{K_1} + \dfrac{d_2}{K_2}\right)}$

    (c) $\dfrac{\varepsilon_0 A K_1 K_2}{d_1 + d_2}$

    (d) $\dfrac{\varepsilon_0 A}{\dfrac{d_1}{K_1} + \dfrac{d_2}{K_2}}$

11. The plates of a charged parallel-plate capacitor are pulled apart. Now

    (a) p.d. will remain unchanged

    (b) p.d. will decrease

    (c) p.d. will increase

    (d) the capacitance will increase

12. A dielectric is placed inbetween two parallel plates of a capacitor as shown in Fig. 6.29. The dielectric constant of the dielectric is K. If the initial capacitance is C, then the new capacitance will be

    (a) KC

    (b) $\dfrac{C (K + 1)}{2}$

    (c) $(K - 1) C$

    (d) $(K + 1) C$

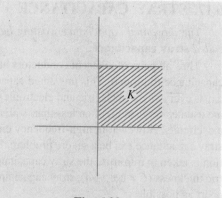

Fig. 6.29

13. Force acting on a charged particle kept between the plates of a charged capacitor is F. If one of the plates of the capacitor is removed, the force acting on the same particle will become

    (a) $F/2$

    (b) 0

    (c) F

    (d) $2F$

14. The capacitance of a parallel plate capacitor is 5 μF. When a glass plate is inserted between its two plates, its potential reduces to 1/8 of the original value. The value of dielectric constant of glass is

    (a) 4

    (b) 8

    (c) 40

    (d) 1.6

15. A parallel-plate capacitor has plate separation t and a capacitance of 100 pF. If a metallic foil of thickness $t/3$ is introduced between the plates, the capacitance would become

    (a) 100 pF

    (b) 180 pF

    (c) 200/3 pF

    (d) 150 pF

16. Five equal capacitors connected in series have a resultant capacitance of 4 μF. When these capacitors are connected in parallel and charged to 400 V d.c., the total energy stored is

    (a) 16 J

    (b) 8 J

    (c) 24 J

    (d) 9 J

17. N drops of mercury of equal radii and possessing equal charges combine to form a bigger drop. The ratio of capacitances of bigger drop to smaller drop is

    (a) $N^{1/3}$

    (b) N

    (c) $N^{2/3}$

    (d) $N^{3/2}$

18. The plates of a capacitor are charged to a potential difference of V volts and then connected across a resistor. The potential difference across the capacitor decreases exponentially w.r.t. time. After one second, the potential difference between the plates is $V/3$. Then after two

seconds from the start, the potential difference between the plates is

(a) 2V/3 (b) V/6

(c) V/3 (d) V/9

19. The equivalent capacitance between points A and B in Fig. 6.30 is

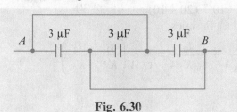

Fig. 6.30

(a) 9 μF

(b) 6 μF

(c) 12 μF

(d) 18 μF

20. Five capacitors of 10 μF capacitance each are connected to a d.c. potential of 100 V as shown in Fig. 6.31. The equivalent capacitance between points A and B is

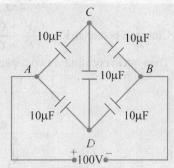

Fig. 6.31

(a) 20 μF (b) 40 μF

(c) 10 μF (d) 30 μF

Answers to Multiple-Choice Questions

1. (a)	**2.** (d)	**3.** (a)	**4.** (d)	**5.** (b)	**6.** (a)	**7.** (b)	**8.** (d)
9. (c)	**10.** (d)	**11.** (c)	**12.** (b)	**13.** (a)	**14.** (b)	**15.** (d)	**16.** (b)
17. (a)	**18.** (d)	**19.** (a)	**20.** (c)				

Hints to Selected Multiple-Choice Questions

2. $\dfrac{C_{mica}}{C_{air}}$ = dielectric constant of mica = **6.**

4. The 3-plate capacitor forms two similar capacitors in parallel. Hence the capacitance of a 3-plate capacitor is **twice** that of a 2-plate capacitor.

5. When two capacitors are connected in series, the total capacitance C_T is given by :

$$C_T = \frac{\text{Product}}{\text{sum}} = \frac{3 \times 6}{3 + 6} = 2\,\mu F$$

6. Due to opposite charges on the two plates of a capacitor, there is a force of attraction between them.

∴   Work done = Energy stored

or $$F \times d = \frac{1}{2}\,CV^2$$

or $$F = \frac{CV^2}{2d}$$

7. $C_P = 12 + 12 = 24$ μF. Now $\dfrac{1}{C_s} = \dfrac{1}{14} + \dfrac{1}{24} + \dfrac{1}{14} = \dfrac{31}{168}$ ∴ $C_S = 168/31 = 5.4$ μF

8. $\dfrac{4}{3}\,\pi R^3\,\rho = 64 \times \left(\dfrac{4}{3}\,\pi r^3\right)\rho$ or $R = (64)^{1/3} \times r = 4r$ ∴ $R/r = 4$

If C_b and C_s are the capacitances of bigger and smaller drops respectively, then $C_b = 4\pi\varepsilon_0 R$ and $C_s = 4\pi\varepsilon_0 r$.

$$\therefore \qquad \frac{C_b}{C_s} = \frac{4\pi\varepsilon_0 R}{4\pi\varepsilon_0 r} = \frac{R}{r} = \frac{4}{1}$$

9. Common potential, $V = \dfrac{C_1 V_1 + C_2 V_2}{C_1 + C_2} = \dfrac{10^{-6}\,(20 \times 500 + 10 \times 200)}{10^{-6}\,(20 + 10)} = \dfrac{12000}{30} = \mathbf{400\ V}$

10. The system constitutes two capacitors C_1 and C_2 in series.

$$\therefore \qquad \frac{1}{C_S} = \frac{1}{C_1} + \frac{1}{C_2} = \frac{d_1}{\varepsilon_0 K_1 A} + \frac{d_2}{\varepsilon_0 K_2 A} = \frac{1}{\varepsilon_0 A}\left(\frac{d_1}{K_1} + \frac{d_2}{K_2}\right)$$

$$\therefore \qquad C_S = \frac{\varepsilon_0 A}{\dfrac{d_1}{K_1} + \dfrac{d_2}{K_2}}$$

11. In order to pull the plates apart, work will have to be done. This work done is stored in the electric field of the capacitor ($U = CV^2/2$). Therefore p.d. across plates **increases.**

12. In the absence of dielectric, capacitances of the two capacitors are $C/2$ and $C/2$. With dielectric present as shown, the capacitances of the two capacitors are $C/2$ and $KC/2$. Since the two capacitors are in parallel,

$$\text{Resultant capacitance} = \frac{C}{2} + \frac{KC}{2} = \frac{C\,(K+1)}{2}$$

13. The electric field will be halved.

14. $C = q/V$. When potential difference is reduced by 8 times, then for the same charge, capacitance increases by 8 times.

$$\therefore \qquad K = \frac{8 \times 5 \times 10^{-6}}{5 \times 10^{-6}} = \mathbf{8}$$

15. The electric field inside the metallic foil is zero. Therefore, the effective separation is now $t - t/3 = 2t/3$.

New capacitance $\qquad = \dfrac{3}{2} \times 100 = \mathbf{150\ pF}$ $\qquad\qquad\qquad (\because\ C \propto 1/t)$

16. Let $C\,\mu F$ be the capacitance of each capacitor. Then,

$$C_S = C/n \quad \text{or} \quad 4 = C/5 \quad \therefore \quad C = 4 \times 5 = 20\ \mu F$$

Total energy stored $\qquad = \dfrac{1}{2}\, C_P V^2 = \dfrac{1}{2} \times (20 \times 5) \times 10^{-6} \times (400)^2 = \mathbf{8\ J}$

17. Let R and r be the radii of bigger and smaller drops respectively. Since total mass is conserved,

$$\therefore \qquad \frac{4}{3}\pi R^3 \rho = N \times \frac{4}{3}\pi r^3 \rho \quad \text{or} \quad \frac{R}{r} = N^{1/3}$$

Let C and c be the capacitances of bigger and smaller drops respectively. Since the capacitance of a spherical drop is directly proportional to its radius.

$$\therefore \qquad \frac{C}{c} = \frac{R}{r} = N^{1/3}$$

18. $v = V\,e^{-t/RC}$ $\qquad$ or $\qquad \dfrac{V}{3} = V e^{-1/RC} \qquad \therefore\ \dfrac{1}{3} = e^{-1/RC}$

After 2s, $\qquad\qquad v' = V e^{-2/RC} = V\,(e^{-1/RC})^2 = V \times \left(\dfrac{1}{3}\right)^2 = \dfrac{V}{9}$

19. It is clear that one plate of each capacitor is connected to point *A* and the other plate of each capacitor is connected to point *B*. Therefore, the three capacitors are in parallel.

$$C_{AB} = 3 + 3 + 3 = 9 \ \mu F$$

20. A little reflection shows that bridge is balanced. It means that points *C* and *D* are at the same potential. Therefore, there can be no charge on the capacitor in the branch *CD*. Hence this capacitor is ineffective and can be removed from the circuit. The circuit then reduces to the one shown in Fig. 6.32.

∴ $$C_{AB} = (10/2) + (10/2)$$
$$= 5 + 5 = 10 \ \mu F$$

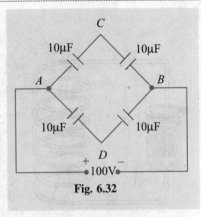

Fig. 6.32

Note that between *A* and *B*, we have two parallel branches each of effective capacitance = 10/2 = 5 μF.

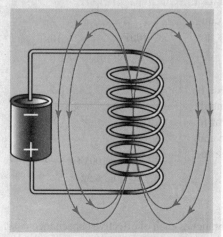

Magnetism and Electromagnetism

INTRODUCTION

In the ancient times, people believed that the invisible force of magnetism was purely a magical quality and hence they showed little practical interest. However, with steadily increasing scientific knowledge over the passing centuries, magnetism assumed a larger and larger role. Today magnetism has attained a place of pride in electrical engineering. Without the aid of magnetism, it is impossible to operate such devices as electric generators, electric motors, transformers, electrical instruments *etc.* Without the use of magnetism, we should be deprived of such valuable assets as the radio, television, telephone, telegraph and the ignition systems of our cars, airplanes, trucks *etc.* In fact, electrical engineering is so much dependent on magnetism that without it a very few of our modern devices would be possible. The purpose of this chapter is to present the salient features of magnetism so that a reader may be able to understand the function of magnetism in the electrical equipment.

7.1. POLES OF A MAGNET

If we take a bar magnet and dip it into iron filings, it will be observed that the iron filings cluster about the ends of the bar magnet. The ends of the bar magnet are apparently points of maximum magnetic effect and for convenience we call them the *poles of the magnet. A magnet has two poles *viz* north pole and south pole. In order to determine the polarity of a magnet, suspend or pivot it at the centre. The magnet will then come to rest in north-south direction. The end of the magnet pointing north is called *north pole* of the magnet while the end pointing south is called the *south pole*. The following points may be noted about the poles of a magnet :

(*i*) The poles of a magnet cannot be separated. If a bar magnet is broken into two parts, each part will be a complete magnet with poles at its ends. No matter how many times a magnet is broken, each piece will contain *n*-pole at one end and *s*-pole at the other.

(*ii*) The two poles of a magnet are of equal strength. The pole strength is represented by *m*.

7.2. LAWS OF MAGNETIC FORCE

(*i*) *Like poles repel each other while unlike poles attract each other.*

(*ii*) *The force between two magnetic poles is directly proportional to the product of their pole strengths and inversely proportional to the square of distance between them.*

Consider two poles of magnetic strength m_1 and m_2 placed at a distance d apart in a medium as shown in Fig. 7.1. According to Coulomb's laws, the force between the two poles is given by ;

$$F \propto \frac{m_1 m_2}{d^2}$$

$$= K \frac{m_1 m_2}{d^2}$$

where K is a constant whose value depends upon the surrounding medium and the system of units employed. In *SI* units, force is measured in newtons, pole strength in weber, distance in metres and the value of K is given by;

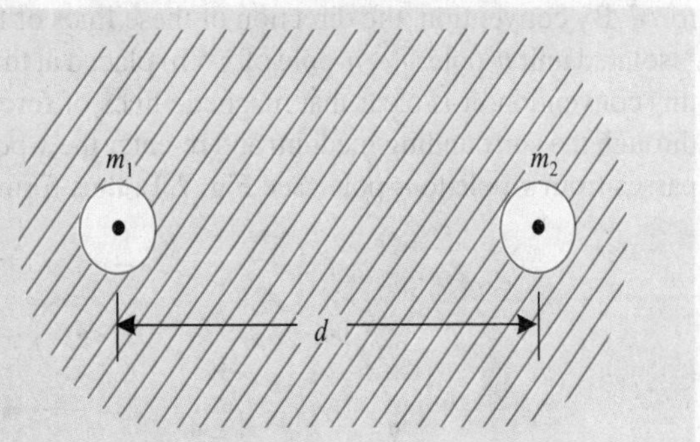

$$K = \frac{1}{4\pi\mu_0\mu_r}$$

Fig. 7.1

where μ_0 = Absolute permeability of vacuum or air

μ_r = Relative permeability of the surrounding medium.

For vacuum or air, its value is 1.

The value of $\mu_0 = 4\pi \times 10^{-7}$ H/m and the value of μ_r is different for different media.

∴ $$F = \frac{m_1 m_2}{4\pi\mu_0\mu_r\, d^2} \text{ newtons} \qquad \text{... in a medium}$$

$$= \frac{m_1 m_2}{4\pi\mu_0\, d^2} \text{ newtons} \qquad \text{...in air}$$

Unit of pole strength. By unit pole strength we mean 1 weber. It can be defined from Coulomb's laws of magnetic force. Suppose two equal point poles placed 1 m apart in *air* exert a force of 62800 newtons *i.e.*

$$m_1 = m_2 = m ; \quad d = 1 \text{ m} ; \quad F = 62800 \text{ N}$$

∴ $$F = \frac{m_1 m_2}{4\pi\mu_0\, d^2} \qquad (\because \text{ For air, } \mu_r = 1)$$

---

* Magnetic poles have no physical reality, but the concept enables us to appreciate magnetic effects more easily.

or $$62800 = \frac{m^2}{4\pi \times 4\pi \times 10^{-7} \times (1)^2}$$

or $$m^2 = (62800) \times (4\pi \times 4\pi \times 10^{-7} \times 1) = 1$$

∴ $$m = \pm 1 \text{ Wb}$$

Hence a **pole of unit strength** *(i.e.1 Wb) is that pole which when placed in air 1 m from an identical pole, repels it with a force of 62800 newtons.*

7.3. MAGNETIC FIELD

Just as electric field exists near a charged object, similarly magnetic field exists around a magnet. If an isolated magnetic pole is brought near a magnet, it experiences a force according to Coulomb's laws. This region near the magnet where forces act on magnetic poles is called a *magnetic field.* The magnetic field is strongest near the pole and goes on decreasing in strength as we move away from the magnet.

The space (or field) in which a magnetic pole experiences a force is called a **magnetic field.**

The magnetic field around a magnet is represented by imaginary lines called *magnetic lines of force.* By convention, the direction of these lines of force at any point is the direction along which an *isolated unit *n*-pole (*i.e. n*-pole of 1Wb) placed at that point would move or tends to move. Following this convention, it is clear that magnetic lines of force would emerge from *n*-pole of the magnet, pass through the surrounding medium and re-enter the *s*-pole. Inside the magnet, each magnetic line of force passes from *s*-pole to *n*-pole (See Fig. 7.2), thus forming a closed loop or magnetic circuit.

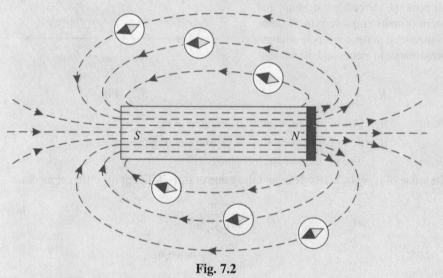

Fig. 7.2

Although magnetic lines of force have no real existence and are purely imaginary, yet they are a useful concept to describe the various magnetic effects.

Properties of Magnetic Lines of Force

(*i*) Each magnetic line of force forms a closed loop *i.e.* outside the magnet, the direction of a magnetic line of force is from north pole to south pole and it continues through the body of the magnet to form a closed loop (See Fig. 7.2).

* Theoretically, it is not possible to get an isolated *n*-pole. However, a small compass needle well approximates to an isolated *n*-pole. The marked end (*n*-pole) of the compass needle indicates the direction of magnetic lines of force as shown in Fig. 7.2.

(ii) The direction of magnetic flux density ($\vec{B}$) at a point is that of the tangent to the magnetic field line at that point.

(iii) No two magnetic lines of force can intersect each other. If two magnetic lines of force intersect, there would be two directions of magnetic field at that point which is not possible.

(iv) Where the magnetic lines of force are close together, the magnetic field is strong and where they are well spaced out, the magnetic field is weak.

(v) The larger the number of magnetic field lines crossing per unit normal area, the larger is the magnetic flux density ($\vec{B}$).

(vi) Magnetic lines of force contract longitudinally and widen laterally.

(vii) Magnetic lines of force are always ready to pass through iron or other magnetic material, in preference to passing through air, even though their closed paths are made longer thereby.

7.4. UNIFORM AND NON-UNIFORM MAGNETIC FIELD

(i) **Uniform magnetic field.** *The magnetic field in a region is uniform if it has the same magnetic flux density* ($\vec{B}$) *and the same direction at all points in the region.*

For example, the earth's magnetic field is nearly uniform. This means that magnitude and direction of magnetic flux density at every point on earth's surface is nearly the same. A uniform magnetic field acting in the plane of the paper is represented by parallel and equidistant magnetic lines of force as shown in Fig. 7.3 (*i*). A uniform magnetic field acting perpendicular to the plane of the paper and directed *downwards* is represented by equally spaced crosses as shown in Fig. 7.3 (*ii*). However, a uniform magnetic field acting perpendicular to the plane of the paper and directed *upwards* is represented by equally spaced dots as shown in Fig. 7.3 (*iii*). It is reminded that crowded magnetic lines of force means stronger magnetic field and vice-versa.

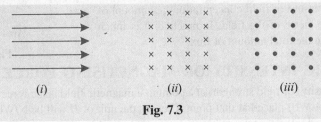

(i)   *(ii)*   *(iii)*

Fig. 7.3

(ii) **Non-uniform magnetic field.** *The magnetic field in a region is non-uniform if the magnitude or/and direction of magnetic flux density varies from point to point in the region.*

For example, the magnetic field due to a bar magnet is non-uniform *i.e.* magnitude and direction of magnetic flux density varies from point to point. A non-uniform magnetic field is represented by converging or diverging magnetic lines of force. Fig. 7.4 (*i*) shows magnetic lines of force due to non-uniform magnetic field where direction of magnetic field varies from point to point. In Fig. 7.4 (*ii*), both magnitude and direction of magnetic field are not constant.

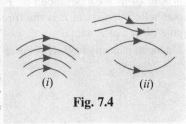

(i)   *(ii)*

Fig. 7.4

7.5. MAGNETIC FLUX

The magnetic field cannot be detected by any of our personal senses but its effects can be observed in many ways. To identify the magnetic field quantitatively (*i.e.* with numbers), we generally use the term magnetic flux.

The amount of magnetic field produced by a magnetic source is called **magnetic flux.**

Magnetic flux is denoted by Greek letter ϕ. If 10 magnetic lines come out of the north pole or enter the south pole of a magnet, then magnetic flux ϕ = 10 lines or maxwells. The *SI* unit of magnetic flux is *weber.*

$$1 \text{ Wb} = 10^8 \text{ lines}$$

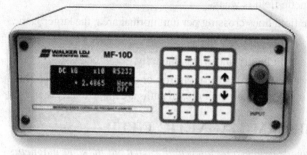

Magnetic Fluxmeters

7.6. MAGNETIC FLUX DENSITY

The magnetic flux density is the flux per unit area at right angles to the flux (See Fig. 7.5) *i.e.*

Magnetic flux density, $B = \dfrac{\phi}{A}$ Wb/m^2

where
ϕ = magnetic flux in Wb

A = area in m^2 normal to flux

The *SI* unit of magnetic flux density is Wb/m^2 or *tesla. Flux density is a measure of field concentration *i.e.* amount of flux in each square metre of the field. In practice, it is much more important than the total amount of flux.

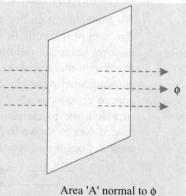

Area 'A' normal to ϕ

Fig. 7.5

7.7. MAGNETIC INTENSITY OR MAGNETISING FORCE (H)

Magnetic intensity (or field strength) at a point in a magnetic field is the force acting on a unit *n*-pole (*i.e. n*-pole of 1 Wb) placed at that point. Clearly, the unit of H will be N/Wb.

Suppose it is desired to find the magnetic intensity at a point P situated at a distance d metres from a pole of strength m webers (See Fig. 7.6). Imagine a unit north pole (*i.e. n*-pole of 1 Wb) is placed at P. Then, by definition, magnetic intensity at P is the force acting on the unit *n*-pole placed at P *i.e.*

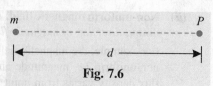

Fig. 7.6

Magnetic intensity at P, H = Force on unit *n*-pole placed at P

or
$$H = \frac{m \times 1}{4\pi\mu_0 \, d^2} \text{ N/Wb} \qquad\qquad [\because \mu_r = 1 \text{ for air}]$$

or
$$H = \frac{m}{4\pi\mu_0 \, d^2} \text{ N/Wb}$$

* Named in honour of Nikola Tesla (1857-1943), an American electrician and inventor.

The reader may note the following points carefully :

(*i*) Magnetic intensity is a vector quantity, possessing both magnitude and direction.

(*ii*) If a pole of *m* Wb is placed in a uniform magnetic field of strength *H* newtons/Wb, then force acting on the pole, $F = mH$ newtons.

7.8. ABSOLUTE AND RELATIVE PERMEABILITY

Permeability of a material means its conductivity for magnetic flux. The greater the permeability of a material, the greater is its conductivity for magnetic flux and *vice-versa*. Air or vacuum is the poorest conductor of magnetic flux. The absolute (or actual) permeability **μ_0 (Greek letter "mu") of air or vacuum is $4\pi \times 10^{-7}$ H/m. The absolute (or actual) permeability μ of magnetic materials is much greater than μ_0. The ratio μ/μ_0 is called the relative permeability of the material and is denoted by μ_r, *i.e.*

$$\mu_r = \frac{\mu}{\mu_0}$$

where μ = absolute (or actual) permeability of the material

μ_0 = absolute permeability of air or vacuum

μ_r = relative permeability of the material

Obviously, the relative permeability for air or vacuum would be $\mu_0/\mu_0 = 1$. The value of μ_r for all non-magnetic materials is also 1. However, relative permeability of magnetic materials is very high. For example, soft iron (*i.e.* pure iron) has a relative permeability of 8000 whereas its value for permalloy (an alloy containing 22% iron and 78% nickel) is as high as 50,000.

Concept of relative permeability. The relative permeability of a material is a measure of the relative ease with which that material conducts magnetic flux compared with the conduction of magnetic flux in air. Fig. 7.7 illustrates the concept of relative permeability. In Fig. 7.7 (*i*), the magnetic flux passes between the poles of a magnet in air. Consider a soft iron ring ($\mu_r = 8000$) placed between the same poles as shown in Fig. 7.7 (*ii*). Since soft iron is a very good conductor of magnetic flux, the flux follows a path entirely within the soft iron itself. The magnetic flux density in the soft iron is much greater than it is in air. In fact, magnetic flux density in soft iron will be 8000 times (*i.e.* μ_r times) the magnetic flux density in air.

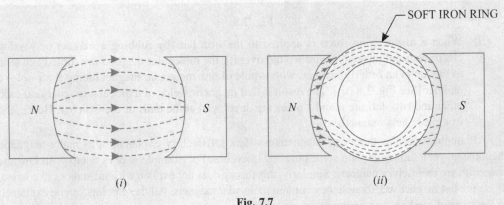

Fig. 7.7

Due to high relative permeability of magnetic materials (*e.g.* iron, steel and other magnetic alloys), they are widely used for the cores of all electromagnetic equipment.

*   The absolute (or actual) permeability of all non-magnetic materials is also $4\pi \times 10^{-7}$ H / m.

7.9. RELATION BETWEEN B AND H

The magnetic flux density B produced in a material is directly proportional to the applied magnetising force H. In other words, the greater the magnetising force, the greater is the magnetic flux density and *vice-versa i.e.*

$$B \propto H$$

or

$$\frac{B}{H} = \text{Constant} = \mu$$

The ratio B/H in a material is always constant and is equal to the absolute permeability μ $(= \mu_0 \mu_r)$ of the material. This relation gives yet another definition of absolute permeability of a material.

Obviously,

$$B = \mu_0 \mu_r H \qquad \qquad \textit{... in a medium}$$
$$= \mu_0 H \qquad \qquad \textit{... in air}$$

7.10. MOLECULAR THEORY OF MAGNETISM

There have been various theories developed from time to time for the explanation of magnetism. The theory proposed by *Weber* in 1852 and modified by Ewing in 1890, is the most popular explanation. According to this theory, *molecules of all substances are basically magnets in themselves, each having a n and s pole.* In other words, every substance consists of a very large number of tiny magnets called *molecular magnets.*

(*i*) Before a piece of iron has been magnetised, these molecular magnets lie in disorderly positions [See Fig. 7.8 (*i*)] so that poles of molecular magnets neutralise each other. Hence, the iron piece does not show any magnetism *i.e.* no poles are developed at the ends.

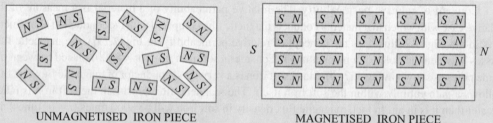

UNMAGNETISED IRON PIECE   MAGNETISED IRON PIECE

(*i*)   (*ii*)

Fig. 7.8

(*ii*) When a magnetising force is applied to the iron bar (by rubbing a magnet or passing electric current through a wire wound over it), the molecular magnets are turned and tend to line up in an orderly manner, with *n*-pole of one molecular magnet facing the *s*-pole of another [See Fig. 7.8 (*ii*)]. The result is that magnetic fields of molecular magnets aid each other and two definite *n* and *s* poles are developed at the ends of the iron bar. Hence, the iron piece gets magnetised.

Although molecular theory of magnetism offers satisfactory explanation to many magnetic phenomena, yet it fails to explain some puzzling questions. For example, it does not explain how the molecules are themselves magnets. Similarly, this theory does not explain why substances like wood, air *etc* are not magnetised, though they contain molecular magnets. All these points can be explained on the basis of modern domain theory of magnetism.

7.11. DOMAIN THEORY OF MAGNETISM

According to this theory, magnetism results from the movement of electrons within the atoms of substances. A moving electron constitutes electric current and magnetic field is always associated with electric current. There are two kinds of electron motions in an atom. First, an electron rotates around the nucleus and secondly it spins around its own axis. The magnetic properties are mainly due to the electron spin.

(*i*) In the atoms of non-magnetic materials, half of the electrons spin in one direction and half in the other. Thus the opposing polarities of the resulting magnetic fields cancel out and the material does not exhibit any magnetism.

(*ii*) In the atoms of magnetic materials (*i.e.* iron, nickel, cobalt *etc.*), more electrons spin in one direction than in the other. Hence the magnetic fields do not cancel out completely and a net external magnetic field is produced. Consider, for example, the magnetic material iron. It has 26 electrons distributed in four orbits as : first orbit contains 2 electrons, second orbit 8 electrons, third 14 electrons and the fourth orbit 2 electrons. In the first, second and fourth orbit, half of the electrons spin in one direction and half in the other. The resulting magnetic fields thus cancel out. However, in the third orbit, 9 electrons spin in one direction and 5 electrons spin in the opposite direction. Thus an atom of iron has a surplus of 4 electron spins in one direction. The result is that each atom of iron has an external magnetic field due to 4 uncancelled electrons in the third orbit *i.e.,* each atom becomes a small magnet.

Domains. In magnetic materials, neighbouring atoms group together in such a way that their magnetic fields aid each other. Such a group of atoms is called a *domain* and contains approximately 10^{15} atoms. Thus a magnetic material contains a large number of domains, each of which is a tiny magnet.

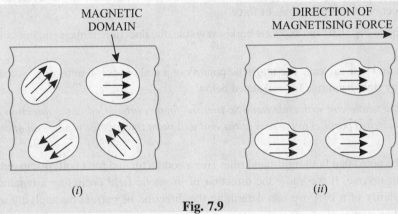

Fig. 7.9

In the unmagnetised magnetic material, these domains are arranged in a disorderly manner as shown in Fig. 7.9 (*i*). Hence their magnetic fields cancel out and the net magnetism is essentially zero. However, when a magnetising force is applied to the magnetic material, the domains are forced to line up in the direction of magnetising force [See Fig. 7.9 (*ii*)]. Hence the magnetic fields of domains aid each other and the material exhibits magnetism *i.e.* the material becomes magnetised.

Except that we now talk of magnetic domains instead of molecular magnets, the explanation offered by Weber's theory for various magnetic phenomena remains unchanged.

7.12. MAGNETIC EFFECT OF ELECTRIC CURRENT

When an electric current flows through a conductor, magnetic field is set up all along the length of the conductor. Fig. 7.10 shows the magnetic field produced by the current flowing in a straight wire. The magnetic lines of force are in the form of *concentric circles around the conductor. The direction of lines of force depends upon the direction of current and may be determined by one of the following methods :

. . . .

*   This can be readily established with a compass needle. If a compass needle is placed near the conductor and it is progressively moved in the direction of its north pole, it will be seen that the paths of magnetic lines of force are concentric circles.

(*i*)   Right-hand rule   (*ii*)   Cork screw rule

(*i*)   **Right-hand rule.** *Hold the conductor in the right hand with the thumb pointing in the direction of current (See Fig. 7.10). Then the fingers will point in the direction of magnetic field around the conductor.*

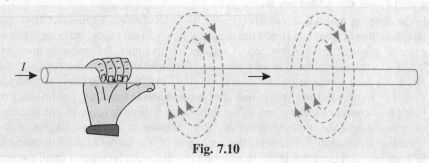

Fig. 7.10

Applying this rule to Fig. 7.10, it is clear that when viewed from left hand side, the direction of magnetic lines of force will be clockwise.

(*ii*)   **Cork screw rule.** Hold the cork screw in your right hand and rotate it in such a way that it advances in the direction of current. Then the direction in which the hand rotates will be the direction of magnetic lines of force.

Referring to Fig. 7.10 and applying cork screw rule, the direction of magnetic lines of force will be clockwise.

Right-hand rule for coil. The magnetic polarity of a coil of several turns or a *solenoid can be determined by right-hand rule for coil stated below :

Grasp the whole coil with right hand so that the fingers are curled in the direction of current. The thumb stretched parallel to the axis of the coil will point towards the n-pole end of the coil (See Fig. 7.11).

It may be noted that both right-hand rules (for a conductor and for a coil) discussed so far can be applied in reverse. If we know the direction of magnetic field encircling a conductor or the magnetic polarity of a coil, we can determine the direction of current by applying appropriate right-hand rule.

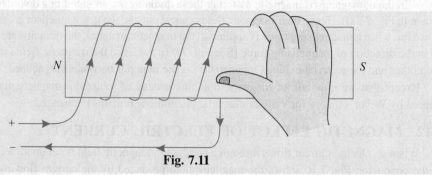

Fig. 7.11

7.13.   CURRENT CARRYING CONDUCTOR IN MAGNETIC FIELD

When a current-carrying conductor is placed at right angles to a magnetic field, it experiences a mechanical force *F* given by;

$$F = BIl \text{ newtons}$$

. . . .

*   Solenoid is a Greek word meaning "tube-like".

where l = length of conductor in metres

                 I = current through conductor in amperes

                 B = magnetic flux density in Wb/m²

The direction of this force can be found by Fleming's left-hand rule.

Fleming's Left-hand Rule. Stretch out the first finger, second finger and thumb of your left hand so that they are at right angles to one another. If the first finger points in the direction of magnetic field (North to South) and second finger (*i.e.* middle finger) points towards the direction of current, then the thumb will point in the direction of motion of the conductor.

Applying Fleming's left-hand rule to Fig. 7.12 (*i*), it is clear that the force F on the conductor will act vertically upwards. Note that if direction of any two of F, B and I is known, the direction of the third can be found by this rule.

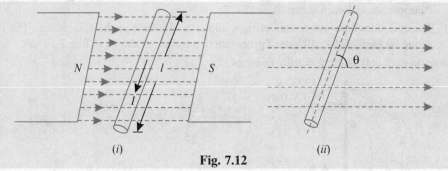

(*i*)   (*ii*)

Fig. 7.12

If the conductor and magnetic field make an angle θ as shown in Fig. 7.12 (*ii*), then effective length (*i.e.* length presented normally to magnetic field) is $l \sin \theta$ and the force is given by;

$$F = BIl \sin \theta \text{ newtons}$$

7.14. MECHANISM OF FORCE PRODUCTION

Consider a conductor carrying current out of the plane of paper and placed at right angles to the magnetic field existing between the poles of a magnet as shown in Fig. 7.13 (*i*). By right-hand rule, the conductor is surrounded by anticlockwise magnetic field. Note that magnetic field around the conductor aids the magnet's field below the conductor but opposes the field above it. The result is that magnetic lines of force are crowded at the bottom of the conductor and thinned at the top as shown in Fig. 7.13 (*ii*). Since magnetic lines of force act somewhat like stretched rubber bands, a force F acts on the conductor from bottom towards top *i.e.* the force moves the conductor upwards.

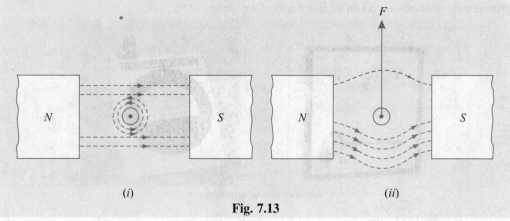

(*i*)   (*ii*)

Fig. 7.13

If the direction of current in the conductor or direction of field is reversed, the direction of force is also reversed. It may be noted that direction of force can also be determined by applying Fleming's left-hand rule.

7.15. TORQUE ON CURRENT-CARRYING COIL IN UNIFORM MAGNETIC FIELD

Consider a rectangular coil, measuring b by l, of N turns carrying a current of I amperes and placed in a uniform magnetic field of B Wb/m². The coil is pivoted about the mid points of the sides b and is free to rotate about an axis in its own plane; this axis being at right angles to the magnetic field density B [See Fig. 7.14 (*i*)]. When current is passed through the coil, forces act on the coil sides.

   (*i*)   The forces developed on each half of coil sides b are equal and are of opposing sense. They, therefore, cancel each other.

   (*ii*)   The coil sides l always remain at right angles to the field as the coil rotates. The force F acting on each of the coil sides l gives rise to a torque as shown in Fig. 7.14 (*ii*).

Force on each coil side l, $F = BIlN$ newtons

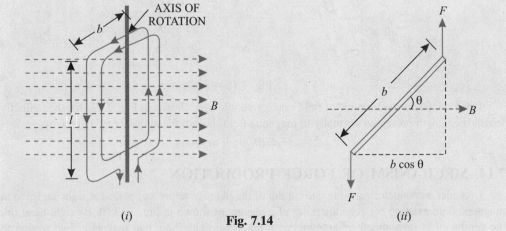

(*i*)   **Fig. 7.14**   (*ii*)

The perpendicular distance between the lines of action of two forces is $b \cos \theta$.

$\therefore$ Torque, $T = F \times b \cos \theta = (BIlN) \, b \cos \theta$

$\therefore$ $T = *BINA \cos \theta$ newton-metre

where $A \, (= l \times b)$ is the area of the coil. By an extension of this reasoning, the expression may be proved quite generally for a coil of area A and of any shape.

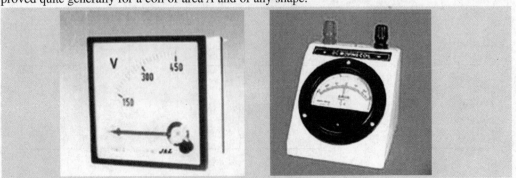

Moving coil voltmeters

*   How to remember ? Torque is equal to *BINA* (name of *girl*) multiplied by $\cos \theta$.

Example 7.1. *In a certain electric motor, wires that carry a current of 5 A are perpendicular to a magnetic field of 0.8 T. What is the force on each cm of these wires?*

Solution. Force on each cm of wires, $F = BIl = (0.8) \times (5) \times (0.01) = $ **0.04 N**

Example 7.2. *A straight wire 0.5 m long carries a current of 100 A and lies at right angles to a uniform magnetic field of 1.5 T. Find the mechanical force on the conductor when (i) it lies in the given position (ii) it lies in a position such that it is inclined at an angle of 30° to be direction of field.*

Solution.

(i) $F = BIl = 1.5 \times 100 \times 0.5 = $ **75 N**

(ii) $F = BIl \sin \theta = 1.5 \times 100 \times 0.5 \times \sin 30° = $ **37.5 N**

Example 7.3. *A conductor of length 100 cm and carrying 100 A is situated in and at right angles to a uniform magnetic field produced by the pole core of an electrical machine. If the pole core has a circular cross-section of 120 mm diameter and the total magnetic flux in the core is 16 mWb, find (i) the mechanical force on the conductor and (ii) power required to move the conductor at a speed of 10 m/s in a plane at right angles to the magnetic field.*

Solution. X-sectional area of pole core $= (\pi/4) \times (0.12)^2 = 0.0113$ m^2

Magnetic flux density of field, $B = \dfrac{\text{Flux}}{\text{Pole core area}} = \dfrac{16 \times 10^{-3}}{0.0113} = 1.416$ Wb/m^2

(i) Force on the conductor, $F = BIl = 1.416 \times 100 \times 1 = $ **141.6 N**

(ii) Power required = Force × distance/second $= 141.6 \times 10 = $ **1416 watts**

Example 7.4. *The plane of a rectangular coil makes an angle of 60° with the direction of a uniform field of magnetic flux density 4×10^{-2} Wb/m^2. The coil is of 20 turns, measuring 20 cm by 10 cm, and carries a current of 0.5A. Calculate the torque acting on the coil.*

Solution. Fig. 7.15 shows the conditions of the problem.

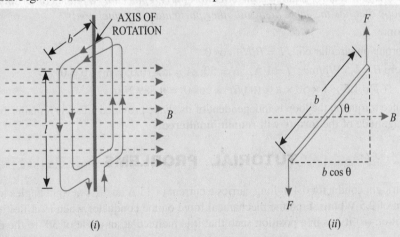

Fig. 7.15

Torque, $T = BINA \cos \theta$ newton-metre

In the given problem :

$B = 4 \times 10^{-2}$ Wb/m^2; $A = 20 \times 10 = 200$ cm$^2 = 2 \times 10^{-2}$ m^2; $I = 0.5$ A ; $\theta = 60°$; $N = 20$

∴ Torque, $T = (4 \times 10^{-2}) \times (0.5) \times (20) \times (2 \times 10^{-2}) \times \cos 60° = $ **4 × 10^{-3} Nm**

Example 7.5. *A d.c. motor consists of an armature winding of 400 turns (equivalent to 800 conductors). The effective length of conductor in the field is 160 mm and the conductors are situated at a radius of 100 mm from the centre of the motor shaft. The magnetic flux density is 0.6 Wb/m^2 and a current of 25 A flows through the winding. Calculate the torque available at the motor shaft.*

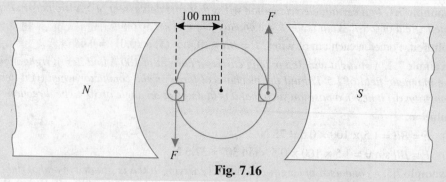

Fig. 7.16

Solution. In a d.c. motor, conductors carrying direct current are wound on an iron core (called armature) placed in a magnetic field. The mechanical forces acting on the conductors rotate the armature. Fig. 7.16 shows a single turn on the armature of the d.c. motor.

Force on each conductor, $F = BIl = (0.6) \times (25) \times (0.16) = 2.4$ N

The perpendicular distance between the two conductors of a turn is twice the radius of armature *i.e.* $2 \times 100 = 200$ mm $= 0.2$ m.

$\therefore$ Torque provided by 1 turn $= 2.4 \times 0.2 = 0.48$ Nm

$$\text{Total torque} = 400 \times 0.48 = \textbf{192 Nm}$$

Example 7.6. *A circular coil of wire of 50 turns and radius 0.05 m carries a current of 1A. The wire is suspended vertically in a uniform magnetic field of 1.5 Wb/m². The direction of magnetic field is parallel to the plane of the coil.*

(i) Calculate the torque on the coil.

(ii) Would your answer change if the circular coil is replaced by a plane coil of some irregular shape that has the same area (all other particulars are unaltered)?

Solution.

(i) Torque on circular coil, $T = BINA \cos \theta$

Here $B = 1.5$ Wb/m² ; $I = 1$ A; $N = 50$; $A = \pi \times (0.05)^2$ m² ; $\theta = 0°$

$\therefore$ $T = 1.5 \times 1 \times 50 \times \pi \times (0.05)^2 \times \cos 0° = \textbf{0.589 Nm}$

(ii) Since torque on the loop is independent of its shape provided area (A) remains the same, the magnitude of the **torque will remain unaltered.**

TUTORIAL PROBLEMS

1. A straight conductor 0.4 m long carries a current of 12 A and lies at right angles to a uniform field of 2.5 Wb/m². Find the mechanical force on the conductor when (*i*) it lies in the given position (*ii*) it lies in a position such that it is inclined at an angle of 30° to the direction of field. **[(*i*) 12 N (*ii*) 6 N]**

2. A conductor of length 100 cm and carrying 100 A is situated in and at right angles to a uniform magnetic field of strength 1 Wb/m². Calculate the force and power required to move the conductor at a speed of 100 m/s in a plane at right angles to the magnetic field.

   [100 N; 1000 watts]

3. A moving coil instrument is to be designed so that when a current of 20 mA passes through the coil, the torque exerted on the coil is 1.2×10^{-3} Nm. The coil is rectangular in shape with effective dimensions 30 mm × 20 mm, and lies in a radial magnetic field of strength 0.8 Wb/m². Calculate the number of turns that should be wound on the coil. **[125 turns]**

4. The control springs of a moving coil instrument provide a resisting torque of 12×10^{-6} Nm per degree. Calculate the torque exerted when the coil deflects through 75°.

   If the coil has effective dimensions 40 mm × 15 mm, is wound with 400 turns, and the deflection of 45° occurs when a current of 5 mA passes through the coil, calculate the strength of radial magnetic field in which the coil lies.   **[900 × 10⁻⁶ Nm; 0.75 Wb/m²]**

5. A d.c. motor is to provide a torque of 540 Nm. The armature winding consists of 600 turns (equivalent to 1200 conductors). The effective length of a conductor in the field is 250 mm and the conductors are situated at a radius of 150 mm from the centre of the motor shaft. Each conductor carries a current of 10 A. Calculate the magnetic flux density which must be provided by the radial magnetic field in which the conductors lie.   **[1.2 Wb/m²]**

7.16. AMPERE'S WORK LAW OR CIRCUITAL LAW

This law relates to work done in a magnetic circuit *i.e.* closed magnetic flux path. Consider N straight conductors, each carrying a current of I amperes as shown in Fig. 7.17. This current carrying conductor arrangement will set up magnetic field. If a unit n-pole is moved in opposition to the lines of force, work will be done *against the magnetic field. The work done on a unit n-pole in moving once round any complete path will be equal to the product of current and number of turns enclosed by that path. This is known as work law and may be stated as under :

The work done on or by a unit n-pole in moving once round any complete path is equal to the product of current and number of turns enclosed by that path i.e.

$$**\oint H_r d_r = NI$$

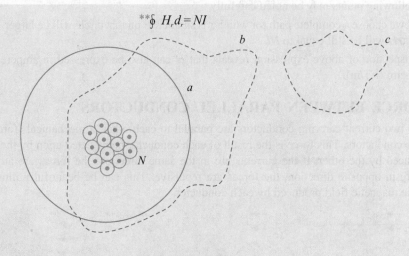

Fig. 7.17

where H_r is the magnetising force at a distance r. The circle round the integral sign indicates that the integral is round a complete path.

The work law is applicable regardless of the shape of complete path. Thus in Fig 7.17, paths a and b completely enclose N conductors. If a unit n-pole is moved once round any of these complete paths, the work done in each case will be equal to NI. Although path c is a complete path, it fails to enclose any current carrying conductor. Hence no work is done in moving a unit n-pole round such a path.

* If the unit n-pole is moved in the direction of magnetic field, work will be done by the magnetic force on whatever force is restraining the movement of the pole.

** This law can also be stated as *the closed line integral of magnetic field intensity (H) is equal to the enclosed ampere turns that produce the magnetic field.*

Applications. The work law can be profitably used to find the field intensity (H) near simple current carrying conductor arrangements. Let us consider the case of a long straight conductor carrying a current of I amperes as shown in Fig. 7.18. The conductor will set up magnetic lines of force which encircle it. Consider a circular path of radius r metres. By symmetry, the field intensity H on all the points of this circular path will be the same. If a unit n-pole is moved once round this circular path, then work done is $2\pi rH$. By work law, this must be equal to the ampere turns enclosed by this circular path.

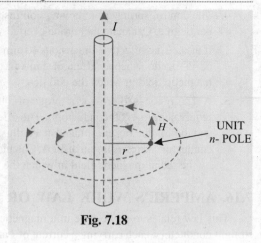

Fig. 7.18

∴ $\qquad 2\pi rH = I \qquad\qquad$ (∵ Number of turns, $N = 1$)

or $\qquad H = \dfrac{I}{2\pi r}$

If there had been N conductors enclosed by the path, then,

$$H = N\,\frac{I}{2\pi r}$$

The following points may be noted carefully :

(i) If we choose a complete path for which r is smaller, H on that circle will be larger. However, $2\pi rH$ will be still equal to NI.

(ii) Inspection of above expression reveals that H can also be expressed in ampere turns per metre (AT/m).

7.17. FORCE BETWEEN PARALLEL CONDUCTORS

When two current-carrying conductors are parallel to each other, a mechanical force acts on each of the conductors. This force is the result of each conductor being acted upon by the magnetic field produced by the other. If the currents are in the same direction, the forces are attractive; if currents are in opposite direction, the forces are repulsive. This can be beautifully illustrated by drawing the magnetic field produced by each conductor.

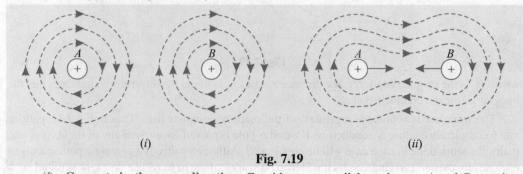

(i)   (ii)

Fig. 7.19

(i) **Currents in the same direction.** Consider two parallel conductors A and B carrying current in the same direction (i.e. into the plane of paper) as shown in Fig. 7.19 (i). Each conductor will set up its own magnetic field as shown. It is clear that in the space between A and B, the two fields are in opposition and hence they tend to cancel each other. However, in the space outside A and B, the two fields assist each other. Hence the resultant field distribution will be as shown in Fig. 7.19 (ii).

Since magnetic lines of force behave as stretched elastic cords, the two conductors are attracted towards each other. Alternatively, the conductors can be viewed as moving away from the relatively strong magnetic field (in the space outside A and B) into the weaker magnetic field between the conductors.

(ii) **Currents in opposite direction.** Consider two parallel conductors A and B carrying currents in the opposite direction as shown in Fig. 7.20. Each conductor will set up its own field as shown. It is clear that in the space outside A and B, the two fields are in opposition and hence they tend to cancel each other. However, in the space between A and B, the two fields assist each other. The lateral pressure between lines of force exerts a force on the conductors tending to push them apart. In other words, the conductors experience a repulsive force.

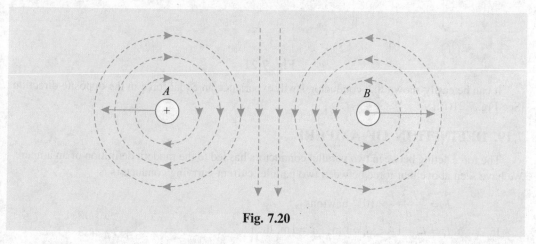

Fig. 7.20

7.18. MAGNITUDE OF MUTUAL FORCE

Fig. 7.21(i) shows two parallel conductors placed in air and carrying current in the same direction.

Let
I_1 = current in conductor 1 in amperes

I_2 = current in conductor 2 in amperes

l = length of each conductor in m

d = distance between conductors in m

It is clear that each of the two parallel conductors lies in the magnetic field of the other conductor. In order to determine the magnitude of force, we can consider conductor 2 placed in the magnetic field produced by conductor 1 as shown in Fig. 7.21(ii). The magnetic flux density B at the centre of conductor 2 due to current I_1 in conductor 1 is

$$B = \frac{\mu_0 I_1}{2\pi d}$$

...*See Art. 7.16*

Force acting on conductor 2 is given by :

$$F = BI_2 l = \left(\frac{\mu_0 I_1}{2\pi d} \right) I_2 l = \frac{4\pi \times 10^{-7} \, I_1 I_2 l}{2\pi d}$$

$$= \frac{2 I_1 I_2 l}{d} \times 10^{-7} \text{ newtons}$$

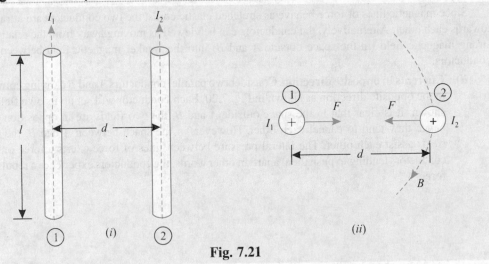

Fig. 7.21

It can be easily shown that conductor 1 will experience an equal force in the opposite direction [See Fig. 7.21(*ii*)].

7.19. DEFINITION OF AMPERE

The force acting between two parallel conductors has led to the modern definition of an ampere. We have seen above that force between two parallel current-carrying conductors is

$$F = \frac{2 I_1 I_2 l}{d} \times 10^{-7} \text{ newtons}$$

If $I_1 = I_2 = 1 \text{A} ; \ l = 1 \text{ m}; \ d = 1 \text{m}$, then,

$$F = \frac{2 \times 1 \times 1 \times 1}{1} \times 10^{-7} = 2 \times 10^{-7} \text{ N}$$

Hence **one ampere** *is that current which, if maintained in two long parallel conductors, and placed 1 m apart in vacuum, would produce between these conductors a force equal to 2×10^{-7} newton per metre of length (See Fig. 7.22).*

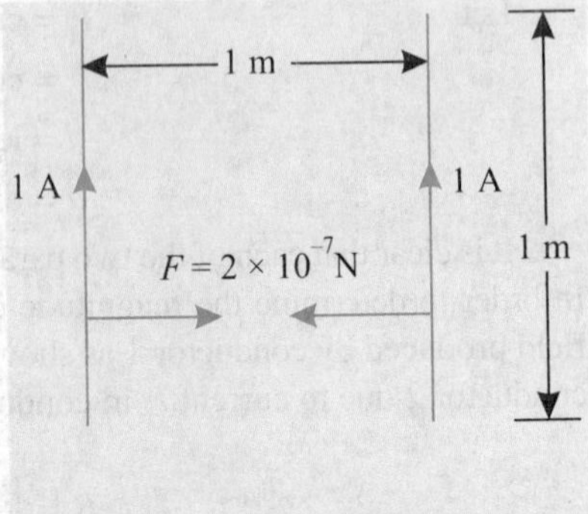

Historically, the ampere was fixed originally in a very different way. The constant 2×10^{-7} that appears in the modern definition was chosen so as to keep the magnitude of ampere the same as formerly.

Example 7.7. *The starting motor of a certain car is connected to a battery by a pair of cables 8 mm apart for a distance of 50 cm. Find the force between the cables when the current in them is 100 A.*

Solution. Force between the cables (See Art. 7.18) is

$$F = \frac{2 I_1 I_2 l}{d} \times 10^{-7} \text{ N}$$

Here $I_1 = I_2 = 100 \text{A}; \ l = 0.5 \text{ m}; \ d = 8 \times 10^{-3} \text{ m}$

∴ $$F = \frac{2 \times 100 \times 100 \times 0.5}{8 \times 10^{-3}} \times 10^{-7} = \textbf{0.125 N}$$

Fig. 7.22

Since the currents are in opposite directions, the force is repulsive.

Example 7.8. *Two bus-bars 80 mm apart are supported by insulators every metre along their length. The busbars each carry a current of 20 kA. What is the force acting on each insulator?*

Solution. Force on each metre of busbar is

$$F = \frac{2I_1 I_2}{d} \times 10^{-7} \text{ N} \qquad\qquad (\because l = 1 \text{ m})$$

$$= \frac{2 \times (20 \times 10^3) \times (20 \times 10^3) \times 10^{-7}}{80 \times 10^{-3}} = 1000 \text{ N}$$

Since busbars are supported by insulators, every metre along their length, this is the force (*i.e.* 1000 N) acting on each insulator. It should be noted that the force will be that of repulsion.

Example 7.9. *Force between two parallel conductors carrying current in opposite direction is 3.2 N/m when they are placed 50 mm apart in air. If current flowing in one conductor is 1000 A, find the current in the other conductor. Mention whether it is a force of attraction or repulsion.*

Solution. Force between the conductors per metre length is

$$F = \frac{2I_1 I_2}{d} \times 10^{-7} \text{ N}$$

Here $\qquad F = 3.2 \text{ N}; \ I_1 = 1000 \text{ A}; \ I_2 = ?; \ d = 50 \times 10^{-3} \text{ m}$

$\therefore \qquad\qquad 3.2 = \dfrac{2 \times 1000 \times I_2}{50 \times 10^{-3}} \times 10^{-7}$

or $\qquad\qquad 3.2 = (40 \times 10^{-4}) I_2$

or $\qquad\qquad I_2 = \dfrac{3.2}{40 \times 10^{-4}} = 800 \text{ A}$

Since the two conductors carry currents in the opposite direction, the force is repulsive.

Example 7.10. *Two long horizontal wires are kept parallel at a distance of 0.2 cm apart in a vertical plane. Both the wires have equal currents in the same direction. The lower wire has a mass of 0.05 kg/m. If the lower wire appears weightless, what is the current in each wire?*

Solution. Let *I* amperes be the current in each wire. The lower wire is acted upon by two forces *viz.* (*i*) upward magnetic force and (*ii*) downward force due to the weight of the wire. Since the lower wire appears weightless, the two forces are equal over 1 m length of the wire.

Upward force/metre length $= \dfrac{2I \times I}{d} \times 10^{-7} = \dfrac{2I^2}{0.002} \times 10^{-7} = 10^{-4} I^2$ newtons

Downward force/metre length $= mg = 0.05 \times 9.8 = 0.49 \text{ N}$

$\therefore \qquad\qquad 10^{-4} I^2 = 0.49$

or $\qquad\qquad I = \sqrt{0.49 \times 10^4} = 70 \text{ A}$

Example 7.11. *A horizontal straight wire 5 cm long of mass 1.2 g/m is placed perpendicular to a uniform magnetic field of 0.6 T. If the resistance of the wire is 3.8 Ω m^{-1}, calculate the p.d. that has to be applied between the ends of the wire to make it just self-supporting.*

Solution. The current (*I*) in the wire is to be in such a direction that magnetic force acts on it vertically upward. To make the wire self-supporting, its weight should be equal to the upward magnetic force *i.e.*

$$BIl = mg \qquad (\because \ \theta = 90°)$$

or $$I = \frac{mg}{Bl}$$

Here $m = 1.2 \times 10^{-3} \ l \, kg; \ B = 0.6 \, T; \ g = 9.8 \, ms^{-2}$

$$\therefore \qquad I = \frac{1.2 \times 10^{-3} \, l \times 9.8}{0.6 \times l} = 19.6 \times 10^{-3} \ A$$

Resistance of wire, $R = 0.05 \times 3.8 = 0.19 \ \Omega$

$\therefore$ Required P.D., $V = IR = (19.6 \times 10^{-3}) \times 0.19 = 3.7 \times 10^{-3} \ V$

TUTORIAL PROBLEMS

1. What is the force on a wire of length 4 cm placed inside a solenoid near its centre making an angle of 60° with the axis? The wire carries a current of 12 A and the magnetic field due to solenoid has a magnitude of 0.25 T. **[0.1 N]**

2. A horizontal wire 0.1 m long carries a current of 5 A. Find the magnitude of field which can support the weight of the wire assuming that its mass is 3×10^{-3} kg m^{-1}. **[5.88 × 10⁻³ T]**

3. A straight horizontal conducting rod of length 0.45 m and mass 60 g is suspended by two vertical wires at its ends. A current of 5 A is set up in the rod through the wires.

   (*i*) What magnetic field should be set up normal to the conductor in order that tension in the wires is zero?

   (*ii*) What will be the total tension in the wires if the direction of current is reversed, keeping the magnetic field the same as before? Neglect the mass of the wires.

   [(*i*) 0.26 T (*ii*) 1.176 N]

4. In Fig. 7.23, X is a very long straight conductor carrying a current of 5 A. A rectangular loop *PQRS* of copper wire is suspended with its longer arm parallel to the conductor X. The various dimensions are shown in the figure. Calculate the net force acting on the loop in magnitude and direction. **[6 × 10⁻⁵ N away from X]**

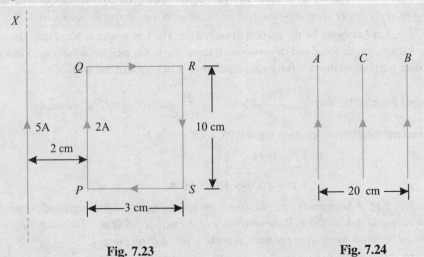

Fig. 7.23   Fig. 7.24

5. In Fig. 7.24, two very long straight parallel wires A and B carry currents of 10 A and 20 A respectively and are at a distance of 20 cm from each other. A third wire C of length 15 cm and carrying a current of 10 A is placed mid-way between them. What is the magnitude and direction of force on wire C? The direction of current in all the three wires is the same.

   [3 × 10⁻⁵ N towards B]

MULTIPLE-CHOICE QUESTIONS

1. When a magnet is heated
   (a) it gains magnetism
   (b) it loses magnetism
   (c) it neither loses nor gains magnetism
   (d) none of the above

2. The magnetic material used in permanent magnets is
   (a) iron
   (b) soft steel
   (c) nickel
   (d) hardened steel

3. The relative permeability of a ferromagnetic material is 10000. Its absolute permeability will be
   (a) 10^6 H/m
   (b) $4\pi \times 10^{-3}$ H/m
   (c) $4\pi \times 10^{-11}$ H/m
   (d) none of the above

4. The absolute permeability of a material having a flux density of 1 Wb/m^2 is 10^{-3} H/m. The value of magnetising force is
   (a) 10^{-3} AT/m
   (b) $4\pi \times 10^{-3}$ AT/m
   (c) 1000 AT/m
   (d) $4\pi \times 10^3$ AT/m

5. The magnetic flux density in an air-cored coil is 10^{-2} Wb/m^2. With a cast iron core of relative permeability 100 inserted, the flux density will become
   (a) 10^{-4} Wb/m^2
   (b) 10^4 Wb/m^2
   (c) 10^{-2} Wb/m^2
   (d) 1 Wb/m^2

6. A magnet is kept in air surrounded by an iron ring. The magnetic lines of force from the magnet will be
   (a) crowded in the ring
   (b) crowded in air
   (c) evenly distributed
   (d) none of the above

7. The distance between two magnetic poles is doubled and their pole strengths are also doubled. The force between them

   (a) increases four times
   (b) decreases four times
   (c) remains unchanged
   (d) none of the above

8. Fig. 7.25 shows a cross-section of a coil. Based on dot and cross notation, which end of the coil is the north pole?

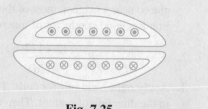

Fig. 7.25

   (a) left
   (b) right
   (c) left or right depending on magnitude of current
   (d) data incomplete

9. Will the two conductors in Fig. 7.26 repel or attract?

Fig. 7.26

   (a) repel
   (b) attract
   (c) neither repel nor attract
   (d) data insufficient

10. Will the two conductors in Fig. 7.27 attract or repel ?

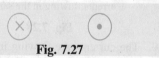

Fig. 7.27

   (a) repel
   (b) attract
   (c) neither repel nor attract
   (d) data insufficient

Answers to Multiple-Choice Questions

1. (b) 2. (d) 3. (b) 4. (c) 5. (d) 6. (a) 7. (c) 8. (b)
9. (b) 10. (a)

Hints to Selected Multiple-Choice Questions

3. $\mu_r = \dfrac{\mu}{\mu_0}$ or $\mu = \mu_0\mu_r = (4\pi \times 10^{-7}) \times 10000 = 4\pi \times 10^{-3}$ **H/m**

4. $\mu = \dfrac{B}{H}$ or $H = \dfrac{B}{\mu} = \dfrac{1}{10^{-3}} = 1000\,\text{AT/m}$

5. $\mu_r = \dfrac{B_{iron}}{B_{air}}$ or $B_{iron} = \mu_r \times B_{air} = 100 \times 10^{-2} = 1\ \text{Wb/m}^2$

6. Magnetic fields are distorted by ferromagnetic materials in their vicinity. If a piece of iron is placed near a magnet, most of the flux lines will be **crowded in the iron piece**. It is because, iron is a good conductor of magnetic flux.

7. $F \propto \dfrac{m_1 m_2}{d^2}$; $F' \propto \dfrac{(2m_1)\,(2m_2)}{(2d)^2}$ $\therefore$ $\dfrac{F'}{F} = 1$

8. Apply right-hand rule for coils. The coil is grasped in the right hand with the fingers pointing in the direction of current. Then thumb points in the direction of north pole.

9. Both the conductors are marked with dots. The currents are both flowing towards the observer. Use your right hand to verify that the field around each conductor travels in a counterclockwise direction (See Fig. 7.28). The fields join in this case, becoming one field. This results in the force of **attraction** between the conductors.

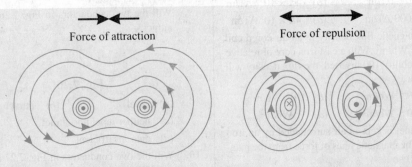

Force of attraction   Force of repulsion

Currents flowing in the same directions   Currents flowing in opposite directions

Fig. 7.28   **Fig. 7.29**

10. The currents are flowing in opposite directions. The fields cannot join in this case and the lines repel each other (See Fig. 7.29). There is a force of **repulsion** between the conductors.

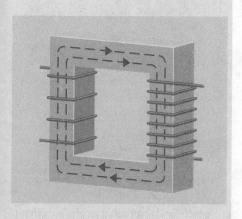

Magnetic Circuits

INTRODUCTION

We have seen that magnetic lines of force form closed loops around and through the magnetic material. The closed path followed by magnetic flux is called a magnetic circuit just as the closed path followed by current is called an electric circuit. Many electrical devices (*e.g.* generator, motor, transformer *etc.*) depend upon magnetism for their operation. Therefore, such devices have magnetic circuits *i.e.* closed magnetic flux paths. In order that these devices function efficiently, their magnetic circuits must be properly designed to obtain the required magnetic conditions. In this chapter, we shall focus our attention on the basic principles of magnetic circuits and methods to obtain their solution.

8.1. MAGNETIC CIRCUIT

The closed path followed by magnetic flux is called a **magnetic circuit**.

In a magnetic circuit, the magnetic flux leaves the *n*-pole, passes through the entire circuit and returns to the starting point. A magnetic circuit usually consists of materials having high permeability *e.g.* iron, soft steel *etc.* It is because these materials offer very small opposition to the 'flow' of magnetic flux. Consider a coil of *N* turns wound on an iron core as shown in Fig. 8.1. When current I is passed through the coil, magnetic flux ϕ is set up in the core. The magnetic flux follows the closed path $ABCDA$ and hence $ABCDA$ is the magnetic circuit.

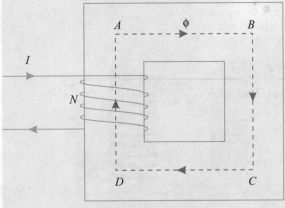

(i) The amount of magnetic flux set up in the core depends upon current (I) and number of turns (N). The product NI is called *magneto-motive force* (m.m.f.) and determines the amount of magnetic flux set up in the magnetic circuit.

$$m.m.f. = NI \text{ ampere turns}$$

Fig. 8.1

It can just be compared to electromotive force (e.m.f.) which sends current in an electric circuit.

(ii) The opposition that the magnetic circuit offers to the magnetic flux is called *reluctance*. It depends upon length of magnetic circuit (*i.e.* length $ABCDA$ in this case), area of x-section of the circuit and the nature of material that makes up the magnetic circuit.

8.2. ANALYSIS OF MAGNETIC CIRCUIT

Consider the magnetic circuit shown in Fig. 8.1. Suppose the mean length of the magnetic circuit (*i.e.* length $ABCDA$) is l metres, cross-sectional area of the core is 'a' m^2 and relative permeability of core material is μ_r. When current I is passed through the coil, it will set up magnetic flux ϕ in the material.

Magnetic flux density in the material, $B = \dfrac{\phi}{a}$ Wb/m^2

Magnetising force in the material, $H = \dfrac{B}{\mu_0 \mu_r} = \dfrac{\phi}{a \mu_0 \mu_r}$ AT/m

According to work law (See Art. 7.16), the work done in moving a unit magnetic pole once round the magnetic circuit (*i.e.* path $ABCDA$ in this case) is equal to the ampere-turns enclosed by the magnetic circuit.

∴ $$*H \times l = NI$$

or $$\dfrac{\phi}{a \mu_0 \mu_r} \times l = NI$$

or $$\phi = \dfrac{NI}{(l / a\, \mu_0 \mu_r)}$$

The quantity NI which produces the magnetic flux is called the magnetomotive force (m.m.f.) and is measured in ampere-turns. The quantity $l/a\, \mu_0 \mu_r$ is called the reluctance of the magnetic circuit. Reluctance is the opposition that the magnetic circuit offers to magnetic flux.

∴ Magnetic flux, $$\phi = \dfrac{\text{m.m.f.}}{\text{reluctance}} \qquad \qquad ...(i)$$

Note that the relationship expressed in eq. (*i*) has a strong resemblance to Ohm's law for electric circuit ($I = E/R$). The m.m.f. is analogous to e.m.f. in the electric circuit, reluctance is analogous to resistance and magnetic flux is analogous to current. Because of this similarity, eq. (*i*) is sometimes referred to as *Ohm's law of magnetic circuit*.

---

* You may recall that H means force acting on a unit magnetic pole. If the unit pole is moved once round the magnetic circuit (*i.e.* distance covered is l), then work done = $H \times l$.

8.3. IMPORTANT TERMS

In the study of magnetic circuits, we generally come across the following terms :

(*i*) **Magnetomotive force (*m.m.f.*).** It is a magnetic pressure which sets up or tends to set up magnetic flux in a magnetic circuit and may be defined as under :

The work done in moving a unit magnetic pole once round the magnetic circuit is called the magnetomotive force (*m.m.f.*). It is equal to the product of current and number of turns of the coil *i.e.*.

$$\text{m.m.f.} = NI \text{ ampere-turns (or AT)}$$

Magnetomotive force in a magnetic circuit corresponds to e.m.f. in an electric circuit.

(*ii*) **Reluctance.** The opposition that the magnetic circuit offers to magnetic flux is called reluctance. Its unit is *AT/Wb.

$$\text{Reluctance, } S = \frac{l}{a \mu_0 \mu_r}$$

Reluctance in a magnetic material corresponds to resistance ($R = \rho\, l/a$) in an electric circuit. Both of them vary as length ÷ area and are dependent upon the nature of material of the circuit. Magnetic materials (*e.g.* iron, steel etc.) have a low reluctance because the value of μ_r is very large in their case. On the other hand, non-magnetic materials (*e.g.* air, wood, copper, brass *etc.*) have a high reluctance because they possess least value of μ_r; being 1 in case of all non-magnetic materials.

(*iii*) **Permeance.** It is the reciprocal of reluctance and is a measure of the ease with which magnetic flux can pass through the material. Its unit is Wb/AT.

$$\text{Permeance} = \frac{1}{\text{reluctance}} = \frac{a \mu_0 \mu_r}{l}$$

Permeance of a magnetic circuit corresponds to conductance (reciprocal of resistance) in an electric circuit.

8.4. COMPARISON BETWEEN MAGNETIC AND ELECTRIC CIRCUITS

Magnetic Circuit   **Electric Circuit**

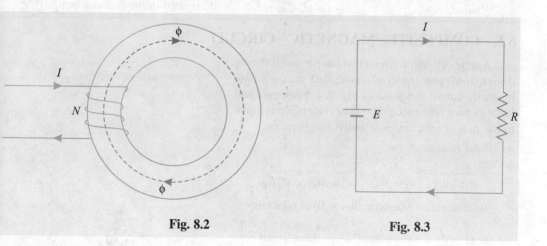

Fig. 8.2   Fig. 8.3

$$\text{Reluctance} = \frac{\text{m.m.f}}{\text{magnetic flux}} = \frac{\text{AT}}{\text{Wb}} = \text{AT/Wb}$$

<table>
<tr><td colspan="2" align="center">**Similarities**</td></tr>
<tr>
<td>

1. The closed path for magnetic flux is called a magnetic circuit.

2. Magnetic flux, $\phi = \dfrac{\text{m.m.f}}{\text{reluctance}}$

3. m.m.f. (ampere-turns)

4. Reluctance, $S = \dfrac{l}{a\mu_0\mu_r}$

5. Magnetic flux density, $B = \dfrac{\phi}{a}$ Wb/m^2

6. m.m.f. drop $= \phi S$

7. Magnetic intensity, $H = NI/l$

</td>
<td>

1. The closed path for electric current is called an electric circuit.

2. Current, $I = \dfrac{\text{e.m.f.}}{\text{resistance}}$

3. e.m.f. (volts)

4. Resistance, $R = \rho\dfrac{l}{a}$

5. Current density, $J = \dfrac{I}{a}$ A/m^2

6. Voltage drop $= IR$

7. Electric intensity, $E = V/d$

</td>
</tr>
</table>

<table>
<tr><td colspan="2" align="center">**Dissimilarities**</td></tr>
<tr>
<td>

1. Truly speaking magnetic flux does not flow.

2. There is no magnetic insulator. For example, magnetic flux can be set up even in air (the best known magnetic insulator) with reasonable m.m.f.

3. The value of μ_r is not constant for a given magnetic material. It varies considerably with magnetic flux density (B) in the material. This implies that reluctance of a magnetic circuit is not constant rather it depends upon B.

4. No energy is expended in a magnetic circuit. In other words, energy is required in creating the magnetic flux, and not in maintaining it.

</td>
<td>

1. The electric current actually flows in an electric circuit.

2. There are a number of electric insulators. For instance, air is a very good insulator and current cannot pass through it.

3. The value of resistivity (ρ) varies very slightly with temperature. Therefore, the resistance of an electric circuit is practically constant. This salient feature calls for different approach to the solution of magnetic and electric circuits.

4. When current flows through an electric circuit; energy is expended so long as the current flows. The expended energy is dissipated in the form of heat.

</td>
</tr>
</table>

8.5. COMPOSITE MAGNETIC CIRCUIT

A series magnetic circuit that has parts of different dimensions and materials is called a composite magnetic circuit as shown in Fig. 8.4. Each part will have its own reluctance. The total reluctance is equal to the sum of reluctances of individual parts *i.e.*

Total reluctance

$$= \frac{l_1}{a_1\mu_0\mu_{r1}} + \frac{l_2}{a_2\mu_0\mu_{r2}} + \frac{l_3}{a_3\mu_0\mu_{r3}} + \frac{l_g{}^*}{a_g\mu_0}$$

Total m.m.f. = Magnetic flux × Total reluctance

$$= \phi\left[\frac{l_1}{a_1\mu_0\mu_{r1}} + \frac{l_2}{a_2\mu_0\mu_{r2}} + \frac{l_3}{a_3\mu_0\mu_{r3}} + \frac{l_g}{a_g\mu_0}\right]$$

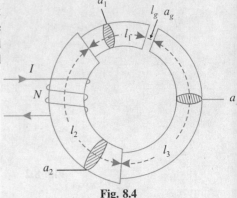

Fig. 8.4

---

* For air, $\mu_r = 1$.

$$= \frac{\phi}{a_1 \mu_0 \mu_{r1}} \times l_1 + \frac{\phi}{a_2 \mu_0 \mu_{r2}} \times l_2 + \frac{\phi}{a_3 \mu_0 \mu_{r3}} \times l_3 + \frac{\phi}{a_g \mu_0} \times l_g$$

$$= \frac{B_1}{\mu_0 \mu_{r1}} \times l_1 + \frac{B_2}{\mu_0 \mu_{r2}} \times l_2 + \frac{B_3}{\mu_0 \mu_{r3}} \times l_3 + \frac{B_g}{\mu_0} \times l_g$$

$$= H_1 l_1 + H_2 l_2 + H_3 l_3 + H_g l_g \qquad\qquad (\because H = B/\mu_0 \mu_r)$$

How to find ampere-turns?

Hence the total ampere-turns required for a series magnetic circuit can be found as under :

(i)   Find H for each part of the series magnetic circuit. For air, $H = B/\mu_0$ whereas for a magnetic material, $H = B/\mu_0 \mu_r$.

(ii) Find the *mean* length (l) of magnetic path for each part of the circuit.

(iii) Find AT required for each part of the magnetic circuit using the relation, $AT = H \times l$.

(iv) The total AT required for the entire series circuit is equal to the sum of AT for various parts.

8.6. PARALLEL MAGNETIC CIRCUITS

A magnetic circuit which has more than one path for magnetic flux is called a parallel magnetic circuit. It can just be compared to a parallel electric circuit which has more than one path for electric current.

The concept of parallel magnetic circuit is illustrated in Fig. 8.5. Here a coil of N turns wounded on limb AF carries a current of I amperes. The magnetic flux ϕ_1 set up by the coil divides at B into two paths, namely ;

(i)   magnetic flux ϕ_2 passes along the path BE

(ii) magnetic flux ϕ_3 follows the path $BCDE$

Clearly, $\phi_1 = \phi_2 + \phi_3$

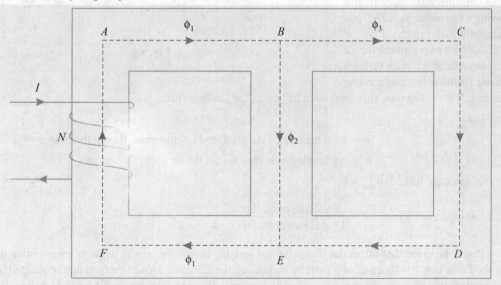

Fig. 8.5

The magnetic paths BE and $BCDE$ are in parallel and form a parallel magnetic circuit. The AT required for this parallel circuit is equal to AT required for any *one of the paths.

---

*   This means that we may consider either path, say path BE, and calculate AT required for it. The same AT will also send the magnetic flux (ϕ_3 in this case) through the other parallel path $BCDE$. The situation is similar to that of two resistors R_1 and R_2 in parallel in an electric circuit. The voltage V required to send currents (say I_1 and I_2) in the resistors is equal to that appearing across either resistor *i.e.* $V = I_1 R_1 = I_2 R_2$.

Let S_1 = reluctance of path *EFAB*

S_2 = reluctance of path *BE*

S_3 = reluctance of path *BCDE*

∴ Total m.m.f. required = m.m.f. for path *EFAB* + m.m.f. for path *BE* or path *BCDE*

or

$$NI = \phi_1 S_1 + \phi_2 S_2$$
$$= \phi_1 S_1 + \phi_3 S_3$$

The reluctances S_1, S_2 and S_3 must be determined from a calculation of $l/a\,\mu_0\mu_r$ for those paths of the magnetic circuit in which ϕ_1, ϕ_2 and ϕ_3 exist respectively.

8.7. LEAKAGE FLUX

The magnetic flux that does not follow the desired path in a magnetic circuit is called a leakage flux.

In most of practical magnetic circuits, a large part of magnetic flux path is through a magnetic material and the remainder part of magnetic flux path is through air. The magnetic flux in the air gap is known as *useful flux* because it can be utilised for various useful purposes. Fig. 8.6 shows an iron ring wound with a coil and having a narrow air gap. The total magnetic flux produced by the coil does not pass through the air gap as some of it *leaks through the air (paths at 'a') surrounding the iron. These magnetic flux lines as at 'a' are called leakage flux.

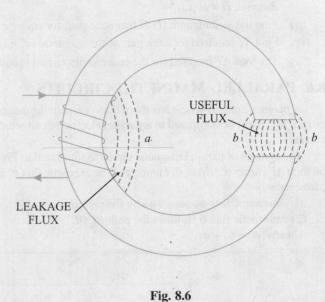

Fig. 8.6

Let

ϕ_i = total magnetic flux produced *i.e.* magnetic flux in the **iron ring

ϕ_g = useful magnetic flux across the air gap

∴ Leakage flux, $\phi_{leak} = \phi_i - \phi_g$

Leakage coefficient, $\lambda = \dfrac{\text{Total magnetic flux}}{\text{Useful magnetic flux}} = \dfrac{\phi_i}{\phi_g}$

It may be noted that the useful magnetic flux passing across the air gap tends to bulge outwards as shown in Fig. 8.6 (lines at *bb*), thereby increasing the effective area of the gap and reducing the magnetic flux density in the gap. This effect is known as *fringing*. The longer the air gap, the greater is the fringing and *vice-versa*.

The value of leakage co-efficient λ for electrical machines is usually about 1.15 to 1.25.

---

* Air is not a good magnetic insulator. Therefore, leakage of magnetic flux from iron to air takes place easily.

** The magnetic flux ϕ_i is not constant all round the ring. However, for reasonable accuracy, it is assumed that the iron carries the whole of the magnetic flux produced by the coil.

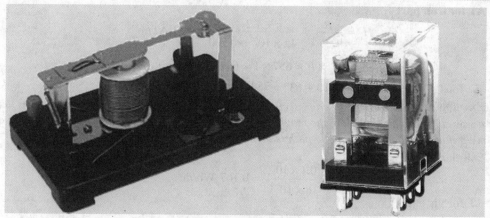

Electromagnetic relays

Example 8.1. *An iron ring has a cross-sectional area of 400 mm² and a mean diameter of 25 cm. It is wound with 500 turns. If the value of relative permeability is 250, find the total magnetic flux set up in the ring. The coil resistance is 474 Ω and the supply voltage is 240 V.*

Solution. The conditions of the problem are represented in Fig. 8.7.

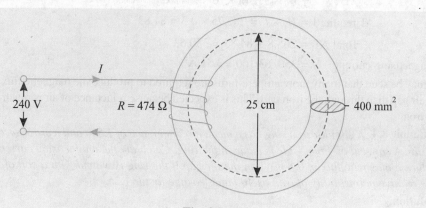

Fig. 8.7

$$I = V/R = 240/474 = 0.506 \text{ A}$$

$$l = \pi D = \pi \times (25 \times 10^{-2}) = 0.7854 \text{ m}$$

$$H = \frac{NI}{l} = \frac{500 \times 0.506}{0.7854} = 322.13 \text{ AT/m}$$

$$B = \mu_0 \mu_r H = 4\pi \times 10^{-7} \times 250 \times 322.13 = 0.1012 \text{ Wb/m}^2$$

∴

$$\phi = B \times a = 0.1012 \times (400 \times 10^{-6}) = \textbf{40.48} \times \textbf{10}^{-6} \textbf{ Wb}$$

Example 8.2. *A magnetic flux density of 1.2 Wb/m² is required in the 2 mm air gap of an electromagnet having an iron path 1 m long. Calculate the m.m.f. required, assuming a relative permeability of iron as 1500. Neglect leakage.*

Solution.

AT for air gap

$$H_g = \frac{B}{\mu_0} = \frac{1.2}{4\pi \times 10^{-7}} = 955 \times 10^3 \text{ AT/m}$$

$$\text{AT required} = H_g \times l_g = (955 \times 10^3)(2 \times 10^{-3}) = 1910$$

AT for iron part

$$H_i = \frac{B}{\mu_0 \mu_r} = \frac{1.2}{4\pi \times 10^{-7} \times 1500} = 637 \text{ AT/m}$$

AT required $= H_i \times l_i = 637 \times 1 = 637$

∴ Total AT required $= 1910 + 637 = \mathbf{2547}$

Example 8.3. *An iron ring of cross-sectional area 6 cm² is wound with a wire of 100 turns and has a saw cut of 2 mm. Calculate the magnetising current required to produce a magnetic flux of 0.1 mWb if mean length of magnetic path is 30 cm and relative permeability of iron is 470.*

Solution.

$$B = \frac{\phi}{a} = \frac{0.1 \times 10^{-3}}{6 \times 10^{-4}} = 0.167 \text{ Wb/m}^2$$

AT for air gap

$$H_g = \frac{B}{\mu_0} = \frac{0.167}{4\pi \times 10^{-7}} = 132.9 \times 10^3 \text{ AT/m}$$

AT required $= H_g \times l_g = 132.9 \times 10^3 \times (2 \times 10^{-3}) = 265.8$

AT for iron part

$$H_i = \frac{B}{\mu_0 \mu_r} = \frac{0.167}{4\pi \times 10^{-7} \times 470} = 282.75 \text{ AT/m}$$

AT required $= H_i \times l_i = 282.75 \times 0.3 = 84.83$

Total AT $= 265.8 + 84.83 = 350.63$

Magnetising current, $I = 350.63/100 = \mathbf{3.51 \text{ A}}$

It may be seen that many more ampere-turns are required to produce the magnetic flux through 2 mm of air gap than through the iron part. This is expected because reluctance of air is much more than that of iron.

Example 8.4. *A circular iron ring has a mean circumference of 1.5 m and a cross-sectional area of 0.01 m². A saw-cut of 4 mm wide is made in the ring. Calculate the magnetising current required to produce a magnetic flux of 0.8 mWb in the air gap if the ring is wound with a coil of 175 turns. Assume relative permeability of iron as 400 and leakage factor 1.25.*

Solution.

$$\phi_g = 0.8 \times 10^{-3} \text{ Wb} ; \quad a = 0.01 \text{ m}^2 ; \quad l_i = 1.5 \text{ m} ; \quad l_g = 4 \times 10^{-3} \text{ m}$$

AT for air gap

$$B_g = \frac{\phi_g}{a} = \frac{0.8 \times 10^{-3}}{0.01} = 0.08 \text{ Wb/m}^2$$

$$H_g = \frac{B_g}{\mu_0} = \frac{0.08}{4\pi \times 10^{-7}} = 63662 \text{ AT/m}$$

∴ $AT_g = H_g \times l_g = 63662 \times (4 \times 10^{-3}) = 254.6 \text{ AT}$

AT for iron path

$$\phi_i = \phi_g \times \lambda = 0.8 \times 10^{-3} \times 1.25 = 10^{-3} \text{ Wb}$$

$$B_i = \phi_i / a = 10^{-3} / 0.01 = 0.1 \text{ Wb/m}^2$$

$$H_i = \frac{B_i}{\mu_0 \mu_r} = \frac{0.1}{4\pi \times 10^{-7} \times 400} = 199 \text{ AT/m}$$

∴ $AT_i = H_i \times l_i = 199 \times 1.5 = 298.5$

$\therefore$ Total $AT = 254.6 + 298.5 = 553.1$

$\therefore$ Magnetising current, $I = 553.1/N = 553.1/175 = \textbf{3.16 A}$

Example 8.5. *An iron ring has a mean diameter of 15 cm, a cross-section of 20 cm² and a radial gap of 0.5 mm cut in it. It is uniformly wound with 1500 turns of insulated wire and a magnetising current of 1 A produces a magnetic flux of 1 mWb. Neglecting the effect of magnetic leakage and fringing, calculate (i) reluctance of the magnetic circuit and (ii) relative permeability of iron.*

Solution.

$$B = \frac{\phi}{a} = \frac{1 \times 10^{-3}}{20 \times 10^{-4}} = 0.5 \text{ Wb/m}^2$$

AT for Air-gap

$$H_g = B/\mu_0 = 0.5/4\pi \times 10^{-7} = 398 \times 10^3 \text{ AT/m}$$

$$AT \text{ required} = H_g \times l_g = (398 \times 10^3) \times 0.5 \times 10^{-3} = 199$$

AT for iron part

$$\text{Total } AT = NI = 1500 \times 1 = 1500$$

$$AT \text{ for iron part, } AT_i = 1500 - 199 = 1301$$

$$H_i = \frac{AT_i}{l_i} = \frac{1301}{0.471} = 2762 \text{ AT/m}$$

(ii) $\therefore \ \mu_r = \dfrac{B}{\mu_0 \, H_i} = \dfrac{0.5}{4\pi \times 10^{-7} \times 2762} = \textbf{144}$

(i)   Reluctance $= \dfrac{\text{Total m.m.f.}}{\text{Magnetic flux}} = \dfrac{1500}{1 \times 10^{-3}} = \textbf{15} \times \textbf{10}^5 \textbf{ AT/Wb}$

Example 8.6. *A steel ring 30 cm mean diameter and of circular section 2 cm in diameter has an air gap 1 mm long. It is wound uniformly with 600 turns of wire carrying current of 2.5 A. Find (i) total m.m.f. (ii) total reluctance and (iii) magnetic flux. Neglect magnetic leakage. The iron path takes 40% of the total m.m.f.*

Solution.

(i)   Total m.m.f. $= NI = 600 \times 2.5 = \textbf{1500 AT}$

(ii)   Let M_1 and M_2 be the m.m.f.s for iron part and air-gap respectively and S_1 and S_2 their corresponding reluctances.

$$M_1 = 40\% \text{ of } 1500 = (40/100) \times 1500 = 600 \text{ AT}$$

$$M_2 = 1500 - 600 = 900 \text{ AT}$$

Now, $M_1 = \phi S_1$ and $M_2 = \phi S_2$

$\therefore$ $\dfrac{S_1}{S_2} = \dfrac{M_1}{M_2} = \dfrac{600}{900} = 0.67$

$$S_2 = \frac{l_g}{a\mu_0} = \frac{1 \times 10^{-3}}{\pi(1 \times 10^{-2})^2 \times 4\pi \times 10^{-7}} = 2.5 \times 10^6 \text{ AT/Wb}$$

$\therefore$ $S_1 = 0.67 \, S_2 = 0.67 \times (2.5 \times 10^6) = 1.675 \times 10^6 \text{ AT/Wb}$

Total reluctance $= S_1 + S_2$

$$= (1.675 + 2.5)10^6 = \textbf{4.175} \times \textbf{10}^6 \textbf{ AT/Wb}$$

(iii)   Magnetic flux $= \dfrac{\text{Total m.m.f.}}{\text{Total reluctance}} = \dfrac{1500}{4.175 \times 10^6}$

$$= 0.36 \times 10^{-3} \text{ Wb} = \textbf{0.36 mWb}$$

Example 8.7. *The magnetic circuit shown in Fig. 8.8 is built up of iron of square cross-section 3 cm side. Each air gap is 2 mm wide. Each coil is wound with 1000 turns and exciting current is 1A. The relative permeability of part A and part B may be taken as 1000 and 1200 respectively. Find (i) reluctance of part A (ii) reluctance of part B (iii) reluctance of two air gaps (iv) total reluctance and (v) total m.m.f.*

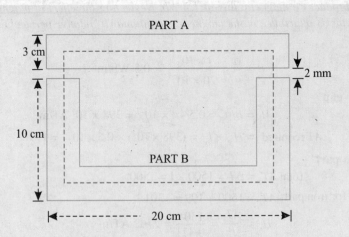

Fig. 8.8

Solution. The dotted line shows the mean path of magnetic flux.

(*i*) **Part A**

Mean length, $l_A = 20 - 1.5 - 1.5 + 1.5 + 1.5 = 20$ cm $= 0.2$ m

Area of X-section, $a = 3 \times 3 = 9$ cm$^2 = 9 \times 10^{-4}$ m^2

Reluctance, $S_A = \dfrac{l_A}{a\mu_0\mu_r} = \dfrac{0.2}{(9 \times 10^{-4}) \times 4\pi \times 10^{-7} \times (1000)} = 176838$ AT/Wb

(*ii*) **Part B**

Mean length, $l_B = (20 - 1.5 - 1.5) + 2(10 - 1.5) = 34$ cm $= 0.34$ m

Reluctance, $S_B = \dfrac{l_B}{a\mu_0\mu_r} = \dfrac{0.34}{(9 \times 10^{-4}) \times (4\pi \times 10^{-7}) \times 1200} = 250521$ AT/Wb

(*iii*) **Air gaps**

Air gap length, $l_g = 2 + 2 = 4$ mm $= 0.004$ m

Reluctance, $S_g = \dfrac{l_g}{a\mu_0} = \dfrac{0.004}{(9 \times 10^{-4}) \times (4\pi \times 10^{-7})} = 3536776$ AT/Wb

(*iv*) Total reluctance $= 176838 + 250521 + 3536776 = 3964135$ AT/Wb

(*v*) Total m.m.f. $= NI = (2 \times 1000) \times 1 = 2000$ AT

Example 8.8. *A magnetic core made of annealed sheet steel has the dimensions as shown in Fig. 8.9. The X-section is 25 cm^2 everywhere. The magnetic flux in branches A and B is 3500 μWb but that in the branch C is zero. Find the required ampere-turns for coil A and for coil C. Relative permeability of sheet steel is 1000.*

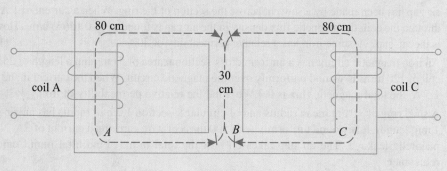

Fig. 8.9

Solution.

AT for coil A

Magnetic flux paths B and C are in parallel. Therefore, AT required for coil A is equal to AT for path A plus AT for path B or path C.

AT for path A = magnetic flux × reluctance = $(3500 \times 10^{-6}) \times \dfrac{0.8}{(25 \times 10^{-4}) \times 4\pi \times 10^{-7} \times 1000}$

$= 891.3$ AT

AT for path B = magnetic flux × reluctance = $(3500 \times 10^{-6}) \times \dfrac{0.3}{(25 \times 10^{-4}) \times 4\pi \times 10^{-7} \times 1000}$

$= 334.2$ AT

Total AT for coil A = $891.3 + 334.2 = $ **1225.5 AT**

AT for coil C

The coil C produces magnetic flux ϕ_C μWb in the opposite direction to that produced by coil A.

$\therefore$ m.m.f. of path B = m.m.f. of path C

or $\qquad\qquad\qquad \phi_B \, S_B = \phi_C \, S_C$

or $\qquad (3500 \times 10^{-6}) \times \dfrac{l_B}{a\mu_0\mu_r} = \phi_C \times \dfrac{l_c}{a\mu_0\mu_r}$

$\therefore \quad \phi_C = (3500 \times 10^{-6}) \times l_B / l_C = (3500 \times 10^{-6}) \times 0.3 / 0.8 = 1312.5 \; \mu\,Wb$

Total AT for coil C = $\phi_C \times$ reluctance

$= (1312.5 \times 10^{-6}) \times \dfrac{0.8}{(25 \times 10^{-4}) \times 4\pi \times 10^{-7} \times 1000} = $ **334.22 AT**

TUTORIAL PROBLEMS

1. A core forms a closed magnetic loop of path length 32 cm. Half of this path has a cross-sectional area of 2 cm^2 and relative permeability 800. The other half has a cross-sectional area of 4 cm^2 and relative permeability 400. Find the current needed to produce a magnetic flux of 0.4 Wb in the core if it is wound with 1000 turns of insulated wire. Ignore leakage and fringing effects.　　　　　　　　　　　　　　　　　　　　　　　　　　　　[636.8 A]

2. An iron ring has a cross-sectional area of 400 mm^2 and a mean diameter of 250 mm. An air gap of 1 mm has been made by a saw-cut across the section of the ring. If a magnetic flux of 0.3 mWb is required in the air gap, find the current necessary to produce this magnetic flux when a coil of 400 turns is wound on the ring. The iron has a relative permeability of 500.　　　　　　　　　　　　　　　　　　　　　　　　　　[3.84 A]

3. An iron ring has a mean circumferential length of 60 cm and a uniform winding of 300 turns. An air gap has been made by a saw cut across the section of the ring. When a current of 1 A flows through the coil, the magnetic flux density in the air gap is found to be 0.126 Wb/m². How long is the air-gap? Assume iron has a relative permeability of 300. **[1 mm]**

4. An iron magnetic circuit has a uniform cross-sectional area of 5 cm² and a length of 25 cm. A coil of 120 turns is wound uniformly over the magnetic circuit. When the current in the coil is 1.5 A, the total magnetic flux is 0.3 Wb. Find the relative permeability of iron. **[663]**

5. A steel ring of 10 cm mean radius and of circular x-section 1 cm in radius has an air-gap of 1 mm length. It is wound uniformly with 500 turns of wire carrying a current of 3A. Neglect magnetic leakage. The air gap takes 60% of the total m.m.f. Find total m.m.f. and total reluctance.

8.8. B-H CURVE

The B/H curve (or magnetisation curve) indicates the manner in which the magnetic flux density (B) varies with magnetising force (H). Fig. 8.10 (i) shows the general shape of B-H curve of a magnetic material. The non-linearity of the curve indicates that the relative permeability μ_r ($= B/\mu_0 H$) of a magnetic material is not *constant but depends very largely upon the magnetic flux density. Fig. 8.10 (ii) shows how relative permeability μ_r of a magnetic material (cast steel) changes with magnetic flux density.

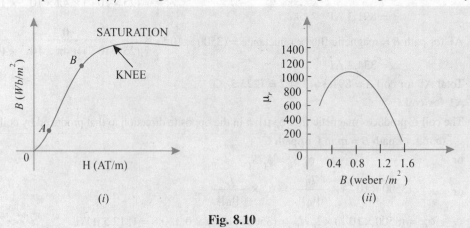

Fig. 8.10

While carrying out magnetic calculations, it should be ensured that the values of μ_r and H are taken at the working magnetic flux density. For this purpose, the B-H curve of the material in question may be very helpful. In fact, the use of B-H curves permits the calculations of magnetic circuits with a fair degree of ease.

8.9. MAGNETIC CALCULATIONS FROM B-H CURVES

The solution of magnetic circuits can be easily obtained by the use of B-H curves. The procedure is as under :

(i) Corresponding to the magnetic flux density B in the material, find the magnetising force H from the B-H curve of the material.

(ii) Compute the magnetic length l.

(iii) m.m.f. required $= H \times l$

* The μ_r for all non-magnetic materials (*e.g.* air, brass etc.) is constant ; being equal to 1. Therefore, for a non-magnetic material $B = \mu_0 H$. Since μ_0 is constant, $B \propto H$ or $B - H$ curve for a non-magnetic material is a straight line passing through the origin.

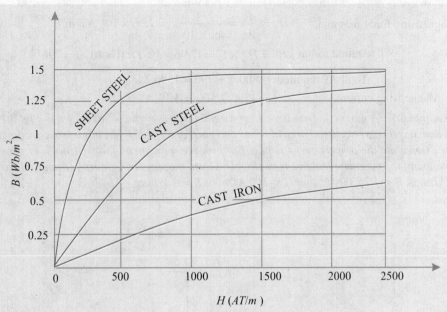

Fig. 8.11

The reader may note that the use of B-H curves for magnetic calculations saves a lot of time. Fig. 8.11 shows the B-H curves for sheet steel, cast steel and cast iron.

Example 8.9. *A cast steel ring of mean diameter 30 cm having a circular cross-section of 5 cm² is uniformly wound with 500 turns. Determine the magnetising current required to establish a magnetic flux of 5 × 10⁻⁴ Wb (i) with no air gap (ii) with a radial air-gap of 1 mm.*

The magnetisation curve for cast steel is given by the following data :

B (Wb/m²)	0.2	0.4	0.6	0.8	1	1.2
H (AT/m)	175	300	400	600	850	1250

Solution. Plot the B-H curve from the given data as shown in Fig. 8.12.

(i) With no air-gap

$$B_i = \frac{\phi}{a} = \frac{5 \times 10^{-4}}{5 \times 10^{-4}} = 1 \text{ Wb/m}^2$$

From the B-H curve, we find that for a magnetic flux density of 1 Wb/m², the value of

$H_i = 850$ AT/m

$l_i = \pi D = \pi \times 30 \times 10^{-2} = 0.942$ m

∴ Total AT required $= H_i \times l_i$

$= 850 \times 0.942 = 800.7$

∴ Magnetising current,

$I = 800.7 / 500 = $ **1.6 A**

(ii) With air-gap of 1 mm

Magnetic flux density in air-gap,

$B_g = 1$ Wb/m² (Same as in steel)

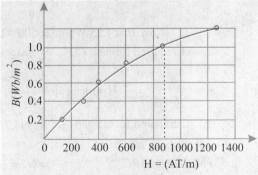

Fig. 8.12

Magnetising force required, $\quad * H_g = \dfrac{B}{\mu_0} = \dfrac{1}{4\pi \times 10^{-7}} = 7.96 \times 10^5$ AT/m

AT required for air gap $= H_g \times l_g = (7.96 \times 10^5) \times (1 \times 10^{-3}) = 796$

Total AT required $= 800.7 + 796 = 1596.7$

$\therefore$ Magnetising current, $\qquad\qquad I = 1596.7/500 = \mathbf{3.19}$ **A**

Example 8.10. *A magnetic circuit made of wrought iron is arranged as shown in Fig. 8.13. The central limb has a cross-sectional area of 8 cm² and each of the side limbs has a cross-sectional area of 5 cm². Calculate the ampere-turns required to produce a magnetic flux of 1 mWb in the central limb, assuming the magnetic leakage is negligible. Given that for wrought iron (from B-H curve), H = 500 AT/m at B = 1.25 Wb/m² and H = 200 AT/m at B = 1 Wb/m².*

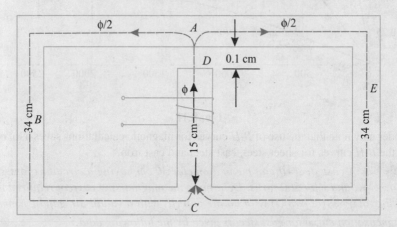

Fig. 8.13

Solution. The magnetic flux ϕ set up in the central limb divides equally into two identical parallel paths *viz.* path *ABC* and path *AEC*. The total m.m.f. required for the entire circuit is the sum of the following three m.m.fs :

(*i*) that required for path *CD*

(*ii*) that required for air gap *DA*

(*iii*) that required for either of parallel paths (*i.e.* path *ABC* or path *AEC*).

(*i*) **AT for path CD**

$$B = \frac{\phi}{a} = \frac{1 \times 10^{-3}}{8 \times 10^{-4}} = 1.25 \text{ Wb/m}^2$$

Now H at 1.25 Wb/m² = 500 AT/m $\qquad$ (*given*)

$\therefore$ AT required for path *CD* $\quad = 500 \times 0.15 = 75$

(*ii*) **AT for air-gap DA**

$$H \text{ in air gap} = \frac{B}{\mu_0} = \frac{1.25}{4\pi \times 10^{-7}} = 994.7 \times 10^3 \text{ AT/m}$$

$\therefore$ AT required for air-gap $\quad = (994.7 \times 10^3) \times (0.1 \times 10^{-2}) = 994.7$

(*iii*) **AT for path ABC**

Flux in path *ABC* $\qquad\qquad = \phi/2 = 1/2 = 0.5$ mWb

$*$ We do not use *B-H* curve to find *AT* for air gap. It is because μ_r for air (in fact for all non-magnetic materials) is constant; being equal to 1 and *AT* can be calculated directly.

Flux density in path ABC $= \dfrac{0.5 \times 10^{-3}}{5 \times 10^{-4}} = 1 \text{ Wb/m}^2$

Now H at 1 Wb/m^2 = 200 AT/m   (*given*)

∴   AT required for path ABC = 200 × 0.34 = 68

∴   Total AT required = 75 + 994.7 + 68 = **1137.7**

The reader may note that air gap "grabs" 87 per cent of the applied ampere-turns.

8.10. MAGNETIC HYSTERESIS

When a magnetic material is subjected to a cycle of magnetisation (*i.e.* it is magnetised first in one direction and then in the other), it is found that magnetic flux density B in the material lags behind the applied magnetising force H. This phenomenon is known as hysteresis.

The phenomenon of lagging of magnetic flux density (B) behind the magnetising force (H) in a magnetic material subjected to cycles of magnetisation is known as *magnetic hysteresis.

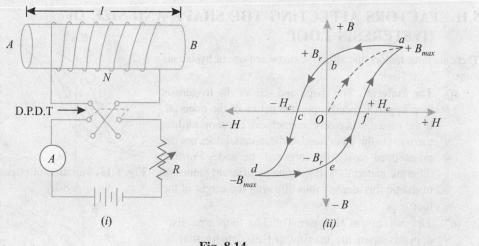

Fig. 8.14

Hysteresis Loop. Consider an unmagnetised iron bar AB wound with N turns as shown in Fig. 8.14 (*i*). The magnetising force H (= NI/l) produced by this solenoid can be changed by varying the current through the coil. We shall see that when the iron piece is subjected to** one cycle of magnetisation, the resultant B-H curve traces a loop *abcdefa* called *hysteresis loop* [See Fig. 8.14 (*ii*)].

(*i*)   When current in the solenoid is zero, $H = 0$ and hence B in the iron is zero. As H is increased (by increasing solenoid current), the magnetic flux density (B) also increases until the point of maximum magnetic flux density (+ B_{max}) is reached. The material is saturated and beyond this point, the magnetic flux density will not increase regardless of any increase in current or magnetising force. Note that B-H curve of iron follows the path *oa*.

(*ii*) If now H is gradually reduced (by reducing solenoid current), it is found that magnetic flux density B does not decrease along *oa* but follows the path *ab*. At point b, the magnetising force H is zero but magnetic flux density in the material has a finite value + B_r (= ob) called

* Hysteresis is derived from the Greek work *hysterein* meaning to lag behind.
** If we start with unmagnetised iron piece, then magnetise it in one direction and then in the other direction and finally demagnetise it (*i.e.* obtain the original condition we started with), the piece is said to go through one cycle of magnetisation. Compare with one cycle of alternating current or voltage.

residual flux density. In other words, *B* lags behind *H*. The greater the lag, the greater is the residual magnetism (*i.e.* ordinate *ob*) retained by the iron piece. The power of retaining residual magnetism is called *retentivity* of the material.

(*iii*) To demagnetise the iron piece (*i.e.* to remove the residual magnetism *ob*), the magnetising force *H* is reversed by reversing the current through the coil. When *H* is gradually increased in the reverse direction, the *B-H* curve follows the path *bc* so that when *H* = *oc*, the residual magnetism is zero. The value of H (= *oc*) required to wipe out residual magnetism is known as *coercive force* (*H_c*).

(*iv*) If *H* is further increased in the negative direction, the material again saturates (point *d*) in the negative direction. Reducing *H* to zero and then increasing it in the positive direction completes the curve *defa*. Thus when an iron piece is subjected to one cycle of magnetisation, the *B-H* curve traces a closed loop *abcdefa* called *hysteresis loop.*

It is clear from the hysteresis loop (*i.e. B-H* curve of iron for one cycle of magnetisation) that *B* lags behind *H*. The two never attain zero value simultaneously.

Note. For one cycle of magnetisation, one hysteresis loop is traced. If a magnetic material is located within a coil through which alternating current (50 Hz) flows, 50 loops will be formed every second.

8.11. FACTORS AFFECTING THE SHAPE AND SIZE OF HYSTERESIS LOOP

There are three factors that affect the shape and size of hysteresis loop.

(*i*) **The material.** The shape and size of the hysteresis loop largely depends upon the nature of the material. If the material is easily magnetised, the loop will be narrow. On the other hand, if the material does not get magnetised easily, the loop will be wide. Further, different materials will saturate at different values of magnetic flux density thus affecting the height of the loop.

Fig. 8.15. Variation of peak flux density

(*ii*) **The maximum flux density.** The loop area also depends upon the maximum flux density that is established in the material. This is illustrated in Fig. 8.15. It is clear that the loop area increases as the alternating magnetic field has progressively greater peak values.

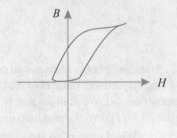

(*iii*) **The initial state of the specimen.** The shape and size of the hysteresis loop also depends upon the initial state of the specimen. To illustrate this point, refer to Fig. 8.16. It is clear that the specimen is

Fig. 8.16. Unsymmetrical characteristic

already saturated to start with. The magnetic flux density is then reduced to zero and finally the specimen is returned to the saturated condition.

8.12. HYSTERESIS LOSS

When a magnetic material is subjected to a cycle of magnetisation (*i.e.* it is magnetised first in one direction and then in the other), an energy loss takes place due to the *molecular friction in the material. That is, the domains (or molecular magnets) of the material resist being turned first in one direction and then the other. Energy is thus expended in the material in overcoming this opposition.

---

* The opposition offered by the magnetic domains (or molecular magnets) to the turning effect of magnetising force is sometimes referred to as the molecular friction.

This loss is in the form of heat and is called *hysteresis loss*. Hysteresis loss is present in all those electrical machines whose iron parts are subjected to cycles of magnetisation. The obvious effect of hysteresis loss is the rise of temperature of the machine.

(*i*) Transformers and most electric motors operate on alternating current. In such devices, the magnetic flux is the iron changes continuously, both in value and direction. Hence hysteresis loss occurs in such machines.

(*ii*) Hysteresis loss also occurs when an iron part rotates in a constant magnetic field *e.g.* d.c. machines.

8.13. CALCULATION OF HYSTERESIS LOSS

We will now show that area of hysteresis loop represents the *energy loss/m³/cycle.

Let l = length of the iron bar

A = area of x-section of bar

N = No. of turns of wire of solenoid

Suppose at any instant the current in the solenoid is i. Then,

$$H = \frac{Ni}{l} \quad \text{or} \quad i = \frac{Hl}{N}$$

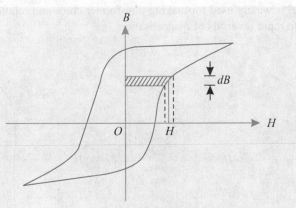

Fig. 8.17

Suppose the current increases by di in a small time dt. This will cause the magnetic flux density to increase by dB and hence an increase in magnetic flux $d\phi$ ($= AdB$). This causes an e.m.f. e to be induced in the solenoid.

$$e = N\frac{d\phi}{dt} = NA\frac{dB}{dt}$$

By Lenz's law, this e.m.f. opposes the current i so that energy dW is spent in overcoming this opposing e.m.f.

∴ $dW = ei\, dt$ joules

$$= \left(NA\frac{dB}{dt}\right) \times \left(\frac{Hl}{N}\right) \times dt \text{ joules}$$

$$= Al \times H \times dB \text{ joules}$$

$$= V \times (H \times dB) \text{ joules}$$

where $Al = V$ = volume of iron bar

* In order to set up magnetic field, certain amount of energy has to supplied which is stored in the field. If the field is in free space, the stored energy is returned to the circuit when the field collapses. If the field is in a magnetic material, not all the energy supplied can be returned; part of it having been converted into heat due to hysteresis effect.

Now $H \times dB$ is the area of the shaded strip (See Fig. 8.17). For one cycle of magnetisation, the area $H \times dB$ will be equal to the area of hysteresis loop.

∴ Hysteresis energy loss/cycle, $W_h = V \times$ (area of loop) joules

If f is the frequency of reversal of magnetisation, then,

Hysteresis power loss, $P_h = W_h \times f = V \times$ (area of loop) $\times f$

Note. While calculating the area of hysteresis loop, proper scale factors of B and H must be considered,

For example, if the scales are : 1 cm $= x$ AT/m ...for H

1 cm $= y$ Wb/m² ...for B

Then, $W_h = xy \times$ (area of loop in cm²) $\times V$ joules

where x and y are the scale factors.

8.14. IMPORTANCE OF HYSTERESIS LOOP

The shape and size of the hysteresis loop *largely depends upon the nature of the material. The choice of a magnetic material for a particular application often depends upon the shape and size of the hysteresis loop. A few cases are discussed below by way of illustration :

(i) The smaller the hysteresis loop area of a magnetic material, the less is the hysteresis loss. The hysteresis loop for silicon steel has a very small area [See Fig. 8.18 (i)]. For this reason, silicon steel is widely used for making transformer cores and rotating machines which are subjected to rapid reversals of magnetisation.

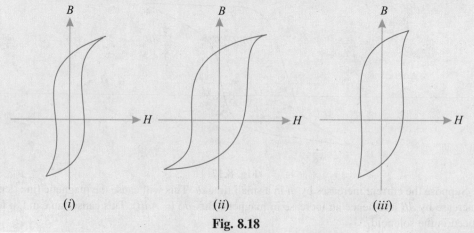

Fig. 8.18

(ii) The hysteresis loop for hard steel [See Fig. 8.18 (ii)] indicates that this material has high retentivity and coercivity. Therefore, hard steel is quite suitable for making permanent magnets. But due to the large area of the loop, there is greater hysteresis loss. For this reason, hard steel is not suitable for the construction of electrical machines.

(iii) The hysteresis loop for wrought iron [See Fig. 8.18 (iii)] shows that this material has fairly good residual magnetism and coercivity. Hence, it is suitable for making cores of electromagnets.

Example 8.11. *A magnetic circuit is made of silicon steel and has a volume of 2×10^{-3} m³. The area of hysteresis loop of silicon steel is found to be 7.25 cm² ; the scales being 1 cm = 10 AT /m and 1 cm = 4 Wb/m². Calculate the hysteresis power loss when the flux is alternating at 50 Hz.*

Solution. Area of hysteresis loop = (Area in cm²) × (Scale factors) = (7.25) × (xy)

= (7.25) × (10 × 4) = 290 J/m³/cycle

* It also depends upon (i) the maximum value of flux density established and (ii) the initial magnetic state of the material.

Hysteresis power loss, P_h = Volume × area of loop × frequency

$$= (2 \times 10^{-3}) \times (290) \times (50) \text{ W} = \textbf{29 W}$$

Example 8.12. *The area of hysteresis loop obtained with a certain magnetic material was 9.3 cm². The co-ordinates were such that 1 cm = 1000 AT/m and 1 cm = 0.2 Wb/m². If the density of the given material is 7.8 g/cm³, calculate the hysteresis loss in watts/kg at 50 Hz.*

Solution.

Volume of 1 kg of material, $V = \dfrac{10^3}{7.8} \times 10^{-6} = 1.282 \times 10^{-4}$ m³

Area of hysteresis loop   = Area in cm² × scale factors

$$= (9.3) \times (1000 \times 0.2) = 1860 \text{ J/m}^3/\text{cycle}$$

Hysteresis energy loss, $W_h = V \times$ (area of loop)

$$= (1.282 \times 10^{-4}) \times 1860 = 0.238 \text{ J/cycle}$$

Hysteresis power loss, $P_h = W_h \times f = 0.283 \times 50 = 11.9$ W

Since we have considered 1 kg of material, ∴ Hysteresis power loss, P_h = **11.9 W/kg**

Example. 8.13. *Calculated the loss of energy caused by hysteresis in 1 hour in 50 kg of iron when subjected to cyclic magnetic changes. The frequency is 25 Hz, the area of hysteresis loop is equivalent in area to 240 J/m³/cycle and the density of iron is 7.8 g/cm³.*

Solution. Hysteresis energy loss   = 240 J/m³/cycle

Volume of iron = $\dfrac{\text{mass}}{\text{density}} = \dfrac{50 \times 10^3}{7.8} \times 10^{-6} = 6.41 \times 10^{-3}$ m³

No. of cycles/hour = $25 \times 60 \times 60 = 9 \times 10^4$

∴   Energy loss/hour = volume × (area of loop) × cycles/hour

$$= (6.41 \times 10^{-3}) \times (240) \times (9 \times 10^4) = \textbf{138456 J}$$

Example 8.14. *The armature of a 4-pole d.c. generator has a volume of 12 × 10⁻³ m³. During rotation, the armature is taken through a hysteresis loop whose area is 20 cm² when plotted to a scale of 1 cm = 100 AT/m, 1 cm = 0.1 Wb/m². Determine the hysteresis loss in watts when the armature rotates at a speed of 900 r.p.m.*

Solution.

Since it is a 4-pole machine, two hysteresis loops will be formed in one revolution of the armature.

∴ No. of loops generated/second, $f = 2 \times 900/60 = 30$

Hysteresis energy loss/cycle   = Area of loop in cm² × scale factors

$$= 20 \times (100 \times 0.1) = 200 \text{ J/m}^3$$

Total hysteresis energy loss/second   = volume × (area of loop in J/m³) × f

$$= (12 \times 10^{-3}) \times 200 \times 30 = 72 \text{ W}$$

i.e. Hysteresis power loss   = **72 W**

TUTORIAL PROBLEMS

1. A hysteresis loop is plotted against a horizontal axis which scales 1 cm = 1000 AT/m and a vertical axis which scales 1 cm = 0.2 Wb/m². If the area of the loop is 9 cm² and the overall height is 14 cm, calculate :
    (*i*) the hysteresis loss in J/m³ /cycle;
    (*ii*) the maximum flux density;
    (*iii*) the hysteresis loss in watt/kg assuming the density of the material to be 7.8 g/cm³.

    [(*i*) **1800** (*ii*) **1.4 Wb/m²** (*iii*) **11.55 W**]

2. The hysteresis loop for a specimen of mass 12 kg is equivalent to 30 W/mm³. Find the loss of energy in kWh in one hour at 50 Hz. The density of the specimen is 7.8 g/cm³. **[0.024 kWh]**

3. A transformer is made of 200 kg of steel plate with a specific gravity of 7.5. It may be assumed that the maximum operating flux density is 1.1 Wb/m² for all parts of the steel. When a specimen of the steel was tested, it was found to have a hysteresis loop of area 100 cm² for a maximum flux density of 1.1 Wb/m². If the scales of the hysteresis loop graph were 1 cm = 50 AT/m and 1 cm = 0.1 Wb/m², calculate the hysteresis power loss when the transformer is operated on 50 Hz mains. **[667 W]**

4. A magnetic core is made from sheet steel, the hysteresis loop of which has an area of 2.1 cm²; the scales being 1 cm = 400 AT/m and 1 cm = 0.4 Wb/m². The core measures 100 cm long and has an average cross-sectional area of 10 cm². The hysteresis loss is 16.8 W. Calculate the frequency of alternating flux. **[50 Hz]**

8.15. STEINMETZ HYSTERESIS LAW

To eliminate the need of finding the area of hysteresis loop for computing the hysteresis loss, Steinmetz devised an empirical law for finding the hysteresis loss. He found that the area of hysteresis loop of a magnetic material is directly proportional to 1.6th power of the maximum flux density established *i.e.*

$$\text{Area of hysteresis loop} \propto {}^{*}B_{max}^{1.6}$$

or $$\text{Hysteresis energy loss} \propto B_{max}^{1.6} \text{ joules/m}^3\text{/cycle}$$

or $$\text{Hysteresis energy loss} = \eta\, B_{max}^{1.6} \text{ joules/m}^3\text{/cycle}$$

where η is a constant called **hysteresis coefficient**. Its value depends upon the nature of material. The smaller the value of η of a magnetic material, the lesser is the hysteresis loss. The armatures of electrical machines and transformer cores are made of magnetic materials having low hysteresis co-efficient in order to reduce the hysteresis loss. The best transformer steels have η values around 130, for cast steel they are around 2500 and for cast iron about 3750.

If V is the volume of the material in m³ and f is the frequency of magnetisation, then,

Hysteresis power loss, $P_h = \eta f\, B_{max}^{1.6}\, V$ J/s or watts.

Example 8.15. *A power transformer has a core material for which hysteresis coefficient is 130 J/m³. Its volume is 8,000 cm³ and the maximum flux density is 1.25 Wb/m². What is the hysteresis loss in watts if the frequency of the alternating current is 50 Hz?*

Solution.

Hysteresis power loss, $P_h = \eta f\, B_{max}^{1.6}\, V = (130) \times (50) \times (1.25)^{1.6} \times (8000 \times 10^{-6}) =$ **74.31 W**

Example 8.16. *The volume of a transformer core built up of sheet steel laminations is 5000 cm³ and the gross cross-sectional area is 240 cm². Because of the insulation between the plates, the net cross-sectional area is 90% of the gross. The maximum value of magnetic flux is 22 mWb and the frequency is 50 Hz. Find (i) the hysteresis loss/m³/cycle and (ii) power loss in watts. Take hysteresis coefficient as 250.*

Solution. $a = 0.9 \times 240 = 216 \text{ cm}^2; \quad B_{max} = \dfrac{22 \times 10^{-3}}{216 \times 10^{-4}} = 1.019 \text{ Wb/m}^2$

(i) Hysteresis energy loss $= \eta B_{max}^{1.6} = 250 \times (1.019)^{1.6} =$ **257.6 J/m³/cycle**

(ii) Hysteresis power loss, $P_h = \eta f\, B_{max}^{1.6} \times V = (257.6) \times (50) \times (5000 \times 10^{-6}) =$ **64.4 W**

- -

*   The index 1.6 is called **Steinmetz index**. In fact, the value of this index depends upon the nature of material and may vary from 1.6 to 2.5. However, reasonable accuracy is obtained if it is taken as 1.6.

Example 8.17. *The area of hysteresis loop obtained with a certain specimen of iron was 9.3 cm². The co-ordinates were such that 1 cm = 1000 AT/m and 1 cm = 0.2 Wb/m². Calculate (i) the hysteresis loss in J/m³/cycle (ii) hysteresis loss in W/m³ at a frequency of 50 Hz (iii) If the maximum flux density was 1.5 Wb/m², calculate the hysteresis loss/m³ for a maximum flux density of 1.2 Wb/m², and a frequency of 30 Hz, assuming the loss to be proportional to $B_{max}^{1.8}$.*

Solution.

(i) Hysteresis energy loss $= (xy) \times$ (area of loop) J/m³/cycle

$\qquad\qquad\qquad\qquad = (1000 \times 0.2) \times 9.3 = $ **1860 J/m³/cycle**

(ii) Hysteresis power loss $= 1860 \times 50 = $ **93,000 W/m³**

(iii) Hysteresis loss/m³ $\qquad = \eta\, f\, (B_{max})^{1.8}$

or $\qquad\qquad 93000 = \eta \times 50 \times (1.5)^{1.8}$

$\therefore \qquad\qquad\qquad \eta = \dfrac{93,000}{50 \times (1.5)^{1.8}} = 896.5$

For $B_{max} = 1.2$ Wb/m² and $f = 30$ Hz,

Hysteresis loss/m³ $= \eta\, f\, (B_{max})^{1.8}$ W $= 896.5 \times 30 \times (1.2)^{1.8} = $ **37342 W**

Example 8.18. *In a certain transformer, the hysteresis loss was found to be 160 watts when the maximum flux density was 1.1 Wb/m² and the frequency 60 Hz. What will be the loss when the maximum flux density is reduced to 0.9 Wb/m² and frequency to 50 Hz?*

Solution. According to Steinmetz hysteresis law,

Hysteresis loss, $\qquad P_h \propto f\,(B_{max})^{1.6}$

For the first case, $\qquad P_1 \propto 60 \times (1.1)^{1.6}$

For the second case, $\qquad P_2 \propto 50 \times (0.9)^{1.6}$

$\therefore \qquad\qquad \dfrac{P_2}{P_1} = \dfrac{50 \times (0.9)^{1.6}}{60 \times (1.1)^{1.6}} = 0.604$

$\therefore \qquad\qquad P_2 = 0.604\, P_1$

$\qquad\qquad\qquad = 0.604 \times 160 = $ **96.64 W**

MULTIPLE-CHOICE QUESTIONS

1. In Fig. 8.19, the magnetic circuit is the path

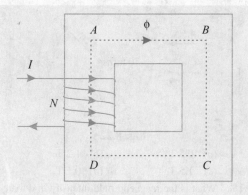

Fig. 8.19

    (a) *DAB*   (b) *ABCDA*

    (c) *ABC*   (d) *ABCD*

2. If *l* is the magnetic path in Fig. 8.19, then magnetising force is

    (a) *NI*   (b) *NI × l*

    (c) *l/NI*   (d) *NI/l*

3. The SI unit of reluctance is

    (a) AT/Wb   (b) AT/m

    (c) AT   (d) N/Wb

4. A 2 cm long coil has 10 turns and carries a current of 750 mA. The magnetising force of the coil is

    (a) 225 AT/m   (b) 675 AT/m

    (c) 450 AT/m   (d) 375 AT/m

5. The reluctance of a magnetic circuit varies as ....

   (a) length × area   (b) length ÷ area

   (c) area ÷ length   (d) (length)^2 + area

6. Permeance of a magnetic circuit is .... area of x-section of the circuit.

   (a) inversely proportional to

   (b) directly proportional to

   (c) independent of

   (d) none of the above

7. A magnetic circuit carries a flux ϕ_i in the iron part and a flux ϕ_g in the air gap. Then leakage co-efficient is .....

   (a) ϕ_i/ϕ_g (b) ϕ_g/ϕ_i

   (c) $\phi_g \times \phi_i$ (d) none of the above

8. The reluctance of a magnetic circuit depends upon .....

   (a) current in the coil

   (b) no. of turns of coil

   (c) flux density in the circuit

   (d) none of the above

9. The B-H curve for ...... will be a straight line passing through the origin.

   (a) air   (b) soft iron

   (c) hardened steel   (d) silicon steel

10. The B-H curve of ...... will not be a straight line.

   (a) air   (b) copper

   (c) wood   (d) soft iron

11. A magnetising force of 800 AT/m will produce a flux density of .... in air.

   (a) 1 mWb/m^2 (b) 1 Wb/m^2

   (c) 10 mWb/m^2 (d) 0.5 Wb/m^2

12. The magnetic material used for ...... should have a large hysteresis loop.

   (a) transformers

   (b) d.c. generators

   (c) a.c. motors

   (d) permanent magnets

13. The magnetic flux density in the core in Fig. 8.20 is ...

   (a) 1 T   (b) 0.5 T

   (c) 1.5 T   (d) 0.8 T

14. If the magnetising force required at the working flux density in Fig. 8.20 is 400 AT/m (from B-H curve), the required number of turns is

   (a) 120   (b) 240

   (c) 180   (d) 320

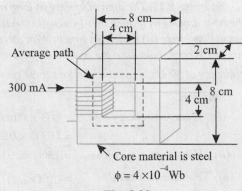

Average path

300 mA →

Core material is steel

$\phi = 4 \times 10^{-4}$ Wb

Fig. 8.20

15. How would the loop in Fig. 8.21 appear for a material with much less retentivity ?

   (a) narrower   (b) wider

   (c) no change   (d) very wide

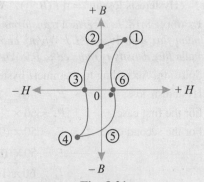

Fig. 8.21

16. At high frequencies, the material used for transformer cores is

   (a) silicon iron   (b) soft iron

   (c) ferrite   (d) none of above

17. The permeability in the core in Fig. 8.22 is 6 × 10^{-5} Wb/AT-m. The flux density in the core is

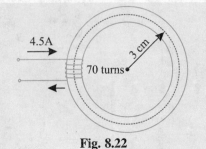

4.5A

70 turns

3 cm

Fig. 8.22

   (a) 0.5 T   (b) 1.2 T

   (c) 1.5 T   (d) 0.1 T

18. What is the magnetic field intensity in a material whose relative permeability is 1 when the flux density is 0.005 T ?

(a) 250 AT/m   (b) 452 AT/m

(c) 3980 AT/m   (d) 1715 AT/m

19. In Fig. 8.23, the cross-section of the core is circular and has radius 1.25 mm. The mean length of the core is 30 cm. If the magnetic flux in the core is 0.6×10^{-5} Wb, then H in air-gap is

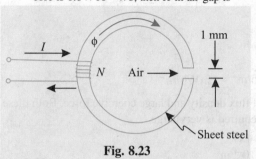

Fig. 8.23

(a) 2.5×10^6 AT/m   (b) 1.5×10^7 AT/m

(c) 8.2×10^4 AT/m   (d) 9.71×10^5 AT/m

20. The current in the winding shown in Fig. 8.24 is 3.2 A. If the winding has 60 turns, the magnetic field intensity in the core is

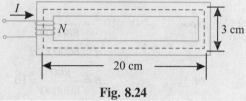

Fig. 8.24

(a) 242.2 AT/m   (b) 417.4 AT/m

(c) 332.8 AT/m   (d) 141.4 AT/m

Answers to Multiple-Choice Questions

1. (b)	**2.** (d)	**3.** (a)	**4.** (d)	**5.** (b)	**6.** (b)	**7.** (a)	**8.** (c)
9. (a)	**10.** (d)	**11.** (a)	**12.** (d)	**13.** (a)	**14.** (d)	**15.** (a)	**16.** (c)
17. (d)	**18.** (c)	**19.** (d)	**20.** (b)				

Hints to Selected Multiple-Choice Questions

3. Unit of reluctance $= \dfrac{\text{Unit of m.m.f.}}{\text{Unit of magnetic flux}} = \textbf{AT/Wb}$

4. Magnetising force, $H = \dfrac{NI}{l} = \dfrac{10 \times (750 \times 10^{-3})}{2 \times 10^{-2}} = \textbf{375 AT/m}$

5. Reluctance $= \dfrac{l}{a \mu_0 \mu_r}$. Therefore, reluctance varies as **length ÷ area.**

6. Permeance $= \dfrac{1}{\text{Reluctance}} = \dfrac{a \mu_0 \mu_r}{l}$

7. Leakage co-efficient $= \dfrac{\phi_i}{\phi_g}$; where ϕ_i = flux in iron part, ϕ_g = flux in air gap

8. Reluctance $= \dfrac{l}{a \mu_0 \mu_r}$. Clearly reluctance depends upon μ_r. Now the value of μ_r is not constant for a magnetic substance; it varies with **flux density.**

9. All non-magnetic materials have B-H curve a straight line passing through the origin. For non-magnetic materials,

$$B = \mu_0 H$$

Since $\mu_0 (= 4\pi \times 10^{-7}$ H/m) is constant, $B \propto H$

or B-H curve is a straight line passing through the origin.

10. For a magnetic material,
$$B = \mu_0 \mu_r H$$
Since μ_r is not a constant quantity, the relation between B and H is non-linear.

11. For air (or any other non-magnetic material),
$$B = \mu_0 H = (4\pi \times 10^{-7}) H$$

Now $$4\pi \times 10^{-7} = \frac{1}{800000}$$

∴ $$H = 800000 B$$

or $$B = \frac{800}{800000} = 10^{-3} \text{ Wb/m}^2 = 1 \text{ mWb/m}^2$$

12. A large hysteresis loop means high residual flux density and large coercive force. Both these features mean that demagnetizing energy required is very large.

13. Area of cross-section of the magnetic circuit is
$$a = 0.02 \times 0.02 = 4 \times 10^{-4} \text{ m}^2$$

Flux density, $$B = \frac{\phi}{a} = \frac{4 \times 10^{-4}}{4 \times 10^{-4}} = 1 \text{ T}$$

14. The average length of magnetic path is
$$l = 6 + 6 + 6 + 6 = 24 \text{ cm} = 0.24 \text{ m}$$
$$\text{m.m.f.} = H \times l = 400 \times 0.24 = 96 \text{ AT}$$

Now $$NI = 96$$

∴ $$N = \frac{96}{I} = \frac{96}{300 \times 10^{-3}} = 320$$

15. Lower retentivity means **narrower** hysteresis loop.

16. At high frequencies, eddy current losses tend to be a serious problem and high retentivity **ferrites** are used.

17. $$H = \frac{NI}{l} = \frac{NI}{2\pi r} = \frac{70 \times 4.5}{2\pi \times 0.03} = 1672 \text{ AT/m}$$

$$B = \mu H = 6 \times 10^{-5} \times 1672 = 0.1 \text{ T}$$

18. $B = \mu_0 \mu_r H$ or $H = \dfrac{B}{\mu_0 \mu_r} = \dfrac{0.005}{4\pi \times 10^{-7} \times 1} = 3980 \text{ AT/m}$

19. Area of X-section, $a = \pi r^2 = \pi (1.25 \times 10^{-3})^2 = 4.91 \times 10^{-6} \text{ m}^2$
Magnetic flux density developed in the core is
$$B = \frac{\phi}{a} = \frac{0.6 \times 10^{-5}}{4.91 \times 10^{-6}} = 1.22 \text{ T}$$

$$H_{air} = \frac{B_{air}}{\mu_0} = \frac{1.22}{4\pi \times 10^{-7}} = 9.71 \times 10^5 \text{ AT/m}$$

20. Mean length of magnetic path is
$$l = 2 (20 + 3) = 46 \text{ cm} = 0.46 \text{ m}$$
Magnetic field intensity in the core is
$$H = \frac{NI}{l} = \frac{60 \times 3.2}{0.46} = 417.4 \text{ AT/m}$$

Electromagnetic Induction

INTRODUCTION

In the beginning of nineteenth century, Oersted discovered that a magnetic field exists around a current carrying conductor. In other words, magnetism can be created by means of an electric current. Can a magnetic field create an electric current in a conductor ? In 1831, Michael Faraday, the famous English scientist discovered that this could be done. He demonstrated that when the magnetic flux linking a conductor changes, an e.m.f. is induced in the conductor. This phenomenon is known as *electromagnetic induction*. The great discovery of electromagnetic induction by Faraday through a series of brilliant experiments has brought a revolution in the engineering world. Most of the electrical devices (*e.g.* electric generator, transformer, telephones *etc.*) are based on this principle. In this chapter, we shall confine our attention to the various aspects of electromagnetic induction.

9.1. ELECTOMAGNETIC INDUCTION

When the magnetic flux *linking a conductor

---

*   Magnetic lines of force form closed loops. Magnetic flux linking the conductor means that the magnetic flux embraces it *i.e.* it encircles the conductor.

changes, an e.m.f. is induced in the conductor. If the conductor forms a complete loop or circuit, a current will flow in it. This phenomenon is known as *electromagnetic induction. Two things are worth noting. First, the basic requirement for electromagnetic induction is the change in magnetic flux linking the conductor (or coil). Secondly, the e.m.f. and hence the current in this conductor (or coil) will persist so long as this change is taking place.

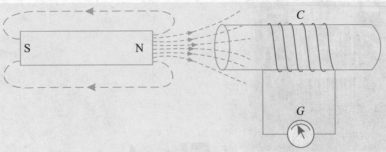

Fig. 9.1

To demonstrate the phenomenon of electromagnetic induction, consider a coil *C* of several turns connected to a centre zero galvanometer *G* as shown in Fig. 9.1. If a permanent magnet is moved towards the coil, it will be observed that the galvanometer shows deflection in one direction. If the magnet is moved away from the coil, the galvanometer again shows deflection but in the opposite direction. In either case, *the deflection will persist so long as the magnet is in motion.* The production of e.m.f. and hence current in coil *C* is due to the fact that when the magnet is in motion (towards or away from the coil), the amount of magnetic flux linking the coil changes—the basic requirement for inducing e.m.f. in the coil. If the movement of the magnet is stopped, though the magnetic flux is linking the coil, there is *no change in magnetic flux* and hence no e.m.f. is induced in the coil. Consequently, the deflection of the galvanometer reduces to zero.

It is emphasised here that the basic requirement for inducting e.m.f. in a coil is not the magnetic flux linking the coil *but* the change in magnetic flux linking the coil. No change in magnetic flux, no e.m.f. is induced in the coil.

9.2. FARADAY'S LAWS OF ELECTROMAGNETIC INDUCTION

Faraday performed a series of experiments to demonstrate the phenomenon of electromagnetic induction. He summed up his conclusions into two laws, known as Faraday's laws of electromagnetic induction.

First law. It states :

When the magnetic flux linking a conductor or coil changes, an e.m.f. is induced in it.

Second law. It states :

The magnitude of induced e.m.f. in a coil is equal to the rate of chage of magnetic flux linkages.

Suppose a coil has N turns and magnetic flux linking the coil increases from ϕ_1 Wb to ϕ_2 Wb in t second. Now magnetic flux linkages means the product of magnetic flux and number of turns.

Initial magnetic flux linkages = $N\phi_1$; Final magnetic flux linkages = $N\phi_2$

$$\therefore \qquad e = \text{Rate of change of magnetic flux linkages} = \frac{N\phi_2 - N\phi_1}{t}$$

or $$e = N\frac{(\phi_2 - \phi_1)}{t}$$

---

* So called because electricity is produced from magnetism (*i.e. electromagnetic*) and that there is no physical connection (*induction*) between the magnetic field and the conductor.

In differential form, we have, $\quad e = N \dfrac{d\phi}{dt}$ volts

It is a usual practice to give a minus sign to the right-hand side expression. The minus sign comes from Lenz's law (See Art. 9.3) and indicates that the voltage is induced in a direction to oppose the change in flux that produced it.

$$\therefore \qquad\qquad e = -N \dfrac{d\phi}{dt} \text{ volts}$$

Example 9.1. *A coil of 100 turns is linked by a magnetic flux of 20 mWb. If this magnetic flux is reversed in a time of 2 ms, calculate the average e.m.f. induced in the coil.*

Solution.

Change in magnetic flux, $\qquad d\phi = 20 - (-20) = 40 \; mWb = 40 \times 10^{-3} \; Wb$

Time taken for the change, $\qquad dt = 2ms = 2 \times 10^{-3} \; s$

$$\therefore \qquad\qquad e = N \dfrac{d\phi}{dt} = 100 \times \dfrac{40 \times 10^{-3}}{2 \times 10^{-3}} = \mathbf{2000 \; V}$$

Example 9.2. *A coil of 200 turns of wire is wound on a magnetic circuit of reluctance 2000 AT/mWb. If a current of 1A flowing in the coil is reversed in 10 ms, find the average e.m.f induced in the coil.*

Solution.

$$\text{Magnetic flux in the coil} = \dfrac{\text{m.m.f}}{\text{reluctance}} = \dfrac{200 \times 1}{2000} = 0.1 \; mWb$$

When current (*i.e.* 1A) in the coil is reversed, magnetic flux through the coil is also reversed.

Now $$e = N \dfrac{d\phi}{dt}$$

Here, $N = 200$; $d\phi = 0.1 - (-0.1) = 0.2 \; mWb$; $dt = 10 \times 10^{-3} \; s$

$$\therefore \qquad\qquad e = 200 \times \dfrac{0.2 \times 10^{-3}}{10 \times 10^{-3}} = \mathbf{4 \; V}$$

Example 9.3. *The field winding of 4-pole d.c. generator consists of 4 coils connected in series, each coil being wound with 1200 turns. When the field is excited, there is a magnetic flux of 0.04Wb/ pole. If the field switch is opened at such a speed that the magnetic flux falls to the residual value of 0.004 Wb/pole in 0.1 second, calculate the average value of e.m.f. induced across the field winding terminals.*

Solution.

Total no. of turns, $\qquad\qquad N = 1200 \times 4 = 4800$

Total initial magnetic flux $\qquad = 4 \times 0.04 = 0.16 \; Wb$

Total residual magnetic flux $\qquad = 4 \times 0.004 = 0.016 \; Wb$

Change in magnetic flux, $\qquad d\phi = 0.16 - 0.016 = 0.144 \; Wb$

Time taken, $\qquad\qquad dt = 0.1 \; second$

$\therefore$ Induced e.m.f., $\qquad\qquad e = N \dfrac{d\phi}{dt} = 4800 \times \dfrac{0.144}{0.1} = \mathbf{6912 \; V}$

TUTORIAL PROBLEMS

1. A square coil of side 5 cm contains 100 loops and is positioned perpendicular to a uniform magnetic field of 0.6 T. It is quickly removed from the field (moving perpendicular to the field) to a region where magnetic field is zero. It takes 0.1 s for the whole coil to reach field-free region. If resistance of the coil is 100 Ω, how much energy is dissipated in the coil ?

[$2.3 \times 10^{-3} \; J$]

2. A flat search coil containing 50 turns each of area 2×10^{-4} m² is connected to a galvanometer; the total resistance of the circuit is 100 Ω. The coil is placed so that its plane is normal to a magnetic field of flux density 0.25 T.

   (*i*) What is the change in magnetic flux linking the circuit when the coil is moved to a region of negligible magnetic field ?

   (*ii*) What charge passes through the galvanometer?   [(*i*) 2.5×10^{-3} Wb   (*ii*) 25 μC]

3. The magnetic flux passing perpendicular to the plane of a coil and directed into the plane of the paper is varying according to the following equation :

$$\phi = 5t^2 + 6t + 2$$

   where ϕ is in *mWb* and *t* in seconds. Find the e.m.f. induced in the coil at $t = 1s$.   [16 *mV*]

4. A coil has an area of 0.04 m^2 and has 1000 turns. It is suspended in a magnetic field of 5×10^{-5} Wb/m^2 perpendicular to the field. The coil is rotated through 90° in 0.2 s. Calculate the average e.m.f. induced in the coil due to rotation.   [**0.01 V**]

5. A gramophone disc of brass of diameter 30 cm rotates horizontally at the rate 100/3 revolutions per minute. If the vertical component of earth's field is 0.01 *T*, calculate the e.m.f. induced between the centre and the rim of the disc.   [**3.9 × 10⁻⁴ V**]

9.3. DIRECTION OF INDUCED E.M.F. AND CURRENT

The direction of induced e.m.f. and hence current in a conductor or coil can be determined by one of the following two methods :

    1. Lenz's law   2. Fleming's Right-hand rule

    1. Lenz's Law. Emil Lenz, a German scientist gave the following simple rule (known as Lenz's law) to find the direction of induced current :

An induced current will flow in such a direction so as to oppose the cause that produces it.

The cause that produces the current is the change of magnetic flux linking the coil. Therefore, the direction of induced current will be such that its own magnetic field opposes the change in flux that produced the induced current. Let us apply Lenz's law to Fig. 9.2. Here N-pole of the magnet is approaching the coil. According to Lenz's law, the direction of induced current will be such that magnetic flux set up by it will oppose the change in original magnetic flux. This is possible only if the left-hand face of the coil becomes N-pole. Once we know the magnetic polarity of the coil face, the direction of induced current can be easily determined by applying Right hand rule for the coil (See Art. 7.12).

It may be noted here that Lenz's law directly follows from the law of conservation of energy *i.e.* in order to set up induced current, some energy must be expended. In the above case, for example, when the N–pole of the magnet is approaching the coil, the induced curent will flow in the coil in such a direction that the left-hand face of the coil becomes N-pole. The result is that motion of the magnet is opposed. The mechanical energy spent in overcoming this opposition is converted into electrical energy which apears in the coil.

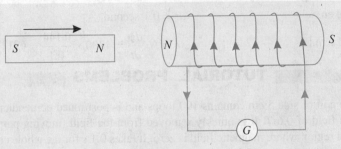

Fig. 9.2

2. Fleming's Right-hand Rule. This rule is particularly suitable to find the direction of induced e.m.f. and hence current when the conductor moves at right angles to a stationary magnetic field. It may be stated as under :

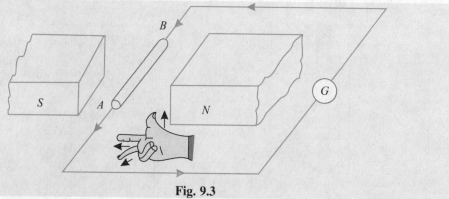

Fig. 9.3

Stretch out the **forefinger, middle finger** *and* **thumb** *of your right hand so that they are at right angles to one another. If the forefinger points in the direction of magnetic field, thumb in the direction of motion of the conductor, then the middle finger will point in the direction of induced current.*

Consider a conductor *AB* moving upwards at right angles to a uniform magnetic field as shown in Fig. 9.3. Applying Fleming's right hand rule, it is clear that the direction of induced current is from *B* to *A*. If the motion of the conductor is downward, keeping the direction of magnetic field unchanged, then the direction of induced current will be from *A* to *B*.

9.4. INDUCED E.M.F.

When the magnetic flux linking a conductor (or coil) changes, an e.m.f. is induced in it. This change in magnetic flux linkages can be brought about in the following two ways :

(*i*)   The conductor is moved in a stationary magnetic field in such a way that the magnetic flux linking it changes in magnitude. The e.m.f. induced in this way is called *dynamically induced e.m.f.* (as in an a.c. or d.c. generator). It is so called because e.m.f. is induced in the conductor which is in motion.

(*ii*) The conductor is stationary and the magnetic field is moving or changing. The e.m.f. induced in this way is called *statically induced e.m.f.* (as in a transformer). It is so called because the e.m.f. is induced in a conductor which is stationary.

It may be noted that in either case the magnitude of induced e.m.f. is given by $Nd\phi/dt$ or derivable from this relation.

9.5. DYNAMICALLY INDUCED E.M.F.

Consinder a single conductor of length *l* metres moving at right angles to a uniform magnetic field of B Wb/m^2 with a velocity of *v* m /s [See Fig. 9.4 (*i*)]. Suppose the conductor moves through a small distance *dx* in *dt* seconds. Then area swept by the conductor is $= l \times dx$.

∴ Magnetic flux cut, $d\phi$ = Flux density × Area swept = $Bldx$ Wb

According to Faraday's laws of electromagnetic induction, e.m.f. *e* induced in the conductor is given by ;

$$e = N\,\frac{d\phi}{dt} = \frac{B\,l\,dx}{dt}$$

$$(\because N = 1)$$

∴ $e = B\,l\,v$ volts

$$(\because dx/dt = v)$$

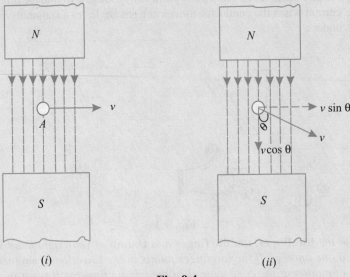

Fig. 9.4

If the conductor moves at angle θ to the magnetic field [See Fig. 9.4 (*ii*)], then the velocity at which the conductor moves across the field is *v sin θ.

∴ $e = Bl\,v\,\sin\theta$

The direction of induced e.m.f. can be determined by Fleming's Right hand rule.

Example 9.4. *A conductor of length 0.5 m situated in and at right angles to a uniform magnetic field of flux density 1 Wb/m² moves with a velocity of 40 m/s. Calculate the e.m.f. induced in the conductor. What will be the e.m.f. induced if the conductor moves at an angle 60° to the field?*

Solution. $e = Bl\,v = 1 \times 0.5 \times 40 = \mathbf{20\ V}$

$e = Bl\,v\sin\theta = 1 \times 0.5 \times 40 \times \sin 60° = \mathbf{17.32\ V}$

Example 9.5. *An aircraft has a wing span of 56 m. It is flying horizontally at a speed of 810 km/hr and the vertical component of earth's magnetic field is 4×10^{-4} Wb/m². Calculate the potential difference between the wing tips of the aircraft.*

Solution. Induced e.m.f. $= Blv$

Here $B = 4 \times 10^{-4}$ Wb/m² ; $l = 56\ m$; $v = 810 \times 10^{3}/3600 = 225\ m/s$

∴ Induced e.m.f. $= (4 \times 10^{-4}) \times 56 \times (225) = 5.04\ V$

or Potential difference $= \mathbf{5.04\ V}$

Example 9.6. *Each field pole of a 4-pole d.c. generator produces a magnetic flux of 20 mWb. The armature conductors rotate at 1200 r.p.m. and may be assumed to cut the magnetic flux at right angles. What is the average value of induced e.m.f. in each armature conductor ?*

Solution. In one revolution, each conductor cuts a total flux of $20 \times 4 = 80$ *mWb*. Since the conductor is rotating at 1200/60 = 20 r.p.s., time taken for one revolution is = 1/20 = 0.05 second.

∴ Average e.m.f. induced in each conductor $= N\dfrac{d\phi}{dt} = 1 \times \dfrac{80 \times 10^{-3}}{0.05} = \mathbf{1.6\ V}$

. . . .

* If the conductor is moved parallel to the magnetic field, there would be no change in magnetic flux and hence no e.m.f. would be induced.

Example 9.7. *A d.c. generator consists of conductors lying on a radius of 10 cm and the effective length of a conductor in a constant radial field of strength 0.9 Wb/m² is 12 cm. The armature rotates at 1400 r.p.m. Given that the generator has 152 conductors in series, calculate the voltage being generated.*

Solution. Since the magnetic field is radial, the conductors cut the magnetic lines of force at right angles.

Velocity, $v = \omega \times r = \dfrac{2\pi N}{60} \times r = \dfrac{2\pi \times 1400}{60} \times 0.1 = 14.66 \, m/s$

Voltage generated in each conductor = $Blv = 0.9 \times 0.12 \times 14.66 = 1.538$ V

Voltage generated in 152 conductors in series = $1.538 \times 152 = $ **240.6 V**

TUTORIAL PROBLEMS

1. A wire 10 cm long is moved at a uniform speed of 4 *m/s* at right angles to its length and to a uniform field. Calculate the density of the field if the e.m.f. generated in the wire is 0.15 V.

   [0.375 Wb/m²]

2. Calculate the e.m.f generated in the axle of a car travelling at 108 km/hr, assuming the length of the axle to be 1.5 m and the vertical component of earth's field to be 320μ Wb/m².

   [14.4 mV]

3. A d.c. generator has 136 conductors in series. Each conductor has an effective length of 15 cm, is constrained to move in a circular path of radius 12 cm and lies in a uniform field of flux density of 1.2 Wb/m². Calculate the e.m.f. generated when the armature rotates at 1400 r.p.m.

   [430 V]

4. In a d.c. generator, the conductors are constrained to move in a circular path of radius 12 cm. Each conductor has an effective length of 20 cm and the magnetic field has a uniform flux density of 0.4 Wb/m². Calculate the speed of roation in r.p.m. so that an e.m.f. of 0.8 V is induced in each conductor.

   [796 r.p.m]

5. An aeroplane with a wing span of 25 m is flying horizontally at a speed of 900 km/hr. Calculate the p.d. between the wing tips if the vertical component of earth's field is 4 × 10⁻⁵ Wb/m².

   [0.25 V]

9.6. STATICALLY INDUCED E.M.F.

When the conductor is stationary and the field is moving or changing, the e.m.f. induced in the conductor is called statically induced e.m.f. A statically induced e.m.f. can be further sub-divided into :

1. Self-induced e.m.f.   2. Mutually induced e.m.f.

1. Self-induced e.m.f. The e.m.f. induced in a coil due to the change of its own magnetic flux linked with it is called *self-induced e.m.f.*

When a coil is carrying current (See Fig. 9.5), a magnetic field is established through the coil. If the current in the coil changes, then magnetic flux linking the coil also changes. Hence by Faraday's laws, an e.m.f. will be induced in the coil. This is knows as self-induced e.m.f. The magnitude of this self-induced e.m.f = $N \, d\phi/dt$. The direction of induced e.m.f. (by Lenz's law) is always such so as to oppose the cause responsible for inducing the e.m.f; namely change of current (and hence field) in the coil.

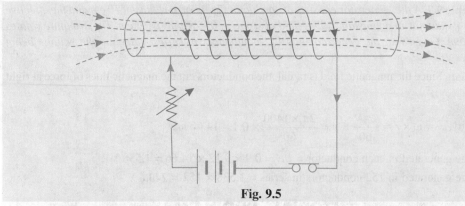

Fig. 9.5

Thus when current in a coil changes, an e.m.f. (self-induced e.m.f.) is induced in it which opposes the change of current in the coil. This propoerty of the coil is called its *self-inductance* or *inductance*. It may be noted that self-induced e.m.f. (and hence inductance) *does not prevent the current from changing*; *it serves only to delay the change*. Thus, after the switch is closed (See Fig. 9.5), the current will rise from zero to final steady value in some time. This delay is due to self-induced e.m.f. or inductance of the coil.

Note. Self-induced e.m.f. (and hence inductance) comes into picture only when current in the coil changes (decreases or increases). When current in the coil is steady or constant, the magnetic field also becomes constant and self-induced e.m.f. drops to zero. Under such condition (*i.e.* constant current), the circuit does not exhibit inductance *i.e.* no self-induced e.m.f.

2. Mutually Induced e.m.f. The e.m.f. induced in a coil due to the changing current in the neighbouring coil is called *mutually induced e.m.f.*

Consider two coils *A* and *B* placed adjacent to each other as shown in Fig. 9.6. A part of the magnetic flux produced by coil *A* passes through or links with coil *B*. This magnetic flux which is common to both the coils *A* and *B* is called *mutual flux* (ϕ_m). If current in coil *A* is varied, the mutual flux also varies and hence e.m.f. is induced in both the coils. The e.m.f. induced in coil *A* is called self-induced e.m.f. as already discussed. The e.m.f. induced in coil *B* is known as *mutually induced e.m.f.*

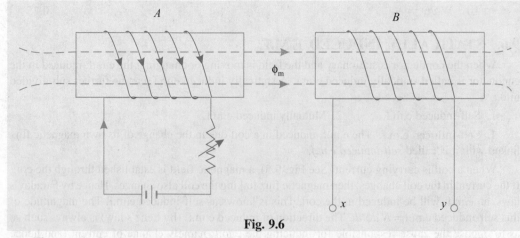

Fig. 9.6

The magnitude of mutually induced e.m.f. is given by Farady's laws *i.e.* $e_M = N_B \, d\phi_m/dt$ where N_B is the number of turns of coil *B* and $d\phi_m/dt$ is the rate of change of mutual flux *i.e.* magnetic flux common to both the coils. The direction of mutually induced e.m.f. (by Lenz's law) is always such so as to oppose the very cause producing it. The cause producing the mutually induced e.m.f. in coil *B* is the changing mutual flux produced by coil *A*. Hence the direction of induced current (when the circuit is completed) in coil *B* will be such that the magnetic flux set up by it will oppose the changing mutual flux produced by coil *A*.

The following points may be noted carefully :

(*i*) The mutually induced e.m.f. in coil *B* persists so long as the current in coil *A* is changing. If current in coil *A* becomes steady, the mutual flux also becomes steady and mutually induced e.m.f. drops to zero.

(*ii*) The property of two neighboruing coils to induce voltage in one coil due to the change of current in the other is called *mutual inductance*.

9.7. SELF-INDUCTANCE (L)

The property of a coil that opposes any change in the amount of current flowing through it is called its **self-inductance** *or* **inductance.**

This property (*i.e.* inductance) is due to the self-induced e.m.f. in the coil itself by the changing current. If the current in the coil is increasing, the self-induced e.m.f. is set up in such a direction so as to oppose the rise of current *i.e.* direction of self-induced e.m.f. is opposite to that of the applied voltage. Similarly, if the current in the coil is decreasing, self-induced voltage will be such so as to oppose the decrease in current *i.e.* self-induced e.m.f. will be in the same direction as the applied voltage. It may be noted that self-inductance does not prevent the current from changing; it serves only to delay the change.

The greater the self-induced e.m.f. $(=Nd\phi/dt)$, the greater the self-inductance of the coil and hence larger is the opposition to the changing current. Hence inductance of a coil depends upon the following factors :

(*i*) Shape and number of turns.

(*ii*) μ_r of the material surrounding the coil

(*iii*) The speed with which magnetic field changes

Expression for L. Consider a coil of *N* turns carrying a current of *I* amperes. If current in the coil changes, the magnetic flux linkages of the coil will also change. This will set up a self-induced e.m.f. *e* in the coil given by;

$$e = N \frac{d\phi}{dt} = \frac{d}{dt}(N\phi)$$

Since magnetic flux is due to current in the coil, it follows that magnetic flux linkages $(= N\phi)$ will be proportional to *I*.

$$\therefore \qquad e \propto \frac{dI}{dt} = \text{constant} \times \frac{dI}{dt}$$

$$\therefore \qquad e = L \frac{dI}{dt} \qquad \qquad ...(i)$$

where *L* is a constant called **self-inductance** or **inductance** of the coil. The unit of inductance is henry (H). If in Eq. (*i*) above, *e* = 1 volt, *dI/dt* = 1A/second, then *L* = 1H.

Hence a coil (or circuit) has an inductance of **1 henry** *if an e.m.f. of 1 volt is induced in it when current through it changes at the rate of 1 ampere per second.*

9.8. OTHER EXPRESSIONS FOR L

Apart from exp. (*i*) above, the value of *L* can be determined by one of the following two ways:

(*i*) **First method.** If the magnetic flux linkages of the coil and current are known, then inductance can be determined as under :

$$e = L \frac{dI}{dt} = \frac{d}{dt}(LI)$$

Also

$$e = N \frac{d\phi}{dt} = \frac{d}{dt}(N\phi)$$

From the two expressions, we have, $LI = N\phi$

∴ $$L = \frac{N\phi}{I}$$ ...(i)

Thus, inductance is the magnetic flux linkages of the coil per ampere. If $N\phi = 1\text{Wb–turn}$ and $I = 1\text{A}$, then $L = 1\text{H}$.

Hence a coil has an inductance of **1 henry** *if a current of 1 A in the coil sets up magnetic flux linkages of 1 Wb-turn.*

(ii) *Second method.* The inductance of a magnetic circuit can be found in terms of its physical dimensions. Consider an iron-cored solenoid of dimensions as shown in Fig. 9.7. Inductance of the solenooid is given by [from exp. (i) above] :

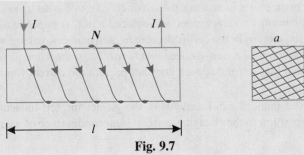

Fig. 9.7

$$L = N \frac{d\phi}{dI}$$

Now

$$\phi = \frac{\text{m.m.f.}}{\text{reluctance}} = \frac{NI}{l/a\mu_0\mu_r}$$

Differentiating ϕ *w.r.t.* I, we get, $\dfrac{d\phi}{dI} = \dfrac{N a \mu_0 \mu_r}{l}$

∴ $$L = N \frac{(N a \mu_0 \mu_r)}{l} \quad \text{or} \quad L = \frac{N^2 a \mu_0 \mu_r}{l}$$ ...(ii)

$$= \frac{N^2}{l/a\mu_0\mu_r} = \frac{N^2}{\text{Reluctance (S)}}$$ ...(iii)

It may be noted that inductance is directly proportional to turns squared and inversely proportional to reluctance of the magnetic path.

Example 9.8. *A wooden toroid of mean diameter 400 mm and cross-sectional area 400 mm^2 is uniformly wound with a coil of 1000 turns which carries a current of 2A. Detemine (i) self-inductance of the coil and (ii) the e.m.f. induced in the coil when the current is uniformly reduced to zero in 10 ms.*

Solution. $l = 0.4\pi \text{ m} ;$ $a = 400 \times 10^{-6} \ m^2$

(i) $$L = \frac{N^2 a \mu_0 \mu_r}{l} = \frac{(1000)^2 \times 400 \times 10^{-6} \times 4\pi \times 10^{-7} \times 1}{0.4\pi} = 0.4 \times 10^{-3} \text{ H}$$

(ii) $$e = L \frac{dI}{dt} = 0.4 \times 10^{-3} \frac{2 - 0}{10 \times 10^{-3}} = \textbf{0.08 V}$$

Example 9.9. *An air-cored solenoid having a diameter of 4 cm and a length of 60 cm is wound with 4000 turns. If a current of 5A flows in the solenoid, calculate (i) the inductance and (ii) energy stored in joules.*

Solution. $a = (\pi/4)\, d^2 = (\pi/4)\, (16 \times 10^{-4}) = 4\pi \times 10^{-4}\ m^2$

(i) $\qquad L = \dfrac{N^2 a \mu_0 \mu_r}{l} = \dfrac{(4000)^2 \times (4\pi \times 10^{-4}) \times 4\pi \times 10^{-7} \times 1}{0.6} = 0.0421\ H$

(ii) Energy stored $= \dfrac{1}{2} LI^2 = \dfrac{1}{2} (0.0421) \times (5)^2 = 0.526\ J$

Example 9.10. *A coil wound on an iron core of permeability 400 has 150 turns and a cross-sectional area of 5 cm². Calculate the inductance of the coil. Given that a steady current of 3mA produces a magnetic field of 10 lines/cm² when air is present as the medium.*

Solution. $\qquad \mu_i = \dfrac{\text{Flux density in iron}}{\text{Flux density in air}} = \dfrac{B_i}{10}$

∴ $\qquad B_i = 10 \times \mu_i = 10 \times 400 = 4000\ \text{lines/cm}^2$

Magnetic flux produced by 3mA current in the iron core,

$$\phi = B_i \times a = 4000 \times 5 = 20{,}000\ \text{lines} = 2 \times 10^{-4}\ Wb$$

∴ $\qquad L = \dfrac{N\phi}{I} = \dfrac{150 \times 2 \times 10^{-4}}{3 \times 10^{-3}} = 10\ H$

Example 9.11. *A 300-turn coil has a resistance of 6 Ω and an inductance of 0.5 H. Determine the new resistance and new inductance if one-third of the turns are removed. Assume all the turns have the same circumference.*

Solution. Since the resistance of a coil is directly proportional to its length,

$$R_1/R_2 = N_1/N_2 \quad \text{or} \quad 6/R_2 = 300/200$$

∴ $\qquad R_2 = \dfrac{200}{300} \times 6 = 4\Omega$

Now $\qquad \dfrac{L_1}{L_2} = \dfrac{N_1^2 / S}{N_2^2 / S}$

Assuming the reuctance of magnetic path to be constant,

$$\dfrac{0.5}{L_2} = \dfrac{(300)^2}{(200)^2} \qquad ∴ \ L_2 = 0.22\ H$$

Example 9.12. *A circuit has 1000 turns enclosing a magnetic circuit 20 cm² in section. With 4A, the flux density is 1Wb/m² and with 9A, it is 1.4 Wb/m². Find the mean value of inductance between these current limits and the induced e.m.f. if the current falls from 9A to 4A in 0.05 second.*

Solution.

Mean inductance, $L = N \dfrac{d\phi}{dI} = N \dfrac{d}{dI}(AB) = NA \dfrac{dB}{dI}$

Here $\quad N = 1000;\ A = 20\ \text{cm}^2;\ dB = 1.4 - 1 = 0.4\ \text{Wb/m}^2;\ dI = 9 - 4 = 5A$

∴ $\qquad L = 1000 \times 20 \times 10^{-4} \times \dfrac{0.4}{5} = 0.16\ H$

Induced e.m.f., $\qquad e = -L \dfrac{dI}{dt} = -0.16 \times \dfrac{4 - 9}{0.05} = 16\ V$

Electromagnetic induction relays

TUTORIAL PROBLEMS

1. A coil has self-inductance of 10 H. If a current of 200 mA is reduced to zero in a time of 1 ms, find the average value of induced e.m.f. across the terminals of the coil.   **[2000 V]**

2. A coil consists of 750 turns and a current of 10A in the coil gives rise to a magnetic flux of 1200 μWb. Calculate the inductance of the coil and determine the average e.m.f. induced in the coil when this current is reversed in 0.01 second.   **[0.09 H; 180 V]**

3. Calculate the inductance of a solenoid of 2000 turns wound uniformly over a length of 50 cm on a cylindrical paper tube 4 cm in diameter. The medium is air.   **[12.62 mH]**

4. An air-cored solenoid 1m long and 10 cm in diameter has 5000 turns. Calculate (i) the inductance and (ii) energy stored in it when a current of 2A passes through it.
    [(i) 0.2468 H (ii) 0.4936 J]

5. A circular iron ring of mean diameter 100 mm and cross-sectional area 500 mm^2 has 200 turns of wire uniformly wound around the circumference. If the relative permeability of iron is assumed to be 1200, find the self-inductance of the coil.   **[96 mH]**

9.9. INDUCTORS

An inductor consists of a large number of turns having either a ferromagnetic core or air-core.

The inductance of an inductor depends on (a) the permeability of the core (b) the number of turns (c) the cross-sectional area of the core and (d) the length of the magnetic circuit.

(i) **Air-core inductor.** The air core has the advantage that it has a linear B/H curve which means that inductance L is the same no matter what current is in the coil. Since the relative permeability of air is 1, the values of inductance obtained are very low. Fig. 9.8 (i) shows the symbol for air-core inductor.

Air-core inductor	Iron-core inductor
(i)	(ii)

Fig. 9.8

(ii) **Iron-core inductor.** The ferromagnetic core has the advantage that it provides very much higher values of inductance. It is because the relative permeability of ferromagnetic material is very large. The disadvantage of ferromagnetic core is that its B/H curve is not linear which means that inductance will vary with current.

Practical Inductor. All inductors are coils that have some winding resistance. Therefore, a practical or real inductor can be represented by a pure inductance L in series with winding resistance R as shows in Fig. 9.9. In many practical applications, the resistance of an inductor must be taken into account while selecting and designing or analysing

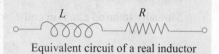

Equivalent circuit of a real inductor

Fig. 9.9

circuits that contain inductors. Where an external resistance is connected in series with an inductor, the resistance of inductor should also be shown as a series component in the equivalent circuit.

Inductors

9.10. MUTUAL INDUCTANCE (M)

The two coils so arranged that a change of current in one coil causes an e.m.f. to be induced in the other are said to have **mutual inductance.**

Consider two coils A and B placed adjacent to each other as shown in Fig. 9.10. If current I_1 flows in the coil A, a magnetic flux is set up and a part ϕ_{12} (*mutual flux*) of this magnetic flux links the coil B. If current in coil A changes, the mutual flux also changes and hence e.m.f. is induced in coil B. This e.m.f. induced in coil B is termed as mutually induced e.m.f. The converse of this action is also true *i.e.*, a change of current in coil B will produce a mutually induced e.m.f. in coil A.

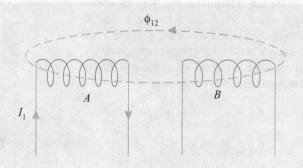

Fig. 9.10

Just as self-induced e.m.f. is responsible for inductance (L), similarly mutually induced e.m.f. is responsible for mutual inductance. Coils A and B have inductances of L_A and L_B respectively. In addition, there is further inductance (called mutual inductance M) between the coils due to mutually induced e.m.f. The effect of mutual inductance is to either increase ($L_A + M$ and $L_B + M$) or decrease ($L_A - M$ and $L_B - M$) the inductance of the two coils; this being decided by the arrangement of the coils.

Expression for M

Mutually induced e.m.f. in coil $B \propto$ Rate of change of current in coil A

or
$$e_M \propto \frac{dI_1}{dt}$$

or
$$e_M = M \frac{dI_1}{dt} \qquad \qquad ...(i)$$

where M is a constant called **mutual inductance** between the two coils. The unit of mutual inductance is henry (H). If in exp. (i), $e_M = 1$ volt, $dI_1/dt = 1$A/sec, then $M = 1$H.

Hence mutual inductance between two coils is **1 henry** *if current changing at the rate of 1A/sec in one coil induces an e.m.f. of 1V in the other coil.*

9.11. OTHER EXPRESSIONS FOR M

Apart from exp. (i) above for M, mutual inductance can also be determined by one of the following two methods :

(i) **First method.** Fig 9.11 shows two magnetically coupled coils A and B.

$$e_M = M \frac{dI_1}{dt} = \frac{d}{dt}(MI_1)$$

Also
$$e_M = N_2 \frac{d\phi_{12}}{dt} = \frac{d}{dt}(N_2\phi_{12})$$

From these two expressions, we have,

$$MI_1 = N_2\phi_{12}$$

or
$$M = \frac{N_2\phi_{12}}{I_1} \qquad \qquad ...(i)$$

If $N_2\phi_{12} = 1$Wb-turn and $I_1 = 1$A, then $M = 1$H.

Hence mutual inductance between two coils is **1 henry** *if a current of 1A flowing in one coil produces magnetic flux linkages of 1Wb-turn in the other.*

(ii) **Second method.** The mutual inductance between the two coils can be determined in terms of physical dimensions of the magnetic circuit. Fig. 9.11 shows two magnetically coupled coils A and B having N_1 and N_2 turns respectively. Suppose l and a are the length and area of cross-section of the magnetic circuit respectively. Let μ_r be the relative permeability of the material of which the magnetic circuit is composed.

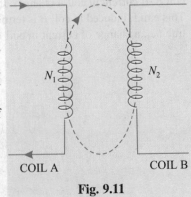

Fig. 9.11

Mutual flux,
$$\phi_{12} = \frac{\text{m.m.f.}}{\text{reluctance}} = \frac{N_1 I_1}{l/a\mu_0\mu_r}$$

or
$$\frac{\phi_{12}}{I_1} = \frac{N_1 a\mu_0\mu_r}{l}$$

Now,
$$M = \frac{N_2\phi_{12}}{I_1}$$

$$\therefore \qquad M = \frac{N_1 N_2 a\mu_0\mu_r}{l} \qquad \qquad ...(ii)$$

$$= \frac{N_1 N_2}{l/a\mu_0\mu_r} = \frac{N_1 N_2}{\text{Reluctance (S)}} \qquad \qquad ...(iii)$$

It may be noted that mutual inductance is inversely proportional to the reluctance of the magnetic circuit.

Example 9.13. *Two identical coils A and B of 1000 turns each lie in parallel planes such that 80% of magnetic flux produced by one coil links with the other. A current of 5A flowing in coil A produces a flux of 0.05 mWb in it. If the current in coil A changes from + 12A to –12A in 0.02 second, calculate (i) the mutual inductance and (ii) the e.m.f. induced in coil B.*

Solution. $*\phi_{12} = 0.8 \times 0.05 \times 10^{-3} = 0.4 \times 10^{-4}$ Wb

(i) $\qquad M = \dfrac{N_2 \phi_{12}}{I_1} = \dfrac{1000 \times 0.4 \times 10^{-4}}{5} = \textbf{0.008 H}$

(ii) $\qquad e_B = M \dfrac{dI_1}{dt} = 0.008 \times \dfrac{12 - (-12)}{0.02} = \textbf{9.6 V}$

Example 9.14. *Two coils A and B having turns 100 and 1000 respectively are wound side by side on a closed iron circuit of cross-sectional area 8 cm² and mean length 80 cm. The relative permeability of iron is 900. Calculate the mutual inductance between the coils. What will be the induced e.m.f. in coil B if current in coil A is increased uniformly from zero to 10A in 0.02 second?*

Solution. $\qquad M = \dfrac{N_1 N_2 a\mu_0\mu_r}{l} = \dfrac{100 \times 1000 \times 8 \times 10^{-4} \times 4\pi \times 10^{-7} \times 900}{0.8} = \textbf{0.113 H}$

$$e_B = M \dfrac{dI_1}{dt} = 0.113 \times \dfrac{10 - 0}{0.02} = \textbf{56.5 V}$$

Example 9.15. *A solenoid 70 cm in length and of 2100 turns has a radius of 4.5 cm. A second coil of 750 turns is wound upon the middle part of the solenoid. Find (i) self-inductance of solenoid (ii) mutual inductance between the two coils.*

Solution. Since μ_r is not given, it will be assumed to be 1.

$$a = \pi r^2 = \pi \, (4.5 \times 10^{-2})^2 \; m^2$$

(i) $\qquad L = \dfrac{N^2 a\mu_0\mu_r}{l} = \dfrac{(2100)^2 \times \pi(4.5 \times 10^{-2})^2 \times 4\pi \times 10^{-7} \times 1}{0.7} = \textbf{51} \times \textbf{10}^{-3} \textbf{ H}$

(ii) As the second coil is wound on the middle part of the solenoid, the co-efficient of coupling is unity *i.e.* the whole of the magnetic flux produced by solenoid links the second coil.

$$M = \dfrac{N_1 N_2 a\mu_0\mu_r}{l} = \dfrac{2100 \times 750 \times \pi(4.5 \times 10^{-2})^2 \times 4\pi \times 10^{-7} \times 1}{0.7} = \textbf{18.2} \times \textbf{10}^{-3} \textbf{ H}$$

Example 9.16. *Two coils A and B are wound side by side on a paper tube former. An e.m.f. of 0.25V is induced in coil A when the flux linking it changes at the rate of 10^{-3} Wb/s. A current of 2A in coil B causes a magnetic flux of 10^{-5} Wb to link coil A. What is the mutual inductance between the coils ?*

Solution. Induced e.m.f. in coil $A = N_1 \dfrac{d\phi}{dt}$

or $\qquad 0.25 = N_1 \times 10^{-3} \qquad \therefore \; N_1 = 0.25/10^{-3} = 250$ turns

Magnetic fllux linkages in coil A due to 2 A in coil B is $= 250 \times 10^{-5}$ *Wb-turns*

$\therefore \qquad M = \dfrac{\text{Magnetic flux linkages in coil } A}{\text{Current in coil } B} = 250 \times 10^{-5}/2 = \textbf{1.25} \times \textbf{10}^{-3} \textbf{ H}$

---

*   Note that 80% of magnetic flux produced in coil A links with coil B. Therefore, mutual flux (ϕ_{12}) is 80% of 0.05 mWb.

9.12. CO-EFFICIENT OF COUPLING

The co-efficient of coupling (k) between two coils is defined as the fraction of magnetic flux produced by the current in one coil that links the other coil.

The co-efficient of coupling has a maximum value of 1 (or 100%) when the entire magnetic flux of one coil links the other. If one-half of the magnetic flux set up in one coil links the other, then co-efficient of coupling is 0.5 or 50%. Suppose the two coils have inductances of L_1 and L_2 and M is the mutual inductance between them. Then it can be shown that :

$$M = k\sqrt{L_1 L_2}$$

Obviouly, M between the two coils will be maximum when $k = 1$.

∴ Maximum mutual inductance between the two coils = $\sqrt{L_1 L_2}$

Example 9.17. *Two magnetically coupled coils have self-inductances, $L_1 = 100$ mH and $L_2 = 400$ mH. If the co-efficient of coupling is 0.8, find the value of mutual inductance between the coils. What would be the maximum possible mutual inductance ?*

Solution. $M = k\sqrt{L_1 L_2} = 0.8 \sqrt{100 \times 10^{-3} \times 400 \times 10^{-3}} = 160 \times 10^{-3}$ H

The value of M will be maximum when $k = 1$.

∴ Maximum $M = \sqrt{L_1 L_2} = \sqrt{100 \times 10^{-3} \times 400 \times 10^{-3}} = 200 \times 10^{-3}$ H

Example 9.18. *An iron ring of cross-sectional area 800 mm² and of mean radius 170 mm has two windings connected in series, one of 500 turns and the other of 700 turns. If the relative permeability of iron is 1200, find (i) the self-inductance of each coil, and (ii) mutual inductance, assuming that there is no leakage.*

Solution.

(i) Reluctance, $S = \dfrac{l}{a\mu_0\mu_r} = \dfrac{2\pi \times 170 \times 10^{-3}}{(800 \times 10^{-6}) \times 4\pi \times 10^{-7} \times (1200)}$

$= 8.85 \times 10^5$ AT/Wb

$$L_1 = \frac{N_1^2}{S} = \frac{(500)^2}{8.85 \times 10^5} = 0.282 \text{ H} \qquad \text{...See Art. 9.8}$$

$$L_2 = \frac{N_2^2}{S} = \frac{(700)^2}{8.85 \times 10^5} = 0.554 \text{ H}$$

(ii) Since there is no leakage flux, it means that the magnetic flux produced by one coil entirely links the other *i.e.* $k = 1$.

∴ $M = k\sqrt{L_1 L_2} = 1\sqrt{0.282 \times 0.554} = 0.395$ H

Example 9.19. *A battery of 24 V is connected to the primary (coil 1) of a two-winding transformer as shown in Fig. 9.12 and the secondary (coil 2) is open-circuited. The coil parameters are :*

$R_1 = 10 \ \Omega, \qquad R_2 = 30 \ \Omega$

$N_1 = 100 \ turns, \qquad N_2 = 160 \ turns$

$\phi_1 = 0.01 \ Wb, \qquad \phi_2 = 0.008 \ Wb$

Calculate (i) the self-inductance of coil 1 (ii) the mutual inductance (iii) the co-efficient of coupling and (iv) the self-inductance of coil 2.

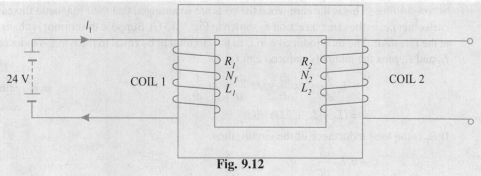

Fig. 9.12

Solution.

(i) $$I_1 = V/R_1 = 24/10 = 2.4 \text{ A}$$

$$\therefore \quad L_1 = \frac{N_1 \, \phi_1}{I_1} = \frac{100 \times 0.01}{2.4} = \mathbf{0.417 \, H}$$

(ii) $$M = \frac{N_2 \, \phi_2}{I_1} = \frac{160 \times 0.008}{2.4} = \mathbf{0.533 \, H}$$

(iii) $$k = 0.008/0.01 = \mathbf{0.8}$$

(iv) $$M = k\sqrt{L_1 \, L_2}$$

or $$0.533 = 0.8\sqrt{0.417 \times L_2} \quad \therefore \quad L_2 = \mathbf{1.064 \, H}$$

TUTORIAL PROBLEMS

1. A solenoid 70 *cm* in length and of 2100 turns has a radius of 4.5 *cm*. A second coil of 750 turns is wound upon the middle part of the solenoid. Find the mutual inductance between the two coils. **[18.2 *mH*]**

2. Two coils having 150 and 200 turns respectively are wound side by side on a closed iron circuit of section 150 *cm²* and mean length of 300 *cm*. Determine the mutual inductance between the coils and e.m.f. induced in the second coil if current changes from zero to 10*A* in the first coil in 0.02 second. Relative permeability of iron = 2000. **[0.377 *H*; 188.5 *V*]**

3. The self-inductance of a coil of 500 turns is 0.25 *H*. If 60% of the flux is linked with a second coil of 10,000 turns, calculate the mutual inductance between the two coils. **[3 *H*]**

4. The windings of a transformer has an inductance of $L_1 = 6 \, H$; $L_2 = 0.06 \, H$ and a coefficient of coupling $k = 0.9$. Find the e.m.f. in both the windings when current in primary increases at the rate of 1000 *A/s*. **[6000 *V*; 540 *V*]**

5. An air-cored solenoid with length 30 *cm*, area of X-section 25 *cm²* and number of turns 500 carries a current of 2.5 A. The current is suddenly switched off in a brief time of 10^{-4} second. How much average e.m.f. is induced across the ends of the open switch in the circuit ? Ignore the variation of magnetic field near the ends of the solenoid.
[6.5 *V*]

9.13. INDUCTANCES IN SERIES

Consider two coils connected in series as shown in Fig. 9.13.

Let $\quad L_1$ = inductance of first coil

$\quad L_2$ = inductance of second coil

$\quad M$ = mutual inductance between the coils

(*i*) **Series-adding.** This is the case when the coils are so arranged that their magnetic fluxes aid each other *i.e.* in the same direction as shown in Fig. 9.13 (*i*). Suppose the current is changing at the rate *di/dt*. The total induced e.m.f. in the circuit will be equal to the e.m.f. s induced in L_1 and L_2 *plus* the mutually induced e.m.f.s, *i.e.*

$$e = L_1 \frac{di}{dt} + L_2 \frac{di}{dt} + M \frac{di}{dt} + M \frac{di}{dt} \qquad \text{... in magnitude}$$

$$= (L_1 + L_2 + 2M) \, di/dt$$

If L_T is the total inductance of the circuit, then,

$$e = L_T \frac{di}{dt}$$

$$\therefore \qquad L_T = L_1 + L_2 + 2M \qquad \text{...magnetic fluxes additive}$$

Energy stored, $W = \dfrac{1}{2} L_T I^2$

$$= \frac{1}{2} (L_1 + L_2 + 2M) \, I^2$$

$$= \frac{1}{2} L_1 I^2 + \frac{1}{2} L_2 I^2 + MI^2$$

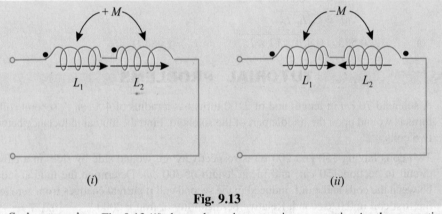

(*i*)　　　　　　　　　　　　(*ii*)

Fig. 9.13

(*ii*) **Series-opposing.** Fig. 9.13 (*ii*) shows the series-opposing connection *i.e.* the magnetic fluxes of the two coils oppose each other. Suppose the current is changing at the rate *di/dt*. The total induced e.m.f. in the circuit will be equal to e.m.f.s induced in L_1 and L_2 minus the mutually induced e.m.f.s.

$$e = L_1 \frac{di}{dt} + L_2 \frac{di}{dt} - M \frac{di}{dt} - M \frac{di}{dt} = (L_1 + L_2 - 2M) \frac{di}{dt}$$

If L_T is the total inductance of the circuit, then,

$$e = L_T \frac{di}{dt}$$

$$\therefore \qquad L_T = L_1 + L_2 - 2M \qquad \text{...magnetic fluxes subtractive}$$

Energy stored, $\quad W = \dfrac{1}{2} L_T I^2$

$$= \frac{1}{2} (L_1 + L_2 - 2M) \, I^2$$

$$= \frac{1}{2} L_1 I^2 + \frac{1}{2} L_2 I^2 - MI^2$$

The negative sign may be interpreted that the electric potential energy due to mutual inductance is in opposition to the electric potential energy due to the self inductance.

Note. If the coils are so positioned that *$M = 0$, then $L_T = L_1 + L_2$.

9.14. INDUCTANCES IN PARALLEL

Consider three inductances L_1, L_2 and L_3 in parallel as shown in Fig. 9.14. Assume for a moment that mutual inductance between the coils is zero. Referring to Fig. 9.14, we have,

$$i_T = i_1 + i_2 + i_3$$

or

$$\frac{di_T}{dt} = \frac{di_1}{dt} + \frac{di_2}{dt} + \frac{di_3}{dt}$$

But

$$e = L\frac{di}{dt} \quad \text{or} \quad \frac{di}{dt} = \frac{e}{L}$$

∴

$$\frac{e}{L_T} = \frac{e}{L_1} + \frac{e}{L_2} + \frac{e}{L_3}$$

or

$$\frac{1}{L_T} = \frac{1}{L_1} + \frac{1}{L_2} + \frac{1}{L_3} \qquad \qquad ...(i)$$

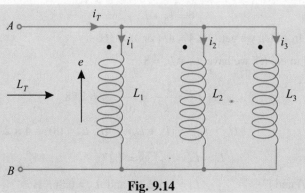

Fig. 9.14

When mutual inductances are present, the values of L_1, L_2 and L_3 will be modified to include the appropriate mutual inductances and then relation (*i*) can be used to find L_T. The mutual inductance between any pair of coils will be +ve or –ve depending upon whether their mutual fluxes add to each other or subtract. **Dot notation on the coils reveals this information. Thus mutual inductance M_{12} between L_1 and L_2 in Fig. 9.14 is positive because their dotted ends are connected to the same terminal A of the supply. Similarly mutual inductance M_{13} between L_1 and L_3 is positive. The result is that value of L_1 is modified and becomes $L_1 + M_{12} + M_{13}$. The same procedure can be followed to find the modified values of L_2 and L_3. By inserting the modified values of L_1, L_2 and L_3 in relation (*i*), we can find L_T.

Example 9.20. *Two identical coils, when connected in series, have total inductance of 12H and 4H depending upon their method of connection. Find (i) self-inductance of the coils and (ii) mutual between the coils.*

* If the coils are so placed that magnetic fluxes produced by them are at right angles to each other, then mutual flux will be zero and hence $M = 0$.

** **Dot notation :** It is generally not possible to state from the figure whether the magnetic fluxes of the two coils are additive or in opposition. Dot notation removes this confusion. The end of the coil through which the current enters is indicated by placing a dot behind it. If the current after leaving the dotted end of coil L_1 enters the dotted end of coil L_2, it means the magnetic fluxes of the two coils are additive otherwise in opposition.

Solution. $L_T = L_1 + L_2 \pm 2M$

For series-aiding, $12 = L + L + 2M$ ...(i)

For series-opposing, $4 = L + L - 2M$ ...(ii)

Solving eqs. (i) and (ii), we get, $L = 4H$ and $M = 2H$

Example 9.21. *Two coils of self-inductances 3H and 2H respectively are connected in series. If the co-efficient of coupling between the coils is 0.5, find the inductance of the circuit when the coils are connected in (i) series-aiding (ii) series-opposing.*

Solution. $L_T = L_1 + L_2 \pm 2M$

          $= L_1 + L_2 \pm 2k\sqrt{L_1 L_2}$ $(\because M = k\sqrt{L_1 L_2})$

(i) For series-aiding, $L_T = 3 + 2 + 2 \times 0.5\sqrt{3 \times 2} = \textbf{7.45 H}$

(ii) For series-opposing, $L_T = 3 + 2 - 2 \times 0.5\sqrt{3 \times 2} = \textbf{2.55 H}$

Example 9.22. *When two coils are connected in series, their effective inductance is found to be 10 H. When the connections of one coil are reversed, the effective inductance is 6 H. If the co-efficient of coupling is 0.6, calculate the self-inductance of each coil and the mutual inductance.*

Solution. $10 = L_1 + L_2 + 2M$ ...(i)

          $6 = L_1 + L_2 - 2M$ ...(ii)

Subtracting (ii) from (i), we get, $4 = 4M$ or $M = 1H$

Putting $M = 1H$ in eq. (i), we have, $L_1 + L_2 = 8$ ...(iii)

Also $^*L_1 L_2 = \dfrac{M^2}{k^2} = \dfrac{1}{(0.6)^2} = 2.78$ ...(iv)

Now $(L_1 - L_2)^2 = (L_1 + L_2)^2 - 4L_1 L_2 = (8)^2 - 4 \times 2.78 = 52.88$

$\therefore$ $L_1 - L_2 = \sqrt{52.88} = 7.27$ ...(v)

Solving eqs. (iii) and (v), $L_1 = \textbf{7.635 H}$ and $L_2 = \textbf{0.365 H}$

Example 9.23. *Two coils of self-inductances 15H and 20H are connected in parallel. If the mutual inductance between the coils is 8H, find the total inductance of the circuit when (i) the mutual fluxes aid each other (ii) the mutual fluxes oppose each other.*

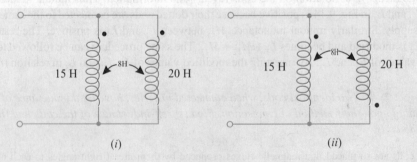

(i)   (ii)

Fig. 9.15

- -

*   Remember $M = k\sqrt{L_1 L_2}$ $\therefore$ $M^2 = k^2(L_1 L_2)$

Solution.

(*i*) When the coils are so arranged that their mutual fluxes aid each other [See Fig. 9.15 (*i*)], the mutual inductance between the coils is positive. The net inductance of each branch becomes :

$$L_1 = 15 + 8 = 23 \text{ H} ; L_2 = 20 + 8 = 28 \text{ H}$$

$$\therefore \qquad \frac{1}{L_T} = \frac{1}{L_1} + \frac{1}{L_2} = \frac{L_1 + L_2}{L_1 L_2}$$

or $$L_T = \frac{L_1 L_2}{L_1 + L_2} = \frac{23 \times 28}{23 + 28} = \textbf{12.63 H}$$

(*ii*) When the coils are so arranged that their mutual fluxes oppose each other [See Fig. 9.15 (*ii*)], the mutual inductance is negative. The net inductance of each branch becomes :

$$L_1 = 15 - 8 = 7\text{H} ; \quad L_2 = 20 - 8 = 12\text{H}$$

$$\therefore \qquad L_T = \frac{L_1 L_2}{L_1 + L_2} = \frac{7 \times 12}{7 + 12} = \textbf{4.42 H}$$

Example 9.24. *Three coils of inductances 30H, 25H and 40H are connected in parallel. The mutual inductances among the coils are as shown in Fig 9.16. Find the total inductance of the circuit.*

Solution. The net branch inductances are :

$$L_1 = 30 + 10 - 15 = 25 \text{ H} ; \quad L_2 = 25 + 10 - 12 = 23 \text{ H} ; \quad L_3 = 40 - 12 - 15 = 13 \text{ H}$$

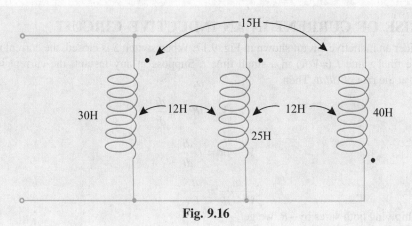

Fig. 9.16

Now $$\frac{1}{L_T} = \frac{1}{L_1} + \frac{1}{L_2} + \frac{1}{L_3} = \frac{1}{25} + \frac{1}{23} + \frac{1}{13}$$

or $$L_T = \textbf{6.24 H}$$

9.15. CLOSING AND BREAKING AN INDUCTIVE CIRCUIT

Consider an inductive circuit shown in Fig. 9.17. When switch *S* is closed, the current increases gradually and takes some time to reach the final value. The reason the current does not build up instantly to its final value is that as the current increases, the self induced e.m.f. in *L* opposes the

....

* The current is zero at the instant the switch is closed because it must start from zero.

Now, self-induced e.m.f., $v_L = L \dfrac{di}{dt}$

If current change (*i.e.*, *di*) is instant, it means *di/dt* = 0. This means that *L* is infinite which is impossible. So it is not possible for current in inductance to change from one value to the other in zero time.

change in current (Lenz's Law). Suppose at any instant, the current is i and is increasing at the rate of di/dt.

Then, $\qquad V = v_R + v_L$

$$= iR + L\frac{di}{dt}$$

As the current increases, $v_R\ (= iR)$ increases and v_L decreases since V is constant. The decrease in $v_L\ (= Ldi/dt)$ means that di/dt decreases because L is constant. The result is that after some time di/dt becomes zero and so does the self-induced e.m.f. $v_L\ (= L\ di/dt)$.

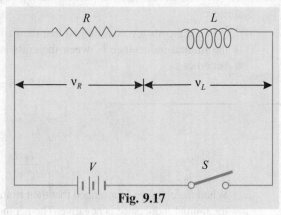

Fig. 9.17

At this stage, the current attains the final fixed value I given by;

$$V = IR + 0$$

or $\qquad I = V/R$

Thus, when a d.c. circuit containing inductance is switched on, the current takes some time to reach the final value $I\ (= V/R)$. Note that the role of inductance is to delay the change; it cannot prevent the current from attaining the final value. Similarly, when an inductive circuit is opened, the current does not jump to zero but falls gradually. In either case, the delay in change depends upon the values of L and R as explained in the next article.

9.16. RISE OF CURRENT IN AN INDUCTIVE CIRCUIT

Consider an inductive circuit shown in Fig. 9.17. When switch S is closed, the current rises from zero to the final value $I\ (=V/R)$ in a small time t. Suppose at any instant, the current is i and is increasing at the rate of di/dt. Then,

$$V = iR + L\frac{di}{dt}$$

or $\qquad V - iR = L\frac{di}{dt}$

or $\qquad \frac{di}{V - iR} = \frac{dt}{L}$

* Multiplying both sides by $-R$, we get,

$$\frac{-R\ di}{V - iR} = \frac{-R}{L}dt$$

Integrating both sides, we get,

$$\int -\frac{R\ di}{V - iR} = -\frac{R}{L}\int dt$$

or $\qquad \log_e (V - iR) = -\frac{R}{L}t + K \qquad\qquad ...(i)$

where K is a constant whose value can be determined from the initial conditions. At $t = 0$, $i = 0$. Putting these values in exp. (i), we have, $\log_e V = K$.

- -

* This step makes the numerator on the L.H.S. a differential of the denominator.

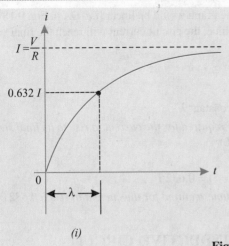

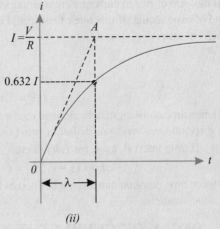

(i)   *(ii)*

Fig. 9.18

$\therefore$ Equation *(i)* becomes : $\log_e (V - iR) = -\dfrac{R}{L} t + \log_e V$

or $\log_e \dfrac{V - iR}{V} = -\dfrac{R}{L} t$

or $\dfrac{V - iR}{V} = e^{-Rt/L}$

or $V - iR = Ve^{-Rt/L}$

or $i = \dfrac{V}{R} (1 - e^{-Rt/L})$

But $V/R = I$, the final value of current attained by the circuit.

$\therefore$ $i = I (1 - e^{-Rt/L})$ ...*(ii)*

Eq. *(ii)* shows that rise of current follows an exponential law (See Fig. 9.18). As *t* increases, the term $e^{-Rt/L}$ gets smaller and current *i* in the circuit gets larger. Theoretically, the current will reach its final value $I (= V/R)$ in an infinite time. However, practically it reaches this value in a short time.

Note. $V = iR + L \, di/dt$

At the instant the switch is closed, $i = 0$. $\therefore$ $V = L \, di/dt$

Initial rate of rise of current, $\dfrac{di}{dt} = \dfrac{V}{L}$ A/sec.

9.17. TIME CONSTANT

Consider the eq. *(ii)* above showing the rise of current *w.r.t.* time *t*.

$$i = I (1 - e^{-Rt/L})$$

The exponent of *e* is Rt/L. The quantity L/R has the dimensions of time so that exponent of *e* (*i.e.* Rt/L) is a number. The quantity L/R is called the *time constant* of the circuit and affects the rise of current in the circuit. It is represented by λ.

$\therefore$ Time constant, $\lambda = L/R$ seconds

Time constant of an inductive circuit can be defined in the following ways :

(i)   Consider the graph showing the rise of current *w.r.t.* time *t* [See Fig. 9.18 *(ii)*]. The initial rate of rise of current (*i.e.* at $t = 0$) in the circuit is

$$\dfrac{di}{dt} = \dfrac{V}{L}$$

If this rate of rise of current were maintained, the graph would be linear [*i.e. OA* in Fig. 9.18 (*ii*)] instead of exponential. If this rate of rise could continue, the circuit current will reach the final value I (= V/R) in time

$$= \frac{V}{R} \div \frac{V}{L}$$

$$= L/R = \text{Time constant } \lambda$$

Hence time constant may be defined *as the time required for the current to rise to its final steady value if it continued rising at its initial rate (i.e. V/L).*

(*ii*)   If time interval, $t = \lambda$ (or L/R), then,

$$\therefore i = I(1 - e^{-Rt/L}) = I(1 - e^{-1}) = 0.632\ I$$

Hence time constant can also be defined *as the time required for the current to reach 0.632 of its final steady value.*

9.18. DECAY OF CURRENT IN AN INDUCTIVE CIRCUIT

Consider an inductive circuit shown in Fig. 9.19. When switch S is thrown to position 2, the current in the circuit starts rising and attains the final value I (= V/R) after some time as explained above. If now switch is thrown to position 1, it is found that current in the $R - L$ circuit does not cease immediately but gradually reduces to zero. Suppose at any instant, the current is i and is decreasing at the rate of di/dt. Then,

$$0 = iR + L\frac{di}{dt}$$

or

$$\frac{di}{i} = -\frac{R}{L}dt$$

Integrating both sides, we get, $\log_e\ i = -\frac{R}{L}t + K$ ...(*i*)

where K is a constant whose value can be determined from the initial conditions. When $t = 0$, then $i = I$ (= V/R).

Putting these values in eq. (*i*), we have,

$$\log_e I = 0 + K \quad \text{or} \quad K = \log_e I$$

$\therefore$ Equation (*i*) becomes : $\log_e\ i = -\frac{R}{L}t + \log_e I$

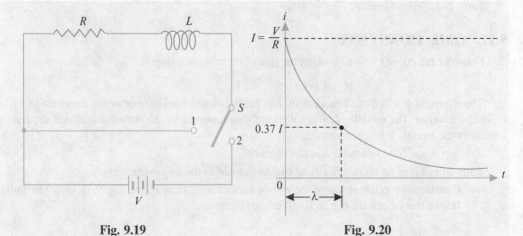

Fig. 9.19   Fig. 9.20

or $$\log_e \frac{i}{I} = -\frac{R}{L}t$$

or $$\frac{i}{I} = e^{-Rt/L}$$

or $$i = Ie^{-Rt/L} \qquad ...(ii)$$

Eq. (*ii*) gives the decay of current in an $R - L$ series circuit with time t and is represented graphically in Fig. 9.20. Note that decay of current follows the exponential law.

Time constant. The quantity L/R in eq. (*ii*) is known as time constant of the circuit. When $t = \lambda \ (= L/R)$,

$$i = I\,e^{-1} = 0.37\,I$$

Hence, time constant may also be defined *as the time taken by the current to fall to 0.37 of its final steady value* ($I = V/R$) *while decaying*.

Example 9.25. *A coil having a resistance of 15 Ω and inductance of 10H is connected to a constant 75 V supply. Find (i) the rate of change of current at the instant of closing the switch (ii) final steady value (iii) time constant of the circuit (iv) the time taken for the current to reach a value of 4A.*

Solution.

(*i*) Initial rate of rise of current is

$$\frac{di}{dt} = \frac{V}{L} = \frac{75}{10} = 7.5 \text{ A/s}$$

(*ii*) Final steady value, $\qquad I = V/R = 75/15 = \textbf{5A}$

(*iii*) Time constant, $\qquad \lambda = L/R = 10/15 = \textbf{0.67s}$

(*iv*) $$i = I\,(1 - e^{-t/\lambda})$$

or $$4 = 5\,(1 - e^{-t/0.67})$$

or $$e^{-t/0.67} = 1 - (4/5) = 0.2$$

or $$e^{t/0.67} = 1/0.2 = 5$$

or $$(t/0.67)\log_e e = \log_e 5$$

∴ $$t = 0.67 \log_e 5 = \textbf{1.078s}$$

Example 9.26. *A coil having L = 2.4H and R = 4Ω is connected to a constant 100V supply source. How long does it take the voltage across the resistance to reach 50V ?*

Solution.

$$i = I\,(1 - e^{-t/\lambda})$$

$$= \frac{V}{R}\,(1 - e^{-t/\lambda})$$

or $$iR = V\,(1 - e^{-t/\lambda})$$

Here $iR = 50$ volts; $V = 100$ volts; $\lambda = L/R = 2.4/4 = 0.6$sec.

∴ $$50 = 100\,(1 - e^{-t/0.6})$$

or $$e^{-t/0.6} = 1 - (50/100) = 0.5$$

or $$e^{t/0.6} = 1/0.5 = 2$$

or $$(t/0.6)\log_e e = \log_e 2$$

∴ $$t = 0.6 \log_e 2 = \textbf{0.416s}$$

Example 9.27. *The field winding of a d.c. machine takes a steady current of 10A when connected to a d.c. source of 230 volts. On switching the voltage to the field, it is observed that it takes 0.3 second to reach 5 A.*

(*i*) *Find the value of inductance of the field winding.*

(*ii*) *Find also the time for the current to fall to 30% of the final steady value if the field terminals are short-circuited.*

Solution.

(*i*) **Growth of current**

$$i = I (1 - e^{-t/\lambda})$$

Here $\qquad\qquad i = 5$ A; $I = 10$ A; $R = 230/10 = 23\Omega$; $t = 0.3$ s

∴ $\qquad\qquad 5 = 10 (1 - e^{-0.3/\lambda})$

or $\qquad\qquad e^{0.3/\lambda} = 1/0.5 = 2$

or $\qquad\qquad (0.3/\lambda) \log_e e = \log_e 2$

∴ $\qquad\qquad \lambda = \dfrac{0.3 \log_e e}{\log_e 2} = 0.433$ s

Now, $\qquad\qquad \lambda = L/R \quad$ or $\quad L = \lambda R = 0.433 \times 23 = \mathbf{9.96}$ **H**

(*ii*) **Decay of current**

$$i = I e^{-t/\lambda}$$

Here $\qquad\qquad i = 30\%$ of 10 A = 3A ; $\lambda = 0.433$ s

∴ $\qquad\qquad 3 = 10 e^{-t/0.433}$

or $\qquad\qquad e^{t/0.433} = 10/3 = 3.33$

or $\qquad\qquad (t/0.433) \log_e e = \log_e 3.33$

∴ $\qquad\qquad t = \dfrac{0.433 \log_e 3.33}{\log_e e} = \mathbf{0.521s}$

Exapmple 9.28. *A coil has a time constant of 1s and an inductance of 10 H. Find (i) the value of current 0.1s after switching to a steady p.d. of 100 V (ii) the time taken for the current to reach half its steady-state value.*

Solution.

$$\lambda = L/R = 1 \qquad \therefore \quad R = L = 10 \ \Omega$$

(*i*) $\qquad\qquad i = I (1 - e^{-t/\lambda})$

Here $\qquad\qquad I = V/R = 100/10 = 10$ A ; $t = 0.1$ s ; $\lambda = 1$s

∴ $\qquad\qquad i = 10 (1 - e^{-0.1/1}) = \mathbf{0.952A}$

(*ii*) $\qquad\qquad i = I (1 - e^{-t/\lambda})$

Here $\qquad\qquad i = 5$ A, $I = 10$ A, $\lambda = 1$s

∴ $\qquad\qquad 5 = 10 (1 - e^{-t/1})$

or $\qquad\qquad e^{-t} = 1 - (5/10) = 0.5$

or $\qquad\qquad e^{t} = 1/0.5 = 2$

or $\qquad\qquad t \log_e e = \log_e 2$

∴ $\qquad\qquad t = \log_e 2/\log_e e = \mathbf{0.693s}$

Example 9.29. *A coil of resistance 200 Ω and inductance 10H is connected to a battery of 100V. Find (i) the current in the coil 40 ms after closing the switch (ii) the rate at which the current will then be increasing.*

Solution.

$$I = 100/200 = 0.5 \text{ A} \; ; \; \lambda = L/R = 10/200 = 0.05 \text{s} \; ; \; t = 0.04 \text{ s}$$

(i)
$$i = I (1 - e^{-t/\lambda}) = 0.5 (1 - e^{-0.04/0.05}) = 0.5 (1 - e^{-0.8}) = \textbf{0.275A}$$

(ii) At the instant the current is 0.275 A,

$$V = iR + L\frac{di}{dt}$$

∴
$$\frac{di}{dt} = \frac{V - iR}{L} = \frac{100 - 0.275 \times 200}{10} = \textbf{4.5A/s}$$

Note. Back e.m.f. at this instant $= L \, di/dt = 10 \times 4.5 = 45V$

Example 9.30. *The time constant of a certain inductive coil was found to be 2.5 ms. With a resistance of 80 Ω added in series, a new time constant of 0.5 ms was obtained. Find the inductance and resistance of the coil.*

Solution. Time constant, $\lambda = L/R$

For the first case, $L/R = 2.5$

For the second case, $L/(R + 80) = 0.5$

∴
$$\frac{R + 80}{R} = \frac{2.5}{0.5} = 5$$

or $\quad R + 80 = 5R \qquad$ ∴ $\quad R = 20Ω$

Now $\qquad L/R = 2.5 \qquad$ ∴ $\quad L = 2.5 \; R = 2.5 \times 20 = \textbf{50 H}$

TUTORIAL PROBLEMS

1. An inductive coil of inductance 1H and resistance 100 Ω is supplied from a 50 V d.c. source of internal resistance 5Ω. Calculate :

   (i) the time constant of the circuit

   (ii) the time elapsed from closing the circuit at which the circuit current has reached 35% of the steady state value. [(i) **9.52 ms** (ii) **4.1 ms**]

2. The current in a d.c. circuit composed of a 10 H coil and 100 Ω resistor in series reached 40% of the maximum value 20 ms after closing the circuit. Calculate the coil resistance.

   [**255.4 Ω**]

3. A coil has a time constant of 1s and an inductance of 10H. What is the value of the current 0.1s after switching on to a d.c. potential of 100 V? Find also the time taken for the current to reach half its steady state value. [**0.952 A; 0.697s**]

4. A coil of inductance 5H and resistance 100Ω carries a steady current of 2A. Calculate the initial rate of fall of current in the coil after a short circuiting switch connected across its terminals has been suddenly closed. What was the energy stored in the coil and in what form was it dissipated ? [**– 40A/s; 10J, heat**]

5. A constant voltage is applied to R–L series circuit at $t = 0$ by closing a switch. The voltage across L is 25 V at $t = 0$ and drops to 5V at $t = 0.025$ second. If $L = 2H$, find (i) the applied voltage and (ii) the value of R. [(i) **25V** (ii) **128.56 Ω**]

6. Determine the value of resistor which when connected in series with a 10H, 200Ω coil will allow the current to change by 50% of the maximum value in 20 ms from the instant of applying the supply voltage. [146.6 Ω]

9.19. ENERGY STORED IN A MAGNETIC FIELD

In order to establish a magnetic field around a coil, energy is *required, though no energy is needed to **maintain it. This energy is stored in the magnetic field and is not used up. When the current is decreased, the magnetic flux surrounding the coil is decreased, causing the stored energy to be returned to the circuit. Consider an inductor connected to a d.c. source as shown in Fig. 9.21 (i). The inductor is equivalent to inductance L in series with a small resistance R as shown in Fig. 9.21 (ii). The energy supplied to the circuit is spent in two ways :

(i) A part of supplied energy is spent to meet I^2R losses and cannot be recovered.

(ii) The remaining part is spent to create magnetic flux around the coil (or inductor) and is stored in the magnetic field. When the field collapses, the stored energy is returned to the circuit.

Mathematical Expression. Suppose at any instant the current in the coil is i and is increasing at the rate of di/dt. Then e.m.f. e across L is given by;

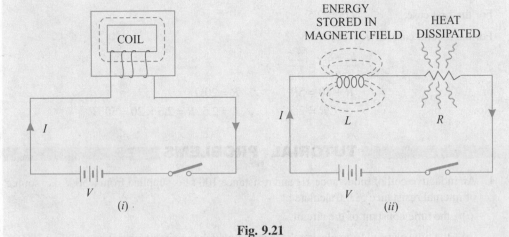

Fig. 9.21

$$e = L\frac{di}{dt}$$

∴ Instantaneous power, $$p = ei = Li\frac{di}{dt}$$

During a short interval of time dt, the energy dw put into the magnetic field is equal to power multiplied by time *i.e.*

$$dw = p.dt = \left(Li\frac{di}{dt}\right)dt = Li\,di$$

. . . .

* When the coil is connected to supply, current increases from zero gradually and reaches the final value I (=V/R) after some time. During this change of current, an e.m.f. is induced in L due to the change in magnetic flux linkages. This induced e.m.f. opposes the rise of current. Electrical energy must be supplied to meet this opposition. This supplied energy is stored in the magnetic field.

** To impart a kinetic energy of $\frac{1}{2}mv^2$ to a body, energy is required but no energy is required to maintain it at that energy level.

The total energy put into the magnetic field from the time current is zero until it has attained the final steady value I is :

$$W = \int_0^I Li \ di = \frac{1}{2} LI^2$$

∴ Energy stored in magnetic field, $E = \frac{1}{2} LI^2$ joules

Note that energy stored will be in joules if inductance (L) and current (i) are in henry and amperes respectively.

Note. If current in an inductor varies, the stored energy rises and falls in step with the current. Thus, whenever current increases, the coil absorbs energy and whenever current falls, energy is returned to the circuit.

Example 9.31. *Calculate the inductance and energy stored in the magnetic field of an air-cored solenoid 50cm long, 5cm in diameter and wound with 1000 turns, if carrying a current of 5A.*

Solution.

$$a = (\pi/4) (5 \times 10^{-2})^2 = 19.63 \times 10^{-4} \ m^2$$

$$L = \frac{N^2 a \mu_0 \mu_r}{l} = \frac{(1000)^2 \times (19.63 \times 10^{-4}) \times 4\pi \times 10^{-7} \times 1}{0.5} = 0.005 \ H$$

$$E = \frac{1}{2} LI^2 = \frac{1}{2} \times 0.005 \times 5^2 = 0.0625 \ J$$

Example 9.32. *The field windings of a d.c. machine consist of eight coils in series, each containing 1200 turns. When the current is 3A, the flux linked with each coil is 20 mWb. Calculate: (i) energy stored (ii) average value of induced e.m.f. if the circuit is broken in 0.1s.*

Solution.

(i)
$$L = \frac{N\phi}{I} = \frac{(1200 \times 8) \times 20 \times 10^{-3}}{3} = 64 \ H$$

$$E = \frac{1}{2} LI^2 = \frac{1}{2} \times 64 \times 3^2 = 288 \ J$$

(ii)
$$e = L \ di/dt = 64 \times \frac{3 - 0}{0.1} = 1920 \ V$$

9.20. MAGNETIC ENERGY STORED PER UNIT VOLUME

It is sometimes desirable to know the energy stored in a unit volume of the magnetic field. Consider a coil of N turns wound over a magnetic circuit of length l metres and uniform X-sectional area of $a \ m^2$.

$$\text{Energy stored} = \frac{1}{2} LI^2 = \frac{1}{2} \left(\frac{N^2 a \mu_0 \mu_r}{l} \right) I^2$$

$$= \frac{1}{2} (a \mu_0 \mu_r) \ l \left(\frac{NI}{l} \right)^2$$

$$= \frac{1}{2} (\mu_0 \mu_r) (al) \ H^2 \qquad\qquad (\because H = NI/l)$$

Now $\qquad al = $ Volume of magnetic field in m^3

∴ $\qquad$ Energy stored/$m^3 = \frac{1}{2} \mu_0 \mu_r \ H^2$

$$= \frac{1}{2} \mu_0 \mu_r \left(\frac{B}{\mu_0 \mu_r} \right)^2 \qquad \left[\because H = \frac{B}{\mu_0 \mu_r} \right]$$

or $\qquad$ Energy stored/$m^3 = \dfrac{B^2}{2\,\mu_0\mu_r}$ joules $\qquad\qquad$ ...in a medium

$$= \dfrac{B^2}{2\,\mu_0} \text{ joules} \qquad\qquad \text{...in air}$$

Note that energy stored will be in joules if flux density B is in Wb/m^2.

9.21. LIFTING POWER OF A MAGNET

Consider two poles, north and south, each of area 'a' square metres as shown in Fig. 9.22. Let P newtons be the force of attraction between the two poles. If one of the poles, say S-pole, is pulled apart through a small distance dx, then work will have to be done against the force of attraction.

$$\text{Work done} = P \times dx \text{ joules}$$

This work done is stored in the additional volume of the magnetic field created. Additional volume of magnetic field created

$$= a \times dx \text{ m}^3$$

∴ Increase in stored energy $\qquad = \dfrac{B^2}{2\,\mu_0} \times a\,dx$

Now, increase in stored energy = Work done

∴ $\qquad\qquad \dfrac{B^2}{2\,\mu_0} \times a\,dx = P \times dx$

or $\qquad\qquad\qquad\qquad P = \dfrac{B^2 a}{2\,\mu_0} \text{ newtons}$

It may be noted that P will be in newtons if B is in Wb/m^2 and 'a' in m^2.

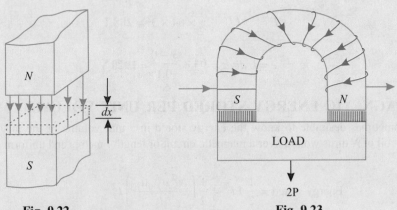

Fig. 9.22 $\qquad\qquad\qquad\qquad\qquad$ Fig. 9.23

Note that P is the force of attraction at each pole. In a practical magnet, there are two poles [See Fig. 9.23] so that the total force of attraction is $2P$. Electromagnets are widely used for commercial lifting jobs such as loading scrap iron into a truck or raising an armature to a higher position.

Example 9.33. *In a telephone receiver, the size of each pole of the electromagnet is 1.2 cm × 0.2 cm and the flux between each pole and the diaphragm is 4 × 10⁻⁶ Wb. With what force is the diaphragm attracted towards the poles ?*

Solution. $\qquad\qquad\qquad\qquad a = 1.2 \times 0.2 = 0.24 \text{ cm}^2 = 0.24 \times 10^{-4} \text{ m}^2$

$$B = \frac{\phi}{a} = \frac{4 \times 10^{-6}}{0.24 \times 10^{-4}} = 0.167 \text{ Wb/m}^2$$

$$P = \frac{B^2 a}{2\mu_0} = \frac{(0.167)^2 \times 0.24 \times 10^{-4}}{2 \times 4\pi \times 10^{-7}} = 0.266 \text{ newtons}$$

Total force $= 2P = 2 \times 0.266 = \textbf{0.532 newtons}$

Example 9.34. *A lifting magnet of inverted U-shape is formed out of an iron bar 60 cm long and 10 cm² in cross-sectional area. Exciting coils of 750 turns each are wound on the two side limbs and are connected in series. Calculate the exciting current necessary for the magnet to lift a load of 60 kg, assuming that the load has negligible reluctance and makes close contact with the magnet. Relative permeability of the material of magnet is 600.*

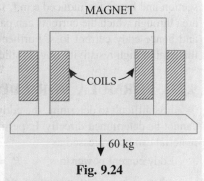

MAGNET

COILS

60 kg

Fig. 9.24

Solution.

$$P = 60 \times 9.81/2 = 294.3 \text{ newtons}$$

Now
$$P = B^2 a / 2\mu_0$$

∴
$$B = \sqrt{\frac{2P\mu_0}{a}} = \sqrt{\frac{2 \times 294.3 \times 4\pi \times 10^{-7}}{10 \times 10^{-4}}} = 0.86 \text{ Wb/m}^2$$

$$H = \frac{B}{\mu_0 \mu_r} = \frac{0.86}{4\pi \times 10^{-7} \times 600} = 1141 \text{ AT/m}$$

Total *AT* required $= H \times l = 1141 \times 0.6 = 684.6$

Magnetising current $= 684.6/N = 684.6/(2 \times 750) = \textbf{0.456A}$

9.22. EDDY CURRENT LOSS

When a magnetic material is subjected to a changing magnetic field, in addition to the hysteresis loss, another loss that occurs in the material is the *eddy current loss*. The changing magnetic flux induces voltages in the material according to Faraday's laws of electromagnetic induction. Since the material is conducting, these induced voltages circulate currents within the body of the material. These induced currents do no useful work and are known as eddy currents. These eddy currents develop $i^2 R$ loss in the material. Like hysteresis loss, the eddy current loss also results in the rise of temperature of the material. The hysteresis and eddy current losses in a magnetic material are sometimes called *core losses* or *iron losses*.

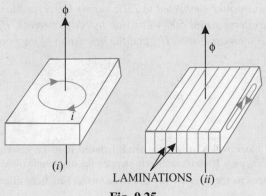

LAMINATIONS (*ii*)

Fig. 9.25

Fig. 9.25 (*i*) shows a solid block of iron subjected to a changing magnetic field. The eddy current power loss in the block will be i^2R where i is the eddy current and R is the resistance of the eddy current path. Since the block is a continuous iron piece of large *x*-section, the magnitude of i will be very *large and hence greater eddy current loss will result. The obvious method of reducing this loss is to reduce the magnitude of eddy current. This can be achieved by splitting the solid block into thin sheets (called *laminations*) in planes parallel to the magnetic flux as shown in Fig. 9.25 (*ii*). Each lamination is insulated from the other by a layer of varnish. This arrangement reduces the area of each section and hence the induced e.m.f. It also increases the resistance of eddy current paths since the area through which the currents can pass is smaller. Both effects combine to reduce the eddy current and hence eddy current loss. Further reduction in this loss can be obtained by using a magnetic material of high resistivity (*e.g.* **silicon steel).

9.23. FORMULA FOR EDDY CURRENT LOSS

It is difficult to determine the eddy current power loss because the current and resistance values cannot be determined directly. Experiments have shown that eddy current power loss in a magnetic material can be expressed as :

Eddy current power loss, $\qquad P_e = k_e \, B_m^2 \, t^2 \, f^2 \, V$ watts

where $\quad k_e$ = eddy-current co-efficient and its value depends upon the nature of the material

$\qquad B_m$ = maximum flux density in Wb/m^2

$\qquad t$ = thickness of lamination in m

$\qquad f$ = frequency of flux in Hz

$\qquad V$ = volume of material in m^3

Example 9.35. *The flux in a magnetic core is alternating sinusoidally at 50Hz. The maximum flux density is 1.5 Wb/m². The eddy current loss then amounts to 140 watts. Find the eddy current loss in the core when the frequency is 75Hz and the flux density 1.2 Wb/m².*

Solution.

Eddy current power loss, $\qquad P_e \propto B_m^2 f^2$

For the first case, $\qquad P_{e1} \propto (1.5)^2 \times (50)^2$

For the second case, $\qquad P_{e2} \propto (1.2)^2 \times (75)^2$

$$\therefore \qquad \frac{P_{e2}}{P_{e1}} = \left(\frac{1.2}{1.5}\right)^2 \times \left(\frac{75}{50}\right)^2 = 1.44$$

or $\qquad P_{e2} = 140 \times 1.44 = \textbf{201.6 W}$

Example 9.36. *A transformer connected to 25Hz supply has a core loss of 1500 watts of which 1000 watts are due to hysteresis and 500 watts due to eddy currents. If the flux density is kept constant and frequency is increased to 50 Hz, find the new value of the core loss.*

Solution.

Hysteresis power loss, $\qquad P_h \propto B_m^{1.6} f$

Eddy current power loss, $\qquad P_e \propto B_m^2 f^2$

---

* The large area of the block will have greater e.m.f. induced in it. Larger *x*-section also means smaller resistance to eddy current path. Both these effects increase the magnitude of eddy current to a great extent.

** Alloying iron with silicon increases resistivity and has a further beneficial effect in reducing the hysteresis loss.

Hysteresis loss

$$\frac{P_{h2}}{P_{h1}} = \left(\frac{B_{m2}}{B_{m1}}\right)^{1.6} \times \frac{f_2}{f_1} = (1)^{1.6} \times 50/25 = 2$$

$$\therefore \qquad P_{h2} = 2 \times 1000 = 2000 \text{ W}$$

Eddy current loss

$$\frac{P_{e2}}{P_{e1}} = \left(\frac{B_{m2}}{B_{m1}}\right)^2 \times \left(\frac{f_2}{f_1}\right)^2 = (1)^2 \times \left(\frac{50}{25}\right)^2 = 4$$

$$\therefore \qquad P_{e2} = 4\, P_{e1} = 4 \times 500 = 2000 \text{ W}$$

$\therefore$ Now core loss $\qquad = P_{h2} + P_{e2} = 2000 + 2000 = \mathbf{4000 \ W}$

9.24. STRAY INDUCTANCE

Since inductance is $L = \Delta\phi/\Delta I$, every current-carrying conductor has some self-inductance and every pair of conductors has inductance. This unwanted inductance is called stray inductance.

The unwanted inductance associated with current-carrying conductor/conductors is called **stray inductance.**

The stray inductance is normally insignificant in d.c. circuits and low-frequency a.c. circuits. However, stray inductance can produce undesirable effect on the performance of high-frequency a.c. circuits. It is because the value of stray inductance can be significant in high-frequency circuits. The stray inductance can be minimised by keeping connecting wires as short as possible.

MULTIPLE-CHOICE QUESTIONS

1. The basic requirement for inducing *e.m.f.* in a coil is that .....

   (*a*) magnetic flux should link the coil

   (*b*) there should be change in magnetic flux linking the coil

   (*c*) coil should form a closed loop

   (*d*) none of the above

2. The e.m.f. induced in a coil is ..... the rate of change of magnetic flux linkages.

   (*a*) directly proportional to

   (*b*) inversely proportional to

   (*c*) independent of

   (*d*) none of the above

3. The e.m.f. induced in a coil of *N* turns is given by ......

   (*a*) $d\phi/dt$ (*b*) $N\, d\phi\, /dt$

   (*c*) $-N\, d\phi\, /\, dt$ (*d*) $N\, dt\, /\, d\phi$

4. In Fig. 9.26, the component of velocity that does not induce any e.m.f. in the conductor is .....

   (*a*) $v \sin\theta$ (*b*) $v \cos\theta$

   (*c*) $v \tan\theta$ (*d*) none of the above

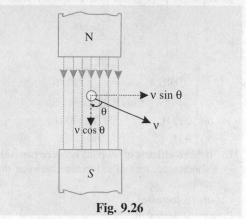

Fig. 9.26

5. If the number of turns of a coil is increased, its inductance.....

   (*a*) remains the same   (*b*) is increased

   (*c*) is decreased   (*d*) none of the above

6. A circuit has inductance of 2H. If the circuit current changes at the rate of 10A/second, then self-induced *e.m.f.* is .....

   (*a*) 5 V   (*b*) 0.2 V

   (*c*) 20 V   (*d*) 10 V

7. A current of 2A through a coil sets up magnetic flux linkages of 4 Wb-turn. The inductance of the coil is .....

   (a) 8 H

   (b) 0.5 H

   (c) 2 H

   (d) 1 H

8. The mutual inductance between two coils is ..... reluctance of magnetic path.

   (a) directly proportional to

   (b) inversely proportional to

   (c) independent of

   (d) none of the above

9. Mutual inductance between two coils is 4H. If current in one coil changes at the rate of 2A/second, then e.m.f. induced in the other coil is .....

   (a) 8 V

   (b) 2 V

   (c) 0.5 V

   (d) none of the above

10. If in Fig. 9.27, $\phi_{12} = 2$ Wb, $N_2 = 20$ and $I_1 = 20$ A, then mutual inductance between the coils is .....

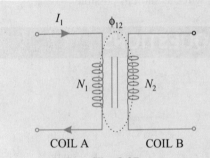

Fig. 9.27

   (a) 200 H   (b) 20 H

   (c) 4 H   (d) 2 H

11. If the co-efficient of coupling between two coils is increased, mutual inductance between the coils .....

   (a) is increased

   (b) is decreased

   (c) remains unchanged

   (d) none of the above

12. The mutual inductance between two unity-coupled coils of 9 H and 4 H is .....

   (a) 36 H

   (b) 13 H

   (c) 2.2 H

   (d) 6 H

13. In Fig. 9.28, the inductance of coil 1 is .....

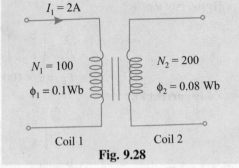

Fig. 9.28

   (a) 2 H

   (b) 5 H

   (c) 50 H

   (d) none of the above

14. In Fig. 9.28, the co-efficient of coupling between the coils is .....

   (a) 1.25

   (b) 0.8

   (c) 0.008

   (d) none of the above

15. In Fig. 9.29, the inductance of coil L_1 will become .....

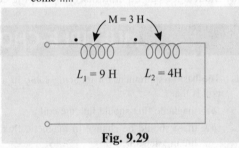

Fig. 9.29

   (a) 9 H

   (b) 6 H

   (c) 12 H

   (d) 3 H

16. Total inductance in Fig. 9.30 is .....

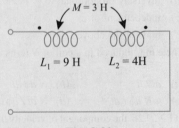

Fig. 9.30

   (a) 5 H   (b) 7 H

   (c) 16 H   (d) 19 H

17. In Fig. 9.31, the rate of change of current at the instant of closing the switch is .....
    (a) 15 A/sec   (b) 7.5 A/sec
    (c) 10 A/sec   (d) none of the above

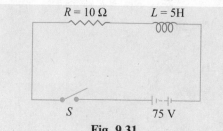

Fig. 9.31

$R = 10\ \Omega$ $L = 5H$ S   75 V

18. The time constant of the circuit shown in Fig. 9.31 is .....
    (a) 2 seconds   (b) 0.5 second
    (c) 5 seconds   (d) 1.5 seconds

19. After closing the switch in Fig. 9.31, the current will reach the steady value in about .....
    (a) 0.5 second   (b) 2.5 seconds
    (c) 5 seconds   (d) 1 second

20. An 8-H choke is carrying a current of 500 mA. The energy stored in the magnetic field is .....
    (a) 1 J   (b) 0.5 J
    (c) 2 J   (d) 4 J

21. A flux $\phi = 1$ m Wb passes a strip having an area $A = 200$ cm^2 and placed at an angle of 60° to the direction of uniform magnetic field. The value of magnetic flux density is
    (a) 0.5 T   (b) 1.2 T
    (c) 0.02 T   (d) 0.058 T

22. The mutual inductance between two coils each of N turns is M. If a current i in the first coil is brough to zero in a time t, then e.m.f. induced in the second coil is
    (a) $\dfrac{M\ N\ i}{t}$ (b) $\dfrac{M\ t}{i\ N}$
    (c) $\dfrac{M\ i}{t}$ (d) $\dfrac{N\ M\ t}{i}$

23. Fig. 9.32 shows two tightly-coupled ($k = 1$) identical coils. If the coils are connected in series - aiding, then total inductance is

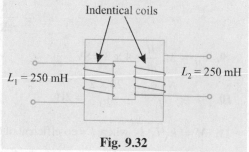

Indentical coils

$L_1 = 250$ mH $L_2 = 250$ mH

Fig. 9.32

   (a) 1 H   (b) 0.5 H
   (c) 4 H   (d) 2 H

24. In the above question, if the coils are connected in series - opposition, then total inductance is
    (a) 1 H   (b) zero
    (c) 2 H   (d) 4 H

25. A coil having 500 square loops each of side 10 cm is placed normal to a magnetic flux which increases at a rate of 1 T/sec. The induced e.m.f. is
    (a) 1 V   (b) 0.5 V
    (c) 0.1 V   (d) 5 V

Answers to Multiple-Choice Questions

1. (b)	2. (a)	3. (c)	4. (b)	5. (b)	6. (c)	7. (c)	8. (b)
9. (a)	10. (d)	11. (a)	12. (d)	13. (b)	14. (b)	15. (c)	16. (b)
17. (a)	18. (b)	19. (b)	20. (a)	21. (d)	22. (c)	23. (a)	24. (b)
25. (d)							

Hints to Selected Multiple-Choice Questions

3.
$$e = -N\frac{d\phi}{dt}$$

The minus sign comes from Lenz's Law and indicates that the current is induced in a direction to oppose the change in magnetic flux that produced it.

4. The component $v \cos \theta$ is parallel to the magnetic field and hence no e.m.f. is induced in the conductor due to this component.

5. $$\text{Inductance of coil} = \frac{N^2}{\text{Reluctance}}$$

6. $$e = L \frac{di}{dt} = 2 \times 10 = 20 \text{ V}$$

7. $$L = \frac{N \phi}{I} = \frac{4}{2} = 2\text{H}$$

8. Mutual inductance between two coils

$$= \frac{N_1 N_2}{\text{reluctance}}$$

9. $e_M = M \dfrac{dI}{dt} = 4 \times 2 = 8\text{V}$

10. $M = \dfrac{N_2 \phi_{12}}{I_1} = \dfrac{20 \times 2}{20} = 2\text{H}$

11. $M = k\sqrt{L_1 L_2}$ where k = co-efficient of coupling between two coils of inductances L_1 and L_2.

12. $M = k\sqrt{L_1 L_2} = 1\sqrt{9 \times 4} = 6\text{H}$

13. Inductance of coil 1 $= \dfrac{N_1 \phi_1}{I_1} = \dfrac{100 \times 0.1}{2} = 5\text{H}$

14. Co-efficient of coupling, $k = \dfrac{\phi_2}{\phi_1} = \dfrac{0.08}{0.1} = 0.8$

15. Since the coils are connected in series-aiding (See dot notation), the inductance of each coil will increase by M (*i.e.* 3H).

16. Total inductance $= L_1 + L_2 - 2M = 9 + 4 - 2 \times 3 = 7\text{H}$

17. Rate of change of current at the instant of closing the switch,

$V/L = 75/5 = 15$ A/sec.

18. Time constant $= L/R = 5/10 = 0.5$ second

19. The current will almost reach the final steady value after time equal to 5 time constants.

$\therefore$ Time to reach final steady value $= 5 \dfrac{L}{R} = 5\,(0.5) = 2.5$ seconds

20. Energy stored $= \dfrac{1}{2} L I^2 = \dfrac{1}{2} \times 8 \times \left(\dfrac{500}{1000}\right)^2 = 1\text{J}$

21. $\phi = BA \cos \theta$ or $B = \dfrac{\phi}{A \cos \theta} = \dfrac{1 \times 10^{-3}}{(200 \times 10^{-4}) \times \cos 30°} = 0.058 \text{ T}$

22. E.M.F. induced in the second coil is

$$e_2 = M \times \frac{dI_1}{dt} = M \times \frac{i}{t} = \frac{M i}{t}$$

23. Fig. 9.33 shows the conditions of the problem.

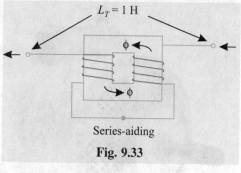

$$M = k\sqrt{L_1 L_2}$$
$$= 1 \times \sqrt{250 \times 250} = 250\,\text{mH}$$

Since the coils are connected in series-aiding, the total inductance L_T is

$$L_T = L_1 + L_2 + 2M$$
$$= 250 + 250 + 2 \times 250$$
$$= 1000\,\text{mH} = \mathbf{1H}$$

Series-aiding

Fig. 9.33

Note that inductance of a coil is directly proportional to the *square* of the number of turns. Connecting the two coils in series doubles the number of turns and the inductance increases by a factor of four.

24. Fig. 9.34 shows the conditions of the problem.

As shown above, $M = 250$ mH

$$\therefore \quad L_T = L_1 + L_2 - 2M$$
$$= 250 + 250 - 2 \times 250 = 0$$

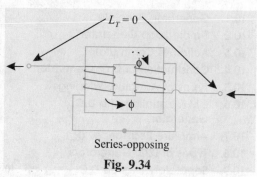

Let us discuss the result physically. The flux from one coil is equal and opposite to the flux produced by the other coil. The cancellation of flux produces a total inductance of 0.

Series-opposing

Fig. 9.34

25. Magnitude of induced e.m.f. is given by;

$$e = N \frac{d}{dt}(\phi)$$

$$= N \frac{d}{dt}(BA) = NA \frac{dB}{dt} = 500 \times (100 \times 10^{-4}) \times 1 = \mathbf{5\ V}$$

10

D.C. Generators

INTRODUCTION

Although a far greater percentage of the electrical machines in service are a.c. machines, the d.c. machines are of considerable industrial importance. The principal advantage of the d.c. machine, particularly the d.c. motor, is that it provides a fine control of speed. Such an advantage is not claimed by any a.c. motor. However, d.c. generators are not as common as they used to be, because direct current, when required, is mainly obtained from an a.c. supply by the use of rectifiers. Nevertheless, an understanding of d.c. generator is important because it represents a logical introduction to the behaviour of d.c. motors. Indeed many d.c. motors in industry actually operate as d.c. generators for a brief period. In this chapter, we shall deal with various aspects of d.c. generators.

10.1. GENERATOR PRINCIPLE

An electric generator is a machine that converts mechanical energy into electrical energy.

An electric generator is based on the principle that whenever magnetic flux is cut by a conductor, an e.m.f. is induced which will cause a current to flow if the conductor circuit is closed. The direction of induced e.m.f. (and hence current) is given by *Fleming's right hand rule. Therefore, the essential components of a generator are:

(*i*)   a magnetic field

(*ii*) conductor or a group of conductors

(*iii*) motion of conductor w.r.t. magnetic field

10.2. SIMPLE LOOP GENERATOR

Consider a single turn loop *ABCD* rotating clockwise in a uniform magnetic field with a constant speed as shown in Fig. 10.1. As the loop rotates, the magnetic flux linking the coil sides *AB* and *CD* changes continuously. Hence the e.m.f. induced in these coil sides also changes but the e.m.f. induced in one coil side ** adds to that induced in the other.

(*i*)   When the loop is in position no. 1 [See Fig. 10.1], the generated e.m.f. is zero because the coil sides (*AB* and *CD*) are cutting no magnetic flux but are moving parallel to it.

(*ii*) When the loop is in position no. 2, the coil sides are moving at an angle to the magnetic flux and, therefore, a low e.m.f. is generated as indicated by point 2 in Fig. 10.2.

(*iii*) When the loop is in position no. 3, the coil sides (*AB* and *CD*) are at right angle to the magnetic flux and are, therefore, cutting the flux at a maximum rate. Hence at this instant, the generated e.m.f. is maximum as indicated by point 3 in Fig. 10.2.

(*iv*) At position 4, the generated e.m.f. is less because the coil sides are cutting the magnetic flux at an angle.

(*v*)   At position 5, no magnetic lines are cut and hence, induced e.m.f. is zero as indicated by point 5 in Fig. 10.2.

(*vi*) At position 6, the coil sides move under a pole of opposite polarity and hence the direction of generated e.m.f. is reversed. The maximum e.m.f. in this direction (*i.e.* reverse direction, See Fig. 10.2) will be when the loop is at position 7 and zero when at position 1. This cycle repeats with each revolution of the coil.

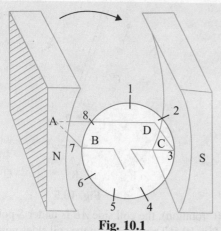

Fig. 10.1

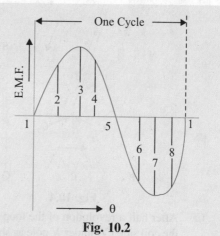

Fig. 10.2

Note that e.m.f. generated in the loop is alternating one. It is because any coil side, say *AB*, has e.m.f. in one direction when under the influence of *N*-pole and in the other direction when under the

---

* *Fleming's Right hand rule.* Stretch the thumb, fore-finger and middle finger of you right hand so that they are at right angles to each other. If the fore-finger points in the direction of field, thumb in the direction of motion of the conductor, then middle finger will point in the direction of induced e.m.f.

** It is because the coil sides always remain under the influence of opposite poles *i.e.* if one coil side is under the influence of the N-pole, then the other coil side will be under the influence of S-pole and *vice-versa*.

influence of S-pole. If a load is connected across the ends of the loop, then alternating current will flow through the load. The alternating voltage generated in the loop can be converted into direct voltage by a device called *commutator* We then have the d.c. generator. In fact, a commutator is a mechanical rectifier.

10.3. ACTION OF COMMUTATOR

If, somehow, connection of the coil side to the external load is reversed at the same instant the current in the coil side reverses, the current through the load will be direct current. This is what a commutator does. Fig. 10.3 shows a commutator having two segments C_1 and C_2. It consists of a cylindrical metal ring cut into two halves or segments C_1 and C_2 respectively separated by a thin sheet of mica. The commutator is mounted on, but insulated from, the rotor shaft. The ends of coil sides AB and CD are connected to the segments C_1 and C_2 respectively as shown in Fig. 10.4. Two stationary carbon brushes rest on the commutator

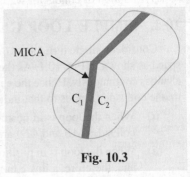

Fig. 10.3

and lead current to the external load. With this arrangement, the commutator at all times connects the coil side under S-pole to the +ve brush and that under N-pole to the –ve brush.

   (i) In Fig. 10.4, the coil sides AB and CD are under N-pole and S-pole respectively. Note that segment C_1 connects the coil side AB to point P of the load resistance R and the segment C_2 connects the coil side CD to point Q of the load. Also note the direction of current through load. It is from Q to P.

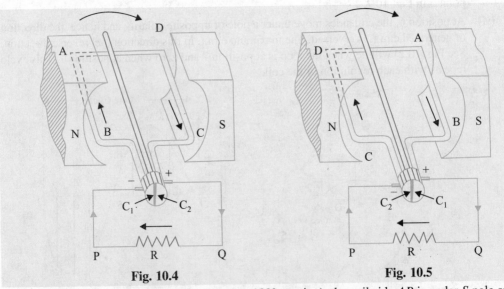

Fig. 10.4   **Fig. 10.5**

  (ii) After half a revolution of the loop (*i.e.* 180° rotation), the coil side AB is under S-pole and the coil side CD under N-pole as shown in Fig. 10.5. The currents in the coil sides now flow in the reverse direction but the segments C_1 and C_2 have also moved through 180° *i.e.* segment C_1 is now in contact with + *ve* brush and segment C_2 in contact with – *ve* brush. Note that commutator has reversed the coil connectios to the load *i.e.* coil side AB is now connected to point Q of the load and coil side CD to the point P of the load. Also note the direction of current through the load. It is *again from Q to P.

* The situation is that currents in the coil sides are reversed and at the same time the connections of the coil sides to the external load are reversed. This means that current will flow in the same direction through the load.

Thus the alternating voltage generated in the loop will appear as direct voltage across the brushes. The reader may note that e.m.f. generated in the armature winding of a d.c. generator is alternating one. It is by the use of commutator that we convert the generated alternating e.m.f. into direct voltage. The purpose of brushes is simply to lead current from the rotating loop or winding to the external stationary load.

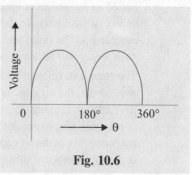

Fig. 10.6

The variation of voltage across the brushes with the angular displacement of the loop will be as shown in Fig. 10.6. This is not a steady direct voltage but has a pulsating character. It is because the voltage appearing across the brushes varies from zero to maximum value and back to zero twice for each revolution of the loop. A pulsating direct voltage such as is produced by a single loop is not suitable for many commercial uses. What we require is the steady direct voltage. This can be achieved by using a large number of coils connected in series. The resulting arrangement is known as *armature winding*.

10.4. CONSTRUCTION OF D.C. GENERATOR

The d.c. generators and d.c. motors have the same general construction. In fact, when the machine is being assembled, the workmen usually do not know whether it is a d.c. generator or motor. Any d.c. generator can be run as a d.c. motor and *vice-versa*. All d.c. machines have five principal components viz (*i*) field system (*ii*) armature core (*iii*) armature winding (*iv*) commutator (*v*) brushes [See Fig. 10.7].

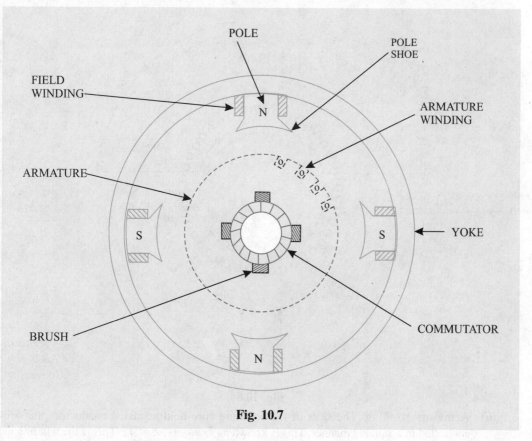

Fig. 10.7

(*i*) **Field system.** The function of the field system is to produce uniform magnetic field within which the armature rotates. It consists of a number of salient poles (of course, even number) bolted to the inside of circular frame (generally called *yoke*). The yoke is usually made of solid cast steel whereas the pole pieces are composed of stacked laminations. Field coils are mounted on the poles and carry the d.c. exciting current. The field coils are connected in such a way that adjacent poles have opposite polarity.

The m.m.f. developed by the field coils produces a magnetic flux that passes through the pole pieces, the air gap, the armature and the frame (See Fig. 10.8). Practical d.c. machines have air gaps ranging from 0.5 mm to 1.5 mm. Since armature and field systems are composed of materials that have high permeability, most of the m.m.f. of field coils is required to set up magnetic flux in the air gap. By reducing the length of air gap, we can reduce the size of field coils (*i.e.* number of turns).

(*ii*) **Armature core.** The armature core is keyed to the machine shaft and rotates between the field poles. It consists of slotted soft-iron laminations (about 0.4 to 0.6 mm thick) that are stacked to form a cylindrical core as shwon in Fig. 10.9. The laminations (See Fig. 10.10) are individually coated with a thin insulating film so that they do not come in electrical contact with each other. The purpose of laminating the core is to reduce the eddy current loss. The laminations are slotted to accommodate and provide mechanical security to the armature winding and to give shorter air gap for the flux to cross between the pole face and the armature "teeth".

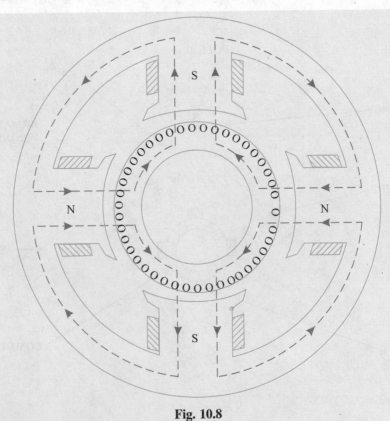

Fig. 10.8

(*iii*) **Armature winding.** The slots of the armature core hold insulated conductors that are connected in a suitable manner. This is known as *armature winding*. This is the winding in which "working" e.m.f. is induced. The armatue conductors are connected in series-parallel; the conductors being connected in series so as to increase the voltage and in parallel paths so as to increase the current. The armature winging of a d.c. machine is a closed-circuit winding; the conductors being connected in a symmetrical manner forming a closed loop or series of closed loops.

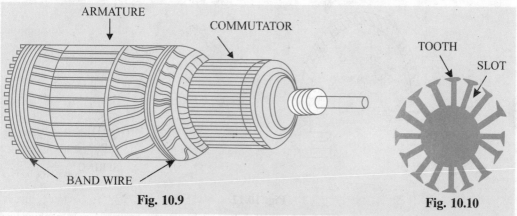

ARMATURE   COMMUTATOR   TOOTH   SLOT

BAND WIRE

Fig. 10.9   **Fig. 10.10**

(*iv*) **Commutator.** A commutator is a mechanical rectifier which converts the alternating voltage generated in the armature winding into direct voltage across the brushes. The commutator is made of copper segments insulated from each other by mica sheets and mounted on the shaft of the machine (See Fig. 10.11). The armature conductors are soldered to the commutator segments in a suitable manner to give rise to the armature winding. Depending upon the manner in which the armature conductors are connected to the commutator segments, there are two types of armature windings in a d.c. machine viz (*a*) lap winding (*b*) wave winding.

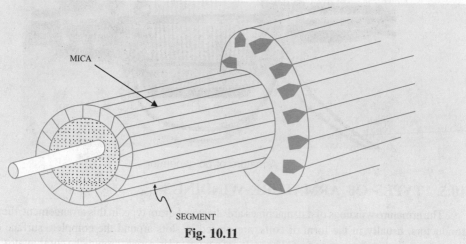

MICA

SEGMENT

Fig. 10.11

Great care is taken in building the commutator because any eccentricity will cause the brushes to bounce, producing unacceptable sparking. The sparks may burn the brushes and overheat and carbonise the commutator.

(*v*) **Brush** The purpose of brushes is to ensure *electrical connections between the rotating

---

* When the machine is acting as a generator, the brushes carry current from the commutator to the external stationary load. In case the machine is acting as a motor, they feed the supply current to the commutator.

commutator and stationary external load circuit. The brushes are made of * carbon and rest on the commutator. The brush pressure is adjusted by means of adjustable springs (See Fig. 10.12). If the brush pressure is very large, the friction produces heating of the commutator and the brushes. On the other hand, if it is too weak, the imperfect contact with the commutator may produce sparking.

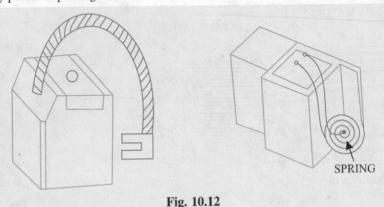

Fig. 10.12

Multipole machines have as many brushes as they have poles. For example, a 4-pole machine has 4 brushes. As we go round the commutator, the successive brushes have positive and negative polarities. Brushes having the same polarity are connected together so that we have two terminals *viz* the +ve terminal and the –ve terminal.

Armature of dc generator

10.5. TYPES OF ARMATURE WINDINGS

The armature windings of d.c. machines are always of drum type. In this arrangement, the armature conductors, usually in the form of coils, are placed in slots around the complete surface of drum-shaped or cylindrical armature core. The coils are connected in series through the commutator segments in such a way that their e.m.f.s add to each other. There are two types of d.c. armature windings *viz* (*i*) Wave winding (*ii*) Lap winding.

    (*i*) **Wave winding.** In this arrangement, the armature coils are connected in series through commutator segments in such a way that *the armature winding is divided into two parallel*

* Because carbon has good electrical conductivity and is soft enough not to scratch the commutator. To improve the conductivity, sometimes we add a small amount of copper.

paths irrespective of the number of poles of the machine. If there are Z armature conductors, then $Z/2$ conductors will be in series in each parallel path as shown in Fig. 10.13. Each parallel path will carry a current $I_a/2$ where I_a is the total armature current.

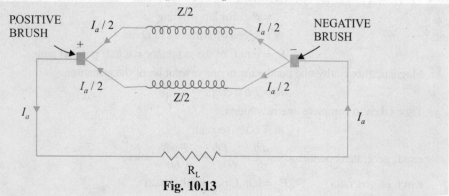

Fig. 10.13

To sum up, in a wave winding;

(*a*) there are two parallel paths irrespective of number of poles of the machine.

(*b*) each parallel path has $Z/2$ conductors in series; Z being total number of armature conductors.

(*c*) e.m.f. generated = e.m.f./parallel path

(*d*) total armature current, $I_a = 2 \times$ current/parallel path

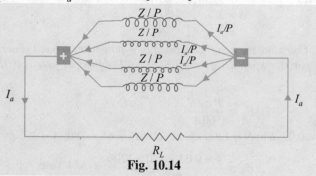

Fig. 10.14

(*ii*) **Lap winding.** In this arrangement, the armature coils are connected in series through commutator segments in such a way that *the armature winding is divided into as many parallel paths as the number of poles of the machine.* If there are Z conductors and P poles, then there will be P parallel paths, each containing Z/P conductors in series as shown in Fig. 10.14. Each parallel path will carry a current of I_a/P where I_a is the total armature current. Here it is assumed that $P = 4$ so that there are 4 parallel paths.

To sum up, in a lap winding;

(*a*) there are as many parallel paths as the number of poles (*P*) of the machine.

(*b*) each parallel path has Z/P conductors in series where Z and P are the total number of armature conductors and poles respectively.

(*c*) e.m.f. generated = e.m.f./parallel path.

(*d*) total armature current, $I_a = P \times$ current/parallel path.

10.6. E.M.F. EQUATION OF A D.C. GENERATOR

We shall now derive an expression for the e.m.f. generated in a d.c. generator.

Let ϕ = magnetic flux/pole in Wb

Z = total number of armature conductors

P = number of poles

A = number of parallel paths = 2....for wave winding

= P ... for lap winding

N = speed of armature in r.p.m.

E_g = e.m.f. of the generator = e.m.f/ parallel path

Magnetic flux cut by one conductor in one revolution of the armature,

$$d\phi = P\phi \text{ webers}$$

Time taken to complete one revolution,

$$dt = 60/N \text{ second}$$

e.m.f. generated/conductor = $\dfrac{d\phi}{dt} = \dfrac{P\phi}{60/N} = \dfrac{P\phi N}{60}$ volts

e.m.f. of generator, $\quad E_g$ = e.m.f. per parallel path

= (e.m.f./conductor) × no. of conductors in series per parallel path

$$= \dfrac{P\phi N}{60} \times \dfrac{Z}{A}$$

∴ $$E_g = \dfrac{P\phi ZN}{60A}$$

where $\qquad A = 2 \qquad\qquad\qquad$ ...for wave winding

$\qquad\qquad\quad = P \qquad\qquad\qquad$ ...for lap winding

Example 10.1. *Calculate the e.m.f. generated by 4-pole wave-wound generator having 65 slots with 12 conductors per slot when driven at 1200 r.p.m. The flux per pole is 0.02 Wb.*

Solution.

$$E_g = \dfrac{P\phi ZN}{60A}$$

Here P = 4; ϕ = 0.02 Wb; N = 1200 r.p.m. ; Z = 12 × 65 = 780; A = 2

∴ $$E_g = \dfrac{4 \times 0.02 \times 780 \times 1200}{60 \times 2} = \textbf{624 volts}$$

Example 10.2. *A 6-pole lap-wound d.c. generator has 600 conductors on its armature. The flux per pole is 0.02 Wb. Calculate (i) the speed at which the generator must be run to generate 300V (ii) What would be the speed if the generator were wave-wound?*

Solution.

(*i*) **Lap wound**

$$E_g = \dfrac{P\phi ZN}{60A}$$

∴ $$N = \dfrac{E_g \times 60A}{P\phi Z} = \dfrac{300 \times 60 \times 6}{6 \times 0.02 \times 600} = \textbf{1500 r.p.m.}$$

(*ii*) **Wave wound**

$$N = \dfrac{E_g \times 60A}{P\phi Z} = \dfrac{300 \times 60 \times 2}{6 \times 0.02 \times 600} = \textbf{500 r.p.m.}$$

Example 10.3. *An 8-pole, lap-wound armature rotated at 350 r.p.m. is required to generate 260 V. The useful magnetic flux per pole is 0.05 Wb. If the armature has 120 slots, calculate the number of conductors per slot.*

Solution.

$$E_g = \dfrac{P\phi ZN}{60A}$$

$$\therefore \qquad Z = \frac{E_g \times 60A}{P\phi N} = \frac{260 \times 60 \times 8}{8 \times 0.05 \times 350} = 890$$

∴ No. of conductors/slot = 890/120 = 7.14

This value must be an even number.

Hence, conductors/slot = 8

Example 10.4. *The armature of a 6-pole, 600 r.p.m. lap-wound generator has 90 slots. If each coil has 4 turns, calculate the flux per pole required to generate an e.m.f. of 288 volts.*

Solution. Each turn has two active conductors and 90 coils are required to fill 90 slots.

$$\therefore \qquad Z = 90 \times 4 \times 2 = 720$$

$$E_g = \frac{P\phi ZN}{60A}$$

or

$$\phi = \frac{E_g \times 60A}{PZN} = \frac{288 \times 60 \times 6}{6 \times 720 \times 600} = 0.04\,\text{Wb}$$

Example 10.5. *The armature of a d.c. generator has 81 slots and the commutator has 243 segments. It is wound to give lap winding having 1 turn per coil. If the flux per pole is 30 mWb, calculate the generated e.m.f. at a speed of 1200 r.p.m. Number of poles = 6.*

Solution. The number of coils is equal to the number of commutator segments. Each turn has 2 active conductors.

$$\therefore \qquad Z = 243 \times 2 = 486; \quad \phi = 30 \times 10^{-3} = 0.03\,\text{Wb}$$

$$E_g = \frac{P\phi ZN}{60A} = \frac{6 \times 0.03 \times 486 \times 1200}{60 \times 6} = \textbf{291.6 volts}$$

10.7. ARMATURE RESISTANCE (R_a)

The resistance offered by the armature circuit is known as armature resistance (R_a) and includes:

(*i*)   resistance of armature winding

(*ii*)   resistance of brushes.

The armature resistance depends upon the construction of machine. Except for small machines, its value is generally less than 1Ω.

10.8. TYPES OF D.C. GENERATORS

The magnetic field in a d.c. generator is normally produced by electromagnets rather than permanent magnets. Generators are generally classified according to their methods of field excitation. On this basis, d.c. generators are divided into the following two classes:

(*i*)   Separately excited d.c. generators

(*ii*)   Self-excited d.c. generators

The behaviour of a d.c. generator on load depends upon the method of field excitation adopted.

10.9. SEPARATELY EXCITED D.C. GENERATORS

A d.c. generator whose field magnet winding is supplied from an independent external d.c. source (*e.g.* a battery *etc.*) is called *a separately excited generator.* Fig. 10.15 shows the connections of a separately excited generator. The voltage output depends upon the speed of rotation of armature and the field current ($E_g = P\phi ZN/60A$). The greater the speed and field current, greater is the generated e.m.f. It may be noted that separately excited d.c. generators are rarely used in practice. The d.c. generators are normally of self-excited type.

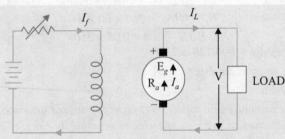

Fig. 10.15

Armature current, $\qquad I_a = I_L$

Terminal voltage, $\qquad V = E_g - I_a R_a$

Electric power developed $\quad = E_g I_a$

Power delivered to load $\qquad = E_g I_a - I_a^2 R_a = I_a (E_g - I_a R_a) = VI_a$

10.10. SELF-EXCITED D.C. GENERATORS

A d.c. generator whose field magnet winding is supplied current from the output of the generator itself is called a *self-excited generator*. There are three types of self-excited generators depending upon the manner in which the field winding is connected to the armature, namely;

(*i*) Series generator

(*ii*) Shunt generator

(*iii*) Compound generator

(*i*) **Series generator.** In a series-wound generator, the field winding is connected in series with armature winding so that whole armature current flows through the field winding as well as the load. Fig. 10.16 shows the connections of a series-wound generator. Since the field winding carries the whole of load current, it has a few turns of thick wire having low resistance. Series generators are rarely used except for special purposes *e.g.* as boosters.

Armature current, $\qquad I_a = I_{se} = I_L = I$ (say)

Terminal voltage, $\qquad V = E_g - I (R_a + R_{se})$

Power developed in armature $\quad = E_g I_a$

Power delivered to load $\qquad = E_g I_a - I_a^2 (R_a + R_{se}) = I_a [E_g - I_a (R_a + R_{se})] = VI_a$ or VI_L

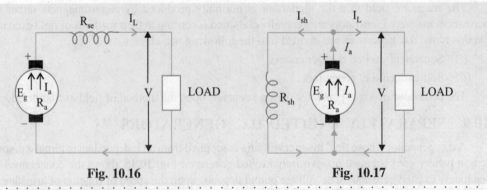

Fig. 10.16 $\qquad\qquad\qquad\qquad\qquad\qquad$ **Fig. 10.17**

* How is self-excitation achieved ? When the armature is rotated, a small voltage is induced in the armature winding due to residual magnetic flux in the poles. This voltage produces a small field current in the field winding and causes the flux per pole to increase. The increased flux increases the induced voltage which further increases the field current. These events take place rapidly and the generator builds up to the rated generated voltage.

(*ii*) **Shunt generator.** In a shunt generator, the field winding is connected in parallel with the armature winding so that terminal voltage of the generator is applied across it. The shunt field winding has many turns of fine wire having high resistance. Therefore, only a part of armature current flows through shunt field winding and the rest flows through the load. Fig. 10.17 shows the connections of a shunt-wound generator.

Shunt field current,	$I_{sh} = V/R_{sh}$
Armature current,	$I_a = I_L + I_{sh}$
Terminal voltage,	$V = E_g - I_a R_a$
Power developed in armature	$= E_g I_a$
Power delivered to load	$= VI_L$

(*iii*) **Compound generator.** In a compound-wound generator, there are * two sets of field windings on each pole—one is in series and the other in parallel with the armature. A compound wound generator may be:

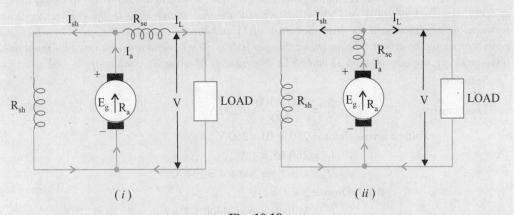

Fig. 10.18

(*a*) **Short Shunt** in which only shunt field winding is in parallel with the armature winding [See Fig. 10.18 (*i*)].

(*b*) **Long shunt** in which shunt field winding is in parallel with both series field and armature winding [See Fig. 10.18 (*ii*)].

Short shunt

Series field current,	$I_{se} = I_L$
Shunt field current,	$I_{sh} = \dfrac{V + I_{se} R_{se}}{R_{sh}}$
Terminal voltage,	$V = E_g - I_a R_a - I_{se} R_{se}$
Power developed in armature	$= E_g I_a$
Power delivered to load	$= VI_L$

Long shunt

Series field current,	$I_{se} = I_a = I_L + I_{sh}$
Shunt field current,	$I_{sh} = V/R_{sh}$

---

* Normally, the majority of m.m.f. is provided by the shunt field. The two windings may be connected to aid each other (*cumulative compounding*) or they may oppose each other (*differential compounding*).

Terminal voltage, $\qquad V = E_g - I_a (R_a + R_{se})$

Power developed in armature $= E_g I_a$

Power delivered to load $= V I_L$

Example 10.6. *A 100 kW, 240V shunt generator has a field resistance of 55 Ω and armature resistance of 0.067 Ω. Find the full-load generated voltage.*

Solution. Fig. 10.19 shows the shunt generator circuit.

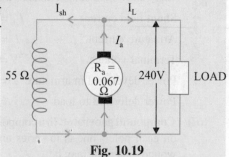

$$I_L = \frac{100 \times 10^3}{240} = 416.7 A$$

$$I_{sh} = 240/55 = 4.36 \ A$$

$$I_a = I_L + I_{sh}$$

$$= 416.7 + 4.36 = 421.1 A$$

$$E_g = V + I_a R_a$$

$$= 240 + 421.1 \times 0.067 = \mathbf{268.2 \ V}$$

Fig. 10.19

Example 10.7. *A 4-pole d.c. shunt generator with a wave-wound armature has to supply a load of 500 lamps each of 100W at 250V. Allowing 10V for the voltage drop in the connecting leads between the generator and the load and drop of 1V per brush, calculate the speed at which the generator should be driven. The magnetic flux per pole is 30 mWb and the armature and shunt field resistances are respectively 0.05 Ω and 65 Ω. The number of armature conductors is 390.*

Solution.

Load current, $\qquad I_L = \dfrac{500 \times 100}{250} = 200 \ A$

Voltage across shunt $= 250 + 10 = 260 \ V$

$$I_{sh} = 260/65 = 4 \ A$$

$$I_a = I_L + I_{sh} = 200 + 4 = 204 \ A$$

Brush Drop $= 2 \times 1 = 2 . V$

$$E_g = \text{Voltage across shunt} + 2 + I_a R_a$$

$$= 260 + 2 + 204 \times 0.05 = 272.2 \ V$$

Now, $\qquad E_g = \dfrac{P \phi Z N}{60 \ A}$

∴ $\qquad N = \dfrac{E_g \times 60 A}{P \phi Z} = \dfrac{272.2 \times 60 \times 2}{4 \times 30 \times 10^{-3} \times 390} = \mathbf{698 \ r.p.m.}$

[For wave winding, A = 2]

Example 10.8. *A 30 kW, 300V d.c. shunt generator has armature and field resistances of 0.05 Ω and 100 Ω respectively. Calculate the total power developed by the armature when it delivers full load output.*

Solution. Fig. 10.20 shows the shunt generator circuit.

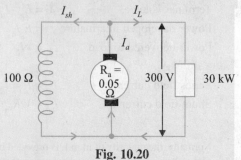

$$I_L = \frac{30 \times 10^3}{300} = 100 \ A$$

$$I_{sh} = 300/100 = 3 \ A$$

$$I_a = I_L + I_{sh} = 100 + 3 = 103 \ A$$

$$E_g = V + I_a R_a$$

$$= 300 + 103 \times 0.05 = 305.15 \ V$$

Power developed by armature $= E_g I_a$

Fig. 10.20

$$= 305.15 \times 103 = 31.43 \times 10^3 \ W = \mathbf{31.43 \ kW}$$

Example 10.9. *A 4-pole lap-wound d.c. shunt generator has a useful flux per pole of 0.07 Wb. The armature winding consists of 220 turns, each of 0.004 Ω resistance. Calculate the terminal voltage when running at 900 r.p.m. if the armature current is 50A.*

Solution.

$$E_g = \frac{P\phi ZN}{60A}$$

Here $\quad\quad\quad Z = 220 \times 2 = 440; \phi = 0.07$ Wb; $N = 900$ r.p.m.; $A = P = 4$

∴ $\quad\quad\quad E_g = \dfrac{4 \times 0.07 \times 440 \times 900}{60 \times 4} = 462$ V

No. of turns per parallel path = 220/4 = 55

Resistance per parallel path = $0.004 \times 55 = 0.22$ Ω

Now $\quad\quad\quad E_g = V + I_a R_a$

or $\quad\quad\quad 462 = V + 50 \times 0.055$

∴ $\quad\quad\quad\quad V = \textbf{459.25 volts}$

Example 10.10 *A d.c. shunt generator runs at 400 r.p.m.and delivers 500 kW to busbars having a constant voltage of 400 V. Assuming the field excitation to be constant at 5A, calculate the speed at which the generator must run if the load on it is to be reduced to 300 kW. The armature resistance is 0.015Ω.*

Solution.

$$* \ E_g \propto \phi N$$

In the present problem, ϕ is given to be constant. Therefore, $E_g \propto N$

Initial conditions

Load current, $\quad\quad I_1 = 500 \times 10^3 / 400 = 1250$ A

Armature current $\quad = 1250 + 5 = 1255$ A

∴ Generated e.m.f., $\quad E_1 = 400 + 1255 \times 0.015 = 418.8$ V

Final conditions

Load current, $\quad\quad I_2 = 300 \times 10^3/400 = 750$ A

Armature current $\quad = 750 + 5 = 755$ A

∴ Generated e.m.f., $\quad E_2 = 400 + 755 \times 0.015 = 411.3$ V

Now $\quad\quad\quad E_2/E_1 = N_2/N_1$

∴ $\quad\quad\quad N_2 = (E_2/E_1) \times N_1 = (411.3/418.8) \times 400 = \textbf{393 r.p.m.}$

Example 10.11. *A compound generator is to supply a load of 250 lamps, each rated at 100 W, 250V. The armature, series and shunt windings have resistances of 0.06 Ω, 0.04 Ω and 50 Ω respectively. Determine the generated e.m.f. when the machine is connected in (i) long shunt (ii) short shunt. Take drop per brush as 1V.*

Solution.

(*i*) Fig. 10.21 shows the connections of the machine when connected in long shunt.

$$I_L = \frac{250 \times 100}{250} = 100 \,\text{A}$$

$I_{sh} = 250/50 = 5$A

$I_a = I_L + I_{sh} = 100 + 5 = 105$ A

$E_g = V + I_a (R_a + R_{se}) + \text{Total brush drop}$

$\quad = 250 + 105 (0.06 + 0.04) + 2 \times 1 = \textbf{262.5 V}$

* *

* $\quad E_g = P\phi ZN/60A$. For a given machine, P, Z and A are constant so that $E_g \propto \phi N$.

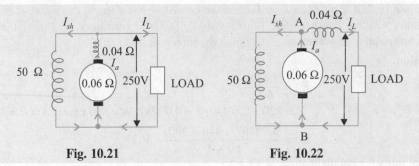

Fig. 10.21	**Fig. 10.22**

(*ii*)   Fig. 10.22 shows the connections when the machine is connected in short shunt.

$$I_L = 100 \text{ A} \qquad\qquad ...same\ as\ before$$

Voltage across shunt, $V_{AB} = 250 + 100 \times 0.04 = 254 \text{ V}$

$$I_{sh} = 254/50 = 5.08 \text{ A}$$

$$I_a = I_L + I_{sh} = 100 + 5.08 = 105.08 \text{ A}$$

$$E_g = V_{AB} + I_a R_a + \text{Total brush drop}$$
$$= 254 + 105.08 \times 0.06 + 2 \times 1 = \textbf{262.3 V}$$

Balancing Armature

10.11. LOSSES IN A D.C. MACHINE

The losses in a d.c. machine (generator or motor) may be divided into three classes *viz* (*i*) copper losses (*ii*) iron or core losses and (*iii*) mechanical losses. All these losses appear as heat and thus raise the temperature of the machine. They also lower the efficiency of the machine.

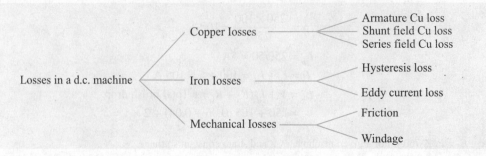

1. Copper losses. These losses occur due to currents in the various windings of the machine.

(*i*)   Armature copper loss = $I_a^2 R_a$

(*ii*) Shunt field copper loss = $I_{sh}^2 R_{sh}$

(*iii*) Series field copper loss = $I_{se}^2 R_{se}$

Note. There is also brush contact loss due to brush contact resistance (*i.e.* resistance between the surface of brush and surface of commutator). This loss is generally included in armature copper loss.

2. Iron or Core losses. These losses occur in the armature of a d.c. machine and are due to the rotation of armature in the magnetic field of the poles. They are of two types *viz* (*i*) hysteresis loss (*ii*) eddy current loss.

(*i*) **Hysteresis loss.** Hysteresis loss occurs in the armature of the d.c. machine since any given part of the armature is subjected to magnetic field reversals as it passes under successive poles. Fig. 10.23 shows an armature rotating in two-pole machine. Consider a small piece *ab* of the armature. When the piece *ab* is under *N*-pole, the magnetic lines pass from *a* to *b*. Half a revolution later, the same piece of iron is under *S*-pole and magnetic lines pass from *b* to *a* so that magnetism in the iron is reversed. In order to reverse continuously the molecular magnets in the armature core, some amount

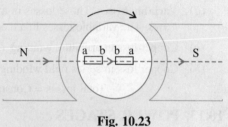

Fig. 10.23

of power has to be spent which is called hysteresis loss. It is given by:

Hysteresis loss, $\qquad P_h = \eta B_{max}^{1.6} f V$ watts

where $\qquad\qquad\qquad B_{max}$ = Maximum magnetic flux density in armature

$\qquad\qquad\qquad\qquad f$ = Frequency of magnetic reversals

$\qquad\qquad\qquad\qquad\quad$ = NP/120 where N is in r.p.m.

$\qquad\qquad\qquad\qquad V$ = Volume of armature in m^3

$\qquad\qquad\qquad\qquad \eta$ = Steinmetz hysteresis co-efficient

In order to reduce this loss in a d.c. machine, armature core is made of such materials which have a low value of steinmetz hysteresis co-efficient *e.g.* silicon steel.

(*ii*) **Eddy current loss.** When armature rotates in the magnetic field of the poles, an e.m.f. is induced in it which circulates eddy currents in the armature core. The power loss due to these eddy currents is called eddy current loss. In order to reduce this loss, the armature core is built up of thin laminations insulated from each other by a thin layer of varnish.

Eddy current loss, $P_e = K_e B_{max}^2 f^2 t^2 V$ watts

where $\qquad\qquad\qquad\quad K_e$ = Constant

$\qquad\qquad\qquad B_{max}$ = Maximum magnetic flux density in the core

$\qquad\qquad\qquad\qquad f$ = Frequency of magnetic reversals

$\qquad\qquad\qquad\qquad t$ = Thickness of lamination

$\qquad\qquad\qquad\qquad V$ = Volume of core in m^3

It may be noted that eddy current loss depends upon the square of lamination thickness. For this reason, lamination thickness should be kept as small as possible.

3. Mechanical losses. These losses are due to friction and windage.

(*i*) friction loss e.g. bearing friction, brush friction etc.

(*ii*) windage loss *i.e.* air friction of rotating armature.

These losses depend upon the speed of the machine. But for a given speed, they are practically constant.

Note. Iron losses and mechanical losses together are called **stray losses**.

10.12. CONSTANT AND VARIABLE LOSSES

The losses in a d.c. generator (or d.c. motor) may be sub-divided into (*i*) constant losses (*ii*) variable losses.

(*i*) **Constant losses.** Those losses in a d.c. generator which remain constant at all loads are known as *constant losses*. The constant losses in a d.c. generator are:

(*a*) iron losses

(*b*) mechanical losses

(*c*) shunt field losses

(*ii*) **Variable losses.** Those losses in a d.c. generator which vary with load are called *variable losses*. The variable losses in a d.c. generator are:

(*a*) Copper loss in armature winding $(I_a^2 R_a)$

(*b*) Copper loss in series field winding $(I_{se}^2 R_{se})$

$$\text{Total losses} = \text{Constant losses} + \text{Variable losses}$$

10.13. POWER STAGES

The various power stages in a d.c. generator are represented diagrammatically in Fig. 10.24.

$$A - B = \text{Iron and friction losses}$$
$$B - C = \text{Copper losses}$$

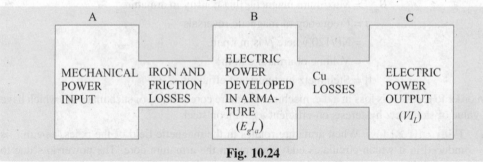

Fig. 10.24

(*i*) **Mechanical efficiency**

$$\eta_m = \frac{B}{A} = \frac{E_g I_a}{\text{Mechanical power input}}$$

(*ii*) **Electrical efficiency**

$$\eta_e = \frac{C}{B} = \frac{VI_L}{E_g I_a}$$

(*iii*) **Commercial or overall efficiency**

$$\eta_c = \frac{C}{A} = \frac{VI_L}{\text{Mechanical power input}}$$

Clearly, $\eta_c = \eta_m \times \eta_e$

Unless otherwise stated, commercial efficiency is always understood.

Now, commercial efficiency, $\eta_c = \dfrac{C}{A} = \dfrac{\text{output}}{\text{input}} = \dfrac{\text{input} - \text{losses}}{\text{input}}$

Eddy current measurement

10.14. CONDITION FOR MAXIMUM EFFICIENCY

The efficiency of a d.c. generator is not constant but varies with load. Consider a shunt generator delivering a load current I_L at a terminal voltage V.

$$\text{Generator output} = VI_L$$

$$\text{Generator input} = \text{Output} + \text{Losses}$$

$$= VI_L + \text{Variable losses} + \text{Constant losses}$$

$$= VI_L + I_a^2 R_a + W_C$$

$$= VI_L + (I_L + I_{sh})^2 R_a + W_C \qquad [\because I_a = I_L + I_{sh}]$$

The shunt field current I_{sh} is generally small as compared to I_L and, therefore, can be neglected.

$\therefore$ $$\text{Generator input} = VI_L + I_L^2 R_a + W_C$$

$\therefore$ $$\eta = \frac{\text{output}}{\text{input}} = \frac{VI_L}{VI_L + I_L^2 R_a + W_C}$$

$$= \frac{1}{1 + \left(\dfrac{I_L R_a}{V} + \dfrac{W_C}{VI_L}\right)} \qquad \qquad ...(i)$$

The efficiency will be maximum when the denominator of eq. (i) is minimum *i.e.*

$$\frac{d}{dI_L}\left(\frac{I_L R_a}{V} + \frac{W_C}{VI_L}\right) = 0$$

or $$\frac{R_a}{V} - \frac{W_C}{VI_L^2} = 0$$

or $$\frac{R_a}{V} = \frac{W_C}{VI_L^2}$$

or $$I_L^2 R_a = W_C$$

i.e. **Variable loss = Constant loss** $\qquad \qquad (\because I_L \approx I_a)$

The load current corresponding to maximum efficiency is given by;

$$I_L = \sqrt{\frac{W_C}{R_a}}$$

Hence, the efficiency of a d.c. generator will be maximum when the load current is such that variable loss is equal to the constant loss.

Example 10.12. *A shunt generator supplies 96A at a terminal voltage of 200 volts. The armature and shunt field resistances are 0.1 Ω and 50 Ω respectively. The iron and frictional losses are 2500 W. Find (i) e.m.f. generated (ii) copper losses (iii) commercial efficiency.*

Solution. Fig. 10.25 shows the connections of shunt generator.

(*i*) $I_{sh} = 200/50 = 4A$

$\quad\quad I_a = I_L + I_{sh} = 96 + 4 = 100$ A

$\quad\quad E_g = V + I_a R_a = 200 + 100 \times 0.1 =$ **210 V**

(*ii*) Armature Cu loss

$\quad\quad = I_a^2 R_a = (100)^2 \times 0.1 = 1000$ W

Shunt Cu loss $\quad = I_{sh}^2 R_{sh} = (4)^2 \times 50 = 800$ W

Total Cu loss $\quad = 1000 + 800 =$ **1800 W**

(*iii*) Total losses $\quad =$ Stray losses + Cu losses

$\quad\quad = 2500 + 1800 = 4300$ W

Output power $\quad = 96 \times 200 = 19200$ W

Input power $\quad = 19200 + 4300 = 23500$ W

$\therefore \quad\quad \eta = \dfrac{19200}{23500} \times 100 =$ **81.7%**

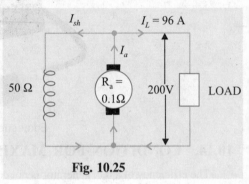

Fig. 10.25

Example 10.13. *The shunt generator delivers full load current of 200A at 240V. The shunt field resistance is 60Ω and full-load efficiency is 90%. The stray losses are 800W. Find (i) armature resistance (ii) current at which maximum efficiency occurs.*

Solution

(*i*) Generator output $\quad = 240 \times 200 = 48000$ W

Generator input $\quad = 48000/0.9 = 53333$ W

Total losses $\quad = 53333 - 48000 = 5333$ W

Shunt field current, $I_{sh}\quad = 240/60 = 4$ A

Armature current, $\quad I_a = 200 + 4 = 204$ A

Shunt Cu loss $\quad = I_{sh}^2 R_{sh} = (4)^2 \times 60 = 960$ W

Constant losses $\quad =$ Stray losses + Shunt Cu loss

$\quad\quad =$ 800 + 960 = 1760 W

$\therefore \quad$ Armature Cu loss = Total losses – Constant losses

$\quad\quad = 5333 - 1760 = 3573$ W

i.e. $\quad\quad I_a^2 R_a = 3573$

or $\quad\quad R_a = 3573 / I_a^2 = 3573/(204)^2 =$ **0.0858 Ω**

(*ii*) For maximum efficiency, the condition is:

$\quad\quad$ Variable losses = Constant losses

or $\quad\quad *I_L^2 R_a = 1760$

$\therefore \quad\quad I_L = \sqrt{\dfrac{1760}{0.0858}} =$ **143.22 A**

- -

* Variable losses in armature are $I_a^2 R_a$. In the derivation of expression for maximum efficiency, I_{sh} was neglected so that $I_a = I_L$.

Example 10.14. *A 10 kW d.c. shunt generator has the following losses at full load:*

Mechanical losses = 290W ; Iron losses = 420 W

Shunt Cu loss = 120 W ; Armature Cu loss = 595 W

Calculate the efficiency at (i) no load (ii) 25% of full-load.

Solution.

(*i*) **At no-load**

The stray losses remain constant at no load or at any other load.

Stray losses = Mechanical losses + Iron losses = 290 + 420 = 710 W

Total losses at no load = 710 + Shunt Cu loss = 710 + 120 = 830 W

The efficiency at no load is **zero** because there is no output.

(*ii*) **At 25% of Full-load**

Constant losses	= 830 W ...*same as before*
Armature Cu loss	= *$(1/4)^2$ of F.L. value = $(1/4)^2 \times 595 = 37$ W
Total losses	= 830 + 37 = 867 W
Output	= $(1/4) \times 10$kW = 2.5 kW = 2500 W
Input	= 2500 + 867 = 3367 W

$$\therefore \quad \eta = \frac{2500}{3367} \times 100 = \mathbf{74\%}$$

Example 10.15. *A 75 kW shunt generator is operated at 230V. The stray losses are 1810W and shunt field circuit draws 5.35A. The armature circuit has a resistance of 0.035 Ω and brush drop is 2.2V. Calculate (i) total losses (ii) input of prime mover (iii) efficiency at rated load.*

Solution.

(*i*) Load current, $I_L = 75 \times 10^3/230 = 326.1$ A

Armature current, $I_a = I_L + I_{sh} = 326.1 + 5.35 = 331.5$ A

Armature Cu loss $= I_a^2 R_a = (331.5)^2 \times 0.035 = 3846$ W

Shunt Cu loss $= VI_{sh} = 230 \times 5.35 = 1230$ W

Brush power loss   = Brush drop $\times I_a = 2.2 \times 331.5 = 729$ W

$\therefore$ Total losses = 1810 + 3846 + 1230 + 729 = **7615 W**

(*ii*) Output power   = 75 kW = 75000W

Input of prime mover   = 75000 + 7615 = **82615 W**

(*iii*) $$\eta = \frac{75000}{82615} \times 100 = \mathbf{90.8\%}$$

TUTORIAL PROBLEMS

1. A 4 pole shunt generator with wave wound armature has 41 slots, each having 12 conductors. The armature resistance is 0.05 Ω and shunt field resistance is 200 Ω.The flux per pole is 25 mWb. If a load resistance of 10 Ω is connected across the armature terminals, calculate the voltage across the load when generator is driven at 1000 r.p.m.   **[389.5V]**

2. A long shunt compound generator has full load output of 100 kW at 250 volts. The armature, series and shunt windings have resistances of 0.05 Ω, 0.03Ω and 55Ω respectively. Find the armature current and generated e.m.f.   **[404.5A, 282.3V]**

---

*   When the generator is loaded to 25% of its normal rating, armature current is 25% (or 1/4) of its full load value. Since Cu loss varies as square of current, we have $(1/4)^2$ term here.

3. A shunt generator supplies 75A at 200V through feeders of resistance 0.08 Ω. The armature and shunt field windings have resistances of 0.04 Ω and 80Ω respectively. Find the terminal voltage and generated e.m.f. **[206V, 209.1V]**

4. A 4-pole short shunt compound generator has armature, shunt field and series field resistances of 0.4 Ω, 160 Ω and 0.2 Ω respectively. The armature is lap connected with 440 conductors and is driven at 600 r.p.m. Calculate the magnetic flux per pole when the machine is delivering 120A at 400V. **[0.108Wb]**

5. The resistance of field circuit of a shunt-excited d.c. generator is 200Ω. When the output of the generator is 100 kW, the terminal voltage is 500V and the generated e.m.f. 525V. Calculated (*i*) the armature resistance (*ii*) the value of generated e.m.f. when the output is 60kW, if the terminal voltage is then 520V. **[(*i*) 0.123 Ω (*ii*) 534.5V]**

10.15. ARMATURE REACTION

So far we have assumed that the only magnetic flux acting in a d.c. machine is that due to the main poles called *main flux*. However, current flowing through armature conductors also creates a magnetic flux (called *armature flux*) that distorts and weakens the magnetic flux coming from the poles. This distortion and field weakening takes place in both generators and motors. The action of armature flux on the main flux is knows as *armature reaction.*

The phenomenon of armature reaction in a d.c. generator is shown in Fig. 10.26. Only one pole is shown for clarity. When the generator is on no-load, a small current flowing in the armature does not appreciably affect the main flux ϕ_1 coming from the pole [See Fig. 10.26 (*i*)]. When the generator is loaded, the current flowing through armature conductors sets up flux ϕ_2. Fig. 10.26. (*ii*) shows flux due to armature current alone. By superimposing ϕ_1 and ϕ_2, we obtain the resulting flux ϕ_3 as shown in Fig. 10.26 (*iii*).

Referring to Fig. 10.26 (*iii*), it is clear that magnetic flux density at the trailing pole tip (point *B*) is increased while at the leading pole tip (point *A*), it is decreased. This unequal field distribution produces the following two effects:

(*i*) The main flux is distorted.

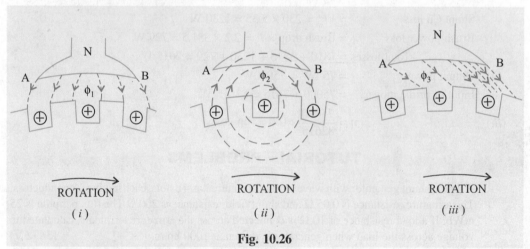

Fig. 10.26

(*ii*) Due to higher flux density at pole tip *B*, saturation sets in. Consequently, the increase in flux at pole tip *B* is less than the decrease in flux under pole tip *A*. Flux ϕ_3 at full load is, therefore, less than flux ϕ_1 at no load.

10.16. PROBLEMS OF ARMATURE REACTION

Armature reaction in a d.c. machine distorts and weakens the main flux. This invites the following two problems:

(*i*) The armature reaction may decrease the main flux by 10%. This causes the generated e.m.f. in a generator to fall with the increase in load current.

(*ii*) To ensure good commutation, the brushes must be placed in the neutral zone. However, due to distortion of flux, neutral zone is shifted. If the load varies frequently, the shifting of brush position is not practicable.

10.17. CORRECTING ARMATURE REACTION EFFECT

There are four main ways of overcoming the armature reaction problem:

(*i*) Rotate the brush hanger mechanism to find the correct neutral zone position. Such a method can be applied only for fixed load current.

(*ii*) Shape or otherwise modify the ends of the field pole shoes so that high flux cannot exist on the ends because of the high reluctance path.

(*iii*) To counter the effect of armature reaction, we usually place a set of *interpoles* or *commutating poles* mid-way between the main poles of a d.c. machine as shown in Fig. 10.27. The polarity of the commutating pole must be that of the main pole just ahead of it (*i.e.* in the direction of rotation) for a generator (See Fig. 10.27) and just behind for a motor.

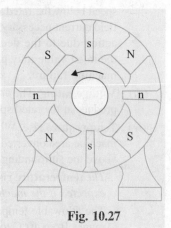

Fig. 10.27

The interpoles set up flux equal and opposite to the armature flux. The commutating-pole windings are connected in series with the armature so that respective fluxes rise and fall together as the load current changes. By cancelling the armature effect in this way, we no longer have to shift the brushes. Commutating poles are now invariably fitted to all d.c. machines except those of the smallest sizes or the lowest speeds.

(*iv*) Some large motors perform a series of rapid heavy-duty operations (*e.g.* motors in steel mills, rolling mills *etc.*). They accelerate, decelerate, stop, reverse, all in a matter of seconds. The corresponding armature current increases, decreases, reverses in stepwise fashion, producing very sudden changes in armature reaction. For such motors, commutating poles do not adequately neutralise the armature flux.

To eliminate this problem, additional *compensating windings* are used. A compensating winding is an auxiliary winding embedded in slots in the pole faces of the main poles. The compensating winding is connected in series with the armature in a manner so that direction of current through the compensating conductors in any one pole face will be opposite to the direction of current through the adjacent armature conductors as shown in Fig. 10.28. The compensating windings produce a flux equal and opposite to the armature flux and thus completely neutralise the armature reaction. The addition of a compensating winding considerably increases the cost of the machine and is justified only for machines intended for unusually severe service.

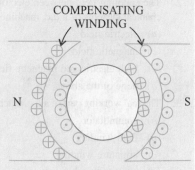

Fig. 10.28

10.18. D.C. GENERATOR RATINGS

The nameplate of a d.c. generator generally contains the following ratings:

(i) Power rating (ii) Speed rating (iii) Voltage rating (iv) Temperature rise

(i) **Power rating.** The power rating of a d.c. generator is the rated full-load output of the generator when the terminal voltage is that specified on the nameplate. It is given in kilowatts (kW). The current rating is generally not included on the nameplate but can be calculated from the power and voltage ratings.

(ii) **Speed rating.** The speed rating of a d.c. generator is the speed at which the machine should be operated in order to deliver rated power at rated voltage without exceeding the specified temperature rise. It is given in revolutions per minute (r.p.m.). If the machine operates at a speed below the rated value, it may result in overheating, not only because of the increased field current necessary to produce rated voltage but also because of the decrease in fanning action due to the decrease in speed. Operation of the machine at speeds higher than the rated value may produce strains in the rotating armature that ultimately may cause machine failure.

(iii) **Voltage rating.** The voltage rating of a d.c. generator is the voltage that the machine should produce at the rated speed. It is given in volts.

(iv) **Temperature rise.** When a d.c. generator is operating, the various losses that occur in the machine are converted into heat. The result is that the temperature of the machine will rise above the surrounding temperature (ambient temperature).

The temperature rise specified on the nameplate of a d.c. generator is usually that to be expected if the machine is operated continuously at rated conditions.

The allowable temperature rise specified on the nameplate of a d.c. generator generally ranges from 40°C to 50°C. The life of insulation of the winding and that of the machine depends on the temperature at which it operates. The high temperatures gradually oxidise and carbonise the insulation materials which reduces their insulation ability. This reduces the life of the machine. It is often said that "the life of a machine is only as good as its insulation".

MULTIPLE-CHOICE QUESTIONS

1. The yoke of a d.c. machine is made of ....
   - (a) silicon steel
   - (b) soft iron
   - (c) aluminium
   - (d) cast steel

2. The coupling field between electrical and mechanical systems of a d.c. machine is.....
   - (a) electric field
   - (b) magnetic field
   - (c) both electric and magnetic fields
   - (d) none of the above

3. The real working part of a d.c. machine is the....
   - (a) commutator
   - (b) field winding
   - (c) armature winding
   - (d) none of the above

4. ....d.c. machines are most common.
   - (a) 2-pole
   - (b) 4-pole
   - (c) 6-pole
   - (d) 8-pole

5. A 4-pole d.c. machine has............magnetic circuits.
   - (a) 2
   - (b) 8
   - (c) 4
   - (d) none of the above

6. The greatest eddy current loss occurs in the .....of a d.c. machine.
   - (a) field poles
   - (b) yoke
   - (c) commutating poles
   - (d) armature

7. The commutator pitch for a simplex lap winding is equal to.......
   - (a) number of poles of the machine
   - (b) pole pairs
   - (c) 1
   - (d) none of the above

8. In a d.c. machine, the number of commutator segments is equal to...........
   (a) number of conductors
   (b) twice the number of poles
   (c) number of coils
   (d) none of the above

9. The nature of armature winding of a d.c. machine is decided by ......
   (a) front pitch
   (b) commutator pitch
   (c) back pitch
   (d) none of the above

10. An 8-pole duplex lap winding will have ....parallel paths.
    (a) 8   (b) 4
    (c) 32   (d) 16

11. A triplex wave winding will have.......parallel paths.
    (a) 6
    (b) 2
    (c) 4
    (d) none of the above

12. A 6-pole lap-wound generator has 300 conductors; the e.m.f. induced per conductor being 5 V. The generated voltage of the generator is ....
    (a) 60 V
    (b) 1500 V
    (c) 360 V
    (d) 250 V

13. For the same rating, a d.c. machine has....... an a.c. machine.
    (a) the same weight as
    (b) more weight than
    (c) less weight than
    (d) none of the above

14. The field winding of a d.c. shunt machine usually carries .... of the rated current of the machine.
    (a) 2 % to 5 %
    (b) 15 % to 20 %
    (c) more than 20%
    (d) less than 0.5%

15. A shunt generator delivers 195 A at a terminal p.d. of 250 V. The armature resistance and shunt field resistance are 0.02Ω and 50Ω respectively. What is the value of generated e.m.f.?
    (a) 246 V
    (b) 270 V
    (c) 254 V
    (d) 282 V

16. In the above question, what is the value of copper losses?
    (a) 825 W   (b) 2050 W
    (c) 1025 W   (d) 960 W

17. If W_c is the constant loss and R_a is the armature resistance of a d.c. generator, then load current I_L corresponding to maximum efficiency is
    (a) $I_L = \sqrt{\dfrac{R_a}{W_c}}$ (b) $I_L = \dfrac{W_c}{\sqrt{R_a}}$
    (c) $I_L = \dfrac{R_a}{\sqrt{W_c}}$ (d) $I_L = \sqrt{\dfrac{W_c}{R_a}}$

18. Stray losses consist of
    (a) magnetic and mechanical losses
    (b) magnetic and copper losses
    (c) mechanical and copper losses
    (d) none of the above

19. A 30 kW, 300 V d.c. shunt generator has armature and field resistances of 0.05 Ω and 100 Ω respectively. What is the generated e.m.f.?
    (a) 295.25 V
    (b) 311.25 V
    (c) 305.15 V
    (d) none of the above

20. In the above question, what is the total power developed when generator delives full output power?
    (a) 16.34 kW   (b) 20.62 kW
    (c) 12.46 kW   (d) 31.43 kW

21. In Fig. 10.29, the electrical efficiency is

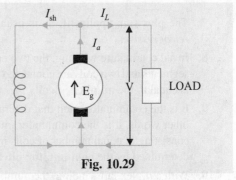

Fig. 10.29

    (a) $\dfrac{VI_a}{E_g I_a}$
    (b) $\dfrac{V\,I_L}{E_g I_a}$
    (c) $\dfrac{E_g I_a}{V\,I_a}$
    (d) none of the above

22. A shunt generator delivers 195 A at a terminal voltage of 250 V. The armature resistance and shunt field resistance are 0.02 Ω and 50 Ω respectively. The iron and friction losses equal 950 W. What are the stray losses?

    (a) 950 W   (b) 3000 W

    (c) 1250 W   (d) 1750 W

23. In Q. 22, what is the output of the prime mover?

    (a) 37.75 kW   (b) 64.25 kW

    (c) 51.75 kW   (d) 48.64 kW

24. In question 22, what is the electrical power produced in the armature?

    (a) 50800 W

    (b) 49600 W

    (c) 47520 W

    (d) none of the above

25. In question 22, what is the mechanical efficiency of the generator?

    (a) 89.4%   (b) 92.6%

    (c) 96.2%   (d) 98.2%

Answers to Multiple-Choice Questions

1. (d)	2. (b)	3. (c)	4. (b)	5. (c)
6. (d)	7. (c)	8. (c)	9. (b)	10. (d)
11. (a)	12. (d)	13. (b)	14. (a)	15. (c)
16. (b)	17. (d)	18. (a)	19. (c)	20. (d)
21. (b)	22. (a)	23. (c)	24. (a)	25. (d)

Hints to Selected Multiple-Choice Questions

5. In a d.c. machine, there are as many magnetic circuits as there are poles. Thus, a 4-pole d.c. machine will have **4 magnetic circuits**. However, m.m.f. acting in each circuit is due to the ampere-turns of a pair of poles.

6. Since every part of the armature sees cyclic reversals in magnetic flux direction, it is potentially subjected to more severe eddy current-losses than the field pole shoes. Hence **armature** is invariably laminated to reduce the eddy current loss.

7. The commutator pitch for a simplex lap winding is given by;

$$Y_c = \pm 1$$

The plus sign applies if, as is usual, the winding is *progressive*; the minus sign, if it is *retrogressive*.

8. In a d.c. armature winding, the two ends of a coil are connected to two different commutator segments and two coils are connected to each segment so that number of commutator segments is equal to the **number of coils**.

9. It is the commutator pitch that determines the grouping of the coils in series and parallel. In other words, it is the commutator pitch that determines as to how many parallel paths, each consisting of equal number of coils in series, will be formed. Hence, the nature of winding is determined by the **commutator pitch**.

10. With a n-plex lap winding, the number of parallel paths is Pn where

    P = number of poles

    n = 2, 3 etc and stand for duplex, triplex etc.

    Hence 8-pole duplex lap winding will have $8 \times 2 = $ **16 parallel paths.**

11. With an n-plex wave winding, the number of parallel paths is $2n$ where n = 2, 3 etc. and stands for duplex, triplex *etc.*

    Hence a triplex wave winding will have $2 \times 3 = $ **6 parallel paths.**

12. Number of conductors per parallel path = 300/6 = 50. Hence the generator voltage = 50 × 5 = **250 V.**

15. $I_{sh} = 250/50 = 5$ A $\qquad \therefore \qquad I_a = I_{sh} + I_L = 5 + 195 = 200$ A

$$\text{Armature drop} = I_a R_a = 200 \times 0.02 = 4 \text{ V}$$

$\therefore \qquad$ Generated e.m.f. $= V + I_a R_a = 250 + 4 = \textbf{254 V}$

16. $\qquad$ Armature Cu loss $= I_a^2 R_a = (200)^2 \times 0.02 = 800$ W

$\qquad$ Shunt Cu loss $= V I_{sh} = 250 \times 5 = 1250$ W

$\qquad$ Total Cu loss $= 1250 + 800 = \textbf{2050 W}$

17. The efficiency of a d.c. generator is maximum when

Variable loss = constant loss

or $\qquad\qquad\qquad I_L^2 R_a = W_c \quad \text{or} \quad I_L = \sqrt{\dfrac{W_c}{R_a}}$

18. Usually **magnetic and mechanical losses** are collectively called stray losses.

19. $I_L = \dfrac{30 \times 10^3}{300} = 100$ A ; $I_{sh} = \dfrac{V}{R_{sh}} = \dfrac{300}{100} = 3$A

$\therefore \qquad\qquad\qquad I_a = I_L + I_{sh} = 100 + 3 = 103$ A

Generated e.m.f., $\qquad E_g = V + I_a R_a = 300 + 103 \times 0.05 = 300 + 5.15 = \textbf{305.15 V}$

20. Power developed in armature $= E_g I_a = \dfrac{305.15 \times 103}{1000} = \textbf{31.43kW}$

21. Electrical efficiency, $\qquad \eta_e = \dfrac{\text{Power in load}}{\text{Total power generated}} = \dfrac{V I_L}{E_g I_a}$.

23. Total losses = Stray losses + Total Cu loss = 950 + 2050 = 3000 W

Generator output $\qquad\qquad = 250 \times 195 = 48750$ W

$\therefore \qquad$ Prime mover's output $= 3000 + 48750 = 51750$ W $= \textbf{51.75 kW}$

24. Electrical power developed in armature

$\qquad\qquad\qquad\qquad$ = Output of prime mover – Stray losses

$\qquad\qquad\qquad\qquad = 51750 - 950 = \textbf{50800 W}$

25. Mechanical efficiency, $\quad \eta_m = \dfrac{\text{Power produced in armature}}{\text{Power produced in armature + Stray losses}} \times 100$

$\qquad\qquad\qquad\qquad = \dfrac{50800}{50800 + 950} \times 100 = \textbf{98.2\%}$

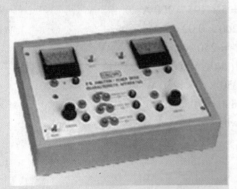

D.C. Generator Characteristics

INTRODUCTION

The speed of a d.c. machine operated as a generator is fixed by the prime mover. For general-purpose operation, the prime mover is equipped with a speed governor so that the speed of the generator is practically constant. Under such condition, the generator performance deals primarily with the relation among excitation, terminal voltage and load. These relations can be best exhibited graphically by means of curves known as generator characteristics. These characteristics show at a glance the behaviour of the generator under different load conditions.

11.1. D.C. GENERATOR CHARACTERISTICS

The following are the three most important characteristics of a d.c. generator :

1. Open Circuit Characteristic (O.C.C.)

This curve shows the relation between the generated e.m.f. at no-load (E_0) and the field current (I_f) at constant speed. It is also known as magnetic characteristic or no-load saturation curve. Its shape is practically the same for all generators whether separately or self-excited.

2. Internal or Total Characteristic (E/I_a)

This curve shows the relation between the generated e.m.f. on load (E) and the armature current (I_a). The e.m.f. E will be less than E_0 due to the effects of armature reaction. Therefore, this curve will lie below the open circuit characteristic.

3. External Characteristic (V/I_L)

This curve shows the relation between the terminal voltage (V) and load current (I_L). The terminal voltage V will be less than E due to voltage drop in the armature circuit. Therefore, this curve will lie below the internal characteristic.

11.2. OPEN CIRCUIT CHARACTERISTIC

The O.C.C. for a d.c. generator is determined as follows. The field winding of the d.c. generator (series or shunt) is disconnected from the machine and is separately excited from an external d.c. source as shown in Fig. 11.1 (*ii*). The generator is run at fixed speed (*i.e.*, normal speed). The field current (I_f) is increased from zero in steps and the corresponding values of generated e.m.f. (E_0) read off on a voltmeter connected across the armature terminals. On plotting the relation between E_0 and I_f, we get the open circuit characteristic as shown in Fig. 11.1 (*i*).

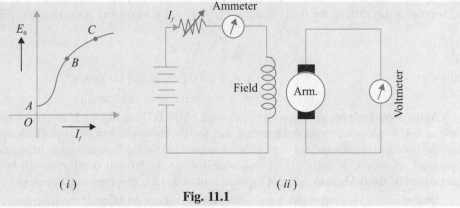

Fig. 11.1

The following points may be noted from O.C.C. :

- (*i*) When the field current is zero, there is some generated e.m.f. *OA*. This is due to the residual magnetism in the field poles.
- (*ii*) Over a fairly wide range of field current (upto point *B* in the curve), the curve is linear. It is because in this range, *reluctance of iron is negligible as compared with that of air gap. The air gap reluctance is constant and hence has linear relationship.
- (*iii*) After point *B* on the curve, the reluctance of iron also comes into picture. It is because at higher flux densities, μ_r for iron decreases and reluctance of iron is no longer negligible. Consequently, the curve deviates from linear relationship.
- (*iv*) After point *C* on the curve, the magnetic saturation of poles begins and E_0 tends to level off.

11.3. GENERATOR BUILD-UP

Let us see how voltage builds up in a self excited d.c. generator. Consider a shunt generator. If the generator is run at a constant speed, some e.m.f. will be generated due to residual magnetism in the main poles. This small e.m.f. circulates a field current which in turn produces additional flux to reinforce the original residual flux (provided field winding connections are correct). This process continues and the generator builds up the normal generated voltage following the O.C.C. shown in Fig. 11.2 (*i*).

* At low flux density, μ_r for iron is high and hence iron path offers negligible reluctance. Remember μ_r for iron depends upon flux density. As flux density increases, μ_r decreases.

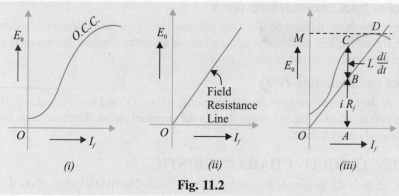

Fig. 11.2

The field resistance R_f can be represented by a straight line passing through the origin as shown in Fig. 11.2 (*ii*). The two curves can be shown on the same diagram as they have the same ordinates [See Fig. 11.2 (*iii*)].

Since the field circuit is inductive, there is a delay in the increase in current upon closing the field circuit switch. The rate at which the current increases depends upon the voltage available for increasing it. Suppose at any instant, the field current is i (= OA) and is increasing at the rate di/dt. Then,

$$E_0 = i\,R_f + L\frac{di}{dt}$$

where

R_f = total field circuit resistance

L = inductance of field circuit

At the considered instant, the total e.m.f. available is AC [See Fig. 11.2 (*iii*)]. An amount AB of the e.m.f. AC is absorbed by the voltage drop $i\,R_f$ and the remainder part BC is available to overcome $L\,di/dt$. Since this surplus voltage is available, it is possible for the field current to increase above the value OA. However, at point D, the available voltage is OM and is all absorbed by iR_f drop. Consequently, the field current cannot increase further and the generator build up stops.

We arrive at a very important conclusion that the voltage build up of the generator is given by the point of intersection of O.C.C. and field resistance line. Thus in Fig. 11.2 (*iii*), D is point of intersection of the two curves. Hence, the generator will build up a voltage OM.

Note : The voltage build up in a series generator is exactly like that of a shunt generator. Here, voltage build up will occur if the whole series circuit is closed.

11.4. CRITICAL FIELD RESISTANCE FOR A SHUNT GENERATOR

We have seen above that voltage build up in a shunt generator depends upon field circuit resistance. If the field circuit resistance is R_1 (line OA), then generator will build up a voltage OM as shown in *Fig. 11.3. If the field circuit resistance is **increased to R_2 (line OB), the generator will build up a voltage OL, slightly less than OM. As the field circuit resistance is increased, the slope of resistance line also increases. When the field resistance line becomes tangent (line OC) to O.C.C., the generator would *just* excite. If the field circuit resistance is

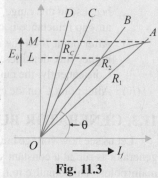

Fig. 11.3

increased beyond this point (say line OD), the generator will †fail to excite. The field circuit resistance

* The effect of residual magnetism has been neglected in drawing O.C.C. so that it starts from the origin.
** Resistance = slope of line = tan θ
  Here θ is the angle which the lines makes with *x*-axis. As θ increases, tan θ and hence resistance increases.
† Since now all the available e.m.f. is immediately absorbed by $i\,R_f$ drop.

represented by line *OC* (tangent to O.C.C.) is called *critical field resistance* R_C for the shunt generator. It may be defined as under :

The maximum field circuit resistance (for a given speed) with which the shunt generator would just excite is known as its **critical field resistance.**

It should be noted that shunt generator will build up voltage only if field circuit resistance is less than critical field resistance.

11.5. CRITICAL RESISTANCE FOR A SERIES GENERATOR

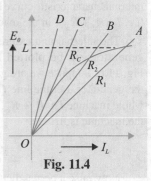

Fig. 11.4

Fig. 11.4 shows the voltage build up in a series generator. Here R_1, R_2 etc. represent the total circuit resistance (load resistance and field winding resistance). If the total circuit resistance is R_1, then series generator will build up a voltage *OL*. The line *OC* is tangent to O.C.C. and represents the critical resistance R_C for a series generator. If the total resistance of the circuit is more than R_C, (say line *OD*), the generator will fail to build up voltage. Note that Fig. 11.4 is similar to Fig. 11.3 with the following differences :

(*i*) In Fig. 11.3, R_1, R_2 etc. represent the total field circuit resistance. However, R_1, R_2 etc. in Fig. 11.4 represent the total circuit resistance (load resistance and series field winding resistance etc.).

(*ii*) In Fig. 11.3, field current alone is represented along *X*-axis. However, in Fig. 11.4, load current I_L is represented along *X*-axis. Note that in a series generator, field current = load current I_L.

11.6. CHARACTERISTICS OF SERIES GENERATOR

Fig. 11.5(*i*) shows the connections of a series wound generator. Since there is only one current (that which flows through the whole machine), the load current is the same as the exciting current.

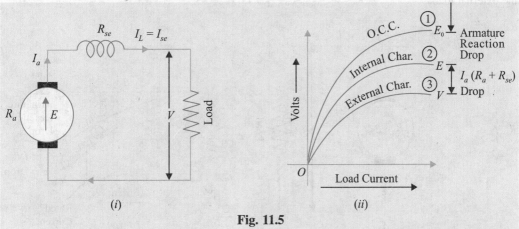

Fig. 11.5

(*i*) **O.C.C.** Curve 1 shows the open circuit characteristic (O.C.C.) of a series generator. It can be obtained experimentally by disconnecting the field winding from the machine and exciting it from a separate d.c. source as discussed in Art. 11.2.

(*ii*) **Internal characteristic.** Curve 2 shows the total or internal characteristic of a series generator. It gives the relation between the generated e.m.f. *E* on load and *armature current. Due to armature reaction, the flux in the machine will be less than the flux at no load. Hence, e.m.f.

---

* In case of series generator, $I_a = I_{se} = I_L$.

E generated under load conditions will be less than the e.m.f. E_0 generated under no load conditions. Consequently, internal characteristic curve lies below the O.C.C. curve; the difference between them representing the effect of armature reaction [See Fig. 11.5 (*ii*)].

(*iii*) **External characteristic.** Curve 3 shows the external characteristic of a series generator. It gives the relation between terminal voltage V and load current I_L.

$$V = E - I_a (R_a + R_{se})$$

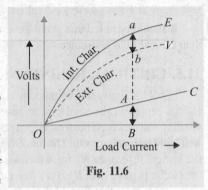

Therefore, external characteristic curve will lie below internal characteristic curve by an amount equal to ohmic drop [*i.e.* $I_a (R_a + R_{se})$] in the machine as shown in Fig. 11.5 (*ii*).

The internal and external characteristics of a d.c. series generator can be plotted from one another as shown in Fig. 11.6. Suppose we are given the internal characteristic of the generator. Let the line OC represent the resistance of the whole machine *i.e.* $R_a + R_{se}$. If the load current is OB, drop in the machine is AB *i.e.*

Fig. 11.6

$$AB = \text{Ohmic drop in the machine}$$
$$= OB (R_a + R_{se})$$

Now raise a perpendicular from point B and mark a point b on this line such that $ab = AB$. Then point b will lie on the external characteristic of the generator. Following similar procedure, other points of external characteristic can be located. It is easy to see that we can also plot internal characteristic from the external characteristic.

11.7. CHARACTERISTICS OF A SHUNT GENERATOR

Fig. 11.7. (*i*) shows the connections of a shunt wound generator. The armature current I_a splits up into two parts; a small fraction I_{sh} flowing through shunt field winding while the major part I_L goes to the external load.

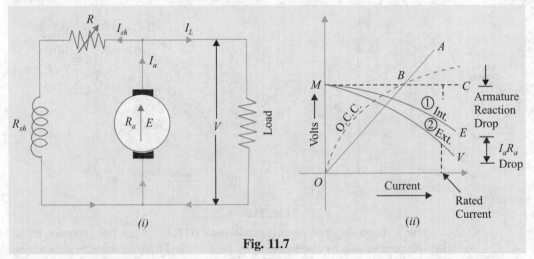

Fig. 11.7

(*i*) **O.C.C.** The O.C.C. of a shunt generator is similar in shape to that of a series generator as shown in Fig. 11.7 (*ii*). The line OA represents the shunt field circuit resistance. When the generator is run at normal speed, it will build up a voltage OM. At no-load, the terminal voltage of the generator will be constant (= OM) represented by the horizontal dotted line MC.

(*ii*) **Internal characteristic.** When the generator is loaded, flux per pole is reduced due to armature reaction. Therefore, e.m.f. E generated on load is less than the e.m.f. generated at no load. As a result, the internal characteristic * (E/I_a) drops down slightly as shown in Fig. 11.7 (*ii*).

(*iii*) **External characteristic.** Curve 2 shows the external characteristic of a shunt generator. It gives the relation between terminal voltage V and load current I_L.

$$V = E - I_a R_a$$
$$= E - (I_L + I_{sh})\, R_a$$

Therefore, external characteristic curve will lie below the internal characteristic curve by an amount equal to drop in the armature circuit [*i.e.*, $(I_L + I_{sh})\, R_a$] as shown in Fig. 11.7 (*ii*).

Note : It may be seen from the external characteristic that change in terminal voltage from no-load to full load is small. The terminal voltage can always be maintained constant by adjusting the field rheostat R automatically.

11.8. CRITICAL EXTERNAL RESISTANCE FOR SHUNT GENERATOR

If the load resistance across the terminals of a shunt generator is decreased, then load current increases. However, there is a limit to the increase in load current with the decrease of load resistance. Any decrease of load resistance beyond this point, instead of increasing the current, ultimately results in **reduced current. Consequently, the external characteristic turns back (dotted curve) as shown in Fig. 11.8. The tangent *OA* to the curve represents the minimum external resistance required to excite the shunt generator on load and is called *critical external resistance*. If the resistance of the external circuit is less than the critical external resistance (represented by tangent *OA* in Fig. 11.8), the machine will refuse to excite or will de-excite if already running. This means that external resistance is so low as virtually to short circuit the machine and so doing away with its excitation.

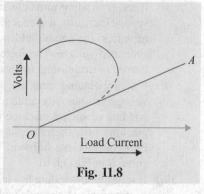

Fig. 11.8

Note : There are two critical resistances for a shunt generator viz. (*i*) critical field resistance (*ii*) critical external resistance.

For the shunt generator to build up voltage, the former should not be exceeded and the latter must not be gone below.

11.9. COMPOUND GENERATOR CHARACTERISTICS

In a compound generator, both series and shunt excitations are combined as shown in Fig. 11.9. The shunt winding can be connected either across the armature only (*short-shunt connection S*) or across armature plus series field (*long-shunt connection G*). The compound generator can be ***cumulatively compounded or differentially compounded generator. The latter is rarely used in practice. Therefore, we shall discuss the characteristics of cumulatively-compounded generator. It may be noted that external characteristics of long and short shunt compound generators are almost identical.

---

* $I_a = I_L + I_{sh}$. As I_{sh} is small, therefore, $I_a \simeq I_L$.

**   Actually on reducing load resistance, the current momentarily increases but this results in the reduction of terminal voltage due to (*i*) armature reaction effect and (*ii*) $I_a R_a$ drop. This decreases the field current and hence the machine flux. By the time steady conditions are obtained, the load current is actually less than before.

***   (*i*) If the series and shunt excitation help each other, it is called cumulatively-compounded generator.

      (*ii*) If shunt and series excitation oppose each other, it is called differentially-compounded generator.

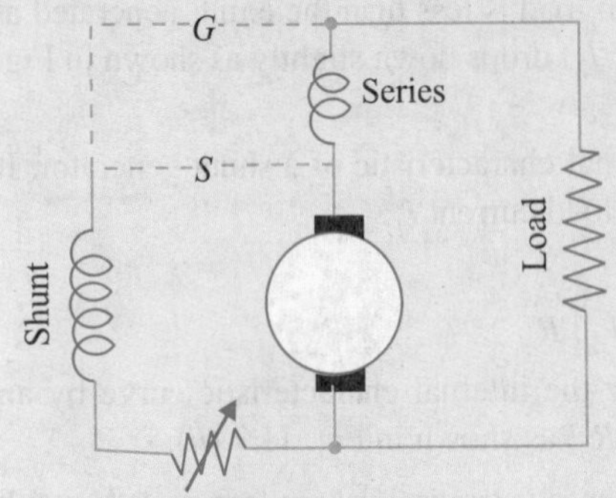

Fig. 11.9 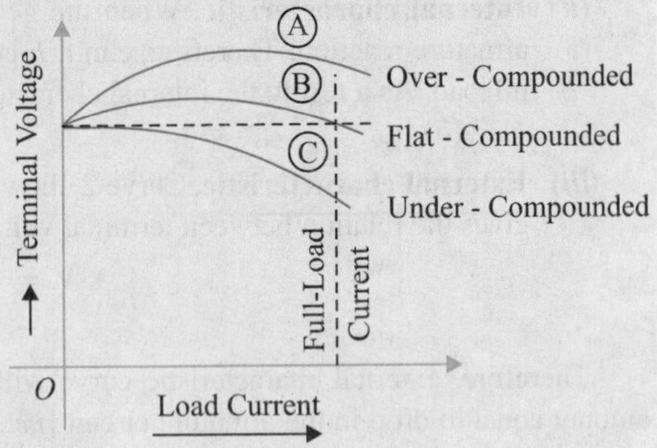   **Fig. 11.10**

External characteristic. Fig. 11.10 shows the external characteristics of a cumulatively compounded generator. The series excitation aids the shunt excitation. The degree of compounding depends upon the increase in series excitation with the increase in load current.

(i) If series winding turns are so adjusted that with the increase in load current, the terminal voltage increases, it is called *over-compounded generator*. In such a case, as the load current increases, the series field m.m.f. increases and tends to increase the flux and hence the generated voltage. The increase in generated voltage is greater than the $I_a R_a$ drop so that instead of decreasing, the terminal voltage increases as shown by curve A in Fig. 11.10.

(ii) If series winding turns are so adjusted that with the increase in load current, the terminal voltage substantially remains constant, it is called *flat-compounded generator*. The series winding of such a machine has lesser number of turns than the one in over-compounded machine and, therefore, does not increase the flux as much for a given load current. Consequently, the full-load voltage is nearly equal to the no-load voltage as indicated by curve B in Fig. 11.10.

(iii) If series field winding has lesser number of turns than that for a flat-compounded machine, the terminal voltage falls with increase in load current as indicated by curve C in Fig. 11.10. Such a machine is called *under-compounded generator*.

11.10. APPLICATIONS OF COMPOUND GENERATORS

In some applications, we can tolerate a reasonable drop in terminal voltage as the load current increases but this is unacceptable in lighting circuits. For example, the distribution system of a ship supplies power to both d.c. machinery and incandescent lamps. The current delivered by the generator changes continuously in response to the varying loads. These current variations produce the corresponding changes in the generator terminal voltage, causing the lights to flicker. To eliminate such voltage fluctuations, we use *over-compounded generators*. In an over-compounded generator, as the load current increases, the generator terminal voltage rises above the no-load value. The rise in voltage compensates for (i) $I_a R_a$ drop in the generator and (ii) the IR drop in the line between the generator and load.

Note : If compounding is too strong, a low resistance can be placed in parallel with the series field winding. This reduces the field current and has the same effect as reducing the number of turns of series winding.

MULTIPLE-CHOICE QUESTIONS

1. A separately excited d.c. generator is not used because.........
   (a) it is costly
   (b) separate d.c. source is required for field circuit

   (c) voltage drops considerably with load
   (d) none of the above
2. A d.c. compound generator having full-load terminal voltage equal to the no-load voltage is called.......... generator.

(*a*) under-compounded

(*b*) over-compounded

(*c*) flat-compounded

(*d*) none of the above

3. The main drawback of a d.c. shunt generator is that...........

(*a*) terminal voltage drops considerably with load

(*b*) shunt field circuit has high resistance

(*c*) generated voltage is small

(*d*) it is expensive

4. D.C. machines which are subjected to abrupt changes of load are provided with...........

(*a*) interpole windings

(*b*) compensating windings

(*c*) equalisers

(*d*) copper brushes

5. Fig. 11.11 shows the external characteristic of .... generator.

(*a*) over-compounded

(*b*) series

(*c*) flat-compounded

(*d*) shunt

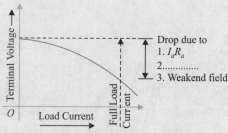

Fig. 11.11

6. Referring to Fig. 11.11, the voltage drop at no. 2 is due to ....

(*a*) friction　　(*b*) armature reaction

(*c*) field circuit　(*d*) none of the above

7. Fig. 11.12 shows the external characteristics of a .... generator.

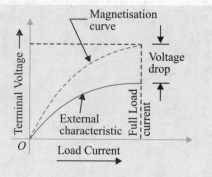

Fig. 11.12

(*a*) shunt　　　(*b*) flat-compounded

(*c*) series　　　(*d*) over-compounded

8. Fig. 11.13 shows the external characteristics of three types of generators having the same rating. Curve 2 represents for .... generator.

(*a*) shunt　　　(*b*) separately-excited

(*c*) compound　(*d*) none of the above

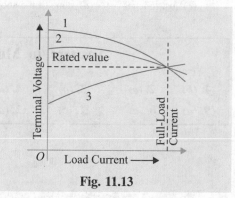

Fig. 11.13

9. Curve 3 in Fig. 11.13 represents the external characteristic of a .... generator.

(*a*) compound　(*b*) separately-excited

(*c*) shunt　　　(*d*) none of the above

10. Curve 1 in Fig. 11.13 represents the external characteristic of a .... generator.

(*a*) shunt　　　　　(*b*) series

(*c*) flat-compounded　(*d*) none of the above

11. The curve *B* in Fig. 11.14 is the external characteristic of a .... generator.

(*a*) shunt　　　　　(*b*) series

(*c*) flat-compounded　(*d*) under-compounded

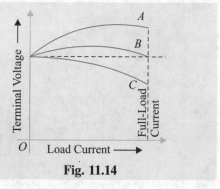

Fig. 11.14

12. The curve *A* in Fig. 11.14 represents the external characteristic of .... generator.

(*a*) shunt

(*b*) flat-compounded

(*c*) under-compounded

(*d*) an over-compounded

13. The terminal voltage of a .... generator varies widely with changes in load current.
    (*a*) series
    (*b*) shunt
    (*c*) flat-compounded
    (*d*) none of the above

14. The line representing the critical resistance of a d.c. generator............... its O.C.C.
    (*a*) intersects
    (*b*) runs parallel to
    (*c*) just touches
    (*d*) none of the above

15. Which of the following generator provides approximately constant voltage from no-load to full-load ?
    (*a*) series
    (*b*) shunt
    (*c*) flat-compounded
    (*d*) over-compounded

Answers to Multiple-Choice Questions

1. (*b*)	**2.** (*c*)	**3.** (*a*)	**4.** (*a*)	**5.** (*d*)	**6.** (*b*)	**7.** (*c*)	**8.** (*b*)
9. (*a*)	**10.** (*a*)	**11.** (*c*)	**12.** (*d*)	**13.** (*a*)	**14.** (*c*)	**15.** (*c*)	

12

D.C. Motors

INTRODUCTION

D.C. motors are seldom used in ordinary applications because all electric supply companies furnish alternating current. However, for special applications such as in steel mills, mines and electric trains, it is advantageous to convert alternating current into direct current in order to use d.c. motors. The reason is that speed/torque characteristics of d.c. motors are much more superior to that of a.c. motors. Like generators, d.c. motors are also of three types viz. series-wound, shunt-wound and compound-wound. The use of a particular d.c. motor depends upon the type of mechanical load it has to drive.

12.1. D.C. MOTOR PRINCIPLE

A machine that converts d.c. power into mechanical power is known as a d.c. motor. Its operation is based on the principle that when a current carrying conductor is placed in a magnetic field, the conductor experiences a mechanical force. The direction of this force is given by Fleming's left hand rule and magnitude is given by ;

$$F = BIl \text{ newtons}$$

Basically, there is no constructional difference between a d.c. motor and a d.c. generator. The same d.c. machine can be run as a generator or motor.

12.2. WORKING OF D.C. MOTOR

Consider a part of a multipolar d.c. motor as shown in Fig. 12.1. When the terminals of the motor are connected to an external source of d.c. supply;

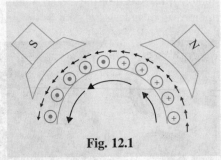

(*i*) the field magnets are excited developing alternate *N* and *S* poles.

(*ii*) the armature conductors carry *currents. All conductors under *N*-pole carry currents in one direction while all the conductors under *S*-pole carry currents in the opposite direction.

Fig. 12.1

Suppose the conductors under *N*-pole carry currents into the plane of the paper and those under *S*-pole carry currents out of the plane of the paper as shown in Fig. 12.1. Since each armature conductor is carrying current and is placed in the magnetic field, mechanical force acts on it. Referring to Fig. 12.1 and applying Fleming's left hand rule, it is clear that force on each conductor is tending to rotate the armature in anticlockwise direction. All these forces add together to produce a driving torque which sets the armature rotating. When the conductor moves from one side of a brush to the other, the current in that conductor is reversed and at the same time it comes under the influence of next pole which is of opposite polarity. Consequently, the direction of force on the conductor remains the same.

12.3. BACK OR COUNTER E.M.F.

When the armature of a d.c. motor rotates under the influence of the driving torque, the armature conductors move through the magnetic field and hence e.m.f. is induced in them as in a generator. The induced e.m.f. acts in opposite direction to the applied voltage *V*(**Lenz's law) and is known as *back or counter e.m.f.* E_b. The back e.m.f. E_b $(= P\phi ZN/60A)$ is always less than the applied voltage *V*, although this difference is small when the motor is running under normal conditions.

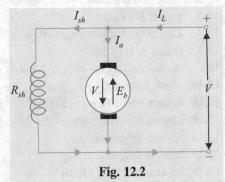

Fig. 12.2

Consider a shunt wound motor shown in Fig. 12.2. When d.c. voltage *V* is applied across the motor terminals, the field magnets are excited and armature conductors are supplied with current. Therefore, driving torque acts on the armature which begins to rotate. As the armature rotates, back e.m.f. E_b is induced which opposes the applied voltage *V*. The applied voltage *V* has to force current through the armature against the back e.m.f. E_b. The electric work done in overcoming and causing the current to flow against E_b is converted into mechanical energy developed in the armature. It follows, therefore, that energy conversion in a d.c. motor is only possible due to the production of back e.m.f. E_b.

Net voltage across armature circuit = $V - E_b$.

If R_a is the armature circuit resistance, then, $I_a = \dfrac{V - E_b}{R_a}$

Since *V* and R_a are usually fixed, the value of E_b will determine the current drawn by the

. . . .

* Since the armature of a motor is the same as that of generator, the current from the supply line must divide and pass through several paths of the armature—2 for wave wound armature and *P* for lap wound armature. As in a generator, currents through all conductors under a pole will be in the same direction.

** According to Lenz's law, the direction of induced e.m.f. is such that it opposes the cause producing it. The cause producing the back e.m.f. E_b is the applied voltage *V*. Hence E_b opposes the applied voltage *V*.

motor. If the speed of the motor is high, then back e.m.f. $E_b(= P\phi ZN/60A)$ is large and hence the motor will draw less armature current and *vice-versa*.

12.4. SIGNIFICANCE OF BACK E.M.F.

The presence of back e.m.f. makes the d.c. motor a *self-regulating* machine i.e., it makes the motor to draw as much armature current as is just sufficient to develop the torque required by the load.

$$\text{Armature current, } I_a = \frac{V - E_b}{R_a}$$

(i) When the motor is running on no load, small torque is required to overcome the friction and windage losses. Therefore, the armature current I_a is small and the back e.m.f. is nearly equal to the applied voltage.

(ii) If the motor is suddenly loaded, the first effect is to cause the armature to slow down. Therefore, the speed at which the armature conductors move through the field is reduced and hence the back e.m.f. E_b falls. The decreased back e.m.f. allows a larger current to flow through the armature and larger current means increased driving torque. Thus, the driving torque increases as the motor slows down. The motor will stop slowing down when the armature current is just sufficient to produce the increased torque required by the load.

(iii) If the load on the motor is decreased, the driving torque is momentarily in excess of the requirement so that armature is accelerated. As the armature speed increases, the back e.m.f. E_b also increases and causes the armature current I_a to decrease. The motor will stop accelerating when the armature current is just sufficient to produce the reduced torque required by the load.

It follows, therefore, that back e.m.f. in a d.c. motor regulates the flow of armature current i.e. it automatically changes the armature current to meet the load requirement.

12.5. VOLTAGE EQUATION OF D.C. MOTOR

Let in a d.c. motor (See Fig. 12.3),

$$V = \text{applied voltage}$$
$$E_b = \text{back e.m.f.}$$
$$R_a = \text{armature resistance}$$
$$I_a = \text{armature current}$$

Since back e.m.f. E_b acts in opposition to the applied voltage V, the net voltage across the armature circuit is $V - E_b$. The armature current I_a is given by ;

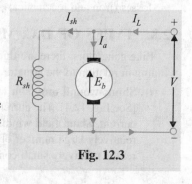

Fig. 12.3

$$I_a = \frac{V - E_b}{R_a}$$

or
$$V = E_b + I_a R_a \qquad \qquad ...(i)$$

This is known as voltage equation of the d.c. motor.

12.6. POWER EQUATION

If eq. (i) above is multiplied by I_a throughout, we get,

$$VI_a = E_b I_a + I_a^2 R_a$$

This is known as power equation of the d.c. motor.

$$VI_a = \text{electric power supplied to armature (*armature input*)}$$
$$E_b I_a = \text{*power developed by armature (*armature output*)}$$
$$I_a^2 R_a = \text{electric power wasted in armature (*armature Cu loss*)}$$

* This will be the mechanical power output in watts.

Thus out of the armature input, a small portion (about 5%) is wasted as $I_a^2 R_a$ and the remaining portion $E_b I_a$ is converted into mechanical power within the armature.

12.7. CONDITION FOR MAXIMUM POWER

The mechanical power developed by the motor is $P_m = E_b I_a$

Now, $$P_m = V I_a - I_a^2 R_a$$

Since V and R_a are fixed, power developed by the motor depends upon armature current. For maximum power, dP_m / dI_a should be zero.

$\therefore$ $$\frac{dP_m}{dI_a} = V - 2 I_a R_a = 0$$

or $$I_a R_a = V/2$$

Now, $$V = E_b + I_a R_a$$

$$= E_b + V/2$$

$\therefore$ $$E_b = V/2 \qquad\qquad [\because I_a R_a = V/2]$$

Hence mechanical power developed by the motor is maximum when back e.m.f. is equal to half the applied voltage.

Limitations. In practice, we never aim at achieving maximum power due to the following reasons :

(i) The armature current under this condition is very large—much excess of rated current of the machine.

(ii) Half of the input power is wasted in the armature circuit. In fact, if we take into account other losses (iron and mechanical), the efficiency will be well below 50%.

12.8. TYPES OF D.C. MOTORS

Like generators, there are three types of d.c. motors characterised by the connections of field winding in relation to the armature viz. :

(i) **Shunt-wound motor** in which the field winding is connected in parallel with the armature [See Fig. 12.4]. The current through the shunt field winding is not the same as the armature current. Shunt field windings are designed to produce the necessary m.m.f. by means of a relatively large number of turns of wire having high resistance. Therefore, shunt field current is relatively small compared with the armature current.

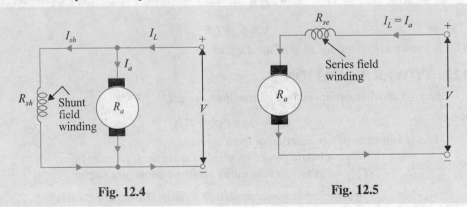

Fig. 12.4   Fig. 12.5

(ii) **Series-wound motor** in which the field winding is connected in series with the armature

[See Fig. 12.5]. Therefore, series field winding carries the armature current. Since the current passing through a series field winding is the same as the armature current, series field windings must be designed with much fewer turns than shunt field windings for the same m.m.f. Therefore, a series field winding has a relatively small number of turns of thick wire and, therefore, will possess a low resistance.

(*iii*) **Compound-wound motor** which has two field windings ; one connected in parallel with the armature and the other in series with it. There are two types of compound motor connections (like generators). When the shunt field winding is directly connected across the armature terminals [See Fig. 12.6], it is called *short-shunt connection*. When the shunt winding is so connected that it shunts the series combination of armature and series field [See Fig. 12.7], it is called *long-shunt connection*.

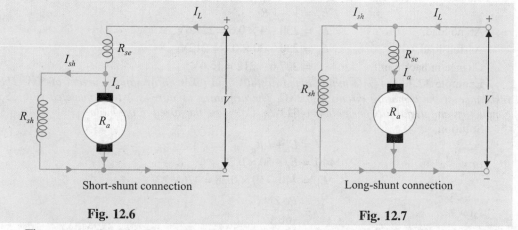

Short-shunt connection	Long-shunt connection
Fig. 12.6	**Fig. 12.7**

The compound machines (generators or motors) are always designed so that the flux produced by shunt field winding is considerably larger than the flux produced by the series field winding. Therefore, shunt field in compound machines is the basic dominant factor in the production of the magnetic field in the machine.

Armature of d.c. motor

Example 12.1. *A 250V shunt motor takes a total current of 20A. The shunt field and armature resistances are 200Ω and 0.3Ω respectively. Determine (i) value of back e.m.f. (ii) gross mechanical power in the armature.*

Solution.

(i) Shunt current, $\qquad I_{sh} = 250/200 = 1.25A$

Armature current, $\qquad I_a = 20 - 1.25 = 18.75 \ A$

Back e.m.f., $\qquad E_b = V - I_a R_a$

$\qquad\qquad\qquad\qquad = 250 - 18.75 \times 0.3 = \textbf{244.4V}$

(ii) Mechanical power developed $= E_b I_a = 244.4 \times 18.75 = \textbf{4582.5W}$

Example 12.2. *A 230V motor has an armature circuit resistance of 0.6Ω. If the full-load armature current is 30A and no load armature current is 4A, find the change in back e.m.f. from no load to full-load.*

Solution.

$$E_b = V - I_a R_a$$

At no load, $\qquad E_b = 230 - 4 \times 0.6 = 227.6V$

At full-load, $\qquad E_b = 230 - 30 \times 0.6 = 212V$

Change in back e.m.f. $\qquad = 227.6 - 212 = \textbf{15.6V}$

Example 12.3. *A 4-pole motor is fed at 440V and takes an armature current of 50A. The resistance of the armature circuit is 0.28Ω. The armature winding is wave-connected with 888 conductors and useful flux per pole is 0.023Wb. Calculate the speed of the motor.*

Solution.

$$V = E_b + I_a R_a$$

or $\qquad 440 = E_b + 50 \times 0.28$

∴ $\qquad E_b = 440 - 50 \times 0.28 = 426V$

Now $\qquad E_b = \dfrac{P\phi ZN}{60A}$

∴ $\qquad N = \dfrac{E_b \times 60A}{P\phi Z} = \dfrac{426 \times 60 \times 2}{4 \times 0.023 \times 888} = \textbf{626 r.p.m.}$

Example 12.4. *The counter e.m.f. of a shunt motor is 227V, the field resistance is 160Ω and field current is 1.5A. If the line current is 39.5 A, find the armature resistance. Also find the armature current when the motor is stationary.*

Solution.

Applied voltage, $\qquad V = I_{sh} R_{sh} = 1.5 \times 160 = 240V$

Armature current, $\qquad I_a = I_L - I_{sh} = 39.5 - 1.5 = 38A$

Now $\qquad V = E_b + I_a R_a$

∴ $\qquad R_a = \dfrac{V - E_b}{I_a} = \dfrac{240 - 227}{38} = 0.342\Omega$

At the moment of start-up, the armature is stationary so that $E_b = 0$.

∴ $\qquad I_a = V/R_a = 240/0.342 = \textbf{701.5A}$

Example 12.5. *A 20kW, 250V d.c. shunt generator has armature and field resistances of 0.1Ω and 125Ω respectively. Calculate the total armature power developed when running (i) as a generator delivering 20kW output (ii) as a motor taking 20kW input.*

Solution.

(i) **As a generator.** Fig. 12.8 (i) shows the connections of shunt generator.

$$I_L = 20 \times 10^3/250 = 80A$$

$$I_{sh} = 250/125 = 2A$$

$$I_a = I_L + I_{sh} = 80 + 2 = 82A$$
$$E_g = V + I_a R_a = 250 + 82 \times 0.1 = 258.2 \ V$$

∴ Power developed in the armature

$$= E_g I_a = 258.2 \times 82 = 21.17 \times 10^3 \ W = \mathbf{21.17 \ kW}$$

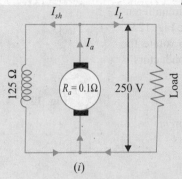 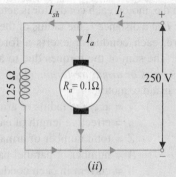

(i) (ii)

Fig. 12.8

(ii) **As a motor.** Fig. 12.8(ii) shows the connections of shunt motor.

$$I_L = 20 \times 10^3 / 250 = 80A$$
$$I_{sh} = 250/125 = 2A$$
$$I_a = I_L - I_{sh} = 80 - 2 = 78A$$
$$E_b = V - I_a R_a = 250 - 78 \times 0.1 = 242.2V$$

Power developed in the armature = $E_b I_a = 242.2 \times 78 = 18.9 \times 10^3 W = \mathbf{18.9kW}$

Example 12.6. *Find the useful flux per pole on no-load of 250V, 6-pole shunt motor having wave-connected armature winding with 110 turns. The armature resistance is 0.2Ω. The armature current is 13.3A at the no-load speed of 908 r.p.m.*

Solution

$$E_b = V - I_a R_a = 250 - 13.3 \times 0.2 = 247.34V$$

Now

$$E_b = \frac{P \phi ZN}{60A}$$

∴ Flux/pole, $$\phi = \frac{E_b \times 60A}{PZN}$$

Here $E_b = 247.34V$; $A = 2$; $P = 6$; $Z = 110 \times 2 = 220$; $N = 908$ r.p.m.

∴ $$\phi = \frac{247.34 \times 60 \times 2}{6 \times 220 \times 908} = 24.8 \times 10^{-3} Wb = \mathbf{24.8mWb}$$

TUTORIAL PROBLEMS

1. A 220V shunt motor takes a total current of 20A. The shunt field resistance is 250Ω while armature resistance is 0.3Ω. Calculate the back e.m.f. **[214.26V]**

2. The armature of a d.c. machine has a resistance of 0.1Ω and is connected to a 230V supply. Calculate the back e.m.f. when it is running (i) as a generator giving 80A (ii) as a motor taking 80A. **[(i) 238V (ii) 222V]**

3. A 4-pole d.c. motor is connected to a 500V d.c. supply and takes an armature current of 80A. The resistance of the armature circuit is 0.4Ω. The armature is wave wound with 522 conductors and useful flux per pole is 0.025Wb. Determine the speed of the motor. **[1075 r.p.m.]**

12.9. ARMATURE TORQUE OF D.C. MOTOR

Torque is the turning moment of a force about an axis and is measured by the product of force (F) and radius (r) at right angle to which the force acts *i.e.*

$$T = F \times r$$

In a d.c. motor, each conductor is acted upon by a circumferential force F at a distance r, the radius of the armature (See Fig. 12.9). Therefore, each conductor exerts a force, tending to rotate the armature. The sum of the torques due to all armature conductors is known as *gross or armature torque* (T_a).

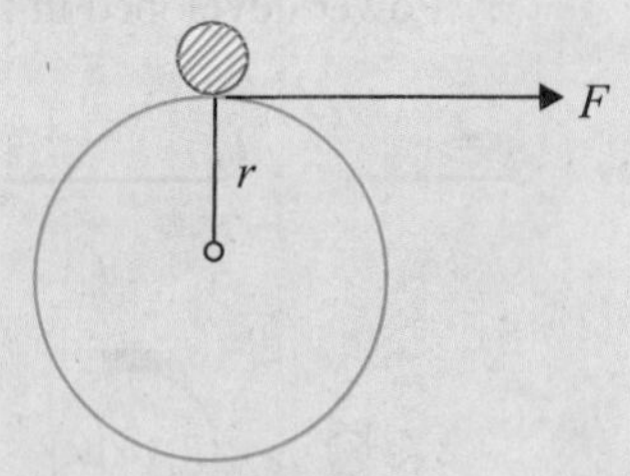

Fig. 12.9

Let in a d.c. motor,

r = average radius of armature in m
l = effective length of each conductor in m
Z = total number of armature conductors
A = number of parallel paths
i = current in each conductor = I_a/A
B = average flux density in Wb/m^2
ϕ = flux per pole in Wb
P = number of poles

Force on each conductor, $F = B\,i\,l$ newtons
Torque due to one conductor $= F \times r$ newton-metre
Total armature torque, $T_a = ZF\,r$ newton-metre
$= Z\,B\,i\,l\,r$

Now $i = I_a/A$, $B = \phi/a$ where a is the x-sectional area of flux path at radius r. Clearly, $a = 2\pi rl/P$.

$\therefore$ $T_a = Z \times (\phi/a) \times (I_a/A) \times l \times r$

$$= Z \times \frac{\phi}{2\pi rl / P} \times \frac{I_a}{A} \times l \times r$$

$$= \frac{Z\,\phi\,I_a\,P}{2\pi\,A}\,Nm$$

or $T_a = 0.159\ Z\phi I_a\ (P/A)Nm$ ...(i)

Since Z, P and A are fixed for a given machine,

$\therefore$ $T_a \propto \phi\,I_a$

Hence *torque in a d.c. motor is directly proportional to flux per pole and armature current.*

(*i*) For a *shunt motor*, flux ϕ is practically constant.

$\therefore$ $T_a \propto I_a$

(*ii*) For a *series motor*, flux ϕ is directly proportional to armature current I_a provided magnetic saturation does not take place.

$\therefore$ $T_a \propto I^2_a$ ...upto magnetic saturation

Alternative expression for T_a

$$E_b = \frac{P\phi Z\,N}{60A}$$

$\therefore$ $\dfrac{P\phi Z}{A} = \dfrac{60 \times E_b}{N}$

From eq.(*i*), we get the expression of T_a as :

$$T_a = 0.159 \times \left(\frac{60 \times E_b}{N}\right) \times I_a$$

or
$$T_a = 9.55 \times \frac{E_b I_a}{N} \, Nm$$

12.10. SHAFT TORQUE (T_{sh})

The torque which is available at the motor shaft for doing useful work is known as *shaft torque*. It is represented by T_{sh}.

Fig. 12.10 illustrates the concept of shaft torque. The total torque T_a developed in armature of a motor is not available at the shaft as a part of it is lost in overcoming the iron and frictional losses in the motor. Therefore, shaft torque T_{sh} is somewhat less than the total armature torque T_a. The difference $T_a - T_{sh}$ is known as lost torque.

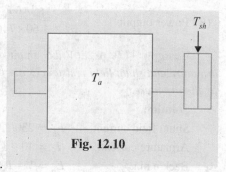

Fig. 12.10

$$T_{sh} = 9.55 \times \frac{\text{Output}}{N} \, Nm$$

12.11. BRAKE HORSE POWER (B.H.P.)

The horse power developed by the shaft torque is known as *brake horse power* (B.H.P.). If the motor is running at N r.p.m. and the shaft torque is T_{sh} newton metres, then,

W.D./revolution = force × distance moved in 1 revolution

$$= F \times 2\pi r = 2\pi \times T_{sh} \, J$$

W.D./minute $= 2\pi N T_{sh} \, J$

W.D./sec. $= \dfrac{2\pi N T_{sh}}{60} \, watts$

$$= \frac{2\pi N T_{sh}}{60 \times 746} \, H.P.$$

∴   Useful output power $= \dfrac{2\pi N T_{sh}}{60 \times 746} \, H.P.$

or $B.H.P. = \dfrac{2\pi N T_{sh}}{60 \times 746}$

Example 12.7. *Calculate the value of torque established by the armature of a 4-pole motor having 774 conductors, two paths in parallel, 24mWb flux per pole, when the total armature current is 50A.*

Solution.

Armature torque, $T_a = 0.159 Z \phi I_a (P/A)$

Here, $Z = 774$; $\phi = 24 \times 10^{-3}$ Wb ; $I_a = 50A$; $P = 4$; $A = 2$

∴ $T_a = 0.159 \times 774 \times 24 \times 10^{-3} \times 50 \times (4/2) =$ **295.35 Nm**

Example 12.8. *An armature of a 6-pole machine 75cm in diameter has 664 conductors each having an effective length of 30cm and carrying a current of 100A. If 70% of total conductors lie simultaneously in the field of average flux density 0.85Wb/m², calculate (i) armature torque (ii) horse power output at 250 r.p.m.*

Solution.

(*i*) Force on one conductor, $F = B \, i \, l = 0.85 \times 100 \times 0.3 = 25.5$ N

Torque due to one conductor $= F \times r = 25.5 \times 0.375 = 9.56$ Nm

No. of effective conductors, $Z = 664 \times 70/100 = 465$

∴ Total armature torque, $T_a = 9.56 \times 465 = \textbf{4445.4 Nm}$

(*ii*) Power output
$$= \frac{2\pi N T_a}{60 \times 746}^* \text{ H.P.} = \frac{2\pi \times 250 \times 4445.4}{60 \times 746} = \textbf{156 H.P.}$$

Example 12.9. *A 230V d.c. shunt motor takes a current of 40A and runs at 1100 r.p.m. If armature and shunt field resistances are 0.25Ω and 230 Ω respectively, find the torque developed by the armature.*

Solution.

Shunt field current, $I_{sh} = 230/230 = 1A$

Armature current, $I_a = 40 - 1 = 39A$

Back e.m.f., $E_b = V - I_a R_a = 230 - 39 \times 0.25 = 220.25 \text{ V}$

Now, $T_a = 9.55 \times E_b I_a/N$ ...See Art. 12.9

$= 9.55 \times (220.25 \times 39/1100)Nm = \textbf{74.66 Nm}$

Example 12.10. *A d.c. motor takes an armature current of 110A at 480V. The armature circuit resistance is 0.2Ω. The machine has 6 poles and the armature is lap-connected with 864 conductors. The flux per pole is 0.05 Wb. Calculate (i) the speed and (ii) the gross torque developed by the motor.*

Solution.

(*i*) $E_b = V - I_a R_a = 480 - 110 \times 0.2 = 458 \text{ volts}$

Now $E_b = \dfrac{P \phi Z N}{60 A}$

or $458 = \dfrac{6 \times 0.05 \times 864 \times N}{60 \times 6}$

∴ $N = \dfrac{458 \times 60 \times 6}{6 \times 0.05 \times 864} = \textbf{636 r.p.m.}$

(*ii*) Gross torque means armature torque T_a.

∴ $T_a = 0.159 \phi Z I_a \times \left(\dfrac{P}{A}\right) = 0.159 \times 0.05 \times 864 \times 110 \times \left(\dfrac{6}{6}\right) = \textbf{756.3 N-m}$

TUTORIAL PROBLEMS

1. A 250V, 4-pole, wave-wound series motor has 782 conductors on its armature. It has armature and series field resistance of 0.75 Ω. The motor takes a current of 40A. Find its speed and gross torque developed if it has a flux per pole of 25mWb. **[338 r.p.m. ; 249 N-m]**

2. A 220V shunt motor takes 105A. The armature resistance is 0.08Ω and shunt field resistance is 44Ω. The motor runs at 950 r.p.m. If iron and friction losses are equal to 2kW, find (*i*) B.H.P. (*ii*) total torque (*iii*) shaft torque.**[(*i*) 25.74 H.P. (*ii*) 212.5 N-m (*iii*) 192.8 N-m]**

3. The armature winding of a 200V, 4-pole series motor is lap-connected. There are 280 slots and each slot has 4 conductors. The current is 45A and the flux per pole is 18mWb. The field resistance is 0.3Ω; the armature resistance 0.5Ω and the iron and friction losses total 800W. The pulley diameter is 0.41m. Find the pull in newtons at the rim of the pulley. **[634 N]**

* Iron and frictional losses are neglected so that $T_a = T_{sh}$.

12.12. SPEED OF A D.C. MOTOR

$$E_b = V - I_a R_a$$

But
$$E_b = P\phi\, ZN/60A$$

$$\therefore \qquad \frac{P\phi Z N}{60A} = V - I_a R_a$$

or
$$N = \frac{(V - I_a R_a)}{\phi}\,\frac{60A}{PZ}$$

or
$$N = K\frac{(V - I_a R_a)}{\phi} \quad \text{where } K = 60A/PZ$$

But
$$V - I_a R_a = E_b$$

$$\therefore \qquad N = K\frac{E_b}{\phi}$$

or
$$N \propto \frac{E_b}{\phi}$$

Therefore, in a d.c. motor, speed is directly proportional to back e.m.f. E_b and inversely proportional to flux per pole ϕ.

12.13. SPEED RELATIONS

If a d.c. motor has initial values of speed, flux per pole and back e.m.f. as N_1, ϕ_1 and E_{b_1} respectively and the corresponding final values are N_2, ϕ_2 and E_{b_2}, then,

$$N_1 \propto \frac{E_{b_1}}{\phi_1} \quad \text{and} \quad N_2 \propto \frac{E_{b_2}}{\phi_2}$$

$$\therefore \qquad \frac{N_1}{N_2} = \frac{E_{b_1}}{E_{b_2}} \times \frac{\phi_2}{\phi_1}$$

(*i*) For a **shunt motor**, flux practically remains constant so that $\phi_1 = \phi_2$.

$$\therefore \qquad \frac{N_1}{N_2} = \frac{E_{b_1}}{E_{b_2}}$$

(*ii*) For a **series motor**, $\phi \propto I_a$ prior to saturation.

$$\therefore \qquad \frac{N_1}{N_2} = \frac{E_{b_1}}{E_{b_2}} \times \frac{I_{a_2}}{I_{a_1}}$$

where
$$I_{a_1} = \text{initial armature current}$$

$$I_{a_2} = \text{final armature current}$$

12.14. SPEED REGULATION

The speed regulation *of a motor is the change in speed from full-load to no load and is expressed as a percentage of the speed at full-load i.e.*

$$\% \text{ Speed regulation} = \frac{N.L.\text{Speed} - F.L.\text{Speed}}{F.L.\text{ Speed}} \times 100$$

$$= \frac{N_0 - N}{N} \times 100$$

where $\qquad N_0 = \text{No} - \text{load speed}$

$\qquad N = \text{Full-load speed}$

Example 12.11. *A 230V d.c. shunt motor takes 5A at no load and runs at 1000 r.p.m. Calculate the speed when loaded and taking a current of 30A. The armature and field resistances are 0.2Ω and 230Ω respectively.*

Solution.

Let N_2 r.p.m. be the speed under loaded conditions.

No load conditions

$$I_{sh} = 230/230 = 1A$$

$$I_{a_1} = I_L - I_{sh} = 5 - 1 = 4A$$

$$E_{b_1} = V - I_{a_1} R_a = 230 - 4 \times 0.2 = 229.2V$$

$$N_1 = 1000 \ r.p.m.$$

Loaded conditions

$$I_{a_2} = I_L - I_{sh} = 30 - 1 = 29A$$

$$E_{b_2} = V - I_{a_2} R_a = 230 - 29 \times 0.2 = 224.2V$$

Since it is a shunt motor,

∴ $\qquad\qquad \dfrac{N_2}{N_1} = \dfrac{E_{b_2}}{E_{b_1}}$ \qquad\qquad ...See Art. 12.13

∴ $\qquad\qquad N_2 = \left(\dfrac{E_{b_2}}{E_{b_1}} \right) N_1 = \dfrac{224.2}{229.2} \times 1000 = \mathbf{978\,r.p.m.}$

Example 12.12. *A 6-pole lap wound shunt motor has 500 conductors. The armature and shunt field resistances are 0.05 Ω and 25Ω respectively. Find the speed of the motor if it takes 120A from a d.c. supply of 100V. Flux per pole is 20mWb.*

Solution.

$$I_{sh} = 100/25 = 4A$$

$$I_a = I_L - I_{sh} = 120 - 4 = 116A$$

$$E_b = V - I_a R_a = 100 - 116 \times 0.05 = 94.2V$$

Now, $\qquad\qquad E_b = \dfrac{P\phi ZN}{60A}$

∴ $\qquad\qquad N = \dfrac{E_b \times 60A}{P\phi Z} = \dfrac{94.2 \times 60 \times 6}{6 \times 20 \times 10^{-3} \times 500} = \mathbf{565\,r.p.m.}$

Example 12.13. *A d.c. shunt generator delivers an output of 100kW at 500V when running at 800 r.p.m. The armature and field resistances are 0.1Ω and 100 Ω respectively. Calculate the speed of the same machine when running as a shunt motor and taking 100kW input at 500V. Allow 1 volt per brush for contact drop.*

Solution.

As a generator. Fig. 12.11 (*i*) shows the connections.

$$I_L = 100 \times 10^3/500 = 200 \ A$$

$$I_{sh} = 500/100 = 5 \ A$$

$$I_{a_1} = I_L + I_{sh} = 200 + 5 = 205 \ A$$

Generated e.m.f., $\quad\quad\quad E_1 = V_1 + I_{a_1} R_a +$ Brush drop

$$= 500 + 205 \times 0.1 + 2 \times 1 = 522.5 \text{ V}$$

$$N_1 = 800 \text{ r.p.m.}$$

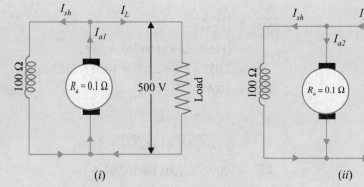

Fig. 12.11

As a motor. Fig. 12.11 (*ii*) shows the connections.

$$I_{a_2} = I_L - I_{sh} = 200 - 5 = 195 \text{ A}$$

Back e.m.f., $\quad\quad\quad E_2 = V - I_{a_2} R_a -$ Brush drop

$$= 500 - 195 \times 0.1 - 2 \times 1 = 478.5 \text{V}$$

Let N_2 be the speed of the machine in r.p.m. when working as a motor.

For a shunt machine, $\dfrac{N_2}{N_1} = \dfrac{E_2}{E_1}$ $\quad\quad\quad\quad$ .... See Art. 12.13

∴ $\quad\quad\quad N_2 = \left(\dfrac{E_2}{E_1}\right)N_1 = \dfrac{478.5}{522.5} \times 800 = \textbf{732.6 r.p.m.}$

Example 12.14. *A 200V series motor takes a current of 100A and runs at 1000 r.p.m. The total resistance of the motor is 0.1 Ω and the field is unsaturated. Calculate :*

(i) *the percentage change in torque and speed if the load is so changed that motor current is 50A.*

(ii) *the motor current and speed if the torque is halved.*

Solution.

(i)

$$T \propto \phi I_a$$

Since the field is unsaturated, $\quad\quad\quad \phi \propto I_a$

Initial armature current, $\quad\quad\quad I_{a_1} = 100 \text{ A}$

New armature current, $\quad\quad\quad I_{a_2} = 50 \text{ A}$

Now $\quad\quad\quad T_1 \propto I_{a_1}^2 \text{ and } T_2 \propto I_{a_2}^2$

∴ $\quad\quad\quad T_2 = T_1\left(\dfrac{I_{a_2}}{I_{a_1}}\right)^2 = T_1\left(\dfrac{50}{100}\right)^2 = 0.25 T_1$

∴ $\quad\quad\quad$ % change in torque $= \dfrac{T_1 - T_2}{T_1} \times 100 = \dfrac{T_1 - 0.25 T_1}{T_1} \times 100 = \textbf{75\%}$

$$E_{b_1} = V - I_{a_1}(^*R_a + R_{se}) = 200 - 100 \times 0.1 = 190V$$

$$E_{b_2} = V - I_{a_2}(R_a + R_{se}) = 200 - 50 \times 0.1 = 195V$$

For series motor prior to saturation,

$$\frac{N_2}{N_1} = \frac{E_{b_2}}{E_{b_1}} \times \frac{I_{a_1}}{I_{a_2}}$$

$$= (195/190) \times (100/50) = 2.052$$

∴

$$N_2 = 2.052 \times N_1 = 2.052 \times 1000 = \mathbf{2052 \ r.p.m.}$$

(ii)

$$E_{b_1} = 190V \qquad\qquad \text{...as before}$$

$$T_1 \propto I_{a_1}^2 \text{ and } T_2' \propto I_{a_2}'^2$$

∴

$$I_{a_2}' = I_{a_1}\sqrt{T_2'/T_1} = 100\sqrt{1/2} = \mathbf{70.7A}$$

$$E_{b_2}' = 200 - 70.7 \times 0.1 = 192.93V$$

$$\frac{N_2'}{N_1} = \left(E_{b_2}'/E_{b_1}\right) \times \left(I_{a_1}/I_{a_2}'\right)$$

$$= (192.93/190) \times (100/70.7) = 1.436$$

∴

$$N_2' = 1.436 \times N_1 = 1.436 \times 1000 = \mathbf{1436 \ r.p.m.}$$

TUTORIAL PROBLEMS

1. A 4.pole 200V d.c. shunt motor has 360 wave connected conductors on its armature. The full load armature current is 30A and flux per pole is 0.03Wb. The armature resistance is 0.2Ω and the contact drop is 1V per brush. Determine the full load speed of the motor. **[672 r.p.m.]**

2. A 4-pole, 460V shunt motor has its armature wave-connected with 880 conductors. The useful flux per pole is 0.02Wb and armature resistance is 0.7Ω. If the armature current is 40A, calculate (i) speed and (ii) torque. **[(i) 730 r.p.m. (ii) 226 Nm]**

3. A 230V d.c. shunt motor takes a no load current of 2A and runs at 1200 r.p.m. If the full-load current is 40A, find (i) speed on full-load (ii) percentage speed regulation. Resistance of armature is 0.25Ω. **[(i) 1150 r.p.m.(ii) 4.35%]**

4. A 230V shunt motor runs at 1000 r.p.m. and takes 5A. The armature resistance of the motor is 0.25Ω and shunt field resistance is 230Ω. Calculate the drop in speed when the motor takes a line current of 41A. **[40 r.p.m.]**

5. A shunt generator has an output of 10kW at 500V; the speed being 1000 r.p.m. The armature circuit resistance is 0.5Ω and the field resistance is 250Ω. Calculate the speed when running as a shunt motor taking 50kW at 500V. **[961 r.p.m.]**

12.15. LOSSES IN A D.C. MOTOR

The losses occurring in a d.c. motor are the same as in a d.c. generator (See Art. 10.11). These are :

    (i) copper losses

    (ii) mechanical losses

    (iii) iron losses

As in a generator, these losses cause (a) an increase of temperature and (b) reduction in efficiency of the d.c. motor.

* Given that $R_a + R_{se} = 0.1 \ \Omega$.

12.16. EFFICIENCY OF A D.C. MOTOR

Like a d.c. generator, the efficiency of a d.c. motor is the ratio of output power to the input power *i.e.*

$$\text{Efficiency, } \eta = \frac{\text{output}}{\text{input}} \times 100 = \frac{\text{output}}{\text{output}+\text{losses}} \times 100$$

As for a generator (See Art. 10.14), the efficiency of a d.c. motor will be maximum when :

Variable losses = Constant losses

12.17. POWER STAGES

The power stages in a d.c. motor are represented diagrammatically in Fig. 12.12.

$A - B$ = Copper losses

$B - C$ = Iron and friction losses

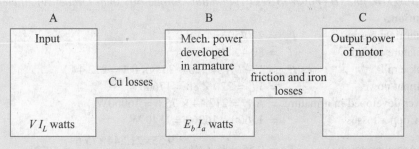

Fig. 12.12

Overall efficiency, $\eta_c = C/A$

Electrical efficiency, $\eta_e = B/A$

Mechanical efficiency, $\eta_m = C/B$

Example 12.15. *A 230V shunt motor takes 5A at no load. The resistances of the armature and field circuit are 0.25Ω and 115Ω respectively. If the motor is loaded so as to carry 40A, determine (i) iron and friction losses and (ii) efficiency.*

Solution.

(*i*) **No load conditions**

Input power $= V I_L = 230 \times 5 = 1150$ W

At no load, the total input power supplied is used up in overcoming (*a*) small armature Cu loss (*b*) shunt field loss and (*c*) iron and friction losses.

$$I_{sh} = 230/115 = 2 \text{ A} ; \qquad I_a = 5 - 2 = 3\text{A}$$

Armature Cu loss $= I_a^2 R_a = (3)^2 \times 0.25 = 2.25$ W

Field Cu loss $= I_{sh}^2 R_{sh} = (2)^2 \times 115 = 460$ W

∴ Iron and friction losses $= 1150 - (2.25 + 460) = \mathbf{687.75W}$

Alternatively. At no load, the power developed in the armature $(E_b I_a)$ is entirely used up in overcoming iron and friction losses.

∴ Iron and friction losses $= E_b I_a = (V - I_a R_a) I_a$

$$= (230 - 3 \times 0.25) \times 3 = \mathbf{687.75 \text{ W}}$$

(*ii*) **Loaded conditions**

Armature current, $I_a = 40 - 2 = 38$ A

Armature Cu loss $= I_a^2 R_a = (38)^2 \times 0.25 = 361$ W

*Constant losses	$= 687.75 + 460 = 1147.75$ W
Total losses	$= 361 + 1147.75 = 1508.75$ W
Input power	$= 230 \times 40 = 9200$ W
Output power	$= 9200 - 1508.75 = 7691.25$ W
∴	$\eta = 7691.25/9200 = 0.836 = \mathbf{83.6\%}$

Alternatively. Under loaded conditions, the power developed in the armature $(E_b I_a)$ consists of (*i*) output power and (*ii*) iron and friction losses.

Power developed in armature	$= E_b I_a = (V - I_a R_a) I_a$
	$= (230 - 38 \times 0.25)\ 38 = 8379\text{W}$
Output power	$= 8379 - 687.75 = 7691.25$ W
∴	$\eta = 7691.25/9200 = 0.836 = \mathbf{83.6\%}$

Example 12.16. *A 220V shunt motor takes a total current of 80A and runs at 800 r.p.m. Shunt field resistance and armature resistance are 50Ω and 0.1Ω respectively. If iron and friction losses amount to 1600W, find (i) copper losses (ii) armature torque (iii) shaft torque (iv) efficiency.*

Solution.

Shunt field current,	$I_{sh} = 220/50 = 4.4\text{A}$
Armature current,	$I_a = 80 - 4.4 = 75.6\text{A}$
Back e.m.f.,	$E_b = V - I_a R_a = 220 - 75.6 \times 0.1 = 212.44$ V
(*i*) Input power	$= V I_L = 220 \times 80 = 17600\text{W}$
Power developed in armature	$= E_b I_a = 212.44 \times 75.6 = 16060\text{W}$
∴ Copper losses	$= 17600 - 16060 = \mathbf{1540\ W}$

(*ii*) Armature torque, $T_a = 9.55 \times E_b I_a / N = \dfrac{9.55 \times 212.44 \times 75.6}{800} = \mathbf{192Nm}$

(*iii*) Output power	$= 16060 - 1600 = 14460$ W
Shaft torque,	$T_{sh} = 9.55 \times \text{output}/N = 9.55 \times 14460/800 = \mathbf{172.6\ Nm}$

(*iv*) Efficiency $= \dfrac{14460}{17600} \times 100 = \mathbf{82.1\%}$

Example 12.17. *A d.c. shunt machine when run as a motor on no-load takes 440 W and runs at 1000 r.p.m. The field current and armature resistance are 1A and 0.5Ω respectively. Calculate the efficiency of the machine when (i) running as a generator delivering 40 A at 220 V and (ii) as a motor taking 40 A from a 220 V supply.*

Solution.

Under no-load

Total motor input $=$ Total no-load losses $= 440$ W

$I_{sh} = 1\text{A}$; $I_{L0} = 440/220 = 2\text{A}$ ∴ $I_{a0} = 2 - 1 = 1$ A

Armature Cu loss $= I_{a_0}^2 \times R_a = (1)^2 \times 0.5 = 0.5\,\text{W}$

Field Cu loss $= 220 \times 1 = 220\text{W}$

∴   Iron and friction loss $= 440 - 220 - 0.5 = 219.5$ W

These losses will be assumed constant.

(*i*) **As a generator**

$I_L = 40\text{A};\ I_a = I_L + I_{sh} = 40 + 1 = 41$ A

Armature Cu loss $= I_a^2 R_a = (41)^2 \times 0.5 = 840.5\,\text{W}$

Field Cu loss $= 220 \times 1 = 220$ W

Iron and friction losses $= 219.5$ W   ...assumed constant

. . . .

* Constant losses = Iron and friction losses + Shunt field losses

$$\text{Total losses} = 840.5 + 220 + 219.5 = 1280 \text{ W}$$
$$\text{Output of generator} = 220 \times 40 = 8800 \text{ W}$$

∴ $\quad$ Efficiency $= \dfrac{\text{Output}}{\text{Output} + \text{Losses}} \times 100 = \dfrac{8800}{8800 + 1280} \times 100 = \mathbf{87.3\%}$

(*ii*) **As a motor**

$$I_L = 40 \text{ A}; \ I_a = I_L - I_{sh} = 40 - 1 = 39 \text{ A}$$
$$\text{Armature Cu loss} = I_a^2 R_a = (39)^2 \times 0.5 = 760.5 \text{ W}$$
$$\text{Field Cu loss} = 220 \times 1 = 220 \text{ W}$$
$$\text{Iron and friction losses} = 219.5 \text{W}$$
$$\text{Total losses} = 760.5 + 220 + 219.5 = 1200 \text{ W}$$
$$\text{Motor input} = 220 \times 40 = 8800 \text{ W}$$

$$\text{Efficiency} = \dfrac{\text{Input} - \text{Losses}}{\text{Input}} \times 100 = \dfrac{8800 - 1200}{8800} \times 100 = \mathbf{86.4\%}$$

Example 12.18. *A 7.46 kW, 250 V shunt motor takes a line current of 5A when running light. Calculate the efficiency as a motor when delivering full-load output, if armature and field resistances are 0.5Ω and 250 Ω respectively. At what output power will the efficiency be maximum?*

Solution.

When running light

$$\text{Total motor input} = \text{Total no-load losses} = 250 \times 5 = 1250 \text{ W}$$
$$I_{sh} = 250/250 = 1\text{A} \ ; \ I_{a0} = I_{L0} - I_{sh} = 5 - 1 = 4\text{A}$$
$$\text{Armature Cu loss} = I_{a0}^2 R_a = (4)^2 \times 0.5 = 8\text{W}$$
$$\text{Field Cu loss} = 250 \times 1 = 250\text{W}$$
$$\text{Iron and friction losses} = 1250 - 8 - 250$$
$$= 992\text{W}$$

The iron and friction losses will be assumed constant.

When delivering full-load output. Let I_a be the full-load armature current (See Fig. 12.13).

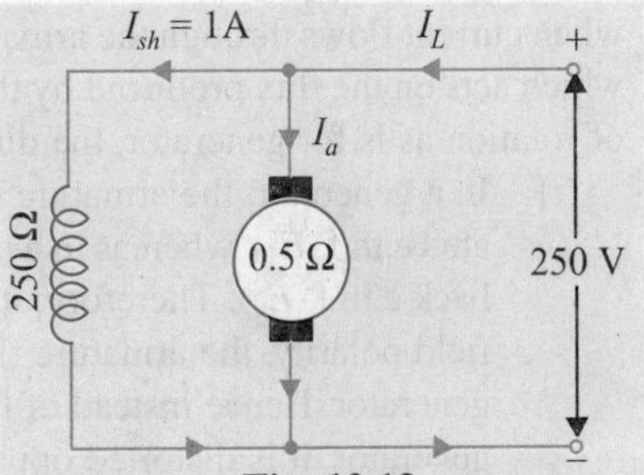

$$\text{Armature input} = (250 \times I_a)\text{W}$$
$$\text{F.L. output} = 7.46 \times 1000 = 7460\text{W}$$

The losses in the armature are :

(*i*) $\quad$ Armature Cu loss $= (I_a^2 \times 0.5)\text{W}$

(*ii*) $\quad$ Iron and friction losses $= 992\text{W}$

∴ $\qquad 250 \, I_a = 7460 + 992 + I_a^2 \times 0.5$

or $\quad 0.5 \, I_a^2 - 250 \, I_a + 8452 = 0$

$$\text{On solving, } I_a = 36.5\text{A}$$
$$\text{F.L. input current, } I_L = I_a + I_{sh} = 36.5 + 1 = 37.5\text{A}$$
$$\text{Motor input} = 250 \times 37.5 = 9375\text{W}$$

$$\text{F.L. efficiency} = \dfrac{\text{F.L. output}}{\text{F.L. input}} \times 100 = \dfrac{7460}{9375} \times 100 = \mathbf{79.6\%}$$

Now efficiency of the motor is maximum when armature Cu loss is equal to constant loss *i.e.*

$$I_a^2 R_a = {}^*1250 - 8$$

Fig. 12.13

---

* $\quad$ Constant losses = Iron and friction losses + Shunt field Cu loss = 1250 − 8 = 1242W

$$\text{or} \qquad I_a = \sqrt{\frac{1242}{R_a}} = \sqrt{\frac{1242}{0.5}} = 49.84 \text{A}$$

$$\text{Armature input} = 250\, I_a = 250 \times 49.84 = 12460 \text{ W}$$

$$\text{Armature Cu loss} = I_a^2\, R_a = (49.84)^2 \times 0.5 = 1242 \text{W}$$

Friction and iron losses $= 992$W   ...assumed constant

$$\text{Armature output} = 12460 - 1242 - 992 = \textbf{10226W}$$

TUTORIAL PROBLEMS

1. A 220V shunt motor is taking a current of 30A. Armature and shunt field resistances are 0.2Ω and 100Ω respectively. Iron and friction losses amount to 500W. Find the efficiency of the motor.   **[82.4%]**

2. A shunt motor running at 600 r.p.m. takes 80A at 250V. The armature and shunt field resistances are 0.1Ω and 50Ω respectively. Iron and friction losses amount to 2188W. Find (*i*) armature torque (*ii*) shaft torque (*iii*) copper losses (*iv*) efficiency.
        [(*i*) 288 Nm (*ii*) 254 Nm (*iii*) 1812 W (*iv*) 80%]

3. The output of certain shunt motor is 3.73 kW when taking 50A at 100 V and running at 750 r.p.m. Armature resistance is 0.06Ω and shunt field resistance is 50Ω. Find (*i*) iron and friction losses (*ii*) armature torque (*iii*) shaft torque.**[(*i*) 932 W (*ii*) 59.2 Nm (*iii*) 47.4 Nm]**

12.18 ARMATURE REACTION IN D.C. MOTORS

As in a d.c. generator, armature reaction also occurs in a d.c. motor. This is expected because when current flows through the armature conductors of a d.c. motor, it produces flux (armature flux) which acts on the flux produced by the main poles. For a motor with the same polarity and direction of rotation as is for generator, the direction of armature reaction field is reversed.

(*i*) In a generator, the armature current flows in the direction of the induced e.m.f. (*i.e.* generated e.m.f. E_g) whereas in a motor, the armature current flows against the induced e.m.f. (*i.e.* back e.m.f. E_b). Therefore, it should be expected that for the same direction of rotation and field polarity, the armature flux of the motor will be in the opposite direction to that of the generator. Hence instead of the main flux being distorted in the direction of rotation as in a generator, it is distorted opposite to the direction of rotation. We can conclude that:

Armature reaction in a d.c. generator weakens the flux at leading pole tips and strengthens the flux at trailing pole tips while the armature reaction in a d.c. motor produces the opposite effect.

(*ii*) In case of a d.c. generator, with brushes along G.N.A. and no commutating poles used, the brushes must be shifted in the direction of rotation (forward lead) for satisfactory commutation. However, in case of a d.c. motor, the brushes are given a negative lead *i.e.*, they are shifted against the direction of rotation.

With no commutating poles used , the brushes are given a forward lead in a d.c. generator and backward lead in a d.c. motor.

(*iii*) By using commutating poles (compoles), a d.c. machine can be operated with fixed brush positions for all conditions of load. Since commutating poles windings carry the armature current, then, when a machine changes from generator to motor (with consequent reversal of current), the polarities of commutating poles must be of opposite sign.

Therefore, in a d.c. motor, the commutating poles must have the same polarity as the main poles directly back of them. This is the opposite of the corresponding relation in a d.c. generator.

12.19 MAGNETIC CIRCUIT OF D.C. MACHINES

In a d.c. machine (generator or motor), the rotor is physically isolated from the stator by the air gap as shown in Fig. 12.14. Thus the magnetic circuit of a d.c. machine consists of magnetic core and air gap. Practically the same flux is present in the magnetic core and the air gap. To maintain the same flux density, the air gap will require much more m.m.f. than the magnetic core.

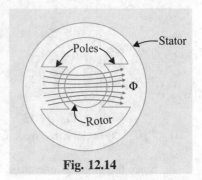

Fig. 12.14

Let l_c = mean length of the magnetic core

l_g = length of the air gap

A = *cross-sectional areas of the core and the air gap

N = number of turns on the field winding

I = current in the field winding

∴ Reluctance of core, $$S_c = \frac{l_c}{\mu_c A}$$

Reluctance of air gap, $$S_g = \frac{l_g}{\mu_0 A}$$

∴ Flux in the magnetic circuit, $$\phi = \frac{NI}{S_c + S_g}$$

Flux density in the magnetic circuit, $B = \dfrac{\phi}{A}$

Although the air gap in a d.c. machine is very small as compared to the length of the core, most of the m.m.f. is used at the air gap. The smaller the air gap in a d.c. machine, the smaller is the current required in the field winding to set up the given flux density in the magnetic circuit of the machine.

12.20. D.C. MOTOR CHARACTERISTICS

The performance of a d.c. motor can be judged from its characteristic curves known as motor characteristics. Following are the three important characteristics of a d.c. motor :

(i) **Torque and Armature current characteristic** (T_a/I_a)
It is the curve between armature torque T_a and armature current I_a of a d.c. motor. It is also known as *electrical characteristic* of the motor.

(ii) **Speed and armature current characteristic** (N/I_a)
It is the curve between speed N and armature current I_a of a d.c. motor. It is very important characteristic as it is often the deciding factor in the selection of the motor for a particular application.

(iii) **Speed and torque characteristic** (N/T_a)
It is the curve between speed N and armature torque T_a of a d.c. motor. It is also known as *mechanical characteristic*.

12.21. CHARACTERISTICS OF SHUNT MOTORS

Fig. 12.15 shows the connections of a d.c. shunt motor. The field current I_{sh} is constant since the field winding is directly connected to the supply voltage V which is assumed to be constant. Hence, the flux in a shunt motor is **approximately constant.

* In the air gap, the magnetic lines bulge outwards somewhat. This is known as *fringing* of the flux. The effect of fringing is to increase the cross-sectional area of the air gap. If the fringing effect is neglected, the cross-sectional areas of the core and the air gap are the same.

** Due to armature reaction, flux decreases a little but the decrease in flux is usually negligible under normal conditions.

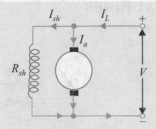

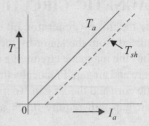

Fig. 12.15	**Fig. 12.16**

(i) T_a/I_a **Characteristic.** We know that in a d.c. motor,

$$T_a \propto \phi I_a$$

Since the motor is operating from a constant supply voltage, flux ϕ is constant (neglecting armature reaction).

$$\therefore \qquad T_a \propto I_a$$

Hence T_a/I_a characteristic is a straight line passing through the origin as shown in Fig. 12.16. The shaft torque (T_{sh}) is less than T_a and is shown by a dotted line. It is clear from the curve that a very large current is required to start a heavy load. Therefore, a shunt motor should not be started on heavy load.

(ii) N/I_a **Characteristic.** The speed N of a motor is given by ;

$$N \propto \frac{E_b}{\phi}$$

The flux ϕ and back e.m.f. E_b in a shunt motor are almost constant under normal conditions. Therefore, speed of a shunt motor will remain constant as the armature current varies (dotted line AB in Fig. 12.17). Strictly speaking, when load is increased, E_b ($= V - I_a R_a$) and ϕ decrease due to the armature resistance drop and armature reaction respectively. However, E_b decreases slightly more than ϕ so that the *speed of the motor decreases slightly with load (line AC).

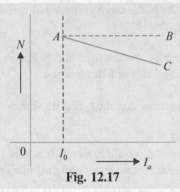

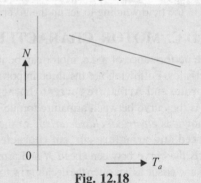

Fig. 12.17	**Fig. 12.18**

(iii) N/T_a **Characteristic.** This curve is obtained by plotting the values of N and T_a for various armature currents (See Fig. 12.18). It may be seen that speed falls somewhat as the load torque increases.

Conclusions : Following two important conclusions are drawn from the above characteristics:

(i) There is slight change in the speed of a shunt motor from no load to full-load. Hence, it is *essentially* a constant-speed motor.

(ii) The starting torque is not high because $T_a \propto I_a$.

. . . .

* It may be noted that characteristic does not have a point of zero armature current because a small current (no load current I_0) is necessary to maintain rotation of the motor at no load.

12.22. CHARACTERISTICS OF SERIES MOTORS

Fig. 12.19 shows the connections of a series motor. Note that current passing through the field winding is the same as that in the armature. If the mechanical load on the motor increases, the armature current also increases. Hence, the flux in a series motor increases with the increase in armature current and *vice-versa*.

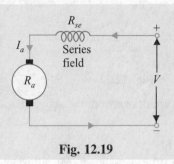
Fig. 12.19

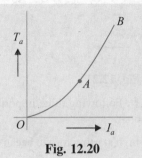
Fig. 12.20

(i) T_a/I_a **Characteristic.** We know that :

$$T_a \propto \phi I_a$$

Upto magnetic saturation, $\phi \propto I_a$ so that $T_a \propto I_a^2$

After magnetic saturation, ϕ is constant so that $T_a \propto I_a$

Thus upto magnetic saturation, the armature torque is directly proportional to the square of armature current. If I_a is doubled, T_a is almost quadrupled. Therefore, T_a/I_a curve upto magnetic saturation is a parabola (portion *OA* of the curve in Fig. 12.20). However, after magnetic saturation, torque is directly proportional to the armature current. Therefore, T_a/I_a curve after magnetic saturation is a straight line (portion *AB* of the curve).

It may be seen that in the initial portion of the curve (*i.e.* upto magnetic saturation), $T_a \propto I_a^2$. This means that starting torque of a d.c. series motor will be very high as compared to a shunt motor (where $T_a \propto I_a$).

(ii) N/I_a **Characteristic.** The speed N of a series motor is given by;

$$N \propto \frac{E_b}{\phi} \text{ where } E_b = V - I_a(R_a + R_{se})$$

When the armature current increases, the back e.m.f. E_b decreases due to $I_a(R_a + R_{se})$ drop while the flux ϕ increases. However, $I_a(R_a + R_{se})$ drop is quite small under normal conditions and may be neglected.

$$\therefore \qquad N \propto \frac{1}{\phi}$$

$$\propto \frac{1}{I_a} \text{ upto magnetic saturation}$$

Thus, upto magnetic saturation, the N/I_a curve follows the hyperbolic path as shown in Fig. 12.21. After saturation, the flux becomes constant and so does the speed.

(iii) N/T_a **Characteristic.** The N/T_a characteristic of a series motor is shown in Fig. 12.22. It is clear that series motor develops high torque at low speed and *vice-versa*. It is because an increase in torque requires an increase in armature current, which is also the field current. The result is that flux is strengthened and hence the speed drops ($\because N \propto 1/\phi$). Reverse happens should the torque be low.

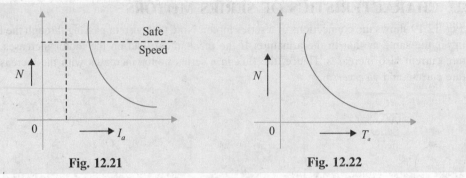

Fig. 12.21   Fig. 12.22

Conclusions : Following three important conclusions are drawn from the above characteristics of series motors :

(i) It has a high starting torque because initially $T_a \propto I_a^2$.

(ii) It is a variable speed motor (See N/I_a curve in Fig. 12.21) *i.e.* it automatically adjusts the speed as the load changes. Thus if the load decreases, its speed is automatically raised and *vice-versa*.

(iii) At no load, the armature current is very small and so is the flux. Hence, the speed rises to an excessive high value $(\because N \propto 1/\phi)$. This is dangerous for the machine which may be destroyed due to centrifugal forces set up in the rotating parts. *Therefore, a series motor should never be started on no load.* However, to start a series motor, mechanical load is first put and then the motor is started.

Note. The minimum load on a d.c. series motor should be great enough to keep the speed within limits. If the speed becomes dangerously high, then motor must be disconnected from the supply.

12.23. COMPOUND MOTORS

A compound motor has both series field and shunt field. The shunt field is always stronger than the series field. Compound motors are of two types :

(i) *Cumulative-compound motors* in which series field aids the shunt field.

(ii) *Differential compound motors* in which series field opposes the shunt field.

Differential-compound motors are rarely used due to their poor torque characteristics at heavy loads.

12.24. CHARACTERISTICS OF CUMULATIVE COMPOUND MOTORS

Fig. 12.23 shows the connections of a cumulative-compound motor. Each pole carries a series as well as shunt field winding; the series field aiding the shunt field.

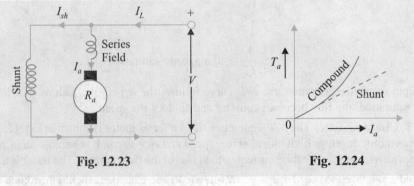

Fig. 12.23   Fig. 12.24

(*i*) *T_a/I_a Characteristic.* As the load increases, the series field increases but shunt field strength remains constant. Consequently, total flux is increased and hence the armature torque

$(\because T_a \propto \phi I_a)$. It may be noted that torque of a cumulative-compound motor is greater than that of shunt motor for a given armature current due to series field [See Fig. 12.24].

(*ii*) *N/I_a Characteristic.* As explained above, as the load increases, the flux per pole also increases. Consequently, the speed ($N \propto 1/\phi$) of the motor falls as the load increases (See Fig. 12.25). It may be noted that as the load is added, the increased amount of flux causes the speed to decrease more than does the speed of a shunt motor. Thus the speed regulation of a cumulative compound motor is poorer than that of a shunt motor.

Note : Due to shunt field, the motor has a definite no load speed and can be operated safely at no load.

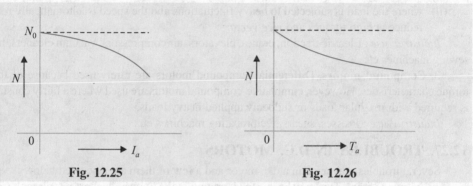

Fig. 12.25   Fig. 12.26

(*iii*) *N/T_a Characteristic.* Fig. 12.26 shows N/T_a characteristic of a cumulative compound motor. For a given armature current, the torque of a cumulative compound motor is more than that of a shunt motor but less than that of a series motor.

Conclusion : A cumulative compound motor has characteristics intermediate between series and shunt motors.

(*i*) Due to the presence of shunt field, the motor is prevented from running away at no load.

(*ii*) Due to the presence of series field, the starting torque is increased.

12.25. COMPARISON OF THREE TYPES OF MOTORS

(*i*) The speed regulation of a shunt motor is better than that of a series motor. However, speed regulation of a cumulative compound motor lies between shunt and series motors (See Fig. 12.27).

(*ii*) For a given armature current, the starting torque of a series motor is more than that of a shunt motor. However, the starting torque of a cumulative compound motor lies between series and shunt motors (See Fig. 12.28).

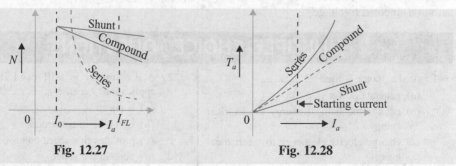

Fig. 12.27   Fig. 12.28

(*iii*) Both shunt and cumulative compound motors have definite no load speed. However, a series motor has dangerously high speed at no load.

12.26. APPLICATIONS OF D.C. MOTORS

1. Shunt motors. The characteristics of a shunt motor reveal that it is an approximately constant speed motor. It is, therefore, used

    (*i*) where the speed is required to remain almost constant from no load to full load.

    (*ii*) where the load has to be driven at a number of speeds and any one of which is required to remain nearly constant.

Industrial use : Lathes, drills, boring mills, shapers, spinning and weaving machines etc.

2. Series motors. It is a variable speed motor *i.e.* speed is low at high torque and *vice-versa*. However, at light or no load, the motor tends to attain dangerously high speed. The motor has a high starting torque. It is, therefore, used

    (*i*) where large starting torque is required *e.g.* in elevators and electric traction.

    (*ii*) where the load is subjected to heavy fluctuations and the speed is automatically required to reduce at high torques and *vice-versa*.

Industrial use : Electric traction, cranes, elevators, air compressors, vacuum cleaners, hair drier, sewing machines etc.

3. Compound motors. Differential-compound motors are rarely used because of their poor torque characteristics. However, cumulative-compound motors are used where a fairly constant speed is required with irregular loads or suddenly applied heavy loads.

Industrial use : Presses, shears, reciprocating machines etc.

12.27. TROUBLES IN D.C. MOTORS

Several troubles may arise in a d.c. motor and a few of them are discussed below :

1. Failure to start. This may be due to (*i*) ground fault (*ii*) open or short-circuit fault (*iii*) wrong connections (*iv*) too low supply voltage (*v*) frozen bearing or (*vi*) excessive load.

2. Sparking at brushes. This may be due to (*i*) troubles in brushes (*ii*) troubles in commutator (*iii*) troubles in armature or (*iv*) excessive load.

    (*i*) Brush troubles may arise due to insufficient contact surface, too short a brush, too little spring tension or wrong brush setting.

    (*ii*) Commutator troubles may be due to dirt on the commutator, high mica, rough surface or eccentricity.

    (*iii*) Armature troubles may be due to an open armature coil. An open armature coil will cause sparking each time the open coil passes the brush. The location of this open coil is noticeable by a burnt line between segments connecting the coil.

3. Vibrations and pounding noises. These may be due to (*i*) worn bearings (*ii*) loose parts (*iii*) rotating parts hitting stationary parts (*iv*) armature unbalanced (*v*) misalignment of machine (*vi*) loose coupling etc.

4. Overheating. The overheating of motor may be due to (*i*) overloads (*ii*) sparking at the brushes (*iii*) short-circuited armature or field coils (*iv*) too frequent starts or reversals (*v*) poor ventilation (*vi*) incorrect voltage.

MULTIPLE-CHOICE QUESTIONS

1. A d.c. motor is used to.................
   - (*a*) generate power
   - (*b*) change mechanical energy to electrical energy
   - (*c*) change electrical energy to mechanical energy
   - (*d*) increase energy put into it

2. A d.c. motor is still used in industrial applications because it....................
   - (*a*) is cheap
   - (*b*) is simple in construction
   - (*c*) provides fine speed control
   - (*d*) none of the above

3. Carbon brushes are preferable to copper brushes because.................
   (a) they have longer life
   (b) they reduce armature reaction
   (c) they have lower resistance
   (d) they reduce sparking

4. The field poles and armature of a d.c. machine are laminated to....................
   (a) reduce the weight of the machine
   (b) decrease the speed
   (c) reduce eddy currents
   (d) reduce armature reaction

5. The back e.m.f.in a d.c. motor................
   (a) opposes the applied voltage
   (b) aids the applied voltage
   (c) aids the armature current
   (d) none of the above

6. The value of back e.m.f. (E_b) in a d.c. motor is maximum at ....
   (a) no load   (b) full load
   (c) half full-load (d) none of the above

7. The motor equation is given by ....
   (a) $V = E_b - I_a R_a$
   (b) $V = E_b + I_a R_a$
   (c) $E_b = I_a R_a - V$
   (d) none of the above

8. Fig. 12.29 shows the d.c. shunt motor on no load. The quantity $E_b I_a$ represents.............
   (a) input power to armature
   (b) copper losses in armature
   (c) core losses
   (d) total friction, windage and core losses

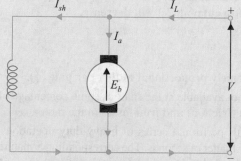

Fig. 12.29. Shunt motor on no load

9. In Fig. 12.29, the quantity VI_a represents..........
   (a) mechanical output of motor
   (b) core losses
   (c) all losses
   (d) friction and windage losses

10. The mechanical power developed in a d.c. motor is maximum when back e.m.f. (E_b) is equal to .... the applied voltage(V).
    (a) twice
    (b) half
    (c) one-third
    (d) none of the above

11. When the speed of a d.c. motor increases, its armature current................
    (a) increases
    (b) decreases
    (c) remains constant
    (d) none of the above

12. The amount of back e.m.f. of a shunt motor will increase when................
    (a) the load is increased
    (b) the field is weakened
    (c) the field is strengthened
    (d) none of the above

13. The speed of a d.c. motor is..............
    (a) directly proportional to flux per pole
    (b) inversely proportional to flux per pole
    (c) inversely proportional to applied voltage
    (d) none of the above

14. The torque developed by a d.c. motor is directly proportional to..........
    (a) flux per pole × armature current
    (b) armature resistance × applied voltage
    (c) armature resistance × armature current
    (d) none of the above

15. The shaft torque (T_{sh}) in a d.c. motor is less than total armature torque (T_a) because of .... in the motor.
    (a) Cu losses
    (b) field losses
    (c) iron and friction losses
    (d) none of the above

16. Armature reaction in a d.c. motor is increased................
    (a) when the armature current increases
    (b) when the armature current decreases
    (c) when the field current increases
    (d) by interpoles

17. With respect to the direction of rotation, interpoles on a d.c. motor must have the same polarity as the main poles................
    (a) ahead of them
    (b) behind them
    (c) none of the above

18. In a d.c. motor, the brushes are shifted from the mechanical neutral plane in a direction opposite to the rotation to...............
    (a) decrease speed
    (b) increase speed
    (c) reduce sparking
    (d) produce flat characteristics

19. In very large d.c. motors with severe heavy duty, armature reaction effects are corrected by ....
    (a) using interpoles only

    (b) using compensatory windings in addition to interpoles
    (c) shifting the brush position
    (d) none of the above

20. The speed of a ....motor is practically constant.
    (a) cumulatively compounded
    (b) series
    (c) differentially compounded
    (d) shunt

Answers to Multiple-Choice Questions

1. (c)	2. (c)	3. (d)	4. (c)	5. (a)	6. (a)	7. (b)	8. (d)
9. (c)	10. (b)	11. (b)	12. (c)	13. (b)	14. (a)	15. (c)	16. (a)
17. (b)	18. (c)	19. (b)	20. (d)				

Hints to Selected Multiple-Choice Questions

2. One potent reason for the widespread use of d.c. motors in industry is that their speed can be changed over a wide range by simple methods. Such a **fine speed control** is not possible with a.c. motors.

3. Since the contact resistance of carbon brushes is very high, **sparking at the brushes can be prevented.**

8. At no load, there is no output. Consequently, the entire power developed in the armature is used up in **overcoming friction, windage and core losses.**

9. At no load, there is no output. Consequently, the motor input (VI_a) is all used up to overcome all the losses.

11. $$I_a = \frac{V - E_b}{R_a}$$

    If the speed of the d.c. motor increases, then the back e.m.f. $E_b \left(= P\phi ZN / 60\,A \right)$ also increases. It is clear from the above equation that **armature current (I_a) will decrease.**

13. $$N \propto \frac{V - I_a R_a}{\phi}$$

    It is clear that speed (N) of a d.c. motor is **inversely proportional to flux per pole (ϕ).**

15. The total torque developed in the armature is not available at the shaft as some percentage of it is used up in overcoming **mechanical losses (friction) and iron losses** in the motor.

19. Some large d.c. motors employed in steel mills perform a series of heavy-duty operations. They accelerate, decelerate, stop, reverse all in a matter of seconds. The corresponding armature current increases, decreases, reverses in stepwise fashion, producing very sudden changes in armature reaction. For such motors, **interpoles do not adequately neutralize the armature m.m.f.** To eliminate this problem, additional *compensating windings* are connected in series with the armature. They are distributed in slots, cut into the pole faces of the main field poles. Like interpoles, these windings produce an m.m.f. equal and opposite to the m.m.f. of the armature.

Speed Control of D.C. Motors

INTRODUCTION

Although a far greater percentage of electric motors in service are a.c. motors, the d.c. motor is of considerable industrial importance. The principal advantage of a d.c. motor is that its speed can be changed over a wide range by a variety of simple methods. Such a fine speed control is generally not possible with a.c. motors. In fact, fine speed control is one of the reasons for the strong competitive position of d.c. motors in modern industrial applications. In this chapter, we shall discuss the various methods of speed control of d.c. motors.

13.1. SPEED CONTROL OF D.C. MOTORS

The speed of a d.c. motor is given by ;

$$N \propto \frac{E_b}{\phi}$$

or $\qquad N = K \dfrac{(V - I_a R)}{\phi}$ r.p.m. $\qquad$ ...(i)

where $\qquad R = R_a \qquad$ *... for shunt motor*

$\qquad\qquad = R_a + R_{se} \qquad$ *...for series motor*

From exp. (*i*), it is clear that there are two main methods of controlling the speed of a d.c. motor, namely;

(*i*) By varying the flux per pole φ. This is known as *flux control method.*

(*ii*) By varying the resistance in the armature circuit. This is known as *armature control method.*

13.2. SPEED CONTROL OF SHUNT MOTORS

The speed of a shunt motor can be changed by (*i*) flux control method (*ii*) armature control method. The former method is frequently used because it is simple and inexpensive.

1. Flux control method. It is based on the fact that by varying the flux φ, the motor speed ($N \propto 1/\phi$) can be changed and hence the name flux control method. In this method, a variable resistance (known as *shunt field rheostat*) is placed in series with shunt field winding as shown in Fig. 13.1.

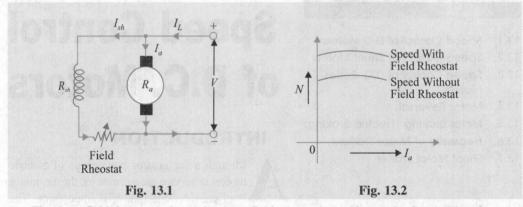

Fig. 13.1   **Fig. 13.2**

The shunt field rheostat reduces the shunt field current I_{sh} and hence the flux φ. Therefore, we can only raise the speed of the motor above the normal speed (See Fig. 13.2). Generally, this method permits to increase the speed in the ratio 3 : 1. Wider speed ranges tend to produce instability and poor commutation.

Advantages

(*i*) This is an easy and convenient method.

(*ii*) It is an inexpensive method since very little power is wasted in the shunt field rheostat due to relatively small value of I_{sh}.

(*iii*) The speed control exercised by this method is independent of load on the machine.

Disadvantages

(*i*) Only speeds higher than the normal speed can be obtained since the total field circuit resistance cannot be reduced below R_{sh}, the shunt field winding resistance.

(*ii*) There is a limit to the maximum speed obtainable by this method. It is because if the flux is too much weakened, commutation becomes poorer.

2. Armature control method. This method is based on the fact that by varying the voltage available across the armature, the back e.m.f. and hence the speed of the motor can be changed. This is done by inserting a variable resistance R_C (known as *controller resistance*) in series with the armature as shown in Fig. 13.3.

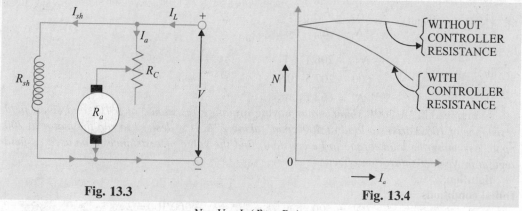

Fig. 13.3   **Fig. 13.4**

$$N \propto V - I_a(R_a + R_C)$$

where R_C = controller resistance

Due to voltage drop in the controller resistance, the back e.m.f. (E_b) is *decreased. Since $N \propto E_b$, the speed of the motor is reduced. The highest speed obtainable is that corresponding to $R_C = 0$ *i.e.*, normal speed. Hence, this method can only provide speeds below the normal speed (See Fig. 13.4).

Disadvantages

(*i*) A large amount of power is wasted in the controller resistance since it carries full armature current I_a.

(*ii*) The speed varies widely with load since the speed depends upon the voltage drop in the controller resistance and hence on the armature current demanded by the load.

(*iii*) The output and efficiency of the motor are reduced.

(*iv*) This method results in poor speed regulation.

Due to above disadvantages, this method is seldom used to control the speed of shunt motors.

Note. The armature control method is a very common method for the speed control of d.c. series motors. The disadvantage of poor speed regulation is not important in a series motor which is used only where varying speed service is required.

Example 13.1. *A 220V d.c. shunt motor having an armature resistance of 0.25Ω carries an armature current of 50A and runs at 600 r.p.m. If the flux is reduced by 10% by field regulator, find the speed assuming load torque remains the same.*

Solution.

Initial conditions

$$N_1 = 600 \text{ r.p.m., } I_{a1} = 50 \text{ A}$$
$$E_{b1} = V - I_{a1}R_a = 220 - 50 \times 0.25 = 207.5 \text{ V}$$

Final conditions

$$\phi_2 = 0.9\phi_1 \text{ so that } \phi_2/\phi_1 = 0.9$$

As the load torque remains unchanged, $\phi_1 I_{a1} = \phi_2 I_{a2}$

∴
$$I_{a_2} = \left(\frac{\phi_1}{\phi_2}\right)I_{a1} = \left(\frac{1}{0.9}\right)50 = 55.6 \text{ A}$$

∴
$$E_{b_2} = V - I_{a2}R_a = 220 - 55.6 \times 0.25 = 206.1 \text{ V}$$

---

* $E_b = V - I_a(R_a + R_C)$. Since V is constant, E_b will decrease.

Using the formula, $\dfrac{N_2}{N_1} = \dfrac{E_{b2}}{E_{b1}} \times \dfrac{\phi_1}{\phi_2}$

or $\dfrac{N_2}{600} = \dfrac{206.1}{207.5} \times \dfrac{1}{0.9}$

$\therefore$ $N_2 = 662$ r.p.m.

Example13.2. *A 200V shunt motor having armature resistance of 0.4Ω and shunt field resistance of 100Ω drives a load at 500 r.p.m. taking 27A. It is desired to run the motor at 700 r.p.m. Assuming the load torque to be constant, find the value of resistance to be used as field regulator. Neglect saturation effect.*

Solution.
Initial conditions

$$N_1 = 500 \text{ r.p.m.}, I_L = 27A \; ; I_{sh1} = 200/100 = 2 \text{ A}$$
$$I_{a1} = I_L - I_{sh1} = 27 - 2 = 25 \text{ A}$$
$$E_{b1} = 200 - 25 \times 0.4 = 190V$$

Final conditions

$$E_{b2} = V - I_{a2} R_a = 200 - 0.4 \, I_{a2}$$

As the load torque is constant , $\phi_1 I_{a1} = \phi_2 I_{a2}$. But $\phi \propto I_{sh}$ so that we have,

$$I_{sh1} I_{a1} = I_{sh2} I_{a2}$$

$\therefore$ $I_{sh2} = \dfrac{I_{sh1} I_{a1}}{I_{a2}} = \dfrac{2 \times 25}{I_{a2}} = \dfrac{50}{I_{a2}}$

Now, $\dfrac{N_1}{N_2} = \dfrac{E_{b1}}{E_{b2}} \times \dfrac{I_{sh2}}{I_{sh1}}$

or $\dfrac{500}{700} = \dfrac{190}{200 - 0.4 I_{a2}} \times \dfrac{(50/I_{a2})}{2}$

or $I_{a2}^2 - 500 I_{a2} + 16625 = 0$

Solving this equation, we get, $I_{a2} = 35$ A

$\therefore$ $I_{sh2} = 50/I_{a2} = 50/35 = 1.43$ A

$\therefore$ $R_{sh2} = V/I_{sh2} = 200/1.43 = 139.86$ Ω

Field rheostat resistance $= 139.86 - 100 = \textbf{39.86 Ω}$

Example13.3. *A shunt motor supplied at 230V runs at 900 r.p.m. while taking armature current of 30A; the resistance of armature circuit being 0.4Ω. Calculate the resistance required in series with the armature circuit to reduce the speed to 500 r.p.m., assuming that the armature current is 25A.*

Solution.
Initial conditions

$$N_1 = 900 \text{ r.p.m.}, I_{a1} = 30 \text{ A}$$
$$E_{b1} = V - I_{a1} R_a = 230 - 30 \times 0.4 = 218 \text{ V}$$

Final conditions

$$N_2 = 500 \text{ r.p.m.}, I_{a2} = 25A, R_t = R_a + R_c$$
$$E_{b2} = V - I_{a2} R_t = 230 - 25 R_t$$

Since excitation is unchanged, $\phi_1 = \phi_2$.

$$\therefore \qquad \frac{N_2}{N_1} = \frac{E_{b2}}{E_{b1}}$$

$$or \qquad \frac{500}{900} = \frac{230 - 25R_t}{218}$$

$$\therefore \qquad R_t = 4.356\Omega$$

∴ Additional series resistance required in the armature

$$R_C = R_t - R_a = 4.356 - 0.4 = \mathbf{3.956\Omega}$$

Example 13.4. *A 250V shunt motor has an armature current of 20A when running at 1000 r.p.m. against full-load torque. The armature resistance is 0.5Ω. What resistance must be inserted in series with the armature to reduce the speed to 500 r.p.m. at the same torque? What will be the speed if the load torque is halved with this resistance in the circuit? Assume the flux to remain constant throughout and neglect brush contact drop.*

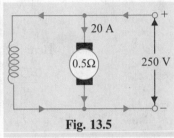

Fig. 13.5

Solution. Figure 13.5 shows shunt motor connections.

At full-load torque. Let R_c be the resistance to be inserted in series with the armature to reduce the speed to 500 r.p.m. Since load torque remains the same and $\phi_1 = \phi_2$,

$$T_a = \phi_1 I_{a1} = \phi_2 I_{a2}$$

$$\therefore \qquad I_{a1} = I_{a2} = 20A$$

$$E_{b1} = V - I_{a1} R_a = 250 - 20 \times 0.5 = 240 \text{ volts}$$

$$E_{b2} = V - I_{a2} R_t = 250 - 20 \times R_t \quad \text{where } R_t = R_a + R_C$$

Now

$$\frac{N_2}{N_1} = \frac{E_{b2}}{E_{b1}} \times \frac{\phi_1}{\phi_2}$$

or

$$\frac{500}{1000} = \frac{250 - 20 R_t}{240} \qquad (\because \ \phi_1 = \phi_2)$$

$$\therefore \qquad R_t = 6.5\Omega \ \text{ or } \ R_C = R_t - R_a = 6.5 - 0.5 = \mathbf{6 \ \Omega}$$

At half full-load. Since load torque is halved and flux remains the same, the armature current is also halved *i.e.*, $I_{a3} = 20/2 = 10A$.

$$E_{b3} = V - I_{a3} R_t = 250 - 10 \times 6.5 = 185 \text{ volts}$$

$$\frac{N_3}{N_1} = \frac{E_{b3}}{E_{b1}} \qquad (\because \ \phi_1 = \phi_3)$$

or

$$\frac{N_3}{1000} = \frac{185}{240}$$

$$\therefore \qquad N_3 = \mathbf{771 \ r.p.m.}$$

Example 13.5. *A 500V, 10 H.P. shunt motor has a full-load efficiency of 85%. With the same shunt field and armature current, it is desired to reduce the speed by 30% by inserting a resistance in the armature circuit. Calculate the value of the inserted resistance. The resistances of the field and armature are 400Ω and 0.25Ω respectively.*

Solution. Let R_C be the required resistance.

$$\text{Input to motor} = \frac{\text{Output}}{\eta} = \frac{10 \times 746}{0.85} = 8776W$$

$$\text{Input current} = \frac{8776}{500} = 17.55\,\text{A}$$

$$\text{Shunt field current} = \frac{500}{400} = 1.25\,\text{A}$$

Armature current, $\quad I_{a1} = 17.55 - 1.25 = 16.3\,\text{A}$

$$E_{b1} = V - I_{a1}R_a = 500 - 16.3 \times 0.25 = 495.9\,\text{volts}$$

Now $\qquad \dfrac{N_2}{N_1} = \dfrac{E_{b2}}{E_{b1}} \times \dfrac{\phi_1}{\phi_2}$

Here $N_2 = 0.7N_1$ and $\phi_1 = \phi_2$.

∴ $\qquad \dfrac{0.7\,N_1}{N_1} = \dfrac{E_{b2}}{495.9} \qquad$ or $\qquad E_{b2} = 347.1\,\text{volts}$

Now $\qquad E_{b2} = V - I_{a2}R_t \qquad$ where $\quad R_t = R_a + R_C$

or $\qquad 347.1 = 500 - 16.3 \times R_t \qquad\qquad (\because I_{a2} = I_{a1} = 16.3\,\text{A})$

∴ $\qquad R_t = 9.37\,\Omega \quad$ or $\quad R_C = R_t - R_a = 9.37 - 0.25 = \mathbf{9.12\,\Omega}$

TUTORIAL PROBLEMS

1. A 200V shunt motor having an armature resistance of $0.2\,\Omega$ carries an armature current of 50A and runs at 960 r.p.m. If the flux is reduced by 10%, find the speed, assuming load torque remains the same. **[1059 r.p.m.]**
2. A shunt motor supplied at 200V runs at 500 r.p.m. while taking armature current of 30A. The armature resistance is $0.5\,\Omega$. Calculate the resistance required in series with the armature to reduce the speed to 300 r.p.m.; assuming the current in the armature remains the same. **[2.47Ω]**
3. A shunt motor connected across 440V supply takes an armature current of 20A and runs at 500 r.p.m. The armature resistance is $0.6\,\Omega$. If the magnitude of flux is reduced by 30% and the torque developed by the armature increases by 40%, what is the speed of the motor? **[695 r.p.m.]**

13.3. SPEED CONTROL OF D.C. SERIES MOTORS

The speed control of d.c. series motors can be obtained by (*i*) flux control method (*ii*) armature-resistance control method. The latter method is mostly used.

1. Flux control method. In this method, the flux produced by the series motor is varied and hence the speed. The variation of flux can be achieved in the following ways:

(*i*) **Field diverters.** In this method, a variable resistance (called *field diverter*) is connected in parallel with series field winding as shown in Fig. 13.6. Its effect is to shunt some portion of the line current from the series field winding, thus weakening the field and increasing the speed

$(\because N \propto 1/\phi)$. The lowest speed obtainable is that corresponding to zero current in the diverter (*i.e.*, diverter is open). Obviously, the lowest speed obtainable is the nor-

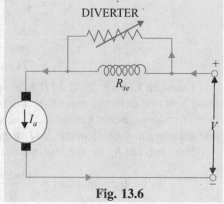

Fig. 13.6

mal speed of the motor. Consequently, this method can only provide speeds above the normal speed. The series field diverter method is often employed in traction work.

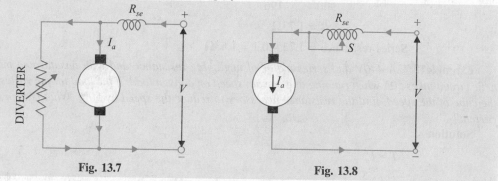

Fig. 13.7   Fig. 13.8

(*ii*) **Armature diverter.** In order to obtain speeds below the normal speed, a variable resistance (called *armature diverter*) is connected in parallel with the armature as shown in Fig. 13.7. The diverter shunts some of the line current, thus reducing the armature current. Now for a given load, if I_a is decreased, the flux ϕ must increase $(\because T \propto \phi I_a)$. Since $N \propto 1/\phi$, the motor speed is decreased. By adjusting the armature diverter, any speed lower than the normal speed can be obtained.

(*iii*) **Tapped field control.** In this method, the flux is reduced (and hence speed is increased) by decreasing the number of turns of the series field winding as shown in Fig. 13.8. The switch S can short circuit any part of the field winding, thus decreasing the flux and raising the speed. With full turns of the field winding, the motor runs at normal speed and as the field turns are cut out, speeds higher than normal speed are achieved.

2. Armature-resistance control. In this method, a variable resistance is directly connected in series with the supply to the complete motor as shown in Fig. 13.9. This reduces the voltage available across the armature and hence the speed falls. By changing the value of variable resistance, any speed below the normal speed can be obtained. This is the most common method employed to control the speed of d.c. series motors. Although this method has poor speed regulation, this has no significance for series motors because they are used

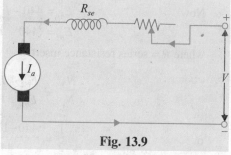

Fig. 13.9

in varying speed applications. The loss of power in the series resistance for many applications of series motors is not too serious since in these applications, the control is utilised for a large portion of the time for reducing the speed under light-load conditions and is only used intermittently when the motor is carrying full load.

Example 13.6. *A 220V d.c. series motor runs at 900 r.p.m. when taking a line current of 40A. The armature resistance and series field resistance are 0.06Ω and 0.04Ω respectively. If current taken remains the same, calculate the series resistance required to reduce the speed to 600 r.p.m.*

Solution.
$$R_a + R_{se} = 0.04 + 0.06 = 0.1\,\Omega$$
$$N_1 = 900 \text{ r.p.m.}; \quad N_2 = 600 \text{ r.p.m.}; \quad I_{a1} = I_{a2} = 40 \text{ A}$$
$$E_{b1} = 200 - 40 \times 0.1 = 196 \text{ V}$$
$$E_{b2} = (200 - 40R) \text{ V}$$

where
$$R = \text{Series resistance} + R_a + R_{se}$$

Now
$$\frac{N_2}{N_1} = \frac{E_{b2}}{E_{b1}} \qquad\qquad (\because \phi_2 = \phi_1)$$

or
$$\frac{600}{900} = \frac{200 - 40\,R}{196}$$

∴
$$R = 1.73\,\Omega$$

∴ Series resistance $= 1.73 - 0.1 = \mathbf{1.63\,\Omega}$

Example 13.7. *A 440V d.c. series motor of negligible resistance and with unsaturated magnetic circuit takes 50A when running at a certain speed on a given load. If the load torque varies as the cube of the speed, find the resistance necessary to reduce the speed by 50%. What is then the current?*

Solution

$$\qquad {}^*T \propto I_a^2$$

Also
$$T \propto N^3 \qquad\qquad\qquad\qquad\qquad ...given$$

For the first case, $\quad I_{a1}^2 \propto N_1^3$

For the second case, $\quad I_{a2}^2 \propto N_2^3$

∴
$$\left(\frac{I_{a2}}{I_{a1}}\right)^2 = \left(\frac{N_2}{N_1}\right)^3 = \left(\frac{1}{2}\right)^3 \qquad\qquad \left(\because \frac{N_2}{N_1} = \frac{1}{2}\right)$$

or
$$I_{a2} = I_{a1}\sqrt{\frac{1}{8}} = 50\sqrt{\frac{1}{8}} = \mathbf{17.68A}$$

Now
$$E_{b1} = 440 - I_{a1} \times 0 = 440 \text{ V}$$
$$E_{b2} = (440 - 17.68\,R)\text{V}$$

where R = series resistance inserted

$$\frac{N_2}{N_1} = \frac{E_{b2}}{E_{b1}} \times \frac{I_{a1}}{I_{a2}} \qquad\qquad (\because \phi \propto I_a)$$

or
$$\frac{1}{2} = \frac{440 - 17.68\,R}{440} \times \frac{50}{17.68}$$

∴
$$R = \mathbf{20.5\,\Omega}$$

Example 13.8. *A 200 V d.c. series motor runs at 800 r.p.m. when taking a line current of 15A. The armature resistance and series field resistance are 0.6Ω and 0.4Ω respectively. Find the speed at which it will run when connected in series with a 5Ω resistance and taking the same current at the same voltage.*

Solution.

$$R_a + R_{se} = 0.6 + 0.4 = 1\,\Omega \; ; \qquad N_1 = 800 \text{ r.p.m.} \; ; \qquad I_{a1} = I_{a2} = 15\text{A} \quad ; N_2 = ?$$

Without 5Ω resistance in series, we have,

$$E_{b1} = V - I_{a1}\,(R_a + R_{se}) = 200 - 15\,(0.6 + 0.4) = 185 \text{ volts}$$

With 5Ω resistance in series, we have,

$$E_{b2} = V - I_{a2}\,(R_a + R_{se} + 5) = 200 - 15\,(0.6 + 0.4 + 5) = 110 \text{ volts}$$

. . . .

* $\quad T \propto \phi I_a$. As the series field is unsaturated, $\phi \propto I_a$.

∴ $T \propto I_a^2$.

Now $\qquad \dfrac{N_2}{N_1} = \dfrac{E_{b2}}{E_{b1}}$ $\qquad\qquad\qquad\qquad\qquad\qquad\qquad$ ($\because$ flux is the same)

or $\qquad \dfrac{N_2}{800} = \dfrac{110}{185}$ $\qquad \therefore\; N_2 = 476$ r.p.m.

Example 13.9. *A 240 V d.c. series motor takes 40A when giving its rated output at 1500 r.p.m. Its resistance is 0.3 Ω. Find what resistance must be added to obtain rated torque (i) at starting (ii) at 1000 r.p.m.*

Solution. Since torque remains the same $(T \propto I_a^2)$, the armature current is same (*i.e.*, 40A) in the two cases.

(*i*) Let R be the series resistance added at starting to obtain the rated torque. Then,

$$40 = \frac{V}{R+0.3} = \frac{240}{R+0.3}$$

$\therefore$ $\qquad\qquad\qquad R = 5.7\ \Omega$

(*ii*) $E_{b1} = V - I_{a1}\,R_a = 240 - 40 \times 0.3 = 228$ volts ; $N_1 = 1500$ r.p.m.

$\qquad E_{b2} = V - I_{a1}\,(R_a + R) = 240 - 40\,(0.3 + R)$ volts ; $N_2 = 1000$ r.p.m.

Now $\qquad \dfrac{N_2}{N_1} = \dfrac{E_{b2}}{E_{b1}}$ $\qquad\qquad\qquad\qquad\qquad\qquad\qquad$ ($\because$ flux is the same)

or $\qquad \dfrac{1000}{1500} = \dfrac{240 - 40\,(0.3 + R)}{228}$ $\qquad \therefore\; R = 1.9\,\Omega$

TUTORIAL PROBLEMS

1. A 220V d.c. series motor takes 10A and runs at 600 r.p.m., its total resistance is 0.8 Ω. At what speed will it run when a 5-ohm resistance is connected in series, the motor is taking the same current at the same supply voltage? [458 r.p.m.]

2. A d.c. series motor with unsaturated field and negligible resistance, when running at a certain speed on a given load takes 60A at 460V. If the load torque varies as the cube of the speed, calculate the series resistance required to reduce the speed by 25%. [6 Ω]

3. A d.c. series motor is connected to a 220V d.c. supply and runs at 500 r.p.m. taking a current of 50A. Calculate the value of series resistance which will reduce the speed to 300 r.p.m.; the load torque then being one-half of its previous value. Resistance of motor is 0.1 Ω. Assume the flux to be proportional to field current. [3,54 Ω]

13.4. MOTOR REVERSAL

The direction of the developed torque in a d.c. motor depends upon the relative directions of the armature current and the field flux. Therefore, the reversal of the developed torque and hence of the rotation of the motor may be accomplished by a reversal of the connections to either the field winding or the armature circuit. Reversal of the connections to both the field winding and the armature circuit does not change the direction of rotation.

13.5. MOTOR BRAKING (ELECTRIC BRAKING)

Sometimes it is desirable to stop a d.c. motor quickly. This may be necessary in case of emergency or to save time if the motor is being used for frequently repeated operations. The motor and its load may be brought to rest by using either (*i*) mechanical (friction) braking or (*ii*) electric braking. In mechanical braking, the motor is stopped due to the friction between the moving parts of the motor and the brake shoe *i.e.* kinetic energy of the motor is dissipated as heat. Mechanical braking has several disadvantages including non-smooth stop and greater stopping time.

In electric braking, the kinetic energy of the moving parts (*i.e.,* motor) is converted into electrical energy which is dissipated in a resistance as heat or alternatively, it is returned to the supply source (Regenerative braking). For d.c. shunt as well as series motors, the following three methods of electric braking are used:

   (*i*) Rheostatic or Dynamic braking

  (*ii*) Plugging

 (*iii*) Regenerative braking

It may be noted that electric braking cannot hold the motor stationary and mechanical braking is necessary. However, the main advantage of using electric braking is that it reduces the wear and tear of mechanical brakes and cuts down the stopping time considerably due to high braking retardation.

(*i*) **Rheostatic or Dynamic braking.** In this method, the armature of the running motor is disconnected from the supply and is connected across a variable resistance R. However, the field winding is left connected to the supply. The armature, while slowing down, rotates in a strong magnetic field and, therefore, operates as a generator, sending a large current through resistance R. This causes the energy possessed by the rotating armature to be dissipated quickly as heat in the resistance. As a result, the motor is brought to standstill quickly.

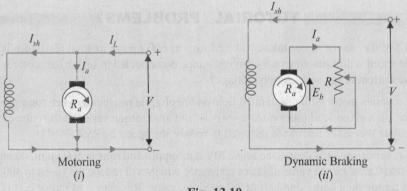

Motoring   Dynamic Braking
(*i*)   (*ii*)

Fig. 13.10

Fig. 13.10 (*ii*) shows dynamic braking of a shunt motor. The braking torque can be controlled by varying the resistance R. If the value of R is decreased as the motor speed decreases, the braking torque may be maintained at a high value. At a low value of speed, the braking torque becomes small and the final stopping of the motor is due to friction. This type of braking is used extensively in connection with the control of elevators and hoists and in other applications in which motors must be started, stopped and reversed frequently.

(*ii*) **Plugging.** In this method, connections to the armature are reversed so that motor tends to rotate in the opposite direction, thus providing the necessary braking effect. When the motor comes to rest, the supply must be cut off otherwise the motor will start rotating in the opposite direction.

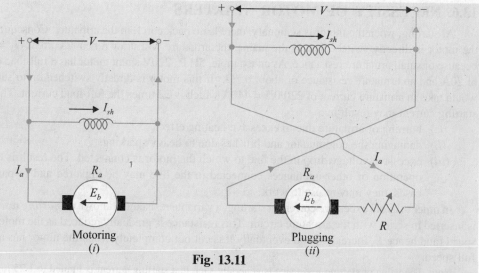

Fig. 13.11

Fig. 13.11 (*ii*) shows plugging of a d.c. shunt motor. Note that armature connections are reversed while the connections of the field winding are kept the same. As a result, the current in the armature reverses. During the normal running of the motor [See Fig. 13.11 (*i*)], the back e.m.f. E_b opposes the applied voltage V. However, when armature connections are reversed, back e.m.f. E_b and V act *in the same direction* around the circuit. Therefore, a voltage equal to $V + E_b$ is impressed across the armature circuit. Since $E_b \simeq V$, the impressed voltage is approximately $2V$. In order to limit the current to safe value, a variable resistance R is inserted in the circuit at the time of changing armature connections.

(*iii*) **Regenerative braking.** In the regenerative braking, the motor is run as a generator. As a result, the kinetic energy of the motor is converted into electrical energy and returned to the supply. Fig. 13.12 shows two methods of regenerative braking for a shunt motor.

(*a*) In one method, field winding is disconnected from the supply and field current is increased by exciting it from another source [See Fig. 13.12 (*i*)]. As a result, induced e.m.f. E exceeds the supply voltage V and the machine feeds energy into the supply. Thus braking torque is provided upto the speed at which induced e.m.f. and supply voltage are equal. As the machine slows down, it is not possible to maintain induced e.m.f. at a higher value than the supply voltage. Therefore, this method is possible only for a limited range of speed.

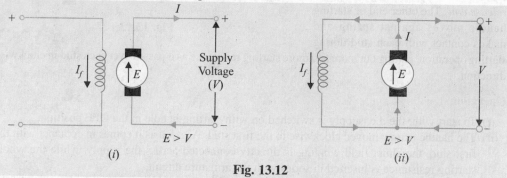

Fig. 13.12

(*b*) In a second method, the field excitation does not change but the load causes the motor to run above the normal speed (*e.g.*, descending load on a crane). As a result, the induced e.m.f. E becomes greater than the supply voltage V [See Fig. 13.12 (*ii*)]. The direction of armature current I, therefore, reverses but the direction of shunt field current I_f remains unaltered. Hence the torque is reversed and the speed falls until E becomes less than V.

13.6. NECESSITY OF MOTOR STARTERS

At starting, when the motor is stationary, there is no back e.m.f. in the armature. Consequently, if the motor is directly switched on to the mains, the armature will draw a heavy current ($I_a = V/R_a$) because of small armature resistance. As an example, 5H.P., 220V shunt motor has a full-load current of 20A and an armature resistance of about 0.5Ω. If this motor is directly switched on to supply, it would take an armature current of 220/0.5 = 440A which is 22 times the full-load current. This high starting current may result in :

(*i*) burning of armature due to excessive heating effect.

(*ii*) damaging the commutator and brushes due to heavy sparking.

(*iii*) excessive voltage drop in the line to which the motor is connected. The result is that the operation of other appliances connected to the line may be impaired and in particular cases, they may refuse to work.

In order to avoid excessive current at starting, a variable resistance (known as *starting resistance*) is inserted in series with the armature circuit. This resistance is gradually reduced as the motor gains speed (and hence E_b increases) and eventually it is cut out completely when the motor has attained full speed.

Note. The value of starting resistance is generally such that starting current is limited to 1.25 to 2 times the full-load current.

13.7. SHUNT MOTOR STARTER

Fig. 13.13 shows the schematic diagram of a shunt motor starter with protective devices. It consists of starting resistance divided into several sections and connected in series with the armature. The tapping points of the starting resistance are brought out to a number of studs. One end of shunt field winding is connected to the first stud and the other end to the far side of the supply. Included in this circuit is the *no-volt release coil*. One end of the starting handle A is connected to one side of supply through *overload release coil*. The other end of starting handle moves against spring and makes contact with each stud during

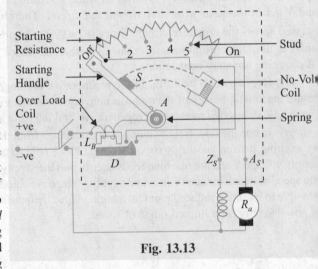

Fig. 13.13

starting operation, cutting out more and more starting resistance as it passes over each stud in clockwise direction.

Operation

(*i*) To start with, the d.c. supply is switched on with starting handle in the OFF position.

(*ii*) The handle is now moved clockwise to the first stud. As soon as it comes in contact with the first stud, the shunt field winding is directly connected across the supply, while the whole starting resistance is inserted in series with the armature circuit.

(*iii*) As the handle is gradually moved over to the final stud, the starting resistance is cut out of the armature circuit in steps. The handle is now held magnetically by the no-volt release coil which is energised by shunt field current.

(iv) If the supply voltage is suddenly interrupted or if the field excitation is accidentally cut, the no-volt release coil is demagnetised and the handle goes back to the OFF position under the pull of the spring. If no-volt release coil were not used, then in case of failure of supply, the handle would remain on the final stud. If then supply is restored, the motor will be directly connected across the supply, resulting in an excessive armature current.

(v) If the motor is overloaded (or a fault occurs), it will draw excessive current from the supply. This current will increase the ampere-turns of the over-load release coil and pull the armature D, thus short-circuiting the no-volt release coil. The no-volt coil is demagnetised and the starting handle is pulled to the OFF position by the spring. Thus, the motor is automatically disconnected from the supply.

DC motor starter

MULTIPLE-CHOICE QUESTIONS

1. A d.c. shunt motor runs at 500 r.p.m. at 220 V. A resistance of 4.5Ω is added in series with the armature for speed control. The armature resistance is 0.5Ω. The current to stall the motor is ....

   (a) 44 A   (b) 50 A

   (c) 60 A   (d) 30 A

2. A d.c. motor runs at 1725 r.p.m. at full-load and 1775 r.p.m. at no load. The speed regulation is ....

   (a) 4.7%   (b) 2.9%

   (c) 7.6%   (d) 1.5%

3. In a shunt motor, the connection of the armature as well as shunt field winding are reversed. Then,

   (a) the direction of rotation is reversed

   (b) the direction of rotation remains unchanged

   (c) the motor will not work

   (d) the motor will run at dangerously high speed

4. A shunt motor runs at 500 r.p.m. on a 200V circuit. Its armature resistance is 0.5Ω and the current taken is 30A in addition to field current. What resistance must be placed in series with armature circuit to reduce the speed to 300 r.p.m.; the current in armature remaining the same ?

   (a) 4.24 Ω   (b) 3.78 Ω

   (c) 6.74 Ω   (d) 2.47 Ω

5. A 200V d.c. series motor runs at 500 r.p.m. when taking a line current of 25A. The resistance of the armature is 0.3Ω and that of the series field 0.5Ω. If current taken remains constant, calculate the resistance necessary to reduce the speed to 350 r.p.m.

   (a) 2.16Ω   (b) 3.42Ω

   (c) 1.56Ω   (d) 4.83Ω

6. A 240V series motor takes 40A when giving its rated output at 1500 r.p.m. Its resistance is 0.3Ω. Find what resistance must be added to obtain rated torque at starting?

   (a) 2.4Ω (b) 1.5Ω

   (c) 3.2Ω (d) 5.7Ω

7. In the above question, what resistance must be added to obtain rated torque at 1000 r.p.m.?

   (a) 1.9Ω (b) 2.3Ω

   (c) 3.2Ω (d) 4.8Ω

8. A series motor of resistance 1Ω between the terminals runs at 800 r.p.m. at 200 V with a current of 15A. Find the speed at which it will run when connected in series with a 5Ω resistance and taking the same current at the same supply voltage.

   (a) 476 r.p.m.   (b) 384 r.p.m.

   (c) 572 r.p.m.   (d) 602 r.p.m.

9. What happens to speed when the flux is reduced by 10% in a 200V d.c. shunt motor having an armature resistance of 0.2Ω, carrying a current of 50A and running at 960 r.p.m. prior to weakening of field? The total torque may be assumed to be constant and iron and friction losses may be neglected.

   (a) 1250 r.p.m.   (b) 1058 r.p.m.

   (c) 920 r.p.m.   (d) 576 r.p.m.

10. By flux control method of speed control of a d.c. shunt motor, we can obtain speeds ....

    (a) above the normal speed only

    (b) below the normal speed only

    (c) above as well as below the normal speed

    (d) none of the above

11. By putting controller resistance in series with the armature of a d.c. motor, we can obtain speeds........

    (a) above the normal speed only

    (b) below the normal speed only

    (c) above as well as below the normal speed

    (d) none of the above

12. The speed of a d.c. motor can be controlled by changing........

    (a) its flux

    (b) armature circuit resistance

    (c) applied voltage

    (d) all of the above

13. Motor starters are essential for........

    (a) accelerating the motor

    (b) starting the motor

    (c) avoiding excessive starting current

    (d) preventing fuse blowing

14. The only disadvantage of field control method for controlling the speed of a d.c. shunt motor is that it........

    (a) gives speeds lower than the normal speed

    (b) is wasteful

    (c) needs a large rheostat

    (d) adversely affects commutation

15. The rheostatic speed control method is very

    (a) economical

    (b) efficient

    (c) unsuitable for rapidly changing loads

    (d) suitable for getting speeds above the normal

Answers to Multiple-Choice Questions

1. (a)	2. (b)	3. (b)	4. (d)	5. (a)	6. (d)	7. (a)	8. (a)
9. (b)	10. (a)	11. (b)	12. (d)	13. (c)	14. (d)	15. (c)	

Hints to Selected Multiple-Choice Questions

1. We can stall the motor (i.e. reduce its speed to zero) by putting more and more load on the shaft. When the motor is stalled, $E_b = 0$.

   $\therefore$ $I_a = \dfrac{220}{4.5+0.5} = 44A$

2. Speed regulation $= \dfrac{N_0 - N_{FL}}{N_{FL}} \times 100 = \dfrac{1775 - 1725}{1725} \times 100 = 2.9\%$

4. $\dfrac{N_2}{N_1} = \dfrac{E_{b2}}{E_{b1}} \times \dfrac{\phi_1}{\phi_2}$. As field current remains same, $\phi_1 = \phi_2$.

$$\therefore \qquad \frac{N_2}{N_1} = \frac{E_{b2}}{E_{b1}}$$

$$E_{b_1} = 200 - 30 \times 0.5 = 185 \text{V} ; \qquad E_{b_2} = 200 - 30 R_t$$

$$\therefore \qquad \frac{300}{500} = \frac{200 - 30 R_t}{185} \qquad \therefore R_t = 2.97 \Omega$$

Additional resistance required = $R_t - R_a = 2.97 - 0.5 = \mathbf{2.47\Omega}$

6. Since torque is same, armature current will be the same. Motor resistance is $R_m = 0.3\Omega$. Let R ohm be the desired resistance to be added in series.

At starting : $\qquad I_a = \dfrac{V - E_b}{R_m + R} = \dfrac{V}{R_m + R} \qquad (\because E_b = 0)$

or $\qquad 40 = \dfrac{240}{0.3 + R} \qquad \therefore R = 5.7\Omega$

7. At 1000 r.p.m., $\dfrac{E_{b_2}}{E_{b_1}} = \dfrac{N_2}{N_1} = \dfrac{1000}{1500} = \dfrac{1}{1.5} \qquad (\because \text{flux is same})$

$$\therefore \qquad E_{b_2} = \frac{E_{b_1}}{1.5} = \frac{240 - 40 \times 0.3}{1.5} = 152 \text{V}$$

If R is the resistance to be added, then,

$$I_a = \frac{V - E_{b_2}}{R_m + R} \quad \text{or} \quad 40 = \frac{240 - 152}{0.3 + R} \quad \therefore R = \mathbf{1.9\Omega}$$

8. $E_b \propto \phi N$ $\qquad$ or $\qquad$ $E_b \propto N$ $\qquad$ ($\because$ Armature current and hence ϕ is the same)

$$E_{b_1} = 200 - 15 \times 1 = 185 \text{V}; \quad E_{b_2} = 200 - 15(5 + 1) = 110 \text{V}$$

Now $\qquad \dfrac{E_{b_2}}{E_{b_1}} = \dfrac{N_2}{N_1} \qquad or \qquad \dfrac{110}{185} = \dfrac{N_2}{800} \qquad \therefore N_2 = \mathbf{476 r.p.m.}$

9. When the flux is decreased, speed ($N \propto E_b / \phi$) of the motor increases.

Now $\qquad \dfrac{N_2}{N_1} = \dfrac{E_{b_2}}{E_{b_1}} \times \dfrac{\phi_1}{\phi_2}$

Also $T_a \propto \phi I_a$. As torque is the same in the two cases,

$$\phi_1 I_{a_1} = \phi_2 I_{a_2} \quad \text{or} \quad \phi_1 \times 50 = 0.9 \phi_1 \times I_{a_2} \quad \therefore I_{a_2} = 50/0.9 = 55.55 \text{A}$$

$$E_{b_1} = 200 - 50 \times 0.2 = 190 \text{V}$$

$$E_{b_2} = 200 - 55.55 \times 0.2 = 188.9 \text{V}$$

$$\therefore \qquad \frac{N_2}{960} = \frac{188.9}{190} \times \frac{\phi_1}{0.9\phi_1} \qquad \therefore N_2 = \mathbf{1058 \text{ r.p.m.}}$$

11. This method gives speeds **below the normal speed** not above it because armature voltage can be decreased (not increased) by the controller resistance.

14. The only disadvantage of this method is that **commutation becomes unsatisfactory** because the effect of armature reaction is greater on a weakened field.

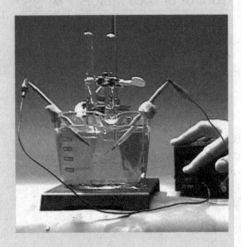

14

Chemical Effects of Electric Current

INTRODUCTION

There are two types of electric conductors *viz.* (*i*) electronic or metallic conductors and (*ii*) electrolytic or ionic conductors. In the former case, current conduction is due to the movement of free electrons and there is no physical or chemical change except the rise in temperature *e.g.*, metals, alloys *etc.* In electrolytic or ionic conductors, current conduction is due to the movement of ions together with the resulting chemical changes *e.g.*, electrolytes. In this chapter, we shall confine our attention to this type of conductors *i.e.*, ionic conductors.

14.1. ELECTROLYTES

A conducting liquid is called an electrolyte *e.g.*, acids (H_2SO_4, HCl *etc.*), solutions of inorganic compounds (*e.g.*, $CuSO_4$, NaCl *etc.*), hydroxides of metals (*e.g.*, KOH, NaOH *etc.*). In an electrolyte, there are no free electrons and current conduction takes place through ions (*i.e.*, charged atoms).

Let us see how an electrolyte provides ions. For example, take the case of $CuSO_4$ (electrolyte). The reader may recall that copper sulphate is an ionic compound *i.e.*, each molecule of $CuSO_4$ is formed due to the attraction between oppositely charged atoms *viz.* Cu^{++} and SO_4^{--}. When dissolved in water, the force of attraction between them is tremendously reduced due to *high permittivity of water. The result is that Cu^{++} and SO_4^{--} get separated. These charged atoms are called ions and the process is called ionisation.

14.2. ELECTROLYSIS

The conduction of electric current through the solution of an electrolyte together with the resulting chemical changes is called electrolysis.

Fig. 14.1 shows the phenomenon of electrolysis. When copper sulphate is dissolved in water, it splits up into its components *viz.* the positive copper ions (Cu^{++}) and negative sulphate ions (SO_4^{--}). This process is called *ionisation*.

If two metal plates, say copper plates, (called *electrodes*) are set at the opposite ends and a **d.c. potential difference is applied to these plates [See Fig. 14.1], an electric field is created between these electrodes. The negative sulphate ions SO_4^{--} move towards the anode (*i.e.*, +ve electrode) and positive copper ions (Cu^{++}) travel towards the cathode (*i.e.*, –ve electrode).

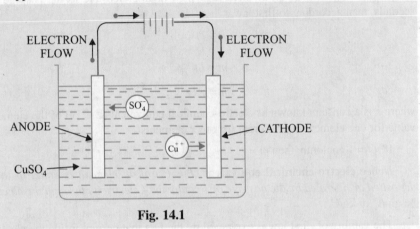

Fig. 14.1

(*i*) A sulphate ion (SO_4^{--}) on reaching the anode gives its two extra electrons to it and becomes sulphate radical. These given up electrons continue their journey towards the cathode *via* the external circuit. Now the sulphate radical cannot exist and, therefore, it acts chemically on the anode material to form copper sulphate according to the following reaction:

$$Cu + SO_4 \longrightarrow CuSO_4$$

Thus, copper from anode continuously dissolves into the solution so long as this action takes place.

(*ii*) At the same time, a copper ion (Cu^{++}) on reaching the cathode takes two electrons from it (these are the same electrons given by the sulphate ion at the anode and have come to cathode *via* the external circuit). The copper ion (Cu^{++}) combines with these two electrons to become copper atom and gets deposited on the cathode.

$$Cu^{++} + 2e \longrightarrow Cu \text{ atom}$$

. . . .

* $F = \dfrac{1}{4\pi} \dfrac{Q_1 Q_2}{\varepsilon_0 \varepsilon_r d^2}$

Relative permittivity of water is 80. It means that when $CuSO_4$ is dissolved in water, attraction force is reduced 80 times than in air.

** Note that d.c. supply must be used to attract ions of only one kind to each electrode.

Thus, copper from the solution $(CuSO_4)$ gets deposited on the cathode.

Two things are worth noting about the conduction of current in electrolytes. First, the electric current in an electrolyte is due to the movement of *ions (Cu^{++} and SO_4^{--} in the present case) unlike metals where current is due to the movement of free electrons. Secondly, the passage of electric current through an electrolyte causes chemical changes. Thus in the present case, the anode material (*i.e.*, copper) continuously dissolves into the solution and gets deposited on the cathode.

14.3. FARADAY'S LAWS OF ELECTROLYSIS

Faraday performed a series of experiments to determine the factors which govern the mass of an element deposited or liberated during electrolysis. He summed up his conclusions into two laws, known as Faraday's laws of electrolysis.

First law. *The mass of an element deposited or liberated at an electrode is directly proportional to the quantity of electricity that passes through the electrolyte.*

If m is the mass of an element deposited or liberated due to the passage of I amperes for t seconds, then according to first law,

$$m \propto Q$$

or $$m \propto I t \qquad (\because Q = It)$$

or $$m = z I t$$

where z is a constant known as electro-chemical equivalent (E.C.E.) of the element. It has the same value for one element but different for other elements.

If $Q = 1$ coulomb, then $m = z$.

Hence **electro-chemical equivalent** (*E.C.E.*) *of an element is equal to the mass of element deposited or liberated by the passage of 1 coulomb of electricity through the electrolyte.* Its unit will be gm/C or kg/C.

The validity of first law is explained by the fact that current inside the electrolyte is carried by the ions themselves. Hence the masses of the chemical substances reaching the anode and cathode are proportional to the quantity of electricity carried by the ions *i.e.*, mass of an ion liberated at any electrode is proportional to the quantity of electricity passed through the electrolyte.

Second law. *The mass of an element deposited or liberated during electrolysis is directly proportional to the chemical equivalent weight of that element i.e.*

$$m \propto \text{Chemical equivalent weight of the element}$$

Faraday's second law is illustrated in Fig. 14.2 where silver and copper voltameters are connected in series. When the same current is passed for the same time through the two voltameters, it will be seen that the masses of silver (Ag) and copper (Cu) deposited on the respective cathodes are in the ratio of 108 : 32. These values of 108 and 32 are respectively the equivalent weights of silver and copper.

$$\frac{\text{Mass of silver deposited}}{\text{Mass of copper deposited}} = \frac{\text{Eq. wt. of Ag}}{\text{Eq. wt. of Cu}} = \frac{108}{32}$$

---

* Note that the flow of current in the external circuit (being metallic wires) is electronic *i.e.*, by electrons. It is only within the electrolyte that conduction is by ions.

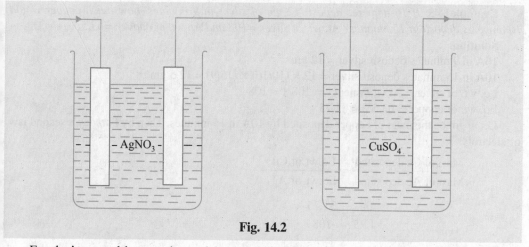

Fig. 14.2

Faraday's second law can be explained as follows. The negative ions (*i.e.*, NO_3^- and SO_4^{--}) from the solutions give up their respective extra electrons to the anodes. These electrons come to cathode *via* the external circuit and are taken up by the positive ions (Ag^+ and Cu^{++}) to become metallic atoms and get deposited on the respective cathodes. Suppose 10 electrons are flowing in the external circuit. Since silver is monovalent (*i.e.*, its valency is 1), 10 silver ions must be liberated at the cathode of silver voltameter. Again copper is bivalent (*i.e.*, its valency is 2) and hence 5 copper ions must be liberated at the cathode of copper voltameter. This means that mass of an element (silver or copper) liberated is directly proportional to the atomic weight and inversely proportional to the valency of that element *i.e.*,

$$\text{Mass liberated, } m \propto \frac{\text{Atomic weight}}{\text{Valency}}$$

$$\propto \text{Chemical eq. wt. of the element}$$

Example14.1. *Find the value of electro-chemical equivalent of chromium if 2.16 gm of chromium are liberated by the passage of a current of 5A for 1 hour and 20 minutes.*

Solution.

Mass of chromium liberated, $m = 2.16$ gm

Current, $I = 5A$

Time for which current flows, $t = 1$ hour, 20 min $= 4800$ s

Now $m = z\,I\,t$ ...See Art. 14.3

$$\therefore \qquad z = \frac{m}{It} = \frac{2.16}{5 \times 4800} = 9 \times 10^{-5} \text{ gm/C}$$

Example14.2. *A current passes through two voltameters in series, one having silver plates and a solution of $AgNO_3$, and the other copper plates and a solution of $CuSO_4$. After the current has ceased to flow, 3.6gm of silver have been deposited. How much copper will have deposited in the other voltameter ? Take E.C.E. of silver as 0.001118 gm/C and that of copper as 328.86×10^{-6} gm/C.*

Solution.

For silver voltameter, $m_1 = z_1 I\,t$

or $It = \dfrac{m_1}{z_1} = \dfrac{3.6}{0.001118}$

For copper voltameter, $m_2 = z_2 I\,t$

$$= (328.86 \times 10^{-6}) \times \frac{3.6}{0.001118} = 1.06 \text{ gm}$$

Example14.3. *If 16 amperes deposit 12 gm of silver in 9 minutes, how much copper would 10 amperes deposit in 15 minutes? At. wt. of silver =108 and At. wt. of copper =63.5.*

Solution.

16A in 9 minutes deposit silver = 12 gm

10A in 15 minutes deposit silver = $12 \times (10/16) \times (15/9) = 12.5$ gm

Eq. wt. of silver = At.wt./Valency = 108/1 = 108

Eq. wt. of copper = 63.5/2 = 31.75

Let m gm be the mass of copper deposited by 10A in 15 minutes. Then by Faraday's second law of electrolysis,

$$\frac{\text{Mass of Cu deposited}}{\text{Mass of Ag deposited}} = \frac{\text{Eq.wt.of Cu}}{\text{Eq.wt.of Ag}}$$

or

$$\frac{m}{12.5} = \frac{31.75}{108}$$

∴

$$m = \frac{31.75}{108} \times 12.5 = 3.67 \,\text{gm}$$

Example14.4. *A coating of nickel 1mm thick is to be deposited on a cylinder 2cm in diameter and 30 cm in length. Calculate the time taken if the current used is 100A. The following data may be taken. Specific gravity of nickel =8.9, At. wt. of nickel =58.7 (divalent), E.C.E. of silver =1.12 mg/C, At. wt. of silver =108.*

Solution.

Area of curved surface of cylinder $= \pi D \times l = \pi \times 2 \times 30 = 188.5 \,\text{cm}^2$

Volume of Ni to be deposited $= 188.5 \times 0.1 = 18.85 \,\text{cm}^3$

Mass of Ni to be deposited, $m = 18.85 \times 8.9 = 167.7$ gm

Eq. wt. of Ni $= 58.7/2 = 29.35$

Eq. wt. of Ag $= 108/1 = 108$

Now

$$\frac{\text{E.C.E of Ni}}{\text{E.C.E.of Ag}} = \frac{\text{Eq.wt.of Ni}}{\text{Eq.wt.of Ag}}$$

∴

$$\text{E.C.E. of Ni} = \frac{29.35}{108} \times 1.12 = 0.304 \,\text{mg/C}$$

Now

$$m = z I t$$

∴

$$t = \frac{m}{zI} = \frac{167.7}{0.304 \times 10^{-3} \times 100} = 5516 \,\text{seconds} = \textbf{91.93 minutes}$$

Example14.5. *A square plate has a side of 10 cm. It is connected to the cathode in a copper electroplating bath and a current of 4A is passed through the bath. Neglecting the thickness of plate, how long does it take to cover both sides of the plate with copper to a thickness of 0.1mm? Take density of copper as 9000 kg/m³ and its E.C.E. as 330×10^{-9} kg/C.*

Solution.

Area of both sides of plates $= 2 \times (10 \times 10^{-2}) \times (10 \times 10^{-2}) = 2 \times 10^{-2} \,\text{m}^2$

Thickness of copper layer $= 0.1 \,\text{mm} = 0.1 \times 10^{-3} \,\text{m}$

Volume of copper to be deposited $= (2 \times 10^{-2}) \times (0.1 \times 10^{-3}) = 2 \times 10^{-6} \,\text{m}^3$

Mass of copper to be deposited, $m = 2 \times 10^{-6} \times 9000 = 18 \times 10^{-3}$ kg

Now, $m = z I t$

∴

$$t = \frac{m}{zI} = \frac{18 \times 10^{-3}}{330 \times 10^{-9} \times 4} = 13636 \,\text{seconds} = \textbf{227 min, 16s}$$

TUTORIAL PROBLEMS

1. A current of 5A flows for 40 minutes through an electrolyte which is a solution of a salt of chromium in water. Calculate the mass of chromium liberated. The electro-chemical equivalent of chromium is 90×10^{-9} kg/C. **[1.08 gm]**

2. How long will it take to deposit, from a copper sulphate solution, a coating of copper 0.05 mm thick on an area of 118 cm^2 if the supply p.d. is 4.5 volts and the total resistance of the circuit is 2.3 Ω? Specific gravity of copper is 8.93 and E.C.E. of copper = 0.329 mg/C. **[2.269 hr]**

3. A metal plate having a surface area of 115 cm^2 is to be silver plated. If a current of 1.5A is passed for 1 hour and 30 minutes, what thickness of copper will be deposited ? Specific gravity of silver = 10.5 and E.C.E. of silver = 1.118 mg/C. **[0.075 mm]**

4. A worn shaft is to be reconditioned by depositing chromium on its curved surface to a thickness of 0.1mm. The shaft has a diameter of 3.5 cm and a length of 80 cm. If a current of 4.4A is passed, calculate how long the process will take. Density of chromium = 6600 kg/m^3 and E.C.E. of chromium = 90×10^{-9} kg/C. **[41 hours, 44 minutes]**

5. Due to an error, a car battery is overcharged with a current of 5A for 10 hours. Given that the electro-chemical equivalents of hydrogen and oxygen are 10.4×10^{-9} kg/C and 83.2×10^{-9} kg/ C respectively, calculate the volume of distilled water which must be added to compensate for the loss. **[16.8 c.c.]**

14.4. CELL

We have seen that when a current passes through the solution of an electrolyte, chemical changes take place *i.e.*, electrical energy is converted into chemical energy. The converse of this is also true *i.e.*, we can convert chemical energy into electrical energy. The device which accomplishes this job is called a cell.

A cell is a source of e.m.f. in which chemical energy is converted into electrical energy.

A cell essentially consists of two metal plates of different materials immersed in a suitable solution. The plates are called electrodes and the solution is called electrolyte. The magnitude of e.m.f. of a cell depends upon (*i*) the nature of material of electrodes used and (*ii*) the nature of electrolyte. For example, if plates of zinc and lead are placed in a solution of sulphuric acid, the e.m.f. developed is about 0.5 V; zinc and copper in sulphuric acid about 1.1V and zinc and silver in sulphuric acid about 1.2 V. It may be noted that the e.m.f. of a cell does not depend upon the size and spacing of the plates. However, with the increase in the size of plates, the capacity of the cell increases *i.e.*, the cell will deliver current for a longer period.

14.5. TYPES OF CELLS

Using various metals and methods of construction, a large variety of cells has been developed. However, the cells can be divided into two main classes *viz.*

      1. Primary cells   2. Secondary cells

    1. Primary cells. A cell in which chemical action is not reversible is called a **primary cell** *e.g.*, voltaic cell, Daniel cell, Lachlanche cell, dry cell *etc*. As a primary cell delivers current, the active materials are used up. When the active materials are nearly consumed, the cell stops delivering current. In order to renew the cell, fresh active materials are provided. Another drawback of a primary cell is that it cannot provide large and steady current for a longer period. This fact makes the primary cell rather an expensive source of electrical energy. Due to these drawbacks, the use of primary cells is limited to torch batteries and for experimental purposes in the laboratories.

2. Secondary cells. A cell in which chemical action is reversible is called a **secondary cell** or **storage cell**. A secondary cell operates on the same principle as a primary cell but differs in the method in which it may be renewed. In a secondary cell, there is no actual consumption of any plate and that the chemical process is reversible. When the cell is delivering current (*i.e.*, *discharging*), the chemical action changes the composition of plates. When the cell is exhausted, the chemical action can be reversed (*i.e.*, plates can be restored to the original condition) by passing current through the cell in the reverse direction to that in which the cell provided current. This process is called *charging*. In other words, charging process reverses the chemical action and enables the plates to acquire original composition. There are several types of secondary or storage cells; the more common ones being:

(*i*) Lead-acid cell

(*ii*) Nickel-iron-alkaline cell (or Edison cell)

(*iii*) Nickel-cadmium-alkaline cell.

As in a primary cell, the e.m.f. of a secondary cell also depends upon the materials used for electrodes and the nature of electrolyte. The e.m.f. of a lead-acid cell is about 2V and that of Nickel-cadmium-alkaline and Edison cells is about 1.2V.

Note. When a secondary cell is charged, electrical energy is converted into chemical energy which is stored in the cell. When the cell discharges, the stored chemical energy starts converting into electrical energy. For this reason, a secondary cell is sometimes called a storage cell.

14.6. LEAD-ACID CELL

The most inexpensive secondary cell is the lead-acid cell and is widely used for commercial purposes. A lead-acid cell when ready for use contains two plates immersed in a dilute sulphuric acid (H_2SO_4) of specific gravity about 1.28. The positive plate (*anode*) is of **lead-peroxide** (PbO_2) which has chocolate brown colour and the negative plate (*cathode*) is **lead** (Pb) which is of grey colour.

(*i*) When the cell supplies current to a load (*i.e.*,discharging), the chemical action that takes place forms lead sulphate ($PbSO_4$) on both the plates with water being formed in the electrolyte. After a certain amount of energy has been withdrawn from the cell, both plates are transformed into the same material (*i.e.*, $PbSO_4$) and the specific gravity of the electrolyte (H_2SO_4) is lowered. The cell is then said to be discharged. There are several methods (See Art. 14.11) to ascertain whether the cell is discharged or not.

(*ii*) To charge the cell, direct current is passed through the cell in the reverse direction to that in which the cell provided current. This reverses the chemical process and again forms a lead peroxide (PbO_2) positive plate and a pure lead (Pb) negative plate. At the same time, H_2SO_4 is formed at the expense of water, restoring the electrolyte (H_2SO_4) to its original condition.

The chemical changes that occur during discharging and recharging of a lead-acid cell are discussed in the articles that follow.

14.7. CHEMICAL CHANGES DURING DISCHARGING

By discharging of a cell, we mean that it is delivering current to the external circuit. Consider a charged lead acid cell with anode of PbO_2 and cathode of Pb; the electrolyte being dilute H_2SO_4 [See Fig. 14.3]. Sulphuric acid splits up into hydrogen ions (H^+H^+) and sulphate ions (SO_4^{--}). The sulphate ions move towards the cathode and hydrogen ions move towards the anode causing the following chemical actions:

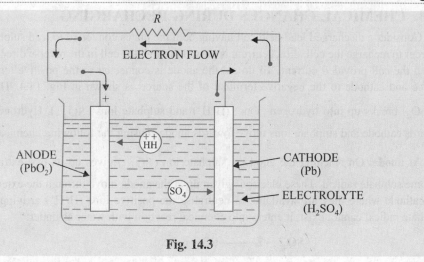

Fig. 14.3

At cathode. On reaching the cathode, a sulphate ion (SO_4^{--}) gives up its two extra electrons to become sulphate radical. These electrons given up at the cathode move through the external circuit to the anode where they are available to neutralise the positive ions (H^+H^+) arriving there. Since sulphate radical cannot exist, it enters into chemical action with cathode material (Pb) to form lead sulphate ($PbSO_4$).

$$SO_4^{--} - 2e \longrightarrow SO_4 \text{ (radical)}$$

$$Pb + SO_4 \longrightarrow PbSO_4$$

(Grey colour)   (Whitish in colour).

At anode. On reaching the anode, each hydrogen ion takes one electron from it to become hydrogen gas. This electron is given by the sulphate ion at the cathode and has come to the anode *via* the external circuit.

$$H^+H^+ + 2e \longrightarrow 2H$$

The hydrogen gas liberated at the anode acts chemically on the anode material (PbO_2) and reduces it to lead oxide (PbO).

$$PbO_2 + 2H \longrightarrow PbO + H_2O$$

Sulphuric acid reacts with PbO to form $PbSO_4$.

$$PbO + H_2SO_4 \longrightarrow PbSO_4 + H_2O$$

The chemical changes that take place during discharging can be summed up as under:

 (*i*) Both the plates are converted into lead sulphate ($PbSO_4$) which is whitish in colour.

 (*ii*) Water is formed which lowers the specific gravity of the electrolyte (H_2SO_4). When the cell is fully discharged, the specific gravity of H_2SO_4 falls to about 1.18.

 (*iii*) The e.m.f. of the cell falls. The lead-acid cell should not be discharged beyond the point where its e.m.f. falls to about 1.8 volts.

 (*iv*) The chemical energy stored in the cell is converted into electrical energy.

It is important to note that e.m.f. of the cell provides little indication to the state of discharge of the cell since it remains close to 2V for 90% of the discharge period. In practice, specific gravity of the electrolyte (H_2SO_4) is used to know the state of discharge. The cell should be recharged when specific gravity of H_2SO_4 falls to 1.18.

14.8. CHEMICAL CHANGES DURING RECHARGING

Consider a discharged lead-acid cell having both the plates converted to lead sulphate ($PbSO_4$). In order to recharge the cell, direct current is passed through the cell in the reverse direction to that in which the cell provided current. To do so, the anode is connected to the positive terminal of d.c. source and cathode to the negative terminal of the source as shown in Fig. 14.4. The electrolyte (H_2SO_4) breaks up into hydrogen ions (H^+H^+) and sulphate ions (SO_4^{--}). Hydrogen ions move towards cathode and sulphate ions move towards anode causing the following chemical reactions:

At anode. On reaching the anode, a sulphate ion (SO_4^{--}) gives up its two extra electrons to become sulphate radical. These electrons given up at the anode move through the external circuit to the cathode where they are available to neutralise the positive ions (H^+H^+) arriving there. Since sulphate radical cannot exist, it enters into chemical reaction with water as under:

$$SO_4^{--} - 2e \longrightarrow SO_4 \text{ (radical)}$$

$$SO_4 + H_2O \longrightarrow H_2SO_4 + O$$

The oxygen in the atomic state (*i.e.* O) is very active and reacts chemically with anode material ($PbSO_4$) to produce the following chemical change:

$$PbSO_4 + O + H_2O \rightarrow PbO_2 + H_2SO_4$$

At Cathode. On reaching the cathode, each hydrogen ion (H^+) takes one electron from it to become hydrogen gas. This electron is given up by the sulphate ion at anode and has come to the cathode *via* the external circuit.

$$H^+H^+ + 2e \longrightarrow 2H$$

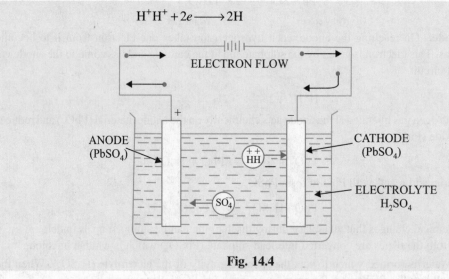

Fig. 14.4

The hydrogen gas liberated at the cathode reacts with cathode material ($PbSO_4$) to reduce it to lead (Pb) as under:

$$PbSO_4 + 2H \longrightarrow Pb + H_2SO_4$$

As the charging process goes on, the anode is converted into PbO_2 and cathode into Pb. The H_2SO_4 produced in the chemical reactions above increases the specific gravity of the electrolyte. The chemical changes that occur during recharging can be summed up as under:

(*i*) The positive plate (anode) is converted into PbO_2 and the negative plate (cathode) into Pb.

(*ii*) H_2SO_4 is formed in the reactions. Therefore, the specific gravity of the electrolyte (H_2SO_4) is raised. When the cell is fully charged, the specific gravity of H_2SO_4 rises to about 1.28.

(*iii*) The e.m.f. of the cell rises. The e.m.f. of a fully charged lead-acid cell is about 2 volts.

(*iv*) Electrical energy supplied is converted into chemical energy which is stored in the cell.

14.9. CONSTRUCTION OF A LEAD-ACID BATTERY

In a 6-volt lead-acid battery, three cells are connected in series whereas for 12-volt type, six cells are series connected. Fig. 14.5 shows the cut-away view of a lead-acid battery.

(*i*) **Container.** The container houses the plates and the electrolyte. It is made of glass or transparent synthetic material or hard rubber depending upon service requirements. The container is sealed off at the top to prevent the spilling of electrolyte.

(*ii*) **Plates.** The capacity of a lead-acid cell *depends upon the plate area. To increase the effective area of plates without increasing the size of the cell, we use a large number of thin plates in the cell instead of two. The alternate positive and negative plates are sandwiched together with insulators called *separators*. The negative plates are connected together as the positive plates. A commercial cell always has odd number of plates such as 11, 13, 15 or 17. The number of negative plates is always one more than the number of positive plates; the outside plates being negative. A separate compartment is provided for each cell and each compartment has large space at the bottom so that any sediment from the plate may collect there.

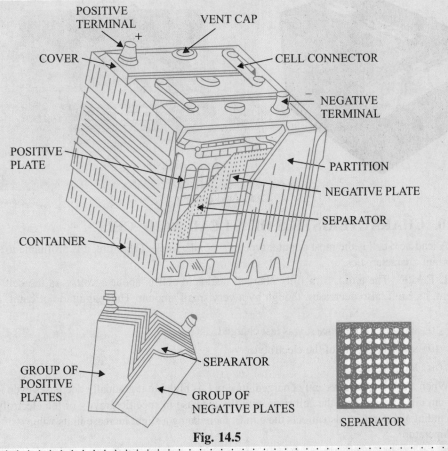

Fig. 14.5

---

* The e.m.f. of a secondary cell does not depend upon the size of its plates. However, the larger the plates, the more the chemical energy that can be stored in the cell and hence greater the current that can be drawn from it.

(*iii*) **Separators.** In order to save space and to reduce the internal resistance of the cell, the plates are placed close together. To prevent the plates touching each other if they wrap or buckle, they are separated by non-conducting materials (*e.g.*, wood, rubber *etc.*) called separators.

(*iv*) **Electrolyte.** The electrolyte is dilute sulphuric acid (H_2SO_4) solution mixed in such a proportion so that with a fully charged battery, its specific gravity is about 1.28. Sometimes, we replace water that has evaporated. To ensure normal battery life, only pure water should be used.

(*v*) **Cell cover.** Each cell compartment has a cover; usually made of moulded hard rubber. Openings are provided in these covers for two terminal posts and vent cap.

(*vi*) **Vent caps.** Each cell has a hole into which is fitted the vent cap. This cap has a vent hole to allow the free exit of the gas formed in the cell. The vent caps can be easily removed for adding water or taking hydrometer reading.

(*vii*) **Inter-cell connector.** It is a lead alloy link that joins the cells in series. The positive terminal of the cell is marked by a large + sign or with a red colour.

(*viii*) **Cell terminals.** Each cell has two terminals. The terminals are generally made of lead as it does not erode due to the acid electrolyte.

Lead Acid Battery

14.10. CHARACTERISTICS OF A LEAD-ACID CELL

A lead-acid cell is the most popular type of secondary cell. Therefore, it is profitable to study its important characteristics.

1. E.M.F. The e.m.f. of a fully charged lead-acid cell is about 2 volts. As the cell delivers current, its e.m.f. also decreases, though by a very small amount. The magnitude of e.m.f. depends upon:

   (*i*) length of time since it was last charged

   (*ii*) specific gravity of the electrolyte

   (*iii*) temperature

When a cell has been recently charged, its e.m.f. is high but it gradually decreases even if left on open-circuit. The e.m.f. of the cell rises with the increase in specific gravity of the electrolyte. The surrounding temperature also affects the e.m.f.; there being a slight increase in its value with the rise in temperature.

2. Terminal voltage. When the cell delivers current, the terminal voltage is less than its e.m.f. due to voltage drop in the internal resistance of the cell. If the discharge is continued, the terminal voltage falls rapidly for a short time, then slowly for some time and again rapidly towards the end of discharge. The chief cause of final rapid fall of voltage is the increase of internal resistance owing to the dilution of the acid in the pores of the plates. It may be noted that when the terminal voltage has fallen to about 1.8 volts, the discharge should be stopped. If it is continued, too much lead sulphate ($PbSO_4$) is formed, clogging the pores of the plates, possibly *damaging them and making the recharging increasingly difficult.

3. Internal resistance. The internal resistance of the cell is due to the resistance of the plates, the active material and the electrolyte. The internal resistance of a lead-acid cell is very small (typical value being 0.01 Ω) and depends upon the following factors:

(*i*) Area of plates—decreases with the increase in plate area

(*ii*) Spacing between plates—decreases with the decrease in spacing

(*iii*) Sp. Gravity of H_2SO_4—decreases with the increase in sp. gravity

The internal resistance of a lead-acid cell should be minimum in order to reduce the internal drop. This is achieved by using multiplate construction in a cell. As explained in Art. 14.9, the negative plates of a cell are connected together as are the positive plates. The effect of this arrangement is as if we have connected a number of cells in parallel. At the same time, the length of electrolyte between the plates is reduced. The result is that internal resistance of the cell is lowered.

4. Capacity. The capacity of a cell is the quantity of electricity which it can give out during single discharge until its terminal voltage falls to 1.8 volts. It is measured by the product of current in amperes and the time in hours *i.e.*

Capacity of cell $= I_d \times T_d$ ampere-hours (or Ah)

where I_d = Steady discharging current in amperes

T_d = Time in hours for which the cell can supply current until its p.d. falls to 1.8 volts.

The capacity of a cell depends upon the following factors :

(*i*) Rate of discharge—Higher the rate of discharge, less the capacity

(*ii*) Temperature—Increases with temperature

(*iii*) Area of plates—Increases with plate area

(*iv*) Sp. gravity of electrolyte—Increases with Sp. gravity

5. Efficiency. There are two ways of expressing the efficiency of a secondary cell *viz*. (*i*)ampere-hour efficiency (*ii*) watt-hour efficiency.

(*i*) Ampere-hour efficiency,

$$\eta_{Ah} = \frac{\text{Ampere - hours provided on discharge}}{\text{Ampere - hours of charge}} \times 100$$

$$= \frac{I_d \times T_d}{I_c \times T_c} \times 100$$

Since ampere-hours is the quantity of electricity, this efficiency is sometimes called *quantity efficiency*. The ampere-hour efficiency of a lead-acid cell is about 90%.

(*ii*) Watt-hour efficiency,

$$\eta_{wh} = \frac{\text{Energy given on discharge}}{\text{Energy input of charge}} \times 100$$

. . . .

* If a cell is discharged excessively (*i.e.*, terminal voltage falls below 1.8 volts), crystalline lead sulphate will be formed. Since this lead sulphate occupies a larger volume than the material from which it is formed, the plates may buckle, the separators may be damaged and the active material may be dislodged.

$$= \frac{V_d \times I_d \times T_d}{V_c \times I_c \times T_c} \times 100$$

$$= \frac{I_d \times T_d}{I_c \times T_c} \times 100 \times \frac{V_d}{V_c}$$

$$= \eta_{Ah} \times \frac{V_d}{V_c}$$

Since average p.d. during discharge (*i.e.*, V_d) is lower than the average p.d. during charge (*i.e.*, V_c) due to the effects of internal resistance and polarisation, η_{wh} is always less than η_{Ah}. The watt-hour (or energy efficiency) of a lead-acid cell is about 75%.

Example 14.6. *A lead-acid cell maintains a constant current of 1.5A for 20 hours before its terminal voltage falls to 1.8 volts. What is the capacity of the cell ?*

Solution. The capacity of a lead-acid cell is the ampere-hours provided by it until its terminal voltage falls to 1.8 volts.

$$\therefore \qquad \text{Capacity of cell} = I_d \times T_d = 1.5 \times 20 = \textbf{30 Ah}$$

Example 14.7. *A lead-acid cell has 13 plates, each 25 cm × 20 cm. The clearance between the neighbouring plates is 1.2 mm. If the resistivity of the acid is 1.6 Ω-cm, find the internal resistance of the cell.*

Solution. Since there are 13 plates, the arrangement constitutes 12 tiny cells in parallel.

Resistance of each tiny cell, $\quad R = \rho \dfrac{l}{a}$

Here $\rho = 1.6$ Ω-cm ; $l = 0.12$ cm ; $a = 25 \times 20 = 500$ cm^2

$\therefore \qquad\qquad\qquad R = 1.6 \times (0.12/500) = 384 \times 10^{-6}$ Ω

Since the cells are connected in parallel, total internal resistance R_T of the cell is :

$$R_T = R/12 = 384 \times 10^{-6}/12 = 32 \times 10^{-6} \, \Omega$$

Example 14.8. *A lead-acid cell is charged at the rate of 18A for 10 hours at an average voltage of 2.26 volts. It is discharged in the same time at the rate of 17.2A ; the average voltage during discharge being 1.98 volts. Calculate (i) ampere-hour efficiency (ii) watt-hour efficiency.*

Solution.

(*i*) Ampere-hour efficiency,

$$\eta_{Ah} = \frac{I_d \times T_d}{I_c \times T_c} \times 100 = \frac{17.2 \times 10}{18 \times 10} \times 100 = \textbf{95.55\%}$$

(*ii*) Watt-hour efficiency,

$$\eta_{wh} = \eta_{Ah} \times \frac{V_d}{V_c} = 95.55 \times \frac{1.98}{2.26} = \textbf{83.71\%}$$

TUTORIAL PROBLEMS

1. A battery can deliver 12 V at 150 mA for 4 days. What is the watt-hour rating? **[173Wh]**
2. What is the watt-hour rating of a battery that averages 12 V output and has a capacity of 100 Ah ? **[1.2kWh]**
3. A completely discharged nickel-cadmium battery is rated at 450 mAh and is to be charged at a constant 45-mA rate. How many hours will be required for a complete recharge? **[14 hours]**

14.11. INDICATIONS OF A FULLY CHARGED CELL

During the charging process, it is very essential that the battery is taken out from the charging circuit as soon as it is fully charged. Overcharging as well as undercharging are undesirable and should always be avoided. The indications of a fully charged cell (or battery) are:

(*i*) Voltage   (*ii*) Specific gravity of electrolyte

(*iii*) Gassing   (*iv*) Colour of plates

(*i*) **Voltage.** During charging, the terminal potential of a cell increases and provides an indication to its state of charge. A fully charged lead-acid cell has a terminal voltage of about 2 volts.

(*ii*) **Specific gravity.** During the charging process, the specific gravity of the electrolyte (H_2SO_4) increases and provides an important indication to the state of charge of the cell. The specific gravity of the electrolyte of a fully charged lead-acid cell is about 1.28. This can be measured by means of a *hydrometer*. It may be noted that the state of charge of a lead-acid cell (or battery) is determined from the specific gravity of the electrolyte (H_2SO_4). The following table may be useful in this regard:

Sp. Gr. of H_2SO_4	State of Charge
1.13	Discharged
1.19	25% charged
1.22	50% charged
1.25	75% charged
1.28	100% charged

(*iii*) **Gassing.** When the cell is fully charged, the charging current starts electrolysis of water. The result is that hydrogen is given off at the cathode and oxygen at the anode; the process being known as *gassing. Gassing at both the plates indicates that the charging current is doing no useful work and hence should be stopped.

(*iv*) **Colour of plates.** The visual examination of colour of the plates of a lead-acid cell provides yet another important indication to its state of charge. When the cell is fully charged, the positive plate gets converted into PbO_2 (chocolate brown) and the negative plate to spongy lead (grey).

14.12. CHARGING OF LEAD-ACID BATTERIES

In order to ensure normal life for a battery, it should be maintained in the charged condition. While charging a battery, the following points may be kept in view :

(*i*) The charging source must be d.c. one. If a.c. supply is available, it must be converted to d.c. before being applied to the battery.

(*ii*) During charging, it should be ensured that polarity is correct. The polarity is correct when the positive terminal of d.c. charging source is connected to the positive terminal of the battery.

(*iii*) The charging voltage must be more than the e.m.f. of the battery to be charged. Approximately 2.5 volts per cell should be applied. For example, if a battery to be charged has 6 cells, then applied direct voltage should be about 15 volts.

(*iv*) The charging current should be set at proper value.

Charging rate. What should be the value of charging current ? The answer is that it may be as high as the battery can take without excessive "gassing" or heat. Too great a charging current may produce excessive heat. This will cause plates to buckle and short circuit may occur. Also the water of

---

*   Gassing is harmless so long as it is not violent enough to dislodge the active material from the plates. However, it leads to waste of energy and the usual practice is to gradually reduce the charging current towards the finish of charge in order to reduce gassing and to avoid overheating of battery.

electrolyte will be lost due to electrolysis and evaporation, raising the concentration of sulphuric acid left behind. The strong acid then may char the separators, causing permanent damage to the battery. The temperature of the electrolyte should not be permitted to rise above 40°C. Efforts should be made to use the charging current value recommended by the manufacturer. In case it is not available, one of the following thumb rules may be applied :

(*i*) The charging current should be 1A for every positive plate of a single cell. Thus, if the cell contains 13 plates, six of them will be positive. The charging current for the battery should, therefore, be 6A.

(*ii*) The charging rate should be such that full charge can be obtained in 8 hours. Thus 100 Ah battery should be charged at the rate of 100/8 = 12.5A. This will ensure the maximum life of the battery.

14.13. BATTERY CHARGING CIRCUIT

Fig. 14.6 shows the battery charging circuit. A d.c. source of suitable magnitude is connected in series with a rheostat *R*, ammeter and the battery to be charged. Ensure that polarity is correct *i.e.* positive terminal of d.c. source should be connected to the positive terminal of the battery. The charging current is adjusted to the required value with the help of rheostat. As the charging process proceeds, the terminal voltage of the battery rises but the charging current is kept constant by adjusting the value of rheostat *R*. The terminal voltage of the battery and specific gravity of electrolyte are checked at regular intervals of time. When the terminal voltage ceases to rise, the specific gravity of electrolyte reaches the value 1.28 and there is enough gassing at the plates, the battery is fully charged. It is then taken out of the charging circuit. The entire charging process may take several hours.

Calculations. When the battery is being charged, its e.m.f. acts in opposition to the applied voltage. The applied voltage *V* sends a charging current *I* against the back e.m.f. E_b of the battery. The input power is *VI* but the power being supplied to the battery is $E_b I$. The power $E_b I$ is converted into chemical energy which is stored in the battery.

Charging current, $$I = \frac{V - E_b}{R + r}$$

where R = resistance of rheostat in the circuit

r = internal resistance of the battery

The charging current is kept constant throughout (by adjusting *R*) except towards the finish of charge.

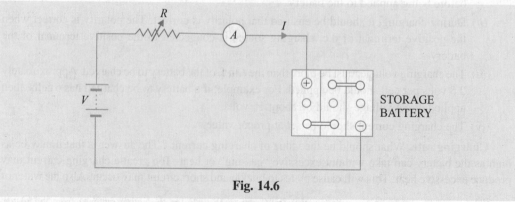

Fig. 14.6

The following points may be kept in mind during charging :

(*i*) When the battery is being charged, the vents must be open so that the gases (H_2 and O_2) may be able to escape. Otherwise the case may be cracked.

(ii) The mixture of hydrogen and oxygen is explosive. Therefore, care must be taken not to carry an open flame or lighted cigarette near a battery being charged.

(iii) The charging current should be such that battery temperature does not exceed 40°C and that violent gassing does not take place. Instead of a constant charging current, the usual practice is to charge the battery at a tapered rate i.e. at high rate at first but at a gradually reduced rate as the battery becomes fully charged.

(iv) After charging, water should be added to compensate for the loss of water by gassing and evaporation. The level of the electrolyte should be 1 cm above the tops of the plates. If water is not added, the excessive concentration of H_2SO_4 may char the separators, causing permanent damage to the battery.

Example 14.9. *A battery of 40 cells is to be charged from a 180V supply. The internal resistance of each cell is 0.05 Ω and the charging current is to be 4A. If the average e.m.f. of each cell during charge is 2.5V, what should be the value of series resistor ?*

Solution.

Applied voltage, $\qquad V = 180$ volts

Charging current, $\qquad I = 4A$

Back e.m.f. of battery, $\qquad E_b = 40 \times 2.5 = 100$ volts

Internal resistance of battery, $\quad r = 40 \times 0.05 = 2\Omega$

Let R ohms be the required value of series resistor.

Charging current, $$I = \frac{V - E_b}{R + r}$$

or $$4 = \frac{180 - 100}{R + 2}$$

$\therefore \qquad\qquad\qquad R = 18\ \Omega$

Example 14.10. *It is desired to charge a 12-V car battery at 6A from a 230-V d.c. source. The d.c. source and battery are connected in series with a group of 60-watt, 220-V bulbs in parallel. How many lamps are required for the purpose ?*

Solution.

Charging current, $$I = \frac{V - E_b}{R} \quad \text{Neglecting internal resistance}$$

or $$6 = \frac{230 - 12}{R}$$

$\therefore$ Required circuit resistance, $\qquad R = 218/6 = 36.33\ \Omega$

Resistance of each bulb $\qquad\qquad = (220)^2/60 = 806.67\ \Omega$

Let N be the required number of bulbs in parallel. It means that N bulbs in parallel should give an equivalent resistance of 36.33 Ω.

$\therefore \qquad\qquad 36.33 = 806.67/N \quad \text{or} \quad N = 806.67/36.33 = \textbf{22 bulbs}$

Example 14.11. *A 6-cell, 12-V battery is to be charged at a constant rate of 10A from a 24-V supply. If the e.m.f. of each cell at the beginning of charge and at the end of charge is 1.9V and 2.4V, what should be the maximum and minimum resistance to be connected in series with the battery ? Resistance of battery is negligible.*

Solution.

Beginning of charge

Back e.m.f. of battery, $\qquad E_b = 6 \times 1.9 = 11.4$ volts

Charging current, $\qquad I = (V - E_b)/R$

or $$R = \frac{V - E_b}{I} = \frac{24 - 11.4}{10} = 1.26\,\Omega$$

End of charging

Back e.m.f of battery, $$E_b = 6 \times 2.4 = 14.4 \text{ volts}$$

$\therefore$ $$R = \frac{V - E_b}{I} = \frac{24 - 14.4}{10} = 0.96\,\Omega$$

Example 14.12. *Calculate the supply voltage necessary for charging a battery of 110 cells at 30A (i) at the beginning of charge and (ii) at the end of the charge, if each cell possesses p.d. of 2.1 volts at the beginning and 2.7 volts at the end of charge. Allow 0.06 Ω for the resistance of the connecting leads.*

Solution. The internal resistance of battery is assumed to be zero.

(i) Beginning of charge

Back e.m.f. of battery, $$E_b = 110 \times 2.1 = 231 \text{ volts}$$

Charging current, $$I = \frac{V - E_b}{0.06}$$

or $$30 = \frac{V - 231}{0.06}$$

$\therefore$ Supply voltage, $$V = 231 + 30 \times 0.06 = \textbf{232.8 volts}$$

(ii) End of charging

Back e.m.f. of battery, $$E_b = 110 \times 2.7 = 297 \text{ volts}$$

$\therefore$ Supply voltage, $$V = 297 + 30 \times 0.06 = \textbf{298.8 volts}$$

Example 14.13. *Thirty-five lead-acid cells, each of discharging capacity 100Ah at the 10-hour rate are to be fully charged at constant current for 8 hours. The d.c. supply is 120 V, the ampere-hour efficiency is 80% and the e.m.f. of each cell at the beginning and end of charge is 1.9V and 2.6V respectively. Calculate the maximum and minimum value of the necessary resistance. Ignore internal resistance of the cells.*

Solution. The output of each cell is 100Ah. Since Ah efficiency is 80%, the input ampere hours will be = 100/0.8 = 125. As the number of hours of charge is 8.

$\therefore$ Charging current, $$I = 125/8 = 15.62 \, A$$

Beginning of charge

Back e.m.f. of battery, $$E_b = 35 \times 1.9 = 66.5 \text{ volts}$$

Charging current, $$I = (V - E_b)/R$$

$\therefore$ External resistance, $$R = \frac{V - E_b}{I} = \frac{120 - 66.5}{15.62} = 3.42\,\Omega$$

The value of external resistance will be maximum at the beginning of charge because then back e.m.f. of the battery is minimum.

End of charging

Back e.m.f. of battery, $$E_b = 35 \times 2.6 = 91 \text{ volts}$$

$\therefore$ External resistance, $$R = \frac{V - E_b}{I} = \frac{120 - 91}{15.62} = 1.86\,\Omega$$

Example 14.14. *A shunt generator is used to charge a battery of 100 cells in series. If each cell has a terminal p.d. of 2.5V at the completion of charge and is of internal resistance 0.001 Ω, calculate the e.m.f. to be generated to give a charging current of 15A at the end of charge.*

Assume that the armature and field resistances are 0.2 Ω and 200 Ω respectively and the cables connecting the generator to the battery have a resistance of 0.6 Ω.

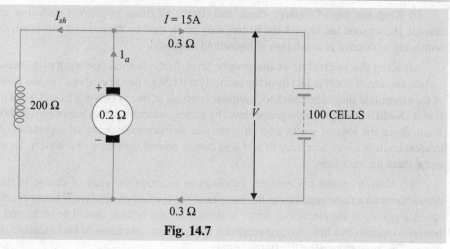

Fig. 14.7

Solution. Fig. 14.7 shows the whole arrangement. The charging current $I = 15A$.

Back e.m.f. of battery,	$E_b = 100 \times 2.5 = 250$ volts
Battery terminal voltage,	$V = 250 +$ Drop in battery
	$= 250 + (15 \times 0.001 \times 100) = 251.5$ volts
Voltage at generator terminals	$= 251.5 +$ Drop in connecting cables
	$= 251.5 + 15 \times 0.6 = 260.5$ volts
Shunt current,	$I_{sh} = 260.5/200 = 1.3\ A$
Armature current,	$I_a = 15 + 1.3 = 16.3\ A$
$\therefore$ E.M.F. of generator	$= 260.5 + 16.3 \times 0.2 = \textbf{263.76 volts}$

TUTORIAL PROBLEMS

1. A battery of accumulators of e.m.f. 50 volts and internal resistance 2Ω is charged on 100-V direct mains. What series resistance will be required to give a charging current of 2A? If the cost of energy is 70 paise per kWh, what will it cost to charge the battery for 8 hours and what percentage of energy supplied will be wasted in the form of heat ? [23Ω ; Rs. 1.12; 50%]

2. A battery of 4 lead-acid cells in series is to be charged and the only available source is 210V d.c. supply. The desired charging current is 0.5 A and each cell on charge has an e.m.f. of 2.5 volts. If an electric lamp is used as the controlling resistance for the circuit, what voltage and size of the lamp will be necessary ? [200V; 100W]

3. A lead-acid battery of 50 cells is to be charged at 25A from a 200V d.c. supply using a series resistor. If the e.m.f. of each cell is 1.95 volts at the commencement of charge and 2.55 volts at the end of the charge, find the range of series resistance value required. The internal resistance of each cell may be assumed to remain constant at 0.002Ω and the resistance of the connecting leads may be neglected. [4Ω to 2.8Ω]

4. Determine the variation in the applied voltage required to charge a battery of 100 lead-acid cells if charged from an e.m.f. of 1.8 volts to 2.6 volts per cell with a constant charging current of 10A. The internal resistance of each cell is 0.01Ω .
   [Initial voltage = 190V; Final voltage = 270 V; Variation = 80V]

14.14. CARE OF LEAD-ACID BATTERIES

The average life of a lead-acid battery is two to four years, depending upon its quality and the kind of care exercised in its use. To get the maximum life out of a lead-acid battery, the following procedures are recommended :

(*i*) **Keep the top of battery clean and dry** at all times to prevent corrosion and leakage of current. If corrosion has started, the battery may be cleaned by the use of a stiff brush and then wiped with a rag moistened in a solution of household ammonia.

(*ii*) **Keep the electrolyte at the proper level.** In the normal operation of a lead-acid battery, a certain amount of water is lost from the electrolyte (H_2SO_4) due to evaporation and gassing. The level of the electrolyte should be checked at regular intervals of one or two weeks and when found to be too low, it should be brought to the proper level by adding water free from impurities. It should always be 1 cm above the tops of plates and separators as this prevents decay of separators. As only water evaporates, it is never necessary to add acid during normal operation of a battery. Be sure to replace and tighten the vent caps.

(*iii*) **Take frequent hydrometer readings** to ascertain the state of charge of the battery. It is advisable to take these readings at the same time the level of electrolyte is being checked. When the specific gravity of the electrolyte drops to about 1.18, the battery should be recharged. Allowing the battery to remain in a low charged condition will produce an excess of lead sulphate ($PbSO_4$) on the plates. This may reduce the life of the battery.

(*iv*) **Do not charge the battery at a high rate.** Charging at too high a rate causes excessive heat and gassing and also a permanent loss in some of the active material of the plates. The battery should be charged at such a rate (See Art. 14.12) that battery temperature does not exceed 40°C and that excessive gassing does not take place.

(*v*) **Do not leave the battery in a discharged condition for a long period.** If left in a discharged condition for a long period, a coating of hard lead sulphate may form on the plates. The sulphate coating cannot be converted to active materials and the battery is permanently damaged. This action is commonly called **sulphation** and may also be caused due to excessive heat and too much concentration of sulphuric acid in the electrolyte.

(*vi*) **If a lead-acid battery is to be stored** for several months, the level of the electrolyte should be periodically checked. After intervals of 4 to 6 weeks, the battery should be given a freshening charge so that it will be kept fully charged at all times.

(*vii*) **Do not short circuit the battery.** Since the internal resistance of a lead-acid battery is very small (typical value being 0.01Ω), a short-circuit will give a damaging current of several hundred amperes. This may cause the plates to buckle, thus ruining the battery.

14.15. APPLICATIONS OF LEAD-ACID BATTERIES

The chief application of lead-acid batteries is at places where a d.c. generator cannot be conveniently installed. Such batteries are employed whenever low-voltage, high-current d.c. source is required. Some of the important applications of lead-acid batteries are given below :

(*i*) Lead-acid batteries are extensively used in automobiles. A d.c. generator, battery and load are connected in parallel. Since the internal resistance of a lead-acid battery is very low, it provides a large output current required for *starting the engine of the car. In addition, the battery furnishes the power of lights, radio *etc.* when the engine is stopped. When the engine is running, it operates the d.c. generator which takes over the duties of the battery. The generator also charges up the battery so that it will be ready when needed.

(*ii*) Railway train lighting system is similar to the above mentioned system. When the train is in motion, axle-driven d.c. generators furnish power for lighting, fans *etc.* When the train runs at slow speeds or is stopped, lead-acid batteries take over the duties of the generators.

* The starting motor of an automobile may require more than 300 A at start. Because of its low internal resistance, a lead-acid battery can furnish currents of such large magnitude but only for a few seconds at a time.

(iii) In a.c. generating plants, lead-acid batteries are used to energise the control apparatus e.g. switching. During shut down of generators, these batteries are used to supply emergency lights.

(iv) Hospitals and other places (e.g. theatres, banks etc.) where continuous supply is absolutely essential often use batteries as an emergency supply.

(v) These are used for lighting purpose in remote rural areas where there are no power lines. The batteries are kept in charge by means of a d.c. generator. When the generator fails, the batteries supply the load.

14.16. NICKEL-IRON CELL OR EDISON CELL

Nickel-iron-alkaline cell was developed by the American scientist Thomas A. Edison in 1909. When the nickel-iron cell is in the charged condition, the active material on the positive plate is nickel oxide (Ni_2O_3) and that on the negative plate is iron (Fe). The electrolyte is 21% solution of potassium hydroxide (KOH) with a small amount of lithium added. When the cell is discharged, the positive plate is reduced to lower oxide of nickel (i.e. NiO) and the negative plate is oxidised to iron oxide (FeO). When the cell is recharged, the chemical process is reversed i.e. positive plate is converted to Ni_2O_3 and the negative plate to Fe. The equation of the chemical action is as under :

$$\underset{\substack{\text{positive}\\\text{plate}}}{Ni_2O_3} + 2KOH + \underset{\substack{\text{negative}\\\text{plate}}}{Fe} \underset{\text{charge}}{\overset{\text{discharge}}{\rightleftharpoons}} \underset{\substack{\text{positive}\\\text{plate}}}{2NiO} + 2KOH + \underset{\substack{\text{negative}\\\text{plate}}}{FeO}$$

The equation is read from left to right for discharging and from right to left for charging. The following points may be noted in these electro-chemical reactions :

(i) There is merely transfer of oxygen from one plate to the other. Thus during discharging, oxygen

(O_2^-) from the positive plate is transferred to the negative plate to form FeO. The reverse happens during charging.

(ii) The specific gravity of the electrolyte (KOH) remains unchanged during charge or discharge.

The e.m.f. of a nickel-iron cell is about 1.2V when charged and falls to 0.9V when discharged. Since the electrolyte does not undergo any change in specific gravity during charge or discharge, the state of charge of this cell cannot be determined by the specific gravity of the electrolyte. Instead, a voltmeter is employed to ascertain whether the cell is charged upto its rated voltage.

Advantages

(i) Since the specific gravity of the electrolyte (KOH) does not change, a nickel-iron cell is not damaged by being left in a fully discharged condition for considerable period of time.

(ii) It is more rugged and can stand more mechanical and electrical abuse than a lead-acid cell.

(iii) It weighs only about half as much as a lead-acid cell of equivalent capacity.

(iv) It does not produce acid fumes that corrode nearby objects.

(v) Its life is much longer than that of a lead-acid cell.

(vi) It can be discharged at a high rate for long periods without danger to the battery and can be recharged safely at a rapid rate.

(vii) It can withstand high temperatures better than a lead-acid cell.

Disadvantages

(i) It is costlier than a lead-acid cell.

(ii) The e.m.f. of a nickel cell is about 1.2 V against 2V of the lead-acid cell. A supply of 12V needs a battery of 10 nickel-iron cells in series but only 6 lead-acid cells in series.

(iii) It has higher internal resistance than the lead-acid cell and cannot provide a large current. For this reason, it is unsuitable for automobile starting service.

(*iv*) The efficiencies of a nickel-iron cell are lower than that of a lead-acid cell. The ampere-hour and watt-hour efficiencies of such a cell are about 80% and 65% respectively.

Applications. Due to their high mechanical strength, lightness, ability to withstand arduous conditions and free from acid fumes, nickel-iron batteries have been found to be more satisfactory for traction purposes, mine locomotives, *submarines *etc*. They are particularly suitable in cases where exceptional vibrations are encountered as on motor cycles *etc*.

14.17. CONSTRUCTION OF NICKEL-IRON CELL

Like a lead-acid cell, a nickel-iron cell also has a multiplate construction. The positive plates consist of a number of perforated steel tubes mounted on a nickel-plated steel grid. Each tube is filled with nickel oxide (Ni_2O_3). The negative plates are constructed of many small perforated steel pockets, each filled with powdered iron (See Fig. 14.8). The perforations in the tubes and pockets of the plates permit the electrolyte to get at the active materials. The alternate positive and negative plates of the cell are sandwiched together with separators. The negative plates are connected together as are the positive plates. The number of negative plates is always one more than the number of positive plates; the outside plates being negative.

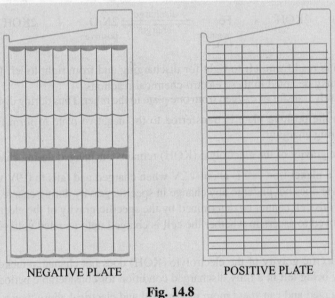

NEGATIVE PLATE   POSITIVE PLATE

Fig. 14.8

A nickel-iron cell embraces the following additional arrangements for better performance :

(*i*) The plates are made thinner than that of a lead-acid cell. For this reason, a nickel-iron cell occupies less volume than the equivalent lead-acid cell.

(*ii*) The assembled plates are housed in a nickel plated steel container. A steel container is used because there is no acid to attack it.

(*iii*) In order to decrease the internal resistance of the cell, nickel oxide is intimately mixed with flakes of pure nickel and the iron with mercuric oxide.

---

* When a submarine is submerged, it cannot use those engines which consume air *e.g.* petrol engine or diesel engine. Hence it runs on electric motors operated by nickel-iron batteries. The lead-acid battery is not suitable because the acid fumes may corrode the equipment. On the surface, the submarine is run by diesel engines. These engines also operate a d.c. generator which recharges the batteries.

14.18. NICKEL-CADMIUM CELL

Nickel-Cadmium cell was developed by Waldermar Junger, a Swede, in 1899. When the nickel-cadmium cell is in the charged condition, the active material on the positive plate is $Ni(OH)_3$ and that on the negative plate is cadmium (Cd). The electrolyte is the same as in the nickel-iron cell *i.e.* potassium hydroxide (KOH). When the cell is discharged, the positive plate is converted to $Ni(OH)_2$ and the negative plate to $Cd(OH)_2$. When the cell is recharged, the chemical process is reversed *i.e.* positive plate is converted to $Ni(OH)_3$ and negative plate to Cd. The equation of chemical action is :

$$\underset{\substack{\text{positive}\\\text{plate}}}{2Ni(OH)_3} + \underset{\substack{\text{negative}\\\text{plate}}}{Cd} \underset{\text{charge}}{\overset{\text{discharge}}{\rightleftharpoons}} \underset{\substack{\text{positive}\\\text{plate}}}{2Ni(OH)_2} + \underset{\substack{\text{negative}\\\text{plate}}}{Cd(OH)_2}$$

The equation is read from left to right for discharging and from right to left when charging. The following points may be noted in these electro-chemical reactions :

(*i*) There is merely transfer of hydroxyl ions ($2OH^-$) from one plate to the other. Thus during discharging, hydroxyl ions from the positive plate are transferred to the negative plate to form $Cd(OH)_2$. The reverse happens during charging.

(*ii*) The specific gravity of the electrolyte (KOH) remains unchanged during charge or discharge.

The e.m.f. of a nickel-cadmium cell is about 1.2V when charged and falls to 1.1V when discharged. Since the specific gravity of the electrolyte (KOH) remains unchanged during charge or discharge, it cannot be used as an indication to the state of charge of the cell. Instead, a voltmeter is employed to determine whether the cell is charged upto its rated voltage.

Advantages. The nickel-cadmium cell combines the best features of both the lead-acid and Edison types.

(*i*) It is rugged and has a very long active life. Periods upto 20 years of service can be expected from nickel-cadmium battery.

(*ii*) It can be stored indefinitely in either a discharged or charged state without suffering any ill effects.

(*iii*) A nickel-cadmium (Ni-Cd) battery can be charged in a short time (say 1 hour).

(*iv*) Its internal resistance is very low which means that it can deliver very large current at constant terminal voltage.

(*v*) It can stand peak rates of discharge and charge upto 20 times the normal operating rate.

The chief disadvantage of a nickel-cadmium cell is that it is expensive.

Nickel Cadmium Batteries

MULTIPLE-CHOICE QUESTIONS

1. The current conduction through the solution of an electrolyte is by ....
   - (a) free electrons
   - (b) ions
   - (c) atoms
   - (d) valence electrons

2. For the process of electrolysis, we require ....
   - (a) d.c. supply
   - (b) a.c. supply
   - (c) varying voltage
   - (d) both d.c. and a.c. supply

3. A positively charged atom is sometimes called............ .
   - (a) donor atom
   - (b) acceptor atom
   - (c) cation
   - (d) anion

4. The mass of an element deposited or liberated at an electrode during electrolysis is .... the quantity of electricity passed through the electrolyte.
   - (a) directly proportional to
   - (b) inversely proportional to
   - (c) independent of
   - (d) none of the above

5. During electrolysis, mass of an element liberated at the electrode is .... of the element.
   - (a) directly proportional to the valency
   - (b) inversely proportional to atomic weight
   - (c) directly proportional to chemical eq. wt.
   - (d) none of the above

6. The most commonly used cell is ....
   - (a) lead-acid cell
   - (b) nickel-iron cell
   - (c) nickel-cadmium cell
   - (d) fuel cell

7. In practice, the state of discharge of a lead-acid cell is determined by ....
   - (a) e.m.f. of the cell
   - (b) specific gravity of the electrolyte
   - (c) colour of plates of the cell
   - (d) none of the above

8. The commercial lead-acid cell has 15 plates. The number of negative plates will be ....
   - (a) 7
   - (b) 9
   - (c) 10
   - (d) 8

9. The life of the positive plates of a lead-acid cell is roughly .... that of negative plates.
   - (a) the same as
   - (b) half
   - (c) twice
   - (d) thrice

10. A lead-acid cell has 13 plates. In the absence of manufacturer's data, the charging current should be ....
    - (a) 13 A
    - (b) 2 A
    - (c) 6 A
    - (d) 3 A

11. The state of charge of a nickel-iron cell is determined by...............
    - (a) the specific gravity of electrolyte (KOH)
    - (b) e.m.f. of the cell
    - (c) colour of plates
    - (d) none of the above

12. In producing chlorine through electrolysis, 100 kW power at 125V is being consumed. How much chlorine per minute is liberated ? E.C.E. of chlorine = 0.367×10^{-6} kg/coulomb.
    - (a) 2.5×10^{-2} kg
    - (b) 17.61×10^{-3} kg
    - (c) 1.2×10^{-3} kg
    - (d) 8.1×10^{-4} kg

13. A brass plate (5 cm × 4 cm) is to be silver plated on both sides with a coating of thickness 0.25 mm. The work is to be completed in 5 hours. What should be the magnitude of current? E.C.E. of silver = 0.00112 g/C; density of silver = 10.5 g/cm^3.
    - (a) 2.1A
    - (b) 0.224 A
    - (c) 1.35 A
    - (d) 0.521 A

14. A battery of e.m.f. 3V and internal resistance 1 Ω is connected to a copper voltameter and a current of 1.5 A flows in the circuit. What is the resistance of the voltameter ?
    - (a) 3 Ω
    - (b) 1 Ω
    - (c) 1.5 Ω
    - (d) 2.5 Ω

15. A certain charge liberates 0.8 g of oxygen. The same charge will liberate how many grams of silver ?
    - (a) 108 g
    - (b) 8 g
    - (c) 10.8 g
    - (d) $\dfrac{108}{0.8}$ g

16. In how much time 1 litre of H_2 will be collected by 5A current if $z = 10^{-8}$ kg/C and density of $H_2 = 0.09$ kg/m^3 ?
    - (a) 30 min
    - (b) 15 min
    - (c) 60 min
    - (d) 45 min

17. A current of 16A flows through molten NaCl for 10 minutes. The amount of metallic sodium that appears at negative electrode would be (F = 96500 C/gram equivalent)
    - (a) 11.5 g
    - (b) 23 g
    - (c) 1.15 g
    - (d) 2.3 g

18. A silver and zinc voltameters are connected in series. A current of I amperes is passed through them for time t. If m gram of zinc is liberated, then the mass of silver deposited is nearly

    (a) m   (b) 3.3 m

    (c) 1.5 m   (d) 2.3 m

19. How much electricity should be passed through an electrolyte solution for one second so that one gram equivalent of the substance is liberated at the electrode ?

    (a) 965 C

    (b) 400 C

    (c) 96500 C

    (d) 550 C

20. A 3 Ω resistor and a silver voltameter of resistance 2 Ω are connected in series across a cell. How will the rate of deposition of silver be effected if a resistance of 2 Ω is connected in parallel with the voltameter ?

    (a) It will decrease by 25%

    (b) It will increase by 25%

    (c) It will increase by 12.5%

    (d) It will decrease by 12.5%

Answers to Multiple-Choice Questions

1. (b)	2. (a)	3. (c)	4. (a)	5.(c)	6.(a)	7.(b)	8.(d)
9. (b)	10. (c)	11. (b)	12. (b)	13.(d)	14.(b)	15.(c)	16.(a)
17. (d)	18. (b)	19. (c)	20. (b)				

Hints to Selected Multiple-Choice Questions

4. $m = z\,Q$

    where z = electrochemical equivalent

               Q = quantity of electricity passed through the electrolyte

5.   Mass liberated $\propto \dfrac{\text{Atomic weight}}{\text{Valency}}$

               $\propto$ **Chemical eq. wt. of the element**

6. Due to relatively low cost, **lead-acid cell** is most widely used.

7. The e.m.f. of a lead-acid cell provides little indication to the state of discharge of the cell since it remains close to 2V for 90% of the discharge period. In practice, **specific gravity of electrolyte** is used to know the state of discharge.

8. The number of negative plates in a lead-acid cell is one more than the number of positive plates; the outside plates being negative.

9. The positive plate active material (*i.e.* PbO_2) undergoes a large change in volume during charge and discharge as compared with negative plate active material (*i.e.* Pb). Therefore, the tendency of PbO_2 to disintegrate and fall to the bottom of the cell is much greater than for Pb. The life of a positive plate is roughly **half** of the negative plate.

10. The charging current should be 1A for every positive plate of a single cell.

11. The specific gravity of the electrolyte (KOH) remains unchanged during charge or discharge.

12. $I = \dfrac{P}{V} = \dfrac{100 \times 10^3}{125} = 800\,\text{A}$

    Mass of chlorine released is

             $m = zIt = 0.367 \times 10^{-6} \times 800 \times 60 = \mathbf{17.61 \times 10^{-3}\,kg}$

13. Mass of coating (both sides) = Volume × density

                      $= 2 \times (5 \times 4 \times 0.025) \times 10.5 = 10.5\,\text{g}$

    $\therefore$ Current, $I = \dfrac{m}{zt} = \dfrac{10.5}{0.00112 \times 5 \times 60 \times 60} = 0.521\,\text{A}$

14. Let R ohm be the resistance of the voltameter. Then,

$$I = \frac{E}{R+1} \quad \text{or} \quad 1.5 = \frac{3}{R+1} \quad \therefore R = 1\Omega$$

15.

$$\frac{m_2}{m_1} = \frac{E_2}{E_1} \quad \text{or} \quad m_2 = m_1 \times \frac{E_2}{E_1} = 0.8 \times \frac{108}{8} = 10.8 \text{g}$$

16. Volume of hydrogen = 1 litre = 1000×10^{-6} m^3 = 10^{-3} m^3
    Mass of hydrogen = Volume × density = $10^{-3} \times 0.09$ kg

$$m = zIt \quad \text{or} \quad t = \frac{m}{zI} = \frac{10^{-3} \times 0.09}{10^{-8} \times 5} = 1800 \text{s} = 30 \text{min}$$

17. Total charge passed = $16 \times 10 \times 60 = 9600$ C
    Now 96500 C of charge liberates 23 g of sodium. Therefore 9600 C of charge will liberate

$$\text{sodium} = \frac{23}{96500} \times 9600 = 2.3 \text{g}$$

18. $\dfrac{m_2}{m_1} = \dfrac{E_2}{E_1}$ or $m_2 = m_1 \times \dfrac{E_2}{E_1} = m \times \dfrac{108}{32.5} = 3.3 \text{m}$

19. Faraday is the quantity of charge required to liberate one gram equivalent of the substance during electrolysis.

20. $m = zIt$. Therefore $m \propto I$. Let E be the e.m.f. of the cell.

For the first case, $\dfrac{E}{5} \propto m_5$;

For the second case, $\dfrac{E}{4} \propto m_2$

$$\therefore \quad \frac{m_2}{m_1} = \frac{E}{4} \times \frac{5}{E} = \frac{5}{4}$$

or

$$\frac{m_2 - m_1}{m_1} = \frac{1}{4}$$

Therefore, the rate of deposition **will increase by 25%**. Note that in the first case total circuit resistance is 5 Ω while in the second case, it is 4 Ω.

15

A.C. Fundamentals

INTRODUCTION

We have dealt so far with cases in which the currents are steady and in one direction; this is called direct current (d.c.). The use of direct currents is limited to a few applications *e.g.* charging of batteries, electroplating, electric traction *etc*. For large-scale power distribution there are, however, many advantages in using alternating current (a.c.). In an a.c. system, the voltage acting in the circuit changes polarity at regular intervals of time and the resulting current (called alternating current) changes direction accordingly. The a.c. system has offered so many advantages that at present, electrical energy is universally generated, transmitted and used in the form of alternating current. Even when d.c. energy is necessary, it is a common practice to convert a.c. into d.c. by means of rotary converters or rectifiers.

Three principal advantages are claimed for a.c. system over the d.c. system. First, alternating voltages can be stepped up or stepped down efficiently by means of a transformer. This permits the transmission of electric power at high voltages to achieve economy and distribute the power at utilization voltages. Secondly, a.c. motors (induction motors) are cheaper and simpler in construction than d.c. motors. Thirdly, the switchgear (*e.g.* switches, circuit breakers *etc*.) for a.c. system is simpler than the d.c. system. In this chapter, we shall confine our attention to the fundamentals of alternating currents.

15.1. SINUSOIDAL ALTERNATING VOLTAGE AND CURRENT

Commercial alternators produce sinusoidal alternating voltage *i.e.* alternating voltage is a sine wave. A sinusoidal alternating voltage can be produced (For proof, refer to Art. 15.3) by rotating a coil with a constant angular velocity (say ω rad/sec) in a uniform magnetic field. The sinusoidal alternating voltage can be expressed by the equation:

$$e = E_m \sin \omega t$$

where
$e =$ Instantaneous value of alternating voltage
$E_m =$ Maximum value of alternating voltage
$\omega =$ Angular velocity of the coil

Sinusoidal voltages always produce sinusoidal currents, unless the circuit is non-linear. Therefore, a sinusoidal current can be expressed in the same way as voltage *i.e.*, $i = I_m \sin \omega t$. Fig. 15.1 (*i*) shows the waveform of sinusoidal voltage whereas Fig. 15.1 (*ii*) shows the waveform of sinusoidal current. Note that sinusoidal voltage or current not only changes direction at regular intervals but the magnitude is also changing continuously.

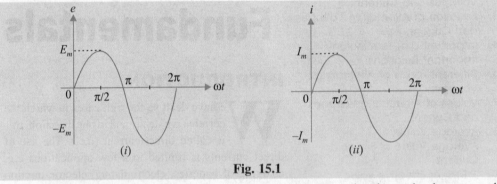

Fig. 15.1

Why Sine Wave form ? Why do we choose sinusoidal wave rather than a simple curve such as a square or triangular wave ? The following are the reasons for doing so :

(*i*) In a.c. machines and transformers, sinusoidal voltages and currents respectively produce the least iron and copper losses for a given output. The efficiency is, therefore, better.

(*ii*) Sinusoidal voltages and currents produce less interference (noise) on telephone lines.

(*iii*) The sine waveform produces the least disturbance in the electrical circuit and is smoothest and efficient waveform.

Due to above advantages, electric supply companies all over the world generate sinusoidal alternating voltages and currents. *It may be noted that alternating voltage and current mean sinusoidal voltage and current unless stated otherwise.*

15.2. GENERATION OF ALTERNATING VOLTAGES AND CURRENTS

An alternating voltage may be generated

(*i*) by rotating a coil at constant angular velocity in a uniform magnetic field as shown in Fig. 15.2.

Or

(*ii*) by rotating a magnetic field at a constant angular velocity within a stationary coil as shown in Fig. 15.3.

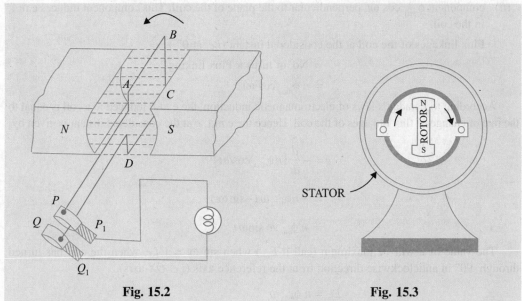

Fig. 15.2   **Fig. 15.3**

In either case, the generated voltage will be of sinusoidal waveform. The magnitude of generated voltage will depend upon the number of turns of coil, the strength of magnetic field and the speed of rotation. The first method is used for small a.c. generators while the second method is employed for large a.c. generators.

15.3. EQUATION OF ALTERNATING VOLTAGE AND CURRENT

Consider a rectangular coil of n turns rotating in anticlockwise direction with an angular velocity of ω rad/sec in a uniform magnetic field as shown in Fig. 15.4. The e.m.f. induced in the coil will be sinusoidal. This can be readily established.

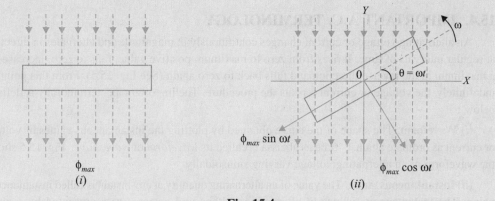

Fig. 15.4

Let the time be measured from the instant the plane of the coil coincides with OX-axis. In this position of the coil [See Fig. 15.4 (i)], the flux linking with the coil has its maximum value ϕ_{max}. Let the coil turn through an angle θ (= ωt) in anticlockwise direction in t seconds and assumes the position shown in Fig. 15.4 (ii). In this position, the maximum flux ϕ_{max} acting vertically downward can be resolved into two perpendicular components $viz.$

(i) component $\phi_{max} \sin \omega t$ parallel to the plane of the coil. This component induces *no e.m.f. in the coil.

. . . .

*   A coil moving parallel to the flux has no change of flux linkage with it or there is no "cutting" of flux.

(ii) component $\phi_{max} \cos \omega t$ perpendicular to the plane of the coil. This component induces e.m.f. in the coil.

∴ Flux linkages of the coil at the considered instant (*i.e.* at $\theta°$)

$$= \text{No. of turns} \times \text{Flux linking}$$

$$= n\, \phi_{max} \cos \omega t$$

According to Faraday's laws of electromagnetic induction, the e.m.f. induced in a coil is equal to the rate of change of flux linkages of the coil. Hence the e.m.f. *e* at the considered instant is given by:

$$e = -\frac{d}{dt}\left(n\phi_{max} \cos\omega t\right)$$

$$= -n\phi_{max}\omega\,(-\sin \omega t)$$

$$= n\,\phi_{max}\omega \sin\omega t$$

The value of *e* will be maximum (call it E_m) when $\sin \omega t = 1$ *i.e.* when the coil has turned through $90°$ in anticlockwise direction from the reference axis (*i.e.* OX-axis).

∴ $$E_m = n\,\phi_{max}\omega$$

or $$e = E_m \sin \omega t = E_m \sin\theta$$

where $$E_m = n\,\phi_{max}\omega$$

It is clear that e.m.f. induced in the coil is sinusoidal *i.e.* instantaneous value of e.m.f. varies as the sine function of time angle (θ or ωt). If this alternating voltage ($e = E_m \sin \omega t$) is applied across a load, alternating current flows through the circuit which would also vary sinusoidally *i.e.*, following a sine law. The equation of the alternating current is given by :

$$i = I_m \sin \omega t \text{ provided the load is *resistive.}$$

15.4. IMPORTANT A.C. TERMINOLOGY

An alternating voltage or current changes continuously in magnitude and alternates in direction at regular intervals of time. It rises from zero to maximum positive value, falls to zero, increases to a maximum in the reverse direction and falls back to zero again (See Fig. 15.5). From this point on indefinitely, the voltage or current repeats the procedure. The important a.c. terminology is defined below :

(i) **Waveform.** The shape of the curve obtained by plotting the instantaneous values of voltage or current as ordinate against †time as abcissa is called its *waveform* or *waveshape*. Fig. 15.5 shows the waveform of an alternating voltage varying sinusoidally.

(ii) **Instantaneous value.** The value of an alternating quantity at any instant is called instantaneous value. The instantaneous values of alternating voltage and current are represented by *e* and *i* respectively. As an example, the instantaneous values of voltage (See Fig. 15.5) at $0°$, $90°$and $270°$are 0, $+E_m$, $-E_m$ respectively.

---

* It will be shown later that if the load is inductive or capacitive, the current equation is changed in time angle.

† We know $\theta = \omega t$. Since ω is constant, $\theta \propto t$. Hence we may take time *t* or θ or ωt along *X*-axis.

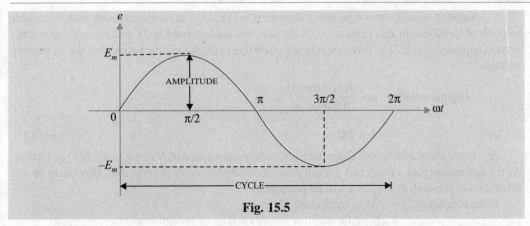

Fig. 15.5

(*iii*) **Cycle.** One complete set of positive and negative values of an alternating quantity is known as a cycle. Fig. 15.5 shows one cycle of an alternating voltage.

A cycle can also be defined in terms of angular measure. One cycle corresponds to 360° *electrical or 2π radians. The voltage or current generated in a conductor will span 360° electrical (or complete one cycle) when the conductor moves past a north and a south pole.

(*iv*) **Alternation.** One-half cycle of an alternating quantity is called an alternation. An alternation spans 180° electrical. Thus in Fig. 15.5, the positive or negative half of alternating voltage is the alternation.

(*v*) **Time period.** The time taken in seconds to complete one cycle of an alternating quantity is called its time period. It is generally represented by T.

(*vi*) **Frequency.** The number of cycles that occur in one second is called the frequency (f) of the alternating quantity. It is measured in cycles/sec (*c/s*) or hertz (*Hz*). One hertz is equal to 1 c/s.

The frequency of power system is low; the most common being 50 *c/s* or 50Hz. It means that alternating voltage or current completes 50 cycles in one second. The 50 Hz frequency is the most popular because it gives the best results when used for operating both lights and machinery.

(*vii*) **Amplitude.** The maximum value (positive or negative) attained by an alternating quantity is called its amplitude or peak value. The amplitude of an alternating voltage or current is designated by E_m (or V_m) or I_m.

15.5. IMPORTANT RELATIONS

Having become familiar with a.c. terminology, we shall now establish some important relations.

(*i*) **Time period and frequency.** Consider an alternating quantity having a frequency of f *c/s* and time period T second.

Time taken to complete f cycles = 1 second   (By definition)

Time taken to complete 1 cycle = 1/f second

But time taken to complete one cycle is the time period T (by definition).

$$\therefore \qquad T = \frac{1}{f} \qquad or \qquad f = \frac{1}{T}$$

* The time required to generate one cycle is divided into 360 divisions called electrical degrees. They differ from mechanical degrees. In one revolution, the coil will always traverse 360°mechanical. However, the electrical degrees spanned will depend upon the number of poles. For a 2-pole generator, electrical degrees spanned in one revolution of the coil are 360° *i.e.*, one cycle is generated. For a 4-pole generator, 2 cycles (*i.e.*720°) will be generated for one revolution of the coil.

(*ii*) **Angular velocity and frequency.** Referring to Fig. 15.4, the coil is rotating with an angular velocity of ωrad/sec. In one revolution of the coil, the angle turned is 2π radians and the voltage wave completes 1 cycle. The time taken to complete one cycle is the time period T of the alternating voltage.

$$\therefore \quad \text{Angular velocity, } \omega = \frac{\text{Angle turned}}{\text{Time taken}} = \frac{2\pi}{T}$$

or $\qquad\qquad\qquad\qquad \omega = 2\pi f \qquad\qquad\qquad\qquad\qquad (\because f = 1/T)$

(*iii*) **Frequency and speed.** Consider a coil rotating at a speed of N r.p.m. in the field of P poles. As the coil moves past a north and a south pole, one complete cycle is generated. Obviously, in one revolution of the coil, $P/2$ cycles will be generated.

Now, Frequency, $f =$ No. of cycles/sec

$\qquad\qquad = $ (No. of cycles/revolution) × (No. of revolutions/sec)

$$= \left(\frac{P}{2}\right)\times\left(\frac{N}{60}\right) = \frac{PN}{120}$$

$$\therefore \qquad\qquad f = \frac{PN}{120}$$

For example, an a.c. generator having 10 poles and running at 600 r.p.m. will generate alternating voltage and current whose frequency is :

$$f = \frac{PN}{120} = \frac{10\times600}{120} = 50\,\text{Hz}$$

Frequency Meters

15.6. DIFFERENT FORMS OF ALTERNATING VOLTAGE

The standard form of an alternating voltage is given by :

$$e = E_m \sin\theta = E_m \sin\omega t$$

$$= E_m \sin 2\pi ft = E_m \sin\frac{2\pi}{T}t$$

Which of the above form of equations is to be used will depend upon the given data. The following points may be noted carefully:

(i) *The maximum value of alternating voltage is given by the co-efficient of sine of the time angle i.e.*

Maximum value of voltage, E_m = Co-efficient of sine of time angle

(ii) *The frequency f of alternating voltage is given by dividing the co-efficient of time in the angle by 2π i.e.*

$$\text{Frequency, } f = \frac{\text{Co-efficient of time in the angle}}{2\pi}$$

For example, suppose the equation of an alternating voltage is given by $e = 100 \sin 314t$. Then the maximum value of voltage, $E_m = 100$ V; frequency, $f = 314/2\pi = 50$ Hz and time period $T = 1/f = 1/50 = 0.02$ second.

Following similar procedure, maximum value, frequency, time period *etc.* can be found out from the various forms of current equation.

Example 15.1. *A rectangular coil measuring 30 cm by 20 cm and having 40 turns is rotated about an axis coinciding with one of its longer sides at a speed of 1500 r.p.m. in a uniform magnetic field of flux density 0.075 Wb/m². Calculate (i) the frequency of the e.m.f. (ii) maximum value of e.m.f. and (iii) the value of e.m.f. when the coil plane makes an angle of 45° with the field direction.*

Solution. The statement of the problem suggests that the number of poles is 2.

(i) Frequency, $f = \dfrac{NP}{120} = \dfrac{1500 \times 2}{120} = $ **25 Hz**

(ii) As proved in Art. 15.3,

Maximum e.m.f., $E_m = n\, \phi_{max} \omega$

Here $\phi_{max} = B \times A = 0.075 \times (30 \times 20 \times 10^{-4}) = 0.0045\text{Wb}$

$\omega = 2\pi f = 2\pi \times 25 = 157\,\text{rad./sec}$

$\therefore$ $E_m = 40 \times (0.0045) \times 157 = $ **28.26 V**

(iii) When the coil plane makes an angle of 45° with the direction of field,

$$e = E_m \sin\theta = 28.26 \sin 45° = \textbf{19.98V}$$

Example 15.2. *An alternating current i is given by :*

$$i = 141.4 \sin 314t$$

Find (i) the maximum value (ii) frequency (iii) time period and (iv) the instantaneous value when t is 3ms.

Solution. Comparing the given equation of alternating current with the standard form $i = I_m \sin \omega t$, we have,

(i) Maximum value, $\qquad\qquad I_m = \textbf{141.4A}$

(ii) Frequency, $\qquad\qquad f = \omega/2\pi = 314/2\pi = \textbf{50 Hz}$

(iii) Time period, $\qquad\qquad T = 1/f = 1/50 = \textbf{0.02s}$

(iv) $\qquad\qquad i = 141.4 \sin 314t$

When $\qquad\qquad t = 3\text{ ms} = 3 \times 10^{-3}\text{s}$

$\qquad\qquad i = 141.4 \sin 314 \times 3 \times 10^{-3} = \textbf{114.35 V}$

Example 15.3. *An alternating current of frequency 60Hz has a maximum value of 120 A.*

(i) *Write down the equation for the instantaneous value.*

(ii) *Reckoning time from the instant the current is zero and becoming positive, find the instantaneous value after 1/360 second.*

(iii) *Time taken to reach 96A for the first time.*

Solution.

(i) The instantaneous value of current is given by ;

$$i = I_m \sin \omega t$$

$$= I_m \sin 2\pi ft = 120 \sin 2\pi \times 60 \times t$$

$$\therefore \qquad i = 120 \sin 120 \, \pi t$$

(ii) Fig. 15.6 shows the wave form of the given alternating current. Since point O has been taken as the reference, the current equation is :

$$i = 120 \sin 120 \, \pi t$$

When $t = 1/360$ second, then,

$$i = 120 \sin 120\pi \times 1/360$$

$$= 120 \sin (\pi/3) = 103.92 A$$

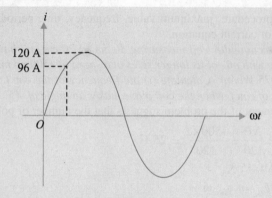

Fig. 15.6

(iii) Suppose the current becomes 96A for the first time after t second as shown in Fig. 15.6.

Then, $96 = 120 \sin 120\pi t$

or $\sin 120 \, \pi t = 96/120 = 0.8$

or $120\pi t = \sin^{-1} 0.8 = 0.927$ rad.

$$\therefore \qquad t = \frac{0.927}{120 \times \pi} = 0.00246 \text{ s}$$

Example 15.4. *A sinusoidal voltage of 50Hz has a maximum value of* $200\sqrt{2}$ *volts. At what time measured from a positive maximum value will the instantaneous voltage be 141.4 volts ?*

Solution. Fig. 15.7 shows the voltage wave-form. The equation of this wave with point O as the reference is given by :

$$e = E_m \sin \omega t = E_m \sin 2\pi ft = 200 \sqrt{2} \sin 2\pi \times 50 \times t$$

$$\therefore \qquad e = 282.8 \sin 314 \, t$$

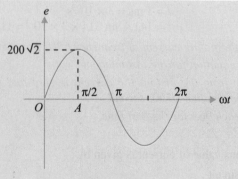

Fig. 15.7

This equation is valid when time is measured from the instant the voltage is zero *i.e.* point O. Since the time is measured from the positive maximum value (point A in Fig. 15.7), the above equation is modified to :

$$e = 282.8 \sin (314t + \pi/2) = 282.8 \cos 314t$$

Let the value of voltage become 141.4 volts t second after passing through the maximum positive value. Then,

$$141.4 = 282.8 \cos 314t$$

or $$\cos 314t = 141.4/282.8 = 0.5$$

or $$314t = \cos^{-1} 0.5 = 1.047 \text{ rad}$$

∴ $$t = 1.047/314 = 3.33 \times 10^{-3} \text{ s} = \mathbf{3.33 \text{ ms}}$$

Example 15.5. *An alternating current of frequency 50Hz has a maximum value of 100A. Calculate (i) its value 1/600 second after the instant the current is zero and its value is decreasing there afterwards (ii) how many seconds after the current is zero and then increasing will attain the value of 86.6A ?*

Solution. Fig. 15.8 shows the current waveform. With O as the origin, the equation of the current is :

$$i = I_m \sin \omega t = 100 \sin 2\pi \times 50 \times t$$

∴ $$i = 100 \sin 100\pi t$$

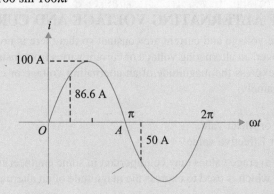

Fig. 15.8

(*i*) Since current is measured from the instant the current is zero and is decreasing there afterwards (point A in Fig. 15.8), the equation of the current with point A as the origin becomes:

$$i = 100 \sin (100\pi t + \pi) = -100 \sin 100\pi t$$

When $$t = 1/600 \text{ second, then,}$$

$$i = -100 \sin 100 \times 180° \times \frac{1}{600} = \mathbf{-50A}$$

(*ii*) When current is measured from the instant the current is zero and is increasing thereafter (*i.e.* point O in Fig. 15.8), the current equation is given by :

$$i = 100 \sin 100\pi t$$

or $$86.6 = 100 \sin 100\pi t$$

or $$\sin 100\pi t = 86.6/100 = 0.866$$

or $$100\pi t = \sin^{-1} 0.866 = 1.047 \text{ rad}$$

∴ $$t = 1.047/100\pi = 3.33 \times 10^{-3}\text{s} = \mathbf{3.33 \text{ ms}}$$

TUTORIAL PROBLEMS

1. An alternating voltage is represented by :
$$e = 141.4 \sin 377\, t$$
Find (i) the maximum value (ii) frequency (iii) time period and (iv) the instantaneous value of voltage when t is 3 ms. [(i) **141.4 V** (ii) **60 Hz** (iii) **16.67 ms** (iv) **127.8V**]

2. An alternating current of frequency 50 Hz has a maximum value of $200\sqrt{2}\,A$. Reckoning the time from the instant the current is zero and becoming positive, find the time taken by the current to reach a value of 141.4 A for a first and second time. [**1.67 ms; 21.67 ms**]

3. An alternating current takes 3.375 ms to reach 15 A for the first time after becoming instantaneously zero. The frequency of current is 40 Hz. Find the maximum value of alternating current. [**20A**]

4. A 50 Hz sinusoidal voltage has a maximum value of 56.56V. Find the value of voltage 0.0025 second after passing through maximum positive value. At what time measured from a positive maximum value will instantaneous voltage be 14.14V ? [**40V; 4.2 ms**]

5. An alternating current of frequency 50Hz has a maximum value of 100A. Calculate its value 1/300 second after the instant the current is zero and its value is decreasing thereafter.
[**– 86.6 A**]

15.7. VALUES OF ALTERNATING VOLTAGE AND CURRENT

In a d.c. system, the voltage and current are constant so that there is no problem of specifying their magnitudes. However, an alternating voltage or current varies from instant to instant. A natural question arises how to express the magnitude of an alternating voltage or current. There are three ways of expressing it, namely;

(i) Peak value
(ii) Average value or Mean value
(iii) R.M.S value or Effective value.

Although peak and average values may be important in some engineering applications, it is the r.m.s. or effective value which is used to express the magnitude of an alternating voltage or current.

15.8. AVERAGE VALUE

The arithmetical average of all the values of an alternating quantity over one cycle is called its average value i.e.
$$\text{Average value} = \frac{\text{Area under the curve}}{\text{Base}}$$

(i) In case of *symmetrical waves (e.g. sinusoidal voltage or current), the average value over one cycle is zero. It is because positive half is exactly equal to the negative half cycle so that net area is zero. However, the average value of positive or negative half is not zero. Hence in case of symmetrical waves, average value means the average value of half-cycle or one alternation.

$$\text{Average value of a symmetrical wave} = \frac{\text{Area of one alternation}}{\text{Base length of one alternation}}$$

$$= \frac{\text{Sum of **mid - ordinates over one alternation}}{\text{No. of mid - ordinates}}$$

* A symmetrical wave is one which has positive half-cycle exactly equal to the negative half-cycle.

** Suppose positive half-cycle is divided into n equal parts. The middle value of each part is the mid-ordinate. The average value will be the sum of mid-ordinates divided by the number of mid-ordinates (i.e. n in this case).

(ii) In case of unsymmetrical waves (*e.g.* half-wave rectified voltage *etc.*), the average value is taken over the full cycle.

$$\text{Average value of an unsymmetrical wave } = \frac{\text{Area over one cycle}}{\text{Base length of 1 cycle}}$$

15.9. AVERAGE VALUE OF SINUSOIDAL CURRENT

The equation of an alternating current varying sinusoidally is given by :
$$i = I_m \sin \theta$$

Consider an elementary strip of width $d\theta$ in the first half-cycle of current wave as shown in Fig. 15.9. Let i be the mid-ordinate of this strip.

Area of strip = $id\theta$

Area of half-cycle

$$= \int_0^\pi i\, d\theta = \int_0^\pi I_m \sin\theta\, d\theta = I_m \left[-\cos\theta \right]_0^\pi = 2I_m$$

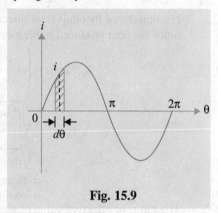

Fig. 15.9

∴ Average value,

$$I_{av} = \frac{\text{Area of half - cycle}}{\text{Base length of half - cycle}} = \frac{2I_m}{\pi}$$

or $\qquad\qquad \mathbf{I_{av} = 0.637\ I_m}$

Similarly, it can be proved that for alternating voltage varying sinusoidally, $E_{av} = 0.637\ E_m$.

15.10. R.M.S. OR EFFECTIVE VALUE

The effective *or r.m.s.* value *of an alternating current is that steady current (d.c.) which when flowing through a given resistance for a given time produces the same amount of heat as produced by the alternating current when flowing through the same resistance for the same time.*

For example, when we say that the r.m.s. or effective value of an alternating current is 5A, it means that the alternating current will do work (or produce heat) at the same rate as 5A direct current under similar conditions.

Illustration. The r.m.s. or effective value of an alternating current (or voltage) can be determined as follows. Consider the half-cycle of a non-sinusoidal alternating current i [See Fig. 15.10 (*i*)] flowing through a resistance $R\Omega$ for t seconds. Divide the time t in n equal intervals of time, each of duration t/n second. Let the mid-ordinates be $i_1, i_2, i_3, ..., i_n$. Each current $i_1, i_2, i_3, ..., i_n$ will produce heating effect when passed through the resistance R as shown in Fig. 15.10 (*ii*). Suppose the heating effect produced by current i in R is the same as produced by some direct current I flowing through the resistance R for the same time t seconds. Then direct current I is the r.m.s. or effective value of alternating current i.

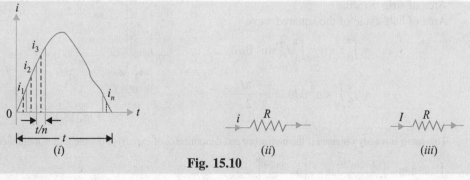

Fig. 15.10

The heating effect of various components of alternating current will be $i_1^2 Rt/n$, $i_2^2 Rt/n,...,i_n^2 Rt/n$ joules. Since the alternating current is varying, the heating effect will also vary.

Total heat produced by alternating current i is

$$= \left(i_1^2 R + i_2^2 R + i_3^2 R + ... + i_n^2 R\right) t/n$$

$$= \left(\frac{i_1^2 R + i_2^2 R + i_3^2 R + ... + i_n^2 R}{n}\right) t \text{ joules}$$

Heat produced by equivalent direct current $I = I^2 Rt$ joules

Since the heat produced in both cases is the same,

∴ $$I^2 Rt = \left(\frac{i_1^2 R + i_2^2 R + i_3^2 R + ... + i_n^2 R}{n}\right) t$$

or $$I = \sqrt{\frac{i_1^2 + i_2^2 + i_3^2 + ... + i_n^2}{n}} \qquad ...(i)$$

$$= \sqrt{\text{mean value of } i^2}$$

= Square **root** of the **mean** of the **squares** of the current

= root-mean-square (r.m.s.) value

The r.m.s. or effective value of alternating voltage can similarly be expressed as :

$$E = \sqrt{\frac{e_1^2 + e_2^2 + e_3^2 + ... + e_n^2}{n}}$$

(*i*) For symmetrical waves, the r.m.s. or effective value can be found by considering half-cycle or full-cycle. However, for unsymmetrical waves, full-cycle should be considered.

(*ii*) The r.m.s. value of a wave can also be expressed as :

$$* \text{R.M.S. value} = \sqrt{\frac{\text{Area of half - cycle wave squared}}{\text{Half - cycle base}}}$$

15.11. R.M.S. VALUE OF SINUSOIDAL CURRENT

The equation of the alternating current varying sinusoidally is given by :

$$i = I_m \sin\theta$$

Consider an elementary strip of width $d\theta$ in the first half-cycle of the squared current wave (shown dotted in Fig. 15.11). Let i^2 be the mid-ordinate of this strip.

Area of strip = $i^2 d\theta$.

Area of half-cycle of the squared wave

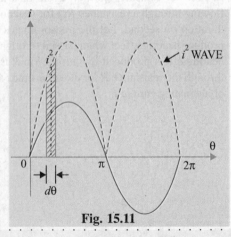

$$= \int_0^\pi i^2 d\theta = \int_0^\pi I_m^2 \sin^2\theta \, d\theta$$

$$= I_m^2 \int_0^\pi \sin^2\theta \, d\theta = ** \frac{\pi I_m^2}{2}$$

Fig. 15.11

∴

* This result is readily obtained if the numerator and denominator of exp. (*i*) under the root is multiplied by t/n.

** $\int_0^\pi \sin^2\theta \, d\theta = \int_0^\pi \frac{1 - \cos 2\theta}{2} d\theta = \frac{1}{2}\left[\theta - \frac{\sin 2\theta}{2}\right]_0^\pi = \frac{\pi}{2}$

$$I_{r.m.s.} = \sqrt{\frac{\text{Area of half - cycle squared wave}}{\text{Half - cycle base}}}$$

$$= \sqrt{\frac{\pi\, I_m^2/2}{\pi}} = \frac{I_m}{\sqrt{2}} = 0.707\, I_m$$

$$\therefore \quad I_{r.m.s.} = 0.707\, I_m$$

Similarly, it can be proved that for alternating voltage varying sinusoidally, $E_{r.m.s.} = 0.707 E_m$.

In a.c. circuits, voltages and currents are normally given in r.m.s. values unless stated otherwise. A.C. ammeters and voltmeters are callibrated to record r.m.s. values.

15.12. FORM FACTOR AND PEAK FACTOR

There exists a definite relation among the peak value, average value and r.m.s. value of an alternating quantity. The relationship is expressed by two factors, namely; form factor and peak factor.

(*i*) **Form factor.** The ratio of r.m.s. value to the average value of an alternating quantity is known as form factor *i.e.*

$$\text{Form factor} = \frac{\text{R.M.S. value}}{\text{Average value}}$$

For a sinusoidal voltage or current,

$$\text{Form factor} = \frac{0.707 \times \text{Max. value}}{0.637 \times \text{Max. value}} = 1.11$$

The form factor is useful in rectifier service because it enables us to find the r.m.s. value from average value and *vice-versa*.

(*ii*) **Peak factor.** The ratio of maximum value to the r.m.s. value of an alternating quantity is known as peak factor *i.e.* $\quad \text{Peak factor} = \dfrac{\text{Max. value}}{\text{R.M.S. value}}$

For a sinusoidal voltage or current : $\quad \text{Peak factor} = \dfrac{\text{Max. value}}{0.707 \times \text{Max. value}} = 1.414$

The peak factor is of much greater importance because it indicates the maximum voltage being applied to the various parts of the apparatus. For instance, when an alternating voltage is applied across a cable or capacitor, the breakdown of insulation will depend upon the maximum voltage. The insulation must be able to withstand the maximum rather than the r.m.s. value of voltage.

Example 15.6. *An alternating current, when passed through a resistor immersed in water for 5 minutes, just raised the temperature of water to boiling point. When a direct current of 4A was passed through the same resistor under indentical conditions, it took 8 minutes to boil the water. Find the r.m.s. value of the alternating current.*

Solution. Let $I_{r.m.s.}$ amperes be the r.m.s. value of the alternating current and R ohms be the value of the resistor.

Heat produced by the alternating current

$$= I_{r.m.s.}^2 \times R \times t$$

$$= I_{r.m.s.}^2 \times R \times 5 \times 60 \text{ joules} \qquad \qquad ...(i)$$

Heat produced by the direct current

$$= 4^2 \times R \times 8 \times 60 \text{ joules} \qquad \qquad ...(ii)$$

As the heat produced in the two cases is the same,

$$\therefore \qquad I_{r.m.s.}^2 \, R \times 5 \times 60 = 4^2 \times R \times 8 \times 60$$

or $\qquad\qquad I_{r.m.s.} = \sqrt{\dfrac{16 \times 8}{5}} = 5.06 \text{ A}$

Example 15.7. *Find the average value, r.m.s. value, form factor and peak factor for (i) half-wave rectified alternating current and (ii) full-wave rectified alternating current.*

Solution.

(*i*) **Half-wave rectified a.c.** Fig. 15.12 shows half-wave rectified a.c. in which one half-cycle is suppressed *i.e.*, current flows for half the time during complete cycle.

$$I_{av} = \frac{\text{Area of one cycle}}{\text{Base}} = \frac{{}^*2I_m + 0}{2\pi} = \frac{I_m}{\pi}$$

$$I_{r.m.s.} = \left[\frac{\text{Area of squared wave over one cycle}}{\text{Base}} \right]^{1/2}$$

$$= \left[\frac{{}^{**}(\pi I_m^2)/2 + 0}{2\pi} \right]^{1/2} = \frac{I_m}{2}$$

Form factor $= \dfrac{I_{r.m.s.}}{I_{av}} = \dfrac{I_m/2}{I_m/\pi} = 1.57$

Peak factor $= \dfrac{I_{max.}}{I_{r.m.s.}} = \dfrac{I_m}{I_m/2} = 2$

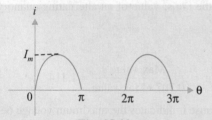

Fig. 15.12

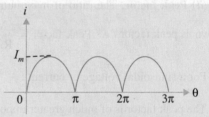

Fig. 15.13

(*ii*) **Full-wave rectified a.c.** Fig. 15.13 shows full-wave rectified a.c. in which both half-cycles appear in the output *i.e.*, current flows in the same direction for both half-cycles. Since the wave is symmetrical, half-cycle may be considered for various computations.

$$I_{av} = \frac{\text{Area of half - cycle}}{\text{Base}} = \frac{2I_m}{\pi}$$

$$I_{r.m.s.} = \left[\frac{\text{Area of squared wave over half - cycle}}{\text{Base}} \right]^{1/2}$$

$$= \left[\frac{\pi \, I_m^2/2}{\pi} \right]^{1/2} = \frac{I_m}{\sqrt{2}}$$

---

* Since the wave is not symmetrical, complete cycle is to be considered. It has been shown by integral method (See Art. 15.9) that the area of a sinusoidal wave over one alternation is $= 2 \times$ Max. value.

** Area of sinusoidal squared wave over one alternation is $= \pi I_m^2 / 2$ (See Art. 15.11).

Form factor $= \dfrac{I_{r.m.s.}}{I_{av}} = \dfrac{I_m/\sqrt{2}}{(2/\pi)I_m} = 1.11$

Peak factor $= \dfrac{I_{max}}{I_{r.m.s.}} = \dfrac{I_m}{I_m/\sqrt{2}} = 1.414$

Example15.8. *An alternating voltage v = 200 sin 314t is applied to a device which offers an ohmic resistance of 20Ω to the flow of current in one direction while entirely preventing the flow of current in the opposite direction. Calculate the r.m.s. value, average value and form factor.*

Solution. It is clear that the device is doing half-wave rectification. The maximum value of the rectified current is

$$I_m = E_m/R = 200/20 = 10 \text{ A}$$

For a half-wave rectified a.c. (See example 15.7),

$$I_{r.m.s.} = I_m/2 = 10/2 = \mathbf{5A}$$
$$I_{av} = I_m/\pi = 10/\pi = \mathbf{3.18A}$$

From factor $= I_{r.m.s}/I_{av} = 5/3.18 = \mathbf{1.57}$

Example15.9. *A moving coil ammeter, a thermal ammeter and a half-wave rectifier are connected in series with a resistor across 110V a.c. supply. The circuit offers a resistance of 50Ω in one direction and an infinite resistance in the reverse direction. Calculate (i) the readings on the ammeters and (ii) the form factor and peak factor of current wave. Assume the supply voltage to be sinusoidal.*

Solution.

Max. value of voltage, $E_m = 110/0.707 = 155.59$ V
Max. value of current, $I_m = 155.59/50 = 3.11$ A

The moving coil instrument will indicate the average value over the whole cycle while the thermal ammeter will show the r.m.s. value over the whole cycle. Since it is a case of half-wave rectified alternating current, the various values are (See example 15.7) :

(i) $I_{av} = I_m/\pi = 3.11/\pi = \mathbf{0.99A}$

Hence, moving coil instrument will read 0.99 A.

$$I_{r.m.s.} = I_m/2 = 3.11/2 = \mathbf{1.555A}$$

Hence, thermal ammeter will read 1.555A.

(ii) Form factor $= 1.555/0.99 = \mathbf{1.57}$
    Peak factor $= 3.11/1.555 = \mathbf{2}$

Example15.10. *A current has the following steady values in amperes for equal intervals of time changing instantaneously from one value to the next:*

0, 10, 20, 30, 20, 10, 0, –10, –20, –30, –20, –10, 0 etc. Calculate (i) average value (ii) r.m.s. value (iii) form factor and (iv) peak factor.

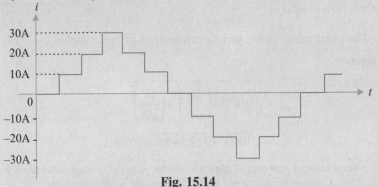

Fig. 15.14

Solution.

(i)
$$I_{av} = \frac{i_1 + i_2 + i_3 + i_4 + i_5 + i_6}{6}$$

$$= \frac{0 + 10 + 20 + 30 + 20 + 10}{6} = \frac{90}{6} = 15A$$

(ii)
$$I_{r.m.s.}^2 = \frac{i_1^2 + i_2^2 + i_3^2 + i_4^2 + i_5^2 + i_6^2}{6} = \frac{1900}{6} = 316.67$$

or
$$I_{r.m.s.} = \sqrt{316.67} = \textbf{17.8 A}$$

(iii) From factor $= \dfrac{I_{r.m.s.}}{I_{av}} = \dfrac{17.8}{15} = \textbf{1.19}$

(iv) Peak factor $= \dfrac{I_m}{I_{r.m.s.}} = \dfrac{30}{17.8} = \textbf{1.68}$

Example 15.11. *A voltage wave is given by equation v = 50 + 30 sin θ volts. Find the r.m.s. value of the wave.*

Solution.

$$E_{r.m.s.}^2 = \frac{1}{2\pi} \int_0^{2\pi} (50 + 30\sin\theta)^2 \, d\theta$$

$$= \frac{1}{2\pi} \int_0^{2\pi} (2500 + 3000\sin\theta + 900\sin^2\theta) \, d\theta$$

$$= \frac{1}{2\pi} \int_0^{2\pi} 2500 \, d\theta + \frac{1}{2\pi} \int_0^{2\pi} 3000\sin\theta \, d\theta + \frac{1}{2\pi} \int_0^{2\pi} 900\sin^2\theta \, d\theta$$

$$= 2500 + *0 + \frac{900}{2} = 2950$$

∴
$$E_{r.m.s.} = \sqrt{2950} = \textbf{54.3V}$$

Another method

$$E_{r.m.s.} = \sqrt{50^2 + (30/\sqrt{2})^2} = \sqrt{2950} = \textbf{54.3V}$$

Note. The r.m.s. value of a complex wave is equal to the square root of the sum of the squares of the r.m.s. values of its individual components.

Example 15.12. *A current wave is given by i = 100 + 25 sin 3θ + 10 sin 5θ amperes. Find the r.m.s. value of this current wave.*

Solution. The r.m.s. values of the various components of this complex wave are 100, $25/\sqrt{2}$ and $10/\sqrt{2}$ amperes.

∴
$$I_{r.m.s.} = \sqrt{(100)^2 + \left(\frac{25}{\sqrt{2}}\right)^2 + \left(\frac{10}{\sqrt{2}}\right)^2}$$

$$= \sqrt{10000 + 312.5 + 50} = \textbf{101.8 A}$$

---

* Remember average value of sinθ over whole cycle is zero. Also the average value of sin²θ over the whole cycle is 1/2. These facts can be ascertained by carrying out the actual integration.

TUTORIAL PROBLEMS

1. An alternating voltage $e = 100 \sin 314t$ is applied to a device which offers an ohmic resistance of 50 Ω in one direction while entirely preventing the flow of current in the opposite direction. Calculate the average and r.m.s. values of current. Also find the form factor.

   [0.637A ; 1A ; 1.57]

2. A hot-wire ammeter, a moving coil ammeter and a rectifier are connected in series. The combination is connected across a sinusoidal source of 50V r.m.s. The forward resistance of rectifier is 20Ω and the reverse resistance is infinite. Calculate the reading on each ammeter.

   [1.767A ; 1.124A]

3. The equation of an alternating current is given by $i = 141.4 \sin 314t$. Find (*i*) r.m.s. current (*ii*) frequency and (*iii*) instantaneous value of current when *t* is 3.6*ms*.

   [(*i*)100A (*ii*) 50Hz (*iii*) 128A]

4. A current has the following steady values (in amperes) for equal intervals of time, changing instantaneously from one value to the next.

   0, 10, 20, 30, 20, 10, 0, –10, –20, –30, –20, –10 etc.

   Calculate the r.m.s. value of current and form factor.

   [17.8A ; 1.18]

15.13. PHASE

Waves of alternating voltage and current are continuous. They do not stop after one cycle is completed but continue to repeat as long as the generator is operating. Consider an alternating voltage wave of time period T second as shown in Fig. 15.15. Note that the time is counted from the instant the voltage is zero and becoming positive. The maximum positive value $(+V_m)$ occurs at $T/4$ second or $\pi/2$ radians. We say that *phase* of maximum positive value is $T/4$ second or $\pi/2$ radians. It means that as the fresh cycle starts, $+ V_m$ will occur at $T/4$ second or $\pi/2$ radians. Similarly, the phase of negative peak $(–V_m)$ is $3T/4$ second or $3\pi/2$ radians.

Hence phase of a particular value of an alternating quantity is the fractional part of time period or cycle through which the quantity has advanced from the selected zero position of reference.

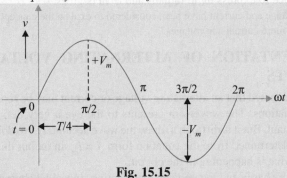

Fig. 15.15

In electrical engineering, we are more concerned with relative phases or phase difference between different alternating quantities rather than with their absolute values.

15.14. PHASE DIFFERENCE

When an alternating voltage is applied to a circuit, an alternating current of the same frequency flows through the circuit. In most of practical circuits, for reasons we will discuss later, voltage and current have different phases. In other words, they do not pass through a particular point, say *zero

---

* We may select any point but it is more convenient to determine the phase difference by considering zero points or positive maximum values or negative maximum values of the two alternating quantities.

point in the same direction at the same instant. Thus voltage may be passing through its zero point while the current has passed or it is yet to pass through its zero point in the same direction. We say that voltage and current have a phase difference.

Hence when two alternating quantities of the same frequency have different zero points, they are said to have a **phase difference**.

The angle between zero points is the angle of phase difference ϕ. It is generally measured in degrees or radians. The quantity which passes through its zero point earlier is said to be leading while the other is said to be lagging. It should be noted that those zero points of alternating quantities are to be considered where they pass in the same direction. Thus if voltage has passed through its zero point and is rising in the positive direction, then zero point considered for the current should have similar situation. Since both alternating quantities have the same frequency, the phase difference between them remains the same.

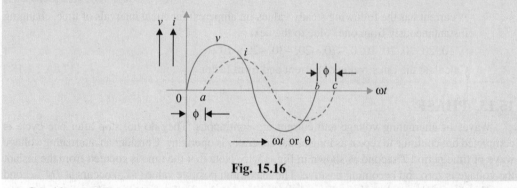

Fig. 15.16

Consider an a.c. circuit in which current i lags behind the voltage v by $\phi°$. This phase relationship is shown by waves in Fig. 15.16. The equations of voltage and current are :

$$v = V_m \sin \omega t$$
$$i = I_m \sin (\omega t - \phi)$$

It is a usual practice to express ωt in radians and ϕ in degrees.

Note. Although voltage and current have been considered to explain the concept of phase difference, it is equally valid for two or more currents or voltages.

15.15. REPRESENTATION OF ALTERNATING VOLTAGES AND CURRENTS

So far we have discussed that an alternating voltage or current may be represented in the form of (*i*) waves and (*ii*) equations. The waveform presents to the eye a very definite picture of what is happening at every instant. But it is difficult to draw the wave accurately. No doubt the current flowing at any instant can be determined from the equation form $i = I_m \sin \omega t$ but this equation presents no picture to the eye of what is happening in the circuit.

The above difficulty has been overcome by representing sinusoidal alternating voltage or current by a line of definite length rotating in *anticlockwise direction at a constant angular velocity (ω) . Such a rotating line is called a **phasor**. The length of the phasor is taken equal to the maximum value (on suitable scale) of the alternating quantity and angular velocity equal to the angular velocity of the alternating quantity. As we shall see presently, this phasor (*i.e.*, rotating line) will generate a sine wave.

15.16. PHASOR REPRESENTATION OF SINUSOIDAL QUANTITIES

Consider an alternating current represented by the equation $i = I_m \sin \omega t$. Take a line *OP* to

* It is a standard convention that the phasor is rotated anticlockwise—a convention that is in harmony with the general use of polar co-ordinates.

represent to scale the maximum value I_m. Imagine the line OP (or *phasor*, as it is called) to be rotating in anticlockwise direction at an angular velocity ω rad/sec about the point O. Measuring the time from the instant when OP is horizontal, let OP rotate through an angle $\theta(=\omega t)$ in the anticlockwise direction. The projection of OP on Y-axis is OM.

$$OM = OP \sin \theta$$
$$= I_m \sin \omega t$$
$$= i, \text{ the value of current at that instant.}$$

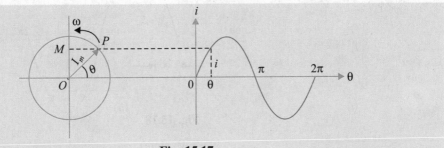

Fig. 15.17

Hence the projection of the phasor OP on Y-axis at any instant gives the value of current at that instant. Thus when $\theta = 90°$, the projection on Y-axis is $OP (= I_m)$ itself. That the value of current at this instant (*i.e.*, at θ or $\omega t = 90°$) is I_m can be readily established if we put $\theta = 90°$ in the current equation. If we plot the projections of the phasor on Y-axis *versus* its angular position point-by-point, a sinusoidal alternating current wave is generated as shown in Fig. 15.17. Thus the phasor represents the sine wave for every instant of time.

The following points are worth noting:

(*i*)   The length of the phasor represents the maximum value and the angle with axis of reference (*i.e.*, X-axis) indicates the phase of the alternating quantity *i.e.*, current in this case.

(*ii*)   The phasor representation enables us to quickly obtain the numerical values and, at the same time, have a picture before the eye of the events taking place in the circuit. Thus in the position of the phasor OP shown in Fig.15.17, the instantaneous value is OM, the phase is θ and frequency is $\omega/2\pi$.

(*iii*)   A phasor diagram permits addition and subtraction of alternating voltages or currents with a fair degree of ease.

Note. Alternating voltages and currents are not vector quantities. Voltage is simply energy or work per coulomb and cannot be classified as a vector. Current is also not a vector quantity because it is merely the flow of electrons through a wire. When we insert an ammeter in a circuit to measure current or connect a voltmeter between two points to measure the potential difference (*i.e.*, voltage), direction with reference to any set of axes is of no consequence. Therefore, neither alternating voltage nor current is a vector quantity. Instead, they are **phasors.

15.17. PHASOR DIAGRAM OF SINE WAVES OF SAME FREQUENCY

Consider a sinusoidal voltage wave v and sinusoidal current i of the same frequency. Suppose the current lags behind the voltage by $\phi°$. The two alternating quantities can be represented on the same

---

*   An arrowhead is drawn at the outer end of phasor OP partly to indicate which end is assumed to move and partly to indicate precise length of the phasor when two or more phasors happen to coincide.

**   Remember that a vector has space co-ordinates while a phasor is derived from the time varying sinusoid.

phasor diagram because the phasors V_m and I_m [See Fig. 15.18 (i)] rotate at the same angular velocity ω^* and hence phase difference ϕ between them remains the same at all times. When each phasor completes one revolution, it generates the corresponding cycle [See Fig. 15.18 (ii)]. The equations of the two waves can be represented as :

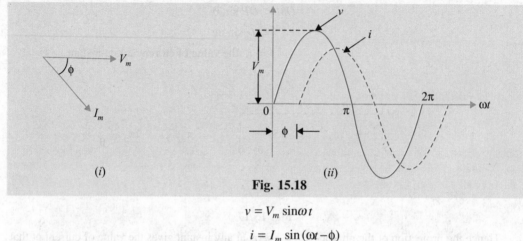

(i)   (ii)

Fig. 15.18

$$v = V_m \sin \omega t$$

$$i = I_m \sin(\omega t - \phi)$$

15.18. ADDITION OF ALTERNATING QUANTITIES

Alternating voltages and currents are phasors. They are added in the same manner as forces are added. Only phasors of the same kind may be added. Common sense tells us that we should not try to add volts to amperes. Addition of alternating currents or voltages can be accomplished by one of the following two methods:

1. Parallelogram method

2. Method of components.

1. Parallelogram method. This method is used for the addition of two phasors at a time. The two phasors are represented in magnitude and direction by the adjacent sides of a parallelogram. Then the diagonal of the parallelogram represents the maximum value of the resultant.

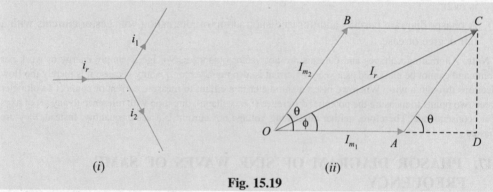

(i)   (ii)

Fig. 15.19

Consider two alternating currents i_1 and i_2 flowing in the two branches of a circuit [See Fig. 15.19 (i)]. Let they be represented by:

$$i_1 = I_{m1} \sin \omega t$$

$$i_2 = I_{m2} \sin(\omega t + \theta)$$

- -

* Remember $\omega = 2\pi f$.

$$OC = \sqrt{(OD)^2 + (CD)^2}$$

$$= \sqrt{(I_{m1} + I_{m2}\cos\theta)^2 + (I_{m2}\sin\theta)^2}$$

$$\therefore \qquad I_r = \sqrt{I_{m1}^2 + I_{m2}^2 + 2I_{m1}I_{m2}\cos\theta}$$

Also $\qquad \tan\phi = \dfrac{CD}{OD} = \dfrac{CD}{OA + AD} = \dfrac{I_{m2}\sin\theta}{I_{m1} + I_{m2}\cos\theta}$

The instantaneous value of resultant current i_r is given by:

$$i_r = I_r \sin(\omega t + \phi)$$

2. Method of Components. This method provides a very convenient means to add two or more phasors. Each phasor is resolved into horizontal and vertical components. The horizontals are summed up algebraically to give the resultant horizontal component X. The verticals are likewise summed up algebraically to give the resultant vertical component Y.

Then, $\qquad$ Resultant $= \sqrt{X^2 + Y^2}$

Phase angle of resultant, $\tan\phi = Y/X$

Thus referring to Fig. 15.19 (*ii*), we have,

$$X = I_{m1} + I_{m2}\cos\theta$$

$$Y = 0 + I_{m2}\sin\theta$$

$\therefore \qquad$ Resultant, $\qquad I_r = \sqrt{(I_{m1} + I_{m2}\cos\theta)^2 + (I_{m2}\sin\theta)^2}$

$$= \sqrt{I_{m1}^2 + I_{m2}^2 + 2I_{m1}I_{m2}\cos\theta}$$

which is the same as derived by parallelogram method.

$$\tan\phi = \frac{Y}{X} = \frac{I_{m2}\sin\theta}{I_{m1} + I_{m2}\cos\theta}$$

$$\therefore \qquad i_r = I_r \sin(\omega t + \phi)$$

15.19. SUBTRACTION OF ALTERNATING QUANTITIES

If difference of two phasors is required, then one of the phasors is reversed and this reversed phasor is then compounded with the other phasor using parallelogram method or method of components.

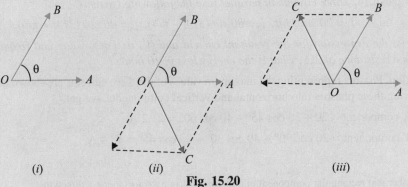

Fig. 15.20

Consider two phasors OA and OB representing two alternating quantities of the same kind

[See Fig. 15.20(*i*)]. The phasor *OB* leads the phasor *OA* by θ. If it is required to subtract the phasor *OB* from *OA*, then *OB* is reversed and is compounded with phasor *OA* as shown in Fig. 15.20 (*ii*). The phasor difference *OA–OB* is given by the phasor – *OC*. In Fig. 15.20 (*iii*), phasor *OC* represents the phasor difference *OB–OA*.

Example 15.13. *The following expressions represent the instantaneous values of e.m.f. in three coils connected in series:* $e_1 = 50 \sin \omega t$; $e_2 = 40 \sin(\omega t + 60°)$; $e_3 = 60 \sin(\omega t - 30°)$. *Find an expression for the resultant e.m.f. when the coils are connected to give the sum of three e.m.f.s.*

Solution. Phasors representing the maximum values of the three e.m.f. s are shown in Fig. 15.21 (*i*). Resolving these phasors into horizontal and vertical components, we get,

X-component = Algebraic sum of components along X-axis
$$= 50 + 40 \cos 60° + 60 \cos 30°$$
$$= 50 + 20 + 51.9 = 121.9 \text{ V}$$

Y-component = Algebraic sum of components along Y-axis
$$= {}^*50 \cos 90° + 40 \cos 30° - 60 \cos 60°$$
$$= 0 + 34.6 - 30 = 4.6 \text{ V}$$

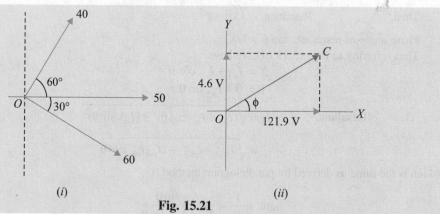

(*i*)   (*ii*)

Fig. 15.21

As shown in Fig. 15.21 (*ii*), *OC* represents the maximum value of the resultant e.m.f.

$$OC = \sqrt{(121.9)^2 + (4.6)^2} = 122 \text{ V}$$

$$\tan \phi = 4.6/121.9 = 0.0377$$

∴ $$\phi = \tan^{-1} 0.0377 = 2.2°$$

∴ The equation of the resultant e.m.f. is $e = 122 \sin(\omega t + 2.2°)$ **Ans.**

Example 15.14. *Three circuits in parallel take the following currents:*

$$i_1 = 20 \sin 314t, \quad i_2 = 30 \sin(314t - \pi/4), \quad i_3 = 40 \cos(314t + \pi/6)$$

Find (i) the expression for the resultant current and (ii) its r.m.s. value and frequency. If the circuit has a resistance of 2Ω, what is the energy loss in 10 hours?

Solution. Phasors representing the maximum values of the three currents are shown in Fig. 15.22 (*i*). Resolving these phasors into horizontal and vertical components, we get,

X-component = $20 + 30 \cos 45° - 40 \cos 60° = 21.2 \text{ A}$

Y-component = $20 \cos 90° + 40 \cos 30° - 30 \cos 45° = 13.4 \text{ A}$

* *

* Remember that rectangular component of a phasor *OA* (or a vector) along a direction
= *OA* × cosine of angle between *OA* and that direction

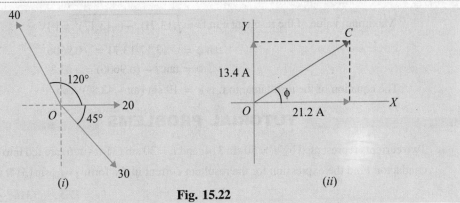

Fig. 15.22

(*i*) As shown in Fig. 15.22 (*ii*), OC represents the maximum value of the resultant current.

$$OC = \sqrt{(21.2)^2 + (13.4)^2} = 25.1 \, \text{A}$$

$$\tan \phi = 13.4/21.2 = 0.632$$

$$\therefore \qquad \phi = \tan^{-1} 0.632 = 32.3°$$

The equation of the resultant current is $i = 25.1 \sin (314t + 32.3°)$ **Ans.**

(*ii*) R.M.S. value of current, $\qquad I_{r.m.s.} = 25.1/\sqrt{2} = \mathbf{17.75 \, A}$

$$\text{Frequency} = \omega/2\pi = 314/2\pi = \mathbf{50 Hz}$$

The frequency of the resultant current is the same as that of the three currents.

Energy loss in 10 hours $\qquad = I_{r.m.s.}^2 \times R \times t$

$$= (17.75)^2 \times 2 \times 10 = \mathbf{6301.25 \, Wh}$$

Example 15.15. *The following four e.m.f.s act together in a circuit:*

$e_1 = 10 \sin \omega t;$ $\qquad\qquad\qquad$ $e_2 = 8 \sin (\omega t + \pi/3)$

$e_3 = 4 \sin (\omega t - \pi/6);$ $\qquad\qquad$ $e_4 = 6 \sin (\omega t + 3\pi/4)$

Calculate the e.m.f. represented by $e_1 - e_2 + e_3 - e_4$.

Solution. Phasors representing the maximum values of the four e.m.f.s are shown in Fig. 15.23 (*i*). In order to determine $e_1 - e_2 + e_3 - e_4$, reverse the phasors representing e_2 and e_4 as shown in Fig. 15.23 (*ii*). Referring to Fig. 15.23 (*ii*) and resolving the phasors into horizontal and vertical components, we get,

$\begin{aligned} X\text{-component} \quad &= 10 \cos 0° + 4 \cos 30° - 8 \cos 60° + 6 \cos 45° \\ &= 10 + 3.464 - 4 + 4.243 = 13.71 \, \text{V} \end{aligned}$

$\begin{aligned} Y\text{-component} \quad &= 10 \cos 90° - 4 \cos 60° - 6 \cos 45° - 8 \cos 30° \\ &= 0 - 2 - 4.243 - 6.928 = -13.17 \, \text{V} \end{aligned}$

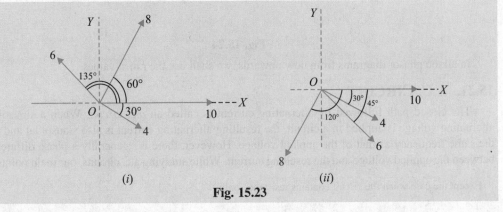

Fig. 15.23

Maximum value of the resultant e.m.f. $= \sqrt{(13.71)^2 + (-13.17)^2} = 19\text{V}$

$$\tan \phi = -13.17/13.71 = -0.9606$$

$\therefore$ $$\phi = \tan^{-1} - (0.9606) = -43.8°$$

The equation of the resultant e.m.f. is $e = 19 \sin(\omega t - 43.8°)$ **Ans.**

TUTORIAL PROBLEMS

1. Two currents represented by $i_1 = 50 \sin 314t$ and $i_2 = 30 \sin(314t - \pi/6)$ are fed into a common conductor. Find the expression for the resultant current in the form $i = I_m \sin(314t \pm \phi)$.

   [$i = 77.5 \sin(314t - 11°10')$]

2. Find the sum of the following two e.m.f.s and express the answer in the similar form:

   $$e_1 = 100 \sin \omega t \; ; \qquad e_2 = 100 \cos \omega t \qquad [e = 141.4 \sin(\omega t + 45°)]$$

3. The following four currents are fed into a common conductor:

   $i_1 = 50 \sin \omega t$ $\qquad ; \qquad$ $i_3 = 40 \cos \omega t$

   $i_2 = 25 \sin(\omega t + \pi/3)$ $\quad ; \qquad$ $i_4 = 30 \sin(\omega t - \pi/2)$

   Find the expression for the resultant in the form $i = I_m \sin(\omega t \pm \phi)$. $\quad$ [$i = 94 \sin(\omega t + 25°)$]

4. The instantaneous voltages across each of four series connected coils are given by:

   $v_1 = 100 \sin \omega t;$ $v_2 = 250 \cos \omega t;$ $v_3 = 150 \sin(\omega t + \pi/6);$ $v_4 = 200 \sin(\omega t - \pi\sqrt{4}).$

   Find the total p.d. and express the answer in the similar form. What will be the resultant p.d. if the polarity of v_2 is reversed ? $\qquad$ [$(v = 414 \sin(\omega t + 26.5°)$; $v = 486 \sin(\omega t - 40°)$]

15.20. PHASOR DIAGRAMS USING R.M.S. VALUES

Instead of drawing the phasor diagram using maximum values, it is a common practice to draw it using r.m.s. values. This does not alter the phase difference (ϕ) between the phasors because only the lengths of the phasors are changed. Fig. 15.24 (*i*) shows the phasor diagram using maximum values while Fig. 15.24 (*ii*) shows the same phasor diagram in terms of r.m.s. equivalent.

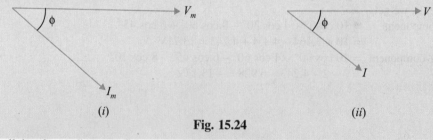

(*i*) $\qquad\qquad\qquad\qquad\qquad\qquad\qquad\qquad$ (*ii*)

Fig. 15.24

In all the phasor diagrams from now onwards, we shall use the r.m.s. values.

15.21. A.C. CIRCUIT

The closed path followed by alternating current is called an *a.c. circuit*. When a sinusoidal alternating voltage is applied in a circuit, the resulting alternating current is also sinusoidal and has the same frequency as that of the applied voltage. However, there is *generally a phase difference between the applied voltage and the resulting current. While studying a.c. circuits, our main points of

---

* Except the case when the circuit contains resistance only.

interest are (*i*) phase difference between applied voltage and circuit current (*ii*) circuit impedance (*iii*) power consumed *etc*. To begin with, we shall study these characteristics for simple a.c. circuits containing one circuit element only (*R* or *L* or *C*) and extend our discussion to the combination of these circuit elements in the later chapters.

15.22. A.C. CIRCUIT CONTAINING RESISTANCE ONLY

Consider a circuit containing a pure resistance of $R\,\Omega$ connected across an alternating voltage source. Let the alternating voltage be given by the equation:

$$v = V_m \sin \omega t \qquad \qquad ...(i)$$

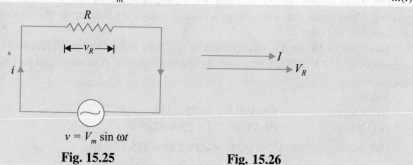

$$v = V_m \sin \omega t$$

Fig. 15.25   **Fig. 15.26**

As a result of this voltage, an alternating current *i* will flow in the circuit. The applied voltage has to overcome the drop in the resistance only *i.e.*,

$$v = iR$$

or
$$i = \frac{v}{R}$$

Substituting the value of *v*, we get,

$$i = \frac{V_m}{R} \sin \omega t \qquad \qquad ...(ii)$$

The value of *i* will be maximum (*i.e.*, I_m) when $\sin \omega t = 1$.

∴
$$I_m = V_m/R$$

∴ Eq. (*ii*) becomes,
$$i = I_m \sin \omega t \qquad \qquad ...(iii)$$

It is clear from eqs. (*i*) and (*iii*) that the applied voltage and circuit current are in phase with each other. This fact is also shown by the phasor diagram in Fig. 15.26 and wave diagram in Fig. 15.27. Note that r.m.s. values have been used in drawing the phasor diagram.

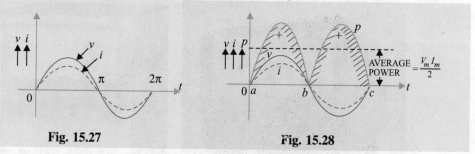

Fig. 15.27   **Fig. 15.28**

Power

Instantaneous power, $p = vi = (V_m \sin \omega t)\,(I_m \sin \omega t) = V_m I_m \sin^2 \omega t$

$$= V_m I_m \frac{(1-\cos 2\omega t)}{2}$$

$$= \frac{V_m I_m}{2} - \frac{V_m I_m}{2} \cos 2\omega t$$

Thus power consists of two parts *viz.* a constant part $(V_m I_m/2)$ and a fluctuating part $(V_m I_m/2)$ cos 2 ω*t*. Since power is a scalar quantity, average power over a complete cycle is to be considered. For a complete cycle, the average value of $(V_m I_m/2)$ cos 2ωt is zero.

∴ Power consumed, $$P = \frac{V_m I_m}{2} = \frac{V_m}{\sqrt{2}} \times \frac{I_m}{\sqrt{2}}$$

or $$P = VI$$

where V = r.m.s. value of the applied voltage
I = r.m.s. value of the circuit current

Fig. 15.28 shows the power curve for a pure resistive circuit. It is clear that power is always positive. This means that the voltage source is constantly delivering power to the circuit which is consumed by the circuit.

Example 15.16. *An a.c. circuit consists of a pure resistance of 10 Ω and is connected across an a.c. supply of 230 V, 50Hz. Calculate (i) current (ii) power consumed and (iii) equations for voltage and current.*

Solution.

(*i*) Current, $I = V/R = 230/10 = $ **23A**

(*ii*) Power, $P = VI = 230 \times 23 = $ **5290 W**

(*iii*) Now, $V_m = \sqrt{2}V = \sqrt{2} \times 230 = 325.27$ volts

$I_m = \sqrt{2}I = \sqrt{2} \times 23 = 32.52$ A

$\omega = 2\pi f = 2\pi \times 50 = 314\ rad\ s^{-1}$

∴ Equations of voltage and current are:

$e = 325.27 \sin 314t$; $i = 32.52 \sin 314t$

Example 15.17. *In a pure resistive circuit, the instantaneous voltage and current are given by:*
$$v = 250 \sin 314t\ ;\ i = 10 \sin 314t.$$
Determine (i) the peak power and (ii) average power.

Solution.

In a pure resistive a.c. circuit,

(*i*) Peak power $= V_m I_m = 250 \times 10 = $ **2500W**

(*ii*) Average power, $P = \dfrac{V_m I_m}{2} = \dfrac{2500}{2} = $ **1250 W**

The reader may note that it is the average power which is consumed in the circuit.

Wattmeters

15.23. A.C. CIRCUIT CONTAINING INDUCTANCE ONLY

When an alternating current flows through a pure *inductive coil, a back e.m.f. (= $L\, di/dt$) is induced due to the inductance of the coil. This back e.m.f. at every instant opposes the change in current through the coil. Since there is no ohmic drop, the applied voltage has to overcome the back e.m.f. only.

Applied alternating voltage = Back e.m.f.

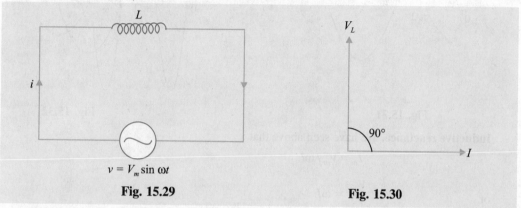

Fig. 15.29   Fig. 15.30

Consider an alternating voltage applied to a pure inductance of L henry as shown in Fig. 15.29. Let the equation of the applied alternating voltage be:

$$v = V_m \sin \omega t \qquad \qquad \ldots(i)$$

Clearly,
$$V_m \sin \omega t = L\frac{di}{dt}$$

or
$$di = \frac{V_m}{L} \sin \omega t\, dt$$

Integrating both sides, we get,

$$i = \frac{V_m}{L} \int \sin \omega t\, dt$$

$$= \frac{V_m}{\omega L}(-\cos \omega t)$$

or
$$i = \frac{V_m}{\omega L} \sin (\omega t - \pi/2) \qquad \qquad \ldots(ii)$$

The value of i will be maximum (i.e., I_m) when $\sin (\omega t - \pi/2)$ is unity.

∴
$$I_m = V_m/\omega L$$

∴ Eq. (ii) becomes, $i = I_m \sin (\omega t - \pi/2)$ where $I_m = V_m/\omega L$ $\qquad \ldots(iii)$

It is clear from eqs. (i) and (iii) that current lags behind the voltage by $\pi/2$ radians or 90°. *Hence in a pure inductance, current lags behind the voltage by 90°.* This fact is also shown in the phasor diagram in Fig. 15.30 and wave diagram in Fig. 15.31.

- -

* Any circuit that is capable of producing flux has inductance as was pointed out in chapter 9. When alternating current flows through such a circuit, there is change in flux linking it and hence back e.m.f. (= Ldi/dt) is induced in the circuit. This e.m.f. opposes the applied voltage at every instant.

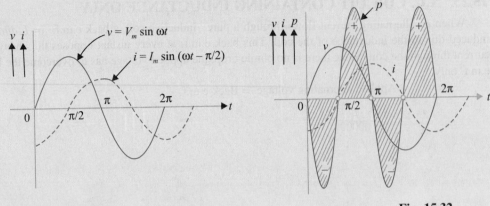

Fig. 15.31   **Fig. 15.32**

Inductive reactance. We have seen above that :

$$I_m = V_m / \omega L$$

or $$* \frac{V_m}{I_m} = \omega L$$

Clearly, the opposition offered by inductance to current flow is ωL. The quantity ωL is called *inductive reactance* X_L of the coil and is measured in Ω. Note that $X_L (= \omega L = 2\pi fL)$ will be in Ω if L is in henry and f in Hz. Since $X_L = 2\pi fL$, $X_L \propto f$. Therefore graph between X_L and f is a straight line passing through the origin as shown in Fig. 15.33.

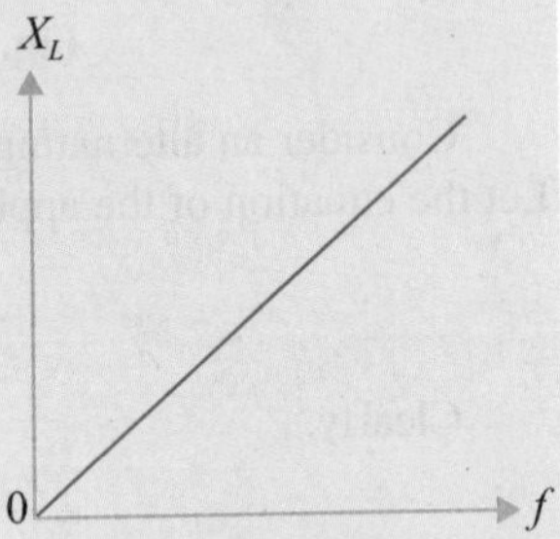

Power

Fig. 15.33

Instantaneous power, $p = vi = V_m \sin \omega t \times I_m \sin (\omega t - \pi / 2)$

$$= -V_m I_m \sin \omega t \cos \omega t = -\frac{V_m I_m}{2} \sin 2\omega t$$

∴   Average power, P = Average of p over one cycle

$$= \frac{1}{2\pi} \int_0^{2\pi} -\frac{V_m I_m}{2} \sin 2\omega t \, d(\omega t) = 0$$

Hence, power absorbed in pure inductance is zero.

Fig. 15.32 shows the power curve for a pure inductive circuit. An examination of power curve over one cycle shows that positive power is equal to the negative power. Hence the resultant power over one cycle is zero *i.e.*, pure inductance consumes no power. The electric power merely flows from the source to the coil and back again.

Example15.18. *A pure inductive coil allows a current of 10A to flow from a 230V, 50Hz supply. Find (i) inductive reactance (ii) inductance of the coil (iii) power absorbed. Write down the equations for voltage and current.*

Solution.

(i)   Circuit current, $I = V/X_L$

∴   Inductive reactance, $X_L = V/I = 230/10 = 23\Omega$

(ii) Now, $X_L = 2\pi fL$

. . . .

* If V and I are the r.m.s. values, $\dfrac{V_m}{I_m} = \dfrac{V}{I} = \omega L$.

$$\therefore \qquad L = \frac{X_L}{2\pi f} = \frac{23}{2\pi \times 50} = 0.073\,\mathrm{H}$$

(*iii*) Power absorbed = **Zero**

$V_m = 230 \times \sqrt{2} = 325.27\,\mathrm{V}$; $I_m = 10 \times \sqrt{2} = 14.14\,\mathrm{A}$; $\omega = 2\pi \times 50 = 314\,\mathrm{rad\,s^{-1}}$

Since in a pure inductive circuit, current lags behind the voltage by $\pi/2$ radians, the equations are:
  $v = 325.27 \sin 314t$; $i = 14.14 \sin(314t - \pi/2)$

Example 15.19. *For the circuit shown in Fig. 15.34, determine L_1 and total inductive reactance X_{L_T}. Assume inductors are ideal.*

Solution. Series inductive circuits are analysed using the same laws and rules as are used with series resistive circuits *if* the inductors are ideal inductors. For series inductors, the total inductive X_{L_T} is

$$X_{L_T} = X_{L_1} + X_{L_2} + \ldots\ldots + X_{L_n}$$

Referring to Fig. 15.34, we have,

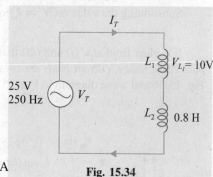

$$X_{L_2} = 2\pi f L_2 = 2\pi \times 250 \times 0.8 = 1256\,\Omega$$

$$V_{L_2} = V_T - V_{L_1} = 25 - 10 = 15\,\mathrm{V}$$

$$I_{L_1} = I_T = I_{L_2} = \frac{V_{L_2}}{X_{L_2}} = \frac{15V}{1256\,\Omega} = 11.94\,\mathrm{mA}$$

Fig. 15.34

$$X_{L_1} = \frac{V_{L_1}}{I_{L_1}} = \frac{10\,\mathrm{V}}{11.94\,\mathrm{mA}} = 837.5\,\Omega$$

$$X_{L_T} = X_{L_1} + X_{L_2} = 837.5 + 1256 = \mathbf{2093.5\,\Omega}$$

$$L_1 = \frac{X_{L_1}}{2\pi f} = \frac{837.5\,\mathrm{V}}{2\pi \times 250} = \mathbf{0.53\,H}$$

15.24. A.C. CIRCUIT CONTAINING CAPACITANCE ONLY

When an alternating voltage is applied across the plates of a capacitor, the capacitor is charged in one direction and then in the other as the voltage reverses. The result is that electrons move to and fro round the circuit, connecting the plates, thus constituting alternating current.

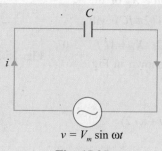

$v = V_m \sin \omega t$

Fig. 15.35

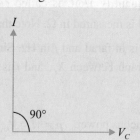

Fig. 15.36

Consider an alternating voltage applied to a capacitor of capacitance C farad as shown in Fig. 15.35. Let the equation of the applied alternating voltage be:

$$v = V_m \sin \omega t \qquad \ldots(i)$$

As a result of this alternating voltage, alternating current will flow through the circuit. Let at any instant i be the current and q be the charge on the plates.

Charge on capacitor, $q = Cv = CV_m \sin \omega t$

∴ Circuit current, $i = \dfrac{d}{dt}(q) = \dfrac{d}{dt}(CV_m \sin \omega t) = \omega C V_m \cos \omega t$

or $i = \omega C V_m \sin(\omega t + \pi/2) \qquad \ldots(ii)$

The value of i will be maximum (i.e., I_m) when $\sin(\omega t + \pi/2)$ is unity.

∴ $I_m = \omega C V_m$

Substituting the value $\omega C V_m = I_m$ in eq. (ii), we get,

$$i = I_m \sin(\omega t + \pi/2) \qquad \ldots(iii)$$

It is clear from eqs. (i) and (iii) that current leads the voltage by $\pi/2$ radians or 90°. *Hence in a pure capacitance, current leads the voltage by 90°.* This fact is also shown in the phasor diagram in Fig. 15.36 and wave diagram in Fig. 15.37.

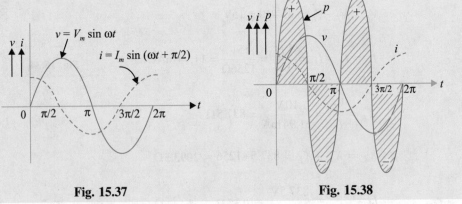

| **Fig. 15.37** | **Fig. 15.38** |

Capacitive reactance. We have seen above that:

$$I_m = \omega C V_m$$

or $\quad *\dfrac{V_m}{I_m} = \dfrac{1}{\omega C}$

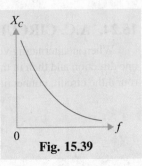

Fig. 15.39

Clearly, the opposition offered by capacitance to current flow is $1/\omega C$. The quantity $1/\omega C$ is called *capacitive reactance* X_C of the capacitor and is measured in Ω. Note that $X_C \,(=1/\omega C = 1/2\pi fC)$ will be in Ω if C is in farad and f in Hz. Since $X_C = 1/2\pi fC$, $X_C \propto 1/f$. Therefore, graph between X_C and f is a hyperbola as shown in Fig. 15.39.

Power

Instantaneous power, $p = vi = V_m \sin \omega t \times I_m \sin(\omega t + \pi/2)$

. . . .

* If V and I are the r.m.s. values, $\dfrac{V_m}{I_m} = \dfrac{V}{I} = \dfrac{1}{\omega C}$.

$$= V_m I_m \sin \omega t \cos \omega t = \frac{V_m I_m}{2} \sin 2\omega t$$

∴   Average power, P = Average of p over one cycle

$$= \frac{1}{2\pi} \int_0^{2\pi} \frac{V_m I_m}{2} \sin 2\omega t \, d(\omega t) = 0$$

Hence, power absorbed in a pure capacitance is zero.

Fig 15.38 shows the power curve for a pure capacitive circuit. The power curve is similar to that for a pure inductor because now current leads the voltage by 90°. It is clear that positive power is equal to the negative power over one cycle. Hence net power absorbed in a pure capacitor is zero.

Example 15.20. *A 318μF capacitor is connected across a 230V, 50Hz system. Determine (i) the capacitive reactance (ii) r.m.s. value of current and (iii) equations for voltage and current.*

Solution.

(*i*) Capacitive reactance, $X_C = \dfrac{1}{2\pi f C} = \dfrac{10^6}{2\pi \times 50 \times 318} = 10\Omega$

(*ii*) R.M.S. value of current, $I = V/X_C = 230/10 = \mathbf{23A}$

(*iii*) $V_m = 230 \times \sqrt{2} = 325.27$ volts; $I_m = \sqrt{2} \times 23 = 32.53A$; $\omega = 2\pi \times 50 = 314 \,\mathrm{rad\,s}^{-1}$

∴   Equations for voltage and current are : $v = 325.27 \sin 314t$; $i = 32.53 \sin(314t + \pi/2)$

Example 15.21. *A 50 μF capacitor is connected across a 230V, 50Hz supply. Determine (i) the maximum instantaneous charge on the capacitor and (ii) the maximum instantaneous energy stored in the capacitor.*

Solution.

(*i*) Maximum instantaneous charge on capacitor

$$= CV_m = (50 \times 10^{-6}) \times (230 \times \sqrt{2}) = \mathbf{16.26 \times 10^{-3} C}$$

(*ii*) Maximum instantaneous energy stored

$$= \frac{1}{2} CV_m^2 = \frac{1}{2}(50 \times 10^{-6}) \times (230 \times \sqrt{2})^2 = \mathbf{2.645 \, J}$$

Example 15.22. *The instantaneous current in a pure inductance of 5H is expressed as $i = 10 \sin (314t - \pi/2)$. A capacitor is connected in parallel with the inductor. What should be the capacitance of the capacitor to receive the same amount of energy as inductance at the same terminal voltage?*

Solution. The current through pure inductance is

$$i = 10 \sin (314t - \pi/2)$$

Here $I_m = 10A$; $\omega = 314$ rad s^{-1}

Maximum energy stored in inductance

$$= \frac{1}{2} LI_m^2 = \frac{1}{2} \times 5 \times 10^2 = 250 \, J$$

Now, $V_m = \omega L I_m = 314 \times 5 \times 10 = 15700$ volts

Maximum energy stored in the capacitor

$$= \frac{1}{2} CV_m^2 = \frac{1}{2} \times C \times (15700)^2$$

$$\therefore \qquad \frac{1}{2} \times C \times (15700)^2 = 250$$

$$or \qquad C = \frac{250 \times 2}{(15700)^2} = 2.028 \times 10^{-6}\,F = \mathbf{2.028\,\mu F}$$

Example 15.23. *Determine the total capacitive reactance for the circuit shown in Fig. 15.40.*

Solution. Capacitive reactances in series follow the same rules as do resistors in series. For series capacitors, the total capacitive reactance X_{C_T} is

$$X_{C_T} = X_{C_1} + X_{C_2} + \ldots\ldots\ldots + X_{C_n}$$

Referring to Fig. 15.40, we have,

$$X_{C_1} = \frac{1}{2\pi f C_1} = \frac{1}{2\pi \times 200 \times 1 \times 10^{-6}} = 796\,\Omega$$

$$X_{C_2} = \frac{1}{2\pi f C_2} = \frac{1}{2\pi \times 200 \times 0.33 \times 10^{-6}} = 2411\,\Omega$$

$$\therefore \qquad X_{C_T} = X_{C_1} + X_{C_2} = 796 + 2411 = \mathbf{3207\,\Omega}$$

Fig. 15.40

Alternatively

$$C_T = \frac{C_1 C_2}{C_1 + C_2} = \frac{1 \times 0.33}{1 + 0.33} = 0.248\,\mu F = 0.248 \times 10^{-6}\,F$$

$$\therefore \qquad X_{C_T} = \frac{1}{2\pi f C_T} = \frac{1}{2\pi \times 200 \times 0.248 \times 10^{-6}} = \mathbf{3207\,\Omega}$$

MULTIPLE-CHOICE QUESTIONS

1. The a.c. system is preferred to d.c. system because ....
   - (a) a.c. voltages can be easily changed in magnitude
   - (b) d.c. motors do not have fine speed control
   - (c) high-voltage a.c. transmission is less efficient
   - (d) d.c. voltage cannot be used for domestic appliances

2. In a.c. system, we generate sinewave form because.................
   - (a) it can be easily drawn
   - (b) it produces least disturbance in electrical circuits
   - (c) it is nature's standard
   - (d) other waves cannot be produced easily

3. .... will work only on d.c.supply.
   - (a) Electric lamp
   - (b) Refrigerator
   - (c) Heater
   - (d) Electroplating

4. .... will produce a.c. voltage.
   - (a) Friction
   - (b) Photoelectric effect
   - (c) Thermal energy
   - (d) Crystal

5. A coil is rotating in the uniform field of an 8-pole generator. In one revolution of the coil, the number of cycles generated by the voltage is ....
    (*a*) one
    (*b*) two
    (*c*) four
    (*d*) eight

6. An alternating voltage is given by $v = 20 \sin 157t$. The frequency of the alternating voltage is...................
    (*a*) 50 Hz
    (*b*) 25 Hz
    (*c*) 100 Hz
    (*d*) 75 Hz

7. An alternating current is given by $i = 10 \sin 314t$. The time taken to generate two cycles of current is..............
    (*a*) 0.02 second
    (*b*) 0.01 second
    (*c*) 0.04 second
    (*d*) 0.05 second

8. An alternating voltage is given by $v = 30 \sin 314t$. The time taken by the voltage to reach – 30V for the first time is..............
    (*a*) 0.02 second
    (*b*) 0.1 second
    (*c*) 0.03 second
    (*d*) 0.015 second

9. A sine wave has a maximum value of 20V. Its value at 135° is ....
    (*a*) 10 V
    (*b*) 14.14 V
    (*c*) 15 V
    (*d*) 5 V

10. A sinusoidal current has a magnitude of 3A at 120°. Its maximum value will be.............. .
    (*a*) $\sqrt{3}$ A
    (*b*) $\sqrt{3}/2$ A
    (*c*) $2\sqrt{3}$ A
    (*d*) 6A

11. An a.c. generator having 10 poles and running at 600 r.p.m. will generate an alternating voltage of frequency.................. .
    (*a*) 25 Hz
    (*b*) 100 Hz
    (*c*) 50 Hz
    (*d*) 200 Hz

12. An alternating voltage is given by $v = 100 \sin 314t$ volts. Its average value will be ....
    (*a*) 70.7 V
    (*b*) 50 V
    (*c*) 63.7 V
    (*d*) 100 V

13. The area of a sinusoidal wave over a half-cycle is ....
    (*a*) max. value ÷ 2
    (*b*) 2 × max. value
    (*c*) max. value ÷ π
    (*d*) max. value ÷ 2π

14. An alternating voltage is given by $v = 200 \sin 314t$. Its r.m.s. value will be ....
    (*a*) 100 V
    (*b*) 282.8 V
    (*c*) 141.4 V
    (*d*) 121.4 V

15. The average value of $\sin^2\theta$ over a complete cycle is ....
    (*a*) + 1
    (*b*) – 1
    (*c*) 1/2
    (*d*) zero

16. The form factor of a sinusoidal wave is ....
    (*a*) 1.414
    (*b*) 1.11
    (*c*) 2
    (*d*) 1.5

17. The form factor of a .... wave is 1.
    (*a*) sinusoidal
    (*b*) square
    (*c*) triangular
    (*d*) saw tooth

18. Out of the following.............:... wave is the peakiest.
    (*a*) sinusoidal
    (*b*) square
    (*c*) rectangular
    (*d*) triangular

19. The peak factor of a sinewave form is ....
    (*a*) 1.11
    (*b*) 1.414
    (*c*) 2
    (*d*) 1.5

20. When a 15-V square wave is connected across a 50-V a.c. voltmeter, it will read ....
    (*a*) 15 V
    (*b*) $15 \times \sqrt{2}$ V
    (*c*) $15/\sqrt{2}$ V
    (*d*) none of the above

Answers to Multiple-Choice Questions

1. (*a*)	2. (*b*)	3. (*d*)	4. (*d*)	5. (*c*)	6. (*b*)	7. (*c*)
8. (*d*)	9. (*b*)	10. (*c*)	11. (*c*)	12. (*c*)	13. (*b*)	14. (*c*)
15. (*c*)	16. (*b*)	17. (*b*)	18. (*d*)	19. (*b*)	20. (*a*)	

Hints to Selected Multiple-Choice Questions

5. For a 2-pole generator, electrical degrees spanned in one revolution of the coil are 360° *i.e.* one cycle is generated. For an 8-pole generator, 4 cycles (*i.e.* 1440° electrical) will be generated for one revolution of the coil.

6. Comparing with standard equation, $v = V_m \sin \omega t$; $\omega = 157$
    or $f = 157/2\pi = 25\,\text{Hz}$

7. $f = 314/2\pi = 50\,\text{Hz}; T = 1/50 = 0.02\,\text{second}$

   $\therefore 2T = 2 \times 0.02 = \textbf{0.04 second}$

8. Time taken $= \dfrac{T}{2} + \dfrac{T}{4} = \dfrac{3T}{4} = \dfrac{3}{4} \times 0.02 = \textbf{0.015 second}$

9. $v = V_m \sin\theta = 20\sin 135° = \textbf{14.14 V}$

10. $i = I_m \sin\theta$ or $3 = I_m \sin 120°$

    $\therefore I_m = \dfrac{3}{\sin 120°} = \dfrac{3}{\sin 60°} = \textbf{2}\sqrt{\textbf{3}}\textbf{ A}$

11. $f = \dfrac{NP}{120} = \dfrac{600 \times 10}{120} = \textbf{50 Hz}$

12. $V_{av} = 0.637\,V_m = 0.637 \times 100 = \textbf{63.7 V}$

13. Area of half-cycle $= \displaystyle\int_0^\pi i\,d\theta = \int_0^\pi I_m \sin\theta\,d\theta = I_m\left[-\cos\theta\right]_0^\pi = \textbf{2}I_m$

14. $V_{r.m.s.} = \dfrac{V_m}{\sqrt{2}} = 0.707\,V_m = 0.707 \times 200 = \textbf{141.4 V}$

15. $\dfrac{1}{2\pi}\displaystyle\int_0^{2\pi} \sin^2\theta\,d\theta = \dfrac{1}{2\pi}\int_0^{2\pi} \dfrac{1-\cos 2\theta}{2}\,d\theta = \dfrac{1}{4\pi}\left[\theta - \dfrac{\sin 2\theta}{2}\right]_0^{2\pi} = \dfrac{1}{2}$

16. Form factor $= \dfrac{\text{R.M.S. value}}{\text{Average value}} = \dfrac{0.707\,I_m}{0.637\,I_m} = \textbf{1.11}$

17. Because the r.m.s. value is equal to the average value.

18. That wave is peakiest which has the greatest form factor.

19. Peak factor $= \dfrac{\text{Max. value}}{\text{R.M.S. value}} = \dfrac{I_m}{0.707\,I_m} = \textbf{1.414}$

20. A voltmeter records the r.m.s. value and the r.m.s. value of 15-V square wave is **15V**.

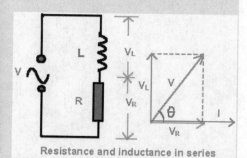

Resistance and inductance in series

16

Series A.C. Circuits

INTRODUCTION

A circuit in which the same alternating current flows through all the circuit elements (*i.e. R, L, C*) is called a series a.c. circuit. Again in the study of these circuits, our points of interest will be (*i*) phase angle ϕ between the applied voltage and circuit current (*ii*) circuit impedance and current and (*iii*) power consumed. Since current is common in a series circuit, it shall be taken as the reference phasor in drawing the phasor diagrams.

16.1. R-L SERIES CIRCUIT

Fig. 16.1 (*i*) shows a pure resistance R ohms connected in series with a coil of pure inductance of *L* henry.

Let　　$V =$ r.m.s. value of the applied voltage

　　　　$I =$ r.m.s. value of the circuit current

∴　　　$V_R = IR$.........where V_R is in phase with I

　　　　$V_L = IX_L$ .... where V_L leads I by 90°

Taking current as the reference phasor, the phasor diagram of the circuit can be drawn as shown in Fig. 16.1 (*ii*). The voltage drop V_R ($= IR$) is in phase with current and is represented in magnitude and direction by the phasor *OA*. The voltage drop V_L (= IX_L)leads current by 90° and is represented in magnitude and direction by the phasor *AB*. The applied voltage V is the phasor sum of these two drops *i.e.*

$$V = \sqrt{V_R^2 + V_L^2} = \sqrt{(IR)^2 + (IX_L)^2} = I\sqrt{R^2 + X_L^2}$$

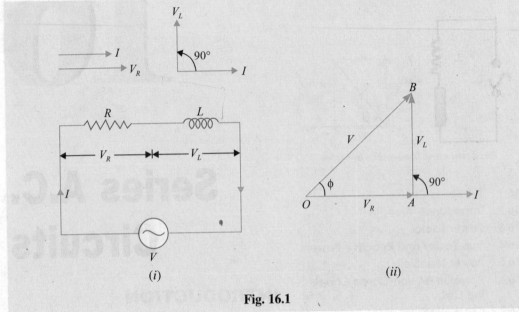

Fig. 16.1

$$\therefore \qquad I = \frac{V}{\sqrt{R^2 + X_L^2}}$$

The quantity $\sqrt{R^2 + X_L^2}$ offers opposition to current flow and is called *impedance* of the circuit. It is represented by Z and is measured in ohms (Ω).

$$\therefore \qquad I = V/Z \text{ where } Z = \sqrt{R^2 + X_L^2}$$

It is clear from the phasor diagram that *circuit current I lags the applied voltage V by $\phi°$*. This fact is also illustrated in the wave diagram shown in Fig. 16.2. The value of phase angle ϕ can be determined from the phasor diagram as :

$$\tan\phi = \frac{V_L}{V_R} = \frac{IX_L}{IR} = \frac{X_L}{R}$$

Since X_L and R are known, the value of ϕ can be calculated.

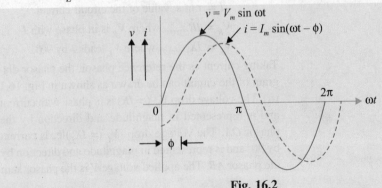

Fig. 16.2

If the applied voltage is $v = V_m \sin \omega t$, then equation for the circuit current will be :

$$i = I_m \sin (\omega t - \phi)$$

where $I_m = V_m / Z$; $\qquad \phi = \tan^{-1} X_L / R$

Power

Instantaneous power, $\qquad p = vi = V_m \sin \omega t \times I_m \sin (\omega t - \phi)$

$$= \frac{1}{2} V_m I_m [2 \sin \omega t \sin (\omega t - \phi)]$$

$$= \frac{1}{2} V_m I_m [\cos \phi - \cos (2 \omega t - \phi)]$$

$$= \frac{1}{2} V_m I_m \cos \phi - \frac{1}{2} V_m I_m \cos (2 \omega t - \phi)$$

Thus instantaneous power consists of two parts :

(i) Constant part $\frac{1}{2} V_m I_m \cos \phi$ whose average value is the same.

(ii) A pulsating component $\frac{1}{2} V_m I_m \cos (2\omega t - \phi)$ whose average value over one complete cycle is zero.

$\therefore$ Average power, $\qquad P = \dfrac{V_m I_m}{2} \cos \phi = \dfrac{V_m}{\sqrt{2}} \times \dfrac{I_m}{\sqrt{2}} \times \cos \phi$

or $\qquad\qquad\qquad\qquad P = VI \cos \phi$

where V and I are the r.m.s. values of voltage and current. The term $\cos \phi$ is called **power factor** of the circuit and its value is given by (from phasor diagram);

Power factor, $\qquad \cos \phi = \dfrac{IR}{IZ} = \dfrac{R}{Z}$

Alternatively $\qquad\qquad P = VI \cos \phi$

$$= (IZ) I (R/Z) \qquad\qquad [\because \cos \phi = R/Z \text{ and } V = IZ]$$

$$= I^2 R$$

This is expected because power is consumed in resistance only; inductance does not consume any power.

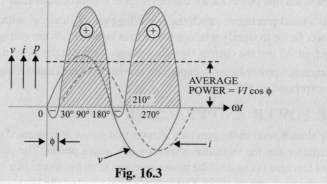

AVERAGE POWER $= VI \cos \phi$

Fig. 16.3

Fig. 16.3 shows the power curve for an R-L series circuit. It is clear that power is negative between 0° and 30° and between 180° and 210°. During the rest of the cycle, the power is positive. This means that power is being consumed by the circuit.

16.2. IMPEDANCE TRIANGLE

The phasor diagram of a R-L series circuit is shown in Fig. 16.4. Dividing each side of the phasor diagram by the same factor I, we get a triangle whose sides represent R, X_L and Z. Such a triangle is known as *impedance triangle* (See Fig. 16.5). Just as in Fig. 16.4, the impedance triangle is also a right-angled triangle.

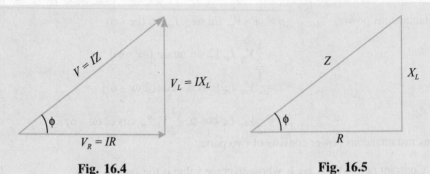

Fig. 16.4   **Fig. 16.5**

Impedance triangle is a useful concept in a.c. circuits as it enables us to calculate,

(i) the impedance of the circuit *i.e.* $Z = \sqrt{R^2 + X_L^2}$

(ii) power factor of the circuit *i.e.* $\cos \phi = R/Z$

(iii) phase angle ϕ *i.e.* $\tan \phi = X_L/R$

(iv) whether current leads or lags the voltage.

Therefore, it is always profitable to draw the impedance triangle while analysing an a.c. circuit.

16.3. POWER FACTOR

The power factor (*i.e.* $\cos \phi$) of a circuit can be defined in one of the following ways :

(i) Power factor = $\cos \phi$ = cosine of angle between V and I

(ii) Power factor $= \dfrac{R}{Z} = \dfrac{\text{Resistance}}{\text{Impedance}}$ [See Fig. 16.5]

(iii) Power factor $= \dfrac{VI \cos \phi}{VI} = \dfrac{\text{True power}}{\text{Apparent power}}$

It may be noted that power factor can never have a value greater than 1.

(a) It is a usual practice to attach the word 'lagging' or 'leading' with the numerical value of power factor to signify whether the current lags or leads the voltage. Thus if a circuit has a p.f. of 0.5 and the current lags the voltage, we generally write p.f. as 0.5 lagging.

(b) Sometimes power factor is expressed as a percentage. Thus 0.8 lagging power factor may be expressed as 80% lagging.

16.4. TRUE POWER AND REACTIVE POWER

We have already seen in the previous chapter that power is consumed only in resistance since neither pure inductor nor the capacitor consumes any active power. The power consumed (or true power) in L and C is zero because all the power received from the source in a quarter-cycle is returned to the source in the next quarter-cycle. This circulating power is called the *reactive power and does no useful work in the circuit. The reader may recall that current and voltage are in phase in a resistance whereas they are 90° out of phase in L or C. Therefore, we come to the conclusion that current

* This is the power that flows back and forth in both directions in the circuit or reacts upon itself. Hence the name.

in phase with voltage produces true or active power whereas current 90° out of phase with voltage contributes to reactive power *i.e.*

True power   = Voltage × Current in phase with voltage

Reactive power   = Voltage × Current 90° out of phase with voltage

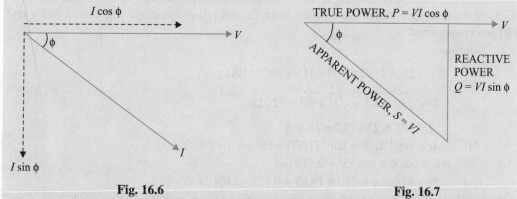

Fig. 16.6   **Fig. 16.7**

Consider an inductive circuit in which current I lags behind the applied voltage V by $\phi°$. The phasor diagram of the circuit is shown in Fig. 16.6. The current I can be resolved into two rectangular components *viz.* (*i*) $I \cos \phi$ in phase with V and (*ii*) $I \sin \phi$; 90° out of phase with V.

∴   True power, $P = V \times I \cos \phi = VI \cos \phi$ watts or kW

           Reactive power, $Q = V \times I \sin \phi = VI \sin \phi$ VAR or kVAR

           Apparent power, $S = V \times I = VI$ VA or kVA

(*i*)   The component $I \cos \phi$ is called the *in phase component or wattful component*. It is this component of total current which contributes to true power (*i.e.* $VI \cos \phi$).

(*ii*)   The component $I \sin \phi$ is called the *reactive component* and contributes to reactive power (*i.e.* $VI \sin \phi$). The reactive power is neither consumed in the circuit nor it does any useful work. It merely flows back and forth in both directions in the circuit. A wattmeter does not measure the reactive power.

(*iii*) The product of voltage (V) and actual current (I) in the circuit is called the *apparent power (i.e. VI)*. To avoid confusion, it is measured in volt-amperes (*VA*).

16.5. POWER TRIANGLE

If we multiply each of the current phasors in Fig. 16.6 by V, we get the power triangle shown in Fig. 16.7. This is a right-angled triangle and indicates the relation among apparent power, true power and reactive power. It reveals the following facts about the circuit :

(*i*)   Power factor, $\cos \phi = \dfrac{\text{True power}}{\text{Apparent power}} = \dfrac{VI \cos \phi}{VI}$

(*ii*)   (Apparent power)^2 = (True power)^2 + (Reactive power)^2

or $S^2 = P^2 + Q^2$

(*iii*) True power, $P =$ Apparent power $\times \cos \phi = VI \cos \phi$

         Reactive power, $Q =$ Apparent power $\times \sin \phi = VI \sin \phi$

Let us illustrate the power relations in an a.c. circuit with an example. Suppose a circuit draws a current of 10A at a voltage of 200V and its p.f. is 0.8 lagging. Then,

           Apparent power, $S = VI = 200 \times 10 = 2000$ VA

           True power, $P = VI \cos \phi = 200 \times 10 \times 0.8 = 1600$ W

           Reactive power, $Q = VI \sin \phi = 200 \times 10 \times 0.6 = 1200$ VAR

The circuit receives an apparent power of 2000VA and is able to convert only 1600 watts into true power. The reactive power of 1200 VAR does no useful work, it merely flows into and out of the circuit periodically. In fact, reactive power is a liability on the source because the source has to supply the additional current (*i.e.*, $I \sin \phi$).

Example 16.1. *A coil having a resistance of 7Ω and an inductance of 31.8 mH is connected to 230V, 50Hz supply. Calculate (i) the circuit current (ii) phase angle (iii) power factor and (iv) power consumed.*

Solution.

(i) $X_L = 2\pi f L = 2\pi \times 50 \times 31.8 \times 10^{-3} = 10\Omega$

$$Z = \sqrt{R^2 + X_L^2} = \sqrt{7^2 + 10^2} = 12.2\Omega$$

∴ $I = V/Z = 230/12.2 = \textbf{18.85A}$

(ii) $\phi = \tan^{-1} X_L/R = \tan^{-1}(10/7) = \textbf{55° } lag$

(iii)   *p.f.* $= \cos \phi = \cos 55° = \textbf{0.573 lag}$

(iv) $P = VI \cos \phi = 230 \times 18.85 \times 0.573 = \textbf{2484.24 W}$

Example 16.2. *A choke coil takes a current of 2.5A when connected across 250V, 50Hz mains and consumes 400 watts. Find (i) the power factor (ii) resistance of the coil and (iii) inductance of the coil.*

Solution.

(i) $P = VI \cos \phi$

∴ $\cos \phi = \dfrac{P}{VI} = \dfrac{400}{250 \times 2.5} = \textbf{0.64 } lag$

(ii) $Z = V/I = 250/2.5 = 100\Omega$

∴ $R = Z \cos \phi = 100 \times 0.64 = \textbf{64}\Omega$

(iii) $X_L = \sqrt{Z^2 - R^2} = \sqrt{100^2 - 64^2} = 76.84\Omega$

∴ $L = \dfrac{X_L}{2\pi f} = \dfrac{76.84}{2\pi \times 50} = \textbf{0.245H}$

Example 16.3. *An e.m.f. given by 326 sin 314t is applied to a certain circuit and current is 2 sin (314 t – 1.3736). Find (i) frequency of voltage (ii) phase angle between voltage and current in degrees and (iii) resistance of the circuit.*

Solution.

(i) $f = \dfrac{\omega}{2\pi} = \dfrac{314}{2\pi} = \textbf{50 Hz}$

(ii) $\phi = 1.3736 \text{ radians} = 1.3736 \times 180°/\pi = \textbf{78.7° } lag$

(iii) $Z = V_m/I_m = 326/2 = 163 \Omega$

∴ $R = Z \cos \phi = 163 \cos 78.7° = \textbf{32.2 } \Omega$

Example 16.4. *A 200V, 50Hz inductive circuit takes a current of 10A, lagging 30°. Find (i) the resistance (ii) reactance and (iii) inductance of the circuit.*

Solution.

(i) $Z = V/I = 200/10 = 20 \Omega$

$R = Z \cos \phi = 20 \cos 30° = \textbf{17.32 } \Omega$

(ii) $X_L = Z \sin \phi = 20 \sin 30° = 10 \, \Omega$

(iii) $L = \dfrac{X_L}{2\pi f} = \dfrac{10}{2\pi \times 50} = 0.0318 \text{H}$

Example 16.5. *In an R-L series circuit, a voltage of 100V at 25 Hz produces one ampere while the same voltage at 75Hz produces half ampere. Find the values of R and L.*

Solution.

$$Z_1 = 100/1 = 100 \, \Omega \; ; Z_2 = 100/0.5 = 200 \, \Omega$$

$\therefore$ $R^2 + (2\pi \times 25L)^2 = 100^2$ ...(i)

and $R^2 + (2\pi \times 75L)^2 = (200)^2$ ...(ii)

From eqs. (i) and (ii), $R = 79\Omega$, $L = 0.39 \text{ H}$

Example 16.6. *Find the inductance of a coil of negligible resistance which when connected in series with a non-inductive resistor of 100 Ω reduces the current to one half of its original value on a supply of frequency 50Hz.*

Solution. The impedance Z of the series combination should be twice that of resistance $R (= 100\Omega)$ *i.e.* $Z = 2R$.

$$Z^2 = R^2 + X_L^2$$

or $4R^2 = R^2 + X_L^2$

or $X_L = \sqrt{3}\, R = \sqrt{3} \times 100 = 173.2\Omega$

$\therefore$ $L = \dfrac{X_L}{2\pi f} = \dfrac{173.2}{2\pi \times 50} = 0.551 \text{ H}$

Example 16.7. *A pure inductance of 318mH is connected in series with a pure resistance of 75 Ω. The circuit is supplied from 50Hz source and the voltage across 75 Ω resistor is found to be 150V. Calculate the supply voltage and the phase angle.*

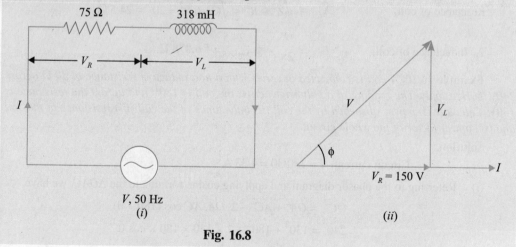

Fig. 16.8

Solution. The circuit diagram and the phasor diagram are shown in Fig. 16.8.

$$I = V_R /R = 150/75 = 2\text{A}$$
$$X_L = 2\pi f L = 2\pi \times 50 \times 318 \times 10^{-3} = 100 \, \Omega$$
$$V_L = IX_L = 2 \times 100 = 200\text{V}$$

Referring to the phasor diagram in Fig. 16.8(*ii*),

Supply voltage, $\qquad V = \sqrt{V_R^2 + V_L^2} = \sqrt{150^2 + 200^2} = \mathbf{250V}$

Phase angle, $\qquad \phi = \tan^{-1}(X_L/R) = \tan^{-1}(100/75) = \mathbf{53.06° \ lag}$

Example 16.8. *A voltage is given by the expression* v = 340 sin ωt *and is applied to a circuit, the current being given by* i = 14.14 sin (ωt −π/6). *Calculate (i) impedance (ii) resistance (iii) reactance and (iv) power consumed.*

Solution.

  (*i*) $Z = V_m/I_m = 340/14.14 = \mathbf{24 \ \Omega}$

  (*ii*) $R = Z \cos \phi = 24 \cos \pi/6 = \mathbf{20.8 \ \Omega}$

  (*iii*) $X_L = Z \sin \phi = 24 \sin \pi/6 = \mathbf{12 \ \Omega}$

  (*iv*) $P = I^2 R = (14.14/\sqrt{2})^2 \times 20.8 = \mathbf{2080 \ W}$

Example 16.9. *A coil when connected across a 100V d.c. supply dissipates 500 W of power. When connected across a 100V a.c. supply of frequency 50Hz, it dissipates 200 W. Calculate the values of resistance and inductance of the coil.*

Solution.

D.C. Supply

 Resistance of coil, $\qquad R = V^2/P = 100^2/500 = \mathbf{20\Omega}$

A.C. supply

Power consumed, $\qquad P = VI \cos \phi = V \times \dfrac{V}{Z} \times \dfrac{R}{Z} = \dfrac{V^2 R}{Z^2}$

Impedance of coil, $\qquad Z = \sqrt{\dfrac{V^2 R}{P}} = \sqrt{\dfrac{100^2 \times 20}{200}} = \mathbf{31.62 \ \Omega}$

Reactance of coil, $\qquad X_L = \sqrt{Z^2 - R^2} = \sqrt{(31.62)^2 - 20^2} = \mathbf{24.5 \ \Omega}$

∴ Inductance of coil, $\qquad L = \dfrac{X_L}{2\pi f} = \dfrac{24.5}{2\pi \times 50} = \mathbf{0.078 \ H}$

Example 16.10. *A coil is connected in series with a non-inductive resistance of 30 Ω across 240V, 50Hz supply. The reading of a voltmeter across the coil is 180V and across the resistance is 130V. Calculate (i) power absorbed by the coil (ii) inductance of the coil (iii) resistance of the coil and (iv) power factor of the whole circuit.*

Solution.

    Circuit current, $I = 130/30 = \mathbf{4.33 \ A}$

 (*i*)   Referring to the phasor diagram and applying cosine formula to the ΔOAC, we have,

$$OC^2 = OA^2 + AC^2 - 2. \ OA. \ AC \cos (180 - \theta)$$

or $\qquad 240^2 = 130^2 + 180^2 + 2 \times 130 \times 180 \times \cos \theta$

∴ $\qquad \cos \theta = \dfrac{240^2 - 130^2 - 180^2}{2 \times 130 \times 180} = \mathbf{0.177 \ lag}$

$$P_{coil} = V_L I \cos \theta = 180 \times 4.33 \times 0.177 = \mathbf{137.95 \ W}$$

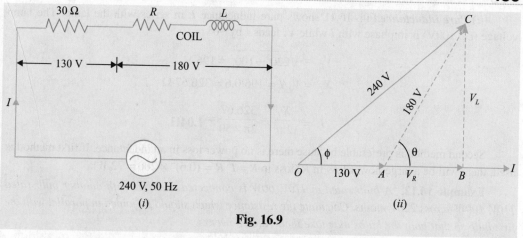

Fig. 16.9

(ii) $V_L = AC \sin \theta = 180 \sqrt{1-(0.177)^2} = 177.16 \, V$

$X_L = V_L / I = 177.16/4.33 = 40.9 \, \Omega$

∴ $L = X_L / 2\pi f = 40.9/2\pi \times 50 = \textbf{0.13 H}$

(iii) $V_R = AC \cos \theta = 180 \times 0.177 = 31.86 \, V$

∴ $R = V_R / I = 31.86/4.33 = \textbf{7.36 } \Omega$

(iv) Circuit p.f. $= \cos \phi = \dfrac{OB}{OC} = \dfrac{130+31.86}{240} = \textbf{0.674} \, lag$

Example 16.11. *A 100V, 60W lamp is to be operated on 220V, 50Hz supply. Find the value of (i) non-inductive resistance (ii) pure inductance in series with the lamp so that the lamp is not over-run. Which would be preferable ?*

Solution.

Rated current of lamp, $I = 60/100 = 0.6 \, A$

(i) *Non-inductive resistance.* Fig. 16.10 shows a resistance R connected in series with the lamp.

$$V_R = 220 - 100 = 120 \, V$$

Both V_R and lamp voltage are in phase with I.

∴ $$R = V_R / I = 120/0.6 = \textbf{200 } \Omega$$

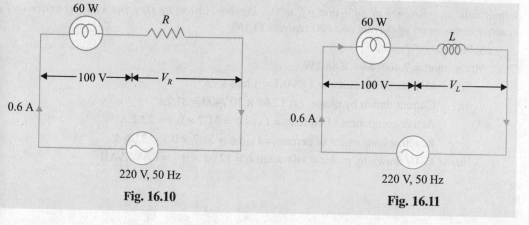

Fig. 16.10

Fig. 16.11

(ii) *Pure inductance.*Fig. 16.11 shows pure inductance L in series with the lamp. The lamp voltage (*i.e.* 100V) is in phase with I while V_L leads I by 90°.

$$\therefore \qquad V_L = \sqrt{220^2 - 100^2} = 196 \text{ V}$$

$$X_L = V_L/I = 196/0.6 = 326.67 \ \Omega$$

$$\therefore \qquad L = \frac{X_L}{2\pi f} = \frac{326.67}{2\pi \times 50} = \textbf{1.04H}$$

Second method is preferable because there is no power loss in an inductance. If first method is used, there will be a large power loss in R (loss in $R = I^2 R = (0.6)^2 \times 200 = 72 \ W$).

Example 16.12. *A bulb rated at 110V, 60W is connected in series with another bulb rated 110V, 100W across 220V mains. Calculate the resistance which should be joined in parallel with the first bulb so that both the bulbs may take their rated power.*

Solution.

Rated current of bulb L_1, $I_1 = 60/110 = 0.545$ A

Rated current of bulb L_2, $I_2 = 100/110 = 0.91$ A

In order that the bulbs take their rated power, they must carry their rated currents. This can be done by connecting a resistance R in parallel with bulb L_1 as shown in Fig. 16.12.

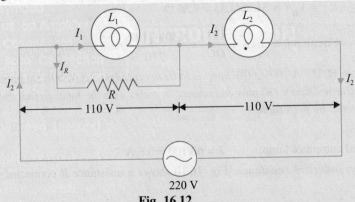

Fig. 16.12

$$I_R = I_2 - I_1 = 0.91 - 0.545 = 0.365 \text{A}$$

$$\therefore \qquad R = 110/0.365 = 301.4 \ \Omega$$

Example 16.13. *A single phase motor operating from 400V, 50Hz supply is developing 7.46 kW output with an efficiency of 84% and p.f. of 0.7 lagging. Calculate (i) input kVA (ii) active and reactive components of current and (iii) reactive kVAR.*

Solution.

Motor input = 7.46/0.84 = 8.88 kW

    (i)   kVA drawn by motor = 8.88/0.7 = **12.68 kVA**

    (ii)   Current drawn by motor, $I = 12.68 \times 10^3/400 = 31.7A$

        Active component of current $= I \cos \phi = 31.7 \times 0.7 = $ **22.2 A**

        Reactive component of current $= I \sin \phi = 31.7 \times 0.7 = $ **22.2 A**

    (iii)   kVAR drawn by motor = kVA × sin ϕ = 12.68 × 0.7 = **8.88 kVAR**

16.6. POWER IN AN IRON-CORED CHOKING COIL

The power P taken by an iron-cored coil has to supply :

(i) power loss in ohmic resistance *i.e.* $I^2 R$ where R is the d.c. resistance or true resistance of the coil.

(ii) the iron loss P_i (*i.e.* hysteresis and eddy current loss).

$$\therefore \qquad P = I^2 R + P_i \qquad \qquad ...(i)$$

The iron loss can be thought as additional resistance in series with the resistance of the coil. Thus the effect of iron core is to increase the effective resistance of the coil. We can say that input to an iron-cored coil is $I^2 R_{eff}$ *i.e.*

$$P = I^2 R_{eff} \qquad \qquad ...(ii)$$

From eqs. (*i*) and (*ii*), we have,

$$I^2 R_{eff} = I^2 R + P_i$$

$$or \qquad \qquad R_{eff} = R + \frac{P_i}{I^2}$$

i.e. Effective resistance = True (or d.c.) resistance + $\dfrac{P_i}{I^2}$

Example 16.14. *An alternating current flows through an iron-cored coil. The d.c. resistance of the coil is 25Ω and the coil takes 10mA and 3.5 mW of power. What is the effective resistance of the coil ?*

Solution.

$$I^2 R_{eff} = P$$

$$or \qquad \qquad R_{eff} = \frac{P}{I^2} = \frac{3.5 \times 10^{-3}}{(10 \times 10^{-3})^2} = 35\Omega$$

The reader may note that with an iron-core, the resistance of the coil is increased from 25Ω to 35 Ω.

Example 16.15. *An iron-cored choking coil has a resistance of 4 Ω when measured by a d.c. supply. On a 240V, 50Hz mains supply, it dissipated 500W, the current taken being 10A. Calculate (i) impedance (ii) the power factor (iii) the iron loss and (iv) inductance of the coil.*

Solution.

(i) Impedance of coil, $\qquad \qquad Z = V/I = 240/10 = 24 \ \Omega$

(ii) Power factor, $\qquad \qquad \cos \phi = \dfrac{P}{VI} = \dfrac{500}{240 \times 10} = 0.208 \ \textbf{lag}$

(iii) $\qquad \qquad$ Total loss = Loss in resistance + Iron loss

$or \qquad \qquad 500 = 10^2 \times 4 + P_i$

$\therefore \qquad \qquad P_i = 500 - 400 = \textbf{100W}$

(iv) Effective resistance, $\qquad R_{eff} = R + P_i/I^2 = 4 + 100/10^2 = 5\Omega$

Reactance of coil, $\qquad X_L = \sqrt{Z^2 - R_{eff}^2} = \sqrt{24^2 - 5^2} = 23.47\Omega$

$\therefore$ Inductance of coil, $\qquad L = \dfrac{X_L}{2\pi f} = \dfrac{23.47}{2\pi \times 50} = \textbf{74.71} \times \textbf{10}^{-3} \textbf{H}$

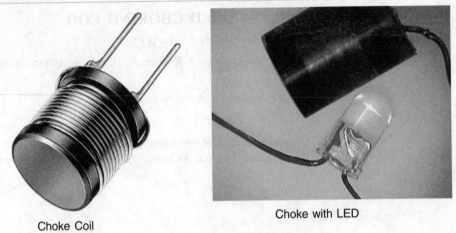

Choke Coil

Choke with LED

16.7. CIRCLE DIAGRAM OF R-L SERIES CIRCUIT

Consider an R-L series circuit supplied from a constant voltage V and fixed frequency. The only variable is R as shown in Fig. 16.13 (i). At any particular value of R, the phasor diagram will be as shown in Fig. 16.13 (ii). As R is varied, the circuit current I also changes. It can be shown that locus of current I is a semi-circle as shown in Fig. 16.13 (iii).

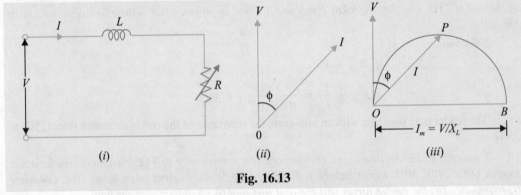

Fig. 16.13

(i)   At a particular value of R, the current in the circuit is OP; the point P lying on a semicircle.

(ii)   As R is decreased, the phase angle ϕ (tan $\phi = X_L/R$) increases and point P shifts towards B. When R becomes zero, the phase angle is 90° lagging and I has the maximum value $I_m = V/X_L$.

(iii)   As R is increased, ϕ decreases and point P moves towards O. When R becomes infinite, the phase angle is zero and point P approaches O. Consequently, circuit current becomes zero.

(iv)   It can be shown that maximum power in the circuit is given by :

$$\text{Max. Power} = \frac{V^2}{2X_L}$$

It will occur when point P is the mid-point of the arc of semicircle *i.e.* $\phi = 45°$.

Example 16.16. *Give vector diagram for 100V, 50Hz R-L series circuit having* $\omega L = 1$ *ohm and variable resistance. Find the maximum power. Draw the locus of current vector.*

Solution.

Fig. 16.14 (i) shows the circuit diagram whereas Fig. 16.14 (ii) shows the locus of circuit current.

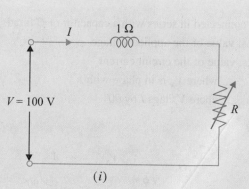

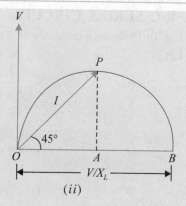

(i)

(ii)

Fig. 16.14

$$\text{Max. Power} = \frac{V^2}{2X_L} = \frac{100^2}{2 \times 1} = 5000\text{W}$$

TUTORIAL PROBLEMS

1. A resistance of 5Ω is connected in series with a pure inductance of 0.01H to a 100V, 50Hz supply. Calculate (i) impedance (ii) current and (iii) power absorbed.

   [(i) 5.9Ω (ii) 16.94A (iii) 1435 W]

2. A 200-V, 50 Hz inductive circuit takes a current of 10A lagging the voltage by 30°. Calculate (i) resistance (ii) reactance and (iii) inductance of the circuit.

   [(i) 10Ω (ii) 17.3Ω (iii) 31.8 mH]

3. An inductive coil connected to a 200V, 50Hz supply takes a current of 10A. If the power dissipated in the coil is 1000 W, calculate (i) inductance of the coil (ii) power factor and (iii) angle of lag. [(i) 0.0552 H (ii) 0.5 (iii) $\phi = 60°$]

4. The p.d. measured across a coil is 20V when a direct current of 2A is passed through it. With an alternating current of 2A at 40Hz, the p.d. across the coil is 140V. If the coil is connected to a 230V, 50Hz supply, calculate (i) current (ii) power and (iii) the power factor. [(i) 2.64A (ii) 69.7 W (iii) 0.1147 lag]

5. An a.c. circuit takes a power of 4.2 kW at a power factor of 0.6 lagging. Find (i) apparent power and (ii) reactive power. [(i) 7 kVA (ii) 5.6 kVAR]

6. A coil is joined in series with a pure resistor of resistance 800 Ω across a 100V, 50Hz supply. The reading of a voltmeter across the coil is 45V and across the pure resistor is 80V. Find (i) inductance and (ii) resistance of the coil. [(i) $L = 1.4$ H (ii) $R = 98.5$ Ω]

7. When a certain inductive coil is supplied at 240V, 50Hz, the current is 6.45A. When the frequency is changed to 40Hz at 240V, the current taken is 7.48A. Calculate the inductance and resistance of the coil. [$L = 0.1$ H ; $R = 20\Omega$]

8. A coil has a resistance of 75Ω and an inductance of 1.4 H. When the applied voltage is 240V a.c., at what frequency is the current 0.3A ? What is the power factor at this frequency ? [90.55 Hz ; 0.0938 lag]

9. When voltage of 240V, 50Hz is applied to a coil P, the current drawn is 10A and power dissipated is 450W. When the same supply is connected to a coil Q, the current is 15A and power dissipated is 950W. Calculate (i) inductive reactance of each coil and (ii) current and power taken when the two coils are connected in series across the above voltage.

   [(i) $X_P = 23.6$ Ω ; $X_Q = 15.4$ Ω (ii) 6A ; 314 W]

10. A metal filament lamp is constructed to take a current of 0.2A at 100V. Calculate the value of inductance which when placed in series with the lamp across 200V, 50Hz supply causes the lamp to work under normal conditions of current and voltage. [2.76 H]

16.8. R-C SERIES CIRCUIT

Fig. 16.15 shows a resistance of R ohms connected in series with a capacitor of C farad.

Let V = r.m.s. value of the applied voltage

I = r.m.s. value of the circuit current

$V_R = IR$ .....where V_R is in phase with I

$V_C = IX_C$ .....where V_C lags I by 90°

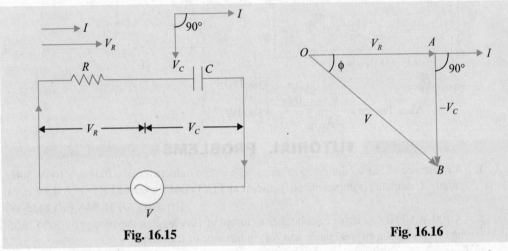

Fig. 16.15   **Fig. 16.16**

The phasor diagram of the circuit is shown in Fig. 16.16. The supply voltage V is the phasor sum of $V_R (= IR)$ and $V_C (= IX_C)$ drops *i.e.*

$$V = \sqrt{V_R^2 + V_C^2} = \sqrt{(IR)^2 + (-IX_C)^2} = I\sqrt{R^2 + X_C^2}$$

$$\therefore \quad I = \frac{V}{\sqrt{R^2 + X_C^2}}$$

The quantity $\sqrt{R^2 + X_C^2}$ offers opposition to current flow and is called *impedance* of the circuit.

$$\therefore \quad I = V/Z \quad \text{where } Z = \sqrt{R^2 + X_C^2}$$

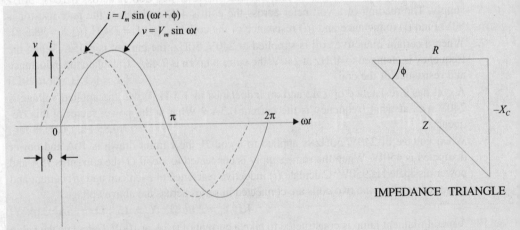

Fig. 16.17   **Fig. 16.18**

It is clear from the phasor diagram that *circuit current I leads the applied voltage V by* $\phi°$ where :

$$\tan \phi = -\frac{V_C}{V_R} = -\frac{IX_C}{IR} = -\frac{X_C}{R}$$

Since current is taken as the reference phasor, negative phase angle implies that voltage lags behind the current. This is the same thing as current leads the voltage [See Fig. 16.17].

Power. The equations for voltage and current are :

$$v = V_m \sin \omega t$$
$$i = I_m \sin (\omega t + \phi)$$

Average power, $\quad P$ = Average of vi

$$= VI \cos \phi \qquad \qquad \text{[By same way as in Art. 16.1]}$$

Alternatively

$$P = \text{Power in } R + \text{Power in } C$$
$$= I^2 R + 0$$

$$= IR \times I = IR \times \frac{V}{Z} = VI \times \frac{R}{Z} = VI \cos \phi$$

Example 16.17. *A capacitor of capacitance 79.5µF is connected in series with a non-inductive resistance of 30 Ω across 100 V, 50 Hz supply. Find (i) impedance (ii) current (iii) phase angle and (iv) equation for the instantaneous value of current.*

Solution.

(*i*) $\quad X_C = \dfrac{1}{2\pi fC} = \dfrac{10^6}{2\pi \times 50 \times 79.5} = 40\Omega$

$\quad\quad Z = \sqrt{R^2 + X_C^2} = \sqrt{30^2 + 40^2} = 50\Omega$

(*ii*) $\quad I = V/Z = 100/50 = \mathbf{2A}$

(*iii*) $\quad \phi = \tan^{-1} X_C/R = \tan^{-1} 40/30 = 53° \ lead$

(*iv*) $\quad I_m = 2 \times \sqrt{2} = 2.828 \text{ A}; \ \omega = 2\pi f = 2\pi \times 50 = 314 \text{ rad s}^{-1}$

$\quad\quad \therefore i = 2.828 \sin (314 \ t + 53°) \textbf{ Ans.}$

Example 16.18. *A capacitor and resistor are connected in series across a 120V, 50Hz supply. The circuit draws a current of 1.144 A. If power loss in the circuit is 130.8W, find the values of resistance and capacitance.*

Solution. Power loss occurs in resistance only as capacitor consumes no power.

$$P = I^2 R$$
$$\therefore \quad R = P/I^2 = 130.8/(1.144)^2 = \mathbf{100\Omega}$$
$$Z = V/I = 120/1.144 = 104.91 \ \Omega$$
$$X_C = \sqrt{Z^2 - R^2} = \sqrt{(104.9)^2 - (100)^2} = 31.7\Omega$$
$$\therefore \quad C = \frac{1}{2\pi fX_C} = \frac{1}{2\pi \times 50 \times 31.7} = 100 \times 10^{-6}\text{F}$$

Example 16.19. *A resistor R in series with a capacitor C is connected to 50Hz, 240V supply. Find the value of C so that R absorbs 300 W at 100 V. Find also the maximum charge and maximum energy stored in C.*

Solution.

R absorbs 300W when connected to 100V so that $R = V^2/P = 100^2/300 = 100/3\,\Omega$

Now,

$$I^2 R = 3000W \qquad \therefore I = \sqrt{300 \times 3/100} = 3A$$

$$Z = V/I = 240/3 = 80\,\Omega$$

$$X_C = \sqrt{Z^2 - R^2} = \sqrt{80^2 - (100/3)^2} = 72.7\,\Omega$$

$\therefore$

$$C = \frac{1}{2\pi f X_C} = \frac{1}{2\pi \times 50 \times 72.7} = 43.7 \times 10^{-6}\,F$$

$$Q_{max} = CV_{max} = (43.7 \times 10^{-6}) \times 240\sqrt{2} = 0.0148C$$

$$E = \frac{1}{2}CV_{max}^2 = \frac{1}{2} \times (43.7 \times 10^{-6}) \times (240 \times \sqrt{2})^2 = 2.5\,J$$

Example 16.20. *A 10 Ω resistor and 400 μF capacitor are connected in series to a 60V sinusoidal supply. The circuit current is 5A. Calculate the supply frequency and phase angle between the current and voltage.*

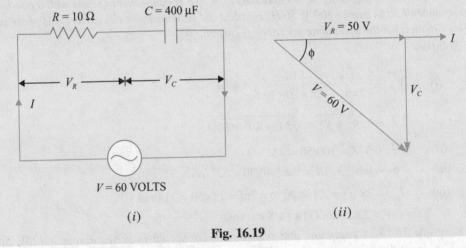

Fig. 16.19

Solution.

$$V_R = IR = 5 \times 10 = 50V$$

$$V_C = \sqrt{V^2 - V_R^2} = \sqrt{60^2 - 50^2} = 33.17\,V$$

$$X_C = V_C/I = 33.17/5 = 6.634\,\Omega$$

$$f = \frac{1}{2\pi CX_C} = \frac{10^6}{2\pi \times 400 \times 6.634} = 60\,Hz$$

$$\phi = \tan^{-1} V_C/V_R = \tan^{-1} 33.17/50 = 33.6°\ lead$$

Example 16.21. *Calculate the capacitance of a condenser to be connected in series with 100V, 80W lamp to enable it to be used on a 200V, 50Hz supply. What is p.f. of the circuit ?*

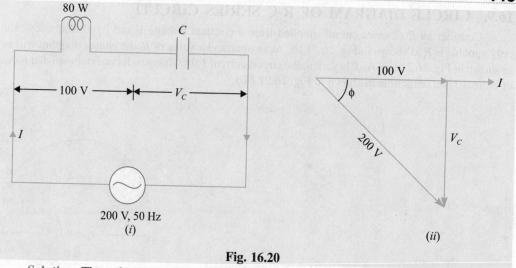

Fig. 16.20

Solution. The voltage across the bulb (pure resistance) should remain 100V for its proper operation. Fig. 16.20 (*i*) shows the required condenser of *C* farad in series with the lamp. The phasor diagram of the circuit is shown in Fig. 16.20 (*ii*).

Rated current of bulb, $I = 80/100 = 0.8A$

$$V_C = \sqrt{200^2 - 100^2} = 173.2\,V$$
$$X_C = V_C/I = 173.2/0.8 = 216.5\,\Omega$$

∴ $$C = \frac{1}{2\pi f X_C} = \frac{1}{2\pi \times 50 \times 216.5} = 14.7 \times 10^{-6}\,F$$

Circuit p.f. $= \cos\phi = V_R/V = 100/200 = 0.5$ lead

Example 16.22. *A load consisting of a capacitor in series with a resistor has an impedance of 50 Ω and power factor 0.707 leading. The load is connected in series with a 40 Ω resistor across an a.c. supply and the resulting current is 3A. Determine the supply voltage and the overall phase angle.*

Solution.

$$R_L = Z_L \cos\phi = 50\cos 45° = 35.35\,\Omega$$
$$X_C = Z_L \sin\phi = 50\sin 45° = 35.35\,\Omega$$
$$R_T = R + R_L = 40 + 35.35 = 75.35\,\Omega$$

$$Z = \sqrt{(75.35)^2 + (35.35)^2} = 83.23\Omega$$
$$V = IZ = 3 \times 83.23 = \mathbf{250V}$$
$$\phi = \tan^{-1} X_C/R_T = \tan^{-1} 35.35/75.35 = \mathbf{25.17°}\ lead$$

TUTORIAL PROBLEMS

1. A circuit when connected to 200V, 50Hz mains takes a current of 10A, leading the voltage by one-twelfth of time period. Calculate (*i*) resistance (*ii*) capacitive reactance and (*iii*) capacitance of the circuit.   [(*i*) 17.32 Ω (*ii*) 10 Ω (*iii*) 318 × 10⁻⁶F]

2. A resistor *R* in series with a capacitance *C* is connected to a 50 Hz, 240V supply. Find the value of *C* so that *R* absorbs 300W at 100V. Find also maximum charge and the maximum stored energy in *C*.   [44μF; 0.0135C; 2.1J]

3. A circuit has a fixed resistance of 2Ω and a capacitive reactance of 10Ω in series with a resistor *R* across 100V constant frequency mains. For what value of *R* is the power consumed in it a maximum?   [10.2 Ω]

16.9. CIRCLE DIAGRAM OF R-C SERIES CIRCUIT

Consider an *R-C* series circuit supplied from a constant voltage *V* and fixed frequency. The only variable is *R* as shown in Fig. 16.21 (*i*). At any particular value of *R*, the phasor diagram will be as shown in Fig. 16.21 (*ii*). As *R* is varied, the circuit current *I* also changes. It can be shown that locus of current *I* is a semicircle as shown in Fig. 16.21 (*iii*).

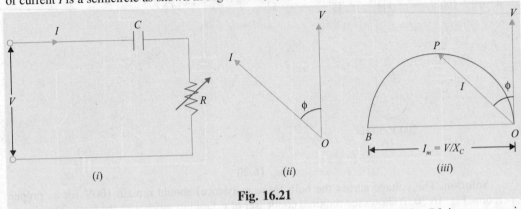

Fig. 16.21

(*i*)   At a particular value of *R*, the current in the circuit is *OP*; the point *P* lying on a semi-circle.

(*ii*)   As *R* is decreased, the phase angle ϕ increases (tan $\phi = X_C/R$) and point *P* shifts towards *B*. When *R* becomes zero, the phase angle is 90° leading and *I* has the maximum value $I_m = V/X_C$.

(*iii*)   As *R* is increased, ϕ decreases and point *P* shifts towards *O*. When *R* becomes infinite, the phase angle is zero and point *P* approaches *O*. Consequently, circuit current becomes zero.

(*iv*)   It can be shown that maximum power in the circuit is given by :

$$\text{Maximum power} = \frac{V^2}{2X_C}$$

It will occur when *P* is the mid-point of the arc of semicircle *i.e.* $\phi = 45°$.

Example 16.23. *Give vector diagram for 100V, 50Hz R-C series circuit having* $\dfrac{1}{\omega C} = 1$ *ohm and variable resistance. Find the maximum power. Draw the locus of current vector.*

Solution. Fig. 16.22 (*i*) shows the circuit diagram whereas Fig. 16.22 (*ii*) shows the locus of circuit current.

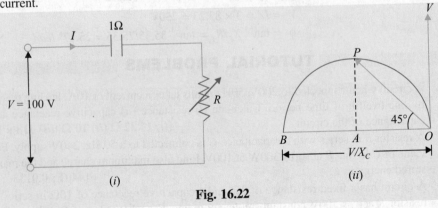

Fig. 16.22

$$\text{Maximum power} = \frac{V^2}{2X_C} = \frac{100^2}{2 \times 1} = 5000 \text{ W}$$

16.10. R-L-C SERIES CIRCUIT

This is a general series a.c. circuit. Fig. 16.23 shows R, L and C connected in series across a supply voltage V (r.m.s.) . The resulting circuit current is I (r.m.s.).

∴ Voltage across R, $V_R = IR$ ... V_R is in phase with I

Voltage across L, $V_L = IX_L$ ... where V_L leads I by 90°

Voltage across C, $V_C = IX_C$ ... where V_C lags I by 90°

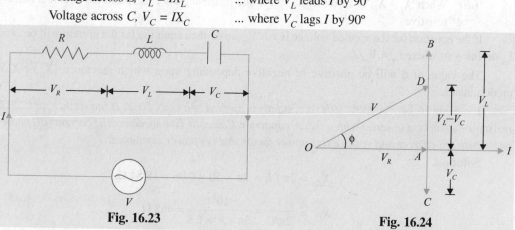

Fig. 16.23   Fig. 16.24

As before, the phasor diagram is drawn taking current as the reference phasor. In the phasor diagram (See Fig. 16.24), OA represents V_R, AB represents V_L and AC represents V_C. It follows that the circuit can either be effectively inductive or capacitive depending upon which voltage drop (V_L or V_C) is predominant. For the case considered, $V_L > V_C$ so that net voltage drop across L-C combination is $V_L - V_C$ and is represented by AD. Therefore, the applied voltage V is the phasor sum of V_R and $V_L - V_C$ and is represented by OD.

$$V = \sqrt{V_R^2 + (V_L - V_C)^2}$$

$$= \sqrt{(IR)^2 + (IX_L - IX_C)^2} = I\sqrt{R^2 + (X_L - X_C)^2}$$

∴ $$I = \frac{V}{\sqrt{R^2 + (X_L - X_C)^2}}$$

The quantity $\sqrt{R^2 + (X_L - X_C)^2}$ offers opposition to current flow and is called *impedance* of the circuit.

Circuit power factor, $$\cos \phi = \frac{R}{Z} = \frac{R}{\sqrt{R^2 + (X_L - X_C)^2}} \qquad ...(i)$$

$$\tan \phi = \frac{V_L - V_C}{V_R} = \frac{X_L - X_C}{R} \qquad ...(ii)$$

Power consumed, $P = VI \cos \phi = *I^2 R$

$P = VI \cos \phi = (IZ) I \times \dfrac{R}{Z} = I^2 R$

This is expected because there is no power loss in L or C.

Three cases of R-L-C series circuit. We have seen that the impedance of a R-L-C series circuit is given by :

$$Z = \sqrt{R^2 + (X_L - X_C)^2}$$

(i) When $X_L - X_C$ is positive (*i.e.* $X_L > X_C$), the phase angle ϕ is positive and the circuit is inductive.

(ii) When $X_L - X_C$ is negative (*i.e.* $X_C > X_L$), the phase angle ϕ is negative and the circuit is capacitive.

(iii) When $X_L - X_C$ is zero (*i.e.* $X_L = X_C$), the phase angle ϕ is zero and the circuit is purely resistive.

If the equation for the applied voltage is $v = V_m \sin \omega t$ then equation for the current will be : $i = I_m \sin (\omega t \pm \phi)$ where $I_m = V_m/Z$.

The value of ϕ will be positive or negative depending upon which reactance (X_L or X_C) predominates.

Example 16.24. *A 230V, 50Hz a.c. supply is applied to a coil of 0.06 H inductance and 2.5Ω resistance connected in series with a 6.8μF capacitor. Calculate (i) impedance (ii) current (iii) phase angle between current and voltage (iv) power factor and (v) power consumed.*

Solution.

$$X_L = 2\pi f L = 2\pi \times 50 \times 0.06 = 18.84\ \Omega$$

$$X_C = \frac{1}{2\pi f C} = \frac{10^6}{2\pi \times 50 \times 6.8} = 468\ \Omega$$

$$X = X_L - X_C = 18.84 - 468 = -449.16\ \Omega$$

(i)
$$Z = \sqrt{R^2 + X^2} = \sqrt{(2.5)^2 + (-449.16)^2} = \textbf{449.2 Ω}$$

(ii)
$$I = V/Z = 230/449.2 = \textbf{0.512 A}$$

(iii)
$$\phi = \tan^{-1}\frac{X}{R} = \tan^{-1}\frac{-449.16}{2.5} = \textbf{−89.7°}$$

The negative sign with ϕ shows that current is leading the voltage.

(iv)
$$p.f. = \cos\phi = R/Z = 2.5/449.2 = \textbf{0.0056}\ \textit{lead}$$

(v)
$$P = VI\cos\phi = 230 \times 0.512 \times 0.0056 = \textbf{0.66 W}$$

Example 16.25. *A resistance R, an inductance L = 0.01H and a capacitance C are connected in series. When an alternating voltage v = 400 sin (3000t −20°) is applied to the series combination, the current flowing is 10 √2 sin (3000t − 65°). Find the values of R and C.*

Solution.

$$\phi = 65° - 20° = 45°\ lag\ i.e.\ \text{circuit is inductive.}$$

$$X_L = \omega L = 3000 \times 0.01 = 30\Omega$$

$$\tan 45° = X/R \quad \therefore \quad X = R$$

$$Z = V_m/I_m = 400/10\sqrt{2} = 28.3\Omega$$

$$Z^2 = R^2 + X^2 = R^2 + R^2 = 2\,R^2$$

$$\therefore \quad R = Z/\sqrt{2} = 28.2/\sqrt{2} = 20\Omega$$

Now
$$X = X_L - X_C$$

$$\therefore \quad X_C = X_L - X = 30 - 20 = 10\Omega$$

$$\therefore \quad C = \frac{1}{\omega X_C} = \frac{1}{3000 \times 10} = 33.3 \times 10^{-6} \, F$$

Example 16.26. *A coil of resistance 8 Ω and inductance 0.03H is connected to an a.c. supply at 240 V, 50 Hz. Calculate the value of capacitance which when connected in series with the above coil, causes no change in the value of current and power taken from the supply.*

Solution.

$$X_L = 2\pi f L = 2\pi \times 50 \times 0.03 = 9.424 \, \Omega$$

To maintain the same current and power, the impedance of the circuit should not change. This is possible if the series capacitor has a capacitive reactance equal to twice the inductive reactance *i.e.*

$$X_C = 2X_L = 2 \times 9.424 = 18.848 \, \Omega$$

$$\therefore \quad C = \frac{1}{2\pi f X_C} = \frac{1}{2\pi \times 50 \times 18.848} = 168.9 \times 10^{-6} \, F$$

Example 16.27. *A coil of p.f. 0.8 is connected in series with a 110 μF capacitor. The supply frequency is 50 Hz. The p.d. across the coil is found to be equal to the p.d. across the capacitor. Calculate the resistance and inductance of the coil.*

Solution.

$$X_C = \frac{1}{2\pi f X_C} = \frac{10^6}{2\pi \times 50 \times 110} = 29 \, \Omega$$

Now
$$I Z_{coil} = I X_C$$
$$\therefore \quad Z_{coil} = X_C = 29 \, \Omega$$
For the coil,
$$\cos \phi = R/Z_{coil}$$
$$\therefore \quad R = Z_{coil} \cos \phi = 29 \times 0.8 = 23.2 \, \Omega$$
Reactance of coil,
$$X_L = Z_{coil} \sin \phi = 29 \times 0.6 = 17.4 \, \Omega$$

$$\therefore \quad L = \frac{X_L}{2\pi f} = \frac{17.4}{2\pi \times 50} = 0.055 \, H$$

Example 16.28. *A resistance of 1 ohm, an inductance of 1 henry and a capacitance of 1 farad are connected in series across a voltage and the line current is 1A. Find the energy consumed in one hour.*

Solution. Energy is only consumed in R since L or C does not consume any energy.

Energy consumed = $I^2 Rt = (1)^2 \times 1 \times 3600 = 3600 \, J$

TUTORIAL PROBLEMS

1. A circuit is made up of 5Ω resistance, 0.2 H inductance and 60 μF capacitance in series. If the circuit current is 20A at a supply frequency of 50Hz, find the applied voltage.[219 V]

2. A series circuit consists of a non-inductive resistor of 10Ω, an inductor having a reactance of 50Ω and a capacitor having a reactance of 30Ω. It is connected to a 230V a.c. supply. Calculate (i) current (ii) the power consumed and (iii) the power factor.

[(i) 10.3A (ii) 1060W (iii) 0.447 lag]

3. A coil of resistance 20Ω is in series with an inductance of 0.04H. A supply of 230V, 50Hz is applied to the combination. Determine the capacitance which when connected in series with the coil causes no change in the magnitude and power taken from the supply.

[67.5 μF]

4. When a certain inductive coil is supplied at 240V, 50Hz, the current is 6.45A. When the frequency is changed to 40Hz at 240V, the current taken is 7.48A. Calculate the inductance and resistance of the coil. [$L = 0.1$H ; $R = 20\Omega$]

5. Two impedances Z_1 and Z_2 when connected separately across a 200V, 50Hz supply consume powers of 100W, 60 W at power factors of 0.5 lagging and 0.6 leading respectively. If the two impedances are now connected together in series across the same supply, calculate (i) circuit current (ii) power absorbed (iii) circuit power factor.
[(i) 0.54 A (ii) 99 W (iii) 0.787 lead]

6. A circuit consists of a resistance of 12Ω, capacitance of 320μF and an inductance of 0.08H, all in series. A supply of 240V, 50Hz is applied to the ends of the circuit. Calculate the frequency at which the circuit power factor would be unity. [32 Hz]

7. A high impedance voltmeter is used to measure the voltage drop across each of the ideal circuit elements of a R-L-C series circuit. If the r.m.s. readings are 40V, 25V and 60V for V_L, V_R and V_C respectively, determine the equation for the applied voltage. The frequency of the applied voltage is 50 Hz. [$v = 45.28 \sin (314t - 38.66°)$]

16.11. RESONANCE IN R-L-C CIRCUIT

A series circuit is said to be in *resonance when circuit power factor is unity i.e. $X_L = X_C$. The frequency f_r at which it occurs is called the *resonant frequency*. The resonance (i.e. $X_L = X_C$) in an R-L-C series circuit can be achieved by changing the supply frequency because X_L and X_C are frequency dependent. At a certain frequency, called the resonant frequency f_r, X_L becomes equal to X_C and series resonance occurs.

At series resonance, $$X_L = X_C$$

or $$2\pi f_r L = \frac{1}{2\pi f_r C}$$

∴ Resonant frequency, $$f_r = \frac{1}{2\pi\sqrt{LC}}$$

If L and C are measured in henry and farad respectively, then f will be in Hz.

16.12. EFFECTS OF SERIES RESONANCE

When series resonance occurs, the effect on the circuit is the same as though neither inductance nor capacitance is present. The current under this condition is dependent solely on the resistance of the circuit and voltage across it.

(i) The impedance of the circuit is minimum and is equal to the resistance of the circuit i.e.
$$Z_r = R$$

(ii) The current in the circuit is maximum as it is limited by the resistance of the circuit alone i.e.,
$$I_r = V/Z_r = V/R$$
As the current is at its maximum value, the power of the circuit will also be at its maximum value.

(iii) Since at series resonance the current flowing in the circuit is very large, the voltage drops across L and C are also very large. In fact, these drops are much greater than the applied voltage. However, voltage drop across $L - C$ combination as a whole will be zero because these drops are equal in magnitude but 180° out of phase with each other.

* Resonance means to be in step with. When in R-L-C series circuit, current is in phase with applied voltage (i.e. circuit p.f. = 1), electrical resonance is said to occur. Clearly, series resonance in R-L-C circuit will occur when $X_L = X_C$.

16.13. RESONANCE CURVE

The curve between current and frequency is known as resonance curve. Fig. 16.25 shows the resonance curve of a typical R-L-C series circuit. Note that current reaches its maximum value at the resonant frequency (f_r), falling off rapidly on either side at that point. It is because if the frequency is below f_r, $X_C > X_L$ and the net reactance is no longer zero. If the frequency is above f_r, then $X_L > X_C$ and the net reactance is again not zero. In both cases, the circuit impedance will be more than the impedance $Z_r (= R)$ at resonance. The result is that the magnitude of circuit current decreases rapidly as the frequency changes from the resonant frequency.

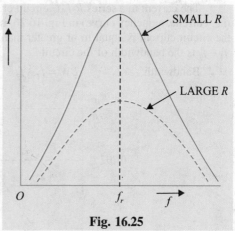

Fig. 16.25

Note also the effect of resistance in the circuit. The smaller the resistance, the greater the current at resonance and sharper is the curve. On the other hand, the greater the resistance, the lower the resonant peak and flatter is the curve (See Fig. 16.25).

16.14. Q-FACTOR OF SERIES RESONANT CIRCUIT

At series resonance, the p.d. across L or C (the two drops being equal and opposite) builds up to a value many times greater than the applied voltage V. This voltage magnification produced by resonance is termed as Q-factor of the series resonant circuit (Q stands for quality) *i.e.*

$$Q\text{-factor} = \frac{\text{Voltage across } L \text{ or } C}{\text{Applied voltage}} = \frac{I_r X_L}{{}^*I_r R} = \frac{X_L}{R}$$

$\therefore \qquad\qquad Q\text{-factor} = \dfrac{\omega_r L}{R} \qquad\qquad\qquad ... (i) \text{ where } \omega_r = 2\pi f_r$

The Q-factor of a series resonant circuit can also be expressed in terms of L and C.

We know, $\qquad\qquad f_r = \dfrac{1}{2\pi\sqrt{LC}} \quad \text{or} \quad 2\pi f_r = \dfrac{1}{\sqrt{LC}}$

or $\qquad\qquad\qquad \omega_r = \dfrac{1}{\sqrt{LC}}$

Substituting the value of ω_r in eq. (i), we get,

$$Q\text{-factor} = \frac{1}{R}\sqrt{\frac{L}{C}} \qquad\qquad\qquad ... (ii)$$

The value of Q-factor depends entirely upon the design of coil (*i.e.* R-L part of the R-L-C series circuit) because resistance arises in this rather than in a capacitor. With a well designed coil, the quality factor can be 200 or more.

Physical meaning of Q-factor. Let us now turn to the physical meaning of Q-factor. The Q-factor of a series circuit indicates how many times the p.d. across L or C is greater than the applied voltage at resonance. For example, consider a R-L-C series circuit connected to a 240 V source. If Q-factor of the coil is 20, then voltage across the coil or capacitor will be $20 \times 240 = 4800$ volts at resonance *i.e.*,

$$V_C = V_L = QV_R = 20 \times 240 = 4800 \text{ Volts.}$$

16.15. BANDWIDTH OF A SERIES RESONANT CIRCUIT

The bandwidth of a series circuit is defined *as the range of frequency over which circuit current is equal to or greater than 70.7% of maximum current (i.e., I_r, current at resonance).*

* At series resonance, applied voltage $V = I_r R$ = voltage across R

The current in a series *R-L-C* circuit changes with frequency. Referring to the resonance curve (*i.e.* current/frequency curve) in Fig. 16.26, it is clear that for any frequency lying between, f_1 and f_2, the circuit current is equal to or greater than 70.7% of maximum current (*i.e.* $I_r = V/R$). Therefore, $f_1 - f_2$ is the bandwidth of the circuit *i.e.*,

Bandwidth, $$BW = f_1 - f_2$$

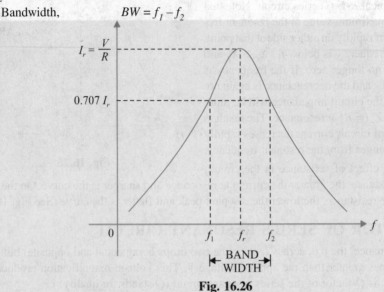

Fig. 16.26

Note that f_1 and f_2 are the limiting frequencies at which current is exactly equal to 70.7% of the maximum value. The frequency f_1 (*i.e.* on the lower side) is called the *lower cut off frequency* and the frequency f_2 (*i.e.* on the higher side) is called the *upper cut off frequency*. The bandwidth of a series resonant circuit means that the circuit will offer low impedance to this frequency range.

The following points may be noted carefully :

(*i*) If the resonant frequency is not centrally located *w.r.t.* lower and upper cut off frequencies, then f_r is the geometric mean of the two *i.e.*,

$$f_r = \sqrt{f_1 f_2}$$

(*ii*) If *Q* of a circuit is ≥ 10 and the resonant frequency is sufficiently centered *w.r.t.* the two cut off frequencies (f_1 and f_2), then,

$$f_2 = f_r + \frac{BW}{2} \qquad \text{For } Q \geq 10$$

$$f_1 = f_r - \frac{BW}{2}$$

(*iii*) It can be proved mathematically that the following relation exists between *Q*-factor and bandwidth of a series resonant circuit :

$$Q = \frac{f_r}{BW}$$

16.16. TUNING FOR RESONANCE

An important application of a series resonant circuit is for tuning purposes in a radio receiver. Fig. 16.27 shows such an application. Here *LC* is the tuning circuit. Resistance *R* represents the resistive component of *L*. By adjusting the value of variable capacitor *C*, the circuit can be made to resonate at any frequency f_r (= $1/2\pi\sqrt{LC}$). Adjusting the value of C is termed as *tuning* the LC circuit and the variable capacitor C is referred to as *tuning capacitor.*

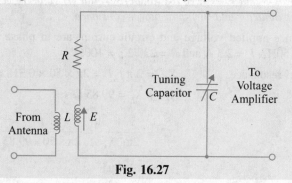

Fig. 16.27

Let us discuss the working of the tuning circuit shown in Fig. 16.27. The radio waves sent into atmosphere by different radio stations have different frequencies. By adjusting the value of capacitor C, the circuit can be made to resonate at the frequency of the desired radio station. The radio wave of the desired station induces a voltage E in L of the series* resonant circuit. The voltage across the capacitor becomes **$V_C = QE$ where Q is the quality factor of the resonant circuit. As the value of Q is generally large, the original signal received by the antenna increases many times in value and appears across C. The value of V_C is much more than that could have been obtained by direct transformer ratio. Thus the voltage amplifier receives a greatly increased signal.

Example 16.29. *A coil of resistance 100 Ω and inductance 100 μH is connected in series with a 100 pF capacitor. The circuit is connected to a 10V variable frequency supply. Calculate (i) the resonant frequency (ii) current at resonance (iii) voltage across L and C at resonance and (iv) Q-factor of the circuit.*

Solution.

(*i*) Resonant frequency,
$$f_r = \frac{1}{2\pi\sqrt{LC}} = \frac{1}{2\pi\sqrt{10^{-4}\times10^{-10}}} = \mathbf{1.59\times10^6\ Hz}$$

(*ii*) Current at resonance,
$$I_r = V/R = 10/100 = \mathbf{0.1\ A}$$

(*iii*) At resonance,
$$X_L = 2\pi f_r L = 2\pi \times 1.59 \times 10^6 \times 10^{-4} = 10000\ \Omega$$

At resonance,
$$V_L = I_r X_L = 0.1 \times 1000 = \mathbf{100\ V}$$

At resonance,
$$V_C = I_r X_C = 0.1 \times 1000 = \mathbf{100\ V}$$

(*iv*) Q-factor,
$$Q = \frac{1}{R}\sqrt{\frac{L}{C}} = \frac{1}{100}\sqrt{\frac{10^{-4}}{10^{-10}}} = \mathbf{10}$$

The reader may note that at resonance, voltage across L or C is Q times the applied voltage.

. . . .

* The circuit has the general appearance of a parallel circuit but actually it is a series circuit. It is because no separate voltage is applied to L, but instead a voltage E is induced in it which is considered as a voltage in series with L and C.

** $\dfrac{V_C}{V_R} = Q$ where V_R is the voltage across R.

But at series resonance, $V_R = E$, the applied voltage (induced voltage E in this case).

∴ $$\frac{V_C}{E} = Q \qquad or \quad V_C = QE$$

Example 16.30. *A series R-L-C circuit consists of resistor of 100 ohms, an inductor of 0.318H and a capacitor of unknown value. When this circuit is energised by 230 ∠0°V, 50Hz sinusoidal supply, the current was found to be 2.3 ∠0° amperes. Find (i) value of capacitor in microfarad (ii) voltage across the inductor and (iii) total power consumed.*

Solution. Since applied voltage and circuit current are in phase, it is a case of series resonance. Here $f_r = 50$ Hz, $I_r = 2.3$ A and $R = 230/2.3 = 100\Omega$.

(i) At series resonance, $\qquad X_L = 2\pi f_r L = 2\pi \times 50 \times 0.318 = 99.85\Omega$

Now $\qquad\qquad\qquad\qquad\qquad X_C = X_L = 99.85\ \Omega$

$$\therefore \qquad\qquad C = \frac{1}{2\pi f_r X_C} = \frac{1}{2\pi \times 50 \times 99.85} = 31.4 \times 10^{-6}\ F$$

$$= 31.4\ \mu F$$

(ii) $\qquad\qquad\qquad V_L = I_r X_L = 2.3 \times 99.85 = 229.6\ V$

(iii) $\qquad\qquad\qquad P = I_r^2 R = (2.3)^2 \times 100 = 529\ W$

Example 16.31. *A choking coil is connected in series with a 20 µF capacitor. With a constant supply voltage of 200V, it is found that the circuit takes its maximum current of 50A when the supply frequency is 100Hz. Calculate (i) resistance and inductance of the choking coil and (ii) voltage across the capacitor. What is the Q-factor of the circuit ?*

Solution. Since current is maximum, the circuit is in resonance *i.e.*, $I_r = 50$A ; $f_r = 100$Hz.

(i) $\qquad\qquad\qquad R = V/I_r = 200/50 = 4\ \Omega$

$\qquad\qquad\qquad X_C = 1/2\pi f_r C = 10^6/2\pi \times 100 \times 20 = 79.62\Omega$

Now $\qquad\qquad\qquad X_C = X_L = 79.62\ \Omega$

$\therefore \qquad\qquad\qquad L = X_L/2\pi f_r = 79.62/2\pi \times 100 = 0.127\ H$

(ii) $\qquad\qquad\qquad V_C = I_r X_C = 50 \times 79.62 = 3981\ V$

$\qquad\qquad Q\text{-factor} = V_C/V = 3981/200 = 19.9$

Example 16.32. *A circuit having a resistance of 4Ω, an inductance of 0.5H and a variable capacitance in series, is connected across a 100V, 50 Hz supply. Calculate (i) the capacitance to give resonance (ii) the voltage across inductance and capacitance and (iii) Q-factor of circuit.*

Solution.

(i) At series resonance, $\quad 2\pi f_r L = \dfrac{1}{2\pi f_r C}$

or $\quad C = \dfrac{1}{4\pi^2 f_r^2 L} = \dfrac{1}{4\pi^2 \times (50)^2 \times 0.5} = 20.26 \times 10^{-6}\ F$

(ii) Current at resonance, $\qquad I_r = \dfrac{V}{R} = \dfrac{100}{4} = 25$A

$\qquad$ P.D. across L, $V_L = I_r X_L = 25\ (2\pi \times 50 \times 0.5) = 3927\ V$

$\qquad$ P.D. across C, $V_C = I_r X_C = 25 \times \dfrac{1}{2\pi \times 50 \times 20.26 \times 10^{-6}} = 3927\ V$

(iii)   Q-factor of the circuit $= \dfrac{1}{R}\sqrt{\dfrac{L}{C}} = \dfrac{1}{4}\sqrt{\dfrac{0.5}{20.26\times10^{-6}}} = 39.27$

Example 16.33. *A series resonant circuit has a Q-factor of 100, an inductance of 10H and a capacitance of 0.1 μF. Calculate the bandwidth of the circuit.*

Solution.

Resonant frequency, $f_r = \dfrac{1}{2\pi\sqrt{LC}} = \dfrac{1}{2\pi\sqrt{10\times0.1\times10^{-6}}} = \dfrac{10^3}{2\pi}$ Hz

Now, $Q = \dfrac{f_r}{BW}$ ∴ Bandwidth, $BW = \dfrac{f_r}{Q} = \dfrac{10^3}{2\pi}\times\dfrac{1}{100} = $ **1.6 Hz**

TUTORIAL PROBLEMS

1. A resistance of 15Ω and an inductance of 4H and a capacitance 25μF are connected in series across 230V a.c. supply. Calculate (*i*) the frequency at which the current shall be maximum (*ii*) current at this frequency and (*iii*) p.d. across inductance.

   [(*i*) **15.9Hz** (*ii*) **15.33A** (*iii*) **6123V**]

2. A 1200Ω resistor, a 0.7 H coil and a 0.001μF capacitor are in series across a 120V source. Determine (*i*) the resonant frequency (*ii*) the voltage across the capacitor at resonance and (*iii*) Q-factor of the circuit at resonance.   [(*i*) **6015Hz** (*ii*) **2646V** (*iii*) **22**]

3. A capacitor C is in series with a 75 Ω resistor and a 12H coil across a 220V, 60Hz supply. Determine the value of *C* that resonates the circuit.   [**0.587μF**]

4. A series circuit consists of a 325Ω resistor, a 0.6 pF capacitor and a coil of 2.93H. Determine the bandwidth if the circuit resonates at 120×10^6 Hz.   [**17.643×10⁶ Hz**]

MULTIPLE-CHOICE QUESTIONS

1. The impedance of an *R-L* series circuit is given by....

   (*a*) $R + X_L$ (*b*) $R^2 + X_L^2$

   (*c*) $\sqrt{R^2 + X_L^2}$ (*d*) none of the above

2. In an *R-L* series circuit, line current.........

   (*a*) leads the applied voltage

   (*b*) lags behind the applied voltage

   (*c*) is in phase with applied voltage

   (*d*) none of the above

3. In an *R-L* series circuit, the phase difference φ between applied voltage and circuit current will increase if ....

   (*a*) X_L is increased

   (*b*) *R* is increased

   (*c*) X_L is decreased

   (*d*) supply frequency is decreased

4. The power consumed in an a.c. circuit is given by ....

   (*a*) $V_m I_m$ (*b*) $\dfrac{V_m I_m}{2}\cos\phi$

   (*c*) $IZ\cos\phi$ (*d*) $V_m I_m \cos\phi$

5. The power factor of an a.c. circuit is given by ....

   (*a*) X_L/R (*b*) Z/R

   (*c*) R/X_L (*d*) R/Z

6. In an *R-L* series circuit, $R = 10\Omega$ and $X_L = 10\Omega$. The phase angle between applied voltage and circuit current is ....

   (*a*) 45°   (*b*) 30°

   (*c*) 60°   (*d*) 36.8°

7. An inductive circuit draws a line current of 10A. If the reactive component of line current is 6 A, then power factor of the circuit is ....

(a) 0.6 lagging   (b) 0.8 lagging

(c) 0.5 lagging   (d) none of the above

8. An R-L series a.c. circuit has 15 V across resistor and 20 V across the inductor. The supply voltage is ....

(a) 35 V   (b) 5 V

(c) 25 V   (d) $\sqrt{175}$ V

9. The power consumed in the circuit shown in Fig. 16.28 is ....

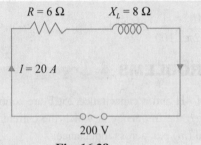

Fig. 16.28

(a) 4000 W   (b) 2400 W

(c) 2000 W   (d) 1200 W

10. The reactive power drawn by the circuit shown in Fig. 16.28 is ....

(a) 2400 VAR   (b) 4000 VAR

(c) 3200 VAR   (d) 2000 VAR

11. The active component of line current in Fig. 16.28 is ....

(a) 12 A   (b) 16 A

(c) 20 A   (d) 4A

12. The active and reactive powers of an inductive circuit are 60 W and 80 VAR respectively. The power factor of the circuit is.........

(a) 0.8 lagging   (b) 0.75 lagging

(c) 0.6 lagging   (d) 0.5 lagging

13. A 200 V, 50 Hz inductive circuit takes a current of 10A, lagging 30°. The inductive reactance of the circuit is ....

(a) 20 Ω   (b) 10 Ω

(c) 17.32 Ω   (d) 16 Ω

14. In Fig. 16.29, the voltmeter will read.........

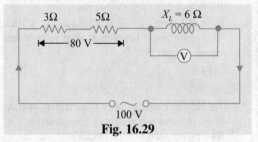

Fig. 16.29

(a) 20 V   (b) 40 V

(c) 120 V   (d) 60 V

15. The reactive component of line current in Fig. 16.29 is ....

(a) 8 A   (b) 6 A

(c) 10 A   (d) 12 A

16. A circuit when connected to 200 V mains takes a current of 20 A, leading the voltage by one-twelfth of time period. The circuit resistance is ....

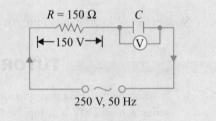

Fig. 16.30

(a) 10 Ω   (b) 8.66 Ω

(c) 20 Ω   (d) 17.32 Ω

17. The power factor of the circuit shown in Fig. 16.30 is ....

(a) 0.6 leading   (b) 0.8 leading

(c) 0.75 leading   (d) 0.5 leading

18. The impedance of an R-C series circuit is 100 Ω. If circuit current leads the applied voltage by 45°, then capacitive reactance is ....

(a) 70.7 Ω   (b) 141.42 Ω

(c) 100 Ω   (d) 50 Ω

19. An a.c series circuit has $R = 6\ \Omega$, $X_L = 20\ \Omega$ and $X_C = 12\ \Omega$. The circuit power factor will be ....

(a) 0.8 lagging   (b) 0.5 leading

(c) 0.6 lagging   (d) 0.6 leading

20. In Fig. 16.31, the supply voltage is...........

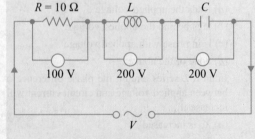

Fig. 16.31

(a) 500 V   (b) 100 V

(c) 200 V   (d) 400 V

Answers to Multiple-Choice Questions

1. (*c*)	**2.** (*b*)	**3.** (*a*)	**4.** (*b*)	**5.** (*d*)	**6.** (*a*)	**7.** (*b*)	**8.** (*c*)
9. (*b*)	**10.** (*c*)	**11.** (*a*)	**12.** (*c*)	**13.** (*b*)	**14.** (*d*)	**15.** (*b*)	**16.** (*b*)
17. (*a*)	**18.** (*a*)	**19.** (*c*)	**20.** (*b*)				

Hints to Selected Multiple-Choice Questions

4. Power Consumed $= \dfrac{V_m I_m}{2} \cos\phi = \dfrac{V_m}{\sqrt{2}} \times \dfrac{I_m}{\sqrt{2}} \cos\phi = VI \cos\phi$

where V and I are the r.m.s. values.

5. Power factor $= \cos\phi = R/Z$ (From impedance triangle)

6. $\tan\phi = X_L/R = 10/10 = 1$ $\therefore$ $\phi = 45°$

Remember, in an R-L series circuit, when $R = X_L$, phase angle will be 45°.

7. Active component $= \sqrt{10^2 - 6^2} = 8$

$$\text{Power factor} = \frac{\text{Active Component}}{\text{Total Current}} = \frac{I\cos\phi}{I} = \frac{8}{10} = 0.8$$

8. $\text{Supply voltage} = \sqrt{V_R^2 + V_L^2} = \sqrt{(15)^2 + (20)^2} = 25 \text{ V}$

9. Power consumed, $P = VI\cos\phi$

$$= VI\,(R/Z) = 200 \times 20\,(6/10) = 2400\text{W}$$

10. Reactive power $= VI\sin\phi$

$$= VI\,(X_L/Z) = 200 \times 20\,(8/10) = 3200 \text{ VAR}$$

11. Active component $= I\cos\phi = 20 \times 0.6 = 12\text{A}$

12. Apparent power $= \sqrt{(60)^2 + (80)^2} = 100 \text{ VA}$

$$\text{Power factor} = \frac{\text{Active power}}{\text{Apparent power}} = \frac{VI\cos\phi}{VI} = \frac{60}{100} = 0.6 \text{ lagging}$$

13. $Z = 200/10 = 20\ \Omega$; $X_L = Z\sin\phi = 20 \times \sin 30° = 10\Omega$

14. $V_L = \sqrt{V^2 - V_R^2} = \sqrt{100^2 - 80^2} = 60 \text{ V}$

15. Circuit current, $I = 8/(3 + 5) = 10 \text{ A}$

Reactive component $= I\sin\phi = I(X_L/Z) = 10(6/10) = 6\text{A}$

16. $Z = 200/20 = 10\Omega$; $\phi = 360°/12 = 30°$

$$R = Z\cos\phi = 10\cos 30° = 8.66\Omega$$

17. Power factor $= V_R/V = 150/250 = 0.6 \text{ leading}$

18. $X_C = Z\sin\phi = 100\sin 45° = 70.7\ \Omega$

19. Net reactance, $X = X_L - X_C = 20 - 12 = 8\ \Omega$ (inductive)

$$Z = \sqrt{R^2 + X^2} = \sqrt{6^2 + 8^2} = 10\Omega$$

$$\cos\phi = R/Z = 6/10 = 0.6 \text{ lagging}$$

20. Since voltage across L is equal to voltage across C, it is a case of series resonance.

$\therefore$ Supply voltage $=$ Voltage across $R = 100 \text{ V}$

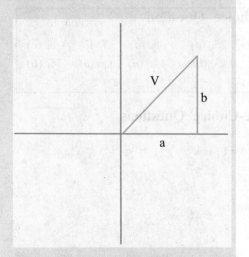

17

Phasor Algebra

INTRODUCTION

So far we used phasor diagrams to solve problems on a.c. circuits. A phasor diagram is a graphical representation of the phasors (*i.e.*, voltages and currents) of an a.c. circuit and may not yield quick results in case of complex circuits. Engineers have developed techniques to represent a phasor in an algebraic (*i.e.*, mathematical) form. Such a technique is known as *phasor algebra or complex algebra*. Phasor algebra has provided a relatively simple but powerful tool for obtaining quick solution of a.c. circuits. It simplifies the mathematical manipulation of phasors to a great extent. In this chapter, we shall discuss the various methods of representing phasors in a mathematical form and their applications to a.c. circuits.

17.1. NOTATION OF PHASORS ON RECTANGULAR CO-ORDINATE AXES

Consider a phasor **V** lying along *OX*-axis as shown in Fig. 17.1. If we multiply this phasor by –1, the phasor is reversed *i.e.*, it is rotated through 180° in the counterclockwise (*CCW*) direction. Let us see with what factor the phasor be multiplied so that it rotates through 90° in *CCW* direction. Suppose this factor is j. As shown in Fig. 17.1, multiplying the phasor by j^2 rotates the phasor through 180° in *CCW* direction. This means that multiplying the phasor by j^2 is the same as multiplying by -1. It follows, therefore, that

$$j^2 = -1$$

or

$$j = \sqrt{-1}$$

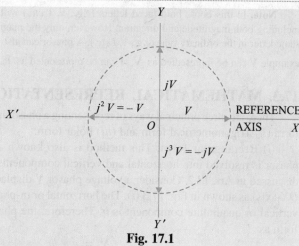

Fig. 17.1

We arrive at a very important conclusion that *when a phasor is multiplied by* $j(=\sqrt{-1})$, *the phasor is rotated through 90° in CCW direction.* Each successive multiplication by j rotates the phasor through an additional 90° in the *CCW* direction. It is easy to see that multiplying a phasor by

$$j = \sqrt{-1} \qquad ... \text{90° } CCW \text{ rotation from } OX\text{-axis}$$

$$j^2 = -1 \qquad ... \text{180° } CCW \text{ rotation from } OX\text{-axis}$$

$$j^3 = j^2 \cdot j = -j \qquad ... \text{270° } CCW \text{ rotation from } OX\text{-axis}$$

$$j^4 = j^2 j^2 = 1 \qquad ... \text{360° } CCW \text{ rotation from } OX\text{-axis}$$

Fig. 17.1 shows the effect of multiplying a phasor by j.

17.2. SIGNIFICANCE OF OPERATOR j

Just as the symbol + indicates the operation of adding two numbers, similarly j indicates an operation of rotating the phasor through 90° in *CCW* direction. The operator j does not change the magnitude of the phasor. Consider a phasor **V** displaced $\theta°$ counterclockwise from *OX*-axis as shown in Fig. 17.2. This phasor can be resolved into two rectangular components *viz.* the horizontal component 'a' along X-axis and the vertical component 'b' along Y-axis. It can be seen that vertical component is displaced 90° *CCW* from *OX*-axis. Therefore, mathematically, we can express this component as jb, meaning that component b is displaced 90° *CCW* from component a (*i.e.*, *OX*-axis).

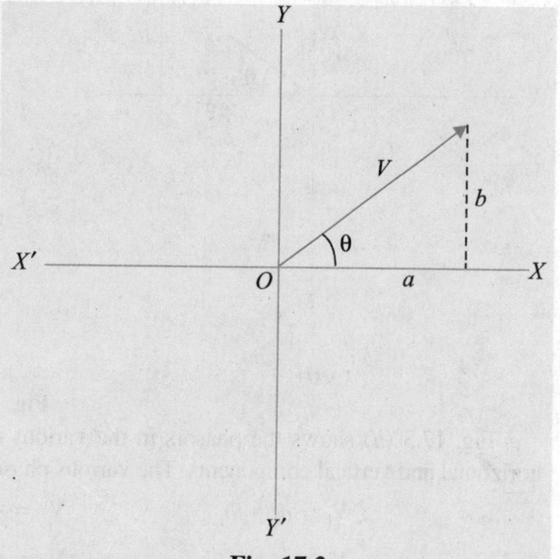

$$\therefore \qquad \mathbf{V} = a + jb$$

Fig. 17.2

Magnitude of **V**, $\qquad V = \sqrt{a^2 + b^2}$

Its angle with *OX*-axis, $\quad \theta = \tan^{-1}(b/a)$

The reader may note that $a + jb$ is the mathematical form of the phasor **V**.

(*i*) The quantity $a + jb$ is called a complex number or complex quantity.

(*ii*) The horizontal component (*i.e.*, a) is called the *in-phase* (or active) component while the vertical component is called *quadrature* (or reactive) component.

Note. In this book, bold-faced letters (*e.g.*, **V, I** *etc.*) will be used to represent the phasor completely, including both magnitude and direction. However, only the magnitude of the phasor will be represented by the same letter in the ordinary type (*e.g.*, *V, I etc.*). A phasor can also be represented by a dot under the symbol. For example **V** can be represented as $\underset{.}{V}$, **I** can be represented as $\underset{.}{I}$, etc.

17.3. MATHEMATICAL REPRESENTATION OF PHASORS

There are three principal ways of representing a phasor in the mathematical form *viz.* (*i*) Rectangular form (*ii*) Trigonometrical form and (*iii*) Polar form.

(*i*) **Rectangular form.** This method is also known as *symbolic notation*. In this method, the phasor is resolved into horizontal and vertical components and is expressed in the complex form as discussed in Art. 17.2. Consider a voltage phasor **V** displaced $\theta°$ *CCW* from the reference axis (*i.e.*, *OX*-axis) as shown in Fig. 17.3 (*i*). The horizontal or in-phase component of this phasor is *a* while the vertical or quadrature component is *b*. Therefore, the phasor can be represented in the rectangular form as:

$$\mathbf{V} = a + jb$$

Magnitude of phasor,

$$V = \sqrt{a^2 + b^2}$$

Its angle *w.r.t. OX*-axis,

$$\theta = \tan^{-1}(b/a)$$

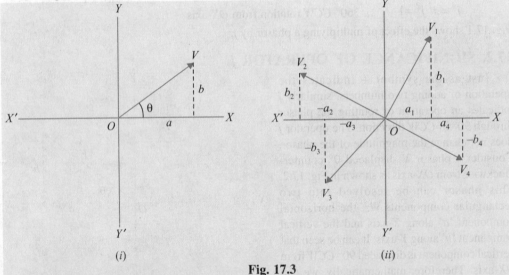

Fig. 17.3

Fig. 17.3 (*ii*) shows the phasors in the various quadrants. The phasors have been resolved into horizontal and vertical components. The various phasors can be represented in the rectangular form as:

$$\mathbf{V}_1 = a_1 + jb_1 \qquad\qquad \mathbf{V}_2 = -a_2 + jb_2$$

$$\mathbf{V}_3 = -a_3 - jb_3 \qquad\qquad \mathbf{V}_4 = a_4 - jb_4$$

The magnitude and phase angles of these phasors can be found out as explained above. Remember phase angles are to be measured from the reference axis *i.e.*, *OX*-axis. If the angle is measured *CCW* from this reference axis, it is assigned a +ve sign. If the angle is measured clockwise from the reference axis, it is assigned a –ve sign.

(*ii*) **Trigonometrical form.** It is similar to the rectangular form except that in-phase and quadrature components of the phasor are expressed in the trigonometrical form. Thus referring to Fig. 17.3 (*i*) above, $a = V\cos\theta$ and $b = V\sin\theta$ where *V* is the magnitude of the phasor **V**. Hence phasor **V** can be expressed in the trigonometrical form as:

$$\mathbf{V} = V(\cos\theta + j\sin\theta)$$

It may be noted that in this form, we express the phasor in terms of its magnitude and phase angle θ.

(iii) **Polar form.** It is a usual practice to write the trigonometrical form $V = V(\cos\theta + j\sin\theta)$ in what is called polar form as:

$$* \mathbf{V} = V \angle \theta$$

where V is the magnitude of the phasor and θ is its angle measured *CCW* from the reference axis *i.e.*, *OX*-axis. A negative angle in the polar form indicates clockwise measurement of the angle from the reference axis. Hence, polar form can be written in general as:

$$\mathbf{V} = V \angle \pm \theta$$

17.4. CONVERSION FROM ONE FORM TO THE OTHER

The reader may see that the above three mathematical forms of representing a phasor convey the same information *i.e.*, magnitude of the phasor and its phase angle. Therefore, it is possible to convert one form to the other. Consider a phasor **V** having in-phase and quadrature components as 3 and 4 respectively as shown in Fig. 17.4 *(i)*.

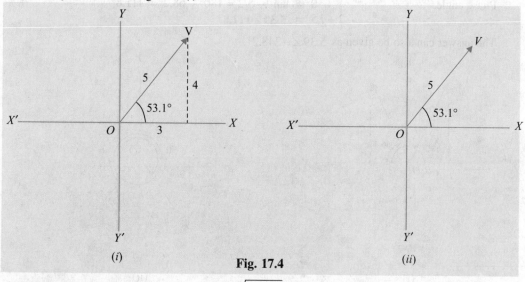

(i)   **Fig. 17.4**   (ii)

Magnitude of the phasor,	$V = \sqrt{3^2 + 4^2} = 5$
Its angle w.r.t. *OX*-axis,	$\theta = \tan^{-1} 4/3 = 53.1°$
In rectangular form,	$\mathbf{V} = 3 + j4$
In trigonometrical form,	$\mathbf{V} = 5(\cos 53.1° + j\sin 53.1°)$
In polar form,	$\mathbf{V} = 5\angle 53.1°$ [See Fig. 17.4 *(ii)*]

This numerical illustrates how one form can be converted to the other.

Example 17.1. *Express the polar form of voltage* **V** $= 50 \angle 36.87°$ *in trigonometrical and rectangular forms.*

Solution.

Trigonometrical form

$$\mathbf{V} = V(\cos\theta + j\sin\theta)$$

$$= 50(\cos 36.87° + j\sin 36.87°) \text{ Ans.}$$

Rectangular form

In-phase component $= V\cos\theta = 50 \times \cos 36.87° = 40$

---

* meaning **V** equals V at angle θ (in *CCW* direction). There is mathematical explanation for this form. It is a shorthand form of trigonometrical form.

Quadrature component $= V \sin \theta = 50 \times \sin 36.87° = 30$

∴ $\qquad\qquad\qquad\qquad \mathbf{V} = 40 + j30$ **Ans.**

Example 17.2. *Express the following in polar form*

(i) $3 + j7$ $\qquad\qquad$ (ii) $-2 + j5$ $\qquad\qquad$ (iii) $-50 - j75$ $\qquad$ and $\qquad$ (iv) $6 - j8$

Solution.

(i) Magnitude $\qquad\qquad\qquad = \sqrt{3^2 + 7^2} = 7.62$

Phase angle, $\qquad\qquad\qquad \theta = \tan^{-1}(7/3) = 66.8°$

∴ $\qquad\qquad\qquad\qquad 3 + j7 = \mathbf{7.62 \angle 66.8°}$

Note that $3 + j\,7$ lies in the first quadrant. As seen in Fig. 17.5 (i), θ measured in *CCW* direction from *OX*-axis is 66.8° and is, therefore, positive. If θ is measured in clockwise direction from *OX*-axis, its value is $= 360° - 66.8° = 293.2°$ and this angle is negative. Hence the above answer can also be given as $7.62 \angle -293.2°$.

(ii) Magnitude $\qquad\qquad\qquad = \sqrt{(-2)^2 + (5)^2} = 5.39$

Phase angle, $\qquad\qquad\qquad \theta = \tan^{-1} -5/2 = 180° - 68.2° = 111.8°$

∴ $\qquad\qquad\qquad\qquad -2 + j\,5 = \mathbf{5.39 \angle 111.8°}$

The answer can also be given as $5.39 \angle -248.2°$.

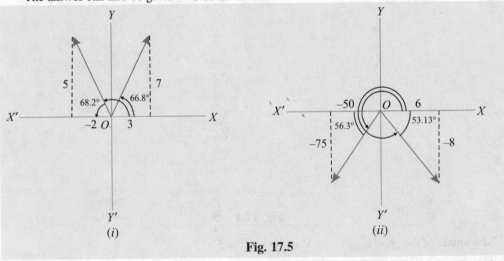

Fig. 17.5

(iii) Magnitude $\qquad\qquad\qquad = \sqrt{(-50)^2 + (-75)^2} = 90.1$

Phase angle, $\qquad\qquad\qquad \theta = \tan^{-1} -75/-50 = 180° + 56.3° = 236.3°$

∴ $\qquad\qquad\qquad\qquad -50 - j\,75 = \mathbf{90.1 \angle 236.3°}$

The answer can also be given as $90.1 \angle -123.7°$.

(iv) Magnitude $\qquad\qquad\qquad = \sqrt{6^2 + (-8)^2} = 10$

Phase angle, $\qquad\qquad\qquad \theta = \tan^{-1} -8/6 = 360° - 53.13° = 306.87°$

∴ $\qquad\qquad\qquad\qquad 6 - j\,8 = \mathbf{10 \angle 306.87°}$

The answer can also be given as $\mathbf{10 \angle -53.13°}$.

17.5. ADDITION AND SUBTRACTION OF PHASORS

The rectangular form is best suited for addition or subtraction of phasors. If the phasors are given in polar form, they should be first converted to rectangular form and then addition or subtraction be carried out.

(*i*) **Addition.** For the addition of phasors in the rectangular form, the in-phase components are added together and the quadrature components are added together. Consider two voltage phasors represented as:

$$\mathbf{V_1} = a_1 + jb_1 \; ; \quad \mathbf{V_2} = a_2 + jb_2$$

Then resultant,
$$\mathbf{V} = \mathbf{V_1} + \mathbf{V_2} = (a_1 + jb_1) + (a_2 + jb_2)$$
$$= (a_1 + a_2) + j(b_1 + b_2)$$

Magnitude of resultant,
$$V = \sqrt{(a_1 + a_2)^2 + (b_1 + b_2)^2}$$

Its angle from *OX*-axis,
$$\theta = \tan^{-1} \frac{(b_1 + b_2)}{a_1 + a_2}$$

(*ii*) **Subtraction.** Like addition, the subtraction of phasors is done by using ordinary rules of phasor algebra.

$$\mathbf{V} = \mathbf{V_1} - \mathbf{V_2} = (a_1 + jb_1) - (a_2 + jb_2)$$
$$= (a_1 - a_2) + j(b_1 - b_2)$$

∴
$$V = \sqrt{(a_1 - a_2)^2 + (b_1 - b_2)^2}$$

Phase angle,
$$\theta = \tan^{-1} \left(\frac{b_1 - b_2}{a_1 - a_2} \right)$$

Example 17.3. *Two current phasors are given in the rectangular form as* $\mathbf{I_1} = 15 + j10$ *and* $\mathbf{I_2} = 12 + j6$. *Perform the operation (i)* $\mathbf{I_1} + \mathbf{I_2}$ *and (ii)* $\mathbf{I_1} - \mathbf{I_2}$.

Solution.

(*i*) Resultant current, $\mathbf{I} = \mathbf{I_1} + \mathbf{I_2} = (15 + j10) + (12 + j6) = \mathbf{27 + j16}$

The magnitude of resultant current is $= \sqrt{27^2 + 16^2} = 31.38$ and it makes an angle $\theta = \tan^{-1} 16/27 = 30.65°$ with *OX*-axis as shown in Fig. 17.6 (*i*).

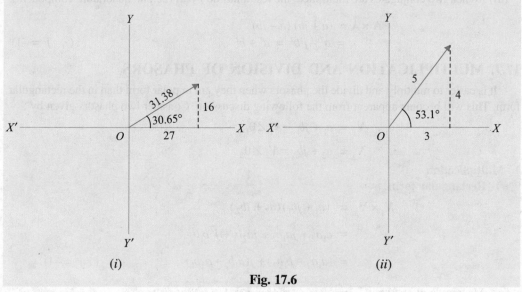

Fig. 17.6

(*ii*) Resultant current, $\mathbf{I} = \mathbf{I_1} - \mathbf{I_2} = (15 + j\,10) - (12 + j\,6) = \mathbf{3 + j4}$

The magnitude of resultant is $= \sqrt{3^2 + 4^2} = 5$ and it makes an angle $\theta = \tan^{-1} 4/3 = 53.1°$ with OX-axis as shown in Fig. 17.6 (*ii*).

Example 17.4. *Determine the resultant voltage of two sinusoidal generators in series whose voltages are* $V_1 = 25 \angle 15°V$ *and* $V_2 = 15 \angle 60°V$.

Solution. We shall first convert polar form to rectangular form and then carry out the addition.

$$V_1 = 25(\cos 15° + j \sin 15°) = (24.15 + j 6.47) \text{ V}$$
$$V_2 = 15 (\cos 60° + j \sin 60°) = (7.5 + j 12.99) \text{V}$$

$\therefore \qquad V = V_1 + V_2 = (24.15 + j 6.47)V + (7.5 + j 12.99)V = (31.65 + j 19.46)V$

$\therefore \qquad V = \sqrt{(31.65)^2 + (19.46)^2} = 37.15$

Phase angle, $\qquad \theta = \tan^{-1} (19.46/31.65) = 31.6°$

$\therefore \qquad V = 37.15 \angle 31.6° V$

17.6. CONJUGATE OF A COMPLEX NUMBER

Two complex numbers (or phasors) are said to be conjugate if they differ only in the algebraic sign of their quadrature components. Thus, the conjugate of $2 + j 3$ is $2 - j 3$. The conjugate of $-4 + j3$ is $- 4 - j3$. In the polar form, conjugate of $5 \angle 30°$ is $5 \angle -30°$ and conjugate of $10 \angle -40°$ is $10 \angle 40°$. It is a usual practice to use an asterik (*)to indicate the conjugate.

Consider a complex number $A = a + jb = A \angle \theta$. Then its conjugate will be $A^* = a - jb = A \angle -\theta$. The conjugate numbers have the following properties:

(*i*) The sum of two conjugate numbers results in in-phase component only (*i.e.*, no *j* part).

$$A + \overset{*}{A} = (a + jb) + (a - jb) = 2a$$

(*ii*) The difference of two conjugate numbers results in quadrature component only.

$$A - \overset{*}{A} = (a + jb) - (a - jb) = j 2b$$

(*iii*) When two conjugates are multiplied, the result has no *j*-part (*i.e.*, no quadrature component).

$$A \times \overset{*}{A} = (a + jb) (a - jb)$$
$$= a^2 - j^2 b^2 = a^2 + b^2 \qquad\qquad (\because j^2 = -1)$$

17.7. MULTIPLICATION AND DIVISION OF PHASORS

It is easier to multiply and divide the phasors when they are in polar form than in the rectangular form. This will become apparent from the following discussion. Consider two phasors given by ;

$$V_1 = a_1 + jb_1 = V_1 \angle \theta_1$$
$$V_2 = a_2 + jb_2 = V_2 \angle \theta_2$$

1. Multiplication
(*i*) **Rectangular form**

$$V_1 \times V_2 = (a_1 + jb_1)(a_2 + jb_2)$$
$$= a_1 a_2 + ja_1 b_2 + ja_2 b_1 + j^2 b_1 b_2$$
$$= (a_1 a_2 - b_1 b_2) + j(a_1 b_2 + a_2 b_1) \qquad\qquad (\because j^2 = -1)$$

Magnitude of resultant $= \sqrt{(a_1 a_2 - b_1 b_2)^2 + (a_1 b_2 + a_2 b_1)^2}$

Its angle *w.r.t.* *OX*-axis, $\theta = \tan^{-1}\left(\dfrac{a_1b_2 + a_2b_1}{a_1a_2 - b_1b_2}\right)$

(*ii*) **Polar form.** To multiply the phasors that are in polar form, multiply their magnitudes and add the angles (algebraically).

$$\mathbf{V}_1 \times \mathbf{V}_2 = V_1 \angle\theta_1 \times V_2 \angle\theta_2 = V_1V_2 \angle\theta_1 + \theta_2$$

The reader may see that multiplication of phasors becomes easier when they are expressed in polar form.

2. Division

(*i*) **Rectangular form**

$$\frac{\mathbf{V}_1}{\mathbf{V}_2} = \frac{a_1 + jb_1}{a_2 + jb_2}$$

$$= \frac{a_1 + jb_1}{a_2 + jb_2} \times \frac{a_2 - jb_2}{a_2 - jb_2} \qquad \left[\begin{array}{l}\text{Rationalising}\\\text{the denominator}\end{array}\right]$$

$$= \frac{(a_1a_2 + b_1b_2) + j(b_1a_2 - a_1b_2)}{a_2^2 + b_2^2}$$

$$= \frac{a_1a_2 + b_1b_2}{a_2^2 + b_2^2} + j\frac{(b_1a_2 - a_1b_2)}{a_2^2 + b_2^2}$$

(*ii*) **Polar form.** To divide the phasors that are in polar form, divide the magnitude of phasors and subtract the denominator angle from the numerator angle.

$$\therefore \qquad \frac{\mathbf{V}_1}{\mathbf{V}_2} = \frac{V_1 \angle\theta_1}{V_2 \angle\theta_2} = \frac{V_1}{V_2} \angle\theta_1 - \theta_2$$

Practically without exception, division is the easiest in the polar form.

Example 17.5. *Two phasors are given in the following form:*
$$\mathbf{V}_1 = 4 + j3; \qquad\qquad \mathbf{V}_2 = 5 + j6$$
Evaluate $\mathbf{V}_1 \times \mathbf{V}_2$ *and* $\mathbf{V}_1/\mathbf{V}_2$ *in* (*i*) *rectangular form* (*ii*) *polar form.*

Solution.

(*i*) **Rectangular form**

$$\mathbf{V}_1 \times \mathbf{V}_2 = (4 + j3)(5 + j6) = 20 + j24 + j15 + j^2 18 = 2 + j39$$

$$\frac{\mathbf{V}_1}{\mathbf{V}_2} = \frac{4 + j3}{5 + j6} = \frac{4 + j3}{5 + j6} \times \frac{5 - j6}{5 - j6}$$

$$= \frac{20 - j24 + j15 - j^2 18}{5^2 - j^2 6^2} = \frac{38 - j9}{61}$$

$$= \frac{38}{61} - j\frac{9}{61} = 0.623 - j0.147$$

(*ii*) **Polar form.** Convert the phasors to polar form.

$$\mathbf{V}_1 = 4 + j3 = 5\angle 36.87°$$

$$\mathbf{V}_2 = 5 + j6 = 7.81\angle 50.19°$$

$$\therefore \qquad \mathbf{V}_1 \times \mathbf{V}_2 = 5\angle 36.87° \times 7.81\angle 50.19°$$

$$= 5 \times 7.81 \angle 36.87° + 50.19° = \mathbf{39.05 \angle 87.06°}$$

$$\frac{\mathbf{V_1}}{\mathbf{V_2}} = \frac{5\angle 36.87°}{7.81\angle 50.19°} = \frac{5}{7.81}\angle 36.87° - 50.19° = 0.64\angle -13.32°$$

The negative angle means that the phasor is below *OX*-axis.

Example 17.6. *The following three phasors are given*:

$$\mathbf{A} = 5 + j5; \quad \mathbf{B} = 50\angle 40°; \quad \mathbf{C} = 4 + j0$$

Perform the following indicated operations:

(*i*) $\dfrac{\mathbf{AB}}{\mathbf{C}}$ (*ii*) $\dfrac{\mathbf{BC}}{\mathbf{A}}$

Solution. Expressing the three phasors in polar form, we have, $\mathbf{A} = 5 + j5 = 7.07\angle 45°$; $\mathbf{B} = 50\angle 40°$; $\mathbf{C} = 4 + j0 = 4\angle 0°$

(*i*) $\dfrac{\mathbf{AB}}{\mathbf{C}} = \dfrac{7.07\angle 45°\times 50\angle 40°}{4\angle 0°} = 88.37\angle 85°$

(*ii*) $\dfrac{\mathbf{BC}}{\mathbf{A}} = \dfrac{50\angle 40°\times 4\angle 0°}{7.07\angle 45°} = 28.29\angle -5°$

Example 17.7. *The applied voltage in a series circuit is given by* $\mathbf{V} = 200\angle 0°$ *volts. The impedance offered by the circuit is* $\mathbf{Z} = 83.3\angle 40°\,\Omega$. *Find the magnitude of current. Is the circuit inductive or capacitive ?*

Solution.

$$\mathbf{I} = \frac{\mathbf{V}}{\mathbf{Z}} = \frac{200\angle 0°}{83.3\angle 40°} = 2.4\angle -40°\,\mathrm{A}$$

The voltage phasor lies along *OX*-axis. The negative angle of circuit current means that current phasor is below *OX*-axis. Hence the circuit is inductive.

17.8. POWERS AND ROOTS OF PHASORS

Powers and roots of complex numbers can be found very conveniently in polar form. If the complex number is not in polar form, it is always advisable to convert the number to this form and then carry out these algebraic operations.

(*i*) **Powers.** Suppose it is required to find the cube of the phasor $2\angle 10°$. For this purpose, the phasor has to be multiplied by itself three times.

∴ $(2\angle 10°)^3 = 2\times 2\times 2 \angle 10° + 10° + 10° = 8\angle 30°$

In general, $\mathbf{A}^n = A^n\angle n\theta$

(*ii*) **Roots.** Let us proceed backward with the above given example. Suppose we are to find the cube root of $8\angle 30°$. It is clear that :

$$\sqrt[3]{8\angle 30°} = 2\angle 10°$$

In general, $\sqrt[n]{\mathbf{A}} = \sqrt[n]{A}\angle \dfrac{\theta}{n}$

Thus the square root of $64\angle 40°$ is $= \sqrt[2]{64}\angle \dfrac{40°}{2} = 8\angle 20°$

17.9. PHASOR ALGEBRA APPLIED TO R-L SERIES CIRCUIT

Fig. 17.7 shows an *R-L* series circuit and its phasor diagram. Since the circuit current is taken as the reference phasor (*i.e.*, along *OX*-axis), we have,

$$\mathbf{I} = I + j0$$

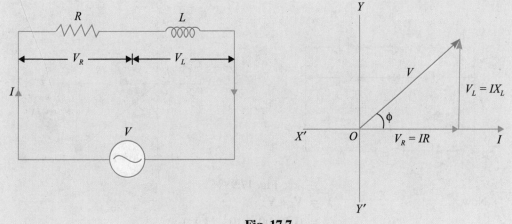

Fig. 17.7

Now,
$$\mathbf{V} = \mathbf{V}_R + \mathbf{V}_L = (IR + j0) + (0 + jIX_L)$$
$$= \mathbf{I}(R + jX_L) = \mathbf{IZ}$$

∴
$$\mathbf{Z} = R + jX_L$$

Magnitude of impedance, $Z = \sqrt{R^2 + X_L^2}$

Phase angle, $\phi = \tan^{-1}(X_L/R)$

It is clear that current lags the voltage by $\phi°$.

Polar form. In the polar form, we have,

$$\mathbf{I} = I + j0 = I\angle 0°$$

$$\mathbf{Z} = R + jX_L = Z\angle\phi°$$

∴
$$\mathbf{V} = \mathbf{IZ} = I\angle 0° \times Z\angle\phi° = IZ\angle\phi°$$

This shows that applied voltage leads the current by $\phi°$. This is the same thing as the current lags the voltage by $\phi°$.

Voltage phasor as reference. In practice, we are given the applied voltage and circuit impedance and it is desired to find the circuit current. It is then profitable to take voltage as the reference phasor (*i.e.*, along *OX*-axis).

$$\mathbf{V} = V + j0 = V\angle 0°$$

$$\mathbf{Z} = R + jX_L = Z\angle\phi°$$

∴
$$\mathbf{I} = \frac{\mathbf{V}}{\mathbf{Z}}$$

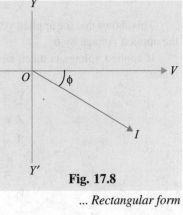

Fig. 17.8

$$= \frac{V + j0}{R + jX_L} \qquad ... \textit{Rectangular form}$$

$$= \frac{V}{Z}\angle -\phi° \qquad ...\textit{Polar form}$$

Fig. 17.8 shows the phasor diagram of the circuit with voltage as the reference phasor.

17.10. R-C SERIES CIRCUIT

Fig. 17.9 shows R-C series circuit and its phasor diagram. Since circuit current is taken as the reference phasor (*i.e.* along *OX*-axis), we have,

$$\mathbf{I} = I + j0$$

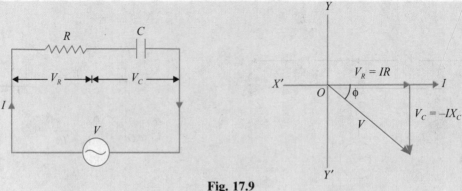

Fig. 17.9

Now, $$\mathbf{V} = \mathbf{V}_R + \mathbf{V}_C$$
$$= (\mathbf{I}\,R + j0) + (0 - j\,\mathbf{I}\,X_C)$$
or $$\mathbf{V} = \mathbf{I}(R - jX_C)$$

But $\mathbf{V} = \mathbf{I}\mathbf{Z}$ where $\mathbf{Z}$ is the impedance of the circuit.

∴ $$\mathbf{Z} = R - jX_C$$

Its magnitude, $$Z = \sqrt{R^2 + X_C^2}\;;\; R = Z\cos\phi \text{ and } X_C = Z\sin\phi$$

Phase angle, $$\phi = \tan^{-1}(-X_C / R)$$

It is clear that current leads the applied voltage by $\phi°$.

Polar form. In the polar form, we have,

$$\mathbf{I} = I + j0 = I\angle 0°$$

$$\mathbf{Z} = R - jX_C = Z\angle-\phi°$$

∴ $$\mathbf{V} = \mathbf{I}\mathbf{Z} = I\angle 0° \times Z\angle-\phi° = IZ\angle-\phi°$$

This shows that the applied voltage lags the current by $\phi°$. This is the same thing as current leads the applied voltage by $\phi°$.

If applied voltage is taken as the reference phasor, then circuit calculations are carried out as under :

$$\mathbf{V} = V + j0 = V\angle 0°$$

$$\mathbf{Z} = R - jX_C = Z\angle-\phi°$$

∴ $$\mathbf{I} = \mathbf{V}/\mathbf{Z}$$

$$= \frac{V + j0}{R - jX_C} \quad \text{... Rectangular form}$$

$$= \frac{V\angle 0°}{Z\angle-\phi°}$$

Fig. 17.10

$$= \frac{V}{Z}\angle\phi° \quad \text{... polar form}$$

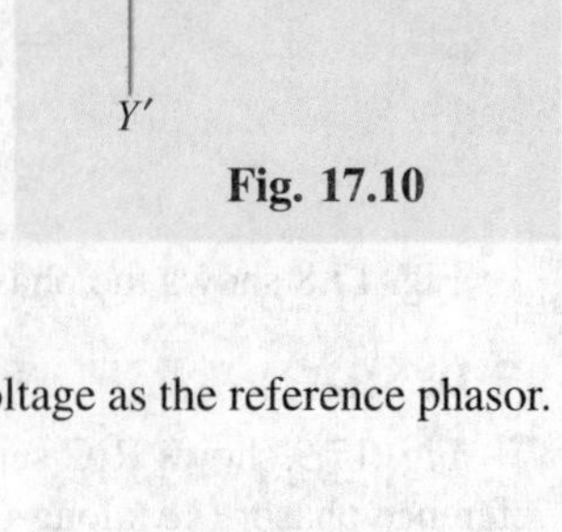

Fig. 17.10 shows the phasor diagram of the circuit with applied voltage as the reference phasor.

17.11. R-L-C SERIES CIRCUIT

Fig. 17.11 shows R-L-C series circuit and its phasor diagram. Since the circuit current is taken as the reference phasor (*i.e.* along *OX*-axis), we have,

$$\mathbf{I} = I + j0$$

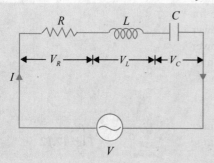 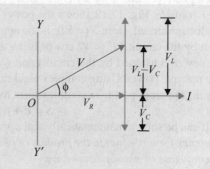

Fig. 17.11

Now,

$$\mathbf{V} = \mathbf{V}_R + j(\mathbf{V}_L - \mathbf{V}_C)$$
$$= IR + j(IX_L - IX_C)$$
$$= I[R + j(X_L - X_C)]$$
$$= \mathbf{IZ}$$

∴

$$\mathbf{Z} = R + j(X_L - X_C)$$

Magnitude of impedance,

$$Z = \sqrt{R^2 + (X_L - X_C)^2}$$

Phase angle,

$$\phi = \tan^{-1}\left(\frac{X_L - X_C}{R}\right)$$

If $X_L > X_C$, then ϕ is positive *i.e.* current lags the voltage. If $X_C > X_L$, then ϕ is negative *i.e.* current leads the voltage.

Polar form. In the polar form, we have,

$$\mathbf{I} = I + j0 = I\angle 0°$$

$$\mathbf{Z} = R + j(X_L - X_C) = Z\angle \pm\phi°$$

∴

$$\mathbf{V} = \mathbf{IZ} = I\angle 0° \times Z\angle \pm\phi° = IZ\angle \pm\phi°$$

The applied voltage will lead or lag the circuit current depending upon whether X_L or X_C is greater.

If applied voltage is taken as the reference phasor, the circuit calculations are carried out as under :

$$\mathbf{V} = V + j0 = V\angle 0°$$

$$\mathbf{Z} = R + j(X_L - X_C) = Z\angle \pm\phi°$$

∴

$$\mathbf{I} = \mathbf{V}/\mathbf{Z}$$

$$= \frac{V + j0}{R + j(X_L - X_C)} \qquad \text{... } Rectangular\ form$$

$$= \frac{V}{Z}\angle \mp\phi° \qquad \text{... } Polar\ form$$

17.12. POWER DETERMINATION USING COMPLEX NOTATION

We have seen in Art. 5 (Chapter 16) that the apparent power, active power and reactive power drawn by a circuit can be represented by a right angled triangle called *power triangle*. Fig. 17.12 shows the power triangle for an inductive circuit. Here S (= VI) is the apparent power drawn by the circuit, P (= $VI \cos \phi$) is the active power (*i.e.*, power consumed by the circuit) and Q (= $VI \sin \phi$) is the reactive power. Using complex algebra, we can express the apparent power in complex form as:

$$S = P + jQ$$

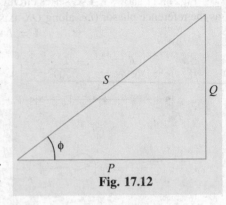

Fig. 17.12

It can be shown mathematically that *apparent power in complex form is equal to the product of phasor voltage and conjugate of phasor current i.e.*

$$S = \text{Phasor voltage} \times \text{Conjugate of phasor current}$$

or
$$P + jQ = \mathbf{V} \times \overset{*}{\mathbf{I}}$$

where **V** is phasor voltage in complex form and $\overset{*}{\mathbf{I}}$ is the conjugate of phasor current **I** in complex form.

Active power, P = In-phase component
Reactive power, Q = Quadrature component

Proof. Fig. 17.13 shows an inductive circuit and its phasor diagram. It is clear from the phasor diagram that phase angle $\phi° = \alpha° - \beta°$.

∴ Active power, $P = VI \cos (\alpha° - \beta°)$
Reactive power, $Q = VI \sin (\alpha° - \beta°)$
Apparent power, $S = VI$
Now $S = P + jQ$

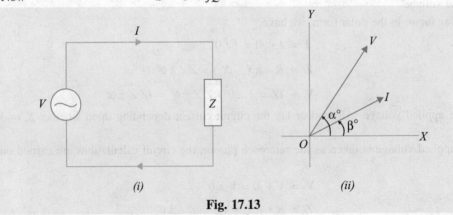

(i)   *(ii)*

Fig. 17.13

Using phasor algebra, we shall prove that product of phasor voltage and conjugate of phasor current is equal to the apparent power in complex form. Referring to the phasor diagram in Fig. 17.13 *(ii)*,

$$\mathbf{V} = V \angle \alpha°; \qquad \mathbf{I} = I \angle \beta°$$

Conjugate of **I** is $\overset{*}{\mathbf{I}} = I \angle -\beta°$

∴ $\mathbf{V} \times \overset{*}{\mathbf{I}} = V \angle \alpha° \times I \angle -\beta°$

$$= VI \angle \alpha° - \beta°$$
$$= VI \cos(\alpha° - \beta°) + jVI \sin(\alpha° - \beta°)$$
$$= P + jQ \qquad Q.E.D.$$

This shows that in-phase component of $\mathbf{V} \times \mathbf{I}^*$ (*i.e.* product of phasor voltage and conjugate of phasor current) gives the active power ($VI \cos \phi$) while quadrature component gives the reactive power ($VI \sin \phi$). Table below indicates the signs that occur for reactive power.

Circuit	Phasors	Reactive Power Q	Complex power S
Inductive	**I** lags **V**	Positive	$P + jQ$
Capacitive	**I** leads **V**	Negative	$P - jQ$

17.13. IMPORTANT POINTS

While solving problems on a.c. circuits by phasor algebra, the following points may be kept in mind :

(*i*) If division and multiplication are involved, use the polar form. This will yield quick results.

(*ii*) The phase angle can be determined from the phasor diagram or complex form (rectangular or polar) of impedance.

(*iii*) The *OX*-axis should be taken as the reference axis. Angles measured in CCW direction from the reference should be assigned positive sign and those measured in CW direction the negative sign.

(*iv*) The impedance phase angle is always the conjugate of current phase angle. If impedance is $45 \angle -30°\Omega$, then current phase angle is $30°$.

Example 17.8. *The current in a circuit is given by (4.5 + j12) A when the applied voltage is (100 + j150) V. Determine (i) the magnitude of impedance and (ii) phase angle.*

Solution.

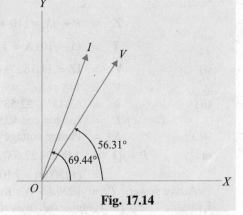

$$\mathbf{V} = (100 + j150)V = 180.28 \angle 56.31° \text{ V}$$

$$\mathbf{I} = (4.5 + j12)A = 12.82 \angle 69.44° \text{ A}$$

(*i*) $\therefore \mathbf{Z} = \mathbf{V/I}$

$$= \frac{180.28 \angle 56.31°}{12.82 \angle 69.44°}$$

$$= 14.06 \angle -13.13°$$

$\therefore$ **Z = 14.06 Ω**

Fig. 17.14

(*ii*) Phase angle, $\phi = \mathbf{13.13°} lead$

Fig. 17.14 shows the phasor diagram. It is clear that current is leading the voltage by 13.13°. Therefore, the circuit is capacitive.

Note. The problem can also be solved using rectangular form. Since division is involved, it is easier to work out in polar form.

Example 17.9. *A resistance and an inductance are connected in series across a voltage of v = 566 sin 314t. The current expression is found to be i = 4 sin (314t − π/4). Find the value of resistance, inductance and power factor. What is the power drawn by the circuit?*

Solution. From the equations of voltage and current, it is clear that:
$$\phi = 45° \text{ lag}; \qquad V_m = 566 \text{ volts}; \qquad I_m = 4A; \qquad \omega = 314 \text{ rad s}^{-1}$$

∴   Power factor $= \cos \phi = \cos 45° = \mathbf{0.707}$ *lag*

Impedance, $Z = V_m/I_m = 566/4 = 141.5 \ \Omega$

Resistance, $R = Z \cos \phi = 141.5 \times 0.707 = \mathbf{100} \ \Omega$

Reactance, $X_L = Z \sin \phi = 141.5 \times 0.707 = 100 \ \Omega$

Inductance, $L = X_L/\omega = 100/314 = \mathbf{0.318 \ H}$

Power, $P = I^2 R = (4/\sqrt{2})^2 \times 100 = \mathbf{800 \ W}$

Example 17.10. *A current of 120 – j 50 flows through a circuit when the applied voltage is 8 + j2. Determine (i) impedance (ii) power factor (iii) power consumed and reactive power.*

Solution. $\mathbf{V} = (8 + j2)\text{V} = 8.25 \angle 14° \ \text{V}$

$\mathbf{I} = (120 - j50)\text{A} = 130 \angle -22.62° \ \text{A}$

(*i*) $\mathbf{Z} = \dfrac{\mathbf{V}}{\mathbf{I}} = \dfrac{8.25 \angle 14°}{130 \angle -22.62°} = 0.0635 \angle 36.62° \ \Omega$

∴ $Z = \mathbf{0.0635 \ \Omega}$

(*ii*) $\phi = 36.62° \ \text{lag}$

∴ $p.f. = \cos \phi = \cos 36.62° = \mathbf{0.803} \ lag$

(*iii*)   As shown in Art. 17.12,

Complex *VA*, $S = $ Phasor voltage × Conjugate of phasor current

or $P + jQ = 8.25 \angle 14° \times 130 \angle 22.62° = 1072.5 \angle 36.62° \ \text{VA}$

$= 1072.5 (\cos 36.62° + j \sin 36.62°) = (860.8 + j639.75) \ \text{VA}$

∴ Power consumed, $P = \mathbf{860.8 \ W}$;   Reactive power, $Q = \mathbf{639.75 \ VAR}$

Example 17.11. *In an R-L series circuit, R = 10Ω and X_L = 8.66 Ω. If current in the circuit is (5 – j 10)A, find (i) the applied voltage (ii) power factor and (iii) active power and reactive power.*

Solution.

$\mathbf{Z} = R + jX_L = (10 + j \ 8.66) \ \Omega = 13.23 \angle 40.9° \ \Omega$

$\mathbf{I} = (5 - j10) \ \text{A} = 11.18 \angle -63.43° \ \text{A}$

(*i*) $\mathbf{V} = \mathbf{IZ} = 11.18 \angle -63.43° \times 13.23 \angle 40.9° = 148 \angle -22.53° \text{V}$

∴ $V = \mathbf{148 \ volts}$

(*ii*) $\phi = 63.43° - 22.53° = 40.9°$

$p.f. = \cos \phi = \cos 40.9° = \mathbf{0.756} \ lag$

(*iii*) $S = $ Phasor voltage × Conjugate of phasor current

or $P + jQ = 148 \angle -22.53° \times 11.18 \angle 63.43° = 1654.64 \angle 40.9° \ \text{VA}$

$= (1250.66 + j \ 1083.36) \ \text{VA}$

∴ Active power, $P = \mathbf{1250.66 \ W}$; Reactive power, $Q = \mathbf{1083.36 \ VAR}$

Example 17.12. *The complex volt amperes in a series circuit are (4330 – j2500) and the current is (25 + j43.3)A. Find the applied voltage.*

Solution. Let the applied voltage be $\mathbf{V} = (a + jb)$.

Complex $VA = $ Phasor voltage × Conjugate of phasor current

or $4330 - j2500 = (a + jb) \times (25 - j43.3)$

$= (25a + 43.3b) + j \ (-43.3a + 25b)$

∴ $25a + 43.3b = 4330$ ...(*i*)

and $-43.3a + 25b = -2500$ ...(*ii*)

Solving eqs. (*i*) and (*ii*), we have, $a = 86.6$ and $b = 50$.

∴ $\mathbf{V} = (86.6 + j50) \ \mathbf{volts}$

Example 17.13. *A coil of resistance 12Ω and inductive reactance of 25 Ω is connected in series with a capacitive reactance of 41Ω. The combination is connected to a supply of 230V, 50Hz. Using phasor algebra, find (i) circuit impedance (ii) current and (iii) power consumed.*

Solution.

(i)
$$\mathbf{Z} = R + j\,(X_L - X_C)$$
$$= 12 + j\,(25 - 41) = (12 - j16)\Omega = 20\angle -53.13°\,\Omega$$
∴ $$\mathbf{Z} = 20\,\Omega$$

(ii) Taking voltage as the reference phasor,
$$\mathbf{V} = (230 + j0)\mathrm{V} = 230\angle 0°\,\mathrm{V}$$

∴
$$\mathbf{I} = \frac{\mathbf{V}}{\mathbf{Z}} = \frac{230\angle 0°}{20\angle -53.13°} = 11.5\angle 53.13°\mathrm{A}$$

∴ $$I = 11.5\,\mathrm{A}$$

(iii) It is clear that current leads the voltage by 53.13° *i.e.*, $\phi = 53.13°$.

∴ Power factor $= \cos\phi = \cos 53.13° = \mathbf{0.6}$ *lead*

∴ Power consumed, $P = VI\cos\phi = 230 \times 11.5 \times 0.6 = \mathbf{1587\ W}$

Example 17.14. *If the potential drop across a circuit be represented by (40 + j25) V with reference to the circuit current and power absorbed by the circuit is 160W, find the complex expression for the impedance. Find also (i) the power factor of the circuit and (ii) the magnitude of the impedance.*

Solution. Fig. 17.15 shows the phasor diagram of the circuit. The drop across resistance $= IR = 40$ volts and that across inductive reactance $= IX_L = 25$ volts.

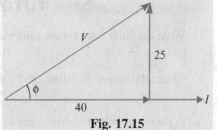

Fig. 17.15

Now, $$IR = 40 \text{ and } I^2R = 160\ \mathrm{W}$$
∴ $$I = I^2R/IR = 160/40 = 4\mathrm{A}$$
Now $$\mathbf{I} = 4\angle 0°\mathrm{A}$$
$$\mathbf{V} = (40 + j25)\mathrm{V} = 47.2\angle 32°\,\mathrm{V}$$

∴
$$\mathbf{Z} = \frac{\mathbf{V}}{\mathbf{I}} = \frac{47.2\angle 32°}{4\angle 0°} = \mathbf{11.8\angle 32°\Omega}$$

(i) Power factor $= \cos\phi = \cos 32° = \mathbf{0.848}$ *lag*

(ii) $$Z = \mathbf{11.8\ \Omega}$$

Example 17.15. *A coil whose resistance and inductance are 60Ω and 318 mH respectively is connected to a 230V, 50Hz supply. Determine the current and power dissipated. Find the current if the 50Hz supply is replaced by a 230 V battery.*

Solution. Since only magnitudes are to be determined, we can find the answer directly without using complex notation.

$$X_L = 2\pi f L = 2\pi \times 50 \times 318 \times 10^{-3} = 100\Omega$$

∴
$$Z = \sqrt{R^2 + X_L^2} = \sqrt{60^2 + 100^2} = 116.62\Omega$$

∴
$$I = \frac{V}{Z} = \frac{230}{116.62} = \mathbf{1.972\,A}$$

Power dissipated, $P^* = I^2R = (1.972)^2 \times 60 = \mathbf{233\ W}$

- -

* Remember $P = VI\cos\phi$ or I^2R. It is because $P = VI\cos\phi = (IZ)\ I \times R/Z = I^2R$.

With battery applied, $f = 0$ so that $X_L = 0$. Hence $Z = R = 60 \Omega$

$$\therefore \qquad I_{dc} = V/Z = V/R = 230/60 = 3.83 \text{ A}$$

Example 17.16. *A high-impedance voltmeter is used to measure voltage drop across each of three series connected ideal circuit elements. If the r.m.s. readings are 25V, 40V and 60V for V_R, V_L and V_C respectively, determine the equation for the voltage wave representing the driving voltage whose frequency is 50 Hz.*

Solution.

Applied voltage,

$$\mathbf{V} = \mathbf{V}_R + j(\mathbf{V}_L - \mathbf{V}_C)$$
$$= 25 + j(40 - 60)$$
$$= (25 - j20)\text{V} = 32\angle -38.66° \text{ V}$$

$$\therefore \qquad V = 32 \text{ volts}$$

$$V_m = 32 \times \sqrt{2} = 45.25 \text{ volts}$$

$$\omega = 2\pi f = 2\pi \times 50 = 314 \, \text{rad s}^{-1}$$

It is clear that voltage lags behind the current by $38.66°$ *i.e.* $\phi = 38.66°$. The equation of the driving voltage is :

$$v = 45.25 \sin(314t - 38.66°)$$

TUTORIAL PROBLEMS

1. Write the polar form for the following:
   (i) $-4 + j6.928$ (ii) $-50 - j75$ [(i) $8\angle 120°$ (ii) $90.1\angle -123.7°$]

2. Obtain the sum of $\mathbf{E}_1 = 100\angle 45°$ and $\mathbf{E}_2 = 80\angle 120°$ in (i) rectangular form and (ii) polar form.

   [(i) $30.7 + j140$ (ii) $143\angle 77.6°$]

3. Perform the indicated operations and express the results in polar form:
   (i) $(5 + j12)^2$

   (ii) Add $10\angle 40°$ to $15\angle 60°$ and divide the result by $(20\angle 45° - 12\angle 180°)$

   (iii) $3\angle 30° + 5\angle -50° - 7\angle 20° + (6 + j5)$

   [(i) $169\angle 134.8°$ (ii) $1.715\angle -29.35°$ (iii) $5.24\angle -3.06°$]

4. Determine the resistance and inductance of series connected elements that will draw a current of $20\angle -30°$ A from a 60 Hz sinusoidal generator whose voltage is $100\angle 0°$ V. [4.35Ω ; 6.6 mH]

5. A coil, a capacitor and a resistor are connected in series and supplied by 1.5kHz generator. The capacitive reactance is 4Ω, the resistor is 4Ω and the coil has a resistance of 3Ω and an inductive reactance of 4Ω. If the current in the circuit is $10\angle 20°$ A, determine (i) complex impedance (ii) voltage drop across coil in polar form. [(i) $7\angle 0°\Omega$; (ii) $50\angle 73.13°$ V]

6. The p.d. across and the current in a circuit are represented by $(100 + j200)$V and $(10 + j5)$A respectively. Calculate the power consumed and the reactive power. [2000W; 1500VAR]

7. In an *R-L-C* series circuit, $L = 25$ mH, $C = 59\mu$F. Find the value of R so that current leads the voltage by $63.4°$ at a supply frequency of $400/2\pi$. [20Ω]

8. The current in a circuit is given by $(4.5 + j12)$A when the applied voltage is $100 + j150$ volts. Determine (i) the complex expression for the impedance (ii) power (iii) the phase angle between voltage and current. [(i) $13.7 - j3.2\Omega$ (ii) 2250 W (iii) $13.9°$]

MULTIPLE-CHOICE QUESTIONS

1. When a phasor is multiplied by $-j$, it is rotated through .... in the counterclockwise direction.
   (a) 90°
   (b) 180°
   (c) 270°
   (d) none of the above

2. The value of j^5 is equal to............
   (a) 1
   (b) $\sqrt{-1}$
   (c) -1
   (d) $-\sqrt{-1}$

3. If two complex numbers are equal, then ....
   (a) only their magnitudes will be equal
   (b) only their angles will be equal
   (c) their in-phase and quadrature components will be separately equal
   (d) none of the above

4. A current of $3 + j4$ amperes is flowing through a circuit. The magnitude of current is...........
   (a) 7 A
   (b) 5 A
   (c) 1 A
   (d) 1.33 A

5. The voltage applied in a circuit is given by $100\angle60°$ volts. It can be written as............
   (a) $100\angle-60°$ volts
   (b) $100\angle240°$ volts
   (c) $100\angle-300°$ volts
   (d) none of the above

6. If the impedance of an a.c. circuit is $10\angle60°\Omega$, then resistance in the circuit is............
   (a) 5 Ω
   (b) 8.66 Ω
   (c) 10 Ω
   (d) none of the above

7. The conjugate of $-4 + j3$ is.................
   (a) $4 - j3$
   (b) $-4 - j3$
   (c) $4 + j3$
   (d) none of the above

8. The sum of two conjugate numbers results in ....
   (a) a complex number
   (b) in-phase component only
   (c) quadrature component only
   (d) none of the above

9. The value of $5\angle40°\times3\angle20°$ is ....
   (a) $15\angle60°$
   (b) $15\angle20°$
   (c) $1.6\angle2°$
   (d) $15\angle800°$

10. The value of $9\angle30°\div3\angle10°$ is
    (a) $27\angle40°$
    (b) $3\angle20°$
    (c) $3\angle40°$
    (d) $3\angle3°$

11. The polar form of the following waveform is
    $$v_1 = 16 \sin (\omega t + 35°)V$$
    $$v_2 = 32 \sin (\omega t - 55°)V$$
    (a) $v_1 = 16\angle70°V; v_2 = 32\angle110°$ V
    (b) $v_1 = 16\angle35°V; v_2 = 32\angle-55°$ V
    (c) $v_1 = 8\angle35°V; v_2 = 32\angle55°$ V
    (d) none of above

12. The current through a 400 Ω resistor is $i = 0.06 \sin (\omega t - 30°)A$. The voltage across the resistor is
    (a) $12\angle30°$ V
    (b) $48\angle45°$ V
    (c) $24\angle30°$ V
    (d) none of above

13. The reciprocal of $12 - j16$ in polar form is
    (a) $0.05\angle53.13°$
    (b) $5\angle53.13°$
    (c) $20\angle31.8°$
    (d) none of above

14. The reciprocal of j is
    (a) j
    (b) $-j$
    (c) j^2
    (d) none of above

15. In Fig. 17.16, $R = 300\ \Omega$, $L = 0.2$H and $v = 17 \sin (2000 t)$ volts. The total equivalent impedance in rectangular form is

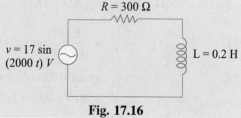

Fig. 17.16

    (a) $(150 + j 200)\ \Omega$
    (b) $(300 - j 400)\ \Omega$
    (c) $(150 - j 200)\ \Omega$
    (d) $(300 + j 400)\ \Omega$

Answers to Multiple-Choice Questions

1. (c)   2. (b)   3. (c)   4. (b)   5. (c)   6. (a)   7. (b)   8. (b)
9. (a)   10. (b)   11. (b)   12. (c)   13. (a)   14. (b)   15. (d)

Hints to Selected Multiple-Choice Questions

2. $j^5 = j^4 \times j = 1 \times j = \sqrt{-1}$

3. Suppose two equal complex numbers are $a + jb$ and $c + jd$.

    $\therefore \qquad\qquad\qquad a + jb = c + jd$

    $\therefore \qquad\qquad\qquad a = c$ and $\quad b = d$

4. $\qquad$ Magnitude $= \sqrt{3^2 + 4^2} = 5A$

5. The angle measured in CCW direction from OX axis is 60°. If the angle is measured in clockwise direction from OX axis, its value is $= 360° - 60° = 300°$ and this angle is negative. Hence $100\angle60°$ can be written as $\mathbf{100\angle-300°}$.

6. $R = Z \cos\phi = 10 \cos 60° = 5\ \Omega$

7. Two complex numbers (or phasors) are said to be conjugate if they differ only in the algebraic sign of their quadrature components. Thus the conjugate of $-4 + j3$ is $-4 - j3$.

8. Suppose a complex number is $2 + j3$. Its conjugate will be $2 - j3$.

    $\qquad\qquad$ Sum $= (2 + j3) + (2 - j3) = 4$

9. $5\angle40° \times 3\angle20° = 5 \times 3 \angle 40° + 20° = 15\angle60°$

10. $9\angle30° \div 3\angle10° = \dfrac{9}{3}\angle30° - 10° = 3\angle20°$

11. Fig. 17.17 shows the solution of the problem.

12. $\qquad\qquad \mathbf{i} = 0.06\angle-30°\,\text{A}; \mathbf{R} = 400\angle0°\,\Omega$

    $\therefore$ Voltage across $R = \mathbf{i} \times \mathbf{R} = 0.06\angle-30° \times 400\angle0°$

    $\qquad\qquad\qquad = 24\angle-30°\,\text{V}$

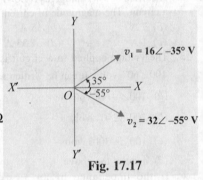

Fig. 17.17

13. $\qquad$ Magnitude $= \sqrt{12^2 + (-16)^2} = 20; \theta = \tan^{-1}\dfrac{-16}{12} = -53.13°$

    $\therefore \qquad \dfrac{1}{12 - j16} = \dfrac{1}{20\angle-53.13°} = \dfrac{1\angle0°}{20\angle-53.13°} = 0.05\angle53.13°$

14. $\qquad \dfrac{1}{j} = \dfrac{1\angle0°}{1\angle90°} = 1\angle-90° = -j$

15. $\qquad X_L = \omega L = 2000 \times 0.2 = 400\Omega \qquad \therefore \mathbf{X_L} = (0 + j400)\,\Omega; \mathbf{R} = (300 + j0)\,\Omega$

    $\therefore \qquad \mathbf{Z} = (0 + j\,400) + (300 + j0) = (300 + j\,400)\ \Omega$

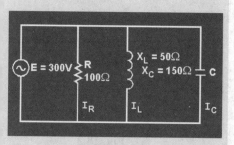

18

Parallel A.C. Circuits

INTRODUCTION

As in parallel d.c. circuits, the voltage across all branches is the same in a parallel a.c. circuit. But current in any branch depends upon the impedance of that branch. The total line current supplied to the circuit is the *phasor sum* of the branch currents. Parallel circuits are used more frequently in electrical systems than are the series circuits. For example, electrical devices and equipment are connected in parallel across a.c. mains. In this chapter, we shall discuss the various methods of solving parallel a.c. circuits.

18.1. SOLVING PARALLEL A.C. CIRCUITS

There are four main methods of solving parallel a.c. circuits, namely;

(*i*) By phasor diagram

(*ii*) By phasor algebra

(*iii*) By equivalent impedance method

(*iv*) By admittance method

The use of a particular method will depend upon the conditions of the problem. However, in general, that method should be used which yields quick results.

18.2. BY PHASOR DIAGRAM

In this method, we draw the phasor diagram of

the parallel circuit taking voltage as the reference phasor. The circuit or line current is determined by the method of components. Consider a parallel circuit consisting of two branches and connected to an alternating voltage of V volts (r.m.s.) as shown in Fig. 18.1.

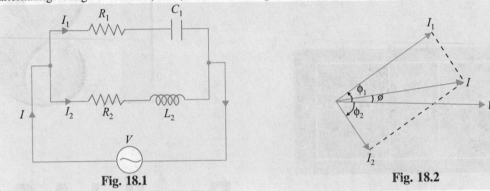

Fig. 18.1   **Fig. 18.2**

Branch 1. $Z_1 = \sqrt{R_1^2 + X_{C_1}^2}$; $I_1 = \dfrac{V}{Z_1}$; $\phi_1 = \tan^{-1}\dfrac{X_{C_1}}{R_1}$

The current I_1 leads the applied voltage V by ϕ_1^0 [See Fig. 18.2].

Branch 2. $Z_2 = \sqrt{R_2^2 + X_{L_2}^2}$; $I_2 = \dfrac{V}{Z_2}$; $\phi_2 = \tan^{-1}\dfrac{X_{L_2}}{R_2}$

The current I_2 lags behind V by ϕ_2° [See Fig. 18.2].

The line current I is the phasor sum of I_1 and I_2. Suppose its phase angle is ϕ as shown in Fig. 18.2. The values of I and ϕ can be determined by resolving the currents into rectangular components.

$$I \cos \phi = \text{Algebraic sum of components of } I_1 \text{ and } I_2 \text{ along X-axis}$$
$$= I_1 \cos \phi_1 + I_2 \cos \phi_2$$
$$I \sin \phi = \text{Algebraic sum of components of } I_1 \text{ and } I_2 \text{ along Y-axis}$$
$$= I_1 \sin \phi_1 - I_2 \sin \phi_2$$

But $I^2 = (I \cos \phi)^2 + (I \sin \phi)^2$

∴ $I^2 = (I_1 \cos \phi_1 + I_2 \cos \phi_2)^2 + (I_1 \sin \phi_1 - I_2 \sin \phi_2)^2$

or $I = \sqrt{(I_1 \cos \phi_1 + I_2 \cos \phi_2)^2 + (I_1 \sin \phi_1 - I_2 \sin \phi_2)^2}$

$$\tan \phi = \frac{I \sin \phi}{I \cos \phi} = \frac{I_1 \sin \phi_1 - I_2 \sin \phi_2}{I_1 \cos \phi_1 + I_2 \cos \phi_2} = \frac{Y - \text{Comp.}}{X - \text{Comp.}}$$

If ϕ is positive, line current I leads the voltage and if ϕ is negative, I lags behind the voltage.

Circuit   *p.f.* $= \dfrac{I \cos \phi}{I} = \dfrac{I_1 \cos \phi_1 + I_2 \cos \phi_2}{I} = \dfrac{X - \text{Comp.}}{I}$

The phasor diagram method is suitable only when the parallel circuit is simple and contains two branches.

Example 18.1. *A capacitor of 50 µF is connected in parallel with a coil that has a resistance of 20Ω and inductance of 0.05 H. If this parallel combination is connected across 200V, 50Hz supply, calculate (i) the line current (ii) power factor and (iii) power consumed.*

Solution.

$$X_C = \frac{1}{2\pi fC} = \frac{10^6}{2\pi \times 50 \times 50} = 63.7\,\Omega$$

$$I_1 = V/X_C = 200/63.7 = 3.14 \text{ A} \qquad\qquad ...leads\ V\ by\ 90°$$

$$X_L = 2\pi fL = 2\pi \times 50 \times 0.05 = 15.7\,\Omega$$

$$Z = \sqrt{20^2 + 15.7^2} = 25.43\,\Omega$$

$$\phi_2 = \tan^{-1} X_L/R = \tan^{-1} 15.7/20 = 38.13° \text{ lag}$$

$$I_2 = V/Z = 200/25.43 = 7.86 \text{ A} \qquad\qquad ...lags\ V\ by\ 38.13°$$

Referring to the phasor diagram in Fig. 18.4, we have,

$$\begin{aligned}
\text{Total } X\text{-component} &= I_1 \cos\phi_1 + I_2 \cos\phi_2 \\
&= 3.14 \cos 90° + 7.86 \cos 38.13° \\
&= 0 + 6.18 = 6.18 \text{ A}
\end{aligned}$$

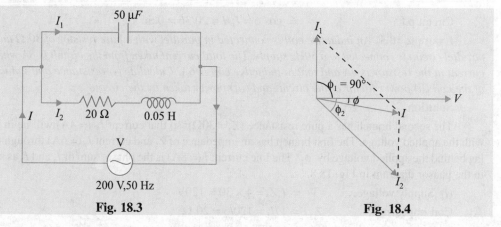

Fig. 18.3   **Fig. 18.4**

$$\begin{aligned}
\text{Total } Y\text{-component} &= I_1 \sin\phi_1 - I_2 \sin\phi_2 \\
&= 3.14 \sin 90° - 7.86 \sin 38.13° \\
&= 3.14 - 4.85 = -1.71 \text{A}
\end{aligned}$$

(*i*) Line current, $I = \sqrt{(6.18)^2 + (-1.71)^2} = \textbf{6.41A}$

Phase angle, $\phi = \tan^{-1}(-1.71/6.18) = -*15.47°$

(*ii*) Power factor $= \cos\phi = \cos(-15.47°) = \textbf{0.964} \textit{ lag}$

(*iii*) Power consumed, $P = VI \cos\phi = 200 \times 6.41 \times 0.964 = \textbf{1235.85 W}$

Example18.2. *A 10 Ω resistor, a 15.9mH inductor and 159 µF capacitor are connected in parallel to a 200V, 50Hz source. Calculate the supply current and power factor.*

Solution. Fig. 18.5 shows the circuit diagram.

$$X_L = 2\pi fL = 2\pi \times 50 \times 15.9 \times 10^{-3} = 5\,\Omega$$

$$X_C = \frac{1}{2\pi fC} = \frac{10^6}{2\pi \times 50 \times 159} = 20\,\Omega$$

---

* In a parallel circuit, voltage is taken as the reference phasor. Therefore, negative phase angle means that circuit current lags behind the applied voltage.

$$I_R = V/R = 200/10 = 20A \qquad \textit{...in phase with V}$$
$$I_L = V/X_L = 200/5 = 40A \qquad \textit{...lags V by 90°}$$
$$I_C = V/X_C = 200/20 = 10A \qquad \textit{...leads V by 90°}$$

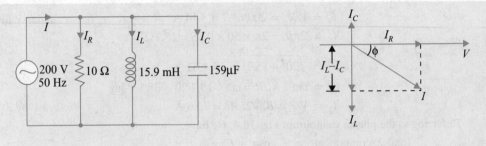

Fig. 18.5   **Fig. 18.6**

Supply current, $\qquad I = \sqrt{I_R^2 + (I_L - I_C)^2} = \sqrt{20^2 + (40 - 10)^2} = \textbf{36A}$

Circuit p.f. $\qquad\qquad = \cos\phi = I_R/I = 20/36 = \textbf{0.56} \textit{ lag}$

Example 18.3. *An inductive coil is connected in parallel with a pure resistor of 30 Ω and this parallel circuit is connected to a 50Hz supply. The total current taken from the circuit is 8A while the current in the resistor is 4A and that in inductive coil is 6A. Calculate (i) resistance and inductance of the coil (ii) power factor of the circuit and (iii) power taken by the circuit.*

Solution.

The second branch has a pure resistance ($Z_2 = 30Ω$) so that current I_2 ($= 4A$) will be in phase with the applied voltage. The first branch has an impedance of Z_1 and current I_1 ($= 6A$) through it will lag behind the applied voltage by $\phi_1°$ The line current I ($= 8A$) is the phasor sum of I_1 and I_2 as shown in the phasor diagram in Fig. 18.8.

(*i*) Supply voltage, $\qquad V = I_2 Z_2 = 4 \times 30 = 120V$

Coil impedance, $\qquad Z_1 = V/I_1 = 120/6 = 20 \ \Omega$

Referring to the phasor diagram in Fig. 18.8, we have,

$$I^2 = I_1^2 + I_2^2 + 2I_1 I_2 \cos\phi_1$$

or $\qquad\qquad 8^2 = 6^2 + 4^2 + 2 \times 6 \times 4 \times \cos\phi_1$

∴ $\qquad\qquad \cos\phi_1 = \dfrac{8^2 - 6^2 - 4^2}{2 \times 6 \times 4} = 0.25 \ \text{ and } \sin\phi_1 = 0.968$

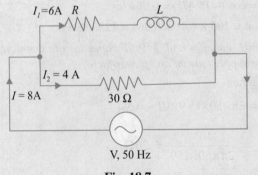   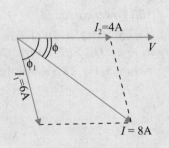

Fig. 18.7   **Fig. 18.8**

∴ Coil resistance, $\qquad R = Z_1 \cos\phi_1 = 20 \times 0.25 = 5\Omega$

Coil reactance, $\qquad X_L = Z_1 \sin\phi_1 = 20 \times 0.968 = 19.36\Omega$

Coil inductance, $\qquad L = \dfrac{X_L}{2\pi f} = \dfrac{19.36}{2\pi \times 50} = 0.0616H$

(*ii*) Resolving the currents along *X*-axis (see Fig. 18.8),

$$I \cos\phi = I_2 + I_1\cos\phi_1$$

∴ Circuit *p.f.*, $\qquad \cos\phi = \dfrac{I_2 + I_1\cos\phi_1}{I} = \dfrac{4 + 6 \times 0.25}{8} = 0.687\,lag$

(*iii*) Power consumed, $\quad P = VI\cos\phi = 120 \times 8 \times 0.687 = 660\ \mathbf{W}$

Example 18.4. *A coil of resistance 50 Ω and inductance 0.318H is connected in parallel with a circuit comprising a 75 Ω resistor in series with a 159 μF capacitor. The circuit is connected to 240V, 50Hz supply. Calculate :*

(*i*) *supply current*

(*ii*) *phase angle between supply current and applied voltage*

Find also the resistance and reactance of series circuit which will take the same current at the same p.f. as the parallel circuit.

Solution.

$$X_L = 2\pi fL = 2\pi \times 50 \times 0.318 = 100\ \Omega$$

$$Z_1 = \sqrt{R_1^2 + X_L^2} = \sqrt{50^2 + 100^2} = 112\Omega$$

$$\phi_1 = \cos^{-1} R_1/Z_1 = \cos^{-1} 50/112 = 63.5°\,lag$$

$$I_1 = V/Z_1 = 240/112 = 2.15A \qquad\qquad \textit{...lags V by } 63.5°$$

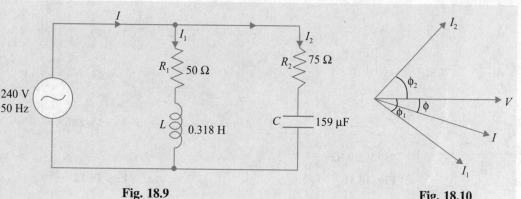

Fig. 18.9   **Fig. 18.10**

$$X_C = \dfrac{1}{2\pi fC} = \dfrac{10^6}{2\pi \times 50 \times 159} = 20\Omega$$

$$Z_2 = \sqrt{R_2^2 + X_C^2} = \sqrt{75^2 + 20^2} = 77.7\Omega$$

$$\phi_2 = \cos^{-1} R_2/Z_2 = \cos^{-1} 75/77.7 = 15°\,lead$$

$$I_2 = V/Z_2 = 240/77.7 = 3.09A \qquad\qquad \textit{... leads V by } 15°$$

Referring to the phasor diagram shown in Fig. 18.10,

Total *X*-comp. $= I_1 \cos\phi_1 + I_2 \cos\phi_2$

$$= 2.15 \cos 63.5° + 3.09 \cos 15° = 3.94 \text{ A}$$

Total Y-comp. $= -I_1 \sin \phi_1 + I_2 \sin \phi_2$

$$= -2.15 \sin 63.5° + 3.09 \sin 15° = -1.13 \text{A}$$

(*i*) Supply current, $\quad I = \sqrt{(3.94)^2 + (-1.13)^2} = \mathbf{4.1A}$

(*ii*) Phase angle, $\quad \phi = \tan^{-1} -1.13/3.94 = \mathbf{-16°}$

Since voltage is the reference phasor, negative angle means that supply current lags the applied voltage, *i.e.*, circuit is inductive.

Circuit impedance, $\quad Z = V/I = 240/4.1 = 58.5\Omega$

Circuit resistance, $\quad R = Z \cos \phi = 58.5 \cos (-16°) = \mathbf{56.2\ \Omega}$

Circuit reactance, $\quad X_L = Z \sin \phi = 58.5 \sin (-16°) = \mathbf{16.12\ \Omega}$

Thus the parallel circuit is equivalent to $56.2\ \Omega$ resistor in series with $16.12\ \Omega$ inductive reactance.

Example 18.5. *A coil of resistance 100 Ω and inductance 0.15H is connected to a 250V, 50Hz supply. Calculate the capacitance of the capacitor to be connected in parallel with the coil so that overall p.f. is unity. Also find the supply current then.*

Solution.

$$X_L = 2\pi fL = 2\pi \times 50 \times 0.15 = 47.1\ \Omega$$

$$Z = \sqrt{R^2 + X_L^2} = \sqrt{(100)^2 + (47.1)^2} = 110.5\Omega$$

$$I_L = V/Z_L = 250/110.5 = 2.26 \text{ A}$$

$$\phi_L = \tan^{-1} X_L/R = \tan^{-1} 47.1/100 = 25.2° lag$$

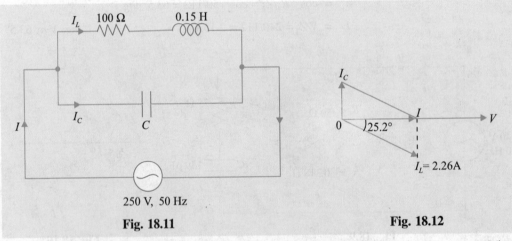

Fig. 18.11   **Fig. 18.12**

Since the overall p.f. has to be unity, the magnitude of I_C should be such that line current I (i.e., phasor sum of I_C and I_L) is in phase with V as shown in Fig. 18.12. In other words, the reactive component of line current should be zero. *i.e.*

$$I_C = I_L \sin\phi_L = 2.26 \sin 25.2° = 0.96 \text{ A}$$

Now $\quad I_C = V/X_C = V \times 2\pi fC$

or $\quad C = \dfrac{I_C}{V \times 2\pi f} = \dfrac{0.96}{250 \times 2\pi \times 50} = \mathbf{12.2 \times 10^{-6} F}$

When the capacitor is connected to the coil,

Line current, $\quad I = I_L \cos \phi_L = 2.26 \cos 25.2° = \mathbf{2.04\ A}$

Example 18.6. *A 230V, 50Hz single phase motor takes 70A and operates at a p.f. 0.75 lagging. If a capacitor of 159 μF is connected in parallel with the motor, find (i) the new line current (ii) circuit p.f.*

Solution.

$$I_m = 70 \text{ A} ; \phi_m = \cos^{-1} 0.75 = 41.4°$$

$$X_C = \frac{1}{2\pi fC} = \frac{10^6}{2\pi \times 50 \times 159} = 20\Omega$$

$$I_C = V/X_C = 230/20 = 11.5 \text{ A} \qquad \text{.....leads } V \text{ by } 90°$$

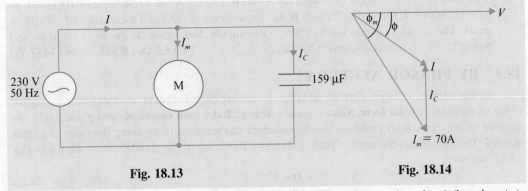

Fig. 18.13   **Fig. 18.14**

As seen from the phasor diagram, the line current I lags the applied voltage by ϕ (less than ϕ_m).

$$\text{Total } X\text{-component} = I_m \cos \phi_m + I_C \cos 90°$$
$$= 70 \times \cos 41.4° + 11.5 \cos 90° = 52.5 \text{ A}$$

$$\text{Total } Y\text{-component} = -I_m \sin \phi_m + I_C \sin 90°$$
$$= -70 \sin 41.4° + 11.5 \sin 90° = -34.8\text{A}$$

(*i*) Line current,
$$I = \sqrt{(52.5)^2 + (-34.8)^2} = \mathbf{63 \text{ A}}$$

(*ii*) Circuit p.f.
$$= \frac{\text{Total } X - \text{component}}{I} = \frac{52.5}{63} = \mathbf{0.833} \, lag$$

Note. Before connecting the capacitor, the line current was 70A and circuit *p.f* = 0.75 lagging. However, when capacitor is connected across the motor, the line current is reduced to 63A and circuit *p.f.* improved to 0.833 lagging.

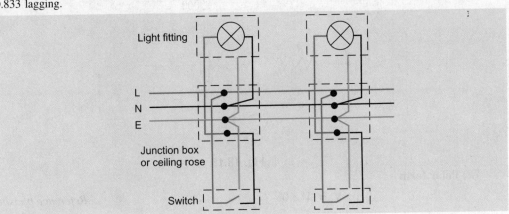

CB Domestic Circuit

TUTORIAL PROBLEMS

1. A resistor of 10 Ω is connected in parallel with an inductor of 31.8 mH. A 200V, 50 Hz supply is connected to the circuit. Determine (*i*) the line current (*ii*) power factor and (*iii*) power consumed by the circuit.   [(*i*) **28.28A**   (*ii*) **0.71** *lag*   (*iii*) **4015.76 W**]

2. A coil of resistance 15 Ω and inductance 0.05H is connected in parallel with a non-inductive resistance of 20Ω. If the circuit is connected to 200V, 50Hz, find (*i*) current in each branch (*ii*) supply current (*iii*) power factor.   [(*i*) **9.22A; 10A** (*ii*) **17.7A** (*iii*) **0.926** *lag*]

3. A 10 Ω resistor, a 31.8 mH inductor and a 318 μF capacitor are connected in parallel and supplied from 200V, 50Hz supply. Determine the supply current and power factor. [**20 A ; 1**]

4. A parallel circuit consists of two branches A and B. Branch A has a resistance of 10Ω and an inductance of 0.1H in series. Branch B has a resistance of 20Ω and a capacitor of 100 μF in series. The circuit is connected to 250V, 50Hz supply. Determine (*i*) the supply current and power factor (*ii*) power consumed by the circuit.   [(*i*) **6.04A ; 0.965** *lag* (*ii*) **1457 W**]

18.3. BY PHASOR ALGEBRA

In this method, voltages, currents and impedances are expressed in the complex form *i.e.*, either in the rectangular or polar form. Since complex form includes both magnitude and phase angle, the solution of parallel-circuit problems can be obtained mathematically by using the rules of phasor algebra. This eliminates the need of phasor diagram. Referring to the parallel circuit shown in Fig. 18.15, we have,

$$\mathbf{V} = V + j0 = V \qquad\qquad \text{... Reference phasor}$$
$$\mathbf{Z}_1 = R_1 + jX_L ; \qquad \mathbf{Z}_2 = R_2 - jX_C$$

(*i*) **Rectangular form**

$$\mathbf{I}_1 = \frac{\mathbf{V}}{\mathbf{Z}_1} = \frac{V}{R_1 + jX_L}$$

$$\mathbf{I}_2 = \frac{\mathbf{V}}{\mathbf{Z}_2} = \frac{V}{R_2 - jX_C}$$

Line current, $\mathbf{I} = \mathbf{I}_1 + \mathbf{I}_2 = \dfrac{V}{R_1 + jX_L} + \dfrac{V}{R_2 - jX_C}$

The solution of **I** can be obtained in the standard form $a \pm jb$ by using the rules of phasor algebra. Then it is an easy task to find the magnitude and phase angle of **I**.

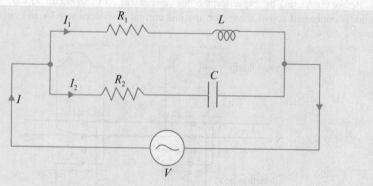

Fig. 18.15

(*ii*) **Polar form**

$$\mathbf{V} = V \angle 0° \qquad\qquad \text{...Reference phasor}$$

$$\mathbf{Z}_1 = Z_1 \angle \phi°_1 \quad \text{where } Z_1 = \sqrt{R_1^2 + X_L^2} \ ; \ \ \phi_1 = \tan^{-1} X_L / R$$

$$\mathbf{Z}_2 = Z_2 \angle{-\phi^\circ}_2 \text{ where } Z_2 = \sqrt{R_2^2 + X_C^2} \; ; \phi_2 = \tan^{-1} X_C / R$$

$$\therefore \quad \mathbf{I}_1 = \frac{\mathbf{V}}{\mathbf{Z}_1} = \frac{V \angle 0^\circ}{Z_1 \angle \phi_1^\circ} = \frac{V}{Z_1} \angle{-\phi_1}^\circ$$

$$\mathbf{I}_2 = \frac{\mathbf{V}}{\mathbf{Z}_2} = \frac{V \angle 0^\circ}{Z_2 \angle{-\phi_2}^\circ} = \frac{V}{Z_2} \angle \phi_2^\circ$$

$$\therefore \quad \mathbf{I} = \mathbf{I}_1 + \mathbf{I}_2 = \frac{V}{Z_1} \angle{-\phi_1^\circ} + \frac{V}{Z_2} \angle \phi_2^\circ$$

Example 18.7. *The voltage applied to a parallel circuit is (68 + j154) volts. The current in one branch is (10 + j14) amperes and the current in the other branch is (2 + j8) amperes. What is the circuit power factor ?*

Solution.

Applied voltage, $\quad \mathbf{V} = (68 + j154) \text{ volts} = 168.34 \angle 66.17^\circ \text{ volts}$

Line current, $\quad \mathbf{I} = \mathbf{I}_1 + \mathbf{I}_2 = (10 + j14) + (2 + j8)$

$$= (12 + j22) \text{ amperes} = 25.06 \angle 61.39^\circ \text{ amperes}$$

$\therefore$ Phase angle, $\quad \phi = 66.17^\circ - 61.39^\circ = 4.78^\circ$

Circuit p.f. $\quad = \cos \phi = \cos 4.78^\circ = \mathbf{0.996} \; lag$

Example 18.8. *Two impedances $Z_1 = 8 + j6$ and $Z_2 = 3 - j4$ are connected in parallel across 230V, 50Hz supply. Calculate (i) current in each branch (ii) line current (iii) circuit p.f. and (iv) power taken by the circuit.*

Solution. Fig. 18.16 shows the conditions of the problem. Taking voltage as the reference phasor, $\mathbf{V} = 230 \angle 0^\circ$ volts.

(i) $\quad \mathbf{Z}_1 = (8 + j6)\Omega = 10 \angle 36.87^\circ \Omega$

$$\mathbf{I}_1 = \frac{\mathbf{V}}{\mathbf{Z}_1} = \frac{230 \angle 0^\circ}{10 \angle 36.87^\circ} = 23 \angle{-36.87^\circ} \text{A}$$

$\therefore \quad I_1 = \mathbf{23A}$

$$\mathbf{Z}_2 = (3 - j4)\Omega = 5 \angle{-53.13^\circ} \Omega$$

$$\mathbf{I}_2 = \frac{\mathbf{V}}{\mathbf{Z}_2} = \frac{230 \angle 0^\circ}{5 \angle{-53.13^\circ}} = 46 \angle 53.13^\circ \text{A}$$

$\therefore \quad I_2 = \mathbf{46A}$

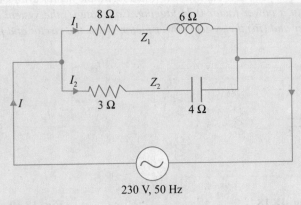

230 V, 50 Hz

Fig. 18.16

(ii)
$$\mathbf{Z_1} + \mathbf{Z_2} = (8 + j6) + (3 - j4) = (11 + j2)\Omega = 11.18\angle10.3° \ \Omega$$

$$\mathbf{Z_T} = \frac{\mathbf{Z_1}\,\mathbf{Z_2}}{\mathbf{Z_1} + \mathbf{Z_2}} = \frac{10\angle36.87° \times 5\angle-53.13°}{11.8\angle10.3°} = 4.23\angle-26.56°\Omega$$

∴
$$\mathbf{I} = \frac{\mathbf{V}}{\mathbf{Z_T}} = \frac{230\angle0°}{4.23\angle-26.56°} = 54.4\angle26.56°\mathrm{A}$$

$$I = 54.4 \ \mathrm{A}$$

(iii) Circuit p.f. $= \cos 26.56° = \mathbf{0.894} \ lead$

(iv) Power taken $= I_1^2 R_1 + I_2^2 R_2 = (23)^2 \times 8 + (46)^2 \times 3 = \mathbf{10580 \ W}$

Example 18.9. *A voltage of* $230\angle30°V$ *is applied to two circuits connected in parallel. The current in the branches are* $20\angle60°A$ *and* $40\angle-30°A$. *Find (i) the total impedance of the circuit (ii) power taken.*

Solution.

$$\mathbf{I_1} = 20\angle60°\mathrm{A} = 20(\cos 60° + j\sin 60°) = (10 + j17.3)\mathrm{A}$$
$$\mathbf{I_2} = 40\angle-30°\mathrm{A} = 40(\cos 30° - j\sin 30°) = (34.6 - j20)\mathrm{A}$$
$$\mathbf{I} = \mathbf{I_1} + \mathbf{I_2} = (10 + j17.3) + (34.6 - j20)$$
$$= (44.6 - j2.7)\mathrm{A} = 44.7\angle-3.46°\mathrm{A}$$

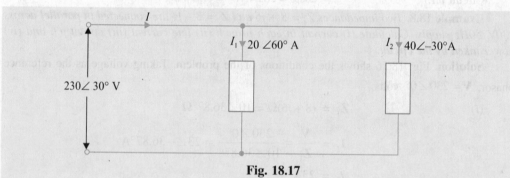

Fig. 18.17

(i) ∴
$$\mathbf{Z} = \frac{\mathbf{V}}{\mathbf{I}} = \frac{230\angle30°}{44.7\angle-3.46°} = \mathbf{5.14\angle33.46°\Omega}$$

(ii)
$$P = VI\cos\phi = 230 \times 44.7 \times \cos 33.46° = \mathbf{8577 \ W}$$

Example 18.10. *A capacitor, an electric resistance heater and an impedance are connected in parallel to 120V, 60Hz system. The capacitor draws 50VAR, the heater draws 100W and the impedance draws 269 VA at a power factor 0.74 lagging. Calculate (i) the system active power (ii) the system reactive power and (iii) the system power factor. Draw the circuit and phasor diagrams.*

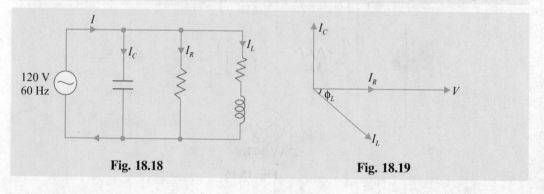

Fig. 18.18   **Fig. 18.19**

Solution. Fig. 18.18 shows the circuit diagram whereas Fig. 18.19 shows the phasor diagram. The circuit current I is the phasor sum of $(I_L \sin \phi_L - I_C)$ and $(I_L \cos \phi_L + I_R)$.

(*i*) **Active Power**

$$\text{Active power taken by capacitor} = 0$$
$$\text{Active power taken by heater} = 100 \text{ W}$$
$$\text{Active power taken by impedance} = \text{VA} \times \cos \phi_L = 269 \times 0.74$$
$$= 199.06 \text{ W}$$
$$\therefore \quad \text{System active power} = 0 + 100 + 199.06 = \mathbf{299.06 \text{ W}}$$

(*ii*) **Reactive power**

$$\text{System reactive power} = Q_C + Q_R + Q_L$$
$$= -50 + 0 + \text{VA} \times \sin \phi_L$$
$$= -50 + 0 + 269 \times 0.67$$
$$= \mathbf{130.23 \text{ VAR}}$$

(*iii*) **Power factor**

$$\text{System apparent power} = \sqrt{(299.06)^2 + (130.23)^2} = 326.18 \text{VA}$$
$$\text{System power factor} = \frac{\text{System active power}}{\text{System apparent power}} = \frac{299.06}{326.18}$$
$$= \mathbf{0.917} \, lag$$

TUTORIAL PROBLEMS

1. An inductive circuit, in parallel with a non-inductive circuit of 20Ω is connected across a 50Hz supply. The inductive current is 4.3A and the non-inductive current is 2.7 A. The total current is 5.8 A. Find (*i*) the power absorbed by the inductive branch (*ii*) its inductance and (*iii*) power factor of the combined circuit.   [(*i*) 78.6 W (*ii*) 0.0376 H (*iii*) 0.719 lag]

2. Two impedances $Z_1 = (10 + j5) \, \Omega$ and $Z_2 = (8 + j6) \, \Omega$ are in parallel and connected to a 200V, 50Hz supply. Calculate (*i*) the supply current (*ii*) circuit power factor and (*iii*) power consumed by the circuit.   [(*i*) 37.74A (*ii*) 0.848 lag (*iii*) 6400W]

3. Two impedances $Z_1 = (10 + j5)\Omega$ and $Z_2 = (25 - j10)\Omega$ are connected in parallel to a 100V, 50Hz supply. Find (*i*) circuit admittance (*ii*) circuit current (*iii*) the phase angle between circuit current and applied voltage.   [(*i*) 0.1174S (*ii*) 11.74A (*iii*) 12.9° lagging]

18.4. EQUIVALENT IMPEDANCE METHOD

In this method, we find the equivalent or total impedance of the parallel circuit. The line current is equal to the applied voltage divided by the equivalent impedance. Consider several impedances connected in parallel as shown in Fig. 18.20.

$$\mathbf{I} = \mathbf{I_1} + \mathbf{I_2} + \mathbf{I_3} + \ldots\ldots\ldots + \mathbf{I_n}$$

or
$$\frac{\mathbf{V}}{\mathbf{Z_T}} = \frac{\mathbf{V}}{\mathbf{Z_1}} + \frac{\mathbf{V}}{\mathbf{Z_2}} + \frac{\mathbf{V}}{\mathbf{Z_3}} + \ldots\ldots\ldots + \frac{\mathbf{V}}{\mathbf{Z_n}}$$

or
$$\frac{1}{\mathbf{Z_T}} = \frac{1}{\mathbf{Z_1}} + \frac{1}{\mathbf{Z_2}} + \frac{1}{\mathbf{Z_3}} + \ldots\ldots\ldots + \frac{1}{\mathbf{Z_n}} \qquad \ldots(i)$$

where $\mathbf{Z_T}$ is the total or equivalent impedance of the parallel circuit.

$$\text{Line current,} \quad \mathbf{I} = \frac{\mathbf{V}}{\mathbf{Z_T}}$$

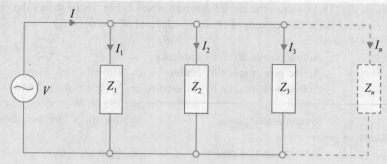

Fig. 18.20

Note that relation (*i*) compares with that for parallel resistors but with one important difference. Here each impedance is in complex form and takes care of magnitude as well as impedance angle. Therefore, all algebraic operations (e.g. addition, division, subtraction etc.) must be in complex form. No attempt should be made to carry out these operations arithmetically.

Special case. If only two impedances are in parallel, then the total or equivalent impedance is given by;

$$\frac{1}{Z_T} = \frac{1}{Z_1} + \frac{1}{Z_2} = \frac{Z_1 + Z_2}{Z_1 Z_2}$$

or

$$Z_T = \frac{Z_1 Z_2}{Z_1 + Z_2}$$

Line current, $\quad I = \dfrac{V}{Z_T} = V\dfrac{Z_1 + Z_2}{Z_1 Z_2}$

Branch current, $\quad I_1 = \dfrac{V}{Z_1} = I\dfrac{Z_2}{Z_1 + Z_2}$

Branch current, $\quad I_2 = \dfrac{V}{Z_2} = I\dfrac{Z_1}{Z_1 + Z_2}$

The reader may note that finding the equivalent impedance in complex form involves lengthy calculations. Such an approach to solve parallel a.c. circuits is not recommended particularly when there are more than two branches in the circuit.

Example 18.11. *Two impedances $Z_1 = (8 + j6)\ \Omega$ and $Z_2 = (3 - j4)\ \Omega$ are in parallel. If the total current of this combination is 25A, find the power taken by each impedance.*

Solution.

$$Z_1 = (8 + j6)\Omega = 10\angle 36.87°\Omega \ ; \ Z_2 = (3 - j4)\Omega = 5\angle -53.13°\Omega$$

$$Z_1 + Z_2 = (8 + j6) + (3 - j4) = (11 + j2)\Omega = 11.18\angle 10.3°\Omega$$

∴

$$I_1 = I\frac{Z_2}{Z_1 + Z_2} = 25 \times \frac{5\angle -53.13°}{11.18\angle 10.3°} = 11.18\angle -63.43°\,A$$

$$I_2 = I\frac{Z_1}{Z_1 + Z_2} = 25 \times \frac{10\angle 36.87°}{11.18\angle 10.3°} = 22.36\angle 26.57°\,A$$

Power taken by first branch $\quad = I_1^2 R_1 = (11.18)^2 \times 8 = \mathbf{1000\ W}$

Power taken by second branch $= I_2^2 R_2 = (22.36)^2 \times 3 = \mathbf{1500\ W}$

18.5. ADMITTANCE (Y)

The **admittance** *is defined as the reciprocal of impedance* just as conductance is the reciprocal of resistance *i.e.*

Admittance, $$\mathbf{Y} = \frac{1}{\mathbf{Z}} = \frac{\mathbf{I}}{\mathbf{V}}$$

The unit of admittance is *siemen* and its symbol is *S*. The admittance of a circuit may be considered as a measure of the ease with which a circuit can conduct alternating current. Thus a circuit with higher value of admittance will have a higher value of current. The reader may wonder about the utility of the new term admittance – the reciprocal of impedance – in the parallel circuit analysis. Soon we shall see its importance. Considering the Fig. 18.20, we have,

$$\frac{1}{\mathbf{Z}_T} = \frac{1}{\mathbf{Z}_1} + \frac{1}{\mathbf{Z}_2} + \frac{1}{\mathbf{Z}_3} + \ldots\ldots\ldots + \frac{1}{\mathbf{Z}_n}$$

Since admittance is the reciprocal of impedance, we have,

$$\mathbf{Y}_T = \mathbf{Y}_1 + \mathbf{Y}_2 + \mathbf{Y}_3 + \ldots\ldots\ldots + \mathbf{Y}_n$$

where $\mathbf{Y}_1, \mathbf{Y}_2, \mathbf{Y}_3 \ldots\ldots\ldots \mathbf{Y}_n$ are the individual admittances of the parallel branches and $\mathbf{Y}_T$ is the total or equivalent admittance of the circuit.

Line current, $$\mathbf{I} = \frac{\mathbf{V}}{\mathbf{Z}_T} = \mathbf{V}\,\mathbf{Y}_T$$

Fig. 18.21 Shows the parallel connected admittances.

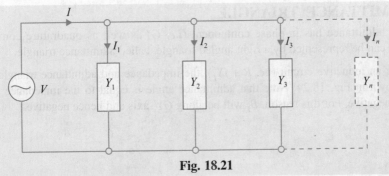

Fig. 18.21

The reader may note that admittances (in complex form) of the parallel branches are added. Thus admittance method in parallel circuits makes the approach somewhat similar to a series circuit where impedances (in complex form) are added.

18.6. COMPONENTS OF ADMITTANCE

The impedance of a circuit can be expressed in the complex form as $\mathbf{Z} = R + jX_L$ or $R - jX_C$ depending upon the nature of reactance. Here R is the resistive or in-phase component of $\mathbf{Z}$ while X_L or X_C is the reactive or quadrature component of $\mathbf{Z}$. The reciprocal of impedance (*i.e.* admittance) will also have a complex form because the reciprocal of a complex number *results in a complex number. Therefore, admittance $\mathbf{Y}$ can be expressed as :

$$\mathbf{Y} = G - jB_L \qquad \text{or} \quad G + jB_C$$

where G is called *conductance* and represents the in-phase component of $\mathbf{Y}$ while B is called the *susceptance* and represents the quadrature component of $\mathbf{Y}$. The susceptance of an inductance is

---

* If we take the reciprocal of a complex number (impedance in this case) and then rationalise the denominator, the result will be another complex number having in-phase and quadrature components.

specially called *inductive susceptance* B_L whereas that of a capacitance is called *capacitive susceptance* B_C. *Note that B_L is always negative while B_C is always positive. However, conductance G is always positive.

Magnitude of admittance,　　$Y = \sqrt{G^2 + B_L^2}$　*or*　$\sqrt{G^2 + B_C^2}$

Phase angle,　　　　　　　　$\phi = \tan^{-1} -B_L/G$ or $\tan^{-1} B_C/G$

Obviously, the units of G and B will also be siemen (S).

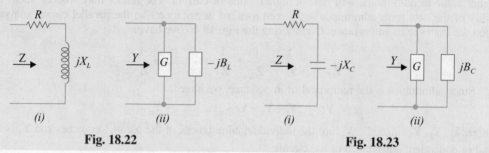

(i)	*(ii)*	*(i)*	*(ii)*
Fig. 18.22		**Fig. 18.23**	

Fig. 18.22 (*i*) shows an impedance $R + jX_L$. The admittance of this circuit consists of conductance component (G) in parallel with inductive susceptance ($- jB_L$) as shown in Fig. 18.22 (*ii*). Similarly, Fig. 18.23 (*ii*) shows the admittance components for the impedence shown in Fig. 18.23(*i*). The reader may see that the conductance and susceptance components of admittance are paralleled elements.

18.7. ADMITTANCE TRIANGLE

Since admittance has in-phase component (*i.e. G*) as well as quadrature component (*i.e.* B_L or B_C), it can be represented by a right angled triangle, called admittance triangle.

(*i*)　For an inductive circuit (*i.e.* $R + jX_L$), the impedance and admittance triangles will be as shown in Fig. 18.24. Note that admittance angle is equal to the impedance angle but is **negative. For this reason, B_L will be along OY'-axis and hence negative.

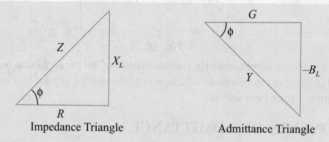

Impedance Triangle	Admittance Triangle

Fig. 18.24

Conductance,　　　　　　　$G = Y \cos \phi = \dfrac{1}{Z} \times \dfrac{R}{Z}$

---

*　This is expected because reciprocal of $R + jX_L$ will result (after rationalising the denominator) in a complex number that will have –ve quadrature component. Therefore, B_L is negative. By similar reasoning, B_C will be positive. However, in each case, the in-phase component (*i.e. G*) will be positive.

**　The reciprocal of a complex number does not change the magnitude of the angle but it changes the sign of the angle.

$$\therefore \qquad\qquad G = \frac{R}{Z^2} = \frac{R}{R^2 + X_L^2}$$

Susceptance, $\qquad\qquad B_L = Y \sin \phi = \frac{1}{Z} \times \frac{X_L}{Z}$

$$\therefore \qquad\qquad B_L = \frac{X_L}{Z^2} = \frac{X_L}{R^2 + X_L^2} \qquad\qquad\qquad (negative)$$

Phase angle, $\qquad\qquad \phi = \tan^{-1} - B_L/G$

(ii) For a capacitive circuit (i.e. $R - jX_C$), the impedance and admittance triangles will be as shown in Fig. 18.25. Note that admittance angle is equal to the impedance angle but of opposite sign. For this reason, B_C will lie along OY-axis and hence positive.

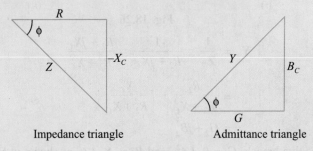

Impedance triangle $\qquad\qquad\qquad\qquad$ Admittance triangle

Fig. 18.25

Following the above procedure, we have,

$$G = \frac{R}{Z^2} = \frac{R}{R^2 + X_C^2}$$

$$B_C = \frac{X_C}{Z^2} = \frac{X_C}{R^2 + X_C^2} \qquad\qquad\qquad (positive)$$

Phase angle, $\qquad\qquad \phi = \tan^{-1} B_C/G$

Note. It is a usual practice to omit the suffix L or C with susceptance B. The positive sign with B indicates capacitive susceptance and the negative sign with B implies inductive susceptance.

18.8 ADMITTANCE METHOD

Consider the parallel circuit shown in Fig. 18.26 (i).

$$\mathbf{Y}_1 = \frac{1}{\mathbf{Z}_1} = \frac{1}{R_1 + jX_L} = {}^* \frac{R_1 - jX_L}{R_1^2 + X_L^2}$$

$$= \frac{R_1}{R_1^2 + X_L^2} - j\frac{X_L}{R_1^2 + X_L^2}$$

$$= G_1 - jB_1 \qquad\qquad\qquad ...(i)$$

Thus for inductive branch, $G_1 = R_1 / Z_1^2$ and $B_1 = X_L / Z_1^2$ as shown in Fig. 18.26 (ii). Note from eq. (i) that *inductive susceptance is negative*.

* After rationalising the denominator.

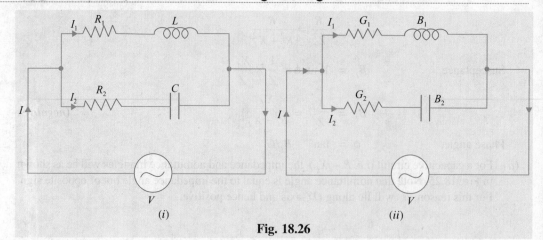

Fig. 18.26

$$\mathbf{Y}_2 = \frac{1}{\mathbf{Z}_2} = \frac{1}{R_2 + jX_C} = \frac{R_2 + jX_C}{R_2^2 + X_C^2}$$

$$= \frac{R_2}{R_2^2 + X_C^2} + j\frac{X_C}{R_2^2 + X_C^2}$$

$$= G_2 + jB_2 \qquad \qquad ...(ii)$$

Thus for capacitive branch, $G_2 = R_2 / Z_2^2$ and $B_2 = X_C / Z_2^2$ as shown in Fig. 18.26 (ii). Note from eq. (ii) that *capacitive susceptance is positive.*

$$\mathbf{Y} = \mathbf{Y}_1 + \mathbf{Y}_2 = (G_1 - jB_1) + (G_2 + jB_2)$$

$$= (G_1 + G_2) + j(-B_1 + B_2)$$

$$\therefore \qquad Y = \sqrt{(G_1 + G_2)^2 + (-B_1 + B_2)^2} \qquad \qquad ...in \ magnitude$$

Line current, $\qquad I = VY$

Phase angle, $\qquad \phi = \tan^{-1}\dfrac{-B_1 + B_2}{G_1 + G_2}$

Power consumed, $\qquad P = VI \cos \phi$

18.9. APPLICATION OF ADMITTANCE METHOD

Consider the parallel circuit shown in Fig. 18.27. The total conductance of the circuit is the sum of conductances of the branches. However, total susceptance is the *algebraic* sum of susceptances of the branches.

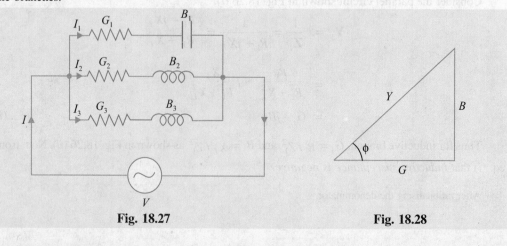

Fig. 18.27   **Fig. 18.28**

(i) Total conductance, $\quad G = G_1 + G_2 + G_3$

(ii) Total susceptance, $\quad B = B_1 - B_2 - B_3$

(iii) Admittance, $\qquad\quad Y = \sqrt{G^2 + B^2}$

(iv) Circuit current, $\qquad I = VY$

(v) Power factor, $\qquad \cos\phi = G/Y$

(vi) Power consumed, $\qquad P = VI\cos\phi = V(VY)(G/Y) = V^2G$

The currents in the individual branches are:

$$I_1 = VY_1 \text{ where } Y_1 = \sqrt{G_1^2 + B_1^2}$$

$$I_2 = VY_2 \text{ where } Y_2 = \sqrt{G_2^2 + (-B_2)^2}$$

$$I_3 = VY_3 \text{ where } Y_3 = \sqrt{G_3^2 + (-B_3)^2}$$

Example 18.12. *A circuit having a resistance of 6Ω and inductive reactance of 8Ω is connected in parallel with another circuit having a resistance of 8Ω and a capacitive reactance of 6Ω. The parallel circuit is connected across 200V, 50Hz supply. Calculate:*

(i) *supply current*

(ii) *power factor of the whole circuit*

(iii) *power consumed*

(iv) *the resistance and reactance of a series circuit which will take the same current at the same p.f. as the parallel circuit.*

Solution.

$$Z_1^2 = 6^2 + 8^2 = 100; \qquad Z_2^2 = 8^2 + 6^2 = 100$$

$$G_1 = R_1/Z_1^2 = 6/100 = 0.06\,\text{S}$$

$$B_1 = X_1/Z_1^2 = 8/100 = -0.08\,\text{S}$$

$$G_2 = R_2/Z_2^2 = 8/100 = 0.08\,\text{S}$$

$$B_2 = X_2/Z_2^2 = 6/100 = 0.06\,\text{S}$$

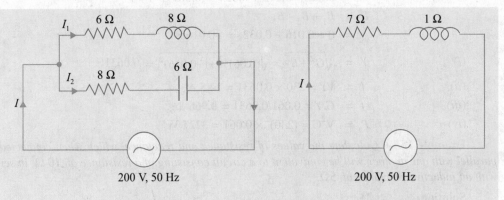

Fig. 18.29   Fig. 18.30

(i) $\qquad\qquad\qquad G = G_1 + G_2 = 0.06 + 0.08 = 0.14\,\text{S}$

$\qquad\qquad\qquad B = -B_1 + B_2 = -0.08 + 0.06 = -0.02\,\text{S} \qquad\qquad (inductive)$

$\qquad\qquad\qquad Y = \sqrt{G^2 + B^2} = \sqrt{(0.14)^2 + (-0.02)^2} = 0.1415\,\text{S}$

$\qquad\qquad\qquad I = VY = 200 \times 0.1415 = \mathbf{28.3A}$

(*ii*) $\qquad\qquad p.f = \cos \phi = G/Y = 0.14/0.1415 = \textbf{0.99} \; lag$

(*iii*) $\qquad\qquad P = V^2 G = (200)^2 \times 0.14 = \textbf{5600 W}$

Also $\qquad\qquad P = VI \cos \phi = 200 \times 28.3 \times 0.99 = 5600 \; W \qquad$ — same as above

(*iv*) Let the equivalent series resistance and reactance be R and X respectively.

$$R = G/Y^2 = 0.14/(0.1415)^2 = \textbf{7 } \Omega$$
$$X = B/Y^2 = 0.02/(0.1415)^2 = \textbf{1}\Omega$$

Since susceptance is negative, the reactance is inductive in nature. Fig. 18.30 shows the equivalent series circuit.

Example 18.13. *In the parallel circuit in Fig. 18.31, find (i) total admittance (ii) line current (iii) circuit p.f. and (iv) power consumed.*

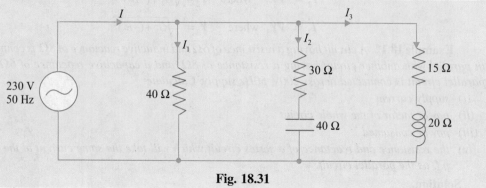

Fig. 18.31

Solution.

$R_1 = 40 \; \Omega \; ; \qquad Z_2^2 = 30^2 + 40^2 = 2500 \; ; \qquad Z_3^2 = 15^2 + 20^2 = 625$

$$\begin{aligned}
G_1 &= 1/40 = 0.025 \; S; & B_1 &= 0 \\
G_2 &= 30/2500 = 0.012 \; S; & B_2 &= 40/2500 = 0.016 \; S \\
G_3 &= 15/625 = 0.024 \; S; & B_3 &= 20/625 = -0.032 \; S
\end{aligned}$$

$\therefore \qquad\qquad G = G_1 + G_2 + G_3$

$\qquad\qquad\qquad = 0.025 + 0.012 + 0.024 = 0.061 \; S$

$\qquad\qquad B = B_1 + B_2 - B_3$

$\qquad\qquad\qquad = 0 + 0.016 - 0.032 = -0.016 \; S$

(*i*) $\qquad\qquad Y = \sqrt{G^2 + B^2} = \sqrt{(0.061)^2 + (-0.016)^2} = \textbf{0.0631S}$

(*ii*) $\qquad\qquad I = VY = 230 \times 0.0631 = \textbf{14.5 A}$

(*iii*) $\qquad\qquad p.f = G/Y = 0.061/0.0631 = \textbf{0.966} \; lag$

(*iv*) $\qquad\qquad P = V^2 G = (230)^2 \times 0.061 = \textbf{3227 W}$

Example 18.14. *Calculate the values of resistance and reactance, which when connected in parallel with one another, will be equivalent to a circuit consisting of a resistance of 10 Ω in series with an inductive reactance of 5Ω.*

Solution.

Conductance of series circuit is

$$G = R/Z^2 = 10/(10^2 + 5^2) = 0.08 \; S$$

Susceptance of series circuit is

$$B = X/Z^2 = 5/(10^2 + 5^2) = -0.04 \; S$$

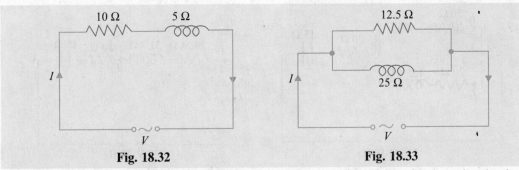

Fig. 18.32   Fig. 18.33

Since the parallel circuit is to have the same conductance and susceptance as the series circuit, the values of parameters of parallel circuit are:

$$R = 1/G = 1/0.08 = 12.5\ \Omega; \qquad X_L = 1/B = 1/0.04 = 25\ \Omega$$

Fig. 18.33 shows the equivalent parallel circuit.

Example 18.15. *A parallel circuit consisting of a 15Ω resistance in parallel with an inductance of 0.06H is connected to 230V, 50Hz source. Find the equivalent series circuit.*

Solution.

Conductance of the parallel circuit is

$$G = 1/R = 1/15 = 0.0667\ S$$

Susceptance of the parallel circuit is

$$B = 1/X_L = 1/2\pi \times 50 \times 0.06 = -0.0531\ S$$

$$Y = \sqrt{G^2 + B^2} = \sqrt{(0.0667)^2 + (-0.0531)^2} = 0.0852\,S$$

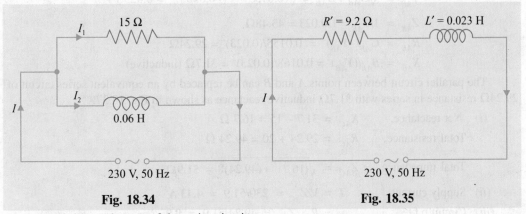

Fig. 18.34   Fig. 18.35

Equivalent resistance of the series circuit

$$R' = G/Y^2 = 0.0667/(0.0852)^2 = 9.2\ \Omega$$

Equivalent inductive reactance of the series circuit

$$X'_L = B/Y^2 = 0.0531/(0.0852)^2 = 7.31\Omega$$

$$\therefore \qquad L' = X'_L/2\pi f = 7.31/2\pi \times 50 = 0.023\ H$$

The equivalent series circuit is shown in Fig. 18.35.

Example 18.16. *For the series-parallel circuit shown in Fig. 18.36, find (i) total impedance (ii) supply current and (iii) circuit p.f.*

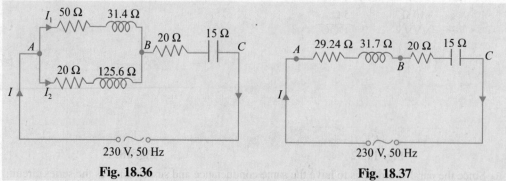

Fig. 18.36   Fig. 18.37

Solution.

$$Z_1^2 = (50)^2 + (31.4)^2 = 3486; \qquad Z_2^2 = (20)^2 + (125.6)^2 = 16170$$

$$G_1 = R_1 / Z_1^2 = 50/3486 = 0.0143 S$$

$$B_1 = X_{L1} / Z_1^2 = 31.4/3486 = -0.009 \ S$$

$$G_2 = R_2 / Z_2^2 = 20/16170 = 0.0012 S$$

$$B_2 = X_{L2} / Z_2^2 = 125.6/16170 = -0.0078 S$$

$$G_{AB} = G_1 + G_2 = 0.0143 + 0.0012 = 0.0155 S$$
$$B_{AB} = -B_1 - B_2 = -0.009 - 0.0078 = -0.0168 S$$

$$Y_{AB} = \sqrt{G_{AB}^2 + B_{AB}^2} = \sqrt{(0.0155)^2 + (-0.0168)^2} = 0.023 S$$

$$Z_{AB} = 1/Y_{AB} = 1/0.023 = 43.48 \Omega$$
$$R_{AB} = G_{AB} / (Y_{AB})^2 = 0.0155/(0.023)^2 = 29.24 \Omega$$
$$X_{AB} = B_{AB} / (Y_{AB})^2 = 0.0168/(0.023)^2 = 31.7 \Omega \text{ (inductive)}$$

The parallel circuit between points A and B can be replaced by an equivalent series circuit of 29.24Ω resistance in series with 31.7Ω inductive reactance as shown in Fig. 18.37.

(i)   Net reactance, $X_{AC} = 31.7 - 15 = 16.7 \ \Omega$

Total resistance, $R_{AC} = 29.24 + 20 = 49.24 \ \Omega$

Total impedance, $Z_{AC} = \sqrt{(16.7)^2 + (49.24)^2} = 51.9\Omega$

(ii) Supply current, $I = V/Z_{AC} = 230/51.9 = \textbf{4.43 A}$

(iii) Circuit p.f. $= R_{AC}/Z_{AC} = 49.24/51.9 = \textbf{0.95} \ lag$

TUTORIAL PROBLEMS

1. An impedance of $(2 + j3)\Omega$ is connected in series with two impedances of $(4 + j2)\Omega$ and $(1 - j5)\Omega$, which are in parallel. Calculate the line current and the circuit power factor when the combined circuit is supplied at 10V.   **[1.71 A ; 0.963 lag]**

2. In a series-parallel circuit, the two parallel branches A and B are in series with C. The impedances are $Z_A = (10 + j8)\Omega$; $Z_B = (9 - j6)\Omega$ and $Z_C = (3 + j2)\Omega$. If the voltage across C is $100\angle 0°V$, determine the values of I_A and I_B.   **[I_A = 15.7A; I_B = 18.6A]**

3. Three impedances $65\angle 45°\Omega$, $42\angle -20°\Omega$ and $30\angle -35°\Omega$ are joined in parallel and connected to 240 V, 60 Hz supply. Determine (*i*) total power (*ii*) circuit power factor (*iii*) series equivalent circuit.   [(*i*) 3613.5 W (*ii*) 0.965 *lead* (*iii*) $R = 15.38\ \Omega$, $X_C = 4.16\ \Omega$]

4. A voltage of $120\angle 60°$ volts is applied to two impedances in parallel. The impedances are $Z_1 = (2 + j3)\Omega$ and $Z_2 = (4 - j8)\ \Omega$. Determine (*i*) current in each branch (*ii*) line current (*iii*) circuit power factor.   [(*i*) $I_1 = 33.2A$; $I_2 = 13.42\ A$ (*ii*) 29A (*iii*) 0.888 *lag*]

5. An impedance of $40\angle 30°\Omega$ is connected in series with four paralleled group of impedances :
   $Z_1 = 3\angle 60°\Omega$; $Z_2 = 5\angle 40°\Omega$; $Z_3 = 8\angle 60°\Omega$ and $Z_4 = 4\angle -25°\Omega$. If the voltage drop across $40\angle 30°$ impedance is $(200 + j0)$ V, determine (*i*) current in Z_3 (*ii*) voltage drop across the paralleled section.   [(*i*) $0.845\angle -55.4°$ A (*ii*) $6.76\angle 4.58°$ V]

18.10. RESONANCE IN PARALLEL CIRCUITS

A parallel circuit containing reactive elements (L and C) is said to be in resonance when the circuit p.f. is unity *i.e.*, the reactive component of line current is zero. The frequency at which it occurs is called the *resonant frequency f_r*.

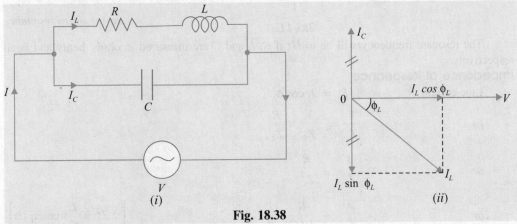

Fig. 18.38

Consider the most common parallel circuit consisting of a coil shunted by a capacitor as shown in Fig. 18.38 (*i*). The phasor diagram of this circuit is shown in Fig. 18.38 (*ii*). The circuit will be in resonance when the reactive component of line current is zero *i.e.* $I_C - I_L \sin \phi_L = 0$. This can be achieved by changing the supply frequency because both I_C and $I_L \sin \phi_L$ are frequency *dependent. At some frequency called resonant frequency f_r, the reactive component of line current will be zero and resonance takes place.

At parallel resonance,

$$I_C - I_L \sin \phi_L = 0$$

or $$I_C = I_L \sin \phi_L$$

or $$\frac{V}{X_C} = \frac{V}{Z_L} \times \frac{X_L}{Z_L}$$

. . . .

* $$I_C = V/X_C = V \times 2\pi f C$$

$$I_L \sin \phi_L = \frac{V}{Z_L} \times \sin \phi_L$$

where $$Z_L = \sqrt{R^2 + (2\pi f L)^2}\ ;\ \phi_L = \tan^{-1} X_L/R$$

or
$$X_L X_C = Z_L^2$$

or
$$\omega L / \omega C = Z_L^2 \qquad \qquad ...(i)$$

or
$$L/C = R^2 + (2\pi f_r L)^2$$

or
$$(2\pi f_r L)^2 = \frac{L}{C} - R^2$$

or
$$2\pi f_r L = \sqrt{\frac{L}{C} - R^2}$$

or
$$f_r = \frac{1}{2\pi L}\sqrt{\frac{L}{C} - R^2}$$

or
$$f_r = \frac{1}{2\pi}\sqrt{\frac{1}{LC} - \frac{R^2}{L^2}}$$

If the coil resistance is small (as is generally the case), then,

$$f_r = \frac{1}{2\pi\sqrt{LC}} \qquad \qquad ...as\ for\ series\ resonance$$

The resonant frequency will be in *Hz* if R, L and C are measured in ohms, henry and farad respectively.

Impedance at Resonance

Line current,
$$I_r = I_L \cos \phi_L$$

or
$$\frac{V}{Z_r} = \frac{V}{Z_L} \times \frac{R}{Z_L}$$

or
$$\frac{1}{Z_r} = \frac{R}{Z_L^2}$$

or
$$\frac{1}{Z_r} = \frac{R}{L/C} \qquad \left[\because Z_L^2 = \frac{L}{C} \text{ from eq.}(i) \right]$$

$$\therefore \qquad Z_r = L/CR$$

The impedance $Z_r (=L/CR)$ at parallel resonance is known as *equivalent* or *dynamic impedance*.

Note that $Z_r (=L/CR)$ is a pure resistance because there is no frequency term present. Further, the value of Z_r is very high because the ratio L/C is very large at parallel resonance.

Line current at resonance

At parallel resonance, the line current I_r is minimum and is given by;

$$I_r = V/Z_r \quad \text{where } Z_r = L/CR$$

Because Z_r is very high, I_r will be very small. The small current I_r is only the amount needed to supply the resistance losses in the circuit.

18.11. GRAPHICAL REPRESENTATION OF PARALLEL RESONANCE

The action of a resonant circuit is best explained by referring to the curves illustrating the variation in the circuit conditions at or near resonance. We shall discuss two such curves viz. impedance-frequency curve and current-frequency curve.

(*i*) **Impedance-frequency curve.** If we plot impedance-frequency graph for a parallel circuit shown in Fig. 18.38 (*i*), the shape of the curve will be as shown in Fig. 18.39. Note that the impedance of the circuit is maximum at resonance. As the frequency changes from resonance, the circuit imped-ance decreases very rapidly. This behaviour can be explained as follows. For frequencies below resonance, the capacitive reactance will be higher and thus *more current will flow through the coil. This causes the line current to lag behind the applied voltage and the circuit appears inductive. For frequencies above resonance, inductive reactance is higher and more current will flow through the capacitor. Consequently, line current leads the applied voltage and circuit appears capacitive. In either case, the circuit impedance is far less than its value at resonance.

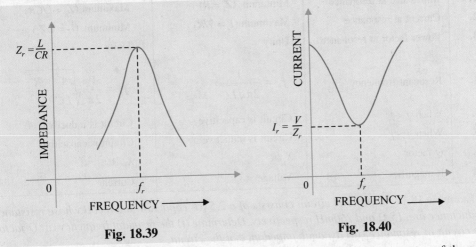

Fig. 18.39   **Fig. 18.40**

   (*ii*) **Current-frequency curve.** Fig. 18.40 shows the current-frequency curve of the parallel circuit shown in Fig. 18.38(*i*). Note that value of line current ($I_r = V/Z_r$) is minimum at resonance. As the frequency changes from resonance, the line current increases rapidly. This action can be ex-plained as follows. For frequencies other than the resonance, the reactive currents in the two branches of the circuit are not equal. The resultant reactive current must be supplied by the line. As the differ-ence of the reactive currents in the two branches increases with the amount of deviation from the resonant frequency, the line current will increase in the same manner.

18.12. Q-FACTOR OF A PARALLEL RESONANT CIRCUIT

   At parallel resonance, the current circulating between the two branches is many times greater than the line current. This current amplification produced by the resonance is termed as Q-factor of the parallel resonant circuit *i.e.*

$$Q\text{-factor} = \frac{\text{Circulating current between } L \text{ and } C}{I_r}$$

Now $I_C = V/X_C = \omega_r CV$ and $I_r = V/(L/CR)$

∴ $Q\text{-factor} = \omega_r CV \div \dfrac{V}{L/CR} = \dfrac{\omega_r L}{R}$

$$= \frac{2\pi f_r L}{R} \qquad \qquad ...same\ as\ for\ series\ circuit$$

   The Q-factor of a parallel resonant circuit can also be expressed in terms of L and C. Neglecting resistance R, the resonant frequency is given by;

$$f_r = \frac{1}{2\pi\sqrt{LC}}$$

. . . .
* In the two parallel branches, more current will flow through that branch which has less impedance.

$$\therefore \qquad Q\text{-factor} = \frac{2\pi f_r L}{R} = \frac{2\pi L}{R} \times \frac{1}{2\pi\sqrt{LC}} = \frac{1}{R}\sqrt{\frac{L}{C}}$$

18.13. COMPARISON OF SERIES AND PARALLEL RESONANT CIRCUITS

S. No.	Particular	Series Circuit	Parallel Circuit
1.	Impedance at resonance	Minimum $(Z_r = R)$	Maximum $(Z_r = L/CR)$
2.	Current at resonance	Maximum $(I_r = V/R)$	Minimum $(I_r = V/Z_r)$
3.	Power factor at resonance	Unity	Unity
4.	Resonant frequency	$f_r = \dfrac{1}{2\pi\sqrt{LC}}$	$f_r = \dfrac{1}{2\pi}\sqrt{\dfrac{1}{LC} - \dfrac{R^2}{L^2}}$
5.	When $f < f_r$	Circuit is capacitive	Circuit is inductive
6.	When $f > f_r$	Circuit is inductive	Circuit is capacitive
7.	Q-factor	X_L/R	X_L/R
8.	It magnifies	Voltage	Current

Example 18.17. *A parallel circuit consists of a 2.5 μF capacitor and a coil whose resistance and inductance are 15 Ω and 260mH respectively. Determine (i) the resonant frequency (ii) Q-factor of the circuit at resonance (iii) dynamic impedance of the circuit.*

Solution.

(*i*) Resonant frequency,

$$f_r = \frac{1}{2\pi}\sqrt{\frac{1}{LC} - \frac{R^2}{L^2}}$$

$$= \frac{1}{2\pi}\sqrt{\frac{10^6}{0.260 \times 2.5} - \frac{(15)^2}{(0.260)^2}} = 197\,\text{Hz}$$

(*ii*) $\qquad Q\text{-factor} = \dfrac{2\pi f_r L}{R} = \dfrac{2\pi \times 197 \times 0.260}{15} = 21.45$

(*iii*) $\qquad Z_r = \dfrac{L}{CR} = \dfrac{0.260}{2.5 \times 10^{-6} \times 15} = 6933\,\Omega$

Example18.18. *A tuned circuit consisting of a coil having an inductance of 200 μH and a resistance of 20 Ω is in parallel with a variable capacitor. This combination is in series with a resistor of 8000 Ω. The entire circuit is connected to a 230V, 1MHz supply. Calculate (i) the value of C to give resonance (ii) the dynamic impedance and Q-factor of the tuned circuit and (iii) the current in each branch.*

Solution.

$$X_L = 2\pi f L = 2\pi \times 10^6 \times 200 \times 10^{-6} = 1256\,\Omega$$

$$Z_L = \sqrt{R^2 + X_L^2} = \sqrt{20^2 + (1256)^2} = 1256.16\,\Omega$$

(*i*) $\qquad Z_L^2 = L/C$

$$\text{...at parallel resonance}$$

$$\therefore \qquad C = \frac{L}{Z_L^2} = \frac{200 \times 10^{-6}}{(1256.16)^2} = 126.6 \times 10^{-12}\,\text{F} = \mathbf{126.6\,pF}$$

(ii)
$$Z_r = \frac{L}{CR} = \frac{200 \times 10^{-6}}{126.6 \times 10^{-12} \times 20} = \mathbf{78957\,\Omega}$$

$$\text{Q-factor} = \frac{2\pi f_r L}{R} = \frac{2\pi \times 10^6 \times 200 \times 10^{-6}}{20} = \mathbf{62.8}$$

(iii)
$$\text{Total impedance} = 8000 + Z_r = 8000 + 78957 = 86957\,\Omega$$
$$\text{Line current, } I = 230/86957 = 2.64 \times 10^{-3}\,\text{A}$$
$$\text{P.D. across tuned ckt.} = IZ_r = 2.64 \times 10^{-3} \times 78957 = 208.4\,\text{V}$$
$$\text{Coil current, } I_L = 208.4/Z_L = 208.4/1256.16 = \mathbf{0.166\,A}$$
$$\text{Capacitor current, } I_C = 208.4/X_C = 208.4 \times 2\pi f_r C$$
$$= 208.4 \times 2\pi \times 10^6 \times 126.6 \times 10^{-12} = \mathbf{0.166\,A}$$

Note that current in each branch is 62.8 times (*i.e.*, Q-factor times) the line current.

TUTORIAL PROBLEMS

1. A coil of $1000\,\Omega$ resistance and 0.15H inductance is connected in parallel with a variable capacitor across a 2V, 10 kHz a.c. supply. Calculate (*i*) the capacitance of the capacitor when the supply current is minimum (*ii*) the dynamic impedance of the network and (*iii*) the supply current at resonance.　　　　　　　　　　　　　　[(*i*) 1690 µF (*ii*) 890 kΩ (*iii*) 2.25 µA]

2. A 0.8 µF capacitor is in parallel with a coil that has a resistance of $4\,\Omega$ and an inductance of 0.2H. Determine (*i*) the resonant frequency (*ii*) Q-factor at resonance (*iii*) input impedance at resonance.　　　　　　　　　　　　　　[(*i*) 398 Hz (*ii*) 125 (*iii*) 62.5 kΩ]

3. A coil that has an inductance L and a resistance of $8\,\Omega$ is in parallel with a variable capacitor. At $\omega = 1.5 \times 10^6$ rad/s, resonance is achieved when $C = 0.0037$ µF. What is the inductance of the coil ?　　　　　　　　　　　　　　[$L = 120$ µH]

4. An inductor for which $L = 40$mH is to be used in parallel with a 1 µF capacitor in a circuit that must have Q-factor atleast as large as 25 when the frequency is 1 kHz. What is the minimum amount of resistance the coil may have? What will the input impedance be when the minimum R is used ?　　　　　　　　　　　　　　[$R = 12.56\ \Omega$; $Z = 3185\ \Omega$]

5. A coil has a resistance of $400\ \Omega$ and inductance of 318 µH. Find the capacitance of a capacitor which, when connected in parallel with the coil, will produce resonance with a supply frequency of 1MHz. If a second capacitor of capacitance 23.5 pF is connected in parallel with the first capacitor, find the frequency at which resonance will occur. 　　[76.5 pF ; 870 kHz]

MULTIPLE-CHOICE QUESTIONS

1. Domestic appliances are connected in parallel across a.c. mains because...................
   (*a*) it is a simple arrangement
   (*b*) operation of each appliance becomes independent of the other
   (*c*) appliances have same currents ratings
   (*d*) this arrangement occupies less space

2. When a parallel a.c. circuit contains a number of branches, then it is convenient to solve the circuit by.......
   (*a*) phasor diagram
   (*b*) phasor algebra
   (*c*) equivalent impedance method
   (*d*) none of the above

3. The power taken by the circuit shown in Fig. 18.41 is ....

    (a) 480 W   (b) 1920 W

    (c) 1200 W   (d) none of the above

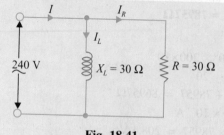

Fig. 18.41

4. The total line current drawn by the circuit shown in Fig. 18.41 is ....

    (a) $8/\sqrt{2}$ A   (b) 16 A

    (c) $8\sqrt{2}$ A   (d) none of the above

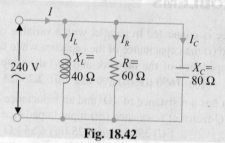

Fig. 18.42

5. The active component of line current in Fig. 18.42 is............

    (a) 6A   (b) 3 A

    (c) 13 A   (d) 4 A

6. The line current drawn by the circuit shown in Fig. 18.42 is ....

    (a) 13 A   (b) 6 A

    (c) 5 A   (d) none of the above

7. The power factor of the circuit shown in Fig. 18.42 is ....

    (a) 0.8   (b) 0.5

    (c) 0.707   (d) none of the above

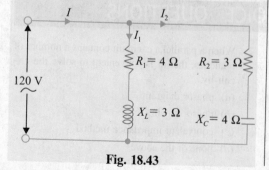

Fig. 18.43

8. If the circuit shown in Fig. 18.43 is connected to 120V d.c., the current drawn by the circuit is ....

    (a) 24 A   (b) 70 A

    (c) 48 A   (d) 30 A

9. If the source frequency in Fig. 18.44 is low, then, ...

    (a) coil takes a high lagging current

    (b) coil takes a low lagging current

    (c) capacitor takes a high leading current

    (d) circuit offers high impedance

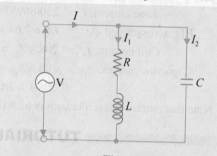

Fig. 18.44

10. The circuit shown in Fig. 18.44 will be in resonance when ....

    (a) $X_L = X_C$

    (b) $I_1 = I_2$

    (c) V and I are in phase

    (d) none of the above

11. The admittance of the circuit shown in Fig. 18.45 is ....

    (a) 10 S   (b) 14 S

    (c) 0.1 S   (d) none of the above

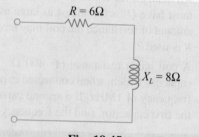

Fig. 18.45

12. The conductance of the circuit shown in Fig. 18.45 is ....

    (a) 14 S   (b) 0.6 S

    (c) 0.06 S   (d) none of the above

13. The inductive susceptance of the circuit shown in Fig. 18.45 is ....

    (a) 8 S   (b) 0.8 S

    (c) 0.08 S   (d) none of the above

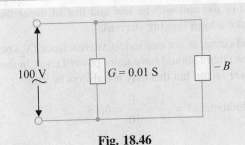

Fig. 18.46

14. The power loss in the circuit shown in Fig. 18.46 is ....
    (a) 100 W   (b) 10,000 W
    (c) 10 W   (d) none of the above

15. The impedance of a circuit is 10 ohms. If the inductive susceptance is 1 S, then inductive reactance of the circuit is ....
    (a) 10 Ω   (b) 1 Ω
    (c) 100 Ω   (d) none of the above

16. A circuit has an impedance of $(1 - j2)\Omega$. The susceptance of the circuit is................
    (a) 0.1 S   (b) 0.2 S
    (c) 0.4 S   (d) none of the above

17. A circuit has admittance of 0.1 S and conductance of 0.08S. The power factor of the circuit is ....
    (a) 0.1   (b) 0.8
    (c) 0.08   (d) none of the above

18. In a parallel a.c. circuit, if the supply frequency is more than the resonant frequency, then the circuit is ....
    (a) resistive   (b) inductive
    (c) capacitive   (d) none of the above

19. At parallel resonance, the circuit draws a current of 2mA. If the Q of the circuit is 100, then current through the capacitor is..........
    (a) 2 mA   (b) 1 mA
    (c) 200 mA   (d) none of the above

20. The Q-factor of a parallel tuned circuit can be increased by ....
    (a) increasing circuit resistance
    (b) decreasing circuit resistance
    (c) decreasing inductance of the circuit
    (d) none of the above

Answers to Multiple-Choice Questions

1. (b)	2. (b)	3. (b)	4. (c)	5. (d)	6. (c)
7. (a)	8. (d)	9. (a)	10. (c)	11. (c)	12. (c)
13. (c)	14. (a)	15. (c)	16. (c)	17. (b)	18. (c)
19. (c)	20. (b)				

Hints to Selected Multiple-Choice Questions

3. Power is consumed only in R as L and C consume no power.
   Current in R = 240/30 = 8A
   ∴ Power consumed = $(8)^2 \times 30$ = **1920 W**

4. Total line current = $\sqrt{8^2 + 8^2}$ = $8\sqrt{2}$ **A**

5. Active component of current = I_R = 240/60 = **4A**

6. Line current = $\sqrt{I_R^2 + (I_L - I_C)^2}$ = $\sqrt{(4)^2 + (6-3)^2}$ = **5A**

7. $I \cos \phi$ = 4 ....active component of current
   ∴ $\cos \phi$ = 4/I = 4/5 = **0.8**

8. D.C. cannot pass through a capacitor. Therefore, R_2 - X_C branch will act as an open for d.c. The direct current will pass through the branch R_1 - X_L. In this branch, only R_1 (= 4 Ω) will offer opposition as $X_L = 0$ for d.c.
   ∴ Circuit current = 120/4 = **30 A**

9. If the frequency is low, the reactance ($= 2\pi fL$) of the coil will be low and that of capacitor ($= 1/2\,\pi\,fC$) will be high. Hence, the **coil will take a high lagging current**.

10. In general, the condition for resonance in parallel circuit is not that inductive reactance (X_L) be equal to the capacitive reactance (X_C) but that the circuit should have unity power factor. In the special case, equal reactances result at unity power factor, but this may not always be true.

11. Circuit impedance, $Z = \sqrt{6^2 + 8^2} = 10\,\Omega$ $\therefore$ Admittance, $Y = \dfrac{1}{Z} = \dfrac{1}{10} = 0.1\,S$

12. Conductance, $G = \dfrac{R}{Z^2} = \dfrac{6}{100} = 0.06\,S$

13. Inductive susceptance, $B = \dfrac{X_L}{Z^2} = \dfrac{8}{100} = 0.08\,S$

14. Power loss in admittance $= V^2 G = (100)^2 \times 0.01 = 100$ W

15. $B = X_L / Z^2$ $\therefore X_L = B \times Z^2 = 1 \times (10)^2 = 100\,\Omega$

16. $B = \dfrac{X_C}{Z^2} = \dfrac{2}{(1)^2 + (2)^2} = \dfrac{2}{5} = 0.4\,S$

17. $G = Y \cos\phi$ $\therefore \cos\phi = G/Y = 0.08/0.1 = 0.8$

18. If the supply frequency is more than the resonant frequency, then:

   (*i*) X_L increases and I_L decreases

   (*ii*) X_C decreases and I_C increases

   (*iii*) the resultant line current will be capacitive and will lead the line voltage.

   Hence the circuit will act as a **capacitive** circuit.

19. $Q = \dfrac{\text{Circulating current between } L \text{ and } C}{\text{Line current}}$

   $100 = \dfrac{\text{Current through } C}{2\text{mA}}$

   $\therefore$ Current through $C = 100 \times 2 = \mathbf{200}$ **mA**

20. $Q = \dfrac{1}{R}\sqrt{\dfrac{L}{C}}$

   Clearly, Q of the circuit can be increased by **decreasing** R in the inductive branch.

19

Three-Phase Circuits

INTRODUCTION

The a.c. circuits discussed so far in the book are termed as single phase circuits because they contain a single alternating current and voltage wave. The generator producing a single phase supply (called single-phase generator) has only one armature winding. But if the generator is arranged to have two or more separate windings displaced from each other by equal electrical angles, it is called a *polyphase generator and will produce as many independent voltages as the number of windings or phases. The electrical displacement between the windings depends upon the number of windings or phases. For example, a 2-phase generator has two separate but identical windings that are 90° electrical apart and rotate in a common magnetic field. Obviously, such a generator will produce two alternating voltages of the same magnitude and frequency having a phase difference of 90°. Similarly, a 3-phase generator has three separate but identical windings that are 120° electrical apart and

---

* The electrical displacement between the windings is determined by the number of phases or windings. For a 2-phase alternator, the two windings are displaced by 90 electrical degrees. For other polyphase systems (*e.g.,* 3-phase, 6-phase), the electrical displacement between different phases or windings is equal to 360/N where N is the number of phases. Thus, for a 3-phase alternator, the three windings are 120 electrical degrees apart.

rotate in a common magnetic field. A 3-phase generator will, therefore, produce three voltages of the same magnitude and frequency but displaced 120° electrical from one another. Although several polyphase systems are possible, the 3-phase system is by far the most popular. In this chapter, we shall confine our attention to 3-phase system.

19.1. POLYPHASE SYSTEMS

Fig. 19.1 shows the generation of single-phase, two-phase and 3-phase voltages.

(i) Fig. 19.1 (i) shows an elementary single-phase alternator. It has one winding or coil A rotating in anticlockwise direction with an angular velocity ω in the 2-pole field. The equation of the e.m.f. induced in the coil is given by;

$$e_{a_1 a_2} = E_m \sin \omega t$$

(ii) Fig. 19.1 (ii) shows an elementary two-phase alternator. It has two identical coils A and B displaced 90° electrical from each other and rotating in anticlockwise direction with an angular velocity ω in the 2-pole field. The wave diagram is shown in Fig. 19.1 (ii). Note that the e.m.f. in coil A leads that in coil B by 90°. The equations of the two e.m.f.s are :

$$e_{a_1 a_2} = E_m \sin \omega t$$
$$e_{b_1 b_2} = E_m \sin (\omega t - 90°)$$

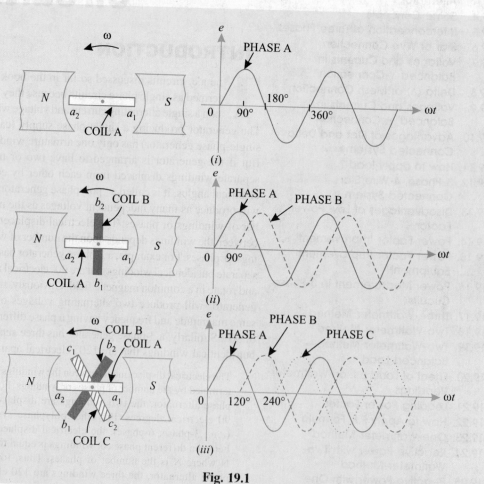

Fig. 19.1

(*iii*) Fig. 19.1 (*iii*) shows an elementary 3-phase alternator. It has three identical windings or coils A, B and C displaced *120 electrical degrees from each other and rotating in anticlockwise direction with angular velocity ω in the 2-pole field. Fig. 19.1 (*iii*) shows the wave diagram. Note that e.m.f. in coil B will be 120° behind that of coil A and e.m.f. in coil C will be 240° behind that of coil A. The equations of the three e.m.f.s can be represented as :

$$e_{a_1 a_2} = E_m \sin \omega t$$

$$e_{b_1 b_2} = E_m \sin (\omega t - 120°)$$

$$e_{c_1 c_2} = E_m \sin (\omega t - 240°)$$

19.2. REASONS FOR THE USE OF 3-PHASE SYSTEM

Electric power is generated, transmitted and distributed in the form of 3-phase power. Homes and small establishments are wired for single phase power but this merely represents a tap-off from the basic 3-phase system. Three-phase power is preferred over single-phase power for the following reasons :

(*i*)   3-phase power has a constant magnitude whereas single-phase power pulsates from zero to peak value at twice the supply frequency.

(*ii*)   A 3-phase system can set up a rotating magnetic field in stationary windings. This cannot be done with a single-phase current.

(*iii*)   For the same rating, 3-phase machines (*e.g.*, generators, motors, transformers) are smaller, simpler in construction and have better operating characteristics than single phase machines.

(*iv*)   To transmit the same amount of power over a fixed distance at a given voltage, the 3-phase system requires only three-fourth the weight of copper that is required by the single-phase system.

(*v*)   The voltage regulation of a 3-phase transmission line is better than that of a single-phase line.

A knowledge of 3-phase power and 3-phase circuits is, therefore, essential to an understanding of power technology. Fortunately, the basic circuit techniques used to solve single-phase circuits can be directly applied to 3-phase circuits. It is because the three phases are identical and one phase (*i.e.*, single phase) represents the behaviour of all the three.

19.3. ELEMENTARY THREE-PHASE ALTERNATOR

In an actual 3-phase alternator, the three windings or coils are stationary and the field **rotates. Fig. 19.2 (*i*) shows an elementary 3-phase alternator. The three identical coils A, B and C are symmetrically placed in such a way that e.m.f.s induced in them are displaced 120 electrical degrees from one another. Since the coils are identical and are subjected to the same rotating field, the e.m.f.s induced in them will be of the same magnitude and frequency. Fig. 19.2 (*ii*) shows the wave diagram of the three e.m.f.s whereas Fig. 19.2 (*iii*) shows the phasor diagram. Note that r.m.s. values have been used in drawing the phasor diagram. The equations of the three e.m.f.s are :

$$e_A = E_m \sin \omega t$$

$$e_B = E_m \sin (\omega t - 120°)$$

$$e_C = E_m \sin (\omega t - 240°)$$

It can be proved in many ways that the sum of the three e.m.f.s at every instant is zero.

(*i*)   Resultant $= e_A + e_B + e_C$

$$= E_m [\sin \omega t + \sin (\omega t - 120°) + \sin (\omega t - 240°)]$$

*   This can be accomplished by placing their start ends (denoted by a_1, b_1 and c_1) 120 electrical degrees apart.
**   This arrangement has many technical and economical advantages.

$$= E_m \left[\sin \omega t + 2 \sin (\omega t - 180°) \cos 60° \right]$$
$$= E_m \left[\sin \omega t - 2 \sin \omega t \cos 60° \right]$$
$$= 0$$

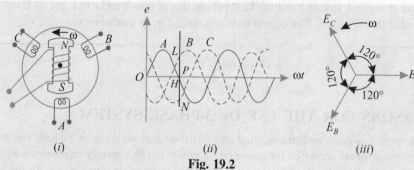

Fig. 19.2

(i)   (ii)   (iii)

(ii) Referring to the wave diagram in Fig. 19.2 (*ii*), the sum of the three e.m.f.s at any instant is zero. For example, at the instant *P*, ordinate *PL* is positive while the ordinates *PN* and *PH* are negative. If you make actual measurements, it will be seen that :

$$PL + (- PN) + (- PH) = 0$$

(iii) Since the three windings or coils are identical, $E_A = E_B = E_C = E$ (in magnitude). As shown in Fig. 19.3, the resultant of E_A and E_B is E_r and its magnitude is $= 2E \cos 60° = E$. This resultant is equal and opposite to E_C. Hence the resultant of the three e.m.f.s is zero.

(iv) Using complex algebra, we can again prove that the sum of the three e.m.f.s is zero. Thus, taking E_A as the reference phasor, we have,

$$\mathbf{E}_A = E \angle 0° = E + j\,0$$
$$\mathbf{E}_B = E \angle - 120°$$
$$= E\,(-0.5 - j\,0.866)$$
$$\mathbf{E}_C = E \angle - 240°$$
$$= E\,(-0.5 - j\,0.866)$$
$$\therefore \mathbf{E}_A + \mathbf{E}_B + \mathbf{E}_C = (E + j\,0) + E\,(-0.5 - j\,0.866)$$
$$+ E\,(-0.5 + j\,0.866) = 0$$

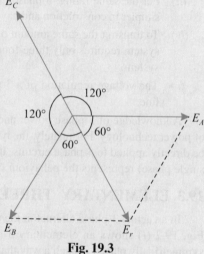

Fig. 19.3

19.4. SOME CONCEPTS

In the analysis of 3-phase system, we often come across the following terms :

(i) Phase sequence. The order in which the voltages in the three phases (or coils) reach their *maximum positive values is called the *phase sequence* or *phase order*. This is determined by the direction of rotation of the alternator. Thus, in Fig. 19.2 (*i*), the three coils *A*, *B* and *C* are producing voltages that are displaced 120 electrical degrees from one another. Referring to the wave diagram in Fig. 19.2 (*ii*), it is easy to see that voltage in coil *A* attains maximum positive value first, next coil *B* and then coil *C*. Hence the phase sequence is *ABC*. If the direction of rotation of the alternator is reversed, then the order in which the three phases attain their maximum positive values would be *ACB*. Hence the phase sequence is now *ACB i.e.*, voltage in coil *A* attains maximum positive value first, next coil *C* and then coil *B*. Since the alternator can be rotated in either clockwise or anticlockwise direction, there can be only two possible phase sequences.

. . . .

* Instead of the positive maximum value, any other instantaneous value can be used to determine the phase sequence.

(ii) **Naming the phases.** The three phases or windings may be numbered (1, 2, 3) or lettered (*A, B, C*). However, it is a usual practice to name the three phases or windings after the three natural colours viz. red (*R*), yellow (*Y*) and blue (*B*). In that case, the phase sequence is *RYB, i.e.* voltage in phase *R* attains maximum positive value first, next phase *Y* and then phase *B*. It may be noted that there are only two possible phase sequences viz *RYB* and *RBY*. By convention, sequence *RYB* is taken as positive and *RBY* as negative. Throughout this book, the phase sequence considered is *RYB* unless stated otherwise.

(iii) **Double-subscript notation.** The double-subscript notation is a very useful concept and may be found advantageous in the analysis of 3-phase system. In this notation, two letters are placed at the foot of the symbol for voltage or current. The two letters indicate the two points between which voltage (or current) exists and the order of the letters indicates the relative polarity of voltage (or current)during *positive half-cycle.

(*a*)　Thus, V_{RY} indicates a voltage *V* between points *R* and *Y* with point *R* being positive *w.r.t.* point *Y* during its positive half-cycle. On the other hand, V_{YR} means that point *Y* is positive *w.r.t.* point *R* during its positive half-cycle.
Obviously,　　　　　$V_{RY} = -V_{YR}$

(*b*)　Again I_{RY} indicates a current *I* between points *R* and *Y* and that its direction is from *R* to *Y* during its positive half-cycle. The advantage of double-subscript notation lies in the fact that a formal description of voltage or current under consideration is not necessary; the subscripts and the order of the subscripts describe the quantity completely.

19.5. INTERCONNECTION OF THREE PHASES

In a 3-phase alternator, there are three windings or phases. Each phase has two terminals viz. start and finish. If a separate load is connected across each winding as shown in Fig. 19.4, 6 conductors are required to transmit power. This will make the whole system complicated and expensive. In practice, the three windings are interconnected to give rise to two methods of connections viz.

　(*i*)　Star or Wye (*Y*) connection　　　　(*ii*)　Mesh or Delta (Δ) connection

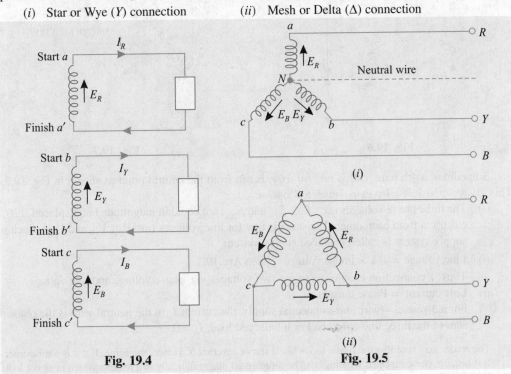

Fig. 19.4　　　　　　　　　　　　　　　**Fig. 19.5**

----

*　　One may consider negative half-cycle. This criterion must be applied to all the three phases.

(*i*) In *Y*-connection, similar ends (start or finish) of the three phases are joined together within the alternator and three lines are run from the other free ends as shown in Fig. 19.5 (*i*). The common point *N* is called neutral point. In *Y*-connection, neutral conductor (shown dotted) may or may not be brought out. If a neutral conductor exists, the system is called *3-phase, 4-wire system*. If there is no neutral conductor, it is called *3-phase, 3-wire system*.

(*ii*) In Δ-connection, dissimilar ends (start to finish) of the phases are joined to form a closed mesh and the three lines are run from the junction points as shown in Fig. 19.5 (*ii*). In a Δ-connection, no neutral point exists and only *3-phase, 3-wire system* can be formed.

Note. The *Y* or delta connection serves substantially all the functions of three separate single phase circuits but with one important advantage that the number of conductors required is reduced. This results in the saving of conductor material and hence leads to economy.

19.6. STAR OR WYE CONNECTION

In this method, *similar ends* (start or finish) of the three phases are joined together to form a common junction *N* as shown in Fig. 19.6. The common junction *N* is called the *star point* or *neutral point*. The three line conductors are run from the three free ends (finish ends *F* in this case) and are designated as *R, Y* and *B*. This constitutes a *3-phase, 3-wire star-connected system*. The voltage between any line and the neutral point (*i.e.*, voltage across each winding) is called the *phase voltage* while the voltage between any two lines is called the *line voltage*. The currents flowing in the phases are called the *phase currents* while those flowing in the lines are called the *line currents*. Note that the phase sequence is *RYB*.

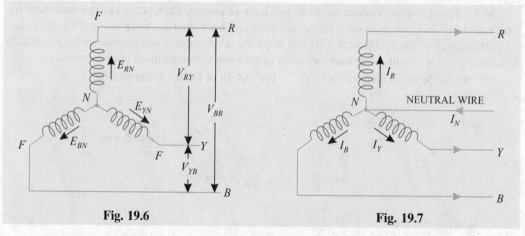

Fig. 19.6   **Fig. 19.7**

Sometimes, a 4th wire, called *neutral wire*, is run from the neutral point as shown in Fig. 19.7. This gives *3-phase, 4-wire star-connected system*.

(*i*) The three phase voltages (*i.e.*, E_{RN}, E_{YN} and E_{BN}) are equal in magnitude but displaced 120° electrical from each other. The same is true for line voltages (*i.e.* V_{RY}, V_{YB} and V_{BR}). Such a supply system is called balanced supply system.

(*ii*) Line voltage = $\sqrt{3}$ × Phase voltage   ... See Art. 19.7.

Thus, *Y* connection enables us to use two voltages viz. phase voltage and line voltage.

(*iii*) Line current = Phase current

(*iv*) For a 3-phase, 4-wire star-connected supply, the current I_N in the neutral wire is the phasor sum of the three line currents. For a balanced load, $I_N = 0$.

* The reader may note that the figure looks like a star or inverted Y. Hence, the name. But it is a misnomer. It is because star-connected windings can be represented diagramatically in a manner which does not look like a star or inverted *Y*.

Note. The arrowheads alongside currents (or voltages) indicate their directions when they are assumed to be *positive* and not their actual directions at a particular instant. At no instant will *all the three line currents flow in the same direction either outwards or inwards*. This is expected because the three line currents are displaced 120° from one another. When one is positive, the other two might both be negative or one positive and one negative. Thus, at any one instant, current flows from the alternator through one of the lines to the load and returns through the other two lines. Or else current flows from the alternator through two of the lines and returns by means of the third.

19.7. VOLTAGES AND CURRENTS IN BALANCED Y-CONNECTION

Fig. 19.8 shows a balanced 3-phase Y-connected system in which the r.m.s. values of the e.m.f.s generated in the three phases are E_{RN}, E_{YN} and E_{BN}. It is clear from the circuit diagram (See Fig. 19.8) that p.d. between any two line terminals (*i.e.,* line voltage) is the phasor difference between the potentials of these terminals *w.r.t.* neutral point *i.e.,*

P.D. between lines R and Y, $*V_{RY} = E_{RN} - E_{YN}$ ... *phasor difference*

P.D. between lines Y and B, $V_{YB} = E_{YN} - E_{BN}$ ... —do—

P.D. between lines B and R, $V_{BR} = E_{BN} - E_{RN}$ ...—do—

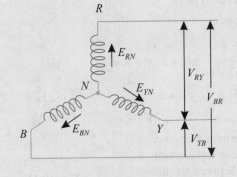

Fig. 19.8

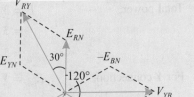
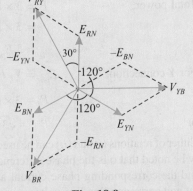

Fig. 19.9

1. Relation between line voltage and phase voltage

Considering the lines R and Y, the line voltage V_{RY} is equal to the phasor difference of E_{RN} and E_{YN}. To subtract E_{YN} from E_{RN}, reverse the phasor E_{YN} and find its phasor sum with E_{RN} as shown in the phasor diagram in Fig. 19.9. The two phasors E_{RN} and $-E_{YN}$ are equal in magnitude ($= E_{ph}$) and are 60° apart.

∴ $V_{RY} = 2E_{ph} \cos (60°/2) = 2E_{ph} \cos 30° = \sqrt{3}\ E_{ph}$

Similarly, $V_{YB} = E_{YN} - E_{BN}$ ... *phasor difference*

         $= \sqrt{3}\ E_{ph}$

and $V_{BR} = E_{BN} - E_{RN}$ ... *phasor difference*

         $= \sqrt{3}\ E_{ph}$

Hence in a balanced 3-phase Y-connection,

(*i*)   Line voltage, $V_L = \sqrt{3}\ E_{ph}$

(*ii*)   All line voltages are equal in magnitude (*i.e.,* $= \sqrt{3}\ E_{ph}$) but displaced 120° apart from one another (See the phasor diagram in Fig. 19.9).

(*iii*)   Line voltages are 30° ahead of their respective phase voltages.

* $V_{RY} = E_{RN} + E_{NY}$ .... phasor sum

     $= E_{RN} - E_{YN}$ .... phasor difference

Between lines R and Y, there is point N (*i.e.,* neutral point). The voltage V_{RY} is the phasor sum of voltages from R to N and N to Y.

2. Relation between line current and phase current

In Y-connection, each line conductor is connected in series to a separate phase as shown in Fig. 19.10. Therefore, current in a line conductor is the same as that in the phase to which the line conductor is connected.

∴ Line current, $\qquad I_L = I_{ph}$

Fig. 19.11 shows the phasor diagram for a balanced lagging load; the phase angle being ϕ.

Hence in a balanced 3-phase Y-connection :

(*i*) Line current, $\qquad I_L = I_{ph}$

(*ii*) All the line currents are equal in magnitude (*i.e.*, $= I_{ph}$) but displaced 120° from one another.

(*iii*) The angle between the line currents and the corresponding line voltages is $30° \pm \phi$; + if p.f. is lagging and − if it is leading.

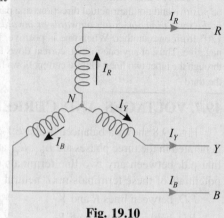

Fig. 19.10

Power

Total power, $\qquad P = 3 \times$ Power in each phase

$\qquad\qquad = 3 \times E_{ph} I_{ph} \cos \phi$

$\qquad\qquad = 3 E_{ph} I_{ph} \cos \phi \qquad\qquad ... (i)$

For Y-connection, $\qquad E_{ph} = V_L / \sqrt{3}; \; I_{ph} = I_L$

∴ $\qquad\qquad P = 3 \times (V_L / \sqrt{3}) \times I_L \times \cos \phi$

or $\qquad\qquad P = \sqrt{3} \, V_L I_L \cos \phi \qquad\qquad ...(ii)$

Either of relations (*i*) and (*ii*) can be used to determine the power. It may be noted that ϕ is the phase difference between a phase voltage and the corresponding phase current and *not* between the line current and corresponding line voltage.

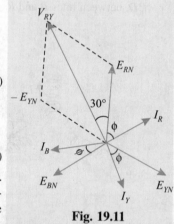

Fig. 19.11

Example 19.1. *Three coils, each having a resistance of 20 Ω and an inductive reactance of 15 Ω, are connected in star to a 400V, 3-phase, 50Hz supply. Calculate (i) the line current, (ii) power factor, and (iii) power supplied.*

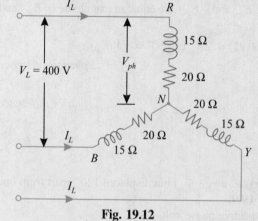

Fig. 19.12

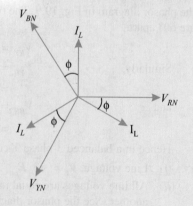

Fig. 19.13

Solution. $\qquad\qquad V_{ph} = V_L / \sqrt{3} = 400/\sqrt{3} = 231V$

$\qquad\qquad\qquad Z_{ph} = \sqrt{20^2 + 15^2} = 25 \; \Omega$

$$I_{ph} = V_{ph}/Z_{ph} = 231/25 = 9.24 \text{ A}$$

(i) $\qquad I_L = I_{ph} = \textbf{9.24 A}$

(ii) $\qquad$ p.f. $= \cos \phi = R_{ph}/Z_{ph} = 20/25 = \textbf{0.8} \; lag$

(iii) $\qquad P = \sqrt{3} V_L I_L \cos \phi = \sqrt{3} \times 400 \times 9.24 \times 0.8 = \textbf{5121 W}$

Alternatively, $\qquad P = 3I_{ph}^2 R_{ph} = 3 \times (9.24)^2 \times 20 = 5121 \text{ W}$

Example 19.2. *Calculate the active and reactive components of current in each phase of a star-connected 10,000 volts, 3-phase generator supplying 5,000 kW at a lagging p.f. 0.8. Find the new output if the current is maintained at the same value but the p.f. is raised to 0.9 lagging.*

Solution. $\qquad P = \sqrt{3} V_L I_L \cos \phi$

or $\qquad I_L = \dfrac{P}{\sqrt{3} V_L \cos \phi} = \dfrac{5000 \times 10^3}{\sqrt{3} \times 10,000 \times 0.8} = 360.8 \text{ A}$

∴ $\qquad I_{ph} = I_L = 360.8 \text{ A}$

Active component $\qquad = I_{ph} \cos \phi = 360.8 \times 0.8 = \textbf{288.64 A}$

Reactive component $\qquad = I_{ph} \sin \phi = 360.8 \times 0.6 = \textbf{216.48 A}$

Power output when p.f. is raised to 0.9 lagging

$$= \sqrt{3} \times 10,000 \times 360.8 \times 0.9 = \textbf{5624} \times 10^3 \text{ W}$$

Example 19.3. *A balanced star-connected load of impedance $(6 + j8)$ ohms per phase is connected to a 3-phase, 230V, 50Hz supply. Find the line current and power absorbed by each phase.*

Solution. $\qquad Z_{ph} = \sqrt{6^2 + 8^2} = 10 \; \Omega$

$$V_{ph} = V_L / \sqrt{3} = 230/\sqrt{3} = 133 \text{ V}$$
$$\cos \phi = R_{ph}/Z_{ph} = 6/10 = 0.6 \; lag$$
$$I_{ph} = V_{ph}/Z_{ph} = 133/10 = 13.3 \text{ A}$$

∴ Line current, $\qquad I_L = I_{ph} = \textbf{13.3 A}$

Power absorbed/phase $\qquad = V_{ph} I_{ph} \cos \phi = 133 \times 13.3 \times 0.6 = \textbf{1061 W}$

Example 19.4. *Three 50-ohm resistors are connected in star across 400V, 3-phase supply.*

(i) *Find phase current, line current and power taken from the mains.*

(ii) *What would be the above values if one of the resistors were disconnected ?*

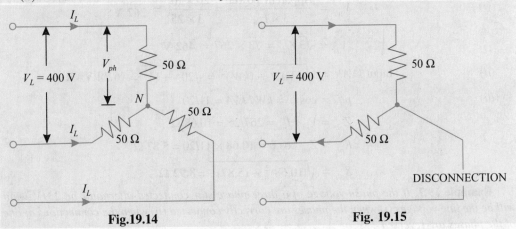

Fig.19.14 $\qquad\qquad\qquad\qquad\qquad$ **Fig. 19.15**

Solution. $\qquad V_L = 400V;\ V_{ph} = 400/\sqrt{3} = 231V;\ R_{ph} = 50\Omega;\ \cos\phi = 1$

(*i*) **When the three resistors are star-connected** [See Fig. 19.14].

$$I_{ph} = V_{ph}/R_{ph} = 231/50 = 4.62\text{ A}$$

$\therefore\qquad\qquad I_L = I_{ph} = 4.62\text{ A}$

Power taken, $\qquad P = \sqrt{3}\ V_L\ I_L\cos\phi = \sqrt{3} \times 400 \times 4.62 \times 1 = 3200\text{ W}$

(*ii*) **When one of the resistors is disconnected.** When one of the resistors is disconnected [See Fig. 19.15], the remaining two resistors behave as if they were connected in series across the line voltage. In fact, the circuit behaves as a single phase circuit.

$\therefore\qquad\qquad I_{ph} = I_L = \dfrac{400}{50 + 50} = 4\text{ A}$

Power taken, $\qquad P = V_L I_L \cos\phi = 400 \times 4 \times 1 = 1600\text{ W}$

Hence, by disconnecting one of the resistors, power consumption is reduced by half.

Example 19.5. *Three similar coils, connected in star, take a total power of 1.5 kW at a p.f. of 0.2 lagging from a 3-phase, 400V, 50Hz supply. Calculate the resistance and inductance of each coil.*

Solution. $\qquad\qquad V_{ph} = V_L/\sqrt{3} = 400/\sqrt{3} = 231\text{ V}$

$$P = \sqrt{3}\ V_L\ I_L\cos\phi$$

$\therefore\qquad I_L = \dfrac{P}{\sqrt{3}\ V_L\cos\phi} = \dfrac{1500}{\sqrt{3} \times 400 \times 0.2} = 10.83\text{ A}$

$I_{ph} = I_L = 10.83\text{ A}$

$Z_{ph} = V_{ph}/I_{ph} = 231/10.83 = 21.33\ \Omega$

$R_{ph} = Z_{ph}\cos\phi = 21.33 \times 0.2 = 4.27\ \Omega$

$X_{ph} = \sqrt{(21.33)^2 - (4.27)^2} = 20.9\ \Omega$

$L_{ph} = X_{ph}/2\pi f = 20.9/2\pi \times 50 = 0.0665\text{ H}$

Example 19.6. *The load to a 3-phase supply comprises three similar coils connected in star. The line currents are 25A and the kVA and kW inputs are 20 and 11 respectively. Find (i) the phase and line voltages (ii) the kVAR input and (iii) resistance and reactance of each coil.*

Solution.

(*i*) $\qquad\qquad V_{ph} = \dfrac{\text{Apparent power}}{3 \times I_{ph}} = \dfrac{20 \times 10^3}{3 \times 25} = 267\text{ V}$

$$V_L = \sqrt{3}V_{ph} = \sqrt{3} \times 267 = 462\text{ V}$$

(*ii*) $\qquad$ Input $kVAR = \sqrt{(kVA)^2 - (kW)^2} = \sqrt{20^2 - 11^2} = 16.7\text{ kVAR}$

(*iii*) $\qquad\qquad p.f. = \cos\phi = kW/kVA = 11/20$

$Z_{ph} = V_{ph}/I_{ph} = 267/25 = 10.68\ \Omega$

$R_{ph} = Z_{ph}\cos\phi = 10.68 \times 11/20 = 5.87\ \Omega$

$X_{ph} = \sqrt{(10.68)^2 - (5.87)^2} = 8.92\ \Omega$

Example 19.7. *If the phase voltage of a three-phase star connected alternator be 231V, what will be the line voltages (i) when the phases are correctly connected (ii) when the connections of one of the phases are reversed?*

Solution.

(*i*) **When the phases are correctly connected.** When the phases are connected correctly (*i.e.*, start or finish ends are joined together), the phasor diagram will be as shown in Fig. 19.9 (Refer back). As proved in Art. 19.7,

$$V_{RY} = V_{YB} = V_{BR} = \sqrt{3} \, E_{ph}$$

Each line voltage, $\qquad V_L = \sqrt{3} \, E_{ph} = \sqrt{3} \times 231 = 400 \text{ V}$

(*ii*) **When one phase connection is reversed.** Suppose connections to phase *B* have been reversed. It simply means that the finished end of phase *B* has been connected to the start ends of the other two phases at *N* as shown in Fig. 19.16. Note that the voltage in phase *B* is now E_{NB} (instead of E_{BN}) acting outwards from *N*. Thus, we have three phase voltages E_{RN}, E_{YN} and E_{NB} 120° apart as shown in Fig. 19.17.

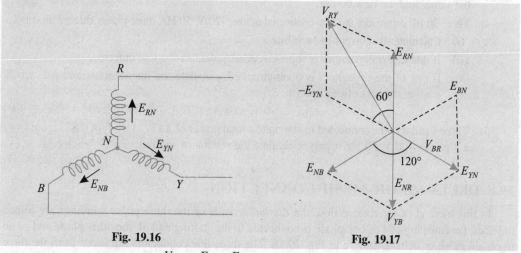

Fig. 19.16	**Fig. 19.17**

$$V_{RY} = E_{RN} - E_{YN} \qquad\qquad \textit{... phasor difference}$$
$$= 2E_{ph} \cos (60°/2) = 2 \times 231 \times \cos 30° = 400 \text{ V}$$
$$V_{YB} = E_{YN} + E_{NB} \qquad\qquad \textit{... phasor sum}$$
$$= 2E_{ph} \cos (120°/2) = 2 \times 231 \times \cos 60° = 231 \text{ V}$$
$$V_{BR} = E_{BN} + E_{NR} \qquad\qquad \textit{... phasor sum}$$
$$= 2E_{ph} \cos (120°/2) = 2 \times 231 \times \cos 60° = 231 \text{ V}$$

Phase Sequence Indicators

TUTORIAL PROBLEMS

1. Three similar coils are star connected to a 3-phase, 400 V, 50 Hz supply. If the inductance and resistance of each coil are 38.2 mH and 16 Ω respectively, determine (*i*) line current, (*ii*) power factor, and (*iii*) power consumed. [(*i*) 11.55 A (*ii*) 0.8 *lag* (*iii*) 6.4 kW]

2. The voltage measured between the terminals of a 3-phase, 3-wire alternator is recorded as 208V. A 3-phase load consisting of three 10-ohm resistors in star is connected to the terminals of the alternator. If one of the resistors should become open-circuited, what would be the current, the voltage and the power of the remaining resistors ? [10.4 A; 104 V; 1081.6 W]

3. A 6600 volts three-phase,star-connected alternator supplies 4000 kW at a p.f. of 0.8 lagging. Calculate the line current. If the load p.f. is raised to 0.95, the total current remaining the same, find the new output. [437.5 A; 4750 kW]

4. Three 20 μF capacitors are star-connected across 420 V, 50 Hz, three-phase, three-wire supply.
   (*i*) Calculate the current in each line.
   (*ii*) If one of the capacitors is short-circuited, calculate the line currents.
   (*iii*) If one of the capacitors is open-circuited, calculate the line currents and p.d. across each of the other two capacitors.
   [(*i*) 1.525 A (*ii*) 2.64 A, 2.64 A, 4.57 A (*iii*) 1.32 A, 132 A, 0A; 210 V]

5. Three similar coils, connected in star, take a total power of 3 kW at a p.f. of 0.8 lagging from a 3-phase, 400 V, 50 Hz supply. Calculate the resistance and reactance of each coil. [33.92 Ω ; 25.68 Ω]

19.8. DELTA (Δ) OR MESH CONNECTION

In this method of interconnection, the *dissimilar ends* of the three phase windings are joined together, *i.e.* finishing end of one phase is connected to the starting end of the other phase and so on to obtain mesh or delta as shown in Fig. 19.18. The three line conductors are taken from the three junctions of the mesh or delta and are designated as *R, Y* and *B*. This is called 3- *phase, 3-wire, delta-connected system.* Since no neutral exists in a Δ-connection, only 3-phase, 3-wire system can be formed.

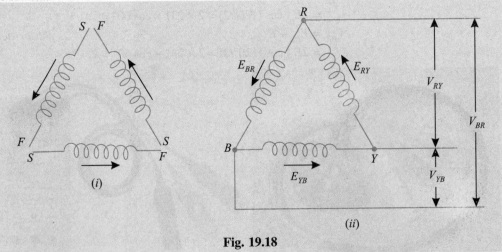

Fig. 19.18

In Fig. 19.18 (*ii*), it may appear that the three phases are short-circuited on themselves. But this is not the case. The finishing end of one phase is connected to the starting end of the other phase so that the resultant voltage round the mesh is the phasor sum of the three phase voltages. Since the three phase voltages are equal in magnitude and displaced 120° from one another, their phasor sum is zero (See Art. 19.3). Consequently, no current can flow round the mesh when the terminals are open.

Note. At no instant will all the three line currents flow in the same direction either outwards or inwards. This is expected because the three line currents are displaced 120° from one another. When one is positive, the other two might both be negative or one positive and one negative. Thus, at any one instant, current flows from the alternator through one of the lines to the load and returns through the other two lines. Or else current flows from the alternator through two of the lines and returns by means of the third. It may be noted that arrows placed alongside currents (or voltages) in the diagram indicate the directions of currents (or voltages) when they are assumed to be positive and *not* their actual directions at a particular instant.

19.9. VOLTAGES AND CURRENTS IN BALANCED Δ CONNECTION

We shall now investigate the characteristics of a balanced Δ-connection.

(*i*) **Line voltage and phase voltage.** Since the system is balanced, the three phase voltages are equal in magnitude (say each equal to V_{ph}, the phase voltage) but displaced 120° from one another. An examination of Fig. 19.19 shows that only one phase winding is included between any pair of lines. Hence in Δ connection, the line voltage is equal to the phase voltage, *i.e.*

$$V_L = V_{ph}$$

Since the phase sequence is *RYB*, the line voltage V_{RY} is 120° ahead of V_{YB} and 240° ahead of V_{BR}. Incidentally, these are also the phase voltages.

(*ii*) **Line current and phase current.** Since the system is balanced, the three phase currents I_R, I_Y and I_B are equal in magnitude (say each equal to I_{ph}, the phase current) but displaced 120° from one another as shown in the phasor diagram in Fig. 19.20. An examination of the circuit diagram in Fig. 19.19 shows that current in any line is equal to the *phasor difference* of the currents in the two phases attached to that line. Thus :

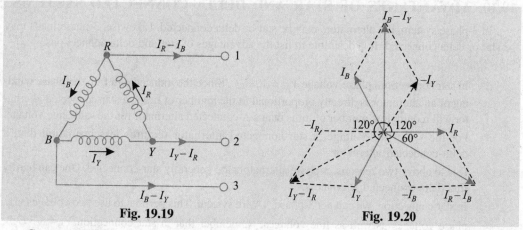

Fig. 19.19   **Fig. 19.20**

Current in line 1, $I_1^* = I_R - I_B$ ... *phasor difference*

Current in line 2, $I_2 = I_Y - I_R$ ... *phasor difference*

Current in line 3, $I_3 = I_B - I_Y$ —do—

The current I_1 in line 1 is the phasor difference of I_R and I_B. To subtract I_B from I_R, reverse the phasor I_B and find its phasor sum with I_R as shown in Fig. 19.20. The two phasors I_R and $-I_B$ are equal in magnitude (= I_{ph}) and are 60° apart.

---

 *   Consider the line current I_1 in line 1 connected to the common point R of red and blue phase windings. It is clear that I_1 is equal to phasor difference of I_R and I_B since positive direction for I_R is towards point R and for I_B it is away from point R.

$$\therefore \qquad I_1 = 2\,I_{ph}\cos(60°/2) = 2\,I_{ph}\cos 30° = \sqrt{3}\,I_{ph}$$

Similarly, $\qquad\qquad\qquad I_2 = I_Y - I_R \qquad\qquad\qquad\qquad$ ... *phasor difference*

$$= \sqrt{3}\,I_{ph}$$

and $\qquad\qquad\qquad\qquad I_3 = I_B - I_Y \qquad\qquad\qquad\qquad$ ... *phasor difference*

$$= \sqrt{3}\,I_{ph}$$

The three line currents I_1, I_2 and I_3 are equal in magnitude; each being equal to $\sqrt{3}\,I_{ph}$.

Hence in a balanced Δ connection :

(a) Line current, $I_L = \sqrt{3}\,I_{ph}$

(b) All the line currents are equal in magnitude (= $\sqrt{3}\,I_{ph}$) but displaced 120° from one another as seen from Fig. 19.20.

(c) Line currents are 30° behind the respective phase currents.

(iii) **Power**

Total power, $\qquad\qquad\qquad P = 3 \times$ Power per phase

$$= 3\,V_{ph}\,I_{ph}\cos\phi \qquad\qquad\qquad\qquad\qquad ...(i)$$

For Δ connection, $\qquad V_{ph} = V_L;\, I_{ph} = I_L / \sqrt{3}$

$$\therefore \qquad\qquad\qquad P = 3 \times V_L \times (I_L / \sqrt{3}) \times \cos\phi$$

$$= \sqrt{3}\,V_L\,I_L \cos\phi \qquad\qquad\qquad\qquad\qquad ...(ii)$$

where $\cos\phi$ is the power factor of each phase. Either of relations (i) and (ii) can be used to determine the power.

19.10. ADVANTAGES OF STAR AND DELTA CONNECTED SYSTEMS

In 3-phase system, the alternators may be star or delta connected. Likewise, 3-phase loads may be star or delta connected. It is desirable to list the advantages of star and delta connections.

Star Connection

(i) In star connection, phase voltage $V_{ph} = V_L / \sqrt{3}$. Since the induced e.m.f. in the phase winding of an alternator is directly proportional to the number of turns, a star-connected alternator will require less number of turns than a Δ-connected alternator for the same line voltage.

(ii) For the same line voltage, a star-connected alternator requires less insulation than a delta-connected alternator.

Due to above two reasons, 3-phase alternators are generally star-connected. One can hardly find delta-connected alternators.

(iii) In star connection, we can get 3-phase, 4-wire system. This permits to use two voltages viz., phase voltages as well as line voltages. Remember that in star connection, $V_L = \sqrt{3}\,E_{ph}$. Single phase loads (e.g., lights, etc.) can be connected between any one line and the neutral wire while the 3-phase loads (e.g., 3-phase motors) can be put across the three lines. Such a flexibility is not available in Δ connection.

(iv) In star connection, the neutral point can be earthed. Such a measure offers many advantages. For example, in case of line to earth fault, the insulators have to bear $1/\sqrt{3}$ (i.e., 57.7%) times the line voltage. Moreover, earthing of neutral permits to use protective devices (e.g., relays) to protect the system in case of ground faults.

Delta Connection

(i) This type of connection is most suitable for rotary convertors.

(ii) Most of the 3-phase loads are Δ-connected rather than Y-connected. One reason for this, at least for the case of an unbalanced load, is the flexibility with which loads may be added or removed on a single phase. This is difficult (or impossible) to do with a Y-connected 3-wire load.

(iii) Most of 3-phase induction motors are delta-connected.

19.11. HOW TO APPLY LOAD?

A natural question arises how to apply load to a 3-phase star-connected supply? One can apply *single phase loads (i.e., loads connected between any line terminal and neutral wire) if the neutral wire is accessible. If the neutral wire is not accessible, the load shall be, quite logically, a 3-phase load. A ** 3-phase load may be star-connected or delta-connected.

(i) For a 3-phase, 3-wire, star-connected supply (i.e., neutral wire not available), there are only three lines. Hence one can connect a 3-phase load (star or delta load) as shown in Fig. 19.21. Most of the 3-phase loads (e.g., 3-phase motors) are **balanced**, i.e. all the three branches have identical impedances—each impedance has same magnitude and power factor. In that case, the three line currents (I_R, I_Y, I_B) are equal in magnitude but 120° apart in phase. Also voltages across the branch impedances are equal in magnitude but 120° apart in phase. Note that problems on balanced loads can be solved by considering one phase only; the conditions in the other two phases being similar. *In this chapter, a 3-phase load means 3-phase balanced load unless stated otherwise.*

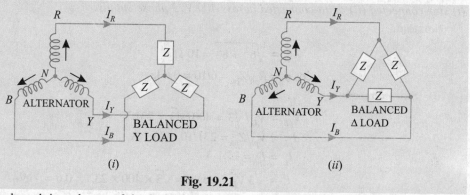

(i)   (ii)

Fig. 19.21

If the branch impedances of the 3-phase load are not identical, it is called *unbalanced 3-phase load*. In such a case, line or phase currents are different and are displaced from one another by unequal angle. Problems on unbalanced 3-phase loads are difficult to handle because conditions in the three phases are different.

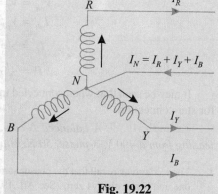

$$I_N = I_R + I_Y + I_B$$

Fig. 19.22

(ii) For a 3-phase, 4-wire star connected supply, both single phase and 3-phase loads can be connected [See Fig. 19.22]. A single phase load can be connected between any line and the neutral wire while a 3-phase load can be applied across the three lines. The current I_N in the neutral wire will be the phasor sum of the three line currents i.e.

$$I_N = I_R + I_Y + I_B \quad \text{...phasor sum}$$

---

* So called because voltage across the load is that due to one (single) phase only i.e. voltage across the load is equal to the phase voltage of the supply.

** Just as the three phases of an alternator can be connected in star or in delta, so the three impedances can also be connected in star or delta. Such a load is called a 3-phase load.

If the loads are balanced (*i.e.*, each of the three phases has the same load), then the three line currents will be equal in magnitude but 120° apart in phase. Consequently, their phasor sum is *zero and the neutral wire carries no current. It may be noted that except as a rare coincidence, 3-phase, 4 -wire supply has **unbalanaced loads.

Example19.8. *A balanced 3-phase, Δ -connected load has per phase impedance of (25 + j40) Ω. If 400V, 3-phase supply is connected to this load, find (i) phase current (ii) line current (iii) power supplied to the load.*

Solution. Fig. 19.23 shows the circuit diagram.

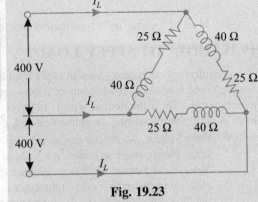

Fig. 19.23

$$Z_{ph} = \sqrt{25^2 + 40^2} = 47.17 \ \Omega$$

(*i*) $I_{ph} = V_{ph}/Z_{ph} = 400/47.17 = \textbf{8.48 A}$

(*ii*) $I_L = \sqrt{3} \ I_{ph} = \sqrt{3} \times 8.48 = \textbf{14.7 A}$

(*iii*) $\cos \phi = R_{ph}/Z_{ph} = 25/47.17 = 0.53 \ lag$

$$P = \sqrt{3} \ V_L I_L \cos \phi = \sqrt{3} \times 400 \times 14.7 \times 0.53 = \textbf{5397.76 W}$$

Example19.9. *A balanced 3-phase load consists of three coils, each of resistance 6 Ω, and inductive reactance of 8 Ω. Determine the line current and power absorbed when the coils are; (i) star-connected (ii) delta-connected across 400 V, 3-phase supply.*

Solution.

$$Z_{ph} = \sqrt{6^2 + 8^2} = 10 \ \Omega$$
$$\cos \phi = R_{ph}/Z_{ph} = 6/10 = 0.6 \ lag$$

(*i*) **Star connection**

$$V_{ph} = V_L /\sqrt{3} = 400/\sqrt{3} = 231 \ V$$
$$I_{ph} = V_{ph}/Z_{ph} = 231/10 = 23.1 \ A$$
∴ $I_L = I_{ph} = \textbf{23.1 A}$
$$P = \sqrt{3} \ V_L I_L \cos \phi = \sqrt{3} \times 400 \times 23.1 \times 0.6 = \textbf{9602.5 W}$$

(*ii*) **Delta connection**

$$V_{ph} = V_L = 400 \ V$$
$$I_{ph} = V_{ph}/Z_{ph} = 400/10 = 40 \ A$$
$$I_L = \sqrt{3} I_{ph} = \sqrt{3} \times 40 = \textbf{69.28 A}$$
$$P = \sqrt{3} \ V_L I_L \cos \phi = \sqrt{3} \times 400 \times 69.28 \times 0.6 = \textbf{28799 W}$$

It may be seen that when connected in Δ, the line current and power drawn are *three times* as that for star connection.

Example 19.10. *A balanced Δ-connected load takes a line current of 18 A at a p.f. of 0.85 leading from a 400 V, 3-phase, 50 Hz supply. Calculate the resistance of each leg of the load.*

* *

*   The reader may recall that the phasor sum of the three phasors equal in magnitude but displaced 120° from one another is always zero (See Art. 19.3). The phasors may be line currents or line voltages or phase currents or phase voltages.

**   No doubt 3-phase loads (*e.g.*, 3-phase motors) connected to this supply are balanced loads but when we add single phase loads (*e.g.*, lights, fans, *etc.*), the balance is lost. It is because it is rarely possible that single phase loads on all the three phases have the same magnitude and power factor.

Solution.

$$V_{ph} = V_L = 400 \text{ V}; I_L = 18 \text{ A}; \cos \phi = 0.85 \text{ lead}$$
$$I_{ph} = I_L / \sqrt{3} = 18 / \sqrt{3} = 10.39 \text{ A}$$
$$Z_{ph} = V_{ph} / I_{ph} = 400 / 10.39 = 38.5 \text{ } \Omega$$

∴
$$R_{ph} = Z_{ph} \cos \phi = 38.5 \times 0.85 = 32.72 \text{ } \Omega$$

Example 19.11. *Three similar resistors are connected in star across 400V, 3-phase supply. The line current is 5A. Calculate the value of each resistance. To what value should the line voltage be changed to obtain the same line current with the resistors connected in delta ?*

Solution.

Star connection

$$V_{ph} = V_L / \sqrt{3} = 400 / \sqrt{3} = 231 \text{ V}$$
$$I_{ph} = I_L = 5 \text{ A}$$

∴
$$R_{ph} = V_{ph} / I_{ph} = 231/5 = 46.2 \text{ } \Omega$$

Delta connection

$$I_L = 5 \text{ A} \qquad \text{... given}$$
$$I_{ph} = I_L / \sqrt{3} = 5 / \sqrt{3} = 2.88 \text{ A}$$
$$V_L = V_{ph} = I_{ph} R_{ph} = 2.88 \times 46.2 = 133 \text{ V}$$

It may be seen that line voltage required is one-third that of star value.

Example 19.12. *Three 40 Ω non-inductive resistances are connected in delta across 400 V, 3-phase lines. Calculate the power taken from the mains. If one of the resistances is disconnected, what would be the power taken from the mains ?*

Solution.

When the three resistances are delta connected [Fig. 19.24].

$$V_{ph} = V_L = 400 \text{ V}; R = 40 \text{ } \Omega$$
$$I_{ph} = V_{ph}/R = 400/40 = 10 \text{ A}$$
$$I_L = \sqrt{3} I_{ph} = \sqrt{3} \times 10 = 17.32 \text{ A}$$
$$P = \sqrt{3} V_L I_L \cos \phi$$
$$= \sqrt{3} \times 400 \times 17.32 \times 1 = 12000 \text{ W}$$

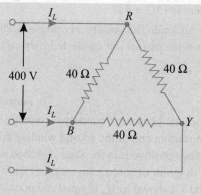

Fig. 19.24

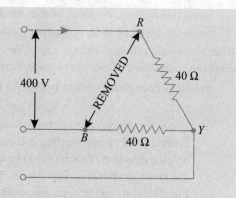

Fig. 19.25

When one resistor is removed. Fig. 19.25 shows the circuit with one resistor removed. In this case, each of the two resistors acts independently as if 400V were applied to 40 Ω.

Current in each resistor, $I = 400/40 = 10$ A

Power consumed in the two $= 2I^2R = 2 \times (10)^2 \times 40 = \textbf{8000 W}$

Hence by disconnecting one resistor, the power consumption is reduced by one-third.

Example 19.13. *Three identical resistances, each of 15 Ω, are connected in delta across 400 V, 3-phase supply. What value of resistance in each leg of balanced star-connected load would take the same line current ?*

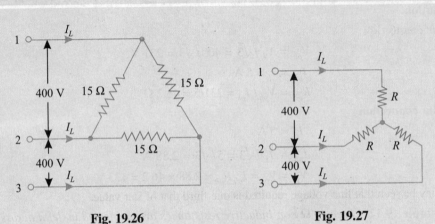

Fig. 19.26   Fig. 19.27

Solution. Let R ohms be the required resistance in each leg of the star-connection (See Fig. 19.27). Since the two circuits have the same line voltage and line current, the resistance between any two corresponding terminals of the two circuits is the same. Considering the terminals 1 and 3,

For delta connection, $R_{13} = 15 \,\|\, (15 + 15) = \dfrac{15 \times 30}{15 + 30} = 10 \,\Omega$

For star connection, $R_{13} = R + R = 2R$

∴ $2R = 10$ or $R = 10/2 = 5 \,\Omega$

Note. Thus, Δ-connected impedances can be replaced by the equivalent Y-connected impedances using the following relation:

$$Z_Y = Z_\Delta/3$$

Using this relation, the value of R in the above problem is $15/3 = 5\,\Omega$.

Example 19.14. *A delta connected alternator is on no load. The voltage per phase is 200 V. What will be the resultant voltage round the mesh (i) when the phases are connected correctly, (ii) when the connections of one of the phases are reversed ?*

Solution. Each phase voltage is 200 V, *i.e.*

$$V_R = V_Y = V_B = V_{ph} = 200 \ V \qquad \qquad ... \ in \ magnitude$$

(*i*) **When the phases are connected correctly.** When the phases are connected correctly (*i.e.*, finishing end of one winding is connected to the starting end of the second winding and so on), the direction of each of the phase voltages when positive is in the same direction round the mesh as shown in Fig. 19.28. The phasor diagram of this arrangement is shown in Fig. 19.29. As can be seen, the resultant of V_R and V_Y, shown as V_a, is equal and opposite to V_B and the resultant voltage round the mesh is zero, *i.e.*

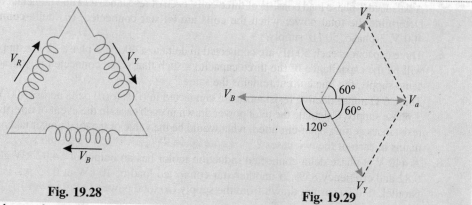

Fig. 19.28   **Fig. 19.29**

Resultant voltage round the mesh = **0V**

(ii) **When one phase connection is reversed.** Suppose connections to phase Y have been reversed. Then the directions of the phase voltages when positive will be as shown in Fig. 19.30. Note that the phasor V_Y will now act in the reversed direction as shown in the phasor diagram in Fig. 19.31. The resultant of V_R and V_Y, shown as V_a, is $= 2V_{ph} \cos 30° = \sqrt{3}\,V_{ph}$. The resultant voltage round the mesh is the phasor sum of V_a and V_B. These two phasors are 90° apart.

∴ Resultant voltage round the mesh

$$= \sqrt{V_a^2 + V_B^2} = \sqrt{(\sqrt{3}\,V_{ph})^2 + (V_{ph})^2} = 2V_{ph} = 2 \times 200 = \mathbf{400\ V}$$

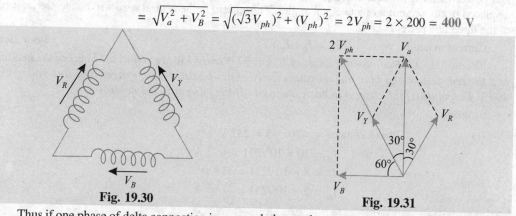

Fig. 19.30   **Fig. 19.31**

Thus if one phase of delta connection is reversed, the resultant voltage round the mesh is equal to *twice* the phase voltage. This high voltage may cause high current to flow through the windings, even without an external load, and may damage the winding.

TUTORIAL PROBLEMS

1. Calculate the phase and line currents in a balanced delta connected load taking 75kW at a power factor 0.8 from a 3-phase 440 V supply.   **[71.02 A; 123 A]**
2. Three identical inductive loads of resistance 15 Ω and reactance of 40 Ω are connected in star to a 440 V, 3-phase supply. Calculate *(i)* phase current, *(ii)* line current, and *(iii)* power absorbed.   **[(i) 5.94 A (ii) 5.94 A (iii) 1589.5 W]**
3. Three identical resistances, each of 18 Ω, are connected in delta across 400V, 3-phase supply. What value of resistance in each leg of balanced star-connected load would take the same line current?   **[6·Ω]**
4. Three similar resistors are connected in star across a 415 V, 3-phase supply. The line current is 10 A. Calculate *(i)* the value of each resistance *(ii)* the line voltage required to give the same line current if the resistors were delta-connected.   **[(i) 23.96 Ω (ii) 138.33 V]**

5. A balanced 3-phase load consists of three coils, each of resistance 4 Ω and inductance 0.0 2 H. Determine the total power when the coils are (i) star-connected, (ii) delta-connected to 400 V, 3-phase, 50 Hz supply. [(i) 11.56 kW (ii) 34.68 kW]

6. Three capacitors each 50 μF, are connected in delta to a 400 V, 3-phase-50 Hz supply. What will be the capacitance of the three capacitors such that when connected in star across the same supply, the line current remains the same ? [150 μF]

7. Three 6 Ω non-inductive resistances are connected in (i) star (ii) delta across 400 V, 50 Hz, 3-phase supply. Calculate the total power drawn in each case. In the event of one of the three resistances getting open-circuited, what would be the value of the total power taken from the mains in each of the two cases ? [star: 26.66 kW; 13.33 kW Delta: 80 kW; 53.33 kW]

8. A 440 V, 3-phase delta-connected induction motor has an output of 14.92 kW at a p.f. of 0.82 and efficiency 85%. If another star-connected load of 10 kW at 0.85 p.f. is added in parallel, find (i) current drawn from the supply (ii) total power. [(i) 43.56 A (ii) 27.6 kW]

19.12. 3-PHASE, 4-WIRE STAR-CONNECTED SYSTEM

3-phase, 4-wire star-connected system is widely used to distribute electric power in domestic, commercial and industrial establishments. The 3-phase loads (e.g., 3-phase induction motors, etc.) are directly connected across the three lines while single-phase loads (e.g., lamps, fans, single-phase motors, etc.) are connected between one of the lines and the neutral wire. Although 3-phase loads on the system are mostly balanced, these are the single-phase loads that introduce the imbalance. This is because it is rarely possible that single-phase loads on all the three phases have the same magnitude and power factor. Consequently, the line currents I_R, I_Y and I_B will be different in magnitude and displaced from one another by unequal angles. The current in the neutral wire will be the phasor sum of the three line currents i.e.,

Current in neutral wire, $\qquad I_N = I_R + I_Y + I_B \qquad\qquad$ ... phasor sum

Example 19.15. *Non-reactive loads of 10 kW, 8 kW and 5 kW are connected between the neutral and the red, yellow and blue phases respectively of a 3-phase, 4-wire system. The line voltage is 400 V. Calculate (i) the current in each line and (ii) the current in the neutral wire.*

Solution.

(i) $\qquad$ Phase voltage $= 400/\sqrt{3} = 231$ V

$\qquad\qquad I_R = 10 \times 10^3/231 = 43.3$ A

$\qquad\qquad I_Y = 8 \times 10^3/231 = 34.6$ A

$\qquad\qquad I_B = 5 \times 10^3/231 = 21.65$ A

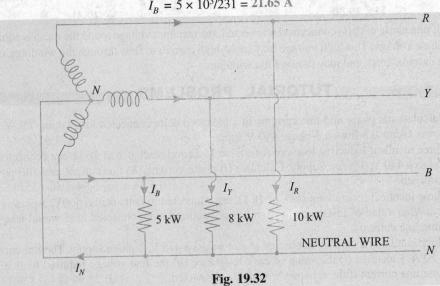

Fig. 19.32

(ii) The three line currents are represented by the respective phasors in Fig. 19.33. Note that the three line currents are of different magnitude but displaced 120° from one another. The current in the neutral wire will be the phasor sum of the three line currents. Resolving the three currents along *X*-axis and *Y*-axis, we have,

Total X-component $= I_Y \cos 30° - I_B \cos 30°$

$$= 34.6 \times 0.866 - 21.65 \times 0.866 = 11.22 \text{ A}$$

Total Y-component $= I_R - I_Y \cos 60° - I_B \cos 60°$

$$= 43.3 - 34.6 \times 0.5 - 21.65 \times 0.5 = 15.2 \text{ A}$$

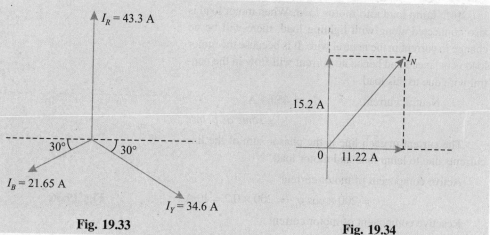

Fig. 19.33   **Fig. 19.34**

As shown in Fig. 19.34, current in the neutral wire,

$$I_N = \sqrt{(11.22)^2 + (15.2)^2} = 18.9 \text{ A}$$

Example 19.16. *A 3-phase, 4-wire system supplies power at 400 V and lighting at 230 V. If the lamps in use require 70, 84 and 33 amperes in each of the three lines, what should be the current in the neutral wire? If a 3-phase motor is now started, taking 200 A from the lines at a p.f. of 0.2 lagging, what should be the total current in each line and the neutral wire? Find also the total power supplied to the lamps and the motor.*

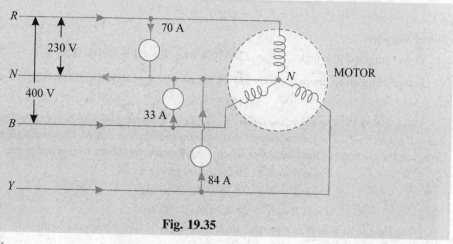

Fig. 19.35

Solution.

Fig. 19.35 shows the lamp load and motor load on 400V/230V, 3-phase, 4-wire supply.

Lamp load alone. If there is lamp load alone, the line currents in phases R, Y and B are 70A, 84A and 33A respectively. These currents will be 120° apart (assuming phase sequence RYB) as shown in Fig. 19.36.

Resultant X-component $= 84 \cos 30° - 33 \cos 30°$

$= 44.17$ A

Resultant Y-component $= 70 - 33 \cos 60° - 84 \cos 60° = 11.5$ A

∴ Neutral current, $I_N = \sqrt{(44.17)^2 + (11.5)^2} = 45.64$ A

Both lamp load and motor load. When motor load is also connected along with lighting load, there will be no change in current in the neutral wire. It is because the motor load is balanced and hence no current will flow in the neutral wire due to this load.

∴ Neutral current, $I_N = 45.64$ A

... same as before

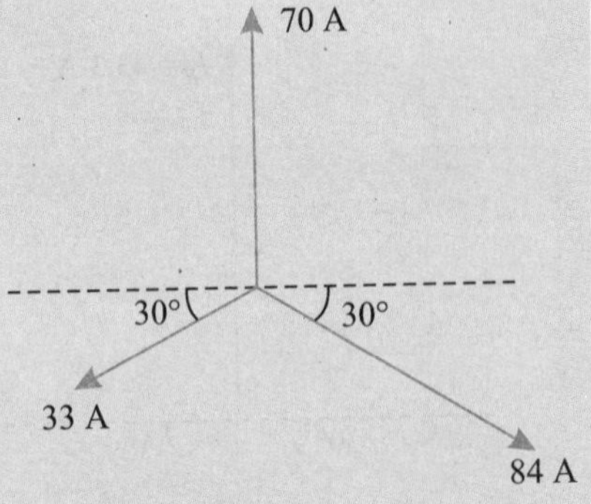

The current in each line is the phasor sum of the line currents due to lamp load and motor load.

Active component of motor current

$= 200 \times \cos \phi_m = 200 \times 0.2 = 40$ A

Reactive component of motor current

$= 200 \times \sin \phi_m = 200 \times 0.98 = 196$ A

$I_R = \sqrt{(\text{sum of active comps.})^2 + (\text{reactive comp.})^2}$

$= \sqrt{(40 + 70)^2 + (196)^2} = 224.8$ A

$I_Y = \sqrt{(40 + 84)^2 + (196)^2} = 232$ A

$I_B = \sqrt{(40 + 33)^2 + (196)^2} = 209.15$ A

Power supplied

Power supplied to lamps $= 230 (70 + 84 + 33) \times 1 = 43010$ W

Power supplied to motor $= \sqrt{3} V_L I_L \cos \phi_m = \sqrt{3} \times 400 \times 200 \times 0.2$ (∵ $\cos \phi_m = 0.2$)

$= 27712$ W

70 A

30°   30°

33 A

84 A

Fig. 19.36

Example 19.17. *The three line leads of a 400/230 V, 3-phase, 4-wire supply are designated as R, Y and B respectively. The fourth wire or neutral wire is designated as N. The phase sequence is RYB. Compute the currents in the four wires when the following loads are connected to this supply :*

From R to N : 20 kW, unity power factor

From Y to N : 28.75 kVA, 0.866 lag

From B to N : 28.75 kVA, 0.866 lead

If the load from B to N is removed, what will be the value of currents in the four wires ?

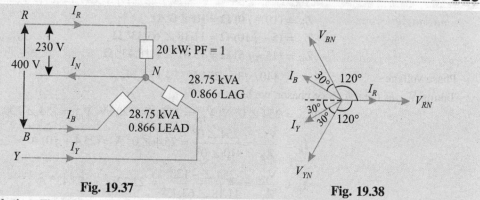

Fig. 19.37   **Fig. 19.38**

Solution. Fig. 19.37 shows the circuit diagram whereas Fig. 19.38 shows its phasor diagram. The current I_R is in phase with V_{RN}, current I_Y lags behind its phase voltage V_{YN} by $\cos^{-1} 0.866 = 30°$ and the current I_B leads its phase voltage V_{BN} by $\cos^{-1} 0.866 = 30°$.

∴
$$I_R = 20 \times 10^3/230 = \mathbf{86.96\ A}$$
$$I_Y = 28.75 \times 10^3/230 = \mathbf{125\ A}$$
$$I_B = 28.75 \times 10^3/230 = \mathbf{125\ A}$$

The current in the neutral wire will be equal to the phasor sum of the three line currents I_R, I_Y and I_B. Referring to the phasor diagram in Fig. 19.38 and resolving these currents along x-axis and y-axis, we have,

Resultant X-component $= 86.96 - 125 \cos 30° - 125 \cos 30°$
$= 86.96 - 108.25 - 108.25 = -129.54\ A$

Resultant Y-component $= 0 + 125 \sin 30° - 125 \sin 30° = 0$

∴ Neutral current, $I_N = \sqrt{(-129.54)^2 + (0)^2} = \mathbf{129.54\ A}$

When load from B to N removed. When load from B to N is removed, the various line currents are :

$$I_R = \mathbf{86.96A}\ \text{in phase with}\ V_{RN}$$
$$I_Y = \mathbf{125A}\ \text{lagging}\ V_{YN}\ \text{by}\ 30°$$
$$I_B = \mathbf{0\ A}$$

The current in the neutral wire is equal to the phasor sum of these three line currents. Resolving the currents along x-axis and y-axis, we have,

Resultant X-component $= 86.96 - 125 \cos 30° = 86.96 - 108.25 = -21.29\ A$
Resultant Y-component $= 0 - 125 \sin 30° = 0 - 125 \times 0.5 = -62.5\ A$

∴ Neutral current, $I_N = \sqrt{(-21.29)^2 + (-62.5)^2} = \mathbf{66.03A}$

Example 19.18. *An unbalanced 4-wire star connected load has balanced voltages of 440 V. The loads are : $Z_R = 10\ \Omega$; $Z_Y = (5 + j\,10)\ \Omega$; $Z_B = (15 - j\,5)\ \Omega$. Calculate the current in the neutral wire and its phase relationship to the voltage across the red phase. The phase sequence is RYB.*

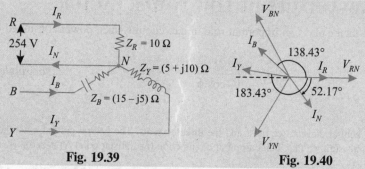

Fig. 19.39   **Fig. 19.40**

Solution.

$$Z_R = (10 + j\,0)\ \Omega = 10\ \angle\ 0°\ \Omega$$
$$Z_Y = (5 + j\,10)\ \Omega = 11.18\ \angle\ 63.43°\ \Omega$$
$$Z_B = (15 - j\,5)\ \Omega = 15.81\ \angle\ -18.43°\ \Omega$$

Phase voltage $= 440/\sqrt{3} = 254$ V

Taking V_{RN} as the reference phasor, we have,

$$V_{RN} = 254\ \angle\ 0°\ V;\ V_{YN} = 254\ \angle\ -120°\ V;\ V_{BN} = 254\ \angle\ 120°\ V$$

$$\therefore \quad I_R = \frac{V_{RN}}{Z_R} = \frac{254\ \angle\ 0°}{10\ \angle\ 0°} = 25.4\ \angle\ 0°\ A = (25.4 + j\,0)\ A$$

$$I_Y = \frac{V_{YN}}{Z_Y} = \frac{254\ \angle\ -120°}{11.18\ \angle\ 63.43°} = 22.72\ \angle\ -183.43°\ A$$

$$= (-22.68 + j\,1.36)\ A$$

$$I_B = \frac{V_{BN}}{Z_B} = \frac{254\ \angle\ 120°}{15.81\ \angle\ -18.43°} = 16.07\ \angle\ 138.43°\ A$$

$$= (-12.02 + j\,10.66)\ A$$

$$\therefore \quad I_N = -\ ^*[I_R + I_Y + I_B]$$

$$= -[(25.4 + j\,0) + (-22.68 + j\,1.36) + (-12.02 + j\,10.66)]$$

$$= -[-9.3 + j\,12.02]$$

$$= (9.3 - j\,12.02)\ A = 15.2\ \angle\ -52.17°\ A$$

Magnitude, $\qquad I_N = \mathbf{15.2\ A}$

Its phase angle w.r.t. V_{RN} is 52.17° as shown in Fig. 19.40.

▌ TUTORIAL PROBLEMS ▌

1. Non-reactive loads of 10 kW, 6 kW and 4 kW are connected between the neutral and red, yellow and blue phases respectively of a 3-phase, 4-wire 400/230 Vsupply. Find the current in each line and in the neutral wire.   [$I_R = 43.3$ A; $I_Y = 26$ A; $I_B = 17.3$ A; $I_N = 22.9$ A]

2. A factory has the following loads with a power factor of 0.9 lagging in each case. Red phase 40 A, yellow phase 50 A and blue phase 60 A. If the supply is 400 V, 3-phase, 4-wire, calculate the current in the neutral wire and the total power.   [17.3 A, 31.2 kW]

3. In a 3-phase, 4-wire system, two phases have currents of 10 A and 6 A at lagging power factors of 0.8 and 0.6 respectively, while the third phase is open-circuited. Calculate the current in the neutral wire.   [7 A]

4. A 3-phase, 4-wire system supplies a lighting load of 40 A, 30 A and 20 A respectively in the three phases. If the line voltage is 400 V, determine the current in the neutral wire. [17.32 A]

19.13. DISADVANTAGES OF LOW POWER FACTOR

The power factor plays an important role in a.c. circuits since power consumed depends upon this factor.

$$I_L = \frac{P}{V_L \cos\phi} \qquad\qquad \textit{... for single phase supply}$$

- -

* To find the neutral current, we must add the three currents. The neutral current must then be equal and *opposite* to this sum, so that total current at the junction (*i.e.*, at star point N) is zero.

$$I_L = \frac{P}{\sqrt{3}\ V_L \cos\phi} \qquad\qquad \textit{... for 3-phase supply}$$

It is clear from above that for fixed power and voltage, the load current is inversely proportional to the power factor. Smaller the power factor, higher is the load current and vice-versa. The large current due to poor power factor results in the following disadvantages:

(*i*) **Large *kVA* rating of equipment.** The electrical machinery (e.g., alternators, transformers, switchgear, etc.) is always rated in *kVA.

Now, $$kVA = \frac{kW}{\cos\phi}$$

It is clear that *kVA* rating of the equipment is inversely proportional to power factor. The smaller the power factor, the larger is the *kVA* rating. Therefore, at low power factor, the *kVA* rating of the equipment has to be made more, making the equipment larger and expensive.

(*ii*) **Greater conductor size.** To transmit or distribute a given amount of power at constant voltage, the conductor will have to carry more current at low power factor. This necessitates large conductor size.

(*iii*) **Large copper losses.** The large current at low power factor causes more I^2R losses in all elements of power system. This results in poor efficiency.

(*iv*) **Poor voltage regulation.** The large current at low lagging power factor causes greater voltage drops in alternators, transformers, transmission lines and distributors. This results in the reduced voltage available to the utilisation devices, impairing their performance, e.g. lighting becomes dimmer, starting torque of motors is reduced, etc. In order to keep the supply voltage within permissible limits, extra equipment (*i.e.*, voltage regulators) is required.

19.14. POWER FACTOR IMPROVEMENT

The low power factor is mainly due to the fact that most of the power loads (e.g., induction motors ,etc.) are inductive in nature and, therefore, take lagging currents. In order to improve the power factor, some device taking leading current should be connected in parallel with the load. One of such devices can be a capacitor. The capacitor draws a leading current and partly or completely neutralises the lagging reactive component of load current. This raises the power factor of the load.

Illustration. To illustrate the power factor improvement by a capacitor, consider a **single phase load taking lagging current *I* at a p.f. of $\cos\phi_1$ as shown in Fig. 19.41 (*i*). The capacitor *C* is connected in parallel with the load and draws current I_C which leads the supply voltage by 90°. The resulting line current *I'* is the phasor sum of *I* and I_C and its angle of lag is ϕ_2 as shown in the phasor diagram in Fig. 19.41 (*iii*). It is clear that ϕ_2 is less than ϕ_1, so that $\cos\phi_2$ is greater than $\cos\phi_1$. Hence, the power factor of the load is increased.

* *

* The electrical machinery is rated in kVA because the power factor is not known when the machinery is manufactured in the factory.

** The treatment can be used for 3-phase balanced loads, *e.g.* 3-phase induction motor. In a balanced 3-phase load, analysis of only one phase leads to the desired results.

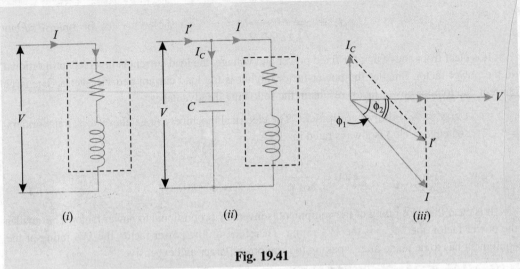

Fig. 19.41

The following points are worth noting :

(i)   The circuit current I' after p.f. correction is less than the original circuit current I.

(ii)   The active or wattful component remains the same before and after p.f. correction because only the lagging reactive component of load is reduced by the capacitor, *i.e.,*

$$I \cos \phi_1 = I' \cos \phi_2$$

or $VI \cos \phi_1 = VI' \cos \phi_2$ (Multiply by V)

Therefore, active power (kW) remains unchanged during p.f. improvement.

(iii)   The original reactive component of load is $I \sin \phi_1$. However, after p.f. correction, it is reduced by I_C and becomes $I' \sin \phi_2$ *i.e.,*

$$I' \sin \phi_2 = I \sin \phi_1 - I_C$$

or $VI' \sin \phi_2 = VI \sin \phi_1 - VI_C$

i.e., Net *kVAR after p.f.* correction = Lagging *kVAR* before p.f. correction – Leading *kVAR* of capacitor

(iv) $$I_C = I \sin \phi_1 - I' \sin \phi_2$$

∴   Capacitance of the capacitor to improve p.f. from $\cos \phi_1$ to $\cos \phi_2$.

$$= \frac{I_C}{\omega V}$$ $(\because X_C = V/I_C = 1/\omega C)$

19.15. POWER FACTOR IMPROVEMENT EQUIPMENT

Power factor improvement may be achieved in the following three principal ways :

(i)   **Static capacitors.** The power factor can be improved by connecting *capacitors in parallel with equipment operating at low lagging power factor. For 3-phase loads, the capacitors can be connected in delta or star as shown in Fig. 19.42.

Since static capacitors are not variable, they tend to overcompensate on light loads. As most of the loads have lagging power factors, this overcompensation is not a problem.

. . . .

*   called static capacitor to distinguish from the so called *synchronous condenser* which is a synchronous motor running at no load and taking leading current.

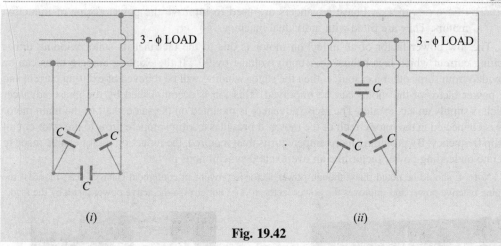

Fig. 19.42

(*ii*) **Synchronous condensers.** A synchronous motor takes a leading current when overexcited and, therefore, behaves as a capacitor. An overexcited synchronous motor running on no load is known as a *synchronous condenser*. When such a machine is connected in parallel with the load, it takes a leading current which partly neutralises the lagging reactive component of the load current. Thus, the p.f. is improved.

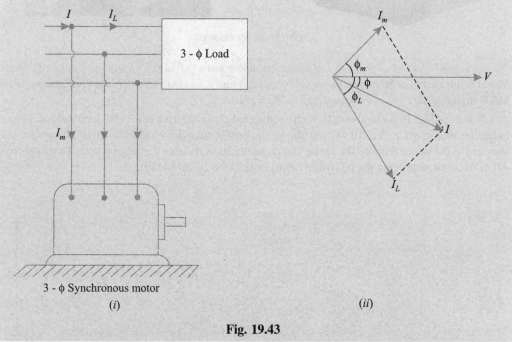

Fig. 19.43

Fig. 19.43 shows the p.f. improvement by synchronous condenser method. The 3-ϕ load takes current I_L at low lagging power factor cos ϕ_L. The synchronous condenser takes a current I_m which leads the voltage by an angle *ϕ_m. The resultant current I is the phasor sum of I_m and I_L and lags behind the voltage by an angle ϕ. It is clear that ϕ is less than ϕ_L so that cos ϕ is greater than cos ϕ_L. Thus, power factor is increased from to cos ϕ_L to cos ϕ.

. . . .

* If the motor is ideal (*i.e.*, there are no losses), then $\phi_m = 90°$. However, in actual practice, losses do occur in the motor even at no load. Therefore, the current I_m leads the voltage by an angle less than 90°.

(*iii*) **Phase advancers.** Phase advancers are used to improve the power factor of induction motors. They are fitted with individual machines.

The low power factor of an induction motor is due to the fact that its stator winding draws exciting current which lags behind the supply voltage by 90°. If the exciting ampere turns can be provided from some other a.c. source, then the stator winding will be relieved of exciting current and the power factor of the motor can be improved. This job is accomplished by the phase advancer which is simply an a.c. exciter. The phase advancer is mounted on the same shaft as the main motor and is connected in the rotor circuit of the motor. It provides exciting ampere turns to the rotor circuit at slip frequency. By providing more ampere turns than required, the induction motor can be made to operate on leading power factor like an overexcited synchronous motor.

Note. It should be noted that although power factor improvement equipment changes (*i.e.*, reduces) the lagging reactive power and improves the power factor, it does not change the active power taken by the load.

Synchronous Condensers

Example 19.19. *A 3-phase, 5 kW induction motor has a p.f. of 0.75 lagging. A bank of capacitors is connected in delta across the supply terminals and p.f. is raised to 0.9 lagging. Determine the kVAR rating of the capacitors connected in each phase.*

Solution. Fig. 19.44 (*i*) shows the delta connected capacitor bank across the terminals of 3-phase induction motor while Fig. 19.44 (*ii*) shows the power triangle. Note that active power (= *OA*) supplied to the motor remains the same. The capacitor bank reduces the lagging reactive power from *AB* to *AC*, thus improving the p.f. from cos ϕ_1 (= 0.75) to cos ϕ_2 (= 0.9).

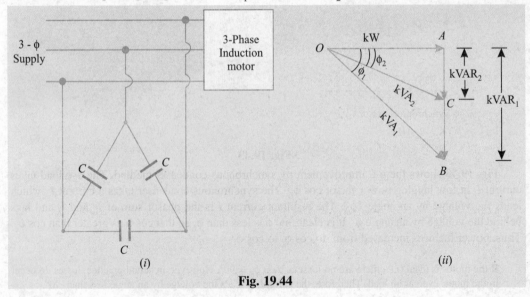

Fig. 19.44

Motor input (*OA*), $\qquad$ P = 5 kW $\qquad$ ... assuming 100% efficiency

Leading *kVAR* supplied by the condenser bank

$$= BC = AB - AC = kVAR_1 - kVAR_2$$
$$= OA\ (\tan \phi_1 - \tan \phi_2) = P\ (\tan \phi_1 - \tan \phi_2)$$

Now, $\qquad \cos \phi_1 = 0.75;\ \phi_1 = \cos^{-1}(0.75) = 41° 24';\ \tan \phi_1 = 0.8819$

$\qquad\qquad \cos \phi_2 = 0.9;\ \phi_2 = \cos^{-1}(0.9) = 25° 50';\ \tan \phi_2 = 0.4843$

∴ Leading *kVAR* supplied by the condenser bank

$$= 5\ (0.8819 - 0.4843) = 1.99\ kVAR$$

∴ Rating of the capacitor connected in each phase

$$= 1.99/3 = 0.663\ \text{kVAR}$$

Example 19.20. *A 3-phase, 50 Hz, 400 V motor develops 100 H.P. (74.6 kW), the power factor being 0.75 lagging and efficiency 93%. A bank of capacitors is connected in delta across the supply terminals and power factor raised to 0.95 lagging. Each of the capacitance unit is built of 4 similar 100 V capacitors. Determine the capacitance of each capacitor.*

Solution. Fig. 19.45 (*i*) shows the delta connected capacitor bank connected across the terminals of 3-phase motor while Fig. 19.45 (*ii*) shows the power triangle. Note that active power (= *OA*) supplied to the motor remains the same. The capacitor bank reduces the lagging reactive power from *AB* to *AC*, thus improving the p.f. from $\cos \phi_1$ (= 0.75) to $\cos \phi_2$ (= 0.95).

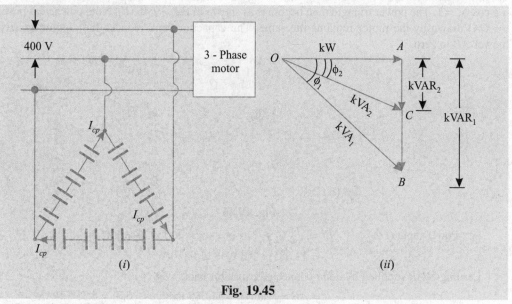

Fig. 19.45

Power input (*OA*), $\qquad$ P = 74.6/η = 74.6/0.93 = 80 kW

Leading *kVAR* supplied by the condenser bank

$$= P\ (\tan \phi_1 - \tan \phi_2)$$

Now, $\qquad \cos \phi_1 = 0.75; \qquad \phi_1 = \cos^{-1}(0.75) = 41° 24'; \qquad \tan \phi_1 = 0.8819$

$\qquad\qquad \cos \phi_2 = 0.95; \qquad \phi_2 = \cos^{-1}(0.95) = 18° 12'; \qquad \tan \phi_2 = 0.3288$

∴ Leading *kVAR* supplied by the condenser bank

$$= 80\ (0.8819 - 0.3288) = 44.25\ kVAR$$

Leading *kVAR* supplied by the capacitor bank/phase

$$= 44.25/3 = 14.75\ kVAR \qquad\qquad\qquad\qquad ...(i)$$

Let C farad be the combined capacitance of 4 capacitors in each phase.

Phase current of capacitor, $I_{cp} = V_{ph}/X_C = 2\pi fCV_{ph}$

$$= 2\pi \times 50 \times C \times 400 = 1,25,600\ C\ \text{amperes}$$

$$kVAR/\text{phase} = \frac{*V_{ph}\ I_{cp}}{1000} = \frac{400 \times 1,25,600\ C}{1000} = 50240\ C \qquad \ldots(ii)$$

Equating exps. (i) and (ii), we get,

$$50240\ C = 14.75$$

$$\therefore \qquad C = 14.75/50240 = 293.4 \times 10^{-6}\ F = 293.4\ \mu\,F$$

Since it is the combined capacitance of four equal capacitors joined in series,

$\therefore$ Capacitance of each capacitor $= 4 \times 293.4 = \textbf{1173.6 μF}$

Example 19.21. *A 3-phase, star-connected motor, connected across a 3-phase, star-connected supply of 400 V, 50 Hz takes a current of 20 A at 0.8 p.f. lagging. Determine :*

(i) the capacitance of the capacitors per phase that are to be connected in delta across the terminals of the motor to raise the p.f. to unity.

(ii) the new value of supply line current with capacitors connected.

Solution. Fig. 19.46 (i) shows the power triangle before the connection of capacitor bank. The active power drawn by the motor is OA while the lagging reactive power is AB; the p.f. being $\cos \phi_1$ $(= 0.8)$. When the capacitor bank is connected across the motor terminals, the p.f. is raised to unity, *i.e* $\cos \phi_2 = 1$. The power triangle then becomes as shown in Fig. 19.46 (ii). Note that active power $(= OA)$ drawn by the motor remains the same. The capacitor bank reduces the lagging reactive power AB to zero.

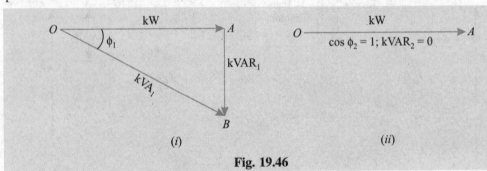

Fig. 19.46

(i) Power input (OA), $P = \sqrt{3}\ V_L\ I_L \cos \phi = \sqrt{3} \times 400 \times 20 \times 0.8$

$$= 11.085 \times 10^3\ W = 11.085\ kW$$

Leading $kVAR$ supplied by delta-connected capacitor bank

$$= AB = P \tan \phi_1 = 11.085 \tan (\cos^{-1} 0.8) = 8.314\ kVAR$$

If I_C is the phase current in the delta-connected bank, then,

$$\text{Total } VAR = 3V_{ph}I_C = 3 \times 400 \times I_C = 1200\ I_C$$

$$\therefore \qquad 1200\ I_C = 8314 \qquad \text{or} \qquad I_C = 8314/1200 = 6.93\ A$$

Capacitive reactance/phase, $X_C = V_{ph}/I_C = 400/6.93 = 57.72\ \Omega$

Capacitance/phase, $C = \dfrac{1}{2\pi f\ X_C} = \dfrac{1}{2\pi \times 50 \times 57.72} = 55.17 \times 10^{-6}\ F = 55.17\ \mu F$

---

*   Since the capacitors are assumed loss-free, $kVAR = kVA$.

(*ii*) Since the p.f. is raised to unity, the new line current I_L' is given by;

$$P = \sqrt{3}\, V_L I_L' \qquad\qquad (\because \cos \phi_2 = 1)$$

$$\therefore \qquad I_L' = \frac{P}{\sqrt{3}\, V_L} = \frac{11.085 \times 10^3}{\sqrt{3} \times 400} = 16\,\text{A}$$

Example 19.22. *A synchronous motor improves the power factor of a load of 200kW from 0.8 lagging to 0.9 lagging. Simultaneously the motor carries a load of 80kW. Find (i) the leading kVAR supplied by the motor, (ii) kVA rating of the motor, and (iii) the power factor at which the motor operates.*

Solution.

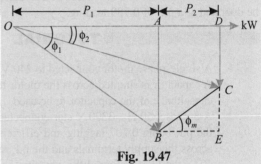

Load, $P_1 = 200$ kW; Motor load, $P_2 = 80\,kW$

p.f. of load, $\cos \phi_1 = 0.8\ lag$

p.f. of combined load, $\cos \phi_2 = 0.9\ lag$

Combined load,

$$P = P_1 + P_2 = 200 + 80 = 280\,kW$$

In Fig. 19.47, Δ *OAB* is the power triangle for load, Δ *ODC* for combined load and Δ *BEC* for the motor.

Fig. 19.47

(*i*) Leading *kVAR* supplied by the motor

$$= CE = DE - DC = AB - DC \qquad (\because AB = DE)$$
$$= P_1 \tan \phi_1 - P^* \tan \phi_2$$
$$= 200 \tan (\cos^{-1} 0.8) - 280 \tan (\cos^{-1} 0.9)$$
$$= 200 \times 0.75 - 280 \times 0.4843 = \textbf{14.4 kVAR}$$

(*ii*) kVA rating of the motor $= BC = \sqrt{(BE)^2 + (EC)^2} = \sqrt{(80)^2 + (14.4)^2} = \textbf{81.28 kVA}$

(*iii*) p.f. of motor, $\quad \cos \phi_m = \dfrac{\text{Motor } kW}{\text{Motor } kVA} = \dfrac{80}{81.28} = \textbf{0.984}\ lead$

Example 19.23. *A supply system feeds the following loads (i) a lighting load of 500 kW, (ii) a load of 400 kW at a p.f. of 0.707 lagging, (iii) a load of 800 kW at a p.f. of 0.8 leading, (iv) a load of 500 kW at a p.f. 0.6 lagging, (v) a synchronous motor driving a 540 kW d.c. generator and having an overall efficiency of 90%. Calculate the power factor of synchronous motor so that the station power factor may become unity.*

Solution.

The lighting load works at unity p.f. and, therefore, its lagging kVAR is zero. The lagging kVAR are supplied by the loads (*ii*) and (*iv*) whereas loads (*iii*) and (*v*) supply the leading *kVAR*. For station power factor to be unity, the total lagging kVAR must be neutralised by the total leading kVAR. We know that kVAR = kW tan ϕ.

∴ Total lagging kVAR taken by loads (*ii*) and (*iv*)

$$= 400 \tan (\cos^{-1} 0.707) + 500 \tan (\cos^{-1} 0.6)$$
$$= 400 \times 1 + 500 \times 1.33 = 1066.6\,\text{kVAR}$$

Leading kVAR supplied by the load (*iii*)

$$= 800 \tan (\cos^{-1} 0.8) = 800 \times 0.75 = 600\,\text{kVAR}$$

* In right angled Δ *OAB*, $AB = P_1 \tan \phi_1$

In right angled Δ *ODC*,

$$DC = OD \tan \phi_2 = (P_1 + P_2) \tan \phi_2 = P \tan \phi_2$$

∴ Leading kVAR to be supplied by synchronous motor

$$= 1066.6 - 600 = 466.6 \text{ kVAR}$$

Motor input = output/efficiency = 540/0.9 = 600 kW

If ϕ is the phase angle of synchronous motor, then,

$$\tan \phi = \text{kVAR/kW} = 466.6/600 = 0.7776$$

∴ $$\phi = \tan^{-1} 0.7776 = 37°52'$$

∴ p.f. of synchronous motor = $\cos \phi = \cos 37°52' = 0.789$ leading

Therefore, in order that the station power factor may become unity, the synchronous motor should be operated at a p.f. of 0.789 leading.

TUTORIAL PROBLEMS

1. A single-phase motor connected to 240 V, 50 Hz supply takes 20 A at a p.f. of 0.75 lagging. A capacitor is shunted across the motor terminals to improve the p.f. to 0.9. Determine the capacitance of the capacitor to be used. [59.8 μF]

2. A 3-phase, 50 Hz, 3300 V star-connected induction motor develops 250 H.P. (186.5 kW), the p.f. being 0.707 lagging and efficiency 0.86. Three capacitors in delta are connected across the supply terminals and the p.f. raised to 0.9 lagging. Calculate :
   (i) the *kVAR* rating of the capacitor bank.
   (ii) the capacitance of each unit. [(i) 111.8 kVAR (ii) 10.9 μF]

3. A 3-phase, 50 Hz, 3000 V motor develops 600 H.P. (447.6 kW), the p.f. being 0.75 lagging and efficiency 0.93. A bank of capacitors is connected in delta across the supply terminals and power factor raised to 0.95 lagging. Each of the capacitance unit is built of five similar 600V capacitors. Determine the capacitance of each capacitor. [156 μF]

4. Three similar coils, each of resistance 20 Ω and inductive reactance 15 Ω are connected in star to a 400 V, 3 – φ, 50 Hz supply. Calculate the line current, power supplied and the power factor. If three capacitors, each of the same capacitance, are connected in delta to the same supply so as to form a parallel circuit with the above impedance coils, calculate the capacitance of each capacitor to obtain an overall p.f. of 0.95 lagging. [9.24A; 5120 W; 0.8 *lag*; 14.31μF]

5. A capacitor bank taking a load of 1200 kVA is necessary to improve the p.f. of a 3-phase balanced load in a factory from 0.75 lagging to 0.95 lagging. Find the factory load in kW and kVA (i) before connection of capacitors (ii) after connection of capacitors. [(i) 2150 kW; 2260 kVA (ii) 2150 kW; 2870 kVA]

19.16. POWER MEASUREMENT IN 3-PHASE CIRCUITS

The following methods are available for measuring power in a 3-phase load (star or delta connected):

(i) **Three-Wattmeter Method.** In this method, three wattmeters are connected in such a way that each has its current coil in one line and its potential coil between that line and some common point. The algebraic sum of the readings of the three wattmeters gives the total power consumed whether the load is balanced or not. If neutral wire is available, the common point should be at the neutral wire.

(ii) **Two-Wattmeter Method.** In this method, the current coils of the two wattmeters are connected in *any* two lines and the potential coil of each joined to the third line. The algebraic sum of their readings gives the total power consumed whether the load is balanced or not. If the neutral wire is available, it should carry no current. Or else the neutral of the load should be isolated from the neutral of the source.

(iii) **One-Wattmeter method.** If the load is balanced, the power in any phase can be measured by a single wattmeter. The total circuit power is given by multiplying the wattmeter reading by three. This method can only be used if the load is balanced. Its principal disadvantage is that it is not always possible to make the required connections.

It may be noted that Two-wattmeter method is a universal method of measuring power in a 3-phase circuit.

19.17. THREE-WATTMETER METHOD

In this method, the three wattmeters are connected in such a way that each has its current coil in one line and its potential coil between that line and some common point *x* as shown in Fig. 19.48. It can be shown mathematically that algebraic sum of their readings gives the total power consumed whether the load is balanced or not, *i.e.*

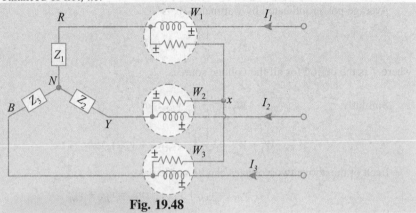

Fig. 19.48

Total power = $W_1 + W_2 + W_3$ *... algebraic sum*

A *caution* if neutral wire is available. Then common point x should be at the neutral wire.

19.18. TWO-WATTMETER METHOD

In this **method, current coils of the two wattmeters are connected in any two lines and the potential coil of each is joined to the third line as shown in Fig. 19.49. It can be proved mathematically that algebraic sum of the readings of the two wattmeters gives the total power consumed whether the load is balanced or not, *i.e.*

Total power = $W_1 + W_2$ *... algebraic sum*

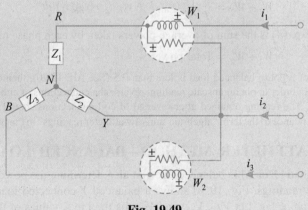

Fig. 19.49

*   The point *x* may be specified point in the three phase system or it may be merely a point in space at which the three potential coils have a common junction.

**   The two-wattmeter method is essentially the three-wattmeter method with common point shifted to one of the lines.

The only precaution in this method is that the neutral wire, if available, should not carry any current. Or else the neutral of the load should be isolated from the neutral of the source. The principal advantage is that the algebraic sum of the readings of the two wattmeters indicates the total power regardless of (*i*) load imbalance (*ii*) source imbalance (*iii*) difference in wattmeters (*iv*) wave-form of the source and (*v*) phase sequence.

Proof. We shall now prove mathematically that the algebraic sum of two wattmeter readings is equal to the total power drawn by the Y load in Fig. 19.49.

Average power indicated by wattmeter W_1 is

$$W_1 = \frac{1}{T} \int_0^T v_{RY}\, i_1\, dt$$

where T is the period for all the voltage sources.

Similarly,
$$W_2 = \frac{1}{T} \int_0^T v_{BY}\, i_3\, dt$$

$$\therefore \qquad W_1 + W_2 = \frac{1}{T} \int_0^T (v_{RY}\, i_1 + v_{BY}\, i_3)\, dt \qquad \qquad ...(i)$$

Each of the above two voltages can be written as :

$$v_{RY} = v_{RN} + v_{NY}; \quad v_{BY} = v_{BN} + v_{NY}$$

Substituting the values of v_{RY} and v_{BY} in exp. (*i*), we get,

$$W_1 + W_2 = \frac{1}{T} \int_0^T (v_{RN}\, i_1 + v_{BN}\, i_3)\, dt + \frac{1}{T} \int_0^T v_{NY}\, (i_1 + i_3)\, dt$$

Since
$$i_1 + i_2 + i_3 = 0; \quad i_1 + i_3 = -i_2$$

$$\therefore \qquad W_1 + W_2 = \frac{1}{T} \int_0^T (v_{RN}\, i_1 + v_{BN}\, i_3)\, dt + \frac{1}{T} \int_0^T v_{NY}\, (-i_2)\, dt$$

$$= \frac{1}{T} \int_0^T (v_{RN}\, i_1 + v_{BN}\, i_3)\, dt + \frac{1}{T} \int_0^T v_{YN}\, i_2\, dt$$

$$\therefore \qquad W_1 + W_2 = \frac{1}{T} \int_0^T (v_{RN}\, i_1 + v_{YN}\, i_2 + v_{BN}\, i_3)\, dt \qquad \qquad ...(ii)$$

The R.H.S. of exp. (*ii*) is the sum of average powers taken by each phase of the load.

$$\therefore \qquad W_1 + W_2 = \text{Total power} \qquad \qquad ...algebraic\ sum$$

Note. If the p.f. of 3-phase balanced load is less than 0.5 (See Art. 19.20), then one of the wattmeters will read down scale. In order to obtain upscale reading, reverse the connections of either potential or current coil of this wattmeter. The reading obtained after reversal of coil connections should be taken as negative. This explains the significance of the term "algebraic sum of wattmeter readings" in the two-wattmeter method.

19.19. TWO-WATTMETER METHOD—BALANCED LOAD

If the 3-phase load (Y or Δ) is balanced, we can also determine the power factor of the load from the wattmeter readings. Fig. 19.50 shows a balanced Y-connected load; the p.f. angle of load impedance being ϕ lag. Let V_{RN}, V_{YN} and V_{BN} be the r.m.s. values of the three load phase voltages (phase sequence being RYB) and I_R, I_Y and I_B the r.m.s. values of phase currents. These currents will lag behind their respective phase voltages by ϕ as shown in the phasor diagram in Fig. 19.51.

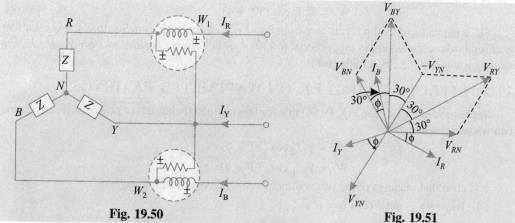

Fig. 19.50   **Fig. 19.51**

Current through current coil of $W_1 = I_R$

P.D. across potential coil of W_1, $V_{RY} = V_{RN} - V_{YN}$ *... phasor difference*

To obtain V_{RY}, find the phasor sum of V_{RN} and $-V_{YN}$ as shown in Fig. 19.51. It is clear from the phasor diagram that phase angle between V_{RY} and I_R is $(30° + \phi)$.

$$\therefore \qquad W_1 = V_{RY} I_R \cos(30° + \phi)$$

Current through current coil of $W_2 = I_B$

P.D. across potential coil of W_2, $V_{BY} = V_{BN} - V_{YN}$ *... phasor difference*

To obtain V_{BY}, find the phasor sum of V_{BN} and $-V_{YN}$ as shown in Fig. 19.51. It is clear from the phasor diagram that phase angle between V_{BY} and I_B is $(30° - \phi)$.

$$\therefore \qquad W_2 = V_{BY} I_B \cos(30° - \phi)$$

Since the load is balanced, $V_{RY} = V_{BY} =$ Line voltage, V_L and $I_R = I_B =$ Line current, I_L

$$\therefore \qquad W_1 = V_L I_L \cos(30° + \phi)$$

and

$$W_2 = V_L I_L \cos(30° - \phi)$$

$$\therefore \qquad W_1 + W_2 = V_L I_L [\cos(30° + \phi) + \cos(30° - \phi)]$$

$$= V_L I_L (2 \cos 30° \cos \phi)$$

$$= \sqrt{3} \, V_L I_L \cos \phi = \text{Total power in the 3-phase load}$$

Hence, the algebraic sum of the two wattmeter readings gives the total power consumed in the 3-phase load.

Power factor

$$W_2 + W_1 = \sqrt{3} \, V_L I_L \cos \phi$$

Also

$$^*W_2 - W_1 = V_L I_L \sin \phi$$

$$\therefore \qquad \tan \phi = \sqrt{3} \, \frac{W_2 - W_1}{W_2 + W_1}$$

Thus, from the two wattmeter readings, we can find ϕ and hence the load power factor $\cos \phi$.

Which is higher-reading wattmeter ? How can we tell which wattmeter reads higher (*i.e.*, W_2) and which reads lower (*i.e.*, W_1) ?

$$W_2 = V_L I_L \cos(30° - \phi)$$

. . . .

$*$ $W_2 - W_1 = V_L I_L [\cos(30° - \phi) - \cos(30° + \phi)]$

$\qquad = V_L I_L [(\cos 30° \cos \phi + \sin 30° \sin \phi) - (\cos 30° \cos\phi - \sin 30° \sin \phi)]$

$\qquad = V_L I_L (2\sin 30° \sin \phi) = V_L I_L \sin \phi$

$$W_1 = V_L I_L \cos (30° + \phi)$$

Since the value of load p.f. can vary from 0 to 1 (*i.e.*, ϕ can vary from 90° to 0°), it is clear that wattmeter whose deflection is proportional to (30° – ϕ) is *always positive and always the higher reading wattmeter (i.e., W_2 in this case).

19.20. EFFECT OF LOAD P.F. ON WATTMETER READINGS

We have seen above (See Fig. 19.50) that for lagging load (balanced) of power factor cos ϕ , the two wattmeter readings are :

$$W_2 = V_L I_L \cos (30° - \phi)$$
$$W_1 = V_L I_L \cos (30° + \phi)$$

It is clear that readings of the two wattmeters depend upon load p.f. angle ϕ.

(*i*) *When p.f. is unity (i.e.,* $\phi = 0°$)

$$W_2 = V_L I_L \cos 30°; \qquad W_1 = V_L I_L \cos 30°$$

Both wattmeters indicate equal and positive (*i.e.*, upscale) readings.

(*ii*) *When p.f. is 0.5 (i.e.,* $\phi = 60°$)

$$W_2 = V_L I_L \cos 30°; \qquad W_1 = V_L I_L \cos 90° = 0$$

Hence, total power is measured by wattmeter W_2 alone.

(*iii*) *When p.f. is less than 0.5 but greater than 0 (i.e., 90° >* ϕ *> 60°).*

$$**W_2 = \text{positive reading}; \qquad W_1 = \text{negative reading}$$

In order to obtain upscale reading on wattmeter W_1, reverse the connections of potential or current coil. *The reading obtained after reversal of coil connections should be taken as negative.*

$$\text{Total power} = W_2 + (- W_1) \qquad\qquad \text{... algebraic sum}$$
$$= W_2 - W_1$$

Thus, if the load p.f. is less than 0.5, then lower reading wattmeter (*i.e.*, W_1 in this case) will give negative reading.

(*iv*) *When p.f. is zero (i.e.* $\phi = 90°$). Such a case will occur when the load consists of pure inductance and/or capacitance.

$$W_2 = V_L I_L \cos (30° - 90°) = V_L I_L \sin 30°$$
$$W_1 = V_L I_L \cos (30° + 90°) = - V_L I_L \sin 30°$$

Thus, the two wattmeters will read equal and opposite.

∴ $$W_1 + W_2 = 0$$

The above facts are summarised below in the tabular form.

ϕ	0°	60°	more than 60°	90°
cos ϕ	1	0.5	< 0.5	0
W_2	positive	positive	positive	positive
W_1	positive	0	negative	negative
Conclusion	$W_1 = W_2$ Total power = $W_1 + W_2$	$W_1 = 0$ Total power = W_2	Total power = $W_2 - W_1$	$W_2 = - W_1$ Totat Power = 0

* Except for the case when load p.f. is unity (*i.e.*, $\phi = 0°$)at which the two wattmeters have equal readings.

** The wattmeter W_2 reads positive (*i.e.*, upscale) because for the given conditions (*i.e.*, 90° > ϕ > 60°), the phase angle between voltage and current will be less than 90°. However, for wattmeter W_1, the phase angle between voltage and current will be more than 90° and hence this wattmeter gives negative (*i.e.*, downscale) reading.

19.21. LEADING POWER FACTOR

In discussing two-wattmeter method for measuring power in a 3-phase balanced load, we have considered lagging load power factor *i.e.*, p.f. angle ϕ is considered positive. For leading power factor, angle ϕ becomes negative. Therefore, by putting the value of load p.f. angle as $-\phi$ in the readings of the wattmeters above, we have,

$$W_2 = V_L I_L \cos (30° + \phi)$$
$$W_1 = V_L I_L \cos (30° - \phi)$$

Note that effect of leading power factor is that the readings of the two wattmeters are interchanged. Now, wattmeter W_1 has become the higher-reading wattmeter.

$$\therefore \qquad \tan \phi = \sqrt{3}\, \frac{W_1 - W_2}{W_1 + W_2}$$

19.22. HOW TO APPLY P.F. FORMULA ?

As shown above, the value of $\tan \phi$ (and hence the p.f. $\cos \phi$) can be determined from the two wattmeter readings.

$$\tan \phi = \sqrt{3}\, \frac{W_2 - W_1}{W_2 + W_1} \qquad \qquad ... \text{lagging p.f.}$$

$$\tan \phi = \sqrt{3}\, \frac{W_1 - W_2}{W_1 + W_2} \qquad \qquad ... \text{leading p.f.}$$

It may be noted that for lagging p.f., W_2 is the higher-reading wattmeter whereas it is W_1 for leading p.f. To avoid any confusion, the reader is well advised to remember the following general formula for both lagging and leading p.f.

$$\tan \phi = \sqrt{3}\, \frac{(\text{Higher reading}) - (\text{Lower reading})}{(\text{Higher reading}) + (\text{Lower reading})}$$

For example, in the two-wattmeter method if the two wattmeter readings are 12.5 kW and –4.8 kW, then,

$$\tan \phi = \sqrt{3}\, \frac{(12.5) - (-4.8)}{(12.5) + (-4.8)} = \sqrt{3}\, \frac{17.3}{7.7} = 3.89$$

$$\therefore \qquad \phi = \tan^{-1} 3.89 = 75.6°$$

$$\therefore \qquad \text{Power factor} = \cos \phi = \cos 75.6° = 0.2487$$

19.23. ONE-WATTMETER METHOD

If the 3-phase load (Y or Δ) is balanced, then one wattmeter is sufficient to measure the power drawn by the load. In this method, two readings of the two-wattmeter method are taken with a single wattmeter as shown in Fig. 19.52. The current coil of the wattmeter is connected in any one line and the pressure coil is connected alternately between this and the other two lines. The algebraic sum of the two readings gives the total power drawn by the balanced 3-phase load.

This method only holds for a balanced load and cannot be applied to an unbalanced load.

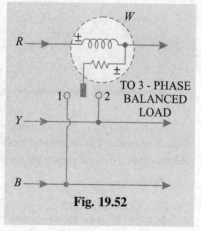

Fig. 19.52

19.24. REACTIVE POWER WITH TWO-WATTMETER METHOD

The reactive power (*i.e.*, *VAR*) in a 3-phase balanced load can be determined from the readings of the two-wattmeter method.

$$W_2 - W_1 = V_L I_L \sin \phi \qquad \text{... See Art. 19.19}$$

Multiplying throughout by $\sqrt{3}$, we get,

$$\sqrt{3}(W_2 - W_1) = \sqrt{3} V_L I_L \sin \phi$$

But $\sqrt{3} V_L I_L \sin \phi$ is equal to the reactive power taken by the 3-phase balanced load.

$$\therefore \qquad \text{Reactive power} = \sqrt{3} \ (*W_2 - W_1) \ VAR$$

Thus, for a balanced load, the reactive power is equal to $\sqrt{3}$ times the algebraic difference of the readings of the two wattmeters.

19.25. REACTIVE POWER WITH ONE WATTMETER

A single wattmeter may be used to read the reactive power in a balanced 3-phase load. The method of connection is shown in Fig. 19.53. The current coil of the wattmeter is connected in one line (say line *R*) and potential coil is connected between the other two lines.

The voltage across the potential coil is V_{YB} (= line voltage V_L) and current though the current coil is I_R (= line current I_L). The phase angle between V_{YB} and I_R is $90° - \phi$ as shown in the phasor diagram in Fig. 19.53.

$$\therefore \quad \text{Wattmeter reading,} \qquad W = V_{YB} I_R \cos(90° - \phi) = V_L I_L \sin \phi$$

But, $$\text{Reactive power} = \sqrt{3} V_L I_L \sin \phi = \sqrt{3} \times \text{wattmeter reading}$$

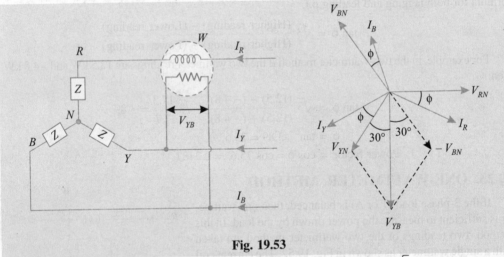

Fig. 19.53

Hence, the reactive power drawn by 3-phase balanced load is equal to $\sqrt{3}$ times the wattmeter reading.

Example 19.24. *Two-wattmeter method is used to measure the power absorbed by a 3-phase induction motor. The wattmeter readings are 12.5 kW and – 4.8 kW. Find (i) the power absorbed by the machine, (ii) load power factor, and (iii) reactive power taken by the load.*

Solution.

$$W_2 = 12.5 \text{ kW}; \quad W_1 = -4.8 \text{ kW}$$

* Note that W_2 is the higher–reading wattmeter. Further $W_2 - W_1$ is the algebraic difference of two wattmeter readings.

(i)   Power absorbed $= W_2 + W_1 = 12.5 + (-4.8) = \textbf{7.7 kW}$

(ii) $\tan \phi = \sqrt{3}\, \dfrac{W_2 - W_1}{W_2 + W_1} = \sqrt{3}\, \dfrac{12.5 - (-4.8)}{(12.5) + (-4.8)} = 3.89$

∴ $\phi = \tan^{-1} 3.89 = 75.6°$

∴   Power factor $= \cos \phi = \cos 75.6° = \textbf{0.2487} \textit{ lag}$

Since the load p.f. is less than 0.5, the lower-reading wattmeter must read downscale as is evident from the data of the problem.

(iii)   Reactive power $= \sqrt{3}\,(W_2 - W_1) = \sqrt{3}\,(12.5 + 4.8) = \textbf{29.96 kVAR}$

Example 19.25. *Two-wattmeter method is used to measure the power taken by a 3-phase induction motor on no load. The wattmeter readings are 375 W and – 50 W. Calculate (i) power factor of the motor at no load (ii) phase difference of voltage and current in two wattmeters.*

Solution.

(i) $\tan \phi = \sqrt{3}\, \dfrac{W_2 - W_1}{W_2 + W_1} = \sqrt{3}\, \dfrac{375 - (-50)}{375 + (-50)} = 2.265$

            $\phi = \tan^{-1} 2.265 = 66.18°$

∴   No load p.f. $= \cos \phi = \cos 66.18° = \textbf{0.404} \textit{ lag}$

(ii)   Phase angle in wattmeter $W_2 = 30° - \phi = 30° - 66.18° = -36.18°$

        Phase angle in wattmeter $W_1 = 30° + \phi = 30° + 66.18° = 96.18°$

Example 19.26. *A 3-phase motor load has a p.f. of 0.397 lagging. Two wattmeters connected to measure power show the input as 30 kW. Find the reading on each wattmeter.*

Solution.

$$W_2 + W_1 = 30 \text{ kW} \hspace{2cm} ...(i)$$

$$\text{p.f. angle, } \phi = \cos^{-1} 0.397 = 66.6°$$

∴ $\tan \phi = \tan 66.6° = 2.311$

Now, $\tan \phi = \sqrt{3}\, \dfrac{W_2 - W_1}{W_2 + W_1}$

or $2.311 = \sqrt{3}\, \dfrac{W_2 - W_1}{30}$

∴ $W_2 - W_1 = 40 \text{ kW} \hspace{2cm} ...(ii)$

Solving eqns. (i) and (ii), we get, $W_2 = \textbf{35 kW}; \; W_1 = \textbf{– 5 kW}$

Since the load p.f. is less than 0.5, the lower-reading wattmeter W_1 gives downscale reading. The upscale reading of this wattmeter can be obtained by reversing the connections of its current or potential coil.

Example 19.27. *Each of the two wattmeters connected to measure the input to a 3-phase induction motor reads 10 kW. If the power factor of the motor be changed to 0.866 lagging, determine the readings of the two wattmeters, the total input power remaining unchanged.*

Solution.

$$\text{Total power} = W_2 + W_1 = 20 \text{ kW} \hspace{1.5cm} .. (i) \text{ regardless of p.f.}$$

$$\text{p.f. angle, } \phi = \cos^{-1} 0.866 = 30°$$

∴ $\tan \phi = \tan 30° = 0.577$

Now, $\tan \phi = \sqrt{3}\, \dfrac{W_2 - W_1}{W_2 + W_1}$

or $0.577 = \sqrt{3}\, \dfrac{W_2 - W_1}{20}$

$$\therefore \qquad W_2 - W_1 = 6.66 \; kW \qquad \qquad \qquad ...(ii)$$

Solving eqs. (i) and (ii), we get, $W_2 = \textbf{13.33 kW}$; $W_1 = \textbf{6.67 kW}$

Example 19.28. *Three indentical coils, each having a resistance of 10 Ω and a reactance of 10 Ω are connected in (i) star (ii) delta, across 400 V, 3-phase supply. Find in each case the line current and the readings on each of the two wattmeters connected to measure the power.*

Solution.

(i) **Star connection**

$$Z_{ph} = \sqrt{10^2 + 10^2} = 10\sqrt{2} \; \Omega$$

$$V_{ph} = V_L/\sqrt{3} = 400/\sqrt{3} = 231 \; V$$

$$I_L = I_{ph} = 231 \div 10\sqrt{2} = \textbf{16.33 A}$$

$$\phi = \tan^{-1} X_{ph}/R_{ph} = \tan^{-1} 10/10 = 45°$$

$$\text{Power factor} = \cos \phi = \cos 45° = \frac{1}{\sqrt{2}} = 0.707$$

$$\text{Total power} = \sqrt{3} V_L I_L \cos \phi = \sqrt{3} \times 400 \times 16.33 \times 1/\sqrt{2} = 8000 \; W$$

Let W_1 and W_2 be the wattmeter readings; W_2 being the higher-reading wattmeter. Since the load p.f. is greater than 0.5, wattmeter W_1 will also read positive.

$$W_2 + W_1 = 8000 \qquad \qquad \qquad ...(i)$$

Also

$$\tan 45° = \sqrt{3} \; \frac{W_2 - W_1}{W_2 + W_1}$$

or

$$1 = \sqrt{3} \; \frac{W_2 - W_1}{8000}$$

$$\therefore \qquad W_2 - W_1 = 4619 \qquad \qquad \qquad ...(ii)$$

Solving eqns. (i) and (ii), we get, $W_2 = \textbf{6309.5 W}$; $W_1 = \textbf{1690.5 W}$

(ii) **Delta connection**

$$Z_{ph} = 10\sqrt{2} \; \Omega \qquad \qquad \qquad \text{... same as for star}$$

$$V_{ph} = V_L = 400 \; V$$

$$I_{ph} = V_{ph}/Z_{ph} = 400 \div 10\sqrt{2} = 28.28 \; A$$

$$I_L = \sqrt{3} \; I_{ph} = \sqrt{3} \times 28.28 = \textbf{48.98 A}$$

$$\text{Power factor} = \cos \phi = \cos 45° = 1/\sqrt{2}$$

$$\text{Total power} = \sqrt{3} \; V_L I_L \cos \phi = \sqrt{3} \times 400 \times 48.98 \times 1/\sqrt{2} = 23995 \; W$$

Now,

$$W_2 + W_1 = 23995 \qquad \qquad \qquad ...(i)$$

Also

$$\tan 45° = \sqrt{3} \; \frac{W_2 - W_1}{W_2 + W_1}$$

or

$$1 = \sqrt{3} \; \frac{W_2 - W_1}{23995}$$

$$\therefore \qquad W_2 - W_1 = 13854 \qquad \qquad \qquad ...(ii)$$

Solving eqns. (i) and (ii), we get, $W_2 = \textbf{18924.5 W}$; $W_1 = \textbf{5070.5 W}$

Example 19.29. *The power input to a 2000 V, 50 Hz, 3-phase motor running on full load at an efficiency of 90% is measured by two wattmeters which indicate 300 kW and 100 kW respectively. Find (i) the input, (ii) the power factor, and (iii) the line current and output.*

Solution.

(*i*)   Input to motor $= W_2 + W_1 = 300 + 100 = $ **400 kW**

(*ii*) $\tan \phi = \sqrt{3} \dfrac{W_2 - W_1}{W_2 + W_1} = \sqrt{3} \dfrac{300 - 100}{300 + 100} = 0.866$

∴ $\phi = \tan^{-1} 0.866 = 40.9°$

∴   Power factor $= \cos \phi = \cos 40.9° = $ **0.756 lag**

(*iii*) $400 \times 10^3 = \sqrt{3} \, V_L I_L \cos \phi$

∴   Line current, $I_L = \dfrac{400 \times 10^3}{\sqrt{3} \times 2000 \times 0.756} = $ **152.74 A**

                         Motor output $=$ Input $\times 0.9 = 400 \times 0.9 = $ **360 kW**

Example 19.30. *The ratio of the readings of the two wattmeters connected to measure power in a 3-phase balanced load is 3 : 1. The load is known to be inductive with a lagging power factor. Calculate the power factor of the load.*

Solution.

                         $W_2/W_1 = 3$; W_2 being the higher reading.

Now, $\tan \phi = \sqrt{3} \dfrac{W_2 - W_1}{W_2 + W_1}$

                         $= \sqrt{3} \dfrac{(W_2/W_1) - 1}{(W_2/W_1) + 1} = \sqrt{3} \dfrac{3 - 1}{3 + 1} = \sqrt{3}/2$

∴ $\phi = \tan^{-1}(\sqrt{3}/2) = 40.9°$

∴   Load p.f. $= \cos \phi = \cos 40.9° = $ **0.756** *lag*

TUTORIAL PROBLEMS

1. Two wattmeters are used to measure power in a 3-phase balanced load. The wattmeter readings are 8.2 kW and 7.5 kW. Calculate (*i*) total power, (*ii*) power factor, and (*iii*) total reactive power.   [(*i*) **15.7 kW** (*ii*) **0.997** (*iii*) **1.21 kVAR**]

2. A balanced 3-phase load takes 10 kW at a p.f. of 0.9 lagging. Calculate the readings on each of the two wattmeters connected to read the input power.   [**6398 W, 3602 W**]

3. A 440 V, 3-phase induction motor has an output of 20.7 kW at a p.f. of 0.82 and efficiency 85%. Calculate the readings on each of the two wattmeters connected to measure input.

                         [**12.35 kW; 5.25 kW**]

4. The power input to a 400 V, 3-phase, 50 Hz induction motor is measured by two-wattmeter method. The readings of the two wattmeters are 40 kW and 10 kW. Calculate (*i*) the input power (*ii*) power factor (*iii*) line current.   [(*i*) **30 kW** (*ii*) **0.327** (*iii*) **132.42 A**]

5. Three identical coils, each having a resistance of 20 Ω and a reactance of 20 Ω are connected in (*i*) star (*ii*) delta across 440 V, 3-phase lines. Calculate for each method of connection the line current and readings on each of the two wattmeters connected to measure the power.

                         [(*i*) **8.98 A; 3817.5 W, 1022.5 W** (*ii*) **26.95 A; 12452.5 W, 3067.5 W**]

MULTIPLE-CHOICE QUESTIONS

1. In a two phase generator, the electrical displacement between the two phases or windings is .... electrical degrees.

   (a) 120   (b) 90

   (c) 180   (d) none of the above

2. In a six-phase generator, the electrical displacement between different phases or windings is .... electrical degrees.

   (a) 60   (b) 90

   (c) 120   (d) 45

3. The torque on the rotor of a 3-phase motor is more constant than that of a single phase motor because ....

   (a) single phase motors are not self-starting

   (b) single phase motors are small in size

   (c) 3-phase power is of constant value

   (d) none of the above

4. For the same rating, the size of a 3-phase motor will be .... single phase motor.

   (a) less than that of

   (b) more than that of

   (c) same as that of

   (d) none of the above

5. To transmit the same amount of power over a fixed distance at a given voltage, the 3-phase system requires............... the weight of copper.

   (a) 3 times

   (b) 3/4th times

   (c) 1.5 times

   (d) 0.5 times

6. The phase sequence of a three-phase system is RYB. The other possible phase sequence can be ....

   (a) BRY

   (b) YRB

   (c) RBY

   (d) none of the above

7. If in Fig. 19.54, the phase sequence is RYB, then, ...

   (a) L_1 will burn more brightly than L_2

   (b) L_2 will burn more brightly than L_1

   (c) both lamps will be equally bright

   (d) none of the above

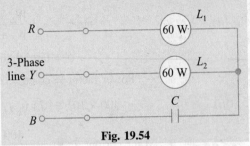

Fig. 19.54

8. In a 3-phase system, if the instantaneous values of phase R and Y are + 60 V and – 40 V respectively, then instantaneous voltage of phase B is

   (a) –120 V   (b) 40 A

   (c) 120 V   (d) none of the above

9. In a 3-phase system, $V_{YN} = 100 \angle -120°$ V and $V_{BN} = 100 \angle 120°$ V. What is V_{YB}?

   (a) $170 \angle 90°$ V   (b) $173 \angle -90°$ V

   (c) $200 \angle 60°$ V   (d) none of the above

10. Three 50-ohm resistors are connected in star across 400 V, 3-phase supply. If one of the resistors is disconnected, then, line current will be ....

    (a) 8A   (b) 4 A

    (c) $8\sqrt{3}$ A   (d) $8/\sqrt{3}$ A

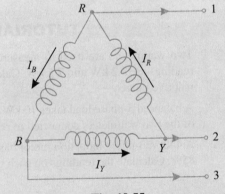

Fig. 19.55

11. Fig. 19.55 shows balanced delta-connected supply system. The current in line 1 is ....

    (a) $I_R - I_B$ ------- phasor difference

    (b) $I_B - I_R$ ------- phasor difference

    (c) $I_Y - I_R - I_B$ -------phasor difference

    (d) none of the above

12. The delta-connected generator shown in Fig. 19.55 has phase voltage of 200 V on no load. If connections of one of the phases is reversed, then, resultant voltage across the mesh is ....

    (a) 200 V

    (b) $200 \times \sqrt{3}$ V

    (c) 400 V

    (d) none of the above

13. The resistance between any two terminals of a balanced delta-connected load is 12 Ω. The resistance of each phase is ....

    (a) 12 Ω

    (b) 18 Ω

    (c) 6 Ω

    (d) 36 Ω

14. The power rating of each resistor in Fig. 19.56 is ....

    (a) 4000 W

    (b) 2300 W

    (c) 4600 W

    (d) 5290 W

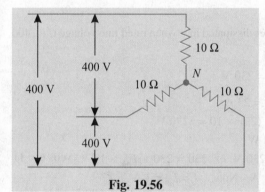

Fig. 19.56

15. The power consumed in the star-connected load shown in Fig. 19.57 is 690 W. The line current is ....

    (a) 2.5 A   (b) 1 A

    (c) 1.725 A   (d) none of the above

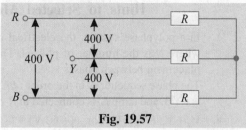

Fig. 19.57

16. If one of the resistors in Fig. 19.57 is open-circuited, power consumption will be ....

    (a) 200 W   (b) 300 W

    (c) 345 W   (d) none of the above

17. The power factor of the star-connected load shown in Fig. 19.58 is ....

    (a) 0.8 lagging   (b) 0.6 lagging

    (c) 0.75 lagging   (d) none of the above

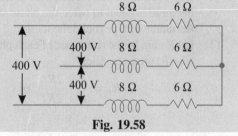

Fig. 19.58

18. Three identical resistances connected in star consume 4000 W. If the resistances are connected in delta across the same supply, the power consumed will be ....

    (a) 4000 W   (b) 6000 W

    (c) 8000 W   (d) 12000 W

19. Three identical resistances, each of 15 Ω, are connected in delta across 400 V, 3-phase supply. The value of resistance in each leg of the equivalent star-connected load would be ....

    (a) 15 Ω   (b) 7.5 Ω

    (c) 5 Ω   (d) 30 Ω

20. In order to measure power in a 3-phase, 4-wire unbalanced load, the minimum number of wattmeters required would be ....

    (a) 1   (b) 2

    (c) 4   (d) 3

Answers to Multiple-Choice Questions

1. (b)	2. (a)	3. (c)	4. (a)	5. (b)	6. (c)	7. (a)	8. (a)
9. (b)	10. (b)	11. (a)	12. (c)	13. (b)	14. (d)	15. (b)	16. (c)
17. (b)	18. (d)	19. (c)	20. (d)				

Hints to Selected Multiple-Choice Questions

1. In a polyphase system, the electrical displacement between phases or windings = $360/N$ where N is the number of phases. The only exception is 2-phase where electrical displacement between phases is **90°**.

7. The phase sequence is in the order : *bright lamp-dim lamp-capacitor.* Since phase sequence is RYB, and lamp L_1 is connected in R-phase, **it will burn more brightly than the lamp L_2.**

8. $V_R + V_Y + V_B = 0$ or $(+ 60 \text{ V}) + (- 40) + V_B = 0$ $\qquad\qquad \therefore V_B = -20\text{V}$

9. $V_{YB} = V_{YN} + V_{NB} = V_{YN} - V_{BN} = 100 \angle - 120° - 100 \angle 120° = 173 \angle - 90° \text{ V}$

10. When one of the resistors is disconnected, the remaining two resistors behave as if they were connected in series across the line voltage (*i.e.*, 400 V).

$$\therefore \quad I_{ph} = I_L = \frac{400}{50 + 50} = 4 \text{ A}$$

11. The current in line 1 is the phasor difference of I_R and I_B since 'positive' direction for I_R is towards point R and for I_B, it is away from point R.

12. It can be shown that if one phase of delta connection is reversed, the resultant voltage round the mesh is equal to twice the phase voltage, *i.e.*
Resultant voltage round the mesh = $2 E_{ph} = 2 \times 200 = 400 \text{ V}$

13. Let R ohm be the resistance of each phase. Between any two terminals of a delta load, R and $(R + R)$ are in parallel.

$$\therefore \quad R_T = \frac{R \times 2R}{R + 2R} \quad \text{or} \quad 12 = \frac{2}{3} R$$

$$\therefore \quad R = \frac{12 \times 3}{2} = 18 \, \Omega$$

14. The power rating of the resistor is the power dissipated in it when rated line voltage (*i.e.*, 400 V) is applied to the 3-phase line.

$$\text{Phase voltage, } E_{ph} = \frac{V_L}{\sqrt{3}} = \frac{400}{\sqrt{3}} = 230 \text{ V}$$

$$\text{Line current, } I_L = I_{ph} = 230/10 = 23 \text{ A}$$

$$\therefore \quad \text{Power rating} = (I_{ph})^2 \times R = (23)^2 \times 10 = 5290 \text{ W}$$

15. $\qquad\qquad$ Power/phase = 690/3 = 230 W
$\qquad$ Phase voltage, $E_{ph} = 400/\sqrt{3} = 230 \text{ V } or\ 230 = 230 \times I_{ph} \times 1$ $\quad (\because \cos \phi = 1)$

$$\therefore \quad I_{ph} = 230/230 = 1 \text{ A} \quad \text{Now,} \quad I_L = I_{ph} = 1 \text{ A}$$

16. By disconnecting one of the resistors, power consumption is halved, *i.e.* 690/2 = 345 W.

17. $\qquad\qquad\qquad Z = \sqrt{8^2 + 6^2} = 10 \, \Omega$

$\therefore \qquad$ Power factor, $\cos \phi = R/Z = 6/10 = 0.6$ **lagging**

18. When three identical impedances (or resistances) are connected in delta, the line current and power drawn are *three times* as that when the same impedances are connected in star across the same supply. Incidentally, this explains the usefulness of delta-connected loads.

19. The Δ-connected impedances can be replaced by the equivalent Y-connected impedances using the following relation :

$$Z_Y = Z_\Delta/3$$

Using this relation, the value of R is 15/3 = 5 Ω

20. According to Blondel's theorem, the minimum number of wattmeters required to measure power in polyphase system is *one less* than the number of wires in the system. Consequently, to measure power in 3-phase, 4-wire system, the minimum number of wattmeters required is = 4 - 1 = 3.

20

Transformers

INTRODUCTION

The transformer is probably one of the most use ful electrical devices ever invented. It can change the magnitude of alternating voltage or current from one value to another. This useful property of transformer is mainly responsible for the widespread use of alternating currents rather than direct currents *i.e.* electric power is generated, transmitted and distributed in the form of alternating current. Transformers have no moving parts, rugged and durable in construction, thus requiring very little attention. They also have a very high efficiency — as high as 99%. In this chapter, we shall study some of the basic properties of transformers.

20.1. TRANSFORMER

A transformer is a static piece of equipment used either for raising or lowering the voltage of an a.c. supply with a corresponding decrease or increase in current. It essentially consists of two windings, the primary and secondary, wound on a common laminated magnetic core as shown in Fig. 20.1. The winding connected to the a.c. source is called *primary winding* (or primary) and the one connected to load is called *secondary winding* (or secondary). The alternating voltage V_1 whose magnitude is to be changed is applied to the primary. Depending upon the number of turns of the primary (N_1) and secondary (N_2), an alternating e.m.f.

E_2 is induced in the secondary. This induced e.m.f. E_2 in the secondary causes a secondary current I_2. Consequently, terminal voltage V_2 will appear across the load. If $V_2 > V_1$, it is called a *step up-transformer*. On the other hand, if $V_2 < V_1$, it is called a *step-down transformer*.

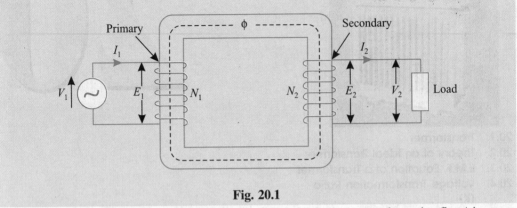

Fig. 20.1

Working. When an alternating voltage V_1 is applied to the primary, an alternating flux ϕ is set up in the core. This alternating flux links both the windings and induces e.m.f.s E_1 and E_2 in them according to Faraday's laws of electromagnetic induction. The e.m.f. E_1 is termed as primary e.m.f. and e.m.f. E_2 is termed as secondary e.m.f.

Clearly,
$$E_1 = - N_1 \frac{d\phi}{dt}$$

and
$$E_2 = - N_2 \frac{d\phi}{dt}$$

∴
$$\frac{E_2}{E_1} = \frac{N_2}{N_1}$$

Note that magnitudes of E_2 and E_1 *depend upon the number of turns on the secondary and primary respectively. If $N_2 > N_1$, then $E_2 > E_1$ (or $V_2 > V_1$) and we get a step-up transformer. On the other hand, if $N_2 < N_1$, then $E_2 < E_1$ (or $V_2 < V_1$) and we get a step-down transformer. If load is connected across the secondary winding, the secondary e.m.f. E_2 will cause a current I_2 to flow through the load. Thus, a transformer enables us to transfer a.c. power from one circuit to another with a change in voltage level.

The following points may be noted carefully:

(*i*) The transformer action is based on the laws of electromagnetic induction.

(*ii*) There is no electrical connection between the primary and secondary. The a.c. power is transferred from primary to secondary through magnetic flux.

(*iii*) There is no change in frequency *i.e.* output power has the same frequency as the input power.

(*iv*) The losses that occur in a transformer are:

    (*a*) core losses—eddy current and hysteresis losses.

    (*b*) copper losses—in the resistance of the windings.

In practice, these losses are very small so that output secondary power is nearly equal to the input primary power. In other words, a transformer has very high efficiency.

- -

*   Since $d\phi/dt$ is common for both the windings.

20.2. THEORY OF AN IDEAL TRANSFORMER

An ideal transformer is one that has

(*i*)   no winding resistance

(*ii*) no leakage flux *i.e.* the same flux links both the windings

(*iii*) no iron losses (*i.e.* eddy current and hysteresis losses) in the core.

Although ideal transformer cannot be physically realised, yet its study provides a very powerful tool in the analysis of a practical transformer. In fact, practical transformers have properties that approach very close to an ideal transformer.

Consider an ideal transformer on no load *i.e.* secondary is open-circuited as shown in Fig. 20.2 (*i*). Under such conditions, the primary is simply a coil of pure inductance. When an alternating voltage V_1 is applied to the primary, it draws a small magnetising current I_m which lags behind the applied voltage by *90°. This alternating current I_m produces an alternating flux ϕ which is proportional to and in **phase with it. The alternating flux ϕ links both the windings and induces e.m.f. E_1 in the primary and e.m.f. E_2 in the secondary. The primary e.m.f. E_1 is, at every instant, equal to and in opposition to V_1 (Lenz's law). Both e.m.f.s E_1 and E_2 lag behind flux ϕ by 90° (See Art. 20.3). However, their magnitudes depend upon the number of primary and secondary turns.

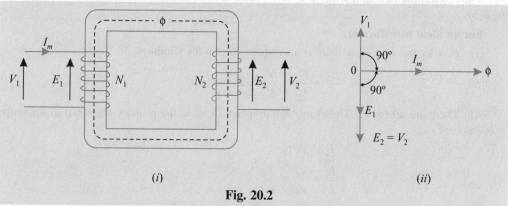

(*i*)   (*ii*)

Fig. 20.2

Fig. 20.2 (*ii*) shows the phasor diagram of an ideal transformer on no load. Since flux ϕ is common to both the windings, it has been taken as the reference phasor. As shown in Art. 20.3, the primary e.m.f. E_1 and secondary e.m.f. E_2 lag behind the flux ϕ by 90°. Note that E_1 and E_2 are in phase. But E_1 is equal to V_1 and 180° out of phase with it.

20.3. E.M.F. EQUATION OF A TRANSFORMER

Consider that an alternating voltage V_1 of frequency f is applied to the primary as shown in Fig. 20.2 (*i*). The sinusoidal flux ϕ produced by the primary can be represented as:

$$\phi = \phi_m \sin \omega t$$

The instantaneous e.m.f. e_1 induced in the primary is

$$e_1 = -N_1 \frac{d\phi}{dt} = -N_1 \frac{d}{dt} (\phi_m \sin \omega t)$$

$$= -\omega N_1 \phi_m \cos \omega t$$

$$= -2\pi f N_1 \phi_m \cos \omega t$$

$$= 2\pi f N_1 \phi_m \sin (\omega t - 90°) \qquad \qquad ...(i)$$

* In a pure inductive circuit, current lags behind the voltage by 90°.

** Since there are no iron losses, flux ϕ is in phase with I_m.

It is clear from the above equation that maximum value of induced e.m.f. in the primary is:

$$E_{m1} = 2\pi f N_1 \phi_m$$

The r.m.s. value E_1 of the primary e.m.f. is

$$E_1 = \frac{E_{m1}}{\sqrt{2}} = \frac{2\pi f N_1 \phi_m}{\sqrt{2}}$$

or $\qquad\qquad E_1 = 4.44 f N_1 \phi_m$

Similarly $\qquad\qquad E_2 = 4.44 f N_2 \phi_m$

∴   In an ideal transformer, $E_1 = V_1$ and $E_2 = V_2$.

Note: It is clear from exp. (*i*) above that e.m.f. E_1 induced in the primary lags behind the flux ϕ by 90°. Likewise, e.m.f. E_2 induced in the secondary lags behind flux ϕ by 90°.

20.4. VOLTAGE TRANSFORMATION RATIO (K)

From the above equations of induced e.m.f., we have,

$$\frac{E_2}{E_1} = \frac{N_2}{N_1} = K$$

The constant K is called *voltage transformation ratio*. Thus if $K = 5$ (*i.e.* $N_2/N_1 = 5$), then $E_2 = 5E_1$.

For an ideal transformer;

(*i*) $E_1 = V_1$ and $E_2 = V_2$ as there is no voltage drop in the windings.

∴ $\qquad\qquad \frac{E_2}{E_1} = \frac{V_2}{V_1} = \frac{N_2}{N_1} = K$

(*ii*)   There are no losses. Therefore, volt-amperes input to the primary are equal to the output volt-amperes *i.e.*

$$V_1 I_1 = V_2 I_2$$

or $\qquad\qquad \frac{I_2}{I_1} = \frac{V_1}{V_2} = \frac{1}{K}$

Hence, currents are in the inverse ratio of voltage transformation ratio. This simply means that if we raise the voltage, there is a corresponding decrease of current.

Example 20.1. *A 2000/200V, 20 kVA transformer has 66 turns in the secondary. Calculate (i) primary turns (ii) primary and secondary full-load currents. Neglect the losses.*

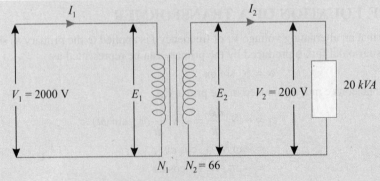

I_1 I_2

$V_1 = 2000$ V E_1 E_2 $V_2 = 200$ V   20 kVA

N_1 $N_2 = 66$

Fig. 20.3

* The e.m.f. E_2 induced in the secondary is produced by the same flux (*i.e.* $\phi = \phi_m \sin \omega t$) that causes e.m.f. E_1. Thus the only difference in the r.m.s. values of the two is the difference in the number of turns.

Solution. Fig. 20.3 represents the conditions of the problem.

$$K = V_2/V_1 = 200/2000 = 1/10$$

(i)
$$\frac{N_2}{N_1} = K = \frac{1}{10}$$

∴
$$N_1 = N_2 \times 10 = 66 \times 10 = \textbf{660 turns}$$

(ii)
$$V_1 I_1 = V_2 I_2 = 20 \times 10^3$$

∴
$$I_2 = \frac{20 \times 10^3}{V_2} = \frac{20 \times 10^3}{200} = \textbf{100 A}$$

$$I_1 = \frac{20 \times 10^3}{V_1} = \frac{20 \times 10^3}{2000} = \textbf{10 A}$$

Alternatively,
$$I_1 = KI_2 = (1/10)\ 100 = 10\ A$$

Example 20.2. *An ideal 25 kVA transformer has 500 turns on the primary winding and 40 turns on the secondary winding. The primary is connected to 3000 V, 50 Hz supply. Calculate (i) primary and secondary currents on full-load (ii) secondary e.m.f. and (iii) the maximum core flux.*

Solution.

$$K = N_2/N_1 = 40/500 = 4/50$$

(i)
$$I_1 = \frac{\text{Volt-amperes}}{V_1} = \frac{25 \times 10^3}{3000} = \textbf{8.33 A}$$

$$I_2 = I_1/K = 8.33 \times 50/4 = \textbf{104.2 A}$$

(ii)
$$E_2/E_1 = K$$

∴
$$E_2 = KE_1 = (4/50) \times 3000 = \textbf{240 V}$$

(iii)
$$E_1 = 4.44\ f N_1\ \phi_m$$

or
$$3000 = 4.44 \times 50 \times 500 \times \phi_m$$

∴
$$\phi_m = \frac{3000}{4.44 \times 50 \times 500} = 27 \times 10^{-3}\ Wb = \textbf{27 mWb}$$

Example 20.3. *A single phase 2200/250 V, 50 Hz transformer has a net core area of 36 cm² and a maximum flux density of 6Wb/m². Calculate the number of turns of primary and secondary.*

Solution.

Here
$$E_1 = 4.44\ f N_1\ \phi_m$$
$$E_1 = 2200\ V;\ f = 50\ Hz;\ \phi_m = B_m \times A = 6 \times 36 \times 10^{-4} = 0.0216\ Wb$$

∴
$$N_1 = \frac{E_1}{4.44\ f\ \phi_m} = \frac{2200}{4.44 \times 50 \times 0.0216} = \textbf{459}$$

Also
$$N_2 = \frac{E_2}{4.44\ f\ \phi_m} = \frac{250}{4.44 \times 50 \times 0.0216} = \textbf{52}$$

Example. 20.4. *A single phase 50 Hz transformer has square core of 20 cm side. The permissible maximum flux density in the core is 1 Wb/m². Calculate the number of turns per limb on the high and low voltage sides for a 3000/220 V ratio. To allow for insulation of stampings, assume the net iron length to be 0.9 × gross iron length.*

Solution. Net iron length
$$= 0.9 \times 20 = 18\ cm$$

Net x-sectional area,
$$A = 18 \times 20 = 360\ cm^2 = 0.036\ m^2$$

Max. flux in core,
$$\phi_m = B_m \times A = 1 \times 0.036 = 0.036\ Wb$$
$$E_1 = 4.44\ f N_1\ \phi_m$$

$$\therefore \qquad N_1 = \frac{E_1}{4.44\, f\, \phi_m} = \frac{3000}{4.44 \times 50 \times 0.036} = 375$$

$$N_2 = \frac{E_2}{4.44\, f\, \phi_m} = \frac{220}{4.44 \times 50 \times 0.036} = 27$$

Note that one length is affected due to stamping.

TUTORIAL PROBLEMS

1. A 50 kVA, 6600/250 V transformer has 52 secondary turns. Find (*i*) the number of primary turns (*ii*) full-load primary and secondary currents. Neglect losses.   [(*i*) 1373 (*ii*) 7.58 A; 200 A]
2. The net cross-sectional area of the core of 400/3000 V, 50 Hz transformer is 600 cm². If the maximum flux density in the core is 1.3 Wb/m², find the number of turns on the primary and secondary.   [24; 180]
3. In a certain 50 kVA transformer, the number of turns on the primary and secondary windings is 834 and 58 respectively. If primary is connected to a 3300 V supply, find (*i*) secondary voltage (*ii*) the primary and secondary currents when the transformer is fully loaded. Neglect the losses.   [(*i*) 230 V (*ii*) 15.2A; 218 A]
4. A single phase transformer has a ratio of 1 : 10 and a secondary winding of 1000 turns. The primary winding is connected to a 25-V sinusoidal supply. If the maximum value of flux in the core is 2.15 mWb, find (*i*) the frequency of the supply (*ii*) the number of primary turns (*iii*) the secondary voltage on open-circuit.   [(*i*) 25 Hz (*ii*) 100 turns (*iii*) 250 V]
5. A single phase 50 Hz transformer has 20 primary turns and 273 secondary turns. The net cross-sectional area of the core is 400 cm². If the primary winding is connected to 230 V supply, find (*i*) peak value of flux density in the core (*ii*) voltage induced in the secondary winding.   [(*i*) 1.24 Wb/m² (*ii*) 3003 V]

20.5. PRACTICAL TRANSFORMER

A practical transformer differs from the ideal transformer in many respects. The practical transformer has (*i*) iron losses (*ii*) winding resistances and (*iii*) magnetic leakage, giving rise to leakage reactances.

(*i*) **Iron losses.** Since the iron core is subjected to alternating flux, there occurs eddy current and hysteresis loss in it. These two losses together are known as *iron losses* or *core losses*. The iron losses depend upon the supply frequency, maximum flux density in the core, volume of the core etc. It may be noted that magnitude of iron losses is quite small in a practical transformer.

(*ii*) **Winding resistances.** Since the windings consist of copper conductors, it immediately follows that both primary and secondary will have winding resistance. The primary resistance R_1 and secondary resistance R_2 act in series with the respective windings as shown in Fig. 20.4.

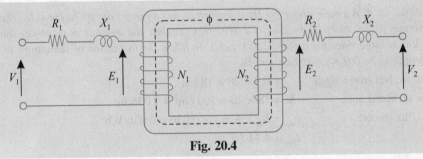

Fig. 20.4

(*iii*) **Leakage reactances.** Both primary and secondary currents produce flux. The flux ϕ which links both the windings is the useful flux and is called mutual flux. However, primary current would produce some flux ϕ_1 which would not link the secondary winding (See Fig. 20.5). Similarly, secondary current would produce some flux ϕ_2 that would not link the primary winding. The flux such as ϕ_1 or ϕ_2 which links only one winding is called *leakage flux*. The leakage flux paths are mainly through the air. The *effect of these leakage fluxes would be the same as though inductive reactance were connected in series with each winding of transformer that had no leakage flux as shown in Fig. 20.4. In other words, the effect of primary leakage flux ϕ_1 is to introduce an inductive reactance X_1 in series with the primary winding as shown in Fig. 20.4. Similarly, the secondary leakage flux ϕ_2 introduces an inductive reactance X_2 in series with the secondary winding.

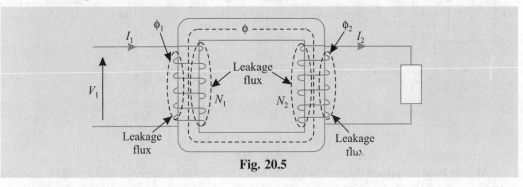

Fig. 20.5

Note: Although leakage flux in a transformer is quite small (about 5% of ϕ) compared to the mutual flux ϕ, yet it cannot be ignored. It is because leakage flux paths are through air of high reluctance and hence require considerable m.m.f. It may be noted that energy is conveyed from the primary winding to the secondary winding by mutual flux ϕ which links both the windings.

Distribution Transformer

. . . .

*   The primary leakage flux ϕ_1 is alternating one and hence induces back e.m.f. e in the primary winding.

∴   Primary leakage inductance, $L_1 = \dfrac{\text{Primary leakage flux linkages}}{\text{Primary current}} = \dfrac{N_1 \phi_1}{I_1}$

∴   Primary leakage reactance, $X_1 = 2\pi f L_1$
Also secondary leakage reactance, $X_2 = 2\pi f L_2$ where $L_2 = N_2 \phi_2 / I_2$

20.6. PRACTICAL TRANSFORMER ON NO LOAD

Consider a practical transformer on no load *i.e.* secondary on open-circuit as shown in Fig. 20.6 (*i*). The primary will draw a small current I_0 to supply (*i*) the iron losses and (*ii*) a very *small amount of copper loss in the primary. Hence the primary no load current I_0 is not 90° behind the applied voltage V_1 but lags it by an angle $\phi_0 < 90°$ as shown in the phasor diagram in Fig. 20.6 (*ii*).

No load input power, $W_0 = V_1 I_0 \cos \phi_0$

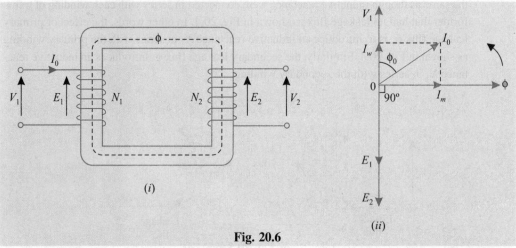

(*i*)

(*ii*)

Fig. 20.6

As seen from the phasor diagram in Fig. 20.6 (*ii*), the no-load primary current I_0 can be resolved into two rectangular components *viz.*

(*i*) The component I_W in phase with the applied voltage V_1. This is known as *active* or *working* or *iron loss component* and **supplies the iron loss and a very small primary copper loss.

$$I_W = I_0 \cos \phi_0$$

(*ii*) The component I_m lagging behind V_1 by 90° and is known as *magnetising component*. It is this component which produces the mutual flux ϕ in the core.

$$I_m = I_0 \sin \phi_0$$

Clearly, I_0 is phasor sum of I_m and I_W.

∴ $$I_0 = \sqrt{I_m^2 + I_W^2}$$

No load p.f., $\cos \phi_0 = I_W/I_0$

It is emphasised here that no load primary copper loss (*i.e.* $I_0^2 R_1$) is very small and may be neglected. Therefore, the no load primary input power is practically equal to the iron loss in the transformer *i.e.*

No load input power, $W_0 = $ Iron loss

Note: At no load, there is no current in the secondary so that $V_2 = E_2$. On the primary side, the drops in R_1 and X_1 due to I_0 are also very small because of the smallness of I_0. Hence, we can say that at no load, $V_1 = E_1$.

Example 20.5. *A transformer takes a current of 0.6 A and absorbs 64 W when primary is connected to its normal supply of 200 V, 50 Hz; the secondary being on open circuit. Find the magnetising and iron loss currents.*

* At no load, copper loss in the primary is $I_0^2 R_1$. Since I_0 is quite small, this loss may be neglected.

** Remember that the component of current in phase with voltage produces the true or real power. However, component 90° out of phase with voltage produces reactive power *i.e.* magnetic flux in this case.

Solution.

No load primary power, $\qquad W_0 = V_1 I_0 \cos \phi_0$

Iron loss component, $\qquad I_W = I_0 \cos \phi_0 = W_0/V_1 = 64/200 = \mathbf{0.32 \ A}$

No load current, $\qquad I_0 = \sqrt{I_m^2 + I_W^2}$

∴ Magnetising current, $\qquad I_m = \sqrt{I_0^2 - I_W^2} = \sqrt{(0.6)^2 - (0.32)^2} = \mathbf{0.507 \ A}$

Example 20.6. *A 230/2300 V transformer takes no load current of 5 A at 0.25 power factor lagging. Find (i) the core loss and (ii) magnetising current.*

Solution.

(*i*) Core loss, $\qquad W_0 = V_1 I_0 \cos \phi_0 = 230 \times 5 \times 0.25 = \mathbf{287.5 \ W}$

(*ii*) Iron-loss current, $\qquad I_W = I_0 \cos \phi_0 = W_0/V_1 = 287.5/230 = \mathbf{1.25 \ A}$

∴ Magnetising current, $\qquad I_m = \sqrt{I_0^2 - I_W^2} = \sqrt{(5)^2 - (1.25)^2} = \mathbf{4.84 \ A}$

Example 20.7. *A 230/2300 V transformer takes a no load current of 6.5 A and absorbs 187 W. If the resistance of primary is 0.06 Ω, find (i) the core loss (ii) no load p.f. (iii) active component of current and (iv) magnetising current.*

Solution.

No-load loss, $\qquad W_0 = 187 \text{ W}$

Primary Cu loss due to no-load current $= I_0^2 R_1 = (6.5)^2 \times 0.06 = 2.5 \text{ W}$

(*i*) Iron loss $\qquad = 187 - 2.5 = \mathbf{184.5 \ W}$

(*ii*) No load p.f., $\qquad \cos \phi_0 = \dfrac{W_0}{V_1 I_0} = \dfrac{187}{230 \times 6.5} = \mathbf{0.125} \ lag$

(*iii*) Active component, $\qquad I_W = W_0/V_1 = 187/230 = \mathbf{0.81 \ A}$

(*iv*) Magnetising current, $\qquad I_m = \sqrt{I_0^2 - I_W^2} = \sqrt{(6.5)^2 - (0.81)^2} = \mathbf{6.4 \ A}$

Example 20.8. *A single-phase transformer on no-load takes 4.5 A at a power factor of 0.25 lagging when connected to a 230 V, 50 Hz supply. The number of turns of the primary winding is 250. Calculate (i) the magnetising current (ii) the core loss and (iii) the maximum value of flux in the core.*

Solution. Fig. 20.7 shows the phasor diagram of the transformer on no-load.

$V_1 = 230$ volts; $N_1 = 250$ turns; $\cos \phi_0 = 0.25$ lag; $I_0 = 4.5$ A

(*i*) Magnetising current, $I_m = I_0 \sin \phi_0 = 4.5 \times 0.968 = \mathbf{4.35 \ A}$

(*ii*) Core loss, $W_0 = V_1 I_0 \cos \phi_0 = 230 \times 4.5 \times 0.25 = \mathbf{259 \ W}$

(*iii*) Since no-load current I_0 is small, $E_1 \approx V_1$.

∴ $\qquad\qquad V_1 = 4.44 \, \phi_m \, f N_1$

or $\qquad\qquad 230 = 4.44 \times \phi_m \times 50 \times 250$

∴ $\qquad\qquad \phi_m = \mathbf{4.14 \times 10^{-3} \ Wb}$

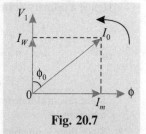

Fig. 20.7

TUTORIAL PROBLEMS

1. A 2200/200 V transformer takes a no load current of 0.6 A and absorbs 400 watts. Find (*i*) the magnetising current and (*ii*) iron-loss current. [(*i*) 0.572 A (*ii*) 0.18 A]

2. A 2200/200 V transformer takes 0.5 A at a p.f. of 0.3 lagging at no load. Find (*i*) the magnetising current and (*ii*) iron-loss current. [(*i*) 0.477 A (*ii*) 0.15 A]

3. The no load current of a transformer is 5 A at 0.3 p.f. lagging when supplied at 230 V, 50 Hz. The number of turns on the primary winding is 200. Calculate (*i*) the maximum value of flux in the core (*ii*) the core loss and (*iii*) the magnetising current.

$$[(i)\ \textbf{5.18 mWb}\ (ii)\ \textbf{345 W}\ (iii)\ \textbf{4.77 A}]$$

20.7. IDEAL TRANSFORMER ON LOAD

Let us connect a load Z_L across the secondary of an *ideal transformer as shown in Fig. 20.8 (*i*). The secondary e.m.f. E_2 will cause a current I_2 to flow through the load.

$$I_2 = {}^{**}\frac{E_2}{Z_L} = \frac{V_2}{Z_L}$$

The angle at which I_2 leads or lags V_2 (or E_2) depends upon the resistance and reactance of the load. In the present case, we have considered inductive load so that current I_2 lags behind V_2 (or E_2) by ϕ_2.

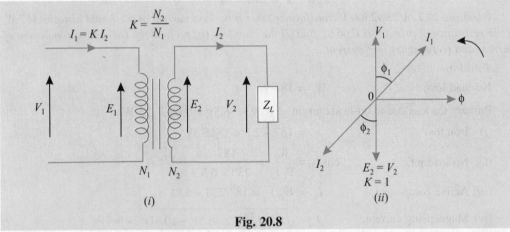

Fig. 20.8

The secondary current I_2 sets up an m.m.f. $N_2 I_2$ which produces a flux in the ***opposite direction to the flux ϕ originally set up in the primary by the magnetising current. This will change the flux in the core from the original value. However, the flux in the core should not †change from the original value. In order to fulfil this condition, the primary must develop an m.m.f. which exactly counterbalances the secondary m.m.f. $N_2 I_2$.

Hence a primary current I_1 must flow such that:

$$N_1 I_1 = N_2 I_2$$

or

$$I_1 = \frac{N_2}{N_1} I_2 = K I_2$$

. . . .

* Since practical transformers have full-load efficiencies well over 99%, they closely approach the ideal transformers.

** Since there is no voltage drop in an ideal transformer, $E_2 = V_2$.

*** Lenz's law states that voltage induced in the secondary (*i.e.* E_2) acts in a direction so as to oppose what is causing it. This means that m.m.f. set up by the secondary current will oppose the mutual flux ϕ which is producing E_2.

† $E_1 = 4.44 f \phi_m N_1$

In an ideal transformer, $V_1 = E_1$. Since applied voltage V_1 is kept fixed, E_1 must remain unchanged. This is possible only if the flux remains fixed. Hence, mutual flux ϕ remains fixed whether a load is connected or not.

Thus when a transformer is loaded and carries a secondary current I_2, then a current I_1 ($= KI_2$) must flow in the primary to maintain the m.m.f. balance. In other words, the primary must draw enough current to neutralise the demagnetising effect of secondary current so that mutual flux ϕ remains constant. Thus as the secondary current increases, the primary current I_1 ($= KI_2$) increases in unison and keeps the mutual flux ϕ constant. The power input, therefore, automatically increases with the output. For example if $K = 2$ and $I_2 = 2A$, then primary will draw a current $I_1 = KI_2 = 2 \times 2 = 4A$. If secondary current is increased to $4A$, then primary current will become $I_1 = KI_2 = 2 \times 4 = 8A$.

Phasor diagram. Fig. 20.8 (*ii*) shows the phasor diagram of an ideal transformer on load. Note that in drawing the phasor diagram, the value of K has been assumed unity so that primary phasors are equal to secondary phasors. The secondary current I_2 lags behind V_2 (or E_2) by ϕ_2. It causes a primary current $I_1 = KI_2 = 1 \times I_2 = I_2$ which is in *antiphase* with it.

(*i*) $\phi_1 = \phi_2$

or $\cos \phi_1 = \cos \phi_2$

Thus, power factor on the primary side is equal to the power factor on the secondary side.

(*ii*) Since there are no losses in an ideal transformer, input primary power is equal to the secondary output power *i.e.*

$$V_1 I_1 \cos \phi_1 = V_2 I_2 \cos \phi_2$$

Example 20.9. *An ideal transformer having 90 turns on the primary and 2250 turns on the secondary is connected to 200 V, 50 Hz supply. The load across the secondary draws a current of 2 A at a p.f. of 0.8 lagging. Calculate (i) the value of primary current and (ii) the peak value of flux linked with the secondary. Draw the phasor diagram.*

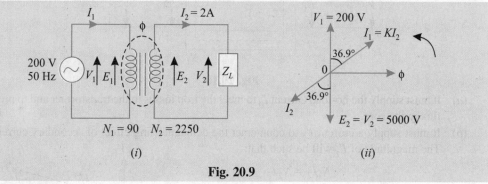

Fig. 20.9

Solution.

The conditions of the problem are represented in Fig. 20.9 (*i*).

$$K = N_2/N_1 = 2250/90 = 25$$

(*i*) $I_1 = KI_2 = 25 \times 2 = 50 \text{ A}$

(*ii*) $E_1 = 4.44 f N_1 \phi_m$

or $200 = 4.44 \times 50 \times 90 \times \phi_m$

∴ $\phi_m = \dfrac{200}{4.44 \times 50 \times 90} = 0.01 \text{ Wb}$

This flux links both the windings.

Phasor diagram. Fig. 20.9 (*ii*) shows the phasor diagram of the transformer.

$$E_2 = KE_1 = 25 \times 200 = 5000 \text{ V}$$

$$\phi = \text{phase angle between } V_2 \text{ and } I_2$$

$$= \cos^{-1} 0.8 = 36.9°$$

The phase angle between V_1 and I_1 is also $36.9°$.

Example 20.10. *An ideal transformer has 1000 turns on its primary and 500 turns on its secondary. The driving voltage on the primary side is 100 V and the load resistance is 5 Ω. Calculate V_2, I_1 and I_2.*

Solution.

$$K = N_2/N_1 = 500/1000 = 1/2$$
$$V_2 = KV_1 = (1/2) \times 100 = 50 \text{ V}$$
$$I_2 = V_2/R_2 = 50/5 = 10 \text{ A}$$
$$I_1 = KI_2 = (1/2) \times 10 = 5 \text{ A}$$

20.8. PRACTICAL TRANSFORMER ON LOAD

We shall consider two cases (*i*) when such a transformer is assumed to have no winding resistance and leakage flux (*ii*) when the transformer has winding resistance and leakage flux.

(*i*) **No winding resistance and leakage flux**

Fig. 20.10 shows a practical transformer with the assumption that resistances and leakage reactances of the windings are negligible. With this assumption, $V_2 = E_2$ and $*V_1 = E_1$. Let us take the usual case of inductive load which causes the secondary current I_2 to lag the secondary voltage V_2 by ϕ_2. The total primary current I_1 must meet two requirements *viz*.

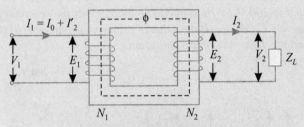

Fig. 20.10

(*a*) It must supply the no-load current I_0 to meet the iron losses in the transformer and to provide flux in the core.

(*b*) It must supply a current I'_2 to counteract the demagnetising effect of secondary current I_2. The magnitude of I'_2 will be such that:

$$N_1 I'_2 = N_2 I_2$$

or

$$I'_2 = \frac{N_2}{N_1} I_2 = KI_2$$

The total primary current I_1 is the phasor sum of I'_2 and I_0 *i.e.*

$$I_1 = I'_2 + I_0$$
$$\qquad\qquad\qquad ... phasor\ sum$$

where

$$I'_2 = -KI_2$$

Note that I'_2 is 180° out of phase with I_2.

Phasor diagram. Fig. 20.11 shows the phasor diagram for the usual case of inductive load. Both E_1 and E_2 lag behind the mutual flux ϕ by 90°. The current I'_2 represents the primary current to neutralise the demagnetising effect of

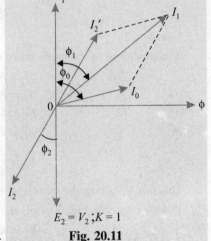

$E_2 = V_2 ; K = 1$

Fig. 20.11

---

*   However, V_1 and E_1 are 180° out of phase.

secondary current I_2. Now $I_2' = KI_2$ and is *antiphase* with I_2. I_0 is the no-load current of the transformer. The phasor sum of I_2' and I_0 gives the total primary current I_1. Note that in drawing the phasor diagram, the value of K is assumed to be unity so that primary phasors are equal to secondary phasors.

Primary p.f. $= \cos \phi_1$; Secondary p.f. $= \cos \phi_2$

Primary input power $= V_1 I_1 \cos \phi_1$; Secondary output power $= V_2 I_2 \cos \phi_2$

Example 20.11. *A single phase transformer with a ratio of 440/110 V takes no-load current of 5 A at 0.2 p.f. lagging. If the secondary supplies a current of 120 A at a p.f. 0.8 lagging, find the current taken by the primary.*

Solution. Fig. 20.12 shows the phasor diagram of the transformer.

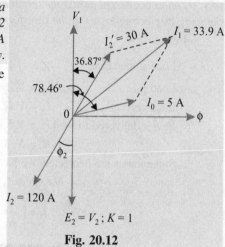

$$\cos \phi_2 = 0.8 \quad \therefore \quad \phi_2 = 36.87°$$
$$\cos \phi_0 = 0.2 \quad \therefore \quad \phi_0 = 78.46°$$

Now $\qquad K = V_2/V_1 = 110/440 = 1/4$

$\therefore$
$$I_2' = KI_2 = (1/4) \times 120 = 30 \text{ A}$$
$$I_0 = 5 \text{ A}$$

Angle between I_2' and I_0
$$= 78.46° - 36.87° = 41.59°$$

Fig. 20.12

Using parallelogram method, we have,

$$I_1 = \sqrt{(I_0)^2 + (I_2')^2 + 2 I_0 I_2' \cos 41.59°}$$

$$= \sqrt{(5)^2 + (30)^2 + 2 \times 5 \times 30 \times \cos 41.59°} = \textbf{33.9 A}$$

Example 20.12. *A single phase transformer has 1000 turns on the primary and 200 turns on the secondary. The no-load current is 3 A at a p.f. of 0.2 lagging. Calculate the primary current and power factor when the secondary current is 280 A at a p.f. of 0.8 lagging.*

Solution. Fig. 20.13 shows the phasor diagram of the transformer.

$$K = \frac{200}{1000} = \frac{1}{5}$$

$\therefore \qquad I_2' = KI_2 = \frac{1}{5} \times 280 = 56 \text{ A}$

$$\cos \phi_2 = 0.8 \quad \therefore \quad \sin \phi_2 = 0.6$$
$$\cos \phi_0 = 0.2 \quad \therefore \quad \sin \phi_0 = 0.98$$

Referring to Fig. 20.13 and resolving the currents along rectangular axes, we have,

$$I_1 \cos \phi_1 = I_2' \cos \phi_2 + I_0 \cos \phi_0$$
$$= (56 \times 0.8) + (3 \times 0.2) = 45.4 \text{ A}$$
$$I_1 \sin \phi_1 = I_2' \sin \phi_2 + I_0 \sin \phi_0$$
$$= (56 \times 0.6) + (3 \times 0.98) = 36.54 \text{ A}$$

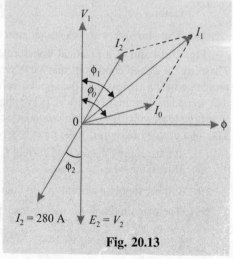

Fig. 20.13

Now, $\qquad I_1 = \sqrt{(I_1 \cos \phi_1)^2 + (I_1 \sin \phi_1)^2}$

$$= \sqrt{(45.4)^2 + (36.54)^2} = \textbf{58.3 A}$$

$$\tan \phi_1 = \frac{I_1 \sin \phi_1}{I_1 \cos \phi_1} = \frac{36.54}{45.4} = 0.805$$

$$\therefore \qquad \phi_1 = \tan^{-1} 0.805 = 38.83°$$

$\therefore$ Primary p.f. = $\cos \phi_1 = \cos 38.83° = $ **0.78** *lag*

Example 20.13. *A single phase transformer with a ratio of 6600/600 V has a load impedance of (4 + j3) ohms connected across the terminals of low voltage winding. Calculate the kW delivered to the load. Neglecting losses in the transformer, find the current taken by it from the supply lines.*

Solution.

Load impedance, $\qquad Z = \sqrt{4^2 + 3^2} = 5\ \Omega$

Load p.f., $\qquad \cos \phi_2 = R/Z = 4/5 = 0.8$ lag

Load current, $\qquad I_2 = V_2/Z = 600/5 = 120$ A

Power delivered to load $= V_2 I_2 \cos \phi_2 = 600 \times 120 \times 0.8 = 57.6 \times 10^3$ W = **57.6 kW**

$$K = V_2/V_1 = 600/6600 = 1/11$$

Since losses are neglected, we have,

$$N_1 I_1 = N_2 I_2$$

or $\qquad I_1 = \left(\dfrac{N_2}{N_1}\right) I_2 = KI_2 = \left(\dfrac{1}{11}\right) \times 120 = $ **10.91 A**

TUTORIAL PROBLEMS

1. A 3300/240 V single phase transformer on no load takes 2 A at a p.f. of 0.25 lagging. Determine the primary current and power factor when the transformer is supplying a load of 60 A at p.f. 0.9 lagging. **[4.43 A, 1]**

2. A 4 : 1 ratio step-down transformer takes 1 A at 0.15 p.f. on no load. Determine the primary current and power factor when the transformer is supplying a load of 2 A at 0.8 p.f. lagging. Neglect voltage drops in the windings. **[7 A; 0.735 *lag*]**

3. A 400/200 V single phase transformer is supplying a load of 50 A at a p.f. of 0.866 lagging. The no-load current is 2 A at 0.208 p.f. lagging. Calculate the primary current and power factor. **[26.4 A; 0.838 *lag*]**

(ii) **Transformer with resistance and Leakage reactance**

Fig. 20.14 shows a practical transformer having winding resistances and leakage reactances. These are the *actual* conditions that exist in a transformer. There is voltage drop in R_1 and X_1 so that primary e.m.f. E_1 is less than the applied voltage V_1. Similarly, there is voltage drop in R_2 and X_2 so that secondary terminal voltage V_2 is less than the secondary e.m.f. E_2. Let us take the usual case of inductive load which causes the secondary current I_2 to lag behind the secondary voltage V_2 by ϕ_2. The total primary current I_1 must meet two requirements *viz.*

(*a*) It must supply the no-load current I_0 to meet the iron losses in the transformer and to provide flux in the core.

(*b*) It must supply a current I_2' to counteract the demagnetising effect of secondary current I_2. The magnitude of I_2' will be such that:

$$N_1 I_2' = N_2 I_2$$

or $\qquad I_2' = \dfrac{N_2}{N_1} I_2 = KI_2$

The total primary current I_1 will be the phasor sum of I_2' and I_0 *i.e.*

$$\mathbf{I}_1 = \mathbf{I}_2' + \mathbf{I}_0 \quad \text{where} \quad \mathbf{I}_2' = -K\mathbf{I}_2$$

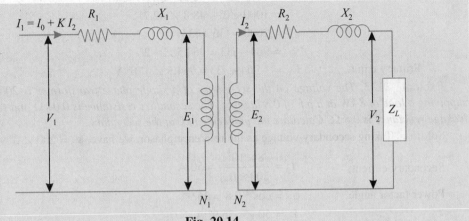

Fig. 20.14

$$\mathbf{V}_1 = -\mathbf{E}_1 + \mathbf{I}_1 (R_1 + jX_1) \quad \text{where} \quad \mathbf{I}_1 = \mathbf{I}_0 + (-K\mathbf{I}_2) \quad \text{... phasor sum}$$
$$= -\mathbf{E}_1 + \mathbf{I}_1 \mathbf{Z}_1 \quad \text{... phasor sum}$$
$$\mathbf{V}_2 = \mathbf{E}_2 - \mathbf{I}_2 (R_2 + jX_2)$$
$$= \mathbf{E}_2 - \mathbf{I}_2 \mathbf{Z}_2$$

Phasor diagram. Fig. 20.15 shows the phasor diagram of a practical transformer for the usual case of inductive load. Both E_1 and E_2 lag the mutual flux ϕ by 90°. The current I_2' represents the primary current to neutralise the demagnetising effect of secondary current I_2. Now $I_2' = KI_2$ and is oppossite to I_2. Also I_0 is the no-load current of the transformer. The phasor sum of I_2' and I_0 gives the total primary current I_1.

Note that counter e.m.f. that opposes the applied voltage $\mathbf{V}_1$ is $-\mathbf{E}_1$. Therefore, if we add $\mathbf{I}_1 R_1$ (in phase with $\mathbf{I}_1$) and $\mathbf{I}_1 X_1$ (90° ahead of $\mathbf{I}_1$) to $-\mathbf{E}_1$, we get the applied primary voltage $\mathbf{V}_1$. The phasor $\mathbf{E}_2$ represents the induced e.m.f. in the secondary by the mutual flux ϕ. The secondary terminal voltage $\mathbf{V}_2$ will be what is left over after subtracting $\mathbf{I}_2 R_2$ and $\mathbf{I}_2 X_2$ from $\mathbf{E}_2$.

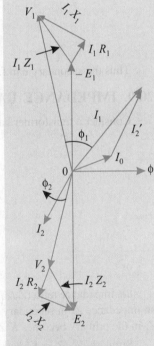

Load power factor $= \cos \phi_2$

Primary power factor $= \cos \phi_1$

Input power to transformer, $P_1 = V_1 I_1 \cos \phi_1$

Output power of transformer, $P_2 = V_2 I_2 \cos \phi_2$

Note: The reader may draw the phasor diagram of a loaded transformer for (*i*) unity p.f. and (*ii*) leading p.f. as an exercise.

Fig. 20.15

Example 20.14. *The primary of a 1000/250 V transformer has a resistance of 0.15 Ω and leakage reactance of 0.8 Ω. Find the primary induced e.m.f when the primary current is 60 A at 0.8 p.f. lagging.*

Solution.

Primary impedance, $\mathbf{Z}_1 = 0.15 + j\,0.8 = 0.814 \angle 79.6° \ \Omega$

Power factor angle, $\phi_1 = \cos^{-1} 0.8 = 36.9°$

Taking applied voltage as the reference phasor, we have, $V_1 = 1000 \angle 0°$ Volts.

Now,
$$-E_1 = V_1 - I_1 Z_1$$
$$= 1000 \angle 0° - 60 \angle -36.9° \times 0.814 \angle 79.6°$$
$$= 1000 \angle 0° - 48.8 \angle 42.7°$$
$$= 1000 - (36 + j33)$$
$$= 964 - j33 = 964.5 \angle -2°$$

∴ Primary e.m.f., $E_1 = -964 + j33 = \mathbf{964.5 \angle 178°}$ **V**

Example 20.15. *The voltage on the secondary of a single phase transformer is 200 V when supplying a load of 8 kW at a p.f. of 0.8 lagging. The secondary resistance is 0.04 Ω and secondary leakage reactance is 0.8 Ω. Calculate the induced e.m.f. in the secondary.*

Solution. Taking secondary voltage as the reference phasor, we have, $V_2 = 200 \angle 0°$ volts.

Secondary current,
$$I_2 = \frac{8 \times 10^3}{200 \times 0.8} = 50 \text{ A}$$

Power factor angle,
$$\phi_2 = \cos^{-1} 0.8 = 36.9°$$

∴
$$I_2 = 50 \angle -36.9° \text{ A}$$
$$Z_2 = 0.04 + j\, 0.8 = 0.8 \angle 87.14° \text{ Ω}$$
$$E_2 = V_2 + I_2 Z_2$$
$$= 200 \angle 0° + 50 \angle -36.9° \times 0.8 \times \angle 87.14°$$
$$= 200 \angle 0° + 40 \angle 50.24°$$
$$= (200 + j\, 0) + (25.58 + j\, 30.75)$$
$$= 225.58 + j\, 30.75 = \mathbf{227.67 \angle 7.8°} \text{ volts}$$

Thus the secondary e.m.f. E_2 leads the secondary terminal voltage V_2 by 7.8°.

20.9. IMPEDANCE RATIO

Consider a transformer having impedance Z_2 in the secondary as shown in Fig. 20.16.

$$Z_2 = \frac{V_2}{I_2}$$

$$Z_1 = \frac{V_1}{I_1}$$

∴
$$\frac{Z_2}{Z_1} = \left(\frac{V_2}{V_1}\right) \times \left(\frac{I_1}{I_2}\right)$$

or
$$\frac{Z_2}{Z_1} = K^2$$

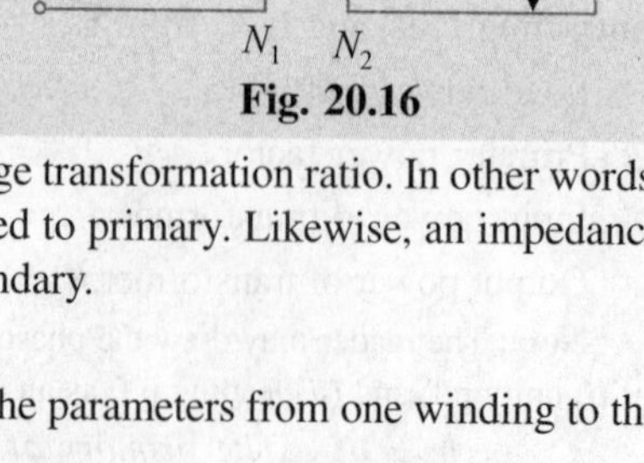

Fig. 20.16

i.e. impedance ratio (Z_2/Z_1) is equal to the square of voltage transformation ratio. In other words, an impedance Z_2 in secondary becomes Z_2/K^2 when transferred to primary. Likewise, an impedance Z_1 in the primary becomes $K^2 Z_1$ when transferred to the secondary.

Similarly, $R_2/R_1 = K^2$ and $X_2/X_1 = K^2$

Note the importance of above relations. We can transfer the parameters from one winding to the other. Thus:

(*i*) A resistance R_1 in the primary becomes $K^2 R_1$ when transferred to the secondary.

(*ii*) A resistance R_2 in the secondary becomes R_2/K^2 when transferred to the primary.

(*iii*) A reactance X_1 in the primary becomes $K^2 X_1$ when transferred to the secondary.

(*iv*) A reactance X_2 in the secondary becomes X_2/K^2 when transferred to the primary.

Note: It is important to remember that :

(i) When transferring resistance or reactance from primary to secondary, *multiply* it by K^2.

(ii) When transferring resistance or reactance from secondary to primary, *divide* it by K^2.

(iii) When transferring voltage or current from one winding to the other, only *K is used.

20.10. SHIFTING IMPEDANCES IN A TRANSFORMER

Fig. 20.17 shows a transformer where resistances and reactances are shown external to the windings. The resistance and reactance of one winding can be transferred to the other by appropriately using the factor K^2. This makes the analysis of the transformer a simple affair because then we have to work in one winding only.

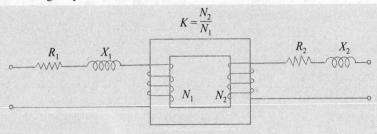

Fig. 20.17

(i) **Referred to primary.** When secondary resistance or reactance in transferred to the primary, it is **divided** by K^2. It is then called *equivalent secondary resistance or reactance referred to primary* and is denoted by R_2' or X_2'.

Equivalent resistance of transformer referred to primary is

$$R_{01} = R_1 + R_2' = R_1 + R_2/K^2$$

Equivalent reactance of transformer referred to primary is

$$X_{01} = X_1 + X_2' = X_1 + X_2/K^2$$

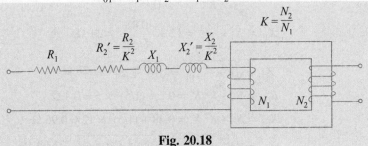

Fig. 20.18

Equivalent impedance of transformer referred to primary is

$$Z_{01} = \sqrt{R_{01}^2 + X_{01}^2}$$

Fig. 20.18 shows the resistance and reactance of the secondary referred to the primary. Note that secondary now has no resistance or reactance.

(ii) **Referred to secondary.** When primary resistance or reactance is transferred to the secondary, it is **multiplied** by K^2. It is then called *equivalent primary resistance or reactance referred to the secondary* and is denoted by R_1' or X_1'.

---

* Thus any voltage V_1 in the primary becomes KV_1 in the secondary. On the other hand, any voltage V_2 in the secondary becomes V_2/K in the primary. Again a current I_1 in the primary becomes I_1/K in the secondary. Any current I_2 in the secondary becomes KI_2 in the primary.

Equivalent resistance of transformer referred to secondary is

$$R_{02} = R_2 + R_1'$$
$$= R_2 + K^2 R_1$$

Equivalent reactance of transformer referred to secondary is

$$X_{02} = X_2 + X_1'$$
$$= X_2 + K^2 X_1$$

Equivalent impedance of transformer referred to secondary is

$$Z_{02} = \sqrt{R_{02}^2 + X_{02}^2}$$

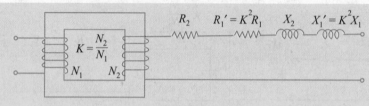

Fig. 20.19

Fig. 20.19 shows the resistance and reactance of the primary referred to the secondary. Note that primary now has no resistance or reactance.

Example 20.16. *A 10 kVA, 2000/400 V single phase transformer has $R_1 = 5\ \Omega$; $X_1 = 12\ \Omega$; $R_2 = 0.2\ \Omega$ and $X_2 = 0.48\ \Omega$. Determine the equivalent impedance of the transformer referred to (i) primary side (ii) secondary side.*

Solution.

$$K = 400/2000 = 1/5$$

(i)
$$R_{01} = R_1 + \frac{R_2}{K^2} = 5 + \frac{0.2}{(1/5)^2} = 10\ \Omega$$

$$X_{01} = X_1 + \frac{X_2}{K^2} = 12 + \frac{0.48}{(1/5)^2} = 24\ \Omega$$

∴
$$Z_{01} = \sqrt{R_{01}^2 + X_{01}^2} = \sqrt{10^2 + 24^2} = 26\ \Omega$$

(ii)
$$R_{02} = R_2 + K^2 R_1 = 0.2 + (1/5)^2 \times 5 = 0.4\ \Omega$$

$$X_{02} = X_2 + K^2 X_1 = 0.48 + (1/5)^2 \times 12 = 0.96\ \Omega$$

∴
$$Z_{02} = \sqrt{R_{02}^2 + X_{02}^2} = \sqrt{(0.4)^2 + (0.96)^2} = 1.04\ \Omega$$

Alternatively;
$$Z_{02} = K^2 Z_{01} = (1/5)^2 \times 26 = 1.04\ \Omega$$

Example 20.17. *A 100 kVA, 2200/440 V transformer has $R_1 = 0.3\ \Omega$; $X_1 = 1.1\ \Omega$; $R_2 = 0.01\ \Omega$ and $X_2 = 0.035\ \Omega$. Calculate (i) the equivalent impedance of the transformer referred to the primary and (ii) total copper losses.*

Solution.

Voltage transformation ratio, $K = 440/2200 = 1/5$

Assuming the efficiency of transformer to be 100%,

Full-load primary current, $I_1 = \dfrac{100 \times 1000}{2200} = 45.45$ A

Full-load secondary current, $I_2 = \dfrac{100 \times 1000}{440} = 227.25$ A

Alternatively;

$$I_2 = I_1/K = 45.45 \times 5 = 227.25 \text{ A}$$

(i)

$$R_{01} = R_1 + \frac{R_2}{K^2} = 0.3 + \frac{0.01}{(1/5)^2} = 0.55 \ \Omega$$

$$X_{01} = X_1 + \frac{X_2}{K^2} = 1.1 + \frac{0.035}{(1/5)^2} = 1.975 \ \Omega$$

$\therefore$

$$Z_{01} = \sqrt{R_{01}^2 + X_{01}^2} = \sqrt{(0.55)^2 + (1.975)^2} = 2.05 \ \Omega$$

(ii) Total Cu losses

$$= I_1^2 R_{01} = (45.45)^2 \times 0.55 = \mathbf{1136.14 \ W}$$

Alternatively: Total Cu losses $= I_1^2 R_1 + I_2^2 R_2$

$$= (45.5)^2 \times 0.3 + (227.25)^2 \times 0.01 = 1136.14 \text{ W}$$

20.11. IMPORTANCE OF SHIFTING IMPEDANCES

If we shift all the impedances from one winding to the other, the transformer is eliminated and we get an equivalent electrical circuit. Various voltages and currents can be readily obtained by solving this electrical circuit.

Consider an *ideal transformer having an impedance Z_2 in the secondary as shown in Fig. 20.20.

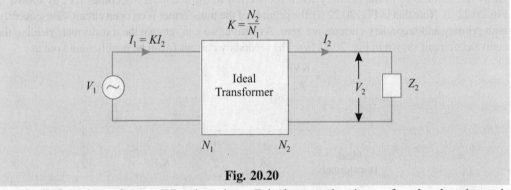

Fig. 20.20

(i) **Referred to primary.** When impedance Z_2 in the secondary is transferred to the primary, it becomes Z_2/K^2 as shown in Fig. 20.21 (i). Note that in Fig. 20.21 (i), the secondary of the ideal transformer is on open-circuit. Consequently, both primary and secondary currents are **zero. We can, therefore, remove the transformer, yielding the equivalent circuit shown in Fig. 20.21 (ii). The primary current can now be readily found out.

$$I_1 = \frac{V_1}{Z_0/K^2}$$

The circuits of Fig. 20.20 and Fig. 20.21 (ii) are electrically equivalent. Thus referring to Fig. 20.20,

$$I_1 = KI_2$$

---

*   A practical transformer consists of an ideal transformer with various resistances and reactances external to it. The treatment will, therefore, be equally valid for a practical transformer.

**   The ideal transformer is located between primary terminals *ab* and secondary terminals *cd* [See Fig. 20.21 (i)]. Terminals *c, d* are open and hence secondary current is zero. Since secondary current is zero, primary current will also be zero *i.e.* no current will flow through terminals *a, b*. The ideal transformer can thus be removed.

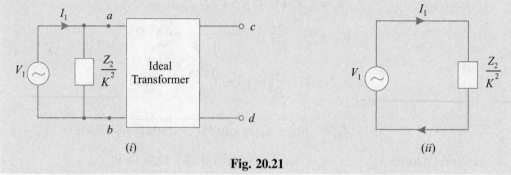

Fig. 20.21

Also if we refer to Fig. 20.21 (*ii*), we have,

$$I_1 = \frac{V_1}{(Z_2/K^2)} = \frac{K^2 V_1}{Z_2} = \frac{K(KV_1)}{Z_2}$$

$$= K\frac{V_2}{Z_2} = KI_2 \qquad\qquad (\because I_2 = V_2/Z_2)$$

Thus the value of primary current I_1 is the same whether we use Fig. 20.20 or Fig. 20.21 (*ii*). Obviously, it is easier to use Fig. 20.21 (*ii*) as it contains no transformer.

(*ii*) **Referred to secondary.** Refer back to Fig. 20.20. There is no impedance on the primary side. However, voltage V_1 in the primary when transferred to the secondary becomes KV_1 as shown in Fig. 20.22 (*i*). Note that in Fig. 20.22 (*i*), the primary of the transformer is on open circuit. Consequently, both primary and secondary currents are zero. As before, we can remove the transformer, yielding the equivalent circuit shown in Fig. 20.22 (*ii*). The secondary current I_2 can be readily found out as :

$$I_2 = \frac{KV_1}{Z_2}$$

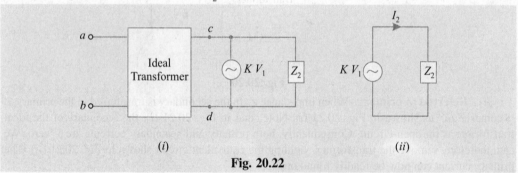

Fig. 20.22

The circuits of Fig. 20.20 and Fig. 20.22 (*ii*) are electrically equivalent. Thus referring back to Fig. 20.20, we have,

$$I_2 = V_2/Z_2$$

Also if we refer to Fig. 20.22 (*ii*), we have,

$$I_2 = \frac{KV_1}{Z_2} = \frac{K(V_2/K)}{Z_2} = \frac{V_2}{Z_2}$$

Thus the value of secondary current I_2 is the same whether we use Fig. 20.20 or Fig. 20.22 (*ii*). Obviously, it is easier to use Fig. 20.22 (*ii*) as it contains no transformer.

Example 20.18. *A single phase 400/2000 V transformer has a resistance of 1 Ω connected in series with primary winding and a 225 Ω resistor connected across its secondary winding. Calculate the primary current when the circuit is supplied at 400 V.*

Solution. The conditions of the problem are represented in Fig. 20.23 (*i*).

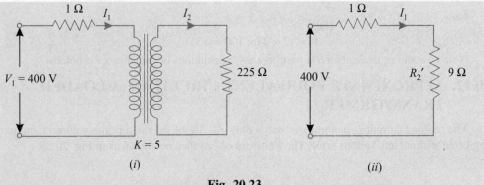

Fig. 20.23

$$K = 2000/400 = 5 \; ; R_1 = 1 \; \Omega \; ; R_2 = 225 \; \Omega$$

Equivalent resistance of transformer referred to primary,

$$R_{01} = R_1 + R_2'$$

$$= R_1 + \frac{R_2}{K^2} = 1 + \frac{225}{(5)^2} = 10 \; \Omega$$

The equivalent circuit of the transformer referred to primary is shown in Fig. 20.23 (*ii*). This is a simple series circuit.

Primary current, $$I_1 = \frac{V_1}{R_{01}} = \frac{V_1}{R_1 + R_2'} = \frac{400}{1 + 9} = 40 \; \text{A}$$

Example 20.19. *Calculate the secondary voltage V and primary current I in the circuit shown in the Fig. 20.24 (i). The transformer has primary to secondary turn ratio of 1 : 100.*

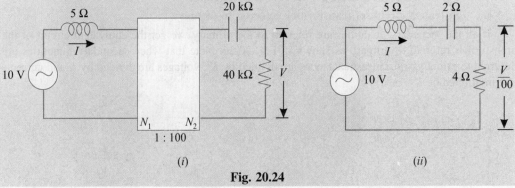

Fig. 20.24

Solution.

$$K = 100/1 = 100; \quad Z_2 = (40000 - j \, 20000) \Omega$$

Equivalent impedance of secondary referred to primary,

$$Z_2' = \frac{Z_2}{K^2} = \frac{1}{(100)^2} (40000 - j \, 20000) = (4 - j2) \Omega$$

The equivalent circuit of the transformer referred to primary is shown in Fig. 20.24 (*ii*). Note that the voltage across 40 kΩ resistance in Fig. 20.24 (*i*) is *V*. But when this resistance is transferred to the primary, the voltage across this resistance becomes *V/K* or *V/100*.

Referring to the equivalent circuit in Fig. 20.24 (*ii*), we have,

Circuit impedance, $$Z = \sqrt{R^2 + (X_L - X_C)^2} = \sqrt{4^2 + (5 - 2)^2} = 5\Omega$$

∴   Primary current, $I = 10/Z = 10/5 = 2\,A$

Now, $\dfrac{V}{100} = I \times 4 = 2 \times 4$

∴ $V = (2 \times 4) \times 100 = \textbf{800V}$

Note how the equivalent circuit permits easy calculations of transformer problems.

20.12. APPROXIMATE EQUIVALENT CIRCUIT OF A LOADED TRANSFORMER

The no-load current I_0 in a transformer is only $1 - 3\%$ of the rated primary current and may be neglected without any serious error. The transformer can then be shown as in Fig. 20.25.

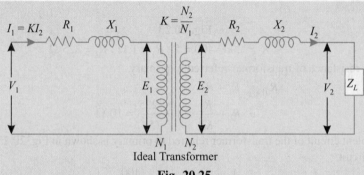

Ideal Transformer

Fig. 20.25

This is an approximate representation because no-load current has been neglected. Note that all the circuit elements have been shown external so that the transformer is an ideal one.

As shown in Art. 20.11, if we refer all the quantities to one side (primary or secondary), the ideal transformer stands removed and we get the equivalent circuit.

(i) **Equivalent circuit of transformer referred to primary**

If all the secondary quantities are referred to the primary, we get the equivalent circuit of the transformer referred to primary as shown in Fig. 20.26. Note that when secondary quantities are referred to primary, resistances/reactances are divided by K^2, voltages are divided by K and currents are multiplied by K.

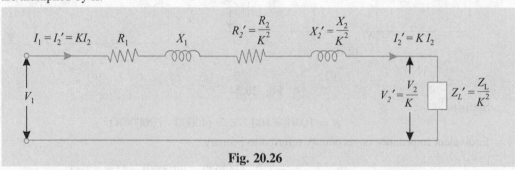

Fig. 20.26

The equivalent circuit shown in Fig. 20.26 is an electrical circuit and can be solved for various currents and voltages. Thus if we find V_2' and I_2', then actual secondary values can be determined as under :

Actual secondary voltage, $V_2 = KV_2'$

Actual secondary current, $I_2 = I_2'/K$

(ii) **Equivalent circuit of transformer referred to secondary**

If all the primary quantities   are referred to secondary, we get the equivalent circuit of the transformer referred to secondary as shown in Fig. 20.27. Note that when primary quantities are referred to secondary, resistances/reactances are multiplied by K^2, voltages are multiplied by K and currents are divided by K.

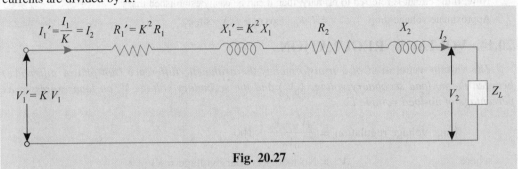

Fig. 20.27

The equivalent circuit shown in Fig. 20.27 is an electrical circuit and can be solved for various voltages and currents. Thus if we find V_1' and I_1', then actual primary values can be determined as under :

Actual primary voltage, $\quad V_1 = V_1'/K$

Actual primary current, $\quad I_1 = KI_1'$

Note. The same final answers will be obtained whether we use the equivalent circuit referred to primary or secondary. The use of a particular equivalent circuit would depend upon the conditions of the problem.

20.13. APPROXIMATE VOLTAGE DROP IN A TRANSFORMER

The approximate equivalent circuit of transformer referred to secondary is shown in Fig. 20.28. At no-load, the secondary voltage is KV_1. When a load having a lagging p.f. $\cos \phi_2$ is applied, the secondary carries a current I_2 and voltage drops occur in $(R_2 + K^2R_1)$ and $(X_2 + K^2X_1)$. Consequently, the secondary voltage falls from KV_1 to V_2. Referring to Fig. 20.28, we have,

$$\mathbf{V_2} = KV_1 - I_2 [(R_2 + K^2R_1) + j (X_2 + K^2X_1)]$$
$$= KV_1 - I_2 (R_{02} + j X_{02})$$
$$= KV_1 - I_2 Z_{02}$$

Drop in secondary voltage $\quad = KV_1 - V_2 = I_2 Z_{02}$

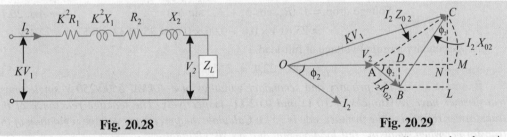

Fig. 20.28   **Fig. 20.29**

The phasor diagram is shown in Fig. 20.29. It is clear from the phasor diagram that drop in secondary voltage is $AC = I_2 Z_{02}$. It can be found as follows. With O as centre and OC as *radius*, draw an arc cutting OA produced at M. Then $AC = AM \simeq AN$. From B, draw BD perpendicular to OA produced. Draw CN perpendicular to OM and draw BL ‖ OM.

Approximate drop in secondary voltage

$$= AN = AD + DN$$
$$= AD + BL \qquad\qquad (\because BL = DN)$$
$$= I_2 R_{02} \cos \phi_2 + I_2 X_{02} \sin \phi_2$$

For a load having a leading p.f. cos ϕ_2, we have,

Approximate voltage drop $= I_2 R_{02} \cos \phi_2 - I_2 X_{02} \sin \phi_2$

Note: If the circuit is referred to primary, then it can be easily established that :

Approximate voltage drop $= I_1 R_{01} \, *\cos \phi_2 \pm I_1 X_{01} \sin \phi_2$

20.14. VOLTAGE REGULATION

The voltage regulation of a transformer is the arithmetic difference (not phasor difference) between the no-load secondary voltage ($_0V_2$) and the secondary voltage V_2 on load expressed as percentage of no-load voltage i.e.

$$\% \text{ age voltage regulation} = \frac{_0V_2 - V_2}{_0V_2} \times 100$$

where $\quad _0V_2 = $ No-load secondary voltage $= KV_1$

$\qquad\qquad V_2 = $ Secondary voltage on load

As shown in Art. 20.13, $_0V_2 - V_2 = I_2 R_{02} \cos \phi_2 \pm I_2 X_{02} \sin \phi_2$

The + ve sign is for lagging p.f. and – ve sign for leading p.f.

It may be noted that %age voltage regulation of the transformer will be the same whether primary or secondary side is considered.

Example 20.20. *A 10 kVA, 2000/400 V single phase transformer has the following data:*

$R_1 = 5 \, \Omega; X_1 = 12 \, \Omega; R_2 = 0.2 \, \Omega; X_2 = 0.48 \, \Omega$

Determine the secondary terminal voltage at full-load, 0.8 p.f. lagging when the primary supply voltage is 2000V.

Solution.

$$K = 400/2000 = 1/5$$
$$R_{02} = R_2 + K^2 R_1 = 0.2 + (1/5)^2 \times 5 = 0.4 \, \Omega$$
$$X_{02} = X_2 + K^2 X_1 = 0.48 + (1/5)^2 \times 12 = 0.96 \, \Omega$$

F.L. secondary current, $\quad I_2 = \dfrac{10 \times 1000}{400} = 25 \text{ A}$

$\cos \phi_2 = 0.8 \qquad \therefore \qquad \sin \phi_2 = 0.6$

Voltage drop $= I_2 (R_{02} \cos \phi_2 + X_{02} \sin \phi_2) \qquad\qquad$ ... *See Art. 20.13*

$\qquad\qquad = 25 (0.4 \times 0.8 + 0.96 \times 0.6) = 25 (0.32 + 0.576) = 22.4 \text{ V}$

$\therefore \quad$ Secondary terminal voltage at full-load,

$$V_2 = 400 - 22.4 = \textbf{377.6 V}$$

Example 20.21. *The primary and secondary windings of a 40kVA, 6600/250 V single phase transformer have resistances of 10 Ω and 0.02 Ω respectively. The leakage reactance of the transformer referred to the primary side is 35 Ω. Calculate the percentage voltage regulation of the transformer when supplying full-load current at a p.f. of 0.8 lagging.*

Solution.

$$K = 250/6600 = 25/660$$

$$R_{01} = R_1 + \frac{R_2}{K^2} = 10 + 0.02 \times (660/25)^2 = 23.93 \, \Omega$$

$$X_{01} = 35 \, \Omega \qquad\qquad\qquad\qquad\qquad\qquad ... \text{ given}$$

---

* Assuming primary p.f., cos ϕ_1 = secondary p.f., cos ϕ_2.

This assumption is quite reasonable because the two values differ by a very small amount.

F.L. primary current, $I_1 = \dfrac{40 \times 1000}{6600} = 6.06$ A

$\cos \phi_2 = 0.8 \quad \therefore \quad \sin \phi_2 = 0.6$

Voltage drop $= I_1 (R_{01} \cos \phi_2 + X_{01} \sin \phi_2)$

$= 6.06 (23.93 \times 0.8 + 35 \times 0.6) = 243$ V

$\therefore$ %age voltage regulation $= \dfrac{243}{6600} \times 100 = 3.7\%$

Example 20.22. *Calculate the % voltage regulation of a transformer in which the percentage resistance drop is 1% and percentage reactance drop is 5% when the power factor is (i) 0.8 lagging (ii) unity and (iii) 0.8 leading.*

Solution.

%age voltage regulation $= \dfrac{I_2 R_{02} \cos \phi_2 \pm I_2 X_{02} \sin \phi_2}{{}_0V_2} \times 100$

$= \dfrac{100 \times I_2 R_{02}}{{}_0V_2} \cos \phi_2 \pm \dfrac{100 \times I_2 X_{02}}{{}_0V_2} \sin \phi_2$

$= v_r \cos \phi_2 \pm v_x \sin \phi_2$

where $v_r = \dfrac{100 \times I_2 R_{02}}{{}_0V_2} =$ Percentage resistive drop

$v_x = \dfrac{100 \times I_2 X_{02}}{{}_0V_2} =$ Percentage reactive drop

(i) When $\cos \phi_2 = 0.8$ lag, regulation $= v_r \cos \phi_2 + v_x \sin \phi_2 = 1 \times 0.8 + 5 \times 0.6 = 3.8\%$

(ii) When $\cos \phi_2 = 1$, regulation $= 1 \times 1 + 5 \times 0 = 1\%$

(iii) When $\cos \phi_2 = 0.8$ lead, regulation $= 1 \times 0.8 - 5 \times 0.6 = -2.2\%$

TUTORIAL PROBLEMS

1. A 500 kVA, 3800/400 V, 50 Hz single phase transformer has the following data :

   $R_1 = 0.114 \, \Omega; \; X_1 = 0.459 \, \Omega; R_2 = 0.00102 \, \Omega; X_2 = 0.00416 \, \Omega$

   Find the percentage voltage regulation of the transformer when supplying full-load current at a p.f. of 0.8 lagging. [2.2 %]

2. A 100kVA transformer has 400 turns on the primary and 80 turns on the secondary. The primary and secondary resistances are 0.3 Ω and 0.1Ω respectively and the corresponding reactances are 1.1 Ω and 0.035 Ω respectively. The supply voltage is 2200 V. Calculate the voltage regulation and secondary terminal voltage for full-load having a p.f. of (i) 0.8 lagging (ii) 0.8 leading. [(i) 3.36 %; 425.2 V (ii) – 1.54%; 446.8 V]

3. The primary and secondary windings of a 30 kVA, 6000/230 V transformer have resistances of 10 Ω and 0.016 Ω respectively. The total reactance of the transformer referred to the primary is 23 Ω. Calculate the percentage voltage regulation of the transformer when supplying full-load current at a p.f. 0.8 lagging. [2.55%]

20.15. TRANSFORMER TESTS

The circuit constants, efficiency and voltage regulation of a transformer can be determined by two simple tests (*i*) *open-circuit test* and (*ii*) *short-circuit test.* These tests are very convenient as they provide the required information without actually loading the transformer. Further, the power required to carry out these tests is very small as compared with full-load output of the transformer.

20.16. OPEN-CIRCUIT OR NO-LOAD TEST

In this test, the rated voltage is applied to the primary (usually *low-voltage winding) while the secondary is left open-circuited. The applied primary voltage V_1 is measured by the voltmeter, the no-load current I_0 by ammeter and no-load input power W_0 by wattmeter as shown in Fig. 20.30.

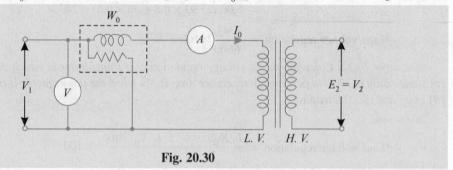

Fig. 20.30

As the normal rated voltage is applied to the primary, therefore, normal iron losses will occur in the transformer core. Hence wattmeter will record the iron losses and small copper loss in the primary. Since no-load current I_0 is very small (usually 2 – 10% of rated current), Cu losses in the primary under no load condition are negligible as compared with iron losses. *Hence, wattmeter reading practically gives the iron losses in the transformer.* It is reminded that iron losses are the same at all loads.

Iron losses, $\qquad\qquad P_i$ = Wattmeter reading = W_0

No-load current $\qquad\qquad$ = Ammeter reading = I_0

Applied voltage $\qquad\qquad$ = Voltmeter reading = V_1

Input power, $\qquad\qquad W_0 = V_1 I_0 \cos\phi_0$

∴ No-load p.f., $\qquad \cos\phi_0 = W_0 / V_1 I_0$

$$I_W = I_0 \cos\phi_0; \qquad I_m = I_0 \sin\phi_0$$

Thus open-circuit test gives P_i, I_0, $\cos\phi_0$, I_W and I_m.

20.17. SHORT-CIRCUIT OR IMPEDANCE TEST

In this test, the secondary (usually ** low-voltage winding) is short-circuited by a thick conductor and variable low voltage is applied to the primary as shown in Fig. 20.31 (*i*). The low input voltage is gradually raised till at voltage V_{SC}, full-load current I_1 flows in the primary. Then I_2 in the secondary also has full-load value since $I_1/I_2 = N_2/N_1$. Under such conditions, the copper loss in the windings is the same as that on full load.

There is no output from the transformer under short-circuit conditons. Therefore input power is all loss and this loss is almost entirely copper loss. It is because iron loss in the core is negligibly †small since the voltage V_{SC} is very small. *Hence, the wattmeter will practically register the full-load*

* The open-circuit test is always made on the low-voltage winding of the transformer. Of course, iron losses will be the same if measured on either winding. But if measurement is made on high-voltage winding, the current I_0 would be inconveniently small and the applied voltage inconveniently large.

** While making a short-circuit test, low-voltage winding is always short-circuited and measurements are made on the high-voltage winding. If measurements are made on the low-voltage winding (of course high-voltage winding being short-circuited), the voltage will be inconveniently low and the current would be inconveniently high.

† Iron loss is proportional to the square of magnetic flux and hence to the square of applied voltage. Since applied voltage V_{SC} under short circuit conditions is about 1/10th of normal voltage, the iron loss will be 1/100th of the normal value. Consequently, the iron loss is negligible under short-circuit conditions.

copper losses in the transformer windings. Fig. 20.31 (*ii*) shows the equivalent circuit of a transformer on short circuit as referred to primary ; the no-load current being neglected due to its smallness.

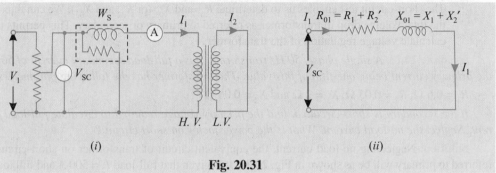

$$(i)$$

$$(ii)$$

Fig. 20.31

Full load Cu loss, P_C = Wattmeter reading = W_S

Applied voltage   = Voltmeter reading = V_{SC}

F.L. primary current   = Ammeter reading = I_1

$$P_C = I_1^2 R_1 + I_1^2 R_2' = I_1^2 R_{01}$$

$$\therefore \qquad R_{01} = P_C / I_1^2$$

where R_{01} is the total resistance of transformer referred to primary.

Total impedance referred to primary, $Z_{01} = V_{SC}/I_1$

Total leakage reactance referred to primary, $X_{01} = \sqrt{Z_{01}^2 - R_{01}^2}$

Short-circuit p.f., $\cos \phi_s = P_C / V_{SC} I_1$

Thus short-circuit test gives full-load Cu loss, R_{01} and X_{01}.

Note: The short circuit test will give full-load Cu loss only if the applied voltage V_{SC} in such so as to circulate full-load currents in the windings. If in a short-circuit test, current value is other than full-load value, then Cu loss will be corresponding to that current value.

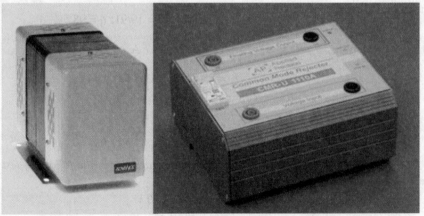

Voltage transformers

20.18. ADVANTAGES OF TRANSFORMER TESTS

The above two simple transformer tests offer the following advantages :

(*i*) The power required to carry out these tests is very small as compared to the full-load output of the transformer. In case of open-circuit test, power required is equal to the iron loss whereas for a short-circuit test, power required is equal to full-load copper loss.

(*ii*) These tests enable us to determine the efficiency of the transformer accurately at any load and p.f. without actually loading the transformer.

(*iii*) The short-circuit test enables us to determine R_{01} and X_{01} (or R_{02} and X_{02}). We can thus find the total voltage drop in transformer as referred to primary or secondary. This permits us to calculate voltage regulation of the transformer.

Example 20.23. *A single phase, 50 Hz transformer has a full-load secondary current of 500 A; the primary current being one-fifth of this value. The transformer has the following parameters:*

$$R_1 = 0.6 \ \Omega; R_2 = 0.03 \ \Omega; X_1 = 2 \ \Omega \text{ and } X_2 = 0.06 \ \Omega$$

If the secondary is short-circuited, find the primary voltage required to circulate full-load current. Neglect the no-load current. What is the power factor on short circuit ?

Solution. Neglecting no-load current, the equivalent circuit of transformer on short-circuit as referred to primary will be as shown in Fig. 20.32. It is given that full-load $I_2 = 500 \ A$ and full load $I_1 = 100 \ A$. Hence $K = I_1/I_2 = 1/5$.

$$R_{01} = R_1 + R_2/K^2 = 0.6 + 0.03 \times 5^2 = 1.35 \ \Omega$$
$$X_{01} = X_1 + X_2/K^2 = 2 + 0.06 \times 5^2 = 3.5 \ \Omega$$

∴ $$Z_{01} = \sqrt{R_{01}^2 + X_{01}^2} = \sqrt{(1.35)^2 + (3.5)^2} = 3.75 \ \Omega$$

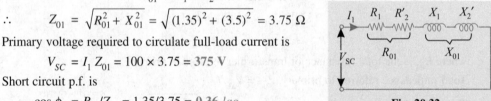

Primary voltage required to circulate full-load current is

$$V_{SC} = I_1 Z_{01} = 100 \times 3.75 = \textbf{375 V}$$

Short circuit p.f. is

$$\cos \phi_s = R_{01}/Z_{01} = 1.35/3.75 = \textbf{0.36} \ lag$$

Fig. 20.32

Example 20.24. *The low-voltage winding of a 300kVA, 11000/2200V, 50Hz transformer has 190 turns and a resistance of 0.06 Ω. The high voltage side has 910 turns and a resistance of 1.6 Ω. When the low-voltage winding is short-circuited, the full-load current is obtained with 550V applied to h.v. side. Calculate the equivalent resistance and leakage reactance referred to high-voltage side. Assume full-load efficiency of 98.5%.*

Solution.

$$V_{SC} = 550 \text{ V}; K = 190/910 = 19/91; \eta = 98.5\%$$

F.L. primary current, $$I_1 = \frac{300 \times 10^3}{11000 \times 0.985} = 27.7 \text{ A}$$

$$Z_{01} = V_{SC}/I_1 = 550/27.7 = 19.8 \ \Omega$$
$$R'_2 = R_2/K^2 = 0.06/(19/91)^2 = 1.38 \ \Omega$$

∴ $$R_{01} = R_1 + R'_2 = 1.6 + 1.38 = \textbf{2.98} \ \Omega$$

$$X_{01} = \sqrt{Z_{01}^2 - R_{01}^2} = \sqrt{(19.8)^2 - (2.98)^2} = \textbf{19.5} \ \Omega$$

Example 20.25. *In a no-load test of a single-phase transformer, the following test data were obtained:*

Primary voltage : 220 V   Secondary voltage : 110 V

Primary current : 0.5 A   Power input : 30 W

Find (i) the turns ratio (ii) the magnetising component of no-load current (iii) the iron-loss component of no-load current (iv) iron loss. The resistance of primary winding is 0.6 Ω.

Solution.

(*i*)   Turns ratio $$= \frac{N_1}{N_2} = \frac{E_1}{E_2} \approx \frac{V_1}{V_2} = \frac{220}{110} = 2$$

(ii) $$W_0 = V_1 I_0 \cos \phi_0$$

∴ No-load p.f., $$\cos \phi_0 = \frac{W_0}{V_1 I_0} = \frac{30}{220 \times 0.5} = 0.273 \; ; \; \sin \phi_0 = 0.962$$

Magnetising current, $I_m = I_0 \sin \phi_0 = 0.5 \times 0.962 = \mathbf{0.48 \; A}$

(iii) Component of no-load current corresponding to core loss is

$$I_W = I_0 \cos \phi_0 = 0.5 \times 0.273 = \mathbf{0.1365 \; A}$$

(iv) Primary Cu loss $= I_0^2 R_1 = (0.5)^2 \times 0.6 = 0.15 \; W$

Iron loss $= 30 - 0.15 = \mathbf{29.85 \; W}$

20.19. LOSSES IN A TRANSFORMER

The power losses in a transformer are of two types, namely;

1. Core or Iron losses
2. Copper losses

These losses appear in the form of heat and produce (i) an increase in temperature and (ii) a drop in efficiency.

1. Core or Iron losses (P_i). These consist of hysteresis and eddy current losses and occur in the transformer core due to the alternating flux. These can be determined by open-circuit test.

$$\text{Hysteresis losses} = k_h f \, B_m^{1.6} \; \text{watts/m}^3$$

$$\text{Eddy current losses} = k_e f^2 \, B_m^2 \, t^2 \; \text{watts/m}^3$$

Both hysteresis and eddy current losses depend upon (i) maximum flus density B_m in the core and (ii) supply frequency f. Since transformers are connected to constant-frequency, constant voltage supply, both f and B_m are constant. Hence, core or iron losses are practically the same at all loads.

Iron or Core losses, P_i = Hysteresis losses + Eddy current losses

= Constant losses

The hysteresis losses can be minimised by using steel of high silicon content whereas eddy current losses can be reduced by using core of thin laminations.

2. Copper losses. These losses occur in both the primary and secondary windings due to their ohmic resistance. These can be determined by short-circuit test.

$$\text{Total Cu losses, } P_C = I_1^2 R_1 + I_2^2 R_2$$

$$= I_1^2 R_{01} \text{ or } I_2^2 R_{02}$$

It is clear that copper losses vary as the square of load current. Thus if copper losses are 400W at a load current of 10A, then they will be $(1/2)^2 \times 400 = 100W$ at a load current of 5A.

Total losses in a transformer $= P_i + P_C$

= Constant losses + Variable losses

It may be noted that in a transformer, copper losses account for about 90% of the total losses.

20.20. EFFICIENCY OF A TRANSFORMER

Like any other electrical machine, the efficiency of a transformer is defined as the ratio of output power (in watts or kW) to input power (watts or kW) i.e.

$$\text{Efficiency} = \frac{\text{Output power}}{\text{Input power}}$$

It may appear that efficiency can be determined by directly loading the transformer and measuring the input power and output power. However, this method has the following drawbacks :

(i) Since the efficiency of a transformer is very high, even 1% error in each wattmeter (output and input) may give ridiculous results. This test, for instance, may give efficiency higher than 100%.

(ii) Since the test is preformed with transformer on load, considerable amount of power is wasted. For large transformers, the cost of power alone would be considerable.

(iii) It is generally difficult to have a device that is capable of absorbing all of the output power.

(iv) The test gives no information about the proportion of various losses.

Due to these drawbacks, direct loading method is seldom used to determine the efficiency of a transformer. In practice, open-circuit and short-circuit tests are carried out to find the efficiency.

$$\text{Efficiency} = \frac{\text{Output}}{\text{Input}} = \frac{\text{Output}}{\text{Output} + \text{Losses}}$$

The losses can be determined by transformer tests.

20.21. EFFICIENCY FROM TRANSFORMER TESTS

$$\text{F.L. Iron loss} = P_i \qquad \qquad \textit{... from open-circuit test}$$
$$\text{F.L. Cu loss} = P_C \qquad \qquad \textit{... from short-circuit test}$$
$$\text{Total F.L. losses} = P_i + P_C$$

We can now find the full-load efficiency of the transformer at any p.f. without actually loading the transformer.

$$\text{F.L. efficiency, } \eta_{F.L.} = \frac{\text{Full–load } VA \times \text{p.f.}}{(\text{Full–load } VA \times \text{p.f.}) + P_i + P_C}$$

Also for *any load equal to $x \times$ full-load,

Corresponding total losses $= P_i + x^2 P_C$

$$\text{Corresponding } \eta_x = \frac{(x \times \text{Full–load } VA) \times \text{p.f.}}{(x \times \text{Full–load } VA \times \text{p.f.}) + P_i + x^2 P_C}$$

Note that iron loss remains the same at all loads.

20.22. CONDITION FOR MAXIMUM EFFICIENCY

$$\text{Output power} = V_2 I_2 \cos \phi_2$$

If R_{02} is the total resistance of the transformer referred to secondary, then,

Total Cu loss, $\qquad\qquad P_C = I_2^2 R_{02}$

Total losses $\qquad\qquad = P_i + P_C$

∴ $\qquad\qquad$ Transformer $\eta = \dfrac{V_2 I_2 \cos \phi_2}{V_2 I_2 \cos \phi_2 + P_i + I_2^2 R_{02}}$

$$= \frac{V_2 \cos \phi_2}{V_2 \cos \phi_2 + P_i/I_2 + I_2 R_{02}} \qquad\qquad ... (i)$$

For a normal transformer, V_2 is approximately constant. Hence for a load of given p.f., efficiency depends upon load current I_2. It is clear from exp. (i) above that numerator is constant and for the efficiency to be maximum, the denominator should be minimum i.e.

$$\frac{d}{dI_2} (\text{denominator}) = 0$$

* Thus if rated VA (i.e. full-load VA) of a transformer is 1000, then half full–load $VA = 500$. Obviously, the value of $x = 1/2$.

or $\qquad \dfrac{d}{dI_2}\,(V_2 \cos\phi_2 + P_i/I_2 + I_2 R_{02}) = 0$

or $\qquad\qquad 0 - \dfrac{P_i}{I_2^2} + R_{02} = 0$

or $\qquad\qquad\qquad P_i = I_2^2\, R_{02}$ $\qquad\qquad\qquad$ ...(ii)

i.e. $\qquad\qquad$ Iron losses = Copper losses

Hence efficiency of a transformer will be maximum when copper losses are equal to constant or iron losses.

From eq. (*ii*) above, the load current I_2 corresponding to maximum efficiency is given by ;

$$I_2 = \sqrt{\dfrac{P_i}{R_{02}}}$$

Note: In a transformer, iron losses are constant whereas copper losses are variable. In order to obtain maximum efficiency, the load current should be such that total Cu losses become equal to iron losses.

20.23. OUTPUT kVA CORRESPONDING TO MAXIMUM EFFICIENCY

Let $\qquad\qquad P_C$ = Copper losses at full-load kVA

$\qquad\qquad P_i$ = Iron losses

$\qquad\qquad x$ = Fraction of full-load kVA at which efficiency is maximum

Total Cu losses $\qquad\qquad = x^2 P_C$

∴ $\qquad\qquad x^2 P_C = P_i$ $\qquad\qquad$ ... *for maximum efficiency*

or $\qquad\qquad x = \sqrt{\dfrac{P_i}{P_C}} = \sqrt{\dfrac{\text{Iron loss}}{\text{F.L. Cu loss}}}$

∴ Output kVA corresponding to maximum efficiency

$$= x \times \text{Full-load kVA} = \text{Full-load kVA} \times \sqrt{\dfrac{\text{Iron loss}}{\text{F.L. Cu loss}}}$$

It may be noted that the value of kVA at which the efficiency is maximum is independant of p.f. of the load.

Example 20.26. *In a 50 kVA transformer, the iron loss is 500W and full-load copper loss is 800W. Find the efficiency at full-load and half full-load at 0.8 p.f. lagging.*

Solution.

Full-load, 0.8 p.f.

Full-load output $\qquad\qquad$ = 50 × 0.8 = 40 kW

Total Full-load losses $\qquad\qquad$ = 500 + 800 = 1300 W = 1.3 kW

Full-load input $\qquad\qquad$ = 40 + 1.3 = 41.3 kW

$$\text{Full-load } \eta = \dfrac{40}{41.3} \times 100 = \mathbf{96.85\%}$$

Half full–load, 0.8 p.f.

Output at half full–load $\qquad\qquad$ = (50 × 1/2) × 0.8 = 20 kW

Total loss at half full–load $\qquad\qquad$ = 500 + (1/2)^2 × 800 = 700W = 0.7 kW

Input at half full–load $\qquad\qquad$ = 20 + 0.7 = 20.7 kW

$$\text{Half full–load } \eta = \dfrac{20}{20.7} \times 100 = \mathbf{96.6\%}$$

Example 20.27. *A 40kVA transformer has iron loss of 450W and full-load copper loss of 850W. If the power factor of the load is 0.8 lagging, calculate (i) full-load efficiency (ii) the load at which maximum efficiency occurs and (iii) the maximum efficiency.*

Solution.

(i) Total F.L. losses $\qquad = 450 + 850 = 1300 \text{ W} = 1.3 \text{ kW}$

F.L. output $\qquad = 40 \times 0.8 = 32 \text{ kW}$

F.L. input $\qquad = 32 + 1.3 = 33.3 \text{ kW}$

F.L. efficiency $\qquad = \dfrac{32}{33.3} \times 100 = \mathbf{96.1\%}$

(ii) Load for max. efficiency $\qquad = \text{F.L. kVA} \times \sqrt{\dfrac{\text{Iron loss}}{\text{F.L. Cu loss}}}$

$\qquad = 40 \times \sqrt{\dfrac{450}{850}} = \mathbf{29.1 \text{ kVA}}$

Corresponding output kW $\qquad = 29.1 \times 0.8 = 23.3 \text{ kW}$

(iii) For maximum efficiency, Cu loss = Iron loss

∴ Total losses $\qquad = 2 \times 450 = 900\text{W} = 0.9 \text{ kW}$

Input $= 23.3 + 0.9 = 24.2 \text{ kW}$

Maximum efficiency $= \dfrac{23.3}{24.2} \times 100 = \mathbf{96.28\%}$

Example 20.28. *The primary and secondary windings of a 50kVA, 6600/220 V transformer have resistances of 7.8 Ω and 0.0085 Ω respectively. The transformer draws no-load current of 0.328A at p.f. of 0.3 lagging. Calculate the efficiency at full-load if the p.f. of the load is 0.8 lagging.*

Solution.

$$K = 220/6600 = 1/30$$

F.L. Iron losses $\qquad = 6600 \times 0.328 \times 0.3 = 650 \text{ W}$

$$R_{01} = R_1 + R_2/K^2 = 7.8 + (0.0085) \times (30)^2 = 15.45 \ \Omega$$

F.L. primary current, $\quad I_1 = 50 \times 10^3/6600 = 7.57 \text{ A}$

F.L. Cu losses $\qquad = I_1^2 R_{01} = (7.57)^2 \times 15.45 = 885.4 \text{ W}$

Total F.L. losses $\qquad = 650 + 885.4 = 1535.4 \text{ W}$

F.L. output $\qquad = 50 \times 10^3 \times 0.8 = 40{,}000 \text{ W}$

F.L. intput $\qquad = 40{,}000 + 1535.4 = 41535.4 \text{ W}$

F.L. efficiency $\qquad = \dfrac{40{,}000}{41535.4} \times 100 = \mathbf{96.3\%}$

Example 20.29. *A 440/110 V transformer has a primary resistance of 0.03 Ω and secondary resistance of 0.02 Ω. Its iron loss at normal input is 150 W. Determine the secondary current at which maximum efficiency will occur and the value of this maximum efficiency at a unity p.f. load.*

Solution.

$$K = 110/440 = 0.25$$

$$R_{02} = R_2 + K^2 R_1 = 0.02 + (0.25)^2 \times 0.03 = 0.022 \ \Omega$$

Cu loss = Iron loss $\hspace{4cm}$ ... *for maximum* η

or $\qquad I_2^2 R_{02} = 150$

∴ $\qquad I_2 = \sqrt{\dfrac{150}{R_{02}}} = \sqrt{\dfrac{150}{0.022}} = \mathbf{82.58 \text{ A}}$

Output at unity p.f.	$= 110 \times 82.58 \times 1 = 9083.8$ W
Total losses	$= 150 + 150 = 300$ W ... *for maximum* η

$$\therefore \quad \text{Maximum efficiency} \quad = \frac{9083.8}{(9083.8 + 300)} \times 100 = 96.8\%$$

Example 20.30. *The efficiency of a 400 kVA, single phase transformer is 98.77% when delivering full-load at 0.8 p.f. lagging and 99.13% at half full–load at unity p.f. Calculate (i) iron loss and (ii) full-load copper loss.*

Solution.

Let	P_i = Iron losses	... constant at all loads
	P_C = F.L. copper losses	

At full-load

F.L. output at 0.8 p.f.	$= 400 \times 0.8 = 320$ kW
F.L. input at 0.8 p.f.	$= 320/0.9877 = 324$ kW
Total F.L. losses	$= 324 - 320 = 4$ kW

i.e. $\qquad\qquad P_i + P_C = 4$ kW $\qquad\qquad\qquad\qquad\qquad\qquad\qquad ...(i)$

At half full–load

Output at unity p.f.	$= (1/2) \times 400 \times 1 = 200$ kW
Input at unity p.f.	$= 200/0.9913 = 201.8$ kW
Total losses at half full-load	$= 201.8 - 200 = 1.8$ kW

i.e. $\qquad\qquad P_i + 0.25 P_C = 1.8$ kW $\qquad\qquad\qquad\qquad\qquad\qquad ...(ii)$

Solving eqs. (*i*) and (*ii*), $P_i = \textbf{1.07 kW}$; $P_C = \textbf{2.93 kW}$

TUTORIAL PROBLEMS

1. In a 100 kVA transformer, the iron loss is 1.2 kW and full-load copper loss is 2 kW. If the load p.f. is 0.8 lagging, find the efficiency at (*i*) full-load and (*ii*) half full-load.

    [(*i*) **96.16 %** (*ii*) **95.94%**]

2. The primary and secondary windings of a 500 kVA, 6600/400 V transformer have resistances of 0.42 Ω and 0.0011 Ω respectively and the iron loss is 2.9 kW. Calculate the efficiency at (*i*) full-load and (*ii*) half full–load, assuming the power factor of the load to be 0.8 lagging.

    [(*i*) **98.27 %** (*ii*) **98.07%**]

3. A 500/250 V, 1-phase transformer has constant losses of 150 W. When delivering an ouput of 8 kW to a load, the transformer takes 21 A at a p.f. of 0.8 lagging from 500 V supply. Calculate the variable losses of the transformer at this load.

4. A 100 kVA transformer has an iron loss of 1 kW and full-load Cu loss of 1.5 kW. Calculate the kVA loading at which the efficiency is maximum and its efficiency at this loading at 0.8 p.f. lagging.   [**82.3 kVA; 97.05%**]

5. A 150 kVA transformer has iron-loss of 1.4 kW and full-load copper loss of 2.8 kW. Calculate (*i*) the efficiency of transformer at full-load (*ii*) the maximum efficiency of the transformer and (*iii*) the output power at the maximum level of efficiency. Assume unity power factor.

    [(*i*) **97.2 %** (*ii*) **98.13%** (*iii*) **106.05 kW**]

20.24. WHY TRANSFORMER RATING IN kVA ?

We have seen that Cu loss depends on current and iron loss depends upon voltage. Hence the total loss in a transformer depends upon volt-ampere (*VA*) only and not on the phase angle between voltage and current *i.e.* it is independent of load power * factor. That is why the raing of a transformer is given in kVA and not in kW. It may be further pointed out that temperature rise of the transformer is directly proportional to the apparent power (*i.e.* kVA) which flows through it. This means that a 500 kVA transformer will get just as hot supplying a 500 kVAR inductive load as a 500 kW resistive load.

20.25. ALL-DAY (OR ENERGY) EFFICIENCY

The ordinary or commercial efficiency of a transformer is defined as the ratio of output power to the input power *i.e.*

$$\text{Commercial efficiency} = \frac{\text{Output power}}{\text{Input power}}$$

There are certain types of transformers whose performance cannot be judged by this efficiency. For instance, distribution transformers used for supplying lighting loads have their primaries energised all the 24 hours in a day but the secondaries supply little or no load during the major portion of the day. It means that a constant loss occurs during the whole day but copper loss occurs only when the transformer is loaded and would depend upon the magnitude of load. Consequently, the copper loss varies considerably during the day and the commercial efficiency of such transformers will vary from a low value (or even zero) to a high value when the load is high. The performance of such transformers is judged on the basis of energy consumption during the whole day (*i.e.* 24 hours). This is known as all-day or energy efficiency.

The ratio of output in kWh to the input in kWh of a transformer over a 24-hour period is known as **all-day efficiency** *i.e.*

$$\eta_{\text{all–day}} = \frac{\text{kWh output in 24 hours}}{\text{kWh input in 24 hours}}$$

All-day efficiency is of special importance for those transformers whose primaries are never open-circuited but the secondaries carry little or no load much of the time during the day. In the design of such transformers, efforts should be made to reduce the iron losses which continuously occur during the whole day.

Note : Efficiency of a transformer means commercial efficiency unless stated otherwise.

Example 20.31. *A 5 kVA distribution transformer has a full-load efficiency of 95% at which Cu loss is equal to the iron loss. The transformer is loaded in 24 hours as under:*

No load for 10 hours, one-fourth full-load for 7 hours, half full-load for 5 hours and full-load for 2 hours.

Calculate the all-day efficiency of the transformer.

Solution. Since a distribution transformer supplies mostly lighting load, it has a load p.f. of unity.

F.L. output	$= 5 \times 1 = 5$ kW
F.L. input	$= 5/0.95 = 5.26$ kW
Total F.L. losses	$= 5.26 - 5 = 0.26$ kW
Iron loss	$=$ F.L. Cu loss $= 0.26/2 = 0.13$ kW
Cu loss at 1/4 F.L.	$= (1/16) \times 0.13 = 0.008$ kW

---

* Rating in $kW = kVA \times$ load p.f.

The load p.f. depends upon the nature of load. Thus, kW rating of a transformer will be different at different load power factors.

Cu loss at 1/2 F.L.	$= (1/4) \times 0.13 = 0.03$ kW
Iron loss in 24 hours	$= 0.13 \times 24 = 3.12$ kWh
Cu loss in 24 hours	$= (0.008 \times 7) + (0.03 \times 5) + (0.13 \times 2)$
	$= 0.056 + 0.15 + 0.26 = 0.466$ kWh
Total losses in 24 hours	$= 3.12 + 0.466 = 3.586$ kWh
Total output in 24 hours	$= (7 \times 5/4) + (5 \times 5/2) + (2 \times 5) = 31.25$ kWh

$$\therefore \quad \text{All-day efficiency} \quad = \frac{31.25}{31.25 + 3.586} \times 100 = 89.7\%$$

Note that commercial efficiency of this transformer is 95% while its all-day efficiency is 89.7%.

Example 20.32. *A 40 kVA distribution transformer has iron loss of 500W and full-load copper loss of 500W. The transformer is supplying a lighting load (unity p.f.). The load cycle is as under:*

Full-load for 4 hours; half full–load for 8 hours and no-load for 12 hours.

Calculate the all-day efficiency of the transformer.

Solution.

Iron loss	$= 500$ W $= 0.5$ kW
F.L. Cu loss	$= 500$ W $= 0.5$ kW
Cu loss at half full–load	$= (1/4) \times 0.5 = 0.125$ kW
Iron loss in 24 hours	$= 0.5 \times 24 = 12$ kWh
Cu loss in 24 hours	$= (0.5 \times 4) + (0.125 \times 8) = 3$ kWh
Total loss in 24 hours	$= 12 + 3 = 15$ kWh
Output in 24 hours	$= (40 \times 4) + (40 \times 1/2 \times 8) = 320$ kWh
All-day efficiency	$= \dfrac{320}{320 + 15} \times 100 = 95.52\%$

20.26. CONSTRUCTION OF A TRANSFORMER

We usually design a power transformer so that it approaches the characteristics of an ideal transformer. To achieve this, following design features are incorporated :

(i) The core is made of silicon steel which has low hysteresis loss and high permeability. Further, core is laminated in order to reduce eddy current loss. These features considerably reduce the iron losses and the no-load current.

(ii) Instead of placing primary on one limb and secondary on the other, it is a usual practice to wind one-half of each winding on one limb. This ensures tight coupling between the two windings. Consequently, leakage flux is considerably reduced.

(iii) The winding resistances R_1 and R_2 are minimised to reduce I^2R loss and resulting rise in temperature and to ensure high efficiency.

20.27. TYPES OF TRANSFORMERS

Depending upon the manner in which the primary and secondary are wound on the core, transformers are of two types *viz* (i) core-type transformer and (ii) shell-type transformer.

(i) **Core-type transformer.** In a core-type transformer, half of the primary winding and half of the secondary winding are placed round each limb as shown in Fig. 20.33. This reduces the leakage flux. It is a usual practice to place the low-votlage winding below the high-voltage winding for mechanical considerations.

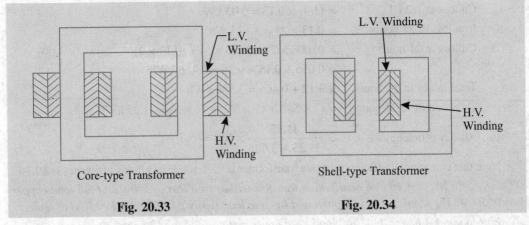

Fig. 20.33   Fig. 20.34

(ii) **Shell-type transformer.** This method of construction involves the use of a double magnetic circuit. Both the windings are placed round the central limb (See Fig. 20.34), the other two limbs acting simply as a low-reluctance flux path.

The choice of type (whether core or shell) will not greatly affect the efficiency of the transformer. The core-type is generally more suitable for high voltage and small output while the shell-type is generally more suitable for low voltage and high output.

20.28. COOLING OF TRANSFORMERS

Heat is produced in a transformer by the iron losses in the core and I^2R loss in the windings. To prevent undue temperature rise, this heat is removed by cooling.

(i) In small transformers (below 50 kVA), natural air cooling is employed *i.e.* the heat produced is carriesd away by the surrounding air.

(ii) Medium size power or distribution transformers are generally cooled by housing them in tanks filled with oil. The oil serves a double purpose, carrying the heat from the windings to the surface of the tank and insulating the primary from the secondary.

(iii) For large transformers, external radiators are added to increase the cooling surface of the oil filled tank. The oil circulates around the transformer and moves through the radiators where the heat is released to surrounding air. Sometimes cooling fans blow air over the radiators to accelerate the cooling process.

20.29. AUTOTRANSFORMER

An autotransformer has a single winding on an iron core and a part of winding is common to both the primary and secondary circuits. Fig. 20.35 (*i*) shows the connections of a step-down autotransformer whereas Fig. 20.35 (*ii*) shows the connections of a step-up autotransformer. In either case, the winding *ab* having N_1 turns is the primary winding and winding *bc* having N_2 turns is the secondary winding. *Note that the primary and secondary windings are connected electrically as well as magnetically.* Therefore, power from the primary is transferred to the secondary conductively as well as inductively (transformer action). The voltage transformation ratio K of an ideal autotransformer is

$$K = \frac{V_2}{V_1} = \frac{N_2}{N_1} = \frac{I_1}{I_2}$$

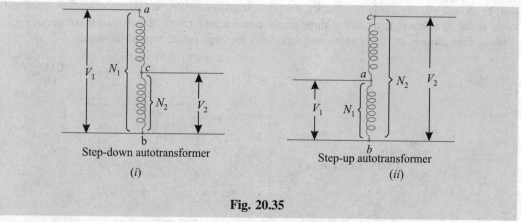

Step-down autotransformer
(i)

Step-up autotransformer
(ii)

Fig. 20.35

Note that in an autotransformer, secondary and primary voltages are related in the same way as in a 2-winding transformer.

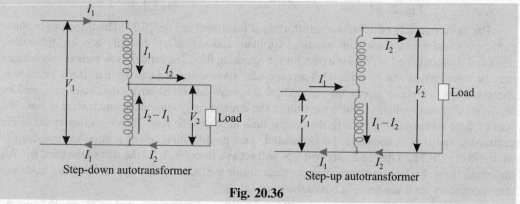

Step-down autotransformer

Step-up autotransformer

Fig. 20.36

Fig. 20.36 shows the connections of a loaded step-down as well as step-up autotransformer. In each case, I_1 is the input current and I_2 is the output or load current. Regardless of autotransformer connection (step-up or step-down), the current in the portion of the winding that is common to both the primary and the secondary is the difference between these currents (I_1 and I_2). The relative direction of the current through the common portion of the winding depends upon the connections of the autotransformer. It is because the type of connection determines whether input current I_1 or output current I_2 is larger. For step-down autotransformer $I_2 > I_1$ (as for 2-winding transformer) so that *$I_2 - I_1$ current flows through the common portion of the winding. For step-up autotransformer, $I_2 < I_1$. Therefore, $I_1 - I_2$ current flows in the common portion of the winding.

In an ideal autotransformer, exciting current and losses are neglected. For such an autotransformer, as K approaches 1, the value of current in the common portion ($I_2 - I_1$ or $I_1 - I_2$) of the winding approaches **zero. Therefore, for value of K near unity, the common portion of the winding can be wound with wire of smaller cross-sectional area. For this reason, an autotransformer requires less copper.

20.30. THREE-PHASE TRANSFORMER

In a three-phase system, the voltage is lowered or raised either by a bank of three single-phase transformers or by one 3-phase transformer. In either case, the windings may be connected in $Y - Y$, Δ

---

* Note that secondary current [($I_2 - I_1$) or ($I_1 - I_2$)] in an autotransformer is less than the load current. This is unlike a two-winding transformer in which secondary current is equal to the load current.

** $I_1 = K I_2$. As $K \rightarrow 1$, $I_1 \simeq I_2$.

$-\Delta$, $Y-\Delta$ or $\Delta-Y$. For the same capacity, a 3-phase transformer weighs less, occupies less space and costs about 20% less than a bank of three single-phase transformers. Because of these advantages, 3-phase transformers are in common use, especially for large power transformations.

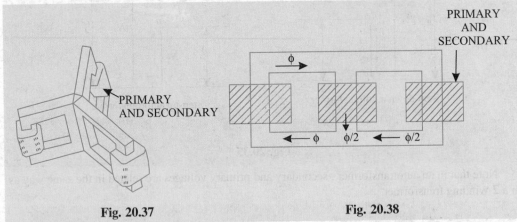

Fig. 20.37   **Fig. 20.38**

The basic principle of a 3-phase transformer is illustrated in Fig. 20.37. The three single phase core-type transformers, each with windings (primary and secondary) on only one leg, have their unwound legs combined to provide a path for the returning flux. The primaries as well as secondaries may be connected in star or delta. This arrangement gives a 3-phase transformer. If the primary is energised from a 3-phase supply, the central limb (*i.e.* unwound limb) carries the fluxes produced by the 3-phase primary winding. Since the sum of the three primary currents at any instant is zero, the sum of three fluxes passing through the central limb must also be zero. Hence no flux exists in the central leg and it may, therefore, be eliminated. This modification gives a three-leg transformer shown in Fig. 20.38. In this case, any two legs will act as a return path for the flux in the third leg. All the connections of a 3-phase transformer are made inside the case so that only three primary leads and three secondary leads are brought out of the case.

Phase transformation ratio (K). It is the ratio of secondary phase voltage to primary phase voltage and is denoted by K.

$$\text{Phase transformation ratio, } K = \frac{\text{Secondary phase voltage}}{\text{Primary phase voltage}}$$

Example 20.33. *A 3-phase, 50 Hz transformer has a delta-connected primary and star-connected secondary, the line voltages being 22000 V and 400 V respectively. The secondary has a star-connected balanced load at 0.8 power factor lagging. The line current on the pirmary side is 5 A. Determine the current in each coil of the primary and in each secondary line. What is the output of the transformer in kW ?*

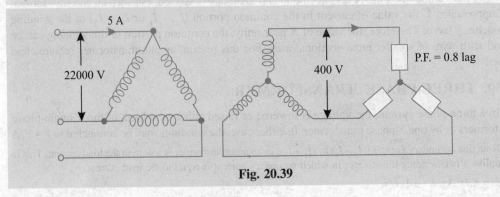

Fig. 20.39

Solution.

Fig. 20.39 shows the conditions of the problem.

Primary phase voltage = 22000 V

Secondary phase voltage = $400 \div \sqrt{3} = 400/\sqrt{3}$ V

∴ $$K = \frac{400/\sqrt{3}}{22000} = \frac{1}{55\sqrt{3}}$$

Primary phase current = $5 \div \sqrt{3} = 5/\sqrt{3}$ A

Secondary phase current = $5/\sqrt{3} \div K = \dfrac{5}{\sqrt{3}} \div \dfrac{1}{55\sqrt{3}} = 275$ A

∴ Secondary line current = **275 A**

Output power = $\sqrt{3} \, V_L I_L \cos\phi$

= $\sqrt{3} \times 400 \times 275 \times 0.8 = 152400$ W = **152.4 kW**

Example 20.34. *The input current to a 3-phase step down transformer connected to an 11 kV supply system is 14 A. Calculate the secondary line voltage and current for (i) star-star and (ii) delta-star if the phase turn ratio is 44.*

Solution.

$$K = \frac{\text{Secondary phase voltage}}{\text{Primary phase voltage}} = \frac{1}{44}$$

(*i*) **Star-Star Connection**

Primary phase voltage = $11000 \div \sqrt{3} = 6351$ V

Secondary phase voltage = $6351 \times K = 6351 \times 1/44 = 144.34$ V

Secondary line voltage = $144.34 \times \sqrt{3} = $ **250 V**

Primary phase current = 14 A

Secondary phase current = $14 \div K = 14 \times 44 = $ **616 A**

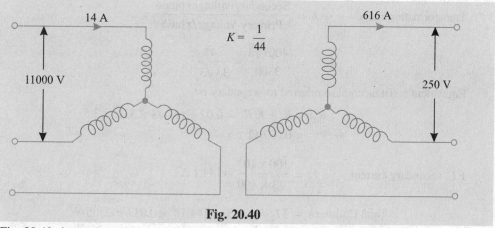

Fig. 20.40

Fig. 20.40 shows the star-star connection.

(*ii*) **Delta-Star Connection**

Primary phase voltage = 11000 V

Secondary phase voltage $= 11000 \times K = 11000 \times 1/44 = 250$ V

Secondary line voltage $= 250 \times \sqrt{3} = \textbf{433 V}$

Primary line current $= 14$ A

Primary phase current $= 14 \div \sqrt{3} = 8.08$ A

Secondary phase current $= 8.08 \div K = 8.08 \times 44 = 355.5$ A

Secondary line current $= \textbf{355.5 A}$

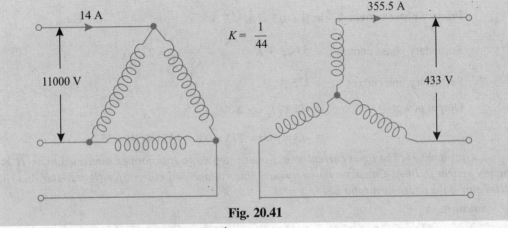

Fig. 20.41

Fig. 20.41 shows the delta-star connection.

Example 20.35. *A 100 kVA, 3-phase, 50 Hz, 3300/400 V transformer is Δ-connected on the h.v. side and Y-connected on the l.v. side. The resistance of the h.v. winding is 3.5 Ω per phase and that of the l.v. winding 0.02 Ω per phase. Calculate the iron losses of the transformer at normal voltage and frequency if its full-load efficiency is 95.8% at 0.8 p.f. (lag).*

Solution.

Full-load output $= 100 \times 0.8 = 80$ kW

Full-load input $= 80/0.958 = 83.5$ kW

Total F.L. losses $= 83.5 - 80 = 3.5$ kW $= 3500$ W

Transformation ratio, $\quad K = \dfrac{\text{Secondary voltage/phase}}{\text{Primary voltage/phase}}$

$$= \frac{400/\sqrt{3}}{3300} = \frac{4}{33\sqrt{3}}$$

Equivalent resistance/phase referred to secondary is

$$R_{02} = R_2 + K^2 R_1 = 0.02 + (4/\sqrt{3} \times 33)^2 \times 3.5$$
$$= 0.037 \ \Omega$$

F.L. secondary current, $\quad I_2 = \dfrac{100 \times 10^3}{\sqrt{3} \times 400} = 144.1$ A

Total Cu losses $= 3 I_2^2 R_{02} = 3 \times (144.1)^2 \times 0.037 = 2305$ W

∴ Iron losses $= 3500 - 2305 = \textbf{1195 W}$

MULTIPLE-CHOICE QUESTIONS

1. A transformer will work on ....
   (a) a.c. only
   (b) d.c. only
   (c) a.c. as well as d.c.
   (d) none of the above

2. The primary and secondary of a transformer are
   .... coupled.
   (a) electrically
   (b) magnetically
   (c) electrically and magnetically
   (d) none of the above

3. A transformer is an efficient device because it
   ....
   (a) is a static device
   (b) uses inductive coupling
   (c) uses capacitive coupling
   (d) uses electric coupling

4. The voltage per turn of the primary of a transformer is .... the voltage per turn of the
   secondary.
   (a) more than   (b) less than
   (c) the same as   (d) none of the above

5. The iron-core is used to .... of the transformer.
   (a) increase the weight
   (b) provide tight magnetic coupling
   (c) reduce core losses
   (d) none of the above

6. The maximum flux produced in the core of a
   transformer is ....
   (a) directly proportional to supply frequency
   (b) inversely proportional to supply frequency
   (c) inversely proportional to primary voltage
   (d) none of the above

7. When the primary of a transformer is connected
   to a d.c. supply, ...
   (a) primary draws small current
   (b) primary leakage reactance is increased
   (c) core losses are increased
   (d) primary may burn out

8. An ideal transformer is one which ....
   (a) has no losses and leakage reactance
   (b) does not work
   (c) has same number of primary and second-
       ary turns
   (d) none of the above

9. A low-voltage outdoor lighting system uses a
   transformer that steps 120 V down to 24 V for
   safety. The equivalent resistance of all low-voltage lamps is 9.6 Ω. What is the current in the
   secondary coil? Assume the transformer is ideal
   and there are no losses in the line.
   (a) 2 A   (b) 2.5 A
   (c) 4.5 A   (d) 1.5 A

10. In the above question, what is the current in
    the primary coil?
    (a) 1.5 A   (b) 4.5 A
    (c) 2.5 A   (d) 0.5 A

11. In Q. 9, how much power is used?
    (a) 30 W   (b) 20 W
    (c) 60 W   (d) 40 W

12. A transformer has an efficiency of 80% and
    works at 100 V, 4 kW. If the secondary voltage
    is 240 V, find the primary current.
    (a) 40 A   (b) 30 A
    (c) 20 A   (d) 10 A

13. In the above question, what is the secondary
    current?
    (a) 12.55 A   (b) 9.42 A
    (c) 11.56 A   (d) 13.33 A

14. A 2000/200 V, 20 kVA ideal transformer has
    66 turns in the secondary. The number of pri-
    mary turns is ....
    (a) 440   (b) 660
    (c) 550   (d) 330

15. In the above question, what is the full-load sec-
    ondary current?
    (a) 50 A   (b) 30 A
    (c) 150 A   (d) 100 A

16. In Q.14, what is the full-load primary current?
    (a) 5 A   (b) 20 A
    (c) 10 A   (d) 30 A

17. The no-load ratio of a 50 Hz single phase trans-
    former is 6000/250 V. The maximum flux in
    the core is 0.06 Wb. What is the number of pri-
    mary turns?
    (a) 450   (b) 900
    (c) 350   (d) 210

18. In the above question, what is the number of secondary turns ?

    (a) 38 (b) 19

    (c) 76 (d) 104

19. A 20-turn iron-cored inductor is connected to a 100 V, 50 Hz source. The maximum flux density in the core is 1 Wb/m^2. The cross-sectional area of the core is

    (a) 0.152 m^2 (b) 0.345 m^2

    (c) 0.056 m^2 (d) 0.0225 m^2

20. Calculate the core area required for a 1600 kVA, 6600/440 V, 50 Hz single phase core-type power transformer. Assume a maximum flux density of 1.2 Wb/m^2 and induced voltage per turn of 30 V.

    (a) 975 cm^2 (b) 1100 cm^2

    (c) 1125 cm^2 (d) 1224 cm^2

Answers to Multiple-Choice Questions

1. (a)	2. (b)	3. (a)	4. (c)	5. (b)	6. (b)	7. (d)	8. (a)
9. (b)	10. (d)	11. (c)	12. (a)	13. (d)	14. (b)	15. (d)	16. (c)
17. (a)	18. (b)	19. (d)	20. (c)				

Hints to Selected Multiple-Choice Questions

1. Transformer action demands only the existence of alternating flux linking the two windings. Since alternating flux can be produced by a.c., a transformer will work **only on a.c.**

3. Since transformer is a **static device**, the friction and windage losses are absent.

4. Since the same mutual flux links both the windings, the voltage per turn of the primary is **the same as** the voltage per turn of the secondary.

5. Iron core ensures **tight magnetic coupling** between the two windings. The co-efficient of coupling between the windings of a practical transformer may be as high as 0.99.

6. The voltage equation of a transformer is given by :

$$V_1 = 4.44 \, N_1 \, \phi_{max} \, f$$

where V_1 = applied primary voltage ; N_1 = number of primary turns

$$\therefore \qquad \phi_{max} = \frac{V_1}{4.44 \, N_1 f}$$

Clearly, maximum flux produced in the core is **inversely proportional to supply frequency**.

7. When the primary of a transformer is connected to a d.c. supply, steady flux is produced in the core. Consequently, no e.m.f. is induced in the primary. The primary winding will draw a large current due to small resistance of primary. This may cause the **primary to burn out**.

8. An ideal transformer is one that has (*i*) **no winding resistance** (*ii*) **no leakage flux** and (*iii*) **no core losses**. An actual transformer has some losses, winding resistance and leakage reactance. It may be noted that losses in an actual transformer are quite small. Moreover, winding resistances and leakage reactances are also small. Consequently, the assumption of ideal transformer is satisfactory for most considerations.

9. Secondary current, $I_2 = \dfrac{V_2}{R} = \dfrac{24}{9.6} = 2.5$ A

10. $V_1 I_1 = V_2 I_2$ or Primary current, $I_1 = \dfrac{V_2 I_2}{V_1} = \dfrac{24 \times 2.5}{120} = 0.5$ A

11. For lamp load, power factor is unity. Therefore $P = V_2 I_2 \cos \phi_2 = 24 \times 2.5 \times 1 = 60$ W. Alternatively, $P = V_1 I_1 \cos \phi_1 = 120 \times 0.5 \times 1 = 60$ W.

12. We shall assume power factor to be unity.

$V_1 I_1 \cos \phi_1 = 4 \times 10^3$ or Primary current, $I_1 = \dfrac{4 \times 10^3}{100 \times 1} = \textbf{40 A}$

13. $V_2 I_2 \cos \phi_2 = 0.8 \times 4 \times 10^3$ or Secondary current, $I_2 = \dfrac{0.8 \times 4 \times 10^3}{240} = \textbf{13.33 A}$

14. A 2000/200 V transformer is one that has normal primary and secondary voltages of 2000 V and 200 V respectively.

$K = \dfrac{E_2}{E_1} = \dfrac{200}{2000} = \dfrac{1}{10}$. Now $\dfrac{N_2}{N_1} = K$ or $\dfrac{66}{N_1} = \dfrac{1}{10}$ $\quad \therefore N_1 = 660$

15. Secondary output = 20 kVA = 20×10^3 VA

$\therefore$ Full-load secondary current, $I_2 = \dfrac{\text{Output}}{V_2} = \dfrac{20 \times 10^3}{200} = \textbf{100 A}$

16. Full-load primary current, $I_1 = \dfrac{20 \times 10^3}{2000} = \textbf{10 A}$

Alternatively : $I_1 = K I_2 = \dfrac{1}{10} \times 100 = \textbf{10 A}$

17. $E_1 = 4.44 f N_1 \phi_m$ or $6000 = 4.44 \times 50 \times N_1 \times 0.06 \therefore N_1 = \textbf{450}$
18. $E_2 = 4.44 f N_2 \phi_m$ or $250 = 4.44 \times 50 \times N_2 \times 0.06 \therefore \quad N_2 = \textbf{19}$

Alternatively: $N_2 = K N_1 = \dfrac{250}{6000} \times 450 = \textbf{19}$

19. $E = 4.44 f N \phi_m$ or $100 = 4.44 \times 50 \times 20 \times \phi_m$ $\therefore \phi_m = 0.0225$ Wb

Max. flux density, $B_m = \dfrac{\phi_m}{a}$ $\therefore$ $a = \dfrac{\phi_m}{B_m} = \dfrac{0.0225}{1} = \textbf{0.0225 m}^2$

20. $E = 4.44 f N \phi_m$ or $E/N = 4.44 f \phi_m$ or $30 = 4.44 \times 50 \times \phi_m$

$\therefore \phi_m = 0.135$ Wb ; Area of x-section $= \dfrac{\phi_m}{B_m} = \dfrac{0.135}{1.2} = \textbf{0.1125 m}^2 = \textbf{1125 cm}^2$

21

Three-Phase Induction Motors

INTRODUCTION

The three-phase induction motors are the most widely used electric motors in industry. They run at essentially constant speed from no-load to full-load. However, the speed is frequency dependent and consequently these motors are not easily adapted to speed control. We usually prefer d.c. motors when large speed variations are required. Nevertheless, the 3-phase induction motors are simple, rugged, low- priced, easy to maintain and can be manufactured with characteristics to suit most industrial requirements. In this chapter, we shall focus our attention on the general principles of 3-phase induction motors.

21.1. THREE-PHASE INDUCTION MOTOR

Like any electric motor, a 3-phase induction motor has a stator and a rotor. The stator carries a 3-phase winding (called stator winding) while the rotor carries a short circuited winding (called rotor winding). *Only the stator winding is fed from 3-phase supply. The rotor winding derives its voltage and power from the externally energised stator winding through

* Unlike a d.c. motor where both stator winding (i.e., field winding) and the rotor winding (i.e., armature winding) are connected to a voltage source.

electromagnetic induction and hence the name. The induction motor may be considered to be a transformer with a rotating secondary and it can, therefore, be described as a "transformer-type" a.c. machine in which electrical energy is converted into mechanical energy.

Advantages:

  (*i*) It has simple and rugged construction.

 (*ii*) It is relatively cheap.

(*iii*) It requires little maintenance.

(*iv*) It has high efficiency and reasonably good power factor.

 (*v*) It has self-starting torque.

Disadvantages:

  (*i*) It is essentially a constant speed motor and its speed cannot be changed easily.

 (*ii*) Its starting torque is inferior to d.c. shunt motor.

21.2. CONSTRUCTION

A 3-phase induction motor has two main parts (*i*) stator and (*ii*) rotor. The rotor is separated from the stator by a small air-gap which ranges from 0.4 mm to 4 mm, depending on the power of the motor.

1. Stator. It consists of a steel frame which encloses a hollow, cylindrical core made up of thin laminations of silicon steel to reduce hysteresis and eddy current loss. A number of evenly spaced slots are provided on the inner periphery of the laminations [See Fig. 21.1]. The insulated conductors are placed in the stator slots and are suitably connected to form a balanced 3-phase star or delta connected circuit. The 3-phase stator winding is wound for a definite number of poles as per requirement of speed. Greater the number of poles, lesser is the speed of the motor and *vice-versa*. When 3-phase supply is given to

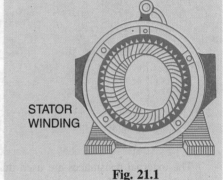

STATOR WINDING

Fig. 21.1

the stator winding, a rotating magnetic field (See Art. 21.3) of constant magnitude is produced. This rotating field induces currents in the rotor by electromagnetic induction.

2. Rotor. The rotor, mounted on a shaft, is a hollow laminated core having slots on its outer periphery. The winding placed in these slots (called rotor winding) may be one of the following two types:

  (*i*) Squirrel cage type 　　　 (*ii*) Wound type

  (*i*) **Squirrel cage rotor.** It consists of a laminated cylindrical core having parallel slots on its outer periphery. One copper or aluminium bar is placed in each slot. All these bars are joined at each end by metal rings called end rings (See Fig. 21.2). This forms a permanently short-circuited winding which is indestructible. The entire construction (bars and end rings) resembles a squirrel cage and hence the name. The rotor is not connected electrically to the supply but has current induced in it by transformer action from the stator.

Those induction motors which employ squirrel cage rotor are called *squirrel cage induction motors.* Most of 3-phase induction motors use squirrel cage rotor as it has a remarkably simple and robust

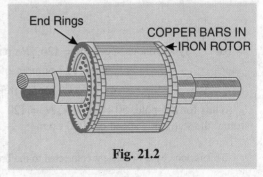

End Rings

COPPER BARS IN
◄IRON ROTOR

Fig. 21.2

construction enabling it to operate in the most adverse circumstances. However, it suffers from the disadvantage of a low starting torque. It is because the rotor bars are permanently short-circuited and it is not possible to add any external resistance to the rotor circuit to have a large starting torque.

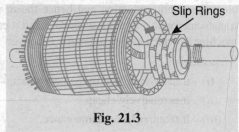

Fig. 21.3

(*ii*) **Wound rotor.** It consists of a laminated cylindrical core and carries a 3-phase winding, similar to the one on the stator (See Fig. 21.3). The rotor winding is uniformly distributed in the slots and is usually star-connected. The open ends of the rotor winding are brought out and joined to three insulated slip rings mounted on the rotor shaft with one brush resting on each slip ring. The three brushes are connected to a 3-phase star-connected rheostat as shown in Fig. 21.4. At starting, the external resistances are included in the rotor circuit to give a large starting torque. These resistances are gradually reduced to zero as the motor runs up to speed.

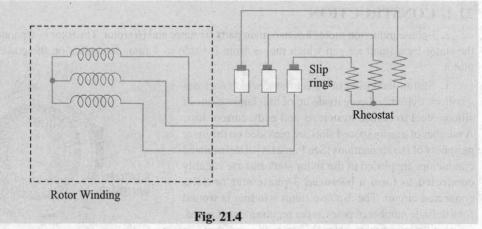

Fig. 21.4

The external resistances are used during starting period only. When the motor attains normal speed, the three brushes are *short-circuited so that the wound rotor runs like a squirrel cage rotor.

21.3. ROTATING MAGNETIC FIELD

When a 3-phase winding is energised from a 3-phase supply, a rotating magnetic field is produced. This field is such that its poles do not remain in a fixed position on the stator but go on shifting their positions around the stator. For this reason, it is called a rotating field. It can be shown that magnitude of this rotating field is constant and is equal to $1.5 \phi_m$ where ϕ_m is the maximum flux due to any phase.

Synchronous speed. The speed at which the revolving flux rotates is called synchronous speed (N_s). Its value depends upon the number of poles and the supply frequency and is given by;

$$f = \frac{N_s P}{120}$$

or   Synchronous speed, $N_s = 120\, f/P$ r.p.m.

where P = number of poles on the stator

f = supply frequency in Hz

Thus for a 6-pole, 50 Hz motor, $N_s = 120 \times 50/6 = 1000$ r.p.m. It means that the flux rotates around the stator at a speed of 1000 r.p.m.

* *

* This is done by a switchgear connected to the brushes.

Note. The direction of rotating flux (i.e., clockwise or anticlockwise) depends upon the phase sequence of supply voltage. If any two of the three lines to the stator winding are reversed, the phase sequence is reversed, thereby reversing the direction of rotating flux.

21.4. PRINCIPLE OF OPERATION

Consider a portion of 3-phase induction motor as shown in Fig. 21.5. The operation of the motor can be explained as under:

(*i*) When 3-phase stator winding is energised from a 3-phase supply, a rotating magnetic field is set up which rotates round the stator at synchronous speed N_s (= 120 f/P).

(*ii*) The rotating field passes through the air-gap and cuts the rotor conductors, which as yet, are stationary. Due to the relative speed between the rotating flux and the stationary rotor, e.m.f.s are induced in the rotor conductors. Since the rotor circuit is short-circuited, currents start flowing in the rotor conductors.

(*iii*) The current-carrying rotor conductors are placed in the magnetic field produced by the stator. Consequently, mechanical force acts on the rotor conductors. The sum of the mechanical forces on all the rotor conductors produces a torque which tends to move the rotor in the *same direction* as the rotating field.

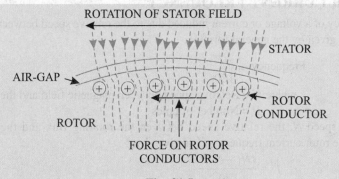

ROTATION OF STATOR FIELD

STATOR

AIR-GAP

ROTOR CONDUCTOR

ROTOR

FORCE ON ROTOR CONDUCTORS

Fig. 21.5

(*iv*) The fact that rotor is urged to follow the stator field (*i.e.*, rotor moves in the direction of stator field) can be explained by Lenz's law. According to this law, the direction of rotor currents will be such that they tend to oppose the cause producing them. Now, the cause producing the rotor currents is the relative speed between the rotating field and the stationary rotor conductors. Hence to reduce this relative speed, the rotor starts running in the same direction as that of stator field and tries to catch it.

Slipring Induction Motors

21.5. SLIP

We have seen above that rotor rapidly accelerates in the direction of rotating field. In practice, the rotor can never reach the speed of stator flux. If it did, there would be no relative speed between the stator field and rotor conductors, no induced rotor currents and, therefore, no torque to drive the rotor. The friction and windage would immediately cause the rotor to slow down. Hence, the rotor speed (N) is always less than the stator field speed (N_s). This difference in speed depends upon load on the motor.

The difference between the synchronous speed N_s of the rotating stator field and the actual rotor speed N is called *slip. It is usually expressed as a percentage of synchronous speed *i.e.,*

$$\% \text{ age slip, } s = \frac{N_s - N}{N_s} \times 100$$

(i) The quantity N_s–N is sometimes called slip speed.

(ii) When the rotor is stationary (*i.e.*, $N = 0$), slip, $s = 1$ or 100%.

(iii) In an induction motor, the change in slip from no-load to full-load is hardly 0.1% to 3% so that it is essentially a constant-speed motor.

21.6. ROTOR CURRENT FREQUENCY

The frequency of a voltage or current induced due to the relative speed between a winding and a magnetic field is given by the general formula;

$$\text{Frequency} = \frac{NP}{120}$$

where N = Relative speed between magnetic field and the winding

P = Number of poles

For a rotor speed N, the relative speed between the rotating flux and the rotor is $N_s - N$. Consequently, the rotor current frequency f' is given by;

$$f' = \frac{(N_s - N)P}{120}$$

$$= \frac{sN_s P}{120} \qquad\qquad \left(\because s = \frac{N_s - N}{N_s} \right)$$

$$= sf \qquad\qquad (\because f = N_s P/120)$$

i.e., Rotor current frequency = Fractional slip × Supply frequency

(i) When the rotor is at standstill or stationary (*i.e.*, $s = 1$), the frequency of rotor current is the same as that of supply frequency ($f' = s f = 1 \times f = f$).

(ii) As the rotor picks up speed, the relative speed between the rotating flux and the rotor decreases. Consequently, the slip s and hence rotor current frequency decreases.

Note: The relative speed between the rotating field and stator winding is N_s–0 = N_s. Therefore, the frequency of induced current or voltage in the stator winding is $f = N_s P/120$—the supply frequency.

Example 21.1. *A 6-pole, 3-phase induction motor is connected to 50 Hz supply. If it is running at 970 r.p.m., find the slip.*

Solution.

Synchronous speed, $N_s = 120 \, f/P = 120 \times 50/6 = 1000$ r.p.m.

$$\text{Slip, } s = \frac{N_s - N}{N_s} \times 100 = \frac{1000 - 970}{1000} \times 100 = 3\% \text{ or } 0.03$$

* The term slip is used because it describes what an observer riding on the stator field sees looking at the rotor—it appears to be slipping backward.

Example 21.2. *A 3-phase induction motor is wound for 4 poles and is supplied from 50 Hz system. Calculate (i) the synchronous speed (ii) the speed of the motor when slip is 4% and (iii) the rotor current frequency when the motor runs at 600 r.p.m.*

Solution.

(i) Synchronous speed, $N_s = 120\, f/P = 120 \times 50/4 = 1500$ **r.p.m.**

(ii) Slip, $s = \dfrac{N_s - N}{N_s} \times 100$

or $4 = \dfrac{1500 - N}{1500} \times 100$

∴ $N = 1440$ **r.p.m.**

(iii) When $N = 600$ r.p.m., $s = \dfrac{1500 - 600}{1500} = 0.6$

∴ Rotor current frequency, $f'' = sf = 0.6 \times 50 = 30$ **Hz**

Example 21.3. *A 6-pole alternator running at 1000 r.p.m. supplies an 8-pole induction motor. Find the actual speed of the motor if the slip is 2.5%.*

Solution. The frequency of 3-phase supply fed to the induction motor is determined from the speed of the alternator and its number of poles.

Supply frequency, $f = NP/120 = 1000 \times 6/120 = 50$ Hz

Synchronous speed, $N_s = 120\, f/P = 120 \times 50/8 = 750$ r.p.m.

Slip, $s = \dfrac{N_s - N}{N_s} \times 100$

or $2.5 = \dfrac{750 - N}{750} \times 100$

∴ $N = 731.25$ **r.p.m.**

Example 21.4. *A 50Hz, 4-pole, 3-phase induction motor has a rotor current of frequency 2Hz. Determine (i) the slip and (ii) speed of the motor.*

Solution.

(i) $f' = s\,f$

or $s = f'/f = 2/50 = 0.04$ or **4%**

(ii) $N_s = 120\, f/P = 120 \times 50/4 = 1500$ r.p.m.

$s = \dfrac{N_s - N}{N_s}$

or $0.04 = \dfrac{1500 - N}{1500}$

∴ $N = 1440$ **r.p.m.**

TUTORIAL PROBLEMS

1. A 2-pole, 3-phase, 50 Hz induction motor is running on no load with a slip of 4%. Calculate (i) the synchronous speed and (ii) speed of the motor. **[(i) 3000 r.p.m. (ii) 2880 r.p.m.]**

2. The frequency of e.m.f. in the stator of a 4-pole, 3-phase induction motor is 50 Hz and that in the rotor is 1.5 Hz. Determine (i) the slip and (ii) speed of the motor.

[(i) 3% (ii) 1455 r.p.m.]

3. A 3-phase, 50 Hz induction motor has 8 poles. If the full-load slip is 2.5%, determine (i) synchronous speed (ii) rotor speed and (iii) rotor frequency.

[(i) 750 r.p.m. (ii) 731 r.p.m. (iii) 1.25 Hz]

21.7. EFFECT OF SLIP ON THE ROTOR CIRCUIT

When the rotor is stationary, $s = 1$. Under these conditions, the per phase rotor e.m.f. E_2 has a frequency equal to that of supply frequency f. At any slip s, the relative speed between stator field and the rotor is decreased. Consequently, the rotor e.m.f. and frequency are reduced proportionally to $s\,E_2$ and $s\,f$ respectively. At the same time, per phase rotor reactance X_2, being frequency dependent, is reduced to $s\,X_2$.

Consider a 6-pole, 3-phase, 50 Hz induction motor. It has synchronous speed $N_s = 120\,f/P = 120 \times 50/6 = 1000$ r.p.m. At standstill, the relative speed between stator flux and rotor is 1000 r.p.m. and rotor e.m.f./phase $= E_2$ (say). If the full-load speed of the motor is 960 r.p.m., then,

$$s = \frac{1000 - 960}{1000} = 0.04$$

(*i*) The relative speed between stator flux and the rotor is now only 40 r.p.m. Consequently, rotor e.m.f./phase is reduced to:

$$^*E_2 \times \frac{40}{1000} = 0.04\,E_2 \text{ or } s\,E_2$$

(*ii*) The frequency is also reduced in the same ratio to:

$$50 \times \frac{40}{1000} = 50 \times 0.04 \text{ or } s\,f$$

(*iii*) The per phase rotor reactance X_2 is likewise reduced to:

$$X_2 \times \frac{40}{1000} = 0.04\,X_2 \text{ or } s\,X_2$$

Thus at any slip s,

$$\text{Rotor e.m.f./phase} \quad = s\,E_2$$
$$\text{Rotor reactance/phase} = s\,X_2$$
$$\text{Rotor frequency} \quad\quad = s\,f$$

where E_2, X_2 and f are the corresponding values at standstill.

Example 21.5. *A 3-phase, 6-pole induction motor is connected to a 60 Hz supply. The voltage induced in the rotor bars is 4 V when the rotor is at standstill. Calculate the voltage and frequency induced in the rotor bars at 300 r.p.m.*

Solution.

Synchronous speed, $\quad N_s = 120\,f/P = 120 \times 60/6 = 1200$ r.p.m.

$$\text{Slip,} \quad s = \frac{N_s - N}{N_s} = \frac{1200 - 300}{1200} = 3/4$$

Corresponding to this slip,

$$\text{Induced voltage} \quad = 4 \times s = 4 \times 3/4 = 3\text{V}$$
$$\text{Frequency} \quad\quad = f \times s = 60 \times 3/4 = 45 \text{ Hz}$$

---

* If the relative speed between stator flux and rotor is 1000 r.p.m., then rotor e.m.f./phase $= E_2$. If the relative speed is now 40 r.p.m., rotor e.m.f./phase is

$$= \frac{40}{1000} \times E_2 \qquad\qquad \textit{... unitary method}$$

21.8. ROTOR CURRENT

Fig. 21.6 shows the circuit of a 3-phase induction motor at any slip s. The rotor is assumed to be of wound type and star connected. Note that rotor e.m.f./phase and rotor reactance/phase are $s\,E_2$ and $s\,X_2$ respectively. The rotor resistance/phase is R_2 and is independent of frequency and, therefore, does not depend upon slip. Likewise, stator winding value R_1 and X_1 do not depend upon slip.

Since the motor represents a balanced 3-phase load, we need consider one phase only; the conditions in the other two phases being similar.

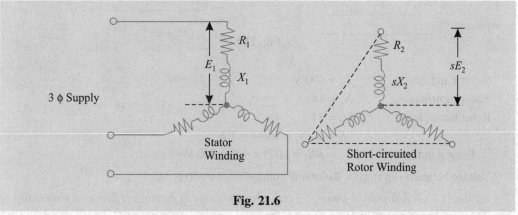

Fig. 21.6

At standstill. Fig. 21.7 (i) shows one phase of the rotor circuit at standstill.

Rotor current/phase, $\qquad I_2 = \dfrac{E_2}{Z_2} = \dfrac{E_2}{\sqrt{R_2^{\,2} + X_2^{\,2}}}$

Rotor p.f., $\qquad \cos\phi_2 = \dfrac{R_2}{Z_2} = \dfrac{R_2}{\sqrt{R_2^2 + X_2^2}}$

When running at slip s. Fig. 21.7 (ii) shows one phase of the rotor circuit when the motor is running at slip s.

Rotor current, $\qquad I_2' = \dfrac{s\,E_2}{Z_2'} = \dfrac{s\,E_2}{\sqrt{R_2^2 + (s\,X_2)^2}}$

Rotor p.f., $\qquad \cos\phi_2' = \dfrac{R_2}{Z_2'} = \dfrac{R_2}{\sqrt{R_2^2 + (s\,X_2)^2}}$

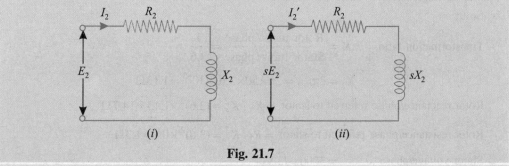

Fig. 21.7

Example 21.6. *A 3-phase, 400 V wound rotor motor has delta-connected stator winding and star-connected rotor winding. The stator has 48 turns/phase while the rotor has 24 turns per phase. Find the standstill open-circuited voltage across the slip rings.*

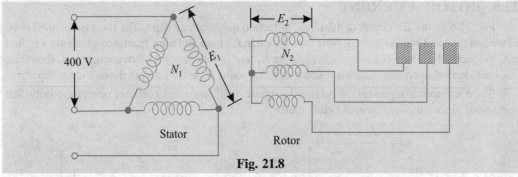

Fig. 21.8

Solution.

Stator e.m.f./phase, $E_1 = 400$ V

Stator turns/phase, $N_1 = 48$

Rotor turns/phase, $N_2 = 24$

∴ $K = N_2/N_1 = 24/48 = 1/2$

∴ Rotor e.m.f./phase $= KE_1 = (1/2) \times 400 = 200$ V

Voltage between slip rings = Rotor line voltage = $\sqrt{3} \times 200 = 346$ V

Example 21.7. *A 6-pole, 3-phase, 50 Hz induction motor is running at full-load with a slip of 4%. The rotor is star-connected and its resistance and standstill reactance are 0.25 Ω and 1.5 Ω per phase. The e.m.f. between slip rings is 100 V. Find the rotor current per phase and p.f., assuming the slip rings are short-circuited.*

Solution.

Rotor e.m.f./phase at standstill, $E_2 = 100/\sqrt{3} = 57.7$ V

Rotor e.m.f./phase at full-load $= s\,E_2 = 0.04 \times 57.7 = 2.31$ V

Rotor reactance/phase at full-load $= s \times X_2 = 0.04 \times 1.5 = 0.06$ Ω

Rotor impedance/phase at full-load $= \sqrt{(0.25)^2 + (0.06)^2} = 0.257\,Ω$

Full-load rotor current/phase $= 2.31/0.257 = 9$ A

Rotor power factor $= 0.25/0.257 = 0.97$ *lag*

Example 21.8. *A 150 kW, 3000 V, 50 Hz, 6-pole, star-connected induction motor has a star-connected slip ring rotor with a transformation ratio of 3.6 (stator/rotor). The rotor resistance is 0.1 Ω per phase and its per phase leakage inductance is 3.61 mH. The stator impedance may be neglected. Find the starting current on rated voltage with short-circuited slip rings.*

Solution.

Transformation ratio, $K = \dfrac{\text{Rotor turns/phase}}{\text{Stator turns/phase}} = \dfrac{1}{3.6}$

$$X_2 = 2\pi f L_2 = 2\pi \times 50 \times 3.61 \times 10^{-3} = 1.13\,Ω$$

Rotor reactance/phase referred to stator $= X_2/K^2 = (3.6)^2 \times 1.13 = 14.7\,Ω$

Rotor resistance/phase referred to stator $= R_2/K^2 = (3.6)^2 \times 0.1 = 1.3\,Ω$

Stator voltage/phase $= 3000/\sqrt{3}$ V

∴ Starting current $= \dfrac{3000/\sqrt{3}}{\sqrt{(1.3)^2 + (14.7)^2}} = 117.4$ A

21.9. ROTOR TORQUE

The torque T developed by the rotor is directly proportional to :

(i)   rotor current

(ii) rotor e.m.f.

(iii) power factor of the rotor circuit.

$$\therefore \qquad\qquad T \propto E_2 I_2 \cos \phi_2$$

or $\qquad\qquad T = KE_2I_2 \cos \phi_2$

where $\qquad\qquad I_2$ = rotor current at standstill

$\qquad\qquad\qquad E_2$ = rotor e.m.f. at standstill

$\qquad\qquad\qquad \cos \phi_2$ = rotor p.f. at standstill

Note. The values of rotor e.m.f., rotor current and rotor power factor are taken for the given conditions.

21.10. STARTING TORQUE (T_s)

Let $\qquad\qquad E_2$ = rotor e.m.f. per phase at standstill

$\qquad\qquad\qquad X_2$ = rotor reactance per phase at standstill

$\qquad\qquad\qquad R_2$ = rotor resistance per phase

Rotor impedance/phase, $\quad Z_2 = \sqrt{R_2^2 + X_2^2}$ *...at standstill*

Rotor current/phase, $\qquad I_2 = \dfrac{E_2}{Z_2} = \dfrac{E_2}{\sqrt{R_2^2 + X_2^2}}$ *...at standstill*

Rotor p.f., $\qquad\qquad \cos\phi_2 = \dfrac{R_2}{Z_2} = \dfrac{R_2}{\sqrt{R_2^2 + X_2^2}}$ *...at standstill*

$\therefore$ Starting torque, $\qquad T_s = KE_2I_2 \cos \phi_2$

$$= KE_2 \times \frac{E_2}{\sqrt{R_2^2 + X_2^2}} \times \frac{R_2}{\sqrt{R_2^2 + X_2^2}}$$

$$= \frac{KE_2^2\, R_2}{R_2^2 + X_2^2}$$

Generally, the stator supply voltage V is constant so that flux per pole ϕ set up by the stator is also fixed. This in turn means that e.m.f. E_2 induced in the rotor will be constant.

$$\therefore \qquad\qquad T_s = \frac{K_1 R_2}{R_2^2 + X_2^2} = \frac{K_1 R_2}{Z_2^2}$$

where K_1 is another constant.

It is clear that the magnitude of starting torque would depend upon the relative values of R_2 and X_2 *i.e.*, rotor resistance/phase and standstill rotor reactance/phase.

21.11. CONDITION FOR MAXIMUM STARTING TORQUE

It can be proved that starting torque will be maximum when rotor resistance/phase is equal to standstill rotor reactance/phase.

Now $\qquad\qquad\qquad\qquad T_s = \dfrac{K_1 R_2}{R_2^2 + X_2^2}$ ...(i)

Differentiating eq. (i) *w.r.t.* R_2 and equating the result to zero, we get,

$$\frac{dT_s}{dR_2} = K_1 \left[\frac{1}{R_2^2 + X_2^2} - \frac{R_2(2R_2)}{(R_2^2 + X_2^2)^2} \right] = 0$$

or $\qquad\qquad\qquad\qquad R_2^2 + X_2^2 = 2R_2^2$

or $\qquad\qquad\qquad\qquad R_2 = X_2$

Hence starting torque will be maximum when:

Rotor resistance/phase = Standstill rotor reactance/phase

Under the condition of maximum starting torque, $\phi_2 = 45°$ and rotor power factor is 0.707 lagging [See Fig. 21.9 (ii)].

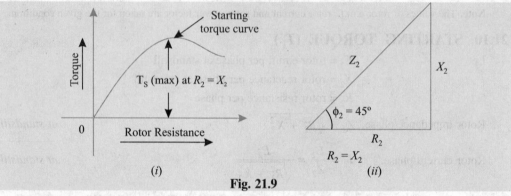

Fig. 21.9

Fig. 21.9 (i) shows the variation of starting torque with rotor resistance. As the rotor resistance is increased from a relatively low value, the starting torque increases until it becomes maximum when $R_2 = X_2$. If the rotor resistance is increased beyond this optimum value, the starting torque will decrease.

21.12. EFFECT OF CHANGE OF SUPPLY VOLTAGE

$$T_s = \frac{KE_2^2 R_2}{R_2^2 + X_2^2}$$

Since $\qquad\qquad\qquad\qquad E_2 \propto$ Supply voltage V

$\therefore \qquad\qquad\qquad\qquad T_s = \frac{K_2 V^2 R_2}{R_2^2 + X_2^2}$

where K_2 is another constant.

$\therefore \qquad\qquad\qquad\qquad T_s \propto V^2$

Therefore, the starting torque is very sensitive to changes in the value of supply voltage. For example, a drop of 10% in supply voltage will decrease the starting torque by about 20%.

21.13. STARTING TORQUE OF 3-PHASE INDUCTION MOTORS

The rotor circuit of an induction motor has low resistance and high *inductance. At starting, the rotor frequency is equal to the stator frequency (i.e., 50 Hz) so that rotor reactance is large compared with rotor resistance. Therefore, rotor current lags the rotor e.m.f. by a large angle, the power factor is low and consequently the starting torque is small. When resistance is added to the rotor circuit, the rotor power factor is improved which results in improved starting torque. This, of course, increases

---

* Because the rotor conductors are embedded in iron.

the rotor impedance and, therefore, decreases the value of rotor current but the effect of improved power factor predominates and the starting torque is increased.

(i) **Squirrel-cage motors.** Since the rotor bars are permanently short-circuited, it is not possible to add any external resistance in the rotor circuit at starting. Consequently, the starting torque of such motors is low. Squirrel-cage motors have starting torque of 1.5 to 2 times the full-load value with starting current of 5 to 9 times the full-load current.

(ii) **Wound rotor motors.** The resistance of the rotor circuit of such motors can be increased through the addition of external resistance. By inserting the proper value of external resistance (so that $R_2 = X_2$), maximum starting torque can be obtained. As the motor accelerates, the external resistance is gradually cut out until the rotor circuit is short-circuited on itself for running conditions.

Example 21.9. *The 3-phase induction motor having star-connected rotor has an induced e.m.f. of 50 V between the slip rings at standstill on open-circuit. The rotor has a resistance and reactance per phase of 0.5 Ω and 4.5 Ω respectively. Find the rotor current per phase and rotor power factor at starting when*

(i) *the slip rings are short-circuited*

(ii) *the slip rings are connected to a star-connected rheostat of 4 Ω per phase.*

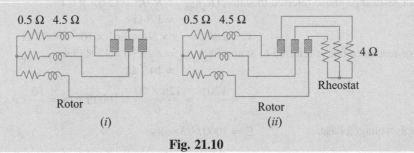

Fig. 21.10

Solution.

Standstill rotor e.m.f./phase, $E_2 = 50/\sqrt{3} = 28.87$ V

(i) **When slip rings are short-circuited** [See Fig. 21.10 (i)].

Rotor impedance/phase $= \sqrt{(0.5)^2 + (4.5)^2} = 4.53\,\Omega$

Rotor current/phase $= 28.87/4.53 = 6.38$ A

Rotor power factor $= 0.5/4.53 = 0.11$ *lag*

(ii) **When slip rings connected to Y-connected rheostat** [See Fig. 21.10 (ii)].

Rotor resistance/phase $= 4 + 0.5 = 4.5\,\Omega$

Rotor impedance/phase $= \sqrt{(4.5)^2 + (4.5)^2} = 6.36\,\Omega$

Rotor current/phase $= 28.87/6.36 = 4.54$ A

Rotor power factor $= 4.5/6.36 = 0.707$ *lag*

It is clear that by inserting additional resistance in the rotor circuit, the p.f. of the rotor circuit is improved, though the rotor current is decreased. However, the effect of improved p.f. predominates the decrease in rotor current. Hence, starting torque is increased.

Example 21.10. *A star-connected rotor winding of a 3-phase induction motor has a resistance of 0.2 Ω per phase and a standstill reactance of 1 Ω per phase. Find the value of external resistance per phase to be added to give maximum starting torque. What is the power factor of the rotor circuit then?*

Solution.

Let R ohm be the external resistance per phase to be added to the rotor circuit to give maximum starting torque. For maximum starting torque,

$$\text{Rotor resistance/phase} = \text{Standstill rotor reactance/phase}$$

or $\qquad\qquad 0.2 + R = 1$

∴ $\qquad\qquad R = 1 - 0.2 = \textbf{0.8 } \Omega$

$$\text{Rotor impedance/phase} = \sqrt{1^2 + 1^2} = \sqrt{2}$$

$$\text{Rotor power factor} = 1/\sqrt{2} = \textbf{0.707 } lag$$

Example 21.11. *A 150 kW, 3000 V, 50 Hz, 6-pole, star-connected induction motor has a star-connected slip-ring rotor with a transformation ratio of 3.6 (stator/rotor). The rotor resistance is 0.1 Ω/phase and its per phase leakage inductance is 3.61 mH. The stator impedance may be neglected. Find the starting torque on rated voltage with short-circuited slip rings.*

Solution.

Transformation ratio, $\qquad K = \dfrac{\text{Rotor turns/phase}}{\text{Stator turns/phase}} = \dfrac{1}{3.6}$

Rotor resistance/phase referred to stator, $(R_2)_{stator} = R_2/K^2 = (3.6)^2 \times 0.1$
$$= 1.3 \ \Omega$$

$$X_2 = 2\pi f L_2 = 2\pi \times 50 \times 3.61 \times 10^{-3} = 1.13 \ \Omega$$

Rotor reactance/phase referred to stator, $(X_2)_{stator} = X_2/K^2 = 1.13 \times (3.6)^2$
$$= 14.7 \ \Omega$$

$$N_s = \frac{120f}{P} = \frac{120 \times 50}{6} = 1000 \text{ r.p.m.} = \frac{50}{3} \text{ r.p.s.}$$

Supply voltage/phase, $\qquad E_1 = 3000/\sqrt{3}$ volts

Starting torque, $\qquad T_s = \dfrac{KE_2^2 R_2}{R_2^2 + X_2^2} = \dfrac{3}{2\pi N_s} \times \dfrac{E_1^{2**}(R_2)_{stator}}{(R_2)^2_{stator} + (X_2)^2_{stator}}$

$$= \frac{3}{2\pi(50/3)} \times \frac{(3000/\sqrt{3})^2 \times 1.3}{(1.3)^2 + (14.7)^2} = \textbf{513 N-m}$$

TUTORIAL PROBLEMS

1. A 3-phase induction motor at standstill has a rotor voltage of 120 V between the slip rings on open-circuit. The rotor winding is star-connected and has reactance of 1 Ω per phase at standstill and a resistance of 0.2 Ω per phase. Find the rotor current per phase and power factor at start.
   [**13.6A**; **0.98** *lag*]

2. A 3-phase induction motor with a star-connected rotor has an induced e.m.f. of 80 V between the slip rings at standstill on open-circuit. The resistance and standstill reactance of the rotor are 0.35 Ω and 2.3 Ω per phase respectively. Calculate the rotor current per phase and the power factor at start with an external resistance of 2 Ω per phase. [**14A**; **0.71** *lag*]

3. If the star-connected rotor winding of a 3-phase induction motor has a resistance of 0.01 Ω per phase and a standstill reactance of 0.08 Ω per phase, what must be the value of external resistance per phase to give maximum starting torque ? What will be the rotor power factor then ? [**0.07 Ω**; **0.707** *lag*]

---

* It can be shown that $K = \dfrac{3}{2\pi N_s}$ where N_s is in r.p.s.

** Since $E_2 \propto E_1$, the supply voltage.

21.14. MOTOR UNDER LOAD

Let us now discuss the behaviour of 3-phase induction motor on load.

(*i*)   When we apply mechanical load to the shaft of the motor, it will begin to slow down and the rotating flux will cut the rotor conductors at a higher and higher rate. The induced voltage and resulting current in rotor conductors will increase progressively, producing greater and greater torque.

(*ii*)   The motor and mechanical load will soon reach a state of equilibrium when the motor torque is exactly equal to the load torque. When this state is reached, the speed will cease to drop any more and the motor will run at the new speed at a constant rate.

(*iii*)   The drop in speed of the induction motor on increased load is small. It is because the rotor impedance is *low and a small decrease in speed produces a large rotor current. The increased rotor current produces a higher torque to meet the increased load on the motor. This is why induction motors are considered to be constant-speed machines. However, because they never actually turn at synchronous speed, they are sometimes called *asynchronous machines*.

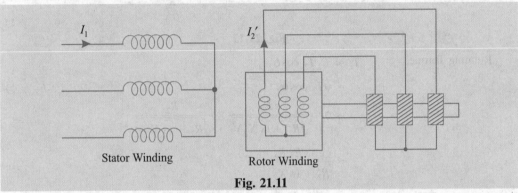

Fig. 21.11

Note that change in load on the induction motor is met through the adjustment of slip. When load on the motor increases, the slip increases slightly (*i.e.*, motor speed decreases slightly). This results in greater relative speed between the rotating flux and rotor conductors. Consequently, rotor current is increased, producing a higher torque to meet the increased load. Reverse happens should the load on the motor decrease.

(*iv*)   With increasing load, the increased load current (I_2') is in such a direction so as to decrease the stator flux (Lenz's law), thereby decreasing the counter e.m.f. in the stator windings. The decreased counter e.m.f. allows motor stator current (I_1) to increase, thereby increasing the power input to the motor. It may be noted that action of the induction motor in adjusting its stator or primary current with changes of current in the rotor or secondary is very much similar to the changes occurring in transformer with changes in load.

21.15. TORQUE UNDER RUNNING CONDITIONS

Let the rotor at standstill have per phase induced e.m.f. E_2, reactance X_2 and resistance R_2. Then under running conditions at slip s,

Rotor e.m.f./phase, $E_2' = s E_2$

Rotor reactance/phase, $X_2' = s X_2$

Rotor impedance/phase, $Z_2' = \sqrt{R_2^2 + (s X_2)^2}$

* Rotor resistance is a fixed small value. The rotor frequency under running conditions is very small ($f' = sf$) and hence rotor reactance is also low. This results in low rotor impedance during running conditions.

Rotor current/phase, $\qquad I_2' = \dfrac{E_2'}{Z_2'} = \dfrac{s\,E_2}{\sqrt{R_2^2 + (s\,X_2)^2}}$

Rotor p.f., $\qquad \cos\phi_2' = \dfrac{R_2}{\sqrt{R_2^2 + (s\,X_2)^2}}$

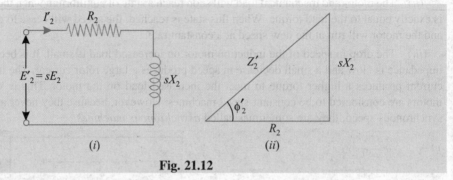

Fig. 21.12

Running Torque, $\qquad T_r \propto E_2'\,I_2'\,\cos\phi_2'$

$$\propto \phi\,I_2'\,\cos\phi_2' \qquad\qquad (\because E_2' \propto \phi)$$

$$\propto \phi \times \dfrac{s\,E_2}{\sqrt{R_2^2 + (s\,X_2)^2}} \times \dfrac{R_2}{\sqrt{R_2^2 + (s\,X_2)^2}}$$

$$\propto \dfrac{\phi\,s\,E_2\,R_2}{R_2^2 + (s\,X_2)^2}$$

$$= \dfrac{K\,\phi\,s\,E_2\,R_2}{R_2^2 + (s\,X_2)^2}$$

$$= \dfrac{K_1\,s\,E_2^2\,R_2}{R_2^2 + (s\,X_2)^2} \qquad\qquad (\because E_2 \propto \phi)$$

If the stator supply voltage V is constant, then stator flux and hence E_2 will be constant.

$$\therefore \qquad T_r = \dfrac{K_2\,s\,R_2}{R_2^2 + (s\,X_2)^2}$$

where K_2 is another constant.

It may be seen that running torque is:

(i) directly proportional to slip *i.e.*, if slip increases (*i.e.*, motor speed decreases), the torque will increase and *vice-versa*.

(ii) directly proportional to square of supply voltage ($\because E_2 \propto V$).

21.16. MAXIMUM TORQUE UNDER RUNNING CONDITIONS

$$T_r = \dfrac{K_2\,s\,R_2}{R_2^2 + s^2\,X_2^2} \qquad\qquad ...(i)$$

In order to find the value of rotor resistance that gives maximum torque under running conditions, differentiate exp. (*i*) *w.r.t.* s and equate the result to zero *i.e.*,

$$\dfrac{dT_r}{ds} = \dfrac{[R_2\,(R_2^2 + s^2\,X_2^2) - 2s\,X_2^2\,(s\,R_2)]}{(R_2^2 + s^2\,X_2^2)^2} = 0$$

or $(R_2^2 + s^2 X_2^2) - 2s^2 X_2^2 = 0$

or $\qquad R_2^2 = s^2 X_2^2$

or $\qquad R_2 = s X_2$

Thus for maximum torque (T_m) under running conditions:

Rotor resistance/phase = Fractional slip × Standstill rotor reactance/phase

Now, $\qquad T_r \propto \dfrac{s R_2}{R_2^2 + s^2 X_2^2}$ ....*from exp. (i) above*

For maximum torque, $R_2 = s X_2$. Putting $R_2 = s X_2$ in the above expression, the maximum torque T_m is given by;

$$T_m \propto \frac{1}{2X_2}$$

Slip corresponding to maximum torque, $s = R_2/X_2$.

21.17. TORQUE-SLIP CHARACTERISTICS

As shown in Art. 21.15, the motor torque under running conditions is given by;

$$T_r = \frac{K_2 s R_2}{R_2^2 + s^2 X_2^2}$$

If a curve is drawn between the torque and slip for a particular value of rotor resistance R_2, the graph thus obtained is called torque-slip characteristic. Fig. 21.13 shows a family of torque-slip characteristics for a slip range from $s = 0$ to $s = 1$ for various values of rotor resistance.

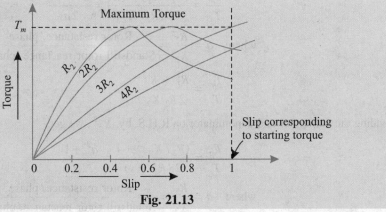

Fig. 21.13

The following points may be noted carefully:

(i)   At $s = 0$, $T_r = 0$ so that torque-slip curve starts from the origin.

(ii) At normal speed, slip is small so that $s X_2$ is negligible as compared to R_2.

∴ $\qquad T_r \propto s/R_2$

$\qquad\qquad \propto s$ ....*as R_2 is constant*

Hence, torque-slip curve is a straight line from zero slip to a slip that corresponds to full-load.

(iii) As slip increases beyond full-load slip, the torque increases and becomes maximum at $s = R_2/X_2$. This maximum torque in an induction motor is called *pull-out torque* or *breakdown torque*. Its value is atleast twice the full-load value when the motor is operated at rated voltage and frequency.

(iv) When slip increases beyond that corresponding to maximum torque, the term $s^2 X_2^2$ increases very rapidly so that R_2^2 may be neglected as compared to $s^2 X_2^2$.

$$\therefore \qquad T_r \propto s/s^2\, X_2^2$$

$$\propto 1/s \qquad\qquad\qquad \text{...as } X_2 \text{ is constant}$$

Thus the torque is now inversely proportional to slip. Hence torque-slip curve is a rectangular hyperbola.

It may be seen from the torque-slip characteristics that *addition of resistance to the rotor circuit does not change the value of maximum torque but it only changes the value of slip at which maximum torque occurs.*

21.18. FULL-LOAD, STARTING AND MAXIMUM TORQUES

$$T_f \propto \frac{s\,R_2}{R_2^2 + (sX_2)^2} \qquad\qquad \text{...See Art. 21.15}$$

$$T_s \propto \frac{R_2}{R_2^2 + X_2^2} \qquad\qquad \text{...See Art. 21.10}$$

$$T_m \propto \frac{1}{2X_2} \qquad\qquad \text{...See Art. 21.16}$$

Note that s corresponds to full-load slip.

(i) $\therefore$
$$\frac{T_m}{T_f} = \frac{R_2^2 + (s\,X_2)^2}{2s\,R_2\,X_2}$$

Dividing the numerator and denominator on R.H.S. by $X_2{}^2$, we get,

$$\frac{T_m}{T_f} = \frac{(R_2/X_2)^2 + s^2}{2s\,(R_2/X_2)} = \frac{a^2 + s^2}{2as}$$

$$\text{where} \quad a = \frac{R_2}{X_2} = \frac{\text{Rotor resistance/phase}}{\text{Standstill rotor reactance/phase}}$$

(ii)
$$\frac{T_m}{T_s} = \frac{R_2^2 + X_2^2}{2\,R_2\,X_2}$$

Dividing the numerator and denominator on R.H.S. by $X_2{}^2$, we get,

$$\frac{T_m}{T_s} = \frac{(R_2/X_2)^2 + 1}{2\,(R_2/X_2)} = \frac{a^2 + 1}{2a}$$

$$\text{where} \quad a = \frac{R_2}{X_2} = \frac{\text{Rotor resistance/phase}}{\text{Standstill rotor reactance/phase}}$$

Example 21.12. *A 50 Hz, 8-pole induction motor has full-load slip of 4%. The rotor resistance and standstill reactance are 0.01 Ω and 0.1 Ω per phase respectively. Find (i) the speed at which maximum torque occurs and (ii) the ratio of maximum torque to full-load torque.*

Solution.

(i) Synchronous speed, $\qquad N_s = 120\, f/P = 120 \times 50/8 = 750$ r.p.m.

Slip at which max. torque occurs $= R_2/X_2 = 0.01/0.1 = 0.1$

$\therefore$ Rotor speed at max. torque $\quad = {}^*(1 - 0.1)\, N_s = (1 - 0.1)750 = $ **675 r.p.m.**

(ii)
$$\frac{T_m}{T_f} = \frac{a^2 + s^2}{2as} \qquad\qquad \text{...See Art. 21.18}$$

- -

$* \quad s = \dfrac{N_s - N}{N_s} = 1 - \dfrac{N}{N_s} \quad \therefore\ N = (1 - s)\, N_s$

where $\quad\quad s$ = full-load slip = 0.04

$$a = R_2/X_2 = 0.01/0.1 = 0.1$$

∴ $\quad\quad\dfrac{T_m}{T_f} = \dfrac{(0.1)^2 + (0.04)^2}{2 \times 0.1 \times 0.04} = 1.45$

Example 21.13. *An 8-pole, 3-phase, 50 Hz induction motor has a rotor resistance of 0.025 Ω/ phase and a rotor standstill reactance of 0.1 Ω/phase. At what speed is the torque maximum ? What proportion of maximum torque is the starting torque?*

Solution.

$$N_s = 120 \, f/P = 120 \times 50/8 = 750 \text{ r.p.m.}$$

$$R_2 = s \, X_2 \quad\quad\quad\quad\quad\quad \text{...for maximum torque}$$

∴ $\quad\quad s = R_2/X_2 = 0.025/0.1 = 0.25$

Corresponding speed, $\quad\quad N = (1 - s) \, N_s = (1 - 0.25)750 = $ **562.5 r.p.m.**

$$\frac{T_s}{T_m} = \frac{2a}{a^2 + 1} \quad\quad\quad\quad \text{...See Art. 21.18}$$

$$a = R_2/X_2 = 0.025/0.1 = 0.25$$

∴ $\quad\quad\dfrac{T_s}{T_m} = \dfrac{2 \times 0.25}{(0.25)^2 + 1} = $ **0.47**

Example 21.14. *A 3-phase, 400/200 V, Y-Y connected wound-rotor induction motor has 0.06 Ω rotor resistance per phase and 0.3 Ω standstill reactance per phase. Find the additional resistance required in the rotor circuit to make the starting torque equal to the maximum torque*

Solution.

$$\frac{T_s}{T_m} = \frac{2a}{a^2 + 1}$$

Since $\quad T_s = T_m, \quad T_s/T_m = 1.$

∴ $\quad\quad 1 = \dfrac{2a}{a^2 + 1} \quad \text{or} \quad a = 1$

Now $\quad\quad\quad\quad\quad a = \dfrac{R_2 + R_x}{X_2}$

where $\quad\quad\quad\quad R_x$ = external resistance/phase added to the rotor circuit

∴ $\quad\quad\quad\quad 1 = \dfrac{0.06 + R_x}{0.3}$

or $\quad\quad\quad\quad R_x = $ **0.24 Ω/phase**

21.19. SPEED REGULATION OF INDUCTION MOTORS

Like any other electrical motor, the speed regulation of an induction motor is given by;

$$\text{\%age speed regulation} = \frac{N_0 - N_{F.L.}}{N_{F.L.}} \times 100$$

where $\quad\quad\quad\quad N_0$ = no-load speed of the motor

$\quad\quad\quad\quad\quad\quad N_{F.L.}$ = full-load speed of the motor

If the no-load speed of the motor is 800 r.p.m. and its full-load speed is 780 r.p.m., then change in speed is 800 – 780 = 20 r.p.m. and percentage speed regulation = 20 × 100/780 = 2.56%.

At no load, only a small torque is required to overcome the small mechanical losses and hence motor slip is small *i.e.*, about 1%. When the motor is fully loaded, the slip increases slightly *i.e.*, motor speed decreases slightly. It is because rotor impedance is low and a small decrease in speed produces a large rotor current. The increased rotor current produces a high torque to meet the full load on the motor. For this reason, the change in speed of the motor from no-load to full-load is small *i.e.*, the speed regulation of an induction motor is low. The speed regulation of an induction motor is 3% to 5%. Although the motor speed does decrease slightly with increased load, the speed regulation is low enough that the induction motor is classed as a constant-speed motor.

Wound Rotor Motors

21.20. SPEED CONTROL OF 3-PHASE INDUCTION MOTORS

$$N = (1 - s) N_s$$

$$= (1 - s) \frac{120 f}{P} \qquad \qquad ...(i)$$

An inspection of eq. (*i*) reveals that the speed *N* of an induction motor can be varied by changing (*i*) supply frequency *f* (*ii*) number of poles *P* on the stator and (*iii*) slip *s*. The change of frequency is generally not possible because the commercial supplies have constant frequency. Therefore, the practical methods of speed control are either to change the number of stator poles or the motor slip.

1. Squirrel cage motors. The speed of a squirrel cage motor is *changed by changing the number of stator poles. Only two or four speeds are possible by this method. Two-speed motor has one stator winding that may be switched through suitable control equipment to provide two speeds, one of which is half of the other. For instance, the winding may be connected for either 4 or 8 poles, giving synchronous speeds of 1500 and 750 r.p.m. Four-speed motors are equipped with two separate stator windings each of which provides two speeds. The disadvantages of this method are:

(*i*) It is not possible to obtain gradual continuous speed control.

(*ii*) Because of the complications in the design and switching of the interconnections of the stator winding, this method can provide a maximum of four different synchronous speeds for any one motor.

2. Wound rotor motors. The speed of wound rotor motors is **changed by changing the motor slip. This can be achieved by:

(*i*) varying the stator line voltage.

---

* The slip of an induction motor can be changed by changing the characteristics of the rotor circuit. Since the bars of a squirrel cage rotor are permanently short-circuited, the motor slip cannot be changed.

** Pole-changing speed control is generally not practicable for wound rotor motors.

$-\Delta$, $Y-\Delta$ or $\Delta-Y$. For the same capacity, a 3-phase transformer weighs less, occupies less space and costs about 20% less than a bank of three single-phase transformers. Because of these advantages, 3-phase transformers are in common use, especially for large power transformations.

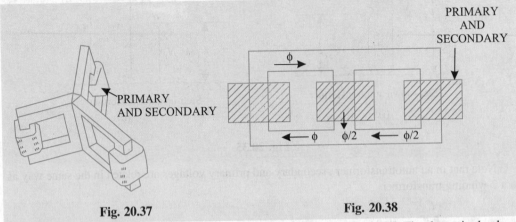

PRIMARY AND SECONDARY

PRIMARY AND SECONDARY

Fig. 20.37   **Fig. 20.38**

The basic principle of a 3-phase transformer is illustrated in Fig. 20.37. The three single phase core-type transformers, each with windings (primary and secondary) on only one leg, have their unwound legs combined to provide a path for the returning flux. The primaries as well as secondaries may be connected in star or delta. This arrangement gives a 3-phase transformer. If the primary is energised from a 3-phase supply, the central limb (*i.e.* unwound limb) carries the fluxes produced by the 3-phase primary winding. Since the sum of the three primary currents at any instant is zero, the sum of three fluxes passing through the central limb must also be zero. Hence no flux exists in the central leg and it may, therefore, be eliminated. This modification gives a three-leg transformer shown in Fig. 20.38. In this case, any two legs will act as a return path for the flux in the third leg. All the connections of a 3-phase transformer are made inside the case so that only three primary leads and three secondary leads are brought out of the case.

Phase transformation ratio (K). It is the ratio of secondary phase voltage to primary phase voltage and is denoted by K.

$$\text{Phase transformation ratio, } K = \frac{\text{Secondary phase voltage}}{\text{Primary phase voltage}}$$

Example 20.33. *A 3-phase, 50 Hz transformer has a delta-connected primary and star-connected secondary, the line voltages being 22000 V and 400 V respectively. The secondary has a star-connected balanced load at 0.8 power factor lagging. The line current on the pirmary side is 5 A. Determine the current in each coil of the primary and in each secondary line. What is the output of the transformer in kW ?*

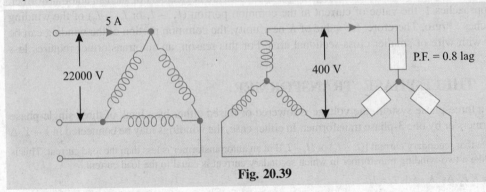

5 A

22000 V

400 V

P.F. = 0.8 lag

Fig. 20.39

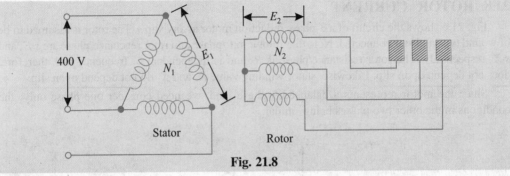

Fig. 21.8

Solution.

Stator e.m.f./phase, $E_1 = 400$ V

Stator turns/phase, $N_1 = 48$

Rotor turns/phase, $N_2 = 24$

∴ $K = N_2/N_1 = 24/48 = 1/2$

∴ Rotor e.m.f./phase $= KE_1 = (1/2) \times 400 = 200$ V

Voltage between slip rings = Rotor line voltage $= \sqrt{3} \times 200 = \mathbf{346 \text{ V}}$

Example 21.7. *A 6-pole, 3-phase, 50 Hz induction motor is running at full-load with a slip of 4%. The rotor is star-connected and its resistance and standstill reactance are 0.25 Ω and 1.5 Ω per phase. The e.m.f. between slip rings is 100 V. Find the rotor current per phase and p.f., assuming the slip rings are short-circuited.*

Solution.

Rotor e.m.f./phase at standstill, $E_2 = 100/\sqrt{3} = 57.7$ V

Rotor e.m.f./phase at full-load $= s\,E_2 = 0.04 \times 57.7 = 2.31$ V

Rotor reactance/phase at full-load $= s \times X_2 = 0.04 \times 1.5 = 0.06$ Ω

Rotor impedance/phase at full-load $= \sqrt{(0.25)^2 + (0.06)^2} = 0.257$ Ω

Full-load rotor current/phase $= 2.31/0.257 = \mathbf{9 \text{ A}}$

Rotor power factor $= 0.25/0.257 = \mathbf{0.97}$ *lag*

Example 21.8. *A 150 kW, 3000 V, 50 Hz, 6-pole, star-connected induction motor has a star-connected slip ring rotor with a transformation ratio of 3.6 (stator/rotor). The rotor resistance is 0.1 Ω per phase and its per phase leakage inductance is 3.61 mH. The stator impedance may be neglected. Find the starting current on rated voltage with short-circuited slip rings.*

Solution.

Transformation ratio, $K = \dfrac{\text{Rotor turns/phase}}{\text{Stator turns/phase}} = \dfrac{1}{3.6}$

$$X_2 = 2\pi f L_2 = 2\pi \times 50 \times 3.61 \times 10^{-3} = 1.13\,\Omega$$

Rotor reactance/phase referred to stator $= X_2 / K^2 = (3.6)^2 \times 1.13 = 14.7\,\Omega$

Rotor resistance/phase referred to stator $= R_2 / K^2 = (3.6)^2 \times 0.1 = 1.3\,\Omega$

Stator voltage/phase $= 3000/\sqrt{3}$ V

∴ Starting current $= \dfrac{3000/\sqrt{3}}{\sqrt{(1.3)^2 + (14.7)^2}} = \mathbf{117.4 \text{ A}}$

or $(R_2^2 + s^2 X_2^2) - 2s^2 X_2^2 = 0$

or $\qquad\qquad\qquad R_2^2 = s^2 X_2^2$

or $\qquad\qquad\qquad R_2 = sX_2$

Thus for maximum torque (T_m) under running conditions:

Rotor resistance/phase = Fractional slip × Standstill rotor reactance/phase

Now, $\qquad\qquad T_r \propto \dfrac{s R_2}{R_2^2 + s^2 X_2^2}$ $\qquad\qquad$ *...from exp. (i) above*

For maximum torque, $R_2 = s X_2$. Putting $R_2 = s X_2$ in the above expression, the maximum torque T_m is given by;

$$T_m \propto \frac{1}{2X_2}$$

Slip corresponding to maximum torque, $s = R_2/X_2$.

21.17. TORQUE-SLIP CHARACTERISTICS

As shown in Art. 21.15, the motor torque under running conditions is given by;

$$T_r = \frac{K_2\, s\, R_2}{R_2^2 + s^2 X_2^2}$$

If a curve is drawn between the torque and slip for a particular value of rotor resistance R_2, the graph thus obtained is called torque-slip characteristic. Fig. 21.13 shows a family of torque-slip characteristics for a slip range from $s = 0$ to $s = 1$ for various values of rotor resistance.

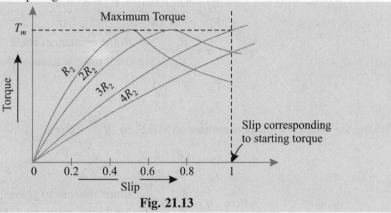

Fig. 21.13

The following points may be noted carefully:

(i) At $s = 0$, $T_r = 0$ so that torque-slip curve starts from the origin.

(ii) At normal speed, slip is small so that $s X_2$ is negligible as compared to R_2.

∴ $\qquad\qquad\qquad T_r \propto s/R_2$

$\qquad\qquad\qquad\qquad \propto s$ $\qquad\qquad\qquad$ *...as R_2 is constant*

Hence, torque-slip curve is a straight line from zero slip to a slip that corresponds to full-load.

(iii) As slip increases beyond full-load slip, the torque increases and becomes maximum at $s = R_2/X_2$. This maximum torque in an induction motor is called *pull-out torque* or *breakdown torque*. Its value is atleast twice the full-load value when the motor is operated at rated voltage and frequency.

(iv) When slip increases beyond that corresponding to maximum torque, the term $s^2 X_2^2$ increases very rapidly so that R_2^2 may be neglected as compared to $s^2 X_2^2$.

(ii) varying the resistance of the rotor circuit.

(iii) inserting and varying a foreign voltage in the rotor circuit.

21.21. POWER FACTOR OF INDUCTION MOTOR

Like any other a.c. machine, the power factor of an induction motor is given by;

$$\text{Power factor, } \cos \phi = \frac{\text{Active component of current } (I \cos \phi)}{\text{Total current } (I)}$$

The presence of air-gap between the stator and rotor of an induction motor greatly increases the reluctance of the magnetic circuit. Consequently, an induction motor draws a large magnetising current (I_m) to produce the required flux in the air-gap.

(i) At no load, an induction motor draws a large magnetising current and a small active component to meet the no-load losses. Therefore, the induction motor takes a †high no-load current lagging the applied voltage by a large angle. Hence, the power factor of an induction motor on no load is low *i.e.*, about 0.1 lagging.

(ii) When an induction motor is loaded, the active component of current increases while the magnetising component remains about the same. Consequently, the power factor of the motor is increased. However, because of the large value of magnetising current, which is present regardless of load, the power factor of an induction motor even at full load seldom exceeds 0.9 lagging.

21.22. POWER STAGES IN AN INDUCTION MOTOR

The input electric power fed to the stator of the motor is converted into mechanical power at the shaft of the motor. The various losses during this energy conversion are:

1. Fixed losses

(i) Stator iron loss *(ii)* Friction and windage loss

The rotor iron loss is negligible because the frequency of rotor currents under normal running condition is small.

2. Variable losses

(i) Stator copper loss *(ii)* Rotor copper loss

Fig. 21.14 shows how electric power fed to the stator of an induction motor suffers losses and finally converted into mechanical power.

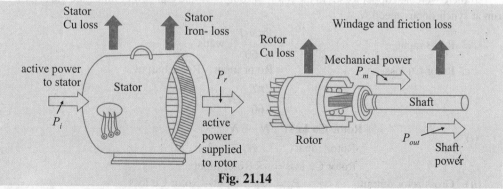

Fig. 21.14

The following points may be noted from the above diagram:

(i) Stator input, P_i = Stator output + Stator losses

= Stator output + Stator Iron loss + Stator Cu loss

† As compared to transformer no-load current.

(*ii*) Rotor input, P_r = Stator output

It is because stator output is entirely transferred to the rotor through air-gap by electromagnetic induction.

(*iii*) Mechanical power available, $P_m = P_r$ – Rotor Cu loss

This mechanical power available is the gross rotor output and will produce a gross torque T_g.

(*iv*) Mechanical power at shaft, $P_{out} = P_m$ – Friction and windage loss

Mechanical power available at the shaft produces a shaft torque T_{sh}.

Clearly, $P_m – P_{out}$ = Friction and windage loss

21.23. INDUCTION MOTOR TORQUE

The mechanical power P available from any electric motor can be expressed as:

$$P = \frac{2\pi NT}{60} \text{ watts}$$

where
N = speed of the motor in r.p.m.

T = torque developed in N – m

∴
$$T = \frac{60}{2\pi} \frac{P}{N} = 9.55 \frac{P}{N} \text{ N–m}$$

If the gross output of the rotor of an induction motor is P_m and its speed is N r.p.m., then gross torque T_g developed is given by;

$$T_g = 9.55 \frac{P_m}{N} \text{ N–m}$$

Similarly,
$$T_{sh} = 9.55 \frac{P_{out}}{N} \text{ N–m}$$

Note. Since windage and friction loss is small, $T_g = T_{sh}$. This assumption hardly leads to any significant error.

21.24. ROTOR OUTPUT

If T_g newton-metre is the gross torque developed and N r.p.m. is the speed of the rotor, then,

Gross rotor output
$$= \frac{2\pi NT_g}{60} \text{ watts}$$

If there were no copper losses in the rotor, the output would equal rotor input and the rotor would run at synchronous speed N_s.

∴ Rotor input
$$= \frac{2\pi N_s T_g}{60} \text{ watts}$$

∴ Rotor Cu loss
= Rotor input – Rotor output

$$= \frac{2\pi T_g}{60} (N_s – N)$$

(*i*)
$$\frac{\text{Rotor Cu loss}}{\text{Rotor input}} = \frac{N_s – N}{N_s} = s$$

∴
Rotor Cu loss = s × Rotor input

(*ii*) Gross rotor output,
P_m = Rotor input – Rotor Cu loss

= Rotor input – s × Rotor input

∴
P_m = Rotor input $(1 – s)$

(*iii*)
$$\frac{\text{Gross rotor output}}{\text{Rotor input}} = 1 – s = \frac{N}{N_s}$$

(iv) $\dfrac{\text{Rotor Cu loss}}{\text{Gross rotor output}} = \dfrac{s}{1-s}$

It is clear that if the input power to rotor is P_r, then s P_r is lost as rotor Cu loss and the remaining $(1 - s) P_r$ is converted into mechanical power. Consequently, induction motor operating at high slip has poor efficiency.

Note.

$$\dfrac{\text{Gross rotor output}}{\text{Rotor input}} = 1 - s$$

If the stator losses as well as friction and windage losses are neglected, then,

$$\text{Gross rotor output = Useful output}$$
$$\text{Rotor input = Stator input}$$

∴ $\dfrac{\text{Useful output}}{\text{Stator input}} = 1 - s = \text{Efficiency}$

Hence the approximate efficiency of an induction motor is 1 – s. Thus if the slip of an induction motor is 0.125, then its approximate efficiency is = 1 – 0.125 = 0.875 or 87.5%.

Example 21.15. *The input power to a 6-pole, 3-phase, 50 Hz induction motor is 42 kW; the speed is 970 r.p.m. The stator losses are 1.2 kW and the friction and windage losses 1.8 kW. Find (i) the rotor Cu loss and (ii) the efficiency of the motor.*

Solution.

Synchronous speed, N_s = 120 f/P = 120 × 50/6 = 1000 r.p.m.

$$\text{Slip,} \quad s = \dfrac{N_s - N}{N_s} = \dfrac{1000 - 970}{1000} = 0.03$$

(i)   Stator output = Stator input – Stator losses

$$= 42 - 1.2 = 40.8 \text{ kW}$$

Rotor input = Stator output = 40.8 kW

Rotor Cu loss = s × Rotor input = 0.03 × 40.8 = **1.224 kW**

(ii)   Useful output, P_{out} = Rotor input – Rotor Cu loss – Windage and friction loss

$$= 40.8 - 1.224 - 1.8 = 37.77 \text{ kW}$$

∴   Motor efficiency = $\dfrac{37.77}{42} \times 100$ = **89.9%**

Example 21.16. *A 7.46 kW, 230 V, 3-phase 50 Hz, 6-pole squirrel cage induction motor operates at full-load slip of 4% when rated voltage and rated frequency are applied. Determine (i) speed of rotation of stator m.m.f. (ii) full-load speed (iii) frequency of rotor current under this condition and (iv) full-load torque in newton-metre.*

Solution.

(i)   The stator m.m.f. revolves at synchronous speed.

$$N_s = 120 \, f/P = 120 \times 50/6 = \mathbf{1000 \text{ r.p.m.}}$$

(ii) $N = (1 - s) \, N_s = (1 - 0.04) \, 1000 = \mathbf{960 \text{ r.p.m.}}$

(iii) $f' = s \, f = 0.04 \times 50 = \mathbf{2 \text{ Hz}}$

(iv)   Neglecting windage and friction loss, $T_g = T_{sh}$

∴ $T_g = 9.55 \dfrac{P_{out}}{N} = 9.55 \times \dfrac{7.46 \times 10^3}{960} = \mathbf{74.2 \text{ N−m}}$

Example 21.17. *The full-load power input to a 3-phase induction motor is 50 kW and the slip is 3%. Neglecting stator losses, calculate (i) the full-load rotor Cu losses per phase and (ii) total mechanical power developed.*

Solution.

(i)   Rotor input = 50 kW   ...*Stator losses neglected*

Rotor Cu loss = s × rotor input = 0.03 × 50 = 1.5 kW

Rotor Cu loss/phase = 1.5/3 = **0.5 kW**

(ii) Total mechanical power developed is

$$P_m = 50 - 1.5 = 48.5 \text{ kW}$$

Example 21.18. *A 6-pole, 50 Hz, 3-phase induction motor runs at 960 r.p.m. when the torque on the shaft is 200 N-m. If the stator losses are 1500 W and friction and windage losses are 500 W, find (i) rotor Cu loss and (ii) efficiency of the motor.*

Solution.

$$N_s = 120 \, f/P = 120 \times 50/6 = 1000 \text{ r.p.m.}$$

$$s = \frac{N_s - N}{N_s} = \frac{1000 - 960}{1000} = 0.04$$

(i)   Rotor output, $P_{out} = \dfrac{2\pi N T_{sh}}{60} = \dfrac{2\pi \times 960 \times 200}{60} = 20096 \text{ W}$

Gross rotor output, $P_m = 20096 + 500 = 20596 \text{ W}$

$$\frac{\text{Rotor Cu loss}}{\text{Gross rotor output}} = \frac{s}{1 - s} \qquad \qquad \text{...See Art. 21.24}$$

∴   Rotor Cu loss $= \dfrac{0.04}{1 - 0.04} \times 20596 = \textbf{858 W}$

(ii)   Rotor input = Stator output = 20596 + 858 = 21454 W

Stator input, $P_i = 21454 + 1500 = 22954 \text{ W}$

∴   Efficiency $= \dfrac{P_{out}}{P_i} \times 100 = \dfrac{20096}{22954} \times 100 = \textbf{87.5\%}$

Example 21.19. *A 25 H.P., 6-pole, 50 Hz slip-ring induction motor runs at 960 r.p.m. on full-load with a rotor current of 35 A. Allowing 250 W for the copper loss in the short-circuiting gear and 1000 W for mechanical losses, find the resistance per phase of the 3-phase rotor winding.*

Solution.

Synchronous speed, $N_s = 120 \, f/P = 120 \times 50/6 = 1000 \text{ r.p.m.}$

Slip, $s = \dfrac{N_s - N}{N_s} = \dfrac{1000 - 960}{1000} = 0.04$

Useful output, $P_{out} = 25 \times 746 = 18650 \text{ W}$

Total mechanical output, $P_m = P_{out} + \text{Losses} = 18650 + 250 + 1000 = 19900 \text{ W}$

∴   Rotor Cu losses $= P_m \times \dfrac{s}{1-s} = 19900 \times \dfrac{0.04}{1 - 0.04} = 830 \text{ W}$

If R_2 is the rotor winding resistance per phase, then,

$$3I_2'^2 R_2 = 830 - \text{Losses in short-circuiting gear}$$

or $\qquad 3 \times (35)^2 \times R_2 = 830 - 250 = 580$

$\therefore \qquad R_2 = \dfrac{580}{3 \times (35)^2} = 0.158 \; \Omega/\text{phase}$

TUTORIAL PROBLEMS

1. A 3-phase, 6-pole, 50 Hz induction motor develops 3.68 kW at 950 r.p.m. If the stator losses are 300 W, find the stator input. [4.17 kW]

2. The power input to a 3-phase induction motor is 40 kW. The stator losses total 1 kW and the mechanical losses are 1.6 kW. Determine (*i*) shaft power (*ii*) rotor Cu loss and (*iii*) efficiency of the motor with a slip of 3.5%. [(*i*) 36 kW (*ii*) 445 W (*iii*) 90%]

3. An 8-pole, 3-phase, 50 Hz induction motor is taking 50 kW and running at 725 r.p.m. Stator losses are 1.2 kW and frictional losses 1.8 kW. Find (*i*) rotor Cu loss and (*ii*) efficiency of the motor. [(*i*) 1.627 kW (*ii*) 90.75%]

4. A 37.3 kW, 4-pole, 50 Hz induction motor has a friction and windage torque of 22 N-m. The stator losses equal rotor Cu loss. Calculate the power input to the stator when delivering full-load output at a speed of 1440 r.p.m. [44 kW]

5. A 50 Hz, 8-pole, 3-phase induction motor delivers an output of 3.1 kW at a slip of 0.02. The losses due to friction and windage are 100 W. Find the value of gross torque in N-m. [41.58 N-m]

21.25. METHODS OF STARTING SQUIRREL CAGE MOTORS

The following four methods are available for starting squirrel cage motors:

(*i*) **Direct on line starting.** This method of starting is just what the name implies—the motor is started by connecting it directly to 3-phase supply. The impedance of the motor at standstill is relatively low and when it is directly connected to the supply system, the starting current will be high (4 to 10 times the full-load current) and at a low power factor. Consequently, this method of starting is suitable for relatively small (upto 7.5 kW) machines.

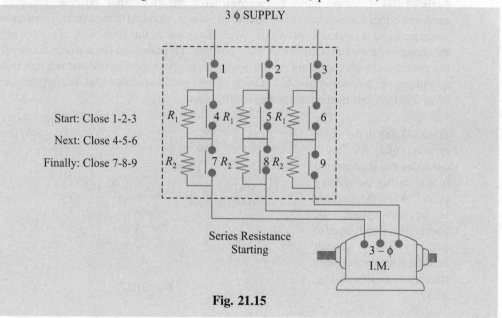

Fig. 21.15

(*ii*) **Stator resistance starting.** In this method, external resistances are connected in series with each phase of stator winding during starting. This causes voltage drop across the resistances so that voltage available across motor terminals is reduced and hence the starting current. The starting resistances are gradually cut out in steps (two or more steps) from the stator circuit as the motor picks up speed. When the motor attains rated speed, the resistances are completely cut out and full line voltage is applied to the motor.

This method suffers from two drawbacks. First, the reduced voltage applied to the motor during the starting period *lowers the starting torque and hence increases the accelerating time. Secondly, a lot of power is wasted in the starting resistances.

(*iii*) **Auto transformer starting.** This method also aims at connecting the induction motor to a reduced supply at starting and then connecting it to the full voltage as the motor picks up sufficient speed. Fig. 21.16 shows the circuit arrangement for autotransformer starting. The tapping on the autotransformer is so set that when it is in the circuit, 65% to 80% of line voltage is applied to the motor.

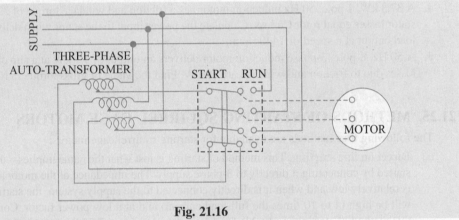

Fig. 21.16

At the instant of starting, the change-over switch is thrown to "start" position. This puts the autotransformer in the circuit and thus reduced voltage is applied to the circuit. Consequently, starting current is limited to safe value. When the motor attains about 80% of normal speed, the change-over switch is thrown to "run" position. This takes out the autotransformer from the circuit and puts the motor to full line voltage. Autotransformer starting has several advantages viz. low power loss, low starting current and less radiated heat. For large machines (over 25 H.P.), this method of starting is often used.

(*iv*) **Star-delta starting.** The stator winding of the motor is designed for delta operation and is connected in star during the starting period. When the machine is up to speed, the connections are changed to delta. The circuit arrangement for star-delta starting is shown in Fig. 21.17.

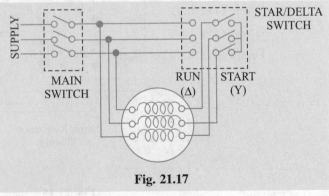

Fig. 21.17

---

* As shown in Art. 21.12, $T_s \propto V^2$ where V is the supply voltage.

The six leads of the stator windings are connected to the change-over switch as shown. At the instant of starting, the change-over switch is thrown to "start" position which connects the stator windings in star. Therefore, each stator phase gets $V/\sqrt{3}$ volts where V is the line voltage. This reduces the starting current. When the motor picks up speed, the change-over switch is thrown to "Run" position which connects the stator windings in delta. Now each stator phase gets full line voltage V. The disadvantages of this method are:

(a) With star-connection during starting, stator phase voltage is $1/\sqrt{3}$ times the line voltage. Consequently, starting torque is $(1/\sqrt{3})^2$ or 1/3 times the value it would have with Δ-connection. This is rather a large reduction in starting torque.

(b) The reduction in voltage is fixed.

This method of starting is used for medium-size machines (upto about 25 H.P.).

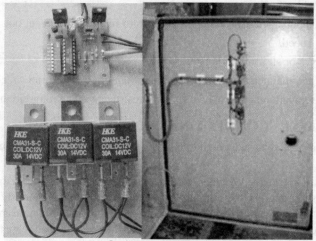

Star-delta starters

21.26. METHODS OF STARTING SLIP RING MOTORS

The following four methods are available for starting slip ring motors:

(i) Direct-on-line starting   (ii) Stator resistance starting

(iii) Auto-transformer starting   (iv) Rotor resistance starting

Methods (i) to (iii) have already been discussed and are equally applicable to slip ring motors. However, slip ring motors invariably employ rotor resistance starting. This gives low starting current and high starting torque.

Rotor resistance starting. In this method, a variable star-connected rheostat is connected in the rotor circuit through slip rings and full voltage is applied to the stator winding as shown in Fig. 21.18.

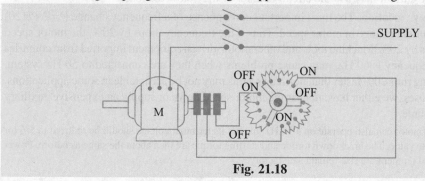

Fig. 21.18

(*i*) At starting, the handle of rheostat is set in the OFF position so that maximum resistance is placed in each phase of the rotor circuit. This reduces the starting current and at the same time starting torque is increased.

(*ii*) As the motor picks up speed, the handle of rheostat is gradually moved in clockwise direction and cuts out the external resistance in each phase of the rotor circuit. When the motor attains normal speed, the change-over switch is in the ON position and the whole external resistance is cut out from the rotor circuit.

21.27. SLIP-RING MOTORS VERSUS SQUIRREL CAGE MOTORS

The slip-ring induction motors have the following advantages over the squirrel cage motors:

(*i*) High starting torque with low starting current.

(*ii*) Smooth acceleration under heavy loads.

(*iii*) No abnormal heating during starting.

(*iv*) Good running characteristics after external rotor resistances are cut out.

(*v*) Adjustable speed.

The disadvantages of slip-ring motors are:

(*i*) The initial and maintenance costs are greater than those of squirrel cage motors.

(*ii*) The speed regulation is poor when run with resistance in the rotor circuit.

21.28. ABNORMAL CONDITIONS

There are a variety of abnormal conditions in the operation of a 3-phase induction motor. Some of them are:

(*i*) **Mechanical overload.** Although standard induction motors can develop twice their rated power for short periods, they should not be allowed to run continuously beyond their rated capacity. Overloads cause overheating which deteriorates the insulation and reduces its useful life. In practice, the higher motor current causes thermal overload relay to trip, bringing the motor to a stop before its temperature gets too high.

(*ii*) **Line voltage variations.** The torque of an induction motor at any speed is directly proportional to the square of the applied voltage. Thus, if the stator voltage decreases by 10%, the torque will drop by 20%. The voltage drop in the line is often produced during start-up due to the large starting current drawn from the line. On the other hand, if the line voltage is too high, the flux per pole will also be high. This increases both the iron losses and the magnetising current. As a result, the temperature increases slightly and the power factor is somewhat lowered.

(*iii*) **Single-phasing.** If one line of a 3-phase line is accidentally broken or if a fuse blows while the motor is running, the machine will continue to run as a single-phase motor. The current drawn from the remaining two lines will almost double and the motor will begin to overheat. This large current may trip the circuit breaker or may blow the fuses.

(*iv*) **Frequency variation.** The most important consequence of a frequency change ($f = NP/120$) is the resulting change in motor speed. Thus if the frequency drops by 20%, the motor speed also drops by 20%. Machine tools and other motor-driven equipment imported from countries where frequency is 60 Hz, may cause problems when they are connected to 50 Hz system. Everything runs 20% faster than normal and this may not be acceptable in some applications. In such cases, we either have to gear the motor speed down or supply an expensive auxiliary 50 Hz source.

Note: A 60 Hz motor can also operate on a 50 Hz line but its terminal voltage should be reduced to 5/6 (or 83%) of its nameplate value. The breakdown torque and starting torque are then about the same as before. Power factor, efficiency and temperature rise remain satisfactory.

21.29. INDUCTION MOTOR AND TRANSFORMER COMPARED

An induction motor may be considered to be a transformer with a rotating short-circuited secondary. The stator winding corresponds to transformer primary and rotor winding to transformer secondary. However, the following differences between the two are worth noting:

(*i*) Unlike a transformer, the magnetic circuit of a 3-phase induction motor has an air gap. Therefore, the magnetising current in a 3-phase induction motor is much larger than that of the transformer. For example, in an induction motor, it may be as high as 30 – 50% of rated current whereas it is only 1 – 5% of rated current in a transformer.

(*ii*) In an induction motor, there is an air gap and the stator and rotor windings are distributed along the periphery of the air gap rather than concentrated on a core as in a transformer. Therefore, the leakage reactances of stator and rotor windings are quite large compared to that of a transformer.

(*iii*) In an induction motor, the inputs to the stator and rotor are electrical but the output from the rotor is mechanical. However, in a transformer, input as well as output is electrical.

(*iv*) *The main difference between the induction motor and transformer lies in the fact that the rotor voltage and its frequency are both proportional to slip s.* If f is the stator frequency, E_2 is the per phase rotor e.m.f. at standstill and X_2 is the standstill rotor reactance/phase, then at any slip s, these values are:

$$\text{Rotor e.m.f./phase, } E_2' = s\,E_2$$
$$\text{Rotor reactance/phase, } X_2' = s\,X_2$$
$$\text{Rotor frequency, } f' = s\,f$$

MULTIPLE-CHOICE QUESTIONS

1. The stator of a 3-phase induction motor produces .... magnetic field.
    (*a*) steady
    (*b*) rotating
    (*c*) alternating
    (*d*) none of the above

2. An induction motor is preferred to a d.c. motor because it.........................
    (*a*) provides high starting torque
    (*b*) provides fine speed control
    (*c*) has simple and rugged construction
    (*d*) none of the above

3. A 3-phase induction motor is...................
    (*a*) essentially a constant-speed motor
    (*b*) a variable speed motor
    (*c*) very costly
    (*d*) not easily maintainable

4. If the frequency of 3-phase supply to the stator of a 3-phase induction motor is increased, then synchronous speed ....
    (*a*) is decreased
    (*b*) is increased
    (*c*) remains unchanged
    (*d*) none of the above

5. The synchronous speed of a 3-phase induction motor having 20 poles and connected to a 50

Hz source is ....
    (*a*) 600 r.p.m.
    (*b*) 1000 r.p.m.
    (*c*) 1200 r.p.m.
    (*d*) 300 r.p.m.

6. The relation among synchronous speed (N_s), rotor speed (N) and slip (s) is...............
    (*a*) $N = (s - 1)\,N_s$
    (*b*) $N = (1 - s)N_s$
    (*c*) $N = (1 + s)N_s$
    (*d*) $N = sN_s$

7. When the rotor of a 3-phase induction motor is blocked, the slip is ....
    (*a*) zero
    (*b*) 0.5
    (*c*) 0.1
    (*d*) 1

8. In Fig. 21.19, the rotor frequency is .... when the motor is at standstill.

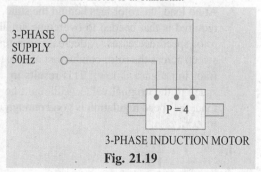

3-PHASE SUPPLY 50Hz

P = 4

3-PHASE INDUCTION MOTOR

Fig. 21.19

(a) zero   (b) 25 Hz
(c) 50 Hz   (d) none of the above

9. If a 4-pole induction motor has a synchronous speed of 1500 r.p.m., then supply frequency is ....
   (a) 50 Hz   (b) 25 Hz
   (c) 60 Hz   (d) none of the above

10. The rotor winding of a 3-phase wound rotor induction motor is generally .... connected.
    (a) star   (b) delta
    (c) partly star and partly delta
    (d) none of the above

11. A wound rotor motor is mainly used in applications where..............
    (a) high starting torque is required
    (b) speed control is required
    (c) less costly motor is not required
    (d) high rotor resistance is required during running

12. A 4-pole, 50 Hz induction motor operates at 5% slip. The frequency of e.m.f. induced in the rotor will be................
    (a) 25 Hz   (b) 50 Hz
    (c) 2.5 Hz   (d) none of the above

13. The reactance of the rotor circuit of a 3-phase induction motor is maximum at.............
    (a) no-load   (b) full-load
    (c) half full-load   (d) starting

14. The rotor current in a 3-phase induction motor is.................. slip.
    (a) inversely proportional to
    (b) directly proportional to
    (c) independent of   (d) none of the above

15. If the slip of a 3-phase induction motor increases, the p.f. of the rotor circuit............
    (a) is increased
    (b) is decreased
    (c) remains unchanged
    (d) none of the above

16. The starting torque of a 3-phase induction motor is............. supply voltage.
    (a) independent of
    (b) directly proportional to
    (c) directly proportional to square of
    (d) none of the above

17. The maximum torque of a 3-phase induction motor under running conditions is...........
    (a) inversely proportional to supply voltage
    (b) inversely proportional to rotor reactance at standstill
    (c) directly proportional to rotor resistance
    (d) none of the above

18. If N_s and N are the speeds of rotating field and rotor respectively, the ratio rotor input/rotor output is equal to.....................
    (a) N/N_s (b) N_s/N
    (c) $N_s - N$ (d) $N - N_s$

19. For higher efficiency of 3-phase induction motor, the slip should be.....................
    (a) large   (b) very large
    (c) as small as possible   (d) 1

20. If a 3-phase induction motor is running at a slip s (in decimal), then approximate efficiency of the motor is ....
    (a) s^2 (b) $1 + s$
    (c) $s - 1$ (d) $1 - s$

Answers to Multiple-Choice Questions

1. (b)	2. (c)	3. (a)	4. (b)	5. (d)	6. (b)	7. (d)	8. (c)
9. (a)	10. (a)	11. (a)	12. (c)	13. (d)	14. (b)	15. (b)	16. (c)
17. (b)	18. (b)	19. (c)	20. (d)				

Hints to Selected Multiple-Choice Questions

3. At no load, the rotor lags behind the stator flux by only a small amount since the only torque required is that needed to overcome small no-load losses. As mechanical load is added, the rotor speed decreases. A decrease in rotor speed allows the constant speed rotating field to sweep across the rotor conductors at a faster rate, thereby inducing larger rotor current (since rotor impedance is low). This results in a large increase in torque which tends to bring the speed to the original value. Although the motor speed does decrease slightly with increased load, the speed regulation is good enough that induction motor is classed as a **constant-speed motor**.

4. $$f = \frac{N_s P}{120}$$

It is clear that $f \propto N_s$ (synchronous speed).

5. $N_s = \dfrac{120 f}{P} = \dfrac{120 \times 50}{20} = 300$ r.p.m.

6. $s = \dfrac{N_s - N}{N_s} = \dfrac{N_s}{N_s} - \dfrac{N}{N_s} = 1 - \dfrac{N}{N_s}$

   $\therefore \quad N = (1 - s)N_s$

7. $s = \dfrac{N_s - N}{N_s}$

   When the rotor is blocked (i.e. rotor cannot rotate), $N = 0$ so that $s = N_s/N_s = 1$.

8. Rotor frequency, $f' = sf$ where f is supply frequency. At standstill, $s = 1$ so that $f' = f = 50$ Hz.

9. $f = \dfrac{N_s P}{120} = \dfrac{1500 \times 4}{120} = 50\,\text{Hz}$

10. So that additional external resistance may be inserted in the rotor circuit at starting to increase the starting torque and decrease the starting current. As the motor gains the speed, these external resistances are cut out of the rotor circuit.

11. At starting, the rotor frequency and reactance are high because $s = 1$. This means that at starting, rotor reactance is very large as compared to rotor resistance. Thus in the highly reactive rotor circuit, the rotor currents lag the rotor e.m.f. by a large angle. This results in high starting currents at low power factor which leads to a low value of starting torque.

    If the rotor circuit has high resistance, rotor p.f. and hence the starting characteristics will improve. This can be easily done in a wound rotor by inserting external resistances in the rotor circuit at the time of starting.

12. $$f' = sf$$

    where $\qquad f' = $ rotor frequency

    $\qquad\qquad f = $ supply frequency (i.e. 50 Hz)

    $\qquad\qquad s = $ decimal slip

    $\therefore \qquad\qquad f' = 0.05 \times 50 = 2.5$ Hz

13. $$X_2' = sX_2$$

    where $\qquad X_2' = $ rotor reactance at slip s

    $\qquad\qquad X_2 = $ rotor reactance at standstill

    Since $s = 1$ at starting, rotor reactance will be maximum under **starting** conditions.

14. $$I_2' = \dfrac{E_2'}{Z_2'} = \dfrac{sE_2}{\sqrt{R_2^2 + (sX_2)^2}}$$

    where $\qquad I_2' = $ rotor current per phase

    $\qquad\qquad E_2 = $ rotor e.m.f./phase at standstill

    $\qquad\qquad X_2 = $ rotor reactance/phase at standstill

    $\qquad\qquad R_2 = $ rotor resistance/phase

    At normal speed, close to synchronism, sX_2 is very small and may be neglected. Since E_2 and R_2 are fixed,

    $$I_2' \propto s$$

15. Rotor p.f., $\qquad\qquad \cos\phi_2' = \dfrac{R_2}{Z_2'}$

An increase in slip causes an increase in rotor frequency and hence the total reactance. This in turn increases the total impedance Z_2'. Since rotor resistance (R_2) is constant, rotor p.f. is **decreased**.

16. Starting torque,
$$T_s = \frac{KE_2^2 R_2}{R_2^2 + X_2^2} \qquad (\because s = 1)$$

Now $E_2 \propto V$, the supply voltage

$\therefore$
$$T_s = \frac{K_1 V^2 R_2}{R_2^2 + X_2^2}$$

or
$$T_s \propto V^2$$

17. The maximum torque (T_{max}) of a 3-phase induction motor is given by:
$$T_{max} = \frac{3}{2\pi N_s} \times \frac{E_2^2}{2X_2}$$

where
$$N_s = \text{synchronous speed}$$
$$E_2 = \text{rotor e.m.f./phase at standstill}$$
$$X_2 = \text{rotor reactance/phase at standstill}$$

It is clear that $T_{max} \propto \dfrac{1}{X_2}$

18.
$$\frac{\text{Rotor output}}{\text{Rotor input}} = 1 - s = 1 - (N_s - N/N_s) = N/N_s$$

$\therefore$
$$\frac{\text{Rotor input}}{\text{Rotor output}} = \frac{N_s}{N}$$

19. Approximate efficiency $= 1 - s$
where s = decimal slip
It is clear that for higher efficiency of 3-phase induction motor, the slip should be **as small as possible**.

20. Turn ratio,
$$k = \frac{\text{Turns per phase on stator}}{\text{Turns per phase on rotor}}$$

Neglecting stator losses, power transferred to the rotor is given by:
$$P_r = \sqrt{3} E_s I_s \cos \phi_s$$
where E_s, I_s and cos ϕ_s represent respectively the voltage, current and power factor of stator.
Rotor induced voltage at slip $s = sE_s/k$
Rotor current $= kI_s$
The stator and rotor power factors are approximately the same (say cos ϕ).

$$\text{Rotor losses} = \sqrt{3}\, \frac{sE_s}{k}\, kI_s \cos \phi = \sqrt{3}\, s\, E_s I_s \cos \phi$$

$$\text{Efficiency} = \frac{\text{Input} - \text{Loss}}{\text{Input}}$$

$$= \frac{\sqrt{3}\, E_s I_s \cos \phi - \sqrt{3}\, E_s I_s\, s \cos \phi}{\sqrt{3}\, E_s I_s \cos \phi}$$

$$= 1 - s \qquad \qquad \dots(i)$$

Since the stator losses are neglected, the actual efficiency is less than that given by eq. (i).

22

Single-Phase Motors

INTRODUCTION

As the name suggests, these motors are used on single-phase supply. Single-phase motors are the most familiar of all electric motors because they are extensively used in home appliances, shops, offices, *etc.* It is true that single-phase motors are less efficient substitute for 3-phase motors but 3-phase power is normally not available except in large commercial and industrial establishments. Since electric power was originally generated and distributed for lighting only, millions of homes were given single-phase supply. This led to the development of single-phase motors. Even where 3-phase mains are present, the single-phase supply may be obtained by using one of the three lines and the neutral. In this chapter, we shall focus our attention on the construction, working and characteristics of commonly used single-phase motors.

22.1. TYPES OF SINGLE-PHASE MOTORS

Single-phase motors are generally built in the fractional-horse power range and may be classified into the following four basic types :

1. **Single-phase induction motors**

   (*i*) Split-phase type (*ii*) Capacitor type
   (*iii*) Shaded-pole type

2. **A.C. series motors or universal motors**
3. **Repulsion motors**
   (*i*) Repulsion-start induction-run motor   (*ii*) Repulsion-induction motor
4. **Synchronous motors**
   (*i*) Reluctance motor   (*ii*) Hysteresis motor

22.2. SINGLE-PHASE INDUCTION MOTORS

A single phase induction motor is very similar to a 3-phase squirrel cage induction motor. It has (*i*) a squirrel-cage rotor identical to a 3-phase motor, and (*ii*) a single-phase winding on the stator.

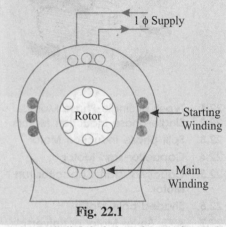

Fig. 22.1

Unlike a 3-phase induction motor, a single-phase induction motor is not self-starting but requires some starting means. The single-phase stator winding produces a magnetic field that pulsates in strength in a sinusoidal manner. The field polarity reverses after each half cycle *but the field does not rotate*. Consequently, the alternating flux cannot produce rotation in a stationary squirrel-cage rotor. However, if the rotor of a single-phase motor is rotated in one direction by some mechanical means, it will continue to run in the direction of rotation. As a matter of fact, the rotor quickly accelerates until it reaches a speed slightly below the synchronous speed. Once the motor is running at this speed, it will continue to rotate even though single-phase current is flowing through the staor winding. This method of starting is generally not convenient for large motors. Nor can it be employed for a motor located at some inaccessible spot.

Making self-starting. To make a single-phase induction motor self-staring, we should somehow produce a revolving stator magnetic field. This may be achieved by converting a single-phase supply into two phase supply through the use of an additional winding. When the motor attains sufficient speed, the starting means (*i.e.*, additional winding) may be removed depending upon the type of the motor. As a matter of fact, single-phase induction motors are classified and named according to the method employed to make them self-starting.

   (*i*) *Split-phase motors*—started by two-phase motor action through the use of an auxiliary or starting winding.
   (*ii*) *Capacitor motors*—started by two-phase motor action through the use of an auxiliary winding and a capacitor.
   (*iii*) *Shaded-pole motors*— started by the motion of the magnetic field produced by means of a shading coil around a portion of the pole structure.

22.3. SPLIT-PHASE INDUCTION MOTOR

The stator of a split-phase induction motor is provided with an auxiliary or starting winding *S* in addition to the main or running winding *M*. The starting winding is located 90° electrical from the main winding [See Fig. 22.2 (*i*)] and operates only during the brief period when the motor starts up. The two windings are so *designed that the starting winding *S* has a high resistance and relatively small reactance while the main winding *M* has relatively low resistance and large reactance as shown in the schematic connections in Fig. 22·2 (*ii*). Consequently, the currents flowing in the two windings have reasonable phase difference α (25° to 30°) as shown in the phasor diagram in Fig. 22.2 (*iii*).

---

* This can be done by having main winding of large diameter and number of turns while starting winding of a fine wire of a small number of turns.

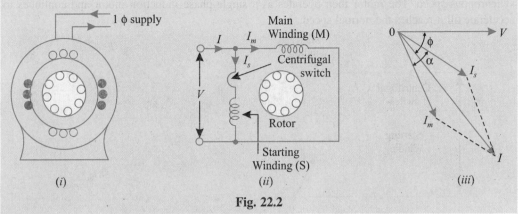

Fig. 22.2

Operation.

(i) When the two stator windings are energised from a single-phase supply, the main winding carries current I_m while the starting winding carries current I_s.

(ii) Since main winding is made highly inductive while the starting winding highly resistive, the currents I_m and I_s have a reasonable phase angle α (25° to 30°) between them as shown in Fig. 22·2 (iii). Consequently, a weak revolving field approximating to that of a 2-phase machine is produced which starts the motor. The starting torque is given by;

$$T_s = k\, I_m\, I_s \sin \alpha$$

where k is a constant whose magnitude depends upon the design of the motor.

(iii) When the motor reaches about 75% of synchronous speed, the centrifugal switch opens the circuit of the starting winding. The motor then operates as a single-phase induction motor and continues to accelerate till it reaches the normal speed. The normal speed of the motor is below the synchronous speed and depends upon the load on the motor.

Characteristics

(i) The starting torque is 1.5 to 2 times the full-load torque and the starting current is 6 to 8 times the full-load current.

(ii) Due to their low cost, split-phase induction motors are most popular single-phase motors in the market.

(iii) Since the starting winding is made of fine wire, the current density is high and the winding heats up quickly. If the starting period exceeds 5 seconds, the winding may burn out unless the motor is protected by built-in-thermal relay. This motor is, therefore, suitable where starting periods are not frequent.

(iv) These motors are suitable where a moderate starting torque is required and where starting periods are infrequent e.g., to drive:

    (a) fans   (b) washing machines   (c) oil burners   (d) small machine tools, etc.

The power rating of such motors generally lies between 60W and 250W.

22.4. CAPACITOR-START MOTOR

The capacitor-start motor is identical to a split-phase motor except that the starting winding has as many turns as the main winding. Moreover, a capacitor C is connected in series with the starting winding as shown in Fig. 22.3. (i). The value of capacitor is so chosen that I_s leads I_m by about 80° (i.e., $\alpha \simeq 80°$) which is considerably greater than 25° found in split-phase motor [See Fig. 22·3 (ii)]. Consequently, starting torque ($T_s = kI_mI_s \sin \alpha$) is much more than that of a split-phase motor. Again, the starting winding is opened by the centrifugal switch when the motor attains about 75% of synchronous speed. The motor then operates as a single-phase induction motor and continues to accelerate till it reaches the normal speed.

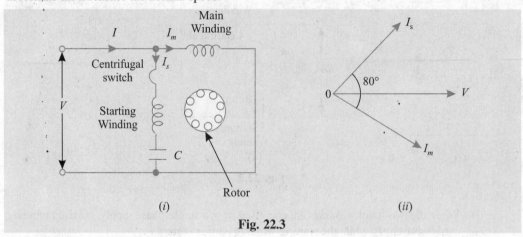

Fig. 22.3

Characteristics

(i) Although starting characteristics of a capacitor-start motor are better than those of a split-phase motor, both machines possess the same running characteristics because the main windings are identical.

(ii) The phase angle between the two currents is about 80° compared to about 25° in a split-phase motor. Consequently, for the same starting torque, the current in the starting winding is only about half that in a split-phase motor. Therefore, the starting winding of a capacitor-start motor heats up less quickly and is well suited to applications involving either frequent or prolonged starting periods.

(iii) Capacitor-start motors are used where high starting torque is required and where the starting period may be long *e.g.*, to drive

    (a) compressors   (b) large fans   (c) pumps   (d) high inertia loads

The power rating of such motors lies between 120W and 7·5 kW.

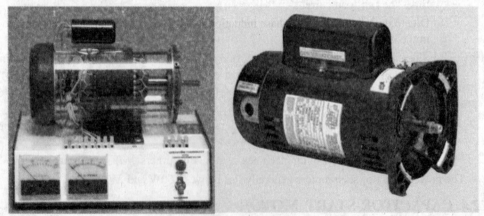

Capacitor start Motors

22.5. CAPACITOR-START CAPACITOR-RUN MOTOR

This motor is identical to a capacitor-start motor except that starting winding is not opened after starting so that both the windings remain connected to the supply when running as well as at starting. Two designs are generally used.

(*i*) In one design, a single capacitor *C* is used for both starting and running as shown in Fig. 22.4 (*i*). This design eliminates the need of a centrifugal switch and at the same time improves the power factor and efficiency of the motor.

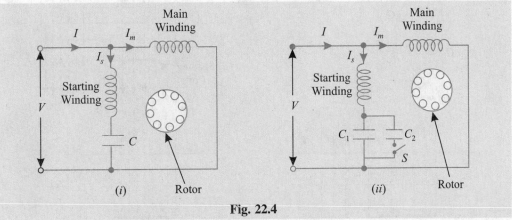

Fig. 22.4

(*ii*) In the other design, two capacitors C_1 and C_2 are used in the starting winding as shown in Fig. 22.4 (*ii*). The smaller capacitor C_1 required for optimum running conditions is permanently connected in series with the starting winding. The much larger capacitor C_2 is connected in parallel with C_1 for optimum starting and remains in the circuit during starting. The starting capacitor C_2 is disconnected when the motor approaches about 75% of synchronous speed. The motor then runs as a single-phase induction motor.

Characteristics

(*i*) The starting winding and the capacitor can be designed for perfect 2-phase operation at any load. The motor then produces a constant torque and not a pulsating torque as in other single-phase motors.

(*ii*) Because of constant torque, the motor is vibration free and can be used in:

(*a*) hospitals   (*b*) studios   and   (*c*) other places where silence is important.

22.6. SHADED-POLE MOTOR

The shaded-pole motor is very popular for ratings below 0.05 H.P. (≃ 40 W) because of its extremely simple construction. It has salient poles on the stator excited by single-phase supply and a squirrel-cage rotor as shown in Fig. 22.5. A portion of each pole is surrounded by a short-circuited turn of copper strip called *shading coil*.

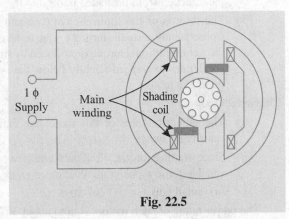

Fig. 22.5

Operation. The operation of the motor can be understood by referring to Fig. 22.6 which shows one pole of the motor with a shading coil.

(*i*) During the portion *OA* of the alternating-current cycle [See Fig. 22.6 (*i*)], the flux begins to increase and an e.m.f. is induced in the shading coil. The resulting current in the shading coil will be in such a direction (Lenz's law) so as to oppose the change in flux. Thus the flux in the shaded portion of the pole is weakened while that in the unshaded portion is strengthened as shown in Fig. 22.6 (*ii*).

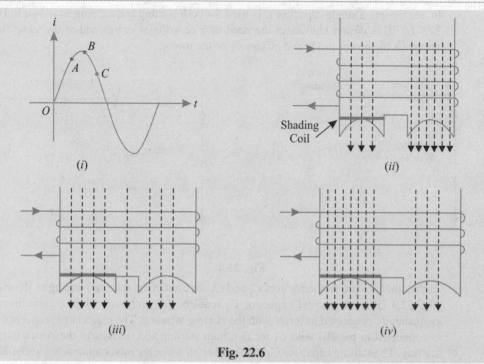

Fig. 22.6

(ii) During the portion AB of the alternating-current cycle, the flux has reached almost maximum value and is not changing. Consequently, the flux distribution across the pole is uniform [See Fig. 22.6 (iii)] since no current is flowing in the shading coil. As the flux decreases (portion BC of the alternating current cycle), current is induced in the shading coil so as to oppose the decrease in current. Thus the flux in the shaded portion of the pole is strengthened while that in the unshaded portion is weakened as shown in Fig. 22.6 (iv).

(iii) The effect of the shading coil is to cause the field flux to shift across the pole face from the unshaded to the shaded portion. This shifting flux is like a rotating weak field moving in the direction from unshaded portion to the shaded portion of the pole.

(iv) The rotor is of the squirrel-cage type and is under the influence of this rotating field. Consequently, a small starting torque is developed. As soon as this torque starts to revolve the rotor, additional torque is produced by single-phase induction-motor action. The motor accelerates to a speed slightly below the synchronous speed and runs as a single-phase induction motor.

Characteristics

(i) The salient features of this motor are extremely simple construction and absence of centrifugal switch.

(ii) Since starting torque, efficiency and power factor are very low, these motors are only suitable for low power applications *e.g.*, to drive

(a) small fans   (b) toys   (c) hair driers   (d) desk fans, *etc*.

The power rating of such motors is upto about 30W.

Example 22.1. *A 4-pole, 50Hz, single-phase induction motor is running with a slip of 3.4%. Calculate the speed of the motor.*

Solution.

Synchronous speed, $N_s = 120\,f/P = 120 \times 50/4 = 1500$ r.p.m.

Motor speed, $N = (1 - s)N_s = (1 - 0.034)\,1500 = \mathbf{1449}$ **r.p.m.**

Example 22.2 *At starting, the windings of a 230V, 50Hz, split-phase induction motor have the following parameters:*

Main winding:	$R = 4\Omega$;	$X_L = 7.5\Omega$
Starting winding:	$R = 7.5\Omega$;	$X_L = 4\Omega$

Find (i) current I_m in the main winding (ii) current I_s in the starting winding (iii) phase angle between I_s and I_m (iv) line current and (v) power factor of the motor.

Solution.

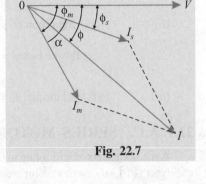

(i)
$$I_m = \frac{V}{Z_m} = \frac{230}{\sqrt{4^2 + (7.5)^2}} = 27A$$

$$\phi_m = \tan^{-1} 7.5/4 = 62°$$

(ii)
$$I_s = \frac{V}{Z_s} = \frac{230}{\sqrt{(7.5)^2 + 4^2}} = 27A$$

$$\phi_s = \tan^{-1} 4/7.5 = 28°$$

(iii) Phase angle between I_s and I_m

$$\alpha = \phi_m - \phi_s = 62° - 28° = 34°$$

Fig. 22.7

(iv) Line current,
$$I = \sqrt{(I_s)^2 + (I_m)^2 + 2\,I_s\,I_m \cos\alpha}$$

$$= \sqrt{(27)^2 + (27)^2 + 2 \times 27 \times 27 \times \cos 34°} = \textbf{51.6 A}$$

(v) Resolving the currents along *OX*-axis, we get,

$$I\cos\phi = I_s \cos\phi_s + I_m \cos\phi_m$$

∴   Motor p.f., $\cos\phi = \dfrac{27\cos 28° + 27\cos 62°}{I} = \dfrac{36.51}{51.6} = \textbf{0.7}\,lag$

Example 22.3. *A 200 W, 230 V, 50 Hz capacitor-start motor has the following winding constants:*

Main winding :	$R = 4.5\ \Omega$;	$X_L = 3.7\ \Omega$
Starting winding:	$R = 9.5\ \Omega$;	$X_L = 3.5\ \Omega$

Find the value of starting capacitance that will result in the maximum starting torque.

Solution. Fig. 22.8 shows the phasor diagram of the motor. The current I_s in the starting winding leads the applied voltage V by ϕ_s while the current I_m in the main winding lags V by ϕ_m. The starting torque will be maximum when phase angle α between I_s and I_m is 90°.

$$\phi_m = \tan^{-1} 3.7/4.5 = 39.6°$$

$$\phi_s = 39.6° - 90° = -50.4°$$

Let *C* farad be the capacitance of the starting capacitor to give maximum starting torque.

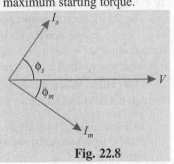

$$\tan(-50.4°) = \frac{3.5 - X_C}{9.5}$$

or
$$-1.21 = \frac{3.5 - X_C}{9.5}$$

or
$$X_C = 15\ \Omega$$

∴
$$C = \frac{1}{2\pi f\, X_C} = \frac{1}{2\pi \times 50 \times 15}$$

$$= 212 \times 10^{-6}F = \textbf{212 μF}$$

Fig. 22.8

Example 22.4. *A 4-pole, 250W, 115V, 60Hz capacitor-start induction motor takes a full load line current of 5.3A while running at 1760 r.p.m. If the full-load efficiency of the motor is 64%, find (i) motor slip (ii) power factor and (iii) full-load torque.*

Solution.

(*i*) $$N_s = 120f/P = 120 \times 60/4 = 1800 \text{ r.p.m.}$$

$$\therefore \qquad s = \frac{N_s - N}{N_s} = \frac{1800 - 1760}{1800} = 0.022$$

(*ii*) $$\text{Input power} = 250/0.64 = 390.6 \text{ W}$$

$$\text{Power factor} = \frac{390.6}{115 \times 5.3} = 0.64 \text{ } lag$$

(*iii*) $$\text{Full-load torque, } T = 9.55 \frac{P_{out}}{N} = 9.55 \frac{250}{1760} = 1.35 \text{ N-m}$$

22.7. A.C. SERIES MOTOR OR UNIVERSAL MOTOR

A d.c. series motor will rotate in the *same direction regardless of the polarity of the supply. One can expect that a d.c. series motor would also operate on a single-phase supply. It is then called an a.c. series motor. However, some changes must be made in a d.c. motor that is to operate satisfactorily on a.c. supply. The changes effected are :

(*i*) The entire magnetic circuit is laminated in order to reduce the eddy current loss. Hence an a.c. series motor requires a more expensive construction than a d.c. series motor.

(*ii*) The series field winding uses as few turns as possible to reduce the reactance of the field winding to a minimum. This reduces the voltage drop across the field winding.

(*iii*) A high field flux is obtained by using a low-reluctance magnetic circuit.

(*iv*) There is considerable sparking between the brushes and the commutator when the motor is used on a.c. supply. It is because the alternating flux establishes high currents in the coils short-circuited by the brushes. When the short-circuited coils break contact from the commutator, excessive sparking is produced. This can be eliminated by using high-resistance leads to connect the coils to the commutator segments.

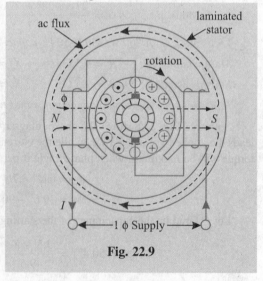

Fig. 22.9

Construction. The construction of an a.c. series motor is very similar to a d.c. series motor except that above modifications are incorporated (See Fig. 22.9). Such a motor can be operated either on a.c. or d.c. supply and the resulting torque-speed curve is about the same in each case. For this reason, it is sometimes called a *universal motor*.

Operation. When the motor is connected to an a.c. supply, the same alternating current flows through the field and armature windings. The field winding produces an alternating flux ϕ that reacts

---
* In a series motor, both armature and field windings are in series. Since the armature current and flux reverse simultaneously, the torque always acts in the same direction regardless of the polarity of the supply.

with the current flowing in the armature to produce a torque. Since both armature current and flux reverse simultaneously, the torque always acts in the same direction. It may be noted that no rotating flux is produced in this type of machines; the principle of operation is the same as that of a d.c. series motor.

Characteristics. The operating characteristics of an a.c. series motor are similar to those of a d.c. series motor.

(*i*)   The speed increases to a high value with a decrease in load. In very small series motors, the losses are usually large enough at no load that limit the speed to a *definite value (1500—15,000 r.p.m.).

(*ii*) The motor torque is high for large armature currents, thus giving a high starting torque.

(*iii*) At full-load, the power factor is about 90%. However, at starting or when carrying an overload, the power factor is lower.

Applications. The fractional horsepower a.c. series motors have high-speed (and corresponding small size) and large starting torque. They can, therefore, be used to drive

(*a*) high-speed vacuum cleaners   (*b*)   sewing machines

(*c*) electric shavers   (*d*)   drills   (*e*)   machine tools *etc.*

22.8. SINGLE-PHASE REPULSION MOTOR

A repulsion motor is similar to an a.c. series motor except that :

(*i*)   brushes are not connected to supply but are short-circuited [See Fig. 22.10]. Consequently, currents are induced in the armature conductors by **transformer action.

(*ii*) the field structure has non-salient pole construction.

By adjusting the position of short-circuited brushes on the commutator, the starting torque can be developed in the motor.

Principle of operation. The principle of operation is illustrated in Fig. 22.10 which shows a two-pole repulsion motor with its two short-circuited brushes. The two drawings of Fig. 22.10 represent a time at which the field current is *increasing* in the direction shown so that the left-hand pole is *N*-pole and the right-hand pole is *S*-pole at the instant shown.

(*i*)   In Fig. 22.10 (*i*), the brush axis is parallel to the stator field. When the stator winding is energised from single-phase supply, e.m.f. is induced in the armature conductors (rotor) by induction. By Lenz's law, the direction of the e.m.f. is such that the magnetic effect of the resulting armature currents will oppose the increase in flux. The direction of current in armature conductors will be as shown in Fig. 22.10 (*i*). With the brush axis in the position shown in Fig. 22.10 (*i*), current will flow from brush *B* to brush *A* where it enters the armature and flows back to brush *B* through the two paths *ACB* and *ADB*. With brushes set in this position, half of the armature conductors under the *N*-pole carry current inward and half carry current outward. The same is true under *S*-pole. Therefore, as much torque is developed in one direction as in the other and the armature remains stationary. The armature will also remain stationary if the brush axis is perpendicular to the stator field axis. It is because even then net torque is zero.

---

*   However, in a d.c. series motor, the speed at no load may rise to a dangerously high value.

**   In an a.c. series motor, the field and armature windings are conductively coupled *i.e.*, the armature current is obtained by conduction from the supply. However, in a repulsion motor, the armature currents are obtained by induction *i.e.*, transformer action.

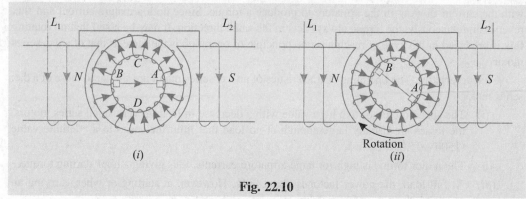

Fig. 22.10

(ii) If the brush axis is at some angle other than 0° or 90° to the axis of the stator field, a net torque is developed on the rotor and the rotor accelerates to its final speed. Fig. 22.10 (*ii*) represents the motor at the same instant as that in Fig. 22.10 (*i*) but the brushes have been shifted clockwise through some angle from the stator field axis. Now e.m.f. is still induced in the direction indicated in Fig. 22.10 (*i*) and current flows through the two paths of the armature winding from brush *A* to brush *B*. However, because of the new brush positions, the greater part of the conductors under the *N*-pole carry current in one direction while the lesser part of conductors under *S*-pole carry current in the opposite direction. With brushes in the position shown in Fig. 22.10 (*ii*), torque is developed in the clockwise direction and the rotor quickly attains the final speed.

(iii) The direction of rotation of the rotor depends upon the direction in which the brushes are shifted. If the brushes are shifted in clockwise direction from the stator field axis, the net torque acts in the clockwise direction and the rotor accelerates in the clockwise direction. If the brushes are shifted in anti-clockwise direction as in Fig. 22.11, the armature current under the pole faces is reversed and the net torque is developed in the anti-clockwise direction. Thus a repulsion motor may be made to rotate

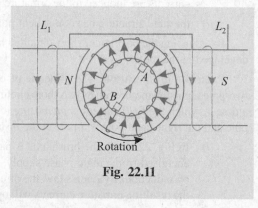

Fig. 22.11

in either direction depending upon the direction in which the brushes are shifted.

(iv) The total armature torque in a repulsion motor can be shown to be:

$$T_a \propto \sin 2\alpha$$

where α = angle between brush axis and stator field axis

For maximum torque, $2\alpha = 90°$ or $\alpha = 45°$

Thus adjusting α to 45° at starting, maximum torque can be obtained during the starting period. However, α has to be adjusted to give a suitable running speed.

Characteristics

(i) The repulsion motor has characteristics very similar to those of an a.c. series motor *i.e.*, it has a high starting torque and a high speed at no load.

(*ii*) The speed which the repulsion motor develops for any given load will depend upon the *position of the brushes.

(*iii*) In comparison with other single-phase motors, the repulsion motor has a high starting torque and relatively low starting current.

22.9. REPULSION-START INDUCTION-RUN MOTOR

Sometimes the action of a repulsion motor is combined with that of a single-phase induction motor to produce repulsion-start induction-run motor (also called repulsion-start motor). The machine is started as a repulsion motor with a corresponding high starting torque. At some predetermined speed, a centrifugal device short-circuits the commutator so that the machine then operates as a single-phase induction motor.

The repulsion-start induction-run motor has the same general construction of a repulsion motor. The only difference is that in addition to the basic repulsion-motor construction, it is equipped with a centrifugal device fitted on the armature shaft. When the motor reaches 75% of its full running speed, the centrifugal device forces a short-circuiting ring to come in contact with the inner surface of the commutator. This short-circuits all the commutator bars. The rotor then resembles squirrel-cage type and the motor runs as a single-phase induction motor. At the same time, the centrifugal device raises the brushes from the commutator which reduces the wear of the brushes and commutator as well as makes the operation quiet.

Characteristics

(*i*) The starting torque is 2.5 to 4.5 times the full-load torque and the starting current is 3.75 times the full-load value.

(*ii*) Due to their high starting torque, repulsion-motors were used to operate devices such as refrigerators, pumps, compressors, *etc.*

However, they posed a serious problem of maintenance of brushes, commutator and the centrifugal device. Consequently, manufacturers have stopped making them in view of the development of capacitor motors which are small in size, reliable and low-priced.

22.10. REPULSION-INDUCTION MOTOR

The repulsion-induction motor produces a high starting torque entirely due to repulsion motor action. When running, it functions through a combination of induction motor and repulsion motor action.

Construction. Fig. 22.12 shows the connections of a 4-pole repulsion-induction motor for 230V operation. It consists of a stator and a rotor (or armature).

(*i*) The **stator** carries a single distributed winding fed from single-phase supply.

(*ii*) The **rotor** is provided with two independent windings placed one inside the other. The inner winding is a squirrel-cage winding with rotor bars permanently short-circuited. Placed over the squirrel cage winding is a repulsion commutator armature winding. The repulsion winding is connected to a commutator on which ride short-circuited brushes. There is no centrifugal device and the repulsion winding functions at all times.

---

* Shifting the brush position has the same effect as changing the number of turns of the series winding of an a.c. series motor *i.e.*, speed of the motor is affected.

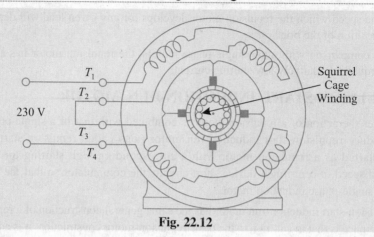

Fig. 22.12

Operation.

(*i*) When single-phase supply is given to the stator winding, the repulsion winding (*i.e.*, outer winding) is *active. Consequently, the motor starts as a repulsion motor with a corresponding high starting torque.

(*ii*) As the motor speed increases, the current shifts from the outer to inner winding due to the decreasing impedance of the inner winding with increasing speed. Consequently, at running speed, the squirrel cage winding carries the greater part of rotor current. This shifting of repulsion-motor action to induction-motor action is thus achieved without any switching arrangement.

(*iii*) It may be seen that the motor starts as a repulsion motor. When running, it functions through a combination of principle of induction and repulsion; the former being predominant.

Characteristics

(*i*) The no-load speed of a repulsion-induction motor is somewhat above the synchronous speed because of the effect of repulsion winding. However, the speed at full-load is slightly less than the synchronous speed as in an induction motor.

(*ii*) The speed regulation of the motor is about 6%.

(*iii*) The starting torque is 2.25 to 3 times the full-load torque; the lower value being for large motors. The starting current is 3 to 4 times the full-load current.

This type of motor is used for applications requiring a high starting torque with essentially a constant running speed. The common sizes are 0.25 to 5 H.P.

22.11. SINGLE-PHASE SYNCHRONOUS MOTORS

Very small single-phase motors have been developed which run at true synchronous speed. They do not require d.c. excitation for the rotor. Because of these characteristics, they are called *unexcited single-phase synchronous motors.* The most commonly used types are:

(*i*) Reluctance motors　　　　(*ii*) Hysteresis motors

The efficiency and torque-developing ability of these motors is low. The output of most of the commercial motors is only a few watts.

- -

* The inner winding (*i.e.*, squirrel cage winding), being nearly surrounded by iron, has a high inductance. At starting, rotor frequency is equal to the supply frequency and the impedance of the outer winding is less than that of the inner winding. This results in a large proportion of rotor current flowing in the outer winding.

22.12. RELUCTANCE MOTOR

It is a single-phase synchronous motor which does not require d.c. excitation to the rotor. Its operation is based upon the following principle:

Whenever a piece of ferromagnetic material is located in a magnetic field, a force is exerted on the material, tending to align the material so that reluctance of the magnetic path that passes through the material is minimum.

Construction. A reluctance motor (also called synchronous reluctance motor) consists of :

- (*i*) a **stator** carrying a single-phase winding along with an auxiliary winding to produce a synchronously-revolving magnetic field.

- (*ii*) a **squirrel-cage rotor** having unsymmetrical magnetic construction. This is achieved by symmetrically removing some of the teeth from the squirrel-cage rotor to produce salient poles on the rotor. As shown in Fig. 22.13 (*i*), 4 salient poles have been produced on the rotor. The salient poles created on the rotor must be equal to the poles on the stator.

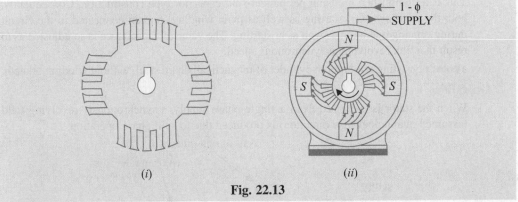

(*i*)   (*ii*)

Fig. 22.13

Note that rotor salient poles offer low reluctance to the stator flux and, therefore, become strongly magnetised.

Operation.

- (*i*) When single-phase stator having an auxiliary winding is energised, a synchronously-revolving field is produced. The motor starts as a standard squirrel-cage induction motor and will accelerate to near its synchronous speed.

- (*ii*) As the rotor approaches synchronous speed, the rotating stator flux will exert **reluctance torque* on the rotor poles tending to align the salient-pole axis with the axis of the rotating field. The rotor assumes a position where its salient poles lock with the poles of the revolving field [See Fig. 22.13 (*ii*)]. Consequently, the motor will continue to run at the speed of revolving flux *i.e.*, at the synchronous speed.

- (*iii*) When we apply a mechanical load, the rotor poles fall slightly behind the stator poles, while continuing to turn at synchronous speed. As the load on the motor is increased, the mechanical angle between the poles increases progressively. Nevertheless, magnetic attraction keeps the rotor locked to the rotating flux. If the load is increased beyond the amount under which the reluctance torque can maintain synchronous speed, the rotor drops out of step with the revolving field. The speed , then, drops to some value at which the slip is sufficient to develop the necessary torque to drive the load by induction-motor action.

* *

*   The reluctance torque arises from the tendency of the rotor to align itself in the minimum reluctance position *w.r.t.* the synchronously-revolving stator flux.

Characteristics

(*i*)   These motors have poor torque, power factor and efficiency.

(*ii*)   These motors cannot accelerate high-inertia loads to synchronous speed.

(*iii*)   The pull-in and pull-out torques of such motors are weak.

Despite the above drawbacks, the reluctance motor is cheaper than any other type of synchronous motor. They are widely used for constant-speed applications such as timing devices, signalling devices, *etc*.

22.13. HYSTERESIS MOTOR

It is a single-phase motor whose operation depends upon the hysteresis effect *i.e.*, magnetisation produced in a ferromagnetic material lags behind the magnetising force.

Construction. It consists of :

(*i*)   a **stator** designed to produce a synchronously-revolving field from a single-phase supply. This is accomplished by using permanent-split capacitor type construction. Consequently, both the windings (*i.e.*, starting as well as main winding) remain connected in the circuit during running operation as well as at starting. The value of capacitance is so adjusted as to result in a flux revolving at synchronous speed.

(*ii*)   a **rotor** consisting of a smooth cylinder of magnetically hard steel, without winding or teeth.

Operation.

(*i*)   When the stator is energised from a single-phase supply, a synchronously-revolving field (assumed in anticlockwise direction) is produced due to split phase operation.

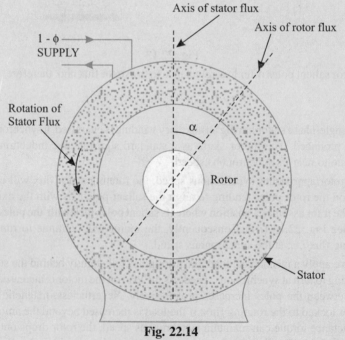

Fig. 22.14

(*ii*)   The revolving stator flux magnetises the rotor. Due to hysteresis effect, the axis of magnetisation of rotor will lag behind the axis of stator field by hysteresis lag angle α as shown in Fig. 22.14. If the rotor is stationary, the starting torque produced is given by;

$$T_s \propto \phi_s \, \phi_r \sin \alpha$$

where ϕ_s = stator flux

ϕ_r = rotor flux

From now onwards, the rotor accelerates to synchronous speed with a *uniform torque.

(*iii*) After reaching synchronism, the motor continues to run at synchronous speed and adjusts its torque angle so as to develop the torque required by the load.

Characteristics

(*i*) A hysteresis motor can synchronise any load which it can accelerate, no matter how great the inertia. It is because the torque is uniform from standstill to synchronous speed.

(*ii*) Since the rotor has no teeth or salient poles or winding, a hysteresis motor is inherently quiet and produces smooth rotation of the load.

(*iii*) The rotor takes on the same number of poles as the stator field. Thus by changing the number of stator poles through pole-changing connections, we can get a set of synchronous speeds for the motor.

Applications. Due to their quiet operation and ability to drive high-inertia loads, hysteresis motors are particularly well suited for driving (*i*) electric clocks (*ii*) timing devices (*iii*) tape-decks (*iv*) turn-tables and other precision audio-equipment.

Stator pole

Reluctance Motors

MULTIPLE-CHOICE QUESTIONS

1. A single-phase induction motor employs .... rotor.

    (*a*) squirrel cage   (*b*) wound

    (*c*) either squirrel cage or wound

    (*d*) none of the above

2. For the same rating, the size of a single-phase induction motor is about............. that of the corresponding 3-phase induction motor.

    (*a*) 3 times   (*b*) the same as

    (*c*) 1.5 times   (*d*) 0.33 times

3. For the same rating, the p.f. of a single-phase induction motor is..........that of 3-phase induction motor.

    (*a*) the same as   (*b*) less than

    (*c*) more than   (*d*) none of the above

4. For the same rating, the efficiency of a single-phase induction motor is........ that of 3-phase induction motor.

    (*a*) less than   (*b*) the same as

    (*c*) more than   (*d*) none of the above

*   Now ϕ_s and ϕ_r are constant. When the rotor accelerates, the lag angle α remains constant since the angle α depends merely upon the hysteresis loop of the rotor and is independent of the rate at which the loop is traversed. The motor, therefore, develops constant torque from standstill to synchronous speed.

5. Most of single-phase induction motors are .... machines.
   (a) 2-pole   (b) 6-pole
   (c) 8-pole   (d) 4-pole

6. The main winding and starting winding of a single-phase induction motor are connected in............across the supply.
   (a) series   (b) parallel
   (c) series-parallel
   (d) none of the above

7. The starting winding of a single-phase induction motor has............that of main winding.
   (a) more poles than
   (b) less poles than
   (c) same number of poles as
   (d) none of the above

8. A 50 Hz, 4-pole single-phase induction motor will have a synchronous speed of......
   (a) 1500 r.p.m.   (b) 750 r.p.m.
   (c) 1200 r.p.m.
   (d) none of the above

9. A 4-pole, 50 Hz single-phase induction motor has a slip of 5%. The speed of the motor will be...........
   (a) 1500 r.p.m.   (b) 1425 r.p.m.
   (c) 1200 r.p.m.
   (d) none of the above

10. The purpose of starting winding in a single phase induction motor is to.............
    (a) reduce losses
    (b) limit temperature rise of the machine
    (c) produce rotating flux in conjunction with main winding
    (d) none of the above

11. In the resistance split-phase induction motor shown in Fig. 22.15, the main winding has.........
    (a) high resistance and high inductance
    (b) high resistance and low inductance
    (c) low resistance and high inductance
    (d) low resistance and low inductance

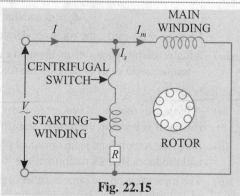

Fig. 22.15

12. At starting, the current I_s in the starting winding shown in Fig. 22.15...........
    (a) lags V by 90°   (b) leads V by 90°
    (c) is nearly in phase with V
    (d) leads V by 75°

13. In the capacitor start induction motor shown in Fig. 22.16, the angle α between I_m and I_s is ....
    (a) exactly 90°   (b) about 30°
    (c) about 40°   (d) about 75°

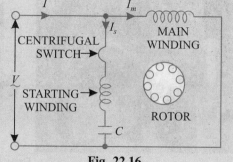

Fig. 22.16

14. The value of current I_s in capacitor-start motor shown in Fig. 22.16 is ..... the current I_m.
    (a) equal to
    (b) less than that of
    (c) more than that of
    (d) none of the above

15. The capacitor C used in the capacitor-start motor shown in Fig. 22.16 is always a ..... capacitor.
    (a) paper   (b) ceramic
    (c) mica   (d) electrolytic

Answers to Multiple-Choice Questions

1. (a)	**2.** (c)	**3.** (b)	**4.** (a)	**5.** (d)	**6.** (b)	**7.** (c)	**8.** (a)
9. (b)	**10.** (c)	**11.** (c)	**12.** (c)	**13.** (d)	**14.** (b)	**15.** (d)	

Hints to Selected Multiple-Choice Questions

1. Structurally, a single phase induction motor resembles the 3-phase squirrel cage motor except that the stator winding is a single phase winding.

7. The stator of a single phase induction motor carries the *main winding* which creates a set of N-S poles. It also carries a small *starting winding* that only operates during the brief period when the motor starts up. The starting winding has the **same number of poles as** the main winding has.

8.
$$N_s = \frac{120\,f}{P} = \frac{120 \times 50}{4} = 1500\,\text{r.p.m.}$$

9.
$$N_s = \frac{120\,f}{P} = \frac{120 \times 50}{4} = 1500\,\text{r.p.m.}$$

$$s = \frac{N_s - N}{N_s} \times 100 \quad \text{or} \quad 5 = \frac{1500 - N}{1500} \times 100$$

$$\therefore \qquad N = 1425\ \text{r.p.m.}$$

10. If a single-phase induction motor has main winding on the stator only, it will not be self-starting. To produce starting torque, we must somehow create a revolving field. This is done by placing an additional auxiliary winding on the stator. Both main and auxiliary windings (also called starting winding) are connected in parallel across the single-phase supply. The currents in the two windings have a phase difference and hence produce a weak revolving field.

11. The main winding of a resistance split-phase motor:

    (*i*) is always made of relatively large wire to reduce I^2R losses.

    (*ii*) has a relatively large number of turns.

    Due to these reasons, the main winding has **low resistance and high inductance**.

12. The starting winding of a resistance split-phase induction motor has a relatively small number of turns of fine wire. Consequently, the starting winding has high resistance and low inductance. The result is that at starting, the current I_s in the starting winding **is nearly in phase with the applied voltage V**.

13. The capacitor C is so chosen that current I_s in the starting winding leads the current I_m in the main winding by **about 75°**.

14. In a capacitor-start motor, the starting winding has about as many turns as the main winding. Furthermore, a capacitor is connected in series with the starting winding. For this reason, the value of I_s is **less than I_m** at starting.

15. Because these capacitors are available in small size and are quite reliable. Moreover, they are also not expensive.

Alternators

INTRODUCTION

A.C. system has a number of advantages over d.c. system. These days 3-phase a.c. system is being exclusively used for generation, transmission and distribution of power. The machine which produces 3-phase power from mechanical power is called an alternator or synchronous generator. Alternators are the primary source of all the electrical energy we consume. These machines are the largest energy converters found in the world. They convert mechanical energy into a.c. energy. In this chapter, we shall discuss the construction and characteristics of alternators.

23.1. ALTERNATOR

An alternator operates on the same fundamental principle of electromagnetic induction as a d.c. generator *i.e.*, when the flux linking a conductor changes, an e.m.f. is induced in the conductor. Like a d.c. generator, an alternator also has an armature winding and a field winding. But there is one important difference between the two. In a d.c. generator, the armature winding is placed on the rotor in order to provide a way of converting alternating voltage generated in the winding to a direct voltage at the terminals through the use of a rotating commutator. The field poles are placed on the stationary part of the machine. Since no commutator is required in an alternator, it is usually more convenient and advantageous to place the field winding on the rotating part (*i.e.*, rotor) and armature winding on the stationary part (*i.e.*, stator).

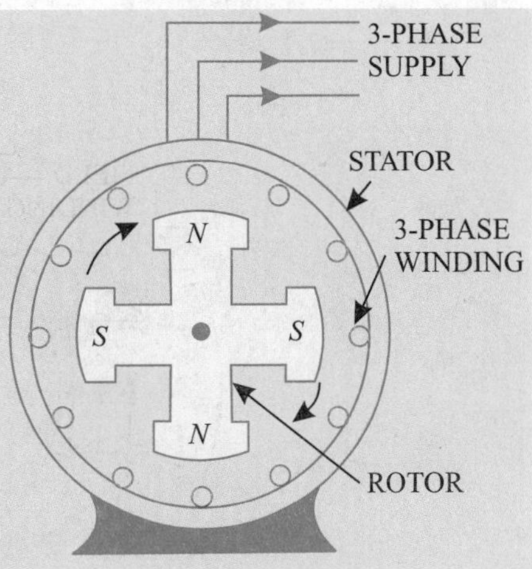

Advantages of stationary armature. The field winding of an alternator is placed on the rotor and is connected to d.c. supply through two slip rings. The 3-phase armature winding is placed on the stator. This arrangement has the following advantages:

Fig. 23.1

(*i*) It is easier to insulate stationary winding for high voltages for which the alternators are usually designed. It is because they are not subjected to centrifugal forces and also extra space is available due to the stationary arrangement of the armature.

(*ii*) The stationary 3-phase armature can be directly connected to load without going through large, unrealiable slip rings and brushes.

(*iii*) Only two slip rings are required for d.c. supply to the field winding on the rotor. Since the exciting current is small, the slip rings and brush gear required are of light construction.

(*iv*) Due to simple and robust construction of the rotor, higher speed of rotating d.c. field is possible. This increases the output obtainable from a machine of given dimensions.

Note: All alternators above 5 kVA employ a stationary armature (or stator) and a revolving d.c. field.

23.2. CONSTRUCTION OF ALTERNATOR

An alternator has 3-phase winding on the stator and a d.c. field winding on the rotor.

1. Stator. It is the stationary part of the machine and is built up of sheet-steel laminations having slots on its inner periphery. A 3-phase winding is placed in these slots and serves as the armature winding of the alternator. The armature winding is always connected in *star and the neutral is connected to **ground.

2. Rotor. The rotor carries a field winding which is supplied with direct current through two slip rings by a separate d.c. source. This d.c. source (called exciter) is generally a small d.c. shunt or compound generator mounted on the shaft of the alternator. Rotor construction is of two types, namely;

(*i*) Salient (or projecting) pole type

(*ii*) Non-salient (or cylindrical) pole type

(*i*) **Salient pole type.** In this type, salient or projecting poles are mounted on a large circular steel frame which is fixed to the shaft of the alternator as shown in Fig. 23.2. The individual field pole windings are connected in series in such a way that when the field winding is energised by the d.c. exciter, adjacent poles have opposite polarities.

---

*   In star connection, phase voltage $V_{ph} = V_L / \sqrt{3}$. Since the induced e.m.f. in the phase winding of an alternator is directly proportional to the number of turns, a star-connected alternator will require less number of turns than a delta-connected alternator for the same line voltage.

**   This permits to use protective devices (*e.g.*, relays) to protect the system in case of ground faults.

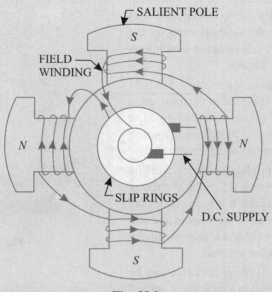

Fig. 23.2

Low and medium-speed alternators (120-400 r.p.m.) such as those driven by diesel engines or water turbines have salient pole type rotors due to the following reasons:

(*a*) The salient field poles would cause an excessive windage loss if driven at high speed and would tend to produce noise.

(*b*) Salient-pole construction cannot be made strong enough to withstand the mechanical stresses to which they may be subjected at higher speeds.

Since a frequency of 50 Hz is required, we must use a *large number of poles on the rotor of slow-speed alternators. Low-speed rotors always posses a large diameter to provide the necessary space for the poles. Consequently, salient-pole type rotors have large diameters and short axial lengths.

(*ii*) **Non-salient pole type.** In this type, the rotor is made of smooth solid forged-steel radial cylinder having a number of slots along the outer periphery. The field windings are embedded in these slots and are connected in series to the slip rings through which they are energised by the d.c. exciter. The regions forming the poles are usually left unslotted as shown in Fig. 23.3. It is clear that the poles formed are non-salient *i.e.*, they do not project out from the rotor surface.

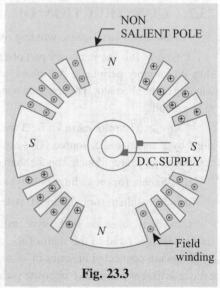

Fig. 23.3

High-speed alternators (1500 or 3000 r.p.m.) are driven by steam turbines and use non-salient type rotors due to the following reasons:

(*a*) This type of construction has mechanical robustness and gives noiseless operation at high speeds.

---

* $f = NP/120$

(*b*) The flux distribution around the periphery is nearly a sine wave and hence a better e.m.f. waveform is obtained than in the case of salient-pole type.

Since steam turbines run at high speed and a frequency of 50 Hz is required, we need a small number of poles on the rotor of high-speed alternators (also called turboalternators). We can use no less than 2 poles and this fixes the highest possible speed. For a frequency of 50 Hz, it is 3000 r.p.m. The next lower speed is 1500 r.p.m. for a 4-pole machine. Consequently, turboalternators possess 2 or 4 poles and have *small diameters and very long axial lengths.

23.3. ALTERNATOR OPERATION

The rotor winding is energised from the d.c. exciter and alternate *N* and *S* poles are developed on the rotor. When the rotor is rotated in anticlockwise direction by a prime mover, the stator or armature conductors are cut by the magnetic flux of rotor poles. Consequently, e.m.f. is induced in the armature conductors due to electromagnetic induction. The induced e.m.f. is alternating since *N* and *S* poles of rotor alternately pass the armature conductors. The direction of induced e.m.f. can be found by Fleming's right hand rule and frequency is given by;

$$f = \frac{NP}{120}$$ ...See Art. 23.4

where N = speed of rotor in r.p.m.

P = number of rotor poles

Fig. 23.4 (*i*) shows star-connected armature winding and d.c. field winding. When the rotor is rotated, a 3-phase voltage is induced in the armature winding. The magnitude of induced e.m.f. depends upon the speed of rotation and the d.c. exciting current. The magnitude of e.m.f. in each phase of the armature winding is the same. However, they differ in phase by 120° electrical as shown in the phasor diagram in Fig. 23.4 (*ii*).

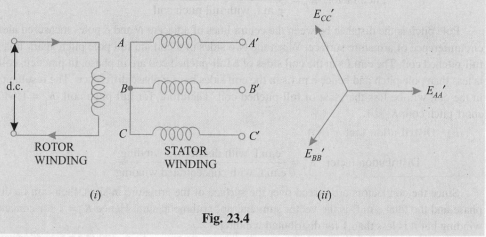

Fig. 23.4

23.4. FREQUENCY

The frequency of induced e.m.f. in the armature conductors depends upon speed and the number of poles.

Let N = rotor speed in r.p.m.

P = number of rotor poles

f = frequency of e.m.f. in Hz

---

*   The high speed of rotation produces strong centrifugal forces which impose an upper limit on the diameter. On the other hand, to build powerful alternators, we have to use massive rotors. Therefore, high-power and high-speed rotors have to be very long.

Consider a stator conductor that is successively swept by the N and S poles of the rotor. If a *positive* voltage is induced when a N-pole sweeps across the conductor, a similar *negative* voltage is induced when a S-pole sweeps by. This means that *one complete cycle* of e.m.f. is generated in the conductor as a pair of poles passes it *i.e.*, one N-pole and the adjacent following S-pole. The same is true for every other armature conductor.

∴   No. of cycles/revolution = No. of pairs of poles = P/2

No of revolutions/second = N/60

∴   No. of cycles/second = *(P/2) (N/60) = NP/120

But number of cycles of e.m.f. per second is its frequency.

$$\therefore \qquad f = \frac{NP}{120}$$

It may be noted that N is the synchronous speed. For a given alternator, the number of rotor poles is fixed and, therefore, the alternator must be run at synchronous speed to give an output of desired frequency. For this reason, an alternator is sometimes called *synchronous generator.*

23.5. PITCH FACTOR AND DISTRIBUTION FACTOR

The armature winding of an alternator is distributed over the entire armature. The distributed winding produces nearly a sine waveform and the heating is more uniform. Likewise, the coils of armature winding are not full-pitched *i.e.*, the two sides of a coil are not at corresponding points under adjacent poles. The fractional pitched armature winding requires less copper per coil and at the same time waveform of output voltage is improved.

   (*i*)   **Pitch factor (K_p)**

$$\text{Pitch factor, } K_p = \frac{\text{e.m.f. with short-pitch coil}}{\text{e.m.f. with full-pitch coil}}$$

Pole pitch is the distance between the centre lines of adjacent N and S poles measured along the circumference of armature surface. When the two sides of a coil are full pole pitch apart, it is called full-pitched coil. The e.m.f.s in the coil sides of a full-pitched coil are in phase. In practice, coil pitch is less than pole pitch and hence e.m.f.s in the coil sides have a phase difference. The resultant e.m.f. in the coil will be less than that of full-pitched coil. Therefore, for full-pitch coil, $K_p = 1$ while for short-pitch coil, $K_p < 1$.

   (*ii*)   **Distribution factor (K_d)**

$$\text{Distribution factor, } K_d = \frac{\text{e.m.f. with distributed winding}}{\text{e.m.f. with concentrated winding}}$$

Since the conductors are spread over the surface of the armature in slots, their e.m.f.s differ in phase and the total e.m.f. is the vector sum and not arithmetic sum. Hence $K_d = 1$ for concentrated winding but it is less than 1 for distributed winding.

23.6. E.M.F. EQUATION OF AN ALTERNATOR

Let   Z = No. of conductors or coil sides in series *per phase*

φ = Flux per pole in webers

P = Number of rotor poles

N = Rotor speed in r.p.m.

---

*   No. of cycle/second = No. of cycles/revolution × No. of revolutions/second.

In one revolution (*i.e.*, 60/N second), each stator conductor is cut by $P\phi$ webers *i.e.*,

$$d\phi = P\phi \; ; \; dt = 60/N$$

∴ Average e.m.f. induced in one stator conductor

$$= \frac{d\phi}{dt} = \frac{P\phi}{60/N} = \frac{P\phi N}{60} \text{ volts}$$

Since there are Z conductors in series per phase,

∴ Average e.m.f./phase $= \dfrac{P\phi N}{60} \times Z$

$$= \frac{P\phi Z}{60} \times \frac{120 f}{P} \qquad\qquad \left(\because N = \frac{120 f}{P}\right)$$

$$= 2 f \phi Z \text{ volts}$$

R.M.S. value of e.m.f./phase = Average value/phase × form factor

$$= 2 f \phi Z \times 1.11 = 2.22 f \phi Z \text{ volts}$$

∴ $E_{\text{r.m.s.}}$/phase $= 2.22 f \phi Z$ volts ...(i)

If K_p and K_d are the pitch factor and distribution factor of the armature winding, then,

$$E_{\text{r.m.s.}}\text{/phase} = 2.22 \, K_p K_d Z f \phi \text{ volts} \qquad\qquad (ii)$$

Example 23.1. *A 3-phase, 50 Hz, star-connected alternator has 180 conductors per phase and flux per pole is 0.0543 Wb. Find (i) e.m.f. generated per phase and (ii) e.m.f. between line terminals. Assume the winding to be full pitched and distribution factor to be 0.96.*

Solution.

(*i*) Generated e.m.f./phase, $\quad E_{ph} = 2.22 \, K_p K_d Z f \phi$

$$= 2.22 \times 1 \times 0.96 \times 180 \times 50 \times 0.0543 = 1041.5 \text{ V}$$

(*ii*) Line voltage, $\quad E_L = \sqrt{3} \, E_{ph} = \sqrt{3} \times 1041.5 = 1803.19 \text{ V}$

Example 23.2. *Find the number of armature conductors in series per phase required for the armature of a 3-phase, 50Hz, 10-pole alternator. The winding is star-connected to give a line voltage of 11000 V. The flux per pole is 0.16 Wb. Assume $K_p = 1$ and $K_d = 0.96$.*

Solution.

Generated e.m.f./phase, $\quad E_{ph} = E_L/\sqrt{3} = 11000/\sqrt{3} = 6352 \text{ V}$

Let Z be the number of conductors in series per phase.

$$E_{ph} = 2.22 \, K_p K_d Z f \phi$$

∴ $\quad Z = \dfrac{E_{ph}}{2.22 \, K_p \, K_d \, f \phi} = \dfrac{6352}{2.22 \times 1 \times 0.96 \times 50 \times 0.16} = 372.5$

Example 23.3. *The armature of an 8-pole, 3-phase, 50Hz alternator has 18 slots and 10 conductors/slot. A flux of 0.04 Wb is entering the armature from one pole. Calculate the induced e.m.f. per phase.*

Solution. Since the values of K_p and K_d are not given, they will be assumed 1.

Total no. of conductors $\quad = 18 \times 10 = 180$

No. of conductors/phase, $\quad Z = 180/3 = 60$

Induced e.m.f./phase, $\quad E_{ph} = 2.22 \, K_p K_d Z f \phi$

$$= 2.22 \times 1 \times 1 \times 60 \times 50 \times 0.04 = 266.4 \text{ V}$$

Example 23.4. *A 3-phase, star-connected alternator on open circuit is required to generate a line voltage of 3600V at 50Hz when driven at 500 r.p.m. The stator has 3 slots per pole per phase and 10 conductors per slot. Calculate (i) the number of poles and (ii) useful flux per pole. Assume all the conductors per phase to be connected in series and the coils to be full-pitched with $K_d = 0.96$.*

Solution.

(i)
$$f = \frac{N_s P}{120}$$

or
$$50 = \frac{500 \times P}{120} \qquad \therefore \qquad P = 12$$

(ii) No. of slots/phase $= 3 \times 12 = 36$

No. of conductors/phase, $Z = 36 \times 10 = 360$

E.M.F./phase, $\qquad E_{ph} = \dfrac{3600}{\sqrt{3}} = 2080$ V

Distribution factor, $\qquad K_d = 0.96$

Pitch factor, $\qquad K_p = 1 \qquad\qquad$ ...for full pitch

Induced e.m.f./phase, $\qquad E_{ph} = 2.22\, K_p K_d Z f\, \phi$

or $\qquad 2080 = 2.22 \times 1 \times 0.96 \times 360 \times 50 \times \phi$

$\therefore \qquad \phi = 0.0543$ **Wb**

23.7. ALTERNATOR ON NO LOAD

When the rotor is rotating and energised, the circuit diagram for an alternator with its stator circuit open (*i.e.*, no load condition) is as shown in Fig. 23.5 (*i*). Each phase generates an e.m.f. *E*. The per phase armature resistance and leakage reactance are R_a and X_L respectively.

It is clear from the e.m.f. equation (See Art. 23.6) that the generated e.m.f. *E* in an alternator depends upon speed and flux per pole. Since most of the alternators are operated at constant speed, the generated e.m.f. would depend upon field excitation. By including a rheostat in the field circuit, the field excitation and hence generated e.m.f. can be changed. It is always convenient to analyse an alternator on single-phase basis; the conditions in the other two phases being similar. Fig 23.5 (*ii*), shows one phase of the alternator. It is clear that at no load, terminal voltage *V* per phase is equal to the generated e.m.f. *E* per phase *i.e.*

$$V = E \qquad\qquad ....at\ no\ load$$

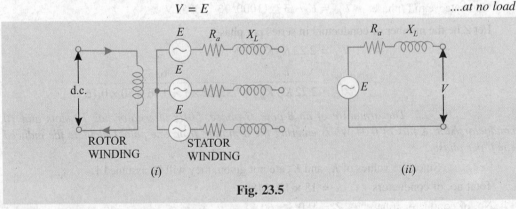

Fig. 23.5

23.8. ALTERNATOR ON LOAD

When load on an alternator changes, the terminal voltage *V* also changes. The change in *V* is due to the following three effects:

(*i*) voltage drop in armature resistance R_a

(*ii*) voltage drop in armature leakage reactance X_L

(*iii*) voltage drop due to armature reaction

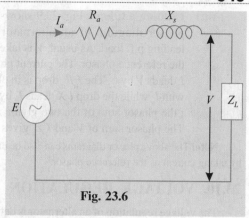

The voltage drop due to armature*reaction is accounted for by assuming a fictitious reactance X_a in the armature winding. The phasor sum of X_L and X_a gives *synchronous reactance* X_s. The per phase equivalent circuit of an alternator on load can be represented as shown in Fig. 23.6.

Synchronous impedance/phase,

$$Z_s = \sqrt{R_a^2 + X_s^2}$$

Fig. 23.6

If V is the terminal voltage/phase and E is the generated e.m.f./phase, then,

$$E = V + I_a (R_a + jX_s) = V + I_a Z_s$$

Note: The value of X_s is 10 to 100 times greater than R_a. Consequently, we can neglect R_a without any serious error.

23.9. PHASOR DIAGRAM OF A LOADED ALTERNATOR

Let
$$E = \text{no-load e.m.f./phase}$$
$$V = \text{terminal voltage/phase}$$
$$I_a = \text{armature current/phase}$$
$$Z_a = \text{synchronous impedance/phase}$$
$$\phi = \text{load p.f. angle}$$

(*i*) **Unity p.f. load.** Fig. 23.7 shows the phasor diagram of an alternator for unity p.f. load. Here V is taken as the reference phasor. The current phasor I_a is in phase with V. The voltage drop $I_a R_a$ is in phase with I_a while the voltage drop $I_a X_s$ leads I_a by 90°; the phasor sum of the two giving $I_a Z_s$. The phasor sum of V and $I_a Z_s$ gives E.

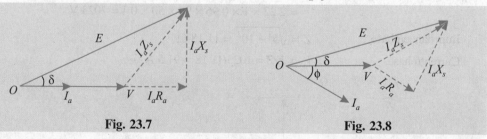

Fig. 23.7   **Fig. 23.8**

(*ii*) **Lagging p.f. load.** Here again V is taken as the reference phasor. The current phasor I_a lags V by ϕ. The $I_a R_a$ drop is in phase with I_a while the drop $I_a X_s$ leads I_a by 90°; the phasor sum of the two giving $I_a Z_s$. The phasor sum of V and $I_a Z_s$ gives E [See Fig. 23.8].

* At no load, only flux ϕ_F due to field excitation exists in the machine. However, when the alternator is loaded, the armature current also produces flux ϕ_A. The action of ϕ_A on ϕ_F is called armature reaction. The actual flux ϕ in a loaded alternator is the phasor sum of ϕ_F and ϕ_A. With lagging power factor loads which usually exist with alternators, the effect of armature reaction is to reduce the resultant flux ϕ and hence the generated e.m.f. The armature reaction effect is accounted for by assuming a fictitious reactance X_a in the armature winding.

(iii) **Leading p.f. load.** Fig. 23.9 shows the phasor diagram of an alternator for leading p.f. load. As usual, V is taken as the reference phasor. The current phasor I_a leads V by ϕ. The $I_a R_a$ drop is in phase with I_a while the drop $I_a X_s$ leads I_a by 90° ; the phasor sum of the two giving $I_a Z_s$. The phasor sum of V and $I_a Z_s$ gives E.

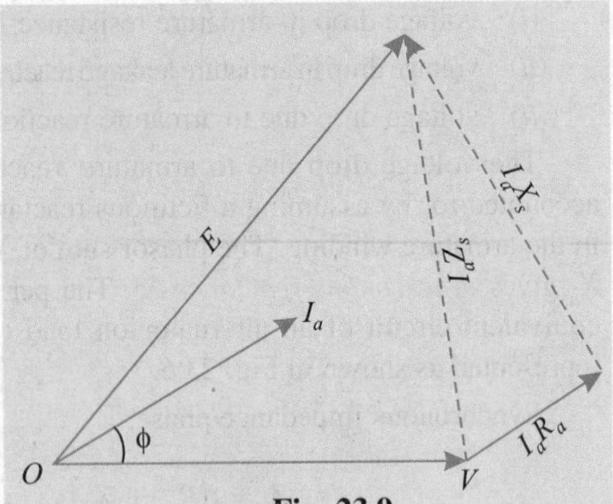

Note: The above phasor diagrams can also be drawn by taking current as the reference phasor.

Fig. 23.9

23.10. VOLTAGE REGULATION

The voltage regulation of an alternator is defined as the percentage rise in terminal voltage when full-load is removed *i.e.*,

$$\% \text{ age voltage regulation} = \frac{E - V}{V} \times 100$$

where

E = no–load voltage per phase

V = full–load voltage per phase

Its value depends upon load current and load power factor.

Example 23.5. *A 3-phase, star-connected, 50Hz alternator has 96 conductors per phase and a flux/pole 0.1 Wb. The alternator winding has a synchronous reactance of 5Ω/phase and negligible resistance. The distribution factor for the stator winding is 0.96.*

Calculate the terminal voltage when three non-inductive resistors, of 10Ω/phase, are connected in star across the terminals.

Solution. Fig. 23.10 *(i)* shows the equivalent circuit for one phase while Fig. 23.10 *(ii)* shows its phasor diagram.

Generated e.m.f./phase, $\quad E = 2.22\, K_P\, K_d\, Z f \phi$
$$= 2.22 \times 1 \times 0.96 \times 96 \times 50 \times 0.1 = 1023 \text{ V}$$

Impedance/phase, $\quad Z = \sqrt{5^2 + 10^2} = 11.18\ \Omega$

Current/phase, $\quad I_a = E/Z = 1023/11.18 = 91.5 \text{ A}$

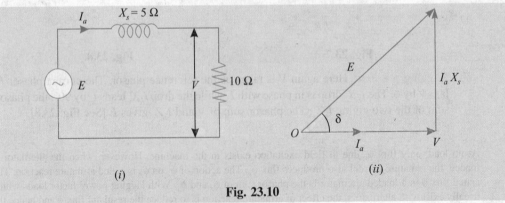

Fig. 23.10

As seen in phasor diagram in Fig. 23.10 *(ii)*,

Terminal voltage/phase, $\quad V = \sqrt{E^2 - (I_a X_s)^2}$

$$= \sqrt{(1023)^2 - (91.5 \times 5)^2} = 915 \, \text{V}$$

Terminal line voltage $\quad = \sqrt{3} \times 915 = \mathbf{1585 \, V}$

Example 23.6. *A 1500 kVA, 6.6kV, 3-phase, star-connected alternator has a resistance of 0.5Ω/ phase and a synchronous reactance of 5Ω/phase. Find its voltage regulation for (i) unity p.f. (ii) 0.8 lagging p.f. and (iii) 0.8 leading p.f.*

Solution.

Line current, $\qquad\qquad I_L = \dfrac{1500 \times 10^3}{\sqrt{3} \times 6600} = 131 \text{A}$

Armature current/phase, $\quad I_a = I_L = 131 \text{A}$

Voltage/phase, $\qquad\qquad V = 6600/\sqrt{3} = 3810 \text{ V}$

$\qquad\qquad\qquad\qquad I_a R_a = 131 \times 0.5 = 65.5 \text{ V}$

$\qquad\qquad\qquad\qquad I_a X_s = 131 \times 5 = 655 \text{ V}$

(*i*) **Unity p.f.** In drawing the phasor diagram for unity p.f. (See fig. 23.11), voltage has been taken as the reference phasor.

$$E = \sqrt{(V + I_a R_a)^2 + (I_a X_s)^2}$$

$$= \sqrt{(3810 + 65.5)^2 + (655)^2} = 3930 \text{ V}$$

$\therefore \quad$ % age voltage regulation $= \dfrac{3930 - 3810}{3810} \times 100 = \mathbf{3.15\%}$

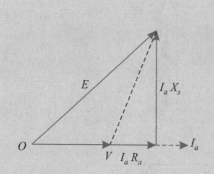

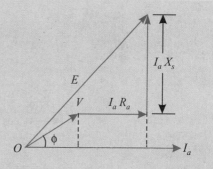

Fig. 23.11	**Fig. 23.12**

(*ii*) **0.8 p.f.. lagging.** In drawing the phasor diagram for 0.8 p.f. lagging (See Fig. 23.12), current has been taken as the reference phasor.

$$\cos \phi = 0.8; \quad \sin \phi = 0.6$$

$$E = \sqrt{(V \cos \phi + I_a R_a)^2 + (V \sin \phi + I_a X_s)^2}$$

$$= \sqrt{(3810 \times 0.8 + 65.5)^2 + (3810 \times 0.6 + 655)^2} = 4283 \text{ V}$$

$\therefore$ % age voltage regulation $= \dfrac{4283 - 3810}{3810} \times 100 = \mathbf{12.4\%}$

(*iii*) **0.8 p.f. leading.** Fig. 23.13 shows the phasor diagram for 0.8 p.f. leading. Note that current has been taken as the reference phasor.

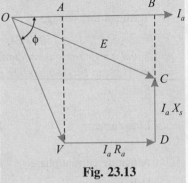

$$OB = OA + AB = V \cos \phi + I_a R_a$$
$$BC = BD - CD = V \sin \phi - I_a X_s$$

In right angled triangle *OBC*,

$$E = \sqrt{(OB)^2 + (BC)^2}$$

$$= \sqrt{(V \cos \phi + I_a R_a)^2 + (V \sin \phi - I_a X_s)^2}$$

$$= \sqrt{(3810 \times 0.8 + 65.5)^2 + (3810 \times 0.6 - 655)^2} = 3515\,V$$

$$\therefore \% \text{age voltage regulation} = \frac{3515 - 3810}{3810} \times 100 = -7.7\%$$

Fig. 23.13

Example 23.7. *A 500 kVA, 3-phase, star-connected alternator has a rated line-to-line voltage of 3300 V. The resistance and synchronous reactance per phase are 0.3 Ω and 4 Ω respectively. Calculate the line value of the e.m.f. generated at full load, 0.8 p.f. lagging.*

Solution.

F.L. output current, $\quad I_a = \dfrac{500 \times 10^3}{\sqrt{3} \times 3300} = 87.5\,A$

Fig. 23.14 shows the phasor diagram of the alternator. Note that current I_a has been taken as the reference phasor. From the phasor diagram, we have,

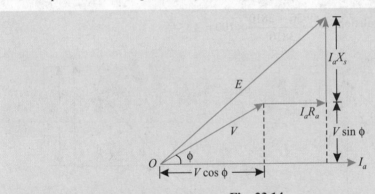

Fig. 23.14

$$E = \sqrt{(V \cos \phi + I_a R_a)^2 + (V \sin \phi + I_a X_s)^2}$$

Now $\quad\quad\quad \cos \phi = 0.8 \quad \therefore \quad \sin \phi = 0.6$

$$I_a R_a \text{ drop} = 87.5 \times 0.3 = 26.25 \text{ volts}$$
$$I_a X_s = 87.5 \times 4 = 350 \text{ volts}$$

Terminal voltage/phase, $\quad V = 3300/\sqrt{3} = 1905 \text{ volts}$

$\therefore$

$$E = \sqrt{(1905 \times 0.8 + 26.25)^2 + (1905 \times 0.6 + 350)^2} = 2152 \text{ volts}$$

$\therefore$ Line e.m.f. $\quad\quad = \sqrt{3}\,E = \sqrt{3} \times 2152 = \textbf{3727 volts}$

TUTORIAL PROBLEMS

1. A 3-phase, 11kV star-connected alternator has armature resistance of 1Ω/phase and a synchronous reactance of 20Ω/phase. Calculate the voltage regulation for a load of 1500 kW at p.f. of (*i*) 0.8 lagging (*ii*) unity (*iii*) 0.8 leading. [(*i*) 22% (*ii*) 4.25% (*iii*) –13.4%]

2. A 3-phase, star-connected alternator is rated at 1500 kVA, 11 kV. The resistance and reactance per phase are 1.5Ω and 30Ω respectively. To what value will the terminal voltage rise when full-load at p.f. 0.8 lagging is switched off ? [13970V]

3. A 3-phase alternator generates an open-circuit line voltage of 6920V. The synchronous reactance per phase is 5Ω while resistance/phase is negligible. Find the terminal voltage if three 12Ω resistors are connected in star across the alternator.

23.11. PARALLEL OPERATION OF ALTERNATORS

It is rare to find a 3-phase alternator supplying its own load independently except under test conditions. In practice, a very large number of 3-phase alternators operate in parallel because the various power stations are interconnected through the national grid. Therefore, the output of any single alternator is small compared with the total interconnected capacity. For example, the total capacity of the interconnected system may be over 40,000 MW while the capacity of the biggest single alternator may be 500 MW. For this reason, the performance of a single alternator is unlikely to *affect appreciably the voltage and frequency of the whole system. An alternator connected to such a system is said to be connected to *infinite busbars*. The outstanding electrical characteristics of such busbars are that they are constant-voltage, constant-frequency busbars.

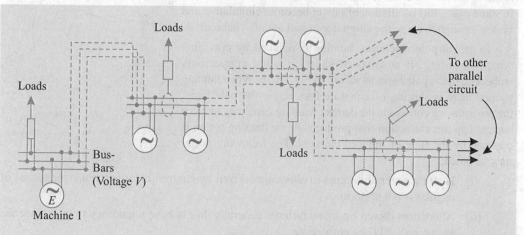

Fig. 23.15

Fig. 23.15 shows a typical infinite bus system. Loads are tapped from the infinite bus at various load centres. The alternators may be connected to or disconnected from the infinite bus, depending on the power demand on the system. If an alternator is connected to infinite busbars, no matter what power is delivered by the incoming alternator, the voltage and frequency of the system remain the same. The operation of connecting an alternator to the infinite busbars is known as *paralleling with the infinite busbars*. It may be noted that before an alternator is connected to an infinite busbars, certain conditions must be satisfied.

. . . .

* Since large number of alternators operate in parallel, the system becomes a constant voltage source of very large inertia. Any change made in the operating conditions of one alternator will make insignificant change in voltage or frequency of the system because of its large size and inertia.

23.12. ADVANTAGES OF PARALLEL OPERATION OF ALTERNATORS

The following are the advantages of operating alternators in parallel:

(*i*) **Continuity of service.** The continuity of service is one of the important requirements of any electrical apparatus. If one alternator fails, the continuity of supply can be maintained through the other healthy units. This will ensure uninterrupted supply to the consumers.

(*ii*) **Efficiency.** The load on the power system varies during the whole day; being minimum during the late night hours. Since alternators operate most efficiently when delivering full-load, units can be added or put off depending upon the load requirement. This permits the efficient operation of the power system.

(*iii*) **Maintenance and repair.** It is often desirable to carry out routine maintenance and repair of one or more units. For this purpose, the desired unit/units can be *shut down* and the continuity of supply is maintained through the other units.

(*iv*) **Load growth.** The load demand is increasing due to the increasing use of electrical energy. The load growth can be met by adding more units without disturbing the original installation.

23.13. HUNTING

Sometimes an alternator will not operate satisfactorily with others due to hunting. If the driving torque applied to an alternator is pulsating such as that produced by a diesel engine, the alternator rotor may be pulled periodically ahead of or behind its normal position as it rotates. This oscillating action is called *hunting*. Hunting causes the alternators to shift load from one to another. In some cases, this oscillation of power becomes cumulative and violent enough to cause the alternator to pull out of synchronism.

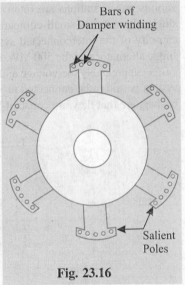

Bars of Damper winding

Salient Poles

Fig. 23.16

In salient-pole machines, hunting is reduced by providing *damper winding*. It consists of short-circuited copper bars embedded in the pole faces as shown in Fig. 23.16. When hunting occurs, there is shifting of armature flux across the pole faces, thereby inducing currents in the damper winding. Since any induced current opposes the action that produces it, the hunting action is opposed by the flow of induced currents. The following points may be noted:

(*i*) Hunting generally occurs in alternators driven by engines because the driving torque of engines is not uniform.

(*ii*) Alternators driven by steam turbines generally do not have a tendency to hunt since the torque applied does not pulsate.

(*iii*) In cylindrical rotor machine, the damper windings are generally not used. It is because the solid rotor provides considerable damping.

Note. Under normal running conditions, damper winding does not carry any current because rotor runs at synchronous speed.

MULTIPLE-CHOICE QUESTIONS

1. Majority of alternators in use have ....
   (*a*) revolving a.c. armature winding
   (*b*) stationary field type construction
   (*c*) revolving field type construction
   (*d*) none of the above.

2. The stator of an alternator is identical to that of a ....
   (*a*) d.c. generator
   (*b*) 3-phase induction motor
   (*c*) 1-phase induction motor
   (*d*) Rosenberg generator

3. The stator of an alternator rarely uses .... slots.
   - (a) wide open type
   - (b) semi-closed type
   - (c) closed type
   - (d) none of the above

4. The a.c. armature winding of an alternator operates at .... the field winding.
   - (a) the same voltage as
   - (b) much lesser voltage than
   - (c) much higher voltage than
   - (d) none of the above

5. The salient-pole construction for field structure of an alternator is generally used for ...... machine.
   - (a) 2-pole
   - (b) 4-pole
   - (c) 8-pole
   - (d) none of the above

6. A turbo-alternator uses ....
   - (a) salient-pole field structure
   - (b) nonsalient-pole field structure
   - (c) rotating a.c. armature winding
   - (d) none of the above.

7. High-speed alternators are driven by ....
   - (a) diesel engines
   - (b) hydraulic turbines
   - (c) steam turbines
   - (d) none of the above

8. Turbo-alternators have rotors of.............
   - (a) small diameter and long axial length
   - (b) large diameter and long axial length
   - (c) large diameter and small axial length
   - (d) same diameter and axial length

9. The speed at which a 6-pole alternator should be driven to generate 50 cycles per second is ....

   - (a) 1500 r.p.m.
   - (b) 1000 r.p.m.
   - (c) 500 r.p.m.
   - (d) none of the above

10. The frequency of e.m.f. generated in an 8-pole alternator running at 900 r.p.m. is ....
    - (a) 50 Hz
    - (b) 60 Hz
    - (c) 120 Hz
    - (d) none of the above

11. The synchronous reactance of an alternator is generally .... armature resistance.
    - (a) 5 times smaller than
    - (b) 5 times greater than
    - (c) 10 to 100 times greater than
    - (d) 10 times smaller than

12. A 3-phase alternator generates an open-circuit phase voltage of 4000 V when exciting current is 50 A; the short-circuit current for the same excitation being 800 A. The synchronous reactance per phase is ....
    - (a) 80 Ω
    - (b) 5 Ω
    - (c) 15 Ω
    - (d) none of the above

13. A 30 MVA, 15 kV alternator will have a per phase nominal impedance of ....
    - (a) 9 Ω
    - (b) 15 Ω
    - (c) 7.5 Ω
    - (d) none of the above

14. The full-load efficiency of an alternator .... with the size of the machine.
    - (a) increases
    - (b) decreases
    - (c) remains unchanged
    - (d) none of the above

15. In the armature winding of an alternator, the coil span falls short of full-pitch by 60° (electrical). The pitch factor is ....
    - (a) 0.866
    - (b) 0.5
    - (c) 0.25
    - (d) none of the above

Answers to Multiple-Choice Questions

1. (c)	2. (b)	3. (c)	4. (c)	5. (c)	6. (b)	7. (c)	8. (a)
9. (b)	10. (b)	11. (c)	12. (b)	13. (c)	14. (a)	15. (a)	

Hints to Selected Multiple-Choice Questions

3. The **closed -type** slots have the following disadvantages:
   - (i) They increase the inductance of the windings.
   - (ii) They are expensive in the initial cost.
   - (iii) They present a problem of end connections.

   Due to these disadvantages, wholly closed slots are not used.

4. The field winding is supplied with direct current, usually at 125V or 250 V. However, voltages as high as 33 kV are generated in the armature winding.

5. The salient pole rotors are driven by low-speed water turbines or diesel engines. It is because the salient-pole type construction is difficult to build to withstand the stresses at high speeds. Because a salient pole rotor turns at low speed (50 to 300 r.p.m.) and because a frequency of 50 Hz is required, we must place a large number of poles on the rotor ($f = NP/120$).

6. High-speed or turbo-alternators have **nonsalient-pole** (*i.e.* cylindrical rotor) rotor to withstand the stresses at high speeds. Because the rotor is driven at a high speed, we require a small number of poles.

7. **Steam turbines** are smaller and more efficient when they turn at high speed. The same is true of alternators.

8. The turbo-alternators run at high speeds. The high speed of rotation produces strong centrifugal forces which impose an upper limit on the diameter of the rotor. In case of a rotor turning at 3600 r.p.m., the elastic limit of the steel requires the manufacturer to limit the diameter to a maximum of 1.2 m. We can double the diameter when the speed is 1800 r.p.m. but because of the transportation problems, we seldom go beyond 1.8m.

9. $$f = \frac{NP}{120} \quad \therefore \quad N = \frac{120\,f}{P} = \frac{120 \times 50}{6} = 1000 \text{ r.p.m.}$$

10. $$f = \frac{NP}{120} = \frac{900 \times 8}{120} = 60 \text{ Hz}$$

11. The value of synchronous reactance is **10 to 100 times greater than** armature resistance. Consequently, we can neglect armature resistance unless we are interested in efficiency or heating effects.

12. Synchronous reactance, $X_s = \dfrac{E_{ph}}{I_{sc}} = \dfrac{4000}{800} = 5\,\Omega$

    where
    E_{ph} = rated open-circuit phase voltage
    I_{sc} = short-circuit current per phase, using the same exciting current that was required to produce E_{ph}.

13. Nominal impedance, $Z_n = \dfrac{E_L^2}{S} = \dfrac{(15000)^2}{30 \times 10^6} = 7.5\,\Omega$

    where
    E_L = rated line voltage in volts
    S = rated power of alternator in VA

14. The efficiency of an alternator automatically improves as the power rating increases. For example, if an alternator of 1 kVA has an efficiency of 50%, a large but similar model having a capacity of 10 MVA will have an efficiency of about 90%.

15. Pitch factor, $K_p = \cos(\alpha/2) = \cos(60°/2) = 0.866$

    where
    α = electrical angle by which coil span falls short of full-pitch.

Synchronous Motors

INTRODUCTION

$\mathbf{I}$t may be recalled that a d.c. generator can be run as a d.c. motor. In like manner, an alternator may op erate as a motor by connecting its armature winding to a 3-phase supply. It is then called a synchronous motor. As the name implies, a synchronous motor runs at synchronous speed $(N_s = 120\ f/P)$ i.e., in synchronism with the revolving field produced by the 3-phase supply. The speed of rotation is, therefore, tied to the frequency of the source. Since the frequency is fixed, the motor speed stays constant irrespective of the load or voltage of 3-phase supply. However, synchronous motors are not used so much because they run at constant speed (i.e., synchronous speed) but because they possess other unique electrical properties. In this chapter, we shall discuss the working and characteristics of synchronous motors.

24.1. CONSTRUCTION

A synchronous motor is a machine that operates at synchronous speed and converts electrical energy into mechanical energy. It is fundamentally an alternator operated as a motor. Like an alternator, a synchronous motor has the following two parts:

    (i)   a **stator** which houses 3-phase armature winding in the slots of the stator core and receives power from a 3-phase supply (See Fig. 24.1).

(*ii*) a **rotor** that has a set of salient poles excited by direct current to form alternate N and S poles. The exciting coils are connected in series to two slip rings and direct current is fed into the winding from an external exciter mounted on the rotor shaft.

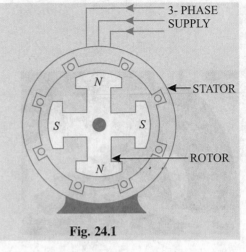

The stator is wound for the same number of poles as the rotor poles. As in the case of an induction motor, the number of poles determines the synchronous speed of the motor:

Synchronous speed, $\qquad N_s = \dfrac{120 f}{P}$

where $\qquad\qquad f =$ frequency of supply in Hz

$P =$ number of poles

Fig. 24.1

An important drawback of a synchronous motor is that it is not self-starting and auxiliary means have to be used for starting it.

24.2. OPERATING PRINCIPLE

The fact that a synchronous motor has no starting torque can be easily explained.

(*i*) Consider a 3-phase synchronous motor having two rotor poles N_R and S_R. Then the stator will also be wound for two poles N_S and S_S. The motor has direct voltage applied to the rotor winding and a 3-phase voltage applied to the stator winding. The stator winding produces a rotating field which revolves round the stator at synchronous speed N_s ($= 120\ f/P$). The direct (or zero frequency) current sets up a two-pole field which is stationary so long as the rotor is not turning. Thus we have a situation in which there exists a pair of revolving armature poles (*i.e.*, $N_S - S_S$) and a pair of stationary rotor poles (*i.e.*, $N_R - S_R$).

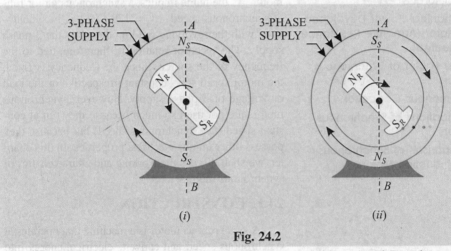

Fig. 24.2

(*ii*) Suppose at any instant, the stator poles are at positions A and B as shown in Fig. 24.2 (*i*). It is clear that poles N_S and N_R repel each other and so do the poles S_S and S_R. Therefore the rotor tends to move in the anticlockwise direction. After a period of half-cycle (or $1/2\ f = 1/100$ second), the polarities of the stator poles are reversed but the polarities of the rotor poles remain the same as shown in Fig. 24.2 (*ii*). Now S_S and N_R attract each other and so do N_S and S_R. Therefore, the rotor tends to move in the clockwise direction. Since the stator poles change their polarities rapidly, they tend to pull the rotor first in one direction and then after a period of half-cycle in the other. Due to high inertia of the rotor, the motor fails to start.

Hence, a synchronous motor has no self-starting torque i.e., a synchronous motor cannot start by itself.

How to get continuous unidirectional torque ? If the rotor poles are rotated by some external means at *such* a speed that they interchange their positions along with the stator poles, then the rotor will experience a continuous unidirectional torque. This can be understood from the following discussion:

(*i*) Suppose the stator field is rotating in the clockwise direction and the rotor is also rotated clockwise by some external means at such a speed that the rotor poles interchange their positions along with the stator poles.

(*ii*) Suppose at any instant the stator and rotor poles are in the position shown in Fig. 24.3 (*i*). It is clear that torque on the rotor will be clockwise. After a period of half-cycle, the stator poles reverse their polarities and at the same time rotor poles also *interchange their positions as shown in Fig. 24.3 (*ii*). The result is that again the torque on the rotor is clockwise. Hence, a continuous unidirectional torque acts on the rotor and moves it in the clockwise direction. Under this condition, *poles on the rotor always face poles of opposite polarity on the stator* and a strong magnetic attraction is set up between them. This mutual attraction locks the rotor and stator together and the rotor is virtually pulled into step with the speed of revolving flux (*i.e.*, synchronous speed).

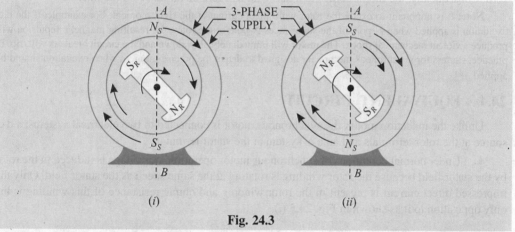

Fig. 24.3

(*iii*) If now the external prime mover driving the rotor is removed, the rotor will continue to rotate at synchronous speed in the clockwise direction because the rotor poles are magnetically locked up with the stator poles. It is due to this magnetic interlocking between stator and rotor poles that a synchronous motor runs at the speed of revolving flux *i.e.*, synchronous speed.

24.3. MAKING SYNCHRONOUS MOTOR SELF-STARTING

A synchronous motor cannot start by itself. In order to make the motor self-starting, a **squirrel cage winding (also called damper winding) is provided on the rotor. The damper winding consists of

---

* Since the rotor poles are being rotated by an external means at such a speed that they interchange their positions along with the stator poles.
** Similar to that in an induction motor.

copper bars embedded in the pole faces of the salient poles of the rotor as shown in Fig. 24.4. The bars are short-circuited at the ends to form in effect a partial squirrel cage winding. The damper winding serves to start the motor.

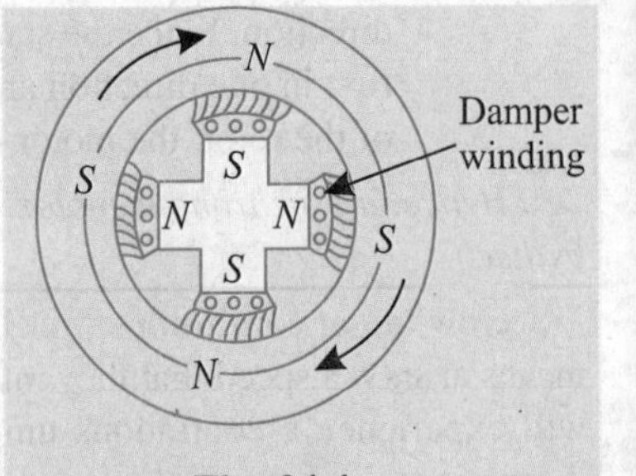

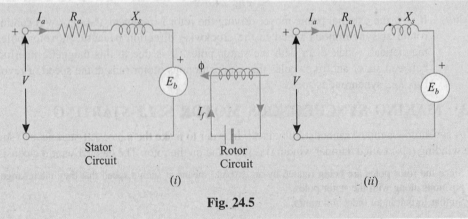

    (*i*)   To start with, 3-phase supply is given to the stator winding while the rotor field winding is left unenergised. The rotating stator field induces currents in the damper or squirrel cage winding and the motor starts as an induction motor.

Fig. 24.4

    (*ii*)   As the motor approaches the synchronous speed, the rotor is excited with direct current. Now the resulting poles on the rotor face poles of opposite polarity on the stator and a strong magnetic attraction is set up between them. The rotor poles lock in with the poles of rotating flux. Consequently, the rotor revolves at the same speed as the stator field *i.e.*, at synchronous speed.

   (*iii*)   Because the bars of squirrel cage portion of the rotor now rotate at the same speed as the rotating stator field, these bars do not cut any flux and, therefore, have no induced currents in them. Hence squirrel cage portion of the rotor is, in effect, removed from the operation of the motor.

It may be emphasised here that due to magnetic interlocking between the stator and rotor poles, a synchronous motor can only run at synchronous speed. At any other speed, this magnetic interlocking (i.e., rotor poles facing opposite polarity stator poles) ceases and the average torque becomes zero. Consequently, the motor comes to a halt with a severe disturbance on the line.

Note: It is important to excite the rotor with direct current at the right moment. For example, if the d.c. excitation is applied when N-pole of the stator faces N-pole of the rotor, the resulting magnetic repulsion will produce a violent mechanical shock. The motor will immediately slow down and the circuit breakers will trip. In practice, starters for synchronous motors are designed to detect the precise moment when excitation should be applied.

24.4. EQUIVALENT CIRCUIT

Unlike the induction motor, the synchronous motor is connected to two electrical systems; a d.c. source at the rotor terminals and an a.c. system at the stator terminals.

1.   Under normal conditions of synchronous motor operation, no voltage is induced in the rotor by the stator field because the rotor winding is rotating at the same speed as the stator field. Only the impressed direct current is present in the rotor winding and ohmic resistance of this winding is the only opposition to it as shown in Fig. 24.5 (*i*).

Fig. 24.5

2. In the stator winding, two effects are to be considered; the effect of stator field on the stator winding and the effect of the rotor field cutting the stator conductors at synchronous speed.

(*i*) The effect of stator field on the stator (or armature) conductors is accounted for by including an inductive reactance in the armature winding. This is called *synchronous reactance* X_s. A resistance R_a must be considered to be in series with this reactance to account for the copper losses in the stator or armature winding as shown in Fig. 24.5 (*i*). This resistance combines with synchronous reactance and gives the synchronous impedance of the machine.

(*ii*) The second effect is that a voltage is generated in the stator winding by the synchronously-revolving field of the rotor as shown in Fig. 24.5 (*i*). This generated e.m.f. E_b is known as back e.m.f. and opposes the stator voltage V. The magnitude of E_b depends upon rotor speed and rotor flux ϕ per pole. Since rotor speed is constant, the value of E_b depends upon the rotor flux per pole i.e., exciting rotor current I_f.

Fig 24.5 (*i*) shows the schematic diagram for one phase of a star-connected synchronous motor while Fig. 24.5 (*ii*) shows its equivalent circuit. Referring to the equivalent circuit in Fig. 24.5 (*ii*),

Net voltage/phase in stator winding,

$$E_r = V - E_b \qquad \text{...phasor differnece}$$

Armature current/phase,
$$I_a = \frac{E_r}{Z_s}$$

where
$$Z_s = \sqrt{R_a^2 + X_s^2}$$

This equivalent circuit helps considerably in understanding the operation of a synchronous motor.

Note: In a synchronous motor, the value of X_s is 10 to 100 times greater than R_a. Consequently, we can neglect R_a unless we are interested in efficiency or heating effects.

24.5. MOTOR ON LOAD

In d.c. motors and induction motors, an addition of load causes the motor speed to decrease. The decrease in speed reduces the counter e.m.f. enough so that additional current is drawn from the source to carry the increased load at a reduced speed. This action cannot take place in a synchronous motor because it runs at a constant speed (*i.e.*, synchronous speed) at all loads.

What happens when we apply mechanical load to a synchronous motor? The rotor poles fall slightly behind the stator poles, while continuing to run at synchronous speed. The angular displacement between stator and rotor poles (called torque angle α) causes the phase of back em.f. E_b to change *w.r.t.* supply voltage V. This increases the net e.m.f. E_r in the stator winding. Consequently, stator current I_a $(= E_r/Z_s)$ increases to carry the load.

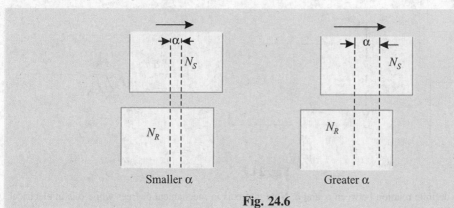

Smaller α Greater α

Fig. 24.6

The following points may be noted in synchronous motor operation:

(*i*)   A synchronous motor runs at synchronous speed at all loads. It meets the increased load not by a decrease in speed but by the relative shift between stator and rotor poles *i.e.*, by the adjustment of torque angle α.

(*ii*)   If the load on the motor increases, the torque angle α also increases (*i.e.*, rotor poles lag behind the stator poles by a greater angle) but the motor continues to run at synchronous speed. The increase in torque angle α causes a greater phase shift of back e.m.f. E_b w.r.t. supply voltage V. This increases the net voltage E_r in the stator winding. Consequently, armature current I_a $(= E_r/Z_s)$ increases to meet the load demand.

(*iii*)   If the load on the motor decreases, the torque angle α also decreases. This causes a smaller phase shift of E_b *w.r.t.* V. Consequently, the net voltage E_r in the stator winding decreases and so does the armature current I_a $(= E_r/Z_s)$.

24.6. PULL-OUT TORQUE

There is a limit to the mechanical load that can be applied to a synchronous motor. As the load increases, the torque angle α also increases so that a stage is reached when the rotor is pulled out of synchronism and the motor comes to a standstill. This load torque at which the motor pulls out of synchronism is called *pull-out* or *breakdown torque*. Its value varies from 1.5 to 3.5 times the full-load torque.

When a synchronous motor pulls out of synchronism, there is a major disturbance on the line and the circuit breakers immediately trip. This protects the motor because both squirrel cage and stator winding heat up rapidly when the machine ceases to run at synchronous speed.

24.7.   MOTOR PHASOR DIAGRAM

Consider an under-excited star-connected synchronous motor supplied with fixed excitation *i.e.*, back e.m.f. E_b is constant.

Let
$$V = \text{supply voltage/phase}$$
$$E_b = \text{back e.m.f./phase}$$
$$Z_s = \text{synchronous impedance/phase}$$

(*i*)   **Motor on no load.** When the motor is on no load, the torque angle α is small as shown in Fig. 24.7. (*i*). Consequently, back e.m.f. E_b lags behind the supply voltage V by a small angle *δ as shown in the phasor diagram in Fig. 24.7 (*iii*). The net voltage/phase in the stator winding is E_r.

Armature current/phase, $I_a = E_r/Z_s$

The armature current I_a lags behind E_r by $\theta = \tan^{-1} X_s/R_a$. Since $X_s >> R_a$, I_a lags E_r by nearly 90°. The phase angle between V and I_a is ϕ so that motor power factor is $\cos \phi$.

Input power/phase = $V I_a \cos \phi$

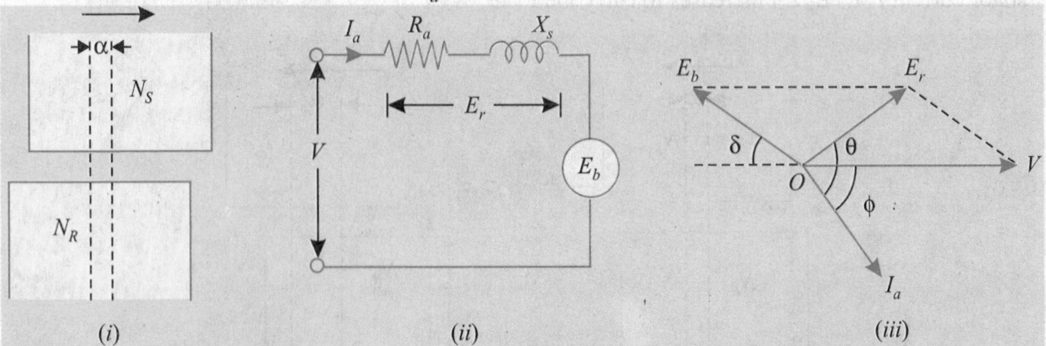

(*i*)   (*ii*)   (*iii*)

Fig. 24.7

---

*   There is a definite relation between α and δ. Note that α is in mechanical degrees while δ is in electrical degrees.

Thus at no load, the motor takes a small power $V I_a \cos \phi$/phase from the supply to meet the no-load losses while it continues to run at synchronous speed.

(*ii*) **Motor on load.** When load is applied to the motor, the torque angle α increases as shown in Fig. 24.8 (*i*). This causes E_b (its magnitude is constant as excitation is fixed) to lag behind V by a greater angle as shown in the phasor diagram in Fig. 24.8 (*ii*). The net voltage/phase E_r in the stator winding increases. Consequently, the motor draws more armature current $I_a \, (= E_r/Z_s)$ to meet the applied load.

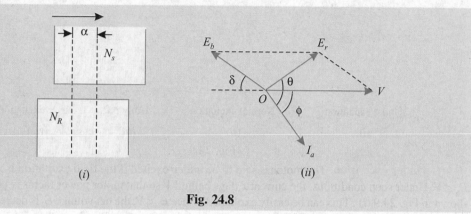

Fig. 24.8

Again I_a lags E_r by about 90° since $X_s >> R_a$. The power factor of the motor is $\cos \phi$.

Input power/phase, $\qquad P_i = V I_a \cos \phi$

Mechanical power developed by motor/phase is

$$P_m = E_b \times I_a \times \text{cosine of angle between } E_b \text{ and } I_a$$
$$= E_b I_a \cos (\delta - \phi)$$

24.8. EFFECT OF CHANGING FIELD EXCITATION AT CONSTANT LOAD

In a d.c. motor, the armature current I_a is determined by dividing the difference between V and E_b by the armature resistance R_a. Similarly, in a synchronous motor, the stator current (I_a) is determined by dividing voltage-phasor resultant (E_r) between V and E_b by the synchronous impedance Z_s.

One of the most important features of a synchronous motor is that by changing the field excitation, it can be made to operate from lagging to leading power factor. Consider a synchronous motor having a fixed supply voltage and driving a constant mechanical load. Since the mechanical load as well as the speed is constant, the power input to the motor (= 3 $V I_a \cos \phi$) is also constant. This means that the in-phase component $I_a \cos \phi$ drawn from the supply will remain *constant. If the field excitation is changed, back e.m.f. E_b also changes. This results in the change of phase position of I_a w.r.t. V and hence the power factor $\cos \phi$ of the motor changes. Fig. 24.9 shows the phasor diagram of the synchronous motor for different values of field excitation. Note that extremities of current phasor I_a lie on the straight line **AB.

* Input power = 3 $V I_a \cos \phi$

Since V and input power are constant, $I_a \cos \phi$ must be constant.

** Since $I_a \cos \phi$ is constant, component of I_a along V is fixed.

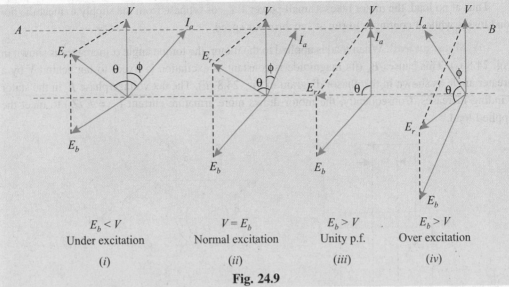

Fig. 24.9

(i) **Under excitation.** The motor is said to be under-excited if the field excitation is such that $E_b < V$. Under such conditions, the current I_a lags behind V so that motor power factor is lagging as shown in Fig. 24.9 (i). This can be easily explained. Since $E_b < V$, the net voltage E_r is decreased and turns clockwise. As angle θ (= 90°) between E_r and I_a is †constant, therefore, phasor I_a also turns clockwise i.e., current I_a lags behind the supply voltage. Consequently, the motor has a lagging power factor.

(ii) **Normal excitation.** The motor is said to be normally excited if the field excitation is such that $E_b = V$. This is shown in Fig. 24.9 (ii). Note that the effect of increasing excitation (i.e., increasing E_b) is to turn the phasor E_r and hence I_a in the anticlockwise direction i.e., I_a phasor has come closer to phasor V. Therefore, p.f. increases though still lagging. Since input power (= $3VI_a \cos \phi$) is unchanged, the stator current I_a must *decrease with increase in p.f.

Suppose the field excitation is increased until the current I_a is in phase with the applied voltage V, making the p.f. of the synchronous motor unity [See Fig. 24.9 (iii)]. For a given load, at **unity p.f. the resultant E_r and, therefore, I_a are minimum.

(iii) **Over excitation.** The motor is said to be overexcited if the field excitation is such that $E_b > V$. Under such conditions, current I_a leads V and the motor power factor is leading as shown in Fig. 24.9 (iv). Note that E_r and hence I_a further turn anticlockwise from the normal excitation position. Consequently, I_a leads V.

From the above discussion, it is concluded that if the synchronous motor is under-excited, it has a lagging power factor. As the excitation is increased, the power factor improves till it becomes unity at normal excitation. Under such conditions, the current drawn from the supply is minimum. If the excitation is further increased (i.e., over excitation), the motor power factor becomes leading.

Note. The armature current (I_a) is minimum at unity p.f. and increases as the power factor becomes poor, either leading or lagging.

† $\quad \theta = \tan^{-1} X_s/R_a$. Since $X_s \gg R_a$ and both are fixed, $\theta = 90°$ and is fixed.

* $\quad I_a = \sqrt{(I_a \cos \phi)^2 + (I_a \sin \phi)^2}$. Since $I_a \cos \phi$ is constant, the lagging reactive component $I_a \sin \phi$ will decrease.

** At unity p.f., $E_b > V$ but the difference is very small so that $E_b \approx V$. Therefore, unity p.f. also corresponds to normal excitation.

24.9. POWER RELATIONS

Consider an under-excited star-connected synchronous motor driving a mechanical load. Fig. 24.10. (i) shows the equivalent circuit for one phase while Fig. 24.10. (ii) shows the phasor diagram.

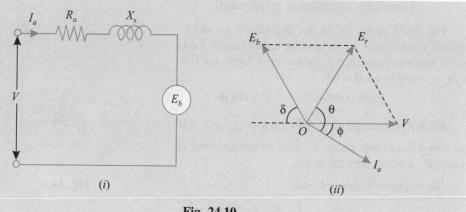

Fig. 24.10

(i)   Input power/phase, $P_i = V I_a \cos \phi$

(ii)   Mechanical power developed by the motor/phase is

$$P_m = E_b \times I_a \times \text{cosine of angle between } E_b \text{ and } I_a$$
$$= E_b I_a \cos (\delta - \phi)$$

(iii)   Armature Cu loss/phase $= I_a^2 R_a = P_i - P_m$

(iv)   Output power/phase, $P_{out} = P_m -$ Iron, friction and excitation loss

Fig. 24.11 shows the power flow diagram of the synchronous motor.

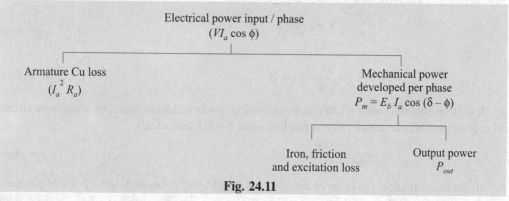

Fig. 24.11

24.10. MOTOR TORQUE

$$\text{Gross torque, } T_g = 9.55 \frac{P_m}{N_s} \text{ N-m}$$

where P_m = Gross motor output in watts = $E_b I_a \cos (\delta - \phi)$

          N_s = Synchronous speed in r.p.m.

$$\text{Shaft torque, } T_{sh} = 9.55 \frac{P_{out}}{N_s} \text{ N-m}$$

It may be seen that torque is directly proportional to the mechanical power because rotor speed (*i.e.*, N_s) is fixed.

24.11. MECHANICAL POWER DEVELOPED BY MOTOR

(*Armature resistance neglected*)

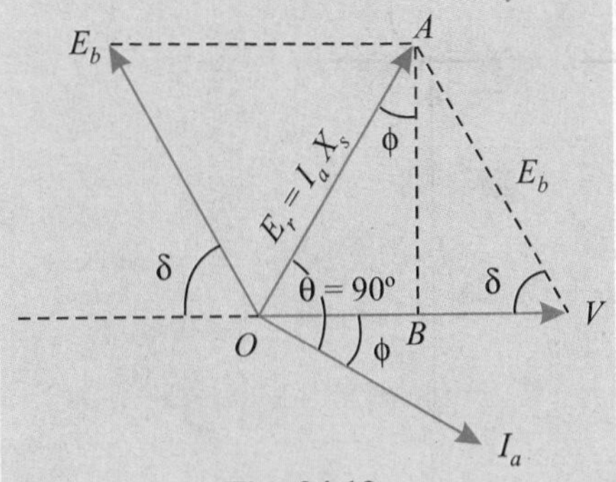

Fig. 24.12 shows the phasor diagram of an under-excited synchronous motor driving a mechanical load. Since armature resistance R_a is assumed *zero, tan θ = $X_s/R_a = \infty$ and hence $\theta = 90°$.

Fig. 24.12

Input power/phase = $V I_a \cos \phi$

Since R_a is assumed zero, stator Cu loss ($I_a^2 R_a$) will be zero. Hence input power is equal to the mechanical power P_m developed by the motor.

Mech. power developed/phase,

$$P_m = V I_a \cos \phi \qquad ...(i)$$

Referring to the phasor diagram in Fig. 24.12,

$$AB = E_r \cos \phi = I_a X_s \cos \phi$$

Also

$$AB = E_b \sin \delta$$

∴

$$I_a X_s \cos \phi = E_b \sin \delta$$

or

$$I_a \cos \phi = \frac{E_b \sin \delta}{X_s}$$

Substituting the value of $I_a \cos \phi$ in exp. (*i*) above,

$$P_m = \frac{V E_b}{X_s} \sin \delta \qquad ...per\ phase$$

$$= \frac{3V E_b}{X_s} \sin \delta \qquad ...for\ 3\text{-}phase$$

It is clear from the above relation that mechanical power increases with torque angle (in electrical degrees) and its maximum value is reached when $\delta = 90°$ (electrical).

∴

$$P_{max} = \frac{V E_b}{X_s} \qquad ...per\ phase$$

Under this condition, the poles of the rotor will be mid-way between N and S poles of the stator.

Example 24.1. *A 2000 V, 3-phase, star-connected motor has resistance and synchronous reactance per phase of 0.2 Ω and 1.9 Ω respectively. Calculate the generated (back) e.m.f. per phase with an input of 800 kW at p.f. 0.8 lagging.*

Solution.

Supply voltage/phase, $V = 2000/\sqrt{3} = 1155$ V

---

* In a practical motor, the value of X_s is 10 to 100 times greater than R_a. Consequently, we can neglect R_a without significant error.

Line current, $\quad I_L = \dfrac{800 \times 10^3}{\sqrt{3} \times 2000 \times 0.8}$

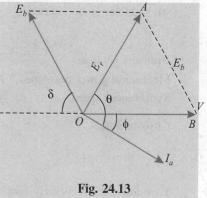

$\quad = 288$ A

Armature current/phase, $I_a = I_L = 288$ A

$\quad \theta = \tan^{-1} 1.9/0.2 = 84°$

$\quad \phi = \cos^{-1} 0.8 = 36.8°$

$\quad Z_s = \sqrt{(0.2)^2 + (1.9)^2} = 1.91\ \Omega$

$\quad E_r = I_a Z_s = 288 \times 1.91 = 550$ V

Fig. 24.13

Refer to the phasor diagram of the motor shown in Fig. 24.13. Applying rule of trigonometry to Δ OAB,

$$AB^2 = OA^2 + OB^2 - 2 \times OA \times OB \times \cos(\theta - \phi)$$

or $\quad E_b^2 = (550)^2 + (1155)^2 - 2 \times 550 \times 1155 \times \cos(84° - 36.8°)$

$\quad\quad = 773296$

$\therefore \quad E_b = \sqrt{773296} = \mathbf{879}$ **V/phase**

Example 24.2. *A 3980 V, 50 Hz, 4-pole, star-connected synchronous motor generates back e.m.f. of 1790 V per phase. The resistance and synchronous reactance per phase are 2.2 Ω and 22 Ω respectively. The torque angle is 30° electrical. Calculate (i) the resultant armature voltage/phase (ii) armature current/phase (iii) power factor of the motor (iv) gross torque developed by the motor.*

Solution. Fig. 24.14 shows the phasor diagram of the motor. Since $V > E_b$, the motor power factor will be lagging.

Armature voltage/phase, $V = 3980/\sqrt{3} = 2300$ V

Back e.m.f./phase, $\quad E_b = 1790$ V

(i) $\quad E_r^2 = V^2 + E_b^2 - 2\,VE_b \cos\delta$

$\quad\quad = (2300)^2 + (1790)^2 - 2 \times 2300 \times 1790 \times \cos 30°$

$\quad\quad = 1363000$

$\therefore \quad E_r = \sqrt{1363000} = \mathbf{1167\,V}$

(ii) $\quad Z_s = \sqrt{R_a^2 + X_s^2} = \sqrt{(2.2)^2 + (22)^2} = 22.1\ \Omega$

$\quad I_a = E_r/Z_s = 1167/22.1 = \mathbf{52.8\ A}$

(iii) $\quad \theta = \tan^{-1} X_s/R_a = \tan^{-1} 22/2.2 = 84.3°$

In right angled Δ ABO, $\angle AOB = \theta - \phi$.

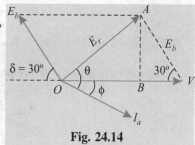

$\therefore \quad \tan(\theta - \phi) = \dfrac{AB}{OB} = \dfrac{E_b \sin 30°}{V - E_b \cos 30°}$

$\quad\quad = \dfrac{1790 \sin 30°}{2300 - 1790 \cos 30°} = 1.193$

Fig. 24.14

or $\quad \theta - \phi = \tan^{-1} 1.193 = 50°$

or $\quad \phi = \theta - 50° = 84.3° - 50° = 34.3°$

$\therefore \quad$ Motor p.f. $= \cos\phi = \cos 34.3° = \mathbf{0.826\ lag}$

(*iv*) Motor input power, $P_i = \sqrt{3}\ V_L I_L \cos \phi$

$$= \sqrt{3} \times 3980 \times 52.8 \times 0.826 = 300647 \text{ W}$$

Armature Cu loss $= 3\ I_a^2 R_a = 3 \times (52.8)^2 \times 2.2 = 18400 \text{ W}$

Mechanical power developed, $P_m = 300647 - 18400 = 282247 \text{ W}$

Synchronous speed, $N_s = 120\ f/P = 120 \times 50/4 = 1500 \text{ r.p.m.}$

Gross torque, $T_g = 9.55 \dfrac{P_m}{N_s}$

$$= 9.55 \frac{282247}{1500} = 1797 \text{ N} - \text{m}$$

Example 24.3. *A 3-phase synchronous motor has 12 poles and operates from 440 V, 50 Hz supply. Calculate its speed. If it takes a line current of 100 A at 0.8 power factor lead, what torque the motor will be developing ? Neglect losses.*

Solution.

Motor speed, $N_s = \dfrac{120\ f}{P} = \dfrac{120 \times 50}{12} = 500 \text{ r.p.m.}$

Input power, $P_i = \sqrt{3}\ V_L I_L \cos \phi$

$$= \sqrt{3} \times 440 \times 100 \times 0.8 = 60966 \text{ W}$$

As losses are neglected, output power, $P_{out} = P_i = 60966 \text{ W}$

∴ Motor torque, $T = 9.55 \dfrac{P_{out}}{N_s}$

$$= 9.55 \frac{60966}{500} = 1165 \text{ N--m}$$

Example 24.4. *A 3-phase, 6000 kW, 4 kV, 180 r.p.m., 50 Hz motor has per phase synchronous reactance of 1.2 Ω. At full load, the torque angle is 20° electrical. If the generated back e.m.f./phase is 2.4 kV, calculate the mechanical power developed. What will be the maximum mechanical power developed?*

Solution.

Voltage/phase, $V = 4/\sqrt{3} = 2.3 \text{ kV}$

$$P_m = \frac{3\ VE_b}{X_s} \sin \delta$$

$$= \frac{3\ (2.3 \times 10^3) \times (2.4 \times 10^3)}{1.2} \times \sin 20°$$

$$= 4.71 \times 10^6 \text{ W} = 4.71 \text{ MW}$$

The mechanical power developed will be maximum when $\delta = 90°$.

∴ $P_{max} = \dfrac{3\ V E_b}{X_s} = \dfrac{3 \times (2.3 \times 10^3) \times (2.4 \times 10^3)}{1.2}$

$$= 13.8 \times 10^6 \text{ W} = 13.8 \text{ MW}$$

Example 24.5. *A 500 V, 1-phase synchronous motor is developing 10 H.P. and operates at 0.9 p.f. lagging. The effective resistance of armature is 0.8 Ω. Iron and frictional losses amount to 500 W and excitation losses are 800 W. Find (i) armature current (ii) total power supplied (iii) commercial efficiency.*

Solution.

Motor input = $V I_a \cos \phi$; Armature Cu loss = $I_a^2 R_a$. If P_m is the total mechanical power developed (includes iron and friction losses), then,

$$P_m = V I_a \cos \phi - I_a^2 R_a$$

or $\quad I_a^2 R_a - V I_a \cos \phi + P_m = 0$

(i) ∴ $\qquad\qquad I_a = \dfrac{V \cos \phi \pm \sqrt{V^2 \cos^2 \phi - 4 R_a P_m}}{2 R_a}$

Here $P_m = 10 \times 746 + 500 = 7960$ W; $R_a = 0.8$ Ω $\cos \phi = 0.9$; $V = 500$ volts

∴ $\qquad\qquad I_a = \dfrac{500 \times 0.9 \pm \sqrt{(500 \times 0.9)^2 - 4 \times 0.8 \times 7960}}{2 \times 0.8}$

$\qquad\qquad = \dfrac{450 \pm \sqrt{(450)^2 - 25472}}{1.6} = \dfrac{450 \pm 420.7}{1.6}$

$\qquad\qquad = \dfrac{29.3}{1.6} = \mathbf{18.31\ A}$

(ii) Power supplied to stator = $V I_a \cos \phi = 500 \times 18.31 \times 0.9 = 8240$ W

Total power supplied to stator and rotor = 8240 + 800 = **9040 W**

(iii) Commercial efficiency, $\eta_c = \dfrac{7460}{9040} \times 100 = \mathbf{82.5\%}$

Synchronous condensers

TUTORIAL PROBLEMS

1. A 2200 V, 3-phase, 50 Hz star-connected synchronous motor has a resistance of 0.6 Ω/phase and a synchronous reactance of 6 Ω per phase. Find the generated e.m.f. when the input is 200 kW at (i) a power factor of unity (ii) a power factor of 0.8 leading.

[(i) 2200 V (ii) 2640 V]

2. A 3-phase, star-connected synchronous motor takes 20 kW at 400 V from 50 Hz supply. The synchronous reactance/phase is 4 Ω/phase and the effective resistance is negligible. If the exciting current is so adjusted that back e.m.f. is 550 V, find the power factor of the motor.

[0.872 lead]

3. In a 3-phase, star-connected 660 V synchronous motor, the synchronous reactance is 2 Ω/phase. When a certain load is applied, the input is 90 kW and the back e.m.f. is 890 V. Neglecting resistance, calculate the power factor.

[0.824 lead]

24.12. POWER FACTOR OF SYNCHRONOUS MOTORS

In an induction motor, only one winding (*i.e.*, stator winding) produces the necessary flux in the machine. The stator winding must draw reactive power from the supply to set up the flux. Consequently, induction motor must operate at lagging power factor.

But in a synchronous motor, there are two possible sources of excitation; alternating current in the stator or *direct current in the rotor. The required flux may be produced either by stator or rotor or both.

(i) If the rotor exciting current is of such magnitude that it produces all the required flux, then no magnetising current or reactive power is needed in the stator. As a result, the motor will operate at unity power factor.

(ii) If the rotor exciting current is less (*i.e.*, motor is under-excited), the deficit in flux is made up by the stator. Consequently, the motor draws reactive power to provide for the remaining flux. Hence motor will operate at a lagging power factor.

(iii) If the rotor exciting current is greater (*i.e.*, motor is over-excited), the excess flux must be counterbalanced in the stator. Now the stator, instead of absorbing reactive power, actually *delivers* reactive power to the 3-phase line. The motor then behaves like a source of reactive power, as if it were a capacitor. In other words, the motor operates at a leading power factor.

To sum up, *a synchronous motor absorbs reactive power when it is under-excited and delivers reactive power to source when it is over-excited.*

24.13. SYNCHRONOUS CAPACITOR

An over-excited synchronous motor running on no load is known as synchronous capacitor.

We have seen that a synchronous motor takes a leading current when over excited and, therefore, behaves as a capacitor. When such a machine is connected in parallel with induction motors or other devices that operate at lagging power factor, the leading kVAR supplied by the synchronous capacitor partly neutralises the lagging reactive kVAR of the loads. Consequently, power factor of the system is improved.

Synchronous capacitors (*i.e.*, unloaded over-excited synchronous motors) are installed in power systems solely for power factor improvement. They are economical in large sizes than the static capacitors.

24.14. APPLICATIONS OF SYNCHRONOUS MOTORS

(i) Synchronous motors are particularly attractive for **low speeds (< 300 r.p.m.) because the power factor can always be adjusted to unity and efficiency is high.

* The rotor produces a d.c. magnetomotive force (m.m.f.). However, as far as the stator is concerned, d.c. m.m.f. appears as an a.c. m.m.f. because the rotor is constantly turning. Moreover, rotor m.m.f. has the same frequency as the stator m.m.f. because the rotor turns at synchronous speed. The total flux in the machine is, therefore, due to the combined action of the two m.m.f.s.

** At low speeds, induction motors become heavy, costly and have relatively low power factor and low efficiency.

(ii) Over-excited synchronous motors can be used to improve the power factor of a plant while carrying their rated loads.

(iii) They are used to improve the voltage regulation of transmission lines.

(iv) High-power electronic converters generating very low frequencies enable us to run synchronous motors at ultra-low speeds. Thus huge motors in the 10 MW range drive crushers, rotary kilns and variable-speed ball mills.

24.15. COMPARISON OF SYNCHRONOUS AND INDUCTION MOTORS

S.No.	Particular	Synchronous Motor	3-phase Induction Motor
1.	Speed	Remains constant (i.e., N_s) from no-load to full-load	Decreases with load.
2.	Power factor	Can be made to operate from lagging to leading power factor.	Operates at lagging power factor
3.	Excitation	Requires d.c. excitation at the rotor.	No excitation for the rotor.
4.	Economy	Economical for speeds below 300 r.p.m.	Economical for speeds above 600 r.p.m.
5.	Self-starting	No self-starting torque. Auxiliary means have to be provided for starting.	Self-starting
6.	Construction	Complicated	Simple
7.	Starting torque	More	less

MULTIPLE-CHOICE QUESTIONS

1. The rotor of a synchronous motor is...........................
   (a) salient-pole type
   (b) nonsalient-pole type
   (c) identical to that of a d.c. motor
   (d) none of the above

2. Damper winding in a synchronous motor.....................
   (a) reduces windage losses
   (b) serves to start the motor
   (c) improves p.f. of the motor
   (d) increases hunting of the motor

3. Small synchronous motors are started by......................
   (a) pony motor
   (b) damper winding
   (c) variable-frequency source
   (d) none of the above

4. A synchronous motor runs at speeds ranging from......................
   (a) 1800 to 3600 r.p.m.
   (b) 3600 to 6000 r.p.m.
   (c) 150 to 1800 r.p.m.
   (d) none of the above

5. The full-load slip of a synchronous motor is........................
   (a) 5%   (b) 1%
   (c) 2%   (d) zero

6. If the supply frequency of synchronous motors is 60 cycles/second, then the rotor must revolve at........................
   (a) 25 cycles/second
   (b) 60 cycles/second
   (c) 100 cycles/second
   (d) none of the above

7. When the synchronous motor runs at synchronous speed, the voltage induced in the damper winding is......................
   (a) maximum
   (b) minimum
   (c) zero
   (d) none of the above

8. A synchronous motor runs at only one speed (*i.e.* synchronous speed) because it.............
   (*a*) has no losses
   (*b*) is a doubly fed machine
   (*c*) has a damper winding
   (*d*) none of the above

9. The speed of a synchronous motor can be changed by varying.......................
   (*a*) mechanical load
   (*b*) field excitation
   (*c*) supply frequency
   (*d*) none of the above

10. If the mechanical angle α between the stator and rotor poles increases, then, stator current...................
    (*a*) is decreased
    (*b*) remains unchanged
    (*c*) is increased
    (*d*) none of the above

11. The pull-out torque of a practical synchronous motor will occur when the torque angle is about...................
    (*a*) 0°
    (*b*) 30°
    (*c*) 45°
    (*d*) 75°

12. For a given load, the normal field excitation of synchronous motor is that which gives......... power factor.
    (*a*) 0.8 leading
    (*b*) 0.8 lagging
    (*c*) unity
    (*d*) none of the above

13. For a given load, the armature current of a synchronous motor will be minimum for............ power factor.
    (*a*) unity
    (*b*) 0.8 leading
    (*c*) 0.8 lagging
    (*d*) none of the above

14. An over-excited synchronous motor behaves as............................
    (*a*) a resistor
    (*b*) an inductor
    (*c*) a capacitor
    (*d*) none of the above

15. An under-excited synchronous motor behaves as...............................
    (*a*) an inductor
    (*b*) a capacitor
    (*c*) a resistor
    (*d*) none of the above

Answers to Multiple-Choice Questions

1. (*a*)	2. (*b*)	3. (*b*)	4. (*c*)	5. (*d*)	6. (*b*)	7. (*c*)	8. (*b*)
9. (*c*)	10. (*c*)	11. (*d*)	12. (*c*)	13. (*a*)	14. (*c*)	15. (*a*)	

Hints to Selected Multiple-Choice Questions

4. Most synchronous motors are rated between 150 kW (200 H.P.) and 15 MW (20,000 H.P.) and turn at speeds ranging from 150 to 1800 r.p.m. Consequently, these machines are used in heavy industry.

5. A synchronous motor runs at one speed only i.e. synchronous speed. Consequently, slip is zero.

6. The primary requirement is that frequency of rotation of the rotor should be such *that stator and rotor fields are stationary with respect to each other*. For this to happen, obviously, the rotor must revolve at 60 cycles/second.

7. When the motor runs at synchronous speed, there is no relative motion between rotor and revolving flux produced by stator currents. Hence e.m.f. in the damper winding placed on the rotor is zero.

8. The significant and distinguishing feature of synchronous motors in contrast to induction motors is that they are doubly fed. Electrical energy is supplied both to the field and the armature windings. When this is done, torque can only be developed at one speed—the

synchronous speed. At any other speed, the torque is zero. In fact, it is this characteristic (*i.e.* doubly fed) which enables the synchronous motor to develop non-zero torque at only one speed (*i.e.* synchronous speed) and hence the name synchronous motor.

9. $f = \dfrac{N_s P}{120}$ ∴ $N_s = \dfrac{120 f}{P}$

For a given machine, the value of P is fixed. Hence, the speed of a synchronous motor can only be changed by varying the **supply frequency**.

10. When synchronous motor is on no-load, the axes of the rotor and stator poles nearly coincide. As the motor is loaded, the rotor poles fall slightly behind the stator poles, while continuing to turn at synchronous speed. The increased power must come from the a.c. source (*i.e.* stator winding). Hence, stator current **increases**.

11. The mechanical power developed by a synchronous motor per phase is given by:

$$P_m = \frac{V E_b}{X_s} \sin \delta$$

where
    P_m = mechanical power of motor per phase
    E_b = phase voltage induced by excitation
    V = phase voltage of a.c. source
    X_s = synchronous reactance per phase
    δ = torque angle (in electrical degrees between E_b and V)

The maximum torque that motor can develop is called the pull-out torque and will occur at $\delta = 90°$. This is true for motors having smooth rotors. Most synchronous motors have salient poles; in this case the pull-out torque occurs at a torque angle of about **75°** (**electrical**).

12. The resultant flux ϕ in a synchronous motor is fixed in value as the applied stator voltage is constant. Since synchronous motor is a doubly excited machine, *both d.c. and a.c. sources may co-operate to produce this fixed resultant flux ϕ. For a given mechanical load, if the entire resultant flux is provided by d.c. excitation alone, the stator will absorb no reactive power (as it is not contributing to the resultant flux). Hence the p.f. of the motor will be **unity**.

13. Since at **unity** power factor the motor draws no reactive power, the stator current will be minimum.

14. An over-excited synchronous motor delivers reactive power to the 3-phase line. The motor then behaves like a source of power, as if it were a **capacitor**.

15. In an under-excited synchronous motor, the resultant fixed flux is (*i*) partly supplied by stator and (*ii*) partly by the rotor. As a result, motor absorbs reactive power from the 3-phase line. Consequently, it behaves as an **inductor**.

---

*   Fortunately, the stator flux has the same frequency as the rotor flux because rotor turns at synchronous speed.

25

Electrical Instruments and Electrical Measurements

INTRODUCTION

Electrical energy is being used in the manufacture of many commodities. In order to ensure quality and efficiency, it is important that we should be able to measure accurately the electrical quantities involved. The instruments used to measure electrical quantities (*e.g.* current, voltage, power, energy etc.) are called electrical instruments. These instruments are generally named after the electrical quantity to be measured. Thus the instruments which measure current, voltage, power and energy are called ammeter, voltmeter, wattmeter and energy meter respectively. The accuracy, convenience and reliability of electrical instruments are mainly responsible for the widespread use of electrical methods of measurements. In this chapter, we shall confine our attention to the construction, working and applications of some important electrical instruments.

25.1. TYPES OF ELECTRICAL INSTRUMENTS

Electrical measuring instruments may be classified according to their functions as (*i*) indicating instruments (*ii*) integrating instruments and (*iii*) recording instruments.

    (*i*) **Indicating instruments.** Those instruments which directly indicate the value of the electrical quantity *at the time* when it is being measured are called indicating instruments e.g. *ammeters, voltmeters* and *wattmeters.* In such instruments, a pointer moving over a graduated scale directly gives the value of the electrical quantity being measured. For example, when an ammeter is connected in the circuit, the pointer of the meter directly indicates the value of current flowing in the circuit at that time.

(*ii*) **Integrating instruments.** Those instruments which measure the total quantity of electricity (in ampere-hours) or electrical energy (in watt-hours) in a given time are called integrating instruments *e.g. ampere-hour meter* and *watt-hour meter.* In such instruments, there are sets of dials and pointers which register the total quantity of electricity or electrical energy supplied to the load.

(*iii*) **Recording instruments.** Those instruments which give a continuous record of the variations of the electrical quantity to be measured are called recording instruments. A recording instrument is merely an indicating instrument with a pen attached to its pointer. The pen rests lightly on a chart wrapped over a drum moving with a slow uniform speed. The motion of the drum is in a direction perpendicular to the direction of the pointer. The path traced out by the pen indicates the manner in which the quantity, being measured, has varied during the time of the record. Recording voltmeters are used in supply stations to record the voltage of the supply mains during the day. Recording ammeters are employed in supply stations for registering the current taken from the batteries.

25.2. PRINCIPLES OF OPERATION OF ELECTRICAL INSTRUMENTS

An electrical instrument essentially consists of a movable element and a scale to indicate or register the electrical quantity being measured. The movable element is supported on jewelled bearings and carries a pointer or sets of dials. The movement of the movable element is caused by utilising one or more of the following effects of current or voltage:

1. Magnetic effect ...... Moving-iron instruments
2. Electrodynamic effect ...... (*i*) Permanent-magnet moving coil
   (*ii*) Dynamometer type
3. Electromagnetic-induction ...... Induction type instruments
4. Thermal effect ...... Hot-wire instruments
5. Chemical effect ...... Electrolytic instruments
6. Electrostatic effect ...... Electrostatic instruments

S.No.	Type	Effect	Suitable for	Instrument
1.	Moving-iron	Magnetic effect	*d.c.* and *a.c.*	Ammeter, Voltmeter
2.	Permanent-magnet moving coil	Electrodynamic effect	*d.c.* only	Ammeter, Voltmeter
3.	Dynamometer type	Electrodynamic effect	*d.c.* and *a.c.*	Ammeter, Voltmeter, Wattmeter
4.	Induction type	Electro-magnetic induction effect	*a.c.* only	Ammeter, Voltmeter, Wattmeter, Energy meter
5.	Hot-wire	Thermal effect	*d.c.* and *a.c.*	Ammeter, Voltmeter
6.	Electrolytic meter	Chemical effect	*d.c.* only	Ampere-hour meter
7.	Electrostatic type	Electrostatic effect	*d.c.* and *a.c.*	Voltmeter only

The principles of operation of electrical instruments are given in the above table for facility of reference.

25.3. ESSENTIALS OF INDICATING INSTRUMENTS

An indicating instrument essentially consists of moving system pivoted in jewel bearings. A pointer is attached to the moving system which indicates on a graduated scale, the value of the electrical quantity being measured. In order to ensure proper operation of indicating instruments, the following three torques are required:

    (*i*)   Deflecting (or operating) torque

    (*ii*) Controlling (or restoring) torque

    (*iii*) Damping torque

The deflecting torque is produced by utilising the various effects of electric current or voltage and causes the moving system (and hence the pointer) to move from zero position. The controlling torque is provided by spring or gravity and opposes the deflecting torque. The pointer comes to rest at a position where these two opposing torques are equal. The damping torque is provided by air friction or eddy currents. It ensures that the pointer comes to the final position without oscillations, thus enabling accurate and quick readings to be taken.

25.4. DEFLECTING TORQUE

One important requirement in indicating instruments is the arrangement for producing deflecting or operating torque (T_d) when the instrument is connected in the circuit to measure the given electrical quantity. This is achieved by utilising the various effects of electric current or voltage mentioned in Art. 25.2. The deflecting torque causes the moving system (and hence the pointer attached to it) to move from zero position to indicate on a graduated scale the value of electrial quantity being measured. The actual method of producing the deflecting torque depends upon the type of instrument and shall be discussed while dealing with particular instrument.

25.5. CONTROLLING TORQUE

If deflecting torque were acting alone, the pointer would continue to move indefinitely and would swing over to the maximum deflected position irrespective of the magnitude of current (or voltage or power) to be measured. This necessitates to provide some form of controlling or opposing torque (T_C). This controlling torque should oppose the deflecting torque and should increase with the deflection of the moving system. The pointer will be brought to rest at a position where the two opposing torques are equal *i.e.*, $T_d = T_C$. The controlling torque performs two functions :

    (*i*) It increases with the deflection of the moving system so that the final position of the pointer on the scale will be according to the magnitude of current (or voltage or power) to be measured.

    (*ii*) It brings the pointer back to zero position when the deflecting torque is removed. If it were not provided, the pointer once deflected would not return to zero position on removing the deflecting torque.

The controlling torque in indicating instruments may be provided by one of the following two methods:

    1. By one or more springs   *... Spring control*

    2. By weight of moving parts   *... Gravity control*

    1. **Spring control.** This is the most common method of providing controlling torque in electrical instruments. A spiral *hairspring made of some nonmagnetic material like phosphor bronze

---

  *   In some instruments, two spiral hairsprings wound in the opposite direction are used. The two springs serve the additional purpose of leading current to the moving system (*i.e.* operating coil).

is attached to the moving system of the instrument as shown in Fig. 25.1. With the deflection of the pointer, the spring is twisted in the opposite direction. This twist in the spring provides the controlling torque. Since the torsion torque of a spiral spring is proportional to the angle of twist, the controlling torque is directly proportional to the deflection of the pointer *i.e.* $T_C \propto \theta$.

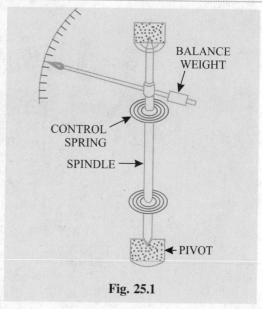

Fig. 25.1

The pointer will come to rest at a position where controlling torque T_C is equal to the deflecting torque T_d *i.e.*, $T_d = T_C$.

In an instrument where the deflecting torque is uniform, spring control provides a linear or evenly-spaced scale over the whole range. For example, in a permanent-magnet moving coil instrument, the deflecting torque is directly proportional to the current flowing through the operating coil *i.e.*,

$$T_d \propto I$$

With spring control, $\qquad T_C \propto \theta$

In the final deflected position, $\quad T_d = T_C$

∴ $\qquad\qquad\qquad \theta \propto I$

Since the deflection is directly proportional to I, scale of such an instrument will be uniform as shown in Fig. 25.2.

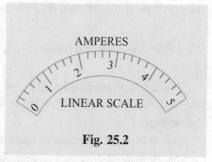

Fig. 25.2

2. **Gravity control.** In this method, a small adjustable weight W is attached to the moving system [See *Fig. 25.3 (*i*)] which provides the necessary controlling torque. In the zero position of the pointer, the control weight hangs vertically downward and therefore provides no controlling torque. However, under the action of deflecting torque, the pointer moves from zero position (from left to right) and control weight moves in the opposite direction. Due to gravity, the control weight would tend to come to original position (*i.e.*, vertical) and thus provides an opposing or controlling torque. The pointer comes to rest at a position where controlling torque is equal to the deflecting torque.

In the deflected position shown in Fig. 25.3 (*ii*), weight W can be resolved into two rectangular components *viz* $W \cos \theta$ and $W \sin \theta$. Only the component $W \sin \theta$ provides the controlling torque T_C.

∴ $\qquad\qquad\qquad T_C = W\,l \sin \theta$

or $\qquad\qquad\qquad T_C \propto \sin \theta \quad$ (for fixed W and l)

Thus, the controlling torque is proportional to the sine of angle of deflection. It may be seen that the value of T_C can be varied by changing l *i.e.*, by changing the position of control weight W on the arm.

* Note that another weight (called balance weight) is attached to counterbalance the weight of the pointer and other parts.

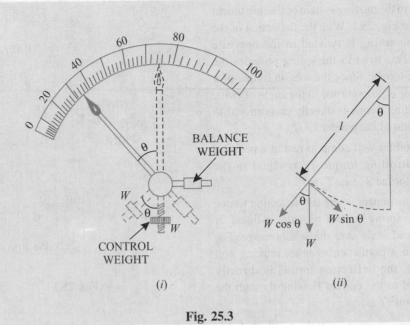

CONTROL
WEIGHT

BALANCE
WEIGHT

(i) (ii)

Fig. 25.3

Taking the case of an instrument in which the deflecting torque is directly proportional to current (*i.e.*, permanent-magnet moving coil instrument), we have for gravity control,

$$T_d \propto I \text{ and } T_C \propto \sin \theta$$

In the final deflected position, $\quad T_d = T_C$

∴ $I \propto \sin \theta$

Since I is proportional to the sine of angle of deflection, gravity-controlled instruments have non-uniform scales; being crowded at the beginning as shown in Fig. 25.3 (i).

Advantages

(*i*)   It is slightly cheaper in manufacturing costs than spring control.

(*ii*) It is unaffected by temperature variations.

(*iii*) It is not subjected to fatigue.

(*iv*) The controlling torque can be changed easily.

Disadvantages

(*i*)   The instrument has to be kept in vertical position.

(*ii*) The control weight increases the weight of the moving system.

(*iii*) Gravity-controlled instruments have non-uniform scale.

Example 25.1. *The deflecting torque of an ammeter is directly proportional to the current passing through it, and the instrument has full scale deflection of 70° for a current of 10 A. What deflection will occur for a current of 5 A when the instrument is (i) spring-controlled (ii) gravity-controlled?*

Solution.

Deflecting torque, $T_d \propto I$

(*i*)   **Spring-controlled**

Controlling torque, $T_C \propto \theta$

∴ $I \propto \theta$

In the first case, $10 \propto 70°$

In the second case, $5 \propto \theta$

∴ $\theta = (5/10) \times 70° = 35°$

(*ii*) **Gravity-controlled**

Controlling torque, $T_C \propto \sin \theta$

∴ $I \propto \sin \theta$

In the first case, $10 \propto \sin 70°$

In the second case, $5 \propto \sin \theta$

∴ $\sin \theta = (5/10) \sin 70° = 0.47$

or $\theta = \sin^{-1} 0.47 = 28°$

25.6. DAMPING TORQUE

If the moving system is acted upon by deflecting and controlling torques alone, then the pointer, due to inertia, will oscillate about its final deflected position for quite some time before coming to rest. This is often undesirable because it makes difficult to obtain quick and accurate readings. In order to avoid these oscillations of the pointer and to bring it quickly to its final deflected position, a damping torque is provided in the indicating instruments. This damping torque acts only when the pointer is in motion and always opposes the motion. The position of the pointer when stationary is, therefore, not *affected by damping.

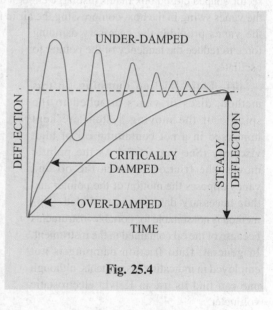

The degree of damping decides the behaviour of the moving system. If the instrument is under-damped, the pointer will oscillate about the final position for some time before coming to rest. On the other hand, if the instrument is over-damped, the pointer will become slow and lethargic. However, if the degree of damping is adjusted to such a value that the pointer comes up to the correct reading quickly without passing beyond it or oscillating about it, the instrument is said to be *dead-beat* or critically damped. Fig. 25.4 shows graph for under-damping, over damping and critical damping (dead-beat). The damping torque in indicating instruments can be provided by (*i*) air-friction (*ii*) fluid friction and (*iii*) eddy currents.

Fig. 25.4

(*i*) **Air friction damping.** Two arrangements of air friction damping are shown in Fig. 25.5 and Fig. 25.6. In the arrangement shown in Fig. 25.5, a light aluminium piston is attached to the spindle that carries the pointer and moves with a very little clearance in a rectangular or circular air chamber closed at one end. The cushioning action of the air on the piston damps out any tendency of the pointer to oscillate about the final deflected position. This method is not favoured these days and the one shown in Fig. 25.6 (*i*) is preferred.

---

* The damping torque acts only when the pointer is in *motion*. When the pointer is in a particular deflected position, though deflecting and controlling torques are acting on the moving system but the damping torque is zero. It is because the pointer is steady and there is no movement of the moving system.

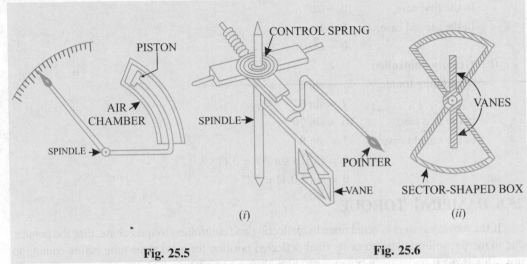

Fig. 25.5   Fig. 25.6

The arrangement shown in Fig. 25.6 (*ii*) is widely used. In this method, one or two light aluminium vanes are attached to the same spindle that carries the pointer. The vanes are permitted to swing in a sector-shaped closed box that is just large enough to accommodate the vanes. As the pointer moves, the vanes swing in the box, compressing the air in front of them. The pressure of compressed air in the vanes provides the necessary damping force to reduce the tendency of the pointer to oscillate.

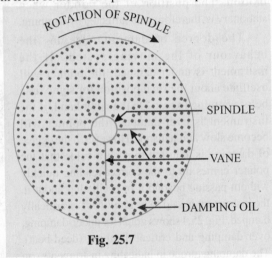

Fig. 25.7

(*ii*) **Fluid friction damping.** In this method, discs or vanes attached to the spindle of the moving system are kept immersed in a pot containing oil of high viscosity (See Fig. 25.7). As the pointer moves, the friction between the oil and vanes opposes the motion of the pointer and thus necessary damping is provided. This method is not suitable for portable instruments because of the oil contained in the instrument. In general, fluid friction damping is not employed in indicating instruments, although one can find its use in Kelvin electrostatic voltmeter.

(*iii*) **Eddy current damping.** Two methods of eddy current damping are shown in Fig. 25.8 and Fig. 25.9. In Fig. 25.8, a thin *aluminium or copper disc attached to the moving system is allowed to pass between the poles of a permanent magnet. As the pointer moves, the disc cuts across the magnetic field and **eddy currents are induced in the disc. These eddy currents react with the field of the magnet to produce a force which opposes the motion (Lenz's Law). In this way, eddy currents provide the damping torque to reduce the oscillations of the pointer.

. . . .
*   The disc must be a conductor but non-magnetic.
**   The currents induced in the disc assume the form of little whirls or eddies and hence the name eddy currents.

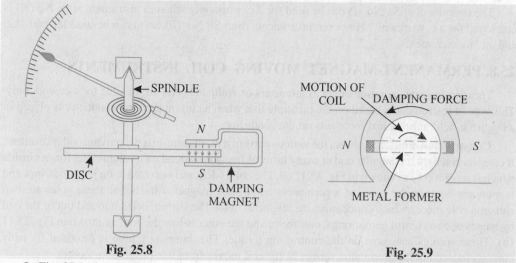

Fig. 25.8   **Fig. 25.9**

In Fig. 25.9, the operating coil (*i.e.* the coil which produces the deflecting torque) is wound on the aluminium former. As the coil moves in the field of the instrument, eddy currents are induced in the aluminium former to provide the necessary damping torque.

25.7. AMMETERS AND VOLTMETERS

(*i*) An ammeter is used to measure the flow of current in a circuit. It is thus connected in series with the circuit under test (See Fig. 25.10) so that current to be measured or a †fraction of it passes through the instrument itself. The ammeter must be capable of carrying this current without injury to itself and without abnormally increasing the resistance of the circuit into which it is inserted. For this reason, an ammeter is designed to have low resistance.

(*ii*) A voltmeter is used to measure the potential difference between two points of a circuit. It is thus connected in parallel with the circuit or some part of the circuit as shown in Fig. 25.10. The voltmeter must have enough resistance so that it will not be injured by the current that flows through it, and so that it will not materially affect the current in the circuit to which it is connected.

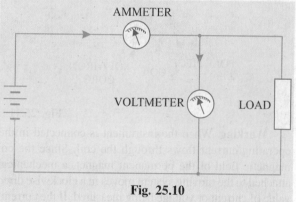

Fig. 25.10

The basic principle of the ammeter and of the voltmeter is the same. Both are current operated devices *i.e.*, deflecting torque is produced when current flows through their operating coils. In the ammeter, the deflecting torque is produced by the current we wish to measure, or a certain fraction of that current. In the voltmeter, the deflecting torque is produced by a current which is proportional to the potential difference we wish to measure. Thus, the same instrument can be used as an ammeter or voltmeter with proper design.

The following types of instruments are used for making voltmeters and ammeters :

(*i*) Permanent-magnet moving coil type   (*ii*) Dynamometer type

(*iii*) Moving-iron type   (*iv*) Hot-wire type

(*v*) Electrostatic type (for voltmeters only)   (*vi*) Induction type

† If the circuit current is large, a shunt is used to divert a major portion of current so that only a small current flows through the instrument.

The instrument at Sr. No. (*i*) can be used for d.c. work only whereas instrument at Sr. No (*vi*) is employed for a.c. work only. However, instruments from Sr. No. (*ii*) to (*v*) can be used for both d.c. and a.c. measurements.

25.8. PERMANENT-MAGNET MOVING COIL INSTRUMENTS

These instruments are used either as ammeters or voltmeters and are suitable for d.c. work only. This type of instrument is based on the principle that when a current carrying conductor is placed in a magnetic field, mechanical force acts on the conductor.

Construction. Fig. 25.11 shows the various parts of a permanent-magnet moving coil instrument. It consists of a light rectangular coil of many turns of fine wire wound on an aluminium former inside which is an iron core as shown in Fig. 25.11 (*i*). The coil is delicately pivoted upon jewel bearings and is mounted between the poles of a permanent horse-shoe magnet. Attached to these poles are two soft-iron pole pieces which concentrate the magnetic field. The current is led into and out of the coil by means of two control hair-springs, one above and the other below the coil, as shown in Fig. 25.11 (*ii*). These springs also provide the controlling torque. The damping torque is provided by eddy currents induced in the aluminium former as the coil moves from one position to another.

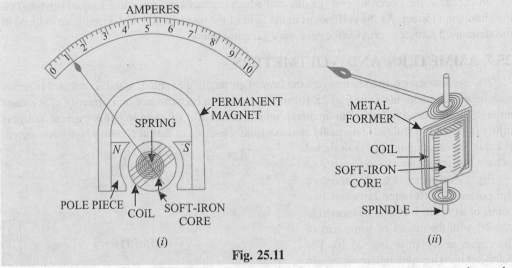

Fig. 25.11

Working. When the instrument is connected in the circuit to measure current or voltage, the operating current flows through the coil. Since the coil is carrying current and is placed in the magnetic field of the permanent magnet, a mechanical force acts on it. As a result, the pointer attached to the moving system moves in a clockwise direction over the graduated scale to indicate the value of current or voltage being measured. If the current in the coil is reversed, the deflecting torque will also be reversed since the direction of the field of the permanent magnet is the same. Consequently, the pointer will try to deflect below zero. Deflection in this direction (*i.e.*, reverse direction) is prevented by a spring "stop". Since the deflecting torque reverses with the reversal of current in the coil, such instruments can be used to measure direct current and voltage *only.

Deflecting torque. The magnetic field in the air gap is radial due to the presence of **soft-iron

* The instrument can be used to measure alternating currents and voltages by using a rectifier. The given alternating quantity is converted to d.c. by using a bridge type rectifier. This d.c. or average value is measured by the permanent-magnet moving coil instrument. Since a.c. meters are calibrated to indicate *effective* or *r.m.s.* values, we must multiply the average value registered on this meter by 1.11 (the form factor of sinusoidal wave) to obtain the r.m.s. values. Some instruments are scaled to read r.m.s. values directly.

** The soft-iron results in the decreased reluctance of the magnetic circuit and in a uniform, radial flux in the air gap.

core. This means that conductors of the coil will always move at right angle to the field. When current is passed through the coil, forces act on its both sides which produce the deflecting torque.

Referring to Fig. 25.12, let,

B = flux density in Wb/m^2

l = length or depth of coil in m

b = breadth of coil in m

N = No. of turns in the coil

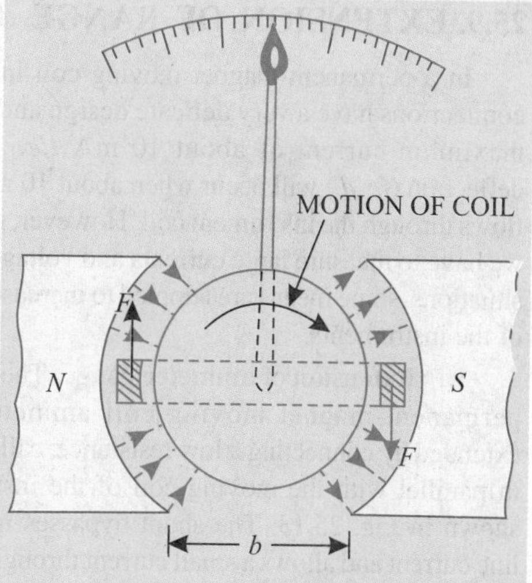

If a current of I amperes flows in the coil, then force acting on each coil side is given by;

Force on each coil side, $F = B I l N$ newtons

Deflecting torque, T_d = Force × perpendicular distance

$$= (B I l N) \times b$$

∴ $T_d = B I N A$ newton-metre

where $A \ (= b \times l)$ is the area of the coil in m^2.

Since the values of B, N and A are fixed,

∴ $T_d \propto I$

The instrument is spring-controlled so that $T_C \propto \theta$

The pointer will come to rest at a position where $T_d = T_C$

∴ $\theta \propto I$

Thus, the deflection is directly proportional to the operating current. Hence, such instruments have uniform scale [See Fig. 25.11 (i)].

Fig. 25.12

Advantages

(i) Uniform scale i.e., evenly divided scale.

(ii) Very effective eddy current damping because the aluminium former moves in an intense magnetic field of the permanent magnet.

(iii) High efficiency as it requires very little power for its operation.

(iv) No hysteresis loss as the magnetic flux is practically constant.

(v) External stray fields have little effect on the readings as the operating magnetic field is very strong.

(vi) Very accurate and reliable.

Disadvantages

(i) Such instruments cannot be used for a.c. measurements.

(ii) About 50% more expensive than moving-iron instruments because of their accurate design.

(iii) Some errors are caused due to variations (with time or temperature) either in the strength of permanent magnet or in the control springs.

Applications. Permanent-magnet moving coil instruments are acknowledged to be the best type for all d.c. measurements. They are very sensitive and maintain a high degree of accuracy over long periods. The chief applications of such instruments are :

(i) In the measurement of direct currents and voltages.

(ii) In d.c. galvanometers to detect small currents.

(iii) In ballistic galvanometers used mainly for measuring changes of magnetic flux linkages.

25.9. EXTENSION OF RANGE

In a permanent-magnet moving coil instrument, the moving coil and the spring used as coil connections have a very delicate design and can carry maximum current of about 10 mA *i.e.*, full-scale deflection (*f.s.d.*) will occur when about 10 mA current flows through the instrument coil. However, in practice, we have to measure large currents and voltages. In such situations, some means are adopted to increase the range of the instruments.

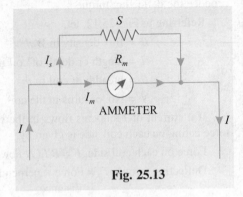

Fig. 25.13

1. **Extension of ammeter range.** The range of a permanent-magnet moving coil ammeter can be extended by connecting a low resistance, called **shunt,* in parallel with the moving coil of the instrument as shown in Fig. 25.13. The shunt bypasses most of the line current and allows a small current through the meter which it can handle without burning.

Let R_m = meter resistance

S = shunt resistance

I_m = full-scale deflection (*f.s.d.*) current

I = Full range current of the meter

Voltage across shunt = Voltage across the meter

or $(I - I_m) S = I_m R_m$

∴ $$S = \frac{I_m R_m}{I - I_m} \qquad \qquad \dots(i)$$

Multiplying power of shunt $= \dfrac{I}{I_m} = \dfrac{R_m + S}{S}$ [From eq. (*i*)]

Suppose the meter has a resistance of 5 Ω and requires 15 mA for full-scale deflection. In order that the meter may read 1A, the value of shunt is given by;

$$S = \frac{I_m R_m}{I - I_m} = \frac{0.015 \times 5}{1 - 0.015} = 0.0761 \ \Omega$$

Multiplying power = I/I_m = 1/0.015 = 66.67

2. **Extension of Voltmeter Range.** The range of a permanent-magnet moving coil voltmeter can be increased by connecting a high resistance R_s called **multiplier**, in **series with it as shown in Fig. 25.14.

Let R_m = meter resistance

R_s = series resistance *i.e.*, multiplier

I_m = full-scale deflection current

V = full-range voltage of the meter

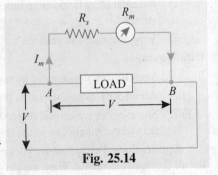

Fig. 25.14

* *

*   Shunts are made of a material such as manganin having low temperature co-efficient of resistance.

** A voltmeter is connected in parallel with the load. Consequently, current through the meter will be proportional to the voltage across the load *i.e.* voltage we wish to measure. In order to restrict the current through the meter (about 10 mA), a high resistance R_s is connected in series with it.

Voltage across AB = Voltage across the meter

or
$$V = I_m (R_s + R_m)$$

$\therefore$
$$R_s = \frac{V}{I_m} - R_m \qquad \qquad \text{...(}i\text{)}$$

$$\text{Voltage amplification} = \frac{\text{Voltage to be measured}}{\text{Voltage across meter}}$$

$$= \frac{V}{I_m R_m} = 1 + \frac{R_s}{R_m} \qquad \qquad \text{[From eq. (}i\text{)]}$$

Suppose the meter has a resistance of 5 Ω and requires 15 mA for full-scale deflection. In order that the meter may read 15 V, the value of series resistance R_s is given by:

$$R_s = \frac{V}{I_m} - R_m = \frac{15}{0.015} - 5 = 995 \, \Omega$$

$$\text{Voltage amplification} = 1 + \frac{R_s}{R_m} = 1 + \frac{995}{5} = 200$$

Clearly, greater the value of R_s, greater is the voltage amplification. For this reason, R_s is called voltage multiplier or simply multiplier.

Example 25.2 *The coil of a permanent-magnet moving coil instrument has 20 turns on a rectangular former of 3.5 cm × 1.5 cm and swings in a uniform field of 0.18 Wb/m². If a steady current of 50 mA is flowing through the coil, calculate the deflecting torque.*

Solution.

Area of coil,
$$A = 3.5 \times 1.5 = 5.25 \text{ cm}^2 = 5.25 \times 10^{-4} \text{ m}^2$$

Deflecting torque,
$$T_d = B I N A \qquad \qquad \textit{... See Art. 25.8}$$
$$= (0.18) \times (50 \times 10^{-3}) \times (20) \times (5.25 \times 10^{-4}) = 945 \times 10^{-7} \text{ Nm}$$

Example 25.3 *The meter element of a permanent-magnet moving coil instrument has a resistance of 5 ohms and requires 15 mA for full-scale deflection. Calculate the resistance to be connected (i) in parallel to enable the instrument to read upto 1A (ii) in series to enable it to read upto 15 V.*

Solution.

Meter resistance,
$$R_m = 5 \, \Omega$$

Full-scale meter current,
$$I_m = 15 \text{ mA} = 0.015 \text{ A}$$

(i) **As Ammeter.**

Full-scale circuit current,
$$I = 1 \text{ A}$$

Let S ohms be the required value of the shunt [See Fig. 25.15].

Now
$$I_m R_m = (I - I_m) S$$

$\therefore$
$$S = \frac{I_m R_m}{I - I_m} = \frac{0.015 \times 5}{1 - 0.015} = 0.0761 \, \Omega$$

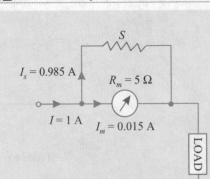

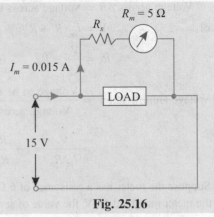

| **Fig. 25.15** | **Fig. 25.16** |

(ii) **As Voltmeter.**

Desired full-scale reading, $V = 15$ volts

Let R_s ohms be the required series resistance [See Fig. 25.16].

Now $$V = I_m (R_s + R_m)$$

or $$R_s = \frac{V}{I_m} - R_m = \frac{15}{0.015} - 5 = \textbf{995} \; \boldsymbol{\Omega}$$

Example 25.4 *A moving coil milliammeter with a resistance of 1.6 Ω is connected with a shunt of 0.228 Ω. What will be the current flowing through the instrument if it is connected in a circuit in which a current of 200 mA is flowing?*

Solution.

Multiplying power of shunt $$= \frac{I}{I_m} = \frac{R_m + S}{S} = \frac{1.6 + 0.228}{0.228} = 8$$

∴ $$I_m = I/8 = 200/8 = \textbf{25 mA}$$

Example 25.5 *What should be the resistance of the moving coil of an ammeter which requires 2.5 mA for full-scale deflection so that it may be used with a shunt having a resistance of 0.0025 Ω for a range of 0 – 10 A?*

Solution.

Multiplying power of shunt $$= \frac{I}{I_m} = \frac{10}{2.5 \times 10^{-3}} = 4000$$

Now, $$4000 = \frac{R_m + S}{S} = \frac{R_m + 0.0025}{0.0025}$$

∴ $$R_m = \textbf{10 } \boldsymbol{\Omega}$$

Example 25.6 *A permanent-magnet moving coil instrument gives full-scale reading of 25 mA when a p.d. across its terminals is 75 mV. Show how it can be used (i) as an ammeter for a range of 0 – 100A (ii) as a voltmeter for a range of 0 – 750 V. Also find the multiplying power of the shunt and voltage amplification.*

Solution.

Meter resistance, $$R_m = 75/25 = 3 \; \Omega$$

Full-scale meter current, $$I_m = 25 \text{ mA} = 0.025 \text{ A}$$

(i) **Ammeter**

Required shunt resistance, $$S = \frac{I_m R_m}{I - I_m} = \frac{0.025 \times 3}{100 - 0.025} = \textbf{0.00075 } \boldsymbol{\Omega}$$

Multiplying power $$= I/I_m = 100/0.025 = \textbf{4000}$$

(*ii*) **Voltmeter**

Required series resistance, $R_s = \dfrac{V}{I_m} - R_m = \dfrac{750}{0.025} - 3 = 29997\ \Omega$

Voltage amplification $= 1 + \dfrac{R_s}{R_m} = 1 + \dfrac{29997}{3} = 10,000$

Alternatively

Voltage amplification $= V/v = 750\ V/(75\ mV) = 10,000$

TUTORIAL PROBLEMS

1. A permanent magnet moving coil instrument gives full-scale deflection with 5 mA and has a resistance of 5 Ω. Calculate the resistance of the necessary components in order that the instrument may be used as (*i*) a 2 A ammeter (*ii*) a 100 V voltmeter.

    [(*i*) **0.0378 Ω in parallel** (*ii*) **6662 Ω in series**]

2. The coil of a permanent-magnet moving coil instrument has a resistance of 25 Ω and gives full-scale deflection when a current of 2 mA passes through it. Calculate the value of shunt required to convert the instrument to an ammeter having a full-scale deflection current of 1.5 A.

    [**0.0334 Ω**]

3. The coil of a permanent-magnet moving coil instrument has 50 turns and its effective length and breadth are 2.8 cm and 2 cm. The control springs have a total torque of 0.8×10^{-6} Nm per degree of deflection. Find the air-gap flux density that will give a full-scale deflection of 100° at 15 mA.

    [**0.19 Wb/m²**]

4. A permanent-magnet moving coil instrument used as a voltmeter has a coil of 50 turns with a width of 3 cm and active length of 3 cm. The gap flux density is 0.15 Wb/m². If the full-scale reading is 150 V and the total resistance is 100 kΩ, find the torque exerted by the springs at full-scale.

    [**8.1×10^{-5} Nm**]

5. A permanent-magnet moving coil instrument has an air-gap flux density of 0.08 Wb/m². There are 60 turns of wire on the moving coil which has an effective length in the gap of 4 cm, a width of 2.5 cm and negligible resistance. The control springs exert a torque of 49.05×10^{-6} Nm at full-scale deflection. Find the resistance to be connected in series with the coil to enable the instrument to be used as a voltmeter reading upto 500 V.

    [**49,000 Ω**]

25.10. DYNAMOMETER TYPE INSTRUMENTS

These instruments are the modified form of permanent-magnet type. Here magnetic field is not produced by a permanent magnet but by two air-cored fixed coils placed on either side of the moving coil. Such instruments can be used as ammeters or as voltmeters but are generally used as wattmeters. They are suitable for d.c. as well as a.c. work.

Principle. These instruments are based on the principle that mechanical force exists between the current carrying conductors.

Construction. It essentially consists of a fixed coil and a moving coil. The fixed coil is split into two equal parts (*F, F*) which are placed close together and parallel to each other. The moving coil (*M*) is pivoted inbetween the two fixed coils and carries a pointer as shown in Fig. 25.17. The current is led into and out of the moving coil by means of two spiral hairsprings which also provide the controlling torque. *Air friction damping is provided by means of the aluminium vanes that move in the sector shaped chamber at the bottom of the instrument.

---

* Since the coils are air-cored, the operating magnetic field is very weak. For this reason, eddy current damping cannot be provided.

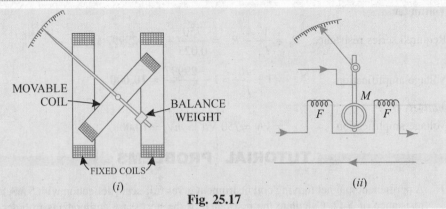

Fig. 25.17

Working. For use as an ammeter or voltmeter, the fixed coils FF and the moving coil M are so connected that the same current flows through the two coils. Due to these currents, mechanical force exists between the coils. The result is that moving coil M moves the pointer over the scale. The pointer comes to rest at a position where deflecting torque is equal to the controlling torque. Since the polarity of the fields produced by both fixed and moving coils is reversed by the reversal of current, the deflection of the moving system is always in the same direction regardless of the direction of current through the coils. For this reason, dynamometer instruments can be used for both d.c. and a.c. measurements.

Deflecting torque. The force of attraction or repulsion between the fixed and moving coils is directly proportional to the product of ampere-turns of fixed coils and the moving coil *i.e.*,

Deflecting torque, $\qquad T_d \propto N_f\, I_f \times N_m I_m$

Since N_m and N_f are constant,

$\therefore \qquad\qquad\qquad T_d \propto I_f I_m$

Since the instrument is spring-controlled, the controlling torque is proportional to the angular deflection θ *i.e.*,

$$T_C \propto \theta$$

In the steady position of deflection, $T_d = T_C$

$\therefore \qquad\qquad\qquad \theta \propto I_f I_m$

Thus deflection (θ) is directly proportional to the product of currents in the fixed coils and the moving coil.

(i) **As ammeter.** When the instrument is used as an ammeter, the fixed coils and the moving coil are connected in series so that the same current flows through the two coils as shown in Fig. 25.18. In that case, $I_f = I_m = I$ so that:

$$\theta \propto I^2$$

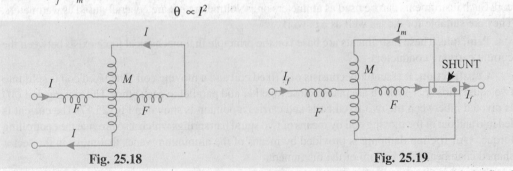

Fig. 25.18   **Fig. 25.19**

For measuring large currents, the moving coil is shunted; the shunt being in series with the fixed coils as shown in Fig. 25.19. The fixed coils carry the main current while the moving coil carries a current proportional to the main current.

(ii) As voltmeter. When the instrument is used as a voltmeter, both fixed coils and the moving coil are connected in series together with a high resistance R_s (called multiplier) having a negligible temperature co-efficient as shown in Fig. 25.20. Therefore, current in both the coils is the same and is proportional to the voltage V being measured.

$$\therefore \qquad \theta \propto V^2$$

MULTIPLIER	
Fig. 25.20	**Fig. 25.21**

It may be seen that whether the instrument is used as an ammeter or voltmeter, the deflection is directly proportional to the square of quantity (current or voltage) being measured. Doubling the current will make the deflection four times as large. Hence, the scale of dynamometer type instruments is *not uniform; being crowded at the beginning and open at the upper end of the scale as shown in Fig. 25.21. The obvious disadvantage of such a scale is that the divisions near the start of the scale are small and cannot be read accurately.

Advantages

   (i)   These instruments can be used for both d.c. and a.c. measurements.

  (ii)   Since air-cored coils are used, they are generally free from hysteresis and eddy current errors when used on a.c. circuits.

Disadvantages

   (i)   Since air-cored coils are used, the operating field of these instruments is so weak that considerable errors may be introduced due to stray magnetic fields and in order to protect them, they must be shielded with cast-iron cases.

  (ii)   Since energy must be used to create two magnetic fields, such instruments are relatively insensitive.

 (iii)   The power required is generally greater than that required by permanent-magnet type owing to the greater weight of the moving parts.

 (iv)   Dynamometer type ammeters and voltmeters have uneven scale. However, dynamometer wattmeters (See Art. 25.30) have uniform scale.

  (v)   They are more expensive than the permanent-magnet type instruments.

    Applications. It is clear from above that dynamometer ammeters and voltmeters are inferior to the permanent-magnet moving coil instruments and are seldom used for d.c. measurements. Their chief sphere of application is in a.c. measurements and particularly when the same instrument is required to read both direct and alternating currents as in the a.c. potentiometer.

25.11. MOVING-IRON AMMETERS AND VOLTMETERS

    This type of instrument is principally used for the measurement of alternating currents and voltages, though it can also be used for d.c. measurements. There are two types of moving-iron instruments.

   (i)   *Attraction type* in which a single soft-iron vane (or moving iron) is mounted on the spindle and is attracted towards the coil when operating current flows through it.

---

  *   For ammeters and voltmeters only. However, dynamometer wattmeters have uniform scale (See Art. 25.30).

    (*ii*)   *Repulsion type* in which two soft-iron vanes are used; one fixed and attached to the stationary coil while the other is movable (*i.e.* moving iron) and mounted on the spindle of the instrument. When operating current flows through the coil, the two vanes are magnetised, developing similar polarity at the same ends. Consequently, repulsion takes place between the vanes and the movable vane causes the pointer to move over the scale.

25.12. ATTRACTION TYPE

    Fig. 25.22 shows the constructional details of an attraction type moving-iron instrument. It consists of a cylindrical coil or solenoid which is kept fixed. An oval-shaped soft-iron is attached to the spindle in such a way that it can move in and out of the coil. A pointer is attached to the spindle so that it is deflected with the motion of the soft-iron piece. The controlling torque is provided by one spiral spring arranged at the top of the moving element. It should be noted that in this instrument, the springs do not carry the current as the same is carried by the stationary coil. The *damping device is an aluminium vane attached to the spindle, as shown in Fig 25.22, which moves in a closed air chamber. In some instruments, damping is provided by the movement of a piston inside the curved chamber [See Fig. 25.23]; the piston being attached to the spindle.

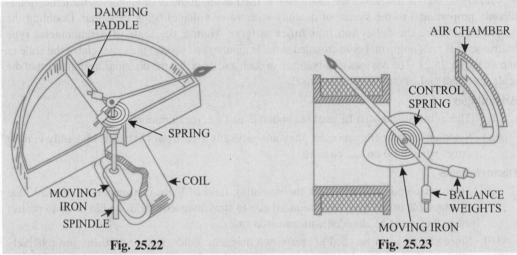

Fig. 25.22   **Fig. 25.23**

    Working. When the instrument is connected in the circuit to measure current or voltage, the operating current flowing through the coil sets up a magnetic field. In other words, the coil behaves like a magnet and therefore it attracts the soft-iron piece towards it. The result is that the pointer attached to the moving system moves from zero position. The pointer will come to rest at a position where deflecting torque is equal to the controlling torque. If current in the coil is reversed, the direction of magnetic field also reverses and so does the magnetism produced in the soft-iron piece. Hence, the direction of the deflecting torque remains unchanged. For this reason, such instruments can be used for both d.c. and a.c. measurements.

    Deflecting torque. The force F pulling the soft-iron piece towards the coil is directly proportional to :

    (*i*)   field strength H produced by the coil

    (*ii*)   pole strength m developed in the iron piece

$$\therefore \qquad\qquad\qquad F \propto m\,H$$

$$\propto H^2 \qquad\qquad\qquad (\because m \propto H)$$

---

*   Eddy current damping is not provided in moving-iron instruments because the presence of the permanent magnet required for the purpose would affect the field due to the coil. This will, in turn, affect the reading of the instrument.

∴   Instantaneous deflecting torque $\propto H^2$

If the permeability of iron is assumed constant, then,

$$H \propto i \text{ where } i \text{ is the instantaneous coil current.}$$

∴   Instantaneous deflecting torque $\propto i^2$

Average deflecting torque, $T_d \propto$ mean of i^2 over a cycle

Since the instrument is spring controlled,

$$T_C \propto \theta$$

In the steady position of deflection, $T_d = T_C$

∴ $\theta \propto$ mean of i^2 over a cycle

$$\propto I^2 \qquad\qquad\qquad .... \text{for d.c.}$$

$$\propto I^2_{r.m.s.} \qquad\qquad .... \text{for a.c.}$$

Since the deflection is proportional to the square of coil current, the scale of such instruments is non-uniform; being crowded in the beginning and spread out near the finish end of the scale.

25.13. REPULSION TYPE

Fig. 25.24 (*i*) shows the constructional details of a repulsion type moving-iron instrument. It consists of two soft-iron pieces or vanes surrounded by a fixed cylindrical hollow coil which carries the operating current. One of these vanes is fixed and the other is free to move as shown in Fig. 25.24 (*ii*). The movable vane is of cylindrical shape and is mounted axially on a spindle to which a pointer is attached. The fixed vane, which is wedge-shaped and has a larger radius, is attached to the stationary coil. The controlling torque is provided by one spiral spring at the top of the instrument. It may be noted that in this instrument, springs do not provide the electrical connections. Damping is provided by air friction due to the motion of a piston in an air chamber.

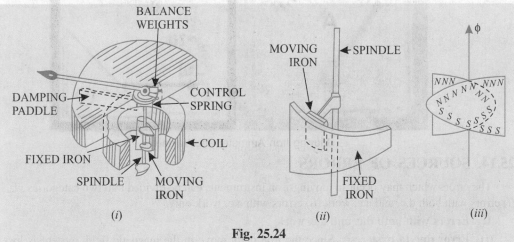

Fig. 25.24

Working. When current to be measured or current proportional to the voltage to be measured flows through the coil, a magnetic field is set up by the coil. This magnetic field magnetises the two vanes in the same direction *i.e.*, similar polarities are developed at the same ends of the vanes as shown in Fig. 25.24 (*iii*). Since the adjacent edges of the vanes are of the same polarity, the two vanes repel each other. As the fixed vane cannot move, the movable vane deflects and causes the pointer to move from zero position. The pointer will come to rest at a position where deflecting torque is equal to the controlling torque provided by the spring. If the current in the coil is reversed, the direction of deflecting torque remains unchanged. It is because reversal of the field of the coil reverses the magnetisation of both iron vanes so that they repel each other regardless of which way the current flows through the coil. For this reason, such instruments can be used for both d.c. and a.c. applications.

Deflecting torque. The deflecting torque results due to the repulsion between the similarly magnetised soft-iron pieces or vanes. If the two pieces develop pole strengths of m_1 and m_2 respectively, then,

Instantaneous deflecting torque $\propto m_1 \, m_2 \propto *H^2$

If the permeability of iron is assumed constant, then,

$$H \propto i \quad \text{where } i \text{ is coil current.}$$

Instantaneous deflecting torque $\propto i^2$

∴ Average deflecting torque, $T_d \propto$ mean of i^2 over a cycle

Since the instrument is spring-controlled,

$$T_C \propto \theta$$

In the steady position of deflection, $T_d = T_C$.

∴ $\qquad\qquad\qquad \theta \propto$ mean of i^2 over a cycle

$$\propto I^2 \qquad\qquad\qquad\qquad\qquad ... for \ d.c.$$

$$\propto I^2_{r.m.s.} \qquad\qquad\qquad\qquad ... for \ a.c.$$

Thus, the deflection is proportional to the square of coil current as is the case with attraction type moving-iron instrument. Therefore, the scale of such instruments is also non-uniform; being crowded in the beginning and spread out near the finish end of the scale. However, the non-linearity of the scale can be corrected to some extent by the accurate shaping (*e.g.* using tongue-shaped vanes) and positioning of iron vanes in relation to the operating coil.

Moving Iron Ammeter and Voltmeter

25.14. SOURCES OF ERRORS

The errors which may occur in moving-iron instruments can be divided into two categories *viz.*, (*i*) errors with both d.c. and a.c. work (*ii*) errors with a.c. work only.

1. **Errors with both d.c. and a.c. work**

(*i*) **Error due to hysteresis.** Since the iron parts move in the magnetic field, hysteresis loss occurs in them. The effect of this error is that the readings are higher when current increases than when it decreases. This error can be reduced by employing vanes of **mumetal and by working it over a low range of flux densities.

---

* Since pole strengths developed are proportional to the field strength H produced by the operating current in the coil.

** Mumetal is a magnetic material having high permeability and low hysteresis loss. However, this material saturates at even medium flux density which affects the deflecting torque. For this reason, working flux density should have a low value.

(*ii*) **Error due to stray fields.** Since the operating field is comparatively weak (say 7×10^{-3} Wb/m^2), such instruments are readily affected by stray fields. This may give rise to wrong readings. This error can be reduced by enclosing the movement in an iron case.

(*iii*) **Error due to temperature.** Change of temperature affects the instrument resistance and stiffness of the control spring.

(*iv*) **Error due to friction.** Due to the friction of moving parts, a slight error may be introduced. This can be avoided by making torque-weight ratio high.

2. **Errors with a.c. work only.** With the change in frequency, the impedance of the instrument coil changes. This will cause a change of current in the coil. This is particularly important in case of voltmeters since these are connected in parallel with the circuit. The indicated voltage *V* is given by :

$$V = I_m \sqrt{(R_m + R_s)^2 + \omega^2 L_m^2}$$

where I_m is the meter current, R_m and L_m are the resistance and inductance of the coil of the meter, and R_s is multiplier. For high frequencies, the meter gives low readings and *vice-versa*. This error can be eliminated by connecting a capacitor of suitable value in parallel with the swamp resistance *r* of the voltmeter. The value of capacitor is given by $C = L_m/r^2$.

25.15. CHARACTERISTICS OF MOVING-IRON INSTRUMENTS

Advantages
(*i*) These are less expensive, robust and simple in construction.
(*ii*) These can be used for both d.c. and a.c. measurements. However, when used with *d.c., they are liable to small errors due to residual magnetism.
(*iii*) These instruments have high operating torque.
(*iv*) These instruments are reasonably accurate.

Disadvantages
(*i*) These instruments have non-linear scales.
(*ii*) These instruments are not as sensitive as the permanent-magnet moving coil instruments.
(*iii*) Errors are introduced due to change in frequency in case of a.c. measurements.

Applications. The moving-iron instruments are primarily used for a.c. measurements *viz.*, alternating currents and voltages. They are not used to measure direct currents and voltages because their characteristics are inferior to permanent-magnet moving coil instruments.

25.16. EXTENDING RANGE OF MOVING-IRON INSTRUMENTS

As explained above, moving-iron instruments are used mainly on a.c. circuits. Therefore, range extension shall be discussed with reference to a.c. measurements.

1. **Ammeter.** Shunts are not used to extend the range of moving-iron a.c. ammeters. It is because the division of current between the operating coil and the shunt varies with frequency (since reactance of the coil depends upon frequency). In practice, the range of moving-iron a.c. ammeter is extended by one of the following two methods:

(*i*) **By changing the number of turns** of the operating coil. For example, suppose that full-scale deflection is obtained with 400 ampere-turns. For full-scale reading with 100A, the number of turns required would be = 400/100 = 4.

Similarly, for full-scale reading with 50 A, the number of turns required is = 400/50 = 8. Thus the ammeter can be arranged to have different ranges by merely having different number of turns on the

---

* A moving-iron instrument can be used to measure direct currents and voltages as long as the effects of a possible residual magnetism in the iron are considered. Thus a second reading should be made with the leads interchanged when the meter is used on d.c. circuits. The average of the two readings gives the true value.

coil. Since the coil carries the whole of the current to be measured, it has a few turns of thick wire. The usual ranges obtained by this method are $0 - 250$ A.

(ii) For ranges above $0 - 250$ A, a **current transformer** is used in conjunction with $0 - 5$ A a.c. ammeter as shown in Fig 25.25. The current transformer is a step-up transformer *i.e.*, number of secondary turns is more than the *primary turns. The primary of this transformer is connected in series with the load and carries the load current. The a.c. ammeter is connected across the secondary of the transformer. Since in Fig 25.25, the current transformer ratio is 10 : 1, it means that the line (or load) current is equal to 10 times the reading on the a.c. meter.

∴   Load current, $I_L = 3 \times 10 = 30$ A

2. **Voltmeter.** The range of a moving-iron a.c. voltmeter is extended by connecting a high resistance (multiplier) in series with it. For ranges higher than $0 - 750$ V, where power wasted in the multiplier would be excessive, a $0 - 110$ V a.c. voltmeter is used in conjunction with a **potential transformer** as shown in Fig. 25.25. The potential transformer is a step-down transformer *i.e.*, number of primary turns is more than the secondary turns. The primary of the transformer is connected across the load across which voltage is to be measured. The a.c. voltmeter is connected across the secondary. Since in Fig. 25.25, the potential transformer ratio is 20 : 1, the load voltage is equal to 20 times the reading on the a.c. voltmeter.

∴   Load voltage, $V_L = 100 \times 20 = 2000$ V

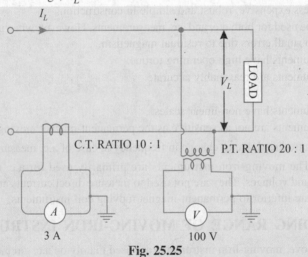

Fig. 25.25

Not that both secondaries of the instrument transformers are grounded as a safety measure.

Example 25.7 *A 15 V moving-iron voltmeter has a resistance of 300 Ω and an inductance of 0.12 H. Assume that the voltmeter reads correctly on d.c., what will be the percentage error when the instrument is placed on 15 V a.c. supply at 100 Hz?*

Solution.

Resistance of meter, $R_m = 300$ Ω

Inductance of meter, $L_m = 0.12$ H

On d.c. circuit.

Meter current, $I_m = V/R_m = 15/300 = 0.05$ A

Since the meter reads correctly on d.c., it means that a current of 0.05 A flowing through the instrument will give a reading of 15 V.

* *

* Usually, the primary winding of the transformer consists of a single turn or at the most a few turns.

On a.c. circuit.

Meter impedance,
$$Z_m = \sqrt{R_m^2 + (2\pi f L_m)^2}$$
$$= \sqrt{(300)^2 + (2\pi \times 100 \times 0.12)^2} = 309.33 \ \Omega$$

∴ Meter current, $\quad I_m' = V/Z_m = 15/309.33 = 0.0485$ A

∴ Meter reading
$$= \frac{15}{0.05} \times 0.0485 = 14.55 \text{ V}$$

% age error
$$= \frac{15 - 14.55}{15} \times 100 = 3\%$$

Example 25.8 *A moving-iron instrument gives full-scale deflection with 200 V. It has a coil of 20,000 turns and a resistance of 2000 Ω. If the instrument is used as an ammeter to give full-scale deflection at 10 A, calculate the number of turns required.*

Solution.

As voltmeter.

Full-scale deflection voltage, $\quad V = 200$ volts

Resistance of instrument coil, $\quad R_m = 2000 \ \Omega$

Full-scale meter current, $\quad I_m = V/R_m = 200/2000 = 0.1$ A

Full-scale AT required $\quad = N I_m = 20,000 \times 0.1 = 2000$

As ammeter. The ampere-turns required to give full-scale deflection should be the same *i.e.* 2000 *AT*. Since the full-scale deflection current is 10 A,

∴ No of turns required = 2000/10 = 200

Example 25.9. *The working coil of a 0 – 400 V moving-iron voltmeter requires 300 ampere-turns to give full-scale deflection. The added resistance is to be three times the coil resistance. Find the diameter of the wire for the coil if the wire be of copper having a resistivity of 1.7×10^{-6} Ω cm; the mean length of one turn = 13.5 cm.*

Solution. The p.d. across the working coil will be one-quarter of the applied voltage, since the added resistance is three times the coil resistance.

∴ Voltage across the coil, $\quad V = \dfrac{400}{4} = 100$ volts

Suppose the number of turns of the coil is N and the full-scale deflection current through the coil is I.

∴ $\qquad\qquad N I = 300 \qquad\qquad\qquad\qquad\qquad$ (given)

Resistance of coil, $\qquad R = \rho \dfrac{*l}{a} = \dfrac{\rho \times l_m \times N}{(\pi/4) d^2}$

or $\qquad\qquad\qquad \dfrac{V}{I} = \dfrac{\rho \times l_m \times N}{(\pi/4) d^2} \qquad\qquad \left[\because R = \dfrac{V}{I} \right]$

∴ Diameter of wire, $\qquad d = \sqrt{\dfrac{4 \times \rho \times l_m \times NI}{\pi \times V}}$

$$= \sqrt{\dfrac{4 \times 1.7 \times 10^{-6} \times 13.5 \times 300}{\pi \times 100}}$$

$$= 0.0094 \text{ cm} = \mathbf{0.094 \text{ mm}}$$

* Length of coil = Mean length of 1 turn × No. of turns = $l_m \times N$

TUTORIAL PROBLEMS

1. A 150 V moving-iron voltmeter is correct at 50 Hz; it has a resistance of 2000 Ω and an inductance of 0.35 H. If it were used on 400 Hz system in an aircraft, what would be its full-scale error ? **[8.25%]**

2. A 50 V moving-iron voltmeter has a resistance of 1000 Ω and an inductance of 0.765 H. Assuming the instrument reads correctly on d.c., what will be the percentage error when the instrument is used to measure alternating voltage of 50 V at 25 Hz? **[0.72%]**

3. A moving-iron voltmeter gives full-scale deflection with 100 V. It has a coil of 10,000 turns and a resistance of 2000 Ω. If the instrument is to be used as an ammeter to give full-scale deflection at 20 A, calculate the number of turns required in the coil. **[25]**

25.17. HOT-WIRE AMMETERS AND VOLTMETERS

The operation of these instruments depends upon the expansion of a wire which is heated due to the passage of electric current. The expansion of the wire is taken up by the moving system which causes the pointer to move over a graduated scale. They are suitable for d.c. as well as a.c. measurements.

Construction. Fig. 25.26 shows the simplified diagram of a hot-wire instrument. It consists of a very thin platinum-iridium wire *AB* stretched between terminals *A* and *B*. The wire *AB* is generally called the hot-wire and carries the operating current of the instrument. A fine phosphor-bronze wire *CD* (called *tension wire*) is attached to the centre *C* of the hot-wire; the other end *D* being fixed to the base of the instrument. A fine silk thread attached to *CD* at *E* passes round a pulley on the spindle and is connected to a spring *F*. The effect of wire *CD* and the silk thread is to *magnify the expansion of the wire *AB*. A pointer is attached to the spindle which moves over the scale as the hot-wire *AB* expands. A thin light aluminium disc is attached to the pulley and moves between the poles of a permanent magnet M. Eddy currents produced in the disc provide the necessary damping. The instrument is generally spring controlled.

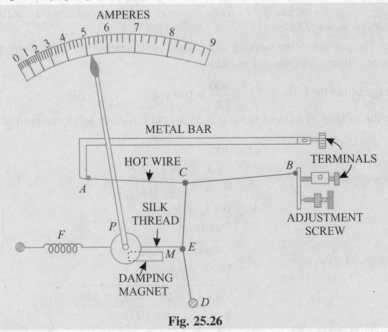

Fig. 25.26

---

* The co-efficient of linear expansion of most metals is quite small, say 0.000015. Therefore, passage of current through the hot-wire will cause a very little expansion of the wire. With this arrangement, we measure the sag (*i.e.*, downward movement of point *C* due to the expansion of the wire *AB*) which would be much larger than the actual expansion of the wire *AB*.

Working. When the instrument is connected in the circuit to measure current or voltage, the operating current flows through the hot-wire *AB*. This causes the hot-wire to expand. The slack in the hot-wire is taken up by the spring *F*, causing the pulley *P* to turn and move the pointer over the scale. When the operating current ceases to flow, the wire *AB* cools and contracts, and the silk thread is pulled to the right causing the pointer to return to zero. Since the tension of wire *AB* changes with temperature, the pointer is set to zero (with adjustment screw) practically each time the instrument is to be used. As the heating effect of electric current is independent of the direction of current flow, therefore, such instruments can be used for both d.c. and a.c. work.

Deflecting torque. The expansion of the hot-wire depends upon $i^2 R$ loss where i is the instantaneous current through the hot wire *AB*.

∴   Average deflecting torque, $T_d \propto$ mean of i^2 over a cycle

Since the instrument is spring-controlled,

$$T_C \propto \theta$$

In the steady position of deflection, $T_d = T_C$

∴ $\theta \propto$ mean of i^2 over a cycle

$$\propto I^2 \qquad\qquad\qquad ... for\ d.c.$$

$$\propto I^2_{r.m.s.} \qquad\qquad ... for\ a.c.$$

Note that deflection is directly proportional to the square of current through the hot-wire. If current is increased two times, the deflection is increased four times. Hence such instruments have square-law scale; being crowded in the beginning and open near the end of the scale.

Advantages

(*i*)   They can be used for both d.c. and a.c. measurements.

(*ii*) Their readings are independent of waveform and frequency.

(*iii*) They are unaffected by stray magnetic fields.

Disadvantages

(*i*)   They have non-uniform scale.

(*ii*) They have a sluggish action since the hot-wire takes some time to reach its final temperature.

(*iii*) Their zero position needs frequent adjustment.

(*iv*) They are liable to burn out or the hot-wire melts, if over-loaded.

(*v*)   They have a high power consumption.

Range extension. The range of a hot-wire voltmeter can be extended by using a high resistance (multiplier) in series with the hot-wire. The ammeter range can be extended by using a shunt. However, for use at radio frequency, special precautions must be observed in the design of the instrument and the shunt; in particular inductance must be avoided as far as possible.

Applications

(*i*)   Hot-wire instruments are particularly useful for a.c. measurements and are as a rule cheaper than instruments based on dynamometer principle.

(*ii*) Hot-wire instruments are used for high-frequency alternating currents (*e.g.* in wireless work) because the inductance of the hot-wire is very small. Dynamometer or moving-iron instruments are unsuitable at such high frequencies.

(*iii*) Hot-wire ammeters are not, however, as accurate as dynamometer ammeters, and must be calibrated by comparison with a d.c. ammeter, say of the moving-coil type.

25.18. ELECTROSTATIC VOLTMETERS

These instruments are based on the fact that an electric force (attraction or repulsion) exists between charged plates or objects. An electrostatic voltmeter is essentially an air condenser; one plate is fixed while the other, which is coupled to the pointer, is free to rotate on jewelled bearings. When p.d. to be measured is applied across the plates, the electric force between the plates gives rise to a deflecting torque. Under the action of deflecting torque, the movable plate moves and causes the deflection of the pointer to indicate the voltage being measured. Such instruments can be used to measure direct as well as alternating voltages.

There are three types of electrostatic voltmeters *viz.*:

(*i*)	Attracted disc type	— usual range from 500 V to 500 kV
(*ii*)	Quadrant type	— usual range from 250 V to 10 kV
(*iii*)	Multicellular type	— usual range from 30 V to 300 V

Two things are worth noting about electrostatic voltmeters. First, the deflecting torque is very small for low voltages. For this reason, they are not very sensitive to measure small voltages. Secondly, the instrument is only available for the measurement of p.d., that is to say as voltmeter. It cannot be used as an *ammeter.

25.19. ATTRACTED DISC TYPE VOLTMETER

Fig. 25.27 shows the simplified diagram of an attracted disc electrostatic voltmeter. It consists of two mushroom-shaped plates *A* and *B*, each mounted on insulated pedestal. The plate *B* is fixed while the plate *A* (negative, for direct voltage) has a movable central portion-the attracted disc. The movable plate *A* is attached to a horizontal rod which is suspended by two phosphor bronze strips. When p.d. to be measured is applied across the plates, the plate *A* moves towards the fixed plate *B* and actuates the pointer *via* a pulley or link mechanism. The control force is provided by gravity and damping force by air dash pot. If the plates are too close together or if the applied voltage is too high, a spark discharge

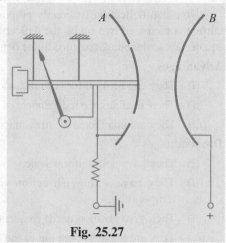

Fig. 25.27

may occur. In order to prevent such a possibility, a **ballast resistor is included in the circuit. The function of this resistor is to limit the current if any sparking-over occurs. If the applied voltage reverses in polarity, there is a simultaneous change in the sign of charge on the plates so that the direction of deflecting force remains unchanged. Hence such instruments can be used for both d.c. and a.c. measurements.

Theory. The force of attraction *F* between the charged plates is given by;

$$F = \frac{1}{2} \frac{dC}{dx} V^2$$

where x = distance between the plates

---

* When used as an ammeter, there will be a few millivolts voltage across the instrument. This extremely small p.d. is insufficient to produce any deflecting torque.

** When direct voltage is being measured, there will be no voltage drop across this resistor. For alternating voltages, the drop will be negligible at low frequencies. Hence, this resistor will not cause any error in the measurement of voltage.

C = capacitance between the plates

V = applied voltage

Since x is always small, dC/dx is practically constant.

∴ $F \propto V^2$

Obviously, the scale of the instrument will be non-uniform.

25.20. QUADRANT TYPE VOLTMETER

Fig. 25.28 shows the simplified diagram of a quadrant electrostatic voltmeter. It consists of a light aluminium vane A suspended by a phosphorbronze string mid-way between two inter-connected quadrant shaped brass plates BB. One terminal is joined to fixed plates BB (positive for direct voltage) and the other to the movable plate A (negative for direct voltage). The controlling torque is provided by the torsion of the suspension string. Damping is provided by air friction due to the motion of another vane in a partially closed box.

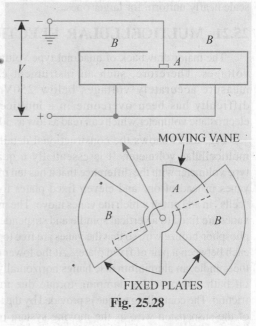

Working. When the instrument is connected in the circuit to measure the p.d., an electric force exists between the plates. Consequently, the movable vane A moves in between the fixed plates and causes the deflection of the pointer. The pointer comes to rest at a position where deflecting torque is equal to the controlling torque. Since the force of attraction between the movable plate A and the fixed plates BB is directly proportional to (p.d.)^2, the

Fig. 25.28

instrument can be used to measure either direct or alternating voltages. When used in an a.c. circuit, it reads the r.m.s. values. More robust but *less accurate voltmeters are made by pivoting the moving system. In pivoted voltmeters, the controlling torque is provided by a spiral spring.

Theory. The capacitance C between the plates depends upon deflection θ *i.e.*, upon the position of the movable plate (or vane) A. Suppose that at any instant, the applied alternating voltage is v.

Electrostatic energy at that instant $= \dfrac{1}{2} Cv^2$

Since the capacitance between the plates depends upon deflection θ, the instantaneous deflecting torque $T_d{'}$ is given by;

$$T_d{'} = \frac{1}{2} \frac{dC}{d\theta} v^2$$

Average deflecting torque, T_d = Average of $T_d{'}$ over a cycle

$$= \frac{1}{T} \int_0^T \frac{1}{2} \frac{dC}{d\theta} v^2 \, dt$$

$$= \frac{1}{2} \frac{dC}{d\theta} \cdot \frac{1}{T} \int_0^T v^2 \, dt$$

---

*   Due to pivot friction, the pivoted voltmeters are less accurate than the suspension type. For this reason, low voltage electrostatic voltmeters are always of suspension type.

$$\therefore \qquad T_d = \frac{1}{2}\frac{dC}{d\theta}V^2$$

where $\qquad\qquad\qquad\qquad V$ = r.m.s. value of alternating voltage.

This equation equally applies to direct voltages. If $dC/d\theta$ were constant, then,

$$T_d \propto V^2$$

Hence the instrument has non-uniform scale. The non-linearity in the scale can be corrected by shaping the movable vane A in such a way as to increase $dC/d\theta$ for small deflections and to make the scale nearly uniform for larger ones.

25.21. MULTICELLULAR ELECTROSTATIC VOLTMETER

The major drawback of quadrant type voltmeter is that deflecting torque is very *small for low voltages. Therefore, such an instrument cannot measure accurately voltages below 250V. This difficulty has been overcome in a multicellular electrostatic voltmeter which can read as low as 30 volts.

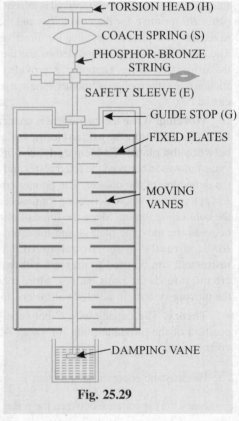

Fig. 25.29 shows the constructional details of a multicellular voltmeter. It is essentially a quadrant type voltmeter with the difference that it has ten moving vanes instead of one and eleven fixed plates forming "cells" in and out of which the vanes move. The moving vanes are fixed to a vertical spindle and suspended by a phosphor-bronze wire so that the vanes are free to move, each between a pair of fixed plates. At the lower end of the spindle, an aluminium disc hangs horizontally in an oil bath and provides damping torque due to fluid friction. The controlling torque is provided by the torsion of the suspension wire as the moving system rotates. The upper end of the suspension wire is attached through a coach spring S to a torsion head H. The torsion head is provided with a tangent screw for zero adjustment. The function of the coach spring is to prevent the suspension wire from breaking when accidentally jerked. Should the moving vanes be jerked downward, then the coach spring yields sufficiently to allow the safety sleeve E to come into contact with the guide stop G before the suspension wire is over strained. The scale is horizontal if the pointer is straight but the indications can be given on a vertical scale by bending the pointer at right angles.

Fig. 25.29

The working principle of multicellular voltmeter is exactly similar to the quadrant type. By using a number of inter-leaved stationary and moving plates, we are able to increase the capacitance and hence the deflecting torque. Consequently, the multicellular voltmeter is much more sensitive than the quadrant type and can accurately measure low voltages.

25.22. CHARACTERISTICS OF ELECTROSTATIC VOLTMETERS

It is worthwhile to mention the advantages, disadvantages and applications of electrostatic voltmeters.

---

* Deflecting torque also depends upon the capacitance between plates $\left[i.e. T_d = \frac{1}{2}(dC/d\theta)\,V^2 \right]$. In a quadrant voltmeter, the capacitance cannot be increased since the number of vanes is limited by space consideration.

Advantages

(*i*) They can be used for both d.c. and a.c. measurements.

(*ii*) They draw *negligible power from the mains. Hence such voltmeters do not alter the conditions of the circuit to which they are connected.

(*iii*) They are free from hysteresis and eddy current losses as no iron is used in their construction.

(*iv*) Their readings are independent of waveform and frequency.

(*v*) They are unaffected by stray magnetic fields, although electrostatic fields (set up, for instance, by such a simple process as rubbing the glass of the case to clean it) may cause considerable errors.

Disadvantages

(*i*) The operating force is very small for low voltages so that they are particularly suitable for the measurement of high voltages.

(*ii*) Since the operating force is generally small, errors due to friction are difficult to avoid.

(*iii*) They are expensive, large in size and are not robust in construction.

(*iv*) Their scale is non-uniform; being crowded in the beginning of the scale.

Applications

(*i*) They are used for the measurement of very high direct voltages at which a permanent magnet moving coil instrument and the multiplier would be unsuitable.

(*ii*) They are used to measure direct low voltages when it is necessary to preserve an open circuit.

(*iii*) They are used to measure very high alternating voltages when the use of a transformer must be avoided.

25.23. RANGE EXTENSION OF ELECTROSTATIC VOLTMETERS

The range of electrostatic voltmeters can be increased by the use of multipliers. Two types of multipliers are employed for this purpose *viz.*

(*i*) Resistance potential divider — for ranges upto 40kV

(*ii*) Capacitance potential divider — for ranges upto 1000 kV

The first method can be used for both direct and alternating voltages whereas the second method is suitable only for alternating voltages.

(*i*) **Resistance potential divider.** This divider consists of a high resistance with tappings taken off at intermediate points. The voltage *V* to be measured is applied across the whole of the potential divider and the electrostatic voltmeter connected across part of it (resistance *r* in this case) as shown in Fig. 25.30. Since the voltmeter **practically carries no current, the p.d. *v* across it is the same fraction of the applied voltage *V* as the resistance across it (*i.e.*, *r*) is of the whole resistance (*i.e. R*) *i.e.*, .

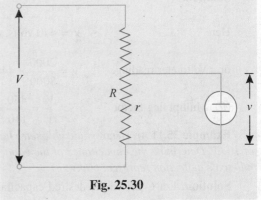

Fig. 25.30

$$\text{Multiplying factor, } \frac{V}{v} = \frac{R}{r}$$

* With direct voltage, the instrument draws only the initial charging current. With alternating voltages, the alternating current drawn is extremely small.

** An electrostatic voltmeter is essentially an air capacitor. For direct voltages, no current can flow through it. For alternating voltages, the current through the voltmeter is extremely small.

Thus if the voltmeter is connected across 1/5 of the whole resistance (*i.e.*, $R/r = 5$), then voltage V to be measured is 5 times the reading of the voltmeter. The advantage of this method is that there is no shunting effect of the voltmeter. The drawback is that there is power loss in the resistance divider.

(*ii*) **Capacitance potential divider.** In this method, a single capacitor of capacitance C is connected in series with the voltmeter and the whole circuit is connected across the voltage V to be measured as shown in Fig. 25.31. Let v volts be the reading of the voltmeter. Since the voltage across a capacitor is inversely proportional to its capacitance,

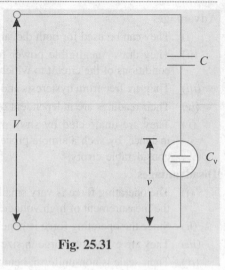

Fig. 25.31

$$\therefore \qquad V \propto \frac{{}^{*}C + C_v}{C \times C_v}$$

and

$$v \propto \frac{1}{C_v}$$

$\therefore$ Multiplying factor,

$$\frac{V}{v} = \frac{C + C_v}{C}$$

$$= 1 + \frac{C_v}{C}$$

By using capacitors of different capacitances, different voltage ranges can be obtained. This method has the advantage that the circuit consumes no power. However, the drawback is that capacitance current taken is greatly increased.

Example 25.10 *A non-inductive coil AB is connected across 440 V mains and an electrostatic voltmeter of negligible capacitance is connected across a portion CD of this coil. The resistance of the coil AB is 8000 Ω and that of portion CD is 2000 Ω. Find (i) the reading of the voltmeter and (ii) multiplying factor.*

Solution. (*i*)
$$\frac{V}{v} = \frac{R}{r}$$

Here $\qquad V = 440$ volts, $R = 8000$ Ω; $r = 2000$ Ω $\qquad \therefore \qquad \dfrac{440}{v} = \dfrac{8000}{2000}$

or Voltmeter reading, $\qquad v = \dfrac{2000}{8000} \times 440 = \textbf{110 volts}$

(*ii*) Multiplying factor $\qquad = \dfrac{V}{v} = \dfrac{440}{110} = \textbf{4}$

Example 25.11 *An electrostatic voltmeter has a capacitance of 0.1 μF and full-scale deflection of 10 kV. Determine the capacitance of the capacitor to be connected in series which will make the full-scale deflection represent 60 kV.*

Solution. Let C μF be the desired capacitance of the capacitor connected in series with the voltmeter.

$$\frac{V}{v} = 1 + \frac{C_v}{C} \qquad\qquad ...See\ Art.\ 25.23$$

$*$ Total circuit capacitance $= \dfrac{C \times C_v}{C + C_v}$ because C and C_v are in series.

Here $\quad\quad V = 60$ kV; $\quad v = 10$ kV; $C_v = 0.1$ μF

∴ $\quad\quad \dfrac{60}{10} = 1 + \dfrac{0.1}{C}$ $\quad$ or $\quad$ $C = 0.02$ μF

Example 25.12 *An electrostatic voltmeter reading upto 1000 volts is controlled by a spring with a torsion constant of 9.81×10^{-8} Nm per degree and has a full-scale deflection of 80°. The capacitance of the voltmeter is 10 μμF when it reads zero. What is the capacitance when the pointer indicates 1000 V?*

Solution.

Deflecting torque, $\quad\quad\quad\quad\quad T_d = \dfrac{1}{2} \dfrac{dC}{d\theta} V^2$ $\quad\quad\quad\quad\quad$ ...See Art. 25.20

Controlling torque, $\quad\quad\quad\quad\quad T_C = k\theta$

In the steady position of deflection, $\quad T_d = T_C$.

∴ $\quad\quad\quad\quad\quad k\theta = \dfrac{1}{2} \dfrac{dC}{d\theta} V^2$

or $\quad\quad\quad\quad\quad \dfrac{dC}{d\theta} = \dfrac{2k\theta}{V^2} = \dfrac{2 \times (9.81 \times 10^{-8}) \times 80}{(1000)^2} = 15.7 \times 10^{-12}$ F per radian

$\quad\quad\quad\quad\quad\quad\quad = 15.7$ μμF per radian $= 0.274$ μμF per degree

Change in capacitance when voltmeter reads 1000 V

$$= \dfrac{dC}{d\theta} \times \theta = 0.274 \times 80 = 21.92 \text{ μμF}$$

Total capacitance of the voltmeter when it reads 1000 V

$$= 10 + 21.92 = 31.92 \text{ μμF}$$

25.24. INDUCTION TYPE INSTRUMENTS

This class of instruments is suitable only for a.c. measurements. These instruments may be used either as ammeter or voltmeter or wattmeter or energy meter. Perhaps the widest application of induction principle is in watt-hour or energy meter.

Principle. Fig. 25.32 illustrates the principle of induction type instruments. Two alternating fluxes ϕ_1 and ϕ_2 (whose magnitudes depend upon the current or voltage to be measured) having a phase difference θ pass through a metallic disc, usually of copper or aluminium. These alternating fluxes induce currents in the disc. The current produced by one flux reacts with the other flux, and *vice-versa*, to produce the deflecting torque that acts on the disc. It can be proved that net deflecting torque on the disc is given by;

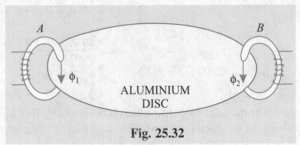

Fig. 25.32

$$T_d \propto \phi_{1m} \phi_{2m} \sin \theta$$

where $\quad\quad\quad \phi_{1m} = $ maximum value of alternating flux ϕ_1

$\quad\quad\quad\quad\quad \phi_{2m} = $ maximum value of alternating flux ϕ_2

Obviously, to obtain maximum deflecting torque, the angle θ (*i.e.* phase angle between ϕ_1 and ϕ_2) should be 90°.

The induction type instruments are worked on single phase. The question arises how to obtain two fluxes having a phase difference θ (= 90° as far as possible) from a single phase supply. This can be achieved in two ways *viz.*

1. Splitting the phase (*i.e.* Ferrari's Principle)

2. Shaded-pole arrangement

1. Splitting the phase. In this method, two flux-producing windings are connected in parallel across a single phase supply; an inductive coil L in series with one and a resistance R in series with the other. The values of R and L are so selected that currents through the two windings [*i.e.* I_R and I_L in Fig. 25.33 (*i*)] have a phase difference of nearly 90°. The result is that we have two alternating fluxes with a relative phase shift of 90°. These fluxes pass through the aluminium disc and induce currents in it to produce the necessary driving torque.

The fluxes produced by the two currents may be represented as:

$$\phi_1 = \phi_{1m} \sin \omega t$$
$$\phi_2 = \phi_{2m} \sin (\omega t + \theta)$$

where θ is the phase angle by which ϕ_2 leads ϕ_1.

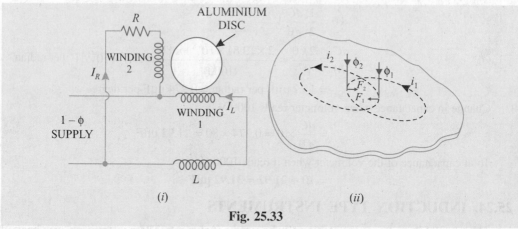

(i)   (ii)

Fig. 25.33

The two fluxes ϕ_1 and ϕ_2 will induce e.m.f.s e_1 and e_2 respectively in the disc. Assuming r to be the resistance offered by the disc to each induced e.m.f., the induced currents are given by;

$$i_1 = \frac{e_1}{r} = \frac{d\phi_1/dt}{r} = \frac{1}{r} \frac{d}{dt} (\phi_{1m} \sin \omega t)$$

$$= \frac{\omega \phi_{1m} \cos \omega t}{r}$$

or $i_1 \propto \phi_{1m} \cos \omega t$ *... as r and ω are constant*

Similarly, $i_2 \propto \phi_{2m} \cos (\omega t + \theta)$

The portion of the disc which is traversed by flux ϕ_1 and carries current i_2 experiences a force F_1 along the direction indicated. The magnitude of this force is given by;

$$F_1 \propto \phi_1 i_2$$

Similarly, $F_2 \propto \phi_2 i_1$

Since the direction of both fluxes and both currents are the same, these forces will be in the opposite directions. This can be easily ascertained by applying left-hand rule.

∴   Resultant force, $F \propto F_2 - F_1$

$$\propto (\phi_2 i_1 - \phi_1 i_2)$$
$$\propto \phi_{1m} \phi_{2m} [\sin (\omega t + \theta) \cos \omega t - \sin \omega t \cos (\omega t + \theta)]$$
$$\propto \phi_{1m} \phi_{2m} \sin \theta$$

This resultant force will produce the deflecting torque T_d which is directly proportional to it.

∴ $T_d \propto \phi_{1m} \phi_{2m} \sin \theta$

(i) If $\theta = 0°$ (*i.e.* the two fluxes are in phase), then deflecting torque is zero. The deflecting torque will be maximum when $\theta = 90°$ *i.e.* when the alternating fluxes have a phase difference of $90°$.

(ii) The deflecting torque is the same at every instant since ϕ_{1m}, ϕ_{2m} and θ are fixed for a given condition.

(iii) The direction of deflecting torque depends upon which flux is leading the other. The deflecting torque acts in such a direction so as to rotate the disc from the point where the leading flux passes the disc towards the point where the lagging flux passes the disc.

2. Shaded-pole arrangement. The shaded-pole structure differs from the split-phase type in that there is only one flux-producing winding connected to a.c. supply. The flux ϕ produced by this winding is split into two portions ϕ_1 and ϕ_2 having a phase difference of θ by shaded-pole arrangement as shown in Fig. 25.34. In this arrangement, one-half of each pole (on the same side) embraces a thick short-circuited copper loop called a *shading coil*. The shading coil acts as a short-circuited secondary and the main winding as a primary. Induced currents in the *shading coil cause the flux ϕ_1 in the shaded portion to lag the flux ϕ_2 in the unshaded portion by θ (= 40° to 50°). This displacement between the two fluxes produces the necessary deflecting torque given by;

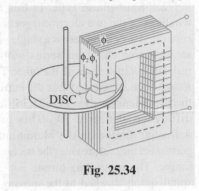

Fig. 25.34

$$T_d \propto \phi_{1m}\, \phi_{2m} \sin \theta$$

25.25. INDUCTION AMMETERS AND VOLTMETERS

Induction ammeters and voltmeters can be used for a.c. measurements only and can be of shaded-pole type or split-phase type.

1. Shaded-pole type. Fig. 25.35 shows the principal parts of a shaded-pole type instrument. It consists of a specially shaped aluminium disc coupled to a pointer and suspended in jewelled bearings. The disc passes through two air-gaps; the first located in an electromagnet having a shading coil and the second in a permanent magnet. The permanent magnet provides the necessary damping torque. The controlling torque is provided by a spiral spring attached to the moving system. As shown above, the deflecting torque is given by;

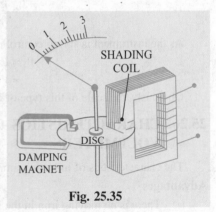

Fig. 25.35

$$T_d \propto \phi_{1m}\, \phi_{2m} \sin \theta$$

(i) When used as an ammeter, the current to be measured or a part of it is passed through the operating coil of the instrument. Since both the fluxes are produced by the same alternating current I (r.m.s. value),

$$\therefore \qquad T_d \propto I^2$$

As the instrument is spring controlled, $T_C \propto \theta$

$$\therefore \qquad \theta \propto I^2$$

* * * * *

* Note that shading coil serves the same purpose as connecting resistance and inductance in split-phase arrangement.

(*ii*) When used as a voltmeter, current proportional to the voltage to be measured is passed through the operating coil.

$$\therefore \qquad\qquad T_d \propto V^2$$

Again the instrument is spring controlled, $T_C \propto \theta$

$$\therefore \qquad\qquad \theta \propto V^2$$

It is clear that shaded-pole instruments have uneven scale, being crowded in the beginning and open near the end of the scale. However, the non-linearity in the scale can be corrected to a considerable extent by modifying the shape of the disc *i.e.*, by using cam-shaped disc.

2. Split-phase type. In this method, the windings of the two electromagnets A and B are connected in parallel across a single phase supply; an inductive coil L in series with one and a resistance R in series with the other. The values of R and L are so selected that the currents through the two windings [See Fig. 25.36] have a phase difference of nearly 90°. This produces the deflecting torque on the aluminium disc. The permanent magnet provides the necessary damping torque. The controlling torque is provided by a spiral spring attached to the moving system. As shown above, the deflecting torque is given by;

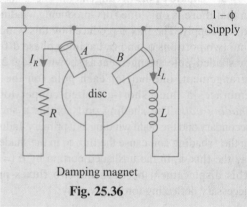

Fig. 25.36

$$T_d \propto \phi_{1m} \; \phi_{2m} \sin \theta$$

Both fluxes are proportional to current or voltage to be measured

$$\therefore \qquad\qquad T_d \propto I^2 \qquad\qquad\qquad \textit{... for ammeter}$$
$$\propto V^2 \qquad\qquad\qquad \textit{... for voltmeter}$$

As the instrument is spring controlled, $T_C \propto \theta$

$$\therefore \qquad\qquad \theta \propto I^2 \qquad\qquad\qquad \textit{... for ammeter}$$
$$\propto V^2 \qquad\qquad\qquad \textit{... for voltmeter}$$

Obviously, the scale of this type of instrument is also non-uniform.

25.26. CHARACTERISTICS OF INDUCTION AMMETERS AND VOLTMETERS

The characteristics of induction ammeters and voltmeters are given below:

Advantages

(*i*) There is no moving iron in the instrument.

(*ii*) The moving element (*i.e.* disc) is not electrically connected to the circuit.

(*iii*) A full-scale deflection of over 250° can be obtained.

(*iv*) They provide very effective damping.

(*v*) They are not easily affected by stray magnetic fields owing to the intense concentration of instrument's own field.

Disadvantages

(*i*) They have high cost.

(*ii*) They have non-linear scales.

(*iii*) They can be used for a.c. measurements only.

(*iv*) They introduce fairly large errors due to temperature, frequency and wave-form variations.

(v) They consume fairly large power because of relatively large power losses in the shading coil.

Range extension. In voltmeters, the operating coil is of fine wire, a non-inductive resistance R being connected in series with it. In ammeters, the coil is comparatively of thick wire. A voltmeter is connected in the circuit either directly or through a potential transformer depending upon the voltage to be measured. An ammeter is connected directly in the circuit for currents upto 10A provided the circuit voltage does not exceed 650 V. Beyond that, it is usual to employ a current transformer.

Applications. The sources of errors in induction ammeters and voltmeters have been considerably reduced by the use of special alloys and modern design. Consequently, they are superseding other types (e.g. moving-iron voltmeters and ammeters) for switchboards and panels.

25.27. OHMMETER

A device that measures the resistance directly is called an ohmmeter. The simplest direct reading ohmmeter is the basic *series ohmmeter* circuit shown in Fig. 25.37 (*i*). It consists of a permanent magnet moving coil (PMMC) instrument in series with a battery and a rheostat R. Note that A and B are the terminals of ohmmeter.

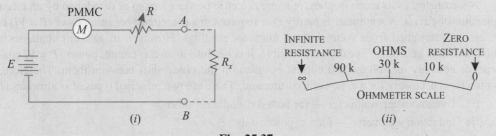

Fig. 25.37

(*i*) With terminals A and B shorted together, R is adjusted for full-scale deflection (f.s.d.). Since terminals A and B are shorted, the ohmmeter should read zero resistance. Thus as shown in Fig. 25.37 (*ii*), the full-scale deflection should read zero resistance.

Full-scale deflection current, $\qquad I_g = \dfrac{E}{R}$ $\qquad\qquad$ (neglecting meter resistance)

(*ii*) When terminals A and B are open-circuited, the pointer should indicate infinity. Therefore, zero deflection point on the scale is marked as infinite resistance [See Fig. 25.37 (*ii*)].

(*iii*) When an unknown resistance R_x is connected to terminals A and B, the meter current I_m is

$$I_m = \frac{E}{R + R_x}$$

Since the value of I_m is more than zero and less than I_g (f.s.d.), the meter will give a reading between zero and infinity. Thus the value of unknown resistance R_x can be determined.

Note: The circuit shown in Fig. 25.37 (*i*) relies upon battery voltage remaining absolutely constant. When the battery terminal voltage falls (as they all do with use), the instrument scale is no longer accurate. Thus some means of adjusting for battery voltage variations must be built in the circuit.

25.28. MEGGER

The megohmmeter (or megger) is an instrument for measuring very high resistance such as the insulation resistance of electrical cables. A megger is essentially an ohmmeter with its own hand-cranked high voltage generator (See Fig. 25.38). The generated voltage may be anything from 100 V to 2.5 kV. The high voltage source is required to pass a measurable current through the high resistance to be measured.

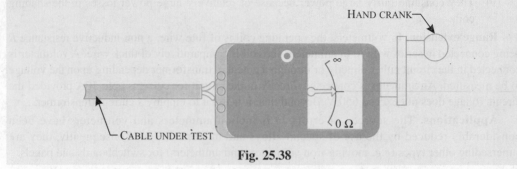

HAND CRANK

CABLE UNDER TEST

Fig. 25.38

As in the case of ohmmeter, the scale of the megger indicates infinity (∞) when its terminals are open-circuited and zero when the megger terminals are shorted. When the unknown resistance is connected to megger terminals, it gives the value of resistance between zero and infinity. The range of the instrument can be changed by switching different values of standard resistor in the circuit.

25.29. WATTMETERS

A wattmeter, as its name implies, measures electric power given to or developed by an electric apparatus or circuit. A wattmeter is hardly ever required in a d.c. circuit because power ($P = VI$) can be easily determined from voltmeter and ammeter readings. However, in an a.c. circuit, such a computation is generally *speaking impossible. It is because in an a.c. circuit, power ($P = VI \cos \phi$) depends not only on voltage and current but also on the phase shift between them. Therefore, a wattmeter is necessary for a.c. power measurement. There are two principal types of wattmeters viz.,

(*i*) Dynamometer wattmeter — for both d.c. and a.c. power

(*ii*) Induction wattmeter — for a.c. power only

Wattmeters

25.30. DYNAMOMETER WATTMETER

A dynamometer wattmeter is almost universally used for the measurement of d.c. as well as a.c. power. It works on the dynamometer principle *i.e.* mechanical force exists between two current carrying conductors or coils.

* Except for the case of pure resistance when $P = VI$ (∵ $\cos \phi$ is 1 for pure resistance).

Construction. When a dynamometer instrument is used as a wattmeter, the fixed coils are connected in series with the load and carry the load current (I_1) while the moving coil is connected across the load through a series multiplier R and carries a current (I_2) proportional to the load voltage as shown in Fig 25.39. The fixed coil (or coils) is called the *current coil* and the movable coil is known as *potential coil*. The controlling torque is provided by two spiral springs which also serve the additional purpose of leading current into and out of the moving coil. Air friction damping is provided in such instruments. A pointer is attached to the movable coil.

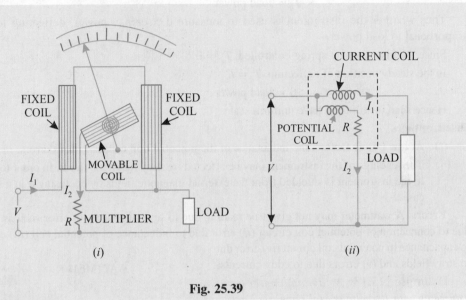

Fig. 25.39

Working. When the wattmeter is connected in the circuit to measure power (See Fig. 25.39), the current coil carries the load current and potential coil carries current proportional to the load voltage. Due to currents in the coils, mechanical force exists between them. The result is that movable coil moves the pointer over the scale. The pointer comes to rest at a position where deflecting torque is equal to the controlling torque. Reversal of current reverses currents in both the fixed coils and the movable coil so that the direction of deflecting torque remains unchanged. Hence, such instruments can be used for the measurement of d.c. as well as a.c. power.

Deflecting torque. We shall now prove that deflecting torque is proportional to load power in a d.c. as well as a.c. circuit.

(i) Consider that the wattmeter is connected in a d.c. circuit to measure power as shown in Fig. 25.39 (ii). The power taken by the load is VI_1.

Deflecting torque, $\qquad T_d \propto I_1 I_2$

Since I_2 is directly proportional to V,

∴ Deflecting torque, $\qquad T_d \propto V I_1 \propto$ load power

(ii) Consider that the wattmeter is connected in an a.c. circuit to measure power. Suppose at any instant, current through the load is i and voltage across the load is v. Let the load power factor be $\cos \phi$ lagging. Then,

$$v = V_m \sin \theta$$
$$i = I_m \sin (\theta - \phi)$$

Instantaneous deflecting torque $\propto v \, i$

The pointer cannot follow the rapid changes in the instantaneous power owing to the large inertia of the moving system. Hence the instrument indicates the mean or average power.

∴   Average deflecting torque, $T_d \propto$ Average of $v\, i$ over a cycle

$$\propto \frac{1}{2\pi} \int_0^{2\pi} V_m I_m \sin \theta \, \sin (\theta - \phi) \, d\theta$$

$$\propto \frac{V_m I_m}{2} \cos \phi$$

$$\propto VI \cos \phi$$

∴ $T_d \propto$ load power

Thus whether the instrument is used to measure d.c. or a.c. power, deflecting torque is proportional to load power.

Since the instrument is spring-controlled, $T_C \propto \theta$

In the steady position of deflection, $T_d = T_C$

∴ $\theta \propto$ load power

Hence such instruments have uniform scale.

Disadvantages

(*i*)   At low power factors, the inductance of the potential coil causes serious errors.

(*ii*) The readings of the instrument may be affected by stray magnetic fields. In order to prevent it, the instrument is shielded from the external magnetic fields by enclosing it in a soft-iron case.

Errors. A wattmeter may not give true reading due to several sources of error such as (*i*) error due to connection of potential coil circuit (*ii*) error due to inductance of potential coil (*iii*) error due to capacitance in potential coil circuit (*iv*) error due to stray fields and (*v*) errors due to eddy currents.

Example 25.13 *A dynamometer type wattmeter with its voltage coil connected across the load side reads 192 W. The load voltage is 208 V and the resistance of the potential coil circuit is 3825 Ω. Calculate (i) true load power and (ii) percentage error due to wattmeter connection.*

Solution. Since the voltage coil of the wattmeter is connected on the load side (See Fig. 25.40), the power consumed by it is also included in the reading of the wattmeter.

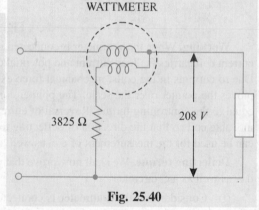

Fig. 25.40

Wattmeter reading = 192 W

Power taken by potential circuit

$$= \frac{(208)^2}{3825}$$

$$= 11.3 \text{ W}$$

(*i*)   True load power   = 192 − 11.3 = **180.7 W**

(*ii*) %age error $= \dfrac{192 - 180.7}{180.7} \times 100 = \mathbf{6.25\%}$

Example 25.14. *The resistances of the two coils of a wattmeter are 0.01 Ω and 1000 Ω respectively and both are non-inductive. The load is taking a current of 20 A at 200 V and 0.8 p.f. lagging. Show the two ways in which the voltage coil can be connected and find the error in the reading of the meter in each case.*

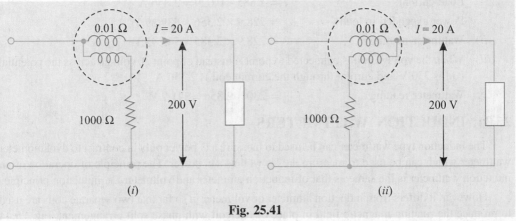

Fig. 25.41

Solution. Fig. 25.41 shows the two possible ways of connecting the voltage coil of the wattmeter.

Load power	$= VI \cos \phi = 200 \times 20 \times 0.8 = 3200$ W

Consider the connections shown in Fig. 25.41 (*i*).

Power loss in current coil	$= I^2 R_C = (20)^2 \times 0.01 = 4$ W
∴ Wattmeter reading	$= 3200 + 4 = 3204$ W
% age error	$= (4/3200) \times 100 = \mathbf{0.125\%}$

Consider the connections shown in Fig. 25.41 (*ii*).

Power loss in voltage coil	$= V^2/R_p = (200)^2/1000 = 40$ W
∴ Wattmeter reading	$= 3200 + 40 = 3240$ W
% age error	$= (40/3200) \times 100 = \mathbf{1.25\%}$

Example 25.15. *In the circuit shown in Fig. 25.42, reading of the voltmeter is 230 V and that of ammeter is 2.5 A. The resistances of the meters are as follows:*

Voltmeter circuit = 2000 Ω; Wattmeter current coil = 0.46 Ω; Wattmeter voltage coil = 8000 Ω; Ammeter circuit = negligible. Calculate (i) the power expended in the load (ii) the reading of the wattmeter and (iii) the reading of the wattmeter if its voltage coil is connected to point A instead of point B.

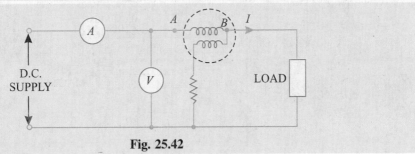

Fig. 25.42

Solution.

(*i*)	Current through voltmeter	$= 230/2000 = 0.115$ A
	Current through current coil	$= 2.5 - 0.115 = 2.385$ A
	Voltage drop in current coil	$= 2.385 \times 0.46 = 1.1$ V
	P.D. across load and voltage coil	$= 230 - 1.1 = 228.9$ V
	Current taken by voltage coil	$= 228.9/8000 = 0.029$ A

Load current, $\qquad I = 2.385 - 0.029 = 2.356$ A

Power expended in load $\qquad = 228.9 \times 2.356 = \mathbf{539.29}$ **W**

(*ii*) Wattmeter reading $\qquad = 228.9 \times 2.385 = \mathbf{545.93}$ **W**

(*iii*) When the voltage coil is connected to point A instead of point B, voltage across the potential coil is 230 V and current through the current coil is 2.356 A.

$\therefore$ Wattmeter reading $\qquad = 230 \times 2.356 = \mathbf{541.9}$ **W**

25.31. INDUCTION WATTMETERS

The induction type wattmeter can be used to measure a.c. power only in contrast to dynamometer wattmeter which can be used to measure d.c. as well as a.c. power. The principle of operation of an induction wattmeter is the same as that of induction ammeter and voltmeter *i.e.* induction principle.

However, it differs from induction ammeter or voltmeter in so far that two separate coils are used to produce the rotating magnetic field in place of one coil with phase split arrangement. Fig. 25.44 shows the physical arrangement of the various parts of an induction wattmeter.

Construction. Fig. 25.43 shows the principal parts of an induction wattmeter.

(*i*) It consists of two laminated electromagnets. One electromagnet, called *shunt magnet* is connected across the supply and carries current proportional to the supply voltage. The coil of this magnet is made highly inductive so that the current (and hence the flux produced) in it lags behind the supply voltage by 90°. The other electromagnet, called *series magnet* is connected in series with the supply and carries the load current. The coil of this magnet is made highly non-inductive so that angle of lag or lead is wholly determined by the load.

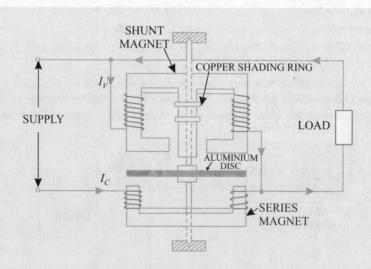

Fig. 25.43

(*ii*) A thin aluminium disc mounted on the spindle is placed between the two magnets so that it cuts the flux of both the magnets. The controlling torque is provided by spiral springs. The damping is electromagnetic and is usually provided by a permanent magnet embracing the aluminium disc (See Fig. 25.44). Two or more closed copper rings (called *shading rings*) are provided on the central limb of the shunt magnet. By adjusting the position of these rings, the shunt magnet flux can be made to lag behind the supply voltage by exactly 90°.

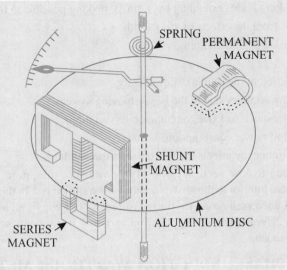

Fig. 25.44

Working. When the wattmeter is connected in the circuit (See Fig. 25.43) to measure a.c. power, the shunt magnet carries current proportional to the supply voltage and the series magnet carries the load current. The two fluxes produced by the magnets induce eddy currents in the aluminium disc. The interaction between the fluxes and eddy currents produces the deflecting torque on the disc, causing the pointer connected to the moving system to move over the scale. The pointer comes to rest at a position where deflecting torque is equal to the controlling torque.

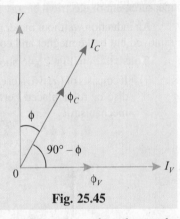

Fig. 25.45

Let
V = supply voltage
I_V = current carried by shunt magnet
I_C = current carried by series magnet
$\cos \phi$ = lagging power factor of the load

The phasor diagram is shown in Fig. 25.45. The current I_V in the shunt magnet lags the supply voltage V by 90° and so does the flux ϕ_V produced by it. The current I_C in the series magnet is the load current and hence lags behind the supply voltage V by ϕ. The flux ϕ_C produced by this current (*i.e.* I_C) is in phase with it. It is clear that phase angle θ between the two fluxes is 90° − ϕ *i.e.*

$$\theta = 90° - \phi$$

∴ Mean deflecting torque,

$$T_d \propto \phi_V \, \phi_C \sin \theta \qquad \qquad ...See\ Art.\ 25.24$$
$$\propto V I \sin (90° - \phi) \qquad [\because \phi_V \propto V \text{ and } \phi_C \propto I]$$
$$\propto V I \cos \phi$$
$$\propto \text{a.c. power}$$

Since the instrument is spring controlled, $T_C \propto \theta$
For steady deflected position, $T_d = T_C$
∴ $\qquad \qquad \theta \propto \text{a.c. power}$
Hence such instruments have uniform scale.

Advantages
(*i*) They have a uniform scale.

(*ii*) They have a long scale (extending over 300°), making possible to take accurate readings.

(*iii*) They are free from the effects of stray fields.

(*iv*) They provide very good damping.

Disadvantages

(*i*) They can be used to measure a.c. power only.

(*ii*) They have low accuracy due to the heavy moving system.

(*iii*) They cause serious errors due to temperature variations.

(*iv*) They have high power consumption.

(*v*) Variation of frequency affects the reactance of the windings.

Applications. Due to low accuracy and high power consumption, the characteristics of induction wattmeters are inferior to those of dynamometer wattmeters. For this reason, dynamometer wattmeters are almost universally used for the measurement of a.c. as well as d.c. power. However, induction wattmeters have their chief application as panel instruments where the variations in frequency are not too much.

25.32. SINGLE PHASE INDUCTION WATTHOUR METER

Single phase induction watthour meters (or energy meters) are extensively used for the measurement of electrical energy in a.c. circuits. One can find such meters installed in homes.

An induction watthour meter is essentially an induction wattmeter with control spring and pointer removed but brake magnet and counting mechanism provided.

Construction. Fig. 25.46 shows the various parts of a single-page induction watthour meter.

(*i*) It consists of (*a*) two a.c. electromagnets; the series magnet and shunt magnet (*b*) an aluminium disc or rotor placed between the two electromagnets (*c*) brake magnet and (*d*) counting mechanism.

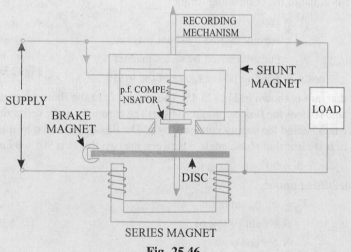

Fig. 25.46

(*ii*) The shunt magnet is wound with a fine wire of many turns and is connected across the supply so that it carries current proportional to the supply voltage. Since the coil of shunt magnet is highly *inductive, the current (and hence the flux) in it lags the supply voltage by 90°.

The series magnet is wound with a heavy wire of few turn and is connected in series with the load

---

* The coil has a very large number of turns and the reluctance of its magnetic circuit is very small due to the presence of small air gaps. This makes the coil highly inductive.

so that it carries the load current. The coil of this magnet is highly non-inductive so that angle of lag or lead is determined wholly by the load.

(*iii*) A thin aluminium disc mounted on the spindle is placed between the shunt and series magnets so that it cuts the fluxes of both the magnets.

(*iv*) The braking torque is obtained by placing a permanent magnet near the rotating disc so that the disc rotates in the field established by the permanent magnet. Eddy currents induced in disc produce a braking or retarding torque that is proportional to the disc speed.

(*v*) A short-circuited copper loop (also known as power factor compensator) is provided on the central limb of the shunt magnet. By adjusting the position of this loop, the shunt magnet flux can be made to lag behind the supply voltage exactly by 90°.

Frictional compensation is obtained by means of two adjustable short-circuited loops placed in the leakage gaps of the shunt magnet. Geared to the rotating element is counting mechanism which indicates the energy consumed directly in kilowatthours (*kWh*).

Theory. When induction watthour meter is connected in the circuit to measure energy, the shunt magnet carries current proportional to the supply voltage and the series magnet carries the load current. Therefore, expression for the driving torque is the same as for induction wattmeter. Referring back to the phasor diagram in Fig. 25.45,

Driving torque, $\qquad T_d \propto \phi_V \phi_C \sin \theta$

$$\propto V I \sin (90° - \phi)$$

$$\propto V I \cos \phi$$

$$\propto \text{power}$$

The braking torque is due to the eddy currents induced in the aluminium disc. Since the magnitude of eddy currents is proportional to the disc speed, the braking torque will also be proportional to the disc speed *i.e.*

Braking torque, $\qquad *T_B \propto n \qquad\qquad\qquad$ (*i.e.* disc speed)

For steady speed of rotation, $\quad T_d = T_B$

∴ $\qquad\qquad$ Power $\propto n$

Multiplying both sides by t, the time for which power is supplied,

$$\text{Power} \times t \propto n\, t$$

or $\qquad\qquad$ Energy $\propto N$

where $N (= n\, t)$ is the total number of revolutions in time t.

The counting mechanism is so arranged that the meter indicates kilowatthours (*kWh*) directly and not the revolutions.

Meter Constant. We have seen above that :

$$N \propto \text{Energy}$$

or $\qquad\qquad N = K \times \text{Energy}$

where K is a constant called *meter constant*.

. . . .

* $\quad$ Let ϕ = flux of permanent magnet; disc speed = n

E.M.F. induced in the disc, $e \propto \phi n$

If R is the resistance of the eddy current path, then,

$$i = e/R \propto \phi n/R$$

Braking torque, $\qquad T_B \propto \phi i \propto \phi^2 n/R$

The braking mecahnism is so designed that ϕ and R are constant.

∴ $\qquad\qquad\qquad T_B \propto n$

$$\therefore \quad \text{Meter constant,} \qquad K = \frac{N}{\text{Energy}} = \frac{\text{No. of revolutions}}{kWh}$$

Hence the number of revolutions made by the disc for 1 kWh of energy consumption is called **meter constant.**

The meter constant is always written on the name plates of the energy meters installed in homes, commercial and industrial establishments. If the meter constant of an energy meter is 1500 rev/kWh, it means that for consumption of 1 kWh, the disc will make 1500 revolutions.

25.33. ERRORS IN SINGLE-PHASE INDUCTION WATTHOUR METERS

The users of electrical energy are charged according to the readings of the energy meters installed in their premises. It is, therefore, very important that construction and design of energy meters should be such as to ensure long-time accuracy *i.e.*, they should give correct readings over a period of several years under normal use conditions. Some of the common errors in energy meters and their remedial measures are discussed below:

(*i*) **Phase error.** The meter will read correctly only if the shunt magnet flux lags behind the supply voltage by exactly 90°. Since the shunt magnet coil has some resistance and is not completely reactive, the shunt magnet flux does not lag the supply voltage by exactly 90°. The result is that the meter will not read correctly at all power factors.

Adjustment. The flux in the shunt magnet can be made to lag behind the supply voltage by exactly 90° by adjusting the position of the shading coil placed round the lower part of the central limb of the shunt magnet. A current is induced in the shading coil by the shunt magnet flux and causes a further displacement of the flux. By moving the shading coil up or down the limb, the displacement between shunt magnet flux and the supply voltage can be adjusted to 90°. This adjustment is known as *lag adjustment or power factor adjustment.*

(*ii*) **Speed error.** Sometimes the speed of the disc of the meter is either fast or slow, resulting in the wrong recording of energy consumption.

Adjustment. The speed of the disc of the energy meter can be adjusted to the desired value by changing the position of the brake magnet. If the brake magnet is moved towards the centre of the spindle, the braking torque is reduced and the disc speed is *increased. Reverse would happen should the brake magnet be moved away from the centre of the spindle.

(*iii*) **Frictional error.** Frictional forces at the rotor bearings and in the counting mechanism cause noticeable error especially at light loads. At light loads, the torque due to friction adds considerably to the braking torque. Since friction torque is not proportional to the speed but is roughly constant, it can cause considerable error in meter reading.

Adjustment. In order to compensate for this error, it is necessary to provide a constant addition to the driving torque that is equal and opposite to the friction torque. This is produced by means of two adjustable short-circuited loops placed in the leakage gaps of the shunt magnet. These loops upset the symmetry of the leakage flux and produce a small torque to oppose the friction torque. This adjustment is known as *light-load adjustment.* The loops are adjusted so that when no current is passing through the current coil (*i.e.* exciting coil of the series magnet), the torque produced is just sufficient to overcome the friction in the system, without actually rotating the disc.

(*iv*) **Creeping.** Sometimes the disc of the meter makes slow but continuous rotation at no load *i.e.*, when potential coil is excited but with no current flowing in the load. This is called *creeping*. This

---

* Moving the brake magnet inwards means that speed of the part of disc under the pole face of brake magnet will be less. This results in the lesser induced voltage in the disc and hence reduced braking torque.

error may be caused due to overcompensation for friction, excessive supply voltage, vibrations, stray magnetic fields *etc*.

Adjustment. In order to prevent this creeping, two diametrically opposite holes are drilled in the disc. This causes sufficient distortion of the field. The result is that the disc tends to remain stationary when one of the holes comes under one of the poles of the shunt magnet.

(*v*) **Temperature error.** Since watthour meters are frequently required to operate in outdoor installations and are subject to extreme temperatures, the effects of temperature and their compensation are very important. The resistance of the disc, of the potential coil and characteristics of magnetic circuit and the strength of brake magnet are affected by the changes in temperature. Therefore, great care is exercised in the design of the meter to eliminate the errors due to temperature variations.

(*vi*) **Frequency variations.** The meter is designed to give minimum error at a particular frequency (generally 50 Hz). If the supply frequency changes, the reactance of the coils also changes, resulting in a small error. Fortunately, this is not of much significance because commercial frequencies are held within close limits.

(*vii*) **Voltage variations.** The shunt magnet flux will increase with an increase in voltage. The driving torque is proportional to the first power of flux whereas braking torque is proportional to the square of the flux. Therefore, if the supply voltage is higher than the normal value, the braking torque will increase much more than the driving torque and *vice-versa*. The result is that the meter has the tendency to run slow at higher than normal voltages and fast at reduced voltages. However, the effect is small for most of the meters and is not more than 0.2% to 0.3% for a voltage change of 10% from the rated value. The small error due to voltage variations can be eliminated by the proper design of the magnetic circuit of the shunt magnet.

 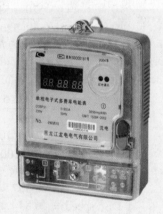

Single-phase Energy meters

Example 25.16 *An energy meter whose constant is 1500 revolutions per kWh makes 20 revolutions in 30 seconds. Calculate the load in kW.*

Solution.

Energy consumed when disc makes 20 revolutions

$$= (1/1500) \times 20 = 1/75 \text{ kWh}$$

Now energy consumed is equal to load in kW multiplied by time in hours *i.e.*,

$$\text{Load} \times \frac{30}{3600} = \frac{1}{75}$$

∴ $$\text{Load} = \frac{1}{75} \times \frac{3600}{30} = \textbf{1.6 kW}$$

Example 25.17. *A 230 V single phase energy meter has a constant load current of 4 A passing through it for 5 hours at unity power factor. If the meter makes 1104 revolutions during this period, what is the meter constant in revolutions per kWh? If the load power factor is 0.8, what number of revolutions the disc will make in the above time ?*

Solution.

$$\text{Energy supplied} \quad = \frac{V I \cos \phi}{1000} \times t = \frac{230 \times 4 \times 1}{1000} \times 5 = 4.6 \,\text{kWh}$$

No. of revolutions = 1104

∴ Meter constant = 1104/4.6 = **240 rev/kWh**

Energy supplied when the load p.f. is 0.8,

$$= \frac{230 \times 4 \times 0.8}{1000} \times 5 = 3.68 \text{ kWh}$$

∴ No. of revolutions = 240 × 3.68 = **883.2**

Example 25.18. *A 50 A, 230 V energy meter on full load test makes 61 revolutions in 37 seconds. If the meter constant is 520 rev/kWh, what is the percentage error ?*

Solution.

Meter constant = 520 rev/kWh

$$\text{Energy supplied} \quad = \frac{230 \times 50}{1000} \times \frac{37}{60 \times 60} = 0.1182 \,\text{kWh}$$

$$\text{No. of rev/kWh} \quad = \frac{61}{0.1182} = 516.07$$

∴ % age error $= \dfrac{520 - 516.07}{520} \times 100 = \mathbf{0.76\%} \textit{ slow}$

Example 25.19. *A 230 V, 50 Hz single phase energy meter has a constant of 1200 rev/kWh. Determine the speed of the disc in r.p.m. for current of 10 A at a p.f. of 0.8 lagging.*

Solution. Energy consumed by the load in 1 minute

$$= \frac{V I \cos \phi}{1000} \times t$$

$$= \frac{230 \times 10 \times 0.8}{1000} \times (1/60) = 0.0307 \text{ kWh}$$

Revolutions made by the disc in 1 minute

$$= 0.0307 \times 1200 = 36.84$$

∴ Disc speed = **36.84 r.p.m.**

Example 25.20. *A single phase energy meter has a constant of 1200 rev/kWh. When a load of 200 watts is connected, the disc rotates at 4.2 r.p.m. If the load is on for 10 hours, how many units are recorded as error ? Also find the percentage error.*

Solution.

Actual energy consumed by the load in 10 hours

$$= (200 \times 10^{-3}) \times 10 = 2 \text{ kWh}$$

No. of revolutions made by the disc in 10 hours

= speed in r.p.m. × minutes in 10 hours

= 4.2 × 10 × 60 = 2520 revolutions

Energy recorded by the energy meter

$$= 2520/1200 = 2.1 \text{ kWh}$$

The meter records 2.1 kWh whereas the actual energy consumed by load during the given period (*i.e.*, 10 hours) is 2 kWh. Therefore, the meter records **0.1 kWh** *or* **0.1 unit** more.

$$\text{\%age error} = \frac{0.1}{2} \times 100 = 5\%$$

Example 25.21. *A 230 V, 10 A single phase energy meter has a meter constant of 600 rev/kWh when correctly adjusted. If the lag adjustment is disturbed so that the phase angle between shunt magnet flux and the applied voltage is 86°, calculate the error introduced at (i) unity p.f. (ii) 0.5 p.f. lagging.*

Solution. As proved in Art. 25.31, the driving torque is given by ;

$$T_d \propto \phi_V \, \phi_C \sin\theta$$

where θ is the phase angle between the two fluxes.

The meter will read correctly if *$\theta = 90° - \phi$. In other words, the meter will register correctly if phase angle between shunt magnet flux and supply voltage is 90°. If this is not so, the meter will give a wrong reading.

(*i*) **At unity p.f.**

Power factor angle, $\phi = \cos^{-1} 1 = 0°$

$\therefore \qquad\qquad \theta = 86° - 0° = 86°$ whereas it should be $90° - 0° = 90°$

$\therefore \qquad \text{\%age error} = \dfrac{\sin 90° - \sin 86°}{\sin 90°} \times 100 = 0.24\%$

(*ii*) **At 0.5 p.f. lagging**

Power factor angle, $\phi = \cos^{-1} 0.5 = 60°$

$\therefore \qquad\qquad \theta = 86° - 60° = 26°$ whereas it should be $= 90° - 60° = 30°$

$\therefore \qquad \text{\%age error} = \dfrac{\sin 30° - \sin 26°}{\sin 30°} \times 100 = 12.32\%$

The reader may note that at low power factors, the error due to shunt magnet flux not being in quadrature with supply voltage is considerable.

TUTORIAL PROBLEMS

1. A meter whose constant is 600 revolutions/kWh makes 5 revolutions in 20 seconds. Calculate the load in kW. **[1.5 kW]**

2. The number of revolutions per kWh for a 230 V, 10 A watthour meter is 900. On test at half full-load, the time for 20 revolutions is found to be 69 seconds. Determine the meter error at half full-load. **[0.82% fast]**

3. A correctly adjusted single phase 240 V energy meter has a meter constant of 600 rev/kWh. Determine the speed of the disc for a current of 10 A at a p.f. 0.8 lagging. **[19.2 r.p.m.]**

4. A single phase energy meter has a meter constant of 200 rev./kWh. When supplying a non-inductive load of 4.4 A at normal voltage, the meter takes 3 minutes for 10 revolutions. Find the percentage error. **[1.186%]**

5. An energy meter has a meter constant of 600 rev/kWh when correctly adjusted. If the lag adjustment is altered so that the phase angle between shunt magnet flux and the supply voltage is 85°, calculate the percentage error at 0.8 p.f. lagging. **[7%]**

---

* In that case, $T_d \propto \phi_V \, \phi_C \sin(90° - \phi)$

$\qquad \propto VI \cos\phi$

$\qquad \propto \text{True power}$

MULTIPLE-CHOICE QUESTIONS

1. An ammeter is .... instrument.
   (a) an indicating
   (b) an integrating
   (c) a recording
   (d) none of the above

2. The controlling torque of an indicating instrument........as the deflection of the moving system increases.
   (a) remains unchanged
   (b) decreases
   (c) increases
   (d) none of the above

3. When the pointer of an indicating instrument comes to rest in the final deflected position,.........
   (a) only controlling torque acts
   (b) only deflecting torque acts
   (c) both deflecting and controlling torques act
   (d) none of the above

4. When the pointer of an indicating instrument is in motion, then deflecting torque is opposed by ....
   (a) controlling torque only
   (b) damping torque only
   (c) both damping & controlling torques
   (d) none of the above

5. The pointer of an indicating instrument is generally made of ....
   (a) copper   (b) aluminium
   (c) silver   (d) soft steel

6. When the pointer of an indicating instrument is in the final deflected position, ...
   (a) deflecting torque is zero
   (b) controlling torque is zero
   (c) damping torque is zero
   (d) both deflecting & controlling torques are zero

7. In general, fluid friction damping is not employed in indicating instruments although one can find its use in ....
   (a) dynamometer wattmeter
   (b) hot-wire ammeter
   (c) induction type energy meter
   (d) Kelvin electrostatic voltmeter

8. The scale of a permanent-magnet moving coil instrument is uniform because ....

   (a) of effective eddy current damping
   (b) external magnetic fields have no effect
   (c) it is spring controlled
   (d) it has no hysteresis loss

9. Shunts are generally made of.............
   (a) copper   (b) aluminium
   (c) silver   (d) manganin

10. The range of a permanent-magnet moving coil instrument is 0-10 A. If the full-scale deflection current of the meter is 2 mA, then multiplying power of the shunt is........
    (a) 2500
    (b) 10000
    (c) 5000
    (d) none of the above

11. A moving coil instrument having meter resistance of 5 Ω is to be used as a voltmeter of range 0-100 V. If the full-scale deflection current is 10 mA, then required series resistance is ....
    (a) 20 Ω (b) 1000 Ω
    (c) 9995 Ω
    (d) none of the above

12. A moving coil voltmeter gives full-scale deflection of 100 V for a meter current of 1 mA. For 45 V reading, the meter current will be ....
    (a) 0.45 mA   (b) 1.45 mA
    (c) 2.22 mA
    (d) none of the above

13. If current through the operating coil of a moving-iron instrument is doubled, the operating force becomes ....
    (a) two times   (b) four times
    (c) one-half time   (d) three times

14. For measuring high values of alternating current with a dynamometer ammeter, we use a ....
    (a) shunt
    (b) multiplier
    (c) potential transformer
    (d) current transformer

15. The best type of meter movement is .... movement.
    (a) iron-vane
    (b) D'Arsonval
    (c) dynamometer
    (d) none of the above

16. The most commonly used induction type instrument is ....
    (a) induction voltmeter
    (b) induction wattmeter
    (c) induction watt-hour meter
    (d) induction ammeter

17. If a wattmeter connected in circuit gives down scale reading, then we normally change connections of ....
    (a) current coil
    (b) potential coil
    (c) both current and potential coils
    (d) none of the above

18. A permanent magnet moving coil ammeter is connected in 50 Hz a.c. circuit in which 5 A current is flowing. The meter will read ....

    (a) 0 A
    (b) 5 A
    (c) 2.5 A
    (d) none of above

19. In the above question, if the meter remains connected in the circuit for some time, ...
    (a) meter pointer gives full-scale deflection
    (b) meter pointer starts oscillating
    (c) meter coil is burnt
    (d) none of the above

20. Out of the following, the most accurate measurement of unknown resistance will be by ....
    (a) potentiometer
    (b) ohmmeter
    (c) voltmeter and ammeter
    (d) Wheatstone bridge

Answers to Multiple-Choice Questions

1. (a)	2. (c)	3. (c)	4. (c)	5. (b)
6. (c)	7. (d)	8. (c)	9. (d)	10. (c)
11. (c)	12. (a)	13. (b)	14. (d)	15. (b)
16. (c)	17. (b)	18. (a)	19. (c)	20. (d)

Hints to Selected Multiple-Choice Questions

5. Because **aluminium** is light and does not increase the weight of the moving system.

6. **Damping torque** acts only when the pointer is in motion and always opposes motion.

7. Most of the indicating instruments are portable. Fluid friction damping is not suitable because of the oil contained in the instrument.

8. In a permanent-magnet moving coil instrument,
$$T_d \propto I \qquad \text{and} \qquad T_C \propto \theta$$
In the final deflected position, $T_d = T_C$.
$$\therefore \qquad \theta \propto I$$
Hence such instruments have uniform scale.

9. Since **manganin** has negligible temperature co-efficient of resistance.

10. Multiplying power of shunt
$$= \frac{I}{I_m} = \frac{10\,A}{2\,mA} = 5000$$
where I is the circuit current and I_m is the meter current. In the present case I is taken equal to 10 A so that I_m will be the full-scale meter current.

11. Series resistance, $\qquad R_s = \dfrac{V}{I_m} - R_m = \dfrac{100\,V}{10\,mA} - 5 = 10000 - 5 = \mathbf{9995\,\Omega}$

12. For full scale deflection (*i.e.* 100 V), the meter current is 1 mA. For 45 V reading, the meter current will be $= (1/100) \times 45 = \mathbf{0.45\,mA}$.

13. In a moving-iron instrument,

$$T_d \propto I^2 \ \ldots\ldots \text{ for d.c.}$$
$$\propto I^2_{r.m.s.} \ \ldots\ldots \text{ for a.c.}$$

If current is doubled, operating torque is increased **four times**.

14. For measuring alternating currents larger than 5A, shunts are not practicable with a dynamometer ammeter. It is because the division of current between the shunt and the coils varies with frequency (since reactance of coils depends upon frequency). Therefore, the instrument will be accurate only at the frequency at which it is calibrated.

15. Because it is very light and accurate. Moreover, the sensitivity of the instrument can be greatly increased by increasing the number of turns of the operating coil.

16. The single phase energy meter used in homes is the **induction watt-hour meter**.

17. It is easier to change connections of **potential coil** than current coil connections.

18. At 50 Hz, the meter pointer would have to rise and fall 50 times in every second. The inertia of the moving system prevents the moving coil from moving this fast. The meter pointer settles at the average level of alternating current. The average value of alternating current is zero.

19. The **meter coil is burnt** due to excessive heat.

20. It is because **Wheatstone bridge** method is independent of the constancy of supply or the calibration of an indicating instrument.

26

Atomic Structure

INTRODUCTION

The study of atomic structure is of considerable importance for electrical engineering. Unfortunately, the size of an atom is so small that it is virtually impossible to see it even with the most powerful microscope. Therefore, we have to employ indirect method for the study of its structure. The method consists of studying the properties of atom experimentally. After this, a *guess* is made regarding the possible structure of atom, which should satisfy the properties studied experimentally.

Various scientists have given different theories regarding the structure of atom. However, for the purpose of studying electrical engineering, the study of Bohr's atomic model is adequate. Although numerous refinements on Bohr's atomic model have since been made, we still believe in the laws that Bohr applied to the atomic world. In this chapter, we shall deal with Bohr's atomic model in order to understand the problems facing the electronic world.

26.1. BOHR'S ATOMIC MODEL

In 1913, Neils Bohr, Danish Physicist gave clear explanation of atomic structure. According to Bohr:

(i) An atom consists of a positively charged

nucleus around which negatively charged electrons revolve in different *circular orbits*.

(ii) *The electrons can revolve around the nucleus only in certain permitted orbits i.e., orbits of certain radii are allowed.*

(iii) The electrons in each permitted orbit have a certain fixed amount of energy. The larger the orbit (*i.e.* larger radius), the greater is the energy of electrons.

(iv) If an electron is given additional energy (*e.g.*, heat, light *etc*), it is lifted to the higher orbit. The atom is then said to be in a state of *excitation*. This state does not last long because the electron soon falls back to the original lower orbit. As it falls, it gives back the acquired energy in the form of heat, light or other radiations.

Neils Bohr
(1885-1962)

Fig. 26.1 shows the structure of silicon atom. It has 14 electrons. Two electrons revolve in the first orbit, 8 in the second orbit and 4 in the third orbit. The first, second, third orbits *etc.*, are also known as *K, L, M* orbits respectively.

These electrons can revolve only in permitted orbits (*i.e.* of *radii r_1, r_2 and r_3) and not in any arbitrary orbit. Thus, all radii between r_1 and r_2 or between r_2 and r_3 are forbidden. Each orbit has fixed amount of energy associated with it. If an electron in the first orbit is to be lifted to the second orbit, just the ** right amount of energy should be supplied to it. When this electron jumps from the second orbit to first, it will give back the acquired energy in the form of electromagnetic radiations.

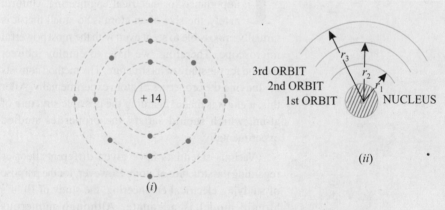

3rd ORBIT
2nd ORBIT
1st ORBIT   NUCLEUS

+14

(i)

(ii)

Fig. 26.1

26.2. ENERGY LEVELS

It has already been discussed that each orbit has fixed amount of energy associated with it. The electrons moving in a particular orbit possess the energy of that orbit. The larger the orbit, the greater is its energy. It becomes clear that outer orbit electrons possess more energy than the inner orbit electrons.

* The values of radii are determined from quantum considerations.
** So that its total energy is equal to that of second orbit.

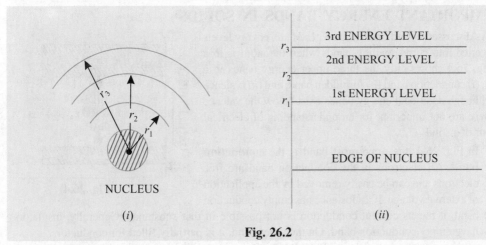

Fig. 26.2

A convenient way of representing the energy of different orbits is shown in Fig. 26.2 (*ii*). This is known as *energy level diagram*. The first orbit represents the first energy level, the second orbit indicates the second energy level and so on. The larger the orbit of an electron, the greater is its energy and higher is the energy level.

26.3. ENERGY BANDS

In case of a single isolated atom, the electrons in any orbit possess definite energy. However, an atom in a solid is greatly influenced by the closely-packed neighbouring atoms. The result is that electron in any orbit of such an atom can have a range of energies rather than a single energy. This is known as *energy band*.

The range of energies possessed by an electron in a solid is known as **energy band.**

The concept of energy band can be easily understood by referring to Fig. 26.3. Fig. 26.3 (*ii*) shows the energy levels of a single isolated atom of silicon. Each orbit of an atom has a single energy. Therefore, an electron can have only single energy corresponding to the orbit in which it exists. However, when the atom is in a solid, the electron in any orbit can have a range of energies. For instance, electrons in the first orbit have slightly different energies because no two electrons in this orbit see exactly the same charge environments. Since there are millions of first orbit electrons, the slightly different energy levels form a band, called first energy band [See Fig. 26.3 (*iii*)]. The electrons in the first orbit can have any energy range in this band. Similarly, second orbit electrons form second energy band and so on.

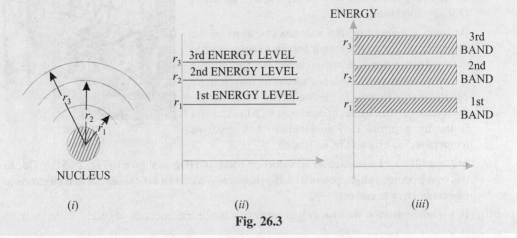

Fig. 26.3

26.4. IMPORTANT ENERGY BANDS IN SOLIDS

As discussed before, individual *K, L, M etc.* energy levels are converted into corresponding bands when the atom is in a solid. Fig. 26.4 shows only the three upper energy bands in a solid *viz*, (*i*) conduction band (*ii*) forbidden band, and (*iii*) valence band. Although additional energy bands exist below the valence band, these are not important for an understanding of electrical behaviour of a solid.

Fig. 26.4

(*i*) In Fig. 26.4, the uppermost band is the **conduction band**. All electrons in the conduction band are free electrons and can be easily removed by the application of external voltage. If a substance has empty conduction band, it means current conduction is not possible in that substance. Generally, insulators have empty conduction band. On the other hand, it is partially filled for conductors.

(*ii*) Below the conduction band is series of energy levels that collectively form the **forbidden band.** Electrons are never found in this band. Electrons may jump back and forth from the bottom valence band to the top conduction band but they never come to rest in the forbidden band.

(*iii*) The range of energies (*i.e.*, band) possessed by valence electrons is the **valence band**. The valence electrons are more or less bound to the individual atoms. Electrons can be moved from the valence band to the conduction band by the application of external energy.

26.5. CLASSIFICATION OF SOLIDS AND ENERGY BANDS

The extent of forbidden band (*i.e.*, separation between conduction and valence bands) will determine whether a substance is an insulator, a conductor or a semiconductor. Fig. 26.5 shows the difference among conductors, insulators and semiconductors in terms of their three energy bands.

(*i*) In an **insulator**, the energy gap between valence and conduction bands is very large $\simeq 15\ eV$ as shown in Fig. 26.5 (*i*). Therefore, a very high electric field is required to push the valence electrons to the conduction band. For this reason, the electrical conductivity of insulators is extremely small and may be regarded as nil under ordinary conditions.

At room temperature, the valence electrons of the insulators do not have enough energy to cross over to the conduction band. However, when the temperature is raised, some of the valence electrons may acquire enough energy to cross to the conduction band. Hence, the resistance of an insulator decreases with the increase in the temperature *i.e.*, an insulator has negative temperature co-efficient of resistance.

Insulators

(*ii*) In a **conductor**, the valence and conduction bands overlap as shown in Fig. 26.5 (*ii*). Due to this overlapping, a slight potential difference across a conductor causes the free electrons to constitute electric current.

(*iii*) In a **semiconductor**, the energy gap between valence and conduction bands is very small $\simeq$

1 *eV* as shown in Fig. 26.5 (*iii*). Therefore, comparatively smaller electric field (smaller than insulators but greater than conductors) is required to push the electrons from valence band to the conduction band.

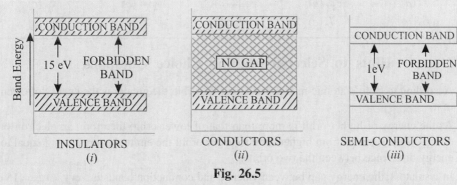

Fig. 26.5

At low temperature, the valence band of a semiconductor is completely full and conduction band is completely empty. Therefore, a semiconductor virtually behaves as an insulator at low temperatures. However, even at room temperature, some electrons (about one electron for 10^{10} atoms) cross over to the conduction band, imparting a little conductivity to the semiconductor. As temperature is increased, more valence electrons cross over to the conduction band and the conductivity increases. This shows that electrical conductivity of a semiconductor increases with the rise in temperature *i.e.*, a semiconductor has negative temperature coefficient of resistance.

MULTIPLE-CHOICE QUESTIONS

1. The electrons in the third orbit of an atom have .... energy than the electrons in the second orbit.

    (*a*) more   (*b*) less

    (*c*) the same   (*d*) none of the above

2. When an electron jumps from higher orbit to a lower orbit, it ..... energy.

    (*a*) absorbs   (*b*) emits

    (*c*) sometimes emits, sometimes absorbs

    (*d*) none of the above

3. Which of the following is quantized according to Bohr's theory of atom ?

    (*a*) linear momentum of electron

    (*b*) linear velocity of electron

    (*c*) angular momentum of electron

    (*d*) angular velocity of electron

4. A semiconductor has .... band.

    (*a*) almost empty valence

    (*b*) almost empty conduction

    (*c*) almost full conduction

    (*d*) none of the above

5. The electrons in the conduction band are known as ....

    (*a*) bound electrons

    (*b*) valence electrons

    (*c*) free electrons

    (*d*) none of the above

6. In insulators, the energy gap between valence and conduction bands is ....

    (*a*) very large   (*b*) zero

    (*c*) very small   (*d*) none of the above

7. In a conductor, the energy gap between valence and conduction bands is ....

    (*a*) large   (*b*) very large

    (*c*) very small   (*d*) none of the above

8. According to Bohr's theory of atom, an electron can move in an orbit of ....

    (*a*) any radius   (*b*) certain radius

    (*c*) some range of radii

    (*d*) none of the above

9. In a semiconductor, the energy gap between valence and conduction bands is about ....

    (*a*) 15 eV   (*b*) 100 eV

    (*c*) 50 eV   (*d*) 1 eV

10. The energy gap between valence and conduction bands in insulators is about ....

    (*a*) 15 eV   (*b*) 1.5 eV

    (*c*) zero   (*d*) 0.5 eV

Answers to Multiple-Choice Questions				
1. (*a*)	2. (*b*)	3. (*c*)	4. (*b*)	5. (*c*)
6. (*a*)	7. (*c*)	8. (*b*)	9. (*d*)	10. (*a*)

Hints to Selected Multiple-Choice Questions

1. According to Bohr's atomic model, the larger the orbit, the greater is the energy of electrons in it.

2. As the energy of higher orbit is more than that of lower orbit, therefore, an electron **emits** energy when it jumps from higher orbit to lower orbit; the emitted energy being equal to the energy difference between the two orbits.

6. In insulators, the energy gap between valence and conduction bands is **very large** $\simeq 15$ eV.

9. In semiconductors, the energy gap between valence and conduction bands is small $\simeq 1$ eV.

27

Semiconductor Physics

INTRODUCTION

Certain substances like germanium, silicon etc. are neither good conductors like copper nor insulator like glass. In other words, the resistivity of these materials lies inbetween conductors and insulators. Such substances are classified as *semiconductors.* Semiconductors have some useful properties and are being extensively used in electronic circuits. For instance, transistor—a semiconductor device— is fast replacing bulky vacuum tubes in almost all applications. Transistors are only one of the family of semiconductor devices; many other semiconductor devices are becoming increasingly popular. In this chapter, we shall focus our attention on different aspects of semiconductors.

27.1. SEMICONDUCTOR

It is not easy to define a semiconductor if we want to take into account all its physical characteristics. However, generally, a semiconductor is defined on the basis of electrical conductivity as under :

A **semiconductor** *is a substance which has resistivity (10^{-4} to 0.5 Ω–m) inbetween conductors and insulators e.g., germanium, silicon, selenium, carbon etc.*

It may be noted that it is not resistivity alone that decides whether a substance is a semiconductor or not. For example, it is just possible to prepare an alloy whose resistivity falls within the range of semiconductors but the alloy cannot be regarded as a semiconductor. In fact, semiconductors have a number of peculiar properties which distinguish them from conductors and insulators. One striking property of a semiconductor is that the forbidden energy gap (*i.e.*, separation between conduction and valence bands) is very *small (≈ 1eV) as shown in Fig. 27.1. Consequently, a semiconductor can be defined much more comprehensively on the basis of energy bands as under :

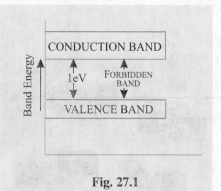

Fig. 27.1

A **semiconductor** *is a substance which has almost filled valence band and nearly empty conduction band with a small energy gap (≈ 1eV) separating the two.*

27.2. PROPERTIES OF SEMICONDUCTORS

(*i*) The resistivity of a semiconductor is less than that of an insulator but more than that of a conductor.

(*ii*) A semiconductor has almost filled valence band and nearly empty conduction band with a small energy gap (≈ 1eV) separating the two.

(*iii*) A semiconductor has *negative temperature co-efficient of resistance i.e.*, the resistance of a semiconductor decreases with the increase in temperature and *vice-versa*. For example, germanium is actually an insulator at low temperatures but becomes a good conductor at high temperatures.

(*iv*) When a suitable metallic impurity (*e.g., arsenic, gallium etc.*) is added to a semiconductor, its current conducting properties change appreciably. This property is most important and is discussed later in detail.

(*v*) A semiconductor is formed by covalent bonds.

(*vi*) A semiconductor has crystalline structure *i.e.*, atoms or molecules of a semiconductor are arranged in an orderly manner.

27.3. BONDS IN SEMICONDUCTORS

The atoms of every element are held together by the bonding action of valence electrons. This bonding is due to the fact that it is the tendency of each atom to complete its last orbit by acquiring 8 electrons in it. However, in most of the substances, the last orbit is incomplete *i.e.*, the last orbit does not have 8 electrons. This makes the atom active to enter into bargain with other atoms to acquire 8 electrons in the last orbit. To do so, the atom may lose, gain or share valence electrons with other atoms. In semiconductors, bonds are formed by sharing of valence electrons. Such bonds are called co-valent bonds. In the formation of a covalent bond, each atom contributes equal number of valence electrons and the contributed valence electrons are shared by the atoms engaged in the formation of the bond.

───

* Unlike conductors (where the two bands overlap) or insulators (where the energy gap is very large).

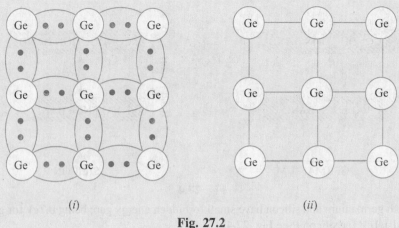

Fig. 27.2

Fig. 27.2 shows the co-valent bonds among germanium atoms. A germanium atom has *4 valence electrons. It is the tendency of each germanium atom to have 8 electrons in the last orbit. To do so, each germanium atom positions itself between four other germanium atoms as shown in Fig. 27.2 (*i*). Each neighbouring atom shares one valence electron with the central atom. In this business of sharing, the central atom completes its orbit by having 8 electrons revolving around the nucleus. This applies equally to any atom in the body of the specimen. Fig. 27.2 (*ii*) shows the bonding diagram.

27.4. COMMONLY USED SEMICONDUCTORS

There are many semiconductors available but very few of them have a practical application in electronics. The two most frequently used materials are *germainum* (*Ge*) and *silicon* (*Si*).

(*i*)   Both germanium and silicon are tetravalent *i.e.*, their atoms have 4 valence electrons as shown in Fig. 27.3.

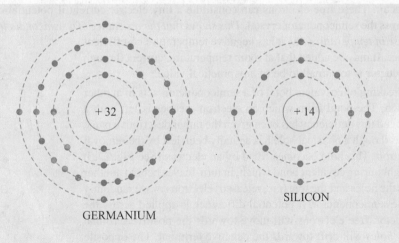

GERMANIUM

SILICON

Fig. 27.3

(*ii*)   Both germanium and silicon are formed through co-valent bonds.

(*iii*) Both germanium and silicon have crystalline structure *i.e.*, their atoms are arranged in an orderly pattern.

* * *

*   A germanium atom has 32 electrons. First orbit has 2 electrons, second 8 electrons, third 18 electrons and the fourth orbit has 4 electrons.

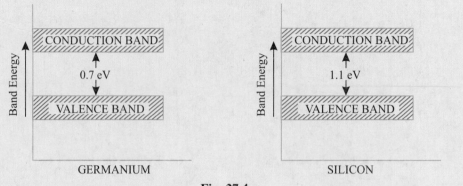

GERMANIUM   SILICON

Fig. 27.4

(*iv*) Both germanium and silicon have small forbidden energy gap; being $0.7 eV$ for germanium and $1.1 eV$ for silicon (See Fig. 27.4).

27.5. EFFECT OF TEMPERATURE ON SEMICONDUCTORS

The electrical conductivity of a semiconductor changes appreciably with temperature. This is a very important point to keep in mind.

(*i*) **At low temperature.** At very low temperature, all the electrons are tightly held by semiconductor atoms. The inner orbit electrons are bound whereas the valence electrons are engaged in co-valent bonding. Consequenetly, no free electrons are available for conduction. A semiconductor in this state is evidently an insulator since voltage applied across its ends can produce no flow of current.

(*ii*) **At room temperature.** At room temperature, some of the covalent bonds of the semiconductor break due to thermal energy. The breaking of bonds sets those electrons *free* which are engaged in the formation of these bonds. The result is that a few free electrons exist in the semiconductor. These free electrons can constitute a tiny electric current if potential difference is applied across the semiconductor crystal. *This shows that the resistance of a semiconductor decreases with the rise in temperature i.e.,* it has negative temperature co-efficient of resistance. It may be added that at room temperature, current through a semiconductor is too small to be of any practical value.

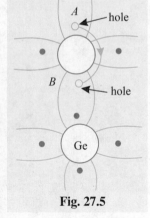

Fig. 27.5

The breaking of co-valent bond of a semiconductor sets in another phenomenon. The bond from which an electron escapes is left with a deficiency and this deficiency has been given the rather descriptive name of "*hole*" as though a physical hole has actually been left by the removal of the electron. This hole becomes filled by an electron (See Fig. 27.5) from a neighbouring covalent bond which, in turn, leaves behind another hole. Thus the holes and the free (*i.e.*, released) electrons move randomly through the semiconductor. If potential difference is applied across the semiconductor, free electrons will move towards the positive terminal while the *holes will drift towards the negative terminal. The opposite movement of these two charges does not cancel each other, as one might suppose. Rather, they aid each other. Therefore, the total current inside the semiconductor is the sum of currents due to free electrons and holes.

27.6. HOLE CURRENT

When a covalent bond breaks due to thermal energy, the removal of electrons leaves a vacancy

* Since hole represents a missing electron, it has a positive charge.

i.e., a missing electrons in the co-valent bond. This missing electron is called a *hole* which acts as a positive charge. For one electron set free, one hole is created. Therefore, thermal energy creates *hole-electron pairs*; there being as many holes as the free electrons. The current conduction by holes can be explained as follows :

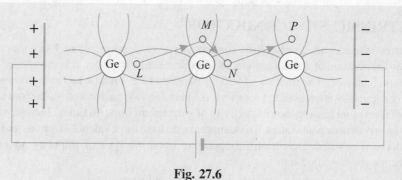

Fig. 27.6

The hole shows a missing electron. Suppose the valence electron at *L* (See Fig. 27.6) has become free electron due to thermal energy. This creates a *hole* in the co-valent bond at *L*. The hole is a strong centre of *attraction for the electron. A valence electron (say at *M*) from nearby co-valent bond comes to fill the hole at *L*. This results in the creation of hole at *M*. Another valence electron (say at *N*) in turn may leave its bond to fill the hole at *M*, thus creating a hole at *N*. Thus, the hole having a positive charge has moved from *L* to *N i.e.*, towards the negative terminal of supply. This constitutes the *hole current*.

It may be noted that hole current is due to the movement of †valence electrons from one co-valent bond to another bond. The reader may wonder why to call it a hole current when the conduction is again by electrons (of course *valence electrons* !). The answer is that the basic reason for current flow is the presence of holes in the co-valent bonds. Therefore, it is more appropriate to consider the current as the movement of holes.

27.7. INTRINSIC SEMICONDUCTOR

*A semiconductor in an extremely pure form is known as an **intrinsic semiconductor**.*

In an intrinsic semiconductor, even at room temperature, hole-electron pairs are created; there being as many holes as the free electrons.

(*i*) If a potential difference is applied across an intrinsic semiconductor (See Fig. 27.7), electrons will move towards the positive terminal while the holes will drift towards the negative terminal. The total current inside the semiconductor is the sum of currents due to free electrons and holes.

(*ii*) If the temperature of the semiconductor increases, the number of hole-electron pairs increases and the current though the specimen rises. Reverse happens, should the temperature fall.

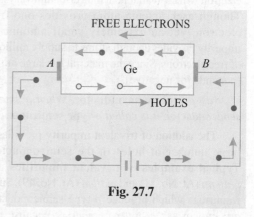

Fig. 27.7

Note. It may be noted that current in the external wire is fully electronic *i.e.*, by electrons. What about

* There is a strong tendency of semiconductor crystal to form covalent bonds. Therefore, a hole attracts an electron from the neighbouring atom.

† Unlike the normal current which is by electrons.

holes ? Referring to Fig. 27.7, holes being positively charged move towards the negative terminal of supply. As the holes reach the negative terminal *B*, electrons enter the semiconductor crystal near the terminal and combine with the holes, thus cancelling them. At the same time, the loosely held electrons near the positive terminal are attracted away from their atoms into the positive terminal. This creates new holes near the positive terminal which again drift towards the negative terminal.

27.8. EXTRINSIC SEMICONDUCTOR

The intrinsic semiconductor has little conductivity at room temperature. Its conductivity can be increased by the addition of a small amount of suitable metallic impurity. It is then called *impurity* or *extrinsic semiconductor*. The process of adding impurity to a semiconductor is known as *doping*. Typically, one impurity atom is added for every 10^8 pure semiconductor atoms. At room temperature, this has the effect of increasing the conductivity of germanium some 46 times. The elements suitable for doping are trivalent or pentavalent. Trivalent elements have three valence electrons and pentavalent materials have five valence electrons. Depending upon the type of impurity added, extrinsic semiconductors are classified into :

(*i*)   *n-type semiconductor*   (*ii*)   *p-type semiconductor*

(*i*)   *n*-**type semiconductor.** *When a small amount of pentavalent impurity is added to a pure semiconductor, it is known as n-type semiconductor.*

The addition of pentavalent impurity provides a large number of free electrons in the semiconductor crystal. Typical examples of pentavalent impurities are *arsenic* (At. No. 33) and *antimony* (At. No. 51). Such impurities which produce *n*-type semiconductors are known as *donor impurities* because they donate or provide free electrons to the semiconductor crystal.

Fig. 27.8 shows the formation of *n*-type semiconductor. Four valence electrons of the impurity atom (*i.e.*, arsenic) form co-valent bonds with four germanium atoms. The *fifth* valence electron of arsenic atom finds no place in the co-valent bonds and is thus free as shown in Fig. 27.8. Therefore, for each arsenic atom added, one free electron will be available in the germanium crystal. Though each arsenic atom provides one free electron, yet an extremely small amount of impurity provides enough atoms to supply millions of free electrons. Since the material has large number of free electrons, it is called *n*-type semiconductor (*n* stands for negative).

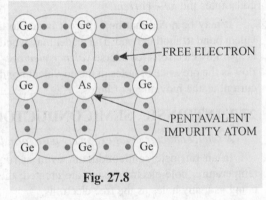

Fig. 27.8

(*ii*)   *p*-**type semiconductor.** *When a small amount of trivalent impurity is added to a pure semiconductor, it is called p-type semiconductor.*

The addtion of trivalent impurity provides a large number of holes in the semiconductor. Typical examples of trivalent impurities are *gallium* (At. No. 31) and *indium* (At. No. 49). Such impurities which produce *p*-type semiconductor are known as *acceptor impurities* because the holes created can accept the electrons.

Fig. 27.9 shows the formation of *p*-type semiconductor. Three valence electrons of the impurity atom (*i.e.*, *gallium*) form co-valent bonds with three germanium atoms. In the fourth co-

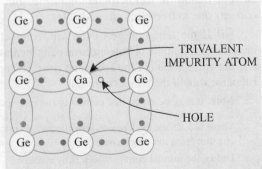

Fig. 27.9

valent bond, only germanium atom contributes one valence electron while gallium has no valence electron to contribute as all its three valence electrons are already engaged in the co-valent *bonds* with the neighbouring germanium atoms. In other words, fourth bond is incomplete, being short of one electron. This missing electron is called a hole. Therefore, for each gallium atom added, one hole is created. A small amount of gallium provides millions of holes. Since the material now has a large number of holes (positive charge), it is called *p*-type *semiconductor* (*p* stands for positive).

27.9. CHARGE ON *n*-TYPE AND *p*-TYPE SEMICONDUCTORS

When viewed as a unit, the extrinsic semiconductor (*n*-type or *p*-type) is electrically neutral. It is because the original germanium atoms are neutral and the atoms of the added impurity are also neutral. The addition of a donor impurity provides more electrons in the valence band for easy elevation into the conduction band. The addition of an acceptor impurity results in the creation of holes in the valence band. No change is made in the net charge in the crystal. *It follows, therefore, that n-type as well as p-type semiconductor is electrically neutral.*

27.10. MAJORITY AND MINORITY CARRIERS

It has already been discussed that due to the effect of impurity, *n*-type material has a large number of free electrons whereas *p*-type material has a large number of holes. However, it may be recalled that even at room temperature, some of the co-valent bonds break, thus releasing an equal number of free electron and holes.

(*i*) An *n*-type material has its share of electron-hole pairs but in addtion has much larger quantity of free electrons due to the effect of impurity. Consequently, an *n*-type material has a large number of free electrons and a small number of holes as shown in Fig. 27.10 (*i*). The free electrons in this case are considered *majority carriers*—since the majority portion of current in *n*-type material is by the flow of free electrons—and the holes are the *minority carriers*.

(*ii*) Similarly, in a *p*-type material, holes outnumber the free electron as shown in Fig. 27.10 (*ii*). Therefore, holes are the *majority carriers* and free electrons are *minority carriers*.

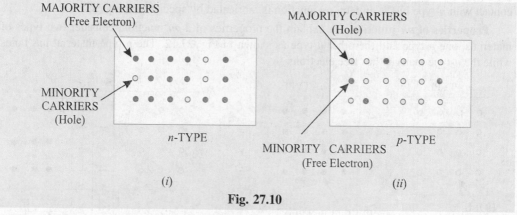

Fig. 27.10

27.11. EXTRINSIC CONDUCTION

The conduction of current in an extrinsic semiconductor (*n*-type or *p*-type) is called extrinsic conduction.

(*i*) **n-type conductivity.** The current conduction in an *n*-type semiconductor is predominantly by free electrons (*i.e.*, negative charges) and is called *n*-type conductivity. Fig. 27.11 (*i*) shows the current conduction in an *n*-type semiconductor. The majority carriers (*i.e.*, free electrons) move towards the positive terminal while the holes move towards the negative terminal. The current due to holes in *n*-type semiconductor is very small and may be neglected.

(ii) **p-type conductivity.** The current conduction in a *p*-type semiconductor is predominantly by holes (*i.e.*, positive charges) and is called *p*-type conductivity. Fig. 27.11 (*ii*) shows the current conduction through a *p*-type semiconductor. The majority carriers (*i.e.*, holes) drift towards the negative terminal while the minority carriers (free electrons) move towards the positive terminal. The current due to minority carriers (*i.e.*, free electrons) in a *p*-type semiconductor is so small that it may be neglected.

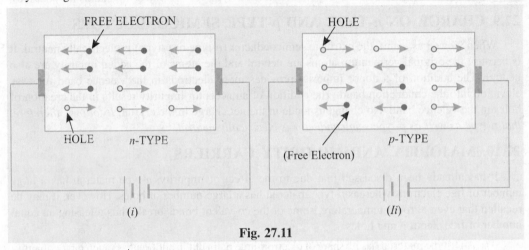

Fig. 27.11

27.12. *pn* JUNCTION

*When a p-type semiconductor is suitably joined to n-type semiconductor, the contact surface is called **pn junction**.*

Most semiconductor devices contain one or more *pn* junctions. The *pn* junction is of great importance because it is, in effect, the *control element* for semiconductor devices. In actual practice, the characteristic properties of *pn* junction will not be apparent if a *p*-type block is just brought in contact with *n*-type block. In fact, *pn* junction is fabricated by special techniques.

Properties of *pn* junction. To explain the properties of a *pn* junction, consider two types of materials, one *p*-type and the other *n*-type as shown in Fig. 27.12. The *p*-type material has holes while the *n*-type material has free electrons.

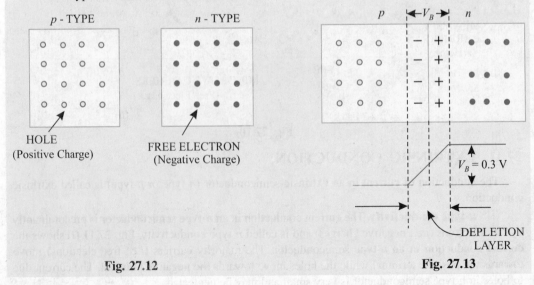

Fig. 27.12   **Fig. 27.13**

Now suppose the two pieces are suitably treated to form *pn* junction. At the junction, there is a tendency for the free electrons from the *n*-type to *diffuse* over to the *p*-side and holes from the *p*-side to the *n*-side. Since both the materials are originally electrically neutral, a positive charge is built up on the *n*-side of the junction and negative charge on the *p*-side of the junction. This situation soon prevents further diffusion. It is because now positive charge on *n*-side repels holes to cross from *p*-type to *n*-type and negative charge on the *p*-side repels free electrons to enter from *n*-type to *p*-type. Thus, a barrier is set up against further movement of charge carriers *i.e.*, holes and free electrons. This is called *potential barrier* or *junction barrier* V_B. The potential barrier is of the order of 0.1 to 0.3 V. The potential distribution diagram is shown in Fig. 27.13. It is clear from the diagram that a potential barrier is set up which gives rise to electric field. This field prevents the majority carriers from crossing the barrier region.

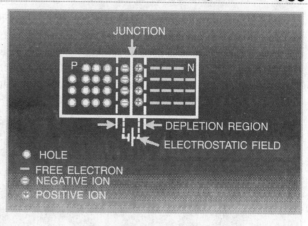

The region in the immediate vicinity of the junction is called the *depletion layer* because the mobile charges (*i.e.*, free electrons and holes) have been depleted (*i.e.*, emptied) in this region. In the *n*-section, the free electrons initially present were lost by combination with the holes on the other side of the junction in the *p*-section.

27.13. APPLYING VOLTAGE ACROSS *pn* JUNCTION

The d.c. potential difference across a *pn* junction can be applied in two ways, namely; *forward biasing* and *reverse biasing*.

(*i*) **Forward biasing.** *When external d.c. voltage applied to the pn junction is in such a direction that it cancels the potential barrier, thus permitting current flow, it is called* **forward biasing.**

To apply forward bias, connect positive terminal of the battery to *p*-type and negative terminal to *n*-type as shown in Fig. 27.14. The applied forward potential establishes an electric field which acts against the field due to potential barrier. As potential barrier voltage is very small (0.1 to 0.3 V), therefore, a small forward voltage is sufficient to completely eliminate the potential barrier. Once the potential barrier is eliminated by the forward voltage, junction resistance becomes almost zero and current flows in the circuit. This is called forward current I_F.

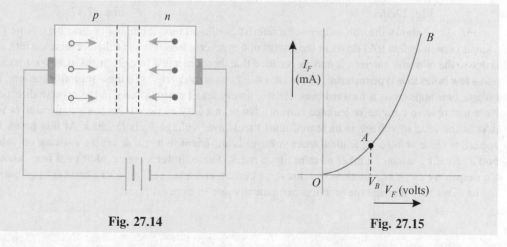

Fig. 27.14   **Fig. 27.15**

Fig. 27.15 shows the volt-ampere curve of a *pn* junction under forward bias. It is seen that at first (portion *OA*), the current increases very slowly and the curve is nonlinear. It is because the external applied voltage is used up in overcoming the potential barrier. However, once the external voltage exceeds the potential barrier voltage, the *pn* junction behaves like an ordinary conductor. Therefore, current rises very sharply with increase in external voltage (portion *AB* on the curve). The curve is now almost linear.

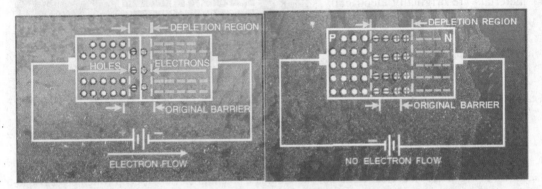

(*ii*) **Reverse biasing.** *When the external d.c. voltage applied to the pn junction is in such a direction that potential barrier is increased, it is called* **reverse biasing.**

To apply reverse bias, connect negative terminal of battery to *p*-type and positive terminal to *n*-type as shown in Fig. 27.16. It is clear that reverse voltage establishes an electric field which acts in the same direction as the field due to potential barrier. The increased potential barrier prevents the flow of charge carriers across the junction. Thus, a high resistance path is established for the entire circuit and hence the current does not flow.

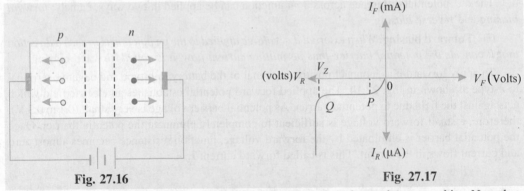

Fig. 27.16   **Fig. 27.17**

Fig. 27.17 shows the volt-ampere characteristics of a *pn* junction under reverse bias. Note that a small current (a few μA) flows in the circuit under reverse bias. This is called reverse current and is due to the minority carriers. It may be recalled that there are a few free electrons in *p*-type material and a few holes in *n*-type material. These are called *minority carriers*. To these minority carriers, the reverse bias appears as a forward bias. Hence, a very small current flows in the reverse direction. Note that reverse current (or leakage current) due to minority carriers stays at a small value (a few μA) as the reverse voltage is increased until breakdown voltage V_Z is reached. At this point, the applied reverse voltage V_Z (called zener voltage) is sufficient to break down the existing co-valent bonds, creating a large number of minority carriers. These, in turn, create additional free carriers. Consequently, there is a sudden rise of reverse current and a sudden fall of the resistance of barrier region. This may damage the junction permanently due to excessive heat.

MULTIPLE-CHOICE QUESTIONS

1. The resistivity of a semi-conductor .... conductors and insulators.

   (*a*) is more than that of

   (*b*) lies between that of

   (*c*) is less than that of

   (*d*) none of the above

2. A semi-conductor is formed by .... bonds.

   (*a*) covalent   (*b*) electrovalent

   (*c*) co-ordinate   (*d*) none of the above

3. The most commonly used semi-conductor is ....

   (*a*) germanium   (*b*) carbon

   (*c*) sulphur   (*d*) silicon

4. In a semi-conductor, the energy gap between valence band and conduction band is about ....

   (*a*) 5 *eV*   (*b*) 10 *eV*

   (*c*) 15 *eV*   (*d*) 1 *eV*

5. A semi-conductor has .... temperature co-efficient of resistance.

   (*a*) negative   (*b*) positive

   (*c*) zero   (*d*) none of the above

6. A semi-conductor generally has .... valence electrons.

   (*a*) 2   (*b*) 3

   (*c*) 4   (*d*) 6

7. The resistivity of pure germanium under standard conditions is about ....

   (*a*) $6 \times 10^4 \, \Omega - \text{cm}$ (*b*) $60 \, \Omega - \text{cm}$

   (*c*) $3 \times 10^{-3} \, \Omega - \text{cm}$ (*d*) $6 \times 10^{-4} \, \Omega - \text{cm}$

8. The resistivity of pure silicon is about ....

   (*a*) $100 \, \Omega - \text{cm}$ (*b*) $6000 \, \Omega - \text{cm}$

   (*c*) $3 \times 10^6 \, \Omega - \text{cm}$ (*d*) $1.6 \times 10^{-8} \, \Omega - \text{cm}$

9. When a pure semi-conductor is heated, its resistance ....

   (*a*) goes down   (*b*) goes up

   (*c*) remains the same   (*d*) none of the above

10. The strength of a semi-conductor crystal comes from ....

    (*a*) forces between nuclei

    (*b*) forces between protons

    (*c*) electron-pair bonds

    (*d*) none of the above

11. When a pentavalent impurity is added to a pure semi-conductor, it becomes .... semi-conductor.

    (*a*) intrinsic   (*b*) *n*-type

    (*c*) *p*-type   (*d*) none of the above

12. Addition of pentavalent impurity to a semi-conductor creates many ....

    (*a*) free electrons   (*b*) holes

    (*c*) valence electrons (*d*) bound electrons

13. A pentavalent impurity has ....

    (*a*) 3 valence electrons

    (*b*) 6 valence electrons

    (*c*) 4 valence electrons

    (*d*) 5 valence electrons

14. An *n*-type semi-conductor is..............

    (*a*) positively charged

    (*b*) electrically neutral

    (*c*) negatively charged

    (*d*) none of the above

15. A trivalent impurity has.............. .

    (*a*) 3 valence electrons

    (*b*) 5 valence electrons

    (*c*) 6 valence electrons

    (*d*) 4 valence electrons

16. Addition of trivalent impurity to a pure semi-conductor creates many ....

    (*a*) free electrons   (*b*) valence electrons

    (*c*) holes   (*d*) bound electrons

17. A hole in a semi-conductor is defined as ....

    (*a*) a free electron

    (*b*) the incomplete part of an electron pair bond

    (*c*) a free proton   (*d*) a free neutron

18. A pentavalent impurity is called ....

    (*a*) donor impurity   (*b*) acceptor impurity

    (*c*) ionic impurity   (*d*) none of the above

19. The charge of a hole is ....

    (*a*) zero

    (*b*) equal to that of a proton

    (*c*) equal to that of an electron

    (*d*) equal to that of a neutron

20. As a general rule, holes are found only in ....

    (*a*) metals   (*b*) semi-conductors

    (*c*) insulators   (*d*) resistance materials

Answers to Multiple-Choice Questions

1. (*b*)	2. (*a*)	3. (*d*)	4. (*d*)	5. (*a*)
6. (*c*)	7. (*b*)	8. (*b*)	9. (*a*)	10. (*c*)
11. (*b*)	12. (*a*)	13. (*d*)	14. (*b*)	15. (*a*)
16. (*c*)	17. (*b*)	18. (*a*)	19. (*b*)	20. (*b*)

Hints to Selected Multiple-Choice Questions

2. In semiconductors, bonds are formed by sharing of valence electrons. Such bonds are called **covalent bonds.**

5. The resistance of a semiconductor decreases with the increase in temperature and *vice-versa.* Therefore, they have **negative** temperature co-efficient of resistance.

10. In a semiconductor crystal, each valence electron of a semiconductor atom forms direct bond with the valence electron of an adjacent semiconductor atom.

12. A pentavalent impurity (*e.g. arsenic, antimony*) has five valence electrons. When it is added to a semiconductor *e.g.* germanium which has four valence electrons, a large number of **free electrons** are available. It is because the four valence electrons of pentavalent impurity atom form covalent bonds with four germanium atoms. However, the fifth valence electron of pentavalent impurity atom becomes free.

14. The *n*-type semiconductor has an excess of electrons but these extra electrons were supplied by pentavalent impurity and each atom of this impurity is **electrically neutral.**

16. A trivalent impurity atom (*e.g. gallium, indium*) has three valence electrons. The three valence electrons of trivalent impurity atom can form only three single covalent bonds with three germanium atoms— a semiconductor. In the fourth co-valent bond only germanium contributes one valence electron while trivalent impurity does not. Thus there is a missing electron in the fourth co-valent bond which is called a **hole.**

28

Semiconductor Diode

INTRODUCTION

It has already been discussed in the previous chapter that a *pn* junction conducts current easily when forward biased and practically no current flows when it is reverse biased. In other words, a *pn* junction behaves like a switch. When forward biased, *pn* junction behaves like a closed switch and when reverse biased, it is like an open switch. This unilateral conduction characteristic of *pn* junction (*i.e.*, semiconductor diode) permits it to do the job of *rectification i.e.,* change alternating current to direct curent . In this chapter, we shall focus our attention on the circuit performance and applications of semiconductor diode.

28.1. SEMICONDUCTOR DIODE

A pn junction is known as a semiconductor or **crystal diode.**

The outstanding property of a crystal diode to conduct current in one direction only permits it to be used as rectifier. Fig. 28.1 (*i*) shows a forward biased diode. A crystal diode is usually represented by the schematic symbol shown in Fig. 28.1 (*ii*). The arrow of the symbol indicates the direction of easier conventional current flow.

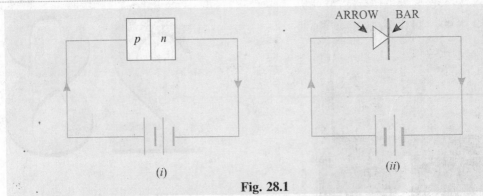

Fig. 28.1

A crystal diode has two terminals. When it is connected in a circuit, one thing to decide is whether the diode is forward or reverse biased. There is an easy rule to ascertain it. If the external circuit is trying to push the conventional current in the direction of arrow, the diode is forward biased. On the other hand, if the conventional current is trying to flow opposite the arrow, the diode is reverse biased . Putting in simple words:

(i) If *arrowhead* of diode symbol is positive *w.r.t. bar* of the symbol, the diode is forward biased.

(ii) If the *arrowhead* of diode symobl is negative *w.r.t. bar*, the diode is reverse biased.

28.2. CRYSTAL DIODE AS A RECTIFIER

Fig. 28.2 shows an *a.c.* supply connected to a load R_L . The output across the load is also a.c.

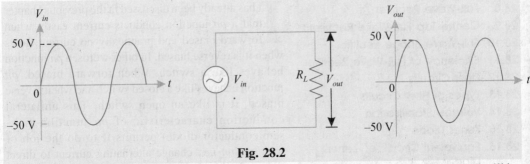

Fig. 28.2

If a diode is connected in this circuit as shown in Fig. 28.3, the output across the load R_L will be d.c.During positive half-cycle of *a.c.* input voltage,the diode is forward biased and conducts current in the circuit. The result is that positive half-cycle of the input voltage appears across the load R_L as shown in Fig. 28.3. However, during the negative half-cycle of input a.c. voltage, the diode is reverse biased and conducts no current. The result is that output consists of positive half-cycles of input a.c. voltage while the negative half-cycles are suppressed. In this way, crystal diode has been able to do rectification *i.e.*, change *a.c.*to *d.c.* It may be seen that output across R_L is pulsating *d.c.*

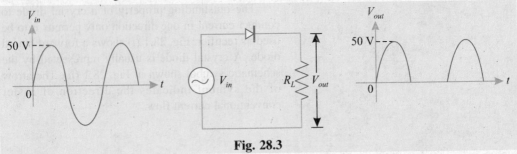

Fig. 28.3

It is interesting to see that behaviour of the diode is like a switch. When the diode is forward biased, it behaves like a closed switch and connects the *a.c.* supply to the load R_L. However, when the diode is reverse biased, it behaves like an open switch and disconnects the *a.c.* supply from the load R_L. This switching action of diode permits only the positive half-cycles of input *a.c.* voltage to appear across R_L.

28.3. RESISTANCE OF CRYSTAL DIODE

It has already been discussed that a forward biased diode conducts easily whereas a reverse biased diode practically conducts no current. It means that *forward resistance* of diode is very small as compared with its *reverse resistance*.

1. Forward resistance. The resistance offered by the diode to forward bias is known as *forward resistance*. This resistance is not the same for direct current as for the changing current. Accordingly, this resistance is of two types, namely; *d.c. forward resistance* and *a.c. forward resistance*.

(i) d.c. forward resistance. It is the resistance offered by the diode to direct current. It is measured by the ratio of direct voltage across the diode to the resulting direct current. Thus referring to the forward characteristic in Fig. 28.4, it is clear that when forward voltage is *OA*, the forward current is *OB*.

∴ d.c. forward resistance, $R_f = \dfrac{OA}{OB}$

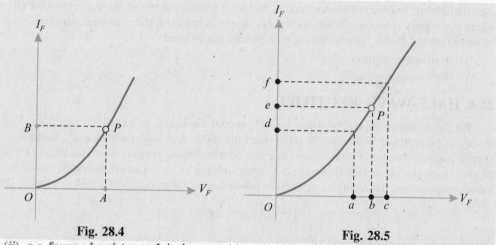

| Fig. 28.4 | Fig. 28.5 |

(ii) a.c. forward resistance. It is the opposition offered by the diode to the changing current. It is measured by the ratio of change in voltage across the diode to the resulting change in forward current *i.e.,*

a.c. forward resistance, $r_f = \dfrac{\text{Change in voltage across diode}}{\text{Corresponding change in current}}$

The a.c. forward resistance is more significant as the diodes are generally used with alternating voltages. Referring to the forward characteristic in Fig. 28.5, if *P* is the operating point, then,

a.c. forward resistance, $r_f = \dfrac{\text{Change in forward voltage}}{\text{Change in forward current}}$

$$= \dfrac{oc - oa}{of - od} = \dfrac{ac}{df}$$

It may be mentioned here that *a.c.* forward resistance of a crystal diode is very small, ranging from 1 to 25 Ω.

2. Reverse resistance. The resistance offered by the diode to reverse bias is known as *reverse resistance*. It can be d.c. reverse resistance or a.c. reverse resistance depending upon whether the reverse bias is direct or changing voltage. Ideally, the reverse resistance of a diode is infinite. However, in practice, the reverse resistance is not infinite because for any value of reverse bias, there does exist a small leakage current. It may be emphasised here that reverse resistance is very large as compared to the forward resistance. In germanium diodes, the ratio of reverse to forward resistance is 40000 : 1 while for silicon diodes, this ratio is 1000000 : 1.

28.4. PEAK INVERSE VOLTAGE (PIV)

The maximum reverse voltage that a diode can withstand without destroying the junction is called **peak inverse voltage** *of the diode.*

If the reverse voltage across a diode exceeds this value, the reverse current increases sharply and breaks down the junction due to excessive heat. Peak inverse voltage (*PIV*) is extremely important when diode is used as a rectifier. In rectifier service, it has to be ensured that reverse voltage across the diode does not exceed its *PIV* rating during the negative half-cycle of input a.c. voltage . As a matter of fact, *PIV* consideration is generally the deciding factor in diode rectifier circuits.

28.5. CRYSTAL DIODE RECTIFIERS

For reasons associated with economics of generation and transmission, electric power available is usually an *a.c.* supply. The supply voltage varies sinusoidally and has a frequency of 50 Hz. It is used for lighting, heating and electric motors. But there are many applications (*e.g.,* electronic circuits) where *d.c.* supply is needed. When such a *d.c.* supply is required, the mains a.c. supply is rectified by using crystal diodes. The following two circuits can be used:

   (*i*)   Half-wave rectifier

   (*ii*)   Full-wave rectifier

28.6. HALF-WAVE RECTIFIER

Fig. 28.6. shows the circuit where a single crystal diode acts as a half-wave rectifier. The a.c. supply to be rectified is applied in series with the diode and load resistance R_L. Generally, a.c. supply is given through a transformer. The use of transformer permits two advantages. Firstly, it allows us to step up or step down the *a.c.* input voltage as the situation demands. Secondly, the transformer isolates the rectifier circuit from power line and thus reduces the risk of electric shock.

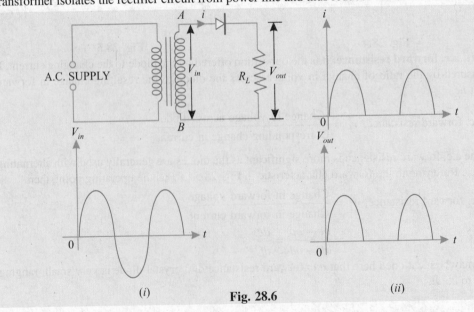

Fig. 28.6

Operation. The *a.c.* voltage across the secondary winding *AB* changes polarity after every half-cycle. During the positive half-cycle of input *a.c.* voltage, end *A* becomes positive *w.r.t.* end *B*. This makes the diode forward biased and hence it conducts current. During the negative half-cycle, end *A* is negative *w.r.t.* end *B*. Under this condition, the diode is reverse biased and it conducts no current. Therefore, current flows through the diode during positive half-cycles of input *a.c.* voltage only; it is blocked during the negative half-cycles. In this way, current flows through the load R_L always in the same direction. Hence *d.c.* output is obtained across R_L. It may be noted that output across the load is pulsating d.c. These pulsations in the output are smoothened with the help of *filter circuits* discussed later.

28.7. EFFICIENCY OF HALF-WAVE RECTIFIER

The ratio of d.c. power output to the applied input a.c. power is known as **rectifier efficiency** *i.e.,*

$$\text{Rectifier efficiency, } \eta = \frac{\text{d.c. power output}}{\text{Input a.c. power}}$$

Consider a half-wave rectifier shown in Fig. 28.6.(*i*). Let $V_{in} = V_m \sin\theta$ be the alternating voltage that appears across the secondary winding *AB*. Let r_f and R_L be the diode resistance and load resistance respectively.

d.c. power. The output current is pulsating direct current. Therefore, in order to find d.c. power, average current has to be found out. It is well known from elementary knowledge of electrical engineering that average current of a half-wave rectified wave is :

Average current, $\qquad I_{dc} = \dfrac{I_m}{\pi} \quad$ where $I_m = \dfrac{V_m}{r_f + R_L}$

Average voltage, $\qquad V_{dc} = \dfrac{V_m}{\pi}$

D.C. power, $\qquad P_{dc} = I_{dc}^2 R_L = (I_m/\pi)^2 \times R_L$

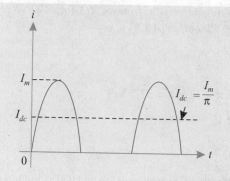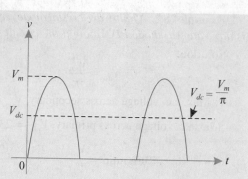

Fig. 28.7

a.c. power input

$$P_{ac} = I_{r.m.s.}^2 \, (r_f + R_L)$$

For a half-wave rectified wave, $I_{r.m.s.} = I_m/2$

∴ $\qquad P_{ac} = (I_m/2)^2 \times (r_f + R_L)$

∴ $\qquad \text{Rectifier } \eta = \dfrac{P_{dc}}{P_{ac}} = \dfrac{(I_m/\pi)^2 \times R_L}{(I_m/2)^2 \times (r_f + R_L)}$

$$= \frac{0.406\,R_L}{r_f + R_L} = \frac{0.406}{1 + (r_f / R_L)}$$

The efficiency will be maximum if r_f is negligible as compared to R_L.

∴ Max. rectifier efficiency = 40.6%

This shows that in half-wave rectification, a maximum of 40.6% of *a.c.* power is converted into *d.c.* power.

Example 28.1. *A crystal diode having internal resistance r_f = 20 Ω is used for half-wave rectification. If the applied voltage is v = 50 sin ωt and load resistance R_L = 800Ω, find (i) I_m, I_{dc}, $I_{r.m.s.}$ (ii) a.c. power input and d.c. power output (iii) d.c. output voltage and (iv) efficiency of rectification.*

Solution.

Maximum voltage, V_m = 50 V

(*i*)
$$I_m = \frac{V_m}{r_f + R_L} = \frac{50}{20 + 800} = 0.061\text{ A} = \textbf{61 mA}$$

$$I_{dc} = I_m/\pi = 61/\pi = \textbf{19.4 mA}$$

$$I_{r.m.s.} = I_m/2 = 61/2 = \textbf{30.5 mA}$$

(*ii*)
$$P_{ac} = I_{r.ms.}^2 \,(r_f + R_L)$$
$$= (30.5 \times 10^{-3})^2 \times (20 + 800) = \textbf{0.763 W}$$

$$P_{dc} = I_{dc}^2 \times R_L = (19.4 \times 10^{-3})^2 \times 800 = \textbf{0.301 W}$$

(*iii*) d.c. output voltage $= I_{dc} \times R_L = 19.4\text{ mA} \times 800\ \Omega = \textbf{15.52 V}$

Alternatively; d.c.output voltage $= V_m/\pi = 50/\pi = 15.52$ V

(*iv*) Efficiency $= \dfrac{0.301}{0.763} \times 100 = \textbf{39.5\%}$

Example 28.2. *A half-wave crystal diode rectifier is transformer-fed from a 230 V line. Calculate (i) turn ratio (ii) diode PIV rating if the circuit provides an output of 12 V d.c.*

Solution.

$$V_{dc} = \frac{V_{sm}}{\pi}$$

∴ Max. a.c. voltage across secondary, $V_{sm} = V_{dc} \times \pi = 12 \times \pi = 37.7$ V

Max a.c. voltage across primary, $V_{pm} = 230 \times \sqrt{2}$ V

(*i*) Turn ratio $= \dfrac{V_{pm}}{V_{sm}} = \dfrac{230 \times \sqrt{2}}{37.7} = \textbf{8.63}$

(*ii*) During the negative half-cycle of a.c. supply, the diode is reverse biased and hence conducts no current. Therefore, the maximum secondary voltage appears across the diode.

∴ PIV $= V_{sm} = \textbf{37.7 V}$

28.8. FULL-WAVE RECTIFIER

In full-wave rectification, current flows through the load in the same direction for both half-cycles of input *a.c.* voltage. Thus a full-wave rectifier utilises both half-cycles of input *a.c.* voltage to produce *d.c.* output. The following two circuits are commonly used for full-wave rectification :

(*i*) Centre-tap full-wave rectifier

(*ii*) Full-wave bridge rectifier

28.9. CENTRE-TAP FULL-WAVE RECTIFIER

The circuit employs two diodes D_1 and D_2 as shown in Fig. 28.8. A centre tapped secondary winding AB is used with diodes connected so that each uses half-cycle of input a.c. voltage. In other words, diode D_1 utilises the *a.c.* voltage appearing across the upper half (OA) of secondary winding for rectification while diode D_2 utilises the lower half winding (OB).

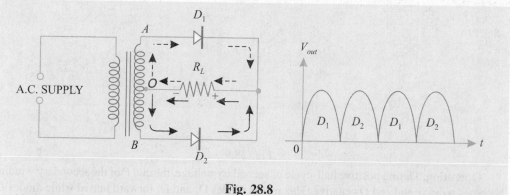

Fig. 28.8

Operation.

(*i*) During the positive half-cycle of secondary voltage, the end A of the secondary winding becomes positive and end B negative. This makes the diode D_1 forward biased and diode D_2 reverse biased. Therefore, diode D_1 conducts while diode D_2 does not. The conventional current flow is through diode D_1, load resistor R_L and the upper half of secondary winding as shown by the dotted arrows.

(*ii*) During the negative half-cycle, end A of the secondary becomes negative and end B positive. Therefore, diode D_2 conducts while diode D_1 does not. The conventional current flow is thorugh diode D_2, load R_L and lower half of secondary winding as shown by solid arrows.

Referring to Fig. 28.8, it may be seen that current in the load is *in the same direction* for both half-cycles of input *a.c.* voltage. Therefore, d.c. output is obtained across the load R_L. Also the polarities of the d.c. output across the load should be noted.

Peak Inverse Voltage. Suppose V_m is the maximum voltage across the half secondary winding. Since at any time one diode conducts while the other does not, the whole secondary voltage would appear across the non-conducting diode. Consequently, peak inverse voltage is twice the maximum voltage across the half secondary winding.

∴ $$PIV = 2V_m$$

Disadvantages

(*i*) It is difficult to locate the centre tap on the secondary winding.

(*ii*) The d.c. output is small as each diode utilises only one-half of the transformer secondary voltage.

(*iii*) The diodes used must have high peak inverse voltage.

28.10. FULL-WAVE BRIDGE RECTIFIER

The need for a centre-tapped transformer is eliminated in the bridge rectifier. It contains four diodes D_1, D_2, D_3 and D_4 connected to form bridge as shown in Fig.28.9 (*i*). The *a.c.* supply to be rectified is applied to the diagonally opposite ends of the bridge through the transformer. Between other ends of the bridge, the load R_L is connected.

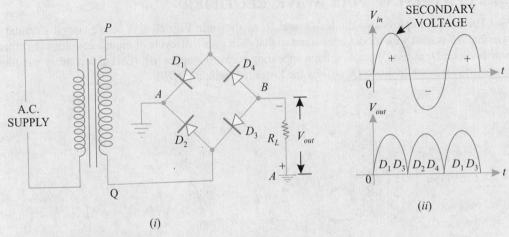

Fig. 28.9

Operation. During positive half-cycle of secondary voltage, the end P of the secondary winding becomes positive and end Q negative. This makes diodes D_1 and D_3 forward biased while diodes D_2 and D_4 are reverse biased. Therefore, only diodes D_1 and D_3 conduct. The two diodes will be in series through the load R_L as shown in Fig. 28.10 (*i*). The conventional current flow is shown by dotted arrows. It may be seen that current flows from A to B through the load R_L.

During the negative half-cycle of the secondary voltage, end P becomes negative and end Q positive. This makes diodes D_2 and D_4 forward biased while diodes D_1 and D_3 are reverse biased. Therefore, only diodes D_2 and D_4 conduct. These two diodes will be in series through the load R_L as shown in Fig.28.10 (*ii*). The current flow is shown by the solid arrows. It may be seen that current flows from A to B through the load R_L *i.e.*, in the same direction as for the positive half-cycle. Therefore, d.c. output is obtained across the load R_L.

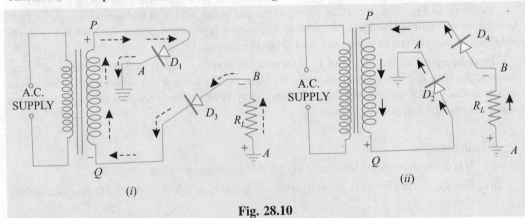

Fig. 28.10

Peak inverse voltage. Referring to Fig.28.9, when end P is positive, diode D_1 conducts (*i.e.*, its resistance is zero) whereas diode D_2 does not conduct. By studying the circuit PD_1D_2Q, it is easy to see that whole of the secondary voltage is applied in the reverse direction across diode D_2. Hence PIV of each diode is equal to the maximum secondary voltage.

Advantages

(*i*) The need for centre-tapped transformer is eliminated.

(*ii*) The output is twice that of the centre-tap circuit for the same secondary voltage.

(iii) For the same d.c. output voltage, *PIV* of bridge circuit is half that of the centre-tap circuit.

Disadvantages

(i) It requires four diodes.

(ii) As during each half-cycle of a.c. input two diodes that conduct are in series, therefore, voltage drop in the internal resistance of the rectifying unit will be twice as great as in the centre-tap circuit. This is objectionable when the secondary voltage is small.

Rectifier

28.11. EFFICIENCY OF FULL-WAVE RECTIFIER

Let $v = V_m \sin \theta$ be the a.c. voltage to be rectified. Let r_f and R_L be the diode resistance and load resistance respectively.

d.c. power output. From the elementary knowledge of electrical engineering,

$$I_{dc} = 2I_m / \pi \quad \text{where } I_m = \frac{V_m}{r_f + R_L}$$

$$V_{dc} = 2 V_m/\pi$$

$$P_{dc} = I_{dc}^2 \times R_L = (2 I_m/\pi)^2 \times R_L$$

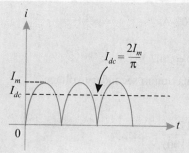 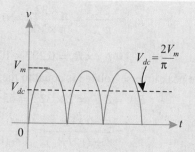

Fig. 28.11

a.c. power input

$$I_{r.m.s.} = I_m / \sqrt{2} \; ; \; P_{ac} = I_{r.m.s}^2 (r_f + R_L) = (I_m / \sqrt{2})^2 \times (r_f + R_L)$$

$\therefore$ Rectifier $\eta = \dfrac{P_{dc}}{P_{ac}} = \dfrac{(2 I_m / \pi)^2 \times R_L}{(I_m / \sqrt{2})^2 \times (r_f + R_L)} = \dfrac{0.812 \, R_L}{r_f + R_L} = \dfrac{0.812}{1 + (r_f / R_L)}$

The efficiency will be maximum if r_f is negligible as compared to R_L.

$\therefore$ Max. efficiency = 81.2%

This is double the efficiency due to a half-wave rectifier. Therefore, a full-wave rectifier is twice as effective as a half-wave rectifier.

Example 28.3. *A full-wave rectifier uses two diodes, the internal resistance of each is assumed constant at 20 Ω. The transformer r.m.s. secondary voltage from centre-tap to each end of secondary is 50 V and load resistance is 980 Ω. Find (i) the mean load current and (ii) the r.m.s. value of load current.*

Solution. The maximum voltage across half secondary winding, $V_m = 50 \times \sqrt{2} = 70.7\text{V}$.

$$I_m = \frac{V_m}{r_f + R_L} = \frac{70.7 \text{ V}}{(20 + 980) \ \Omega} = 70.7 \text{ mA}$$

(i) $\quad I_{dc} = 2 \ I_m/\pi = 2 \times 70.7/\pi = \textbf{45 mA}$

(ii) $\quad I_{r.m.s.} = I_m / \sqrt{2} = 70.7 / \sqrt{2} = \textbf{50 mA}$

Example 28.4. *In the centre-tap circuit shown in Fig. 28.12, the diodes are assumed to be ideal i.e., having zero internal resistance. Find (i) d.c. output voltage (ii) peak inverse voltage and (iii) rectification efficiency.*

Solution. (i) The *r.m.s.* secondary voltage = $230 \times (1/5) = 46$ V. The maximum voltage across the secondary = $46 \times \sqrt{2} = 65$ V. Hence maximum voltage across half secondary winding $V_m = 65/2 = 32.5$ V.

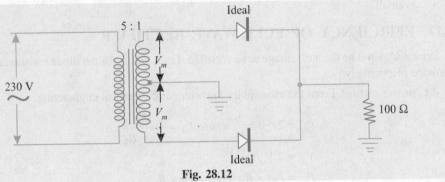

Fig. 28.12

$$I_{dc} = \frac{2V_m}{\pi \ R_L} = \frac{2 \times 32.5}{\pi \times 100} = 0.207 \text{ A}$$

$$V_{dc} = I_{dc} \times R_L = 0.207 \times 100 = \textbf{20.7 V}$$

(ii) The peak inverse voltage is equal to the maximum secondary voltage.

∴ $\quad PIV = 2 \ V_m = 2 \times 32.5 = \textbf{65 V}$

(iii) $\quad \eta = \frac{0.812}{1 + (r_f / R_L)} = \frac{0.812}{1 + (0/100)} = \textbf{81.2\%}$

Example 28.5. *The four diodes used in a bridge rectifier circuit have forward resistances which may be considered constant at 1Ω and an infinite reverse resistance. The alternating supply voltage is 240 V r.m.s. and resistive load is 48 Ω. Calculate (i) mean load current (ii) rectifier efficiency and (iii) power dissipated in each diode.*

Solution.

(i) Max. load current, $\quad I_m = \frac{V_m}{*2r_f + R_L} = \frac{\sqrt{2} \times 240}{2 \times 1 + 48} = 6.79 \text{ A}$

∴ Mean load current, $\quad I_{dc} = \frac{2 \ I_m}{\pi} = \frac{2 \times 6.79}{\pi} = 4.32 \text{ A}$

(ii) R.M.S. value of load current, $I_{r.m.s.} = \frac{I_m}{\sqrt{2}} = \frac{6.79}{\sqrt{2}} = 4.8 \text{ A}$

* At any instant in the bridge rectifier, two diodes in series are conducting. Therefore, the total forward resistance is $2r_f$.

$$\text{Rectifier } \eta = \frac{P_{dc}}{P_{ac}} = \frac{(2\,I_m/\pi)^2 \times R_L}{(I_m/\sqrt{2})^2 \times (2r_f + R_L)}$$

$$= \frac{(4.32)^2 \times 48}{(4.8)^2 \times 50} = 0.779 = 77.9\%$$

(*iii*) Since each diode conducts for only half a cycle, therefore, diode *r.m.s.* current

$$= \frac{I_m}{2} = \frac{6.79}{2} = 3.39 \text{ A}.$$

∴ Power dissipated in each diode = $(3.39)^2 \times 1 = $ **11.5 W**

28.12. FILTER CIRCUITS

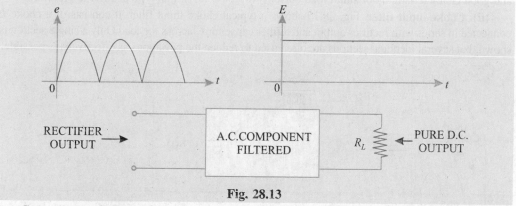

Fig. 28.13

Generally, a rectifier is required to produce pure *d.c.* supply for using at various places in electronic circuits. However, the output of a rectifier has pulsating character *i.e.,* it contains *a.c.* and *d.c.* components. The *a.c.* component is undesirable and must be kept away from the load. To do so, a *filter circuit* is used which removes (or *filters out*) the a.c. component and allows only the *d.c.* component to reach the load.

A **filter circuit** *is a device which removes the a.c. component of rectifier output but allows the d.c. component to reach the load.*

Obivously, a filter circuit should be installed between the rectifier and the load as shown in Fig. 28.13. A filter circuit is generally a combination of inductors (*L*) and capacitors (*C*). The filtering action of *L* and *C* depends upon the basic electrical principles. A capacitor passes *a.c.* readily but does not pass *d.c.* at all. On the other hand, an inductor opposes *a.c.* but allows *d.c.* to pass through it. It then becomes clear that suitable network of *L* and *C* can effectively remove the *a.c.* component, allowing the *d.c.* component to reach the load.

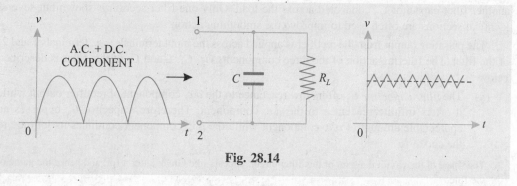

Fig. 28.14

28.13. TYPES OF FILTER CIRCUITS

The most commonly used filter circuits are *capacitor filter, choke input filter* and *capacitor input or π filter.*

(*i*) **Capacitor filter.** Fig. 28.14 shows the capacitor filter circuit. It consists of a capacitor C placed across the rectifier output in parallel with the load R_L. The pulsating direct voltage of the rectifier output is applied across the capacitor *i.e.,* across terminals 1 and 2. As discussed earlier, the pulsating output of rectifier contains *a.c.* and *d.c.* components. The low reactance of capacitor C bypasses the *a.c.* component but prevents the d.c. component to flow through it. Therefore, only *d.c.* component reaches the load. In this way, the filter circuit (*i.e.,C*) has filtered out the *a.c.* component from the rectifier output, allowing the *d.c.*component to reach the load.

The capacitor filter circuit is extremely popular because of its low cost, small size, little weight and good characteristics. For small load currents (upto 50 mA), this type of filter is preferred.

(*ii*) **Choke input filter.** Fig. 28.15 shows a typical choke input filter. It consists of a choke L connected in series with rectifier output and a filter capacitor C across the load.Only a single section is shown, but several identical sections are often used to reduce the pulsations as effectively as possible.

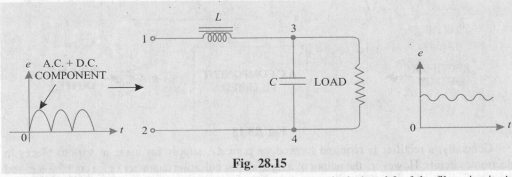

Fig. 28.15

The pulsating output of the rectifier is applied across terminals 1 and 2 of the filter circuit. As discussed before, the pulsating output of the rectifier contains *a.c.*and *d.c* components. The choke offers high opposition to the passage of *a.c.* component but negligible opposition to the *d.c.* component. The result is that most of the *a.c.* component appears across the choke while whole of the d.c. component passes through the choke on its way to load. This results in reduced pulsations at terminal 3.

At terminal 3, the rectifier output contains d.c. component and the remaining *a.c.*component which has managed to pass through the choke. Now the low reactance of filter capacitor C bypasses the *a.c.* component but prevents the *d.c.* component to flow through it. Therefore, only *d.c.* component reaches the load.

(*iii*) **Capacitor input or π-filter.** Fig. 28.16 shows a typical capacitor input filter or *π- filter. It consists of a filter capacitor C_1 connected across the rectifier output, a choke L in series and another filter capacitor C_2 connected across the load. Only one filter section is shown but several identical sections are often used to improve the smoothing action.

The pulsating output from the rectifier is applied across the input terminals (*i.e.,* terminals 1 and 2) of the filter. The filtering action of the three components *viz.* C_1, L and C_2 of this filter is described below :

(*a*)   The *filter capacitor* C_1 offers low reactance to the *a.c.* component of rectifier output while it offers infinite reactance to the *d.c.* component. Therefore, capacitor C_1 bypasses an appreciable amount of *a.c.* component while the d.c. component continues its journey to the choke L.

---

*   The shape of the circuit diagram of this filter circuit appears like Greek letter π (pi) and hence the name of the filter.

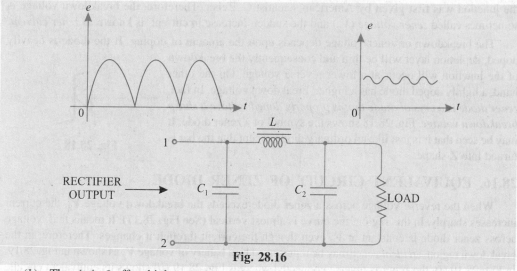

Fig. 28.16

(b) The *choke L* offers high reactance to the *a.c.* component but it offers almost zero opposition to the *d.c.*component. Therefore, it allows the *d.c.* component to flow through it while the *unbypassed *a.c.* component is blocked.

(c) The *filter capacitorC₂* bypasses the *a.c.* component which the choke has failed to block. Therefore, only *d.c.* component appears across the load and that is what we desire.

28.14. VOLTAGE STABILISATION

A rectifier with an appropriate filter serves as a good source of *d.c.* output. However, the major disadvantage of such a power supply is that the output voltage changes with the variations in the input voltage or load. Thus, if the input voltage increases, the *d.c.* output voltage of the rectifier also increases. Similarly, if the load current increases, the output voltage is decreased due to the voltage drop in the rectifying element, filter chokes, transformer windings *etc*. In many electronic applications, it is desired that output voltage should remain constant regardless of the variations in the input voltage or load. In order to ensure this, a voltage stabilising device called voltage stabiliser is used. Several stabilising circuits have been designed but only zener diode as a voltage stabiliser will be discussed.

28.15. ZENER DIODE

A **zener diode** *is a silicon junction diode which is operated under reverse bias and arranged to break down when a specific reverse-bias voltage is applied to it.*

It has already been discussed that when the reverse bias on a crystal diode is increased, a critical voltage, called *breakdown voltage* is reached where the reverse current increases sharply to a high value. The breakdown region is the knee of the reverse characteristic as shown in Fig. 28.17. The satisfactory explanation of this breakdown of

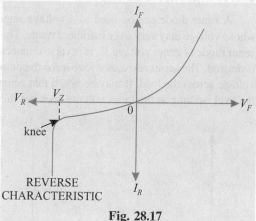

REVERSE
CHARACTERISTIC

Fig. 28.17

---

*   The part of *a.c.* component which could not be bypassed by capacitor C_1.

the junction was first given by American scientist C. Zener. Therefore, the breakdown voltage is sometimes called *zener voltage* (V_Z) and the sudden increase in current is known as *zener current*.

The breakdown or zener voltage depends upon the amount of doping. If the diode is heavily doped, depletion layer will be thin and consequently the breakdown of the junction will occur at a lower reverse voltage. On the other hand, a lightly doped diode has a higher breakdown voltage. In fact, *zener diode is a crystal diode that is properly doped to have a sharp breakdown voltage*. Fig. 28.18 shows the symbol of a zener diode. It may be seen that it is just like an ordinary diode except that the bar is turned into Z-shape.

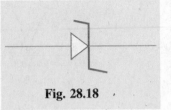

Fig. 28.18

28.16. EQUIVALENT CIRCUIT OF ZENER DIODE

When the reverse voltage across a zener diode exceeds the breakdown voltage V_Z, the current increases sharply. In this region, the curve is almost vertical (See Fig. 28.17). It means that voltage across zener diode is constant at V_Z even though the current through it changes. Therefore, in the breakdown region, an *ideal* zener may be represented by a battery of voltage V_Z as shown in Fig. 28.19. In Fig. 28.19 (*i*), the zener is reverse connected whereas Fig. 28.19 (*ii*) shows its equivalent circuit.

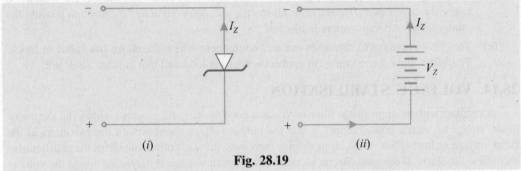

Fig. 28.19

In our further discussion, we shall assume that in the breakdown region, the zener diode can be replaced by a battery of voltage V_Z. This simplified picture makes the analysis of zener diode quite understandable.

28.17. ZENER DIODE AS VOLTAGE REGULATOR

A zener diode can be used as a voltage regulator to provide a constant voltage from a source whose voltage may vary over sufficient range. The circuit arrangement is shown in Fig. 28.20 (*i*). The zener diode of zener voltage V_Z is reverse connected across the load R_L across which constant output is desired. The series resistance R absorbs the output voltage fluctuations so as to maintain a constant voltage across the load. It may be noted that zener will maintain a constant voltage V_Z (= E_0) across the load so long as the input voltage does not fall below V_Z.

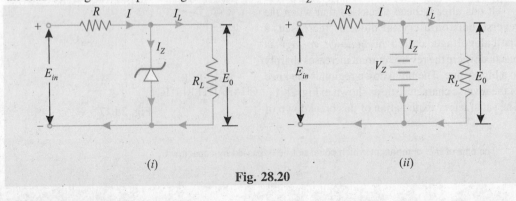

Fig. 28.20

Working. When the circuit is properly designed, the load voltage E_0 remains essentially constant ($= V_Z$) even though the input voltage E_{in} and load resistance R_L may vary over a wide range.

(*i*) Suppose the input voltage increases. Since the zener diode is in the breakdown region, the zener diode is equivalent to a battery V_Z as shown in Fig. 28.20 (*ii*). It is clear that output voltage remains constant at V_Z ($= E_0$).The excess voltage is dropped across the series resistance R. This will cause an increase in the value of total current I. The zener will conduct the increase of current while the load current remains constant.Hence output voltage E_0 remains constant irrespective of the changes in the input voltage E_{in}.

(*ii*) Now suppose the input voltage is constant but the load resistance R_L decreases. This will cause an increase in load current. The extra current cannot come from the source because drop in R (and hence source current I) will not change as the zener is within its regulating range. The additional load current will come from a decrease in zener current I_Z. Consequently, the output voltage stays at a constant value.

28.18. TYPES OF DIODES

The most common application of diodes is rectification. The rectifier diodes are used in power supplies to convert *a.c.* voltage into d.c. voltage . But rectification is not all that a diode can do. A number of specific types of diodes are manufactured for specific applications in this fast developing world. Some of the more common special purpose diodes are :

(*i*) Zener diode   (*ii*) Light-emitting diode (LED)   (*iii*) Photo-diode

(*iv*) Tunnel diode   (*v*) Varactor diode   (*vi*) Shockley diode

(*i*) A properly doped crystal diode which has a sharp breakdown voltage is known as a *zener diode.* They are used as voltage regulators. For detailed discussion on zener diodes, the reader may refer to articles 28.15, 28.16 and 28.17.

(*ii*) A **light-emitting diode (LED)** is a diode that gives off visible light when forward biased. They are not made from silicon or germanium but are made by using special materials. By the use of these special materials, it is possible to produce light of different wavelengths with colours that include red, green, yellow and blue. For example, when a LED is manufactured using gallium arsenide, it will produce a red light. If the LED is made with gallium phosphide, it will produce a green light. They are used as power indicators, in seven segment display etc.

(*iii*) A **photo-diode** is a reverse-biased silicon or germanium *pn* junction in which reverse current increases when the junction is exposed to light. The reverse current in a photo-diode is directly proportional to the intensity of light falling on its *pn* junction. This means that greater the intensity of light falling on the *pn* junction of photo-diode, the greater will be the reverse current. They are used in an alarm circuit, to count items on a conveyor belt etc.

(*iv*) A **tunnel diode** is a *pn* junction that exhibits negative resistance in certain regions of forward voltage. It is made of silicon or germanium. A conventional diode exhibits *positive resistance when it is forward biased or reverse biased. However, if a semiconductor junction diode is heavily doped with impurities, it exhibits negative resistance *i.e.,* current decreases as the voltage is increased. They are used in oscillators to produce undamped oscillations.

(*v*) A junction diode which acts as a variable capacitor under changing reverse bias is known as a **varactor diode.** Under reverse biased conditions, the diode may be considered as a capacitor with *n*-region and *p*-region forming oppositely charged plates and with depletion zone between them acting as a dielectric. They are made of germanium or silicon. They are used in circuits which require voltage controlled tuning.

* If current flowing through a circuit or device increases as the applied voltage is increased, we say that the circuit or device has positive resistance.

(*vi*) **Shockley diode** is a *PNPN* device having two terminals and consists of four alternate *P*-type and *N*-type layers in a single crystal. When proper voltage is applied, the shockley diode behaves like a switch. It is also known as *PNPN* diode or four layer diode or reverse-blocking diode thyristor.

MULTIPLE-CHOICE QUESTIONS

1. A crystal diode has..............
   (*a*) two *pn* junctions
   (*b*) one *pn* junction
   (*c*) three *pn* junctions
   (*d*) none of the above

2. A crystal diode has forward resistance of the order of..............
   (*a*) Ω   (*b*) kΩ
   (*c*) MΩ   (*d*) none of the above

3. If the arrow of a crystal diode symbol is positive *w.r.t.* bar, then diode is .... biased.
   (*a*) reverse   (*b*) forward
   (*c*) none of the two (*d*) forward or reverse

4. The reverse current in a diode is of the order of..............
   (*a*) μA   (*b*) mA
   (*c*) A   (*d*) kA

5. The forward voltage drop across a silicon diode is about..............
   (*a*) 2.5 V   (*b*) 3 V
   (*c*) 0.7 V   (*d*) 10 V

6. A crystal diode is used as..............
   (*a*) an amplifier   (*b*) a rectifier
   (*c*) an oscillator   (*d*) a voltage regulator

7. The *d.c.* resistance of a crystal diode is ....that of its *a.c.* resistance.
   (*a*) the same as   (*b*) more than
   (*c*) less than   (*d*) none of the above

8. An ideal crystal diode is one which behaves as a perfect.............. when forward biased.
   (*a*) conductor   (*b*) insulator
   (*c*) resistance material (*d*) none of the above

9. The reverse resistance and forward resistance of crystal diode have a ratio of about..............
   (*a*) 1 : 1   (*b*) 1000 : 1
   (*c*) 100 : 1   (*d*) 2 : 1

10. The leakage current in a crystal diode is due to..............
    (*a*) minority carriers
    (*b*) majority carriers
    (*c*) junction capacitance
    (*d*) none of the above

11. If temperature of a crystal diode increases, leakage current..............
    (*a*) remains the same
    (*b*) decreases
    (*c*) increases
    (*d*) becomes zero

12. The *PIV* rating of a crystal diode is .... that of equivalent vacuum diode.
    (*a*) lower than   (*b*) more than
    (*c*) the same as   (*d*) none of the above

13. If the doping level of a crystal diode is increased, the breakdown voltage..............
    (*a*) remains the same (*b*) is decreased
    (*c*) is increased   (*d*) none of the above

14. A crystal diode is a ....device.
    (*a*) non-linear   (*b*) linear
    (*c*) amplifying   (*d*) none of the above

15. A crystal diode utilises..............characteristic for rectification.
    (*a*) reverse   (*b*) forward
    (*c*) forward or reverse
    (*d*) none of the above

16. When a crystal diode is used as a rectifier, the most important consideration is..............
    (*a*) doping level   (*b*) *PIV*
    (*c*) forward resistance
    (*d*) none of the above

17. If doping level in a crystal diode is increased, the width of depletion layer..............
    (*a*) remains the same (*b*) is increased
    (*c*) is decreased   (*d*) none of above

18. A zener diode has..............
    (*a*) one *pn* junction (*b*) two *pn* junctions
    (*c*) three *pn* junctions (*d*) none of the above

19. A zener diode is used as..............
    (*a*) an amplifier   (*b*) a rectifier
    (*c*) a voltage regulator (*d*) a multivibrator

20. The doping level in a zener diode is..............that of a crystal diode.
    (*a*) more than   (*b*) less than
    (*c*) the same as   (*d*) none of the above

Answers to Multiple-Choice Questions

1. (b)	2. (a)	3. (b)	4. (a)	5. (c)
6. (b)	7. (c)	8. (a)	9. (b)	10. (a)
11. (c)	12. (a)	13. (b)	14. (a)	15. (b)
16. (b)	17. (c)	18. (a)	19. (c)	20. (a)

Hints to Selected Multiple-Choice Questions

2. The forward resistance of a crystal diode is very small, ranging from 1 to 25Ω.

3. If arrowhead of diode symbol is positive *w.r.t.* bar of the symbol, the diode is **forward** biased.

6. The unilateral conduction capability of a crystal diode makes it similar to that of a vacuum diode. Therefore, like a vacuum diode, it can also accomplish the job of rectification.

8. For an ideal diode, forward resistance $r_f = 0$ and potential barrier V_0 is negligible. Therefore, such a diode behaves as a perfect **conductor** under forward biased conditions.

12. Crystal diodes can handle low inverse voltages as compared to vacuum diodes.

16. The most important consideration is *PIV* when using crystal diode as a rectifier. If the reverse voltage across diode exceeds its *PIV*, it may be destroyed due to excccessive heat.

29

Transistors

INTRODUCTION

When a third doped element is added to a crystal diode in such a way that two *pn* junctions are formed, the resulting device is known as a *transistor*. The transistor—an entirely new type of electronic device— is capable of achieving amplification of weak signals in a fashion comparable and often superior to that realised by vacuum tubes. Transistors are far smaller than vacuum tubes, have no filament and hence need no heating power and may be operated in any position. They are mechanically strong, have practically unlimited life and can do some jobs better than vacuum tubes. In this chapter, we shall focus our attention on the various aspects of transistors and their increasing applications in the fast developing electronics industry.

FIRST SILICON TRANSISTOR

29.1. TRANSISTOR

A **transistor** *consists of two pn junctions formed by* *sandwiching either p-type or n-type semiconductor between a pair of opposite types.* Accordingly, there are two types of transistors, namely;

(*i*) *n-p-n* transistors

(*ii*) *p-n-p* transistors

An *n-p-n* transistor is composed of two *n*-type semiconductors separated by a thin section of *p*-type as shown in Fig. 29.1 (*i*). However, a *p-n-p* transistor is formed by two sections of *p*-type separated by a thin section of *n*-type as shown in Fig. 29.1 (*ii*).

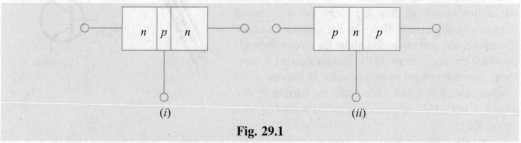

Fig. 29.1

In each type of transistor, the following points may be noted :

(*i*) There are two *pn* junctions.Therefore, a transistor may be regarded as a combination of two diodes connected back to back.

(*ii*) There are three terminals, taken from each type of semiconductor.

(*iii*) The middle section is very thin. This is the most important factor in the function of a transistor.

29.2. SOME FACTS ABOUT THE TRANSISTOR

(*i*) A transistor (*pnp* or *npn*) has three sections of doped semiconductors. The section on one side is the **emitter** and the section on the opposite side is the **collector**. The middle section is called the **base** and forms two junctions between the emitter and collector.

(*ii*) *The emitter-base junction is always forward biased whereas collector-base junction is always reverse biased* (See Fig. 29.2). This is the basic condition for the proper functioning of the transistor.

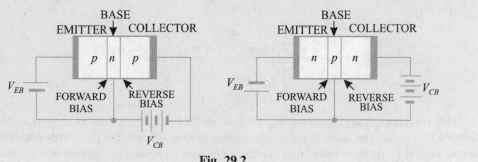

Fig. 29.2

(*iii*) The resistance of the forward-biased junction is very small as compared to that of reversed-biased junction. Therefore, forward bias applied to the emitter-base junction (*i.e.* V_{EB}) is very small whereas reverse bias on the collector-base junction is much higher (*i.e.* V_{CB}).

(*iv*) The emitter is heavily doped so that it can supply a large number of charge **carriers (holes

---

*   In practice, three blocks *p*, *n*, *p* are grown out of the same crystal by adding corresponding impurities in turn.

**   Holes if emitter is p-type and electrons if emitter is n-type.

or electrons) to the base. The base is lightly doped and very thin; it passes most of the emitter injected charge carriers to the collector. The collector is moderately doped.

(*v*) The base is much thinner than the emitter while *collector is wider than both. However, for the sake of convenience, it is customary to show emitter and collector to be of equal size.

29.3. TRANSISTOR ACTION

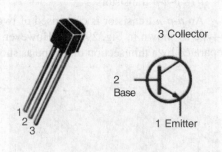

3 Collector

2
Base

1 Emitter

The emitter-base junction of a transistor is forward biased whereas collector-base junction is reverse biased. The forward bias on the emitter-base junction causes the emitter current to flow. It is seen that this emitter current *almost* entirely flows in the collector circuit. Therefore, the current in the collector circuit depends upon the emitter current. If the emitter current is zero, then collector current is *nearly* zero. However, if the emitter current is 1 *mA*, then collector current is also about 1 *mA*. This is precisely what happens in a transistor.

(*i*) **Working of npn transistor.** Fig. 29.3 shows the *npn* transistor with forward bias to emitter-base junction and reverse bias to collector-base junction. The forward bias causes the electrons in the *n*-type emitter to flow towards the base. This constitutes the emitter current I_E. As these electrons flow through the *p*-type base, they tend to combine with holes. As the base is lightly doped and very thin, therefore, only a few electrons (less than 5%) combine with the holes to constitute base current †I_B. The remainder (††more than 95%) cross over into the collector region to constitute collector current I_C. In this way, almost the entire emitter current flows in the collector circuit.

It is clear that emitter current is the sum of collector and base currents *i.e.*,

$$I_E = I_B + I_C$$

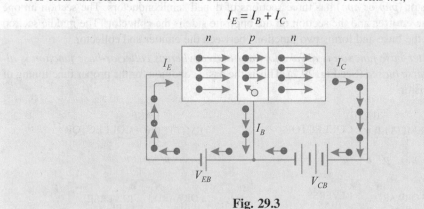

Fig. 29.3

(*ii*) **Working of pnp transistor.** Fig. 29.4 shows the basic connections of a *pnp* transistor. The forward bias causes the holes in the *p*-type emitter to flow towards the base. This constitutes the emitter current I_E. As these holes cross into the *n*-type base, they tend to combine with the electrons.

* During transistor operation, much heat is produced at the collector. The collector is made larger to dissipate the heat.

† The electrons which combine with holes become valence electrons. Then as valence electrons, they flow down through holes and into the external base lead. This constitutes base current I_B.

†† The reasons that most of the electrons from emitter continue their journey through the base to collector to form collector current are :

(*i*) The base is lightly doped and thin. Therefore, there are a few holes which find enough time to combine with electrons.

(*ii*) The reverse bias on the collector is quite high and exerts attractive forces on these electrons.

As the base is lightly doped and very thin, therefore, only a few holes (less than 5%) combine with the electrons. The remainder (more than 95%) cross into the collector region to constitute collector current I_C. In this way, almost the entire emitter current flows in the collector circuit. It may be noted that current conduction within *pnp* transistor is by holes. However, in the external wires, the current is still by electrons.

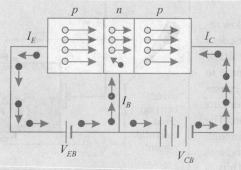

Fig. 29.4

Again, emitter current is the sum of collector and base currents *i.e.*

$$I_E = I_B + I_C$$

29.4. TRANSISTOR SYMBOLS

The symbols used for *npn* and *pnp* transistors are shown in Fig. 29.5. The emitter has an arrowhead, the base is a straight line and collector is shaped like the emitter but without an arrowhead.

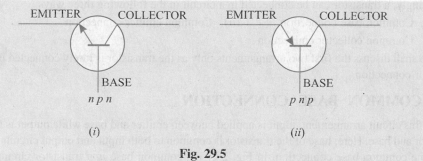

Fig. 29.5

The arrow on the emitter indicates the direction of conventional current in the emitter with forward bias. Checking (refer back to Fig. 29.3) for *npn* connection, it is clear that electrons flow into the emitter. This means that conventional current flows out of the emitter as indicated by the outgoing arrow in Fig. 29.5 (*i*). Similarly, it can be shown that for *pnp* connection (refer back to Fig. 29.4), the conventional current flows into the emitter as indicated by the inward arrow in Fig. 29.5 (*ii*).

29.5. TRANSISTOR AS AN AMPLIFIER

A transistor raises the strength of a weak signal and thus acts as an amplifier. Fig. 29.6 shows the basic circuit of a transistor amplifier. The weak signal is applied between emitter-base junction and output is taken across the load R_C connected in the collector circuit. In order to achieve faithful amplification, emitter-base junction should always remain forward biased. To do so, a *d.c.* voltage V_{EE} is applied in the input circuit in

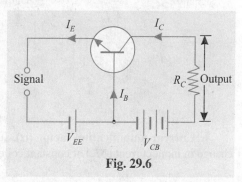

Fig. 29.6

addition to the signal as shown. This *d.c.* voltage is known as *bias voltage* and its magnitude is such that it always keeps emitter-base junction forward biased regardless of the polarity of the signal.

As the input circuit has low resistance (being forward biased), a small change in signal voltage causes an appreciable change in emitter current. This almost causes the same change in collector current due to transistor action. The collector current flowing through a high load resistance R_C produces a large voltage across it. Thus, a

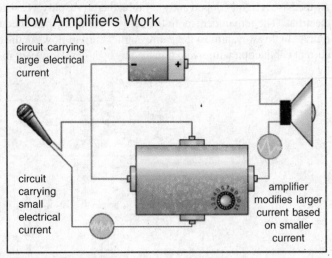

How Amplifiers Work

circuit carrying large electrical current

circuit carrying small electrical current

amplifier modifies larger current based on smaller current

weak signal applied in the input circuit appears in the amplified form in the collector circuit. It is in this way that a transistor acts as an amplifier.

29.6. TRANSISTOR CONNECTIONS

There are three leads in a transistor *viz.*, *emitter, base* and *collector* terminals. However, when a transistor is to be connected in a circuit, we require four terminals; two for the input and two for the output. This difficulty is overcome by making one terminal common to both input and output circuits. Accordingly; a transistor can be connected in a circuit in the following three ways:

(*i*)   Common base connection   (*ii*)   Common emitter connection

(*iii*)   Common collector connection

We shall discuss the first two arrangements only as the transistor is rarely connected in common collector connection.

29.7. COMMON BASE CONNECTION

In this circuit arrangement, input is applied between emitter and base while output is taken from collector and base. Here, base of the transistor is common to both input and output circuits and hence the name common base connection. In Fig. 29.7 (*i*), common base *npn* transistor circuit is shown whereas Fig. 29.7 (*ii*) shows the common base *pnp* transistor circuit.

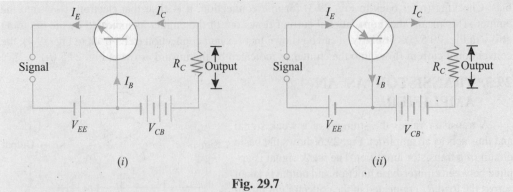

Fig. 29.7

1. **Current amplification factor** (α). It is the ratio of change in output current (ΔI_C) to the change in input current (ΔI_E) at constant collector-base voltage (*i.e.* V_{CB}).

$$^*\alpha = \frac{\Delta I_C}{\Delta I_E} \text{ at constant } V_{CB}$$

It is clear that current amplification factor α is less than unity. This value can be increased (but not more than unity) by decreasing the base current. This is achieved by making the base thin and doping it lightly. Practical values of α in commercial transistors range from 0.9 to 0.99.

2. Total collector current

(i) If switch S of Fig. 29.8 (i) is open (i.e. $I_E = 0$), the circuit is that of a reverse biased diode and the only current in the collector is leakage current I_{CBO} (meaning collector to base current when emitter is open) as shown in Fig 29.8 (i). This is due to the movement of minority carriers across the **reverse biased collector-base junction.

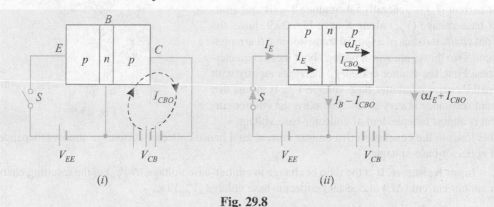

Fig. 29.8

(ii) When switch S is closed, the emitter current I_E divides between collector and base; the current flowing in collector is αI_E ($\because \alpha = I_C/I_E$) and current in base is I_B [$= (1-\alpha) I_E$] as shown in Fig. 29.8 (ii).

$\therefore$ Total collector current = $\qquad \alpha I_E \qquad + \qquad I_{CBO}$

$\qquad\qquad\qquad\qquad\qquad$ Due to majority carriers $\qquad$ Due to minority carriers

The leakage current in a transistor is very small (of the order of μA compared to mA due to majority carriers) and may be ignored.

It may be noted that leakage current is very much temperature dependent. Therefore, leakage current (I_{CBO}) must be taken into account when applications of wide temperature ranges are considered.

Example 29.1. *In a common base connection, current amplification factor is 0.9. If the emitter current is 1 mA, determine the base current.*

Solution.

$$\alpha = I_C/I_E$$

or $\qquad\qquad I_C = \alpha I_E = 0.9 \times 1 = 0.9 \text{ mA}$

Also $\qquad\qquad I_E = I_B + I_C$

$\therefore \qquad\qquad I_B = I_E - I_C = 1 - 0.9 = 0.1 \text{ mA}$

Example 29.2. *In a common base connecion, the emitter current is 1 mA. If the emitter circuit is open, the collector current is 50 μA. Find the total collector current. Given that $\alpha = 0.92$.*

. . . .

* $\quad$ If only d.c. values are considered, then $\alpha = I_C/I_E$.

** $\quad$ It may be recalled that there are present some holes in n-type base and free electrons in p-type collector as minority carriers. To these minority carriers, the reverse bias acts as a forward bias. Consequently, a very small current (of the order of μA) flows across the reverse biased collector-base junction.

Solution.

Here $\qquad I_E = 1\ mA;\ \alpha = 0.92;\ I_{CBO} = 50\ \mu A$

∴ Total collector current, $I_C = \alpha\ I_E + I_{CBO}$

$$= 0.92 \times 1 + 50 \times 10^{-3} = 0.97\ mA$$

29.8. CHARACTERISTICS OF COMMON BASE CONNECTION

The most important characteristics of common base connection are *input characteristics* and *output characteristics*.

(*i*) **Input Characteristics.** It is the curve between emitter current I_E and emitter-base voltage V_{EB}. The emitter current (I_E) is generally taken along Y-axis and emitter-base voltage (V_{EB}) along X-axis. Fig. 29.9 shows the input characteristics of a typical transistor in *CB* arrangement. Two things are worth noting about these characteristics. First, the emitter current I_E increases rapidly with small increase in emitter-base voltage V_{EB}. It means that input resistance is very small. Secondly, the emitter current is almost independent of collector-base voltage V_{CB}. This leads to the conclusion that emitter current (and hence collector current) is almost independent of collector-base voltage.

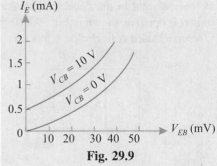

Fig. 29.9

Input resistance. It is the ratio of change in emitter-base voltage (ΔV_{EB}) to the resulting change in emitter current (ΔI_E) at constant collector-base voltage (V_{CB}) *i.e.*,

Input resistance, $r_i = \dfrac{\Delta V_{EB}}{\Delta I_E}$ at constant V_{CB}

In fact, input resistance is the opposition offered to the signal current. As a very small V_{EB} is sufficient to produce a large flow of emitter current I_E, therefore, input resistance is quite small, of the order of a few ohms.

(*ii*) **Output Characteristics.** It is the curve between collector current I_C and collector-base voltage V_{CB} at constant emitter current I_E. Generally, *collector current is taken along Y-axis and collector-base voltage along X-axis. Fig. 29.10 shows the output characteristics of a typical transistor in *CB* arrangement.

The following points may be noted from the characteristics:

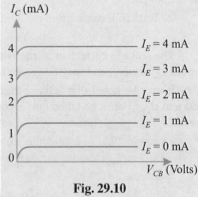

Fig. 29.10

(*i*) The collector current I_C varies with V_{CB} only at very low voltages (< 1V). The transistor is *never operated* in this region.

(*ii*) When the value of V_{CB} is raised above 1–2 V, the collector current becomes constant as indicated by straight horizontal curves. It means that now I_C is independent of V_{CB} and depends upon I_E only. This is consistent with the theory that emitter current flows *almost* entirely to the collector terminal. The transistor is always operated in this region.

(*iii*) A very large change in collector-base voltage produces only a tiny change in collector current. This means that output resistance is very high.

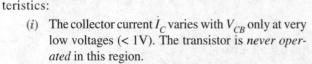

* I_E has to be kept constant because any change in I_E will produce corresponding change in I_C. Here, we are interested to see how V_{CB} influences I_C.

Output resistance. It is the ratio of change in collector-base voltage (ΔV_{CB}) to the resulting change in collector current (ΔI_C) at constant emitter current *i.e.*

Output resistance, $r_o = \dfrac{\Delta V_{CB}}{\Delta I_C}$ at constant I_E

The output resistance of *CB* circuit is very high, of the order of several tens of kilo-ohms. This is not surprising because the collector current changes very slightly with the change in V_{CB}.

29.9. COMMON EMITTER CONNECTION

In this circuit arrangement, input is applied between base and emitter and output is taken from collector and emitter. Here, emitter of the transistor is common to both input and output circuits and hence the name common emitter connection. Fig. 29.11 (*i*) shows common emitter *npn* transistor circuit whereas Fig. 29.11 (*ii*) shows common emitter *pnp* transistor circuit.

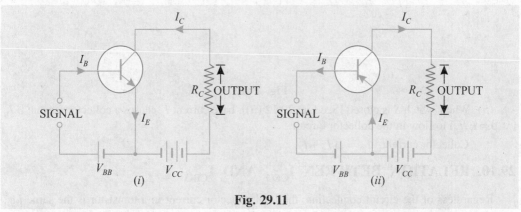

Fig. 29.11

1. Base current amplification factor (β). It is the ratio of change in output current (ΔI_C) to the change in input current (ΔI_B) *i.e.*,

$$*\beta = \frac{\Delta I_C}{\Delta I_B}$$

In almost any transistor, less than 5% of emitter current flows as the base current. Therefore, the value of β is generally greater than 20. Usually, its value ranges from 20 to 500. This type of connection is frequently used as it gives appreciable current gain as well as voltage gain.

Relation between β and α. A simple relation exists between β and α. This can be derived as follows :

$$I_E = I_B + I_C$$

or

$$\Delta I_E = \Delta I_B + \Delta I_C$$

Now,

$$\beta = \frac{\Delta I_C}{\Delta I_B} = \frac{\Delta I_C}{\Delta I_E - \Delta I_C}$$

$$= \frac{\Delta I_C / \Delta I_E}{(\Delta I_E / \Delta I_E) - (\Delta I_C / \Delta I_E)} = \frac{\alpha}{1 - \alpha}$$

$$\therefore \qquad \beta = \frac{\alpha}{1 - \alpha}$$

It is clear that as α approaches unity, β approaches infinity. In other words, the current gain in common emitter connection is very high. It is due to this reason that this circuit arrangement is used in about 90 to 95% of all transistor applications.

* If *d.c.* values are considered, $\beta = I_C / I_B$.

2. Collector current

(i)   If switch S of Fig. 29.12 is open (*i.e.*, $I_B = 0$), the leakage current flows from collector to emitter as shown in Fig. 29.12 (*i*). This leakage current is due to the minority carriers and is designated as I_{CEO}—meaning collector to emitter current when base is open.

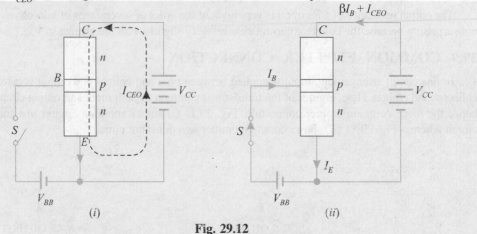

Fig. 29.12

(ii)   When switch S is closed [See Fig. 29.12 (*ii*)], base current I_B causes a collector current βI_B ($\because \beta = I_C/I_B$) to flow in the collector circuit.

∴   Collector current, $I_C = \beta I_B + I_{CEO}$

29.10. RELATION BETWEEN I_{CEO} AND I_{CBO}

Regardless of the circuit connection, the total collector current in a transistor is the same *i.e.*,

Total collector current in *CE*, I_C = Total collector current in *CB*

$$= \alpha I_E + I_{CBO}$$

$$= \alpha (I_B + I_C) + I_{CBO}$$

or $\qquad\qquad (1-\alpha) I_C = \alpha I_B + I_{CBO}$

or $\qquad\qquad I_C = \dfrac{\alpha}{1 - \alpha} I_B + \dfrac{I_{CBO}}{1 - \alpha}$

or $\qquad\qquad I_C = \beta I_B + \dfrac{I_{CBO}}{1 - \alpha}$ ...(*i*)

Also $\qquad\qquad I_C = \beta I_B + I_{CEO}$ ...(*ii*)

From eqs. (*i*) and (*ii*), we have, $I_{CEO} = \dfrac{I_{CBO}}{1 - \alpha}$

Clearly, leakage current in *CE* arrangement is more than in *CB* arrangement because α is less than 1.

Example 29.3. *Find the value of β if (i) $\alpha = 0.9$, (ii) $\alpha = 0.98$ and (iii) $\alpha = 0.99$.*

Solution.

(*i*) $\beta = \dfrac{\alpha}{1 - \alpha} = \dfrac{0.9}{1 - 0.9} = 9$

(*ii*) $\beta = \dfrac{\alpha}{1 - \alpha} = \dfrac{0.98}{1 - 0.98} = 49$

(iii) $\quad \beta = \dfrac{\alpha}{1-\alpha} = \dfrac{0.99}{1-0.99} = \mathbf{99}$

Example 29.4. *The base current in a transistor is 0.01 mA and emitter current is 1 mA. Calculate the values of α and β.*

Solution. $\qquad\qquad I_E = I_B + I_C$

$\therefore \qquad\qquad\qquad I_C = I_E - I_B = 1 - 0.01 = 0.99 \text{ mA}$

$\therefore \qquad\qquad\qquad \alpha = I_C/I_E = 0.99/1 = \mathbf{0.99}$

and $\qquad\qquad\qquad \beta = I_C/I_B = 0.99/0.01 = \mathbf{99}$

Example 29.5. *The collector leakage current in a transistor is 300 μA in CE arrangement. If the transistor is now connected in CB arrangement, what will be the leakage current ? Given that $\beta = 120$.*

Solution.

$$I_{CEO} = 300 \ \mu A; \ \beta = 120$$

Now, $\qquad\qquad \alpha = \dfrac{^* \beta}{\beta + 1} = \dfrac{120}{120 + 1} = 0.992$

$$I_{CEO} = \dfrac{I_{CBO}}{1 - \alpha}$$

$\therefore \qquad\qquad I_{CBO} = (1 - \alpha) \, I_{CEO} = (1 - 0.992) \, 300 = \mathbf{2.4 \ \mu A}$

Note that leakage current in CE arrangement is much more than in CB arrangement.

Example 29.6. *For a certain transistor, $I_B = 20 \ \mu A$, $I_C = 2 \ mA$ and $\beta = 80$. Calculate I_{CBO}.*

Solution.

$$I_C = \beta \, I_B + I_{CEO}$$

$$2 = 80 \times 0.02 + I_{CEO}$$

$\therefore \qquad\qquad I_{CEO} = 2 - 80 \times 0.02 = 0.4 \text{ mA}$

Now, $\qquad\qquad \alpha = \dfrac{\beta}{\beta + 1} = \dfrac{80}{80 + 1} = 0.988$

$\therefore \qquad\qquad I_{CBO} = (1 - \alpha) \, I_{CEO} = (1 - 0.988) \times 0.4 = \mathbf{0.0048 \ mA}$

29.11. CHARACTERISTICS OF COMMON EMITTER CONNECTION

The most important characteristics of this circuit arrangement are *input characteristics* and *output characteristics*.

. . . .

$*$ $\qquad\qquad \beta = \dfrac{\alpha}{1 - \alpha}$

or $\qquad\qquad \dfrac{1}{\beta} = \dfrac{1 - \alpha}{\alpha} = \dfrac{1}{\alpha} - 1$

or $\qquad\qquad \dfrac{1}{\alpha} = \dfrac{1}{\beta} + 1 = \dfrac{\beta + 1}{\beta}$

$\therefore \qquad\qquad \alpha = \dfrac{\beta}{\beta + 1}$

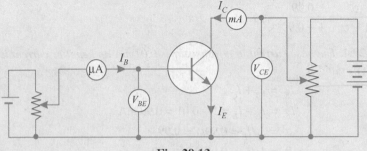

Fig. 29.13

1. Input characteristics. It is the curve between base current I_B and base-emitter voltage V_{BE} at constant collector-emitter voltage V_{CE}. The input characteristics of a *CE* connection can be determined by the circuit shown in Fig. 29.13. Keeping V_{CE} constant (say at 10 V), note the base current I_B for various values of V_{BE}. Then plot the readings obtained on the graph, taking I_B along *Y*-axis and V_{BE} along *X*-axis. This gives the input characteristic at $V_{CE} = 10$ V as shown in Fig. 29.14. Following a similar procedure, a family of input characteristics can be drawn. The following points may be noted from the characteristics :

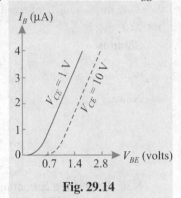

Fig. 29.14

- (*i*) The characteristics resemble those of a forward biased diode curve. This is expected since the base-emitter section of the transistor is a diode that is forward biased.

- (*ii*) As compared to *CB* arrangement, I_B increases less rapidly with V_{BE}. Therefore, input resistance of a *CE* circuit is higher than that of *CB* circuit.

Input resistance. It is the ratio of change in base-emitter voltage (ΔV_{BE}) to the resulting change in base current (ΔI_B) at constant V_{CE} *i.e.*,

$$\text{Input resistance, } r_i = \frac{\Delta V_{BE}}{\Delta I_B} \text{ at constant } V_{CE}$$

The value of input resistance for a *CE* circuit is of the order of a few hundred ohms.

2. Output characteristics. *It is the curve between collector current I_C and collector-emitter voltage V_{CE} at constant base current I_B.*

The output characteristics of a *CE* circuit can be drawn with the help of circuit shown in Fig. 29.13. Keeping the base curent I_B fixed at some value say 5 μA, note the collector current I_C for various values of V_{CE}. Then plot the readings on a graph, taking I_C along *Y*-axis and V_{CE} along *X*-axis. This gives the output characteristic at $I_B = 5$ μA as shown in Fig. 29.15 (*i*). Following similar procedure, a family of output characteristics can be drawn as shown in Fig. 29.15 (*ii*).

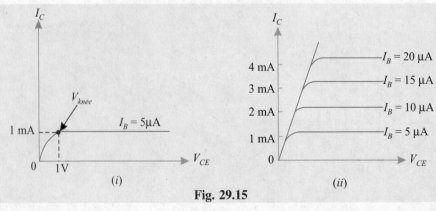

Fig. 29.15

The following points may be noted from the characteristics :

(*i*) The collector current I_C varies with V_{CE} for V_{CE} between 0 and 1 V only. After this, collector current becomes *almost* constant and independent of V_{CE}. This value of V_{CE} upto which collector current I_C changes is called the *knee voltage* (V_{knee}). *The transistors are always operated in the region above knee voltage.*

(*ii*) Above knee voltage, I_C is almost constant. However, a small increase in I_C with increasing V_{CE} is caused by the collector depletion layer getting wider and capturing a few more majority carriers before electron-hole combinations occur in the base area.

(*iii*) For any value of V_{CE} above knee voltage, the collector current I_C is approximately equal to $\beta \times I_B$.

Output resistance. It is the ratio of change in collector-emitter voltage (ΔV_{CE}) to the resulting change in collector current (ΔI_C) at constant I_B i.e.,

Output resistance, $r_o = \dfrac{\Delta V_{CE}}{\Delta I_C}$ at constant I_B

The value of output resistance of a transistor in this arrangement (*i.e.*, *CE* arrangement) is of the order of 50 kΩ.

29.12. TRANSISTOR AS AN AMPLIFIER IN CE ARRANGEMENT

Fig. 29.16 shows the common emitter *npn* amplifier circuit. Note that a battery V_{BB} is connected in the input circuit in addition to the signal voltage. This *d.c.* voltage is known as *bias voltage* and its magnitude is such that it always keeps the emitter-base junction forward biased regardless of the polarity of the signal source.

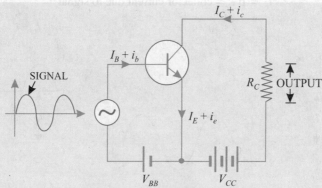

Fig. 29.16

Operation. During the positive half-cycle of the signal, the forward bias across the emitter-base junction is increased. Therefore, more electrons flow from the *n*-type emitter to the collector via the base. This causes an increase in collector current. The increased collector current causes a greater voltage drop across the collector load resistance R_C. However, during the negative half-cycle of the signal, the forward bias across emitter-base junction is decreased. Therefore, collector current decreases. This results in the decreased output voltage (in the opposite direction). Hence amplified output is obtained across the load.

Various currents. In a transistor amplifier, there is a *d.c.* bias as well as *a.c.* signal. Therefore, a transistor amplifier carries direct current as well as alternating current.

(*i*) **Base current.** When no signal is applied in the base, a *d.c.* base current I_B [See Fig. 29.17 (*i*)] flows due to bias battery V_{BB}. When *a.c.* signal is applied, *a.c.* base current i_b also flows [See Fig. 29.17 (*ii*)]. Therefore, with the application of signal, the total base current i_B [See Fig. 29.17 (*iii*)] is given by;

$$i_B = I_B + i_b$$

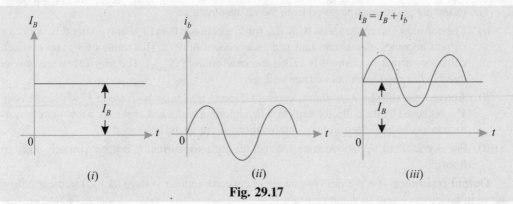

Fig. 29.17

Note that *a.c.* base current i_b rides on a *d.c.* base current I_B. The magnitude of *d.c.* base current I_B is such that base current always flows during all parts of the signal *i.e.*, base-emitter junction remains forward biased during all parts of the input a.c. signal.

(*ii*) **Collector current.** When no signal is applied, a *d.c.* collector current I_C (= βI_B) flows due to bias battery V_{BB} as shown in Fig. 29.18 (*i*). When *a.c.* signal is applied, *a.c.* collector current i_c (= βi_b) also flows as shown in Fig. 29.18 (*ii*). Therefore, the total current i_C [See Fig. 29.18 (*iii*)] is given by;

$$i_C = I_C + i_c$$

where
$$I_C = \beta I_B = \text{zero signal collector current}$$
$$i_c = \beta i_b = \text{collector current due to signal}$$

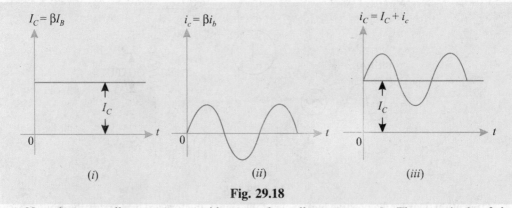

Fig. 29.18

Note that *a.c.* collector current i_c rides on a *d.c.* collector current I_C. The magnitude of *d.c.* collector current I_C (*i.e.*, zero signal collector current) is such that collector current flows during all parts of the input *a.c.* signal.

29.13. TRANSISTOR AS A SWITCH

We have already discussed that a crystal diode behaves like a switch. When the diode is forward biased, it conducts current easily and behaves like a closed switch. However, when diode is reverse biased, it practically conducts no current and behaves like an open switch. A transistor can also be used as a switch by driving it back and forth between *saturation* and *cut off*. This is illustrated in the discussion below.

(*i*)   When the base input voltage is enough negative, the transistor is *cut off* and no current flows in collector load R_C [See Fig. 29.19 (*i*)]. As a result, there is no voltage drop across R_C and the output is ideally V_{CC} *i.e.*

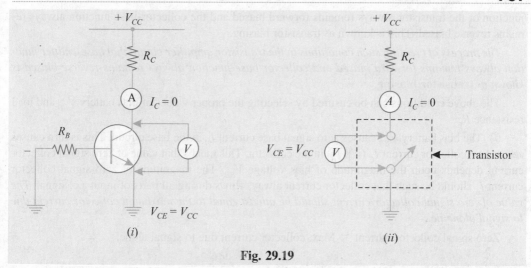

Fig. 29.19

$$I_C = 0 \text{ and } V_{CE} = V_{CC}$$

This condition is similar to that of an open switch (*i.e. OFF* state) as shown in Fig. 29.19 (*ii*).

(*ii*)When the input base voltage is positive enough that transistor saturates, then $I_{C(sat)}$ will flow through R_C. Under such conditions, the entire V_{CC} will drop across collector load R_C and output voltage is ideally zero *i.e.*

$$I_C = I_{C(sat)} = \frac{V_{CC}}{R_C} \text{ and } V_{CE} = 0$$

This condition is similar to that of a closed switch (*i.e. ON* state) as shown in Fig. 29.20 (*ii*).

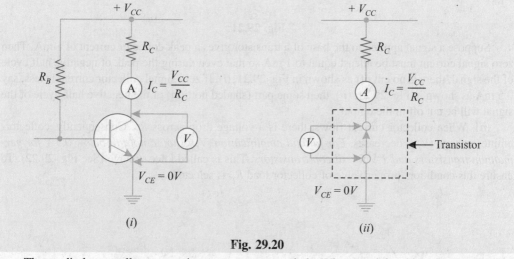

Fig. 29.20

Thus a diode as well as a transistor can act as a switch. When used for this purpose, they are called electronic switches. Electronic switches have become very popular because of their high speed and absence of sparking.

29.14. TRANSISTOR BIASING

The basic function of a transistor is to do amplification. One important requirement during amplification is that only the magnitude of the signal should increase and there should be no change in signal shape. This increase in magnitude of the signal without any change in its shape is known as *faithful amplification*. In order to achieve this, means are provided to ensure that base-emitter junction of the transistor always remains forward biased and the collector-base junction always remains reverse biased. This is known as transistor biasing.

The process of creating such conditions in the transistor amplifier circuit that base-emitter junction always remains forward biased and collector-base junction always remains reverse biased is known as **transistor biasing**.

The above conditions can be ensured by selecting the proper values of bias battery V_{BB} and load resistance R_C.

(*i*) The bias battery V_{BB} causes zero signal base current I_B in the base circuit. This is turn causes zero signal collector current $I_C (= \beta I_B)$ in the collector. This means that value of zero signal collector current depends upon the magnitude of bias voltage V_{BB}. The magnitude of zero signal collector current I_C should be such that collector current always flows during all parts of input a.c. signal. *The value of zero signal collector current should be atleast equal to the maximum collector current due to signal alone i.e.,*

Zero signal collector current $\gtrless$ Max. collector current due to signal alone.

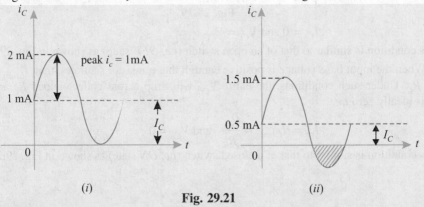

(*i*) Fig. 29.21 (*ii*)

Suppose a signal applied to the base of a transistor gives a peak collector current of 1 mA. Then zero signal current must be atleast equal to 1 mA so that even during the peak of negative half cycle of the signal, there is no cut off as shown in Fig. 29.21. (*i*). If zero signal collector current is less, say 0.5 mA as shown in Fig. 29.21. (*ii*), then some part (shaded portion) of the negative half-cycle of the signal will be cut off in the output.

(*ii*) When collector current flows, there is a voltage drop across R_C. Consequently, collector-emitter voltage (V_{CE}) decreases. *For faithful amplification, V_{CE} should not fall below 0.5 V for germanium transistors and 1 V for silicon transistors.* This is called knee voltage (See Fig. 29.22). To ensure this condition, proper value of collector load R_C is selected.

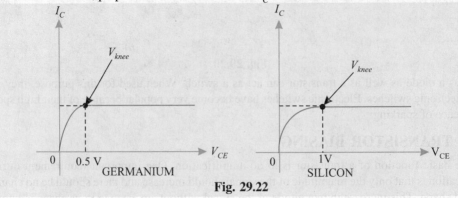

Fig. 29.22

When V_{CE} is too low (less than 0.5 V for *Ge* transistors and 1 V for *Si* transistors), the collector-base junction is not properly reverse biased. This upsets the transistor action and unfaithful amplification results.

29.15. OPERATING POINT

The zero signal values of I_C and V_{CE} in a transistor are known as **operating point**.

For the proper operation of transistor amplifier, it is necessary to set up fixed *d.c.* level of current through the transistor with fixed *d.c.* voltage drop across it. These *d.c.* values (*i.e.*, zero signal values) are known as operating point. Thus, in Fig. 29.23, the transistor has an operating point of 6 V, 2 mA *i.e.*, *d.c.* collector-emitter voltage $V_{CE} = 6$ V and *d.c.* collector current $I_C = 2$ mA. The operating point of the transistor is shown on its output characteristics in Fig. 29.23 (*ii*).

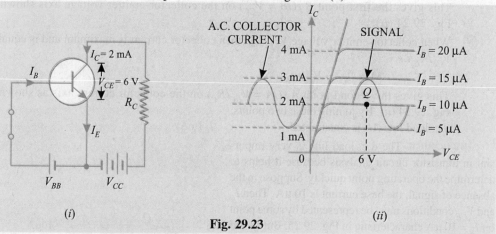

Fig. 29.23

When signal is applied to the input of the transistor, then current through and voltage across the transistor varies about this point as shown in Fig. 29.23 (*ii*). The point Q is called operating point because the variations of collector current and collector-emitter voltage take place about this point when signal is applied. It is also called *quiescent point* (silent) because it is the point on $V_{CE} - I_C$ characteristics when the transistor is silent *i.e.*, in the absence of the signal. The setting up of proper operating point in a transistor circuit is known as *biasing*. Clearly, biasing means setting up of proper *d.c.* values of V_{CE} and I_C in a transistor.

29.16. D.C LOAD LINE

Consider a common emitter *npn* transistor circuit shown in Fig. 29.24 (*i*) where no signal is applied. Therefore, *d.c.* conditions prevail in the circuit. The output characteristics of this circuit are

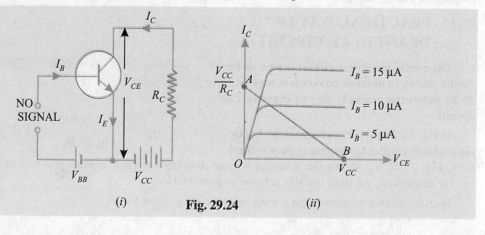

Fig. 29.24

shown in Fig. 29.24 (*ii*). The value of collector-emitter voltage V_{CE} is given by;

$$V_{CE} = V_{CC} - I_C R_C$$

As V_{CC} and R_C are fixed values, therefore, it is a first degree equation and can be represented by a straight line on the output characteristics. This is known as **d.c. *load line** and determines the locus of V_{CE} and I_C points for any load R_C. To draw *d.c.* load line, we require two end points. These two end points can be located as under :

(*i*) When the collector current $I_C = 0$, then collector-emitter voltage is maximum and is equal to V_{CC} i.e.,

$$\text{Max. } V_{CE} = V_{CC} - 0 \times R_C$$
$$= V_{CC}$$

This gives the first point B ($OB = V_{CC}$) on the collector-emitter voltage axis shown in Fig. 29.24 (*ii*).

(*ii*) When collector-emitter voltage $V_{CE} = 0$, then collector current is maximum and is equal to V_{CC}/R_C i.e.

$$\text{Max. } I_C = V_{CC}/R_C$$

This gives the second point A ($OA = V_{CC}/R_C$) on the collector current axis as shown in Fig. 29.24 (*ii*). By joining these two points, *d.c.* load line AB is constructed.

Importance. The d.c. load line is very important in transistor circuit analysis because it helps to determine the operating point quickly. Suppose in the absence of signal, the base current is 10 µA. Then I_C and V_{CE} conditions must be represented by some point on $I_B = 10$ µA characteristic in Fig. 29.25. But I_C and V_{CE} conditions in the circuit are also represented by some point on the *d.c.* load line AB. The point Q where the load line and $I_B = 10$ µA characteristic intersect is the only point which satisfies both these conditions. Thus, for $I_B = 10$ µA, the zero signal values are:

$$V_{CE} = OC \text{ volts}$$

and

$$I_C = OD \text{ mA}$$

It follows, therefore, that zero signal values of I_C and V_{CE} (*i.e.*, operating point) are determined by the point where *d.c.* load line intersects the proper base current curve.

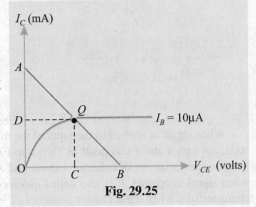

Fig. 29.25

29.17. PRACTICAL WAY OF DRAWING CE CIRCUIT

The common emitter circuit drawn so far can be shown in another convenient way. Fig. 29.26 shows the practical way of drawing *CE* circuit.

In Fig. 29.26 (*i*), the practical way of drawing common emitter *npn* circuit is shown. Simi-

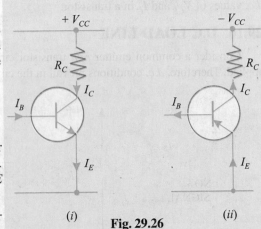

(*i*)   **Fig. 29.26**   (*ii*)

larly, Fig. 29.26 (*ii*) shows the practical way of drawing common emitter *pnp* circuit. In our further discussion, we shall use this scheme of presentation.

*   So called because the slope of this line depends upon the collector load R_C.

29.18. METHODS OF TRANSISTOR BIASING

In the transistor amplifier circuits drawn so far, biasing was done with the aid of battery V_{BB} which was separate from the battery V_{CC} used in the output circuit. However, in the interest of simplicity and economy, it is desirable that transistor circuit should have a single source of supply—the one in the output circuit (*i.e.*, V_{CC}). The following are the most commonly used methods of obtaining biasing from one source of *d.c.* supply (*i.e.*, V_{CC}):

(*i*)   Base resistor method

(*ii*) Biasing with feedback resistor

(*iii*) Voltage-divider bias

In all these methods, the same basic principle is employed *i.e.*, required value of base current (and hence I_C) is obtained from V_{CC} in the zero signal conditions. The value of collector load R_C is selected keeping in view that V_{CE} does not fall below 0.5 V for germanium transistors and 1 V for silicon transistors.

29.19. BASE RESISTOR METHOD

In this method, a high resistance R_B (several hundred kΩ) is connected between the base and +ve end of supply for *npn* transistor (See Fig. 29.27) and between base and negative end of supply for *pnp* transistor. Here, the required zero signal base current is provided by V_{CC} and it flows through R_B. It is because now base is positive *w.r.t.* emitter *i.e.*, base-emitter junction is forward biased. The required value of zero signal base current I_B (and hence $I_C = \beta I_B$) can be made to flow by selecting the proper value of base resistor R_B.

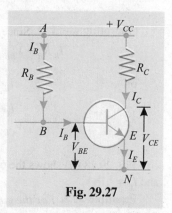

Fig. 29.27

Circuit analysis. It is required to find the value of R_B so that required collector current flows in the zero signal conditions. Let I_C be the required zero signal collector current.

$$\therefore \qquad I_B = I_C/\beta$$

Considering the closed circuit ABENA and applying Kirchoff's voltage law, we get,

$$V_{CC} = I_B R_B + V_{BE}$$

$$\therefore \qquad R_B = \frac{V_{CC} - V_{BE}}{I_B} \qquad\qquad ...(i)$$

As V_{CC} and I_B are known and V_{BE} can be seen from the transistor manual, therefore, the value of R_B can be readily found from exp. (*i*). For germanium transistors, $V_{BE} = 0.3$ V and for silicon transistors $V_{BE} = 0.7$ V. The disadvantage of this method is that there is poor stabilisation *i.e.*, operating point changes due to variation in temperature or transistor parameters.

Example 29.7. *Fig. 29.28 (i) shows a silicon transistor with* $\beta = 100$ *biased by base resistor method. Draw the d.c. load line and determine the operating point.*

Solution.

$$V_{CC} = 6 \text{ V}; R_B = 530 \text{ k}\Omega; R_C = 2 \text{ k}\Omega$$

D.C. load line. Referring to Fig. 29.28 (*i*),

$$V_{CE} = V_{CC} - I_C R_C$$

When $I_C = 0$; $V_{CE} = V_{CC} = 6$ V. This locates the first point B (OB = 6 V) of the load line on the collector-emitter voltage axis as shown in Fig. 29.28 (*ii*).

When $V_{CE} = 0$; $I_C = V_{CC}/R_C = 6$ V/2 kΩ = 3 mA. This locates the second point A (OA = 3 mA) of the load line on the collector current axis as shown in Fig. 29.28 (*ii*). By joining points *A* and *B*, d.c. load line *AB* is constructed.

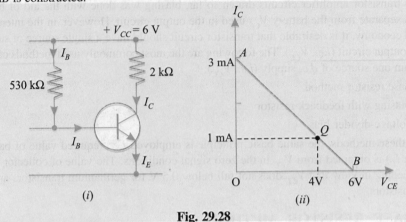

Fig. 29.28

Operating point Q. Since it is a silicon transistor, $V_{BE} = 0.7$ V. Referring to Fig. 29.28 (*i*),

$$I_B R_B + V_{BE} = V_{CC}$$

or

$$I_B = \frac{V_{CC} - V_{BE}}{R_B} = \frac{(6 - 0.7)V}{530 \, k\Omega} = 10 \mu A$$

$$\therefore \quad I_C = \beta I_B = 100 \times 10 = 1000 \, \mu A = 1 \, mA$$

$$\therefore \quad V_{CE} = V_{CC} - I_C R_C$$

$$= 6 - 1 \, mA \times 2 \, k\Omega = 6 - 2 = 4 \, V$$

Fig. 29.28 (*ii*) shows the operating point *Q* on the d.c. load line. Its co-ordinates are $V_{CE} = 4$ V and $I_C = 1$ mA.

Example 29.8. *For the circuit shown in Fig. 29.29, find the operating point. Given that* $\beta = 100$. *Neglect* V_{BE}.

Solution. This is fixed bias circuit with an emitter resistance. This arrangement provides better thermal stability than the fixed bias without R_E. Note that capacitors behave as open to d.c.

$$V_{CC} = I_B R_B + V_{BE} + I_E R_E$$

$$= I_B R_B + 0 + (\beta + 1) I_B R_E$$

$$[\because I_E = (\beta + 1) I_B]$$

$$\therefore \quad I_B \simeq \frac{V_{CC}}{R_B + \beta R_E} = \frac{20 \, V}{(400 + 100 \times 1) \, k\Omega} = 0.04 \, mA$$

$$\therefore \quad I_C = \beta I_B = 100 \times 0.04 = 4 \, mA$$

and

$$V_{CE} = V_{CC} - I_C (R_C + R_E)$$

$$= 20 - 4 \, mA (2 + 1) \, k\Omega = 20 - 12 = 8 \, V$$

Fig. 29.29

$\therefore$ Operating point is **8 V, 4 mA.**

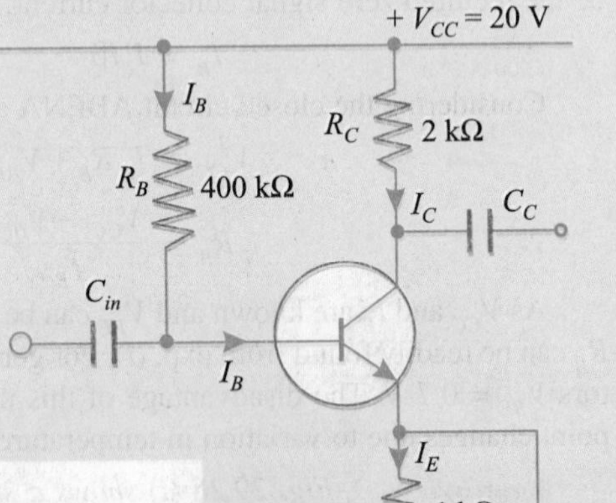

Note that emitter resistance appears as βR_E in the base circuit. In fact, it is this effect which increases the thermal stability.

Example 29.9. *Fig. 29.30 shows a two-stage transistor amplifier biased by base resistor method. What are collector-emitter voltages ? Assume* β = 100 *and* V_{BE} = 0.7 V.

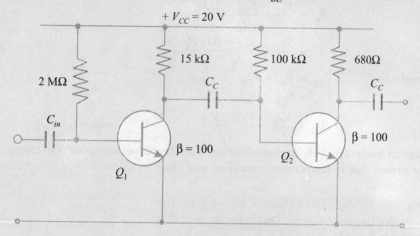

Fig. 29.30

Solution. Since no signal is applied, d.c. conditions prevail in the circuit. Since capacitors offer infinite reactance to d.c., they may be considered open to d.c. Consequently, d.c. currents in one transistor have no effect upon the other.

Transistor Q₁

$$I_B = \frac{V_{CC} - V_{BE}}{R_B} = \frac{20 - 0.7}{2 \times 10^6} = 9.65 \ \mu A$$

$$I_C = \beta I_B = 100 \times 9.65 = 965 \ \mu A = 0.965 \ mA$$

∴ $$V_{CE} = V_{CC} - I_C R_C = 20 - (0.965 \ mA) \times (15 \ k\Omega)$$
$$= 20 - 14.47 = \mathbf{5.53 \ V}$$

Transistor Q₂

$$I_B = \frac{V_{CC} - V_{BE}}{R_B} = \frac{20 - 0.7}{100 \times 10^3} = 0.193 \ mA$$

$$I_C = \beta I_B = 100 \times 0.193 = 19.3 \ mA$$

∴ $$V_{CE} = V_{CC} - I_C R_C = 20 - (19.3 \ mA) \times (0.68 \ k\Omega)$$
$$= 20 - 13.12 = \mathbf{6.88 \ V}$$

29.20. BIASING WITH FEEDBACK RESISTOR

In this method, one end of R_B is connected to the base and the other end to the collector as shown in Fig. 29.31. Here the required zero signal base current is determined *not* by V_{CC} but by the collector-base voltage V_{CB}. It is clear that V_{CB} forward biases the base-emitter junction and hence base current I_B flows through R_B. This causes the zero signal collector current to flow in the collector circuit.

Circuit analysis. The required value of R_B needed to give zero signal collector current I_C can be determined as follows. Referring to Fig. 29.31,

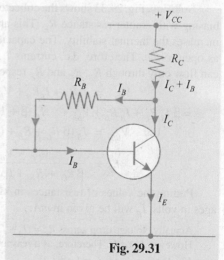

Fig. 29.31

$$V_{CC} = {}^*I_C R_C + I_B R_B + V_{BE}$$

or $$R_B = \frac{V_{CC} - V_{BE} - I_C R_C}{I_B}$$

$$= \frac{V_{CC} - V_{BE} - \beta I_B R_C}{I_B} \qquad (\because I_C = \beta I_B)$$

Alternatively : $$V_{CE} = V_{BE} + V_{CB}$$

or $$V_{CB} = V_{CE} - V_{BE}$$

$$\therefore \qquad R_B = \frac{V_{CB}}{I_B} = \frac{V_{CE} - V_{BE}}{I_B} \qquad \text{where } I_B = I_C/\beta$$

This circuit does not provide good stabilisation. It is because operating point does change, although to a lesser extent, due to temperature variations and other effects.

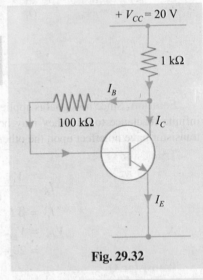

Fig. 29.32

Example 29.10. *Fig. 29.32 shows a silicon transistor biased by feedback resistor method. Determine the operating point. Given that β = 100.*

Solution. Since it is a silicon transistor, $V_{BE} = 0.7$ V. Taking I_B to be in mA and resistance in kΩ, we have,

$$R_B = \frac{V_{CC} - V_{BE} - \beta I_B R_C}{I_B}$$

or $$100 \times I_B = 20 - 0.7 - 100 \times I_B \times 1$$

or $$200\, I_B = 19.3$$

$$\therefore \qquad I_B = 19.3/200 = 0.096 \text{ mA}$$

$$\therefore \qquad I_C = \beta I_B = 100 \times 0.096 = 9.6 \text{ mA}$$

$$V_{CE} = V_{CC} - I_C R_C$$

$$= 20 - 9.6 \text{ mA} \times 1 \text{ k}\Omega = 10.4 \text{ V}$$

∴ Operating point is **10.4V, 9.6 mA**.

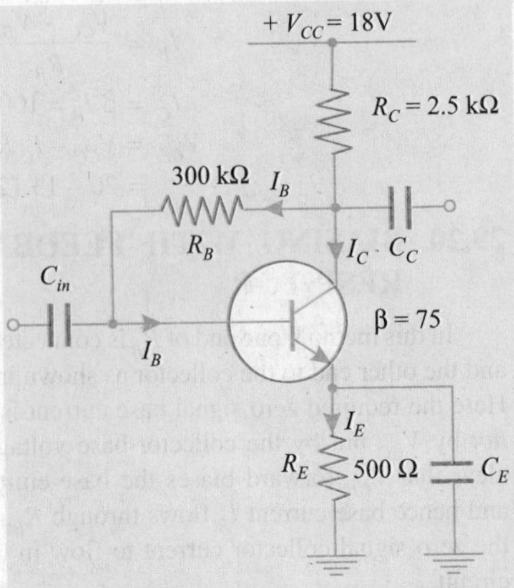

Example 29.11 *Find the operating point in the circuit shown in Fig. 29.33. Assume β = 75 and V_{BE} = 0.7 V.*

Solution. Fig. 29.33 shows the collector feedback biasing with emitter resistance R_E. This arrangement increases the thermal stability. The capacitors appear as open to d.c. Therefore, d.c. currents I_B, I_C and I_E can flow only through R_B, R_C and R_E respectively.

$$V_{CC} = I_C R_C + I_B R_B + V_{BE} + I_E R_E$$

$$= \beta I_B R_C + I_B R_B + V_{BE} + {}^{**}I_B (\beta + 1) R_E$$

or $$V_{CC} - V_{BE} = I_B [\beta R_C + R_B + (\beta + 1) R_E]$$

$$\therefore \qquad I_B = \frac{V_{CC} - V_{BE}}{\beta R_C + R_B + (\beta + 1) R_E}$$

Putting the values of resistances in kΩ and voltages in volts, I_B will be given in *mA*.

Fig. 29.33

* Actually, voltage drop across $R_C = (I_B + I_C) R_C$
However, $I_B \ll I_C$. Therefore, as a reasonable approximation, we can say that drop across $R_C = I_C R_C$.
** $I_E = I_B + I_C = I_B + \beta I_B = I_B (\beta + 1)$

$\therefore$ $$I_B = \frac{18 - 0.7}{(75 \times 2.5) + 300 + (75 + 1)\,0.5} = 32.92 \times 10^{-3}\ \text{mA}$$

$\therefore$ $$I_C = \beta\,I_B = 75 \times (32.92 \times 10^{-3}) = 2.47\ \text{mA}$$

and $$V_{CE} = V_{CC} - I_C R_C - I_E R_E$$

$$= V_{CC} - I_C(R_C + R_E) \qquad\qquad (\because I_E \simeq I_C)$$

$$= 18 - (2.47\ \text{mA})(3\ \text{k}\Omega) = 10.59\ \text{V}$$

$\therefore$ Operating point is **10.59 V, 2.47 mA**.

Example 29.12. *Fig. 29.34 shows biasing by feedback resistor method. Calculate (i) collector current, and (ii) collector voltage. Given that $\beta = 100$ and transistor is made of silicon.*

Solution. (*i*) Since it is a *silicon transistor, $V_{BE} = 0.7$ V. Taking I_B to be in mA and resistance in k Ω, we have,

$$R_B = \frac{V_{CC} - V_{BE} - \beta\,I_B\,R_C}{I_B}$$

or $$200 = \frac{15 - 0.7 - 100 \times I_B \times 1}{I_B}$$

or $$200\,I_B = 14.3 - 100\,I_B$$

or $$300\,I_B = 14.3$$

$\therefore$ $$I_B = \frac{14.3}{300} = 0.0476\ \text{mA}$$

$\therefore$ Collector current, $I_C = \beta\,I_B = 100 \times 0.0476 = \mathbf{4.76\ mA}$

(*ii*) Collector voltage, $V_C = V_{CC} - I_C R_C = 15 - (4.76\ \text{mA})(1\ \text{k}\Omega)$

$$= 10.24\ \text{V}$$

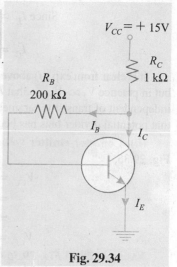

$V_{CC} = +\,15\text{V}$

R_C 1 kΩ

R_B 200 kΩ

I_B I_C

I_E

Fig. 29.34

29.21. VOLTAGE DIVIDER BIAS METHOD

This is the most widely used method of providing biasing and stabilisation to a transistor. In this method, two resistances R_1 and R_2 are connected across the supply voltage V_{CC} (See Fig. 29.35) and provide biasing. The emitter resistance R_E provides stabilisation. The name "voltage divider" comes from the voltage divider formed by R_1 and R_2. The voltage drop across R_2 forward biases the base-emitter junction. This causes the base current and hence collector current to flow in the zero signal conditions.

Circuit analysis. Suppose the current flowing through R_1 is I_1. As the base current I_B is very small, therefore, it can be assumed with reasonable accuracy that current flowing through R_2 is also I_1.

(*i*) **Collector current I_C**

$$I_1 = \frac{V_{CC}}{R_1 + R_2}$$

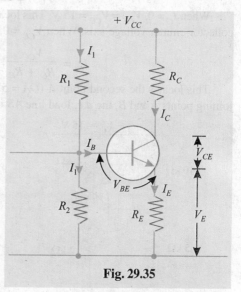

$+\,V_{CC}$

I_1 R_C

R_1 I_C

I_B V_{CE}

I_1 V_{BE} I_E

R_2 R_E V_E

Fig. 29.35

* In numerical problems if it is not given whether the transistor is of silicon or germanium, it is understood that it is a silicon transistor.

Voltage across R_2, $V_2 = \left(\dfrac{V_{CC}}{R_1 + R_2}\right)R_2$

Applying Kirchoff's voltage law to the base circuit of Fig. 29.35,

$$V_2 = V_{BE} + V_E$$
$$= V_{BE} + I_E R_E$$

$\therefore$ $I_E = \dfrac{V_2 - V_{BE}}{R_E}$

Since $I_E \simeq I_C$,

$\therefore$ $I_C = \dfrac{V_2 - V_{BE}}{R_E}$ ...(i)

It is clear from exp. (i) above that I_C does not at all depend upon β. Though I_C depends upon V_{BE} but in practice $V_2 \gg V_{BE}$ so that I_C is practically independent of V_{BE}. Thus I_C in this circuit is almost independent of transistor parameters and hence good stabilisation is ensured. It is due to this reason that potential divider bias has become universal method of providing transistor biasing.

(ii) **Collector-emitter voltage V_{CE}**. Applying Kirchhoff's voltage law to the collector side of Fig. 29.35,

$$V_{CC} = I_C R_C + V_{CE} + I_E R_E$$
$$= I_C R_C + V_{CE} + I_C R_E \qquad (\because I_E \simeq I_C)$$
$$= I_C (R_C + R_E) + V_{CE}$$

$\therefore$ $V_{CE} = V_{CC} - I_C (R_C + R_E)$

Example 29.13 *Fig. 29.36 (i) shows the voltage divider bias method. Draw the d.c. load line and determine the operating point. Assume the transistor to be of silicon.*

Solution.

D.C. load line. Referring to Fig. 29.36 (i),

$$V_{CE} = V_{CC} - I_C (R_C + R_E)$$

When $I_C = 0$, $V_{CE} = V_{CC} = 15$ V. This locates the first point B ($OB = 15$ V) of the load line on the collector-emitter voltage axis. When $V_{CE} = 0$,

$$I_C = \dfrac{V_{CC}}{R_C + R_E} = \dfrac{15V}{(1 + 2)\ k\Omega} = 5\,\text{mA}$$

This locates the second point A ($OA = 5$ mA) of the load line on the collector current axis. By joining points A and B, the *d.c. load line AB* is constructed as shown in Fig. 29.36 (ii).

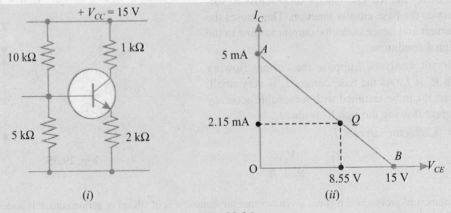

(i)   (ii)

Fig. 29.36

Operating point. For silicon transistor, $V_{BE} = 0.7$ V.

Voltage across 5 kΩ, $V_2 = \left(\dfrac{V_{CC}}{10+5}\right)5 = \dfrac{15\times5}{10+5} = 5\ V$

Emitter current, $I_E = \dfrac{V_2 - V_{BE}}{R_E} = \dfrac{5-0.7}{2\ k\Omega} = 2.15$ mA

Collector current, $I_C \simeq I_E = 2.15$ mA

$$V_{CE} = V_{CC} - I_C\,(R_C + R_E)$$
$$= 15 - 2.15\ \text{mA} \times 3\ k\Omega$$
$$= 15 - 6.45 = 8.55\ V$$

∴ Operating point is **8.55 V, 2.15 mA**.

Fig. 29.36 (*ii*) shows the operating point Q on the *d.c.* load line. Its co-ordinates are $V_{CE} = 8.55$ V and $I_C = 2.15$ mA.

Example 29.14. *An npn transistor circuit (See Fig. 29.37) has* $\alpha = 0.985$ *and* $V_{BE} = 0.3$ V. *If* $V_{CC} = 16$ V, *calculate* R_1 *and* R_C *to place Q point at* $I_C = 2$ mA, $V_{CE} = 6$ V.

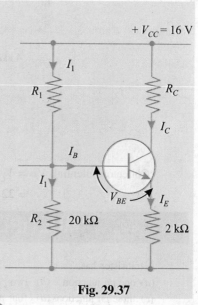

Fig. 29.37

Solution. $\beta = \dfrac{\alpha}{1-\alpha} = \dfrac{0.985}{1-0.985} = 66$

Base current, $I_B = I_C/\beta = 2\ \text{mA}/66 = 0.03$ mA

Voltage across R_2, $V_2 = V_{BE} + V_E$
$$= 0.3 + 2\ \text{mA} \times 2\ k\Omega = 4.3\ V$$

∴ Voltage across $R_1 = V_{CC} - V_2 = 16 - 4.3 = 11.7$ V

Current through R_1 and R_2,
$$I_1 = V_2/R_2 = 4.3\ \text{V}/20\ k\Omega = 0.215\ \text{mA}$$

∴ $R_1 = \dfrac{\text{Voltage across } R_1}{I_1} = \dfrac{11.7\ V}{0.215\ \text{mA}} = \mathbf{54.4\ k\Omega}$

Voltage across $R_C = V_{CC} - V_{CE} - V_E$
$$= 16 - 6 - 2 \times 2 = 6\ V$$

∴ $R_C = \dfrac{\text{Voltage across } R_C}{I_C} = \dfrac{6\ V}{2\ \text{mA}} = \mathbf{3\ k\Omega}$

Example 29.15. *In the circuit shown in Fig. 29.38, find the operating point. What is the collector potential? Assume silicon transistor (i.e.* $V_{BE} = 0.7$ V).

Solution.

Voltage across R_2, $V_2 = \dfrac{V_{CC}}{R_1 + R_2} \times R_2 = \dfrac{22}{40+4} \times 4 = 2\ V$

∴ $I_C = \dfrac{V_2 - V_{BE}}{R_E} = \dfrac{(2-0.7)V}{1.5\ k\Omega} = 0.867$ mA

$$V_{CE} = V_{CC} - I_C\,(R_C + R_E)$$
$$= 22 - (0.867\ \text{mA})\,(11.5\ k\Omega)$$
$$= 12.03\ V$$

∴ operating point is **12.03 V, 0.867 mA**.

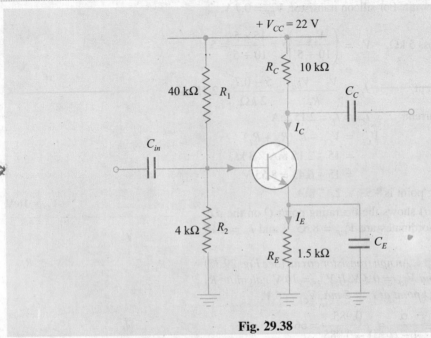

Fig. 29.38

Collector potential, $V_C = V_{CC} - I_C R_C$

$$= 22 - (0.867 \text{ mA}) (10 \text{ k}\Omega) = 13.33 \text{ V}$$

MULTIPLE-CHOICE QUESTIONS

1. A transistor has.............................
   (a) one *pn* junction   (b) two *pn* junctions
   (c) three *pn* junctions (d) four *pn* junctions

2. The number of depletion layers in a transistor is..............
   (a) three   (b) two
   (c) one   (d) four

3. In an *npn* transistor, *p* region is called............
   (a) collector   (b) emitter
   (c) base   (d) none of the above

4. The base of a transistor is....................... doped.
   (a) lightly   (b) moderately
   (c) heavily   (d) none of the above

5. The element that has the biggest size in a transistor is............................
   (a) base   (b) emitter
   (c) collector
   (d) collector-base junction

6. In a *pnp* transistor, the current carriers are.............................
   (a) holes   (b) electrons
   (c) acceptor ions   (d) donor ions

7. The collector of a transistor is...................... doped.
   (a) heavily   (b) lightly
   (c) moderately   (d) none of the above

8. The emitter of a transistor is .... doped.
   (a) lightly   (b) heavily
   (c) moderately   (d) none of the above

9. A transistor is a .... operated device.
   (a) current
   (b) voltage
   (c) both voltage and current
   (d) none of the above

10. In an *npn* transistor, ... are the minority carriers.
    (a) electrons   (b) holes
    (c) donor ions   (d) acceptor ions

11. Biasing represents....................conditions.
    (a) *a.c.*   (b) *d.c.*
    (c) both *d.c.* and *a.c.* (d) none of the above

12. Biasing is done to keep..................... in the circuit.
    (a) proper direct current
    (b) proper alternating current
    (c) the base current small
    (d) collector current small

13. Operating point represents.......................
    (a) values of I_C and V_{CE} when signal is applied
    (b) the magnitude of signal
    (c) zero signal values of I_C and V_{CE}
    (d) none of the above

14. If biasing is not done in an amplifier circuit, it results in....................
    (a) decrease in base current
    (b) unfaithful amplification
    (c) excessive collector bias
    (d) none of the above

15. Biasing is generally provided by a...............
    (a) biasing circuit   (b) bias battery
    (c) transistor   (d) none of the above

16. For faithful amplification, the value of V_{BE} should............... for silicon transistor.
    (a) be zero
    (b) be 0.01 V

    (c) not fall below 0.7 V
    (d) be between 0 V and 0.1 V

17. For proper operation of the transistor, its collector should have................
    (a) proper forward bias
    (b) proper reverse bias
    (c) very small thickness
    (d) none of the above

18. For faithful amplification, the value of V_{CE} should................. for silicon transistors.
    (a) be zero   (b) not fall below 1 V
    (c) be 0.2 V   (d) none of the above

19. The circuit that provides best stabilisation of operating point is..............
    (a) base resistor bias
    (b) collector feedback bias
    (c) potential divider bias
    (d) none of the above

20. The operating point is determined graphically by.............
    (a) intersection of a.c. load line and the given base current curve
    (b) intersection of d.c. and a.c. load lines
    (c) none of the two
    (d) either (a) or (b)

Answers to Multiple-Choice Questions

1. (b)	2. (b)	3. (c)	4. (a)	5. (c)	6. (a)	7. (c)	8. (b)
9. (a)	10. (b)	11. (b)	12. (a)	13. (c)	14. (b)	15. (a)	16. (c)
17. (b)	18. (b)	19. (c)	20. (b)				

Hints to Selected Multiple-Choice Questions

2. A transistor is formed by sandwiching either p-type or n-type semiconductor between a pair of opposite types. Therefore, a transistor has **two** depletion layers.

4. The base of a transistor is **lightly** doped and thin so that it passes most of the emitter injected charge carriers (holes or electrons) to the collector.

5. During transistor operation, much heat is produced at the collector junction. The **collector** is made larger than either base or emitter to dissipate the heat.

9. A transistor is a **current** operated device; the input current controls the output current.

11. Biasing is carried out either with a separate bias battery V_{BB} or by utilising the supply battery V_{CC} in the output circuit; the latter being more common and efficient and is frequently employed. Since both V_{BB} and V_{CC} are batteries, therefore, biasing represents **d.c.** conditions.

14. The basic function of a transistor is to do amplification. One important requirement during amplification is that magnitude of signal should change without any change in its shape. This is known as faithful amplification. This is achieved with the help of a biasing circuit.

19. **Potential divider bias** method provides the best stabilisation of operating point. It is because in this circuit I_C is independent of transistor parameters such as β, V_{BE}.

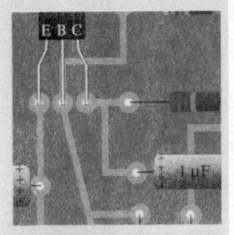

EBC

1 μF

30

Transistor Amplifiers

INTRODUCTION

It has been discussed in the previous chapter that a properly biased transistor raises the strength of a weak signal and thus acts as an amplifier. Almost all electronic equipments must include means for amplifying electrical signals. For instance, radio receivers amplify very weak signals — sometimes a few millionth of a volt at the antenna — until they are strong enough to fill a room with sound. In fact, electronic amplifiers have become a constant and important ingredient of electronics systems. Since common emitter arrangement provides maximum current and voltage gains, we shall use this arrangement in the discussion of amplifiers.

30.1. PRACTICAL CIRCUIT OF A TRANSISTOR AMPLIFIER

It is important to note that a transistor can accomplish faithful amplification only if proper associated circuitry is used with it. Fig. 30.1 shows a practical *single stage transistor amplifier. The various circuit elements and their functions are described below :

---

* When only one transistor with associated circuitry is used for amplifying a weak signal, it is called a single stage transistor amplifier.

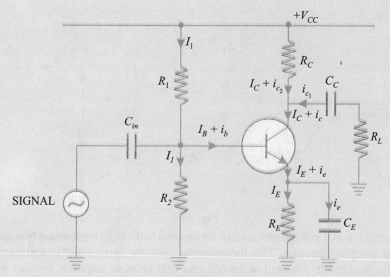

Fig. 30.1

(i) **Biasing circuit.** The resistances R_1, R_2 and R_E form the biasing and stabilisation circuit. The biasing circuit must establish a proper operating point otherwise a part of negative half-cycle of the signal may be cut off in the output.

(ii) **Input capacitor C_{in}.** An electrolytic capacitor C_{in} ($\simeq 10\ \mu F$) is used to couple the signal to the base of the transistor. If it is not used, the signal source resistance will come across R_2 and thus change the bias. The capacitor C_{in} allows only a.c. signal to flow but isolates the signal source from R_2*.

(iii) **Emitter bypass capacitor C_E.** An emitter bypass capacitor C_E ($\simeq 100\ \mu F$) is used in parallel with R_E to provide a low reactance path to the amplified a.c. signal. If it is not used, then amplified a.c. signal flowing through R_E will cause a voltage drop across it, thereby reducing the output voltage.

(iv) **Coupling capacitor C_C.** The coupling capacitor C_C ($\simeq 10\ \mu F$) couples one stage of amplification to the next stage. If it is not used, the bias conditions of the next stage will be drastically changed due to the shunting effect of R_C. This is because R_C will come in parallel with the upper resistance R_1 of the biasing network of the next stage, thereby altering the biasing conditions of the latter. In short, coupling capacitor C_C isolates the d.c. of one stage from the next but allows the passage of a.c. signal.

Note that both d.c. and a.c. conditions prevail in the transistor amplifier. The useful output is the voltage drop across collector load R_C due to the a.c. component. The purpose of zero signal collector curent and collector-emitter voltage (i.e. operating point) is to ensure faithful amplification.

30.2. PHASE REVERSAL

In common emitter connection, there is a phase difference of 180° between the input and output voltages. This is called **phase reversal**. Consider a common emitter amplifier circuit shown in Fig. 30.2. The total instantaneous voltage v_{CE} is given by ;

$$v_{CE} = V_{CC} - i_C R_C \qquad \qquad ...(i)$$

* It may be noted that a capacitor offers infinite reactance to d.c. and blocks it completely while it allows a.c. to pass through it.

** This is so if output is taken from the collector and emitter end of supply as is always done. However, if the output is taken across R_C, it will be in phase with the input.

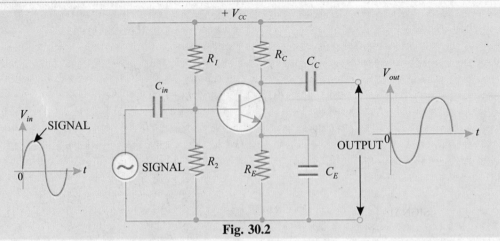

Fig. 30.2

(*i*) When the signal voltage increases in the positive half-cycle, the forward bias on the emitter-base junction increases. This increases the collector current and hence the voltage drop $i_C R_C$. As a result, potential at the collector will be more negative. In other words, as the signal voltage is increasing in the positive half-cycle, the output voltage is increasing in the negative sense *i.e.*, output is 180° out of phase with the input. Likewise, negative half-cycle of the signal will appear as amplified positive half cycle. It may be noted that amplification is not affected by this phase reversal.

(*ii*) The fact of phase reversal can be readily proved mathematically. Thus, differentiating exp. (*i*), we get,

$$dv_{ce} = 0 - di_c R_C$$
$$= - di_c R_C$$

The negative sign shows that output voltage is 180° out of phase with the input voltage.

30.3. D.C. AND A.C. EQUIVALENT CIRCUITS

In a transistor amplifier, both *d.c.* and *a.c.* conditions prevail as shown in Fig. 30.3. The *d.c.* source sets up direct currents and voltages whereas the *a.c.* source (*i.e.* signal) sets up alternating currents and voltages. Therefore, a simple way to analyse the action of a transistor amplifier is to split the analysis into parts *viz.*, (*i*) *d.c.* equivalent circuit and (*ii*) *a.c.* equivalent circuit.

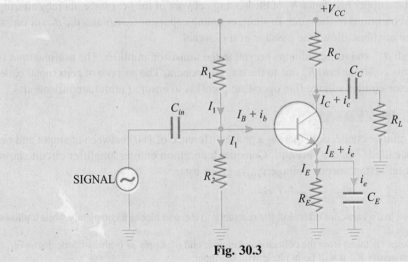

Fig. 30.3

(i) **D.C. equivalent circuit.** In the *d.c.* equivalent circuit of a transistor amplifier, only *d.c.* conditions are to be considered *i.e.*, it is presumed that no signal is applied. As direct current cannot flow through a capacitor, therefore, *all the capacitors look like open circuits in the d.c. equivalent circuit.* It follows, therefore, that in order to draw the *d.c.* equivalent circuit of the transistor amplifier, the following two steps are applied :

   (a) Reduce all the *a.c.* sources to zero.

   (b) Open all the capacitors.

Applying these two steps to the transistor amplifier circuit shown in Fig. 30.3, we get the *d.c.* equivalent circuit shown in Fig. 30.4. We can easily calculate the direct voltages and currents in the circuit. In other words, operating point (*i.e.,* zero signal I_C and V_{CE}) can be found out.

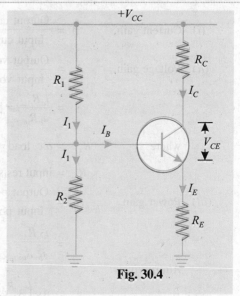

Fig. 30.4

$$I_C = \frac{V_2 - V_{BE}}{R_E} \quad \text{where} \quad V_2 = \left(\frac{V_{CC}}{R_1 + R_2}\right) R_2$$

and

$$V_{CE} = V_{CC} - I_C (R_C + R_E)$$

(ii) **A.C. equivalent circuit.** In the *a.c.* equivalent circuit of a transistor amplifier, only *a.c.* conditions are to be considered. Obviously, the *d.c.* voltage is not important for such a circuit and may be considered zero. The capacitors are generally used to couple or bypass the *a.c.* signal. The designer intentionally selects capacitors that are large enough to appear as *short circuits* to the *a.c.* signal. It follows, therefore, that in order to draw the *a.c.* equivalent circuit of a transistor amplifier, the following two steps are applied :

   (a) Reduce all *d.c.* sources to zero (*i.e.,* $V_{CC} = 0$)

   (b) Short all the capacitors.

Applying these two steps to the transistors amplifier circuit shown in Fig. 30.3, we get the *a.c.* equivalent circuit shown in Fig. 30.5.

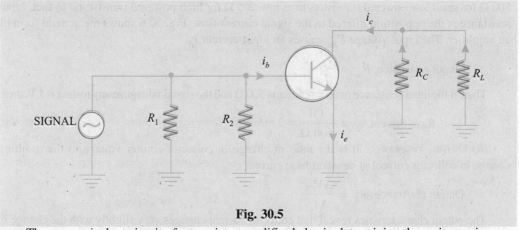

Fig. 30.5

The *a.c.* equivalent circuit of a transistor amplifier helps in determining the various gains.

(i) Current gain, $\beta = \dfrac{\text{Output current}}{\text{Input current}} = \dfrac{i_c}{i_b}$

(ii) Voltage gain, $A_v = \dfrac{\text{Output voltage}}{\text{Input voltage}}$

$$= \frac{i_c R_{AC}}{i_b R_{in}} = \beta \times \frac{R_{AC}}{R_{in}} \qquad \left(\because \frac{i_c}{i_b} = \beta \right)$$

where $R_{AC} = \text{a.c. load} = R_C \parallel R_L = \dfrac{R_C \times R_L}{R_C + R_L}$

$R_{in} = $ input resistance of the amplifier

(iii) Power gain, $A_p = \dfrac{\text{Output power}}{\text{Input power}}$

$$= \frac{i_c^2 \, R_{AC}}{i_b^2 \, R_{in}} = \beta^2 \times \frac{R_{AC}}{R_{in}}$$

Alternatively;

Power gain $= \beta \times \left(\beta \dfrac{R_{AC}}{R_{in}} \right)$

$= \text{Current gain} \times \text{Voltage gain}$

30.4. COMMONLY USED TERMS

In the analysis of transistor amplifier circuit, the following terms are commonly used.

(i) **Input resistance.** It is the ratio of small change in base-emitter voltage to the resulting change in base current at constant collector -emitter voltage *i.e.,*

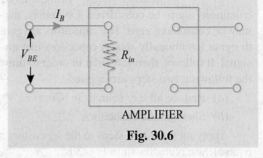

AMPLIFIER

Fig. 30.6

Input resistance, $R_{in} = \dfrac{\Delta V_{BE}}{\Delta I_B}$

The value of input resistance is quite small because input circuit is forward biased. It ranges from 500 Ω for small low powered transistors to as low as 5 Ω for high powered transistors. In fact, input resistance is the opposition offered to the signal current flow. Fig. 30.6 shows the general form of an amplifier. The input voltage V_{BE} causes an input current I_B.

∴ Input resistance, $R_{in} = \dfrac{V_{BE}}{I_B}$

Thus, if the input resistance of an amplifier is 500 Ω and the signal voltage at any instant is 1 *V*, then,

Base current, $i_b = \dfrac{1 V}{500 \, \Omega} = 2$ mA

(ii) **Output resistance.** It is the ratio of change in collector-emitter voltage to the resulting change in collector current at constant base current *i.e.,*

Output resistance, $R_o = \dfrac{\Delta V_{CE}}{\Delta I_C}$

The output characteristics reveal that collector current changes very slightly with the change in collector-emitter voltage. Therefore, output resistance of a transistor is very high, of the order of several hundred kilo-ohms. The physical explanation of high output resistance is that collector-base junction is reverse biased.

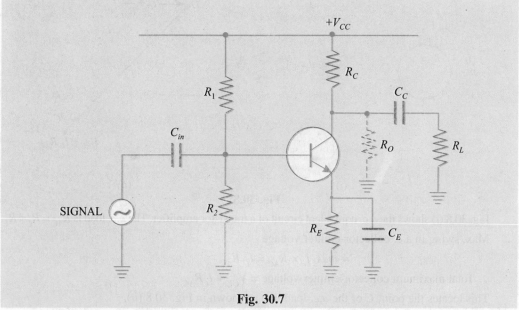

Fig. 30.7

(*iii*) **d.c. load.** The load 'seen' by the transistor under *d.c.* conditions (*i.e.*, zero signal conditions) is known as *d.c.* load. Referring to Fig. 30.7, it is *clear that :

$$d.c. \text{ load } = R_C + R_E$$

The *d.c.* load is important in drawing the *d.c.* load line and determining the operating point.

(*iv*) **a.c. load.** The load 'seen' by the transistor under *a.c.* conditions is known as *a.c.* load R_{AC}. It is clear that *a.c.* load consists of resistances R_C, R_O, and R_L in parallel *i.e.*,

$$a.c. \text{ load, } R_{AC} = R_C \| R_O \| R_L$$

The value of R_O (*i.e.*, output impedance of transistor) is several times more than R_C or R_L.

$$\therefore \qquad **a.c. \text{ load, } R_{AC} = R_C \| R_L = \frac{R_C R_L}{R_C + R_L}$$

The a.c. load is important to draw a.c. load line and to find the voltage or power gain.

30.5. A.C. LOAD LINE

When no signal is applied, V_{CE} and I_C are the collector-emitter voltage and collector current respectively. When an *a.c.* signal is applied, it causes changes to take place about the operating point (*i.e.*, V_{CE} and I_C). For faithful amplification, the maximum *a.c.* collector current can be I_C *i.e.*,

$$\text{Maximum } i_c = I_C = \text{zero signal collector current}$$

. . . .

*   This will be more obvious if you refer to d.c. equivalent circuit of amplifier circuit (Refer back to Fig. 30.4).

**   Consider three resistances of 1 kΩ, 1MΩ and 2 kΩ in parallel. The parallel combination of 1kΩ and 1MΩ is essentially equivalent to a resistance of 1kΩ. Likewise, 1MΩ ‖ 2kΩ ≃ 2 kΩ.

∴ Total resistance = 1 kΩ ‖ 2 kΩ.

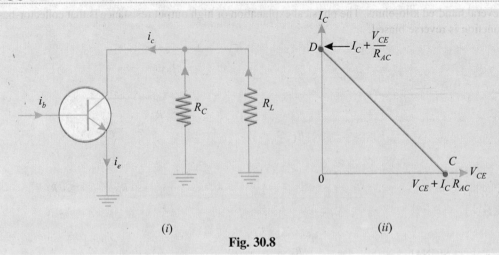

(i)   (ii)

Fig. 30.8

Fig. 30.8 (*i*) shows the *a.c.* equivalent circuit of a transistor amplifier. The *a.c.* load is $R_{AC} = R_C \| R_L$.
Max. swing in a.c. collector-emitter voltage

$$= max. \; i_c \times R_{AC} = I_C R_{AC}$$

∴ Total maximum collector-emitter voltage $= V_{CE} + I_C R_{AC}$

This locates the point *C* of the *a.c.* load line as shown in Fig. 30.8 (*ii*).

$$\text{Max collector current} = \frac{\text{Max. Collector-emitter voltage}}{a.c. \text{ load}}$$

$$= \frac{V_{CE} + I_C R_{AC}}{R_{AC}} = I_C + \frac{V_{CE}}{R_{AC}}$$

This locates the point *D* of the *a.c.* load line. By joining points *C* and *D*, the a.c. load line *CD* is
constructed [See Fig. 30.8 (*ii*)].

Example 30.1. *In Fig. 30.9, the transistor has* β = 60. *Find the voltage gain if input resistance*
$R_{in} = 0.5 \; k\Omega$.

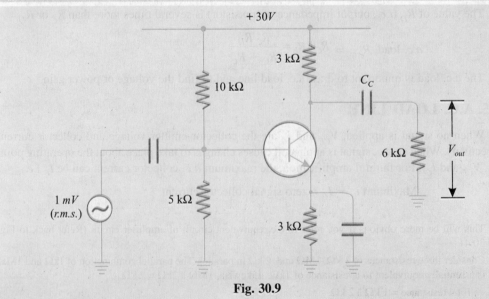

Fig. 30.9

Solution. So far as voltage gain of the circuit is concerned, we need only R_{AC}, β and R_{in}.

Effective load, $R_{AC} = \dfrac{R_C \times R_L}{R_C + R_L} = \dfrac{3 \times 6}{3 + 6} = 2\,k\Omega$

Voltage gain $= \beta \times \dfrac{R_{AC}}{R_{in}}$

$= \dfrac{60 \times 2\,k\Omega}{0.5\,k\Omega} = \mathbf{240}$

Example 30.2. *In the transistor amplifier shown in Fig. 30.10, $R_C = 10\,k\Omega$, $R_L = 30\,k\Omega$ and V_{CC} = 20 V. The values of R_1 and R_2 are such so as to fix the operating point at 10 V, 1 mA. Draw the d.c. and a.c. load lines. Assume R_E to be negligible. What is the voltage gain if R_{in} = 1 kΩ and β = 100 ?*

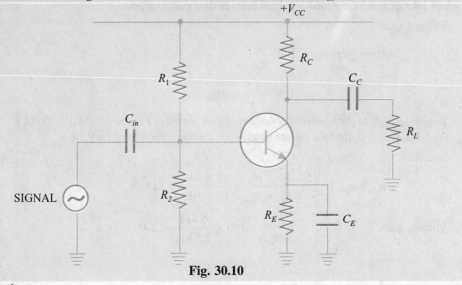

Fig. 30.10

Solution.

d.c. load line. To draw the *d.c.* load line, we require two end points *viz.*, maximum V_{CE} point and maximum I_C point.

Max. $V_{CE} = V_{CC} = 20$ V

This locates the point B ($OB = 20$ V) of the *d.c.* load line on the V_{CE} axis.

Max. $I_C = \dfrac{V_{CC}}{R_C + R_E} = \dfrac{20\,V}{10\,k\Omega} = 2mA$

This locates the point A ($OA = 2$mA) of the *d.c.* load line on the I_C axis. By joining points A and B, *d.c.* load line AB is constructed (See Fig. 30.11).

a.c. load line. To draw *a.c.* load line, we require two end points *viz.*, maximum collector-emitter voltage point and maximum collector current point when signal is applied.

a.c. load, $R_{AC} = R_C \| R_L$

$= \dfrac{10 \times 30}{10 + 30} = 7.5\,k\Omega$

Max. collector-emitter voltage = $V_{CE} + I_C R_{AC}$

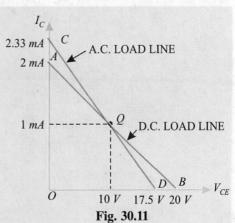

Fig. 30.11

$$= 10 + 1\text{mA} \times 7.5 \text{ k}\Omega$$

$$= 10 + 7.5 = 17.5 \text{ V}$$

This locates the point D (OD = 17.5 V) of the *a.c.* load line on the V_{CE} axis.

Max. collector current = $I_C + V_{CE}/R_{AC}$

$$= 1\text{mA} + 10\text{V}/7.5 \text{ k}\Omega = 1\text{mA} + 1.33 \text{ mA} = 2.33 \text{ mA}$$

This locates the point C (OC = 2.33 mA) of the *a.c.* load line on the I_C axis. By joining points C and D, *a.c.* load line CD is constructed (See Fig. 30.11).

Comments. The reader may see that the operating point lies on both *a.c.* and *d.c.* load lines. This is not surprising because signal is *a.c.* and it becomes zero after every half-cycle. When the signal is zero, we have the exact *d.c.* conditions. Therefore, key point to keep in mind is that the point of intersection of *d.c.* and *a.c.* load lines is the operating point.

Voltage gain

Voltage gain, $A_v = \beta \times \dfrac{R_{AC}}{R_{in}}$

$$= 100 \times \frac{7.5}{1} = 750$$

Example 30.3. *In the transistor amplifier circuit shown in Fig. 30.10, if R_C = 10 kΩ, R_L = 10 kΩ, R_{in} = 2.5 kΩ, β = 100, find the output voltage for an input voltage of 1mV r.m.s.*

Solution.

a.c. load, $R_{AC} = \dfrac{R_C \times R_L}{R_C + R_L} = \dfrac{10 \times 10}{10 + 10} = 5 \text{ k}\Omega$

Voltage gain, $A_v = \beta \dfrac{R_{AC}}{R_{in}} = 100 \times \dfrac{5 \text{ k}\Omega}{2.5 \text{ k}\Omega} = 200$

or $\dfrac{V_{out}}{V_{in}} = 200$

∴ $V_{out} = 200 \times V_{in} = 200 \times 1\text{mV} = \mathbf{200 \ mV}$

Example 30.4. *Fig. 30.12 shows the common emitter transistor amplifier circuit. Draw the d.c. and a.c. load lines for the circuit. Assume V_{BE} = 0.7 V.*

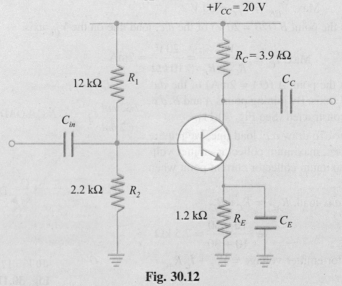

Fig. 30.12

Solution.

d.c. load line

$$V_{CE} = V_{CC} - I_C(R_C + R_E)$$
$$\text{Max. } V_{CE} = V_{CC} = 20 \text{ V} \qquad \text{... when } I_C = 0$$

This locates the point B (20 V, 0mA) of the *d.c.* load line.

$$\text{Max. } I_C = \frac{V_{CC}}{R_C + R_E} \qquad \text{...when } V_{CE} = 0$$

$$= \frac{20}{3.9 + 1.2} = \frac{20 \text{ V}}{5.1 \text{ k}\Omega} = 3.92 \text{ mA}$$

This locates the point A (0V, 3.92 mA) of the *d.c.* load line. Joining A and B, *d.c.* load line AB is constructed as shown in Fig. 30.13.

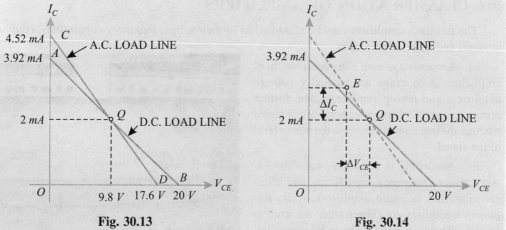

Fig. 30.13   **Fig. 30.14**

a.c. load line. To draw *a.c.* load line, we must first find the operating point.

Voltage across R_2, $V_2 = \dfrac{V_{CC}}{R_1 + R_2} \times R_2 = \dfrac{20}{12 + 2.2} \times 2.2 = 3.1 \text{ V}$

$$I_E = \frac{V_2 - V_{BE}}{R_E} = \frac{(3.1 - 0.7)V}{1.2 \text{ k}\Omega} = 2 \text{ mA}$$

$$\therefore \qquad I_C \simeq I_E = 2 \text{ mA}$$

$$V_{CE} = V_{CC} - I_C(R_C + R_E)$$

$$= 20 - (2 \text{ mA})(5.1 \text{ k}\Omega)$$

$$= 9.8 \text{ V}$$

Max. collector-emitter voltage $= V_{CE} + I_C R_C{}^*$

$$= 9.8 + (2 \text{ mA}) \times (3.9 \text{ k}\Omega)$$

$$= 17.6 \text{ V}$$

This locates point D (17.6 V, 0 mA) of the *a.c.* load line.

Max. collector current $= I_C + V_{CE}/R_C$

$$= 2 + 9.8/3.9$$

$$= 4.52 \text{ mA}$$

....

* $R_{AC} = R_C$

This locates point C (0V, 4.52 mA) of the *a.c.* load line. Joining points C and D, *a.c.* load line CD is constructed as shown in Fig. 30.13.

Alternate method to draw a.c. load line. The *a.c.* load line can be drawn in another way also. First find the operating point Q. It has already been calculated as 9.8 V, 2 mA. Mark the point Q (See Fig. 30.14) on the d.c. load line at $I_C = 2$ mA. This locates one point of *a.c.* load line because point Q lies on both *d.c.* and *a.c.* load lines.

$$\text{a.c. load, } R_{AC} = R_C = 3.9 \text{ k}\Omega$$

If we change collector current by 1 mA (*i.e.*, $\Delta I_C = 1$mA), then change in collector-emitter voltage will be $\Delta V_{CE} = -\Delta I_C^* \times R_{AC} = (-1\text{mA}) \times (3.9 \text{ k}\Omega) = -3.9$ V. Therefore, in order to locate the second point E of the *a.c.* load line, increase I_C by 1mA (from Q point) and decrease V_{CE} by 3.9 V as shown in Fig. 30.14. Joining E and Q and extending E to Y-axis and Q to X-axis along paths QE and EQ respectively, we obtain the desired a.c. load line.

30.6. CLASSIFICATION OF AMPLIFIERS

The transistor amplifiers may be classified as to their *usage, frequency capabilities, coupling methods* and *mode of operation*.

(*i*) **According to use.** The classification of amplifiers as to usage are basically *voltage amplifiers* and *power amplifiers*. The former primarily increase the voltage level of the signal whereas the latter mainly increase the power level of the signal.

(*ii*) **According to frequency capabilities.** According to frequency capabilities, amplifiers are classified as *audio amplifiers, radio frequency amplifiers etc*. The former are used to amplify the signals lying in the audio range (*i.e.*, 20Hz to 20 kHz) whereas the latter are used to amplify signals having very high frequency (*e.g.*, radio waves).

Radio amplifiers

(*iii*) **According to coupling methods.** The output from a single stage amplifier is usually insufficient to meet the practical requirements. Additional amplification is often necessary. To do so, output of one stage is coupled to the input of next stage. Depending upon the coupling device used, amplifiers are classified as *R-C coupled amplifiers, transformer coupled amplifiers, direct coupled amplifiers etc*.

(*iv*) **According to mode of operation.** The amplifiers are frequently classified according to their mode of operation as *class A, class B, class C amplifiers etc*. This classification depends on the portion of the input signal cycle during which collector current is expected to flow. Thus, class A amplifier is one in which collector current flows for the entire *a.c.* signal. Class B amplifier is one in which collector current flows for half-cycle of input *a.c.* signal. Finally, class C amplifier is one in which collector current flows for less than half-cycle of *a.c.* signal.

30.7. VOLTAGE AMPLIFIER VERSUS POWER AMPLIFIER

A transistor amplifier is basically either a voltage amplifier or a power amplifier. Other specifications such as frequency capability, coupling method, mode of operation *etc*. would depend upon service requirements. For example, an amplifier raising the voltage level of audio signal and em-

minus comes because of phase reversal.

ploying *R-C* coupling and operating in class *A* operation would be named as class *A*, *R-C* coupled audio voltage amplifier. Similar remarks apply to a power amplifier. Therefore, it is profitable to distinguish between the two.

1. Voltage amplifier. The voltage gain of an amplifier is given by ;

$$A_v = \beta \times \frac{R_C}{R_{in}}$$

In order to achieve high-voltage amplification, the following design features are incorporated in such amplifiers :

(*i*) The transistor with high β (> 100) is used in the circuit. In other words, those transistors are employed which have thin base.

(*ii*) The input resistance R_{in} of the transistor is sought to be quite low as compared to the collector load R_C.

(*iii*) A relatively high load R_C is used in the collector. To permit this condition, voltage amplifiers are always operated at low collector currents. If collector current is small, we can use large R_C in the collector circuit.

Since voltage amplifiers handle small signals, they are sometimes called *small-signal amplifiers.*

2. Power amplifier. A power amplifier is required to deliver a large amount of power and as such it has to handle large current. In order to achieve high power amplification, the following features are incorporated in such amplifiers:

(*i*) The size of power transistor is usually made considerably larger in order to dissipate the heat produced during operation.

(*ii*) The base of the transistor is made thicker to handle large currents. In other words, transistors with comparatively smaller β are used.

(*iii*) Transformer coupling is used for impedance matching.

Since power amplifiers handle large signals, they are sometimes called *large-signal amplifiers.*

30.8. MULTISTAGE AMPLIFIER

A practical amplifier is a multistage amplifier. In a multistage amplifier, a number of single amplifiers are connected in *cascade arrangement i.e.,* output of first stage is connected to the input of the second stage through a suitable *coupling device* and so on. The purpose of coupling device (*e.g.,* a capacitor, transformer *etc.*) is (*i*) to transfer *a.c.* output of one stage to the input of the next stage and (*ii*) to isolate the d.c. conditions of one stage from the next stage. Fig. 30.15 shows the block diagram of a 3-stage amplifier. Each stage consists of one transistor and associated circuitry and is coupled to the next stage through a coupling device. The name of the amplifier is usually given after the type of coupling used *e.g.*

Name of coupling	Name of multistage amplifier
R-C coupling	*R-C* coupled amplifier
Transformer coupling	Transformer-coupled amplifier
Direct coupling	Direct-coupled amplifier

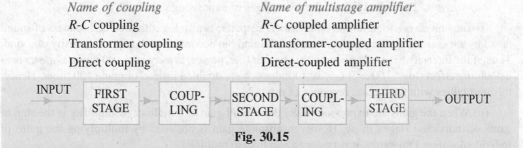

Fig. 30.15

It may be noted here that first few stages in a multistage amplifier have the function of only voltage amplification and employ voltage amplifiers. However, the last stage is designed to provide maximum power in order to operate the output device *e.g.*, speaker. This final stage is called power stage and employs power amplifier.

30.9. FREQUENCY RESPONSE

The voltage gain of an amplifier varies with signal frequency. It is because reactance of the capacitors in the amplifier circuit changes with signal frequency and hence affects the output voltage. The curve between voltage gain and signal frequency of an amplifier is known as *frequency response*. Fig. 30.16 shows the frequency response of a typical amplifier. The gain of the amplifier increases as the signal frequency increases from zero till it becomes maximum at f_r, called *resonant frequency*. If the frequency of signal increases beyond f_r, the gain decreases. The performance of an amplifier depends to a considerable extent upon its frequency response. While designing an amplifier, appropriate steps must be taken to ensure that gain is essentially constant over a specified frequency range.

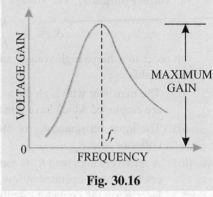

Fig. 30.16

30.10. DECIBEL GAIN

Although the gain of an amplifier can be expressed as a number, yet it is of great practical importance to assign it a unit. The assigned unit is *bel* or *decibel* (*db*).

The common logarithm (log to the base 10) of power gain is known as bel power gain i.e.,

$$\text{Power gain} = \log_{10} \frac{P_{out}}{P_{in}} \text{ bel}$$

Since 1 bel = 10 db

40 decibles phone

∴　　　$$\text{Power gain} = 10 \log_{10} \frac{P_{out}}{P_{in}} \text{ db}$$

As $P \propto V^2$ or I^2, therefore, the voltage and current gains are expressed in *db* as :

$$\text{Voltage gain} = 20 \log_{10} \frac{V_{out}}{V_{in}} \text{ db}$$

$$\text{Current gain} = 20 \log_{10} \frac{I_{out}}{I_{in}} \text{ db}$$

Advantages. The following are the advantages of expressing gain in *db* :

(*i*) The unit *db* is a logarithmic unit. Our ear response is also logarithmic *i.e.*, loudness of sound heard by ear is not according to the intensity of sound but according to the log of intensity of sound. Thus, if the intensity of sound given by the speaker (*i.e.*, power) is increased 100 times, our ears hear a doubling effect ($\log_{10} 100 = 2$) *i.e.*, as if loudness were doubled instead of made 100 times. Hence, this unit tallies with the natural response of our ears.

(*ii*) When the gains are expressed in *db*, the overall gain of a multistage amplifier is the sum of gains of individual stages in *db*. However, absolute gain is obtained by multiplying the gains of individual stages. Obviously, it is easier to add than to multiply.

30.11. BANDWIDTH

*The range of frequency over which the voltage gain is equal to or greater than *70.7% of the maximum gain is known as* **bandwidth.**

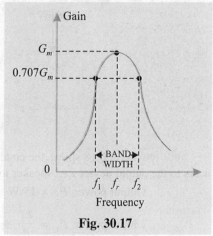

The voltage gain of an amplifier changes with frequency. Referring to the freuqency response in Fig. 30.17, it is clear that for any frequency lying between f_1 and f_2, the gain is equal to or greater than 70.7% of the maximum gain. Therefore, $f_1 - f_2$ is the bandwidth. It may be seen that f_1 and f_2 are the limiting frequencies. The former (f_1) is called *lower cut-off frequency* and the latter (f_2) is known as *upper cut-off frequency*. For distortionless amplification, it is important that signal frequency range must be within the bandwidth of the amplifier. Consider an amplifier that has a maximum voltage gain of 2000 at 2 kHz. Suppose the gain of the amplifier falls to 1414 at 10 kHz and 50 Hz. It is clear that 70.7% of 2000 = 1414.

∴ Lower cut-off frequency, f_1 = 50 Hz

Upper cut-off frequency, f_2 = 10 kHz

Resonant frequency, f_r = 2 kHz

Bandwidth,   BW = 50 Hz to 10 kHz

As the bandwidth of the amplifier is 50 Hz to 10 kHz, therefore, it will amplify the signal frequencies lying in this range without any distortion. However, if signal frequency is not in this range, then there will be distortion in the output.

Example 30.5. *Express the following gains as a number :*

(i) Power gain of 40 db   (ii) Power gain of 43 db.

Solution.

(i) Power gain   = 40 *db* = 4.0 bel

∴ Gain   = Antilog 4

= 10^4 = **10,000**

(ii) Power gain   = 43 *db* = 4.3 bel

∴ Gain   = Antilog 4.3

= 2×10^4 = **20,000**

Example 30.6. *A three-stage amplifier has a first stage voltage gain of 100, second stage voltage gain of 200 and third stage gain of 400. Find the total voltage gain in db.*

Solution.

First stage gain in *db* = $20 \log_{10} 100 = 20 \times 2 = 40$

Second stage gain in *db* = $20 \log_{10} 200 = 20 \times 2.3 = 46$

Third stage gain in *db* = $20 \log_{10} 400 = 20 \times 2.6 = 52$

Total voltage gain = 40 + 46 + 52 = **138 db**

Example 30.7. *A microphone delivers 36 mV at 300 ohms into an amplifier which delivers 15 watts into a 16-ohm speaker system at full power. Find the decibel gain of the amplifier.*

* The human ear is not a very sensitive hearing device. It has been found that if the gain falls to 70.7% of the maximum gain, the ear cannot detect the change. However, if the gain falls below 70.7% of the maximum gain, the ear will hear clear distortion.

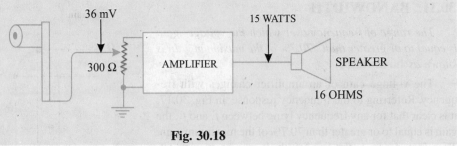

Fig. 30.18

Solution. Fig. 30.18 shows the conditions of the problem. The audio amplifier is delivering 15 watts to the output device *i.e.*, speaker in this case.

Output power, P_2 = 15 W

Input power, $P_1 = \dfrac{E_1^2}{R_1} = \dfrac{(0.036)^2}{300} = 4.3 \times 10^{-6}$ W

∴   Decibel gain $= 10 \log_{10} \dfrac{P_2}{P_1} = 10 \log_{10} \dfrac{15}{4.3 \times 10^{-6}}$

          = 65.41 db

30.12. R-C COUPLED TRANSISTOR AMPLIFIER

This is the most popular type of coupling because it is cheap and has excellent frequency response. It is usually employed for voltage amplification. Fig. 30.19 shows two stages of *R-C* coupled amplifier. A coupling capacitor C_C is used to connect the output of first stage to the base (*i.e., input*) of the second stage and so on. As the coupling from one stage to the next stage is achieved by a coupling capacitor followed by a connection to a shunt resistor, therefore, such amplifiers are called *resistance-capacitance coupled amplifiers.*

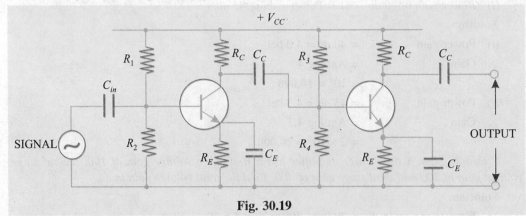

Fig. 30.19

The resistances R_1, R_2 and R_E form the biasing and stabilisation network. The emitter bypass capacitor C_E offers low reactance path to the signal. Without it, the voltage gain of each stage would be lost to some extent. The coupling capacitor C_C transmits *a.c.* signal but blocks *d.c.* This prevents *d.c.* interference between various stages and the shifting of operating point.

Operation. When a.c. signal is applied to the base of the first transistor, it appears in the amplified form across its collector load R_C. The amplified signal developed across R_C is given to the base of next stage through coupling capacitor C_C. The second stage does further amplification of the signal. In this way, the *cascaded* (one after another) stages amplify the signal and overall gain is considerably increased.

First stage gain, $G_1 = \beta \times \dfrac{R_{AC}}{R_{in}}$

where $R_{AC} = R_C \| R_{in} = \dfrac{R_C \times R_{in}}{R_C + R_{in}}$

R_{in} = input resistance of second stage

Second stage gain, $G_2 = \beta \times \dfrac{R_C}{R_{in}}$

Total gian, $G = G_1 \times G_2$

RC Coupled Amplifiers

Note that gain of the first stage is reduced due to the loading effect of the input resistance of second stage.

Frequency response. Fig. 30.20 shows the frequency response of a typical *R-C* coupled amplifier. It is clear that voltage gain falls at low (< 50 Hz) and high (>20 kHz) frequencies whereas it is uniform over mid-frequency range (50 Hz to 20 kHz). Thus *R-C* coupled amplifier has an excellent frequency response. The gain is constant over the audio frequency range (20 Hz to 20 kHz) which is the region of most importance for speech, music *etc.*

Applications. The *R-C* coupled amplifiers have excellent audio fidelity over a wide range of frequency. Therefore, they are widely used as voltage amplifiers *e.g.*, in the initial stages of a public address system. If other coupling (*e.g.*, transformer coupling) is employed in the initial stages, this results in frequency distortion which may be amplified in the next stages.

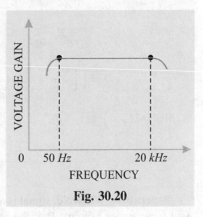

Fig. 30.20

One serious drawback of an *R-C* coupled amplifier is that it has poor impedance matching. It is because the output impedance of *R-C* coupled amplifier is several hundred ohms whereas that of speaker is only a few ohms. Hence, little power is transferred to the speaker. Because of poor impedance matching, *R-C* coupling is rarely used in the final stages.

Example 30.8. *A single stage amplifier has a gain of 60. The collector load $R_C = 1\ k\Omega$ and the input impedance is 500 Ω. Calculate the overall gain when two such stages are cascaded through R-C coupling.*

Solution. The gain of second stage remains 60 because it has no loading effect of any stage. However, the gain of first stage is less than 60 due to the loading effect of input impedance of second stage.

∴ Gain of second stage = 60

Effective load of first stage, $R_{AC} = R_C \| R_{in} = \dfrac{1000 \times 500}{1000 + 500} = 333\ \Omega$

∴ Gain of first stage = $60 \times 333/500 = 39.96$

Total gain = $60 \times 39.96 = \mathbf{2397}$

The gain of the individual stage is 60. But when two stages are coupled, the gain is *not* 60×60 = 3600 as might be expected rather it is less and is equal to 2397.

30.13. TRANSFORMER-COUPLED AMPLIFIER

The main reason for low voltage and power gain of *R-C* coupled amplifier is that the effective load (R_{AC}) of each stage is *decreased due to the low resistance presented by the input of each stage to the preceding stage. If the effective load resistance of each stage could be increased, the voltage and power gain could be increased. This can be achieved by transformer coupling. By the use of **impedance changing properties of transformer, the low resistance of the stage (or load) can be reflected as a high load resistance to the previous stage.

Transformer coupling is generally employed when the load is small. It is mostly used for power amplification. Fig. 30.21 shows two stages of transformer coupled amplifier. A coupling transformer is used to feed the output of one stage to the input of the next stage. The primary P of this transformer is made the collector load and its secondary S gives input to the next stage.

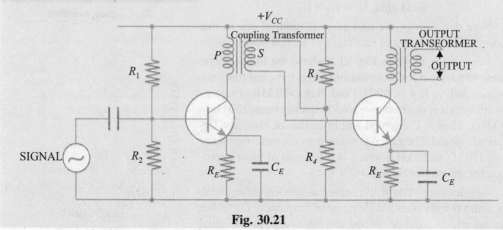

Fig. 30.21

Operation. When a.c. signal is applied to the base of the first transistor, it appears in the amplified form across primary P of the coupling transformer. The voltage developed across primary is transferred to the input of the next stage by the secondary as shown in Fig. 30.21. The second stage renders amplification in an exactly similar manner.

Frequency response. The frequency response of a transformer coupled amplifier is shown in Fig. 30.22. It is clear that frequency response is rather poor *i.e.*, gain is constant only over a small range of frequency. The output voltage is equal to the collector current multiplied by reactance of the primary. At low frequencies, the reactance of the primary begins to fall, resulting in decreased gain. At high frequencies, the capacitance between turns of windings acts as a bypass capacitor to reduce the output voltage and hence gain. It follows, therefore, that there will be disproportionate amplification of freuqencies in a complete signal such as music, speech *etc*. Hence, transformer-coupled amplifiers introduce *frequency distortion*.

Applications. Transformer coupling is mostly employed for *impedance matching*. In general, the last stage of a multistage amplifier is the *power stage*. Here a concentrated effort is made to transfer maximum power to the output device *e.g.*, a loudspeaker. For maximum power transfer, the impedance of the power source

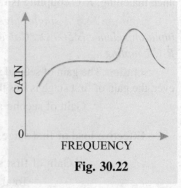

Fig. 30.22

. . . .

*   The input impedance of an amplifier is low while its output impedance is very high. When they are coupled to make a multistage amplifier, the high output impedance of one stage comes in parallel with the low input impedance of next stage. Hence effective load (R_{AC}) is decreased.

**   The resistance on the secondary side of a transformer reflected on the primary depends upon the turn ratio of the transformer.

should be equal to that of load. Usually, the impedance of an output device (*i.e.*, loudspeaker) is a few ohms whereas the output impedance of transistor is several times this value. In order to match the impedance, a step-down transformer of proper turn ratio is used. The impedance of secondary of the transformer is made equal to the output impedance of transistor.

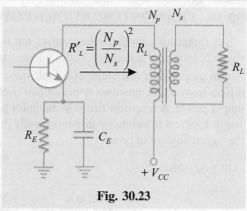

Fig. 30.23

Fig. 30.23 illustrates the impedance matching by a step-down transformer. The output device (*e.g.*, speaker) connected to the secondary has a small resistance R_L. The load R'_L appearing on the primary side will be (See Art. 20.9) :

$$R'_L = \left(\frac{N_p}{N_s}\right)^2 R_L$$

For instance, suppose the transformer has turn ratio $N_p/N_s = 10$. If $R_L = 100\ \Omega$, then load R'_L appearing on the primary is :

$$R'_L = (10)^2 \times 100 = 10\ k\Omega$$

Thus, the load on the primary side is comparable to the output impedance of the transistor. This results in maximum power transfer from transistor to the primary of the transformer. This shows that low resistance of the load (*e.g.*, speaker) can be "stepped-up" to a more favourable value at the collector of transistor by using a step-down transformer of appropriate turn ratio.

Example 30.9. *Determine the necessary transformer turn ratio for transferring maximum power to a 16 Ω load from a source that has an output impedance of 10 kΩ. Also calculate the voltage across the load if the terminal voltage of the source is 10V r.m.s.*

Solution. For maximum power transfer, the impedance of the primary should be equal to the output impedance of the source.

Primary impedance, $R'_L = 10\ k\Omega = 10,000\ \Omega$

Load impedance, $R_L = 16\Omega$

Let the turn ratio of the transformer be $n\ (= N_p/N_s)$.

$$\therefore \qquad R'_L = \left(\frac{N_p}{N_s}\right)^2 R_L$$

or $\qquad \left(\frac{N_p}{N_s}\right)^2 = \frac{R'_L}{R_L} = \frac{10,000}{16} = 625$

or $\qquad n^2 = 625$

$\therefore \qquad n = \sqrt{625} = 25$

Now, $\qquad \dfrac{V_s}{V_p} = \dfrac{N_s}{N_p}$

$\therefore \qquad V_s = \left(\dfrac{N_s}{N_p}\right) V_p = \dfrac{1}{25} \times 10 = 0.4\ V$

30.14. TRANSISTOR AUDIO POWER AMPLIFIER

A transistor amplifier which raises the power level of the signals that have audio frequency range is known as **transistor audio power amplifier.**

In general, the last stage of a multistage amplifier is the *power stage.* The power amplifier differs from all the previous stages in that here a concentrated effort is made to obtain maximum output power. A transistor that is suitable for power amplification is generally called a *power transistor.* It differs from other transistors mostly in size; it is considerably larger to provide for handling the great amount of power.

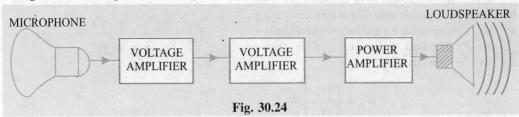

MICROPHONE · LOUDSPEAKER

VOLTAGE AMPLIFIER → VOLTAGE AMPLIFIER → POWER AMPLIFIER

Fig. 30.24

Fig. 30.24 shows the block diagram of an audio power amplifier. The early stages build up the voltage level of the signal and employ *R-C* coupling. However, the last stage builds up power to a level sufficient to operate the loudspeaker. The power stage employs transformer coupling to achieve this objective.

Collector efficiency. An amplifier converts *d.c.* power from supply into *a.c.* power output. Therefore, the ability of a power amplifier to convert *d.c.* power from supply into *a.c.* output power is a measure of its effectiveness. This is known as collector efficiency and may be defined as under :

The ratio of a.c. output power to the zero signal power (i.e. d.c. power) supplied by the battery of a power amplifier is known as **collector efficiency.**

Collector efficiency means as to how well an amplifier converts *d.c.* power from the battery into a.c. power output. For instance, if the d.c. power supplied by the battery is 10W and a.c. output power is 2 W, then collector efficiency is 20%. The greater the collector efficiency, larger is the a.c. power output. It is obvious that for power amplifiers, maximum collector efficiency is the desired goal.

30.15. CLASSIFICATION OF POWER AMPLIFIERS

Transistor power amplifiers handle large currents. Many of them are driven so hard by the input large signal that collector current is either cut-off or is in the saturation region during a large portion of the input cycle. Therefore, such amplifiers are generally classified according to their mode of operation *i.e.,* the portion of the input cycle during which collector current is expected to flow. On this basis, they are classified as :

(*i*)   Class *A* power amplifier

(*ii*)   Class *B* power amplifier

(*iii*)   Class *C* power amplifier

(*i*)   **Class A power amplifier.** *If the collector current flows at all times during the full cycle of the signal, the power amplifier is known as* **Class A power amplifier.**

Obviously for this to happen, the power amplifier must be biased in such a way that no part of the signal is cut-off. Fig. 30.25 (*i*) shows the circuit of class *A* power amplifier. Note that collector has transformer as the load which is most

Transistor Audio Power Amplifiers

common for all classes of power amplifiers. The use of transformer permits impedance matching, resulting in the transference of maximum power to the load *e.g.*, loudspeaker.

Fig. 30.25 (*ii*) shows the class A operation in terms of *a.c.* load line. The operating point Q is so selected that collector current flows at all times throughout the full cycle of the applied signal. As the output wave shape is exactly similar to the input wave shape, therefore, such amplifiers have least distortion. However, they have the disadvantages of low power output and low collector efficiency (about 35%).

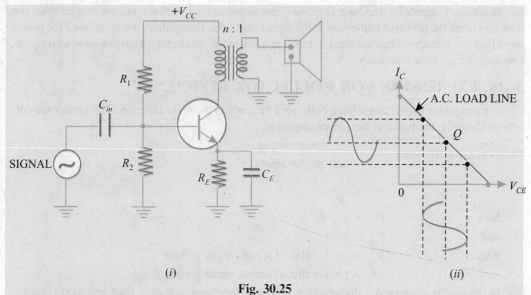

(*i*)   (*ii*)

Fig. 30.25

(*ii*) Class B power amplifier. *If the collector current flows only during the positive half-cycle of the input signal, it is called* **Class B power amplifier.**

In *class B* operation, the transistor bias is so adjusted that zero signal current is zero *i.e.*, no biasing circuit is needed at all. During the positive half-cycle of the signal, the input circuit is forward biased and hence collector current flows. However, during the negative half-cycle of the signal, the input circuit is reverse biased and no collector current flows. Fig. 30.26 shows the *class B* operation in terms of a.c. load line. Obviously, the operating point Q shall be located at collector cut-off voltage. It is easy to see that output from a *class B* amplifier is amplified half-wave rectification.

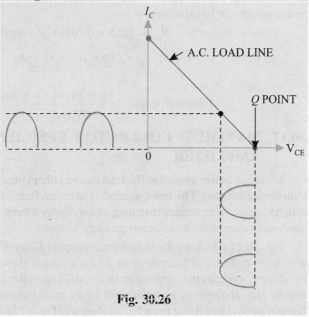

Fig. 30.26

In a class B amplifier, the negative half-cycle of the signal is cut off and hence a severe distortion occurs. However, class B amplifiers provide higher power output and collector efficiency (50–60%). Such amplifiers are mostly used for power amplification in push-pull arrangement. In such an arrangment,

2 transistors are used in *class B* operation. One transistor amplifies the positive half-cycle of the signal while the other amplifies the negative half-cycle.

Note : Voltage amplifiers are always operated in *class A* operation. However, power amplifiers are either operated in class A operation or *class B* operation. In the former arrangement, one transistor is used while for the latter operation, two transistors are used in push-pull arrangement.

(*iii*) **Class C power amplifier.** *If the collector current flows for less than half-cycle of the input signal, it is called* **Class C power amplifier.**

In a class C amplifier, the base is given some negative bias so that collector current does not flow just when the postitive half-cycle of the signal starts. Such amplifiers are never used for power amplification. However, they are used in tuned amplifiers *i.e.*, to amplify a narrow band of frequencies near the resonant frequency.

30.16. EXPRESSION FOR COLLECTOR EFFICIENCY

For comparing power amplifiers, collector efficiency is the main criterion. The greater the collector efficiency, the better is the power amplifier.

Now, collector efficiency,
$$\eta = \frac{a.c. \text{ power output}}{d.c. \text{ power input}}$$

$$= \frac{P_{ac}}{P_{dc}}$$

Now, $P_{dc} = V_{CC} I_C$

and $P_{ac} = V_{ce} I_c$

where V_{ce} = r.m.s. value of signal output voltage

I_c = r.m.s. value of output signal current

In terms of peak-to-peak values (which are often convenient values in load-line work), the a.c. power output can be expressed as :

$$*P_{ac} = [(0.5 \times 0.707)\, v_{ce}\, (p-p)]\, [(0.5 \times 0.707)\, i_c\, (p-p)]$$

$$= \frac{v_{ce}\, (p-p) \times i_c\, (p-p)}{8}$$

∴ Collector $\eta = \dfrac{v_{ce}\, (p-p) \times i_c\, (p-p)}{8 V_{CC}\, I_C}$

30.17. MAXIMUM COLLECTOR EFFICIENCY OF CLASS A POWER AMPLIFIER

In class *A* power amplifier, the load can be either connected directly in the collector or it can be transformer coupled. The latter method is often preferred for two main reasons. First, transformer coupling permits impedance matching and secondly it keeps the *d.c.* power loss small because of the small resistance of the transformer primary winding.

Fig. 30.27 (*i*) shows the transformer-coupled Class A power amplifier. In order to determine maximum collector efficiency, refer to the diagram shown in Fig. 30.27 (*ii*). Under zero signal conditions, the effective resistance in the collector circuit is that of the primary winding of the transformer. The primary resistance has a very small value and is assumed zero. Therefore, *d.c.* load line is a vertical line rising from V_{CC} as shown in Fig. 30.27 (*ii*). When signal is applied, the collector current will vary about the operating point *Q*.

- -

*   r.m.s. value $= \dfrac{1}{2}\dfrac{\text{(peak-to-peak value)}}{\sqrt{2}} = (0.5 \times 0.707) \times$ peak-to-peak value.

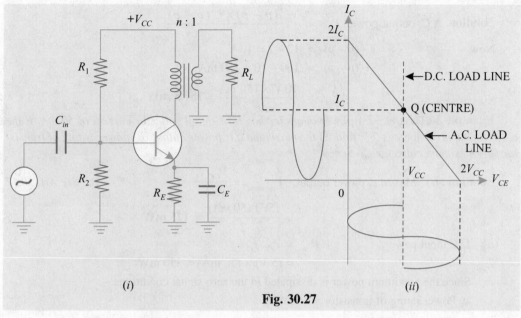

Fig. 30.27

In order to get maximum *a.c.* power output (and hence collector η), the peak value of collector current due to signal alone shoud be equal to the zero signal collector current I_C. In terms of *a.c.* load line, the operating point Q should be located at the centre of *a.c.* load line.

During the peak of the posititive half-cycle of the signal, the total current is $2I_C$ and $v_{ce} = 0$ [See Fig. 30.27 (*ii*)]. During the negative peak of the signal, the *collector* current is zero and $v_{ce} = 2V_{CC}$.

∴ Peak-to-peak collector-emitter voltage, $v_{ce} (p-p) = 2V_{CC}$

Peak-to-peak collector current, $i_c (p-p) = 2 I_C$

$$= \frac{v_{ce} (p-p)}{R'_L} = \frac{2V_{CC}}{R'_L}$$

where R'_L is the reflected value of load R_L and appears in the primary of the transformer. If n (= N_p/N_s) is the turn ratio of the transformer, then $R'_L = n^2 R_L$.

$$\text{d.c. power input,} \qquad P_{dc} = V_{CC} I_C$$

$$= I_C^2 R'_L \qquad\qquad (\because V_{CC} = I_C R'_L)$$

$$\text{Max. } \textit{a.c.} \text{ power output, } P_{ac\,(max)} = \frac{v_{ce} (p-p) \times i_c (p-p)}{8}$$

$$= \frac{2V_{CC} \times 2I_C}{8} = \frac{1}{2} V_{CC} I_C = \frac{1}{2} I_C^2 R'_L \qquad ...(i)$$

$$\text{Max. collector } \eta = \frac{P_{ac(max)}}{P_{dc}} \times 100$$

$$= \frac{(1/2) I_C^2 R'_L}{I_C^2 R'_L} \times 100 = 50\%$$

Hence the maximum collector efficiency of transformer coupled *class A* power amplifier is 50%. However, in practice the efficiency is less than 50% (about 35%) due to power loss in the primary of transformer.

Example 30.10. *In a certain transistor power amplifier,* $i_{C(max)}$ = *160 mA,* $i_{C(min)}$ = *10 mA,* $v_{CE\,(max)}$ = *12 V and* $v_{CE(min)}$ = *2 V. Calculate the a.c. output power.*

Solution. A.C. output power, $P_{ac} = \dfrac{v_{ce}\ (p-p) \times i_c\ (p-p)}{8}$

Now

$$v_{ce}\ (p-p) = 12 - 2 = 10 \text{ V}$$

$$i_c\ (p-p) = 160 - 10 = 150 \text{ mA}$$

∴ $\qquad\qquad\qquad P_{ac} = \dfrac{10\ V \times 150\ mA}{8} = 187.5 \text{ mW}$

Example 30.11. *A class A power amplifier has zero signal collector current of 50 mA. If the collector supply voltage is 5 V, find (i) the maximum a.c. power output (ii) power rating of transistor (iii) maximum collector efficiency.*

Solution *(i)* Max. *a.c.* power output, $P_{ac\ (max)} = \dfrac{V_{CC}\ I_C}{2}$ $\qquad$ *... See Art. 30.17*

$$= \dfrac{(5V)\ (50\ mA)}{2} = 125 \text{ mW}$$

(ii) D.C input power, $\qquad\qquad P_{dc} = V_{CC}\ I_C$

$$= (5\ V) \times (50 \text{ mA}) = 250 \text{ mW}$$

Since the maximum power is dissipated in the zero signal conditions,

∴ Power rating of transistor = **250 mW**

(iii) $\qquad\qquad$ Max. collector η $= \dfrac{P_{ac(max)}}{P_{dc}} \times 100$

$$= \dfrac{125 \text{ mW}}{250 \text{ mW}} \times 100 = 50\%$$

30.18. HEAT SINKS

As power transistors handle large currents, they always heat up during operation. Since transistor is a temperature dependent device, the heat generated must be dissipated to the surroundings in order to keep the temperature within permissible limits. Generally, the transistor is fixed on a metal sheet (usually aluminium) so that additional heat is transferred to the alumimium sheet.

The metal sheet that serves to dissipate the additional heat from the power transistor is known as **heat sink.**

Most of heat within the transistor is produced at the *collector junction. The heat sink increases the surface area and allows heat to escape from the collector junction easily. The result is that temperature of the transistor is sufficiently lowered. As a matter of fact, modern power transistors are generally mounted in thermal contact with the chassis. Now, chassis is a heat conducting body, therefore, entire chassis becomes the heat sink.

30.19. OUTPUT STAGE

The output stage essentially consists of a power amplifier and its purpose is to transfer maximum power to the output device (*e.g.,* speaker). If a single transistor is used in the output stage, it can only be employed as class A amplifier for faithful amplification. Unfortunately, the collector efficiency of class A amplifier is very low (≃ 35%). As transistor amplifiers are operated from batteries, which is a costly source of power, therefore, such a low efficiency cannot be tolerated.

In order to obtain high output power at high efficiency, push-pull arrangement is used in the output stage. In this arrangement, we employ two transistors in class B operation. One transistor

---

* Most of power is dissipated at the collector-base junction. This is because collector-base voltage is much higher than base-emitter voltage, although currents through the two junctions are alomost the same.

amplifies the positive half-cycle of the signal while the other transistor amplifies the negative half-cycle of the signal. In this way, output voltage is a complete sine wave. At the same time, the circuit delivers high output power to the load due to class B operation.

30.20. PUSH-PULL AMPLIFIER

The push-pull amplifier is a power amplifier and is frequently used in the output stages of electronic circuits. It is used whenever high output at high efficiency is required. Fig. 30.28 shows the circuit of a push-pull amplifier. Two transistors Q_1 and Q_2 placed back to back are employed. Both transistors are operated in class B operation $i.e.,$ collector current is nearly zero in the absence of the signal. The centre-tapped secondary of the *driver transformer T_1 supplies equal and opposite voltages to the base-circuits of the two transistors. The output transformer T_2 has the centre-tapped primary winding. The supply voltage V_{CC} is connected between the bases and this centre-tap. The loudspeaker is connected across the secondary of this transformer.

Circuit operation

(i) The input signal appears across the secondary AB of the driver transformer. Suppose during the first half-cycle (marked 1) of the signal, end A becomes positive and end B negative. This will make the base-emitter junction of Q_1 reverse biased and that of Q_2 forward biased. The circuit will conduct current due to Q_2 only and is shown by solid arrows. Therefore, this half-cycle of the signal is amplified by Q_2 and appears in the lower half of the primary of output transformer.

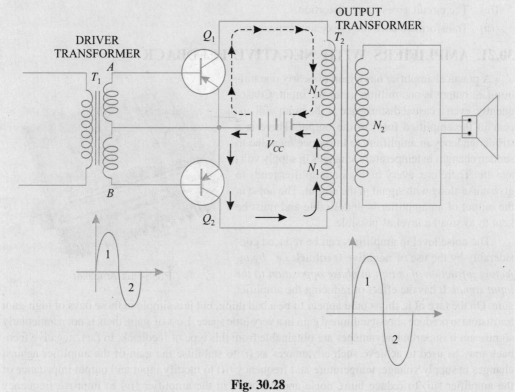

Fig. 30.28

(ii) In the next half-cycle of the signal, Q_1 is forward biased whereas Q_2 is reverse biased. Therefore, circuit conducts current due to Q_1 and is shown by dotted arrows. Consequently, this

* The stage that immediately precedes the output stage is called driver stage. It operates as class A power amplifier and supplies the drive for the output stage.

half-cycle of the signal is amplified by Q_1 and appears in the upper half of the primary of output transformer. The centre-tapped primary of the output transformer combines two collector currents to form a sine wave output in the secondary.

It may be noted here that push-pull arrangement also permits a maximum transfer of power to the load through impedance matching. If R_L is the resistance appearing across secondary of output transformer, then this resistance will be reflected as R'_L in the primary and is given by;

$$R'_L = \left[\frac{2N_1}{N_2}\right]^2 R_L$$

where N_1 = number of turns between either end of primary winding and centre-tap
$\quad\quad\;\; N_2$ = number of secondary turns

Advantages
    (*i*)   The efficiency of the circuit is quite high ($\approx 75\%$) due to class *B* operation.
   (*ii*)   A high a.c. output power is obtained.

Disadvantages
    (*i*)   Two transistors have to be used.
   (*ii*)   It requires two equal and opposite voltages at the input. Therefore, push-pull circuit requires the use of driver stage to furnish these signals.
  (*iii*)   If the parameters of the two transistors are not the same, there will be unequual amplification of the two halves of the signal.
  (*iv*)   The circuit gives more distortion.
   (*v*)   Transformers used are bulky and expensive.

30.21. AMPLIFIERS WITH NEGATIVE FEEDBACK

A practical amplifier has a gain of nearly one million *i.e.,* output is one million times the input. Consequently, even a casual disturbance at the input will appear in the amplified form in the output. There is a strong tendency in amplifiers to introduce *hum* due to sudden changes in temperature, changes in supply voltage *etc.* Therefore, every high gain amplifier tends to give noise along with signal in the output. The noise in the output of an amplifier is undesirable and must be kept to as small a level as possible.

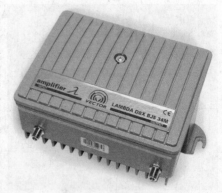

The noise level in amplifiers can be reduced considerably by the use of **negative feedback** *i.e., by injecting a fraction of outupt in phase opposition to the input signal.* It has the effect of reducing the amplifier

Push-Pull Amplifier

gain. On the face of it, this would appear to be a bad thing, but it is simple in these days of high-gain transistors to produce almost unlimited gain in a very little space. Loss of gain, then, is not paraticularly significant if important advantages are obtainable from this type of feedback. In fact, negative feedback may be used to achieve such advantages as (*i*) to stabililse the gain of the amplifier against changes in supply voltage, temperature and frequency (*ii*) to modify input and output impedance of the amplifier (*iii*) to reduce hum, noise and distorion in the amplifier (*iv*) to improve frequency response of the amplifier *etc.* In the light of these advantages, the loss in gain is alomost trivial.

30.22. PRINCIPLES OF NEGATIVE FEEDBACK IN AMPLIFIERS

A feedback amplifier has two parts *viz.* an amplifier and a feedback circuit. The feedback circuit consists of resistors and returns a fraction of output energy back to the input. Fig. 30.29 *shows the principles of negative feedback in an amplifier. Typical values have been assumed to make the treatment more illustrative. The output of the amplifier is 10V. The fraction m of this output (*i.e.,* 100 mV) is fedback to the input where it is applied in series with the input signal of 101 mV. As the feedback is negative, therefore, only 1 mV appears at the input terminals of the amplifier.

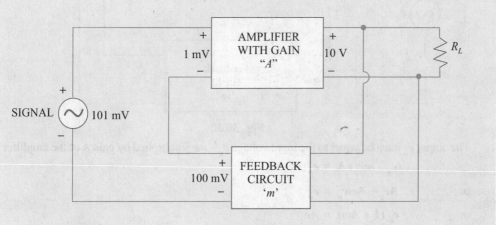

Fig. 30.29

Referring to Fig. 30.29,

Gain of amplifier without feedback, $A = \dfrac{10\ V}{1\ mV} = 10,000$

Fraction of output fedback, $m = \dfrac{100\ mV}{10\ V} = 0.01$

Gain of the amplifier with negative feedback, $A_{fb} = \dfrac{10\ V}{101\ mV} = 100$

The following points are worth noting :

(*i*)   When negative feedback is employed, the gain of the amplifier is reduced. Thus, the gian of above amplifier without feedback is 10,000 whereas with negative feedback, it is only 100.

(*ii*)   When negative feedback is employed, the voltage *actually* applied to the ampifier is extermely small. In this case, the signal voltage is 101 *mV* and the negative feedback is 100*mV* so that voltage applied at the input of the amplifier is 1*mV.*

(*iii*)   In a negative feedback circuit, the feedback fraction m is always between 0and 1.

(*iv*)   The gain with feedback is sometimes called *closed-loop gian* while the gian without feedback is called *open-loop gain.*

30.23. GAIN OF NEGATIVE FEEDBACK AMPLIFIER

Consider the negative feedback amplifier shown in Fig. 30.30. The gain of the amplifier without feedback is A. Negative feedback is then applied by feeding a fraction m of the output voltage (e_o) back to amplifier input. Therefore, the actual input to the amplifier is equal to the signal voltage e_g minus feedback voltage me_o *i.e.,*

$$\text{Actual input to amplifier} = e_g - me_o$$

---

* Note that amplifier and feedback circuits are connected in *series-parallel.* The inputs of amplifier and feedback circuits are in *series* but the outputs are in *parallel.* In practice, this circuit is widely used.

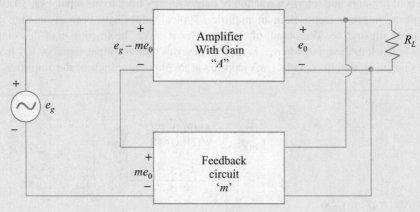

Fig. 30.30

The output e_o must be equal to the input voltage $e_g - me_o$ multiplied by gain A of the amplilfer *i.e.*,

$$(e_g - me_o)\, A = e_o$$

or $\qquad Ae_g - Ame_o = e_o$

or $\qquad e_o\,(1 + Am) = Ae_g$

or $\qquad \dfrac{e_o}{e_g} = \dfrac{A}{1 + Am}$

But e_o/e_g is the gain of the amplifier with negative feedback.

∴ Voltage gain with negative feedback is

$$A_{fb} = \frac{A}{1 + Am}$$

It may be seen that gain of the amplifier without feedback is A. However, when negative feedback is applied, the gain is reduced by a factor $1 + Am$.

30.24. FEEDBACK CIRCUIT

The function of the feedback circuit is to return a fraction of the output voltage to the input of the amplifier. Fig. 30.31 shows the feedback circuit of negative feedback amplifier. It is essentially a potential divider consisting of resistances R_1 and R_2. The output voltage of the amplifier is fed to this potential divider which gives the feedback voltage to the input.

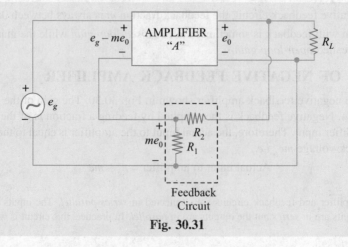

Feedback
Circuit

Fig. 30.31

Referring to Fig. 30.31, it is clear that :

$$\text{Voltage across } R_1 = \frac{R_1}{R_1 + R_2} e_0$$

$$\text{Feedback fraction,} \quad m = \frac{\text{Voltage across } R_1}{e_0} = \frac{R_1}{R_1 + R_2}$$

Example 30.12. *The voltage gain of an amplifier without feedback is 3000. Calculate the voltage gain of the amplifier if negative feedback is introduced in the circuit. Given that feedback fraction m = 0.01.*

Solution.

$$A_{fb} = \frac{A}{1 + Am}$$

Here $\qquad A = 3000; m = 0.01; A_{fb} = ?$

$$\therefore \qquad A_{fb} = \frac{3000}{1 + 3000 \times 0.01} = 97$$

Example 30.13. *With a negative feedback, an amplifier gives an output of 10V with an input of 0.5V. When feedback is removed, it requires 0.25V input for the same output. Calculate (i) gain without feedback (ii) feedback fraction m.*

Solution.

(*i*) Gain without feedback, $\quad A = 10/0.25 = 40$

(*ii*) Gain with feedback, $\quad A_{fb} = 10/0.5 = 20$

Now $\qquad A_{fb} = \frac{A}{1 + Am}$

or $\qquad 20 = \frac{40}{1 + 40\,m}$

$\therefore \qquad m = 0.025$

Example 30.14. *Calculate the gain of a negative feedback amplifier with an internal gain A = 100 and feedback factor m = 0.09. What will be the gain if A doubles ?*

Solution. $\qquad A = 100; m = 0.09; A_{fb} = ?$

$$\therefore \qquad A_{fb} = \frac{A}{1 + Am} = \frac{100}{1 + 100 \times 0.09} = 10$$

$$A = 200; m = 0.09; A_{fb} = ?$$

$$\therefore \qquad A_{fb} = \frac{A}{1 + Am} = \frac{200}{1 + 200 \times 0.09} = 10.5$$

Inspite of the fact that internal gain *A* is doubled up, the change in A_{fb} is negligible . This is a distinct advantage of negative feedback *i.e.,* it provides gain stability

Example 30.15. *An amplifier is having a gain of 500 without feedback. If negative feedback is applied, the gain is reduced to 100. Calculate the fraction of the output fed back. If, due to ageing of components, the gain without feedback falls by 20%, calculate the percentage fall in gain with feedback.*

Solution. $\qquad A = 500; A_{fb} = 100; m = ?$

$$\therefore \qquad A_{fb} = \frac{A}{1 + Am}$$

or
$$100 = \frac{500}{1 + 500m}$$

∴
$$m = 0.008$$

Now
$$A = \frac{80}{100} \times 500 = 400; \ m = 0.008; \ A_{fb} = ?$$

∴
$$A_{fb} = \frac{A}{1 + Am}$$

$$= \frac{400}{1 + 400 \times 0.008} = \frac{400}{4.2} = 95.3$$

$$\% \text{ fall in } A_{fb} = \frac{100 - 95.3}{100} \times 100 = 4.7\%$$

Note that without feedback, the change in gain is 20%. However, when feedback is applied, the change in gain (4.7%) is much less. This shows that negative feedback provides gain stability.

30.25. ADVANTAGES OF NEGATIVE FEEDBACK

The loss in gain due to negative feedback goes to the background when we study the advantages of negative feedback in amplifiers.

(*i*) **Gain stability**

$$A_{fb} = \frac{A}{1 + Am}$$

For negative feedback in an amplifier to be effective, the designer deliberately makes $Am \gg 1$. Therefore, the above relation becomes :

$$A_{fb} = \frac{1}{m}$$

This means that gain now depends upon feedback fraction *m* *i.e.,* characteristics of feedback circuit. As feedback circuit is usually a potenital divider (a resistive network), the gain of the amplifier becomes independent of ageing of transistor, variation in supply voltage, temperature and frequency.

(*ii*) **Reduces non-linear distortion.** The negative feedback reduces the non-linear distortion in large signal amplifiers. It can be proved mathematically that :

$$D_{fb} = \frac{D}{1 + Am}$$

where
D = Distortion in amplifier without feedback

D_{fb} = Distortion in amplifier with negative feedback

It is clear that by applying negative feedback to an amplifier, the distortion is reduced by a factor $1 + Am$.

(*iii*) **Improves frequency response.** As shown above, $A_{fb} = 1/m$. This means that voltage gain of the amplifier is independent of signal frequency. The result is that voltage gain of the amplifier will be substantially constant over a wide range of signal frequency. The negative feedback, therefore, improves the frequency response of the amplifier.

(*iv*) **Modifies input and output impedances.** The negative feedback increases the input impedance and decreases the output impedance of the amplifier. Such a change is profitable in practice as the amplifier can then serve the purpose of impedance matching.

(*a*) It can be shown mathematically that with negative feedback:

$$Z'_{in} = Z_{in} (1 + Am)$$

where Z_{in} = input impedance without feedback

Z'_{in} = input impedance with negative feedback

(*b*) It can be shown mathematically that with negative feedback :

$$Z'_{out} = \frac{Z_{out}}{1 + Am}$$

where Z_{out} = output impedance without feedback

Z'_{out} = output impedance with negative feedback

30.26. TRANSISTOR TUNED AMPLIFIERS

Most of the audio amplifiers we have discussed so far will also work at radio frequencies *i.e.*, above 50 kHz. However, they suffer from two drawbacks. First, they become less efficient at radio frequencies. Secondly, such amplifiers have mostly resistive loads and consequently their gain is independent of signal frequency over a large bandwidth. In other words, an audio amplifier amplifies a wide band of frequencies equally well and does not permit the selection of a particular desired frequency while rejecting all other frequencies.

However, sometimes it is desired that an amplifier should be selective *i.e.*, it should select a desired frequency or narrow band of frequencies for amplification. For instance, radio and television transmission are carried on a specific radio frequency assigned to the broadcasting station. The radio receiver is required to pick up and amplify the radio frequency desired while discriminating all others. To achieve this, the simple resistive load is replaced by a parallel tuned circuit whose impedance strongly depends upon frequency. Such a tuned circuit becomes very selective and amplifies very strongly signals of resonant frequency and narrow band on either side. Therefore, the use of tuned circuit in conjunction with a transistor makes possible the selection and efficient amplification of a particular desired frequency. Such an amplifier is called a *tuned amplifier.*

30.27. TUNED AMPLIFIER CIRCUIT

Amplifiers which amplify a specific frequency or narrow band of frequencies are called tuned amplifiers.

Fig. 30.32. shows the circuit of a simple transistor tuned amplifier. Here, instead of load resistor we have a parallel tuned circuit in the collector. The impedance of this tuned circuit strongly depends upon frequency. It offers a very high impedance at *resonant frequency* and very small impedance at all other frequencies. If the

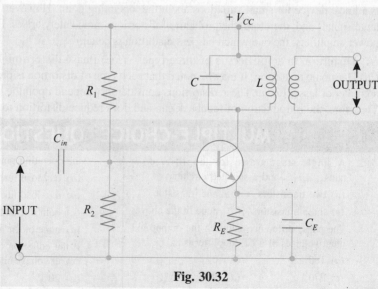

Fig. 30.32

signal has the same frequency as the resonant frequency of the parallel *LC* circuit, large amplification will occur due to high *impedance of *LC* circuit at this frequency.

* It has already been discussed in Art. 18.10 that a parallel *LC* circuit offers high impedance at resonant frequeucy. However, the circuit offers very low impedance to frequencies other than the resonant frequency.

When signals of many frequencies are present at the input of the tuned amplifier, it will select and strongly amplify the signals of resonant frequency while rejecting all others. Therefore, such amplifiers are very useful in radio receivers to select the signal from one particular broadcasting station when signals of many other frequencies are present at the receiving aerial.

30.28. ADVANTAGES OF TUNED AMPLIFIERS

In high frequency applications, it is generally required to amplify a single frequency, while rejecting all other frequencies present. For such purposes, tuned amplifiers are used. These amplifiers use tuned parallel circuit as the collector load and offer the following advantages:

(*i*) **Small power loss.** A tuned parallel circuit employs reactive elements L and C. Consequently, the power loss in such a circuit is quite low. On the other hand, if a resistive load is used in the collector, there will be considerable loss of power. Therefore, tuned amplifiers are highly efficient.

(*ii*) **High selectivity.** A tuned circuit has the property of selectivity *i.e.,* it can select the desired frequency for amplification out of a large number of frequencies simultaneously impressed upon it. For instance, if a mixture of frequencies including f_r (*i.e.,* resonant frequency of LC circuit) is fed to the input of a tuned amplifier, then maximum amplification occurs for f_r. For all other frequencies, the tuned circuit offers very low impedance and hence these are amplified to a little extent and may be thought as rejected by the circuit. On the other hand, if we use resistive load in the collector, all the frequencies will be amplified equally *i.e.,* the circuit will not have the ability to select the desired frequency.

30.29. DISTORTION IN AMPLIFIERS

The change of output wave shape from the input wave shape of an amplifier is known as **distortion.** A transistor like other electronic devices, is essentially a non-linear device. Therefore, whenever a signal is applied to the input of the transistor, the output signal is not exactly like the input signal *i.e.,* distortion occurs. Distortion is not a problem for small signals (*i.e.,* voltage amplifiers) since transistor is a linear device for small variations about the operating point. However, a power amplifier handles large signals and, therefore, the problem of distortion immediately arises. For the comparision of two power amplifiers, the one which has less distortion is better.

Distortion in amplifiers is of three types *viz* (*i*) Phase distortion (*ii*) Amplitude distortion (*iii*) Harmonic distortion. It may be noted that each type of distortion is present in most amplifiers to a greater or lesser extent.These distortions considerably depend upon the basic gain of the amplifier. Therefore, the introduction of feedback can and does reduce distortion to a large extent.

MULTIPLE-CHOICE QUESTIONS

1. A single stage transistor amplifier contains............... and associated circuitry.
   (*a*) two transistors (*b*) one transistor
   (*c*) three transistors (*d*) none of the above

2. The phase difference between the output and input voltages of a *CE* amplifier is...............
   (*a*) 180° (*b*) 0°
   (*c*) 270° (*d*) 90°

3. It is generally desired that a transistor should have .... input impedance.
   (*a*) low (*b*) high
   (*c*) very low (*d*) very high

4. When an *a.c.* signal is applied to an amplifier, the operating point moves along...............
   (*a*) *d.c.* load line
   (*b*) *a.c.* load line
   (*c*) both *d.c.* and *a.c.* load lines
   (*d*) none of the above

5. If the collector supply is 10 V, then collector cut off voltage under *d.c.* conditions is...............
   (*a*) 20 V (*b*) 5 V
   (*c*) 2 V (*d*) 10 V

6. In the zero signal conditions, a transistor sees...............load.
   (*a*) *d.c.* (*b*) *a.c.*
   (*c*) both *d.c.*and *a.c.* (*d*) none of the above

7. A radio receiver has ....of amplification.

   (*a*) one stage

   (*b*) two stages

   (*c*) three stages

   (*d*) more than three stages

8. A multistage amplifier uses atleast...............

   (*a*) one transistor   (*b*) two transistors

   (*c*) none of the two   (*d*) either (*a*) or (*b*)

9. *RC* coupling is used for..............amplification.

   (*a*) voltage   (*b*) current

   (*c*) power   (*d*) none of the above

10. In a *RC* coupled amplifier, the voltage gain over mid-frequency range...............

    (*a*) changes abruptly with frequency

    (*b*) is constant

    (*c*) varies linearly with frequency

    (*d*) none of the three

11. In obtaining the frequency response curve of an amplifier, the ....

    (*a*) generator output level is kept constant

    (*b*) amplifier output is kept constant

    (*c*) generator frequency is held constant

    (*d*) amplifier frequency is held constant

12. An advantage of *RC* coupling scheme is...............

    (*a*) good impedance matching

    (*b*) economy

    (*c*) high efficiency

    (*d*) none of the above

13. The output stage in an amplifier is also called...............

    (*a*) mixer stage   (*b*) power stage

    (*c*) detector stage   (*d*) R.F. stage

14. ....coupling is generally employed in power amplifiers.

    (*a*) Transformer   (*b*) *RC*

    (*c*) Direct   (*d*) Impedance

15. A class A power amplifier uses...............

    (*a*) two transistors   (*b*) three transistors

    (*c*) one transistor   (*d*) none of the above

16. The maximum collector efficiency of a resistance loaded class *A* power amplifier is...............

    (*a*) 50%   (*b*) 25%

    (*c*) 78.5%   (*d*) 30%

17. The maximum collector efficiency of transformer coupled class *A* power amplifier is...............

    (*a*) 30%   (*b*) 45%

    (*c*) 80%   (*d*) 50%

18. Class...............power amplifier has the highest collector efficiency.

    (*a*) *A*   (*b*) *B*

    (*c*) *C*   (*d*) *AB*

19. When negative feedback is applied to an amplifier, its gain...............

    (*a*) is increased   (*b*) is reduced

    (*c*) remains the same   (*d*) none of the above

20. The value of negative feedback fraction is always...............

    (*a*) less than 1   (*b*) more than 1

    (*c*) equal to 1   (*d*) none of the above

21. If the output of an amplifier is 10 V and 100 mV from the output is fed back to the input, then feedback fraction is...............

    (*a*) 10   (*b*) 0.01

    (*c*) 0.1   (*d*) 0.15

22. The gain of an amplifier without feedback is 100 db. If a negative feedback of 3 *db* is applied, the gain of the amplifier will become...............

    (*a*) 103 db   (*b*) 101.5 db

    (*c*) 300 db   (*d*) 97 db

23. If the feedback fraction in an amplifier is 0.01, then gain with negative feedback is approximately...............

    (*a*) 10   (*b*) 100

    (*c*) 1000   (*d*) 500

24. A feedback circuit usually employs .... network.

    (*a*) resistive   (*b*) capacitive

    (*c*) inductive   (*d*) none of the above

25. The gain of an amplifier with feedback is known as...............gain.

    (*a*) closed loop   (*b*) open loop

    (*c*) resonant   (*d*) none of the above.

Answers to Multiple-Choice Questions

1. (*b*)	2. (*a*)	3. (*b*)	4. (*b*)	5. (*d*)	6. (*a*)	7. (*d*)	8. (*b*)
9. (*a*)	10. (*b*)	11. (*a*)	12. (*b*)	13. (*b*)	14. (*a*)	15. (*c*)	16. (*b*)
17. (*d*)	18. (*c*)	19. (*b*)	20. (*a*)	21. (*b*)	22. (*d*)	23. (*b*)	24. (*a*)
25. (*a*)							

Hints to Selected Multiple-Choice Questions

2. In a *CE* amplifier, when the input signal voltage increases in the positive sense, the output voltage increases in the negative direction and vice-versa *i.e.*, there is a phase difference of 180°. Two points are worth noting here:

   (a) Phase reversal (*i.e.*, phase difference of 180° between input and output voltages) occurs if output is taken from collector and emitter end of supply as is always done. However, if the output is taken across R_C, there will be no phase reversal.

   (b) Amplification is not affected by phase reversal.

4. When an *a.c.* signal is applied, the co-ordinates of collector current (i_C) and collector emitter voltage (v_{CE}) are on the *a.c.* load line. Therefore, the operating point moves along the *a.c.* load line.

6. Under zero signal conditions, there is no *a.c.* signal. The capacitors connected are assumed open as for *d.c.* a capacitor offers infinite resistance. It is because under zero signal conditions, only *d.c.* flows and the currents and voltages calculated are *d.c.* Therefore, the load seen by a transistor is *d.c.*

10. In the mid-frequency range, the voltage gain of a *RC* coupled amplifier **is constant**. Incidently, this frequency range (50 Hz to 20 kHz) is also the audio frequency range which is the region of most importance for speech, music etc. The constant voltage gain results in uniform amplification of the whole signal.

12. *RC* coupling employs resistors and capacitors which are cheap.

14. Power amplifiers are required to deliver a large amount of power. Therefore, **transformer coupling** is used to permit impedance matching, which is turn , allows maximum power output.

20. In negative feedback circuit, the value of negative feedback fraction is between 0 and 1.

21. $$m = \frac{100 \ mV}{10 \ V} = \frac{100 \ mV}{10000 \ mV} = 0.01$$

23. $$A_{fb} = \frac{A}{1 + Am}$$

   If $Am^* \gg 1$, then,

   $$A_{fb} = \frac{A}{Am} = \frac{1}{m} = \frac{1}{0.01} = 100$$

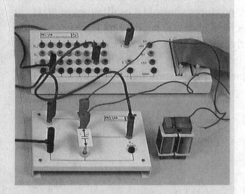

31

Sinusoidal Oscillators

INTRODUCTION

Many electronic devices require a source of energy at a specific frequency which may range from a few Hz to several MHz. This is achieved by an electronic device called an *oscillator*. Oscillators are extensively used in electronic equipment. For example, in radio and television receivers, oscillators are used to generate high frequency wave (called *carrier wave*) in the tuning stages. Audio frequency and radio frequency signals are required for the repair of radio, television and other electronic equipment. Oscillators are also widely used in radar, electronic computers and other electronic devices. In this chapter, we shall discuss about the various aspects of oscillators.

31.1. SINUSOIDAL OSCILLATOR

An electronic device that generates sinusoidal oscillations of desired frequency is known as a sinusoidal oscillator.

Although we speak of an oscillator as "generating" a frequency, it should be noted that it does not create energy, but merely acts as an energy converter. It receives *d.c.* energy and changes it into *a.c.* energy of desired frequency. The frequency of oscillations depends upon the constants of the device.

It may be mentioned here that although an alternator produces sinusoidal oscillations of 50 Hz, it cannot be called an oscillator. Firstly, an alternator is a mechanical device having rotating parts whereas an oscillator is a non-rotating electronic device. Secondly, an alternator converts mechanical energy into *a.c.* energy while an oscillator converts *d.c.* energy into *a.c.* energy. Thirdly, an alternator cannot produce high frequency oscillations whereas an oscillator can produce oscillations from a few Hz to several MHz.

31.2. PRINCIPLE OF AN OSCILLATOR

An oscillator employs *positive feedback* for its operation. Whereas negative feedback tends to reduce the magnitude of the signal applied to the amplifier, positive feedback has the opposite effect.

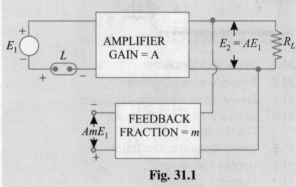

Consider the block diagram of Fig. 31.1. Here A is the voltage gain of the amplifier and m is the feedback fraction. The output voltage is $E_2 = AE_1$ where E_1 is the input voltage. Clearly, feedback voltage = $m E_2$ = $A m E_1$. If the link L were removed and

Fig. 31.1

the feedback circuit output connected to the input circuit with +*ve* to +*ve* and –*ve* to –*ve*, the feedback would be positive. This means that feedback voltage (= $A m E_1$) is in phase with the input voltage. Since E_1 is the required input voltage to produce the output voltage E_2, it means that for continuous output (*i.e.*, oscillations), the feedback voltage must be equal to the input voltage *i.e.*,

$$\text{Feedback voltage} = E_1$$
or $$A m E_1 = E_1$$
or $$A m = 1$$

Under these conditions (*i.e.*, $A m = 1$), even if there were no input generator (*i.e.*, E_1), a continuous output will be obtained across R_L immediately after connecting the necessary power supplies (*i.e.*, V_{CC}). The general layout of an oscillator is shown in Fig. 31.2.

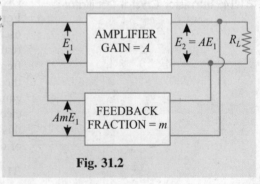

It is clear from Fig. 31.2 that continuous output (E_2) will be obtained with no externallly applied input signal. It provides its own input signal *via* the feedback circuit. Thus, output voltage $E_2 = AE_1$ and feedback voltage = $A m E_1 = E_1$ (because $A m$ = 1).

Fig. 31.2

Mathematical explanation. The gain of a positive feedback amplifier is given by ;

$$A_{fb} = \frac{A}{1 - Am}$$

For continuous undamped output, $Am = 1$

$$\therefore \qquad A_{fb} = \frac{A}{0} = \infty$$

---

* When the feedback energy (voltage or current) is in phase with the input signal and thus aids it, it is called positive feedback.

An amplifier with infinite gain is one that can produce an output signal without any externally applied input signal. It provides its own input signal *via* the feedback circuit. Such a circuit is known as an *oscillator*. In order to produce an output of desired frequency, the circuit is so arranged that *Am* = 1 at that frequency. It may be noted that the condition *Am* = 1 must be satisfied in magnitude and phase. In other words, the feedback circuit must produce this magnitude (*i.e.*, *A m* = 1) and its phase must be the same as that of the input signal E_1 (*i.e.*, positive feedback).

31.3. ESSENTIALS OF TRANSISTOR OSCILLATOR

Fig. 31.3 shows the block diagram of an oscillator. Its essential components are :

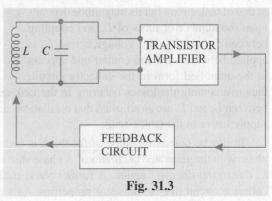

Fig. 31.3

(*i*) **Frequency-determining circuit.** It consists of either parallel tuned circuit (*LC*) or *RC* circuit. The radio-frequency oscillators generally employ the former while the audio frequency oscillators use the latter. The frequency of oscillations in the circuit depends upon these circuit elements.

(*ii*) **Transistor Amplifier.** The transistor amplifier receives *d.c.* power from the battery and changes it into *a.c.* power of desired frequency for supplying to the frequency determining circuit. The oscillations occuring in the frequency-determining circuit are applied to the input of the transistor amplifier. Because of amplifying properties of the transistor, we get increased output of these oscillations. The output of the transistor is supplied to the frequency-determining circuit to meet the losses.

(*iii*) **Feedback Circuit.** The feedback circuit supplies a part of output energy to the frequency-determining circuit satisfying the relation *Am* = 1. The entire circuit arrangement is so designed that energy fed back is in phase with oscillations in the frequency-determining circuit *i.e.*, positive feedback is provided.

31.4. DIFFERENT TYPES OF TRANSISTOR OSCILLATORS

A transistor can work as an oscillator to produce continuous undamped oscillations of any desired frequency if frequency-determining and feedback circuits are properly connected to it. All oscillators under different names have similar function *i.e.*, they produce continuous undamped output. However, the major differences between these oscillators lie in :

    (*i*) the frequency determining elements.

    (*ii*) the method of providing positive feedback.

We shall discuss some important transistor oscillators.

31.5. TUNED COLLECTOR OSCILLATOR

Fig. 31.4 shows the circuit of tuned collector oscillator. It contains tuned circuit $L_1 - C_1$ in the collector and hence the name. The frequency of oscillations depends upon the values of L_1 and C_1 and is given by ;

$$f = \frac{1}{2\pi\sqrt{L_1 C_1}} \qquad \qquad ...(i)$$

The feedback coil L_2 in the base circuit is magnetically coupled to the tank circuit coil L_1. In practice, L_1 and L_2 form the primary and secondary of the transformer. The biasing is provided by potential divider arrangement. The capacitor C connected in the base circuit provides low reactance path to the oscillations.

Circuit operation. When switch S is closed, collector current starts increasing and charges the capacitor C_1. When this capacitor is fully charged, it discharges through coil L_1, setting up oscillations of the frequency given by exp. (*i*). These oscillations induce some voltage in the coil L_2 by mutual induction. The frequency of voltage in the coil L_2 is the same as that of tank circuit but its magnitude depends upon the number of turns of L_2 and coupling between L_2 and L_1. The voltage across L_2 is applied between base and emitter and appears in the amplified form in the collector circuit,

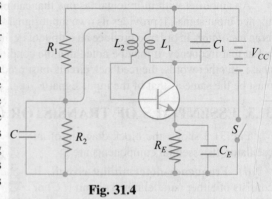

Fig. 31.4

thus overcoming the losses occuring in the tank circuit. The number of turns of L_2 and coupling between L_1 and L_2 are so adjusted that oscillations across L_2 are amplified to a level just sufficient to supply losses to the tank circuit.

It may be noted that phase of feedback is correct *i.e.*, energy supplied to the tank circuit is in phase with the generated oscillations. A phase shift of 180° is created between the voltages of L_1 and L_2 due to transformer *action. A further phase shift of 180° takes place between base-emitter and collector circuit due to transistor properties. As a result, energy fed back to the tank circuit is in phase with the generated oscillations.

31.6. HARTLEY OSCILLATOR

Hartley oscillator is very popular in applications where substantial radio-frequency power is needed as in radio transmitters, induction and dielectric heating and remote control systems. Fig. 31.5 shows the circuit of Hartley oscillator. The tank circuit is made up of C_T, L_1 and L_2. The coil L_1 is inductively coupled to coil L_2, the combination functions as an auto-transformer. The resistance R_b between collector and base provides the necessary biasing. The capacitor C blocks the d.c. component. The frequency of oscillations is determined by the values of L_1, L_2 and C_T and is given by ;

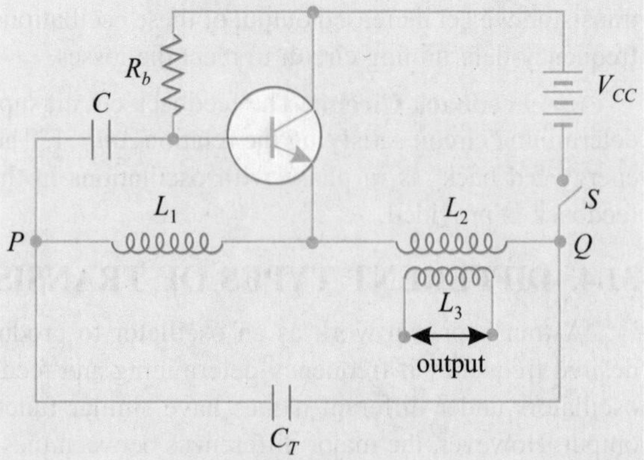

Fig. 31.5

$$f = \frac{1}{2\pi\sqrt{C_T\,(L_1 + L_2)}} \quad ...(i)$$

Circuit operation. When switch S is closed, the collector current starts rising and charges the capacitor C_T. When this capacitor is fully charged, it discharges through coils L_1 and L_2, setting up oscillations of frequency determined by exp. (*i*). The oscillations across L_1 are applied to the base-emitter junction and appear in the amplified form in the collector circuit. The coil L_2 couples the collector circuit energy back into the tank circuit by means of mutual inductance between L_1 and L_2. In this way, energy is being continuously supplied to the tank circuit to overcome the losses occuring in it. Consequently, continuous undamped output is obtained.

. . . .

* All transformers introduce a phase shift of 180° between primary and secondary.

It may be seen that energy supplied to the tank circuit is of correct phase. The ends P and Q of the auto-transformer $L_1 - L_2$ are $180°$ out of phase. A further phase-shift of $180°$ is produced by base and collector circuit of the transistor. In this way, energy fed back to the tank circuit is in phase with the generated oscillations.

31.7. COLLPITT'S OSCILLATOR

The Collpitt's oscillator is similar to Hartley oscillator with minor modifications. Whereas Hartley oscillator uses two coils and a capacitor for frequency selection, Collpitt's oscillator uses two capacitors and a coil as shown in Fig. 31.6. The tank circuit is made up of C_1, C_2 and L. The frequency of the oscillations is determined by the values of C_1, C_2 and L and is given by ;

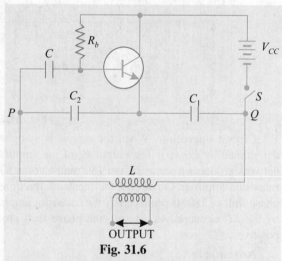

$$f = \frac{1}{2\pi\sqrt{LC_T}} \qquad ...(i)$$

where $C_T = \dfrac{C_1 C_2}{C_1 + C_2}$

Fig. 31.6

Circuit operation. When switch S is closed, the capacitors C_1 and C_2 are charged. These capacitors are discharged through coil L, setting up oscillations determined by exp. (*i*). The oscillations across C_2 are applied to the base-emitter junction and will appear in the amplified form in the collector circuit and supply losses to the tank circuit. The amount of feedback depends upon the relative capacitance values of C_1 and C_2. The smaller the capacitance C_1, the greater the feedback. It is easy to ascertain that energy fed back to tank circuit is of correct phase. The capacitors C_1 and C_2 act as a simple alternating voltage divider. Therefore, points P and Q are $180°$ out of phase. A further phase shift of $180°$ is produced by the transistor. In this way, feedback is properly phased to produce continuous undamped oscillations.

31.8. PHASE SHIFT OSCILLATOR

These oscillators are used as *signal generators* from the lowest audio range upto around 10 MHz. Fig. 31.7 shows the circuit of a phase shift oscillator. It consists of a conventional single transistor amplifier and a RC phase shift network. The phase shift network consists of three sections $R_1 C_1$, $R_2 C_2$ and $R_3 C_3$. At some frequency f_0, the *phase shift produced by each section is $60°$ so that total phase shift produced by the RC network is $180°$. The frequency of oscillations is given by ;

$$f_0 = \frac{1}{2\pi RC\sqrt{6}} \qquad ...(i)$$

where $R_1 = R_2 = R_3 = R$

$C_1 = C_2 = C_3 = C$

Because the capacitive reactance of the network changes at different frequencies, $180°$ phase shift required occurs only at one frequency. If R or C is made variable, however, a range of frequencies can be obtained. The reader may note carefully that in R - C phase shift oscillators, R and C are the frequency determining elements.

* The phase shift comes about in RC section because R and C in series produce a current that leads the applied voltage by a certain angle. The value of angle depends upon the values of R and C. By properly selecting R and C, $60°$ phase shift per section can be obtained.

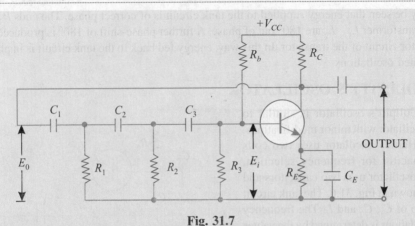

Fig. 31.7

Circuit operation. When the circuit is switched on, it produces oscillations of frequency determined by exp. (*i*). The output E_0 of the amplifier is fedback to *RC* feedback network. This network produces a phase shift of 180° and a voltage E_i appears at its output which is applied to the transistor amplifier. Obviously, the feedback fraction $m = E_i/E_0$. The feedback phase is correct. A phase shift of 180° is produced by the transistor amplifier. A further phase shift of 180° is produced by the *RC* network. As a result, the phase shift around the entire loop is 360° *i.e.*, feedback is positive.

Advantages

  (*i*) It does not require transformers or inductors.

  (*ii*) It can be used to produce very low frequencies.

  (*iii*) The circuit provides good frequency stability.

Disadvantages

  (*i*) It is difficult for the circuit to start oscillations.

  (*ii*) The circuit gives small output.

31.9. WIEN BRIDGE OSCILLATOR

The Wien bridge oscillator is the standard oscillator circuit for all low frequencies in the range of 10 Hz to about 1 MHz. It is the most frequently used type of audio oscillator as the output is free from circuit fluctuations and ambient temperature.

Circuit detail. Fig. 31.8 shows the circuit of Wien bridge oscillator. It is essentially a 2-stage amplifier with $R - C$ bridge circuit. The bridge circuit (Wien bridge) has the arms R_1C_1, R_3, R_2C_2 and tungsten lamp L_P. Resistances R_3 and L_P are used to stabilise the amplitude of the output. The transistor T_1 serves as an oscillator and amplifier while the other transistor T_2 serves as an inverter (*i.e.*, produces a phase shift of 180°). The circuit uses positive and negative feedbacks. The positive feedback is through R_1C_1, R_2C_2 to the transistor T_1. The negative feedback is through the voltage divider to the input transistor T_2. At a particular frequency f, the arms of the bridge are balanced. Under such conditions ;

$$f = \frac{1}{2\pi\sqrt{R_1 C_1 R_2 C_2}}$$

If $R_1 = R_2 = R$ and $C_1 = C_2 = C$, then,

$$f = \frac{1}{2\pi RC} \qquad \qquad ...(i)$$

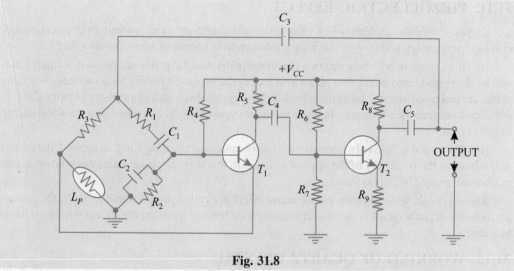

Fig. 31.8

Operation. When the circuit is started, bridge circuit produces oscillations of frequency determined by exp. (*i*). The two transistors produce a total phase shift of 360° so that proper positive feedback is ensured. The negative feedback in the circuit ensures constant output. This is achieved by the temperature sensitive lamp L_p. Its resistance increases with current. Should the amplitude of output tend to increase, more current would provide more negative feedback. The result is that output would return to the original value. A reverse action would take place if the output tends to decrease.

Advantages

(*i*) It gives constant ouptut.

(*ii*) The circuit works quite easily.

(*iii*) The overall gain is high because of two transistors.

(*iv*) The frequency of oscillations can be changed easily by using a potentiometer.

Disadvantages

(*i*) The circuit requires two transistors and a large number of components.

(*ii*) It cannot generate very high frequencies.

31.10. LIMITATIONS OF *LC* AND *RC* OSCILLATORS

The *LC* and *RC* oscillators discussed so far have their own limitations. The major problem in such circuits is that their frequency of operation does not remain strictly constant. It is because the values of resistors and inductors, which are the frequency determining elements in these circuits, change with temperature. This causes the change in the frequency of the oscillator. However, in many applications, it is desirable and necessary to maintain the frequency constant with extreme low tolerances. For example, it is desired that frequency of the broadcasting station should not change due to change in temperature or any other reason.

In order to maintain constant frequency, *piezoelectric crystals* are used in place of *LC* or *RC* circuits. Oscillators of this type are called crystal oscillators. The frequency of a crystal oscillator changes by less than 0.1% due to temperature or other changes. Therefore, such oscillators offer the most satisfactory method of stablising the frequency and are used in great majority of electronic applications.

31.11. PIEZOELECTRIC EFFECT

Certain crystalline materials (*e.g.*, Rochelle salt, quartz *etc.*) can convert mechanical energy into electrical energy and *vice-versa*. This phenomenon is known as *piezoelectric effect*.

(*i*) If a crystal is held between two flat metal plates and the plates are pressed, a small e.m.f. will be developed between the two plates as if the crystal became a battery for a moment. When the plates are realeased, the crystal springs back to its original shape and an opposite polarity e.m.f. is developed between the two plates. In this way, mechanical energy is converted into electrical energy by the crystal.

(*ii*) If a crystal is held between two metal plates and an alternating e.m.f. is applied, the crystal will vibrate at the frequency of the applied voltage. In this way, electrical energy is converted into mechanical energy by the crystal.

Those crystals which exhibit piezoelectric effect are called *piezoelectric crystals*. Of various piezoelectric crystals, quartz is the most commonly used because it is inexpensive and readily available in nature.

31.12. WORKING OF QUARTZ CRYSTAL

In order to use crystal in an electronic circuit, it is placed between two metal plates. The arrangement then forms a capacitor with crystal as the dielectric as shown in Fig. 31.9 (*i*). If the

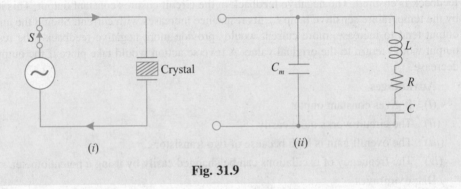

Fig. 31.9

crystal between the paltes is *shock-excited, it will vibrate mechanically at its natural frequency for a short while and at the same time produce an e.m.f. between the two plates. The frequency of oscillations depends upon the crystal dimensions. This action of the crystal is somewhat similar to a shock-excited oscillator. If all mechanical losses are overcome, the vibrations at this natural frequency will sustain themselves and generate electrical oscillations of constant frequency. Accordingly, a crystal can be substituted for the tank circuit in an electronic oscillator.

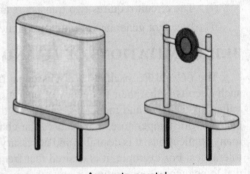

A quartz crystal

Fig. 31.9 (*ii*) shows the equivalent circuit of a vibrating crystal.

C_m = mounting capacitance

**$R - L - C$ = electrical equivalent of vibrating characteristic of crystal

* Voltage is applied across the plates for a moment.

** When the crystal is vibrating, L is the electrical equivalent of crystal mass, C is the electrical equivalent of elasticity and R is the electrical equivalent of the mechanical friction.

Note that Q of the crystal is very high. It may go as high as half a million when special care is taken in the mounting. This is the main reason for high frequency stability of crystal oscillators.

31.13. CRYSTAL RESONANCE CURVE

A piezoelectric crystal acts like a high Q tuned circuit. Fig. 31.10 shows the crystal resonance curve. Note that there are two resonant conditions; a series resonance closely followed by a parallel resonance. The series resonant frequency f_s is due to the R-L-C part of the equivalent circuit. However, parallel resonant frequency f_p is due to the presence of C_m. The frequency of oscillations will be in the narrow range of f_s and f_p *i.e.*, frequency will be nearly constant. The resonant frequency of piezoelectric crystal normally varies with temperature but by careful selection of the axes at which the crystal cut is made, an almost zero temperature co-efficient crystal may be obtained in the range 0°C to 100°C.

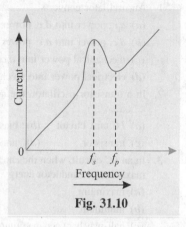

Fig. 31.10

31.14. TRANSISTOR CRYSTAL OSCILLATOR

Fig. 31.11 shows the circuit of a transistor crystal oscillator. A tank circuit $L_1 - C_1$ is placed in the collector and the piezoelectric crystal is connected in the base circuit. Feedback is obtained by the coil L_2 inductively coupled to coil L_1. The crystal is connected in series with the feedback winding. The natural frequency of LC circuit is made nearly equal to the natural frequency of the crystal.

Circuit operation. When the power is turned on, capacitor C_1 is charged. When this capacitor discharges, it sets up oscillations. The voltage across L_1 is fed to coil L_2 due to mutual inductance. This positive feedback causes the oscillator to produce oscillations. The frequency of oscillations in the circuit is controlled by the crystal. It is because the crystal is connected in the base circuit and hence its influence on the frequency of the circuit is much

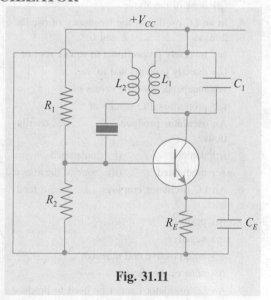

Fig. 31.11

more than LC circuit. Consequently, the entire circuit vibrates at the natural frequency of the crystal. As the frequency of the crystal is independent of temperature *etc.*, therefore, the circuit generates a constant frequency.

Advantages

(*i*) They have a high order of frequency stability.

(*ii*) The quality factor (Q) of the crystal is very high. The Q factor of the crystal may be as high as 10,000 compared to about 100 of L-C tank.

Disadvantages

(*i*) They are fragile and consequently can only be used in low power circuits.

(*ii*) The frequency of oscillations cannot be changed appreciably.

MULTIPLE-CHOICE QUESTIONS

1. An oscillator converts ....
   - (a) a.c. power into d.c. power
   - (b) d.c. power into a.c. power
   - (c) mechanical power into a.c. power
   - (d) electrical power into mechanical power

2. In a transistor oscillator, the active device is ....
   - (a) LC tank circuit
   - (b) biasing circuit
   - (c) transistor
   - (d) none of the above

3. In an LC circuit, when the capacitor energy is maximum, the inductor energy is ....
   - (a) maximum
   - (b) minimum
   - (c) half-way between maximum and minimum
   - (d) none of the above

4. In an LC oscillator, the frequency of oscillations is .... L and C.
   - (a) inversely proportional to square root of
   - (b) directly proportional to
   - (c) independent of the values of
   - (d) proportional to square of

5. An oscillator produces .... oscillations.
   - (a) damped
   - (b) undamped
   - (c) modulated
   - (d) none of the above

6. An LC oscillator employs .... feedback.
   - (a) positive
   - (b) negative
   - (c) both positive and negative
   - (d) none of the above.

7. An LC oscillator cannot be used to produce .... frequencies.
   - (a) high
   - (b) audio
   - (c) very high
   - (d) very low

8. Hartley oscillator is commonly used in ....
   - (a) radio receivers
   - (b) radio transmitters
   - (c) TV receivers
   - (d) none of the above

9. The frequency stability of the oscillator output is maximum in ....
   - (a) LC oscillators
   - (b) phase-shift oscillators
   - (c) crystal oscillators
   - (d) Wien bridge oscillator

10. In a phase-shift oscillator, we generally use .... RC sections.
    - (a) three
    - (b) two
    - (c) four
    - (d) none of the above

11. In a phase-shift oscillator, the frequency determining elements are ....
    - (a) L and C
    - (b) R and C
    - (c) R, L and C
    - (d) none of the above

12. A Wien bridge oscillator uses .... feedback.
    - (a) positive
    - (b) negative
    - (c) both positive and negative
    - (d) none of the above

13. The piezoelectric effect in a crystal is ....
    - (a) a voltage developed because of mechanical stress
    - (b) a change in resistance because of temperature
    - (c) a change of frequency because of temperature
    - (d) none of the above

14. The axis connecting the corners of a crystal is the ....
    - (a) X
    - (b) Y
    - (c) mechanical
    - (d) none of the above

15. If the crystal frequency increases with temperature, we say that the crystal has .... temperature co-efficient.
    - (a) positive
    - (b) zero
    - (c) negative
    - (d) none of the above

16. The crystal oscillator frequency is very stable due to .... of the crystal.
    - (a) rigidity
    - (b) high Q
    - (c) vibrations
    - (d) low Q

17. The application where one would most likely find a crystal oscillator is ....
    - (a) radio transmitter
    - (b) radio receiver
    - (c) AF sweep generator
    - (d) none of the above

18. In a Colpitts's oscillator, feedback is obtained ....
    - (a) by magnetic induction
    - (b) by a tickler coil
    - (c) from the centre of split capacitors
    - (d) none of the above

19. When *CE* configuration is used for an oscillator, the voltage fed back must ....
    (a) be inverted by 180°
    (b) have a 0° phase shift
    (c) be taken from a capacitor
    (d) none of the above

20. To sustain oscillations, the power gain of the amplifier may be ....
    (a) between 0.1 to 0.5
    (b) any value from 0.5 upward
    (c) equal to or greater than 1
    (d) none of the above

Answers to Multiple-Choice Questions

1. (b)	2. (c)	3. (b)	4. (a)	5. (b)	6. (a)	7. (d)	8. (a)
9. (c)	10. (a)	11. (b)	12. (c)	13. (a)	14. (a)	15. (a)	16. (b)
17. (a)	18. (c)	19. (a)	20. (c)				

Hints to Selected Multiple-Choice Questions

1. An oscillator merely acts as an energy converter. It receives d.c. energy (power) and changes it into a.c. energy (power) of desired frequency.

4. The natural or resonant frequency of oscillations of an oscillator is given by;

$$f_r = \frac{1}{2\pi\sqrt{LC}}$$

or
$$f_r \propto \frac{1}{\sqrt{LC}}$$

6. A transistor amplifier with proper **positive** feedback acts as an oscillator *i.e.* it can generate oscillations without any external signal source.

11. In a phase-shift oscillator, the frequency of oscillations is given by;

$$f_0 = \frac{1}{2\pi RC\sqrt{6}}$$

Clearly, f_0 depends on the values **R and C**.

13. Certain crystalline materials like Rochelle salt, quartz etc. when compressed or placed under mechanical strain to vibrate; they produce an a.c. voltage. This is known as piezoelectric effect.

16. The Q of a crystal is very high. At such a **high** Q, frequency is primarily determined by L and C. Since L and C remain fixed for a crystal, the frequency is very stable.

19. The *CE* configuration produces a phase shift of 180°. Now for the circuit to act as an oscillator, the input voltage should be in phase with voltage fed back. This is possible only if the voltage fed back is **inverted by 180°** by the feedback network.

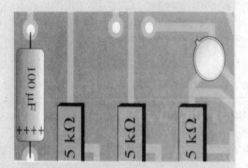

32

Field Effect Transistors

INTRODUCTION

In the previous chapters, we have discussed the circuit applications of an ordinary transistor. In this type of transistor, both holes and electrons play part in conduction. For this reason, it is sometimes called a *bipolar transistor*. The ordinary or biopolar transistor has two principal drawbacks. First, it has low input impedance because of forward biased emitter-base junction. Secondly, it has considerable noise level. Although low input impedance problem may be improved by careful design and use of more than one transistor, yet it is difficult to achieve input impedance more than a few megaohms. The field effect transistor (*FET*) has, by virtue of its construction and biasing, large input impedance which may be more than 100 megaohms. The *FET* is generally much less noisy than the ordinary or biopolar transistor. In this chapter, we shall focus our attention on the construction, working and circuit applications of field effect transistors.

32.1. FIELD EFFECT TRANSISTORS

A field effect transistor is a three terminal semiconductor device in which current conduction is by one type of carrier i.e., electrons or holes.

The *FET* was developed about the same time as the transistor but it came into use only in the late 1960s. In a *FET*, the current conduction is either by electrons or holes (*i.e.*, majority carriers) and is controlled by an electric field. For this reason, a *FET* is called a *unipolar transistor*. There are two basic types of field effect transistors *viz.*,

(*i*)   Junction Field Effect Transistor (*JFET*)

(*ii*) Metal-Oxide Semiconductor *FET* (*MOSFET*)

The need for *FET* arose because there were many functions in which biopolar transistors were unable to replace vacuum tubes. Owing to their extremely high input impedance, *FET* devices are more like vacuum tubes than are biopolar devices and hence are able to take over many vacuum-tube functions.

32.2. JUNCTION FIELD EFFECT TRANSISTOR (*JFET*)

A *JFET* consists of a *p*-type or *n*-type bar containing two *pn* junctions at the sides as shown in Fig. 32.1. The bar forms the conducting channel for the charge carriers. If the bar is of *n*-type, it is called *n-channel JFET* as shown in Fig. 32.1 (*i*) and if the bar is of *p*-type, it is called *p-channel JFET* as shown in Fig. 32.1 (*ii*). The two *pn* junctions forming diodes are connected internally and a common terminal called *gate* is taken out. Other terminals are *source* and *drain* taken out from the bar as shown. Thus a *JFET* has essentially three terminals *viz.*, gate (*G*), source (*S*) and drain (*D*).

JFET Polarities. Fig. 32.2 (*i*) shows *n*-channel *JFET* polarities whereas Fig. 32.2 (*ii*) shows *p*-channel *JFET* polarities. Note that in each case, the voltage between the gate and source is such that the gate is reverse biased. This is the normal way of *JFET* connection. The drain and source terminals are interchangeable *i.e.*, either end can be used as source and the other end as drain.

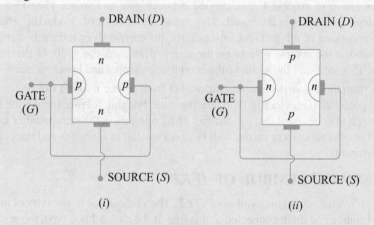

Fig. 32.1

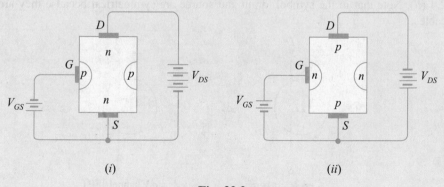

Fig. 32.2

32.3. WORKING PRINCIPLE OF *JFET*

Fig. 32.3 shows the circuit of *n*-channel *JFET* with normal polarities. The circuit action is as under:

(*i*) When a voltage V_{DS} is applied between drain and source terminals and voltage on the gate is zero [See Fig. 32.3 (*i*)], the two *pn* junctions at the sides of the bar establish depletion layers. The electrons will flow from source to drain through a channel between the depletion layers. The size of these layers determines the width of the channel and hence the amount of current conduction through the channel.

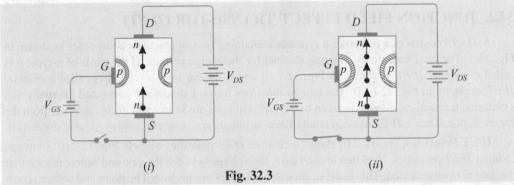

Fig. 32.3

(*ii*) When a reverse voltage V_{GS} is applied between gate and source [See Fig. 32.3 (*ii*)], the width of the depletion layers is increased. This reduces the width of conducting channel, thereby increasing the resistance of *n*-type bar. Consequently, the current from source to drain is decreased. On the other hand, if the reverse voltage on the gate is decreased, the width of the depletion layers also decreases. This increases the width of the conducting channel and hence source to drain current.

It is clear from the above discussion that current from source to drain can be controlled by the application of potential (*i.e.*, electric field) on the gate. For this reason, the device is called *field effect transistor*. It may be noted that a *p*-channel *JFET* operates in the same manner as an *n*-channel *JFET* except that channel current carries will be holes instead of electrons and the polarities of V_{GS} and V_{DS} are reversed.

32.4. SCHEMATIC SYMBOL OF *JFET*

Fig. 32.4 shows the schematic symbol of *JFET*. The vertical line in the symbol may be thought as channel and source and drain connected to this line. If the channel is *n*-type, the arrow on the gate is given as shown in Fig. 32.4 (*i*) whereas for *p*-type channel, the arrow on the gate is as shown in Fig. 32.4 (*ii*). Note that in the symbol, drain and source are symmetrical because they are interchangeable.

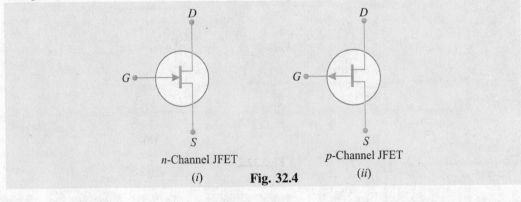

n-Channel JFET   *p*-Channel JFET

(*i*)   **Fig. 32.4**   (*ii*)

32.5. IMPORTANCE OF *JFET*

A *JFET* acts like a voltage controlled device *i.e.,* input voltage (V_{GS}) controls the output current. This is different from ordinary transistor (or bipolar transistor) where input current controls the output current. Thus *JFET* is a semiconductor device acting *like a vacuum tube.

The need for *JFET* arose because as modern electronic equipment became increasingly transistorised, it became apparent that there were many functions in which biopolar transistors were unable to replace vacuum tubes. Owing to their extremely high input impedance, *JFET* devices are more like vacuum tubes than

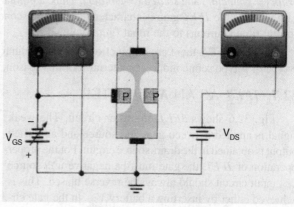

JFET biased for conduction

are the biopolar devices and are hence able to take over many vacuum-tube functions. Thus, because of the *JFET*, electronic equipment is closer today to being completely solid state.

The *JFET* devices have not only taken over the functions of vacuum tubes but they now also threaten to depose the bipolar transistors as the most widely used semiconductor devices. As an amplifier, the *JFET* provides a higher input impedance than a conventional transistor, generates less self-noise and has greater resistance to nuclear radiations.

32.6. DIFFERENCE BETWEEN *JFET* AND BIPOLAR TRANSISTOR

The *JFET* differs from an ordinary or bipolar transistor in the following ways :

(*i*) In a *JFET*, there is only one type of carrier, holes in *p*-type channel and electrons in *n*-type channel. For this reason, it is also called a unipolar transistor. However, in an ordinary transistor, both holes and electrons play part in conduction. Therefore, an ordinary transistor is sometimes called a bipolar transistor.

(*ii*) As the input circuit (*i.e.,* gate to source) of a *JFET* is reverse biased, therefore, the device has high input impedance. However, the input circuit of an ordinary

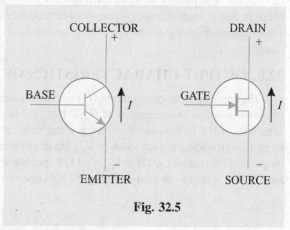

Fig. 32.5

transistor is forward biased and hence has low input impedance.

(*iii*) As the gate is reverse biased, therefore, it carries very small current. Obviously, *JFET* is just like a vacuum tube where control grid (corresponding to gate in *JFET*) carries extremely small current and input voltage controls the output current. For this reason, *JFET* is essentially a *voltage driven device.* However, an ordinary transistor is a current driven device *i.e.,* input current controls the output current.

. . . .

* The gate, source and drain of a *JFET* correspond to grid, cathode and anode of a vacuum tube.

(*iv*) A bipolar transistor uses a current into its base to control a large current between collector and emitter, whereas a *JFET* uses voltage on the *gate* (= *base*) terminal to control the current between *drain* (= *collector*) and *source* (= *emitter*). Thus, a bipolar transistor gain is characterised by current gain whereas the *JFET* gain is characterised as a transconductance *i.e.*, the ratio of change in output current (drain current) to the input (*gate*) voltage.

(*v*) In a *JFET*, there are no junctions as in an ordinary transistor. The conduction is through an *n*-type or *p*-type semiconductor material. For this reason, noise level in *JFET* is very small.

32.7. *JFET* AS AN AMPLIFIER

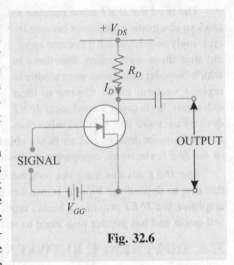

Fig. 32.6

Fig. 32.6 shows *JFET* amplifier circuit. The weak signal is applied between gate and source and amplified output is obtained in the drain-source circuit. For the proper operation of *JFET*, the gate must be negative *w.r.t* source *i.e.*, input circuit should always be reverse biased. This is achieved either by inserting a battery V_{GG} in the gate circuit or by a circuit known as biasing circuit. In the present case, we are providing biasing by the battery V_{GG}.

Operation. A small change in the reverse bias on the gate produces a large change in drain current. This fact makes *JFET* capable of raising the strength of a weak signal. During the positive half-cycle of the signal, the reverse bias on the gate decreases. This increases the channel width and hence the drain current. During negative half-cycle of the signal, the reverse bias on the gate increases. Consequently, the drain current decreases. The result is that a small change in gate voltage produces a large change in drain current. These large variations in drain current produce large output across the load R_D. In this way, *JFET* acts as an amplifier.

32.8. OUTPUT CHARACTERISTICS OF *JFET*

The curve between drain current (I_D) and drain-source voltage (V_{DS}) at constant gate voltage (V_{GS}) is known as output characteristics of *JFET*. Fig. 32.7 shows the circuit for determining the output characteristics of *JFET*. Keeping V_{GS} fixed at some value, say – 1V, the drain-source voltage is changed in steps. Corresponding to each value of V_{DS}, the drain current I_D is noted. A plot of these values gives the output characteristics of *JFET* at $V_{GS} = -1V$. Repeating similar procedure, output characteristics at other gate-source voltages can be drawn. Fig. 32.8 shows a family of output characteristics.

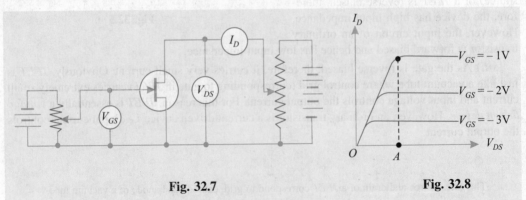

Fig. 32.7   **Fig. 32.8**

The following points may be noted from the characteristics :

(i) At first, the drain current I_D rises rapidly with drain-source voltage V_{DS} but then becomes constant. The drain-source voltage above which the drain current becomes constant is known as *pinch off voltage*. Thus, in Fig. 32.8, *OA* is the pinch off voltage.

(ii) After pinch off voltage, the channel width becomes so narrow that depletion layers almost touch each other. The drain current passes through the small passage between these layers. Therefore, increase in drain current is very small with V_{DS} above pinch off voltage. Consequently, drain current remains constant.

(iii) The characteristics resemble those of a pentode valve.

32.9. IMPORTANT TERMS

In the analysis of a *JFET* circuit, the following terms are often used :

1. Shorted-gate drain current (I_{DSS})
2. Pinch off voltage (V_P)
3. Gate-source cut off voltage [$V_{GS}(off)$]

1. Shorted-gate drain current (I_{DSS}). *It is the drain current with source short-circuited to gate (i.e. $V_{GS} = 0$) and drain voltage (V_{DS}) equal to pinch off voltage.* It is sometimes called zero-bias current.

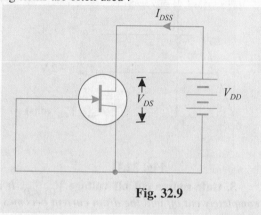

Fig. 32.9

Fig. 32.9 shows the *JFET* circuit with $V_{GS} = 0$ *i.e.*, source short-circuited to gate. This is normally called shorted-gate condition. Fig. 32.10 shows the graph between I_D and V_{DS} for the shorted gate condition. The drain current rises rapidly at first and then levels off at pinch off voltage V_P. The drain current has now reached the maximum value I_{DSS}. When V_{DS} is increased beyond V_P, the depletion layers expand at the top of the channel. The channel now acts as a current limiter and *holds drain current constant at I_{DSS}.

The following points may be noted carefully :

(i) Since I_{DSS} is measured under shorted gate conditions, it is the maximum drain current you can get with normal operation of *JFET*.

(ii) There is a maximum drain voltage [$V_{DS\ max}$] that can be applied to a *JFET*. If the drain voltage exceeds $V_{DS\ max}$, *JFET* would breakdown as shown in Fig. 32.10.

(iii) The region between V_P and $V_{DS\ max}$ is called *active region*. For proper working of *JFET*, it must be operated in the active region. Note that in the active region, the *JFET* behaves like a constant-current source.

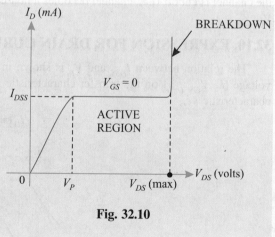

Fig. 32.10

---

* When drain voltage equals V_P, the channel becomes narrow and the depletion layers almost touch each other. The channel now acts as current limiter and holds drain current at a constant value of I_{DSS}.

2. Pinch off voltage V_P. *It is the minimum drain-source voltage at which the drain current essentially becomes constant.*

Fig. 32.11 shows the drain curves of a *JFET*. Note that pinch off voltage is V_p. The highest curve is for $V_{GS} = 0$, the shorted-gate condition. For values of V_{DS} greater than V_P, the drain current is almost constant. It is because when V_{DS} equals V_P, the channel is effectively closed and does not allow any further increase in drain current. It may be noted that for proper function of *JFET*, it is always operated for $V_{DS} > V_P$. However, V_{DS} should not exceed $V_{DS\,max}$ otherwise *JFET* may breakdown.

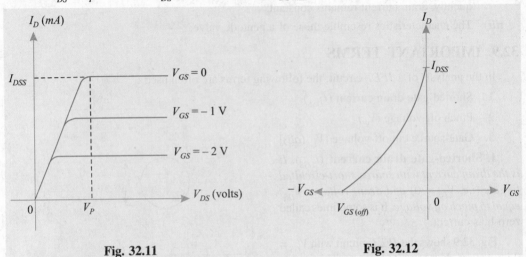

Fig. 32.11   Fig. 32.12

3. Gate-source cut off voltage $V_{GS\,(off)}$. *It is the gate-source voltage where the channel is completely cut off and the drain current becomes zero.*

The idea of gate-source cut off voltage can be easily understood if we refer to the transfer characteristic of a *JFET* shown in Fig. 32.12. As the reverse gate-source voltage is increased, the cross-sectional area of the channel decreases. This in turn decreases the drain current. At some reverse gate-source voltage, the depletion layers extend completely across the channel. In this condition, the channel is cut off and the drain current reduces to zero. The gate voltage at which the channel is cut off (*i.e.*, channel becomes a non-conductor) is called gate-source cut off voltage $V_{GS\,(off)}$.

32.10. EXPRESSION FOR DRAIN CURRENT (I_D)

The relation between I_{DSS} and V_P is shown in Fig. 32.13. We note that gate-source cut off voltage [*i.e.* $V_{GS\,(off)}$] on the transfer characteristic is equal to pinch off voltage V_P on the drain characteristic *i.e.*,

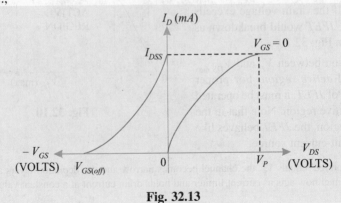

Fig. 32.13

$$V_P = |V_{GS\,(off)}|$$

For example, if a *JFET* has $V_{GS\,(off)} = -4V$, then $V_P = 4V$.

The transfer characteristic of *JFET* shown in Fig. 32.13 is part of a parabola. A rather complex mathematical analysis yields the following expression for drain current :

$$I_D = I_{DSS}\,[1 - V_{GS}/V_{GS\,(off)}]^2$$

where

I_D = drain current at given V_{GS}

I_{DSS} = shorted-gate drain current

V_{GS} = gate-source voltage

$V_{GS\,(off)}$ = gate-source cut off voltage

Example 32.1. *Fig. 32.14 shows the transfer characteristic of a JFET. Write the equation for drain current.*

Solution. Referring to the transfer characteristic in Fig. 32.14, we have,

$$I_{DSS} = 12\ mA$$
$$V_{GS\,(off)} = -5\ V$$

∴
$$I_D = I_{DSS}\,[1 - V_{GS}/V_{GS\,(off)}]^2$$

or
$$I_D = 12\,[1 + V_{GS}/5]^2\ mA$$

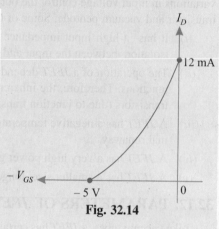

Fig. 32.14

Example 32.2. *A JFET has the following parameters :*

$$I_{DSS} = 32\ mA;\ V_{GS\,(off)} = -8\ V;\ V_{GS} = -4.5\ V$$

Find the value of drain current.

Solution.
$$I_D = I_{DSS}\,[1 - V_{GS}/V_{GS\,(off)}]^2$$
$$= 32\,[1 - (-4.5)/-8]^2$$
$$= \mathbf{6.12\ mA}$$

Example 32.3. *A JFET has a drain current of a 5 mA. If $I_{DSS} = 10\ mA$ and $V_{GS(off)} = -6V$, find the value of (i) V_{GS} and (ii) V_P.*

Solution. (i)
$$I_D = I_{DSS}\,[1 - V_{GS}/V_{GS\,(off)}]^2$$

or
$$5 = 10\,[1 + V_{GS}/6]^2$$

or
$$1 + V_{GS}/6 = \sqrt{5/10} = 0.707$$

∴
$$V_{GS} = \mathbf{-1.76V}$$

(ii)
$$V_P = V_{GS\,(off)} = \mathbf{6V}$$

Example 32.4. *In Fig. 32.15, what is the drain source voltage when V_{GS} is zero ?*

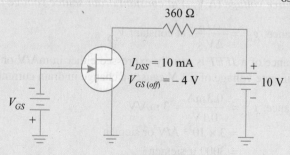

Fig. 32.15

Solution. Assume *JFET* to be a constant current source.

As $V_{GS} = 0$, the drain current is maximum and is equal to 10 mA. The circuit then reduces to the one shown in Fig. 32.16. This circuit consists of a current source of 10 mA in series with a resistance of 360 Ω and a battery of 10 V.

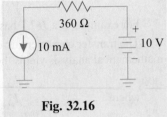

$$\therefore \qquad V_{DS} = 10\text{ V} - (10\text{ mA})(360\ \Omega) = \textbf{6.4 V}$$

Now $\qquad V_{GS\,(off)} = -4\text{V} \qquad \therefore V_P = 4\text{ V}$

As $V_{DS} > V_P$, therefore, the assumption of *JFET* as a constant current source is correct.

Fig. 32.16

32.11. ADVANTAGES OF *JFET*

A *JFET* is a voltage controlled, constant current device (similar to a pentode valve) in which variations in input voltage control the output current. It combines many advantages of both bipolar transistor and vacuum pentode. Some of them are :

(i) It has a high input impedance (of the order of 100*M* Ω). This permits high degree of isolation between the input and output circuits.

(ii) The operation of a *JFET* depends upon the bulk material current carriers that do not cross junctions. Therefore, the inherent noises of tubes (due to high temperature) and those of transistors (due to junction transitions) are not present in a *JFET*.

(iii) A *JFET* has a negative temperature co-efficient of resistance. This avoids the risk of thermal runaway.

(iv) A *JFET* has a very high power gain. This eliminates the necessity of using driver stages.

(v) A *JFET* has a smaller size, longer life and high efficiency.

32.12. PARAMETERS OF *JFET*

Like vaccum tubes, a *JFET* has certain parameters which determine its performance in a circuit. The main parameters of a *JFET* are (i) a.c. drain resistance (ii) transconductance and (iii) amplification factor.

(i) *a.c. drain resistance* (r_d). *It is the ratio of change in drain-source voltage* (ΔV_{DS}) *to the corresponding change in drain current* (ΔI_D) *at constant gate-source voltage i.e.,*

$$\text{a.c. drain resistance, } r_d = \frac{\Delta V_{DS}}{\Delta I_D} \text{ at constant } V_{GS}$$

For instance, if a change in drain voltage of 2*V* produces a change in drain current of 0.02 *mA*, then $r_d = 2$ V/0.02 mA = 100 kΩ. The drain resistance of a *JFET* has a large value, ranging from 10 kΩ to 1 MΩ.

(ii) **Transconductance** (g_m). *It is the ratio of change in drain current* (ΔI_D) *to the corresponding change in gate-source voltage* (ΔV_{GS}) *at constant drain-source voltage i.e.,*

$$\text{Transconductance, } g_m = \frac{\Delta I_D}{\Delta V_{GS}} \text{ at constant } V_{DS}$$

The transconductance of a *JFET* is usually expressed either in mA/V or microsiemens. As an example, if a change in gate voltage of 0.1 V causes a change in drain current of 0.3 mA, then,

$$\text{Transconductance, } g_m = \frac{0.3\,\text{mA}}{0.1\,\text{V}} = 3\text{ mA/V}$$
$$= 3 \times 10^{-3}\text{ A/V or siemen}$$
$$= 3000\ \mu\text{ siemen}$$

(iii) **Amplification factor** (μ). *It is the ratio of change in drain-source voltage* (ΔV_{DS}) *to the change in gate-source voltage* (ΔV_{GS}) *at constant drain current i.e.,*

Amplification factor, $\mu = \dfrac{\Delta V_{DS}}{\Delta V_{GS}}$ at constant I_D

Amplification factor of a *JFET* indicates how much more control the gate voltage has over drain current than has the drain voltage. For instance, if the amplification factor of a *JFET* is 50, it means that gate voltage is 50 times as effective as the drain voltage in controlling the drain current.

32.13. RELATION AMONG *JFET* PARAMETERS

The relationship among the above three parameters of *JFET* can be established as under :

We know, $\qquad\qquad \mu = \dfrac{\Delta V_{DS}}{\Delta V_{GS}}$

Multiplying the numerator and denominator on R.H.S. by ΔI_D, we get,

$$\mu = \dfrac{\Delta V_{DS}}{\Delta V_{GS}} \times \dfrac{\Delta I_D}{\Delta I_D}$$

$$= \dfrac{\Delta V_{DS}}{\Delta I_D} \times \dfrac{\Delta I_D}{\Delta V_{GS}}$$

$\therefore \qquad\qquad \mu = r_d \times g_m$

i.e., Amplification factor = A.C. drain resistance × Transconductance

32.14. GRAPHICAL MEANING OF TRANSCONDUCTANCE (g_m)

Fig. 32.17 shows the transfer characteristic of a *JFET*. To calculate g_m at any operating point, we select two nearby points like A and B on either side of the operating point (See Fig. 32.17). The ratio of change in I_D to the change in V_{GS} gives g_m at the chosen point. Similarly, we can select another pair of points like C and D and find the value of g_m between these points. Since transfer characteristic is a parabola, the value of g_m will be different at different points on the curve. The value of transconductance at $V_{GS} = 0$ (*i.e.,* value of g_m between points like C and D) is designated as g_{mo}. It can be proved mathematically that g_m at any operating point is given by;

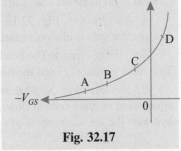

Fig. 32.17

$$g_m = g_{mo} [1 - V_{GS}/V_{GS\,(off)}]$$

Also $\qquad\qquad V_{GS\,(off)} = -\dfrac{2\,I_{DSS}}{g_{mo}}$

$$|V_{GS\,(off)}| = |V_P|$$

Example 32.5. *The following readings were obtained experimentally from a JFET:*

V_{GS}	0 V	0 V	– 0.2 V
V_{DS}	7 V	15 V	15 V
I_D	10 mA	10.25 mA	9.65 mA

Determine (i) a.c. drain resistance (ii) transconductance and (iii) amplification factor.

Solution.

(i) With V_{GS} constant at 0 V, the increase in V_{DS} from 7 V to 15 V increases the drain current from 10 mA to 10.25 mA *i.e.,* $\Delta V_{DS} = 15 - 7 = 8$ V and $\Delta I_D = 10.25 - 10 = 0.25$ mA.

$\therefore$ A.C. drain resistance, $r_d = \dfrac{\Delta V_{DS}}{\Delta I_D} = \dfrac{8V}{0.25\,mA} = 32\ k\Omega$

(ii) With V_{DS} constant at 15V, drain current changes from 10.25 mA to 9.65 mA as V_{GS} changes from 0 to – 0.2 V *i.e.,* $\Delta I_D = 10.25 - 9.65 = 0.6$ mA and $\Delta V_{GS} = 0.2$ V.

Transconductance, $g_m = \dfrac{\Delta I_D}{\Delta V_{GS}} = \dfrac{0.6\,\text{mA}}{0.2\,\text{V}}$

$= 3\ \text{mA/V} = 3000\ \mu\ \text{mho or } 3000\ \mu\text{S}$

Note that the symbol S is for the unit *siemens* formerly referred to as *mho*.

(*iii*) Amplification factor, $\mu = r_d \times g_m$

$= (32 \times 10^3) \times (3000 \times 10^{-6}) = 96$

Example 32.6. *For an n-channel JFET, $I_{DSS} = 32$ mA, $V_{GS\,(off)} = -8V$, $V_{GS} = -4.5V$. Find the values of (i) I_D (ii) g_{mo} and (iii) g_m.*

Solution.

(*i*)
$$I_D = I_{DSS}\left[1 - \frac{V_{GS}}{V_{GS\,(off)}}\right]^2$$

$$= 32\left[1 - \frac{-4.5}{-8}\right]^2 = 6.12\ \text{mA}$$

(*ii*)
$$g_{mo} = \frac{-2\,I_{DSS}}{V_{GS\,(off)}} = \frac{-2 \times 32}{-8} = 8\ \text{mS}$$

(*iii*)
$$g_m = g_{mo}\left[1 - \frac{V_{GS}}{V_{GS\,(off)}}\right] = 8\left(1 - \frac{-4.5}{-8}\right) = 3.5\ \text{mS}$$

32.15. *JFET* BIASING

For the proper operation of *JFET*, gate must be negative *w.r.t.* source. This can be achieved either by inserting a battery in the gate circuit or by a circuit known as biasing circuit. The latter method is prefered because batteries are costly and require frequent replacement.

1. Bias battery. Fig. 32.18 shows the biasing of a *JFET* by a bias battery V_{GG}. This battery ensures that gate is always negative *w.r.t.* source during all parts of the signal.

2. Biasing circuit. The biasing circuit uses supply voltage V_{DD} to provide the necessary bias. Two most commonly used methods are (*i*) self-bias (*ii*) potential divider method.

(*i*) **Self-bias.** Fig. 32.19 shows the self-bias method. The resistor R_S is the bias resistor. The d.c. component of drain current flowing through R_S produces the desired bias voltage. The capacitor C_S bypasses the *a.c.* component of the drain current.

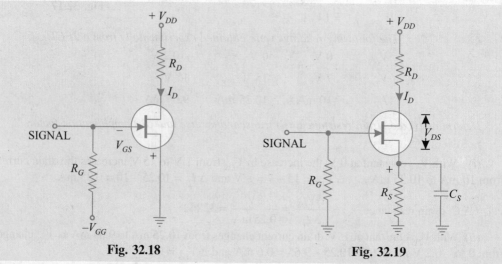

Fig. 32.18   **Fig. 32.19**

Voltage across R_S, $V_S = I_D R_S$

Since gate current is negligibly small, the gate terminal is at *d.c.* ground *i.e.*, $V_G = 0$.

∴ $$V_{GS} = V_G - V_S = 0 - I_D R_S$$

or $$V_{GS} = -I_D R_S$$

Thus, bias voltage V_{GS} keeps gate negative *w.r.t.* source.

Operating point. The *d.c.* operating point (*i.e.*, zero signal I_D and V_{DS}) can be easily determined. Since the parameters of *JFET* are usually known, zero signal I_D can be calculated from the following relation :

$$I_D = I_{DSS} \left[1 - \frac{V_{GS}}{V_{GS(off)}} \right]^2$$

Also $$V_{DS} = V_{DD} - I_D (R_D + R_S)$$

Thus, *d.c.* conditions of *JFET* amplifier are fully specified.

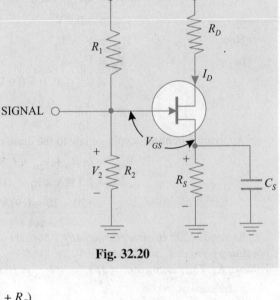

(ii) **Potential divider method.** Fig. 32.20 shows potential divider method of biasing a *JFET*. This circuit is identical to that used for a transistor. The resistors R_1 and R_2 form a voltage divider across drain supply V_{DD}. The voltage V_2 across R_2 provides the necessary bias.

$$V_2 = \frac{V_{DD}}{R_1 + R_2} \times R_2$$

Now $$V_2 = V_{GS} + I_D R_S$$

or $$V_{GS} = V_2 - I_D R_S$$

The circuit is so designed that $I_D R_S$ is larger than V_2 so that V_{GS} is negative. This provides correct bias voltage. We can find the operating point as under :

$$I_D = \frac{V_2 - V_{GS}}{R_S}$$

and $$V_{DS} = V_{DD} - I_D (R_D + R_S)$$

Fig. 32.20

32.16. *JFET* CONNECTIONS

There are three leads in a *JFET viz.*, source, gate and drain terminals. However, when a *JFET* is to be connected in a circuit, we require four terminals; two for the input and two for output. This difficulty is overcome by making one terminal of the *JFET* common to both input and output terminals. Accordingly; a *JFET* can be connected in a circuit in the following three ways :

(i) Common source connection

(ii) Common gate connection

(iii) Common drain connection

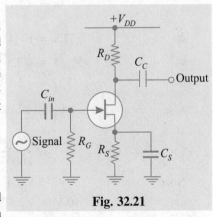

Fig. 32.21

The common source connection is the most widely used arrangement. It is because this connection provides high input impedance, good voltage gain and a moderate output impedance. However, the circuit produces phase reversal *i.e.*, output signal is 180° out of phase with the input signal. Fig. 32.21 shows a common source *n*-channel *JFET* amplifier. Note that source terminal is common to both input and output.

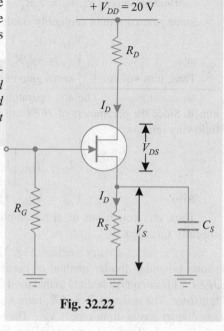

Example 32.7. *In a self-bias n-channel JFET circuit, the operating point is to be set at $I_D = 1.5$ mA and $V_{DS} = 10V$. The JFET parameters are $I_{DSS} = 5$ mA and $V_{GS(off)} = -2V$. Find the values of R_S and R_D. Given that $V_{DD} = 20$ V.*

Solution.

$$I_D = I_{DSS}\left[1 - \frac{V_{GS}}{V_{GS(off)}}\right]^2$$

or $\qquad 1.5 = 5\,(1 + V_{GS}/2)^2$

or $\qquad 1 + V_{GS}/2 = \sqrt{1.5/5} = 0.55$

or $\qquad V_{GS} = -0.9$ V

Now $\qquad V_{GS} = V_G - V_S$

or $\qquad V_S = V_G - V_{GS}$

$\qquad\qquad = 0 - (-0.9) = 0.9$ V

$\therefore \qquad R_S = \dfrac{V_S}{I_D} = \dfrac{0.9\,\text{V}}{1.5\,\text{mA}} = 0.6\,\text{k}\Omega$

Fig. 32.22

Applying Kirchhoff's voltage law to the drain circuit,

$$V_{DD} = I_D R_D + V_{DS} + I_D R_S$$
$$20 = 1.5\ \text{mA} \times R_D + 10 + 0.9$$

$\therefore \qquad R_D = \dfrac{(20 - 10 - 0.9)\,\text{V}}{1.5\,\text{mA}} = 6\,\text{k}\Omega$

Example 32.8. *In an n-channel JFET biased by potential divider method, it is desired to set the operating point at $I_D = 2.5$ mA and $V_{DS} = 8V$. If $V_{DD} = 30$ V, $R_1 = 1M\,\Omega$ and $R_2 = 500\,k\,\Omega$, find the value of R_S. The parameters of JFET are $I_{DSS} = 10$ mA and $V_{GS(off)} = -5$ V.*

Solution.

$$I_D = I_{DSS}\left[1 - \frac{V_{GS}}{V_{GS(off)}}\right]^2$$

or $\qquad 2.5 = 10\,(1 + V_{GS}/5)^2$

or $\qquad 1 + V_{GS}/5 = \sqrt{2.5/10} = 0.5$

or $\qquad V_{GS} = -2.5$ V

Now, $\qquad V_2 = \dfrac{V_{DD}}{R_1 + R_2} \times R_2$

$\qquad\qquad = \dfrac{30}{1000 + 500} \times 500 = 10$ V

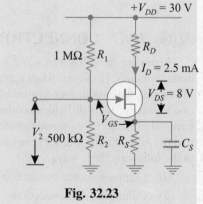

Fig. 32.23

Now $\qquad V_2 = V_{GS} + I_D R_S$

or $\qquad 10\,\text{V} = -2.5\,\text{V} + 2.5\,\text{mA} \times R_S$

$\therefore \qquad R_S = \dfrac{10\,\text{V} + 2.5\,\text{V}}{2.5\,\text{mA}} = \dfrac{12.5\,\text{V}}{2.5\,\text{mA}} = 5\text{k}\,\Omega$

Example 32.9. *Draw the d.c. load line for the JFET amplifier shown in Fig. 32.24.*

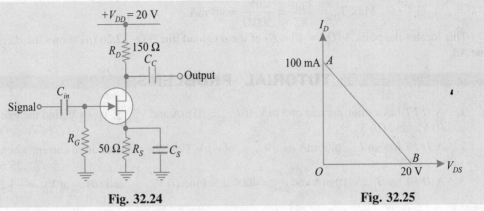

Fig. 32.24   Fig. 32.25

Solution. Consider the d.c. conditions in the circuit.

$$V_{DS} = V_{DD} - I_D (R_D + R_S)$$

This is a first degree equation and can be represented by a straight line on the drain characteristics. This is known as d.c. *load line* and determines the locus of I_D and V_{DS} (*i.e.*, operating point) in the absence of the signal. To draw *d.c.* load line, we require two end points *viz.* max. V_{DS} and max. I_D points.

$$\text{Max. } V_{DS} = V_{DD} = 20 \text{ V} \qquad\qquad \text{(putting } I_D = 0)$$

This locates the point *B* (*OB* = 20 V) of the d.c. load line.

$$\text{Max. } I_D = \frac{V_{DD}}{R_D + R_S} \qquad\qquad \text{(putting } V_{DS} = 0)$$

$$= \frac{20V}{(150 + 50)\Omega} = 100 \text{ mA}$$

This locates the points *A* (*OA* = 100 mA) of the *d.c.* load line. Joining *A* and *B*, we get *d.c.* load line *AB* [See Fig. 32.25].

Example 32.10. *Draw the d.c. load line for the JFET amplifier shown in Fig. 32.26 (i).*

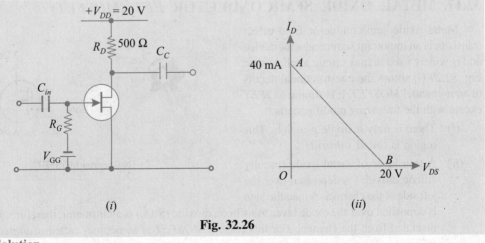

(*i*)   (*ii*)

Fig. 32.26

Solution.

$$\text{Max. } V_{DS} = V_{DD} = 20 \text{ V}$$

This locates the point B ($OB = 20$ V) of the *d.c.* load line.

$$\text{Max. } I_D = \frac{V_{DD}}{R_D} = \frac{20V}{500\Omega} = 40 \text{ mA}$$

This locates the point A ($OA = 40$ mA) of the d.c. load line. Fig. 32.26 (*ii*) shows the *d.c.* load line *AB*.

<hr>

TUTORIAL PROBLEMS

1. A *JFET* has a drain current of 5 mA. If $I_{DSS} = 10$ mA and $V_{GS\,(off)}$ is -6 V, find the value of (*i*) V_{GS} and (*ii*) V_P.   [(*i*) -1.5 V (*ii*) 6 V]

2. A *JFET* has an I_{DSS} of 9 mA and $V_{GS(off)}$ of -3 V. Find the value of drain current when V_{GS} $= -1.5$ V.   [2.25 mA]

3. A *JFET* has $I_{DSS} = 10$ mA and $g_{mo} = 4000$ μ S. Find (*i*) $V_{GS\,(off)}$ and (*ii*) g_m at $V_{GS} = -1.25$ V.   [(*i*) -5 V (*ii*) 3000 μ S]

4. In the *JFET* circuit shown in Fig. 32.27, if $I_D = 1.9$ mA, find V_{GS} and V_{DS}.   [(*i*) -1.56 V , 13.5 V]

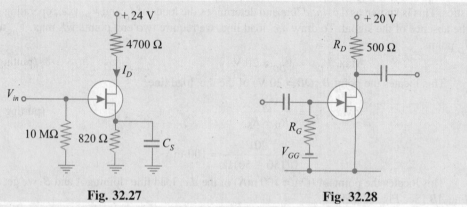

Fig. 32.27   **Fig. 32.28**

5. For the *JFET* amplifier shown in Fig. 32.28, draw the d.c. load line.

32.17. METAL OXIDE SEMICONDUCTOR *FET (MOSFET)*

Metal oxide semiconductor field effect transistor is an important semiconductor device and is widely used in may circuit applications. Fig. 32.29 (*i*) shows the constructional details of an *n*-channel *MOSFET*. It is similar to *JFET* except with the following modifications :

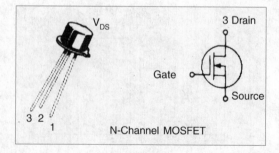

(*i*) There is only a single *p*-region. This region is called *substrate*.

(*ii*) A thin layer of metal oxide (usually silicon dioxide) is deposited over the left side of the channel. A metallic gate is deposited over the oxide layer. As silicon dioxide (SiO_2) is an insulator, therefore, gate is insulated from the channel. For this reason, *MOSFET* is sometimes called *insulated gate FET*.

(*iii*) Like a *JFET*, a *MOSFET* has three terminals *viz. source, gate,* and *drain*.

n-channel MOSFET. Fig. 32.29 (*i*) shows the various parts of an *n*-channel *MOSFET*. The *p*-type substrate constricts the channel between the source and drain so that only a small passage remains at the left side. Electrons flowing from source (when drain is positive *w.r.t.* source) must pass through this narrow channel.

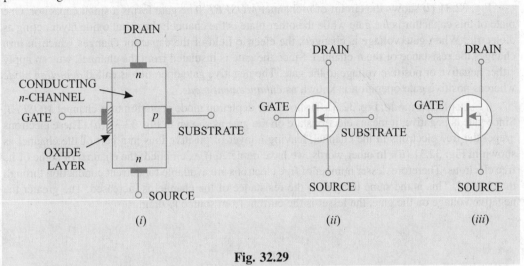

Fig. 32.29

The symbol for *n*-channel *MOSFET* is shown in Fig. 32.29 (*ii*). The gate appears like a capacitor plate. Just to the right of the gate is a thick vertical line representing the channel. The drain lead comes at the top of the channel and the source lead connects to the bottom. The arrow is on the substrate and points to the *n*-material, therefore, we have *n*-channel *MOSFET*. It is a usual practice to connect the substrate internally as shown in Fig. 32.29 (*iii*). This gives rise to a three terminal device.

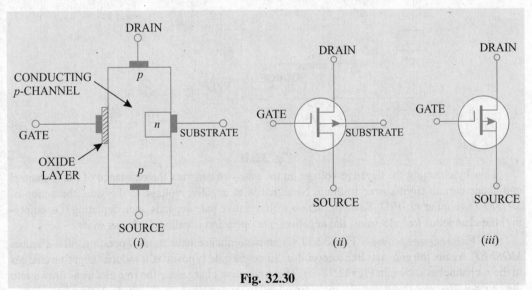

Fig. 32.30

p-channel MOSFET. Fig. 32.30 (*i*) shows the various parts of *p*-channel *MOSFET*. The *n*-type substrate constricts the channel between the source and drain so that only small passage remains at the left side. The conduction takes place by the flow of holes from source to drain through this narrow channel.

The symbol for *p*-channel *MOSFET* is shown in Fig. 32.30 (*ii*). It is a usual practice to connect the substrate to source internally as shown in Fig. 32.30 (*iii*). This results in a three terminal device.

32.18. WORKING OF MOSFET

Fig. 32.31 (*i*) shows the circuit of *n*-channel *MOSFET*. The gate forms a small capacitor. One plate of this capacitor is the gate while the other plate is the channel; the metal oxide layer acting as dielectric. When gate voltage is changed, the electric field of the capacitor changes which in turn changes the resistance of the *n*-channel. Since the gate is insulated from the channel, we can apply either negative or positive voltage to the gate. The negative gate operation is called *depletion mode* whereas positive gate operation is known as *enhancement mode*.

(*i*)   **Depletion mode.** Fig. 32.31 (*i*) shows the depletion mode operation of *n*-channel *MOSFET*. Since gate is negative, it means electrons are on the gate as shown in Fig. 32.31 (*ii*). These electrons *repel the free electrons in the channel, leaving a layer of positive ions in a part of the channel as shown in Fig. 32.31 (*ii*). In other words, we have depleted (*i.e.*, emptied) the channel of some of its free electrons. Therefore, lesser number of free electrons are available for current conduction through the channel. This is the same thing as if the resistance of the channel is increased. The greater the negative voltage on the gate, the lesser is the current from source to drain.

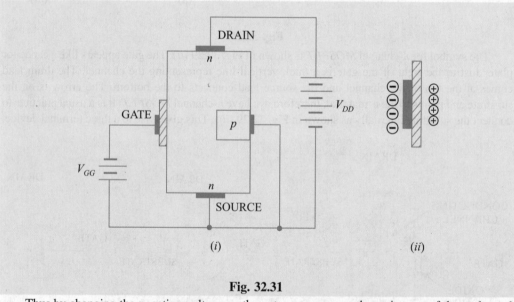

Fig. 32.31

Thus by changing the negative voltage on the gate, we can vary the resistance of the *n*-channel and hence current from source to drain. Note that with negative voltage to the gate, the action of *MOSFET* is similar to *JFET*. Since the action with negative gate depends upon depleting (*i.e.* emptying) the channel of free electrons, the negative-gate operation is called *depletion mode*.

(*ii*)   **Enhancement mode.** Fig. 32.32 (*i*) shows enhancement mode operation of *n*-channel *MOSFET*. Again, the gate acts like a capacitor. Since the gate is positive, it induces negative charges in the *n*-channel as shown in Fig. 32.32 (*ii*). These negative charges are the free electrons drawn into the channel. Because these free electrons are added to those already in the channel, the total number of free electrons in the channel is increased. Thus, a positive gate voltage *enhances* or increases the conductivity of the channel. The greater the positive voltage on the gate, greater is the current conduction from source to drain.

* *

*   If one plate of the capacitor is negatively charged, it induces positive charge on the other plate.

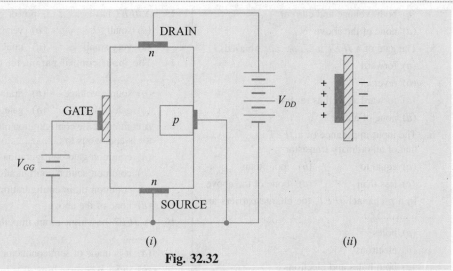

Fig. 32.32

Thus by changing the positive voltage on the gate, we can change the conductivity of the channel. The main difference between *MOFSET* and *JFET* is that we can apply positive gate voltage to *MOSFET* and still have essentially *zero current. Because the action with a positive gate depends upon *enhancing* the conductivity of the channel, the positive-gate operation is called *enhancement mode*.

Note. Because the device can be operated in depletion mode as well as enhancement mode, it is sometimes called Depletion-enhancement *MOSFET* (*i.e.*, *DE-MOSFET*). There is another kind of *MOSFET* which operates in enhancement mode only. It is known as *enhancement-only MOSFET*.

32.19. IMPORTANT POINTS ABOUT DE-MOSFET

The following points are worth noting about *MOSFET* operation :

(*i*) In a *MOSFET*, the source to drain current is controlled by the electric field of capacitor formed at the gate.

(*ii*) The gate of a *JFET* behaves as a reverse-biased junction whereas the gate of a *MOSFET* acts like a capacitor. For this reason, it is possible to operate a *MOSFET* with positive or negative gate voltage.

(*iii*) As the gate of *MOSFET* forms a capacitor, therefore, negligible gate current flows whether positive or negative voltage is applied to the gate. For this reason, the input impedance of *MOSFET* is very high, ranging from 10,000MΩ to 10,000,00MΩ.

MULTIPLE-CHOICE QUESTIONS

1. A *JFET* has three terminals, namely ....
   (*a*) cathode, anode, grid
   (*b*) emitter, base, collector
   (*c*) source, gate, drain
   (*d*) none of the above
2. A *JFET* is similar in operation to .... valve.

   (*a*) triode   (*b*) tetrode
   (*c*) pentode   (*d*) diode
3. A *JFET* is also called .... transistor.
   (*a*) bipolar   (*b*) unipolar
   (*c*) unijunction   (*d*) none of the above
4. A *JFET* is a .... driven device.
   (*a*) voltage   (*b*) current

---

* Note that gate of a *JFET* is always reverse biased for proper operation. However, in a *MOSFET*, because of insulating layer, a negligible gate current flows whether we apply negative or positive voltage to the gate.

(c) both voltage and current

(d) none of the above

5. The gate of a *JFET* is .... biased.

(a) forward

(b) reverse

(c) forward as well as reverse

(d) none of above

6. The input impedance of a *JFET* is .... that of an ordinary transistor.

(a) equal to

(b) more than

(c) less than

(d) none of the above

7. In a *p*-channel *JFET*, the charge carriers are ....

(a) holes

(b) electrons

(c) both holes and electrons

(d) ions

8. A *JFET* is characterised by .... gain.

(a) voltage

(b) current

(c) resistance

(d) none of the above

9. When drain voltage equals the pinch-off voltage, then drain current .... with the increase in drain voltage.

(a) decreases

(b) increases

(c) remains constant

(d) none of the above

10. If the reverse bias on the gate of a *JFET* is increased, then width of conducting channel ....

(a) remains the same

(b) is decreased

(c) is increased

(d) none of the above

11. A *MOSFET* has .... terminals.

(a) two

(b) five

(c) four

(d) three

12. A *MOSFET* can be operated with ....

(a) negative gate voltage only

(b) positive gate voltage only

(c) with both positive and negative gate voltage

(d) none of the above

13. A *JFET* has .... power gain.

(a) small

(b) very high

(c) very small

(d) none of the above

14. The input control parameter of a *JFET* is ....

(a) source voltage

(b) drain voltage

(c) gate voltage

(d) gate current

15. A common base configuration of a *pnp* transistor is analogous to .... of a *JFET*.

(a) common gate configuration

(b) common source configuration

(c) common drain configuration

(d) none of the above

16. A *JFET* has high input impedance because ....

(a) it is made of semiconductor material

(b) input is reverse biased

(c) of the impurity atoms

(d) none of the above

17. In a *JFET*, when drain voltage is equal to pinch-off voltage, the depletion layers ....

(a) almost touch each other

(b) have large gap

(c) have moderate gap

(d) none of the above

18. In a *JFET*, I_{DSS} is known as ....

(a) drain to source current

(b) drain to source current with gate shorted

(c) drain to source current with gate open

(d) none of the above

19. The two important advantages of a *JFET* are ....

(a) high input impedance and square-law property

(b) inexpensive and high output impedance

(c) low input impedance and high output impedance

(d) none of the above

20. .... has the least noise-level.

(a) Triode

(b) Ordinary transistor

(c) Tetrode

(d) *JFET*

Answers to Multiple-Choice Questions

1. (c)	2. (c)	3. (b)	4. (a)	5. (b)	6. (b)	7. (a)	8. (a)
9. (c)	10. (b)	11. (d)	12. (c)	13. (b)	14. (c)	15. (a)	16. (b)
17. (a)	18. (b)	19. (a)	20. (d)				

Hints to Selected Multiple-Choice Questions

2. The output characteristics of a *JFET* resemble to that of a pentode valve. Therefore it is similar in operation to a **pentode** valve.

3. In a *JFET*, there is only one type of carrier, holes in *p*-type channel and electrons in *n*-type channel. For this reason, it is also called a **unipolar** transistor.

4. In a *JFET*, the output characteristics are controlled by input voltage (*i.e.*, electric field). In other words, input voltage controls the output current. Therefore it is essentially a **voltage driven** device.

6. As the input circuit (*i.e.*, gate to source) of a *JFET* is reverse biased, therefore, the device has high input impedance greater than an ordinary transistor.

9. When V_{DS} equals V_p, the channel is effectively closed and does not allow further increase in drain current. Even if V_{DS} is increased *w.r.t.* V_p, the drain current is almost constant.

12. Unlike the *JFET*, a *MOSFET* has no gate diode. Therefore it is possible to operate the device with positive or negative gate voltage.

14. A small change in voltage at the gate produces a large change in drain current. Therefore it is the **gate voltage** which controls the amount of drain current flowing through *JFET*.

17. When drain voltage becomes equal to pinch off voltage, the depletion layers **almost touch each other**. The drain current passes through a small passage between these layers and essentially remains constant thereafter.

20. The operation of a *JFET* depends upon the bulk material current carriers that do not cross junctions. Therefore, the inherent noise of tubes (due to high-temperature operation) and those of transistors (due to junctions **transitions**) is not present in a *JFET*.

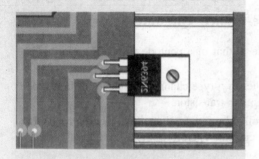

Power Electronics

INTRODUCTION

One major field of application of semiconductor devices in the recent years has been to control large blocks of power flow in a system. The branch of electronics which deals with the control of 50 Hz power flow in a system is called *power electronics*. Power electronics essentially deals with those semiconductor devices which can act as controlled switches. These devices can perform the duties of rectification, inversion, and regulation of power flow in a load. The important semiconductor switching devices are (*i*) Silicon controlled rectifier (*SCR*) (*ii*) Triac (*iii*) Diac and (*iv*) Unijuntion transistor (*UJT*). The purpose of this chapter is to deal with these important switching devices much used in power electronics.

33.1. SILICON CONTROLLED RECTIFIER

A silicon controlled rectifier is a semiconductor device that acts as a true electronic switch. It can change alternating current into direct current and at the same time can **control the amount of power fed to the load.

. . . .

*   The frequency of our power system is 50 Hz. Power electronics essentially deals with the control of 50Hz power and hence the name.

** It got this name because it is a silicon device and is used as a rectifier and that rectification can be controlled.

Thus, *SCR* combines the features of a rectifier and a transistor.

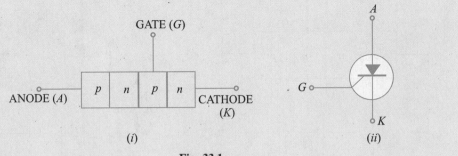

Fig. 33.1

Constructional details. When a *pn* junction is added to a junction transistor, the resulting three *pn* junction device is called a silicon controlled rectifier. Fig. 33.1 (*i*) shows its construction. It is clear that it is essentially an ordinary rectifier (*pn*) and a junction transistor (*npn*) combined in one unit to form *pnpn device*. Three terminals are taken; one from the outer *p*-type material and is called *anode A*, second from the outer *n*-type material called *cathode K* and the third from the base of the transistor section and is called *gate G*. In the normal operating conditions of *SCR*, anode is held at high positive potential *w.r.t.* cathode. Fig. 33.1 (*ii*) shows the symbol of *SCR*. The *SCR* is also known by the name *thyristor*.

Note. The device is made of silicon and not of germanium. It is because leakage current in silicon is very small as compared to germanium. Since the device is used as a switch, it will carry leakage current in the off condition which should be as small as possible.

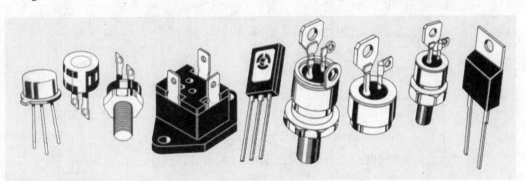

Typical SCR Packages

33.2. WORKING OF *SCR*

In a silicon controlled rectifier, load is connected in series with anode. The anode is always kept at positive potential *w.r.t.* cathode. The working of *SCR* can be studied under two headings :

(*i*) **When gate is open.** Fig. 33.2 shows the *SCR* circuit with gate open *i.e.* no voltage applied to the gate. Under this condition, junction J_2 is reverse biased while junctions J_1 and J_3 are forward biased. Since one of the three juctions (*i.e.*, junction J_2 in this case) is reverse biased, no current flows through the load R_L and the *SCR* is *cut off*. However, if the applied voltage is gradually increased, a stage is reached when * reverse biased junction J_2 breaks down. The *SCR* now conducts **heavily and is said to be in the *ON* state. The applied voltage at which *SCR* conducts heavily without gate voltage is called *Breakover voltage*.

---

*   The whole applied voltage *V* appears as reverse voltage across junction J_2 as junctions J_1 and J_3 are forward biased.

**   Because junctions J_1 and J_3 are forward biased and junction J_2 has broken down.

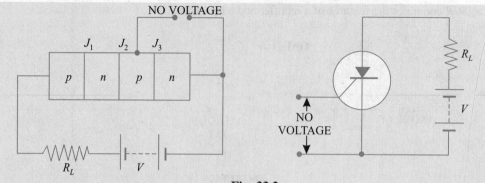

Fig. 33.2

(ii) When gate is positive w.r.t. cathode. The *SCR* can be made to conduct heavily at smaller applied voltage by applying a small positive potential to the gate as shown in Fig. 33.3. Now junction J_3 is forward biased and junction J_2 is reverse biased. The electrons from *n*-type material start moving across junction J_3 towards left whereas holes from *p*-type towards the right. Consequently, the electrons from junction J_3 are attracted across junction J_2 and gate current starts flowing. As soon as gate current flows, anode current increases. The increased anode current in turn makes more electrons available at junction J_2. This process continues and in an extremely small time, junction J_2 breaks down and the *SCR* starts conducting heavily. *Once SCR starts conducting, the gate* (the reason for this name is obvious) *loses all control.* Even if gate voltage is removed, the anode current does not decrease at all. The only way to stop conduction (*i.e.*, bring *SCR* in the off condition) is to reduce the applied voltage to zero.

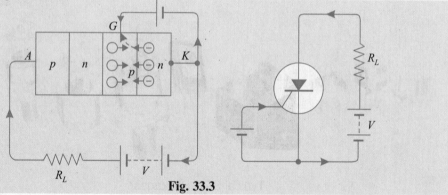

Fig. 33.3

Conclusion. The following conclusions are drawn from the working of *SCR* :

(i) An *SCR* has two states *i.e.*, either it does not conduct or it conducts heavily. There is no state inbetween. Therefore, *SCR* behaves like a switch.

(ii) There are two ways to turn on the *SCR*. The first method is to keep the gate open and make the supply voltage equal to the breakover voltage. The second method is to operate *SCR* with supply voltage less than breakover voltage and then turn it on by means of a small positive voltage (typically 1.5V, 30mA) applied to the gate.

(iii) *Applying small positive voltage to the gate is the normal way to close an SCR because the breakover voltage is usually much greater than supply voltage.*

(iv) To open the *SCR* (*i.e.*, to make it non-conducting), reduce the supply voltage to zero.

33.3. IMPORTANT TERMS

The following terms are much used in the study of *SCR* :

(i) Breakover voltage (ii) Peak inverse voltage (iii) Holding current (iv) Forward current rating.

(*i*) **Breakover voltage.** *It is the minimum forward voltage, gate being open, at which SCR starts conducting heavily i.e., turned on.*

Thus, if the breakover voltage of an *SCR* is 200V, it means that it can block a forward voltage (*i.e.*, *SCR* remains open) as long as the supply voltage is less than 200V. If the supply voltage is more than this value, then *SCR* will be turned on. In practice, *SCR* is operated with supply voltage less than breakover voltage and it is then turned on by means of a small positive voltage applied to the gate. Commercially available *SCRs* have breakover voltages from about 50V to 500V.

(*ii*) **Peak reverse voltage (*PRV*).** *It is the maximum reverse voltage (cathode being positive w.r.t. anode) that can be applied to an SCR without conducting in the reverse direction.*

Peak reverse voltage (*PRV*) is an important consideration while connecting an *SCR* in an a.c. circuit. During the negative half of a.c. supply, reverse voltage is applied across the *SCR*. If the *PRV* is exceeded, there may be avalanche breakdown and *SCR* will be damaged if the external circuit does not limit the current. Commercially available *SCRs* have *PRV* ratings upto 2.5kV.

(*iii*) **Holding current.** *It is the maximum anode current, gate being open, at which SCR is turned OFF from ON condition.*

As discussed earlier, when *SCR* is in the conducting state, it cannot be turned *OFF* even if gate voltage is removed. The only way to *turn off* or open the *SCR* is to reduce the supply voltage to almost zero at which point the internal transistor comes out of saturation and opens the *SCR*. The anode current under this condition is very small (a few mA) and is called *holding current.* Thus, if an *SCR* has a holding current of 5mA, it means that if anode current is made less than 5mA, then *SCR* will be *turned off.*

(*iv*) **Forward current rating.** *It is the maximum anode current that an SCR is capable of passing without destruction.*

Every *SCR* has a safe value of forward current which it can conduct. If the value of current exceeds this value, the *SCR* may be destroyed due to intensive heating at the junctions. For example, if an *SCR* has a forward current rating of 40*A*, it means that *SCR* can safely carry only 40*A*. Any attempt to exceed this value will result in the destruction of the *SCR*. Commercially available *SCRs* have forward current ratings from about 30*A* to 100*A*.

33.4. *V-I* CHARACTERISTICS OF *SCR*

It is the curve between anode-cathode voltage (*V*) and anode current (*I*) of an *SCR* at constant gate current. Fig. 33.4 shows the *V-I* characteristics of a typical *SCR*.

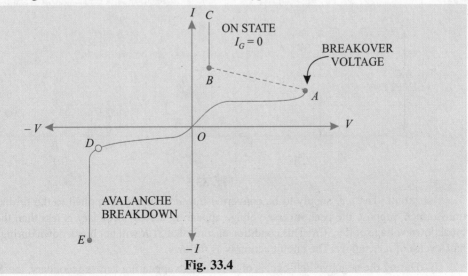

Fig. 33.4

(*i*) **Forward characteristics.** When anode is positive *w.r.t.* cathode, the curve between *V* and *I* is called the forward characteristic. In Fig. 33.4, *OABC* is the forward characteristic of *SCR* at $I_G = 0$. If the supply voltage is increased from zero, a point is reached (point *A*) when the *SCR* starts conducting. Under this condition, the voltage across *SCR* suddenly drops as shown by the dotted curve *AB* and most of the supply voltage appears across the load resistance R_L. If proper gate current is made to flow, *SCR* can close at much smaller supply voltage.

(*ii*) **Reverse characteristics.** When anode is negative *w.r.t.* cathode, the curve between *V* and *I* is known as reverse characteristic. The reverse voltage does come across *SCR* when it is operated with a.c. supply. If the reverse volage is gradually increased, at first the anode current remains small (*i.e.*, leakage current) and at some reverse voltage, avalanche breakdown occurs and the *SCR* starts conducting heavily in the reverse direction as shown by the curve *DE*. This maximum reverse voltage at which *SCR* starts conducting heavily in the reverse direction is known as *reverse breakdown voltage*.

33.5. SCR IN NORMAL OPERATION

In order to operate the *SCR* in normal operation, the following points are kept in view :

(*i*) The supply voltage is generally much less than the breakover voltage of the *SCR*.

(*ii*) The *SCR* is turned on by passing appropriate amount of gate current (a few mA) and not by breakover voltage.

(*iii*) When *SCR* is operated from a.c. supply, the peak reverse voltage which comes during negative half-cycle should not exceed the reverse breakdown voltage.

(*iv*) When *SCR* is to be turned *OFF* from the *ON* state, anode current should be reduced to holding current.

(*v*) If gate current is increased above the required value, the *SCR* will close at much reduced supply voltage.

33.6. *SCR* HALF-WAVE RECTIFIER

One important application of an *SCR* is the controlled half-wave rectification. Fig. 33.5 (*i*) shows the circuit of an *SCR* half-wave rectifier. The *a.c.* supply to be rectified is supplied through the transformer. The load resistance R_L is connected in series with the anode. A variable resistance *r* is inserted in the gate circuit to control the gate current.

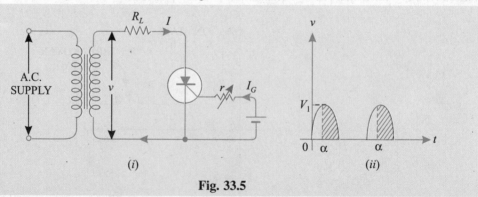

Fig. 33.5

Operation. The *a.c.* supply to be converted into *d.c.* supply is applied to the primary of the transformer. Suppose the peak inverse voltage appearing across secondary is less than the reverse breakdown voltage of the *SCR*. This condition ensures that *SCR* will not break down during negative half-cycles of *a.c.* supply. The circuit action is as follows.

(*i*) During the negative half-cycles of *a.c.* voltage appearing across secondary, the *SCR* does not conduct regardless of the gate voltage. It is because in this condition, anode is negative *w.r.t.* cathode and also *PIV* is less than the reverse breakdown voltage.

(*ii*) The *SCR* will conduct during the positive half-cycles provided proper gate current is made to flow. The greater the gate current, the lesser the supply voltage at which *SCR* is turned *ON*. The gate current can be changed by the variable resistance *r* as shown in Fig. 33.5 (*i*).

(*iii*) Suppose that gate current is adjusted to such a value that *SCR* closes at a positive voltage V_1 which is less than the peak voltage V_m. Referring to Fig. 33.5 (*ii*), it is clear that *SCR* will start conducting when secondary *a.c.* voltage becomes V_1 in the positive half-cycle. Beyond this, the *SCR* will continue to conduct till voltage becomes zero at which point it is turned *OFF*. Again at the start of the next positive half-cycle, *SCR* will start conducting when secondary voltage becomes V_1.

(*iv*) Referring to Fig. 33.5 (*ii*), it is clear that firing angle is α *i.e.*, at this angle in the positive half-cycle, *SCR* starts conduction. The conduction angle is = φ = 180° – α.

It is worthwhile to distinguish between an ordinary half-wave rectifier and *SCR* half-wave rectifier. Whereas an ordinary half-wave rectifier will conduct full positive half-cycle, an *SCR* half-wave rectifier can be made to conduct full or part of a positive half-cycle by proper adjustment of gate current. Therefore, an *SCR* can control power fed to the load and hence the name *controlled rectifier*.

Mathematical treatment. Referring to Fig. 33.5 (*i*), let $v = V_m \sin\theta$ be the alternating voltage that appears across the secondary. Let α be the firing angle. It means that rectifier will conduct from α to 180° during the positive half-cycle.

∴ Average voltage output, $V_{av} = \dfrac{1}{2\pi} \int_{\alpha}^{180°} V_m \sin\theta \, d\theta = \dfrac{V_m}{2\pi} \int_{\alpha}^{180°} \sin\theta \, d\theta$

$$= \frac{V_m}{2\pi} [-\cos\theta]_{\alpha}^{180°}$$

$$= \frac{V_m}{2\pi} (\cos\alpha - \cos 180°)$$

∴ $\qquad V_{av} = \dfrac{V_m}{2\pi} (1 + \cos\alpha)$

Average current, $\qquad I_{av} = \dfrac{V_{av}}{R_L} = \dfrac{V_m}{2\pi R_L} (1 + \cos\alpha)$

The following points may be noted :

(*i*) If the firing angle α = 0°, then full positive half-cycle will appear across the load R_L and the output current becomes ;

$$I_{av} = \frac{V_m}{2\pi R_L} (1 + \cos 0°) = \frac{V_m}{\pi R_L}$$

This is the value of average current for ordinary half-wave rectifier. This is expected since the full positive half-cycle is being conducted.

(*ii*) If α = 90°, then average current is given by :

$$I_{av} = \frac{V_m}{2\pi R_L} (1 + \cos 90°) = \frac{V_m}{2\pi R_L}$$

This shows that greater the firing angle α, the smaller is the average current and *vice-versa*.

Example 33.1. *A half-wave rectifier circuit employing an SCR is adjusted to have a gate current of 1mA. The forward breakdown voltage of SCR is 100V for* $I_G = 1mA$*. If a sinusoidal voltage of 200V peak is applied, find :*

(i) firing angle   (ii) conduction angle   (iii) average current.

Assume load resistance = 100Ω and the holding current to be zero.

Solution. $v = V_m \sin \theta$

Here, $v = 100 \text{ V}, V_m = 200 \text{ V}$

(i) ∴ $100 = 200 \sin \theta$

or $\sin \theta = \dfrac{100}{200} = 0.5$

∴ $\theta = \sin^{-1}(0.5) = 30°$ i.e., Firing angle, $\alpha = \theta = 30°$

(ii) Conduction angle, $\phi = 180° - \alpha = 180° - 30° = 150°$

(iii)   Average voltage $= \dfrac{V_m}{2\pi}(1 + \cos\alpha) = \dfrac{200}{2\pi}(1 + \cos 30°) = 59.25 \text{ V}$

∴   Average current $= \dfrac{\text{Average voltage}}{R_L} = \dfrac{59.25}{100} = 0.5925 \text{ A}$

Example 33.2. *Power (brightness) of a 100 W, 110 V tungsten lamp is to be varied by controlling the firing angle of an SCR in a half-wave circuit supplied with 110 V a.c. What r.m.s. voltage and current are developed in the lamp at firing angle* $\alpha = 60°$?

Solution. The a.c. voltage is given by;

$$v = V_m \sin \theta$$

Let α be the firing angle as shown in Fig. 33.6. This means that *SCR* will fire (*i.e.*, start conducting) at $\theta = \alpha$. Clearly, the *SCR* will conduct from α to 180°.

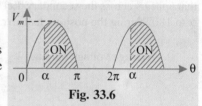

Fig. 33.6

$$E_{r.m.s.}^2 = \frac{1}{2\pi}\int_{\alpha}^{\pi} V_m^2 \sin^2\theta \, d\theta$$

$$= V_m^2 \, {}^{*}\frac{2(\pi - \alpha) + \sin 2\alpha}{8\pi}$$

∴ $E_{r.m.s.} = V_m \sqrt{\dfrac{2(\pi - \alpha) + \sin 2\alpha}{8\pi}}$

Here, $V_m = \sqrt{2} \times 110 = 156 \text{V}; \quad \alpha = 60° = \pi/3$

∴ $E_{r.m.s.} = 156\sqrt{\dfrac{2(\pi - \pi/3) + \sin 120°}{8\pi}} = 70 \text{ V}$

Lamp resistance, $R_L = \dfrac{V^2}{P} = \dfrac{(110)^2}{100} = 121 \, \Omega$

∴ $I_{r.m.s.} = \dfrac{E_{r.m.s.}}{R_L} = \dfrac{70}{121} = 0.58 \text{ A}$

Comments. The load current can be decreased by increasing the firing angle. The larger the value of α, the smaller is the load current and *vice-versa*. This method of controlling power is very efficient because other methods, such as added resistance, waste much power in the added control element.

. . . .

*   On carrying out the integration.

33.7. *SCR* FULL-WAVE RECTIFIER

Fig. 33.7 (*i*) shows the circuit of *SCR* full-wave rectifier. It is exactly like an ordinary centre-tap circuit except that the two diodes have been replaced by two *SCRs*. The gates of both *SCRs* get their supply from two gate controls. One *SCR* conducts during the positive half-cycle and the other during the negative half-cycle. Consequently, full-wave rectified output is obtained across the load.

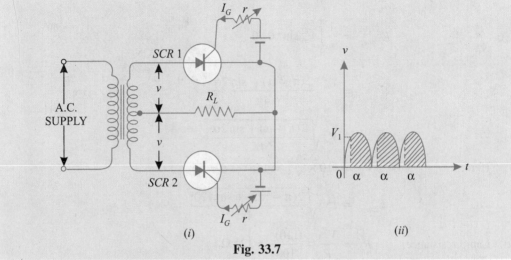

(*i*)   (*ii*)

Fig. 33.7

Operation. The angle of conduction can be changed by adjusting the gate currents. Suppose the gate currents are so adjusted that *SCRs* conduct as the secondary voltage (across half winding) becomes V_1. During the positive half-cycle of *a.c.* across secondary, the upper end of secondary is positive and the lower end negative. This will cause *SCR* 1 to conduct. However, the conduction will start only when the voltage across the upper half of secondary becomes V_1 as shown in Fig. 33.7 (*ii*). In this way, only shaded portion of positive half-cycle will pass through the load.

During the negative half-cycle of a.c. input, the upper end of secondary becomes negative and the lower end positive. This will cause *SCR* 2 to conduct when the voltage across the lower half of secondary becomes V_1. It may be seen that current through the load is in the same direction (*d.c.*) on both half -cycles of input a.c. The obvious advantage of this circuit over ordinary full-wave rectifier circuit is that by adjusting the gate currents, we can change the conduction angle and hence the output voltage.

Mathematical treatment. Referring to Fig. 33.7 (*i*), let $v = V_m \sin\theta$ be the alternating voltage that appears between centre tap and either end of secondary. Let α be the firing angle.

Average voltage output, $V_{av} = \dfrac{1}{\pi}\displaystyle\int_\alpha^{180°} V_m \sin\theta\, d\theta = \dfrac{V_m}{\pi}\displaystyle\int_\alpha^{180°} \sin\theta\, d\theta$

$$= \frac{V_m}{\pi}[-\cos\theta]_\alpha^{180°} = \frac{V_m}{\pi}(\cos\alpha - \cos 180°)$$

$$\therefore \qquad V_{av} = \frac{V_m}{\pi}(1 + \cos\alpha)$$

This is double that of a half-wave rectifier. It is expected since now negative half-cycle is also rectified.

Average currrent, $\qquad I_{av} = \dfrac{V_{av}}{R_L} = \dfrac{V_m}{\pi R_L}(1 + \cos\alpha)$

Example 33.3. Power (brightness) of a 100W, 110 V lamp is to be varied by controlling firing angle of SCR full-wave circuit; the r.m.s. value of a.c. voltage appearing across each SCR being 110V. Find the r.m.s. voltage and current in the lamp at firing angle of 60°.

Solution. Let $v = V_m \sin \theta$ be the alternating voltage that appears between centre tap and either end of secondary. Let α be the firing angle as shown in Fig. 33.8. This means that SCR will conduct at $\theta = \alpha$. Clearly, SCR circuit will conduct from α to 180°.

$$E_{r.m.s.}^2 = \frac{1}{\pi} \int_\alpha^\pi V_m^2 \sin^2 \theta \, d\theta$$

$$= V_m^2 * \frac{2(\pi - \alpha) + \sin 2\alpha}{4\pi}$$

∴ $$E_{r.m.s.} = V_m \sqrt{\frac{2(\pi - \alpha) + \sin 2\alpha}{4\pi}}$$

Here, $$V_m = 110 \times \sqrt{2} = 156V; \quad \alpha = 60°$$

∴ $$E_{r.m.s.} = 156 \sqrt{\frac{2(\pi - \pi/3) + \sin 120°}{4\pi}} = 98.9 \text{ V}$$

Lamp resistance, $$R_L = \frac{V^2}{P} = \frac{(110)^2}{100} = 121 \, \Omega$$

∴ $$I_{r.m.s.} = \frac{E_{r.m.s.}}{R_L} = \frac{98.9}{121} = 0.82 \text{ A}$$

Fig. 33.8 (with labels: V_m, $\alpha = 60°$, ON, ON, 0, α, π, α, 2π, θ)

33.8. APPLICATIONS OF SCR

The ability of an SCR to **control large currents in a load by means of small gate current makes this device useful in switching and control applications. Two important applications of SCR are given below by way of illustration.

(*i*) *SCR for power control.* It is often necessary to control power delivered to some load such as the heating element of a furnace. Series resistances or potentiometers cannot be used because they waste power in high power circuits. Under such conditions, silicon controlled rectifiers are used which are capable of adjusting the transmitted power with little waste.

Fig. 33.9 shows a common circuit for controlling power in the load R_L. During the positive half-cycle of *a.c.* supply, end A is positive and end B is negative. Therefore, capacitor C_2 is charged through $AD_1 RC_2 D_4 B$. The charge on capacitor C_2 depends upon the value of potentiometer R. When capacitor C_2 is charged through a sufficient voltage, it discharges through the zener Z. This gives a pulse to the primary and hence secondary of transformer T_2. This turns on SCR 2 which

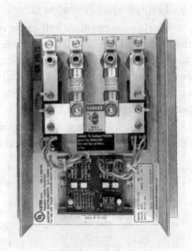

SCR Power Control

---

* On carrying out the integration.

** When the SCR is in the *OFF* state, current through it is negligible and when it in the *ON* state, voltage across it is very small. This means that power loss in the device is very small. Since SCR is highly efficient controlled switch, it is widely used in switching applications.

conducts current through the load. During negative half-cycle of *a.c.* supply, end *A* is negative and end *B* positive. Therefore, capacitor C_1 is charged. It discharges through the zener and fires *SCR* 1 which conducts current through the load.

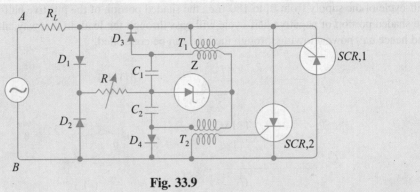

Fig. 33.9

The angle of conduction can be controlled by the potentiometer *R*. The greater the resistance of *R*, lesser is the voltage across C_1 or C_2 and hence smaller will be the time during which *SCR* 1 and *SCR* 2 will conduct in a full-cycle. In this way, we can control a large power of several kW in the load R_L with the help of a small potentiometer *R*.

(*ii*) *SCRs for speed control of d.c. shunt motor.* The conventional method of speed control of *d.c.* shunt motor is to change the field excitation. But change in field excitation changes the motor torque also. This drawback is overcome in *SCR* control as shown in Fig. 33.10. Diodes D_1, D_2, D_3, and D_4 form the bridge. This bridge circuit converts *a.c.* into d.c. and supplies it to the field winding of the motor. During the positive half-cycle of a.c. supply, *SCR* 1 conducts because it gets gate current from bridge circuit as well as its anode is positive *w.r.t.* cathode. The armature winding of the motor gets current. The angle of conduction

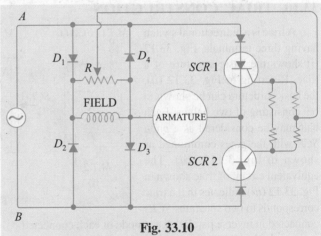

Fig. 33.10

can be changed by varying the gate current. During the negative half cycle of *a.c.* supply, *SCR* 2 provides current to the armature winding. In this way, the voltage fed to the motor armature and hence the speed can be controlled.

33.9. THE TRIAC

The major drawback of an *SCR* is that it can conduct current in one direction only. Therefore, an *SCR* can only control *d.c.* power or forward biased half-cycles of *a.c.* in a load. However, in an *a.c.* system, it is often desirable and necessary to exercise control over both positive and negative half-cycles. For this purpose, a semiconductor device called *triac* is used.

A *triac is a three terminal semiconductor switching device which can control alternating current in a load.*

Triac is an abbreviation for triode *a.c.* switch. 'Tri' indicates that the device has three terminals and *a.c.* means that the device controls alternating current or can conduct current in either direction.

The key function of a triac may be understood by referring to the simplified Fig. 33.11. The *control circuit of triac can be adjusted to pass the desired portions of positive and negative half cycles of a.c. supply through the load R_L. Thus, referring to Fig. 33.11 (*ii*), the triac passes the positive half-cycle of the supply from θ_1 to 180° *i.e.*, the shaded portion of the positive half-cycle. Similarly, the shaded portion of negative half-cycle will pass through the load. In this way, alternating current and hence *a.c.* power flowing through the load can be controlled.

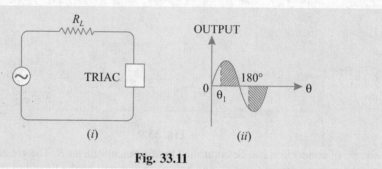

(*i*)　　　　　　　　　　　　　(*ii*)

Fig. 33.11

Since a triac can control conduction of both positive and negative half-cycles of a.c. supply, it is sometimes called a bidirectional semi-conductor triode switch. The above action of a triac is certainly not a rectifying action (as in an **SCR) so that the triac makes no mention of rectification in its name.

33.10. TRIAC CONSTRUCTION

A triac is a bidirectional switch having three terminals. Fig. 33.12 (*i*) shows the basic structure of a triac. Referring to Fig. 33.12 (*ii*), the basic structure can be shown to be consisting of two halves. Each half may be considered as a *pnpn* SCR with the gates commoned as shown in Fig. 33.12 (*iii*). The equivalent circuit of triac shown in Fig. 33.12 (*iii*) indicates that a triac corresponds to two spearates SCRs connected in inverse parallel (*i.e.*, anode of each connected to the cathode of the other) with gates commoned.

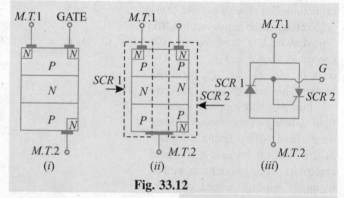

(*i*)　　　　　　(*ii*)　　　　　　(*iii*)

Fig. 33.12

Fig. 33.13 shows the symbol of a triac. The control terminal as with SCR is called the gate G. The other two terminals are MT 1 and MT 2 respectively called main terminal 1 and main terminal 2. With a proper gate current, the triac can be made to conduct when MT 2 is either positive or negative w.r.t. MT 1. It can be seen that even symbol of triac indicates that it can conduct for either polarity of voltage across the main terminals. The gate provides control over conduction in either direction.

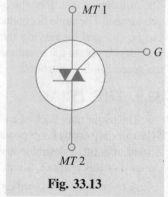

Fig. 33.13

---

*　　Although it appears that 'triac' has two terminals, there is also third terminal connected to the control circuit.

**　　SCR is a controlled rectifier. It is a unidirectional switch and can conduct only in one direction. Therefore, it can control only one half-cycle (positive or negative) of a.c. supply.

33.11. TRIAC OPERATION

Fig. 33.14 shows the simple triac circuit. The a.c. supply to be controlled is connected across the main terminals of triac through a load resistance R_L. The gate circuit consists of battery, a current limiting resistor R and a switch S. The circuit action is as follows :

(*i*) When switch S is open, there will be no gate current and the *triac* is cut off. Even with no gate current, the triac can be turned on provided the supply voltage becomes equal to breakover voltage of triac. However, the normal way to turn on a triac is by introducing a proper gate current.

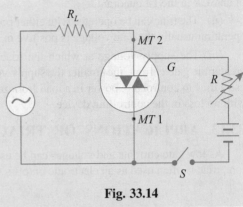

Fig. 33.14

(*ii*) When switch S is closed, the gate current starts flowing in the gate circuit. In a similar manner to *SCR*, the breakover voltage of triac can be varied by making proper gate current to flow. With a few milliamperes introduced at the gate, the triac will start conducting whether teminal *MT* 2 is positive or negative *w.r.t.* *MT* 1.

(*iii*) If terminal *MT* 2 is positive *w.r.t.* *MT* 1, the triac turns on and the conventional current will flow from *MT* 2 to *MT* 1. If the terminal *MT* 2 is negative *w.r.t.* *MT* 1, the triac is again turned on but this time the conventional current flows from *MT* 1 to *MT* 2.

The above action of triac reveals that it can act as an a.c. contactor to switch on or off alterating current to a load. The additional advantage of triac is that by adjusting the gate current to a proper value, any portion of both positive and negative half-cycles of *a.c.* supply can be made to flow through the load. This permits to adjust the transfer of *a.c.* power from the source to the load.

33.12. TRIAC CHARACTERISTICS

Fig. 33.15 shows the *V-I* characteristics of triac. Because the triac essentially consists of two *SCRs* of opposite orientation fabricated in the same crystal, its operating characteristics in the first and third quadrants are the same except for the direction of applied voltage and current flow.

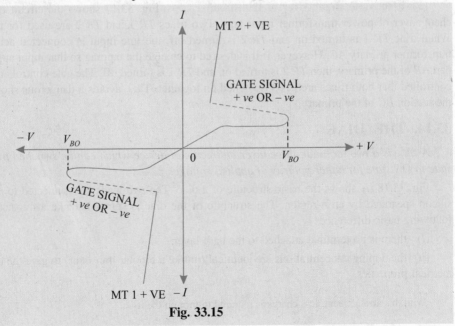

Fig. 33.15

(*i*) The *V-I* charateristics for triac in the Ist and IIIrd quadrants are essentially identical to those of an *SCR* in the Ist quadrant.

(*ii*) The triac can be operated with either positive or negative gate control voltage but in *normal operation usually the gate voltage is positive in quadrant I and negative in quadrant III.

(*iii*) The supply voltage at which the triac is turned *ON* depends upon the *gate* current. The greater the gate current, the smaller the supply voltage at which the triac is turned on. This permits to use a triac to control *a.c.* power in a load from zero to full power in a smooth and continuous manner with no loss in the controlling device.

33.13. APPLICATIONS OF TRIAC

As low gate currents and voltages can be used to control large load currents and voltages, therefore, triac is often used as an electronic on/off switch controlled by a low-current mechanical switch.

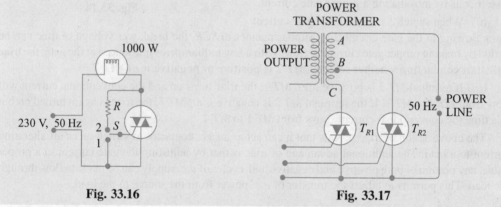

Fig. 33.16   **Fig. 33.17**

(*i*) **As a high-power lamp switch.** Fig. 33.16 shows the use of a triac as an a.c. on/off switch. When switch *S* is thrown to position 1, the triac is cut off and the output power of lamp is zero. But as the switch is thrown to position 2, a small gate current (a few mA) flowing through the gate turns the triac on. Consequently, the lamp is switched on to give full output of 1000 watts.

(*ii*) **Electronic changeover of transformer taps.** Fig. 33.17 shows the circuit of electronic changeover of power transformer input taps. Two triacs *TR* 1 and *TR* 2 are used for the purpose. When triac *TR* 1 is turned on and *TR* 2 is turned off, the line input is connected across the full transformer primary *AC*. However, if it is desired to change the tapping so that input appears across part *AB* of the primary, then *TR* 2 is turned on and *TR* 1 is turned off. The gate control signals are so controlled that both triacs are never switched on together. This avoids a dangerous short circuit on the section *BC* of the primary.

33.14. THE DIAC

A diac is a two terminal, three layer bidirectional device which can be switched from its OFF state to ON state for either polarity of applied voltage.

Fig. 33.18 (*i*) shows the basic structure of a diac. The two leads are connected to *p*-regions of silicon spearated by an *n*-region. The structure of the diac is somewhat like a transistor with the following basic differences :

(*i*) there is no terminal attached to the base layer.

(*ii*) the doping concentrations are identical (unlike a bipolar transistor) to give the device symmetrical properties.

---

*   With this arrangement, less charge is required to turn on the triac.

Fig. 33.18 (*ii*) shows the symbol of a diac.

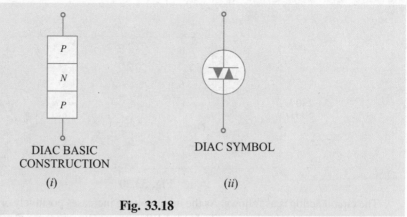

DIAC BASIC
CONSTRUCTION

(*i*)

DIAC SYMBOL

(*ii*)

Fig. 33.18

Operation. When a positive or negative voltage is applied across the terminals of a diac, only a small leakage current I_{BO} will flow through the device. As the applied voltage is increased, the leakage current will continue to flow until the voltage reaches the breakover voltage V_{BO}. At this point, avalanche breakdown on the reverse biased junction occurs and the device exhibits negative resistance *i.e.*, current through the device increases with the decreasing values of applied voltage. The voltage across the device then drops to 'breakback' voltage V_W.

Fig. 33.19 shows the *V-I* characteristics of a diac. For applied positive voltage less than $+V_{BO}$ and negative voltage less than $-V_{BO}$, a small leakage curent $(+I_{BO})$ flows through the device. Under such conditions, the diac blocks the flow of current

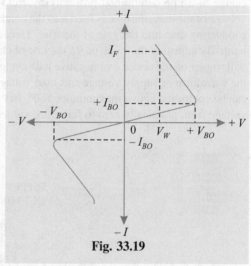

Fig. 33.19

and effectively behaves as an open circuit. The voltages $+V_{BO}$ and $-V_{BO}$ are the breakdown voltages and usually have a range of 30 to 50 volts.

When the positive or negative applied voltage is equal to or greater than the breakdown voltage, diac begins to conduct and the voltage drop across it becomes a few volts.

Diacs are used primarily for triggering of triacs in adjustable phase control of a.c. mains power. Some of the circuit applications of diac are (*i*) light dimming (*ii*) heat control and (*iii*) universal motor speed control.

33.15. APPLICATIONS OF DIAC

Although a triac may be fired into the conducting state by a simple resistive triggering circuit, more reliable and faster turn-on may be had if a switching device is used in series with the gate. One of the switching devices that can trigger a triac is the diac. This is illustrated in the following applications.

(*i*) **Lamp dimmer.** Fig. 33.20 shows a typical circuit that may be used for smooth control of a.c. power fed to a lamp. This permits to control the light output from the lamp. The basic control is by an *RC* variable gate voltage arrangement. The series $R_4 - C_1$ circuit across the triac is designed to limit the rate of voltage rise across the device during switch off.

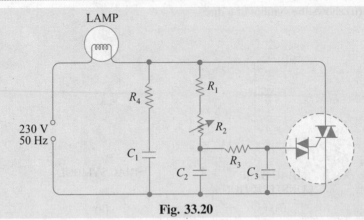

Fig. 33.20

The circuit action is as follows. As the input voltage increases positively or negatively, C_1 and C_2 charge at a rate determined primarily by R_2. When the voltage across C_3 exceeds the breakover voltage of the diac, the diac is fired into the conducting state. The capacitor C_3 discharges through the conducting diac into the gate of the triac. Hence, the triac is turned on to pass the a.c. power to the lamp. By adjusting the value of R_2, the rate of charge of capacitors and hence the point at which triac will trigger on the positive or negative half-cycle of input voltage can be controlled. Fig. 33.21 shows the waveform of supply voltage and load voltage in the diac-triac control circuit. The firing of triac can be controlled upto a maximum of 180°. In this way, we can provide a continuous control of load voltage from practically zero to full *r.m.s.* value.

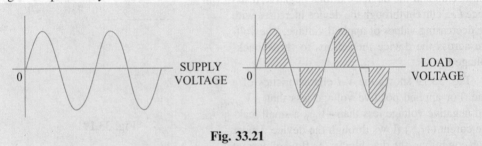

Fig. 33.21

(*ii*) **Heat control.** Fig. 33.22 shows a typical diac-triac circuit that may be used for the smooth control of *a.c.* power in a heater. This is similar to the circuit shown in Fig. 33.20. The capacitor C_1 in series with choke L across the triac helps to slow-up the voltage rise across the device during switch-off. The resistor R_4 in parallel with the diac ensures smooth control at all positions of variable resistance R_2.

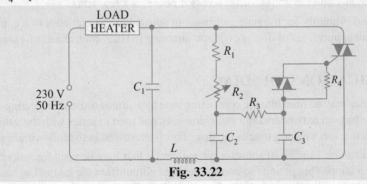

Fig. 33.22

The circuit action is as follows. As the input voltage increases positively or negatively, C_1 and C_2 charge at a rate determined primarily by R_2. When the voltage across C_3 exceeds the breakover voltage of the diac, the diac conducts. The capacitor C_3 discharges through the conducting diac into the gate of the triac. This turns on the triac and hence *a.c.* power to the heater. By adjusting the value of R_2, any portion of positive and negative half-cycles of the supply voltage can be passed through the heater. This permits a smooth control of the heat output from the heater.

33.16. UNIJUNCTION TRANSISTOR (*UJT*)

A *unijunction transistor (abbreviated as *UJT*) is a three terminal semiconductor switching device. This device has unique characteristic that when it is triggered, the emitter current increases regeneratively until it is limited by emitter power supply. Due to this characteristic, the unijunction transistor can be employed in a variety of applications *e.g.*, switching pulse generator, saw-tooth generator.

Construction. Fig. 33.23 (*i*) shows the basic structure of a unijunction transistor. It consists of an *n*-type silicon bar with an electrical connection on each end. The leads to these connections are called base leads-*base-one* B_1 and *base-two* B_2. Part way along the bar between the two bases, near to B_2 than B_1, a *pn* junction is formed between a *p*-type emitter and the bar. The lead to this junction is called the *emitter* lead *E*. Fig. 33.23 (*ii*) shows the symbol of unijunction transistor. Note that emitter is shown closer to B_2 than B_1. The following points are worth noting ;

(*i*) Since the device has one *pn* junction and three leads, it is commonly called a unijunction transistor (*uni* means single).

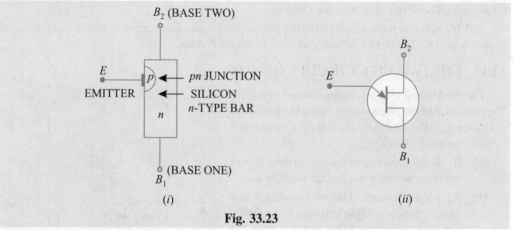

Fig. 33.23

(*ii*) With only one *pn* junciton, the device is really a form of diode. Because the two base terminals are taken from one section of the diode, this device is also called *double-based diode*.

(*iii*) The emitter is heavily doped having many holes. The *n* region, however, is lightly doped. For this reason, the resistance between the base terminals is very high (5 to 10kΩ) when emitter lead is open.

Operation. Fig. 33.24 shows the basic circuit operation of a unijunction transistor. The device has normally B_2 positive *w.r.t.* B_1.

(*i*)   If voltage V_{BB} is applied with emitter open [See Fig. 33.24 (*i*)], a voltage gradient is established along the *n*-type bar. Since the emitter is located nearer to B_2, more than **half of V_{BB} appears between the emitter and B_1. The voltage V_1 between emitter and B_1, establishes a reverse bias on the *pn* junction and the emitter current is cut off. Of course, a small leakage current flows from B_2 to emitter due to minority carriers.

---

*   In package form, a *UJT* looks very much like a small signal transistor. As a *UJT* has only one *pn* junction, therefore, naming it a 'transistor' is really a misnomer.

**   The *n*-type silicon bar has a high resistance. The resistance between emitter and B_1 is greater than between B_2 and emitter. It is because emitter is nearer to B_2 than B_1.

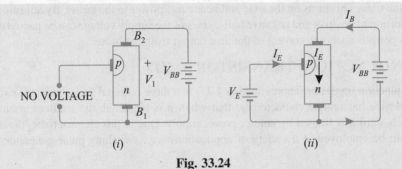

Fig. 33.24

(*ii*) If a positive voltage is applied at the emitter [See Fig. 33.24 (*i*)], the *pn* junction will remain reverse biased so long as the input voltage is less than V_1. If the input voltage to the emitter exceeds V_1, the *pn* junction becomes forward biased. Under these conditions, holes are injected from *p*-type material into the *n*-type bar. These holes are repelled by positive B_2 terminal and they are attracted towards B_1 terminal of the bar. This accumulation of holes in the emitter to B_1 region results in the decrease of resistance in this section of the bar. The result is that internal voltage drop from emitter to B_1 is decreased and hence the emitter current I_E increases. As more holes are injected, a condition of saturation will eventually be reached. At this point, the emitter current is limited by emitter power supply only. The device is now in the *ON* state.

(*iii*) If a negative pulse is applied to the emitter, the *pn* junction is reverse biased and the emitter current is cut off. The device is then said to be in the *OFF* state.

33.17. EQUIVALENT CIRCUIT OF *UJT*

Fig. 33.25 shows the equivalent circuit of a *UJT*. The resistance of the silicon bar is called the inter-base resistance R_{BB}. The inter-base resistance is represented by two resistors in series *viz*.

(*a*) R_{B2} is the resistance of the bar between B_2 and the point at which the emitter junction lies.

(*b*) R_{B1} is the resistance of the bar between B_1 and emitter junction. This resistance is shown variable because its value depends upon the bias voltage across the *pn* junction.

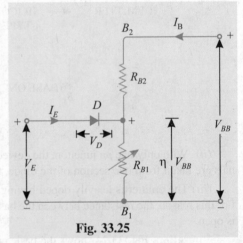

The *pn* junction is represented in the emitter by a diode *D*.

The circuit action of a *UJT* can be explained more clearly from its equivalent circuit.

Fig. 33.25

(*i*) With no voltage applied to the *UJT*, the inter-base resistance is given by;

$$R_{BB} = R_{B1} + R_{B2}$$

The value of R_{BB} generally lies between 4 kΩ and 10kΩ.

(*ii*) If a voltage V_{BB} is applied between the bases with emitter open, the voltage will divide up across R_{B1} and R_{B2}.

$$\text{Voltage across } R_{B1}, V_1 = \frac{R_{B1}}{R_{B1} + R_{B2}} V_{BB}$$

or

$$V_1/V_{BB} = \frac{R_{B1}}{R_{B1} + R_{B2}}$$

The ratio V_1/V_{BB} is called *intrinsic stand-off ratio* and is represented by Greek letter η.

Obviously, $$\eta = \frac{R_{B1}}{R_{B1} + R_{B2}}$$

The value of η usually lies between 0.51 and 0.82.

∴   Voltage across R_{B1} = η V_{BB}

The voltage η V_{BB} appearing across R_{B1} reverse biases the diode. Therefore, the emitter current is zero.

(*iii*) If now a progressively rising positive voltage is applied to the emitter, the diode will become forward biased when input voltage exceeds ηV_{BB} plus V_D, the forward voltage drop across the silicon diode *i.e.*,

$$V_P = \eta \ V_{BB} + V_D$$

where V_P = peak point voltage

V_D = forward voltage drop across silicon diode (≈ 0.7 V)

When the diode *D* starts conducting, holes are injected from *p*-type material to the *n*-type bar. These holes are swept down towards the terminal B_1. This decreases the resistance between emitter and B_1 (indicated by variable resistance symbol for R_{B1}) and hence the internal drop from emitter to B_1. The emitter current now increases regeneratively until it is limited by the emitter power supply.

Conclusion. The above discussion leads to the conclusion that when input positive voltage to the emitter is less than peak-point voltage V_P, the *pn* junction remains reverse biased and the emitter current is practically zero. However, when the input voltage exceeds V_P, R_{B1} falls from several thousand ohms to a small value. The diode is now forward biased and the emitter current quickly reaches to a saturation value limited by R_{B1} (about 20 Ω) and forward resistance of *pn* junction (about 200 Ω).

33.18. CHARACTERISTICS OF *UJT*

Fig. 33.26 shows the curve between emitter voltage (V_E) and emitter current (I_E) of a *UJT* at a given voltage V_{BB} between the bases. This is known as the emitter characteristic of *UJT*. The following points may be noted from the characteristic :

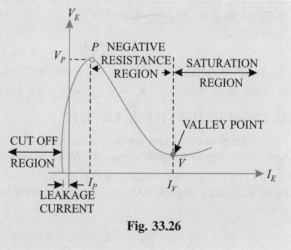

(*i*) Initially, in the cut-off region, as V_E increases from zero, slight leakage current flows from terminal B_2 to the emitter. This current is due to the minority carriers in the reversed biased diode.

(*ii*) Above a certain value of V_E, emitter current I_E begins to flow, increasing until the peak voltage V_P and current I_P are reached at point *P*.

Fig. 33.26

(*iii*) After the peak point *P*, an attempt to increase V_E is followed by a sudden increase in emitter current I_E with a corresponding decrease in V_E. This is a *negative resistance* portion of the curve because with increase in I_E, V_E decreases.

(*iv*) The negative portion of the curve lasts until the point *V* is reached with valley-point voltage V_V and valley-point current I_V. After the valley point, the device is driven to saturation.

Fig. 33.27 shows the typical family of V_E/I_E characteristics of a *UJT* at different voltages between the bases. It is clear that peak-point voltage ($= \eta\, V_{BB} + V_D$) falls steadily with reducing V_{BB} and so does the valley-point voltage V_V. The difference $V_P - V_V$ is a measure of the switching efficiency of *UJT* and can be seen to fall off as V_{BB} decreases. For a general purpose *UJT*, the peak-point current is of the order of 1 µA at $V_{BB} = 20$V with a valley-point voltage of about 2.5V at 6 mA.

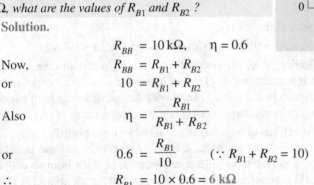

Fig. 33.27

Example 33.4. *The intrinsic stand-off ratio for a UJT is determined to be 0.6. If the inter-base resistance is 10kΩ, what are the values of R_{B1} and R_{B2} ?*

Solution.

$$R_{BB} = 10 \text{ k}\Omega, \qquad \eta = 0.6$$

Now,
$$R_{BB} = R_{B1} + R_{B2}$$
or
$$10 = R_{B1} + R_{B2}$$

Also
$$\eta = \frac{R_{B1}}{R_{B1} + R_{B2}}$$

or
$$0.6 = \frac{R_{B1}}{10} \qquad (\because R_{B1} + R_{B2} = 10)$$

$\therefore$
$$R_{B1} = 10 \times 0.6 = 6 \text{ k}\Omega$$
and
$$R_{B2} = 10 - 6 = 4 \text{ k}\Omega$$

Example 33.5. *A unijunction transistor has 10V between the bases. If the intrinsic stand off ratio is 0.65, find the value of stand off voltage. What will be the peak-point voltage if the forward voltage drop in the pn-junction is 0.7V ?*

Solution.

$$V_{BB} = 10 \text{ V}; \qquad \eta = 0.65; V_D = 0.7 \text{ V}$$

Stand off voltage
$$= \eta\, V_{BB} = 0.65 \times 10 = 6.5 \text{ V}$$
Peak-point voltage,
$$V_P = \eta\, V_{BB} + V_D = 6.5 + 0.7 = 7.2 \text{ V}$$

33.19. APPLICATIONS OF *UJT*

Unijunction transistors are used extensively in oscillators, pulse and voltage sensing circuits. Some of the important applications of *UJT* are discussed below :

(i) **UJT relaxation oscillator.** Fig. 33.28 shows *UJT* relaxation oscillator where the discharging of a capacitor through *UJT* can develop a saw-tooth output as shown.

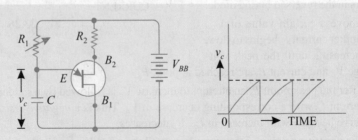

Fig. 33.28

When battery V_{BB} is turned on, the capacitor C charges through resistor R_1. During the charging period, the voltage across the capacitor rises in an exponential manner until it reaches the peak-point voltage. At this instant of time, the *UJT* switches to its low resistance conducting mode and the capacitor is discharged between E and B_1. As the capacitor voltage flys back to zero, the emitter ceases to conduct and the *UJT* is switched off. The next cycle then begins, allowing the capacitor C to charge again. The frequency of the output saw-tooth wave can be varied by changing the value of R_1 since this controls the time constant R_1C of the capacitor charging circuit.

(*ii*) **Overvoltage detector.** Fig. 33.29 shows a simple d.c. over-voltage indicator. A warning pilot-lamp L is connected between the emitter and B_1 circuit. So long as the input voltage is less than the peak-point voltage (V_p) of the *UJT*, the device remains switched off. However, when the input voltage exceeds V_P, the *UJT* is switched on and the capacitor discharges through the low resistance path between terminals E and B_1. The current flowing in the pilot lamp L lights it, thereby indicating the overvoltage in the circuit.

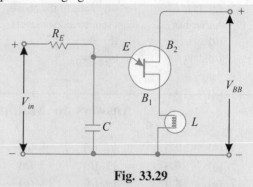

Fig. 33.29

MULTIPLE-CHOICE QUESTIONS

1. An *SCR* has .... *pn* junctions.
   - (*a*) two
   - (*b*) three
   - (*c*) four
   - (*d*) five
2. An *SCR* is a solid state equivalent of ....
   - (*a*) triode
   - (*b*) pentode
   - (*c*) gas-filled triode
   - (*d*) tetrode
3. An *SCR* has three terminals *viz,* ....
   - (*a*) anode, cathode, grid
   - (*b*) anode, cathode, drain
   - (*c*) cathode, anode, gate
   - (*d*) none of the above
4. An *SCR* has .... semi-conductor layers.
   - (*a*) four
   - (*b*) three
   - (*c*) two
   - (*d*) none of the above
5. An *SCR* behaves as a .... switch.
   - (*a*) bidirectional
   - (*b*) unidirectional
   - (*c*) mechanical
   - (*d*) none of the above
6. An *SCR* is sometimes called a ....
   - (*a*) triac
   - (*b*) thyristor
   - (*c*) diac
   - (*d*) unijunction transistor
7. An *SCR* is made of ....
   - (*a*) silicon
   - (*b*) germanium
   - (*c*) carbon
   - (*d*) none of the above
8. In the normal operation of an *SCR*, anode is .... *w.r.t.* cathode.
   - (*a*) negative
   - (*b*) at zero potential
   - (*c*) positive
   - (*d*) none of the above
9. In the normal operation of an *SCR*, gate is .... *w.r.t.* cathode.
   - (*a*) positive
   - (*b*) negative
   - (*c*) at zero potential
   - (*d*) none of the above
10. An *SCR* combines the features of ....
    - (*a*) a rectifier and resistance
    - (*b*) a rectifier and capacitor
    - (*c*) a rectifier and transistor
    - (*d*) none of the above
11. A triac has three terminals *viz.* ....
    - (*a*) drain, source, gate
    - (*b*) two main terminals and a gate terminal
    - (*c*) cathode, anode, gate
    - (*d*) none of the above
12. A triac is equivalent to two *SCRs* ....
    - (*a*) in parallel
    - (*b*) in series
    - (*c*) in inverse-parallel
    - (*d*) none of the above
13. A triac is a .... switch.
    - (*a*) unidirectional
    - (*b*) bidirectional
    - (*c*) mechanical
    - (*d*) none of the above
14. The *V-I* characteristics for a triac in the first and third quadrants are essentially identical to those of .... in the first quadrant.
    - (*a*) SCR
    - (*b*) transistor
    - (*c*) UJT
    - (*d*) none of the above

15. A triac can pass a portion of .... half-cycle through the load..
    (a) only positive   (b) only negative
    (c) both positive and negative
    (d) none of the above

16. A diac has .... terminals.
    (a) two   (b) three
    (c) four   (d) none of the above

17. A triac has .... semiconductor layers.
    (a) two   (b) three
    (c) four   (d) one

18. A diac has ....
    (a) one *pn* junction
    (b) two *pn* junctions
    (c) three *pn* junctions
    (d) none of the above

19. The device that does not have a gate terminal is ....
    (a) triac   (b) *FET*
    (c) *SCR*   (d) diac

20. A diac has .... semiconductor layers.
    (a) three   (b) two
    (c) four   (d) none of above

Answers to Multiple-Choice Questions

1. (b)	2. (c)	3. (c)	4. (a)	5. (b)	6. (b)	7. (a)	8. (c)
9. (a)	10. (c)	11. (b)	12. (c)	13. (b)	14. (a)	15. (c)	16. (a)
17. (c)	18. (b)	19. (d)	20. (a)				

Hints to Selected Multiple-Choice Questions

2. The *SCR* is a solid state equivalent of **gas-filled triode** (thyratron). The gate, anode and cathode of *SCR* correspond to the grid, plate and cathode of thyratron.

5. During negative half cycle of a.c. voltage, the *SCR* does not conduct irrespective of the gate voltage. It is because anode is negative *w.r.t.* cathode and *PRV* is less than the reverse break-down voltage. However, during the positive half cycle the *SCR* conducts provided proper gate current is made to flow. Thus it acts as a **unidirectional** switch.

7. The device is made of **silicon** because leakage current in silicon is very small as compared to germanium. Thus during the *OFF* condition, the leakage current is very small in a *SCR*. As a result, it can be used more effectively as a switch.

10. An *SCR* can change alternating current into direct current and at the same time control the amount of power fed to the load. Thus *SCR* combines the features of **a rectifier and a transistor**.

13. A triac consists of three terminals gate (*G*), main terminal 1 (*MT* 1) and main terminal 2 (*MT* 2). In triac operation when *MT* 1 is positive *w.r.t. MT* 2, the conventional current flows from *MT* 1 to *MT* 2 indicating that triac is *ON*.

    However, when *MT* 1 becomes negative *w.r.t. MT* 2, the triac is again turned on but now the conventional current flows from *MT* 2 to *MT* 1. Thus, a triac conducts in both directions and acts as a **bidirectional** switch.

15. A triac is a bidirectional switch. As a result it can pass portions of **both positive and negative** half-cycles.

19. In a diac, there is no terminal attached to the base lead. Therefore, a **diac** does not have a gate terminal.

34

Vacuum Tubes and Gas-Filled Tubes

INTRODUCTION

V acuum tubes depend for their operation on the movement of electrons in an evacuated space.

For this purpose, the free electrons are ejected from the surface of a metallic conductor by supplying sufficient energy from some external source. This is known as *electron emission*. The emitted electrons can be made to move in vacuum under the influence of an electric field, thus constituting electric current in vacuum. Since 1950, solid state devices like crystal diode, bipolar transistor and *FET* have taken over the duties previously performed by *vacuum tubes. If some inert gas (*e.g.*, argon, neon, helium) at low pressure is introduced in a vacuum tube, it is called a gas-filled tube. The gas-filled tubes were used for voltage regulation and switching applications. However, the discovery of zener diode and *SCR* has eliminated the gas-filled tubes from the mainstream of electronics. Although the future of vacuum tubes and gas-filled tubes is fast shrinking, yet their study may be necessary to compare them with the counterpart solid state devices.

* Vacuum tubes are still used in very high power applications *e.g.*, high-power amplifiers, microwave amplifiers, TV picture tubes etc.

34.1. ELECTRON EMISSION

The liberation of electrons from the surface of a substance is known as electron emission.

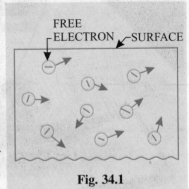

Fig. 34.1

For electron emission, metals are used because they have many free electrons. If a piece of metal is investigated at room temperature, the random motion of free electrons is as shown in Fig. 34.1. However, these electrons are free only to the extent that they may transfer from one atom to another within the metal but they cannot leave the metal surface to provide electron emission. It is because the free electrons that start at the surface of metal find behind them positive nuclei pulling them back and none pulling forward. Thus, at the surface of a metal, a free electron encounters forces that prevent it to leave the metal. In other words, the metallic surface offers barrier to free electrons and is known as *surface barrier.*

However, if sufficient external energy is given to the free electron, its kinetic energy is increased and thus, electron will cross over the surface barrier to leave the metal. This additional energy required by an electron to overcome the surface barrier of the metal is called *work function* of the metal.

The amount of additional energy required to emit an electron from a metallic surface is known as work function *of that metal.*

Thus, if the total energy required to liberate an electron from a metal is 4 e V and the energy already possessed by the electron is 0.5 eV, then additional energy required (*i.e.*, work function) is 4 − 0.5 = 3.5 eV. The work function of pure metals varies roughly from 2 to 6 eV. It depends upon the nature of metal, its purity and the conditions of its surface. It may be noted that it is desirable that metal used for electron emission should have low work function so that a small amount of energy is required to cause emission of electrons.

34.2. TYPES OF ELECTRON EMISSION

The electron emission from the surface of a metal is possible only if sufficient additional energy (*equal to the work function of the metal*) is supplied from some external source. This external energy may come from a variety of sources such as heat energy, energy stored in electric field, light energy or kinetic energy of the electric charges bombarding the metal surface. Accordingly, there are following four principal methods of obtaining electron emission from the surface of a metal :

(*i*) Thermionic emission. In this method, the metal is heated to sufficient temperature (about 2500°C) to enable the free electrons to leave the metal surface. The number of electrons emitted depends upon the temperature. The higher the temperature, the greater is the emission of electrons. This type of emission is employed in vacuum tubes.

* *

* Work function is the additional energy required for the liberation of electrons. Therefore, it should have the conventional unit of energy *i.e.*, joules. But this unit is very large for computing electronics work. Therefore, in practice, a smaller unit called *electron volt* (abbreviated as eV) is used.

One electron-volt is the amount of energy acquired by an electron when it is accelerated through a potential difference of 1V.

Thus, if an electron moves from a point of 0 potential to a point of +10V, then amount of energy acquired by the electron is 10eV.

Since charge on an electron = 1.602×10^{-19} C

and   voltage = 1V,

∴   1 electron–volt = $QV = (1.602 \times 10^{-19}) \times 1$ J

or   1 eV = 1.602×10^{-19} J

(*ii*) **Field emission.** In this method, a strong electric field (*i.e.*, a high positive voltage) is applied at the metal surface which pulls the free electrons out of metal because of the attraction of positive field. The stronger the electric field, the greater is the electron emission.

(*iii*) **Photo-electric emission.** In this method, the energy of light falling upon the metal surface is transferred to the free electrons within the metal to enable them to leave the surface. The greater the intensity (*i.e.*, brightness) of light beam falling on the metal surface, the greater is the photo-electric emission.

(*iv*) **Secondary emission.** In this method, a high velocity beam of electrons strikes the metal surface and causes the free electrons of the metal to be knocked out from the surface.

34.3. THERMIONIC EMISSION

The process of electron emission from a metal surface by supplying thermal energy to it is known as **thermionic emission.**

At ordinary temperatures, the energy possessed by free electrons in the metal is inadequate to cause them to escape from the surface. When heat is applied to the metal, some of heat energy is converted into kinetic energy, causing accelerated motion of free electrons. When the temperature rises sufficiently, these electrons acquire additional energy equal to the work function of the metal. Consequently, they overcome the restraining surface barrier and leave the metal surface.

Metals *with lower work function* will require less additional energy and, therefore, will emit electrons at lower temperatures. The commonly used materials for electron emission are *tungsten, thoriated tungsten* and *metallic oxides of barium and strontium*. It may be added here that high temperatures are necessary to cause thermionic emission. For example, pure tungsten must be heated to about 2300°C to get electron emission. However, oxide coated emitters need only 750°C to cause thermionic emission.

The amount of thermionic emission increases rapidly as the emitter temperature is raised. The emission current density is given by Richardson-Dushman equation given below :

$$J_s = AT^2 e^{-\frac{b}{T}} \text{ amp/m}^2$$

where, J_s = emission current density *i.e.*, current per square metre of the emitting surface.

T = absolute temperature of emitter in *K*

A = constant, depending upon the type of emitter and is measured in amp/m^2/K^2

b = a constant for the emitter

e = natural logarithmic base

34.4. THERMIONIC EMITTER

The substance used for electron emission is known as an *emitter* or *cathode*. The cathode is heated in an evacuated space to emit electrons. If the cathode were heated to the required temperature in open air, it would burn up because of the presence of oxygen in the air. A cathode should have the following properties :

(*i*) **Low work function.** The substance selected as cathode should have low work function so that electron emission takes place by applying small amount of energy *i.e.*, at low temperatures.

(*ii*) **High melting point.** As electron emission takes place at very high temperatures (> 1500°C), therefore, the substance used as a cathode should have high melting point. For a material such as copper, which has the advantage of low work function, it is seen that it cannot be used as cathode because it melts at 810°C. Consequently, it will vapourise before it begins to emit electrons.

(*iii*) **High mechanical strength.** The emitter should have high mechanical strength to withstand the bombardment of positive ions. In any vacuum tube, no matter how careful the evacuation, there are always present some gas molecules which may form ions by impact with electrons when current flows. Under the influence of electric field, the positive ions strike the cathode. If high voltages are used, the cathode is subjected to considerable bombardment and may be damaged.

34.5. CATHODE CONSTRUCTION

As cathode is sealed in vacuum, therefore, the most convenient way to heat it is by electrical method. On this basis, the thermionic cathodes are divided into two types *viz.*, directly heated cathode and indirectly heated cathode.

(*i*) **Directly heated cathode.** In this type, the cathode consists of oxide coated nickel ribbon, called the **filament*. The heating current is directly passed through this ribbon which emits the electrons. Fig. 34.2 (*i*) shows the structure of directly heated cathode whereas Fig. 34.2 (*ii*) shows its symbol.

The directly heated cathode is more efficient in converting heating power into thermionic emission. Therefore, it is generally used in power tubes that need large amount of emission and in small tubes operated from batteries where efficiency and quick heating are important. The principal limitation of this type of cathode is that any variation in heater voltage affects the electron emission and thus produces *hum* in the circuit.

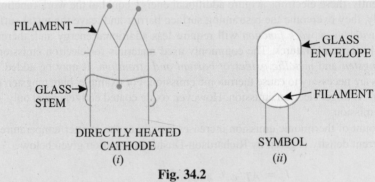

Fig. 34.2

(*ii*) **Indirectly heated cathode.** In this type, the cathode consists of a thin metal sleeve coated with barium and strontium oxides. A filament or heater is enclosed within the sleeve and insulated from it. There is no electrical connection between the heater and the cathode. The heating current is passed through the heater and the cathode is heated indirectly through heat transfer from the heater element. Fig. 34.3 (*i*) shows the structure of indirectly heated cathode whereas Fig. 34.3 (*ii*) shows its symbol.

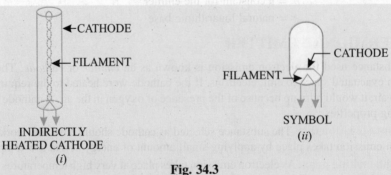

Fig. 34.3

Indirectly heated cathode has many advantages. As cathode is completely separated from the heating circuit, therefore, it can be readily connected to any desired potential as needed, independent of the heater potential. Furthermore, because of relatively large mass of cylindrical cathode, it

---

*   Filament. The term filament (literally means a thin wire) denotes the element through which the cathode heating current flows. In case of directly heated, cathode is itself the filament. If indirectly heated, heater is the filament.

takes time to heat or cool and as such does not introduce *hum* due to heater voltage fluctuations. Finally, a.c. can be used in the heater circuit to simplify the power requirements. Almost all modern receiving tubes use this type of cathode.

34.6. TYPES OF VACUUM TUBES

An electronic device in which the flow of electrons is through a vacuum is known as a *vacuum tube*. There are two principal electrodes, namely ; *cathode* and *anode* present in every tube. The cathode is the electron emitter while anode (also called *plate*) is the electron collector. The other electrodes, if any, are called *grids*. One of them *control grid* is used to control the flow of electrons between cathode and anode. The others are called *screen grids* and are generally held at some constant potential and serve to alter the characteristics of the tube. According to the number of electrodes, vacuum tubes are classified as :

(*i*)   vacuum diode   (*ii*)   vacuum triode

(*iii*)   vacuum tetrode   (*iv*)   vacuum pentode

The diode, triode, tetrode and pentode contain 2, 3, 4 and 5 electrodes respectively. It may be noted that the heater is not counted as electrode because it is merely an incandescent filament to heat the cathode electrically.

34.7. VACUUM DIODE

A vacuum diode consists of two electrodes, a *cathode* and an *anode* (or *plate*) enclosed in a highly evacuated glass envelope. The cathode is in the form of nickel cylinder coated with barium and strontium oxides and is heated electrically to provide electron emission. The anode is generally a hollow cylinder made of nickel and surrounds the cathode. Fig. 34.4 (*i*) shows the symbol of vacuum diode. Note the symbol of diode where plate is represented by straight line, cathode by a straight line with sides folded down and heater by inverted *V*.

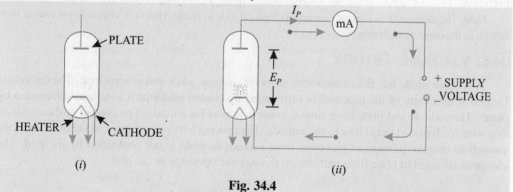

Fig. 34.4

Working. When the cathode is heated by passing electric current through the heater, it emits a large number of electrons. These emitted electrons are then in the vacuum between cathode and anode. If anode is held at positive potential *w.r.t.* cathode [See Fig. 34.4 (*ii*)], the emitted electrons are attracted by the plate to constitute plate current I_P. On the other hand, if anode is negative *w.r.t.* cathode, the emitted electrons are repelled back and no current flows in the circuit. Thus, a vacuum diode, like a crystal diode, behaves as a switch . When the vacuum diode is forward biased (*i.e.*, plate is positive *w.r.t.* cathode), it conducts current and be-

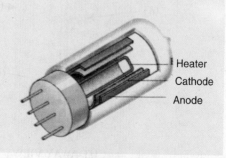

Vacuum tube diode

haves like a closed switch. However, when vacuum diode is reverse biased (*i.e.*, plate is negative *w.r.t.* cathode), it conducts no current and behaves like an open switch.

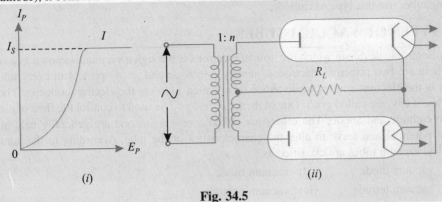

Fig. 34.5

Plate characteristic. The relation between plate voltage (E_P) and plate current (I_P) of a diode at constant temperature is known as its plate characteristic. Fig. 34.5 (*i*) shows the plate characteristic of a typical vacuum diode at cathode temperature T. As the plate voltage is increased, plate current also increases till it becomes maximum, called *saturation current*. Under such conditions, the entire supply of emitted electrons (for a given cathode temperature) is attracted to the plate. Unlike the crystal diode, a vacuum diode has no potential barrier. Consequently, the plate current I_P appears as soon as plate is made positive *w.r.t.* cathode.

As a rectifier. Like a crystal diode, a vacuum diode behaves as a switch . Consequently, we can use vacuum diodes in any of the rectifier circuits discussed in chapter 28. As an example, Fig. 34.5 (*ii*) shows full-wave centre-tapped circuit using vacuum diodes. Note that step up transformer has been used. This is expected because vacuum tubes require high voltages (>300 V) for their operation.

Note. The electron flow in a vacuum tube is from cathode to anode. However, conventional current flow will be in the opposite direction.

34.8. VACUUM TRIODE

A vacuum triode has three electrodes, namely; *cathode, plate* and *control grid*. The cathode is located at the centre of the tube and is surrounded by control grid which is in turn surrounded by plate. The cathode and plate have similar construction as for a diode. The control grid consists of fine wire mesh placed very close to the cathode. The spacing between the turns of the mesh are wide enough so that the passage of electrons from cathode to plate is not obstructed by the grid. The electrons attracted to plate from cathode go through the openings in the grid.

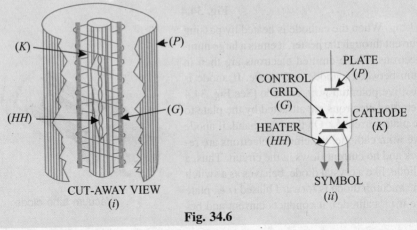

CUT-AWAY VIEW
(*i*)

SYMBOL
(*ii*)

Fig. 34.6

Fig. 34.6 (*i*) shows the cut-away view of triode whereas Fig. 34.6 (*ii*) shows its symbol. The dotted line between plate and cathode in the symbol represents the control grid.

Working. Like any other vacuum tube, the plate of a triode is held positive *w.r.t* cathode. In the normal operation of a triode, the control grid is held at *negative potential *w.r.t.* cathode as shown in Fig. 34.7 (*i*). The electrons emitted by the cathode pass through the openings of contol grid to reach the plate. As the control grid is much closer to the cathode than the plate, therefore, a small change in control grid potential brings about a large change in plate current. This **behaviour of a triode may be compared to that of a transistor where a small change in base current produces a large change in collector current (*CE* arrangement). Thus, like a transistor, a triode also acts as an amplifier; raising the strength of a weak signal inserted in the grid circuit.

Plate characteristics. Fig. 34.7 (*ii*) shows a family of plate characteristics of a vacuum triode. Keeping the grid voltage fixed, say at 0 V, the plate voltage is varied in steps and the corresponding values of plate currents are noted. This gives the plate characteristic of triode at $E_C = 0$ V. Likewise, plate characteristics for triode at $E_C = -1$ V, $E_C = -2$ V *etc.* can be drawn.

Vacuum triode

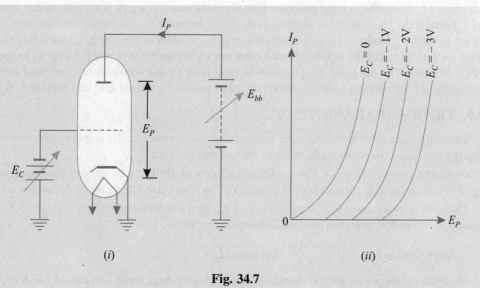

| (*i*) | (*ii*) |

Fig. 34.7

Biasing of triode. The triode should be biased in such a way that control grid is negative *w.r.t.* cathode at all times. This can be achieved by a battery E_C in the grid circuit. However, the use of such a grid bias battery is undesirable because of its high cost and frequent replacement. Therefore, in practice, the *d.c.* component of plate current of triode is itself used for obtaining grid bias voltage. Under such conditions, the triode is said to be self-biased.

---

* If the control grid is driven positive *w.r.t.* cathode, there will be current in the grid circuit. The input signal is too weak to supply this power. Consequently, distorted amplification would result.

** The vacuum triode (or any other grid controlled tube like tetrode or pentode) is a voltage driven device *i.e.*, input voltage controls the output current. However, a transistor is a current operated device *i.e.* input current controls the output current.

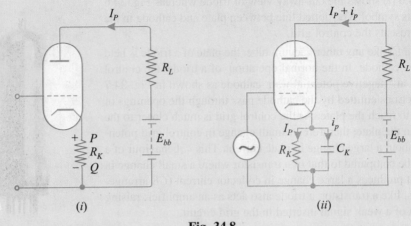

Fig. 34.8

Fig. 34.8 shows the common method of self-biasing a triode. This is known as cathode bias. A resistance R_K (called *cathode resistor*) is placed in series with the cathode circuit as shown in Fig. 34.8 (*i*). The d.c. plate current I_P flowing through R_K produces a d.c. voltage drop $I_P R_K$, making control grid negative *w.r.t.* cathode. It is very important that grid bias voltage ($I_P R_K$) should remain constant whether the signal is applied or not. When no signal is applied [See Fig. 34.8 (*i*)], the d.c. plate current I_P establishes a fixed grid bias. However, when an *a.c.* signal is applied, an *a.c.* component i_p flows in the plate circuit in addition to the d.c. component I_P. The total plate current ($I_P + i_p$) flowing through R_K produces varying grid bias across R_K. In order to keep the grid bias voltage fixed during the application of the signal, a bypass capacitor C_K is connected in parallel with R_K as shown in Fig. 34.8 (*ii*). The capacitor C_K provides an easy path for *a.c.* component i_p of plate current whereas the d.c. component I_P flows through R_K, thus producing a fixed grid bias voltage $I_P R_K$.

34.9. TRIODE PARAMETERS

There are three most important tube constants or parameters *viz.*, (*i*) amplification factor (*ii*) a.c. plate resistance (*iii*) transconductance or mutual conductance.

(*i*) **Amplification factor (μ).** The amplification factor of a tube is a measure of the effectiveness of grid voltage relative to plate voltage in controlling the plate current and may be defined as under :

The ratio of small change in plate voltage (ΔE_P) to a small change in grid voltage (ΔE_C) at constant plate current in known as **amplification factor** *i.e.,*

$$\text{Amplification factor, } \mu = \frac{\Delta E_P}{\Delta E_C} \text{ at constant } I_P.$$

For instance, suppose a 40 volt change in plate voltage brings about a change of 1 mA in plate current and the same plate current change (1 mA) is obtained by changing the grid voltage by 2V. Then it becomes clear that the effect of grid voltage on the plate current is 20 times as large as the plate voltage effect. In other words, amplification factor of the tube = 40/2 = 20. If the amplification factor of a tube is more, it means that effect of grid voltage on the plate current is greater relative to the plate voltage.

(*ii*) *a.c. plate resistance (r_p).* It is the opposition offered by the tube to the flow of electrons from cathode to plate when varying voltages are applied to the electrodes. It may be defined as under :

---

* A tube has *d.c.* plate resistance also which is the opposition by the tube to direct current. However, *a.c.* plate resistance is more significant in a practical circuit.

The ratio of small change in plate-voltage (ΔE_p) *to the resulting change in plate current* (ΔI_p) *at constant grid voltage is known as* **a.c. plate resistance** *i.e.,*

a.c. plate resistance, $r_p = \dfrac{\Delta E_P}{\Delta I_P}$ at constant E_C

The *a.c.* plate resistance indicates how the plate voltage influences the plate current at constant grid voltage. For example, if 20V change of plate voltage brings about 2.5 mA change in plate current at consant grid voltage, then $r_p = 20$ V/2.5 mA = 8000 Ω.

(*iii*) **Transconductance or mutual conductance** (g_m). The transconductance or mutual conductance indicates the effectiveness of grid potential in changing the plate current and may be defined as under ;

The ratio of small change in plate current (ΔI_p) *to the small change in grid voltage* (ΔE_C) *at constant plate voltage is known as* **transconductance or mutual conductance** *i.e.,*

Mutual conductance, $g_m = \dfrac{\Delta I_P}{\Delta E_C}$ at constant E_P.

As g_m is a ratio of current to voltage, therefore, it should be expressed in the units of siemens. However, this unit is too large for practical purposes and hence a smaller unit called microsiemen (μ S) is generally used. Note that $1S = 10^6$ μS. Thus, if a 1 V change of grid voltage in a valve produces 3 mA (= 0.003 A) change in plate current, then,

Transconductance, $g_m = \dfrac{0.003\,\text{A}}{1\text{V}} \times 10^6 = 3000$ μS

34.10. RELATIONSHIP AMONG μ, r_p AND g_m

We know $\mu = \dfrac{\Delta E_P}{\Delta E_C}$

Multiplying and dividing the numerator and denominator on R.H.S. by ΔI_p, we get,

$$\mu = \dfrac{\Delta E_P}{\Delta E_C} \times \dfrac{\Delta I_P}{\Delta I_P}$$

$$= \dfrac{\Delta E_P}{\Delta I_P} \times \dfrac{\Delta I_P}{\Delta E_C}$$

$\therefore$ $\mu = r_p \times g_m$

i.e., amplification factor = *a.c.* plate resistance × mutual conductance

It is clear from the above relation that if we know any two values, we can find the third.

Example 34.1. *Find the mutual conductance of a triode if* $\mu = 20$ *and* $r_p = 8000$ Ω.

Solution.

$\mu = r_p \times g_m$

or $20 = 8000 \times g_m$

$\therefore$ $g_m = \dfrac{20}{8000}$ siemen $= \dfrac{20}{8000} \times 10^6$ μS = **2500 μS**

Example 34.2. *The plate resistance of a triode is 8000 Ω and transconductance is 3000 μS. If the plate voltage is increased by 40 V, what is the increase in plate current, assuming the grid voltage is maintained constant ?*

Solution.

$$\mu = r_p \times g_m$$
$$= (8000) \times (3000 \times 10^{-6}) = 24$$

Now, $$\mu = \frac{\Delta E_P}{\Delta E_C}$$

$$\therefore \quad \Delta E_C = \frac{\Delta E_P}{\mu} = \frac{40}{24} = \frac{5}{3}$$

Also $$g_m = \frac{\Delta I_P}{\Delta E_C}$$

$$\therefore \quad \Delta I_P = g_m \times \Delta E_C = (3000 \times 10^{-6}) \times \frac{5}{3} = 5 \times 10^{-3} \text{ A}$$
$$= 5 \text{ mA}$$

34.11. TRIODE AS AN AMPLIFIER

Fig. 34.9 shows the basic triode amplifier circuit. The weak signal e_g is applied in the grid circuit and useful output is obtained across R_L connected in
the plate circuit. The biasing is provided
by $R_K - C_K$ and ensures the grid to be
always negative *w.r.t.* cathode. The weak
signal produces a large change in plate
current. As the value of R_L is quite high,
therefore, a large voltage drop occurs
across it. Thus a weak signal applied in
the grid circuit appears in the amplified
form in the plate circuit. In this way, a
triode acts as an amplifier.

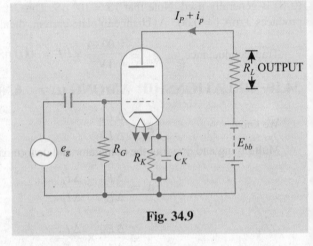

Fig. 34.9

When no signal is applied, *d.c.* plate
current I_P flows in the circuit due to grid
bias. However, when the signal is applied, a large *a.c.* plate current i_p also flows in addition to the
d.c. plate current I_P. The total plate current in the circuit is $I_P + i_p$. The useful output of the tube is the
voltage drop across R_L due to *a.c.* component i_p *i.e.*

Useful output, $e_o = i_p R_L$

Voltage gain $= \dfrac{i_p R_L}{\text{signal voltage}}$

Voltage gain. So far as the flow of *a.c.* in the tube is concerned, the equivalent circuit is as
shown in Fig. 34.10. The signal voltage e_g appears as μe_g in the plate circuit where μ is the amplification factor of the tube. Therefore, between plate and cathode, an imaginary *a.c.* generator of
voltage μe_g can be incorporated. The *a.c.* plate resistance r_p is in series with plate load R_L. The *a.c.*
output e_o is obtained across load R_L.

$$i_p = \frac{\mu e_g}{r_p + R_L}$$

Now $$e_o = i_p R_L = \left(\frac{\mu e_g}{r_p + R_L} \right) R_L$$

or
$$\frac{e_o}{e_g} = \left(\frac{\mu R_L}{r_p + R_L}\right)$$

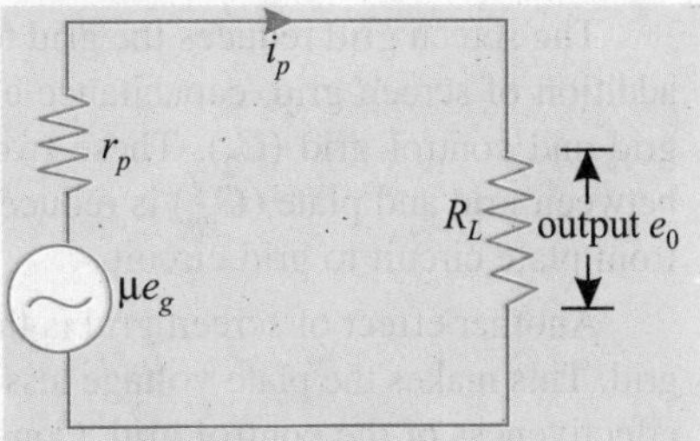

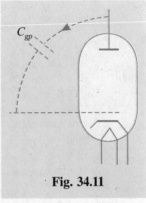

Fig. 34.10

But e_o/e_g is the voltage gain of the amplifier.

∴ Voltage gain, $\quad A_v = \dfrac{\mu R_L}{r_p + R_L}$

Example 34.3. *A triode used as an amplifier has an amplification factor of 20 and a.c. plate resistance of 10 kΩ. The load resistance is 15 kΩ. Find the voltage gain of the amplifier.*

Solution.
$$\mu = 20; \; r_p = 10 \text{ k}\Omega \; ; R_L = 15 \text{ k}\Omega$$

Voltage gain, $\quad A_v = \dfrac{\mu R_L}{r_p + R_L} = \dfrac{20 \times 15}{10 + 15} = 12$

34.12. LIMITATIONS OF TRIODE

The triode electrodes are made of metals and space between any two of them presents insulation. Therefore, capacitance exists between the electrodes of a triode. This is called inter-electrode capacitance. In particular, the capacitance between grid and plate C_{gp} (See Fig. 34.11) limits the frequency range of the triode. At low frequencies, its effect is negligible. However, at high frequencies, grid to plate reactance (X_{cgp}) is so low that a part of plate energy is fed back to the grid circuit through C_{gp}. This capacitive feedback is negative and reduces the amplification at high frequencies. It is due to this reason that triodes are generally used for amplifying low frequency (< 20 kHz) signals. Another drawback is that the amplification factor (μ) of a triode is low ; it is generally less than 100.

Fig. 34.11

34.13. TETRODE VALVE

The drawbacks of triode can be overcome by inserting an additional grid, called *screen grid* between control grid and plate. Such a four-electrode valve is known as tetrode. The construction of screen grid is somewhat similar to control grid and is operated at fixed positive potential *w.r.t.* cathode, but somewhat lower than the plate voltage. Fig. 34.12 (*i*) shows the symbol of tetrode.

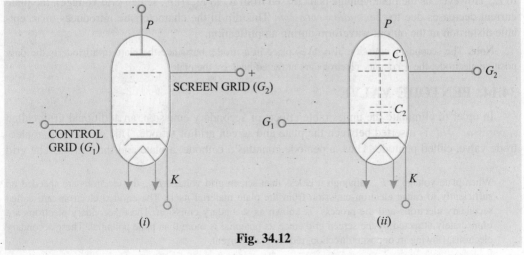

(*i*)   (*ii*)

Fig. 34.12

The screen grid reduces the grid to plate capacitance (C_{gp}) as shown in Fig. 34.12 (*ii*). With the addition of screen grid, capacitance exists between plate and screen grid (C_1) and between screen grid and control grid (C_2). These two capacitances are in series and, therefore, total capacitance between grid and plate (C_{gp}) is reduced. The reduced C_{gp} nearly eliminates the capacitive feedback from plate circuit to grid circuit.

Another effect of screen grid is that it acts as *electrostatic shield* between the plate and control grid. This makes the plate voltage less effective in controlling the plate current without affecting the effectiveness of the control grid. Consequently, amplification factor is increased.

Tetrode charateristics. Fig. 34.13 (*i*) shows the tetrode circuit for the determination of plate characteristics of tetrode. With control grid voltage held constant, say – 2 V, and screen grid voltage at some positive value (say $E_{SG} = 100$ V), the plate voltage is varied from zero to maximum. Corresponding to each value of plate voltage, the plate current is noted. The variations of plate current with plate voltage are then plotted on a graph. This gives the plate characteristic of tetrode at $E_C = – 2$ V and screen grid voltage $E_{SG} = 100$ V as shown in Fig. 34.13 (*ii*).

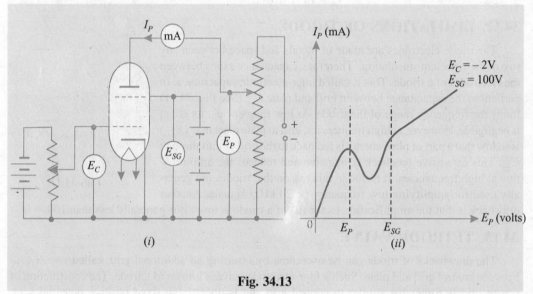

(*i*)   (*ii*)

Fig. 34.13

Note that plate current increases with the increase in the plate voltage upto plate voltage equal to E_P. However, as the plate voltage is increased from E_P to E_{SG} (*i.e.*, screen grid voltage), the plate current decreases due to *secondary emission. This dip in the characteristic introduces unacceptable distortion in the output waveform during amplification.

Note. The secondary emission also takes place in a triode, but since the plate in a triode is the only positive electrode, the secondary electrons are attracted back by the plate.

34.14. PENTODE VALVE

In order to eliminate the undesirable effects of secondary emission, an additional grid, called *suppressor grid* is inserted between the plate and screen grid of tetrode. This gives the five electrode valve, called pentode. Thus, a pentode contains a cathode, a plate and three grids. The grid

---

* When plate voltage is E_P, although it is less than screen grid voltage E_{SG}, the electrons are speeded up sufficiently to cause electron emission from the plate material itself. The emitted electrons are called secondary electrons and the process is known as secondary emission. These secondary electrons are immediately attracted by the screen grid since its potential is more than plate potential. These secondary electrons, flowing in opposite direction, reduce plate current.

closest to the cathode is the control grid G_1, and next is the screen grid G_2 and then the suppressor grid G_3. The suppressor grid is connected to the cathode and serves to suppress the effects of secondary emission. Fig. 34.14 shows the symbol of a pentode valve.

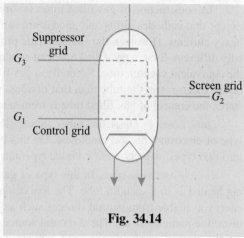

Fig. 34.14

The effects of secondary emission are overcome in the following manner. As the suppressor grid is connected to the cathode, therefore, it is at substantial negative potential *w.r.t.* plate. The electrons from cathode produce secondary emission as they hit the plate with high speeds. But now the secondary electrons are no longer attracted by the screen grid. As soon as the secondary electrons are emitted by the plate, they are repelled back by the negative suppressor grid. Thus, the effects of secondary emission are *suppressed and dip in the plate characteristic of tetrode is eliminated.

Another advantage of suppressor grid is that it provides further shielding between plate and control grid. This reduces grid to plate capacitances (C_{gp}) and completely eliminates the feedback action. Further, the amplification factor of the tube is increased.

Plate characteristics. The plate characteristics of a pentode can be obtained by using the same circuit as for tetrode. Fig. 34.15 shows a family of plate characteristics of a typical pentode valve.

Note that over the major portion of the characteristics, plate current is largely independent of plate voltage. This means that the device exhibits constant current characteristics above the knee votlage. Therefore, a.c. plate resistance is high ; it may be 1MΩ or more. The mutual conductance g_m is about the same as for triode or tetrode. Consequently, the amplification factor μ (= $r_p \times g_m$) of a

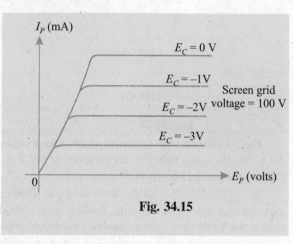

Fig. 34.15

pentode is very high; it may range from 1000 to 5000. Because of these qualities, a pentode is the most commonly used device in vaccum tube amplifiers.

34.15. GAS-FILLED TUBES OR VALVES

In the vacuum tubes we have been discussing so far, the electrons flow from cathode to anode in vacuum. If gas is present even in small amount, the electrons flowing from cathode to anode will cause ionisation of the gas. The ionised molecules would interfere with the control and make the device useless as an amplifier. In certain applications, fine control within the valve is of less importance than efficient handling and turning on and off of heavy currents. In such situations, some inert gas (argon, neon, helium) at low pressure (10 mm of Hg to 50 mm) is purposely introduced into the valve envelope. Such a tube is known as *gas-filled tube.*

* *

* The reader may note that suppressor grid does not prevent secondary emission by the plate. Rather it eliminates the effects of secondary emission.

The construction of gas-filled tubes is similar to that of vacuum tubes, except that cathodes, grids and anodes are usually larger in order to carry heavy currents. However, the characteristic properties of the two are markedly different. First, a gas-filled tube can conduct much *more current than the equivalent vacuum tube. Secondly, a gas-filled tube has far less control on the electrons in the tube than that of vacuum tube. Once the ionisation starts, the control of gas-filled tube is tremendously reduced.

Classification. Gas-filled tubes are usually classified according to the type of electron emission employed. On this basis, they may be classified into two types, namely; *cold-cathode type* and *hot-cathode type*.

(*i*) **Cold-cathode type.** In this type of gas-filled tubes, the cathode is not heated as in a vacuum tube. The ionisation of the gas is caused by the energy available from natural sources such as cosmic rays, sun rays or radioactive particles in air. These natural sources are the underlying reasons for the start of conduction in cold-cathode gas tubes. Most cold cathode tubes are used as diodes.

Gas-filled tube

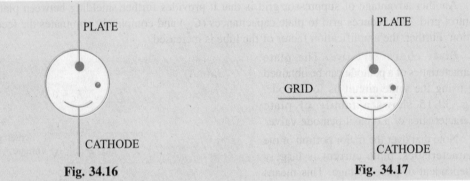

| Fig. 34.16 | Fig. 34.17 |

Fig. 34.16 shows the schematic symbol for a cold-cathode gas diode, known as *glow tube*. The dot within the circle indicates the presence of gas. Fig. 34.17 shows the schematic symbol of cold-cathode gas triode, known as *grid flow tube*.

(*ii*) **Hot-cathode type.** In this type of gas-filled tubes, the cathode is heated just as in an ordinary vacuum tube. The electrons flowing from cathode to plate cause ionisation of the gas molecules. Such tubes are used as diodes, triodes and tetrodes.

Fig. 34.18 shows the schematic symbol of a hot-cathode gas diode, known as *phanotron* whereas Fig. 34.19 shows the symbol of hot-cathode gas triode, known as *thyratron*.

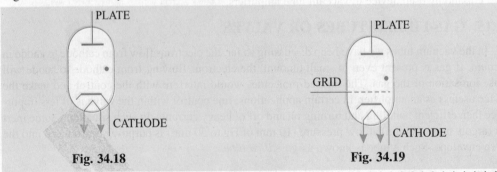

| Fig. 34.18 | Fig. 34.19 |

***

* It is because the electrons from cathode to anode collide with gas molecules and ionise them *i.e.*, knock out electrons from them. The additional electrons flow to the anode together with the original electrons, resulting in the increase in plate current.

34.16. CONDUCTION IN A GAS

A gas under ordinary pressure is a perfect insulator and cannot conduct current. However, if the gas pressure is low, it is possible to produce a large number of free electrons in the gas by the process of ionisation and thus cause the gas to become a conductor. This is precisely what happens in gas-filled tubes. The current conduction in a gas at low pressure can be beautifully illustrated by referring to the hot-cathode gas diode shown in Fig. 34.20. The space between cathode and anode of the tube contains gas molecules. When cathode is heated, it emits a large number of electrons. These electrons form a cloud of electrons near the cathode, called space charge. If anode is made positive *w.r.t.* cathode, the electrons (magenta dots) from the space charge speed towards the anode and collide with gas molecules (cyan circles) in the tube.

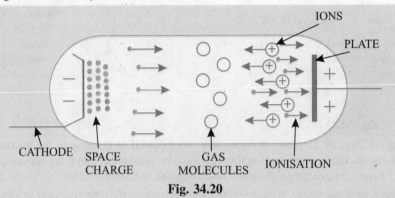

Fig. 34.20

If the anode-cathode voltage is low, the electrons do not possess the necessary energy to cause ionisation of the gas. Therefore, the plate current flow in the tube is only due to the electrons emitted by the cathode. As the anode-cathode voltage is increased, the electrons acquire more speed and energy and a point, called *ionisation voltage* is reached, where ionisation of the gas starts. The ionisation of gas produces free electrons and positive gas ions (cyan circles with +ve signs). The additional free electrons flow to the anode together with the original electrons, thus increasing plate current. However, the increase in plate current due to these added electrons is practically negligible. But, the major effect is that the positive gas ions slowly drift towards the cathode and neutralise the space charge. Consequently, the resistance of the tube decreases, resulting in large plate current. *Hence, it is due to the neutralisation of space charge by the positive gas ions that plate current in a gas tube is too much increased.*

The following points may be noted regarding the condution in a gas at low pressure :

(*i*) At low anode-cathode voltage, the ionisation of the gas does not occur and the plate current is about the same as for a vacuum tube at the same anode voltage.

(*ii*) At some anode-cathode voltage, called ionisation voltage, ionisation of the gas takes place. The plate current increases dramatically to a large value due to the neutralisation of space charge by the positive gas ions. The ionisation voltage depends upon the type and pressure of gas in the tube.

(*iii*) Once ionisation has started, it is maintained at anode-cathode voltage much lower than ionisation voltage. However, minimum anode-cathode voltage, called *deionising voltage,* exists below which ionisation cannot be maintained. Under such conditions, the positive gas ions combine with electrons to form neutral gas molecules and conduction stops. Because of this switching action, a gas-filled tube can be used as an electronic switch.

34.17. COLD-CATHODE GAS DIODE OR GLOW TUBE

Fig. 34.21 shows the cut-away view of cold cathode gas diode or glow tube. It essentially consists of two electrodes, cathode and anode, mounted fairly close together in an envelope filled with some inert gas at low pressure. The anode is in the form of a thin wire whereas cathode is a cylindrical metallic surface having oxide coating. The anode is always held at positive potential *w.r.t.* cathode.

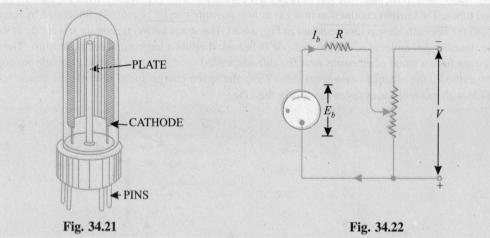

| **Fig. 34.21** | **Fig. 34.22** |

—— **Operation.** Fig. 34.22 shows a circuit that can be used to investigate the operation of cold-cathode gas diode. Electric conduction through the tube passes through three successive discharge phases *viz.*, Townsend discharge, the glow discharge and the arc discharge.

(*i*) **Townsend discharge.** At low anode-cathode voltage, the tube conducts an extremely small current (1 μA). It is because the cathode is cold and as such no source of electrons is present. However, natural sources (*e.g.*, cosmic rays *etc.*) cause some ionisation of the gas, creating a few free electrons. These electrons move towards the anode to constitute a small current. This stage of conduction is known as *Townsend discharge*. In this phase of conduction, no visible light is associated.

(*ii*) **Glow discharge.** As the anode-cathode voltage is increased, the electrons acquire more and more energy. At some voltage, known as *ionisation voltage*, ionisation of the gas starts and the tube current rises to a large value. The voltage across the tube drops to a low value, which remains constant regardless of the plate current. At the same time, glow is seen in the gas and on a portion of the cathode. This phase of conduction is known as *glow discharge*.

The fact that glow tube maintains constant voltage across it in the glow discharge region needs some explanation. In this region, any increase in supply voltage causes more current to flow ; the drop across series resistance R increases but the voltage E_b across the tube remains constant. As the current increases, the degree of ionisation increases and the glow covers a greater part of cathode surface and hence the ionised gas path between cathode and anode has greater area of cross-section. As resistance is inversely proportional to the area of cross-section, therefore, resistance of the tube decreases. Hence the voltage across the tube remains constant. Reverse is also true should the supply voltage decrease. Thus, in the glow discharge region, the resistance of the tube changes so as to maintain constant voltage across it.

(*iii*) **Arc discharge.** Once the cathode glow covers the entire surface of the cathode, the X-sectional area of gas path cannot increase further. This region is known as abnormal glow. If the current density is further increased, the discharge becomes an arc.

* The voltage-ampere characteristic of glow tube were first investigated by J.S. Townsend in 1901 and hence the name.

34.18. CHARACTERISTICS OF COLD-CATHODE GAS DIODE

The volt-ampere characteristic of a cold-cathode diode is shown in Fig. 34.23. At low anode-cathode voltage, the tube current is very small (1 µA) and is due to the ionisation of gas molecules by the natural sources. This stage of conduction upto voltage B is known as *Townsend discharge* and is non-self maintained discharge because it requires an external source to cause ionisation. At some critical voltage such as *B*, the tube fires and the voltage across the tube drops (from *B* to *C*) and remains constant regardless of plate current. This is the start of second conduction and is known as *glow discharge*. In this region (*C* to *D*), voltage across the tube remains constant even if the plate current increases.

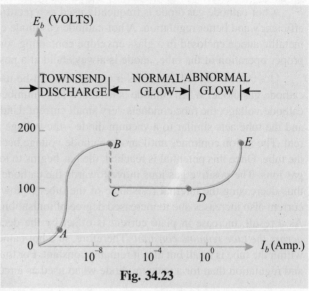

Fig. 34.23

After the glow discharge, the voltage across the tube no longer remains constant. Now, if the supply voltage is raised, not only will the circuit current increase but the voltage across the tube will start to rise again. This stage of conduction (*D* to *E*) is known as abnormal glow.

34.19. APPLICATIONS OF GLOW TUBES

The outstanding characteristic of a cold-cathode gas diode (or glow tube) to maintain constant voltage across it in the glow discharge region renders it suitable for many industrial and control applications. A few of such applications are mentioned below.

(*i*) **As a voltage regulating tube.** A glow tube maintains constant voltage across it in the glow discharge region. This characteristic permits it to be used as a voltage regulating tube. Fig. 34.24 shows a simple circuit commonly used to maintain constant voltage across a load. The glow tube (*VR* tube) is connected in parallel with the load R_L across which constant voltage is desired. So long as the tube operates in the glow discharge region, it will maintain constant voltage (= 150 V) across the load. The extra voltage is dropped across the series resistance *R*.

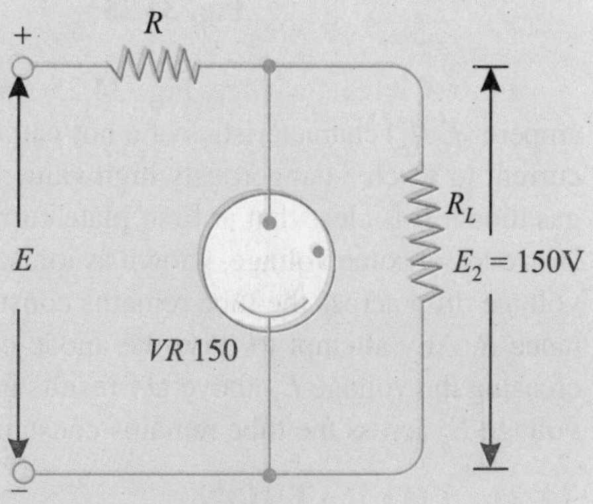

(*ii*) **As a polarity indicator.** As the cathode is surrounded by a characteristic glow, therefore, it can be useful to indicate the polarity of a direct voltage.

Fig. 34.24

(*iii*) **As an electronic switch,** which closes at ionisation potential, permitting a large current to flow, and opens at the deionising voltage, blocking the current flow.

(*iv*) **As a radio frequency field detector.** A strong radio-frequency field is capable of ionising the gas without direct connection to the tube. Therefore, the tube can indicate the presence of radio frequency field.

34.20. HOT CATHODE GAS DIODE

A hot-cathode gas diode is frequently used as a rectifier for moderate voltages because of high efficiency and better regulation. A hot-cathode gas diode consists of an oxide-coated cathode and a metallic anode enclosed in a glass envelope containing some inert gas under reduced pressure. For proper operation of the tube, anode is always held at a positive potential *w.r.t.* cathode.

Operation. Fig. 34.25 shows a circuit that can be used to investigate the operation of a hot-cathode gas diode. When cathode is heated, a large number of electrons are emitted. At low anode-cathode voltage, the tube conducts very small current. Under such conditions, the gas is not ionised and the tube acts similar to a vacuum diode—the voltage across the tube increases with plate current. The action continues until anode-cathode voltage becomes equal to the ionisation potential of the tube. Once this potential is reached, the gas begins to ionise, creating free electrons and positive gas ions. The positive gas ions move towards the cathode and tend to neutralise the space charge, thus decreasing the internal resistance of the tube. If now the plate voltage is increased, the plate current also increases due to increased degree of ionisation. This further reduces the tube resistance. As a result, increase in plate current is offset by the decrease in tube resistance and *the voltage across the tube remains constant.* Therefore, in a hot-cathode gas diode, not only the internal drop within the tube is small but also it remains constant. For this reason, a gas diode has better efficiency and regulation than for a vacuum diode when used as a rectifier.

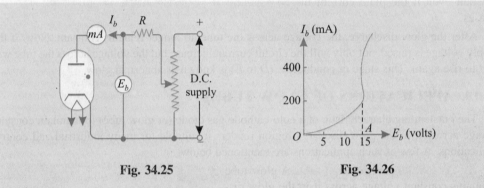

| **Fig. 34.25** | **Fig. 34.26** |

Plate Characteristics. Fig. 34.25 shows the circuit that can be used to determine the volt-ampere (E_b/I_b) characteristics of a hot-cathode gas diode. The series resistance R is used to limit the current to reach a dangerously high value. Fig. 34.26 shows the plate characteristic of hot-cathode gas diode. It is clear that at first, plate current rises slowly with increase in anode-cathode voltage. However, at some voltage, known as ionisation voltage (*OA*), the plate current rises sharply and the voltage drop across the tube remains constant. The extra voltage is dropped across the series resistance R. Any attempt to raise the anode-cathode voltage above the ionising value is fruitless. Increasing the voltage E_b above *OA* results in higher plate current (I_b) and large drop across R but the voltage E_b across the tube remains constant.

34.21. THYRATRON

A hot-cathode gas triode is known by the trade name thyratron. As discussed before, a gas diode fires at a fixed plate potential, depending upon the type of gas used and gas pressure. Very often it is necessary to control the plate potential at which the tube is to fire. Such a control is obviously impossible with a gas diode. However, if a third electrode, known as *control grid* is introduced in a gas diode, this control is possible. The tube is then known as hot-cathode gas triode or thyratron. By controlling the negative potential on the control grid, the tube can be fired at any plate potential.

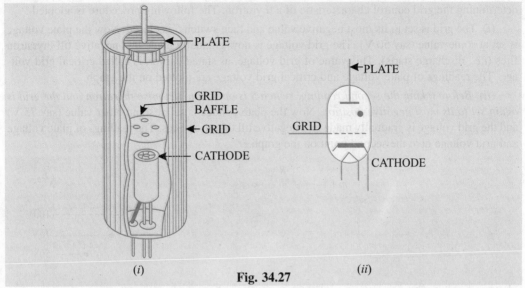

PLATE

PLATE

GRID
BAFFLE

GRID

GRID

CATHODE

CATHODE

(i)

Fig. 34.27

(ii)

Construction. Fig.34.27 (*i*) and Fig. 34.27 (*ii*) respectively show the cut-away view and schematic symbol of a thyratron. It consists of three electrodes, namely ; *cathode, anode* and *control grid* enclosed in a glass envelope containing some inert gas at low pressure. The cathode and anode are approximately planar. The control grid of thyratron has a special structure quite different from that of a vacuum tube. It consists of a metal cylinder surrounding the cathode with one or more perforated discs known as *grid baffles* near the centre.

Operation. When cathode is heated, it emits plenty of electrons by thermionic emission. If the control grid is made sufficiently negative, the electrons do not have the necessary energy to ionise the gas and the plate current is substantially zero. As the negative grid voltage is reduced, the electrons acquire more speed and energy. At some grid voltage, called *critical grid voltage,* ionisation of the gas occurs and the plate current rises to a large value.

The negative grid voltage, for a given plate potential, at which ionisation of the gas starts is known as **critical grid voltage.**

At critical grid voltage, gas ionises, creating free electrons and positive gas ions. The positive ions tend to neutralise the space charge, resulting in large plate current. In addition, these positive ions are attracted by the negative grid and neutralise the normal negative field of the grid, thereby preventing the grid from exerting any further control on the plate current of the tube. The grid now loses all control and the tube behaves as a diode. *Therefore, the function of control grid is only to start the conduction of anode current.* Once the conduction is started, the tube acts as a gas diode. It is important to realise the usefulness of control grid. We have seen that the ionisation does not start at low values of plate current. In a gas diode, it requires that the plate potential shoud be increased until sufficient plate current is flowing to cause ionisation. However, by adjusting the negative voltage on the grid, the desired plate current can be obtained to cause ionisation.

It may be mentioned here that once the thyratron fires, the only way to stop conduction is to reduce plate voltage to zero for a period long enough for deionisation of the gas in the tube.

34.22. GRID CONTROL CHARACTERISTIC

The curve between plate voltage and critical grid voltage (*i.e.*, grid voltage at which firing takes place) is known as *grid control characteristic.* Fig. 34.28 (*i*) *shows the experimental set up for

* A safety resistance is included in series with the anode. The grid resistance is included for the same reason.

determining the grid control characteristic of a thyratron. The following procedure is adopted :

(*i*) The grid is set to its most negative value and then switch *S* is closed. Now the plate voltage is set at some value (say 50 V). The grid voltage is now gradually made less negative till thyratron fires (*i.e.*, discharge starts). This value of grid voltage, as stated earlier, is called critical grid voltage. The readings of plate voltage and critical grid voltage are plotted on the graph.

(*ii*) *Before taking the second reading, switch S is opened to deionise thyratron and the grid is again set to its most negative position.* Now the plate voltage is set at some other value (say 75 V) and the grid voltage is gradually made less negative till thyratron fires. The readings of plate voltage and grid voltage give the second point on the graph.

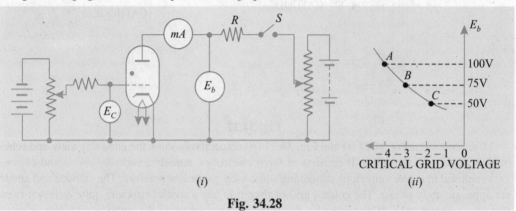

(i)   *(ii)*

Fig. 34.28

(*iii*) Following similar procedure, a number of anode voltage and corresponding critical grid voltage readings can be plotted on the graph. This gives grid control characteristic as shown in Fig. 34.28 (*ii*).

Information. The grid control characteristics convey the following information :

(*i*)   Any point on the curve specifies a combination of grid and plate voltage at which "firing" will take place.

(*ii*) There is a different value of critical grid voltage for each value of plate voltage.

(*iii*) The slope of the characteristic gives the value of control ratio. The control ratio is defined as the change in plate voltage divided by the change in critical grid voltage.

MULTIPLE-CHOICE QUESTIONS

1. The amount of additional energy required to emit an electron from the surface of a metal is called ....

    (*a*) surface barrier (*b*) work function

    (*c*) threshold level (*d*) none of the above

2. Work function of metals is generally measured in ....

    (*a*) joules   (*b*) electron volt

    (*c*) watt-hour   (*d*) watt

3. In practice, ... emission is most widely used.

    (*a*) field   (*b*) thermionic

    (*c*) secondary   (*d*) photo

4. .... emitter is most commonly used in the tubes of a radio receiver.

    (*a*) tungsten   (*b*) thoriated tungsten

    (*c*) oxide coated   (*d*) nickel

5. The work function of an oxide coated cathode is ....

    (*a*) 4.0 electron-volts (*b*) 4.52 electron-volts

    (*c*) 2.63 electron-volts (*d*) 1.1 electron-volts

6. The two principal electrodes in every tube are ....

    (*a*) plate and control grid

    (*b*) cathode and screen grid

    (*c*) plate and cathode

    (*d*) screen grid and control grid

7. A vacuum tube will conduct only if its plate is .... *w.r.t.* cathode.

    (*a*) positive   (*b*) negative

    (*c*) at zero potential (*d*) none of the above

8. A vacuum diode can be used as ....
   (a) an amplifier   (b) a rectifier
   (c) an oscillator   (d) none of the above

9. The negative resistance characteristic of tetrode is due to ....
   (a) secondary emission
   (b) plate being positive w.r.t. cathode
   (c) control grid being negative w.r.t. cathode
   (d) screen grid being negative w.r.t. cathode

10. The grid to plate capacitance is least in .... valve.
    (a) triode   (b) pentode
    (c) tetrode   (d) none of the above

11. A vacuum diode acts as a rectifier because of its .... conduction.
    (a) unidirectional   (b) bidirectional
    (c) controlled   (d) none of the three

12. A vacuum diode can act as ....
    (a) an amplifier   (b) a rectifier
    (c) an oscillator   (d) a multivibrator

13. The output of a rectifier is ....
    (a) pulsating d.c.   (b) pure d.c.
    (c) pure a.c.   (d) none of the above

14. A vacuum diode can act as a .... switch.
    (a) bidirectional   (b) controlled
    (c) unidirectional   (d) none of the above

15. The maximum efficiency of a full-wave rectifier is ....
    (a) 40.6%   (b) 20.3%
    (c) 90%   (d) 81.2%

16. Every grid controlled vacuum tube can act as ....
    (a) an amplifier
    (b) a rectifier
    (c) a controlled switch
    (d) none of the above

17. For faithful amplification, the control grid should be .... w.r.t. cathode.
    (a) positive   (b) at zero potential
    (c) negative   (d) none of the above

18. The actual voltage gain of a triode amplifier is less than μ due to ....
    (a) grid being negative w.r.t. cathode
    (b) voltage drop in a.c. resistance of the tube
    (c) plate being positive w.r.t. cathode
    (d) none of the above

19. The output and input voltages of a grounded-cathode amplifier have a phase difference of ....
    (a) 90°   (b) 270°
    (c) 360°   (d) 180°

20. Transformer coupling provides ....
    (a) impedance matching
    (b) good frequency response
    (c) step-up in voltage
    (d) none of the above

21. A gas diode can conduct .... the equivalent vacuum diode for the same plate voltage.
    (a) less current than   (b) more current than
    (c) same current as   (d) none of the above

22. A gas-filled tube has a .... resistance before ionisation.
    (a) very high   (b) small
    (c) very small   (d) zero

23. The PIV of hot cathode gas diode is .... the equivalent vacuum diode.
    (a) the same as that of
    (b) more than
    (c) less than
    (d) none of the above

24. The anode-to-cathode potential of a gas-filled tube at which gas deionises and stops conduction is called .... potential.
    (a) extinction   (b) striking
    (c) ionising   (d) none of the above

25. A thyratron can be used as ....
    (a) an oscillator
    (b) an amplifier
    (c) a controlled switch
    (d) a multi-vibrator

Answers to Multiple-Choice Questions

1. (b)	2. (b)	3. (b)	4. (c)	5. (d)	6. (c)	7. (a)	8. (b)
9. (a)	10. (b)	11. (a)	12. (b)	13. (a)	14. (c)	15. (d)	16. (a)
17. (c)	18. (b)	19. (d)	20. (a)	21. (b)	22. (a)	23. (c)	24. (a)
25. (c)							

Hints to Selected Multiple-Choice Questions

2. Work function is the amount of additional energy required to emit an electron from the surface of metal. Therefore, it should have the conventional unit of energy i.e. joules. But this is a very large unit for computing electronics work. Therefore, in practice, smaller unit of energy called **electron volt (eV)** is used.

$$1eV = 1.602 \times 10^{-19} \text{ J}$$

4. An oxide coated emitter has low work function (1.1eV), operates at low temperature (750°C) and has high emission efficiency (200 mA/watt) as compared to other types of emitters. However, it cannot withstand high voltages. Therefore, it is mostly used in the tubes of radio receiver.

7. If the plate is made positive *w.r.t.* cathode (electron emitter), the electrons are attracted towards the positively charged plate in a vacuum tube. Thus, the electrons flow from cathode to plate to constitute what is known as *plate current* and the vacuum tube conducts current.

9. In the negative resistance characteristic of tetrode, the increase in plate voltage causes a decrease in plate current. In this region, the plate potential is less than screen grid potential. However, the electrons are speeded up sufficiently to cause electron emission from the plate itself. These emitted electrons (called secondary electrons) are attracted by screen grid because its voltage is more positive than plate. The secondary electrons flow in opposite direction to plate current. As a result, plate current decreases though plate potential is increasing. This phenomenon is called secondary emission.

10. In a pentode valve in addition to control grid and screen grid, there is a third grid called suppressor grid. The suppressor grid further reduces grid to plate capacitance as compared to other valves.

11. In a vacuum diode, current flows in plate circuit when plate is positive *w.r.t.* cathode whereas no current flows when plate is negative *w.r.t.* cathode. Due to unidirectional flow of current, only positive half cycles appear across the load while negative half cycles are suppressed. This permits it to be used as a rectifier *i.e.* it converts *a.c.* into *d.c.*

13. The output from a rectifier is pulsating *d.c.* These pulsations are removed with the help of filter circuits to obtain steady *d.c.* output.

15. Rectification efficiency of a full-wave rectifier is given by;

$$\eta = \frac{0.812}{1 + r_p / R_L}$$

If $R_L \gg r_p$, then efficiency will be maximum and is equal to 81.2 %.

17. In order to achieve faithful amplification *i.e.* the magnitude of signal should increase without any change in its general shape, the control grid should be kept at negative potential *w.r.t.* cathode. To do so, a *d.c.* voltage is applied in the grid circuit or *d.c.* component of plate current is itself used in addition to the signal voltage. This d.c. voltage or *d.c.* component of plate current provides grid bias. Its magnitude is such that it always keeps the grid negative *w.r.t.* cathode regardless of the polarity of the signal.

20. Transformer coupled amplifiers provide impedance matching. This enables maximum power to be transferred from source to load *i.e.* from amplifier to speaker.

22. Prior to ionisation, the anode-cathode voltage is low and the electrons emitted by cathode do not have necessary energy to cause ionisation of the gas. The plate current flow is only due to electrons emitted by cathode. Therefore, as such, a gas-filled tube has very high resistance before ionisation.

25. In a thyratron, a third electrode called *control grid* is introduced. By controlling the negative potential on the grid, it can be made to fire at any plate potential. Once the thyratron fires, the only way to stop conduction is to reduce plate voltage to zero for a period long enough for deionisation of the gas in the tube. Thus due to its triggering action it can act as a controlled switch.

INDEX

A

B

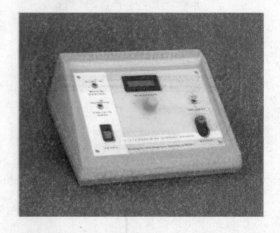

D

E

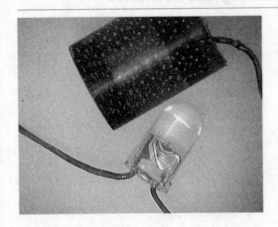

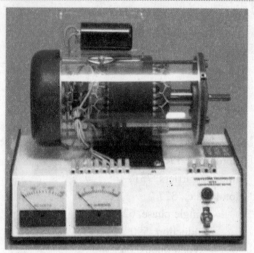

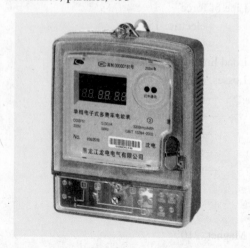

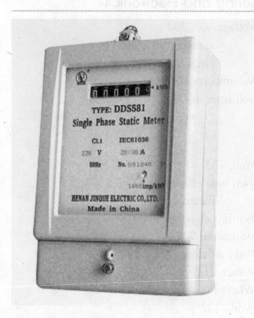

S

T

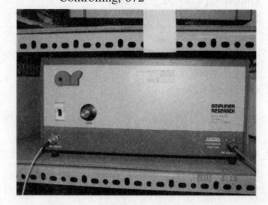

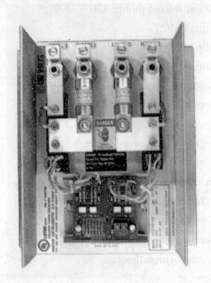

—Damping, 675
—deflecting, 672
Transformer, 547
—ideal, 549
—losses, 575
—practical, 552
Transistors, 754
—common base, 758
—common emitter, 761
Triode, vacuum, 870
Trivalent atom, 730
Two-phase circuit, 504
Two-wattmeter method, 535

U

Unbalanced 3-phase system, 522
Undercompounded generator, 324
Units, 131
—energy, 132
—power, 133
—work, 132
Universal motor 628

V

Valence electrons, 3
Valves, electronic, 869
VAR, 431

Voltage, a.c., 394
—average value, 402
—r.m.s. value, 403
Voltamperes, 431
Voltmeter, 677

W

Watt, 133
Watt hour efficiency, 379
—meter, 710
Wattless component, 431
Wattmeter, 704
Wave winding, 298
Weber, 211
Wheatstone bridge, 56
Work, 132
—Law, 223
Wound rotor, 592
Wye connection, 508

Y

Y-connection, 508
Yoke, 296

Z

Zener diode, 749

Win Prizes !

Attention: Students

We request you, for your frank assessment, regarding some of the aspects of the book, given as under:

10 324   Principles of Electrical Engineering and Electronics
V.K. Mehta and Rohit Mehta   **Reprint 2012**

Please fill up the given space in neat capital letters. Add additional sheet(s) if the space provided is not sufficient, and if so required.

(i)   What topic(s) of your syllabus that are important from your examination point of view are not covered in the book ?

....
....
....
....

(ii)   What are the chapters and/or topics, wherein the treatment of the subject-matter is not systematic or organised or updated?

....
....
....
....

(iii)   Have you come across misprints/mistakes/factual inaccuracies in the book? Please specify the chapters, topics and the page numbers.

....
....
....
....
....

(iv)   Name top three books on the same subject (in order of your preference - 1, 2, 3) that you have found/heard better than the present book? Please specify in terms of quality (in all aspects).

1 ....
....
2 ....
....
3 ....
....

(v) Further suggestions and comments for the improvement of the book:

....

....

....

....

....

Other Details:

(i) Who recommended you the book? (Please tick in the box near the option relevant to you.)

☐ Teacher ☐ Friends ☐ Bookseller

(ii) Name of the recommending teacher, his designation and address:

....

....

....

(iii) Name and address of the bookseller you purchased the book from:

....

....

....

(iv) Name and address of your institution (Please mention the University or Board, as the case may be)

....

....

....

(v) Your name and complete postal address:

....

....

....

(vi) Write your preferences of our publications (1, 2, 3) you would like to have

....

....

The best assessment will be awarded half-yearly. The award will be in the form of our publications, as decided by the Editorial Board, amounting to Rs. 300 (total).

Please mail the filled up coupon at your earliest to:
Editorial Department
S. CHAND & COMPANY LTD.,
Post Box No. 5733, Ram Nagar,
New Delhi 110 055